INTERNATIONAL GUIDE TO STUDENT ACHIEVEMENT

The *International Guide to Student Achievement* brings together and critically examines the major influences shaping student achievement today. There are many, often competing, claims about how to enhance student achievement, raising the questions of "What works?" and "What works best?" World-renowned bestselling authors, John Hattie and Eric M. Anderman have invited an international group of scholars to write brief, empirically supported articles that examine predictors of academic achievement across a variety of topics and domains.

Rather than telling people what to do in their schools and classrooms, this guide simply provides the first-ever compendium of research that summarizes what is known about the major influences shaping students' academic achievement around the world. Readers can apply this knowledge base to their own school and classroom settings. More than 150 entries serve as intellectual building blocks to creatively mix into new or existing educational arrangements and aim for quick, easy reference. Chapter authors follow a common format that allows readers to more seamlessly compare and contrast information across entries, guiding readers to apply this knowledge to their own classrooms, their curriculums and teaching strategies, and their teacher training programs.

John Hattie is Professor and Director of the Melbourne Education Research Institute at the University of Melbourne, Australia and Honorary Professor at the University of Auckland. The author of the international bestsellers, *Visible Learning* and *Visible Learning for Teachers*, he has served as President of the International Text Commission, and associate editor of the *British Journal of Educational Psychology*. He has published and presented over 550 papers and has supervised 160 theses students.

Eric M. Anderman is Professor of Educational Psychology and the Interim Director of the School of Educational Policy and Leadership at the Ohio State University. In 1999 he was awarded the Richard E. Snow Early Career Achievement Award from the American Psychological Association (APA) and he served as President of Division 15 of APA in 2008. In addition to authoring and editing several books, he has served on the editorial boards of several major journals and as the Associate Editor of the *Journal of Educational Psychology* from 2002–2009.

D1568737

Educational Psychology Handbook Series

Series Editor: Patricia A. Alexander

Following is a list of volumes published or currently in development.

New editions of the first three volumes are currently in the early stages of development.

Persons interested in organizing handbooks around similar topics should contact Patricia Alexander at the following address.

Dr. Patricia Alexander
Dept. of Human Development
College of Education
University of Maryland
College Park, MD 20742
Pa34@mail.umd.edu

INTERNATIONAL GUIDE TO STUDENT ACHIEVEMENT

Edited by

John Hattie

University of Melbourne

Eric M. Anderman

Ohio State University

 Routledge
Taylor & Francis Group

NEW YORK AND LONDON

First published 2013
by Routledge
711 Third Avenue, New York, NY 10017

Simultaneously published in the UK
by Routledge
2 Park Square, Milton Park, Abingdon, Oxon OX14 4RN

Routledge is an imprint of the Taylor & Francis Group, an informa business

Library of Congress Cataloging in Publication Data
International guide to student achievement / [edited by] John Hattie, Eric M. Anderman.
   p. cm.
   strategies, and their teacher training programs"— Provided by publisher.
   Includes bibliographical references and index.
   1. Academic achievement—Cross-cultural studies. I. Hattie, John. II. Anderman, Eric M.
   LB1062.6.I72 2012
   370.15'4—dc23
   2012022523

ISBN: 978-0-415-87898-2 (hbk)
ISBN: 978-0-415-87901-9 (pbk)
ISBN: 978-0-203-85039-8 (ebk)

Typeset in Times
by EvS Communication Networx, Inc.

Printed and bound in the United States of America by Sheridan Books, Inc. (a Sheridan Group Company).

To Lane Akers — for his initiation, support, friendship, and many contributions to the field of education and publishing

Contents

Acknowledgments

As noted in the Dedication, the idea for this guide came from Lane Akers, and he has been instrumental in ensuring it has come to fruition. His passion for this volume has led to wonderful meetings and dinners, the extensive use of Skype, and a set of standards and structures which is evident throughout. His team at Taylor and Francis have added to the pleasure of completing this book: thanks to Julie Ganz, Lynn Goeller, Lori Kelly, Andrew Weckenman, and their teams.

One of our first tasks was to select editors for each section, and this is one task where it became evident we had made great choices Each editor recommended entry titles, world-class scholars, attended to the details, and added so much value to the total corpus. Thanks to Mimi Bong, Andrew Martin, Catherine Bradshaw, Julianne Turner, Anita Woolfolk Hoy, Rayne Sperling, Christine Rubie-Davies, and Julian Elliott for their outstanding work. We also are deeply indebted to Ashley Marietta-Brown, who spent countless hours communicating with the editors and authors, and keeping us organized.

Close to 250 authors contributed to this guide, and every one of them responded to our sometimes many requests. Asking academics to write less than about 2,000 words on their passion and, in some cases, their life work requires remarkable discipline and sometimes good humor—these attributes were consistently evident in all interactions.

For both of us, the learning has been enormous—we have learned about the main ideas from the best in the world, we have found new friends and colleagues in our section editors, and we have enjoyed working together across continents in forming and creating this volume. We met (Skyped) Sunday nights, and once again the time for creating books comes out of family time, hence our gratitude to our families for supporting us—thanks to Janet, Joel, Kyle, Kieran, Bobbi and Jimmy (from John) and to Lynley, Sarah, and Jacob (from Eric).

Introduction

John Hattie and Eric M. Anderman

The purposes of schooling have been debated from the early days of Plato to the divergent prescriptions put forth by modern day political parties. Some want to foster the development of 21st century skills while others urge greater attention to basic literacy and numeracy. Given the ubiquitous presence of the Web, there are calls for schools to develop critical thinking and evaluation skills. Likewise there are expectations that schools will develop positive attitudes, physical fitness, belongingness, respect, citizenship, and the love of learning; that is, the attributes of character development. Perhaps the most common expectation, however, is the development of achievement, and that is the focus of this book.

For as long as schools have existed, enhanced student achievement has been the most important outcome of schooling at any level. While there are many definitional contests about what "achievement" means (see Guskey, entry 1), there are also many, often competing, claims about how to enhance student achievement. Often it seems that the various claims are talking across each other, that there is evidence to defend almost any method (short of unethical ones). Every teacher seems to have a recipe for enhancement, and the variability among these recipes is enormous. This has led to an "everything goes" attitude toward interventions where permissive policies allow each teacher to introduce his or her own methods and interventions.

Likewise, school leaders will sometimes introduce some innovation or "new idea" to enhance achievement knowing that these methods have not worked elsewhere. The proverbial argument is that "it is different here" and just needs some local adaptation. To quote Thomas (1979, p. 159) "virtually anything that could be thought up for treatment was tried out at one time or another and, once tried, lasted decades or even centuries before being given up. It was, in retrospect, the most frivolous and irresponsible kind of human experimentation, based on nothing but trial and error, and usually resulting in precisely that sequence." Thomas was referring to the study of medicine and noted how evidence-based medicine was the mechanism for driving out dogma, as dogma does not destroy itself.

One of us (Hattie, 2009, 2012) has documented the effects from over 900 meta-analyses related to achievement. The evidence shows that if the bar is set at the standard of, "Can we enhance student achievement?" then 95%+ of all interventions are successful! The question thus is not "What works?" but "What works best?" Fortunately, there is a massive amount of evidence with which to address this question. The 165 entries in this book provide a reasonable sample of this evidence. Later editions will provide even more.

Given the many influences that can have positive effects on student achievement, the constant question every system, school, and teacher should ask is *how much* each influence impacts on achievement growth. The impact can then be compared to typical effects and can be used as a benchmark to seek even greater impact. Furthermore, there may be critical moderators to the claims about what are the best influences on achievement. For example, is there a need for different programs for boys and girls, for gifted and nongifted, for minority and majority, for low and high socioeconomic status? Despite the hunt for moderators, the evidence for their presence is often difficult to document, particularly in a replicable manner. There is no doubt, however, that the search for these moderators is critical. The entries in this book note some moderators, but they are not as prevalent as many believe. There is little evidence, generally, for local adaptations, that is, for modifications based on "we are different here." While the search for moderators is legitimate and should not cease, the search for evidence is the key, not a belief in moderators. Thus the mission of this book is to assemble and to critically examine the many possible influences shaping student achievement, to seek evidence where there are moderators, and to consider the implications for school and classroom practice.

This book is termed a *guide* and a major reason is to distinguish it from the many handbooks that are available. Handbooks typically have denser, 20+ page chapters whereas this Guide aims more for quick, easy reference. It aims to provide guidance based on the best available evidence in this Guide, and to this end we have invited an international group of scholars to write brief, empirically supported articles that examine predictors of academic achievement across a variety of topics and domains. As readers will see, achievement is operationalized somewhat differently across domains. Thus achievement in literacy may not be measured in the same way as achievement in physical education. Chapter authors represent an array of prominent scholars who provide up-to-date empirical examinations of variables that are related to academic achievement.

In all but the first and last sections, authors follow a common format that allows readers to more easily compare and contrast information across entries. Each chapter begins with a brief "Introduction" to the topic. This is followed by the main "Research Evidence" section that summarizes empirical research related to achievement in that particular domain. The final section concludes with a "Summary and Recommendations" section that summarizes the main takeaway messages from the chapter and offers recommendations for practice, policy, and possible future research.

A brief overview of the book's nine sections follows.

Section 1: Understanding Achievement:
Edited by Eric M. Anderman (Ohio State University) and John Hattie (University of Melbourne)

Achievement is not a straightforward concept. As Guskey notes in the first entry, student achievement is the basis of nearly every aspect of education, but there is no shared understanding of what it is. The current debates about "curricula" indicate this contestation. Achievement can differ across subjects, in complexity (e.g., from surface to deep understanding), in forms of evidence (e.g., essays, performances, constructions), can be seen from an attainment versus improvement perspective, can relate to what we know, do, and care about, and can change in meaning as students progress from early childhood to elementary, high school, higher education, and into adulthood. It is also the case that achievement does not exist in isolation. Attitudes can affect achievement just as achievement affects attitudes. The search for causes, influences, and effects of achievement are voluminous, as the entries in this book illustrate.

Guskey opens with a discussion of the many, hotly contested meanings of achievement and shows how the lack of a shared definition often defaults to some standardized test. He then focuses our discussion of achievement on what takes place in established instructional environments, specifically in classrooms and schools. Of the many dimensions of achievement the most commonly used demarcations are between cognitive, affective, and psychomotor. These, however, are also multifaceted. For example, cognitive can relate to subject matter knowledge and understanding (e.g., history, science), to understanding critical or civics thinking, to knowing about one's culture, society, and social mobility, to participating in learning events (e.g., raising rabbits, watching falling stars), and to the development of key competencies (e.g., managing self and collaborating with others). And hovering above everything are debates related to the uses of achievement (e.g., in developing character) and their use in examinations which can open or close future opportunities for the student.

There are also important distinctions between attainment and improvement or between proficiency and progress. Currently, there is pressure throughout the world to demonstrate that all or most students reach prescribed levels of attainment. In any large cohort of students (especially at the national level), it is common to find that achievement in school subjects is normally distributed; that is, as many above as below the cohort mean. Expecting most or all students below the mean to subsequently perform above the mean is unrealistic because standards tend to be set above the average. Schools that do not have all their students above the mean are often identified as problematic and in need of intervention. Further, it is not uncommon for these schools to include a heavy population of students from lower socioeconomic areas thus making it more difficult to achieve a common high standard. Conversely, if improvement or growth is featured, then schools with a heavy population of students from lower socioeconomic backgrounds may be much more successful. It may also be the case that schools with a heavy population of students from higher socioeconomic backgrounds may have many above the the mean but show few who make adequate progress.

Each of the subsequent sections contains entries on the major influences on achievement. The term *major* refers here to the most often discussed or used influences and does not imply greater impact. Entry writers were advised not to overuse meta-analyses and effect sizes, but to be inclusive in their review of studies across many methodologies (including qualitative studies). Being unable to include every possible influence, we have focused on those that seem to have a significant impact on achievement.

Section 2: Influences from the Student:
Edited by Mimi Bong (Korea University)

This section focuses on what the learner brings to the achievement situation; that is, their phases of development, their health, gender, personality, and attitudes. Not only are their goals, levels of concentration, and persistence important in terms of how, when, and how often they engage in learning, but these elements can also be significantly modified by schools. Some students have greater opportunities to learn based on the success of their prior learning experiences, their cultural aspirations and influences, and their physical and developmental differences. Entries in this section focus on students' developmental characteristics, their motivation (e.g., self-efficacy, attributions, and social motivation), and on students with special needs.

Section 3: Influences from the Home:
Edited by Andrew Martin (University of Sydney)

There is much debate about the influence of the home, and the entries in Section 3 outline many of the most important ones. Whereas these factors may be critical to many students' academic success, it is noted that their effects are variable. Further, once students arrive at school, schools are asked to make improvements in attainment and growth notwithstanding home differences. When schools were made compulsory, the argument was that experts (educators) could enhance learning in what societies considered valuable ways, as expressed in the curriculum. Now, however, there is recognition of the need for home–school partnership and parents are being asked to take more responsibility for the success of their child's learning. Questions are often asked, for example, about the effects of different family compositions (e.g., single, two parent, resident or nonresident fathers), the influence of resources in the home (e.g., socioeconomic influences, home environment, maternal employment, television), and the various ways parents can interact with the school. The entries in this section address those issues and should be of interest to all stakeholders in education, including concerned parents.

Section 4: Influences from the School:
Edited by Catherine Bradshaw (Johns Hopkins University)

The influence of variability among schools can be quite different across countries. For example, the variance between schools in New Zealand and Australia is among the lowest in the world, while the variance between schools in Germany and South Africa is much higher. Given two students of similar abilities, it matters very little what schools they might attend should they move between New Zealand and Australia, whereas school differences can be quite critical when moving between Germany and South Africa. In some countries (e.g., the United States), variability in students' school performance is used as a marketing tool by realtors to lure families into neighborhoods known for having high achieving schools.

Within all countries there are major policy debates about the nature of schools, especially about initiatives concerning their mission, direction, and use of finances. School leaders and policy makers tend to show special interest in the *visible* arrangements of their schools such as their physical configuration, class sizes, within or between ability groupings, single sex vs. co-ed enrollments, the extent of summer classes, the climate of a school, the presence of para-professionals, extracurricular and service learning programs, and grade retention or promotion standards. National and district debates also center around alternative forms of schooling such as those found in charter schools, private schools, inclusive schooling, and faith based schooling. The entries in this section offer rich information for school leaders to work through as they seek to maximize student achievement and teacher development.

Section 5: Influences from the Classroom:
Edited by Julianne Turner (University of Notre Dame)

Perhaps the greatest concern of educators is how to organize their classrooms to ensure effective instruction for all students. Thomas Good and Jere Brophy noted in their classic text that classrooms are one of the most important entities to consider when thinking about students' education (Good & Brophy, 1987). There are many configurations when setting up classrooms, such as tracking and acceleration, and within each, the management of classrooms is critical—maintaining control and a high sense of fairness are necessary but often not sufficient conditions for learning to occur. When students are grouped in classrooms, this leads to important questions as to the peer effects on learning, and the ways teachers can develop collaboration as well as maximize students' motivation to maximize learning among peers. In addition, the instructional practices that are selected for any particular group of students and implemented at the classroom level have powerful effects on student achievement.

Section 6: Influences from the Teacher:
Edited by Anita Woolfolk Hoy (Ohio State University)

After accounting for the variance among students, the next most powerful influence on student achievement is the teacher. This means that there is considerable variation in the effects that teachers have on students' academic achievement. Every student is aware of these differences, but school policy often assumes that teacher variance is not sufficient to be incorporated into policies. This leads to policies in which all teachers are grouped together as if they were all similar in their effects.

Research relating to the training of teachers and their subsequent impact on students' learning is an underresearched topic. Levine (2006, p. 109) described teacher education as the "the Dodge City of the education world. Like the fabled Wild West town, it is unruly and disordered." There are many claims about the importance of teacher content knowledge, intelligence, professional identities, beliefs about achievement and teaching, motivation, enthusiasm, efficacy, and expectations. Certainly the relationship between teachers and students lies at the heart of the learning experience in most situations. This section examines how these factors relate to the quality of teaching and also looks at some of the methods for studying teacher effectiveness, including the National Board for Professional Teaching Standards.

Section 7: Influences from the Curriculum:
Edited by Rayne Sperling (Pennsylvania State University)

The stated curriculum is important but, as noted in the introductory section, there are many other outcomes of schooling not included in most curricula. Although reading and numeracy are central in most countries' stated curricula, there are well debated and contentious issues as to what is to be included within these domains. Other curricula include writing, languages (native and bilingual), social skills, values, social studies, drama and the arts, health, and various extracurricula domains. Debates also include how best to implement major curricula, such as activity learning, individualized instruction, and creativity methods.

Section 8: Influences from Teaching Strategies: Edited by Christine Rubie-Davies (University of Auckland)

Most teachers develop a method of teaching that seems to work for them and then continue to refine this method over their careers. This does not stop those responsible for faculty development programs from introducing alternative methods, and in some cases, requiring the use of a single school-wide method. Some of these methods relate to specific teaching programs such as mastery learning, problem-based learning, reciprocal teaching, direct instruction, simulations, cooperative learning, programmed instruction, inquiry based teaching, or co- or team teaching. Other less programmatic methods include concept mapping, peer tutoring, multimedia learning, problem solving, individual instruction, computer-based learning, and adjunct aids.

Another set of teacher influences includes specific actions such as questioning, use of worked examples, metacognitive strategies, use of feedback, cognitive task analysis, and matching methods or styles of learning to specific groups of students. And finally, teacher influences include teaching students how to learn on their own via study skills, time on task, frequent testing, goal setting, spaced vs. massed practice, self-verbalization, and self-questioning. This lengthy section examines the most prevalent of these methods knowing that the list will only grow longer as the learning sciences continue to broaden.

Section 9: Influences from an International Perspective: Edited by Julian G. Elliot (Durham University)

Among the major influences on achievement, not only in terms of how it is conceived and measured, are the international methods of evaluating achievement impact across countries. There are many systems for such cross-country comparison and their importance in making policy directives is increasing. Because it is not possible to cover achievement in all countries, this section includes a carefully selected sample based on countries with highly variable systems: South Africa, Finland, Singapore, the Russian Federation, Nepal, Taiwan, Canada, South Korea, Ghana, Nigeria, Israel, and South America.

Audience and Presentation

The audience for this book is enormous. It includes anyone who is a serious stakeholder in education: politicians, superintendents, regional officers, school board members, school principals, teachers, professional support staff, academic researchers and their graduate students, and involved parents. In order to be accessible to such a large and divergent audience, entries have been kept as nontechnical as possible and follow a common structure: (a) a brief introduction, (b) major research findings, and (c) implications for practice. The sections have been organized according to their point of origin: student, home, school, classroom, teacher, curriculum, and teaching approach.

This book does not attempt to tell people what to do in their schools and classrooms. It simply provides them with the first ever compendium of research that summarizes what is known about the major influences shaping students' academic achievement across the world. Readers can then creatively apply this knowledge base to their own school and classroom organizational patterns, their curricula and teaching strategies, and their teacher training programs. The entries can, therefore, be viewed as intellectual building blocks to be creatively mixed into new or existing educational arrangements.

We appreciate that it is not inclusive of everything we know about influencing achievement. There are many handbooks that delve far more deeply into the topics presented here. A large number of these can be found on the Routledge website: www.routledge/education.

References

Good, T. L., & Brophy, J. E., (1987). *Looking in classrooms*. New York: Harper & Row.
Hattie, J. A. C. (2009). *Visible learning: A synthesis of 800+ meta-analyses on achievement*. Abingdon, England: Routledge.
Hattie, J. A. C. (2012). *Visible learning for teachers: Maximizing impact on achievement*. Abingdon, England: Routledge.
Levine, A. (2006). *Educating school teachers*. New York: Education Schools Project.
Thomas, L. (1979). *The medusa and the snail: More notes of a biology watcher*. New York: Viking Press.

---

1. Note: An entry entitled "Cognitive Task Analysis" by Kenneth A. Yates and Richard E. Clark was inadvertently omitted from Section 8 and can be found on the Routledge Website at www.routledge.com/9780415879019.

Yates, K. A., and Clark R. E. (2012). Cognitive task analysis. In J. Hattie and E. M. Anderman (Eds.), *International guide to student achievement*. New York: Routledge.

Section 1

Understanding Achievement

EDITORS: ERIC M. ANDERMAN
Ohio State University

JOHN HATTIE
Melbourne University

1.1

Defining Student Achievement

Thomas R. Guskey
University of Kentucky

Introduction

Student achievement is the basis of nearly every aspect of education. It gives direction to all educational improvement efforts, provides the foundation for education accountability programs, and serves as the primary outcome variable in most educational research studies. The phrase *student achievement* is included in the titles of over 2,000 research studies and reports listed in the Education Resources Information Center (ERIC) system—more than any other phrase. Google Scholar lists nearly 5,000 resources published within the past decade with "student achievement" in the title.

Given the prominence of student achievement in education policy, practice, and research, one might assume that we have a shared understanding of what it means. Unfortunately, that is not the case. Not only do policy makers, legislators, school leaders, teachers, parents, and researchers often define student achievement differently, tremendous variation exists in the definitions of individuals within each of these groups (Guskey, 2007). This lack of a common definition confounds efforts to determine the effectiveness of education improvement initiatives and thwarts attempts to develop consensus regarding the success of education reforms.

The Concept of Achievement

In simplest terms, "achievement" implies "the accomplishment of something." In education, that "something" generally refers to articulated learning goals. Although learning can occur in a wide variety of contexts, the focus of educators rests more narrowly on the learning that takes place in established instructional environments, specifically in classrooms and schools. Educators interact with students in these environments in purposeful and intentional ways to help students acquire explicit knowledge and skills.

Because learning goals are typically multifaceted and involve different kinds of learning in different subject areas, "student achievement" must be considered a multifaceted construct. To be accurate, therefore, discussions of student achievement should always include descriptors that clarify the specific learning goals that were the focus of instructional activities and that students were expected to attain.

Domains of Learning. Learning goals in education have long been classified in three broad domains: *cognitive, affective,* and *psychomotor.* Cognitive goals (Bloom, Englehart, Furst, Hill, & Krathwohl, 1956) provide the basis of most forms of academic achievement and come first to mind when we think about the purposes of formal education. They describe the concepts and skills educators strive to have students gain through planned instructional activities. Cognitive goals also provide the foundation of every school's academic curriculum. Although some cognitive goals apply across multiple content areas (e.g., problem solving and critical thinking), most are subject area specific. Hence, "student achievement in language arts" may be distinct from "student achievement in mathematics" or "student achievement in science."

The curriculums of most countries throughout the world consider a broad range of content areas. Australia's national curriculum, for example, focuses on reading, spelling, writing, and numeracy skills, as well as science literacy, civics and citizenship, and information and communication technology (Ministerial Council on Education, Employment, Training and Youth Affairs, 2006). In Japan the Education Ministry highlights creating well-rounded students in the national curriculum by emphasizing subjects such as music, arts and handicrafts, and homemaking, physical education, and moral education, as well as math and science. Their curriculum also devotes a large amount of time to Japanese language and life activities that give younger students personal life experiences in preparation for classroom-oriented science. In life activities class, students participate in activities such as picking flowers, raising rabbits, catching frogs and insects, and watching falling stars (Wu, 1999).

Furthermore, because cognitive goals span a broad range of subdomains and topics in each subject area, student achievement within a subject area can vary in its breadth. The *Common Core State Standards Initiative* (Council of Chief State School Officers and National Governors' Association [CCSSO & NGA, 2010) in the United States, for example, divides student learning goals (standards) in language arts into the subdomains of Reading, Writing, Speaking/Listening, and Language. Mathematics subdomains consist of Operations and Algebraic Thinking, Number and Operations—Base Ten, Number and Operations—Fractions, Measurement and Data, Geometry, and Mathematical Practices. Researchers concerned with the content validity of measures of student achievement in a subject area must ensure adequate sampling of concepts and skills across these subdomains (Sireci, 1998).

Within each subdomain, cognitive goals also can vary in intellectual complexity or depth. They can range from simple goals that require only recall of factual information, to more complex goals that call for sophisticated reasoning and higher mental processes, such as the ability to make applications, analyze relationships, or draw inferences. Recent criticism of mathematics instruction in the United States, for example, focused on these issues of depth. Noting that U.S. teachers tend to cover a wider range of topics than do teachers in other developed countries, but explore few topics in great depth, researchers described the U.S. mathematics curriculum as "a mile wide and an inch deep" (Duffrin, 1998). The current emphasis on 21st century skills (Larson & Miller, 2011) comes largely from concerns about the lack of depth in many established curriculums.

Affective goals (Krathwohl, Bloom, & Masia, 1964) refer to students' attitudes, interests, feelings, beliefs, and dispositions. They relate to how students feel and what they believe about the subjects they are studying, their teachers, school, learning, and themselves as learners. Affective goals also relate to the development of responsibility, consideration, empathy, respect for others, self-confidence, motivation, and self-regulation. Some researchers, teachers, and parents believe that affective goals are just as important as cognitive goals, although they seldom hold the same prominence in school curriculums (Guskey & Anderman, 2008). Affective goals tend to be emphasized more in elementary grades than in secondary grades, and student report cards at the elementary level often include teachers' evaluations of students' achievement of specific affective goals (Guskey & Bailey, 2010).

Psychomotor learning goals (Simpson, 1966) typically require student performances or demonstrations of specific skills or behaviors. In certain technical fields, like the performing arts and physical education, these skills and behaviors are the focus of instruction and a vital aspect of student achievement. In other instances psychomotor

goals involve student learning behaviors such as participation or engagement, attendance, persistence, punctuality, work habits, and effort. The life activities in the Japanese curriculum described earlier reflect largely psychomotor goals.

Relations among Domains. Over the years researchers have debated the relations among the cognitive, affective, and psychomotor domains. Studies consistently yield positive but moderate correlations among measures of student achievement in each domain (e.g., Knuver & Brandsma, 1993), but cause-and-effect relations have been difficult to confirm. Some researchers consider affective and psychomotor goals to be "enabling" traits or behaviors that facilitate student achievement of cognitive outcomes (McMillan, 2001). Students with interest in the content, confidence in their ability to learn, and who actively engage in instructional activities, for example, tend to perform well on associated cognitive tasks. Other researchers contend, however, that cognitive results prompt affective and psychomotor responses. Students who succeed on cognitive tasks tend to like the content, experience increased confidence, and are more likely to engage in subsequent, related learning experiences (Creemers, & Kyriakides, 2010). Significant differences among students in these relations are also known to exist. The best that can be said, therefore, is that measures of student achievement in these three domains tend to be moderately related, and those relations appear to be reciprocal.

Attainment versus Improvement. Further complicating efforts to define "student achievement" is the distinction between "attainment" and "improvement." "Attainment" describes students' level of achievement at a particular point in time. It provides a time-specific snapshot of what students have accomplished. Individual measures of attainment may be interpreted in comparison to the performance on the same items or tasks of a large, normative group of students who are similar in age or at the same grade level. When we say that a student is "on grade level" or "scored at the 60th percentile," we are making these kinds of "norm-referenced" comparisons. Attainment measures also may be described in terms of the particular learning criteria that students have met at a grade level or in a specific course of study. Such "criterion-referenced" comparisons are use when we say that a student has "reached proficiency" or has "met grade level expectations." Attainment measures provided the basis for accountability in the U.S. No Child Left Behind Act, which required schools to record the percent of students in various subgroups at each grade level that reached a predetermined level of proficiency on state assessments.

"Improvement" describes what a student or group of students gain as a result of their learning experiences in school. Because it is based on documented change in performance, "improvement" requires two, parallel or "linked" measures of student learning: one administered at the beginning of an instructional sequence and another at the end. Measures of improvement provide the basis for "growth trajectories" in education and "value-added" models of accountability (Martineau, 2010; see also, Harris, 2010).

Most educators have assumed that attainment and improvement measures of student achievement would be comparable because both are based on similar assessment results. But the relation between measures of attainment and improvement tends to be quite modest (Weiss, 2008). Certain students might make significant learning progress and improve greatly on measures of their achievement during an academic term, but still not reach the predetermined level of proficiency expected for their grade level or course. Students with learning disabilities and those from disadvantaged backgrounds frequently fall into this category. Other students, especially those with exceptional ability, may attain the same high level of performance on initial and final measures of their achievement but demonstrate little or no improvement. Thus, examining attainment and improvement might yield very different conclusions about what students have achieved.

Instructional Sensitivity. Another factor confounding the way we interpret measures of student achievement is the "instructional sensitivity" of the measurement (Popham, 2007). All tests and assessments are designed for a specific purpose. Some are developed to measure the competence or proficiency students gain as a result of their learning experiences in school. Such "instructionally sensitive" assessments must be well aligned with established learning goals in order to provide evidence of the effectiveness of instructional activities. As the quality of instruction improves, measures of student achievement based on "instructionally sensitive" assessments also would be expected to improve. Having many students do well on such an assessment is a good thing. It shows that the instruction was effective and succeeded in having lots of students learn well.

Other measures of student achievement are designed for selection purposes. College entrance exams such as the ACT and SAT, for example, help colleges and universities decide whom to admit. Some standardized assessments similarly help educators identify and sort students into various educational programs or tracks. Having many students do well on a selection assessment is not so good. Instead, such measures of student achievement must yield widely varied scores that separate students and allow for clear ranking in order to make the selection process easier.

To serve these different purposes, proficiency and selection assessments include different types of items or tasks. Proficiency assessments contain items related to the most essential knowledge and skills that all competent students would be expected to answer correctly. Selection assessments, on the other hand, cannot include items that all or nearly all students answer correctly, regardless of their importance. Such items do not discriminate among students and make ranking more difficult. For this reason, tests like the ACT and SAT are labeled "instructionally

insensitive." If instruction helps most students answer an item correctly or perform a task well, then that item or task is eliminated from the assessment, for it no longer serves its purpose.

This is why results from selection assessments tend to be more strongly related to social and economic factors than are those from proficiency assessments (Barton & Coley, 2009). Aspects other than those influenced by instruction often account for the differences among students. It is also why it makes little sense to use an "instructionally insensitive," selection assessment like the ACT or SAT as a measure of the quality of instructional programs. Doing so would be analogous to using a ruler to measure a person's weight. The most meaningful results from purposeful instructional programs always come from "instructionally sensitive" measures.

Conclusion

Student achievement is a multifaceted construct that can address different domains of learning, often measured in many different ways, and for distinctly different purposes. To ensure the accuracy and validity of statements made about student achievement, therefore, researchers must be specific in the way they describe this important construct. In particular, they must identify the domain of the learning goals involved and the way student achievement is determined (e.g., attainment vs. improvement). In addition, they must include detailed information about the breadth, the depth, and the purpose (instructional sensitivity) of the instruments used to measure student achievement. All of these factors bear on interpretations of student achievement results.

Researchers also must be mindful of the critical balance between accuracy and efficiency when interpreting measures of student achievement. In many instances, for example, measures of student achievement are based on students' responses to multiple-choice items because they offer a fast and easy way to gather reliable information on a broad array of learning outcomes. Although performance-based items and tasks that require critical thinking, analysis, and synthesis are considered superior, especially in measuring these higher-order learning goals, they are also more costly and time-consuming to create, maintain, and score (Robelen, 2009).

Finally, policy makers, legislators, school leaders, teachers, parents, and researchers alike must recognize that students' scores on tests and assessments are "indicators" of achievement, and that these indicators are only as accurate as the measures themselves. All measures include some degree of error, both random and systematic. Therefore, decisions made about students, teachers, or schools based on measures of student achievement must always be made with caution, taking into account the fallibility of the measure or measures. The higher the stakes involved and the greater the consequences of these decisions, the more caution and care are required.

References

Barton, P. E., & Coley, R. J. (2009). *Parsing the achievement gap* (Vol. 2). Princeton, NJ: Policy Information Center, Educational Testing Service. http://www.ets.org/Media/Research/pdf/PICPARSINGII.pdf

Bloom, B. S., Englehart, M. D., Furst, E. J., Hill, W. H., & Krathwohl, D. R. (1956). *Taxonomy of educational objectives: Handbook 1. The cognitive domain.* New York: McKay.

Council of Chief State School Officers & National Governors Association, Center for Best Practices. (2010). *Common core state standards initiative.* Washington, DC: Author. Retrieved from http://www.corestandards.org/the-standards

Creemers, B., & Kyriakides, L. (2010). School factors explaining achievement on cognitive and affective outcomes: Establishing a dynamic model of educational effectiveness. *Scandinavian Journal of Educational Research, 54*(3), 263–294.

Duffrin, E. (1998, September). Math teaching in U.S. "inch deep, mile wide." *Catalyst, 10*(1). Retrieved from http://www.catalyst-chicago.org/arch/09-98/098toc.htm

Guskey, T. R. (2007). Multiple sources of evidence: An analysis of stakeholders' perceptions of various indicators of student learning. *Educational Measurement: Issues and Practice, 26*(1), 19–27.

Guskey, T. R., & Anderman, E. M. (2008). Students at bat. *Educational Leadership, 66*(3), 8–14.

Guskey, T. R., & Bailey, J. M. (2010). Developing standards-based report cards. Thousand Oaks, CA: Corwin.

Harris, D. N. (2010). Clear away the smoke and mirrors of value-added. *Phi Delta Kappan, 91*(8), 66–69.

Knuver, A. W. M., & Brandsma, H. (1993). Cognitive and affective outcomes in school effectiveness research. *School Effectiveness and School Improvement, 3*, 189–204.

Krathwohl, D. R., Bloom, B. S., & Masia, B. B. (1964). *Taxonomy of educational objectives: Handbook 2. The affective domain.* New York: McKay.

Larson, L. C., & Miller, T. N. (2011). 21st century skills: Prepare students for the future. *Kappa Delta Pi Record, 47*(3), 121–123.

Martineau, J. A. (2010). The validity of value-added models. *Phi Delta Kappan, 91*(7), 64–67.

McMillan, J. H. (2001). Secondary teachers' classroom assessment and grading practices. *Educational Measurement: Issues and Practice, 20*(1), 20–32.

Ministerial Council on Education, Employment, Training and Youth Affairs. (2006). *Assessing student achievement in Australia.* Canberra ACT, Australia: Author. Retrieved from http://www.mceetya.edu.au/verve/_resources/Assess_student_achievement.pdf

Popham, J. W. (2007). Instructional insensitivity of tests: Accountability's dire drawback. *Phi Delta Kappan, 89*(2), 146–150.

Robelen, E. W. (2009, October 6). Budget woes putting squeeze on state testing, GAO reports. *Education Week.* Retrieved from http://www.edweek.org/ew/articles/2009/10/06/07gao_ep.h29.html

Simpson, E. J. (1966). *The classification of educational objectives: Psychomotor domain.* Urbana: University of Illinois.

Sireci, S. G. (1998). Gathering and analyzing content validity data. *Educational Assessment, 5*(4), 299–321.

Weiss, M. J. (2008, March). *Examining the measures used in the federal growth model pilot program.* Paper presented at the annual meeting of the Society for Research on Educational Effectiveness, Washington, DC.

Wu, A. (1999). *The Japanese education system: A case study summary and analysis.* Washington, DC: National Institute on Student Achievement, Curriculum, and Assessment, Office of Educational Research and Improvement, U.S. Department of Education. Retrieved from http://www2.ed.gov/pubs/ResearchToday/98-3038.html

1.2

Academic Achievement

An Elementary School Perspective

ALAN BATES, RENA SHIFFLET, AND MIRANDA LIN
Illinois State University

Introduction

Achievement is the determination of a student's academic competencies in related content areas; abilities necessary to succeed in school and real-world contexts. However, there is some variance as to what is considered academic achievement, how it can be measured, and what may influence this determination at the elementary school level, typically represented by children between the ages of 5 and 11.

Both nationally and internationally, academic achievement is typically measured using a students' grades or standardized test scores; both measures present some unique challenges. Teacher-assigned grades are subjective by nature and can vary at the teacher, school, and district level. An assigned "A" in fifth grade mathematics may be based on higher standards and expectations than a similar grade from another teacher or school. Yet the same letter grade promotes the assumption that the amount and sophistication of mathematical knowledge would be equivalent for both students. While standardized tests utilize the same testing procedures, materials, and scoring methods, they are often rebuked for their inability to assess more complex levels of understanding, as their purpose is to determine the content students know rather than their potential or aptitude for learning. One must also consider that achievement can only be inferred from the test results, since the student's ability to perform the task cannot be directly observed. To address this issue, states like Vermont and Kentucky have explored the use of portfolios as evidence of achievement. However, reliability in scoring made their use impractical as a standardized means of assessing achievement (Wiliam, 2010).

Research Evidence

Children who do well on standardized tests or have a high grade point average (GPA) tend to do well across childhood. On the other hand, low achievement is often associated with dropping out of school. There have been many research studies that have examined student achievement at the elementary level. These studies have focused on predictors of academic achievement as well as various influences such as family, socioeconomic status, community, and school. The different factors associated with academic achievement can be viewed as individual factors including intelligence and motivation or contextual factors such as family and school.

Current international research findings support previous research which states that intelligence is the one of the strongest predictors of academic achievement. Lu, Weber, Spinath, and Shi (2011) examined the predictive ability of intelligence and working memory on academic achievement using a Chinese sample. The results showed that intelligence was a strong predictor of children's academic achievement but working memory, as measured by various sorting and memory tasks, was an even stronger predictor of academic achievement. Laidra, Pullmann, and Allik (2007) also examined the relation between intelligence and academic achievement with 1,400 second, third, and fourth graders in Estonian schools and concluded that intelligence was the best predictor of academic achievement in the elementary school grades.

Other research has examined motivation as an influence on academic achievement, although research at the elementary level is limited. Lu et al. (2011) examined the relation of motivation and academic achievement and found no relation between academic achievement and children's reports on self-perceived ability and intrinsic values. However, Matthews, Ponitz, and Morrison (2009) found that elementary school children's ability to self-regulate predicted math achievement over the academic year. Related to self-regulation is children's ability to pay attention. Rudasill, Gallagher, and White (2010) found that children whose parents rated them higher in attention at 4.5 years of age possessed higher reading and mathematics achievement in third grade.

Individual differences such as intelligence, motivation, and self-regulation may be important predictors of academic achievement; however, other research shows that academic achievement is difficult to separate from children's home environment, school, and community. There is a direct link between a community's sense of cohesiveness in regards to the efficacy and socialization of children and the academic experience of those children in that community. Children who live in neighborhoods with high expectations for educational attainment tend to have higher passing rates for both math and reading (Emory, Caughy, Harris, & Franzini, 2008). Another study found a link between academic achievement and violence experienced by children (Baker-Henningham, Meeks-Gardner, Chang, & Walker, 2009). Using a sample of 1,300 fifth graders in Jamaica, the authors found that children who encountered high levels of violence had the lowest academic achievement and that children encountering moderate levels of violence had lower achievement than those children who encountered little or no violence.

Parents also can have a strong influence on children's academic achievement by being involved in their children's education. Parental involvement activities, such as volunteering at school; helping children with their homework; attending school functions; visiting the child's classroom; and taking on leadership roles in the school, has been associated with higher math and reading scores (LaRocque, Kleiman, & Darling, 2011). More specifically, instructional interactions in the home can positively influence student achievement (Schlee, Mullis, & Shriner, 2009). For example, children who participate in literacy activities, such as visiting the library and reading frequently in the home displayed higher academic achievement compared to children who did not have those opportunities.

In addition to the effects of the community and parents, schools and teachers play a role in academic achievement. School attendance is associated with student achievement (Pil & Leana, 2009). Students with better attendance are more likely to have higher achievement. Also important to achievement at the elementary school level are the experiences children receive prior to entering that level. In their study of 30 Bangladesh preschools, Aboud and Hossain (2011) found that students who attended one year of preschool (the equivalent of kindergarten in the United States) before entering first and second grades show increased academic achievement in both literacy and mathematics as compared to those students who did not attend preschool. The effects were still significant in second grade mathematics but not literacy. In their comprehensive meta-analysis of preschool enrollment effects in the United States, Camilli, Vargas, Ryan, and Barnett (2010) revealed a positive effect from such experiences on children's cognitive development as measured by achievement test scores. Their analysis also revealed significant lasting benefits although there is an initial decline upon entrance to elementary school.

In regards to curriculum, researchers in British Columbia (Richards, Vining, & Weimer, 2010) and Hong Kong (Lam & Phillipson, 2009) both concluded that teachers who are sensitive to children's needs, and who also provide different avenues for students to understand the materials/content, could increase academic achievement in low-achieving students. Elementary schools should also consider the importance of physical fitness to academic achievement as many studies demonstrate a relation between the two. For example, results of one study of close to 4,000 elementary aged students in an urban city in the United States indicated strong relations between physical fitness and academic achievement (Chomitz et al., 2009). Students who did well on physical fitness tests also scored high on mathematics and reading achievement tests.

Teachers have also been found to influence academic achievement. Myrberg (2007) found positive effects of teacher competence on third graders' reading achievement in Sweden. Furthermore, students display higher achievement when their teachers have adequate education, not just in terms of pedagogical knowledge, but in regards to their knowledge of learners. In the United States, Pil and Leana (2009) propose that teachers' teaching experience that is specific to the setting (years teaching the same grade level) and task (ability to teach a subject) have a positive effect on children's academic achievement. Their findings also suggest that teachers who work closely with colleagues have children who perform better. In their study of third graders in the United States, Rudasill et al. (2010) examined the effect of emotional support that teachers provide on children's academic achievement. Emotional support included teacher attachment, classroom climate, productive use of instructional time, and teacher sensitivity. The authors found that the higher levels of emotional support in the third grade classroom were related to children's higher reading and mathematics achievement. In addition, research shows that teachers' participation in professional development can have an effect on students' achievement. Wallace (2009) analyzed data from six databases, which included math and reading scores of students as well as professional development hours completed by teachers, to examine the effect of professional development on students' academic achievement. She found that professional development had small but significant effects on student achievement, with the highest effect in the area of reading. This finding is also supported by Jarrett, Evans, Dai, Williams, and Rogers (2010) who found that second and third graders' reading achievement was increased partially as a result of the high level of professional development required by teachers in a professional development school.

Summary and Recommendations

The literature has revealed several influential variables that are related to academic achievement. Some factors, such as culturally responsive teaching, teacher professional development, parental education, student motivation, and classroom environment can be controlled or manipulated; while others such as innate ability, community violence, and accessibility to financial support can be more difficult to address. Even the simple level of awareness of the benefits of these factors can work to initiate improvement of academic achievement. It is also important to note that the variables mentioned above could be influenced by culture or country of origin. Cultures have different values and expectations that are placed on students, parents, and teachers so the effect of the variables may vary based on these cultural expectations.

Although teachers have limited influence on students' intelligence, teachers can play a strong role in developing students' working memory by providing opportunities for rehearsal, mnemonic devices, and other techniques to take maximum of advantage of working memory space to assist with retention of information. Teachers can also help with their student's self-regulation by providing opportunities to make choices and to reflect on their thinking.

To enhance academic achievement, teachers should strive to provide a positive learning environment that is respectful, caring, safe, and sensitive to children's academic and emotional needs. In order to be culturally responsive, teachers need to make sure the curriculum content reflects the cultural, ethnic, linguistic, and gender diversity of their students and society. Teachers should seek professional development to improve their content knowledge as well as instructional strategies. Collaboration between teachers and their colleagues regarding instructional practices should be encouraged and supported by administrators by offering incentives and time.

Teachers should also make a strong effort to involve parents in their child's learning, emphasizing the importance of its effects on academic achievement. For example, teachers can encourage parents to take an interest in what their children are doing in school by being involved in their schoolwork, exposing their children to cultural experiences at the local library, museums, theater, and zoo, and inviting them to get involved at classroom or school level. When necessary, teachers can provide information on community resources to assist for parents in need.

There is no doubt that academic achievement is an important consideration during the elementary school years. The suggested recommendations can act as a springboard to enhance current instructional efforts. However, the effect of these recommendations on academic achievement will only be realized through continued efforts, support, and evaluation by all parties involved.

References

Aboud, F. E., & Hossain, K. (2011). The impact of preprimary school on primary school achievement in Bangladesh. *Early Childhood Research Quarterly, 26,* 237–246.

Baker-Henningham, H., Meeks-Gardner, J., Chang, S., & Walker, S. (2009). Experiences of violence and deficits in academic achievement among urban primary school children in Jamaica. *Child Abuse & Neglect, 33,* 296–306.

Camilli, G., Vargas, S., Ryan, S., & Barnett, W.S. (2010). Meta-analysis of the effects of early education interventions on cognitive and social development. *Teachers College Record, 112*(3), 579–620.

Chomitz, V. R., Slining, M. M., McGowan, R. J., Mitchell, S. E., Dawson, G. F., & Hacker, K. A. (2009). Is there a relationship between physical fitness and academic achievement? Positive results from public school children in the Northeastern United States. *Journal of School Health, 79*(1), 30–37.

Emory, R., Caughy, M., Harris, R., & Franzini, L. (2008). Neighborhood social processes and academic achievement in elementary school. *Journal of Community Psychology, 36,* 885–896.

Jarrett, C., Evans, C., Dai, Y., Williams, D., & Rogers, K. (2010). Effect of specialized in-service professional development activities on elementary school students' reading achievement. *National Forum of Teacher Education Journal, 20*(3). Retrieved from http://www.eric.ed.gov

Laidra, K., Pullmann, H., & Allik, J. (2007). Personality and intelligence as predictors of academic achievement: A cross-sectional study from elementary to secondary school. *Personality and Individual Differences, 42*(3), 441–551.

Lam, B., & Phillipson, S. (2009). What are the affective and social outcomes for low-achieving students within an inclusive school in Hong Kong? *Educational Research for Policy and Practice, 8,* 135–150.

LaRocque, M., Kleiman, I., & Darling, S. M. (2011). Parental involvement: The missing link in school achievement. *Preventing School Failure: Alternative Education for Children and Youth, 55*(3), 115–122.

Lu, L., Weber, H. S., Spinath, F. M., & Shi, J. (2011). Predicting school achievement from cognitive and non-cognitive variables in a Chinese sample of elementary school children. *Intelligence, 39,* 130–140.

Matthews, J., Ponitz, C., & Morrison, F. (2009). Early gender differences in self-regulation and academic achievement. *Journal of Educational Psychology, 101,* 689–704.

Myrberg, E. (2007). The effect of formal teacher education on reading achievement of 3rd grade students in public and independent schools in Sweden. *Educational Studies, 33,* 145–162.

Pil, F., & Leana, C. (2009). Applying organizational research to public school reform: The effects of teacher human and social capital on student performance. *Academy of Management Journal, 52,* 1101–1124.

Richards, J., Vining, A., & Weimer, D. (2010). Aboriginal performance on standardized tests: Evidence and analysis from provincial schools in British Columbia. *The Policy Studies Journal, 38,* 47–67.

Rudasill, K. M., Gallagher, K. C., & White, J. M. (2010). Temperamental attention and activity classroom emotional support and academic achievement in third grade. *Journal of School Psychology, 48*(2), 113–134.

Schlee, B., Mullis, A., & Shriner, M. (2009). Parents social and resource capital: Predictors of academic achievement during early childhood. Children and Youth Services Review, *31,* 227–234.

Wallace, M. R. (2009). Making sense of the links: Professional development, teacher practices, and student achievement. *Teachers College Record, 111*(2), 573–596.

Wiliam, D. (2010). What counts as evidence of educational achievement? The role of constructs in the pursuit of equity in assessment. *Review of Research in Education, 34*(1), 254–284.

1.3

Academic Achievement

An Adolescent Perspective

R. TRENT HAINES
Morgan State University

CHRISTIAN E. MUELLER
University of Memphis

Introduction

In recent decades, there has been an increasing worldwide emphasis on adolescents' academic achievement because local and national governments have recognized that high levels of achievement are required for students to become successful in an increasingly competitive global market-place (Carnoy & Rhoten, 2002). As many nations wrestle with the best ways to prepare their students, they often rely on standardized test scores as indicators of student success, which are often compared between nations to determine which students are most prepared and able to compete in the global economy. On a more local level, students, families, and teachers rely on classroom grades to monitor student performance on a regular basis. Although these indicators vary between locales, they are often the types of assessments that are used to determine which students are successful and which are not.

In an ongoing effort to improve student performance, it is important for policy makers, teachers, and parents to understand that adolescence is a period of time when students go through a number of significant developmental changes that subsequently impact their achievement. Whereas government policies can affect adolescent achievement on a macrolevel, the influence of culture, families, and teachers can have an even more important and direct impact (Hill & Tyson, 2009). Within this context, then, our goal is to explain how adolescent growth, development, and achievement are intertwined and how research-driven teacher and parent practices can lead to high levels of achievement among adolescents. We will focus our attention on how the development of adolescents' thought processes can be nurtured to increase achievement, how student interest and engagement contribute to achievement, and how supportive environments can improve academic outcomes even in the face of adverse circumstances. Although the cognitive and social changes we discuss in this chapter are common among adolescents, we believe they are expressed through the lens of culture, which is why we have used examples from around the world to demonstrate how research-driven instructional and social support strategies can impact achievement in different settings.

Research Evidence

Cognitive Development and Instructional Strategies.

Developments in the research literature over the last few decades suggest that the education of adolescents is most successful when they are challenged to think for themselves, to dialogue with their teachers and peers, and to engage in interesting and appropriately challenging course work. Much of the research on effective instructional strategies for adolescents emerged from the theories of French psychologist Jean Piaget and Russian psychologist Lev Vygotsky. For example, Piaget (1972) argued that about the time children enter adolescence, they begin to develop the ability to think more abstractly about real-life and hypothetical ideas. Through a process of absorbing new information and then trying to make sense of it, especially when it runs contrary to information they already possess, adolescents are able to engage in more complex thought processes and develop new insights by working to resolve the discrepancies between two sets of information. Similarly, Vygotsky (1978) argued that adolescents should be challenged by new material and learn best when they are presented with material they cannot yet grasp on their own, but can master with the assistance of someone who is more advanced in understanding. Both perspectives have been manifested in different educational systems around the world, such as in the implementation of student–teacher dialogues in some Ugandan biology classrooms (Mutonyi, Nashon, & Nielsen, 2010).

In Uganda, students and teachers typically follow a traditional lecture format whereby teachers are viewed as having the ultimate authority and are afforded a great deal of respect, which often results in passive student participation in the classroom. In this project, however, adolescent students were encouraged to dialogue with their teachers and peers in order to construct a more complex understanding of HIV transmission that did not rely solely on messages communicated through the media and social interactions. As a result, the students were able to integrate new scientific knowledge with cultural, religious, and political perspectives they had previously come to accept. Through this process, the students maintained their traditional values by respecting their teachers as authority figures who provide educational guidance while simultaneously interacting with their peers to resolve discrepancies between their prior beliefs and new information (Mutonyi et al., 2010).

In a similar example, students in the United Kingdom have been encouraged to debate and form a more detailed understanding of British history. The teacher in a study by Deaney, Chapman, and Hennessy (2009) encouraged early adolescent students to develop historical thinking processes by encouraging collaborative activities within the classroom setting. Students formed interdependent learning relationships with their peers as they worked together to annotate historical images and corresponding texts that described critical events in British history. In addition to forming peer relationships, the students learned from their teacher, who modeled the types of thinking processes that were desired and provided ongoing support in the collaborative process. Many researchers (e.g., Fisher, Frey, & Lapp, 2011; Mayer & Tucker, 2010) have found that the types of instructional strategies found in the studies from Uganda and the United Kingdom, such as student–teacher interactions, group work, teacher modeling, and scaffolding, are effective approaches to enhance achievement among adolescents because they draw upon developing cognitive abilities.

Student Interest and Engagement. Similarly, authentic learning activities that involve creativity, group work, and student interaction often lead to heightened student interest and engagement (Certo, Cauley, Moxley, & Chafin, 2008), which have been shown to increase student performance (Wang & Holcombe, 2010) by increasing adolescents' motivations to achieve in the classroom. In a recent study on instructional strategies in Korean classrooms, for example, House (2009) found that eighth grade students who conducted their own research activities and watched their teachers demonstrate science experiments were more engaged with the material and achieved at higher levels than students who reported that they only listened to lectures about course content. In Sweden, school officials have adopted a different approach in which they require adolescents to develop their own course of study that is based on individual academic interests. This effort to maximize adolescents' interest in

education has resulted in students who perceive themselves as having higher levels of autonomy and personal control (Nordgren, 2002). Just as the previous examples demonstrated that student–teacher interaction, scaffolding, and engagement are important, these types of authentic learning activities and a sense of autonomy often lead to higher levels of achievement among adolescents (Ross & Broh, 2000).

Parental and Teacher Support. Outside the classroom, parents can have a great deal of influence on achievement by remaining involved in adolescents' academic pursuits. Based on the work of Baumrind (1971), researchers have shown that parental involvement in their adolescents' education is an important predictor of high academic achievement. For example, among Latino immigrants in the United States, adolescents were more likely to achieve in school when they shared their parents' emphasis on academic success (Fuligni & Fuligni, 2007) and when they felt supported by their parents (Coatsworth, Pantin, & Szapocznik, 2002). Despite a common emphasis on achievement, however, there are times when adolescents also feel an obligation to spend more time helping with household duties than studying and completing homework, especially in some immigrant Latino and Asian communities (Telzer & Fuligni, 2009). In order to help students balance both familial and individual needs, parents and teachers can work together by providing flexible workloads and deadlines as well as time and space that allow students to focus on their school work (Kao & Tienda, 1995). Although some parents do not have the knowledge required to help their adolescents with homework or other study habits, they can remain involved in adolescents' academic lives by maintaining a supportive attitude toward school work and showing interest in adolescents' educational activities. Even when adolescents do not perform as expected, parents' academic support produces better results than attempts to control behavior through restrictive or harsh disciplinary actions, which have been shown to decrease student motivation and achievement (Duchesne & Ratelle, 2010). Collectively, this research reflects the important roles parents and teachers have as they guide and support adolescents who continue to develop the skills they need to achieve at high levels.

Summary and Recommendations

Research findings overwhelmingly suggest that both parents and teachers play crucial roles in enhancing academic achievement during adolescence and that achievement is influenced by developmentally appropriate and culturally relevant instruction and support. Parents and teachers should work together to communicate and foster high expectations about the value and utility of educational achievement, while at the same time allowing adolescents to take an increasingly active role in guiding their own academic paths. At home, parents should relate school work to real-world pursuits, provide time and support for academic endeavors, and help adolescents as they plan for their futures. In the classroom, teachers should hold high expectations for students, provide choices when appropriate, and foster collaborative interactions and engagement to increase achievement. Combined, these approaches have been shown to have a profound impact on adolescent academic achievement. Similarly, local, national, and international educational systems and policies need to reflect that education and achievement in the 21st century should increasingly prepare students to think creatively, become their own problems solvers, and work cooperatively within an increasingly diverse global society (Nordgren, 2002).

References

Baumrind, D. (1971). Current patterns of parental authority. *Developmental Psychology Monographs, 4*, 1–102.

Carnoy, M., & Rhoten, D. (2002). What does globalization mean for educational change? A comparative approach. *Comparative Education Review, 46*(1), 1–9.

Certo, J. L., Cauley, K. M., Moxley, K. D., & Chafin, C. (2008). An argument for authenticity: Adolescents' perspectives on standards-based reform. *The High School Journal, 91*(4), 26–39.

Coatsworth, J. D., Pantin, H., & Szapocznik, J. (2002). Familias Unidas: A family-centered ecodevelopmental intervention to reduce risk for problem behavior among Hispanic adolescents. *Clinical Child and Family Psychology Review, 5*, 113–132.

Deaney, R., Chapman, A., & Hennessy, S. (2009). A case-study of one teacher's use of an interactive whiteboard system to support knowledge co-construction in the history classroom. *The Curriculum Journal, 20*, 365–387.

Duchesne, S., & Ratelle, C. (2010). Parental behaviors and adolescents' achievement goals at the beginning of middle school: Emotional problems as potential mediators. *Journal of Educational Psychology, 102*, 497–507.

Fisher, D., Frey, N., & Lapp, D. (2011). Focusing on the participation and engagement gap: A case study on closing the achievement gap. *Journal of Education for Students Placed at Risk, 16*, 56–64.

Fuligni, A. J., & Fuligni, A. S. (2007). Immigrant families and the educational development of their children. In J. E. Lansford, K. Deater-Deckard, & M. H. Bornstein (Eds.), *Immigrant families in contemporary society* (pp. 231–249). New York: Guilford.

Hill, N. E., & Tyson, D. F. (2009). Parental involvement in middle school: A meta-analytic assessment of the strategies that promote achievement. *Developmental Psychology, 45*(3), 740–763.

House, J. D. (2009). Classroom instructional strategies and science career interest for adolescent students in Korea: Results from the TIMSS 2003 assessment. *Journal of Instructional Psychology, 36*, 13–19.

Kao, G., & Tienda, M. (1995). Optimism and achievement: The educational performance of immigrant youth. *Social Science Quarterly, 76*(1), 1–19.

Mayer, A. P., & Tucker, S. K. (2010). Cultivating students of color: Strategies for ensuring high academic achievement in middle and secondary schools. *Journal of School Leadership, 20*, 470–490.

Mutonyi, H., Nashon, S., & Nielsen, W. S. (2010). Perceptual influence of Ugandan biology students' understanding of HIV/AIDS. *Research in Science Education, 40*, 573–588.

Nordgren, R. D. (2002). Globalization and education: What students will need to know and be able to do in the global village. *The Phi Delta Kappan, 84*(4), 318–321.

Piaget, J. (1972). *The psychology of the child*. New York: Basic Books.

Ross, C. E., & Broh, B. A. (2000). The roles of self-esteem and the sense of personal control in the academic achievement process. *Sociology of Education, 73*, 270–284.

Telzer, E. H., & Fuligni, A. J. (2009). A longitudinal daily diary study of family assistance and academic achievement among adolescents from Mexican, Chinese, and European backgrounds. *Journal of Youth and Adolescence, 38*, 560–571.

Vygotsky, L. S. (1978). *Mind in society: The development of higher psychological processes*. Cambridge, MA: Harvard University Press.

Wang, M., & Holcombe, R. (2010). Adolescents' perceptions of school environment, engagement, and academic achievement in middle school. *American Educational Research Journal, 47*, 633–662.

1.4

Adult Education and Achievement

M Cecil Smith
Northern Illinois University

Introduction

Adult education is a worldwide phenomenon. It encompasses a broad range of learner activities, educational programs and institutions, and populations. Adult education includes all manner and types of adult learners, including those persons who are seeking to

- develop literacy skills in adult basic literacy education (ABE) programs;
- earn a high school equivalency diploma through general educational development (GED) test programs (in the United States) or similar secondary education equivalencies in other countries;
- participate in informal (and, often, self-directed) learning programs offered by educational institutions or community organizations that provide lessons on a variety of topics or skills covering a broad range of vocational interests and pastimes (e.g., gardening; sailing);
- obtain vocational training or credentials for entry into or advancement within specific occupations (e.g., cosmetology; radiology technology);
- earn a college degree; or
- achieve advanced degrees in fields ranging from law and medicine to nanoscience.

Clearly, then, adult education is a diverse and complex enterprise. It has been characterized as an "open system" (Knowles, 1962) that must be responsive to rapidly changing social needs.

Adult education occurs in settings that include career training and technical schools, the workplace and military installations, proprietary schools, prisons, hospitals and clinics, and both public and private higher education institutions, including 2- and 4-year colleges and universities. Other settings for adult education include cultural institutions such as churches and community centers, museums and libraries, and parks and zoos (E. W. Taylor, Parrish, &

Banz, 2010). Although these public or private cultural and educational institutions have broadly recognized standards for learning and achievement, it should not be inferred that these are the only settings where adult education can be obtained or where academic achievement is valued.

Adults seeking further education are not always motivated by academic goals and achievements, such as grades or diplomas, however. Adult education is also often informal and unstructured with no set curriculum, and desired learner outcomes may not be clearly specified. Whereas adult education may nonetheless be pursued within the confines of formal institutions, such as universities, public libraries, or museums, it may also be taken up privately by individuals or groups without any obvious connection to an educational or cultural institution. In these and other situations, it is largely up to individual adult learners (sometimes in consultation with their teachers or mentors) to determine how and to what extent they have "achieved" some level of knowledge or skill. Thus, the task of describing what academic achievement means in the context of adult education is daunting.

In formal education institutions, however, adult learners' academic achievement is typically defined and determined by indicators such as course grades and accumulated grade point average (GPA), and the earning of diplomas or degrees, certificates, vocational licenses, or other such education credentials. A somewhat narrower view of achievement localizes on standardized (norm-referenced) test scores within specific disciplines of study. Achievement in many educational contexts, including adult education, is synonymous with academic learning, but broadly speaking academic accomplishments may also pertain to growth in individual learners' cognitive abilities, skill development (physical and/or social), or affect (attitudes and values).

Other, broader approaches to determining achievement in adult education indicate students' success in making a successful transition to higher (postsecondary) education, and their abilities to transfer what they have learned in the classroom to other settings and situations (i.e., the workplace). Both transition and transfer are related to the concept of return-on-investment (ROI), an economic indicator of educational achievement. ROI compares the "costs" (direct or indirect, fixed or variable, short- or long-term) to various entities, including individual students, employers, educational institutions, or the state, and the "benefits" of educational programming, such as increased skills and knowledge, greater self-confidence, and increased employability for individuals, more skilled workers for employers, and increased tax revenues for the state, as better-skilled workers are paid higher wages.

Research Evidence

Data on adults' academic achievement in adult education settings is difficult to ascertain due to the great diversity of institutions that provide educational programs for adults, and lack of consensus about what sorts of data are indicative of such achievement. The U.S. National Center for Education Statistics (NCES) is the data-gathering arm of the U.S. Department of Education. NCES reported that approximately 57% of first-time, full-time students seeking a bachelor's degree or its equivalent who were attending 4-year higher education institutions in 2001 to 2002 had completed a bachelor's degree or its equivalent at that same institution in 6 years or less (U.S. Department of Education, 2010). In addition to higher education achievement, NCES also reports on the "participation" of adults, ages 16 and older, in various adult education programs (e.g., adult basic education and GED classes, work-related courses, and personal interest courses). The Department of Education tracks adults' literacy proficiencies (i.e., reading prose, documents, and materials with quantitative information) as an "outcome" that is loosely related to educational attainment. In general, adults having more education outperform those with less education on literacy measures (NCES, 2005). International comparisons show that U.S. adults' literacy skills lag slightly below that of several other industrialized nations.

Achievement is often indexed in terms of degree completion. Here, census data indicate that, in the United States, 84.5% of the adult population, ages 25 years and older, had earned a high school diploma or equivalency, 54.4% had earned some college credits, 27.5% held a bachelor's degree, and 10.1% had attained an advanced degree (U.S. Bureau of the Census, 2009). Internationally, one-third (33%) of young adults, ages 25 to 34, have attained tertiary (postsecondary) education among 38 Organization for Economic Co-Operation and Development (OECD) countries (OECD, 2010a,b), although the attainment rate varies considerably by country. Data on adult education participation in most Third World nations (i.e., many parts of Africa and South-Central Asia) is lacking.

The U.S. government considers postsecondary education students who are enrolled in college or graduate school to be "adult learners." Of the 18.5 million adults so enrolled in 2008, 12% were part-time attendees at 2-year institutions

(community colleges) and 17% were part-time attendees at 4-year schools. Enrollment figures for the broad range of other types of adult education programs throughout the United States are more difficult to obtain. However, in 2007, there were 2.3 million adults enrolled in state-administered adult basic education, adult secondary education (GED), and English as a Second Language programs. No achievement or other outcome data are available for these students. There were 13.3 million employed persons, ages 17 years and older, participating in various career-related adult education courses or programs in 2005. In 2003 (the latest year for which data are available), 22.7% of the participants in formal work-related courses received a certificate (e.g., continuing education credits) to earn or retain a state or industry certificate or license for their occupation. All data were reported by the U.S. National Center for Education Statistics.

Adult education systems vary greatly from one country to another; thus, comparisons regarding adult learners' participation, performance, and achievement in adult basic education programs are difficult. The OECD provides the best available data on adult education participation in 34 countries, including the United States, Canada, the United Kingdom and 23 European nations, Australia, Israel, and Turkey, among others. According to OECD's 2010 Indicators on Education, 29% of adults in OECD countries have attained education that is below the upper secondary (i.e., high school) level. Presumably, a significant portion of these adults will be likely to pursue adult basic literacy education at some point in their lives to improve their literacy skills (and obtain better paying work). The OECD reports that, on average, 28% of adults have attained tertiary (i.e., postsecondary) education in OECD nations.

Transition from Adult Basic Education to Higher Education. Earning a high school equivalency diploma (GED) enables adults who choose to do so to enter college or other tertiary education or training programs. Many adult basic education programs in the United States, including GED, provide services (e.g., academic and financial counseling) to assist adult learners in their transition to higher education—an educational passage that is difficult for many academically underprepared students (Zafft, Kallenbach, & Spohn, 2006). Despite having earned a high school equivalency diploma, many adult learners may not have the necessary literacy skills to be successful in college. In the United States, for example, less than 2% of GED recipients enter 4-year colleges and universities, although of those who do, 40% have earned a degree or are still enrolled and pursuing a degree 5 years after matriculating (Reder, 2000).

Return on Investment. Return on investment (ROI) studies consistently demonstrate the economic benefits of greater educational attainment for adults (McLendon, Jones, & Rosin, 2011). Simply put, better educated adults earn more than do less educated ones. Data from the U.S. Census Bureau (2009) show, for example, that adults ages

25 and older with less than a high school diploma earned, in 2008, a median annual income = ~$20,000, whereas those with a high school degree earned ~$29,000. Those with some college experience, an associate or technical degree earned ~$37,000, whereas college graduates earned a median income = ~$52,000. In Europe, one additional year of education yields an average 8% wage increase, according to an analysis by London Economics (2005).

Transfer of Learning from Classroom to Workplace. Transfer of learning from school to work is a component of ROI (M. Taylor, 1998). Being able to take what one has learned in the classroom and apply this knowledge to life outside of the classroom or training situation is important to being a more competent individual, an effective parent, a capable worker, and a participating citizen. In the context of work, transfer of learning occurs when individuals can apply the skills and knowledge gained from an educational or training program to their jobs (Broad, 1997). Studies show, however, that the transfer of knowledge and skills is frequently difficult to accomplish (Driscoll, 2005). The transfer of skills and knowledge is accomplished more easily when tasks and situations are similar between classroom and workplace than when they are very different from one another. Learner characteristics (i.e., motivation), the design and goals of the instructional training program, and the work environment (i.e., degree of supervisory support) all interact to determine the degree to which transfer occurs (Merriam & Leahy, 2005). Instructional practices in adult education that incorporate real-world learning, simulations, feedback, and apprenticeships, among other activities, may promote learners' abilities to transfer what they have learned.

Summary and Recommendations

Academic achievement in adult education means different things to different people. There are numerous ways to think about and measure adult education achievement. In general, particularly in higher education, academic achievement is indicated by course grades and earned degrees. The abilities of adult learners to successfully transition from one level of education to another, their skill at transferring what they have learned in the classroom to the workplace, and the rate of return on the individual's, the employer's, or society's investment in adult education are other important indicators of achievement. Thus, any effort to standardize "achievement" in the context of adult education should be avoided.

The richness, variety, and complexity of adult education cannot be meaningfully reduced to simple formulas, letter grades, or economic indicators.

References

Broad, M. (1997). *Transferring learning to the workplace.* Alexandria, VA: American Society for Training and Development.

Driscoll, M. (2005). *Psychology of learning for instruction* (3rd ed.). Needham Heights, MA: Allyn & Bacon.

Knowles, M. (1962). *The adult education movement in the United States.* Boston, MA: Holt, Rinehart & Winston.

London Economics. (2005, December). *Study on "The returns to various types of investments in education and training": Final report.* European Commission, Director General Education and Culture. Retrieved from http://ec.europa.eu/education/policies/2010/studies/invest05_en.pdf.

McLendon, L., Jones, D., & Rosin, M. (2011). *The return on investment (ROI) from adult education and training: Measuring the impact of a better educated and trained U.S. workforce.* Boston, MA: McGraw-Hill Research Foundation. Retrieved from http://www.mcgraw-hillresearchfoundation.org/roi-adult-ed-and-training.

Merriam, S. B., & Leahy, B. (2005). Learning transfer: A review of the research in adult education and training. *PAACE Journal of Lifelong Learning, 14,* 1–24.

National Center for Education Statistics. (2005). *National assessment of adult literacy* (NAAL). Washington, DC: NCES. Retrieved from http://nces.ed.gov/naal/.

Organization for Economic Co-operation and Development (2010a). *Education at a glance: OECD indicators 2008.* Paris: Author.

Organization for Economic Co-operation and Development (OECD). (2010b). *Education at a glance: OECD indicators 2010.* Paris: Author.

Reder, S. (2000). Adult literacy and postsecondary education students: Overlapping populations and learning trajectories. In J. Comings, B. Garner, & C. Smith (Eds.), *Annual review of adult learning and literacy* (Vol. 1, pp. 111–157). San Francisco, CA: Jossey-Bass.

Taylor, E. W., Parrish, M. M., & Banz, R. (2010). Adult education in cultural institutions. In C. E. Kasworm, A. D. Rose, & J. M. Ross-Gordon (Eds.), *Handbook of adult and continuing education* (pp. 219–231). Los Angeles, CA: Sage.

Taylor, M. (1998). *Partners in transfer of learning: A resource manual for workplace literacy instructors.* Ottawa, ON: Partnership in Learning.

U.S. Bureau of the Census. (2009, January). *Educational attainment in the United States: 2007. Population characteristics.* Washington, DC: U.S. Department of Commerce. Retrieved from http://www.census.gov/prod/2009pubs/p20-560.pdf.

U.S. Department of Education. (2010). *The condition of education 2010* (NCES 2010-028). Washington, DC: National Center for Education Statistics.

Women's Funding Network. (2011). *Securing access to education.* Retrieved from http://www.womensfundingnetwork.org/impact/education.

Zafft, C., Kallenbach, S., & Spohn, J. (2006, December). *Transitioning adults to college: Adult basic education program models* (NCSALL Occasional Paper). Cambridge, MA: National Center for the Study of Adult Learning and Literacy.

1.5

Academic Achievement

A Higher Education Perspective

TERRELL L. STRAYHORN
Ohio State University

Introduction

Democratic systems of higher education, like the one found in North America, espouse an abiding, and oftentimes public, commitment to access and equity. Such deeply held beliefs are reflected in the diversity of institutions, the heterogeneity of mission statements, as well as the radically egalitarian policies that distinguish such countries from their peers, one of which is equal opportunity in education (Thelin, 2004).

Strictly interpreted, equal opportunity in education refers to granting the same type and level of access to higher education for all people. Countries like the United States and Great Britain, for instance, pride themselves on taking all necessary steps to ensure that virtually anyone who desires access to higher education is afforded an opportunity to pursue a college degree. This has not always been the case. "In 1955, one half of the nation's colleges and universities had some type of selective admissions policies in place"; but today, very few do so (Lucas, 1994, p. 290). Other countries, such as Ireland, South Korea, and Portugal, operate hierarchical systems of education that offer increasingly fewer persons an opportunity to ascend to higher levels. Typically, high achievement on rigorous "exit" exams, which are taken during and upon graduation from secondary school, determine one's odds for accessing higher education in such contexts.

There can be no question that higher education plays an essential role in global society. Benefits that flow from higher education include, but are not limited to, generating new and testing existing knowledge, transferring cultural norms and expectations to society's youth, and inciting innovation that may likely lead to new solutions for perennial problems (Thelin, 2004). Consequently, a college education, in most countries, is a prerequisite for positions in business and high-status professions. Individuals who complete a bachelor's degree earn about 62% more per year than their counterparts with a high school diploma (Baum & Payea,

2004). And decades of empirical evidence demonstrate that earning a college degree is, in part, a function of academic achievement.

Intuitively, the relation between academic achievement and attainment[1] of a college degree makes sense. That is, students who earn good grades in college are more likely to maintain good standing according to academic standards set by most universities (Strayhorn, 2010). Those who remain in good standing are generally eligible to remain enrolled semester to semester, year to year—generally referred to as retention in the literature. Students who fail to meet academic standards, however, may be dismissed involuntarily, although academic dismissals represent only 15 to 20% of all institutional departures. There are other nuances to academic achievement in higher education that deserve clarification.

Academic Achievement Defined in Higher Education. Academic achievement is one term with several meanings in the extant literature on postsecondary education. The concept has eluded precise definitions for centuries, especially since there are no national or international standards for academic achievement in higher education (Guskey, Entry 1.1 this volume; Lucas, 1994). To some, academic achievement is in obvious contrast with academic failure. To others, academic achievement is closely related to grades or test performance, typically measured by one's cumulative grade point average (GPA) or scores on standardized achievement tests such as the SAT or ACT (Kuh & Hu, 1999). Still, another conception of academic achievement in higher education is defined as mastery of subject matter (i.e., learning) or persistence, which generally refers to the length of time a student remains enrolled at an institution in pursuit of a college degree (Braxton, 2000). Whether measured in GPA, SAT score, perceived learning gains, or retention status, increasing academic achievement among all students is critically important for those of us charged with supporting and enabling the success of students in higher education. A significant, and growing, line of inquiry provides empirical support for the impact of college on student success, as well as the determinants of college students' academic achievement (e.g., Astin, 1993; Pascarella & Terenzini, 2005). It is toward this body of research that the next section turns.

Research Evidence

Astin (1993) noted that academic achievement is the most widely researched among all college outcomes. Academic achievement in higher education has been investigated using various predictors, including precollege characteristics, traditional assessments of one's cognitive abilities, and a battery of psychological and noncognitive variables. For instance, the weight of empirical research, to date, focuses on traditional measures such as GPA and aptitude test scores (e.g., Camara & Echternacht, 2000). For instance, Baron and Norman (1992) studied 3,816 undergraduate students at a northeastern university and found that SAT scores contributed to the prediction of students' grades in college. While important, the weight of empirical evidence suggests that traditional indicators of cognitive skills account for less than 25% of the variance when predicting first-year college GPA (Adelman, 1999), thereby providing empirical support for the argument that academic achievement in higher education is determined, in large part, by factors unaccounted for in traditional models.

To investigate the unexplained variance in postsecondary academic achievement, scholars have examined social psychological determinants of college success. There is compelling evidence that the amount of time and quality of effort that students devote to academic tasks positively affects their achievement in college. For example, if we know anything at all, we know that it matters how students use their out-of-class time in college. Research has consistently shown that students who spend more time studying in preparation for class and examinations, engaged in educationally purposeful activities such as faculty–student mentoring, or interacting with individuals whose backgrounds are different from their own, earn higher grades, on average, than those who devote little to no time to such activities (Pike, 1991). Further, we know that "student involvement leads to greater integration into the academic and social systems of college and promotes institutional commitment," which is a strong predictor of retention (Berger & Milem, 1999, p. 644). It's important to note that these findings are generalizable internationally.

For students who may be less well prepared for college or those who do not perform well on standardized tests, psychological determinants may be critical. A segment of existing research indicates that at least three types of psychological variables—self-efficacy, motivation, sense of belonging—can play an important role in academic achievement for higher education students. For example, evidence exists that, at least for some, academic achievement is the result of high levels of self-efficacy in academic-oriented

domains (DeWitz, Woolsey, & Walsh, 2009). Self-efficacy is defined as individuals' confidence in their ability to successfully complete a task. Specifically, Bandura and Locke (2003) explained that "self-efficacy beliefs are rooted in the core beliefs that one has the power to produce desired effects" (p. 87). Interpreted directly, college students with greater self-efficacy in a particular domain of academic functioning (e.g., writing an essay, using a computer, carrying out an experiment) are more likely to approach that activity and complete the task successfully. There is compelling evidence to suggest that these findings are generalizable internationally (Poyrazil, Arbona, Nora, McPherson, & Pisecco, 2002).

Another conceptual framework that has been offered as an alternative to traditional measures of academic achievement is Sedlacek's (2004) noncognitive variables (NCVs). He outlined eight NCVs that relate to academic achievement in higher education: (a) positive self-concept, (b) realistic self-appraisal, (c) understanding of and an ability to deal with racism, (d) preference for long-term goals over more immediate, short-term needs, (e) availability of strong support person, (f) successful leadership experience, and (g) demonstrated community service. These variables are empirically linked to college GPA, retention, and persistence (e.g., Kim & Sedlacek, 1996). Some data suggest that NCVs can be more important than traditional measures (e.g., SAT) in predicting academic achievement among nontraditional undergraduates such as women, athletes, and racial/ethnic minorities. In fact, the weight of empirical evidence, to date, suggests that the effect of social psychological variables on academic achievement in higher education varies depending on students' race and gender, which tend to have moderating effects on grades and subsequent persistence to degree. Relatively little is known about the extent to which these findings are generalizable internationally; for instance, while realistic self-appraisal and self-concept may hold universal relevance, the ability to deal with racism is likely applicable in countries where race plays a major role in shaping students' social relations.

Despite evidence of the salience of these factors, much remains to be learned about the role they play in various campus contexts and whether and how college student educators can draw upon such information to promote high academic achievement among students.

Summary and Recommendations

This chapter was designed to provide researchers and practitioners around the world with state of the art information regarding academic achievement in higher education. To this point, I have provided a short history on academic achievement in postsecondary education, identified how achievement is operationalized in the higher education literature, and summarized what is currently known from research about this important topic. To aide practitioners in the use of this information, I offer the following recommendations for future practice and policy.

A consistent finding from the literature is that academic preparation is the most significant predictor of academic achievement in higher education. Thus, practices and policies that facilitate students' readiness for college are likely to improve student achievement in higher education. Several strategies may be particularly effective in promoting students' preparation for higher, or tertiary, education including, but not limited to, access to rigorous high school curricula, early exposure to advanced math and science courses that nurture one's critical thinking skills, and counseling about college options and student financial aid.

Data reviewed in this chapter suggest that one way to improve student achievement in higher education is to raise students' confidence or self-efficacy toward academic tasks. Thus, efforts to raise academic self-efficacy would seem warranted. Theory suggests four primary ways to raise self-efficacy: mastery experiences, vicarious experiences, verbal persuasion, and emotional states. Simply put, success in a task begets confidence in a domain. Offering students multiple opportunities to utilize their skills to complete successfully an academic task (e.g., homework, test, or experiment) will raise their confidence, which in turn, will likely raise academic achievement. Praise or positive encouragement also goes a long way in improving student performance. There are more formal mechanisms that can be used to enhance achievement in higher education.

Recall that, according to research, the more effort higher education students expend in using the resources and opportunities an institution provides for their learning and development, the more they benefit. Several examples were previously mentioned ranging from time spent studying to faculty-student mentoring. Practitioners should ensure the continued provision of these types of programs, as well as establish new programs that offer students opportunities for meaningful engagement with faculty and peers. Suggested strategies could include living-learning communities (LLCs), peer tutoring partnerships, study abroad, and even first-year seminars, as the first year is the period of time in which students develop the habits of mind on which their subsequent success will depend.

It is certainly true that a few of these strategies may be difficult to mount given the amount of time and resources needed to implement them effectively. Establishing new residence hall configurations (e.g., LLCs) or first-year seminars is hard work, but hard work is no excuse for retreat. Using information from this volume, educators worldwide can take intentional steps toward improving academic achievement in higher education and beyond.

Note

1. In this chapter, "attainment" refers to the goal of completing one's degree, while "persistence" refers to the continuous enrollment that leads to graduation (Braxton, 2000).

References

Adelman, C. (1999). *Answers in the toolbox: Academic intensity, attendance patterns, and bachelor's degree attainment*. Washington, DC: U.S. Department of Education, Office of Educational Research and Improvement.

Astin, A. W. (1993). *What matters in college: Four critical years revisited*. San Francisco, CA: Jossey-Bass.

Bandura, A., & Locke, E. A. (2003). Negative self-efficacy and goal effects revisited. *Journal of Applied Psychology, 38*(1), 87–99.

Baron, J., & Norman, F. (1992). SATs, achievement tests, and high-school class rank as predictors of college performance. *Educational and Psychological Measurement, 52*, 1047–1055.

Baum, S., & Payea, K. (2004). *Education pays 2004*. New York: The College Board.

Berger, J. B., & Milem, J. F. (1999). The role of student involvement and perceptions of integration in a causal model of student persistence. *Research in Higher Education, 40*(6), 641–664.

Braxton, J. M. (2000). Introduction: Reworking the student departure puzzle. In J. M. Braxton (Ed.), *Reworking the student departure puzzle* (pp. 1–8). Nashville, TN: Vanderbilt University Press.

Camara, W. J., & Echternacht, G. (2000). The SAT I and high school grades: Utility in predicting success in college. *The College Board Research Notes* (RN-10), 1–12.

DeWitz, S. J., Woolsey, M. L., & Walsh, W. B. (2009). College student retention: An exploration of the relationship between self-efficacy beliefs and purpose in life among college students. *Journal of College Student Development, 50*(1), 19–34.

Kim, S. H., & Sedlacek, W. E. (1996). Gender differences among incoming African American freshmen on academic and social expectations (Research Report 7-94). *Journal of the First-Year Experience & Students in Transition, 8*(1), 25–37.

Kuh, G. D., & Hu, S. (1999). Unraveling the complexity of the increase in college grades from the mid-1980s to the mid-1990s. *Educational Evaluation and Policy Analysis, 21*, 1–24.

Lucas, C. (1994). *American higher education: A history*. New York: St. Martin's Griffin.

Pascarella, E. T., & Terenzini, P. T. (2005). *How college affects students: A third decade of research* (Vol. 2). San Francisco, CA: Jossey-Bass.

Pike, G. R. (1991). The effects of background, coursework, and involvement on students' grades and satisfaction. *Research in Higher Education, 32*(1), 15–30.

Poyrazil, S., Arbona, C., Nora, A., McPherson, R., & Pisecco, S. (2002). Relation between assertiveness, academic self-efficacy, and psychosocial adjustment among international graduate students. *Journal of College Student Development, 43*(5), 632–642.

Sedlacek, W. E. (2004). *Beyond the big test: Noncognitive assessment in higher education*. San Francisco, CA: Jossey-Bass.

Strayhorn, T. L. (2010). When race and gender collide: The impact of social and cultural capital on the academic achievement of African American and Latino males. *The Review of Higher Education, 33*(3), 307–332.

Thelin, J. R. (2004). *A history of American higher education*. Baltimore, MD: Johns Hopkins University Press.

1.6

Developmental Education for Adults and Academic Achievement

Joshua D. Hawley
The Ohio State University

Shu Chen Chiang
National Taiwan Normal University

Introduction

Many nations have significant drop-out rates for higher education. Across 18 Organization of Economic Co-operation and Development (OECD) nations surveyed in 2009, 31% of higher education enrollees do not complete college. This can vary from a high of 40% in the United States to under 15% in Japan, Korea, or Denmark (OECD, 2010). Reasons for student dropout vary by nation, with students in the United States leaving due mostly to academic difficulties, whereas students in France often move to vocational education. Students in Russia, where roughly a quarter of students drop out, often do so because of a lack of academic success, whether due to individual problems or the result of poor education within the college is unclear (Gury 2010; Hawley & Chiang, 2011).

Gaps in college achievement in the United States persist for ethnic and racial minorities, just as the population of the United States is poised to dramatically diversify. Moreover, there are worrying signs that college education does not necessarily imply high skills. Whereas there are no standard tests across nations for individuals in college as there are for elementary and secondary schooling (e.g., PISA and TIMSS), the National Assessment of Educational Progress (NAEP) scores in the United States for 17 year olds show essentially no improvement since 1999 on the average mathematics scores across the entire country.

Developmental education, also known as remediation, is a series of courses designed for students who fail to achieve school-based cutoff scores on placement tests. Colleges can also assign students to developmental education without using test scores (Martorell & McFarlin, 2011). In general, remediation is concentrated in core academic skills, such as math, writing, and reading. Remediation is present in many nations, particularly those such as the United States,

New Zealand, Australia, and Canada, where there is a policy priority to increase access to higher education for disadvantaged groups such as adults, immigrants, or youth.

By increasing the pressure on colleges to improve student achievement, colleges are facing similar accountability pressures that have impacted the K-12 sector. More focus on achievement in college, however, clearly makes it more difficult to ignore lagging skills in school. In this chapter we will first define achievement in college, focusing on the role of developmental or remedial education. We will then provide a summary of recent research in this area, and conclude with some recommendations.

Research Evidence

How Developmental Education Impacts Academic Achievement for Adults. In the context of developmental education, academic achievement is generally defined as mastery of lagging math or language skills, enabling students to proceed to regular credit-bearing courses. However, it is difficult to monitor changes in the skills or those in math or language arts in college because there is no mandate across the United States or other nations that we are aware of that requires colleges to measure changes in skills as students progress through school (Boylan, 2008). Therefore, researchers normally define academic achievement in developmental education as the completion of developmental education courses and the successful transfer to regular academic courses.

Many schools in the United States now use the metrics defined by the Achieving the Dream Initiative, which measures academic success as achievement of specific milestones along the pathway to completion of an academic degree. In the context of international practice, success is measured differently. In both the Russian and French systems, it appears that success is defined more by not transferring from one degree program to another or moving from the academic to the vocational track (Gury, 2010; Hawley & Koltova, 2010). For instance, intermediary measures such as continuous enrollment or attainment of a portion of degree credits are important to long-run academic completion.

Consequently, the requirement to take developmental education inevitably prolongs students' progress toward earning a degree. Another detrimental impact is the intimidating effect, indicating that many students fail to pass remediation simply because they do not enroll in the first place (Bailey, Jeong, & Cho, 2010). Remediation can also become a cyclical event because many students are not successful on their first attempts.

It is the tremendous cost but mixed effects that makes developmental education a thrust of research. Specifically, the expenditure for developmental education is estimated to be at least $1 billion annually for nationwide public colleges (Martorell & McFarlin, 2011), given that almost half of all community colleges students participate (Aud et al., 2011). In this sense, state governments struggle to intervene in the market for developmental education to reduce costs as well as increase academic outcomes. The issue internationally, however, is different in that many colleges in Europe view student failure as a natural result of poor performance. Therefore, student attrition is beneficial in maintaining the quality of the higher education output.

Various programmatic interventions have been developed to help students be successful and strengthen developmental education. For instance, in the United States, intensive counseling services have been implemented in Ohio (Scrivener & Weiss, 2009), and Washington state has piloted the Integrated Basic Education and Skill Training (I-BEST) programs (Jenkins, Zeidenberg, & Kienzl, 2009).

Math remediation has attracted much attention. In Texas, the state has used "high touch" mentoring services to target students in lower-level math courses. Math remediation has attracted considerable attention given the fact that participants in math remediation outnumber students participating in English remediation (Biswas, 2007; Visher, Butcher, & Cerna, 2010). Schools in Connecticut, Colorado, and Virginia designed nontraditional structures to provide flexible, self-paced learning opportunities to help student progress (Biswas, 2007). As a part of these efforts, a report from Texas revealed that developmental education instructors lack credentials or professional development, illustrating the barriers to successfully improve the quality of teaching in developmental education (Neeley & Paredes, 2007). Besides investigating the best practices in the classroom, more researchers make efforts to examine the relationship between developmental education and student outcomes from a quasi-experimental approach (Scrivner & Weiss, 2009).

Table 1.1 lists 10 studies representing findings from six states—Florida, Ohio, Virginia, California, Tennessee, and Texas, as well as datasets on a national scale—all studies are listed chronologically. As indicated, the impact of de-velopmental education is divided into short- and long-term outcomes. Short-term outcomes include the first college-level courses completed and persistence through college. The long-term outcomes we highlight include credential attainment, transfer between a 2- and 4-year colleges, and transition to the labor market. We have chosen these particular studies because they use student level records, and attempt to make some corrections for sample selection bias.

Short-Term Outcomes. For the findings related to short-term measures, three are positive, three are negative, whereas four do not come to a consistent conclusion. To clarify, positive outcomes indicate remediated students perform better compared with their nonremediated counterparts in various outcomes. Negative results imply that remediated students performed at levels below those without remediation.

Attewell and his colleagues report remediation increases the possibility of completing credits and persisting through college (Attewell, Lavin, Domina, & Levey, 2006). Several studies have found that remediation does not help and has no discernible impact on intermediate measures such as courses or persistence (Boatman & Long, 2010; Martorell & McFarlin, 2011).

Long-Term Outcomes. As the column on the far right of Table 1.1 indicates, studies that examine the long-term outcomes of remediation provide no consistent evidence to support that remediation positively or negatively influences student degree receipt, transfer, or economic success. Three studies refer to positive outcomes related to participation in remediation, three are indifferent, one is negative, and one is mixed.

As for mixed effects, Boatman and Long (2010) found the likelihood of degree attainment varies among remediated students depending on the subject of remediation. Writing remediation has positive effects on long-term outcomes, but negative effects are evident with math remediation. In terms of studies indicating positive effects, findings from a national dataset show that remediation in reading and writing specifically can improve the possibility of earning credentials for community college entrants (Attewell et al., 2006). Also in the case of California, positive effects of developmental education are strongly supported in terms of credential attainment and transfer to 4-year degree programs (Bahr, 2010). Moreover, findings from Ohio data indicate that students who complete remediation courses successfully are more likely to complete a bachelor's degree in 6 years (Bettinger & Long, 2009). However, no discernible influence was found by Hawley and Chiang (2011).

Findings from Florida convey different outcomes in the long run. The work of Calcagno and his colleagues suggests developmental education decreases the possibility of graduation for all (Calcagno, Crosta, Bailey, & Jenkins, 2007a,b). Yet interestingly enough, they found that students who were over age 25 are less affected by remediation than younger undergraduates. In contrast, other studies found no evidence that developmental education impacts completion of transfer (Calcagno & Long, 2008).

Efforts to Eliminate Self-Selection Bias. In essence, sophisticated statistical techniques used in these empirical studies aim to provide evidence that remediation is related to student achievement. Researchers spend significant time addressing the impact of remediation in the context of self-selection bias, and attempt to eliminate it from research discussed (Schneider, Carnoy, et al., 2007). To clarify, self-selection bias indicates that subjects choose to participate in certain programs, suggesting they differ from nonparticipants on certain unobserved characteristics. For example, adults who enroll in remediation in community colleges may have different levels of motivation from nonparticipants. However, the impact of developmental education is still difficult to describe, since findings yield mixed results.

Summary and Recommendations

Recent research allows us to describe the basic impacts of remediation across different schools, although we lack definitive evidence of the impact on student achievement. First, participation in remediation helps students maintain enrollment for college, and leads to an increase in credits earned, although these credits may not count toward a degree (Calcagno & Long, 2008). Therefore, individual student academic achievement may improve, at least in terms of short-term measures, over time.

As previous studies reveal, intensive interaction with remediated students or more flexible designs of instruction can further improve student outcomes (Visher et al., 2010). It is critical to stress that ongoing studies are investigating the possible impact of a range of academic improvements designed to keep students enrolled and therefore increase the likelihood of academic achievement.

For example, researchers are currently expanding and studying new interventions systematically. Russian scholars, for example, are beginning a long-term study to investigate the long-run impact of school-level factors such as faculty quality and curriculum on student success (Hawley & Koltova, 2011). Second, states such as Texas are experimenting with access to summer school for students that qualify for remediation. Initial evidence (Wathington et al., 2011) indicates some positive outcomes for students randomly assigned to remediation during the summer before entering college. States such as Ohio are taking a different approach by attempting to better serve adults who are at the lowest levels of skills in math and English through linking developmental education to adult basic education and literacy programs at the college campuses. Finally, schools continue to experiment with technological solutions, offering students a wide range of computer-based alternatives to college level remediation that might cost less and assist those students that are comfortable with the technology.

Whereas many studies are in process, it is important to note that keeping students enrolled is not the same as graduation (Hawley & Chiang, 2011). Developmental education

Table 1.6.1 Empirical Studies on the Effect of Developmental Education on Short and Long Term Academic Achievement

Study	Data Source	Early Outcomes	Long-term Outcomes
Attelwell, Lavin, & Levey (2006)	National Education Longitudinal Study (NELS:88) (1988–2000)	(–)	(+)
Calcagno, Crosta, Bailey & Jenkins (2007)	28 community colleges in Florida (1998–2004)	N/A	(–)
Calcagno & Long (2008)	28 community colleges in Florida (1997–2000)	(+)	(~)
Bettinger& Long (2009)	Two-year and four-year public colleges in Ohio (1998–2003)	(+)	(+)
Hawley & Chiang (2011)	10 community colleges in Ohio (2003–2009)	(+)	(~)
Jenkins, Jaggars, & Roska (2009)	Virginia Community College System (VCCS) (2005–2008 school year)	(~)	N/A
Bahr (2010)	104 community colleges in California (1995–2001)	N/A	(+)
Bailey, Jeong, & Cho (2010)	Achieving the Dream initiative (AtD) (2004–2006)	(–)	N/A
Boatman& Long (2010)	Two-year and four-year public colleges in Tennessee (2000–2006)	(–)	Mixed
Martorell & McFarlin (2011)	Two-year and four-year public colleges in Texas (1999–2005)	(~)	(~)

Notes:
N/A not applicable (+) positive (–) negative (~) indifferent
Short-term outcomes: Earning 10 or fewer credits/ first college-level course-taking / total credits completed / 1st & 2nd term (year) persistence/
Long-term outcomes: Associate's or higher degree attainment/ upward transfer (two-year to four-year institutions)

is a critical part of a college's capacity to serve students that need additional help if they are to be successful. It is not possible, however, for all college systems, especially in advanced European countries, to discuss college access through developmental education without first studying the underlying purpose of college. If college is supposed to develop access for disadvantaged groups, more sound and powerful interventions should be implemented to help students succeed in remediation to complete a degree.

Results from large-scale datasets and innovative strategies reflect the need to focus on institutions of higher learning. Indeed, colleges should take the initiative to conduct school-based research to clarify the effects of developmental education, as a way to improve student success since those institutions know what "fits" their students. The research should involve stakeholders such as administrators, instructors, and students, in particular, given that developmental education is such a costly investment.

References

Aud, S., Hussar, W., Kena, G., Bianco, K., Frohlich, L., Kemp, J., Tahan, K. (2011). *The condition of education 2011* (NCES 2011-033). U.S. Department of Education, National Center for Education Statistics. Washington, DC: U.S. Government Printing Office.

Attewell, P., Lavin, D., Domina, T., & Levey, T. (2006). New evidence on college remediation. *Journal of Higher Education, 77*(5), 886–924.

Bahr, P. R. (2010). Revisiting the efficacy of postsecondary remediation: The moderating effects of depth/breadth of deficiency. *The Review of Higher Education, 33*(2), 177–205.

Bailey, T., Jeong, D. W., & Cho, S.-W. (2010). Referral, enrollment, and completion in developmental education sequences in community colleges. *Economics of Education Review, 29*, 255–270

Bettinger, E. P., & Long, B. T. (2009). Addressing the needs of underprepared students in higher education: Does college remediation work? *Journal of Human Resources, 44*(3), 736–771.

Biswas, R. R. (2007). *Accelerating remedial math education: How institutional innovation and state policy interact*. Boston, MA: Jobs for the Future.

Boatman, A., & Long, B. T. (2010). *Does remediation work for all students? How the effects of postsecondary remedial and developmental courses vary by level of academic preparation* (NBER Working Paper). Cambridge, MA: National Bureau of Economic Research

Boylan, H. R (2008). How research contributes to access and opportunity around the world. *Journal of Developmental Education, 32*(1), 2–4.

Calcagno, J. C., Crosta, P., Bailey, T. R., & Jenkins, D. (2007a). Does age of entrance affect community college completion probabilities? Evidence from a discrete-time hazard model. *Educational Evaluation and Policy Analysis, 29*(3), 218–235.

Calcagno, J. C., Crosta, P., Bailey, T., & Jenkins, D. (2007b). Stepping stones to a degree: The impact of enrollment pathways and milestones on community college student outcomes. *Research in Higher Education, 48*(7), 775–801.

Calcagno, J. C., & Long, B. T. (2008). *The impact of postsecondary remediation using a regression discontinuity approach: addressing endogenous sorting and noncompliance* (NCPR Working Paper. No. 14194). Cambridge, MA: National Bureau of Economic Research.

Gury, N. (2010). Dropping out of higher education in France: A micro economic approach using survival analysis. *Education Economics, 19*(1), 51–64.

Hawley, J. D., & Chiang, S.-C. (2011). *Does developmental education help?* Columbus, OH: Ohio State University.

Hawley, J. D., & Koltova, E. (2011). *Exploring the incidence and charactieristics of student dropout in the Russian higher education sector.* Paper presented at the Comparative and International Education Society Conference, Montreal, Canada.

Jenkins, D., Zeidenberg, M., & Kienzl (2009). *Educational outcomes of I-Best, Washington State community and technical college system's integrated basic education and skills training program: Findings from a multivariate analysis*. New York, Columbia University, Community College Research Center.

Lee, J. M. J., & Rawls, A. (2010). *The college completion agenda 2010*. New York: College Board Advocacy and Policy Center.

Martorell, P., & McFarlin, I. (2011). Help or hindrance? The effects of college remediation on academic and labor market outcomes. *Review of Economic & Statistics, 93*(2), 436–454.

Neeley, S. J., & Paredes, R. A. (2007). *Texas P-16 Council developmental education report: A report on recommendations produced FY 2005–2006*. Austin, TX: P-16 Council.

OECD. (2010). *Education at a glance 2010: OECD indicators*. Paris: Organization for Economic Cooperation and Development

Scrivener, S., & Weiss, M. J. (2009). *More guidance, better results? Three-year effects of an enhanced student services program at two community colleges*. New York: MDRC.

Schneider, B., Carnoy, M., Kilpatrick, J., Schmidt, W. H., & Shavelson, R. J. (2007). *Estimating causal effects using experimental and observational designs*. Washington D.C., American Educational Research Association.

Visher, M. G., Butcher, K. F., & Cerna, O. S. (2010). *Guiding developmental math students to campus services*. New York: MDRC.

Wathington, H. D., Barnett, E. A., Weissman, E., Teres, J., Pretlow, J., & Nakanishi, A. (2011). *Getting ready for college: An implementation and early impacts study of eight Texas developmental summer bridge programs*. New York: MDRC.

Section 2

Influences from the Student

EDITOR: MIMI BONG
Korea University

2.1

Entry to School

COLLETTE TAYLER
University of Melbourne

Introduction

Early parenting practices and preschool preparation, as well as the process of transitioning into school, have been shown to have long-term positive influences on children's cognitive and social development. This is particularly important because government policy and industry standards can have a direct impact on preschool environments including child care centres, Head Start agencies, and prep programs.

Research Evidence

Early intervention in cognitive development is a key component of an effective entry to school program. For example, one seminal North Carolina program beginning in 1972 and working with infants from the time they were 6 weeks old, emphasises language development. Activities are designed to enhance perceptual-motor, cognitive, language, and social development and involved simple, age-appropriate, adult–child interactions such as talking to an infant, showing toys or pictures, and offering infants a chance to react to sights or sounds in their environment. As children grew, the educational content became more conceptual and skill-based. The intervention, known as the Abecedarian Project, monitored the children until they were 21 years old and reported an effect size of 1.40 for reading achievement and 0.86 for mathematics, when comparing the children who participated in the project to a control group. Moreover, the experimental group was half as likely to need special education services and their IQ scores were five points higher on average than those in the control group (Campbell & Ramey, 1995). The clear effects of this early intervention program highlight the importance of designing comprehensive cognitive development programs that begin at birth.

Parental involvement is another critical component in early entry-to-school interventions. One British study of over 3,000 children found that parental participation in activities such as reading to their child, teaching songs and nursery rhymes, playing with letters and numbers, visiting the library, and painting and drawing with their child accounted for differences in children's social behavioural development at the start of primary school. The researchers compared the group receiving the highest amount of support in their home environment with the group receiving the least home support. They found that home support was linked to significantly better cognitive and language outcomes at primary school entry (effect size = 0.58; Sammons et al., 2003). For this group, the home learning environment in the preschool period remained important for mathematics (effect size = 0.42) and English achievement (effect size 0.69) at age 11 (Sylva et al., 2008). In other words, what parents do *does* matter.

Preschool Programs and Academic Achievement: The Effects. Research connecting preschool programs to academic achievement began in the 1960s and 1970s when three seminal studies compared experimental and control groups of low-SES, African American children in the United States: the aforementioned Abecedarian Project, High/Scope Perry Preschool, and the Child–Parent Center program. The Abecedarian Project was the most intensive, providing full-day, year-round care for 5 years. The other two began at age 3–4: the Perry Preschool Program had the most established curriculum, while the Child–Parent Centers included parent involvement and wraparound health and nutrition services. All three studies found that, compared to a random control group of children from a similar demographic, an intensive preschool experience—beginning as early as 3 months—led to higher graduation rates, higher achievement levels on standardised tests, and lower unemployment rates (Campbell & Ramey, 1995; Reynolds & Temple, 2008; Schweinhart et al., 2005).

Even when examining the general population, the effect sizes of preschool program participation on school readiness range from 0.26 to 0.58 (Reynolds & Temple, 2008).

Indeed, multiple meta-analyses conducted over the past 25 years have found preschool education to have an effect size of half a standard deviation in cognitive development, which is equivalent to about eight points on an IQ test (Camilli, Vargas, Ryan, & Barnett, 2010). Regardless of socioeconomic standing, getting the right programs in place (i.e., involving cognitive and social development) during the first 5 years of a child's life can make a real difference to later academic success.

Research in developing countries reports similar results. In the first non-U.S. meta-analysis of early childhood interventions, Nores and Barnett (2010) observed that educational or mixed interventions—including health care or cognitive stimulation—had the largest cognitive effects (0.31) compared to cash transfers or solely nutritional interventions. Their analysis of 56 non-U.S. studies across 23 countries in Europe, Asia, Africa, and Central and South America, found the average effect sizes of early interventions for poor countries (0.25) was lower than that of middle- and high-income countries (0.31). Across countries, the effect of early interventions on cognitive development was significant, but declined over time: 0.69 for immediate impact, 0.35 from ages 5 to 10, and 0.28 beyond age 10.

The evidence is also supportive from a cost-benefit perspective. For example, participants in the Child–Parent Center program spent an average of 0.7 fewer years in special education, which translates to an average savings of $5,317 per program participant. Overall, the program was found to have a $10.15 return for each dollar invested; the Perry Preschool Program had a return of $16.14 per dollar invested, and the Abecedarian a return of $2.49 (Reynolds, Temple, & White, 2010). Analyses of several other large-scale evaluations yielded a median of $2.81 per dollar invested. No study found a negative return.

Transitions to School and Academic Achievement. Since the 1990s, in addition to focusing on best practices in pre-schools, researchers have broadened their entry-to-school focus to include the specific period of transition to school as a critical factor in children's academic achievement (Ramey & Ramey, 1999). For instance, in a national survey of problems identified by 10,071 teachers during the transition to kindergarten, teachers reported that 48% of all children had difficulty adjusting to school (Rimm-Kaufman, Pianta, & Cox, 2000). Dockett and Perry (2001) synthesised interview data to find that effective transitions include: positive relationships between the parent, child, and teacher; dedicated funding with a range of stakeholders; and individually tailored attention to students (see also Birch & Ladd, 1997).

Pianta and Kraft-Sayre (2003) synthesised qualitative evaluations and noted the importance of schools being ready to receive their new children via collaboration, partnering, and building relationships. They developed a model that recommended schools reach out to preschool families and help foster connections to preschool settings. The model focuses on family strengths, tailoring outreach practices to individual students, and promoting personal connections before a child's first day of school. Transition-to-school experiences are most positive when educators acknowledge children's strengths and abilities, families are encouraged to share information about the child including their aspirations, and children are given the opportunity to provide their own views about what they need to prepare and adapt to their new school.

The link connecting positive preschool transition experiences with cognitive development and academic achievement at the end of kindergarten can be shown by a Duke University research team involving evidence from over 21,000 children (Schulting, Malone, & Dodge, 2005). Kindergarten teachers were asked to identify which of the following seven transition practices were implemented at their school to ease children's transition to kindergarten: (a) information about the kindergarten program is phoned or sent home to parents, (b) preschoolers spend time in the kindergarten classrooms, (c) school days are shortened at the beginning of the school year, (d) parents and children visit kindergarten prior to the start of the school year, (e) teachers visit students' homes at the beginning of the school year, (f) parents attend an orientation session prior to the school year, or (g) other transition activities are provided. Using hierarchical linear modelling and controlling for SES, the researchers found that effects were stronger for low- and mid-SES children than high SES children. Achievement on cognitive assessments increased by 0.21 standard deviations for children from low-SES backgrounds exposed to seven transition practices. In brief, the impact of transition practices is greatest for low-SES children.

Summary and Recommendations

Early child development sets the foundation for learning, behaviour, and health, and helps build social capital and equality in both the developed and developing world. Given the critical nature of early childhood and the proven effectiveness of preschool intervention programs, it becomes important for policy makers to disseminate best practices in preschool education in order to maximise both student affective gains *and* academic achievement. That is, attention should move beyond the mere provision of services and focus more on the nature and quality of preschool interventions.

Although there is no one set prescription for high-quality cognitive interventions, effective preschool programs share the following characteristics: they target multiple factors (education, health, and parenting); they start early and are ongoing (although they need not be full-day); and parents and local communities are involved and respected.

Policy makers also need to determine what types of interventions are cost-effective. A few parameters are known: programs for children living in highly disadvantaged circumstances should begin at birth; programs that begin at age 3 should be coordinated with the school system; teaching staff should be well trained and compensated; cognition and school readiness need to be components of the preschool curriculum; comprehensive family services are included; and programs are evaluated and improved upon (Reynolds et al., 2010). Although these are clear components of a cost-effective program, there is debate about the exact manifestation of these components.

In addition to looking at preschool practices, policy makers need to ask: What can schools do to assist transitions? In order to have an effective impact on academic achievement, entry to school must go beyond orientation and focus on promoting communication. A common finding emphasises the importance of teacher professional development regarding transition practices (Dockett & Perry, 2003). Other best practices in transitions include buddy programs between new and older children, advance parent-teacher-principal meetings in which both social and academic information is shared, and programs involving nonteaching staff, even the bus driver, in improving communication between students, teachers, and parents. Continuity of experience is critical: governments need to implement these practices and act to better understand the long-term implications for children, families, and society.

References

Birch, S. H., & Ladd, G. W. (1997). The teacher–child relationship and children's early school adjustment. *Journal of School Psychology, 35*(1), 61–79.

Camilli, G., Vargas, S., Ryan, S., & Barnett, W. S. (2010). Meta-analysis of the effects of early education interventions on cognitive and social development. *Teachers College Record, 112*(3), 579–620.

Campbell, F. A., & Ramey, C. T. (1995). Cognitive and school outcomes for high-risk African-American students at middle adolescence: Positive effects of early intervention. *American Educational Research Journal, 32*(4), 743–772.

Dockett, S., & Perry, B. (Eds.). (2001). *Beginning school together: Sharing strengths*. Watson, ACT: Australian Early Childhood Association.

Dockett, S., & Perry, B. (2003). *Transition to school: Development and evaluation of guidelines and programs for best practice*. Sydney, Australia: University of Western Sydney. Unpublished report.

Nores, M., & Barnett, W. S. (2010). Benefits of early childhood interventions across the world: (Under) investing in the very young. *Economics of Education Review, 29*(2), 271–282.

Pianta, R., & Kraft-Sayre, M. (2003). *Successful kindergarten transition*. Baltimore, MD: Brookes.

Ramey, C. T., & Ramey, S. L. (1999). Beginning school for children at risk. In R. C. Pianta & M. J. Cox (Eds.), *In the transition to kindergarten* (pp. 89–96). Baltimore, MD: Brookes.

Reynolds, A. J., & Temple, J. A. (2008). Cost-effective early childhood development programs from preschool to third grade. *Annual Review of Clinical Psychology, 4*(1), 109.

Reynolds, A. J., Temple, J. A., & White, B. (2010). Cost-effective early childhood development programs from preschool to third grade. *Annual International Encyclopedia of Education* (Vol. 3, pp. 38–48). New York, NY: Elsevier.

Rimm-Kaufman, S., Pianta, R., & Cox, M. (2000). Teachers' judgments of problems in the transition to kindergarten. *Early Childhood Research Quarterly, 15*, 147–166.

Sammons, P., Sylva, K., Melhuish, E., Siraj-Blatchford, I., Taggart, B., & Elliot, K. (2003). *The effective provision of pre-school education (EPPE) project: Technical Paper 8b—Measuring the impact of pre-school on children's social/behavioural development over the pre-school period*. London: Institute of Education, University of London.

Schulting, A. B., Malone, P. S., & Dodge, K. A. (2005). The effect of school-based kindergarten transition policies and practices on child academic outcomes. *Developmental Psychology, 41*(6), 860–871.

Schweinhart, L. J., Montie, J., Xiangm, Z., Barnett, W. S., Belfield, C. R., & Nores, M. (2005). *Lifetime effects: The high/scope Perry preschool study through age 40*. Ypsilanti, MI: High/Scope Press.

Sylva, K., Melhuish, E., Sammons, P., Siraj-Blatchford, I., & Taggart, B. (2008). *Final report from the primary phase: Pre-school, school and family influences on children's development during key stage 2 (Age 7–11)*. Nottingham, England: DCFS.

2.2

Piagetian Approaches

Philip Adey and Michael Shayer
King's College, London

Introduction

Of the over 800 meta-analyses synthesised by Hattie (2009) reporting the effect sizes of various educational approaches on achievement, "Piagetian Approaches" ranked number 2 out of 138 influences. This is a remarkable effect by any standards, and makes one wonder why educational establishments internationally are not beating a path to the door of this apparent elixir. Part of the reason must lie in the ambiguity of the term *Piagetian Approaches* and the first task of this section must be to clarify what a Piagetian approach might look like. A necessary precursor of that task must be to summarise the essentials of Piagetian theory.

Research Evidence

The most memorable contribution of Jean Piaget (1896–1980) to our understanding of learning was a rich and detailed description, based on many hundreds of hours of practical interviews, of how children's thinking develops qualitatively through successive stages under the influence of maturation and of the social and physical environment. Descriptions of the sort of thinking available to children at different stages in their cognitive development provide a uniquely reliable tool for teachers grappling with question of what is "difficult" for their students, why it is difficult (Shayer & Adey, 1981), and, perhaps less certainly, what they might be able to do about it.

The most basic possible meaning of a Piagetian approach, which is the one that Hattie (2009, p. 43) seems to be investing in the term, is simply the high correlation found between measured levels of cognitive development in Piagetian terms and educational achievement. This itself is simply a description of a situation which leaves wide open possible interpretations of what teachers and curriculum planners might do about it. In the worst case interpretation of such a correlation there would actually be little that teachers could do about it except recognise the reasons why

some of their students had persistent difficulty in mastering their work. This would be the determinist (one might say, "helpless") position.

But from the correlation between levels of cognitive development and educational achievement a somewhat more active response by teachers may be hypothesised. Having become cognizant of their students' levels of cognitive development (individually or as a class mean), they would be able to choose their teaching material and approach accordingly, in an attempt to avoid undue difficulties or dissonances between the learners and what is to be learned. This may described as a "matching" approach. We have found no examples of research which have operationalised this matching Piagetian approach in a systematic way, comparing educational achievement or cognitive gains of groups who have had learning experiences matched to their measured levels of development, compared with a control group taught the same material without regard to levels of difficulty. It is true that in the 1970s some science curriculum projects such as the Australian Science Education Project and the UK's Nuffield Science 5-13 adopted an explicit Piagetian matching strategy but these were based on suppositions about the ages at which stages were typically attained rather than actual data on mean levels in the population. Such comprehensive data only became available toward the end of that decade following the large scale survey of the Concepts in Secondary Mathematics and Science project at Chelsea College, University of London (Shayer, Küchemann, & Wylam, 1976; Shayer & Wylam, 1978) and by that time the appetite for Piagetian approaches to education was retreating in the face of a fashion for addressing student "alternative conceptions."

There is, however, a far more active interpretation of a Piagetian approach to education, and that is to pay attention to what Piaget postulated were the drivers of cognitive development, and to attempt to operationalise those drivers as an educational intervention to maximise the rate of cognitive development of every child. This is the approach

adopted by a series of Cognitive Acceleration projects ema-
nating from King's College London from the mid-1980s to
the present day (Shayer & Adey, 1981). This approach of
course goes way beyond either the deterministic/fatalistic
approach or the simple matching approach in that it assumes that cognitive development can be accelerated, an
assumption in line with generally accepted understanding
of the intimate interaction between genetic endowment
and a nurturing environment (Adey, Csapo, Demteriou,
Hautamäki, & Shayer, 2007; Ridley, 2003) and, as we will
show, fully justified by empirical results.

Cognitive Acceleration (CA) identifies three main drivers of cognitive development. From Piaget we have the
ideas (a) that the mind develops in response to challenge,
or to disequilibrium, so the intervention must provide
some cognitive conflict; and (b) of reflective abstraction,
the mind's growing ability to become conscious of and so
take control of its own processes, so the intervention must
encourage students to be metacognitive. CA also draws from
Piaget's contemporary, Vygotsky, the idea (c) that cognitive
development is a social process promoted by high quality
discussion amongst peers scaffolded by a teacher or other
more mature person, thus the intervention must encourage
social construction (Shayer, 2003), as much as individual
thinking and creativity. Driver 1 is key to the structuring of
classroom activities within the curriculum, while driver 2 is
key to classroom pedagogy for any activity, however structured. Driver 3 applies to the two others for optimal effects:
metacognition usually occurs toward the end of the activity but will in the end become a part of the student's own
strategies while considering how to approach a problem.

The first intervention program designed to incorporate
these drivers was Cognitive Acceleration through Science
Education (CASE), which consisted of 30 activities (Adey,
Shayer, & Yates, 2001) designed to be taught over 2 years
to grade 6 and 7 classes at the rate of one activity every 2
weeks. The materials were introduced to teachers through
an extensive professional development programme (Adey,
Hewitt, Hewitt, & Landau, 2004). Effect sizes on long-term
follow-up and transfer to subject areas outside science (the
subject context of the intervention) ranged from 0.3 to
1.0 (Adey & Shayer, 1993, 1994). Follow-up evaluations
(Shayer, 1999a, 1999b) confirmed that students in schools
which used the CASE programme scored significantly
higher (d = 0.60 for 11 schools) in public measures of
educational achievement for science than those in matched
non-CASE schools. Evidence that the CASE intervention
had affected the learning ability of students in general, and
was not specific to science, comes from the effect sizes of
d = 0.50 for mathematics and d = 0.57 for English: these
three sets of results coming from the GCSE exams taken
by all students at 16.

In 1999 CA projects started in primary schools with
kindergarten children and gradually extended through to six
grades of elementary education in the UK. The most recent
results from a 2-year intervention with children aged 5 to
7 in the context of mathematics (Shayer & Adhami, 2007,

2010) show post-test effects of d = 0.71 on a Piagetian test,
d = 0.65 and 0.43 on national tests of maths and English
at age 7 and d = 0.24 and 0.34 on National tests taken 4
years later at age 11, without any further teaching in the
CA manner (Shayer & Adhami, 2010).

One aspect of causation which may be relevant to such
work is the evidence on brain growth. In his summary
Epstein (1986) described two major brain-growth stages
of children: the first at about 6 years of age, the second at
10/11. Presumably the brain growths are in preparation
for major changes in adaption of the growing child to the
world they inhabit. As described by Piaget these are the
development of "concrete thinking" starting between 5
and 7 years, and the development of "formal thinking"
beginning at age 11. The shift is from use of descriptive
models of the world, with causality limited to simultaneous
occurrences—if this, then that—to interpretative models
where some hypothesised mechanism is included between
the "if" and the "then"—often a mathematical expression—which then needs to be tested against reality. Given
appropriately stimulating environments the new brain wir-
ing will take place. But the results of the CSMS survey on
10,000 children between the ages of 10 and 16 (Shayer et
al., 1976; Shayer & Wylam, 1978) show that by the age
of 16 only 30% of the population have developed formal
thinking: indeed already by the age of 7 something like a
6-year development gap has opened up between the least
and most able: at 11 it is more like a 12-year gap. It may
well be that the choice of ages 11 to 13 and 5 to 7 as ages
to supplement children's learning environments may have
been a choice most likely to maximise success.

Summary and Recommendations

We believe that there are two major changes in teacher
behaviours that the success of this interventionist research
points to—each as important and essential as the other, but
one much more difficult to induce as the thinking behind it
is both unfashionable and unfamiliar. To take the easier one
first: the idea that teaching is a direct giving by the teacher
to the student, verbally or as demonstration, is a long time
a-dying. But both for motivation and for the learning of the
student the most important source of his or her learning is
the groping and stumbling proto-learning performance of
their fellow students, to which he or she is also contributing. As Vygotsky said:

> Functions are first formed in the collective as relations
> among children and then become mental functions for the
> individual. (Wertsch, 1979, p. 165)

and, 5 lines later:

> Research shows that reflection [by the individual] is
> spawned from argument [in the collective]. (Wertsch,
> 1979, p. 165)

The individuals have to construct new concepts for
themselves otherwise it is merely rote learning, yet the

activity of their fellow students is more important for their learning than that of their teacher, who is no longer in the same river as the students are swimming in. Some teachers find this very easy to realise, but many feel as though they have something to lose in the respect of their students if they refrain from trying to "tell" them. Yet in the long run the more sophisticated art of arranging learning experiences for students so that they have to create their learning for themselves with each other is far more worthy of respect, and students soon realise this for themselves, and prefer to learn this way. Our research suggests that not only do students learn their subjects better if taught this way: they also learn how better to learn better in general—a possible definition of intelligence?

But the other aspect of the cognitive activity art is, we are sure, equally important and essential, but far less often mediated well by tutors to teachers. Although we have cited CA publications with appropriate lesson material, specimen "good" lessons don't do it: they aren't enough on their own to change teachers' behaviours. In order to find suitable lessons we had first to analyse the hierarchical steps in the subject matter of science and mathematics through Piagetian eyes, finding first contexts that contained at least two or three steps of learning of the important concepts, and then plan the lessons in such a way that every student, whatever his or her initial level, would have some possible achievement during the lesson activity, and that there was also enough of a challenging conflict even for the most able later on. This means that, as researchers, we were also looking at the learning behaviour of the students through Piagetian eyes during the classes, seeing at every point what the match must be between the thinking demand of each step in the lesson context and the thinking level of each student, determining their responses. Unless teachers can also learn to do this for themselves they can neither plan a lesson adequately nor mediate the peer-peer learning during the course of the lesson. Indeed collaborative learning can just as easily degenerate into the blind leading the blind: teachers must know how to intervene on the spot to keep the learning process heading upwards all the time, and for that they need to be able to see where each of the students are in relation to the learning demands of the subject matter.

Lastly, we have found that for adequate professional development of the teacher skills required, teachers have to construct their own practice through the same kind of collaborative learning they are being asked to mediate with their own students' learning. Their tutors' mediative performance with the teachers—an art quite new to many of them—must develop in parallel with that which the teachers are asked to use with their students.

References

Adey, P., Csapo, B., Demteriou, A., Hautamäki, J., & Shayer, M. (2007). Can we be intelligent about intelligence? Why education needs the concept of plastic general ability. *The Educational Research Review, 2*(2), 75–97.

Adey, P., Hewitt, G., Hewitt, J., & Landau, N. (2004). *The professional development of teachers: Practice and theory.* Dordrecht, Netherlands: Kluwer Academic.

Adey, P., & Shayer, M. (1993). An exploration of long-term far-transfer effects following an extended intervention programme in the high school science curriculum. *Cognition and Instruction, 11*(1), 1–29.

Adey, P., & Shayer, M. (1994). *Really raising standards: cognitive intervention and academic achievement.* London: Routledge.

Adey, P., Shayer, M., & Yates, C. (2001). *Thinking science: The curriculum materials of the CASE project* (3rd ed.). London: Nelson Thornes.

Epstein, H. T. (1986). Stages in human brain development. *Developmental brain research, 30,* 114–119.

Hattie, J. (2009). *Visible learning.* Oxford, England: Routledge.

Ridley, M. (2003). *Nature via nurture.* London: Harper Perennial.

Shayer, M. (1999a). Cognitive acceleration through science education II: Its effect and scope. *International Journal of Science Education, 21*(8), 883–902.

Shayer, M. (1999b). *GCSE 1999: Added-value from schools adopting the CASE Intervention.* London: Centre for the Advancement of Thinking.

Shayer, M., & Adey, P. (1981). *Towards a science of science teaching.* London: Heinemann.

Shayer, M., & Adhami, M. (2007). Fostering cognitive development through the context of mathematics: Results of the CAME Project. *Educational Studies in Mathematics, 64*(3), 265–291.

Shayer, M., & Adhami, M. (2010). Realizing the cognitive potential of children 5 to 7 with a mathematics focus: Post-test and long-term Effects of a two-year intervention. *British Journal of Educational Psychology, 80,* 363–369.

Shayer, M., Küchemann, D., & Wylam, H. (1976). The distribution of Piagetian stages of thinking in British middle and secondary school children. *British Journal of Educational Psychology, 46,* 164–173.

Shayer, M., & Wylam, H. (1978). The distribution of Piagetian stages of thinking in British middle and secondary school children. II- 14- to 16-year olds and sex differentials. *British Journal of Educational Psychology, 48,* 62–70.

Wertsch, J. V. (Ed.). (1979). *The concept of activity in Soviet psychology.* Armonk, NY: M.E. Sharpe.

2.3

Entry to Tertiary Education

EMER SMYTH
Economic and Social Research Institute, Dublin, Ireland

Introduction

Across many different contexts, students with higher levels of educational achievement are found to be more likely to go on to tertiary education. This is an important issue because inequalities in achievement at primary and secondary levels will serve to further reinforce social differences in later educational attainment.

Research Evidence

Prior achievement can influence entry to tertiary education in direct or indirect ways. In certain systems such as Ireland, England, and Australia, the grades achieved in state examinations are used, wholly or partly, to determine entry to higher education institutions. As a result, higher achieving young people are more likely to enter tertiary education. In other countries such as the United States, Israel, and Sweden, standardised tests are frequently used to determine access to tertiary institutions. Even in these systems which use standardised testing to determine entry, prior achievement in terms of high school grades is strongly associated with access to higher education (Roksa, Grodsky, Arum, & Gamoran, 2007). Other systems such as France and Italy allow open entry to higher education, provided that students have taken a specific qualification or track. Still, the association of entry to tertiary education with academic achievement at school level remains evident.

Nevertheless, international research clearly indicates that higher education entry processes cannot simply be read off prior student achievement. Two sets of factors have been found to have a significant effect on entry to tertiary education, even after controlling for prior achievement: social background characteristics and school factors.

Social Background Factors and Higher Education Entry. Empirical studies have indicated a consistently significant effect of social background, usually conceptualised in terms of social class or parental education, on educational outcomes. Comparative studies have shown that the pattern of association between social class background and educational attainment tends to be similar across countries with very different educational systems (Shavit & Blossfeld, 1993). Such class inequalities reflect differences between social classes in academic "ability" or achievement (primary effects) or the level of educational participation, while controlling for prior academic performance (secondary effects) (Boudon, 1974). From this perspective, young people from middle-class backgrounds are more likely to enter higher education than similarly qualified working-class young people. This direct effect of social background on tertiary participation has been variously attributed to the differential economic, social, and cultural resources across classes (Bourdieu & Passeron, 1977) or to the relative costs and benefits attached to educational participation for different social groups (Erikson & Jonsson, 1996).

Researchers have reached different conclusions about the relative importance of achievement and social class in college entry. In the United States, Roksa and coauthors (2007) show that only part of the social background effect is mediated by academic achievement and all else being equal, students with highly educated parents remain advantaged in college entry. In contrast, Chowdry and coauthors (Chowdry, Crawford, Dearden, Goodman, & Vignoles, 2010) indicate that social class inequalities in higher education entry in England are almost wholly due to differences in secondary school achievement, with no direct social class effects evident when academic performance is taken into account.

There has been a long-standing debate in many countries on the extent to which social background influences have declined in the face of higher education expansion. In the absence of significant changes in the distribution of economic and cultural resources, it has been argued that educational inequality will only decrease when the demand for education among the upper middle classes has been saturated, a situation termed *maximally maintained inequality* by Raftery and Hout (1993). So far, expansion to the point of saturation has been associated with declining inequality in tertiary education entry in only two countries, Italy and Israel. Rapid expansion of higher education has also resulted in reduced inequality in Japan and Taiwan (Shavit et al., 2007). However, studies in other countries have shown increasing social inequality in college entry. Astin and Oseguera (2004) highlight increasing stratification in higher education entry, especially to élite institutions, in the United States in the 1980s and 1990s, although Roksa et al. (2007) point to stable levels of inequality. In the UK, Blanden and Machin (2004) report increasing stratification by family income over time as higher education expands in numbers.

School Factors and Higher Education Entry.   School factors also affect the entry to higher education in two ways: by influencing levels of student achievement and by influencing the propensity to enter higher education. A large body of research on school effectiveness shows the ways in which student achievement differs significantly across schools, even controlling for prior academic ability, gender, social background, and other relevant factors (see Teddlie & Reynolds, 2000, for a review). Thus, schools differentially enhance the chances of their students' entry to tertiary education. Entry to tertiary education does, in fact, vary significantly according to the secondary school attended (Smyth & Hannan, 2007). Such variation is not fully accounted for by between-school differences in student achievement. The concept of *institutional habitus* has increasingly been used to indicate the way in which schools can shape the educational pathways of their students. The institutional habitus of the school reflects the social mix of the student body as well as historical factors and is reflected in teacher expectations and the kind of guidance provided to students (McDonough, 1997). In this way, the social composition of the school can influence young people's likelihood of going on to higher education, over and above the effect of their own social background.

Increasingly, the focus has shifted from exploring the factors that influence overall entry to higher education to examining differences in the type of tertiary education pursued, distinguishing between élite and other colleges (see Shavit, Arum, & Gamoran, 2007). Young people with higher achievement levels are not only more likely to enter tertiary education but, when they do so, are more likely to attend more prestigious institutions. Achievement overall and in particular subject domains also influences the field of study taken within tertiary education (van de Werfhorst, Sullivan, & Cheung, 2003).

Summary and Recommendations

In sum, prior achievement is associated with entry to tertiary education across very different national contexts. Entry to tertiary education as a consequence, rather than a cause, of achievement shows the way in which achievement at earlier stages of the schooling career is linked to later transitions. The relationship between achievement and higher education entry is moderated by social background and school factors. Social inequalities in tertiary entry are thus found to reflect inequalities in prior achievement and in the type of school attended. Existing research therefore points to the importance of early intervention in enhancing young people's access to higher education. Investments in preschool education and in school-based literacy and numeracy initiatives have been found to reduce inequalities in educational outcomes (Levin, 2009) and are therefore likely to have a longer term impact on participation in tertiary education. Furthermore, inequality in access to tertiary education will be influenced by the broader distribution of economic and social resources, thus reflecting, and reinforcing, inequalities within the wider society.

References

Astin, A.W., & Oseguera, L. (2004). The declining "equity" of US higher education. *The Review of Higher Education, 27*(3), 321–341.

Blanden, J., & Machin, S. (2004). Educational inequality and the expansion of UK higher education. *Scottish Journal of Political Economy, 51*(2), 230–249.

Boudon, R. (1974). *Education, opportunity, and social inequality*. New York: Wiley.

Bourdieu, P., & Passeron, J. (1977). *Reproduction in education, society and culture*. London: Sage.

Chowdry, H., Crawford, C., Dearden, L., Goodman, A., & Vignoles, A. (2010). *Widening participation in higher education: Analysis using linked administrative data*. Bonn, Germany: IZA Working Paper.

Erikson, R., & Jonsson, J. O. (1996). *Can education be equalised? The Swedish case in comparative perspective*. Boulder, CO: Westview Press.

Levin, H. M. (2009). The economic payoff to investing in educational justice. *Educational Researcher, 38*(1), 5–20.

McDonough, P. M. (1997). *Choosing colleges: How social class and schools structure opportunity*. Albany, NY: State University of New York Press.

Raftery, A., & Hout, M. (1993). Maximally maintained inequality: Expansion, reform, and opportunity in Irish education, 1921–75. *Sociology of Education, 66*(1), 41–62.

Roksa, J., Grodsky, E., Arum, R., & Gamoran, A. (2007). United States: Changes in higher education and social stratification. In Y. Shavit, R. Arum, & A. Gamoran (Eds.), *Stratification in higher education: A comparative study* (pp. 165–191). Stanford, CA: Stanford University Press.

Shavit, Y., & Blossfeld, H. (Eds.). (1993). *Persistent inequalities: A comparative study of educational attainment in thirteen countries*. Boulder, CO: Westview Press.

Shavit, Y., Arum, R., & Gamoran, A. (Eds.). (2007). *Stratification in higher education: A comparative study*. Stanford, CA: Stanford University Press.

Smyth, E., & Hannan, C. (2007). School process and the transition to higher education. *Oxford Review of Education, 33*(2), 175–194.

Teddlie, C., & Reynolds, D. (Eds.). (2000). *The international handbook of school effectiveness research*. London: Falmer.

Van De Werfhorst, H. G., Sullivan, A., & Cheung, S. Y. (2003). Social class, ability and choice of subject in secondary and tertiary education in Britain. *British Educational Research Journal, 29*(1), 41–62.

2.4

Physical Activity

Janet Clinton
University of Melbourne

Introduction

Physical activity levels for young people are declining in many Western countries and sedentary behaviours are on the increase. Further, throughout the world many children are affected by the effects of poor nutrition which can severely affect children's brain development, brain functioning, behaviour, and thence psychological and social functioning, all of which can impact on their ability to learn (Clinton, Rensford, & Willing, 2007). These trends are of concern because physical inactivity and poor diet also are key risk factors for obesity and associated chronic conditions.

This has led to the development of many school health programs, which typically have three components: enhancing the school's environment, curriculum, and health services; recognizing the relationship between the quality of a school's physical and psychosocial environment; and optimizing the health of students and staff. The health promoting school recognises that health is not only developed through the taught curriculum, but extends to learning in and through the school, home, and community. In addition, such schools aim to enable pupils, staff, and the community they serve to take action for a healthier life, school, and society.

A recent proliferation of programs in schools targeting different health and well-being areas, ranging from physical health (e.g., nutrition, physical activity, smoking), mental health, to social well-being have helped to raise the profile of school health promotion. There is, however, a dearth of evidence about the effectiveness of these programs, usually because of insufficient monitoring and evaluation systems.

Research Evidence

Although educators would agree that healthy children are in a better position to learn, it is difficult to isolate the relationship that exists between nutrition, physical activity, and academic achievement. Benham-Deal and Hudson (2006) claimed that education reform goals and public health initia-

tives reinforce and support one another, a proposition that is supported by research on the relationship between readiness to learn and healthful nutrition and physical activity (Clinton et al., 2007). As a consequence, schools are increasingly seen as an important vehicle via which health related objectives can be achieved, most commonly through school based health education and health promotion activities.

On the whole, many studies find a weak but positive association between physical activity and academic performance (Keeley & Fox, 2009). The cause and strength of the effect that physical activity has on academic performance remain difficult to determine, but there is, at minimum, consensus on the lack of detrimental effect on academic performance even where academic class durations are shortened in compensation for increased in-school physical activity (Active Living Research, 2009; Keeley & Fox, 2009; Murray, Low, Hollis, Cross, & Davis, 2007; Trudeau & Shephard, 2008).

Reviews which attempted to establish the causal link between physical activity and academic performance have reviewed studies in domains of physical education, physical activity, and school sports (Trudeau & Shephard, 2008). Many studies have found positive (but small) relationships between physical activity and academic performance. Improvements in academic performance have been reported by Dwyer, Sallis, Blizzard, Lazarus, and Dean (2001), Keeley and Fox (2009), and Wachs (1995).

Fox, Barr-Anderson, Neumark-Sztainer, and Wall (2010) attempted to separate the effects of physical activity and team participation that school sports has on academic performance and found inconsistent results.

> For high school girls, both physical activity and sports team participation were each independently associated with a higher GPA. For high school boys, only sports team participation was independently associated with a higher GPA. For middle school students, the positive association between physical activity and GPA could not be separated from the relationship between sports team participation and a higher GPA. (p. 31)

Reviews by Active Living Research (2009), which summarises the latest peer-reviewed research on the relationship between physical activity and academic performance among children and adolescents, also provide evidence for the positive effect increased time spent in physical education has on academic performance. Similarly, Trudeau and Shephard (2008) reported that physical activity

> can be added to the school curriculum by taking time from other subjects without risk of hindering student academic achievement. On the other hand, adding time to "academic" or "curricular" subjects by taking time from physical education programmes does not enhance grades in these subjects and may be detrimental to health. (8)

There have also been many studies that have attempted to understand the relationship between physical activity and academic performance by determining how physical activity influences established factors known to influence academic performance. In this respect, focus has been placed on cognitive function—brain development, memory, and decision making and behavioural impacts (Ploughman, 2008). For example, an academic review of educational benefits claimed for physical education and school sports (Bailey et al., 2009) found support for the claim physical activity can improve children's concentration and arousal, which might indirectly benefit academic performance (see also Keeley & Fox, 2009). Others have pointed to the connections between physical activity and brain functioning (Etnier & Landers, 1995) and increased neural connections (Jensen, 1998).

There is support for positive effects derived from physical activity on student behaviour, particularly behavioral compliance (e.g., Dwyer, Coonan, Leitch, Hetzel, & Baghurst, 1983), improved attitudes to learning, and overall discipline (Keays & Allison, 1995). Many studies that have investigated the effects of increasing physical activity in schools report a positive effect on students' classroom behaviour including attitudes, creativity, and discipline (Keays & Allison, 1995). Improved behaviour and attention in the classroom then enables students to absorb what they hear and see in the classroom (Putnam, Tette, & Wendt, 2004). Trudeau and Shephard (2009) found that moderate (20 minutes) physical activity reduced disruptive behaviour and increased on-task behaviour during core academic classes as well as improved perceptual and decision-making capacity that was not apparent in less physical activities such as music playing.

Increased physical activity has also been associated with improvements in the emotional health of children. Children who are physically fit generally have higher levels of self-esteem, self-efficacy, confidence, a sense of optimism, and decreased anxiety, stress, and depression (Gruber, 1986, Tremblay, Inman, & Willms, 2000, Scully, Kremer, Meade, Graham, & Dudgeon, 1998, Strauss, Rodzilsky, Burack, & Colin, 2001; Kirkcaldy, Shephard, & Siefen, 2002).

Aligned to the learning process, children's motivation to learn has been directly linked to improving factors which then lead to positive effects on the learning. Trudeau and Shephard (2008) found that children who participated in physical activity have better self-esteem, self-image, body image, and confidence. School satisfaction and school connectedness are also higher, they claim, which leads to improved academic performance by reducing school dropout rates and absenteeism. Emotional well-being

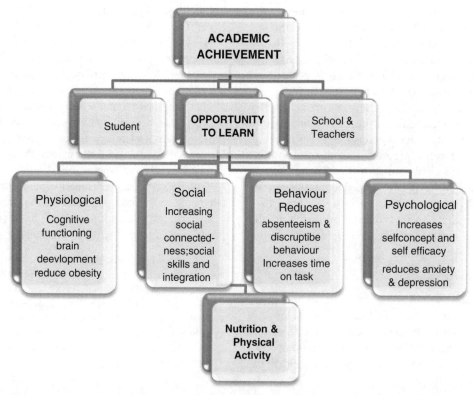

Figure 2.4.1

(absence of depressive mood state), better future expectations, spirituality were also factors linked to improved academic motivation and achievement that can be brought about through increased physical activity, especially with support by parental involvement.

Summary and Recommendations

This review has suggested that physical activity has a number of interrelated and complex implications for children's physiological, behavioural, psychological, and social health and well-being, all of which can influence their opportunity to learn. The reality, however, is that these relations are relatively small, the causal connections often overstated, and the evidence not so convincing that schools embrace physical activities.

Achievement in school is dependent on a number of factors ranging from the quality of teaching and the school environment to the intellectual capability of the child, their investment in learning, as well as their opportunity to learn. Students' health and well-being can either contribute to or undermine this opportunity to learn, and therefore their ability to achieve academically. Although there is no clear evidence that improving physical activity will directly result in improved academic achievement, it is suggested that an indirect link may be more likely between physical activity and academic achievement due to improvements in physiological, behavioural, psychological, and social well-being. Overall, these improvements lead children to a state where they have greater opportunity to learn. It is health and well-being combined with the intellectual capability of children that brings them to a position to be able to learn. Many students may, however, find ways to compensate and overcome the potential effects of their physical or health issues. Figure 2.4.1 provides a potential pathway from physical activity to achievement effects and it can be seen that the effects are probably indirect, can be compensated or affected by many moderators, and overall the effects are likely to be small.

References

Active Living Research. (2009). Active education: Physical education, physical activity and academic performance research brief. Retrieved from http://www.activelivingresearch.org/files/Active_Ed_Summer2009.pdf.

Bailey, R., Armour, K., Kirk, D., Jess, M., Pickup, I., Sandford, R., ... BERA Physical Education and Sport Pedagogy Special Interest Group. (2009). The educational benefits claimed for physical education and school sport: An academic review. *Research Papers in Education, 24*(1), 1–27.

Benham-Deal, T. & Hudson, N., (2006). Are health educators in denial or

facing reality? Demonstrating effectiveness within a school accountability system. *American Journal of Health Education, 37*(3) 154–158.

Clinton, J., Rensford, A., & Willing, E. (2007). Literature review of the relationship between physical activity, nutrition and academic achievement. Auckland Centre for Health Services, Research and Policy, University of Auckland, New Zealand.

Dwyer, T., Coonan, W., Leitch, D., Hetzel, B., & Baghurst, R. (1983). An Investigation of the effects of daily physical activity on the health of primary school students in South Australia. *International Journal of Epidemiology. 12*(3), 308–313.

Dwyer, T., Sallis, J. F., Blizzard, L., Lazarus, R., & Dean, K. (2001). Relation of academic performance to physical activity and fitness in children. *Pediatric Exercise Science, 13,* 225–237.

Etnier, J. L., & Landers, D. M. (1995). Brain function and exercise. *American Journal of Sports Medicine, 19*(2), 81–85.

Fox, C. K., Barr-Anderson, D., Neumark-Sztainer, D., & Wall, M. (2010). Physical activity and sports team participation: Associations with academic outcomes in middle school and high school students. *Journal of School Health, 80*(1), 31–37.

Gruber, J. J. (1986). Physical activity and self-esteem development in children. In A. G. Stull & H. M. Eckert (Eds.), *Effects of physical activity and self-esteem development in children.* The Academy Papers No 19, 30–48.

Jensen, E. (1998). *Teaching with the brain in mind.* Alexandria. VA: Association for Supervision & Curriculum Development.

Keays, J. J. & Allison, K. R. (1995). The effects of regular moderate to vigorous physical activity on student outcomes: A review. *Canadian Journal of Public Health, 86*(1), 62–65.

Keeley, T. J. H., & Fox, K. R. (2009). The impact of physical activity and fitness on academic achievement and cognitive performance in children. *International Review of Sport and Exercise Psychology, 2*(2), 198–214.

Kirkcaldy, B. D., Shephard, R. J., & Siefen, R. G. (2002).The relationship between physical activity and self-image and problem behaviour among adolescents. *Social Psychiatry and Psychiatric Epidemiology, 37*(11), 544–550.

Murray, N. G., Low, B. J., Hollis, C., Cross, A. W., & Davis, S. M. (2007). Coordinated school health programs and academic achievement: A systematic review of the literature. *Journal of School Health, 77*(9), 589–600.

Ploughman, M. (2008). Exercise is brain food: The effects of physical activity on cognitive function. *Developmental Neurorehabilitation, 11*(3), 236–240.

Putnam, S. C., Tette, J., & Wendt, M. (2004) Exercise: a prescription for at-risk students. *American Journal of Health Education, 75*(9), 25–27.

Scully, D., Kremer, J., Meade, M., Graham, R. & Dudgeon, K. (1998). Physical exercise and psychological well being: A critical review. *Journal of Sports Medicine, 32*(2), 11–120.

Strauss, R. S., Rodzilsky, D., Burack, G., & Colin, M. (2001). Psychosocial correlates of physical activity in healthy children. *Archives of Paediatrics and Adolescent Medicine,155*, 897–902.

Tremblay, M. S., Inman, J. W., & Willms, J. D. (2000). The relationship between physical activity, self-esteem, and academic achievement in 12-year-old children. *Pediatric Exercise Science, 12*, 312–324.

Trudeau, F., & Shephard, R. (2008). Physical education, school physical activity, school sports and academic performance. *International Journal of Behavioral Nutrition and Physical Activity, 5*(1), 5–10.

Wachs, T. D. (1995). Relation of mild-to-moderate malnutrition to human development: Correlational studies. *Journal of Nutrition, 125*(8) 2245S–2254S.

2.5

Gender Influences

Judith Gill
University of South Australia

Introduction

Few topics have generated such vigorous and ongoing debates in recent decades as have those concerning the relationship between gender and achievement. In the 1970s, when the talk was about sex differences in learning outcomes, it seemed that many educationists were inclined to believe the nostrums of early psychology wherein young people were understood to have innate and inevitable differences in their capacity to learn that were reliably demonstrable in learning outcomes. This thinking was about to undergo rapid and fundamental change with the move from thinking of "sex" as fixed and innate to "gender," which was seen as produced by the learner's social context in conjunction with his or her innate potentials. By 2011, the term *sex* had virtually disappeared from the public lexicon and been replaced by *gender* on forms for individual inscription. This change in terminology followed from research results demonstrating that the old truths were no longer universally applicable in terms of male and female differences in learning outcomes, along with science's incapacity to account for the differences that were seen to occur. The following text will offer a broad overview of what we now know about gender and achievement, and what we still do not know.

Research Evidence

In the mid-1970s, the first major review was conducted into sex differences in thinking. Based on hundreds of preceding American studies on the topic, Maccoby and Jacklin (1974) produced their analysis of the combined results and concluded that there were very few reliable and consistent differences in mental functioning between boys and girls, so few in fact that they advised great caution in restating them for fear of perpetuating some of the myths. The researchers insisted that there was far greater variation *within* either population of girls or boys than between them. The one item they cautiously identified

concerns the superior performance of boys from age 10 in mental spatial rotation—a feature often associated with superior mathematical performance in males although its explanatory capacity is much more limited. Subsequently, a prominent British researcher published his review of the British studies of sex differences in cognition and came to the same conclusion (Fairweather, 1976). In this case, he added that the differences were least likely to appear the younger the population tested, giving support to the idea that what was still called sex differences in thinking were socially produced rather than innately given. Despite the clarity of these findings, the high repute of the researchers, and the fact that the finding of no or very little difference continues to be demonstrated (Halpern & Mamay, 2000; Hyde & Lin, 2006), these results did not indicate the end of the story.

The decades following the 1970s produced many examples of research investigating gender differences in schooling outcomes in terms of the subjects girls and boys chose to study, the scores they obtained, their proceeding to tertiary education, and their capacity to engage in the highest levels of intellectual life. Initially, this research typically showed girls trailing boys in a range of performance measures, most notably math and science. Increasingly, it was noticed that the gender gaps in student achievement were seen to increase with age, suggesting that schooling treatments may work to increase the gender differences in achievement rather than reduce them. This perception led to many studies of classroom treatments in the attempt to identify ways in which teaching practice might be implicated in the construction of gender difference (Gill, 1992; Sadker & Sadker, 1994).

During the 1980s and 1990s, there was much activity inspired by feminist efforts to address gender inequity in girls' schooling. Classroom research was dedicated to monitoring the inclusion of girls and their interests, teaching materials were scrutinized to avoid featuring males at the expense of females across the broad spectrum of adult roles, girls were targeted and encouraged to enroll in nontraditional subject areas, especially math and science. In many respects the movement to improve girls' educational outcomes was successful: girls now are seen to get higher grades than boys and more of them complete school than boys. Girls are enrolling in math and science in significant numbers in high school, albeit not quite as commonly as are boys, and they progress to university and choose courses not open to women of previous generations.

While the success story holds true for many middle class girls if less so for girls from disadvantaged backgrounds, by the mid-1990s the situation for boys had become a cause for widespread concern. Boys began to emerge as significantly less successful than girls in terms of learning outcomes. Researchers write of a "small but pervasive tendency for females to score better on standardized tests and to achieve more post school qualifications" (Gibb, Fergusson, & Horwood, 2008, p. 63). Increasing numbers of research papers appeared addressing what became known as the "crisis" in boys' education. Studies have shown that boys are more likely than girls to get referrals for behavioural issues, to present with reading problems, to be identified with ADHD, and to drop out of school before completion. For example, U.S. statistics for the 2003–2004 school year show that 26% of female students became school dropouts compared to 34% of male students. Reports of male underachievement have come from across the developed world (Thiessen & Nickerson, 1999; Tinklin, Croxford, Ducklin, & Frame, 2001; Weaver-Hightower, 2003; Younger & Warrington, 2005). Tallies of high school graduations show girls as the more successful group, more of them go on to university, more of them gain undergraduate degrees—albeit in the fields of education and health, which are not renowned for providing access to the status and power of some other professions. By 2009 for the first time in the United States more women than men graduated with master's degrees. As New Zealand researchers Gibb et al. concluded, "The trend of male underachievement has been evident for at least the last decade" (Gibb et al., 2008, p. 63). However, it is also the case that middle-class boys continue in the main to do well in school. Male underachievement is particularly prevalent among boys from disadvantaged backgrounds whose situation is made more evident with the demise of ready employment in unskilled trades and manufacturing. However the media hype around the "boys' crisis" continues to reproduce a gender wars scenario as though all girls are doing well and all boys are not.

While girls appear to have established themselves as more reliable in terms of passing grades than their male peers, the one area that stands out in the research and popular understanding of gender differences in achievement is science, engineering, technology, and mathematics (STEM). Numerous studies have attempted to demonstrate and explain gender differences in achievement in these areas and have led to a mixed bag of conclusions. For example, it has been alleged that girls' lower achievements in these areas are largely due to their choosing against these courses

in high school and consequently having less experience with numerical and scientific ways of thinking. Conversely, when senior school results for these subjects are compared, a higher proportion of girls is frequently found among the high performers which is explained in terms of the more selective group of girls who form the minority enrolment in these areas. On the other hand, studies continue to show that among the very high performers as evidenced by competitions such as the Mathematics Olympiad and industry led country specific prizes, boys are consistently more likely than girls to be among the winners (Ellison & Swanson, 2009).

One interesting outcome of the Programme for International Student Assessment (PISA) analyses is that the variation in student performance *within* the participating European countries is many times larger than the variation *between* countries. However, differences in test items and survey methodologies make generalizations extremely difficult, with at least one study showing that the gender difference in reading is a product of the test items rather than the individual responses (Lafontaine & Monseur, 2008). Moreover, PISA results suggest that the most consistent and visible gender difference relates to girls' advantage in reading, a gender gap that emerges early and is maintained with age, such that by age 15 there were "significant differences in favour of females reported for virtually all European countries" (Eurydice, 2010, p. 34). There is some indication in this work that the recorded differences result from different patterns of school attendance, with boys tending to start school later and being more likely to be required to repeat a year. Thus testing that records achievement against age should also account for difference in schooling patterns and treatments.

In mathematics, the gender differences were less pronounced and less stable than those for reading. A 1995 survey showed that gender difference in mathematics in the 4th year of schooling was small or nonexistent. A similar "no difference" outcome was found at year 8. It was not until the final year of secondary school that the males emerged with significantly higher mathematical achievement in all countries except Hungary (Eurydice, 2010, p. 35). Other comparable tests found similarly inconsistent results, with gender gaps visible only intermittently across age and culture.

A more promising line of research has been carried out by Hyde and colleagues who argue that there is a much more consistent and demonstrable *similarity* between males and females in mathematics and science capabilities than there is difference (Hyde & Linn, 2006). Based on a meta-analysis of gender differences in mathematics across a sample of 100 studies testing more than 3 million students, Hyde's team was able to show the traditional gap in favour of males had disappeared, an outcome that had been predicted by neuroscientist researchers for some time (Rogers, 2001). This latter case repeats a theme from analyses of the gender and achievement research; that is, the differences that used to be understood as a result of the genetic makeup of males and females have in reality been produced by their different treatment within the social context. Hyde notes that the lack of gender difference in math achievement does not explain the ongoing gender disparity in STEM enrolments which continue to favour males. She suggests that teachers and parents retain stereotypical views of gender related abilities which contribute to this disparity.

Summary and Recommendations

Much has been learned in recent years from the research on gender and achievement. We now know that the older generalizations have little basis in hard evidence and that boys and girls are much more likely to have similar abilities than to be divided in terms of capacity. If we must talk of gender differences in educational outcomes—and we take seriously the warnings of researchers about not wishing to further the difference case!—we should say only that girls as a group emerge as the more reliable scholars in terms of passing grades whereas there are some indications that boys are more spread across the scale, with some found among the very high achievers as well as many others at the lowest underachieving end. By and large, however, the evidence that there is a far greater area of similarity than of difference between girls and boys in terms of learning capacities appears most compelling.

The implications for teaching that follow are that teachers should encourage the young people in their charge to explore and learn unhampered by outdated gender roles. The research shows that gender differences are more often developed in terms of the learner's social context than as a result of innate propensities. The challenge for teachers is to develop all students in ways that maximize potential. This is surely best done by using teaching methods and materials that include men and women as equal active participants in the world beyond school.

References

Ellison, G., & Swanson, A. (2009). The gender gap in secondary school mathematics at high achievement levels. *Journal of Economic Perspectives, 24*(2), 109–128.

Eurydice. (2010). *Gender differences in educational outcomes.* European Commission. Retrieved from http://eacea.ec.europa.eu/education/eurydice/documents/thematic_reports/120EN.pdf.

Fairweather, H. (1976). Sex differences in cognition. *Cognition, 4*(3), 231–280.

Gibb, S. J., Fergusson, D., & Horwood, L. J. (2008). Gender differences in educational achievement to age 25. *Australian Journal of Education, 52*(1), 63–78.

Gill, J. (1992). *Differences in the making: The construction of gender in Australian schooling* (Unpublished doctoral dissertation). Adelaide University, Australia.

Halpern, D. F., & Mamay, M. L. (2000). The smarter sex: A critical review of sex differences in intelligence. https://springerlink3.metapress.com/behavioral-science/*Educational Psychology Review, 12*(2), 229–246.

Hyde, J. S., & Linn, M. (2006, October 27). Gender similarities in mathematics and science. *Science, 314,* 599–600.

Lafontaine, D., & Monseur, C. (2009). Gender gap in comparative studies of reading comprehension: To what extent do the test characteristics make a difference? *European Educational Research Journal, 8*(1), 69–79.

Maccoby, E., & Jacklin, C. N. (1974). *The psychology of sex differences.* Stanford, CA: Stanford University Press.

Rogers, L. (2001). *Sexing the brain.* New York: Columbia University Press.

Sadker, M., & Sadker, D. (1994). *Failing at fairness: How our schools cheat girls.* New York: Simon & Schuster.

Thiessen, V., & Nickerson, C. (1999). *Canadian gender trends in education and work.* Ottawa, Canada: Human Resources Development.

Tinklin, T., Croxford L., Ducklin, A., & Frame, B. (2001). *Gender and pupil performance in Scotland's schools.* Edinburgh, Scotland: Edinburgh University Press.

Weaver-Hightower, M. (2003). The "boy turn" in research on gender and education. *Review of Educational Research, 73*(4), 471–498.

Younger, M., & Warrington, M. (2005). *Raising boys' achievement.* London: Department for Education and Skills.

2.6

Engagement and Opportunity to Learn

PHILLIP L. ACKERMAN
Georgia Institute of Technology

Introduction

Student engagement in academic contexts, both in and out of the classroom, is a relatively recent construct, having only appeared in the literature since the 1980s (Mosher & MacGowan, 1985). Although the core construct is readily understood (e.g., in distinguishing between a student who is engaged in the academic situation as opposed to one who is disengaged), there is substantial disagreement about the breadth of the construct (Appleton, Christenson, & Furlong, 2008). Some researchers limit their consideration of student engagement to the student's motivation to learn or the student's effort in class, whereas other researchers consider the student's interest in a topic, the student's completion of homework or other assignments, the student's attitudes toward the school experience, and even whether or not the student engages in school- related extracurricular activities.

Student engagement can be considered from a "customer" or student perspective. From this perspective, when the student is happily involved in school activities, he or she could be considered to be highly engaged. In contrast, a student who is frequently absent and who is inattentive and uninvolved in school activities could be considered to be disengaged. Student engagement can also be considered from a "medical" perspective. From this perspective, a student's disengagement from the school would be considered a disorder that has a variety of symptoms (e.g., lack of enthusiasm, low motivation to learn, absenteeism, etc.). A student who is positively engaged at school would be considered healthy or normal.

The fundamental underlying assumption is that a student who is positively engaged at school will both achieve more and be more satisfied with the school experience than a student who is disengaged. However, one can also consider a more nuanced approach; that is, that disengaged students do not succeed at school or even have high rates of drop-out, either in high school or in postsecondary study; but once

a threshold level of engagement is reached, higher levels of engagement may have little effect on academic achievement. The more nuanced approach is consistent with the results of an analysis of student engagement (in terms of a "sense of belonging" and "participation") in the large-scale cross-national Programme for International Student Assessment (PISA) survey (Wilms, 2003). In this study, five clusters of students were found, referred to as "Top students," "Engaged students," "Students feeling isolated," "Absentee students," and "Non-academic students." When compared on both engagement measures and reading and math literacy performance, the top students and engaged students outperformed the students in the other three less engaged groups of students. However, the top students had substantially lower "sense of belonging" than the engaged students, yet the top students had much higher levels of reading and math literacy.

Research Evidence

The personal attributes that make up the myriad descriptions of student engagement has been referred to as a "meta-construct" (Frederiks, Blumenfeld, & Paris, 2004; Marks, 2000) or "trait complex" (Ackerman & Heggestad, 1997). Trait complexes are groups of cognitive (ability), affective (personality), and conative (motivation, volition, interests) traits that have significant degrees of shared variance; that is, the traits are substantially positively correlated with one another, and are generally unrelated to other traits. One overarching consideration is needed for this discussion, and that is Thorndike's notion that all "good" characteristics tend to be positively correlated with one another (Ackerman, 1997). There is substantial evidence that positively framed traits (e.g., well-being, intelligence, interest in a wide variety of activities, etc.) are positively correlated with one another. For example, a student who is engaged at school is more likely to have, all other things being equal, higher ability levels, higher levels of self-concept, higher educational aspirations, and so on, compared to a student who is disengaged at school.

Trait Complexes. Two trait complexes that are likely to be highly related to student engagement are the Intellectual/Cultural trait complex, and the Science/Math trait complex (Ackerman & Heggestad, 1997). The Intellectual/Cultural trait complex includes abilities of crystallized intelligence (knowledge and skills across many domains, verbal knowledge, vocabulary, fluency, verbal self-concept, and so on), the personality traits of openness to experience and absorption, and the vocational interests identified as artistic and investigative themes. The Science/Math trait complex includes math and spatial abilities, and both realistic and investigative vocational interest themes, but does not include any specific personality characteristics. In a series of empirical studies of young and middle-aged adults, these two trait complexes tend to be correlated relatively modestly, meaning that being engaged in one domain is not highly related to being engaged in the other domain. In addition, both the Intellectual/Cultural and Science/Math trait complexes are significantly positively related to academic achievement at the postsecondary level (e.g., see Ackerman et al., 2001).

One variable that is an integral component to the Intellectual/Cultural trait complex is called Typical Intellectual Engagement (Goff & Ackerman, 1992). Students who score high on this scale report a higher degree of interest in and engagement with intellectually demanding activities. Scores on this measure have been positively associated with school grades and domain knowledge, especially in social sciences and humanities areas. However, it is important to note that although high-scoring individuals are likely to be more engaged at school, they also tend to be more intellectually engaged in situations that are not specifically educational in context. Thus, such individuals are likely to seek opportunities to learn, even when not required to do so.

Another trait complex that might be expected to have mixed relations with student engagement is the Social trait complex. The Social trait complex is composed of personality traits of extraversion and well-being and enterprising and social vocational interests but this trait complex is not associated with any traditional measures of intellectual abilities. The reason that one can expect mixed relations of the Social trait complex with student engagement is that individual differences in the Social trait complex are likely to be negatively associated with achievement measures in academic courses (e.g., math, science, English, history) but have positive relations with the student's social interactions in the classroom and in school-related extracurricular activities. In general, scores on the Social trait complex are negatively associated with academic performance at the postsecondary level (e.g., see Ackerman, Chamorro-Premuzic, & Furnham, 2001).

Educational Aspirations and Life Goals. Individual differences in educational aspirations and life goals are also expected to be associated with measures of student engagement. In general, these variables make up either a vicious circle or a virtuous circle, as the child develops into adolescence and early adulthood, much in the way that self-concept and interests develop (Holland, 1973). That is, early successes in a particular domain, such as math, lead to increases in math self-concept and math self-efficacy, which in turn lead to increases in interest in math topics, engagement in math classes, and an increase in domain knowledge and skills. Each additional success, in turn, leads to increased engagement and further successes. In contrast, failures encountered by the student will lead to decreases in self-concept and interests, which lead to disengagement in math classes and thus limit acquisition of new domain knowledge and skills. Eventually, after encountering repeated failures and accumulating associated losses of self-efficacy and motivation, one would expect that the student will be more likely to "leave the field of conflict" (after Lewin) and thus be at risk for dropping out. In this context, efforts to ameliorate student disengagement may be seen as valuable, even in the absence of concerns with achievement per se (Marks, 2000).

Summary and Recommendations

In the PISA study (Wilms, 2003) the correlation between student engagement and reading/math/ science literacy at the individual student level was relatively modest (*r*s = .07 and .14, for "sense of belonging" and "participation," respectively). However, when the data were examined at the school level, the relationship was much stronger (*r* = .50). That is, schools where students have higher levels of overall engagement also are likely to have higher levels of overall achievement. Although there are external variables that influence this relationship (e.g., socioeconomic status), students tended to be "more engaged in schools where there is a strong disciplinary climate, positive student-teacher relations, and high expectations for student success" (p. 57). From this perspective, student engagement is a complex function of individual traits, teacher behaviors, school and curricular characteristics, and community characteristics. Schools that provide more opportunities for engagement appear to have students who report higher levels of a sense of belonging and participation.

Because the field of student engagement research is still relatively new, it is as yet unknown to what degree teacher and school interventions can lead to changes in individual student engagement. Based on the extant empirical research and theory, it appears that when academic achievement is the main criterion variable, student engagement is not a critical concern for the highly talented students, as they appear to succeed even when they have relatively moderate levels of engagement. The more critical issue is determining the interventions that are maximally effective for the group of at-risk students who are both relatively disengaged and who perform below average on achievement measures. Such a perspective is consistent with an aptitude–treatment interaction, where the greatest benefits will come from classroom interventions that are aimed at both the schools and individuals that are low-achieving and low in engagement measures. Because the relations among student engagement and academic achievement appear to be reciprocal (Skinner & Belmont, 1993), it may be most appropriate to focus on improving both achievement and engagement simultaneously, rather than focusing only on one or the other variable.

References

Ackerman, P. L. (1997). Personality, self-concept, interests, and intelligence: Which construct doesn't fit? *Journal of Personality, 65*(2), 171–204.

Ackerman, P. L., Chamorro-Premuzic, T., & Furnham, A. (2001). Trait complexes and academic achievement: Old and new ways of examining personality in educational contexts. *British Journal of Educational Psychology, 81*(1), 27–40.

Ackerman, P. L., & Heggestad, E. D. (1997). Intelligence, personality, and interests: Evidence for overlapping traits. *Psychological Bulletin, 121*, 219–245.

Appleton, J. J., Christenson, S. L., & Furlong, M. J. (2008). Student engagement with school: Critical conceptual and methodological issues of the construct. *Psychology in the Schools, 45*, 369–386.

Frederiks, J. A., Blumenfeld, P. C., & Paris, A. H. (2004). School engagement: Potential of the concept, state of the evidence. *Review of Educational Research, 74*, 59–109.

Goff, M., & Ackerman, P. L. (1992). Personality-intelligence relations: Assessing typical intellectual engagement. *Journal of Educational Psychology, 84*, 537–552.

Holland, J. L. (1973). *Making vocational choices: A theory of careers.* Englewood Cliffs, NJ: Prentice Hall.

Marks, H. M. (2000). Student engagement in instructional activity: Patterns in the elementary, middle, and high school years. *American Educational Research Journal, 37*, 153–184.

Mosher, R., & MacGowan, B. (1985). *Assessing student engagement in secondary schools: Alternative conceptions, strategies of assessing, and instruments.* Madison, WI: University of Wisconsin, Research and Development Center. Retrieved from ERIC database. (ERIC Document Reproduction Service No. ED 272812)

Skinner, E. A., & Belmont, M. J. (1993). Motivation in the classroom: Reciprocal effects of teacher behavior and student engagement across the school year. *Journal of Educational Psychology, 85*, 571–581.

Willms, J. D. (2003). *Student engagement at school: A sense of belonging and participation, Results from Pisa 2000.* Paris: Organisation for Economic Co-Operation and Development.

2.7

Behavioral Engagement in Learning

Jennifer Fredricks
Connecticut College

Introduction

There is a long history of research on behavioral engagement in learning that grew out of earlier studies on attention, time-on-task, and classroom participation. Studies conducted in the 1960 and 1970s demonstrated that paying attention, responding to teachers' direction, and time on task was positively related achievement (Finn, 1989). More recently, there has been an explosion in interest in engagement as a construct and a key contributor to students' academic success. Increasing engagement has been seen as a potential answer to problems of declining motivation and achievement, high levels of student alienation, and high dropout rates (Fredricks, Blumenfeld, & Paris, 2004). In a review of the literature, Fredricks and her colleagues (2004) outlined three different ways that behavioral engagement has been defined, including positive conduct (e.g., following the rules, attendance, absence of disruptive behavior), involvement in learning and academic tasks (e.g., effort, persistence, concentration, and attention), and involvement in school-related activities. Some definitions contrast the positive aspects of behavioral engagement in learning with inattentive behavior, off-task behavior, and behavioral disaffection.

Research Evidence

A growing body of research shows a positive correlation between behavioral engagement and achievement (Fredricks et al., 2004). The majority of these findings have been based on cross-sectional and short-term longitudinal studies during the elementary school years. In addition, several studies have documented a link between disruptive and problem behavior (i.e., behavioral disengagement) and lower academic performance (Fredricks et al., 2004).The strength of the relation between behavioral engagement and achievement varies across these studies as a function of differences in the measures of achievement (i.e., grades,

standardized achievement tests) and variations in age, types of students, and types of schools (Fredricks et al., 2004). It is possible for some students to score high on achievement tests but not be behaviorally engaged in learning because some tests require only superficial understanding and short-term retention. In addition, there may only be a modest relation between behavioral engagement and achievement in some studies because some low-achieving students are highly engaged in learning because they find schoolwork difficult, while high-achieving students can succeed and be less behaviorally engaged because prior achievement makes it easier for them to achieve school success (Newmann, Wehlage, & Lamborn, 1992).

Behavioral patterns in the early years can persist and have long-term behavioral consequences. Evidence from the Beginning School Study showed that teachers' behavioral ratings in the first grade were related to achievement score gains, grades over the first four years, and the decision to drop out of high school (Fredricks et al., 2004). According to the participation-identification model (Finn, 1989), behavioral engagement (i.e. participation) in learning in the early years leads to higher emotional engagement (i.e., identification with school). In contrast, students with non-participatory behaviors are at increased risk for emotional and physical withdrawal over time. Concerns about high dropout rates have led to an increased focus on identifying the factors that lead students to disengage from school. Child attributes such as low socioeconomic status, low achievement, and externalizing behaviors place children at higher risk for disengagement and school problems.

Several scholars have posited that behavioral engagement is the link between contextual factors (or what teachers do) and achievement (or what students learn in the classroom; Fredricks et al., 2004). There is growing empirical support for a mediation model of engagement (see, for example, Hughs, Luo, Kwok, & Loyd, 2008). That is, behavioral engagement is likely to lead to higher achievement because a student is involved in the behaviors related to learning such as concentrating, exerting effort, taking initiative, and being persistent in the face of failure. Students who are behaviorally engaged follow the rules and interact positively with the teacher and their peers. In contrast, students who are behaviorally disengaged do not participate in the academic behaviors that can increase achievement. These students have higher antisocial behaviors which can disrupt the teacher and other students and make it harder to learn.

There is a growing literature on the aspects of the school and classroom context that promote behavioral engagement (Fredricks et al., 2004). Several studies have linked aspects of the social environment, including teacher support (i.e., caring, quality relationships) and positive peer relations to higher behavioral engagement. Moreover, behavioral engagement is higher in classrooms where tasks are varied, interesting, meaningful, and challenging, and where there is an adequate level of structure and rules and routines to maintain time on task (Fredricks et al., 2004). High-quality instruction also has been linked to higher behavioral engagement (Pianta, La Paro, Payne, Cox, & Bradley, 2002). In these classrooms, teachers form personal relationships with students, encourage autonomy, establish clear rules for instruction, apply concepts to the real world, and provide a variety of activities to sustain students' interest and attention.

The level of behavioral engagement varies across instructional contexts, though the findings on which contexts are most engaging differ across methodologies and cultures. Evidence from studies using experience sampling techniques shows that behavioral engagement is higher in classrooms where students perceive instruction as challenging and where youth are in cooperative group activities as opposed to large group discussions (Shernoff & Csikszentmihalyi, 2009). In contrast, observational studies in the United States show that behavioral engagement is higher in structured teacher-directed settings than in other activities with less teacher direction, such as centers, seatwork, and free time (Rimm-Kaufman, La Paro, Downer, & Pianta, 2005). In addition, in an observational study, behavioral engagement was higher in both Chinese and American classrooms in large-group than in small-group settings (Lan et al., 2009).

There are also international differences that may be critical. An evaluation of the Program for International Assessment data (PISA) demonstrated large variation in both the level of behavioral engagement (i.e., participation) and in the number of disengaged youth (Wilms, 2003). In a study of behavioral engagement in Chinese and American classroom, Lan and colleagues (2009) found that engagement declined over time but the decline was significantly larger in American than in Asian classrooms. Other studies have examined cross-cultural differences in opportunities to learn as it relates to behavioral engagement. For example, Clarke-Stewart and colleagues (Clarke-Stewart, Lee, Allhusen, Kim, & McDowell, 2006) found that Korean children exhibited greater sustained attention and engagement than did American children in early childhood settings. Finally,

in a study of New Zealand classrooms, Anderson, Hamilton, and Hattie (2004) found that the level of affiliation was positively related to teacher and self-reports of behavioral engagement.

Summary and Recommendations

Although research on behavioral engagement in learning has proliferated, the large variation in the conceptualization of this construct has made it challenging to compare findings on the effects of behavioral engagement on achievement (Fredricks et al., 2004). Recently, scholars have proposed a multidimensional conceptualization of engagement that includes behavioral, emotional, or cognitive engagement, arguing that this provides a richer characterization of learning than examining each component in isolation (Fredricks et al., 2004). Establishing greater clarity in the conceptualization and measurement of behavioral engagement and how it relates to both emotional and cognitive engagement is a critical area of future work. In addition, there is a need for longitudinal studies about how each type of engagement develops, influences each other over time, and differentially relates to achievement.

In sum, research indicates that behavioral engagement is positively related to both academic achievement and school retention. Some scholars study behavioral engagement as a mediator between contextual factors and desired learning outcomes and others have examined it as outcome in its own right (Fredricks et al., 2004). An important message for educators is that the contexts matter and it is possible to increase behavioral engagement by changing aspects of the environment. Teachers can increase behavioral engagement in learning by: (a) showing students that they care about them, (b) creating a positive social environment, (c) having clear expectations, rules, and routines to maximize time on task, and (d) including a variety of activities that have real world applications and sustain students' attention (Fredricks, 2011). A person-environment fit should be applied to both future research and practice. It is critical to identify instructional environments that can increase behavioral engagement in learning and tailor these environments to the individual needs of children.

References

Anderson, A., Hamilton, R. J., & Hattie, J. (2004). Classroom climate and motivated behaviour in secondary schools. *Learning Environment Research, 7,* 211–225.

Clarke-Stewart, A., Lee, Y., Allhusen, V. D., Kim, M. S., & McDowell, D. J. (2006). Observed differences between early childhood programs in the U.S. and Korea: Reflections of developmentally appropriate practices in two cultural contexts. *Journal of Applied Developmental Psychology, 27,* 427–443.

Finn, J. D. (1989). Withdrawing from school. *Review of Educational Research, 59,* 117–142.

Fredricks, J. A. (2011). Engagement in school and out of school contexts: A multidimensional view of engagement. *Theory Into Practice, 50,* 327–335.

Fredricks, J. A., Blumenfeld, P. C., & Paris, A. (2004). School engagement:

Potential of the concept: State of the evidence. *Review of Educational Research, 74,* 59–119.

Hughs, J. N., Luo, W., Kwok, O-M., & Loyd, L. K. (2008). Teacher–student support, effortful engagement, and achievement: A 3-year longitudinal study. *Journal of Educational Psychology, 100,* 1–14.

Lan, X., Pointz, C. C., Miller, K. M., Li, S., Cortina, K., Perry, M., & Fang, G. (2009). Keeping their attention: Classroom practices associated with behavioral engagement in first grade mathematics classes in China and the United States. *Early Childhood Research Quarterly, 24,* 198–211.

Newmann, F., Wehlage, G. G., & Lamborn, S. D. (1992). The significance and sources of student engagement. In F. Newmann (Ed.), *Student engagement and achievement in American secondary schools* (pp. 11–39). New York: Teachers College Press.

Pianta, R. C, La Paro, K. M., Payne, C., Cox, M. J., & Bradley, R. (2002). The relation of kindergarten classroom environment to teacher, family, and school characteristics and child outcomes. *Elementary School Journal, 102,* 225–238.

Rimm-Kaufman, S. E., La Paro, K. M., Downer, J. T., & Pianta, R. C. (2005). The contribution of classroom setting and quality of instruction to children's behavior in the kindergarten classroom. *Elementary School Journal, 105,* 377–394.

Shernoff, D. J., & Csikszentmihalyi, M. (2009). Flow in schools: Cultivating engaged learners and optimal learning environments. In R. Gilman, E. S. Huebner, & M. J. Furlong (Eds.), *Handbook of positive psychology in schools* (pp. 131–146). New York: Routledge.

Wilms, J. D. (2003). *Student engagement at school: A sense of belonging and participation. Results from PISA 2000.* Paris: OECD. Retrieved from http://www.oecd.org/dataoecd/42/35/33689437.pdf

2.8

Goal Setting and Academic Achievement

DOMINIQUE MORISANO
Centre for Addiction and Mental Health and Univeristy of Toronto, Ontario, Canada

EDWIN A. LOCKE
University of Maryland

Introduction

Goals have been shown to be reliable, powerful, and proximal determinants of action (Locke & Latham, 2002). They have the strongest effect on action when they are both specific and challenging. In the field of education, it has been found that "grade goals" (best measured as "the minimum grade you would be satisfied with" or "the lowest grade you would not be dissatisfied with") are consistent predictors of actual grades (e.g., Locke & Bryan, 1968; Wood & Locke, 1987; cf. Locke & Latham, 2002). Zimmerman and Bandura (1994) had students rate the strength of their belief that they could achieve each of 12 grades ranging from A to F (- and +) on a 7-point scale. They, as well, found that grade goals correlated with final course grades, and that perceived self-efficacy affected goals. Goal-intervention programs have also been found to improve student performance (Morisano, Hirsh, Peterson, Pihl, & Shore, 2010), thus providing strong evidence of the causal effect of goals (supporting Locke & Latham, 2002).

Research Evidence

Goals affect action through specific mechanisms. First, individuals who set goals are better able to direct attention toward goal-relevant activities while avoiding distractions. Second, if goals are challenging, they arouse effort in accordance with difficulty level. Third, goals increase persistence, because people keep working until they have reached the goal (assuming commitment—see below). Lastly, well-defined goals motivate people to search for and apply strategies that will help goal attainment.

Goals for outcomes do not always work, however. When assigning new and complex tasks in a classroom context, it might work best to also provide students with initial learning goals so that they can focus on discovering effective strategies. Once they know what to do, setting performance goals

can be effective, given the following boundary conditions. First, there must be feedback so that people can monitor goal progress. If progress is poor, this feedback might signal them to work harder or try new strategies. Second, there must be goal commitment. The main factors fostering commitment are the attractiveness or importance of the goal and an individual's confidence regarding his or her ability to make goal progress (i.e., self-efficacy).

Self-efficacy not only influences one's chosen goal's difficulty level, but also one's goal commitment, strategy choice, and failure response. It often has a direct effect on performance and student retention rates. Like goals, self-efficacy affects effort and persistence, and can mediate the effect of other variables (e.g., skill acquisition) on achievement. Both goals and self-efficacy are mediators of feedback effects (cf. Locke & Latham, 2002). As a student experiences goal attainment, self-efficacy increases; this in turn enhances goal commitment and mobilizes the self-regulation of cognitive and motivational resources to facilitate subsequent achievement. Proximal academic achievement is affected by an interconnected set of causal factors that includes goals, self-efficacy, and their mediators and moderators as well as emotions; these all change dynamically as different milestones are reached (see Covington, 2000, for a review).

Mastery and Performance Goals. Goal-setting theory stresses the use of quantitative versus general "do your best" goals. However, within educational psychology there has been considerable research on general achievement goals. An "achievement goal" represents the underlying purposes for engaging in achievement-related behavior. Achievement-goal theory surmises that individual differences impact how goals influence school performance, via variations in cognitive self-regulation (e.g., quality, timing, and appropriateness of cognitive strategies; Covington, 2000).

Two major categories of achievement goals have been established: mastery goals (also called learning or task goals) and performance goals (also called ego-, ego-involved, ability, competitive, and self-enhancing goals). Mastery goals, which focus on the acquisition of new knowledge or skills, have been associated with several outcomes: (a) deeper and more strategic processing of information and classroom materials (see Covington, 2000); (b) persistence and effort in the face of obstacles; and (c) motivation and interest in the course material. When a course involves sustained challenge and complexity, or when the task is personally motivating, mastery goals can positively impact academic performance as well as intrinsic motivation, even in the face of setbacks and low self-efficacy (Grant & Dweck, 2003). With regard to performance goals, these can refer to many things. Performance goals may focus on relieving self-doubt or gaining rewards (Covington, 2000). They are also sometimes viewed as things one does to impress others, which could lead to trying for low goals that lead to ready success; such goals would not necessarily motivate high performance. They also might involve competitive motivation (beating others). This variation can make it hard to evaluate studies using performance goals. Linnenbrink-Garcia and colleagues (Linnenbrink-Garcia, Tyson, & Patall, 2008) addressed the mastery/performance goal debate with a review of over 90 articles, and found that 40% of reported effects showed a positive relation between both mastery and performance goals with achievement; less than 5% showed a negative relation. But they did not report which measures of performance goals were used.

Some have suggested that classroom context is important in achievement-goal orientation. Harackiewicz, Barron, Carter, Lehto, and Elliot (1997) found that students in a large lecture class adopting mastery-oriented goals (self-set and generalized) showed more interest in the class, but those with performance goals had higher course grades. Although mastery and performance goals can both lead to important positive outcomes, performance-goal orientations might be more facilitative of objective performance in large classes with multiple-choice exams and normative grading structures, due to the performance-oriented nature of the class context.

To achieve greater conceptual clarity regarding achievement goals, some have distinguished between performance and mastery "approach" or "avoidance" goals. Approach goals typically focus on attaining or sustaining desired ends, while avoidance goals involve evading or abolishing unwanted ends. Approach goals of either type are better for achievement than avoidance goals (Daniels et al., 2008). Performance-approach goals that aim to validate ability level (e.g., "show others that I do well in school") promote frequent rehearsal and good grades, but also produce superficial levels of processing. Performance-avoidance goals aim to avoid exposing low ability (Grant & Dweck, 2003), and ultimately foster disorganized study strategies, anxiety, and poor grades (Okun, Fairholme, Karoly, Ruehlman, & Newton, 2006). Similarly, mastery-approach goals are associated with positive outcomes (grades, deeper processing of material, well-being); mastery-avoidance goals are not, although their outcomes have been deemed less harmful than performance-avoidance outcomes. In keeping with these subcategories, some have endorsed a "multiple goals" framework (e.g., Pintrich, Conley, & Kempler, 2003), suggesting that students benefit most from a combination of performance-approach and mastery-approach goals.

Durik, Lovejoy, and Johnson (2009) found, after controlling for ability, that performance-approach goals positively predicted 2-year GPA among first-semester university students, while performance-avoidance goals negatively predicted performance; mastery goals had no predictive power. In turn, Diseth and Kobbeltvedt (2010) found that among Norwegian undergraduate students, grades were positively correlated with performance-approach and mastery goals, and negatively correlated with performance-avoidance goals. Harackiewicz's group (Harackiewicz, Durik, Barron, Linnenbrink-Garcia, & Tauer, 2008) similarly showed that performance-approach goals in a single course predicted overall long-term GPA.

Daniels and colleagues (2008) showed that individuals with multiple (high mastery-approach/high performance-approach), performance-approach, or mastery-approach goal clusters had similar levels of achievement (measured by a single course grade and overall GPA), but students in the performance-goal cluster were more emotionally vulnerable (note that avoidance goals were not measured). The results suggested that approach goals are better than no goals. However, the authors implied the need for a multiple-goal perspective, suggesting that performance goals undermine positive affect unless coupled with mastery goals. They concluded that mastery goals, on their own or in combination with performance goals, promoted the most positive set of emotions, cognitive appraisals, and achievement, except when performance goals were heavily weighted (in which case anxiety rose).

Brief Research Critiques.   Many universities offer mentoring programs, freshman-interest groups, seminars or learning communities, and service-learning programs to ease the transition to university. Although these programs might broadly improve student experience, little rigorous, randomized, and controlled experimental research has been done to assess whether they actually impact general student outcomes, let alone whether they improve overall grade-point averages (GPAs). Furthermore, of the studies that have been done on specific targeted interventions, many focused on students with several elements of risk (e.g., subgroups of minority students in community colleges), leaving it difficult to generalize any successful results to other student populations.

In contrast, there is solid, ever-growing, experimental evidence (see above) that helping students to set academic goals improves grades. We have even found some preliminary evidence that taking the time to write in detail about one's "life goals" (or personal goals) can impact school success. In the Morisano et al. (2010) study noted earlier, it was investigated whether an online personal goal-setting program would have positive effects on achievement among academically struggling university students. Students were recruited to participate in a randomized, controlled intervention, with half completing the goal-setting program, and half completing a control "intervention." After a 4-month follow-up, students who set personal goals displayed significant improvements in academic performance (semester GPA) compared with the control group.

In spite of the evidence for goal setting, however, there are always caveats. With some of the studies that have specifically focused on performance versus mastery goals, for example, associations between outcomes and goal type have been correlational and not causal. Harackiewicz, Barron et al. (1997) suggested that particular types of people might be more likely to adopt certain types of goals; for example, academically successful students might be more prone to adopt performance goals, while students with a keen interest in a topic might adopt mastery goals in studying that topic. And this begs the question: Is there such a thing as general goal orientation versus orientation for specific task goals? In order to get at the role of individual differences, future studies could allow individuals to set their own goals. Furthermore, with studies showing a relationship between student-reported performance goals and higher exam grades, it is possible that the higher grades might be related to exam format and goodness-of-fit of information processing. In other words, according to Okun et al. (2006), performance goals might be associated with shallower information processing that aligns more closely with exam formats such as multiple-choice, used often for exams in large classes. They suggested that further research should acknowledge the conflict between information processing and exam formats when reporting outcomes. Mastery goals could be more beneficial without multiple-choice formats.

Culture also needs consideration in goal-setting research. Values of autonomy, independence, and healthy (or unhealthy) competition are often associated with the Western Hemisphere. In turn, most studies that have been done on goal setting and academic achievement have also come out in the Western Hemisphere. In this context, Covington (2000) has suggested that we aim to understand more fully the nature and costs of the disconnect between cultural values and achievement structures. For example, how do social goals interact with academic goals (mastery vs. performance), and what are the associated motivational aspects of these types of goals? How do school and cultural reward structures impact the goals that students develop? It would be a fascinating global exercise to see how goal setting (personal or academic) impacts academic (or other) achievement in a non-American or European context.

Furthermore, many of the articles that were reviewed when putting together this chapter mentioned problems with goal definitions (especially performance goals) and making proper distinctions. Pintrich et al. (2003) called attention to the measurement issues involved in studying goal defini-

tions and the role of contextual factors. Taking the time to further distinguish between major and minor types of goals could enhance research findings and resolve conflicts that have arisen (Grant & Dweck, 2003). Is a two- (mastery, performance), three- (mastery, performance-approach, and performance-avoidance), or four-goal (mastery-approach/avoidance and performance-approach/avoidance) model more appropriate for future research? Pintrich and colleagues offered the following questions (p. 331): "Do students operate according to the one goal that is most salient to them, or do we need to look more carefully at the dynamics involved when individuals adopt multiple goals? Second, what is the difference between goals that arise from the individual and goals that arise from the context? Further, is there an important distinction between perceived and actual contextual goals?"

Moving forward, we should also consider other avenues of practical but experimentally rigorous research in the context of goal setting and academic achievement. For instance, how do different levels of perfectionism impact outcomes? How does age impact general goal orientation and goal choice? How do subconscious goals impact outcomes, and how do we study this?

Summary and Recommendations

Numerous factors, such as a lack of goal clarity or low motivation, are potential contributors to poor grades. Without proper intervention, subpar school performance can precede demotivation, which can lead to poorer grades, which can result in course failures, which can give rise to ultimate school departure or expulsion. It is a vicious cycle. Regardless of the point in time that the performance drop occurs or the reason for the difficulty, intervention is key, and teaching our students academic goal-setting is a simple and reasonable solution.

Diseth and Kobbeltvedt (2010) and Pintrich et al. (2003) have recommended the use of a multiple-goal approach including both performance-approach and mastery goals. They suggested that teachers foster opportunities for mastery experiences among students, for example, by engendering intrinsic interest in course topics and limiting excessive workloads. Zimmerman and Bandura (1994) proposed that due to the relationship between self-efficacy, goal-setting, and academic achievement, teachers should also consider making diagnostic assessments of students' self-regulatory efficacy at the outset of courses, in order to reveal specific areas where each student feels inadequate (e.g., time management) and to highlight appropriate solutions.

High school teachers, guidance counselors, and parents should consider encouraging students to choose and reflect on personally important short- and long-term goals as they prepare for college. Universities, in turn, are recommended to focus on prematriculation writing assignments on goal clarification (e.g., Morisano et al., 2010); university instructors might include writing about personal goals as an in-class or take-home assignment.

What is the bottom line? So far, high academic performance coupled with positive well-being is best achieved with a combination of cognitive ability, high grade goals, high mastery-approach and performance-approach goals focused on individually chosen outcomes, high self-efficacy, feedback, and commitment. None of this denies the great importance of outstanding teaching and institutional support.

References

Covington, M. V. (2000). Goal theory, motivation, and school achievement: An integrative review. *Annual Review of Psychology, 51,* 171–200.

Daniels, L. M., Haynes, T. L., Stupnisky, R. H., Perry, R. P., Newall, N., & Pekrun, R. (2008). Individual differences in achievement goals: A longitudinal study of cognitive, emotional, and achievement outcomes. *Contemporary Educational Psychology, 33,* 584–608.

Diseth, A. & Kobbeltvedt, T. (2010). A mediation analysis of achievement motives, goals, learning strategies, and academic achievement. *British Journal of Educational Psychology, 80,* 671–687.

Durik, A. M., Lovejoy, C. M., & Johnson, S. J. (2009). A longitudinal study of achievement goals for college in general: Predicting cumulative GPA and diversity in course selection. *Contemporary Educational Psychology, 34,* 113–119.

Grant, H., & Dweck, C. (2003). Clarifying achievement goals and their impact. *Journal of Personality and Social Psychology, 85,* 541–553.

Harackiewicz, J. M., Barron, K. E., Carter, S. M., Lehto, A. T., & Elliot, A. J. (1997). Predictors and consequences of achievement goals in the college classroom: Maintaining interest and making the grade. *Journal of Personality and Social Psychology, 73,* 1284–1295.

Harackiewicz, J. M., Durik, A. M., Barron, K. E., Linnenbrink-Garcia, L., & Tauer, J. M. (2008). The role of achievement goals in the development of interest: Reciprocal relations between achievement goals, interest and performance. *Journal of Educational Psychology, 100*(1), 105–122.

Linnenbrink-Garcia, L., Tyson, D. E., & Patall, E. A. (2008). When are achievement goal orientations beneficial for academic achievement? A closer look at main effects and moderating factors. *International Review of Social Psychology, 21,* 19–70.

Locke, E. A., & Bryan, J. F. (1968). Grade goals as determinants of academic achievement. *Journal of General Psychology, 79,* 217–228.

Locke, E. A., & Latham, G. P. (2002). Building a practically useful theory of goal setting and task motivation: A 35-year odyssey. *American Psychologist, 57,* 705–717.

Morisano, D., Hirsh, J. B, Peterson, J. B., Pihl, R. O., & Shore, B. M. (2010). Setting, elaborating, and reflecting on personal goals improves academic performance. *Journal of Applied Psychology, 95*(2), 255–264.

Okun, M. A., Fairholme, C., Karoly, P., Ruehlman, L. S., & Newton, C. (2006). Academic goals, goal process cognition, and exam performance among college students. *Learning and Individual Differences, 16,* 255–265.

Pintrich, P. R., Conley, A. M., & Kempler, T. M. (2003). Current issues in achievement goal theory and research. *International Journal of Educational Research, 39,* 319–338.

Wood, R. E., & Locke, E. A. (1987). The relation of self-efficacy and grade goals to academic performance. *Educational and Psychological Measurement, 47,* 1013–1024.

Zimmerman, B. J., & Bandura, A. (1994). Impact of self-regulatory influences on writing course attainment. *American Educational Research Journal, 31,* 845–862.

2.9

Self-Reported Grades and GPA

MARCUS CREDÉ
University of Albany

NATHAN R. KUNCEL
University of Minnesota

Introduction

Educational researchers often gather information on participants' high school grade point average (GPA) as an indicator of prior academic performance and summaries of student learning. Given the practical difficulties associated with obtaining participants' consent and subsequent access to their high school or university academic records, many researchers use self-reported GPA as a proxy for actual GPA (e.g., the GPA reported in academic transcripts). Although self-reported GPA is strongly correlated with actual GPA in general, there are several sources of systematic errors associated with it.

Research Evidence

The reliance on self-reported GPA is based on the dual assumption that any errors in the reporting of GPA are both small and nonsystematic. It is assumed that most individuals report their GPA with a great deal of accuracy and there is no tendency for a certain type of individuals to report their GPA with a greater or lesser degree of accuracy than other individuals.

Previous meta-analytic reviews of the validity of self-reported academic performance indicators (Kuncel, Credé, & Thomas, 2005) have shed some light on these two assumptions. Specifically, self-reported high school GPA is relatively strongly correlated with actual high school GPA ($r = .82$, $k = 17$, $N = 44,176$) but there is also a general tendency for students to overreport their high school GPA ($d = .32$, $k = 12$, $N = 4,566$). Further, students with low grades tend to overreport their level of achievement more than students with medium or high grades. Therefore, there is a relatively high level of correspondence between self-reported and actual GPA but there are nontrivial errors in reporting that are not randomly distributed.

Discrepancies between self-reported and actual high school GPAs are largely due to three factors, each of which has a unique effect on the construct validity of self-reported GPA.

- First, participants simply do not remember their high school GPA with a high degree of accuracy. The influence of this factor increases with the amount of time that has elapsed since the participant graduated high school. This effect implies that self-reported GPA has some amount of random error added to it.

- Second, participants base their report on performance in classes that are not taken into account for the calculation of "official" high school GPA, such as grades in classes outside the core curriculum or where grades tend to be uniformly high (e.g., a physical education class). Similarly, some universities use GPAs constructed on the basis of their own admissions rules (e.g., academic classes only) and even an accurately self-reported high school GPA does not necessarily reflect the numbers used for decision-making purposes by the institution. This factor accounts for the general overreporting of high school GPA evident when relying on self-reports. This factor also represents a possible source of systematic error (construct-irrelevant variance; Messick, 1995) because the inclusion of grades from noncore classes in the calculation of high school GPA would affect the average of the students with low grades more than the average of the students who already have high average grades and whose average therefore cannot be substantially improved by including the grades from noncore classes.

- Third, self-reported high school GPA is inflated by high self-esteem, impression management, or a need for self-enhancement—an influence particularly evident for students with relatively low GPA. This factor is a second possible source of systematic error or construct-irrelevant variance in self-reported GPA because it primarily inflates the reported GPA for students with low actual GPA. Students with high GPA are unable to inflate their reported grades substantially due to a ceiling effect.

Because high school GPA is so widely used to make college admissions decisions and as a predictor of college GPA in research settings, the relationship of self-reported high school GPA with college GPA is reviewed quantitatively in this chapter. The review used the Hunter and Schmidt's (2004) interactive meta-analytic method and corrected the unreliability in college GPA using artifact distributions based on four published reliability estimates of college GPA (e.g., Barritt, 1966). Data sources were identified via keyword searches of the PsycINFO and ERIC databases as well as targeted Internet and hand searches of the issues of 14 prominent education and measurement journals published over a 10-year period (2000–2010). These searches produced a database of 33 correlations, representing 112,589 students.

The meta-analytic results indicate moderate relationships between self-reported high school GPA and both college GPA ($k = 33$, $N = 112,589$, $r = .37$, $\rho = .41$, $SD\rho = .04$), and freshman GPA ($k = 10$, $N = 104,291$, $r = .36$, $\rho = .40$, $SD\rho = .03$). These validity coefficients are nearly identical to those reported in other large-scale studies on self-reported high school GPA (Berry & Sackett, 2009) and somewhat lower than those reported in large-scale reviews of the validity of actual high school GPA (e.g., Hezlett et al., 2001).

Together, these findings have important implications for whether or not self-reported GPA can be used as a reasonable substitute for actual GPA, particularly in settings where GPA information is used as a predictor, outcome, or control variable in regression-based analyses. The relatively high correlation between self-reported GPA and actual GPA suggests that self-reported GPA can act as a reasonable substitute for actual GPA. However, two variables can exhibit much higher correlations than those observed between self-reported and actual GPAs and still exhibit substantially different correlations with other variables. For example, if variables A and B are correlated at $r = .94$ and A correlates $r = .50$ with variable C, then the possible correlations between variables B and C range from $r = .17$ to $r = .77$ (McCornack, 1956). Thus, the substantial correlation between self-reported and actual GPAs does not guarantee that the two GPAs will exhibit similar relationships with other variables. Indeed, given the apparent systematic error influences on self-reported GPA, we would expect that the relationships with other variables are likely to be dissimilar.

Summary and Recommendations

Self-reported GPA correlates with actual GPA to a substantial degree. However, the nontrivial influence of systematic error suggests that self-reported GPA should only be used with caution as a proxy for actual GPA. As such, it is recommended that researchers access participants' academic records whenever feasible. While the administrative burden of obtaining this information is often substantial, the impact on the validity of research findings may well be substantial. Researchers who are required to rely on self-reported GPA should increase the accuracy of such self-reported GPA and, particularly, decrease the amount of systematic error in self-reported GPA. Two relatively easy methods are particularly effective. First, researchers should specifically highlight the need for accurate information and simultaneously acknowledge the possible desire to inflate reported GPA above actual GPA. Second, instructions to participants should be clear as to which "version" of GPA is requested. For example, instructions may ask participants to report the high school GPA that the university has used to admit the student to college. Alternately, participants could be asked to report their grades in specific subjects and the researcher could then form a composite of this information.

References

Barritt, L. S. (1966). Note: The consistency of first-semester college grade point average. *Journal of Educational Measurement, 3*, 261–262.

Berry, C. M., & Sackett, P. R. (2009). Individual differences in course choice result in underestimation of the validity of college admission systems. *Psychological Science, 20*, 822–830.

Hezlett, S. A., Kuncel, N. R., Vey, M. A., Ahart, A., Ones, D. S., Campbell, J. P., & Camara, W. (2001, April). The predictive validity of the SAT: A comprehensive meta-analysis. In D. S. Ones & S. A. Hezlett (Chairs), *Predicting performance: The interface of I/O psychology and educational research*. Symposia presented at the annual conference of the Society for Industrial and Organizational Psychology, San Diego, CA.

Hunter, J. E., & Schmidt, F. L. (2004). *Methods of meta-analysis: Correcting error and bias in research findings* (2nd ed.). Newbury Park, CA: Sage.

Kuncel, N. R., Credé, M., & Thomas, L. L. (2005). The reliability of self-reported grade point averages: A meta-analysis and summary of the literature. *Review of Educational Research, 75*, 63–82.

McCornack, R. L. (1956). A criticism of studies comparing weighting methods. *Journal of Applied Psychology, 40*, 343–345.

Messick, S. (1995). Validity of psychological assessment: Validation of inferences from persons' responses and performances as scientific inquiry into score meaning. *American Psychologist, 50*, 741–749.

2.10

Conceptual Change

Stella Vosniadou and Panagiotis Tsoumakis
National and Kapodistrian University of Athens

Introduction

Conceptual change research investigates knowledge acquisition processes in cases where the new, to-be-learned information conflicts with what is already known. Many concepts are difficult to understand because they violate people's intuitive beliefs and require substantial reorganization of prior knowledge. The beginnings of this type of research can be traced to physics education but it is by no means restricted to this subject. Rather, it makes a larger claim about learning that transcends many domains of knowledge and can apply, for example, to biology, psychology, political science, medicine, environmental learning, and mathematics. Conceptual change research has flourished in the last decade and constitutes an important area of educational psychology.

Research Evidence

An overwhelming body of educational research has documented the considerable learning difficulties students encounter in many subject-matter areas, difficulties which can result in the absence of critical thinking, knowledge fragmentation, lack of transfer, and the formation of misconceptions. These difficulties are present even in the case of the brighter students attending the most prestigious universities. The problem of conceptual change appears to be one of the major reasons behind such widespread learning failures (Chi, 2008; diSessa, 1993; Vosniadou, Vamvakoussi, & Skopeliti, 2008).

Consider, for example, the case of fraction understanding in mathematics. Only 50% of a nationally representative sample of U.S. eighth graders were found to be able to correctly order three fractions on the National Assessment of Educational Progress (National Council of Teachers of Mathematics, 2007), while a recent study of sixth graders with a mean IQ of 116 reported only 59% correct ordering of a set of fractions (Mazzocco & Delvin, 2008). Many researchers have argued that students' difficulties with fractions are related to the problem of conceptual change. This is the case because fractions violate some of the important principles that apply to natural numbers, such as that between two successive numbers there is no other number, that every number has a unique symbolic representation, and that multiplication always makes "bigger" and division always makes "smaller" (Vamvakoussi & Vosniadou, 2010).

There are various theories that attempt to explain students' difficulties in situations where conceptual change is required. According to diSessa (1993), the knowledge system of novices consists of an unstructured collection of many subconceptual elements which become organized into a larger system of complex knowledge structures in experts. This approach emphasizes the importance of knowledge integration.

Other researchers argue that even young children can form relatively coherent naive theories based on their everyday observations and cultural experiences well before they are exposed to systematic instruction. When exposed to counterintuitive scientific explanations, students use the usual constructive, implicit learning mechanisms to incorporate the new, incompatible information to their background knowledge, in the process creating fragmentation and misconceptions (Vosniadou et al., 2008). This approach emphasizes the importance of knowledge revision in conceptual change processes.

In addition to cognitive factors, conceptual change also seems to be affected by various motivational factors such as goals, self-efficacy, interest, and academic emotions. Although research is still scarce, some findings indicate that students who adopt a mastery goal orientation engage in more elaborative cognitive and metacognitive self-regulatory strategies than students who do not adopt a mastery goal orientation and are thus more likely to achieve conceptual change (Linnenbrink & Pintrich, 2002). Confidence in one's ability to perform well in a particular task or domain may also influence performance through a more effective processing of the material to be learned. However, high self-efficacy may also have detrimental effects on conceptual change, as high confidence in erroneous beliefs often generates commitment to current conceptions and resistance to revision.

Recommendations

Despite their theoretical differences, most researchers agree that conceptual change is a gradual and time-consuming affair that is difficult to achieve and that requires both extensive revision of prior knowledge as well as knowledge integration. Instruction for conceptual change requires substantial changes in curricula so that they take into consideration students' prior knowledge and misconceptions. It is important for teachers to identify the areas where new information is likely to violate what students already know and alert the students of the possibility of negative transfer through explicit instruction. Argumentation, collaboration, and classroom discussion can be also used to create prolonged motivation for change, metaconceptual awareness, and deep comprehension activity, all of which are important facilitators of conceptual change that promote knowledge integration (Hatano & Inagaki, 2003). Finally, students must become familiar with the use of new learning mechanisms, such as the deliberate use of analogies and models, to help them restructure what they already know (Wiser & Smith, 2008).

Instruction for conceptual change is often associated with the use of cognitive conflict, which can be produced by asking students to make predictions or give explanations of phenomena and then presenting them with contradictory experimental evidence or some other kind of anomalous data. Research shows that a combination of cognitive conflict with knowledge building strategies (such as the use of analogies) can be fruitful in promoting conceptual change (Clement, 2008). In recent years, cognitive conflict has been used in a particular type of text structure known as refutational text. A refutational text states readers' alternative conceptions about a topic explicitly and then directly refutes them introducing the scientific concept as a viable alternative. The superiority of refutational, compared to traditional expository text has been documented in many studies (Guzzetti, Snyder, Glass, & Gamas, 1993).

Other interventions which have been found to promote conceptual change involve the use of instructional analogies (Dagher, 1994; Duit, 1991); that is, explicit analogies in which an unfamiliar concept or explanation is introduced by appealing to its relational similarity to a familiar concept from a different domain. Several models of how to teach with analogies have been developed, all of which emphasize, amongst others, the need to (a) use well-planned analogies from a base domain highly familiar to students, (b) make the mapping between the base analog and the target concept clear and explicit, and (c) indicate where the analogy breaks down to avoid the creation of misconceptions.

Some researchers argue that explanatory models and qualitative model construction are an important mechanism for conceptual change (Clement, 2008; Wiser & Smith, 2008). By constructing explanatory models, students translate the verbal, abstract theories and explanations of science into concrete representations that can be explored and examined. A number of innovative curricula have been developed that start with children's views and help them construct new representations through model building activities (e.g., Lehrer, Shauble, Strom, & Pligge, 2001; Vosniadou, Ionnades, Dimitrakopoulou, & Papademitriou, 2001). These approaches have been consistently more effective in bringing about conceptual change compared to standard physical activities in science.

Finally, the evaluation of students' achievement of conceptual change is a challenging issue. Standard achievement tests and school grades may not always capture students' failures to achieve a qualitative understanding of many science and mathematics concepts. Often, misconceptions become obvious only when in-depth investigations are conducted, usually involving open questionnaires and interview studies. The assessment procedure must highlight the transformation of students' preexisting understandings through instruction. Formative assessments designed to make students' thinking visible to both teachers and students are essential. In those curricular areas where research has uncovered students' detailed learning progressions, these progressions can be used to provide a basis for the development of formative assessments that can inform instruction.

Conclusions

In conclusion, instruction-based conceptual change research investigates learning processes which require the substantial revision of prior knowledge under conditions of systematic instruction. Conceptual change research has shown that many concepts are difficult to understand because they violate people's intuitive beliefs constructed on the basis of observational experience in the context of lay culture. Conceptual change is difficult to achieve and requires many years of concentrated instruction and the design of innovative curricula that build on students' learning progressions. This type of instruction also requires extensive sociocultural support. Engagement in contextually appropriate classroom discourse is a necessary component of a learning environment that creates metaconceptual awareness and intentional learning and promotes conceptual change.

References

Chi, M. T. H. (2008). Three types of conceptual change: Belief revision, mental model transformation, and categorical shift. In S. Vosniadou (Ed.), *The international handbook of research on conceptual change* (pp. 61–82). New York: Routledge.

Clement, J. (2008). The role of explanatory models in teaching for conceptual change. In S. Vosniadou (Ed.), *The international handbook of research on conceptual change* (pp. 417–452). New York: Routledge.

Dagher, Z., R. (1994). Does the use of analogies contribute to conceptual change? *Science Education, 78,* 601–614.

diSessa, A. (1993). Toward an epistemology of physics. *Cognition and Instruction, 10,* 105–225.

Duit, R. (1991). On the role of analogies and metaphors in learning science. *Science Education, 75,* 649–672.

Guzzetti, B. J., Snyder, T. E., Glass, G. V., & Gamas, W. S. (1993). Promoting conceptual change in science: A comparative meta-analysis of instructional interventions from reading education and science education. *Reading Research Quarterly, 28*(2), 116–159.

Hatano, G., & Inagaki, K. (2003). When is conceptual change intended? A cognitive-sociocultural view. In G. M. Sinatra & P. R. Pintrich (Eds.), *Intentional conceptual change* (pp. 407–427). Mahwah, NJ: Erlbaum.

Lehrer, R., Schauble, L., Strom, D., & Pligge, M. (2001). Similarity of form and substance: Modeling material kind. In S. Carver & D. Klahr (Eds.), *Cognition and instruction: Twenty-five years of progress* (pp. 39–74). Mahwah, NJ: Erlbaum.

Linnenbrink, E. A., & Pintrich, P.R (2002). The role of motivational beliefs in conceptual change. In M. Limon & L. Mason (Eds.), *Reconsidering conceptual change: Issues in theory and practice* (pp. 115–135). Dordrecht, Netherlands: Kluwer.

Mazzocco, M. M., & Devlin, K. T. (2008). Parts and "holes": Gaps in rational number sense among children with vs. without mathematical learning disabilities. *Developmental Science, 11,* 681–691.

National Council of Teachers of Mathematics. (2007). *The learning of mathematics: 69th NCTM yearbook.* Reston, VA: Author.

Vamvakoussi, X., & Vosniadou, S. (2010). How many decimals are there between two fractions? Aspects of secondary school students' reasoning about rational numbers and their notation. *Cognition and Instruction, 28*(2), 181–209.

Vosniadou, S., Ioannides, Ch., Dimitrakopoulou, A., & Papademitriou, E. (2001). Designing learning environments to promote conceptual change in science. *Learning and Instruction, 11*(4–5), 381–419.

Vosniadou, S., Vamvakoussi, X., & Skopeliti, I. (2008). The framework theory approach to the problem of conceptual change. In S. Vosniadou (Ed.), *International handbook of research on conceptual change* (pp. 3–34). New York: Routledge.

Wiser, M., & Smith, C. L. (2008). Learning and teaching about matter in grades K-8: When should the atomic-molecular theory be introduced? In S. Vosniadou (Ed.), *The international handbook of research on conceptual change* (pp. 205–239). New York: Routledge.

2.11

Social Motivation and Academic Motivation

TIM URDAN
Santa Clara University

Introduction

Fifty years ago, James Coleman identified a phenomenon that American teachers and parents still find troubling today. In his study of the social dynamics of adolescents in 10 high schools, Coleman (1961) found that popularity with peers depended more on athletic prowess (for boys) and physical appearance (for girls) than on academic achievement. Coleman went so far as to argue that social motivation—the desire for popularity—is inversely related to achievement motivation. Indeed, for several decades motivation researchers argued that the need for affiliation (social motives) undermined academic achievement (Atkinson & Feather, 1966).

More recent research has demonstrated that the actual association between social motives and academic achievement is more complex than the simple inverse relationship posited by Coleman, Murray, and others. Examinations of social goals, affiliation needs from the self-determination theory perspective, variations between individualistic and collectivist cultures, and the dynamics of social groups have all contributed to a more nuanced understanding of the association between social motivation and academic motivation and achievement. In the remainder of this chapter, each of these conceptualizations of social motivation is examined in turn.

Research Evidence

Social Goals. Urdan and Maehr (1995) argued that research on students' achievement goals should be broadened to include social goals, which had been largely ignored up to that point. This argument was based on the recognition that within the domain of school, students' social concerns are often as strong, if not stronger, than their academic concerns. In addition, there was growing evidence at that time that the assumed negative association between academic and social motivations was too simplistic. Led by the work

of Wentzel (1989), researchers have examined a variety of social goals that students pursue in school. Some of these can, indeed, undermine academic focus and achievement. For example, social interaction goals, where the primary focus of the student is to interact with other students during class time, may distract students from their work. On the other hand, social responsibility goals include the desire to be a good citizen of the classroom, get class work done on time, and help the classroom function smoothly, are positively associated with academic achievement. Additional research on social goals has identified over a dozen types of these goals, all of which may influence academic motivation and achievement in different ways (Rodkin & Ryan, 2011).

Perhaps the most important factors to consider when trying to understand the effects of social goals on academic motivation and achievement are the academic values and behaviors of the social target. The goal of gaining acceptance from peers can undermine academic motivation and achievement if those peers devalue academic success. In contrast, if a student has high-achieving friends who are annoyed by behavior that distracts them from their academic goals, the social goal of maintaining bonds with these friends is likely to bolster academic motivation and achievement. In general, social goals that involve pleasing teachers or parents will be positively associated with academic motivation, because teachers and parents value academic achievement. The pursuit of social goals involving peers can undermine or enhance academic motivation and achievement depending on the academic values of the peers one is trying to impress.

Affiliation Needs. Despite the view of achievement and affiliation needs as negatively correlated constructs that was presented by Atkinson and colleagues in the 1960s, there is actually quite a long history in psychology of viewing these two needs as complementary. Erikson (1950) argued that the successful resolution of affiliation stages, both early in life (trust) and later in life (intimacy) were prerequisite for achievement in other domains of life. Similarly, Maslow's hierarchy of needs posits that the affiliation needs of love and security must be met before the healthy pursuit of academic and career success can be accomplished.

Currently, self-determination theory (SDT; Deci & Ryan, 1985) is one of the most prominent theories of motivation. According to SDT, the need for affiliation is a basic and universal human need. For optimal motivation and psychological well-being, individuals must be autonomous. When people feel that their actions are coerced and not engaged in freely, they experience a lack of perceived control over their actions. This lack of autonomy has psychological costs that reduce motivation and achievement. In order to feel autonomous, individuals must have their basic needs satisfied. These needs include the need to feel competent and the need to feel connected to others. When one feels competent and socially secure, she is able to autonomously pursue learning and achievement goals. Research on attachment theory supports the SDT perspective that without secure social bonds, the ability to undertake intellectual pursuits (i.e., exploratory behavior) is undermined.

Cultural Variations.   Any attempt to understand the association between social motivation and academic motivation would be incomplete without a consideration of differences between cultures in the meaning and function of social motives. The most commonly discussed cultural difference is the individualist-collectivist distinction (Triandis, 1989). According to this perspective, some cultures (e.g., the United States, several Western European countries) place a greater emphasis on individuation and individual accomplishment. In contrast, collectivist cultures (most often represented by Asian countries such as China and Japan) tend to emphasize social relatedness purposes for achievement. Rather than viewing academic success as a means of distinguishing oneself from others to pursue one's own interests and goals, in collectivist cultures academic success is more likely to be viewed as a vehicle for bringing honor to one's in-group (e.g., the family, community, or even country) and helping to further the interests of that group (Triandis, 1989).

Clearly, this individualist–collectivist distinction has implications for the association between social and academic motives. Whereas social goals such as gaining popularity or spending time with friends may distract students from their academic pursuits, in a collectivist culture the social goals are more likely to be goals that enhance the reputation and living conditions of the family, and these goals are likely to increase students' focus on doing well in school. One reason that social and academic goals are viewed as competing in U.S. samples of adolescent students is that part of the developmental process of individuation from parents involves opposing parental (and other adult) values. Antisocial behaviors that oppose adult norms and values actually increase popularity with peers for many teenagers in the United States (Juvonen & Ho, 2008). Because parents and other adults value academic achievement, American adolescents who look like they are trying too hard to succeed academically risk sacrificing popularity with their peers.

In collectivist cultures, where the emphasis on separation and individuation from parents is much weaker, there is little social reward for opposing parental values (Arnett, 2009). Indeed, disrespecting parents by purposely undermining their values has social costs with adults and adolescent peers alike, so there is little to be gained socially by performing poorly in school. The cultural differences between individualistic and collectivist cultures explain, at least partially, why social and academic motives may compete with each other for some samples of students but complement each other in other samples.

Social Dynamics.   The idea that children and adolescents are strongly influenced by peer pressure is so widespread that it is rarely even questioned. But documenting the effects of peer pressure has been difficult for researchers. As Epstein (1983) noted, children and adolescents select their friends partly on the basis of similarity. Although it is tempting for parents to believe that their child became a delinquent because he "fell in with the wrong crowd," it is actually quite likely that he chose to associate with that group of friends due to their similar interest in, and enjoyment of, delinquent behavior.

To distinguish between the effects of peer influence and friend selection, researchers have increasingly focused on the social dynamics within peer or friendship groups (e.g., Berndt & Keefe, 1992). This research generally indicates that students within a given peer network tend to become more similar over time in terms of their attitudes and achievement in school. For example, Kindermann (2007) found that children who associated with academically engaged peers became more academically engaged themselves over time. In a study of Chinese school children, Chen, Chang, Liu, and He (2008) found that children who affiliated with higher achieving students tended to become more academically engaged and performed better in school over time. Of course, this effect of peer group affiliation can work in the opposite direction as well. Research has revealed a particularly strong effect of the peer network on deviant behavior. Specifically, adolescents who are affiliated with peers who engage in deviant behavior are more likely to develop deviant behavior patterns themselves.

The group of peers with which students identify and spend time creates a set of perceived norms regarding academic behaviors, aspirations, and motivation. In addition, the relative position of each student within the status hierarchy of the group affects how much one is influenced by the social network, with higher status peers influencing the academic motivation and behavior of less powerful or popular members of the group. Although peer group membership involves a process of self-selection, and students tend to choose to associate with peers who share similar attitudes and motivation toward school, there is also convincing evidence that, over time, students who share an affiliation network tend to become more similar in their academic motivation and behavior over time.

Summary and Recommendations

Although early research supported the common perception that students' social motives undermines their academic motivation, more recent research reveals a more complex association between these two motives. Social motivation can undermine or enhance academic motivation. The type of social goal one is hoping to achieve, the values and behaviors of the person or group from whom one hopes to gain approval, and situational factors combine to determine whether social and academic motivations work with or against each other.

References

Arnett, J. J. (2009). *Adolescence and emerging adulthood: A cultural approach* (4th ed.). New York: Prentice Hall.

Atkinson, J. W., & Feather, N. T. (1966). *A theory of achievement motivation.* New York: Wiley.

Berndt, T. J., & Keefe, K. (1992). Friends' influence on adolescents' perceptions of themselves at school. In D. Schunk & J. Meece (Eds.), *Student perceptions in the classroom* (pp. 51–73). Hillsdale, NJ: Erlbaum.

Chen, X., Chang, L., Liu, H., & He, Y. (2008). Effects of the peer group on the development of social functioning and academic achievement: A longitudinal study in Chinese children. *Child Development, 79,* 235–251.

Coleman, J. (1961). *The adolescent society.* Glencoe, IL: Free Press.

Deci, E. L., & Ryan, R. M. (1985). *Intrinsic motivation and self-determination in human behavior.* New York: Plenum.

Epstein, J. L. (1983). *Friends in school: Patterns of selection and influence in secondary schools.* New York: Academic Press.

Erikson, E. (1950). *Childhood and society.* New York: Norton.

Juvonen, J., & Ho, A. Y. (2008). Social motives underlying antisocial behavior across middle school grades. *Journal of Youth and Adolescence, 37,* 747–756.

Kindermann, T. A. (2007). Effects of naturally existing peer groups on changes in academic engagement in a cohort of sixth graders. *Child Development, 74,* 1186–1203.

Rodkin, P. C., & Ryan, A. (2011). Child and adolescent peer relations in educational context. In T. Urdan (Ed.), *APA Educational Psychology Handbook* (Vol. 2, pp. 336–369). Washington, DC: American Psychological Association.

Triandis, H. C. (1989). The self and social behavior in differing social contexts. *Psychological Review, 96,* 506–520.

Urdan, T., & Maehr, M. L. (1995). Beyond a two-goal theory of motivation: A case for social goals. *Review of Educational Research, 65,* 213–244.

Wentzel, K. R. (1989). Adolescent classroom goals, standards for performance, and academic achievement: An interactionist perspective. *Journal of Educational Psychology, 81,* 131–142.

2.12

Attitudes and Dispositions

ROBERT D. RENAUD
University of Manitoba

Introduction

For most people in education, the relationship between student attitudes, dispositions, and academic achievement seems rather obvious. Students who have positive feelings about education or learning in particular subjects are likely to do well. Perhaps this is one reason why it has received a relatively limited amount of attention in the broader area of research on attitudes and dispositions. For example, one major review noted that attitude is assessed mostly as a dependent variable and that few studies have examined the relation between attitude and achievement (Silverman & Subramaniam, 1999).

At this point, it would be useful to clarify the distinction between attitude and disposition. Dispositions are more general and enduring characteristics (Buss & Craik, 1983). For example, someone with a gregarious disposition is likely to behave in a corresponding manner in a variety of situations such as preferring to work as part of a team or inviting friends over for dinner. In comparison, attitude is "a tendency or state internal to the person. This internal state biases or predisposes a person toward evaluative responses of some degree of favorability or unfavorability—that is, toward favorable responses if the attitude is positive and toward unfavorable responses if the attitude is negative" (Eagly, 1992, p. 694). Moreover, an attitude is usually directed toward a particular entity, which could be anything that a person may evaluate such as learning math, extracurricular activities, or the general notion of going to school. These definitions suggest that dispositions may be more difficult to modify compared to attitudes, which may explain why there seem to be fewer published studies that compare academic achievement with dispositions than with attitudes.

Research Evidence

A search through ERIC and PsycInfo that included the terms *attitude or disposition* and *achievement or learning* and *review or analysis* in the title of the paper revealed five reviews or meta-analyses that examined the relation between attitude and academic achievement, published between 1983 and 2003. The same search terms, but without *review or analysis*, revealed 26 published studies in peer-reviewed journals over the last 10 years, with about half of these studies focusing on math and science, and only a single study that examined the relation between dispositions and achievement. Given that very little of the research of interest here focuses on dispositions, the remainder of this review will focus on the link between attitude and achievement.

Overall, the relation between attitude and academic achievement appears to be somewhat weak. For example, in two meta-analyses, the mean correlation between attitude and achievement across grade levels was .16 in science (Willson, 1983) and .12 in mathematics (Ma & Kishor, 1997a). While these relationships do not appear to be of much practical value in classrooms, more notable effects have been found in specific contexts. The relationship between attitude and achievement generally appears to be strongest in upper elementary grades. For example, in grades 7 through 9 the correlation averages .25 (Ma & Kishor, 1997a). The stronger relationship in upper elementary grades has been noted in other subjects including second language learning (Masogret & Gardner, 2003), science (Willson, 1983), and physical education (Silverman & Subramaniam, 1999).

The relations between attitudes and achievement do not appear to vary dramatically as a function of how they were measured. Ma and Kishor (1997b) analyzed studies that compared self-concept about mathematics, family support, and gender role in mathematics as indicators of attitude with achievement in mathematics. They found that while each indicator was related to achievement, the largest mean correlation (.23) was found between self-concept and achievement. Similarly, it seems that the measure of academic achievement made little difference. Willson (1983) included studies that measured science achievement in several ways: tests of general science, biology, chemistry, physics, process of science knowledge, science course grade, general intelligence, science GPA, overall GPA, and number of science credits. The studies analyzed by Masgoret and Gardner (2003) assessed achievement with either grades, objective measures, or self-ratings.

Taking a closer look at the association between attitude and achievement, Masgoret and Gardner (2003) found that achievement is more closely related to motivation than with attitude, which supports the interpretation that attitude influences achievement indirectly through motivation. A relatively small proportion of studies examined in these reviews looked at the causal link between attitude and achievement. Both Ma and Kishor (1997a) and Willson (1983) found that the effect of each causal direction (i.e., attitude influencing achievement vs. achievement influencing attitude) was fairly small. For example, Ma and Kishor (1997a) found a marginally stronger effect from attitude to achievement at only .08, which they interpret as not practically meaningful.

Summary and Recommendations

Back to the main question in this chapter: How much is attitude related to academic achievement? While one may not consider even the stronger correlations in the upper elementary grades as outstanding, it would not be unreasonable to argue that they are indeed worth noting. As Masgoret and Gardner (2003) point out, correlations such as these can be considered substantial when the variables are quite distinct from one another, such as attitude and achievement. A similar point is made by Prentice and Miller (1992). When data is collected in a context with several inherent limitations such as using limited measures, lack of control, and a short time span, it would seem unfair to expect two variables such as attitude and achievement to be strongly associated.

Perhaps the biggest challenge in learning how attitudes are associated with academic achievement lies in how validly attitudes are assessed in education. Two of the reviews cited in this chapter provide useful information on quantitative and qualitative approaches and psychometric issues (Masgoret & Gardner, 2003; Silverman &

Subramaniam, 1999). Regarding validity, Silverman and Subramaniam emphasize that attitudes would be more accurately measured as a multidimensional construct rather than as a single dimension. With more detailed measures of attitude, it should be easier to ensure that the definitions and measures of attitudes are more comparable across studies of interest (Masgoret & Gardner, 2003).

While teaching strategies at any grade level should include ways to help foster a positive student attitude toward learning, it appears that the most crucial period is from about grades 6 to 9. Given that the direction of causality question remains unclear (i.e., attitude influences achievement, the reverse, or reciprocal), it may be worthwhile for teachers to provide students with many opportunities to have a successful learning experience. Generally, one possibility is to assess the students' learning frequently and in varied formats. Finally, future research with larger samples should consider using advanced statistical techniques such as structural equation modeling (SEM) to better explore the reciprocal association between attitude and achievement, and hierarchical linear modeling (HLM) to disentangle the effects of classes and schools (Ma & Kishor, 1997a).

References

Buss, D. M., & Craik, K. H. (1983). The act frequency approach to personality. *Psychological Review, 90*(2), 105–126.

Eagly, A. H. (1992). Uneven progress: Social psychology and the study of attitudes. *Journal of Personality and Social Psychology, 63*(5), 693–710.

Ma, X., & Kishor, N. (1997a). Assessing the relationship between attitude toward mathematics and achievement in mathematics: A meta-analysis. *Journal for Research in Mathematics Education, 28*(1), 26–47.

Ma, X., & Kishor, N. (1997b). Attitude toward self, social factors, and achievement in mathematics: A meta-analytic review. *Educational Psychology Review, 9*(2), 89–120.

Masgoret, A. M., & Gardner, R. C. (2003). Attitudes, motivation, and second language learning: A meta-analysis of studies conducted by Gardner and Associates. *Language Learning, 53*(1), 123–163.

Prentice, D. A., & Miller, D. T. (1992). When small effects are impressive. *Psychological Bulletin, 112,* 160–164.

Silverman, S., & Subramaniam, P. R. (1999). Student attitude toward physical education and physical activity: A review of measurement issues and outcomes. *Journal of Teaching in Physical Education, 19,* 97–125.

Willson, V. L. (1983). A meta-analysis of the relationship between science achievement and science attitude: Kindergarten through college. *Journal of Research in Science Teaching, 20*(9), 839–850.

2.13

Personality Influences

MEERA KOMARRAJU
Southern Illinois University, Carbondale

Introduction

Student success is a central goal of educational organizations worldwide. In achieving this objective, educators are encouraged to look beyond cognitive ability and investigate psychosocial factors that influence academic achievement. A spotlight on nonintellectual factors is needed particularly at the college level where students' ability within a cohort is restricted by admission criteria (Furnham, Monsen, & Ahmetoglu, 2009). In highly selective programs that enroll students who are more homogeneous in intellectual ability, differences in student achievement at the time of graduation are more likely to be explained by noncognitive factors. For instance, two students entering a college or university may have similar standardized test scores and high school grade point averages (GPA); yet, the degree of success they achieve in college is likely to be influenced by noncognitive variables such as personality, motivation, self-efficacy, information processing style, intellectual engagement, or effort-regulation. This chapter focuses mainly on untangling the relationship between the Big Five personality traits and academic achievement.

Research Evidence

Over the past two decades, the Big Five theory of personality has emerged as a robust and parsimonious conceptual framework of personality. Empirical evidence establishes it as an important predictor of academic achievement such as course grades, overall exam scores, or college GPA (O'Connor & Paunonen, 2007). Of the Big Five personality traits, conscientiousness is the single most consistent and strongest significant predictor of academic performance, beyond cognitive ability (Conard, 2006). Regarding the relationship between the four other Big Five traits (openness, agreeableness, extraversion, and neuroticism) and academic achievement, research findings are inconsistent or nonexistent (Chamorro-Premuzic & Furnham, 2003). For instance, in a meta-analysis that included about 25 studies, O'Connor and Paunonen (2007) report a mean correlation of .24 between conscientiousness and academic performance and mixed results for openness and extraversion. This body of research suggests that although cognitive ability scores inform us about what students can do, their personality unveils what they are likely to do. For example, students who score high on conscientiousness are more likely to be hardworking, thorough, disciplined, and achievement-oriented, whereas those who score high on neuroticism are more likely to be anxious, worried, and inclined to give up or avoid coming to class if they think they are not doing well (Chamorro-Premuzic & Furnham, 2008). In attempting to unravel the relationship between personality traits and academic achievement, researchers have focused on four intermediate or causal mechanisms including achievement motivation, self-regulation, deep processing of information, and regular class attendance.

A comprehensive meta-analysis of 65 studies by Judge and Ilies (2002) revealed that the link between personality and motivation is complex. They found consistent associations between three types of performance motivation (goal-setting, expectancy, and self-efficacy) and two personality traits, conscientiousness (in a positive direction) and neuroticism (in a negative direction). On further scrutiny, Chamorro-Premuzic and Furnham (2003) state that although some of the broad personality traits (conscientiousness positively, and extraversion and neuroticism negatively) explain 15% of the variance in exam grades, the narrower facets (achievement striving, self-discipline, and activity) have a stronger relationship and explain much more (about 30%) variance in exam scores. Since conscientiousness and achievement motivation (the capacity to persist in the face of difficulties, obstacles, or failures) are both significant predictors of GPA, even after controlling for scores on standardized entrance exam test scores (Richardson & Abraham, 2009), some researchers have examined their interrelationship more closely. Conscientiousness seems to include a component of achievement motivation, as highly conscientious students seem to be motivated to succeed (Higgins, Peterson, Pihl, & Lee, 2007). This is supported by Noftle and Robins's (2007) results; these demonstrate that the relationship between conscientiousness and GPA is mediated by students' self-report of how much effort they put into their studying and their perceptions of their overall academic ability as well as verbal ability. There is also support for the notion that students who are driven to accomplish are more likely to obtain higher GPAs if they are also more conscientious; they need to be disciplined, organized, follow through, and remain persistent despite facing difficulties (Komarraju, Karau, & Schmeck, 2009). As conscientiousness is associated with both intrinsic and extrinsic motivation, highly conscientious students might remain internally motivated despite fluctuations in environmental rewards (Hart, Stasson, & Mahoney, 2007). This empirical evidence draws attention to the achievement motivation component of personality traits (particularly conscientiousness) in explaining academic achievement.

In addition to achievement motivation, self-regulation has emerged as a causal mechanism that influences student performance and achievement. A decade ago, Pintrich (2000) noted that effort regulation fully mediated the individual relationships between GPA and the personality traits of conscientiousness and agreeableness. He found that highly conscientious individuals tend to be better self-managers and able to regulate themselves more effectively. Conscientious students also display proactive and initiating behavior as they plan, monitor, gather feedback, and reflect on whether or not their learning strategies are working (Bidjerano & Dai, 2007). They are responsible, disciplined, achievement oriented, organized, and proactive as they are driven to achieve their goals (Higgins et al., 2007). This quality of being organized, self-disciplined, and self-directed is very crucial in college because, unlike in high school, parents and teachers no longer offer constant reminders or monitoring and students have to self-regulate and manage themselves.

The extent to which students process information deeply and meaningfully also appears to be an important determinant of their academic achievement. Highly conscientious students appear to use deep and strategic learning styles that help them achieve higher academic performance (Duff, Boyle, Dunleavy, & Ferguson, 2004). In addition, Chamorro-Premuzic and Furnham (2008) note that 40% of the variance in academic performance measured through end-of-year comprehensive essay exams was explained incrementally by ability, two personality traits (conscientiousness and openness), and learning style. What is interesting about this study is the finding that conscientiousness was positively linked to performance but negatively with ability, suggesting that students who are lower in ability might compensate by being more diligent and disciplined and thus achieving higher academic performance. By the same token, some of those who are of higher ability may be less conscientious and obtain lower exam grades.

What is most noteworthy is the finding that individuals with high ability performed well because they were more open (displayed intellectual curiosity) and those who were more open performed well because they processed information more deeply. Other researchers also support the importance of elaborative and meaningful processing of information for academic performance. To illustrate, in a study predicting national secondary school exam performance for 212 secondary school students, Furnham et al. (2009) found that although intelligence tests predicted a majority of the variance in the academic performance test, a deep processing and achieving learning style was a significant predictor of exam scores. Thus, empirical evidence certainly highlights the importance of a deep and thoughtful learning style as a link between personality traits and academic achievement.

Classroom behaviors that are associated with personality traits, such as attending classes, conforming to task directions, and participating in group discussions appear to have an important role in achieving academic success. For example, class absences incrementally predict final course grade beyond intelligence and the Big Five traits; conscientious and agreeable students are more likely to attend class seminars and those attending regularly achieve better performance (Conard, 2006). Dollinger, Matyja, and Huber (2008) offer similar empirical support through their findings that the variance in exam scores is predicted not only by factors that are not under the control of students such as verbal ability, personality traits, and past performance, but also by factors such as attendance and hours spent working or studying that are under the control of students. In taking a closer look at the facets of the Big Five, McCann, Duckworth, and Roberts, (2009) report that industriousness was a stronger predictor of classroom absenteeism compared to the broad conscientiousness factor and perfectionism was a stronger predictor of cognitive test scores and attaining high academic honors compared to the broad conscientiousness factor. These results are supported by Kappe and van der Flier (2010) who found that conscientiousness was positively associated with attending lectures, acquiring skills, working on group projects, obtaining on-the-job training, and completing a thesis. They also found that extraversion was positively associated with performance on tasks that involved interacting with others and expressing or articulating ideas, neuroticism was negatively associated with performance under time pressure or being observed, and openness was negatively associated with conforming to group project deadlines. Thus, these results suggest that the Big Five personality traits influence preferred ways of behaving that influence task accomplishment and academic achievement.

Summary and Recommendations

Personality traits have a distal influence on academic achievement through mechanisms such as motivation, self-regulation, deep processing, and attendance behavior that are more proximal to achievement. Schools and teachers could utilize this information to construct syllabi, curriculum, and learning environments that foster and reward achievement motivation, self-regulatory efforts, deep processing, and conscientious behavior. Future researchers could further our understanding of the link between the Big Five personality traits (specifically conscientiousness) and academic achievement by exploring other causal mechanisms.

References

Bidjerano, T., & Dai, D. Y. (2007). The relationship between the big-five model of personality and self-regulated learning strategies. *Learning and Individual Differences, 17,* 69–81.

Chamorro-Premuzic, T., & Furnham, A. (2003). Personality traits and academic examination performance. *European Journal of Personality, 17,* 237–250.

Chamorro-Premuzic, T., & Furnham, A. (2008). Personality, intelligence and approaches to learning as predictors of academic performance. *Personality and Individual Differences, 44,* 1596–1603.

Conard, M. A. (2006). Aptitude is not enough: How personality and behavior predict academic performance. *Journal of Research in Personality, 40,* 339–346.

Dollinger, S. J., Matyja, A. M., & Huber, J. L. (2008). Which factors best account for academic success: Those which college students can control or those they cannot? *Journal of Research in Personality, 42,* 872–885.

Duff, A., Boyle, E., Dunleavy, K., & Ferguson, J. (2004). The relationship between personality, approach to learning and academic performance. *Personality and Individual Differences, 36,* 1907–1920.

Furnham, A., Monsen, J., & Ahmetoglu, G. (2009). Typical intellectual engagement, big five personality traits, approaches to learning and cognitive ability predictors of academic performance. *British Journal of Educational Psychology, 79,* 769–782.

Hart, J. W., Stasson, M. F., & Mahoney, J. M. (2007). The big five and achievement motivation: Exploring the relationship between personality and a two-factor model of motivation. *Individual Differences Research, 5,* 267–274.

Higgins, D. M., Peterson, J. B., Pihl, R. O., & Lee, A. G. M. (2007). Prefrontal cognitive ability, intelligence, Big Five personality, and the prediction of advanced academic and workplace performance. *Journal of Personality and Social Psychology, 93*(2), 298–319.

Judge, T. A., & Ilies, R. (2002). Relationship of personality to performance motivation: A meta-analytic review. *Journal of Applied Psychology, 87,* 797–807.

Kappe, R., & van der Flier, H. (2010). Using multiple and specific criteria to assess the predictive validity of the big five personality factors on academic performance. *Journal of Research in Personality, 44,* 142–145.

Komarraju, M., Karau, S. J., & Schmeck, R. R. (2009). Role of the big five personality traits in predicting college students' academic motivation and achievement. *Learning and Individual Differences, 19,* 47–52.

McCann, C., Duckworth, A. L., & Roberts, R. D. (2009). Empirical identification of the major facets of conscientiousness. *Learning and Individual Differences, 19,* 451–458.

Noftle, E .E., & Robins, R. W. (2007). Personality predictors of academic outcomes: Big five correlates of GPA and SAT scores. *Journal of Personality and Social Psychology, 93*(1), 116–130.

O'Connor, M. C., & Paunonen, S. V. (2007). Big Five personality predictors of post-secondary academic performance. *Personality and Individual Differences, 43,* 971–990.

Pintrich, P. R. (2000). Multiple goals, multiple pathways: The role of goal orientation in learning and achievement. *Journal of Educational Psychology, 92*(3), 544–555.

Richardson, M., & Abraham, C. (2009). Conscientiousness and achievement motivation predict performance. *European Journal of Personality, 23,* 589–605.

2.14

Academic Self-Concept

HERBERT W. MARSH
University of Oxford and University of Western Sydney

MARJORIE SEATON
University of Western Sydney

Introduction

Self-concept has a long and distinguished history, spanning the centuries from Socrates and Plato to Bandura and Rogers in the present day (see Hattie, 1992). Academic self-concept, one's knowledge and perceptions about one's academic ability (Bong & Skaalvik, 2003), can be considered as one of the principal components of self-concept (Shavelson, Hubner, & Stanton, 1976).

Research Evidence

Domain Specificity.   Much of the early literature investigating the relation between academic self-concept and academic achievement demonstrated that higher levels of academic self-concept were associated with higher levels of achievement (see Marsh & Craven, 1997). In their meta-analysis, Hansford and Hattie (1982) reported that the average correlation between measures of general self-concept and academic achievement was moderately low, but positive (.21). However, when measures of academic self-concept were examined, this correlation rose to .42. Hence, not only does there appear to be a strong positive association between academic self-concept and academic achievement, but this relationship appears to be domain specific: Self-concepts in one domain (e.g., math self-concept) are more strongly associated with achievement in that domain (e.g., math achievement) than in other domains.

Reciprocal Effects Model.   An important question is the causal relation between academic self-concept and academic achievement: Did a more positive academic self-concept cause higher achievement, did higher achievement cause a more positive academic self-concept, or did each one have a causal effect on the other? This question and its subsequent answer have substantive practical implications for educational interventions and teaching practice. If academic self-concept has a causal effect on academic achievement (known as the self-enhancement model), then interventions or teacher feedback based on enhancing self-concept would presumably result in higher achievement. Focusing on ways to improve performance would be the better option if achievement fosters higher academic self-concept (the skill development model) (Calsyn & Kenny, 1977). But, if academic self-concept and academic achievement shared a reciprocal relation, then the superior approach would be to address both academic self-concept and academic achievement simultaneously (Marsh & Craven, 2005, 2006).

In recent years, support for the reciprocal effects model (REM) has grown steadily (e.g., Marsh, Trautwein, Lüdtke, Köller, & Baumert, 2005). A meta-analysis of relevant research further supported the REM, whereby it was concluded that academic self-concept had a significant effect on academic achievement and vice versa (Valentine, DuBois, & Cooper, 2004). Moreover these results generalised over age, gender, ethnicity, and countries. This reciprocal relation has also been demonstrated to be valid cross-culturally.

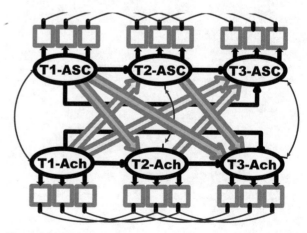

Figure 2.14.1 Reciprocal Effects Model. (Adapted from Marsh, 2007)

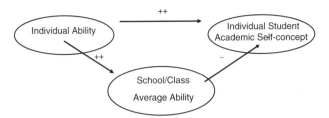

Figure 2.14.2 The Big-Fish-Little-Pond Effect (Marsh & Hau, 2003)

The Big-Fish-Little-Pond Effect (BFLPE). The BFLPE model predicts that students who attend high-ability environments will have lower academic self-concepts than equally able students who attend average- and low-ability environments. In effect, a high class- or school-achievement level may have a negative impact on students' academic self-concepts. The BFLPE has been shown to exist in classes and schools where students are segregated according to ability (e.g., Craven, Marsh, & Print, 2000) and to generalise across cultures (e.g., Seaton, Marsh, & Craven, 2009). The results from BFLPE studies are cause for concern: If high-ability students in academically segregated schools have lower academic self-concepts, then they may not be reaching their full academic potential. Similarly, academically disadvantaged students in support units showed gains in their academic self-concepts while the academic self-concepts of those in the mixed-ability classes dropped (Tracey, Marsh, & Craven, 2003). While there have been criticisms of the BFLPE (Dai & Rinn, 2008), there have been many studies showing that BFLPE is highly generalizable and robust (Seaton et al., 2010).

Summary and Recommendations

There are many implications from these findings. First, results from REM research suggest that simultaneously improving both academic self-concept and academic achievement may be the optimal method for improving performance. To achieve synergy between these two, teachers could use strategies such as: (a) providing constructive feedback to students; (b) assisting students in formulating suitable success and failure attributions; and (c) reinforcing students when they engage in positive self-talk (see Marsh & Craven, 2006). Second, results from studies that have demonstrated the domain specificity of academic self-concept suggest that these strategies should also be domain specific. For example, to aid in improvement in math, constructive feedback should be targeted specifically at work done in math. Finally, we must not forget students at both ends of the academic spectrum. In order to ensure that high-ability students and those who are academically disadvantaged reach their full potential, teachers should not overlook strategies to improve their academic self-concepts.

References

Bong, M., & Skaalvik, E. M. (2003). Academic self-concept and self-efficacy: How different are they really? *Educational Psychology Review, 15*(1), 1–40.

Calsyn, R. J., & Kenny, D. A. (1977). Self-concept of ability and perceived evaluation of others: Cause or effect of academic achievement? *Journal of Educational Psychology, 69*(2), 136–145.

Craven, R. G., Marsh, H. W., & Print, M. (2000). Gifted, streamed and mixed-ability programs for gifted students: Impact on self-concept, motivation, and achievement. *Australian Journal of Education, 44*(1), 51–75.

Dai, D. Y., & Rinn, A. N. (2008). The big-fish–little-pond effect: What do we know and where do we go from here? *Educational Psychological Review, 20,* 283–317.

Hansford, B. C., & Hattie, J. A. (1982). The relationship between self and achievement / performance measures. *Review of Educational Research, 52*(1), 123–142.

Hattie, J. (1992). *Self-concept.* Hillsdale, NJ: Erlbaum.

Marsh, H. W., & Craven, R. G. (1997). Academic self-concept: Beyond the dustbowl. In G. Phye (Ed.), *Handbook of classroom assessment: Learning, achievement, and adjustment* (pp. 131–198). Orlando, FL: Academic Press.

Marsh, H. W., & Craven, R. G. (2005). A reciprocal effects model of the causal ordering of self-concept and achievement: New support for the benefits of enhancing self-concept. In H. W. Marsh, R. G. Craven, & D. M. McInerney (Eds.), *The new frontiers of self-research* (Vol. 2). Greenwich, CT: Information Age.

Marsh, H. W., & Craven, R. G. (2006). Reciprocal effects of self-concept and performance from a multidimensional perspective: Beyond seductive pleasure and unidimensional perspectives. *Perspectives on Psychological Science, 1*(2), 133–163.

Marsh, H. W., & Hau, K. T. (2003). Big-Fish--Little-Pond effect on academic self-concept: A cross-cultural (26-country) test of the negative effects of academically selective schools. *American Psychologist, 58*(5), 364–376.

Marsh, H. W., Trautwein, U., Lüdtke, O., Köller, O., & Baumert, J. (2005). Academic self-concept, interest, grades, and standardized test scores: Reciprocal effects models of causal ordering. *Child Development, 76*(2), 397–416.

Seaton, M., Marsh, H. W., & Craven, R. G. (2009). Earning its place as a pan-human theory: Universality of the big-fish-little-pond effect (BFLPE) across 41 culturally and economically diverse countries. *Journal of Educational Psychology, 101*(2), 403–419.

Seaton, M., Marsh, H. W., & Craven, R. G. (2010). Big-fish-little-pond-effect: Generalizability and moderation—Two sides of the same coin. *American Educational Research Journal, 47(2),* 390–433.

Shavelson, R. J., Hubner, J. J., & Stanton, G. C. (1976). Self-concept: Validation of construct interpretations. *Review of Educational Research, 46*(3), 407–441.

Tracey, D. K., Marsh, H. W. & Craven, R. G. (2003). Self-concepts of preadolescent students with mild intellectual disabilities: Issues of measurement and educational placement. In H. W. Marsh, R. G. Craven, & D. M. McInerney (Eds.), *International advances in self research* (Vol. 1, pp. 203–230). Charlotte, NC: Information Age.

Valentine, J. C., DuBois, D. L., & Cooper, H. (2004). The relations between self-beliefs and academic achievement: A systematic review. *Educational Psychologist, 39,* 111–133.

2.15

Self-Efficacy

Mimi Bong
Korea University

Introduction

Self-efficacy refers to the subjective conviction that one can successfully execute the courses of action required to obtain a desired outcome. Bandura (1977) first coined the term after his experiments on phobia treatment. A group of individuals suffering from severe snake phobia participated in a treatment program. One group of these individuals directly engaged in fearful encounters with a boa constrictor, which involved mastery of progressively more fearful interactions with the snake. Another group observed a model successfully demonstrating a range of approach behaviors toward the snake. The other group did not receive any treatment. Repeated mastery experiences of the first group and repeated observations of the model's successes in handling the boa constrictor by the second group increased the participants' self-efficacy beliefs that they could handle the snake successfully. The greater were the changes in their self-efficacy beliefs, the greater the changes in their behaviors toward the snake. The group that did not receive treatment failed to reach target performance.

Self-efficacy has been proven to initiate and sustain behavioral changes in a wide array of domains including pain coping, exercise behavior, smoking cessation, alcohol abstinence, weight management, career choice, decision making, organizational behavior, sport performance, problem solving, and academic achievement. Academic self-efficacy, in particular, refers to the belief that one can successfully carry out the tasks and behaviors necessary to reach a designated level of academic achievement (Schunk, 1991a,b). Self-efficacy has proved to be one of the most essential precursors of students' academic performance and persistence (Multon, Brown, & Lent, 1991).

Research Evidence

Self-Efficacy and Student Achievement   Self-efficacy influences almost every aspect of students' learning and performance, including cognitive, affective, motivational, and selection processes (Bandura, 1989). Students armed with a strong sense of academic self-efficacy display greater willingness to choose challenging tasks, more effective use of learning strategies, less anxiety, enhanced effort, and improved academic achievement compared to those with a weaker sense of self-efficacy (Pintrich & De Groot, 1990). Self-efficacy also shows significant positive relations to persistence measures such as the amount of time spent on tasks and the number of problems and tasks attempted or completed (Multon, Brown, & Lent, 1991). Self-efficacy predicts academic performance particularly well when self-efficacy is assessed after instructional treatments, performance indexes comprise basic skills measures, and the students are low-achieving.

Self-efficacy is also a key component in self-regulated learning. Self-regulated learning consists of three highly interdependent subprocesses: Self-observation, self-judgment, and self-reaction. Self-observation refers to systematic monitoring of one's own performance; self-judgment refers to comparison of one's performance to a known standard; and self-reaction refers to responses to the evaluation of one's own performance (Zimmerman, 1989; Zimmerman, Bandura, & Martinez-Pons, 1992). Self-efficacy influences all of these processes and mediates effects of goal-setting on subsequent achievement strivings.

Sources of Self-Efficacy.   Students form efficacy expectations by cognitively appraising self-efficacy information from four major sources (Bandura, 1997). Direct mastery experience is the most reliable source. Success with the task raises self-efficacy toward it, whereas failure lowers it. Vicarious experience is the second powerful source. Observing others succeed or fail at tasks raises or lowers observers' self-efficacy toward those tasks. Effects of vicarious experience increase as observers perceive greater similarity between the model and themselves. The third source is verbal persuasion. Self-efficacy is modified by

the persuasion of significant others, especially when the persuader is perceived to be credible and knowledgeable. Finally, physiological indexes function as the fourth source of efficacy information. Bodily reactions and emotional arousals such as nervousness, sweating, and faster heart rates signal to the students that they lack competence for successfully performing the task and hence lower their self-efficacy.

Nature of Self-Efficacy. Self-efficacy is formed in reference to a specific task, activity, or domain. It is thus critically important that tasks and activities used to assess self-efficacy closely approximate the prediction target in terms of specificity and correspondence (Pajares, 1996). If teachers want to predict how well students will perform on the next physics test covering gravity, they need to assess students' self-efficacy for successfully solving problems on gravity, rather than their self-efficacy for dealing with acceleration and velocity problems or physics in general. Mismatch between the tasks and activities used to assess self-efficacy and those used to assess target performance diminishes self-efficacy's prediction power.

Beliefs of self-efficacy can also differ in strength, level, and generality (Bandura, 1997). Students with a strong sense of math self-efficacy built on their repeated successes in math in the past would not despair upon receiving a poor score on a single difficult math test (i.e., strength). Likewise, students may feel confident for correctly solving multiplication problems consisting of only one- and two-digit numbers, whereas others may feel confident for successfully solving multiplication problems involving up to six-digit numbers (i.e., level). Further, students who feel highly self-efficacious in algebra may feel comparably efficacious for learning calculus (i.e., generality). The same success or failure experiences do not guarantee self-efficacy beliefs of the same strength, level, or generality for different students because what matters is how these experiences are cognitively weighed, interpreted, and combined by each student. Two students who received the same test score could reach different conclusions regarding their self-efficacy.

Differences of Self-Efficacy from Other Constructs. First and foremost, self-efficacy is a predictive construct. Whereas self-esteem, self-concept, and self-efficacy are all formed on the basis of one's past experiences, self-efficacy uniquely concerns the belief regarding what one will be able to do in the upcoming future with whatever skills, knowledge, and capabilities one possesses. "I will be able to do excellent work in math" is a self-efficacy statement, whereas "I'm good at math" is a self-concept statement. Second, self-efficacy is context-specific. One's self-efficacy for successfully delivering a public speech, for example, would differ greatly depending on the familiarity of the topic, knowledgeableness and size of the audience, and language used to deliver the speech (Bandura, 1997). Third, self-efficacy is estimated largely in relation to performance goals. Although social comparison also affects judgments

of self-efficacy, students judge their competence in relation to the goals and standards first. "How confident are you that you can successfully achieve an A in English?" is a self-efficacy question but "Do you think you are better than other students in English?" is not. Finally, self-efficacy is a producer and a product of affective reactions but does not include them as part of its definition (Bong & Skaalvik, 2003). Whether students are satisfied with the way they are, deem themselves worthy, or feel hopeless when it comes to certain domains, are important in global self-esteem, self-worth, or academic self-concept. In contrast, self-efficacy concerns mainly one's perceived competence against the target performance.

Self-efficacy should be distinguished from outcome expectancy, which represents the belief that certain actions will lead to a particular outcome. In comparison, self-efficacy is about whether or not individuals believe that they can successfully execute the very behavior that will result in the expected outcome. For example, most students have outcome expectancy that study behaviors such as paying attention during class, finishing homework in time, reviewing course materials regularly, and preparing for tests well ahead of time will produce a decent grade on an upcoming test. Nonetheless, not all of them have sufficiently strong self-efficacy that they could successfully engage in all of these behaviors to attain the desired grade. Self-efficacy belief plays a more critical role than outcome expectancy because efficacy expectation is what makes people initiate and sustain the behaviors necessary for acquiring a desired outcome (Bandura, 1977).

Summary and Recommendations

To better understand the role of self-efficacy in student achievement and help them develop a stronger sense of academic self-efficacy, the following recommendations are offered:

Goals and Goal-Setting. Goals provide students with criteria against which to compare their academic performance and progress. When students realize that the gap between their goal and performance is gradually decreasing, they feel more motivated to keep exerting effort until they reach the goal. Goal properties are important in moderating the effects of goals on self-efficacy. Goals that are too general (e.g., "Do your best"), too difficult (e.g., "Get 100% of the problems correct in AP physics"), or too distal (e.g., "Master the content of the course by the end of this academic year") are not as effective as goals that are specific (e.g., "obtain a letter grade of B or better"), moderately challenging (e.g., "Get at least 80% of the problems correct"), and proximal (e.g., "Complete two lessons in each study session") (Bandura & Schunk, 1981).

Skills Training. Providing gradual mastery experience to students is most effective for arming them with a heightened sense of self-efficacy. In "guided" mastery experience, teachers help students to conquer personal challenges and develop academic skills to see the gap between the goals and their own performance progressively narrows. Teachers then gradually reduce instructional scaffolding as students' competencies develop. When providing performance feedback to students, teachers should provide progress feedback because it helps students monitor the degree of their goal attainments and witness their own improvements (Schunk & Swartz, 1993). It is also important to ensure that teachers present students with multiple opportunities to experience success. Repeated successes can help build a resilient sense of self-efficacy that does not dissipate upon occasional setbacks. These successes must be authentic mastery experiences and not easy successes on superficial tasks that do not require effort.

Modeling. Students can become more self-efficacious about their own learning and performance by observing a model. Cartoons and fictitious characters can be models as well. Students can also function as their own models by videotaping themselves during task performance and watching the tape afterwards. Perceived similarity of the model to observers determines how much benefit will be gained from the observation. Therefore, peer models are a lot more effective than teacher models for demonstrating problem-solving procedures. For the same reason, coping models who overcome initial and occasional difficulties through effort and persistence are better at instilling efficacy beliefs in the observers than are mastery models. Students find coping models more similar in competence to themselves than mastery models who put up a flawless task performance from the very beginning (Schunk, Hanson, & Cox, 1987). Coping models are also more helpful because these models present students with favorable social comparison results about their own competence.

Attributional Feedback. Attribution plays a critical role in the cognitive appraisal processes leading to self-efficacy. Successes attributed to unstable, external factors will have their significance diminished and will not augment students' self-efficacy much. However, successes attributed to internal factors will help boost students' self-efficacy. Two students with similar achievements arrive at drastically different conclusions regarding their own competence in the domain, depending on whether they ascribe their superb performance to pure luck and easy tasks or their own ability and effort. For students who have acquired differentiated conceptions of ability, successes achieved with minimum effort signify high ability and hence most reliably raise self-efficacy. Having to exert a lot of effort to enjoy the same level of success is interpreted as lack of ability and is not as effective as ability attribution for strengthening self-efficacy (Schunk, 1983).

Perceived Task Difficulty. Even among students who make the same ability attributions for their successes on a recent test, strengths of their resultant self-efficacy could still differ. Self-efficacy would be the strongest for those who view the test to have been difficult. Successes at only easy tasks will not help improve students' self-efficacy because they do not provide enough new information regarding competence. Conversely, successes at difficult tasks indicate noticeable improvement in competence from the past and hence are much more potent for strengthening self-efficacy (Bandura, 1977).

Reward-Performance Contingency. When providing rewards, teachers should be mindful about the reward-performance contingency. Rewards that are not contingent upon performance could have undermining effects on students' self-efficacy, if students believe that teachers give out the rewards simply for participation because they lack the capability to accomplish the goal. Like the progress feedback, rewards that correspond to the level and quality of performance convey information to students regarding how much they have improved and how well they are progressing toward the goal. This information is useful for strengthening students' self-efficacy beliefs that they will be able to perform successfully at a designated level to attain a desired academic outcome.

References

Bandura, A. (1977). Self-efficacy: Toward a unifying theory of behavioral change. *Psychological Review, 84,* 191–215.

Bandura, A. (1989). Human agency in social cognitive theory. *American Psychologist, 44,* 1175–1184.

Bandura, A. (1997). *Self-efficacy: The exercise of control.* New York: Freeman.

Bandura, A., & Schunk, D. H. (1981). Cultivating competence, self-efficacy, and intrinsic interest through proximal self-motivation. *Journal of Personality and Social Psychology, 41,* 586–598.

Bong, M., & Skaalvik, E. M. (2003). Academic self-concept and self-efficacy: How different are they really? *Educational Psychology Review, 15,* 1–40.

Multon, K. D., Brown, S. D., & Lent, R. W. (1991). Relation of self-efficacy beliefs to academic outcomes: A meta-analytic investigation. *Journal of Counseling Psychology, 38,* 30–38.

Pajares, F. (1996). Self-efficacy beliefs in academic settings. *Review of Educational Research, 66,* 543–578.

Pintrich, P. R., & De Groot, E. V. (1990). Motivational and self-regulated learning components of classroom academic performance. *Journal of Educational Psychology, 82,* 33–40.

Schunk, D. H. (1983). Ability versus effort attributional feedback: Differential effects on self-efficacy and achievement. *Journal of Educational Psychology, 75,* 848–856.

Schunk, D. H. (1991a). Goal setting and self-evaluation: A social cognitive perspective on self-regulation. *Advances in Motivation and Achievement, 7,* 85–113.

Schunk, D. H. (1991b). Self-efficacy and academic motivation. *Educational Psychologist, 26,* 207–231.

Schunk, D. H., Hanson, A. R., & Cox, P. (1987). Peer-model attributes and children's achievement behaviors. *Journal of Educational Psychology, 79,* 54–61.

Schunk, D. H., & Swartz, C. W. (1993). Goals and progress feedback: Effects on self-efficacy and writing achievement. *Contemporary Educational Psychology, 18,* 337–354.

Zimmerman, B. J. (1989). A social cognitive view of self-regulated academic learning. *Journal of Educational Psychology, 81,* 329–339.

Zimmerman, B. J., Bandura, A., & Martinez-Pons, M. (1992). Self-motivation for academic attainment: The role of self-efficacy beliefs and personal goal setting. *American Educational Research Journal, 29,* 663–676.

2.16

Motivation

DALE H. SCHUNK AND CAROL A. MULLEN
The University of North Carolina at Greensboro

Introduction

Motivation is the process whereby goal-directed activities are instigated and sustained (Schunk, Pintrich, & Meece, 2008). We do not directly observe motivation but rather its outcomes: selection of activities, effort, persistence, and achievement. Because motivation always involves goals, it is necessary to characterize one's level of motivation relative to those goals. To illustrate, imagine that high school students Kevin and Alex have a test tomorrow. Kevin's goal is to make a good grade, so he studies for 4 hours. In contrast, Alex's goal is to pass the test, so he studies for 30 minutes, spending the bulk of his evening social networking with friends. While both students are motivated, Kevin has higher academic motivation in contrast with Alex whose social motivation is relatively higher.

Research Evidence

Theoretical perspectives explain motivation differently (Schunk et al., 2008). Historical theorists viewed motivation as reflecting processes such as instincts, needs, and drives. Humanistic psychologists such as Abraham Maslow and Carl Rogers emphasized the need for personal growth, achieving wholeness, and self-actualization. Conversely, behavioral psychologists contended that motivation was superfluous because reinforcement strengthened behavior and punishment weakened it. Motivation reflected the rate and duration of behavior. These historical views construed motivation as something that affected the performance of previously-learned behaviors more than new learning.

As cognitive theories of learning gained ascendance in the 1960s, researchers began investigating cognitive and affective variables that can influence learning and performance (Shuell, 1986). Thus, one can have a goal to learn a skill (learning goal) or to demonstrate a learned skill (performance goal). Researchers currently explore the conditions, variables, and attitudes that affect motivated learning.

Motivation can influence what, when, and how people learn (Schunk et al., 2008). Students approach learning tasks with different goals, self-efficacy (perceived capabilities) for learning, values (perceived importance of learning), and affects (e.g., excitement, fear). They decide how they will work on the task (i.e., their learning strategy). While engaged in learning, learners are influenced by instructional (e.g., materials, feedback) and contextual variables (e.g., peers, environmental conditions). They monitor their understanding and gauge their learning progress. Perceptions of progress build self-efficacy and sustain motivation. When difficulties arise, they may seek help or alter their strategy. Following task engagement, they may reflect and make attributions (perceived causes) for their outcomes (e.g., success due to hard work). Students who believe they are progressing toward valued goals are apt to sustain their motivation, self-efficacy, and positive affect.

Reviews of motivational research support the influence of these processes on learning and achievement. Goal properties have motivational effects (Locke & Latham, 2002). Goals that incorporate specific standards of performance, can be attained relatively quickly, and are moderately difficult, are more likely to sustain motivation and lead to better performance than are goals that are general (e.g., "Do your best"), long-term, and overly easy or difficult. Self-evaluations of goal progress build self-efficacy and propel motivation (Schunk et al., 2008).

Self-efficacy influences learning and achievement through effort and persistence (Pajares, 1996). Multon, Brown, and Lent (1991) found that self-efficacy related positively to academic outcomes and accounted for 14% of their variance. Effects were stronger for older (high school, college) students and when self-efficacy and performance measures reflected specific tasks rather than general tasks (e.g., standardized tests).

Values have been shown to relate positively to achievement-related choices including course enrolments, occupational choices, college majors, and sports participation

(Eccles, Wigfield, & Schiefele, 1998). Pekrun (1992) reported that positive affective states influence motivation and learning through their effects on cognitive engagement and use of learning strategies.

Attribution research shows that successes ascribed to internal and stable causes such as ability (e.g., "I'm good at this") result in higher expectancies for future successes than attributions to external and unstable causes such as luck (e.g., "I made lucky guesses"; Weiner, 1985). For difficulties, more-adaptive attributions are those to unstable and controllable causes, such as low effort (e.g., "I didn't study enough") and poor strategy (e.g., "I used the wrong method"; Försterling, 1985).

Studies on the effects of interventions designed to promote motivation have shown that motivation and achievement are enhanced by the following: having learners pursue proximal and specific goals: teaching them to set their own goals, having students observe peer models who learn by expending effort and persisting: showing students video recordings of their own performances demonstrating learning: rewarding students for their performance improvements: stressing the value of learning to students: and providing them with feedback linking their improved performances to increased effort (Schunk et al., 2008).

Certain variables can moderate the influence of motivation on learning and achievement. Children's cognitive capacity limits their abilities to represent distant goals in thought, segment long-term goals into short-term goals, and evaluate their progress (Schunk et al., 2008). They also tend to overestimate what they can do. They are motivated by goals that can be attained quickly and by immediate consequences of actions. With cognitive development, children's capabilities for goal setting and self-evaluation improve.

Cultural factors also affect motivation. Researchers have found that self-efficacy often is lower among non-Western students (e.g., Asian) than for students from Western Europe, Canada, and the United States (Klassen, 2004); however, the former students' self-efficacy aligns more closely with their actual performances, whereas the Western students overestimate what they can do. How students interpret perceived causes may vary due to culture (Hau & Salili, 1993). In some cultures, ability may be thought of as uncontrollable (similar to intelligence), whereas individuals in other cultures may interpret it more akin to specific skills that can be learned. Academic motivation may suffer when the practices of schools and students' cultures conflict (e.g., individual versus group learning; Kumar & Maehr, 2010).

Student differences in mindsets and interests can affect motivation. Persons with *fixed* mindsets assume that capabilities are set and that one cannot change much, whereas those holding *growth* mindsets equate ability with learning (Dweck, 2006). Students with growth mindsets may be more motivated to set learning goals and evaluate their progress, believing they can improve their skills.

Students also vary in their interests. Some may be *intrinsically* motivated to engage in activities for their own sake, whereas others may be *extrinsically* motivated to engage

in activities as means toward ends (e.g., praise, rewards). Whether offering students rewards decreases their intrinsic motivation is a source of debate (Cameron & Pierce, 2002). Research shows that rewards given commensurate with performance improvements convey that students are becoming more capable and can foster motivation and self-efficacy (Schunk et al., 2008).

Motivation is a complex topic and questions remain. One is whether motivation—which presumably operates before, during, and after task engagement—is distinct from *volition,* or the processes that protect concentration and effort from distractions while a student is working on a task (Schunk et al., 2008). Whether motivation and volition are separate or overlap, it is useful to think of motivation at different phases of task engagement. Thus, choice of activities is a motivational outcome but often is not relevant because students may not be able to decide whether to engage in particular learning.

A second question is how motivation fits with cognitive accounts of learning. Motivational processes have cognitive referents (e.g., self-efficacy beliefs), which presumably are stored along with other cognitive information. Early cognitive learning theorists were not settled on this score, but recent cognitive theories have begun to address motivation (Winne & Hadwin, 2008).

Summary and Recommendations

Research on academic motivation has implications for educational practice. Motivation is improved when students set goals and evaluate their progress. If rewards are used, they should be given contingent on students' improving their capabilities. It is also helpful to show students how learning will help them perform better. Learners can be taught to attribute learning difficulties to causes they can control, such as low effort or poor use of strategies. Lastly, linking learning to students' interests can improve motivation. For example, teachers' use of technology should appeal to today's students, thereby increasing their motivation to learn.

References

Cameron, J., & Pierce, W. D. (2002). *Rewards and intrinsic motivation: Resolving the controversy.* Westport, CT: Bergin & Garvey.

Dweck, C. S. (2006). *Mindset: The new psychology of success.* New York: Random House.

Eccles, J. S., Wigfield, A., & Schiefele, U. (1998). Motivation to succeed. In N. Eisenberg (Ed.), *Handbook of child psychology: Vol. 3. Social, emotional, and personality development* (5th ed., pp. 1017–1095). New York: Wiley.

Försterling, F. (1985). Attributional retraining: A review. *Psychological Bulletin, 98,* 495–512.

Hau, K., & Salili, F. (1993). Measurement of achievement attribution: A review of instigation methods, question contents, and measurement formats. *Educational Psychology Review, 5,* 377–422.

Klassen, R. M. (2004). Optimism and realism: A review of self-efficacy from a cross-cultural/perspective. *International Journal of Psychology, 39,* 205–230.

Kumar, R., & Maehr, M. L. (2010). Schooling, cultural diversity, and student motivation. In J. L. Meece & J. S. Eccles (Eds.), *Handbook of research on schools, schooling, and human development* (pp. 308–324). New York: Routledge.

Locke, E. A., & Latham, G. P. (2002). Building a practically useful theory of goal setting and task motivation: A 35-year odyssey. *American Psychologist, 57,* 705–717.

Multon, K. D., Brown, S. D., & Lent, R. W. (1991). Relation of self-efficacy beliefs to academic outcomes: A meta-analytic investigation. *Journal of Counseling Psychology, 38,* 30–38.

Pajares, F. (1996). Self-efficacy beliefs in achievement settings. *Review of Educational Research, 66,* 543–578.

Pekrun, R. (1992). The impact of emotions on learning and achievement: Towards a theory of cognitive/motivational mediators. *Applied Psychology: An International Review, 41,* 359–376.

Schunk, D. H., Pintrich, P. R., & Meece, J. L. (2008). *Motivation in education: Theory, research, and applications* (3rd ed.). Upper Saddle River, NJ: Merrill/Prentice Hall.

Shuell, T. J. (1986). Cognitive conceptions of learning. *Review of Educational Research, 56,* 411–436.

Weiner, B. (1985). An attributional theory of achievement motivation and emotion. *Psychological Review, 92,* 548–573.

Winne, P. H., & Hadwin, A. F. (2008). The weave of motivation and self-regulated learning. In D. H. Schunk & B. J. Zimmerman (Eds.), *Motivation and self-regulated learning: Theory, research, and applications* (pp. 297–314). New York: Taylor & Francis.

2.17

Friendship in School

ANNEMAREE CARROLL
The University of Queensland

STEPHEN HOUGHTON
University of Western Australia

SASHA LYNN
The University of Queensland

Introduction

School is an important place for children and adolescents. When young people reach pre- and early adolescence, the influence of family and parenting seems to decrease and the environment, especially school, becomes increasingly important (Liljeberg, Eklund, Fritz, & Klinteberg, 2011). Consequently, children and adolescents spend more time with nonfamily members (i.e., friends), who in turn become more central in their daily lives. The development and maintenance of friendships can therefore impact on the current and long-term adjustment and maturity of young people. In most cases, this results in positive academic and social outcomes for children and adolescents (Véronneau & Dishion, 2011) both in the short and long term. In some instances, however, friendships or a lack of friendships in school leads to adversity (Carroll, Houghton, Durkin, & Hattie, 2009). Within the dynamic of friendships there are two categories of peer relationships. These are: peer group relations (e.g., peer acceptance or rejection) and dyadic peer relationships (e.g., friendships). While peer acceptance may assist entry to play and work groups and contribute to classroom inclusion and competence, friendships in school provide emotional support and companionship to children. However, in both categories, it is not just the presence or number of friends but the quality and personality characteristics of friends that contribute to students' adjustment, particularly academic adjustment.

Research Evidence

Although in its infancy in developmental research, the stage-specific transactional model has been used to investigate the links between peer relationships and academic achievement across different developmental stages (Véronneau, Vitaro,

Brendgen, Dishion, & Tremblay, 2010). What is evident from this research is that there are different influences in terms of friendships on academic achievement across the developmental periods of early childhood through adolescence.

The Early Years. Establishing positive relationships with other children and understanding the emotions of oneself and others are the first key skills in friendship making to emerge during early childhood. The ability to be able to label emotions and respond appropriately to emotional situations has a close association with positive peer interactions in the early years: Children who are more emotionally competent are more liked by their peers and rated as more prosocial by their teachers. Moreover, there is also evidence to suggest that a positive association exists between emotion knowledge and academic success (Rhodes, Warren, Domitrovich, & Greenberg, 2011). It has been argued that children who do not learn the important skills of friendship making in these formative years (especially before the age of 8 years) may be at high risk of experiencing academic problems and antisocial behavior and eventual school dropout.

Early friendships, which are clearly evident in toddler and preschool children, begin through play. These friendships are quite stable over time, with the strength of these friendships being demonstrated through a greater number of play initiations and social interactions and more complex play. Preschool children with more friends have higher peer and teacher social ratings than children with few or no friends. Moreover, it is during the early childhood years that peer group reputations as being liked or disliked are also formed. These reputations can be long-lasting and can result in either peer acceptance or peer rejection. Once formed, these peer reputations have more influence than social behavior and can be hard to transform. Children who experience peer rejection but have one reciprocal friend, however, find it easier to enter play groups and activities.

Middle Childhood.

Friendships during the middle childhood years serve six key functions, namely, companionship, stimulation, physical support, ego support, social comparison, and intimacy/affection. These functions provide the grounds for successful development of social competence. The ability to establish satisfactory peer relationships and the development of academic achievement are key milestones during the childhood period (Véronneau et al., 2010). Important skills that contribute to the success of making friends during middle childhood include engaging in conversations with other children, solving interpersonal conflicts, initiating play with others, and being able to regulate emotions when frustrating experiences occur (Crick & Dodge, 1994).

For children between the ages of 7 and 10 years, peer group status and peer acceptance have a strong influence on academic achievement, with high academic achievement inflating the students' peer status and acceptance (Véronneau et al., 2010). The views of parents and teachers are also highly influential. Children's perceptions are affected by these views more than at any other stage in development. High-achieving children, therefore, tend to associate with high-achieving friends, either by desire or design. This association predicts children's own academic achievement over time (Wentzel, 2005). High-achieving friends can provide a number of positive mutual outcomes including: Being positive role models for efficient study and coping skills; engaging in cooperative school work that is cognitively challenging; enhancing self-esteem through positive feedback; verbal and nonverbal reinforcement of positive behaviors and attitudes to academic success; and providing social comparisons for aspiring to high academic standards (Bissell-Havran & Loken, 2009).

On the other hand, children who are rejected by their peers have been found to have lower academic achievement, with compounding issues such as a disinterest in school, negative attitudes to teachers and schoolwork, lack of participation in school activities, school refusal, poor academic performance, and internalizing problems such as depressed mood and loneliness (Mercer & DeRosier, 2008). This is particularly so for boys who place greater importance on being popular.

Early Adolescence.

Early adolescence (between the ages of 11 and 13 years) is a critical stage in the development of friendships. Young people at this stage spend less time with family and more time with peers who undoubtedly become powerfully influential for long-term developmental trajectories. It is at this time that adolescents embrace their freedom to actively select their own friends who are similar with regard to academic characteristics and be able to spend more time alone with these friends than during childhood. The potential for influence is extremely high during the early adolescent years especially with regard to academic achievement, school engagement, and problem behaviors. It is well established that friends play a positive role with regard to academic achievement. For example, students may learn important study habits through observing and modeling the behaviors of their friends. Friends may offer each other valuable support in homework and school assignment completion, and the interactions that they have with each other may be more academically engaging and stimulating because of the hobbies and interests that they share. Similarly, friends are often like-minded in the extracurricular and school-based activities in which they engage. Those who are highly involved in sport, music, creative arts, or public speaking, for example, will most likely have friends who share these pastimes. School engagement equates with rule compliance, peer and teacher cooperation, and high motivation and effort, and these attributes will also indirectly influence friends' academic achievement (Appleton, Christenson, & Furlong, 2008).

Unfortunately, the powerful influence of friends during early adolescence is also evident in terms of deviant behavior. Students who have friends with higher levels of delinquent involvement have been found to have lower levels of academic achievement, with an escalation of problematic behaviors and substance use by antisocial peers' encouragement to engage in such activities (Carroll et al., 2009). Why engagement with antisocial peers occurs is a complex issue. However, both parental and school factors appear to play contributing roles. Parental monitoring is a highly salient factor with regard to academic achievement and antisocial peers. Low levels of parents' knowledge about their early adolescent's homework completion, unsupervised activities, time spent with friends, and the unsupervised activities of friends, has been found to predict delinquency in middle and late adolescence (Lahey, Van Hulle, D'Onofrio, Rodgers, & Waldman, 2008). Moreover, there are a myriad of school factors that enhance the establishment of antisocial peer networks. According to Carroll et al. (2009), one of the most effective strategies that students use in schools to enhance their antisocial peer identities is through the display of highly visible antisocial behavior in response to the behavior management strategies that teachers and schools employ. For example, ensuring that teachers publicly reprimand them, being sent out of class so that they can communicate their misbehavior to passers-by, and being put in detention or sent to the deputy principal's office (which is always sited in a very busy public area of the school) are all strategies deliberately taken to enhance reputations among peers (friends and nonfriends). Such manipulation of behavior management strategies actually facilitates the making of new antisocial friends.

Adolescence.

During the period marking adolescence, young people seek out social contexts within which the likelihood of social success is high, a process referred to as niche finding. This process ensures the continued potential to select friends who are similar to oneself. Academic success can therefore provide an important venue for interacting with other peers who also engage in school, complete homework, and receive high grades. Groups of similarly high-achieving peers are known to develop and establish their own dynamics, and in this context, academic functioning plays a stronger role in friends' academic functioning (see Frank et al., 2008).

High school adolescents who value academic success appear to be more attracted to peers who focus on academic tasks and this provides an opportunity for mutual help in developing academic skills. That is, high-achieving adolescents build networks of similarly high-achieving friends through a process involving deliberate selection to maintain or improve their academic results.

Adolescence may therefore be the period when young people are more aware of and deliberate in their friendship choices than at any other developmental period, primarily because of the self-serving purposes such actions provide. The extensive research evidence demonstrating that deliberate choice of friendships extends to those involved in delinquent activities adds support to this conjecture (see Carroll et al., 2009, for a comprehensive review). According to reputation enhancement theory (Emler, 1984), a reputation for bad behavior is a deliberate choice made by the individual concerned. Delinquent action is not only a means of creating a tough reputation among outsiders but also a means of proving one's credentials to the in-group to sustain one's self-identity. As was the case with the friends of academically achieving adolescents, the friends of delinquent adolescents provide selective, positive reinforcement for deviant behavior.

Summary and Recommendations

Interventions to Support Friendship Issues. Recommendations pertaining to preventive programs and intervention strategies are not straightforward, as demonstrated by the research evidence presented here. For example, children and adolescents tend to find their own friends whether in conformity or crime. Schools that direct children and adolescents into friendship groups may therefore be making a rod for their own back. Similarly, interventions that focus primarily on social skills or academic achievement may be underestimating or not paying due respect to other social psychological factors which young people hold as important in their choice of friendships. Thus, future research might undertake a growth curve modeling approach to examine the changing dynamics of friendships and friendship groups across the school experience. In this way, a more targeted approach to intervention might be possible, especially at critical times in the developmental life span. A number of recommendations can be made:

* *Early to Middle Childhood*: For all children, early friendships, begin through play. Therefore, providing frequent and appropriate play experiences with compatible agemates may help young children to enhance peer relationships, especially among those with limited or poor social behaviors (Turnbull, Pereira, & Blue-Banning, 2000);
* To foster young children's friendships, provide appropriate training programs for parents and early years educators (Quinn & Hennessy, 2010);
* Initiate preventive interventions that target social-emotional skills and children's abilities to regulate their emotional arousal and attention. This may improve children's academic achievement (Rhodes et al., 2011) and offset the possible risks due to the child's biology, environment, temperament, and learning or emotional problems;
* *Early Adolescence through Adolescence*: Dyadic friendship affiliations may be more malleable than social status in the peer group. Therefore, dyadic friendship experiences should be targeted rather than working directly on peer status within the groups because friendships are more amenable to change (Véronneau et al., 2010);
* Assisting students to achieve academically may improve their academic achievement and hence peer status (Véronneau et al., 2010);
* Revise school policies so that problem adolescents are guided toward adult-supervised extracurricular activities with well-adjusted peers. This may prevent school failure and improve friendships (Véronneau & Dishion, 2011);
* Provide school-based extracurricular activities that are supervised by adults. This provides opportunities for young people to meet others and make friends with the students who enact prosocial behaviors and have a healthy school connection.

References

Appleton, J. J., Christenson, S. L., & Furlong, M. J. (2008). Student engagement with school: Critical conceptual and methodological issues of the construct. *Psychology in the Schools, 45*, 369–386.

Bissell-Havran, J. M., & Loken, E. (2009). The role of friends in early adolescents' academic self-competence and intrinsic value for math and English. *Journal of Youth and Adolescence, 38*, 41–50.

Carroll, A., Houghton, S., Durkin, K., & Hattie, J. (2009). *Adolescent reputations and risk: Developmental trajectories to delinquency.* New York: Springer.

Crick, N. R., & Dodge, K. A. (1994). A review and reformulation of social information processing mechanisms in children's social adjustment. *Psychological Bulletin, 115*, 74–101.

Emler, N. (1984). Differential involvement in delinquency: Towards an interpretation in terms of reputation management. In B. A. Mahler & W. B. Maher (Eds.), *Progress in experimental personality research* (Vol. 13, pp. 173–237). New York: Academic Press.

Frank, K. A., Muller, C., Schiller, K. S., Riegle-Crumb, C., Mueller, A. S., Crosnoe, R., & Pearson, J. (2008). The social dynamics of mathematics course taking in high school. *American Journal of Sociology, 113*, 1645–1696.

Lahey, B. B., Van Hulle, C. A., D'Onofrio, B. M., Rodgers, J. L., & Waldman, I. D. (2008). Is parental knowledge of their adolescent offspring's whereabouts and peer associations spuriously associated with offspring delinquency? *Journal of Abnormal Child Psychology, 36*, 807–823.

Liljeberg, J. F., Eklund, J. M., Fritz, M. V., & Klinteberg, B. (2011). Poor school bonding and delinquency over time: Bidirectional effects and sex differences. *Journal of Adolescence, 34*, 1–9.

Mercer, S. H., & DeRosier, M. E. (2008). Teacher preference, peer rejection, and student aggression: A prospective study of transactional influence and independent contributions to emotional adjustment and grades. *Journal of School Psychology, 46*, 661–685.

Quinn, M., & Hennessy, E. (2010). Peer relationships across the preschool to school transition. *Early Education and Development, 21*, 825–842.

Rhodes, B. L., Warren, H. K., Domitrovich, C. E., & Greenberg, M. T. (2011). Examining the link between preschool social-emotional competence and first grade academic achievement: The role of attention skills. *Early Childhood Research Quarterly, 26*, 182–191.

Turnbull, A. P., Pereira, L., & Blue-Banning, M. J. (2000). Teachers as friendship facilitators. *Teaching Exceptional Children, 32*(5), 66–70.

Véronneau, M-H., & Dishion, T. J. (2011). Middle school friendships and academic achievement in early adolescence: A longitudinal analysis. *Journal of Early Adolescence, 31*, 99–124.

Véronneau, M-H., Vitaro, F., Brendgen, M., Dishion, T. J., & Tremblay, R. E. (2010). Transactional analysis of the reciprocal links between peer experiences and academic achievement from middle childhood to early adolescence. *Developmental Psychology, 46*, 773–790.

Wentzel, K. R. (2005). Peer relationships, motivation, and academic performance at school. In A. J. Elliott & C. S. Dweck (Eds.), *Handbook of competence and motivation* (pp. 279–296). New York: Guilford.

2.18

Indigenous and Other Minoritized Students

RUSSELL BISHOP
University of Waikato

Introduction

A seemingly intractable problem that besets modern education in the Western world is how to raise the achievement levels of indigenous and other minoritized students so that the educational disparities that afflict these students can be addressed. The term *minoritized* refers to a people who have been ascribed the characteristics of a minority (Shields, Bishop, & Mazawi, 2005). To be minoritized, one does not need to be in the numerical minority but only to be treated as if one's position and perspective are of less worth; to be silenced or marginalised. Hence, for example, in schools on the Navajo reservation with over 95% of the population being Navajo or in Bedouin schools, we find characteristics of the students similar to those we may find among Māori in mainstream schools in which they are actually in the numerical minority. Also included in this category are the increasing number of migrants into European countries, populations of color or poverty, and those whose abilities and sexual persuasions do not belong to the perceived mainstream.

There are numerous explanations about why indigenous and other minoritized groups from around the world continue to suffer from the immediate and long term effects of educational disparities on employment, social well-being, and health. These theories range from deficit notions about the paucity of literature in the children's homes; the lack of positive educational experiences and expertise among their families; lack of motivation among particular groups of students; the negative impacts of peer cultures; the impact of the generally low socioeconomic status of the families; the impact of child poverty and abuse; the lack of positive role models (including those of successful members of indigenous and other minoritized groups in schools); and the neocolonial nature of the school system. It is a feature of most of these theories that they focus either on the problems that the child and their families present to the school or that the school presents to the families. Less common are

explanations that focus on what actually happens between the participants of education; that is, the relationships that exist within the school's classrooms and between the school and the families within the wider society; or the impact of the power imbalances that exist in the wider society that are reflected and reproduced within the nation's classrooms.

Research Evidence

Fundamental to this analysis of explanatory theories about the phenomena of low achievement among indigenous and other minoritized students is the understanding that when teaching occurs, progress is decided upon and practices are modified as "a direct reflection of the beliefs and assumptions the teacher holds about the learner" (Bruner, 1996, p. 47). This means that "our interactions with others are deeply affected by our everyday intuitive theorizing about how other minds work" (Bruner, 1996, p. 45). To Foucault (1972), such theorising is seen in the images that teachers create in their minds when explaining their experiences of interacting with indigenous and other minoritized students. These images are expressed in the metaphors they use that are part of the language or the discourses around education that already exist for considerable periods of time and which struggle against each other for explanatory power. It is through these metaphors that teachers subsequently organise classroom relationships and activities. Hence, discourses have a powerful influence on how teachers, and those with whom they interact, understand or ascribe meaning to particular experiences and what eventually happens in practice. In short, particular discourses will provide teachers with a complex network of explanatory images and metaphors, which are then manifest in their positioning, which then will determine, in large part, how they think and act in relation to indigenous and other minoritized students.

The impact of teachers' discursive positioning on indigenous and other minoritized student achievement is seen when it is understood that some discourses hold solutions

74

to problems that affect these students, while others do not. For example, if the discourse that the teacher is drawing from explains indigenous and other minoritized students' achievement problems in their classroom as being due to inherent or culturally based deficiencies of the children or of their parents and families, then the relationships and interactions that teachers develop with these children will be negative and they will engage students in low quality pedagogic content and skill programmes such as remedial activities or resort to traditional transmission strategies. In addition, and perhaps not surprisingly, indigenous and other minoritized students will react to this experience negatively with consequent negative implications for their attendance (they will often vote with their feet), engagement and motivation for learning (they will be met with behaviour modification programmes and assertive discipline), and achievement (which remains lower than children of the majority cultural groups in the classroom, and in many cases in the world, the gaps continue to widen).[1] Conversely, if the discourse offers positive explanations and solutions, then teachers will more likely be able to act in an agentic manner, seeing themselves as being able to develop quality caring and learning pedagogic relationships with indigenous and other minoritized students. When such contexts for learning are developed, as evidenced in the Te Kotahitanga project (Bishop, Berryman, Powell, & Teddy, 2007; Bishop, Berryman, Tiakiwai, & Richardson, 2003) that focuses on improving the achievement of indigenous Māori students in mainstream, public secondary schools in New Zealand, Māori students respond positively with measurable increases in engagement, attendance, retention, motivation (Bishop, Berryman, Powell et al., 2007; Meyer et al., 2010), and achievement (Bishop, Berryman, Wearmouth, Peter, & Clapham, 2011; Meyer et al., 2010).

Further studies support this conclusion. The first example considered the determinants of student leadership in schools thereby determining the keys to improving student achievement (Dempster, 2011). The argument is that "it is the immediacy of the sense of connection and belonging they experience with their teachers and their peers that governs the sense of identification students have with their schools. Only then is engagement in all aspects of learning, curricular and cocurricular, enhanced, and once this occurs, the desire to take on leadership responsibilities in matters of school citizenship is elevated" (p. 97). Dempster continues by suggesting that

> how well children and young people are treated by their families, teachers and peers is a fundamental influence on how well they become connected to their schools. Furthermore, there is support for the proposition that experience of reasonable empowerment and a climate of participatory social engagement (both factors influencing leadership), are known to develop in students the very social, emotional and cognitive attributes that facilitate improvements in academic achievement. (p. 97)

The second example is a meta-analysis by Corneluius-White (2007, cited in Hattie, 2009) based on 119 studies with 1,450 effects, which was based on 355,325 students, 14,851 teachers, and 2,439 schools. In this analysis, there was a correlation of 0.34 ($d = 0.72$) across all person-centered teacher variables and all student outcomes (achievement and attitudes). Hattie (2009) uses these results to argue that in classrooms "with person-centered teachers, there are more engagements, more respect of self and others, there are fewer resistant behaviours, there is greater non-directivity (student initiative and student-regulated activities), and there are higher student achievement outcomes" (p. 119).

The third example is our own research into means of changing teacher theorising and practice in ways that will bring about improvements in the schooling experiences and achievement of Māori students in mainstream, public schools. In 2001, we began the research for Te Kotahitanga by talking with groups of Years 9 and 10 Māori students, together with members of these students' families, school principals, and teachers, about their collective schooling experiences. From these interviews, a series of narratives of experience were developed (Bishop & Berryman, 2006). In contrast to the majority of their teachers who tended to dwell upon the problems that the children's deficiencies caused them, the children clearly identified that the main influence on their educational achievement was the quality of the in-class relationships and interactions they had with their teachers. They also explained how teachers could create a context for learning in which Māori students' educational achievement could improve by teachers changing the ways they related and interacted with Māori students in their classrooms. It was clear from their experiences that if Māori students are to achieve at higher levels and educational disparities are to be reduced, then teachers must relate to and interact with these students in a different manner from the most commonly occurring approaches.

From these interviews, we developed an Effective Teaching Profile (ETP; Bishop, Berryman, Tiakiwai et al., 2003) that formed the basis of the Te Kotahitanga professional development innovation, which is now running in 49 secondary schools in New Zealand. In these schools, the most effective implementers of the ETP are those who see Māori student schooling experiences improve dramatically and achievement rise to the highest levels in norm-referenced standardised tests.

Fundamental to the ETP are teachers' understandings of the need to explicitly reject deficit theorising as a means of explaining Māori students' educational achievement levels and their taking an agentic position in their theorising about their practice. In order for teachers to attain these understandings, teachers need to be provided with learning opportunities for critically evaluating where they discursively position themselves when constructing their own images, principles, and practices in relation to Māori and other minoritized students in their classrooms. They also need an opportunity to consider the implications of their discursive positioning on their own agency and for Māori students' learning. Practitioners need to be able to express their professional commitment and responsibility to bringing about change in indigenous and other minoritized students' educational achievement by accepting professional responsibility for the learning of all of their students, not just those who they can relate to readily. These central understandings are then manifested in these teachers' classrooms when effective teachers demonstrate on a daily basis: that they care for the students as culturally located individuals; they have high expectations for students' learning; they are able to manage their classrooms and curriculum so as to promote learning; they are able to engage in a range of discursive learning interactions with students or facilitate students to engage with others in these ways; they know a range of strategies that can facilitate learning interactions; they collaboratively promote, monitor, and reflect upon student's learning outcomes so as to modify their instructional practices in ways that will lead to improvements in Māori student achievement; and they share this knowledge with the students.

Summary and Recommendations

Positive classroom relationships and interactions are built upon positive, nondeficit, agentic thinking by teachers about students and their families. Agentic thinking views the students as having many experiences that are relevant and fundamental to classroom interactions. This agentic thinking by teachers means they see themselves as being able to solve problems that come their way and as having recourse to skills and knowledge that can help all of their students and they believe that all of their students can achieve, no matter what. Agentic thinking is fundamental to the creation of learning contexts in classrooms where young Māori people are able to be themselves as Māori, to bring whom they are into the classroom, where Māori students' humour is acceptable, where students can care for and learn with each other, where being different is acceptable, and where the power of Māori students' own self-determination is fundamental to classroom relations and interactions. Indeed, the interdependence of self-determining participants in the classroom creates vibrant learning contexts, which in turn are characterised by the growth and development of quality learning relations and interactions, increased student attendance, and engagement and achievement both in school and on nationally based measures.

Fundamental to these classrooms is teachers' discursive (re)positioning, which is a necessary but often overlooked condition for educational reform; the sufficient conditions are the skills and experience teachers need to develop effective caring and learning relationships. In this way, theorising from within a relational discourse addresses the limitations of the culturalist position that promotes quality teaching but gives limited consideration to the impact of power differentials within the classroom, school, and society such as those that manifest themselves in teachers drawing upon deficit discourses to explain their use of ineffective pedagogies. It also is preferable to the structuralist position that promotes a redistribution of resources and wealth in society, yet gives only limited consideration to the agency of teachers and

school leaders and policy makers at all levels of education, allowing them to abrogate their responsibilities. While both of these considerations are necessary, what is missing from much current debate about the influences on (indigenous and other minoritized) students' achievement is a model that promotes effective and sustainable educational reform drawn from a relational discourse.

Note

1. It is interesting that when challenged over their "closing the gaps" policy in the early 1990s, the then New Zealand government chose to abandon the policy and instead focus on "realising Māori student potential." However, there are a number of problems with this new focus. First, it is a much more elusive target and is extremely difficult to define, and in fact is left undefined, in government policy documents (Ministry of Education, 2008) other than statements about Māori students having unlimited potential and abilities. Second, most teachers that we interviewed during our research used deficit terms when they spoke of Māori students (Bishop et al., 2003). This means that the power of defining what constitutes Māori potential is, in practice, left to a group of people who think Māori potential is limited, not unlimited. In policy terms, to leave the determination of Māori potential in the hands of what is essentially a non-Māori teaching force, most of whom see Māori potential as being limited, can only be described as careless. Rather, it is essential to have an outcome measure that is not open to sabotage by deficit thinking, which does not go away just because antideficit thinking is suggested in a policy document.

References

Bishop, R., & Berryman, M. (2006). *Culture speaks: Cultural relationships and classroom learning.* Wellington, NZ: Huia.

Bishop, R., Berryman, M., Powell, A., & Teddy, L. (2007). *Te Kotahitanga: Improving the educational achievement of Māori students in mainstream education Phase 2: Towards a whole school approach.* Report to the Ministry of Education. Wellington, NZ: Ministry of Education.

Bishop, R., Berryman, M., Tiakiwai, S., & Richardson, C. (2003). *Te Kotahitanga: The experiences of year 9 and 10 Māori students in mainstream classrooms. Final report to Ministry of Education.* Wellington, NZ: Ministry of Education.

Bishop, R., Berryman, M., Wearmouth, J., Peter, M., & Clapham, S., (2011). *Te Kotahitanga: Improving the educational achievement of Māori students in English-medium schools: Report for Phase 3 and Phase 4: 2008–2010.* Report to the Ministry of Education. Wellington, NZ: Ministry of Education. 1-228. http://www.educationcounts.govt.nz/publications/maori/english-medium-education/9977

Bruner, J. (1996). *The culture of education.* Cambridge, MA: Harvard University Press.

Dempster, N. (2011). Leadership and learning: Making connections down under. In Townsend T. & J. MacBeath (Eds.), *International handbook: Leadership for learning* (pp. 89–102). Springer, Dortrecht, The Netherlands.

Foucault, M. (1972). *The archaeology of knowledge.* New York: Pantheon.

Hattie, J. (2009). *Visible learning: A synthesis of over 800 meta-analyses relating to achievement.* New York: Routledge.

Meyer, L., Penetito, W., Hynds, A., Savage, C., Hindle, R., & Sleeter, C. (2010). *Evaluation of Te Kotahitanga: 2004–2008.* Wellington, NZ: Jessie Hetherington Centre for Educational Research, Victoria University. www.educationcounts.govt.nz/publications/maori_education/78910

Ministry of Education. (2008). *Ka Hikitia—Managing for success: The Māori education strategy 2008–2012.* Wellington, NZ: Ministry of Education.

Shields, C. M., Bishop, R., & Mazawi, A. E. (2005). *Pathologizing practices: The impact of deficit thinking on education.* New York: Peter Lang.

2.19

Low Academic Success

David A. Bergin
University of Missouri

Introduction

Low academic success is indicated by low school grades, low standardized test scores, and retention in grade. Low academic success tends to be stable; that is, students who are low achievers at one age tend to be low achievers at a later age. Early achievement may be particularly important because students who experience less academic success in kindergarten and first grade tend to have lower achievement in high school.

Research Evidence

Major predictors of low academic success include child attributes, parent behavior, and group membership. Child attributes include low intelligence, poor executive function, low conscientiousness, and low self-control. A study of over 70,000 English children found that those with relatively low intelligence at age 11 had low achievement on national examinations at age 16 (Deary, Strand, Smith, & Fernandes, 2007). A component of intelligence is executive functioning, and students with poor executive functioning have trouble shifting from one task to another and controlling their attention; they have trouble solving math problems and comprehending what they read, and they have lower standardized test scores. The personality factor known as "conscientiousness" also predicts achievement. Students with low conscientiousness tend to be poorly organised and unreliable, to pursue goals weakly, to give up easily, and to act impulsively. They tend to exhibit low achievement (Poropat, 2009).

Students with low self-control have trouble paying attention, staying on task, and ignoring distractions; this often leads to low academic success. The achievement of children with poor self-control tends to decline across the school years. Indeed data suggest that self-control may predict GPA better than intelligence. Preschoolers who exhibit poor self-control tend to have lower SAT scores

many years later, and as young adults they have fewer years of education.

Parents who have low achievement aspirations for their children, who do not socialize their children toward understanding the goals of education, and who do not communicate the value of achievement, tend to have children with low academic success (Hill & Tyson, 2009). Children whose parents do not read to them tend to have low achievement, regardless of socioeconomic status (SES) (average effect size=-.59; Bus, Van IJzendoorn, & Pellegrini, 1995). Parents who hold high standards for behavior while also showing warmth and acceptance tend to have children whose achievement is higher than children of parents who are permissive or neglectful. In addition, stable families foster higher achievement than families that experience divorce, out-of-wedlock birth, frequent moves, or familial conflict.

Group membership, such as gender, social class, and ethnicity, also predicts low academic success. When measured by school grades, boys consistently have lower academic success than girls. Across hundreds of studies, low SES predicts low academic success. A meta-analysis (Sirin, 2005) shows an effect size of .28 between SES and academic achievement. The SES achievement gap occurs across countries. The effects of SES emerge and grow in the preschool years. By the time they enter school, impoverished children have lower math and reading abilities, and do not catch up to nonpoor children. SES influences children through quality of parenting and opportunities that parental income and education make possible, such as exposure to cognitively stimulating talk and materials, and experiences like books, writing materials, museum visits, and travel.

Across countries, members of oppressed ethnic groups tend to have low academic success due to factors such a cultural mismatch, language differences, low teacher expectations, and low SES. For example, in the United States, African Americans and Latinos have a history as oppressed minorities and tend to have particularly low achievement levels. Nationwide, the high school graduation rate is about

50% for African American students, 53% for Hispanic students, and 75% for White students. Schools with predominantly minority students tend to be overcrowded, lack textbooks, and have fewer qualified teachers, all of which affect student success. Minority students tend to report less caring from school personnel.

What Does Low Academic Success Predict? Low academic success predicts low social success during childhood. Children with low achievement are more likely than high achievers to experience low peer popularity, and even social rejection. The link between social and academic success may be bidirectional. Peer victimization predicts lack of academic success in North America, Europe, and Asia, but the correlation is small (r = -.10; Nakamoto & Schwartz, 2010).

A meta-analysis of over 50 longitudinal studies found that low academic success predicts less education, lower-level occupations, and lower income in adulthood than high academic success (average correlation = .33; Strenze, 2007). This may be partly explained through the effects of retention and dropping out, both of which are predicted by low academic success. Low academic achievement is a significant predictor of retention in grade and of dropping out of school (but retention is more likely the direct cause of dropping out because similarly low success students not retained have lower dropout rates). Retention is associated with later dropping out, even when retention occurs in first grade. Dropping out, in turn, is associated with lower wages, higher rates of welfare dependency, and greater criminality (Alexander, Entwisle, & Kabbani, 2001). Most research on grade retention shows that retention does not improve the achievement of low achieving youth. A meta-analysis (Jimerson, 2001) showed that retained youth achieve about .39 standard deviations below promoted comparison groups, though a more recent meta-analysis suggests that the negative effects of retention may not be as great as is generally believed (Allen, Chen, Willson, & Hughes, 2009).

Summary and Recommendations

Low academic success predicts many negative outcomes that include further low academic success, dropping out, and poor life prospects. Parents can pursue specific behaviors that improve achievement such as reading to young children, expressing high expectations for success, and communicating that success comes through effort and persistence. Teachers can improve academic success by using effective, evidence-based curricula, holding high expectations for success, and communicating that success comes

through effort and persistence. They should be sure that time spent in the classroom is focused on learning and not on diversions that detract from academic engagement. They should use motivational techniques that engage all students, not just a few. For example, competition among individual students might engage the top students in a class, but most students will not try hard because their previous experience has demonstrated that they will not compete successfully.

Teachers need to be careful not to fall prey to myths that parents of minority students do not care about school or achievement. While such parents may not manifest their interest in education through frequent contact with teachers or administrators, there is considerable evidence they do care about their children's education. Cultural and language barriers can interfere with teachers' understanding of their students and their students' parents. Teachers and students benefit when they understand each other's cultural backgrounds. When teachers and school personnel communicate caring to all students and foster an emotional bond to the school, students tend to experience higher achievement than when they feel that no one at the school cares about them. Successful interventions pay attention to emotional well-being as a foundation for academic success.

References

Alexander, K. L., Entwisle, D. R., & Kabbani, N. (2001). The dropout process in life course perspective: Early risk factors at home and school. *Teachers College Record, 103*, 760–822.

Allen, C., Chen, Q., Willson, V., & Hughes, J. N. (2009). Quality of research design moderates effects of grade retention on achievement: A meta-analytic, multi-level analysis. *Educational Evaluation and Policy Analysis, 31*, 480–499.

Bus, A. G., Van IJzendoorn, M. H., & Pellegrini, A. D. (1995). Joint book reading makes for success in learning to read: A meta-analysis on intergenerational transmission of literacy. *Review of Educational Research, 65*, 1–21.

Deary, I. J., Strand, S., Smith, P., & Fernandes, C. (2007). Intelligence and educational achievement. *Intelligence, 35*, 13–21.

Hill, N. E., & Tyson, D. F. (2009). Parental involvement in middle school: A meta-analytic assessment of the strategies that promote achievement. *Developmental Psychology, 45*, 740–763.

Jimerson, S. R. (2001). Meta-analysis of grade retention research: Implications for practice in the 21st century. *School Psychology Review, 30*, 420–437.

Nakamoto, J., & Schwartz, D. (2010). Is peer victimization associated with academic achievement: A meta-analytic review. *Social Development, 19*, 221–242.

Poropat, A. E. (2009). A meta-analysis of the five-factor model of personality and academic performance. *Psychological Bulletin, 135*, 322–338.

Sirin, S. R. (2005). Socioeconomic status and academic achievement: A meta-analytic review of research. *Review of Educational Research, 75*, 417–453.

Strenze, T. (2007). Intelligence and socioeconomic success: A meta-analytic review of longitudinal research. *Intelligence, 35*, 401–426.

2.20

Learning Difficulties in School

R. Allan Allday
University of Kentucky

Mitchell L. Yell
University of South Carolina

Introduction

Learning difficulties present a myriad of academic and behavioral challenges to schools and teachers due to their effect on achievement. Numerous factors are associated with learning difficulties; however, these factors typically funnel into similar outcomes that are often linked to low academic achievement and poor social functioning. Identifying factors that lead to learning difficulties requires pinpointing the primary sources of influence within schools.

Three distinct groups (i.e., students, teachers, and schools) contain specific factors and characteristics that impact school achievement. For example, student factors, such as presence of a disability, socioeconomic status, or family involvement can affect achievement. Teachers who lack training in effective practices for struggling learners and effective classroom and behavior management strategies can magnify learning difficulties. Finally, school factors can affect student achievement through the established school-wide climate and expectations. Each of these groups (i.e., student, teacher, and school) influences achievement and they are interconnected; therefore, focusing on these three groups can help identify effective practices that can increase success of students with learning difficulties.

Research Evidence

Understanding and defining school achievement is necessary before addressing how student, teacher, and school factors can impact academic and behavioral success. Defining school achievement requires consideration of a school's role in a student's life. That is, schools function as mediators to prepare students for successful competitive employment and a socially well-adjusted adult life. In order to prepare students to achieve these goals, schools must focus on the attainment of academic and behavioral skills necessary for productive and socially engaged adults. For the purpose of this discussion, achievement is defined as success within the school environment in the areas of academic functioning (e.g., reaching skill mastery, performing at or above expected levels) and behavioral functioning (e.g., exhibiting appropriate social skills, engaging in school-appropriate behavior).

Student Factors. There are a number of causal mechanisms that affect students ***prior*** to entering primary school. The presence of a disability, whether physical, intellectual, or behavioral, can impact school success (Lane, Carter, Pierson, & Glaeser, 2006). Other mechanisms, such as socioeconomic status (Perry & McConney, 2010; Yang-Hansen, 2008) and familial structures affect student outcomes (Hill & Tyson, 2009). Considering these mechanisms, it is clear that individual students enter primary school with different skills and experiences that will impact academic successes as well as social productivity (e.g., social skills, behavioral regulation).

Academic and behavioral challenges often occur simultaneously within the student and impact school success (Algozzine, Wang, & Violette, 2011). Nowicki (2003) conducted a meta-analysis of social competence of students with learning disabilities and students who were low- and high achievers. Results suggested that students with learning disabilities and students who were low achievers were more likely to experience problems with social functioning. Similar results have been found in studies conducted in the United Kingdom (Walker & Nabuzoka, 2007) and China (Chen, Rubin, & Li, 1997). Each of these studies suggested that learning difficulties directly impact achievement and social successes.

Schools and teachers can only plan for student characteristics, but are limited in what they can control outside of school functions. For example, schools cannot control presence of a disability, socioeconomic status, or familial structures; however, schools can control experiences a student has when he or she enters the school building. Providing students with effective teachers and a school environment that supports learning is vital to negate the effects of student characteristics. The following sections relate to how teacher and school characteristics can improve academic achievement and limit learning difficulties.

Teacher Characteristics. Teachers are the most important mediators of knowledge within schools. They must understand how to initiate learning so that the full spectrum of students can be successful. As inclusion of students with academic and behavioral difficulties increases in the general education classroom (i.e., mainstreaming), teachers must be effective in providing instruction to students with a wide spectrum of skills. Woolfson and Brady's (2009) research surmised that many teachers do not believe they can positively impact students with learning difficulties through their instruction. This belief has a drastic impact on student–teacher relationships and interactions (Jordan & Stanovich, 2001), as well as student achievement.

Instructional practices and classroom/behavior management strategies are two primary factors that can hinder a teacher's ability to address learning difficulties effectively. Jordan and Stanovich (2001) found that teachers who viewed learning difficulties as a problem they could not control were less likely to interact with students with exceptionalities or students who are at risk. This suggests that some teachers are ill prepared to instruct students who learn at slower paces or require additional academic or behavioral supports. Teachers who are well trained to instruct students with learning difficulties understand that effective instructional practices can be successful with *any* student. Furthermore, un- or underprepared teachers may avoid students with learning difficulties for lack of understanding of how to remedy the challenges. For example, students who struggle with new concepts tend to slow the pace of instruction. This slowing of instruction can cause the struggling learner to be overlooked or unintentionally ignored by teachers. It helps in maintaining lesson pacing to overlook low performing students; however, it does not address those students' learning difficulties.

A solid foundation in classroom and behavior management is a second factor that can limit teacher effectiveness in improving achievement. Teachers who do not have good management skills are more likely to remove students from the classroom. The likelihood of a student gaining academic skills decreases when that student is removed from the learning environment. Teachers with a strong foundational understanding of management principles know that students who struggle academically may be more apt to exhibit problem behaviors in order to escape task demands. The teacher with the effective management system in place can combat these types of behaviors. Another challenge for teachers with poor management skills is stopping instruction to address problem behavior. The more frequently a teacher stops the lesson, the less content that can be covered during instruction. Proximity control and effective questioning are two strategies effective class-

room managers use to continue lessons while addressing problem behavior.

Moving forward in reducing or eliminating learning difficulties, teachers must better prepare to teach students who have academic and behavioral challenges. Specifically, teachers must embrace teaching methods known to be effective (e.g., direct instruction) and be more hesitant to use unproven methods. Often, teachers can use simple techniques such as guided notes or response cards to assist students with learning difficulties. For example, Konrad, Joseph, and Eveleigh (2009) conducted a meta-analysis supporting the use of guided notes in improving academic achievement of students with learning difficulties. Randolph (2007) found in his meta-analysis that the use of response cards could increase test and quiz achievement. When teachers utilize research-validated methods, they increase the likelihood of maximum content coverage and overcoming academic deficits.

Teachers must learn strategies to reduce challenging behavior, while promoting socially appropriate alternative behaviors. As with academics, teachers can use simple management strategies (e.g., proximity control, effective questioning) to address student behavior. When teachers employ proven methods to increase positive behaviors, they should see an increase in academic achievement.

School Characteristics. Effective schools provide environments that encourage academic growth and reinforce socially appropriate behaviors. Effective schools meet student needs through hard work and staff perseverance, and overcome many factors that potentially impede school effectiveness. For instance, learning can be affected by issues posed by low socioeconomic status in a school, as well as urban or rural challenges. Schools, however, can focus on factors in which they have more control, such as developing a learning climate and collaborative teamwork that builds upon student success.

Historically, schools have taken a punitive approach to managing behavior that disrupts the learning environment. Although this approach is effective with many students, it is less effective in reducing problem behaviors of students with chronic behavior problems. Often students with consistent problem behaviors receive progressively more intense levels of punishment (e.g., from office referrals to suspensions to expulsions). Students who receive suspensions and expulsions are disadvantaged in academic achievement because of removal from the learning environment. For schools to address the learning difficulties of students with challenging behaviors, it is necessary to address student engagement in the learning environment.

A second school-wide factor that can affect achievement is an atmosphere of collaborative teamwork with the school. Schools that fail to create effective communication between administration and staff limit their effectiveness. Students with learning difficulties may exhibit different behaviors with different teachers. When teachers fail to communicate effective strategies for particular students, they may decrease the likelihood of student success in all classes. An additional challenge in communication among school staff is the sharing of academic and behavioral data. If teachers view data as "my data" versus "our data" then they may be less likely to work collaboratively in analyzing the data and developing interventions.

Addressing learning difficulties at a school-wide level requires individual schools and districts to be prepared to address their students' various academic and behavioral issues. School-wide positive behavior supports and interventions (PBIS) has proven to be a successful method of addressing some of these issues (Sugai & Horner, 2008). PBIS has been an endeavor aimed at creating a welcoming learning environment that promotes socially appropriate behavior. Within the system of PBIS, there are several effective practices that can help schools better meet the needs of students with learning difficulties. Specifically, school staff must collaboratively define common objectives, develop teaching methods for expectations, follow-through with set procedures, and evaluate program effectiveness (Sugai & Horner, 2002). Lassen, Steele, and Sailor (2006) studied the effects of PBIS in an urban middle school over multiple years. The authors noted that office discipline referrals and school suspensions decreased throughout the study, while standardized scores on reading and math tests increased. This approach addresses student and teacher behavior through encouraging positive behavior and requires that schools train their teachers in effective practices.

Summary and Recommendations

Identifying factors that support and maintain learning difficulties in school is a challenge that researchers, educators, and school administrators must continue to resolve. These factors can be numerous and complex, but present themselves in various forms of academic and behavior problems. It is unknown if academic or behavior problems arise first; therefore, teachers and schools should work to *teach* academic skills and to *teach* behavior skills (Algozzine et al., 2011). Two goals can be reached through teaching academic and behavior skills. First, learning difficulties in schools can be reduced when students are presented with effective instruction. Second, academic achievement can be increased when schools and teachers reinforce positive student behaviors.

References

Algozzine, B., Wang, C., & Violette, A. S. (2011). Reexamining the relationship between academic achievement and social behavior. *Journal of Positive Behavior Interventions, 13,* 3–16.

Chen, X., Rubin, K. H., & Li, D. (1997). Relation between academic achievement and social adjustment: Evidence from Chinese children. *Developmental Psychology, 33,* 518–525.

Hill, N. B., & Tyson, D. F. (2009). Parental involvement in middle school: A meta-analytic assessment of the strategies that promote achievement. *Developmental Psychology, 45,* 740–763.

Jordan, A., & Stanovich, P. (2001). Patterns of teacher-student interaction in inclusive elementary classrooms and correlates of student self-concept. *International Journal of Disability, Development and Education, 48,* 33–52.

Konrad, M., Joseph, L. M., & Eveleigh, E. (2009). A meta-analytic review of guided notes. *Education and Treatment of Children, 32,* 421–444.

Lane, K., Carter, E., Pierson, M., & Glaeser, B. (2006). Academic, social, and behavioral characteristics of high school students with emotional disturbances or learning disabilities. *Journal of Emotional and Behavioral Disorders, 14,* 108–117.

Lassen, S. R., Steele, M. M., & Sailor, W. (2006). The relationship of school-wide positive behavior support to academic achievement in an urban school. *Psychology in the Schools, 43,* 701–712.

Nowicki, E. A. (2003). A meta-analysis of the social competence of children with learning disabilities compared to classmates of low and average to high achievement. *Learning Disability Quarterly, 26,* 171–188.

Perry, L., & McConney, A. (2010). School socio-economic composition and student outcomes in Australia: Implications for educational policy. *Australian Journal of Education, 54,* 72–85.

Randolph, J. J. (2007). Meta-analysis of the research on response cards: Effects on test achievement, quiz achievement, participation and off-task behavior. *Journal of Positive Behavior Interventions, 9,* 113–128.

Sugai, G., & Horner, R. (2002). The evolution of discipline practices: School-wide positive behavior supports. *Child and Family Behavior Therapy, 24,* 23–50.

Sugai, G, & Horner, R. (2008). What we know and need to know about preventing problem behavior in schools. *Exceptionality, 16,* 67–77.

Walker, A., & Nabuzoka, D. (2007). Academic achievement and social functioning of children with and without learning difficulties. *Educational Psychology, 27,* 635–654.

Woolfson, L. M., & Brady, K. (2009). An investigation of factors impacting on mainstream teachers' beliefs about teaching students with learning difficulties. *Educational Psychology, 29,* 221–238.

Yang-Hansen, K. (2008). Ten-year trend in SES effects on reading achievement at school and individual levels: A cross-country comparison. *Educational Research and Evaluation, 14,* 521–537.

Section 3

Influences from the Home

EDITOR: ANDREW MARTIN
University of Sydney

3.1

Resident and Nonresident Fathers

WILLIAM JEYNES

The Witherspoon Institute, Princeton, NJ and California State University, Long Beach

Introduction

Over a period of several decades American leaders, social scientists, parents, and teachers have reached a greater understanding of the multifarious factors that influence academic achievement, first and foremost of which is the role that family factors play in helping determine academic outcomes. The factor that people have tended to focus on the most is family structure (Wallerstein & Blakeslee, 1989). This focus has been especially salient due to two seminal reports that each had a major impact on how people perceive the significance of academic outcomes. First, the Coleman Report in 1966 indicated that parental family structure had a prodigious effect on scholastic achievement (U.S. Center for Education Statistics, 1966). Second, in the report, *On Further Examination*, the Educational Testing Service thoroughly examined the decline of SAT scores in the 17 consecutive years from 1963 to 1980 (Wirtz, 1977). They concluded that in spite of the temptation the citizenry might have to immediately blame teachers for the precipitous drop in test scores, there are other variables that played prominent roles in contributing to the decline (Jeynes, 2007; Wirtz, 1977). Specifically, the Educational Testing Service noted that family and moral changes (including decline of father involvement) in the United States during the 1963 to 1980 period played a major role in causing the decline in test scores (Wirtz, 1977). These two reports were arguably among the most important educational reports of the 1960s and the 1970s, respectively. To the extent that this is true, it is particularly significant that these two reports came to essentially the same conclusion regarding the salience of family structure.

The challenges faced by children from single-parent family structures have been a concern of parents and educators for many centuries (Jeynes, 2002). In the period from the 1600s until the early 1960s, most of this concern revolved around children who had lost one of their parents (Jeynes,

1999, 2007). In the majority of cases children had lost their father, either due to a health-related death or because he had died in a war (McLanahan & Sandefur, 1994). The first studies of the impact of father absence were directed at one or both of the causes of father absence (health and war) (Jeynes, 2002). Sutherland (1930) was the first social scientist to compare the intellectual output of youth from father absent families versus their counterparts in two-parent biological parent families and found that the average IQ of the latter group was higher. Sutherland's work played a significant role in causing Fortes (1933) to examine the relationship between father absence and juvenile delinquency. His findings that father absence was associated with elevated rates of juvenile delinquency have been supported repeatedly in the nearly eight decades since publication of Fortes's work. Today, social scientists understand that one of the most reliable predictors of gang membership is coming from a father absent family. About 85% of gang members come from a father absent family structure (Bellair & McNulty, 2009).

World War II created a new pool of single-parent families because of the plethora of young men who died in battle (McLanahan & Sandefur, 1994). For 20 years following the conclusion of World War II in 1945, there was a surge in the number of studies on the effects of father absence (Jeynes, 2002). Smith (1945) wrote on the unique psychological adjustments that stepchildren need to make, and Nye (1952) undertook the most comprehensive study of fatherless families, by addressing a wide array of variables including gender, psychological attributes, and their interplay. Carlsmith (1964, 1973), undertook studies that examined the effects of father absence resulting from military duty, found that such absence was associated with lower school achievement only if the father absence was for an extended period of time. Since that time there have been a copious number of studies that have reaffirmed the academic disadvantages that accrue when the father is absent from the family and the detrimental effects when there is a lack of quality involvement when the father is present (Jeynes, 2002).

Research Evidence

Amato and Keith (1991) conducted the first sophisticated meta-analysis on the relationship between father absence and scholastic outcomes, although they limited their study to children of divorce. They found that there was a consistent relationship between father absence and depressed academic outcomes (Amato & Keith, 1993). Wallerstein and Blakeslee (1989) found that the effects of divorce were longer lasting than most social scientists had previously hypothesized. Additional studies have examined a wider range of father-less families than Amato had included and found a general pattern that appears to make comprehensible the differing effect sizes that emerge for various family structures (Jeynes, 2000). The general pattern that emerged is that where there is not a two-biological-parent family, then the greater the negative impact family structure has on educational out-comes. In addition, a meta-analysis was undertaken that examined both single-parent and blended father-absent families (Jeynes, 2006). This meta-analysis confirmed the finding mentioned above and also divulged another trend that was suggested in the first study. That is, the larger the number of family transitions that a child has encountered, the more of a negative impact this has on the school outcomes of that child (although more research is needed comparing one-parent father with one-parent mother families).

The studies that have measured the relationship between father absence and academic outcomes have examined myriad types of scholastic measures that include standardized tests assessing skills in all the major academic disciplines; grade point average; teacher ratings; rate of grade reten-tion; high school dropout rate; whether a student took the basic core set of courses that are generally associated with college preparation; teacher ratings; and other measures. The effects of father absence appear to be quite consistent across the various academic measures examined (Amato & Keith, 1991; Jeynes, 1999, 2003b).

One of the most remarkable findings regarding the salience of father absence relates to the achievement gap. That is, if one examines the role of father absence with regard to the achievement gap that exists between African American and Hispanic students in the United States on the one hand and White students on the other, an intriguing trend emerges. That is, if one examines African American and Hispanic children who are from two-biological-parent families and compares them with White students, the achievement gap disappears even when one controls for socioeconomic status (Jeynes, 1999, 2003b).

There are a variety of causal mechanisms at work that help explain the influence of being from a single-parent fatherless family structure. The first mechanism is the direct effects of psychological loss that results from the relatively sudden absence of a father. Human beings do not generally

fare well when they are victimized by the trauma that results from the sudden removal of a person who is a source of love and strength, and that is particularly the case in a child's life (Biofield, 2006). Second, a good deal of the results of father absence stem from the reduction in the degree of access that a child has to the father (Pui-Ha Yong & Yuk-Linook, 2005). On average, in terms of time and emotional support, youth have less access to a noncustodial father than they do to a father that resides in the home. Third, research has shown that father absence causes a reduction in the socioeconomic status (SES) of families. The income component of SES declines, particularly when a father leaves, resulting in the breakup of a previously intact family. The occupational and educational components of SES might also decline.

A variety of factors can either intensify or reduce the ef-fects of father absence. It is the case, that some students are terribly affected by paternal absence, while other children appear to fare quite well. Part of the reason for this variation stems from the dynamics of moderators and conditionals. The list of these factors is in its fullest expression prodigious in size, but some of the more important include whether the child knows the identity of the father, the timing of the father's departure, and the degree to which the child has contact with the father. Generally speaking, if children do not know who their father is this has more of a deleterious influence on their academic achievement than if they can identify their father. The timing of the father's departure is somewhat more complicated because there is a rather com-plex relationship between the extent a child has had access to the father and the degree to which a deep relationship has had a chance to develop between the parent and the child. On the one hand, the degree to which a child had a close relationship before a father's departure, then the more negative the effect. On the other hand, the less access a child has to a father over time also has a detrimental effect on educational outcomes. A third factor is the extent to which the child has contact with the father when the father is a noncustodial parent. When fathers continue to cherish their relationship with their children and embrace them as valu-able parts of their lives, this tends to diminish the otherwise generally negative effect of father absence (McLanahan & Sandefur, 1994; Wallerstein & Blakeslee, 1989). A variety of studies have indicated that the degree to which a child has access to his or her father is particularly strong in its relationship to that youth's academic achievement (Jeynes, 2002; McLanahan & Sandefur, 1994). Research also in-dicates that children who continued to have contact with their noncustodial fathers fared better in their educational outcomes than children who had no contact (Wallerstein & Lewis, 1998). Other studies support the notion that the other factors listed in this paragraph can also have an impact (Wallerstein & Lewis, 1998).

Summary and Recommendations

There are a number of recommendations that one can make based on the results of research on the effects of father absence that can apply to teachers, parents, social scientists, and society at large. The most prominent include the following: First, there needs to be a more complete understanding that father absence generally hurts the scholastic output of children. Society needs to do more to support two-parent marriages out of compassion for children, who generally are those who suffer the most from divorce. Some states, like the state of Missouri, are considering waiving marriage fees when couples receive premarital counseling either from a member of the clergy or a marriage counselor. Schools might also consider offering their facilities so that family and couple counselors can offer their advice to a wider audience, not only on marriage but also on parenting.

Second, schools need to be more sensitive to those families with an absent father. They need to be more cognizant of the challenges faced by these families. Teachers therefore need to demonstrate love and support for students that are consistent with being a type of surrogate parent. Teachers also need to be more sensitive to the fact that children often visit their noncustodial father well away from their homes. As a result, these children often have less time to do their homework than most children and they may sometimes leave their homework at the nonresident father's home. Naturally, this does not mean that teachers show favoritism toward children who have nonresident fathers, but it does mean these youth will appreciate it when teachers demonstrate empathy and sensitivity regarding family-based challenges that they may face (Pui-Ha Yong & Yuk-Linook, 2005).

Third, it is important to remember that there is a preponderance of evidence that indicates that children fare best academically if both biological parents are present in the home (Jeynes, 1999, 2003b; Pui-Ha Yong & Yuk-Linook, 2005). It is interesting to note, however, that schools often do little to involve parents in the educational process (Jeynes, 2003a, 2005, 2010). Moreover, as much as mothers are engaged, it is clear that educators generally do even less to involve fathers (Mapp, Johnson, Strickland, & Meza, 2008; Potter & Carpenter, 2008). And as much as social scientists frequently highlight the advantages of marriage and the presence of two biological parents, it is puzzling why educators do not know more about ways that they can involve fathers. Admittedly, part of this should not be surprising given that the majority of teachers are female. It follows that these educators will feel more comfortable reaching out to women and are more cognizant of what it takes to involve mothers in the schools than they are about how to involve fathers. Numerous schools, for example, offer aerobics and sewing classes at schools to make parents feel more connected with and comfortable in the school, but these gatherings are generally appealing to mothers more than fathers. Recently, however, the Sure Start program in Great Britain has shown that many fathers are drawn in when vigorous workout programs that involve weights and boxing are offered (Potter & Carpenter, 2008). Teachers also need to become more familiar with what the research indicates are the most salient components of

parental involvement. If educators can help supply families with this vital information, parents can more fully utilize the advantages of resident fathers. There are many steps that teachers and principals can take to help fathers from a wide variety of family structures become more engaged in their children's education. It is important that school officials do their best to make it easier for fathers to take the right steps to become more involved in their children's schooling. Research indicates that many youths will achieve at higher levels in school if these actions are taken.

References

Amato, P. R., & Keith, B. (1991). Parental divorce and adult well-being: A meta-analysis. *Journal of Marriage & the Family, 53*(1), 43–58.

Bellair, P., & McNulty, T. (2009). Gang membership, drug selling, and violence in a neighborhood context. *Justice Quarterly, 26*(4), 644–669.

Biofield, M. (2006). *The politics of moral sin: Abortion and divorce in Spain, Chile, and Argentina.* London: Routledge.

Carlsmith, L. (1964). Effect of early father-absence on scholastic aptitude. *Harvard Educational Review, 34,* 3–21.

Carlsmith, L. (1973). Some personality characteristics of boys separated from their fathers during World War II. *Ethos, 1,* 466–477.

Fortes (1933). Notes on juvenile delinquency: ii. Step-parenthood and delinquency. *The Sociological Review, 25*(2), 153–159.

Jeynes, W. (1999). The effects of religious commitment on the academic achievement of Black and Hispanic children. *Urban Education, 34*(4), 458–479.

Jeynes, W. (2000). The effects of several of the most common family structures on the academic achievement of eighth graders. *Marriage and Family Review, 30*(1–2), 73–97.

Jeynes, W. (2002). *Divorce, family structure, and the academic success of children.* Binghamton, NY: Haworth Press.

Jeynes, W. (2003a). A meta-analysis: The effects of parental involvement on minority children's academic achievement. *Education & Urban Society, 35*(2), 202–218.

Jeynes, W. (2003b). The effects of Black and Hispanic twelfth graders living in intact families and being religious on their academic achievement. *Urban Education, 38*(1), 35–57.

Jeynes, W. (2005). A meta-analysis of the relation of parental involvement to urban elementary school student academic achievement. *Urban Education, 40*(3), 237–269.

Jeynes, W. (2006). The impact of parental remarriage on children: A meta-analysis. *Marriage and Family Review, 40*(4), 75–102.

Jeynes, W. (2007). *American educational education: School, society, and the common good.* Thousand Oaks, CA: Sage.

Jeynes, W. (2010). The salience of the subtle aspects of parental involvement and encouraging that involvement: Implications for school-based programs. *Teachers College Record, 112*(3), 747–774.

Mapp, K. L., Johnson, V. R., Strickland, C. S., & Meza, C. (2008). High school family centers: Transformative spaces linking schools and family in support of student learning. *Marriage & Family Review, 43*(1–2), 338–368.

McLanahan, S., & Sandefur, G. (1994). *Growing up with a single parent: What hurts, what helps.* Cambridge, MA: Harvard University Press.

Potter, C., & Carpenter, J. (2008). Something in it for dads: Getting fathers involved in Sure Start. *Early Child Development & Care, 18*(7–8), 761–772.

Pui-Ha Yong, K. & Yuk-Linook A. (2005). *Marriage, divorce, and remarriage: Professional practice in Hong Kong.* Hong Kong, China: Hong Kong University Press.

Smith, W. C. (1945). The stepchild. *American Sociological Review, 10,* 237–242.

Sutherland, H. E. G. (1930). The relationship between IQ and size of family In the case of fatherless families. *Journal of Genetic Psychology, 38,* 161–170.

U.S. Center for Education Statistics. (1966). *Equality of educational opportunity.* Washington, DC: U.S. Center for Education Statistics.

Wallerstein, J. S., & Blakeslee, S. (1989). *Second chances: Men, women, and children a decade after divorce.* New York: Ticknor & Fields.

Wallerstein, J. S., & Lewis, J. (1998). The long-term impact of divorce on children: A first report from a 25-year study. *Family and Conciliation Courts Review, 36*(3), 368–383.

Wirtz, W. (1977). *On further examination.* New York: College Entrance Examination Board.

3.2

Home Environment

BURKHARD GNIEWOSZ
University of Jena

JACQUELYNNE S. ECCLES
University of Michigan

Introduction

Theoretical and empirical approaches to the investigation of learning processes and educational achievement have been profoundly enriched by adding an ecological perspective, which examines the multiple effects and interrelatedness of social elements in an environment. Learning and its outcomes do not occur in a vacuum. Processes leading to positive or negative academic outcomes are embedded in multiple contexts. The school is one, admittedly very important, context among others, such as the peer group or the home environment. Educators probably have experienced the difficulties emerging in the family or peer context that can often hamper their influences on learners. It is important to understand the complex interactions working within and between the contexts to provide an optimal learning environment. In this entry, the focus is on the home environment as being an important context for students' academic achievement (see also Eccles, 2007; Wigfield, Eccles, Schiefele, Roeser, & Davis-Kean, 2006).

Research Evidence

Who the Parents/Caregivers Are. When we look at the parental background characteristics that affect children's academic achievement, the socioeconomic background is of tremendous importance. A meta-analysis based on the review of 74 samples (>100,000 students) by Sirin (2005) provided strong evidence for the link between (a) parental income, education, and occupation and (b) various academic achievement outcomes (domain-specific grades, GPA, general, and domain-specific achievement). The aim was to explain achievement differences between students by the parental social background. About 9% of these differences were due to differences in the social status of the parents. One interpretation of this association is that the financial and social background of a family determines the opportunity structure through which parents can positively affect their

children's academic development. Many of the ways in which parents might benefit their children are a lot easier to provide if the parents have financial and social resources. Moreover, if the parents have to work two jobs to support their family, the stress level can be increased and the time available to support the children becomes limited. Both stressors are linked to a less supportive home environment.

The parents' socioeconomic background is linked to educational transitions, such as the change from elementary to secondary school, as well. In ability tracked systems, such as the German school system, these transitions serve as selective filters for college-bound or vocational educational tracks. There is evidence that parental socioeconomic status is related to the probability of being admitted for the college-bound school track, even if achievement, migration status, and other student characteristics are the same (Ditton, Krüsken, & Schauenberg, 2005). The likelihood of attending the college-bound track is higher for students from better-off families, independent of their grades and achievements.

Although largely ignored by educators, parents affect their children through genetic transmission, as well. Academic success is to a considerable extent explained by interindividual differences in cognitive competences and personality characteristics—all of them highly heritable (Petrill & Wilkerson, 2000). Johnson, McGue, and Iacono (2006), for example, showed strong genetic influences on achievement development through adolescence. However, this genetic predisposition interacts with the environment. There is no deterministic relationship of genetic predisposition and academic success. Students' academic outcomes can be promoted, regardless of genetics. Nonetheless, the initial differences between students can be explained, in part, by within-family genetic transmission.

What Parents Believe. Parents' general attitudes, beliefs, and values play a very important role as effects on students' academic development within the home environment. If parents think that education is important and useful their offspring are more likely to also value schooling (e.g., Jodl, Michael, Malanchuk, Eccles, & Sameroff, 2001; Noack, 2004). Social learning processes are assumed to lead to this intergenerational transmission of values. Parents can communicate their beliefs in several ways. They can directly communicate the importance of doing homework and learning. Furthermore, if parents behave in ways consistent with their values, they communicate by being a role model and social learning processes can result in the intergenerational transmission of academic values. Subsequently, if students' value education highly they will engage more in learning activities and thus achievement can be improved.

Parents' child-specific beliefs and expectations can also affect students' academic development through their impact on their children's developing self-perceptions. Students at the same achievement level whose parents hold positive competence perceptions about their children will have more favorable competence beliefs themselves than students with less confident parents (e.g., Gniewosz, 2010). In turn, these competence beliefs are strongly linked to subsequent academic engagement and achievement (see Wigfield et al., 2006).

The beliefs held by the parents are affected by their gender-related domain-specific stereotypes. Oftentimes, parents expect higher performances in the mathematical domain for their sons, while they consider daughters as more competent in the verbal domain, independent of the children's actual performances (e.g., Tiedemann, 2000). Considering the above mentioned impact of the parental child-specific beliefs on the students' self-perceptions, parents' stereotypes influence the students' academic development. The same processes are likely to be associated with other socially defined group memberships.

What Parents Do.   Parents' values and beliefs are strongly linked to the extent to which parents get involved in their children's' school matters. If parents value academics highly, they will spend more time with their children in academic activities (Noack, 2004). In addition to these indirect effects, parental behaviors directly affect students' motivation and achievement through the provision of important resources. One example is that parents provide learning materials or private tutoring if needed. Here, the parental financial background becomes an obvious factor in a child's academic success. It is much easier for better-off families to pay for these materials or the tutoring. In this case, the question about "what parents do" becomes the question "what parents can afford to do."

Not all of the resources that are provided by the parents are tangible. The way parents interact with their children can be understood as resource, as well. An authoritative parenting style, characterized by warmth, support for the child's autonomy, and clear rules, enhances students' motivation and strategy use in learning activities (Aunola, Stattin, & Nurmi, 2000). Providing students with a supportive home environment in a general sense satisfies the students' need for autonomy. This basic need is of tremendous importance for the students' motivation to learn, especially during adolescence. If the general parenting style supports the students' needs then the students will be more academically engaged, which consequently will result in better achievement in terms of grades or test results.

Moreover, the direct involvement of parents in their children's schooling and learning is important for their academic outcomes. Parents differ in the nature of their involvement. This involvement of parents can be categorized into personal, cognitive, and behavioral (Grolnick & Slowiaczek, 1994). *Personal involvement* means that the parents can elicit the affective experience in their children that their parents care about education and school matters. The children of personally involved parents enjoy parent–child interactions around school leading to a positive feeling toward school. Parents who show a high *cognitive involvement* expose their children to intellectually stimulating activities, such as book reading, museum trips, or solving Sudoku puzzles. This can covey the intrinsically rewarding qualities of education-related activities. Moreover, students can have mastery experiences in these stimulating activities, improving their ability and value beliefs within an out-of-school setting. These decontextualized educational experiences are important for the development of students' valuing of intellectual academic activities and thus subsequently affect achievement. Parents who are *behaviorally involved* participate in parent–teacher interactions, join the PTA, take part in school activities, and so on. Thus, parental involvement in school matters conveys a notion about their valuing of education. High parental involvement indicates that the parents value school, which can be linked to the students valuing school through intergenerational value transmission. In terms of social learning, the parental academic involvement can serve as a positive role model, and thus reinforce the students' academic involvement that, in turn, affects academic engagement and performance.

Summary and Recommendations

A meta-analysis by Jeynes (2007) combined the results of 52 studies (in sum > 300,000 students) on home environment predictors of students' academic achievement (operationalized as grades and test scores in secondary school). Several dimensions were compared regarding their association with academic achievement outcomes. Unfortunately, this study did not distinguish between longitudinal and cross-sectional studies. Therefore, it is not possible to determine if home environment variables affect achievement or vice versa. However, comparing the effect sizes allows for a differential evaluation of the strength of association. Parental educational expectations turned out to be the best predictor of academic achievement. If the student's parents maintained high expectations of the student's ability to achieve at high levels, students' showed better performances. The second strongest source of influence was parenting style (see above) followed by homework support (an indicator of *personal involvement*). The communication between parents and students about school activities predicted the achievement as well. Furthermore, whether and how frequently parents attended and participate in school functions and activities was associated with higher achievement levels of the students, as well (indicators of *behavioral involvement*). The associations of the home environment characteristics and the achievement outcomes were by and large the same for European American and minority students.

As outlined above, there are several ways for the home environment to affect students' academic development. The described routes of influence are not independent of each other or independent of influences from other contexts. For example, if schools do not provide opportunities for parents to participate in school activities or teacher–parent interaction, then there will be little chance to influence the students' academic development positively through behavioral involvement. On a macrolevel, there are societal factors that determine the ways parents can be part of students' education. Societies differ in their social norms about the extent that parents should participate in their children's education. Thus, values that are shared within a society affect the parents' values, which in turn predict their individual involvement. Finally, as noted at the start of this entry, if parents' have few economic resources and their lives are stressed due to other factors linked to their health, their socioeconomic or historical constraints, or to characteristics of their children or other family-related constraints, then their ability to provide opportunities for their children are likely to be constrained as well.

References

Aunola, K., Stattin, H., & Nurmi, J. (2000). Parenting styles and adolescents' achievement strategies. *Journal of Adolescence, 23*(2), 205–222.

Ditton, H., Krüsken, J., & Schauenberg, M. (2005). Bildungsungleichheit—der Beitrag von Familie und Schule [Educational disparities and the contribution of family and school]. *Zeitschrift für Erziehungswissenschaft, 8*(2), 285–304.

Eccles, J. S. (2007). Families, schools, and developing achievement-related motivations and engagement. In J. E. Grusec & P. D. Hastings (Eds.), *Handbook of socialization* (pp. 665–691). New York: Guilford.

Gniewosz, B. (2010). Die Konstruktion des akademischen Selbstkonzeptes: Eltern und Zensuren als Informationsquellen [The construction of the academic self-concept: Parents and grades as sources of information]. *Zeitschrift für Entwicklungs- und Pädagogische Psychologie, 42*(3), 133–142.

Grolnick, W., & Slowiaczek, M. L. (1994). Parents' involvement in children's schooling: A multidimensional conceptualization and motivational model. *Child Development, 65*(1), 237–252.

Jeynes, W. H. (2007). The relationship between parental involvement and urban secondary school student academic achievement. *Urban Education*, 82–110.

Jodl, K. M., Michael, A., Malanchuk, O., Eccles, J. S., & Sameroff, A. (2001). Parents' roles in shaping early adolescents' occupational aspirations. *Child Development, 72*(4), 1247–1265.

Johnson, W., McGue, M., & Iacono, W. G. (2006). Genetic and environmental influences on academic achievement trajectories during adolescence. *Developmental Psychology, 42*(3), 514–532.

Noack, P. (2004). The family context of preadolescents' orientations toward education: Effects of maternal orientations and behavior. *Journal of Educational Psychology, 96*(4), 714–722.

Petrill, S. A., & Wilkerson, B. (2000). Intelligence and achievement: A behavioral genetic perspective. *Educational Psychology Review, 12*(2), 185–199.

Sirin, S. R. (2005). Socioeconomic status and academic achievement: A meta-analytic review of research. *Review of Educational Research, 75*(3), 417–453.

Tiedemann, J. (2000). Parents' gender stereotypes and teachers' beliefs as predictors of children's concept of their mathematical ability in elementary school. *Journal of Educational Psychology, 92*(1), 144–151.

Wigfield, A., Eccles, J. S., Schiefele, U., Roeser, R. W., & Davis-Kean, P. (2006). Development of achievement motivation. In N. Eisenberg (Ed.), *Handbook of child psychology* (Vol. 3, 6th ed., pp. 933–1002). New York: Wiley.

3.3

Socioeconomic Status and Student Achievement

ERIN BUMGARNER AND JEANNE BROOKS-GUNN
Columbia University

Introduction

Decades of research have confirmed that socioeconomic status (SES) plays a significant role in children's academic achievement (Bradley & Corwyn, 2002; Duncan, Ziol-Guest, & Kalil, 2010; Sirin, 2005; Smith, Brooks-Gunn, & Klebanov, 1997). SES is a comprehensive, multifaceted construct, which extends beyond poverty status alone to describe social stratification within a given society (Mueller & Parcel, 1981). Therefore, the most sophisticated measures of SES often combine aspects of income, education, and occupation (Duncan & Magnuson, 2003).

Research Evidence

A majority of research examining the pathways between SES and children's achievement scores has drawn on two models. First, the parental investment model (Becker & Tomes, 1986), posits that economic hardship prevents parents from purchasing materials, experiences, and resources for their children because they must invest more in immediate, basic needs (Mayer, 1997). As a consequence, children of these parents are less likely to have access to resources that foster positive development, such as child care, cognitively stimulating activities in the home, and medical insurance (Yeung, Linver & Brooks-Gunn, 2002). A second model, the family stress model (Conger & Elder, 1994), proposes that economic hardship causes significant strain on parents' emotional well-being and increases marital conflict. As a result, parents are less likely to provide warm, responsive, and consistent parenting (Smith & Brooks-Gunn, 1997). This is problematic because these parenting skills have significant, positive implications for a child's cognitive, language, and social development (Collins, Maccoby, Steinberg, Hetherington, & Bornstein, 2000).

While these two models focus exclusively on family processes as the direct pathway, more current literature has begun exploring how other contexts serve as pathways. For example, the literature suggests that neighborhoods also serve as a pathway between SES and achievement (Kohen, Brooks-Gunn, Leventhal, & Hertzman, 2002; Leventhal & Brooks-Gunn, 2000, 2004). This literature finds poor parents are restricted in their choice of neighborhoods, and are therefore more likely to live in areas characterized by social disorganization and limited resources for child development. Other pathways include physical health, teaching quality, and school environment (Sirin, 2005).

Beyond the pathways that connect SES to achievement, research has explored how various mechanisms determine the strength of this association. Using income as a proxy of SES, research has found achievement scores to be particularly sensitive to poverty during the first few years of life (Smith, Brooks-Gunn, & Klebanov, 1997). This can be explained by the cumulative nature of skill development, such that a solid foundation of skills makes subsequent learning easier and more efficient (Heckman, 2006). In addition to timing, both the length and depth of poverty influence how severely SES impacts achievement outcomes (Duncan et al., 1998).

As we move forward in our understanding of the relation between SES and achievement, it is important to keep in mind several critiques and recommendations that have been made thus far. First, the majority of research on SES has focused on economic aspects of SES. Several studies have begun looking at the unique contribution of parental education and occupation as predictors of children's academic achievement (Brooks-Gunn, Han, & Waldfogel, 2010; Magnuson, 2007). Nevertheless, future research will need to explore how parental education, occupation and income work in isolation and in various configurations to predict children's academic achievement (Conger, Conger, & Martin, 2010). With that said, however, singular measures of SES likely overestimate its effect achievement, and so care should be used when interpreting results (Siren, 2005).

Second, the majority of literature looking at the relation between SES and academic achievement has been based on cross-sectional analyses of large datasets. The most convincing studies, however, are longitudinal, use fixed effects models, and include a rich array of controls. Randomized trials are always preferable; however, as of yet there are only a few that have explored this line of research (Costello, Compton, Keeler, & Angold, 2003). Despite this limitation, however, the effect sizes in many studies are modest and consistent, thus confirming that SES has important implications for children's academic achievement (Dearing, McCartney, & Taylor, 2001; Siren, 2005).

Third, caution should be used when generalizing results because the relative impact of pathways between SES and academic outcomes may vary depending on the context and culture. For example, in the United States, research has indicated that two of the most significant mediating pathways are the cognitive stimulation provided within the home as well as parenting style (Guo & Harris, 2000). In other countries, however, particularly the poorest, SES may have the most impact on academic outcomes via pathways such as nutrition and access to health care (Grantham-McGregor et al., 2007).

Finally, despite the need for more research, researchers, policy makers, and schools must continue developing more effective policies and interventions. Without them, the impact of SES on academic achievement is often sustained into adulthood (Schweinhart et al., 2005). In the presence of limited resources, the decision regarding which type of intervention to implement is critical. There is no single intervention or policy that can inoculate against the negative effects of SES on children (Brooks-Gunn, 2003). Nevertheless, current research suggests that high quality, early investments in young children's experiences can be a cost effective method for protecting against long-term, negative consequences of poverty on academic outcomes later in life (Barnett, 1995; Heckman, 2006).

Summary and Recommendations

In sum, the literature has found that SES has important implications for children's academic achievement (Bradley & Corwyn, 2002; Duncan et al., 2010; Smith et al., 1997). There are multiple causal pathways through which SES exerts its influence on academic achievement, including the home learning environment, parenting, health, teaching methods, and neighborhood conditions (Sirin, 2005). The depth, duration, and timing of poverty are determinants of how severely SES impacts children's academic performance (Smith et al., 1997). In the face of limited resources it is critical that all parties come together to develop more effective policies that are cost effective, of high quality, and able to provide an equal playing field for young children (Currie, 1997; Heckman, 2006).

References

Barnett, S. (1995). Long-term effects of early childhood programs on cognitive and school outcomes. *The Future of Children, 5*(3), 25–50.

Becker, G. S., & Tomes, N. (1986). Human capital and the rise and fall of families. *Journal of Labor Economics, 4,* S1–S139.

Bradley, R., & Corwyn, R. (2002). Socioeconomic status and child development. *Annual Review of Psychology, 53,* 371–399.

Brooks-Gunn, J. (2003). Do you believe in magic? What we can expect from early childhood intervention programs. *Social Policy Report, Society for Research in Child Development, 17,* 3–13.

Brooks-Gunn, J., Han, W.-J., & Waldfogel, J. (2010). First-year maternal employment and child development in the first seven years. *Monographs of the Society for Research in Child Development, 75*(2), 1–19.

Collins, W., Maccoby, E., Steinberg, L., Hetherington, E., & Bornstein, M. (2000). Contemporary research on parenting: The case of nature and nurture. *American Psychologist, 55,* 215–232.

Conger, R. D., Conger, K. J., & Martin, M. J. (2010). Socioeconomic status, family processes, and individual development. *Journal of Marriage and Family, 72,* 685–704.

Conger, R. D., & Elder, G. H. (1994). *Families in troubled times: Adapting to change in rural America.* Hawthorne, NY: Aldine de Gruyter.

Costello, J., Compton, S., Keeler, G., & Angold, A. (2003). Relationships between poverty and psychopathology: A natural experiment. *Journal of the American Medical Association, 290,* 2023–2029.

Currie, J. (1997). Choosing among alternative programs for poor children. *Children and Poverty, 7*(2), 113–131.

Dearing, E., McCartney, K., & Taylor, B. (2001). Change in family income-to-needs matters more for children with less. *Child Development, 72,* 1779–1793.

Duncan, G. J., & Magnuson, K. A. (2003). Off with Hollingshead: Socioeconomic resources, parenting and child development. In M. H. Bornstein & R. H. Bradley (Eds.), *Socioeconomic status, parenting and child development* (pp. 83–106). Mahwah, NJ: Erlbaum.

Duncan, G. J., Ziol-Guest, K., & Kalil, A. (2010). Early-childhood poverty and adult attainment, behavior, and health. *Child Development, 81,* 306–325.

Grantham-McGregor, S., Cheung, Y., Cueto, S., Glewwe, P., Richter, L., Strupp, B., & The International Child Development Steering Group. (2007). Developmental potential in the first 5 years for children in developing countries. *The Lancet, 369,* 60–70.

Guo, G., & Harris, K. M. (2000). The mechanisms mediating the effects of poverty on children's intellectual development. *Demography, 37,* 431–447.

Heckman, J. (2006). Skill formation and the economics of investing in disadvantaged children. *Science, 312,* 1900–1902.

Kohen, D. E., Brooks-Gunn, J., Leventhal, T., & Hertzman, C. (2002). Neighborhood income and physical and social disorder in Canada: Associations with young children's competencies. *Child Development, 73,* 1845–1860.

Leventhal, T., & Brooks-Gunn, J. (2000). The neighborhoods they live in: The effects of neighborhood residence upon child and adolescent outcomes. *Psychological Bulletin, 126,* 309–337.

Leventhal, T., & Brooks-Gunn, J. (2004). A randomized study of neighborhood effects on low-income children's educational outcomes. *Developmental Psychology, 40,* 488–507.

Magnuson, K. (2007). Maternal education and children's academic achievement during middle childhood. *Developmental Psychology, 43,* 1497–1512.

Mayer, S. (1997). *What money can't buy: Family income and children's life chances.* Cambridge, MA: Harvard University Press.

Mueller, C. W., & Parcel, T. L. (1981) Measures of socioeconomic status: Alternatives and recommendations. *Child Development, 52,* 13–30.

Schweinhart, L., Montie, J. Xiang, Z. Barnett, W., Belfield, C., & Nores, M. (2005). *Lifetime effects: The High/Scope Perry Preschool Study through age 40.* Ypsilanti, MI: High/Scope Press.

Sirin, S. (2005) Socioeconomic status and academic achievement: A meta-analytic review of research. *Review of Educational Research, 75*(3), 417–453.

Smith, J. R., & Brooks-Gunn, J. (1997). Correlates and consequences of harsh discipline for young children. *Archives of Pediatric and Adolescent Medicine, 151,* 777–786.

Smith, J. R., Brooks-Gunn, J., & Klebanov, P. K. (1997). The consequences of living in poverty for young children's cognitive and verbal ability and early school achievement. In G. J. Duncan & J. Brooks-Gunn (Eds.), *Consequences of growing up poor* (pp. 132–189). New York: Russell Sage.

Yeung, J., Linver, M., & Brooks-Gunn, J. (2002). How money matters for young children's development: Parental investment and family processes. *Child Development, 73*(6), 1861–1879.

3.4

Welfare Policies

Lisa A. Gennetian
The Brookings Institution

Pamela A. Morris
New York University

Introduction

A variety of U.S. work and income security policies target resources to improve parent's ability to be involved and invest in their children'spositive development. For example, in the United States, one of the most significant contemporary policy reforms for poor families was the replacement of Aid to Families with Dependent Children with Temporary Assistance for Needy Families (AFDC), upon the passage of the Personal Responsibility and Work Opportunity Reconciliation Act in 1996. From 1935 to 1996, AFDC was initially designed to support widowed mothers as an entitlement program financed by a federal matching grant. The 1996 reform law transformed welfare into federally funded block grants whose main purpose is to promote self-sufficiency by requiring and supporting work that included policies such as time limits, work requirements, and work supports such as child care and transportation assistance (Moffitt, 2003). Debates ensued about subsequent effects on the development of children. Transitions from welfare to work may benefit children by placing them in stimulating child care settings, creating positive maternal role models, promoting maternal self-esteem and sense of control, introducing productive daily routines into family life, and in turn, fostering improved child achievement. On the other hand, efforts to promote employment may overwhelm already stressed parents, force young children into substandard child care, reduce parents' abilities to monitor the behavior of their older children, and, for those unable to sustain steady employment, deepen family poverty, undermining the achievement of children who are already at high risk.

Research Evidence

The research on this topic indicates that welfare reforms appear to have increased work participation, earnings, and family income (see Haskins, 2006, for an overview), though debate remains about the extent to which the effects were additionally fueled by a forgiving economy with a high demand for labor (Blank & Haskins, 2001). Moreover, the income gains may have been confined to those with higher levels of education (Blank & Schoeni, 2003). The effects on children are harder to judge, although most agree that the dire predictions about child poverty and children's well-being that were made in the wake of welfare reform did not come to pass. In the absence of national longitudinal data that convincingly separates out the effects of welfare reform from other contextual changes occurring concomitantly, we turn to two lines of research that inform our understanding of the effects of welfare policies and children's achievement (for a review of research conducted on welfare reform effects across the prior decade see Grogger & Karoly, 2005; Ziliak 2009, and for commentary on the effects of the recent recession on the well-being of children, see Isaacs, 2011).

The first line of research comes from experimental studies that predated the 1996 changes in welfare reform policy at the federal level, but tested many of the policies that emerged in the post-1996 period. Pooling data from seven random assignment studies evaluating 13 welfare-to-work programs in the United States and Canada, Morris, Gennetian, and Duncan (2005) estimated the impacts of these types of programs on parents' earnings and income, and on outcomes for children. These programs fall under two broad categories: (a) earnings supplements programs that provided generous monthly cash supplements to earnings up to a certain income threshold, or disregarded earnings for those recipients who were receiving public assistance, and (b) mandatory employment services programs with no earnings supplements, some with time limits (Michalopoulos & Bloom, 2001). Using this categorization of the programs, Morris et al. show that, for their sample of parents of young children, the earnings supplements programs increased average earnings by $926 and total family income by $1,703 per year (14%). The programs with no earnings supplements increased earnings by $645, but this increase was offset by a decrease in welfare payments, resulting in no statistical difference in family income. The employment programs with earnings supplements that increased average family annual income by about $1,700 did have positive, albeit small, statistically significant effects on young children's achievement. The analysis finds no effect on children's achievement in middle childhood of these same models and small unfavorable effects on the schooling performance of adolescents (Gennetian et al., 2004). All programs ended after 3 years, and the effects of parents' economic outcomes faded soon after. In the absence of these increases in income, the positive effects on achievement faded as well (Morris et al., 2005). By contrast, those programs that increased earnings but not income had few and inconsistent effects on children's achievement (Morris et al., 2005).

The second line of research comes from observational studies drawing on samples undergoing welfare and work transitions over this same period of time in specific cities in the United States. A disadvantage of experimental evidence is that it is strong on internal validity, being based on a sample that represents a population specific to the policy context and the time period in which the experiment was conducted, and low on external validity. For example, it may not be possible to generalize evidence from the set of welfare-to-work experiments to all low-income families, as the experiments included mostly single-parent families receiving welfare in the 1990s.

The nonexperimental research generally finds neutral to small benefits of welfare reform transitions on children's achievement. Chase-Lansdale et al. (2003) showed that parents' transitions into employment had few effects, positive or negative, on changes in reading and math skills for very young children or for adolescents, although adolescents whose parents had entered or remained in employment showed somewhat better mental health than those whose parents were unemployed. Dunifon, Hines, and Peters (2006) found few effects of state level welfare policy effects on measures of suspensions and expulsions in school. Using a decade of national math achievement data and controlling for contemporaneous changes in education policy and environment, Miller and Zhang (2009) associated welfare reform with relative test score improvements for low-income students with greater gains occurring in states with larger initial welfare caseloads and larger caseload reductions.

Turning to questions about why welfare policies might make a difference for children, the evidence most strongly points to the roles of income and child care. Maternal education may play some role, but these programs did not substantially increase formal education, nor were they intended to do so (although notably, if they were to do so, the effects might indeed be more positive; Gennetian, Magnuson, & Morris, 2008). With regard to income, a separate analysis of this experimental data by Duncan, Morris, and Rodrigues (2011) leveraged the exogenous variation in income and achievement that arises from random assignment to the treatment group to estimate the causal effect of income on child achievement. They find that a $1,000 increase in

annual income is expected to increase child achievement by 6% of a standard deviation. This is consistent with an earlier paper using the same analytic technique by Morris and Gennetian (2003), finding positive effects of income on school engagement and positive social behavior but no statistically significant effects on achievement and problem behavior. Dahl and Lochner (2008) used a nonexperimental, but quite rigorous approach and found positive, and surprisingly similar effects of income on children's achievement. With regard to child care, Crosby, Gennetian, and Huston (2005) separated those experimental welfare programs that expanded child care assistance from those that did not and found that the former statistically increased use of center-based settings whereas the latter increased use of home-based settings. Estimates of this increased use of center-based care on achievement suggest small beneficial effects on children's achievement, controlling for income (Morris, Gennetian, Duncan, & Huston, 2009). The experimental research does not find evidence for improved parent–child interactions, quality of home environment, or maternal mental health. The reason may be partly poor measurement, but these programs may have had more effects on the family management aspects of parenting (i.e., parents' placement of children in child care) than on families' psychosocial features.

One remaining open question is the effects of welfare policies on very young children. Current law permits states to require mothers to participate in work-related activities when their children are very young infants. The studies reviewed above includes few infants younger than a year old, but other research investigating the effects of maternal employment on such young children raises questions about possible negative effects of full-time employment (Waldfogel, 2006). A National Academy of Science panel specifically recommended that welfare policies should not require full-time maternal employment when children were less than a year old (Smolensky & Gootman, 2001).

Research on the effects of welfare (or social assistance) policies on children are more limited when looking at other industrialized nations, though researchers do engage in comparative descriptions of child poverty levels and social safety net systems (Burtless & Smeeding, 2007; Danziger & Danziger, 2009). The UK implemented a number of changes in welfare policy benefits, while also implementing changes in parental leave policies, child care and education, and schools (Waldfogel, 2006, 2007, 2010). Low-income children have made progress on a number of well-being measures over this same time period, but it is difficult to be certain how much this progress is due to welfare reform changes, per se, as compared to these other policy changes (Waldfogel, 2007).

Summary and Recommendations

Welfare policies target parents, and it is through their effects on parents' economic behavior that children will be affected, for good or for bad. Both the experiments and observational studies show that many families remain in poverty, even when parents are employed full time. Without increases in income, it is unlikely that movements from welfare to employment are likely to benefit children's achievement in school. Of course, a number of questions remain regarding the effects of welfare reform in differing economic conditions, and whether some policies might exacerbate, rather than promote, income volatility (Gennetian, Castells, & Morris, 2010). That said, these findings pose a choice for policymakers deciding which welfare reforms and poverty-reduction programs to support. They can increase parental employment and save government money with mandatory employment service programs but have little effect on the already low levels of school performance for children in low-income families. Or they can increase parental employment, raise family income, and increase government spending with earnings supplement and child care subsidy programs, better neighborhoods and improved schools, with the likely result that young children will do better in school.

References

Blank, R. M., & Haskins, R. (2001). *The new world of welfare.* Washington, DC: The Brookings Institution Press.

Blank, R. M., & Schoeni, R. F. (2003). Changes in the distribution of children's family income over the 1990's. *American Economic Review, 93*(2), 304–308.

Burtless, G., & Smeeding, T. (2007). Poverty, work and policy: The United States in comparative perspective. Testimony prepared for Subcommittee on Income Security and Family Support, Committee on Ways and Means, U.S. House of Representatives, 110th Congress of the United States.

Chase-Lansdale, P. L., Moffitt, R. A., Lohman, B. J., Cherlin, A. J., Coley, R. L., Pittman, L. ... Votruba-Drzal, E. (2003). Mothers' transitions from welfare to work and the well-being of preschoolers and adolescents. *Science, 299*(5612), 1548–1552.

Crosby, D., Gennetian, L., & Huston, A. (2005). Child care assistance policies can affect the use of formal care for children in low-income families. *Applied Developmental Science, 9*(2), 86–106

Dahl, G., & Lochner, L. (2008). *The impact of family income on child achievement: Evidence from the earned income tax credit* (NBER Working Paper Series: Working Paper No. 14599). Cambridge, MA: National Bureau of Economic Research.

Danziger, S., & Danziger, S. H. (2009). Child poverty and antipoverty policies in the U.S.: Lessons from research and cross-national policies. In S. B. Kamerman, S. Phipps, & A. Ben-Arieh (Eds.), *From child welfare to child well-being: An international perspective on knowledge in the service of making policy* (pp. 255–274). New York: Springer.

Duncan, G., Morris, P., & Rodrigues, C. (2011). Does money really matter? Estimating impacts of family income on children's achievement with data from social policy experiments. *Developmental Psychology 47*(5), 1263–1279.

Dunifon, R., Hines, K., & Peters, E. H. (2006). Welfare reform and child well-being. *Children and Youth Services Review, 28,* 1273–1292.

Gennetian, L., Castells, N., & Morris, P. (2010). *Meeting the basic needs of children: Does income matter? Children and Youth Services Review, 32*(9), 1138–1148.

Gennetian, L., Duncan, G., Knox, V., Vargas, W., Clark-Kauffman, E., & London, A. (2004). How welfare policies can affect adolescents: A synthesis of evidence from experimental studies. *Journal of Research on Adolescence, 14*(4), 399–423.

Gennetian, L., Magnuson, K., & Morris, P. (2008). From statistical association to causation: What developmentalists can learn from instrumental variables techniques coupled with experimental data. *Developmental Psychology, 44*(2), 381–394.

Grogger, J., & Karoly, L. (2005). *Welfare reform: The effects of a decade of change.* Cambridge, MA: Harvard University Press.

Haskins, R. (2006, July 19). The Outcomes of 1996 Welfare Reform. Testimony given to the U.S. House of Representatives, Committee on Ways and Means.110th Congress of the United States

Isaacs, Julia (2011). *The recession's ongoing impact on America's children: Indicators of children's economic well-being through 2011.* Washington, DC: The Brookings Institution.

Michalopoulos, C., & Bloom, D. (2001). *How welfare and work policies affect employment and income: A synthesis of research.* New York: MDRC.

Miller, A., & Zhang, L. (2009). The effects of welfare reform on the academic performance of children in low income families. *Journal of Policy Analysis and Management, 28*(4), 577–599.

Moffitt, R. (2003). The negative income tax and the evolution of U.S. welfare policy. *Journal of Economic Perspectives, 17*(3), 119–140.

Morris, P., & Gennetian, L. (2003). Identifying the effects of income on children's development: Using experimental data. *Journal of Marriage and Family, 65*(3), 716–729.

Morris, P., Gennetian, L., & Duncan, G. (2005). Long term effects of welfare and work policies on children's school achievement: A synthesis from policy experiments conducted in the 1990s. *Social Policy Report, 19*(2).

Morris, P., Gennetian, L., Duncan, G., & Huston, A. (2009). How welfare policies affect child and adolescent school performance: Investigating pathways of influence with experimental data. In J. P. Ziliak (Ed.), *Welfare reform and its long-term consequences for America's poor.* Cambridge, England: Cambridge University Press.

Smolensky & Gootman (2001). *Working families and growing kids: Caring for children and adolescents.* Washington, DC: National Academies Press.

Waldfogel, J. (2006). *What children need.* Cambridge, MA: Harvard University Press.

Waldfogel, J. (2007). Welfare reforms and child well-being in the US and UK. *Swedish Economic Policy Review, 14*(2), 137–168.

Waldfogel, J. (2010). *Britain's war on poverty.* New York: Russell Sage Foundation.

Ziliak, J. (2009). *Welfare reform and its long term consequences for America's poor.* Cambridge, England: Cambridge University Press.

3.5

Family–School Partnerships and Academic Achievement

ANDREW J. MARTIN
University of Sydney

Introduction

Parental[1] involvement in a child's academic life can be broadly demarcated into that which is home based (e.g., help with homework, reading to the child, discussion of subject matter) and that which is school based. The focus of this chapter is on the latter, referred to as the family–school partnership, and its links with students' academic achievement. Family–school partnerships emphasize the active involvement of both home and school, whereas home-based involvements tend to be centered on the home and people and processes within it. Examples of family–school partnerships include attending teacher–parent conferences, attending school meetings, home visits by teachers, volunteering to help in the classroom, attending school events (e.g., open days, fairs), and being involved in school governance (e.g., parent and teacher association, school board). The most common form of school-based involvement is attendance at teacher–parent conferences and involvement in school meetings, with relatively few parents involved in higher level activities such as school governance (Grolnick & Slowiaczek, 1994; Pomerantz & Moorman, 2010).

A number of theoretical perspectives and operational frameworks have been developed to characterize family–school partnerships. Epstein (2001), for example, identified six forms of involvement in school partnership programs: parenting (helping families to support the child), communicating (developing effective home–school and school-home communication channels), volunteering (recruiting parent help), learning at home (providing information to families to help with schoolwork), decision making (including parents in school decision making), and community collaboration (integrating community resources to foster family–school partnerships).

Others have extended Epstein's work by suggesting additional focus on the nature of family–school partnerships. For example, Reschly and Christenson (2009) emphasize the importance of congruence between school and home and working with the home to develop consistency in rules, expectations, standards, and activities to assist students' academic development. Similarly, Hattie (2009) emphasized the importance of a common language between home and school, suggesting that high socioeconomic status (SES) parents are better able to speak the language of school, curriculum, and learning than low SES parents who leave their children to attempt to resolve the dissonance between home-school, negatively impacting their academic outcomes.

Ecological systems theory (Bronfenbrenner, 1992) also speaks to the issue of family–school partnerships. The "mesosystem" in Bronfenbrenner's theory explicitly maps the interactions between school and home and emphasizes the importance of this interaction for child development. Indeed, it has been proposed that academic risk is distributed across the layers of the ecology such that a lack of congruence between school and home is a source of academic risk—and good congruence between the two reflects low risk (Pianta & Walsh, 1996). In line with the ecological systems concept are arguments that family–school partnerships provide a context for child development that provide the supportive resources to positively impact academic achievement (Pomerantz & Moorman, 2010).

Reciprocal interactions emphasized by ecological systems theory are also a basis for considering family–school partnerships and school–family partnerships; the former reflecting family involvement at the school and the latter reflecting school involvement with the home (e.g., teacher visits) (Pomerantz & Moorman, 2010; Reschly & Christenson, 2009). Further, part of an effective partnership is the recognition that quality links are based on *family*–school partnerships (that recognize diverse family roles and structures) more than *parent*–school partnerships (that are a narrower form of partnership centering on the parent; Reschly & Christenson, 2009). Another differentiation important to recognize are family–school partnerships that are focused on academic dimensions (e.g., teacher–parent conferences) and those that are not academically focused (e.g., volunteering at the school fair).

When seeking to understand exactly how family–school partnerships affect achievement, it seems that at least two mechanisms are at work. The first is characterized as a skill development mechanism such that family–school partnerships provide positive skill-related resources that underpin achievement. These include: (a) parents gaining knowledge about school subjects that can assist their instruction to the child, (b) parents receiving accurate information about the child that enables them to provide better support for achievement, and (c) teachers providing students with greater achievement-related attention when they know the parents are also involved in the process (Pomerantz & Moorman, 2010). The second is a motivation development mechanism such that family–school partnerships provide positive motivation-related resources. These include: (a) school and parents jointly highlighting the value of school to the child and the child internalizing this valuing, and (b) parents modeling active engagement and agency with the school that the child then emulates. Through these mechanisms and processes, family–school partnerships provide a basis for students' academic achievement.

Research Evidence

In the main, research suggests that family–school partnerships have positive impacts on academic achievement (Alton-Lee, 2003; Epstein, 2001; Pomerantz & Moorman, 2010). Effect sizes are generally small to medium, becoming larger when particular moderators (see below) are considered (Hattie, 2009). Effects are derived in cross-sectional studies as well as in longitudinal research demonstrating achievement gains for elementary and high school students, lower and upper income students, ethnically diverse samples, and for mathematics and literacy-based outcomes (Pomerantz & Moorman, 2010)

Research reviewing various forms of family–school partnerships has found effect sizes of 1.81 for parent–teacher intervention programs, 1.38 for teachers designing homework in collaboration with parents, 0.93 for incorporating family/community knowledge into curriculum and teaching, and 0.63 for interventions (e.g., school workshops) to help parents support their child's learning (Robinson, Hohepa, & Lloyd, 2009). Smaller effects are found for parents volunteering in the school (0.35), a null effect is generally found for parent involvement in school governance, and a slightly negative effect exists for frequency of teacher–parent interaction (-0.04; possibly because greater frequency signals wider problems) (Robinson et al., 2009; Mansour & Martin, 2009). Other results summarized in Hattie (2009) include small positive effects for family participation in school activities (0.14), communication with school and teachers (0.14), and moderate effect sizes for home visits by teachers (0.48), including positive effects on cognitive gains from home visits by teachers for children with learning disabilities (0.39).

There is also evidence that a number of factors moderate the impact of family–school partnerships on achievement. For example, the active involvement and contribution of the teacher is beneficial whereas teachers' deficit assumptions and negative expectations of the student or family can be a barrier to positive impacts (Epstein, 2001). It also seems that the curriculum area is important to consider, with relatively greater impacts on reading than mathematics achievement (not surprising as parents are more likely to read to or with their child) (Epstein, 2001; Hattie, 2009). Also, family–school interactions focusing on processes (e.g., mastery, effort) yield more positive results than those focusing on the student's attributes (e.g., ability) (Pomerantz & Moorman, 2010). Further, family–school partnerships focused on student learning yield greater achievement effects than activities not academically related (e.g., school governance) (Alton-Lee, 2003).

Other moderators include SES, age, and race with larger effect sizes for high SES students, higher levels of parental education, elementary school students, and Euro-American (relative to Latino and African American) students (Ceballo, Huerta, & Epstein-Ngo, 2010; Hattie, 2009; Pomerantz & Moorman, 2010). In relation to race, there may be some dependence on where the parental involvement takes place, with parental involvement at home (more than at school) associated with achievement for Latino students (Ceballo et al., 2010). Gender may also be a factor given that boys can be lower than girls in terms of self-regulation, aspects of achievement, and motivation—and thus possibly greater beneficiaries of positive family–school partnerships (Ceballo et al., 2010; Pomerantz & Moorman, 2010).

The role of student perception is another factor to consider. It seems that student reports of parental involvement explain more variance in achievement than parent reports of involvement (Ceballo et al., 2010). Some have also suggested a mediating role of parental expectation (with a main effect size of 0.88 on achievement) between school involvement and achievement (Hattie, 2009). That is, constructive involvements with the school provide a basis for more positive expectations on the part of parents. To the extent that this is the case, family–school partnerships may have direct and indirect effects on student achievement.

Interestingly, intervention studies that seek to develop family-school partnerships have yielded mixed effects on achievement. For example, although meta-analyses do identify small effect sizes for interventions, they also demonstrate significant variability between studies (Pomerantz & Moorman, 2010). Meta-analysts suggest higher quality intervention research is needed before concluding on the merits of intervention for family-school partnerships. Others have suggested greater attention to moderators of intervention effectiveness. For example, is it the case, as some have suggested (Pomerantz & Moorman, 2010), that intervention focusing on processes (e.g., mastery, effort) is more effective than intervention focusing on attributes (e.g., ability)? Or, do different effects emerge when differentiating intervention as a function of high and low achieving students (where the nature of family–school interactions is likely to be quite different)?

Summary and Recommendations

Taken together, family–school partnerships are associated with students' academic achievement. Importantly, research has identified specific aspects of these partnerships that are most likely to promote achievement. It seems partnerships focused on learning and behavior yield more significant effects, as do partnerships aimed at increasing parents' expectations for their children. It may also be the case that parents' own confidence to work with the school needs to be addressed, as fear and uncertainty (perhaps based on their own negative experiences as a student or a lack of adequate prior education) may be a prevalent aspect of their orientation to school and teachers (Ceballo et al., 2010; Reschly & Christenson, 2009). Research also suggests the importance of genuine partnerships between school and family, being mindful not to assert inappropriate authority when true collaboration is needed, and also being mindful of the key differentiation between parent attendance (a low form of engagement) and parent participation (a rich form of engagement) (Reschly & Christenson, 2009).

Research identifies specific groups requiring greater effort from schools, including low SES students and disadvantaged or minority ethnic groups. The issues of SES and race require close consideration as there are some major barriers to initiating and sustaining family–school partnerships on these fronts, including: poor language proficiency to effectively communicate with the school, little educational experience or familiarity with the school system, long work hours that make attending school difficult, problems with transport to the school, few staff at the school of the same ethnic/language background, and moving areas (hence, schools) to gain employment (Ceballo et al., 2010). These must be addressed to foster more and better family–school partnerships amongst low SES students and disadvantaged ethnic groups.

There are some other areas where gaps are apparent. For example, most family–school partnerships and the majority of related research involve mothers, not fathers. Research and practice might look to more active involvement of fathers in research and practice (Pomerantz & Moorman, 2010). It is also the case that teachers may need professional development (in-servicing) on family–school partnerships

as many are not trained or prepared for this aspect of their work (Reschly & Christenson, 2009). Part of this professional development might also address deficit perspectives held by some teachers (e.g., about low SES families) that might be a barrier to family involvement. Here the aim would be to encourage educators to focus on processes and strengths rather than personal attributes and vulnerabilities (Reschly & Christenson, 2009). As a result of such actions, family–school partnerships are strengthened, leading to enhanced achievement through school and beyond.

Note

1. Throughout the discussion, the term *parent* refers to parent and caregiver roles.

References

Alton-Lee, A. (2003). *Quality teaching for diverse students in schooling: Best evidence synthesis.* Wellington, New Zealand: Ministry of Education.

Bronfenbrenner, U. (1992). Ecological systems theory. In R. Vasta (Ed.), *Six theories of child development: Revised reformulations and current issues* (pp. 187–249). London: Jessica Kingsley.

Ceballo, R., Huerta, M., & Epstein-Ngo, Q. (2010). Parental and school influences promoting academic success among Latino students. In J. L. Meece & J. S. Eccles (Eds.), *Handbook of research on schools, schooling, and human development* (pp. 293–307). New York: Routledge.

Epstein, J. L. (2001). *School, family and community partnerships: Preparing educators and improving schools.* Boulder, CO: Westview Press.

Grolnick, W., & Slowiaczek, M. L. (1994) Parents' involvement in children's schooling: A multidimensional conceptualization and motivational model. *Child Development, 65,* 237–252.

Hattie, J. A. (2009). *Visible learning.* New York: Routledge.

Mansour, M., & Martin, A. J. (2009). Home, parents, and achievement motivation: A study of key home and parental factors that predict student motivation and engagement. *Australian Educational and Developmental Psychologist, 26,* 111–126.

Pianta, R. C., & Walsh, D. J. (1996). *High-risk children in schools: Constructing sustaining relationships.* New York: Routledge.

Pomerantz, E. M., & Moorman, E. A. (2010). Parents' involvement in children's schooling. In J. L. Meece & J. S. Eccles (Eds.), *Handbook of research on schools, schooling, and human development* (pp. 398–416). New York: Routledge.

Reschly, A. L., & Christenson, S. L. (2009). Parents as essential partners for fostering students' learning outcomes. In R. Gilman., E. S. Huebner, & M. J. Furlong (Eds.), *Handbook of positive psychology in schools* (pp. 257–272). New York: Routledge.

Robinson, V., Hohepa, M., & Lloyd, C. (2009). *School leadership and student outcomes: Identifying what works and why.* Iterative Best Evidence Synthesis Project, Ministry of Education, Wellington, New Zealand. Retrieved from http://www.educationcounts.govt.nz/publications/series/2515/60169/60170

3.6

Parent Involvement in Learning

Wendy S. Grolnick, Jacquelyn N. Raftery-Helmer, and Elizabeth S. Flamm
Clark University

Introduction

There has been increasing interest by educators, psychologists, and policy makers in parent involvement in children's learning. Increasing parent involvement has been identified as a key mechanism for closing achievement gaps between more and less advantaged and majority and minority youth (Dearing, Kreider, Simpkins, & Weiss, 2006; Hara, 1998). Further, facilitating parent involvement has been included as a major goal in the proposed reauthorization of the Elementary and Secondary Education Act (U.S. Department of Education, 2010). These moves reflect our understanding that parent involvement is a significant factor in students' achievement and school adjustment.

Parent involvement in children's learning is typically defined broadly. For example, Grolnick and Slowiaczek (1994) defined involvement as the dedication of resources by the parent to the child in a given domain. Gonzalez-DeHass, Willems, and Holbein (2005) defined parent involvement in children's schooling as "parenting behaviors directed toward children's education" (p. 101). Hill and Taylor (2004) defined involvement as "parents' interaction with schools and with their children to promote academic success" (p. 1491). These definitions are purposefully broad to include the many ways that parents can be involved in their children's educations.

Research Evidence

A burgeoning literature supports the importance of parent involvement in children's learning for children's achievement across a range of ages and populations. In particular, Jeynes's (2005) meta-analysis of 41 studies, which included over 20,000 elementary age students, addressed the relations between parent involvement and academic achievement, and showed large effects of parent involvement on both children's grades and standardized test scores. These results held when controlling for socioeconomic status, race, and other demographic factors. In a second meta-analysis of 52 studies of secondary school children (Jeynes, 2007) there were also positive effects of parent involvement on both grades and standardized test scores. Though the effects were somewhat smaller for the older students than those for the elementary students, they were still appreciable. Finally, in a meta-analysis of 50 studies of middle school students, Hill and Tyson (2009) found a highly significant effect of parent involvement on children's achievement. Thus, across all age groups and in a variety of populations there appears to be a robust connection between parent involvement and children's achievement.

While research has clearly supported overall relations between parent involvement and children's achievement, it is crucial to understand what parents are doing that effectively supports children's achievement. Thus, researchers have divided parent involvement into different types. Notably, Epstein's (1986) home–school partnership model identified six types of involvement; (a) basic responsibilities of families to provide a supportive environment for children's adequate health, safety, and well-being; (b) school–home communication such as through conferences, notes, and report cards; (c) involvement at school including volunteering and attending school events; (d) involvement in learning activities at home including helping with homework; (e) involvement in advocacy, governance, or decision making such as in school councils or PTOs; and (f) family collaboration with other stakeholders such as businesses or agencies in the community that can facilitate children's learning.

Several studies have attempted to examine the efficacy of some of these different types of involvement. Jeynes (2005, 2007) divided the studies in his meta-analyses into communication, homework, parental expectations, reading, attendance, and participation at school. He found the strongest effects for parental expectations. McWayne, Hampton, Fantuzzo, Cohen, and Sekino (2004) divided parent involvement into a supportive home learning environment that included behaviors such as talking about school and structuring the home environment to support learning; direct involvement, including involvement in school activities and direct communication between families and school; and inhibited involvement, including time and language constraints and competing responsibilities that interfere with involvement. They found the strongest effects for the supportive environment involvement, particularly for kindergarten children. In their meta-analysis of studies of middle school children, Hill and Tyson (2009) examined school-based involvement, home based strategies, and academic socialization such as communicating expectations for the value of education. There were no significant effects of home-based involvement, significant effects for school-based involvement, and the strongest effects for academic socialization on children's achievement (class grades, test scores, track placement, and other measures of achievement). Overall, research suggests that the strongest parent involvement findings are for the attitudes, expectations, and values parents convey to their children, especially their older children.

The strength of findings for parents' socialization of attitudes and values for education brings up the question of how parent involvement is associated with children's achievement. Grolnick and Slowiaczek (1994) differentiated between two models for such effects. The direct effects model suggests that parent involvement affects children's achievement by helping them to attain the academic skills they need to succeed; for example, math and reading skills. A second model suggests that parent involvement affects children's achievement by facilitating children's motivation (i.e., their confidence in their abilities, their sense that they can control their own successes and failures in school, and their engagement in school for more autonomous versus controlled reasons). In a study of 203 middle school students, these authors tested this model by examining relations between three types of parent involvement; behavior at school, cognitive/intellectual activities with their children, and personal involvement, which was asking about and keeping up on children's school activities and progress and children's motivation and school performance. For both mothers and fathers, the results supported the motivational model indicating that involvement at school and in cognitive/intellectual activities facilitated students' perceived competence and perceived control which were then associated with children's school performance.

The findings for the motivation model are supported by other studies that have shown relations between parental involvement and children's motivation. For example, Sanders (1998) found positive relations between parent encouragement of academic endeavors and achievement and children's positive academic self-concept, school behavior, and perception of the importance of achievement for future success. Fan and Williams (2010) showed that parents' educational aspirations for their children as well as their school-based involvement were positively associated with children's academic self-efficacy, school engagement,

and intrinsic motivation. A review of multiple studies by Gonzalez-DeHass et al., (2005) concluded that that there is ample support for the view that parent involvement facilitates children's perceived competence, perceived control, and value for the educational endeavor.

Summary and Recommendations

Given evidence of the strength and breadth of effects of parent involvement, it is not surprising that boosting parent involvement is a key goal for educational policies and school reform. While research has clearly shown that characteristics of parents such as education and income predict involvement, with, for example, levels of involvement being higher for more educated and higher income families (e.g., Grolnick et al., 1997; Horvat, Weininger, & Lareau, 2003) there is also evidence that teachers and schools can make a difference in parents' levels of involvement. For example, Epstein (1986) showed that parents whose children's teachers believed strongly in parent involvement reported that they received the most ideas for home learning activities from the teacher and felt they had an increased understanding of what their child was learning in school relative to those of teachers who were not "leaders in involvement." Beyond what teachers can do, there are many school-wide efforts that are successfully increasing parent involvement. For example, schools that are members of the National Network of Partnership Schools (NNPS; Sanders & Epstein, 2000) set goals for implementing family–school partnerships and monitoring progress toward these goals. Schools with these partnership programs have more parent involvement both at home and at school than non-partnership schools (Sheldon & Van Voorhis, 2004).

In sum, parents' involvement in children's learning is a major resource for children's academic achievement. Facilitating this crucial resource will require the active efforts of all stakeholders who have children's success and well-being as their goal.

References

Dearing, E., Kreider, H., Simpkins, S., & Weiss, H. B. (2006). Family involvement in school and low-income children's literacy: Longitudinal association between and within families. *Journal of Educational Psychology, 98*, 653–664

Epstein, J. L. (1986). Parents' reactions to teacher practices of parent involvement. *The Elementary School Journal, 86*, 277–294.

Fan, W. & Williams, C. M. (2010). The effects of parental involvement on students' academic self-efficacy, engagement and intrinsic motivation. *Educational Psychology, 30*, 53–74

Gonzalez-DeHass, A. Willems, P., & Holbein, M. (2005). Examining the relationship between parental involvement and student motivation. *Educational Psychology Review, 17*(2), 99–123.

Grolnick, W. S., Benjet, C., Kurowski, C. O., & Apostoleris, N. (1997). Predictors of parent involvement in children's schooling. *Journal of Educational Psychology, 89*, 538–548

Grolnick, W. S., & Slowiaczek, M. L. (1994). Parents' involvement in children's schooling: A multidimensional conceptualization and motivational model. *Child Development, 65*, 237–252

Hara, S. R. (1998). Parent involvement: The key to improved student achievement. *School Community Journal, 8*(2), 9–19

Hill, N. E., & Taylor, L. C. (2004). Parental school involvement and children's academic achievement: Pragmatics and issues. *Current Directions in Psychological Science, 13,* 161–164

Hill, N. E., & Tyson, D. F. (2009). Parental involvement in middle school: A meta-analytic assessment of the strategies that promote achievement. *Developmental Psychology, 45*(3), 740–763.

Horvat, E. M., Weininger, E. B., & Lareau, A. (2003). From social ties to social capital: Class differences in the relations between schools and parent networks. *American Educational Research Journal, 40,* 319–351

Jeynes, W. H. (2005). A meta-analysis of the relation of parental involvement to urban elementary school student academic achievement. *Urban Education, 40,* 237–269

Jeynes, W. H. (2007). The relationship between parental involvement and urban secondary school student academic achievement: A meta-analysis. *Urban Education, 42,* 82–110.

McWayne, C., Hampton, V., Fantuzzo, J., Cohen, H. L., & Sekino, Y. (2004). A multivariate examination of parent involvement and the social and academic competencies of urban kindergarten children. *Psychology in the Schools, 41,* 363–377.

Sanders, M. G. (1998). The effects of school, family, and community support on the academic achievement of African American adolescents. *Urban Education, 33,* 385–409.

Sanders, M. G., & Epstein, J. L. (2000). The National Network of Partnership Schools: How research influences educational practice. *Journal of Education for Students Placed at Risk, 5,* 61–76.

Sheldon, S. B., & Van Voorhis, F. L. (2004). Partnership programs in U. S. schools: Their development and relationship to family involvement outcomes. *School Effectiveness and School Improvement, 15,* 125–148.

U.S. Department of Education. (2010). *A blueprint for reform: The reauthorization of the Elementary and Secondary Education Act.* Washington, DC: Author.

3.7

Maternal Employment and Achievement

RACHEL G. LUCAS-THOMPSON
Macalester College

WENDY A. GOLDBERG
University of California, Irvine

Introduction

In the last 50 to 60 years, a dramatic social revolution has occurred: more and more women, particularly those with children, have been employed outside the home. In 1950, only about one in three U.S. women were employed; by 2009, more than half of the U.S. labor force was women (U.S. Census Bureau, 2002). Although employment rates for women have leveled off in recent years, they are especially high for women with children under age 18. Indeed, the majority of mothers with children are employed, most of them full-time. These days, only 20% of married couples with children fit the stereotype of dad working and mom at home full-time (Treas & Drobnic, 2010). Along with the changes in the rates of women working have occurred changes in the social perceptions of the risks versus benefits of women's work outside the home (Pew Research Center, 2009). Although in the late 1970s only 48.9% of American adults endorsed the idea that working women can be good mothers, by the mid-2000s, 67% of men and 80% of women agreed with the same statement. What remains more controversial, however, is work when children are young. In fact, views about the employment of mothers with young children have changed very little over the decades. The vast majority of adults think that mothers with young children should not work full-time. Because of the changing rates and social ideas about maternal work, decades of research have aimed to determine how that work matters for children's development. The focus of the current chapter is on how maternal work is associated with a critical domain of development: children's achievement.

Research Evidence

Why is it that scholars, parents, and policy makers been concerned with the effects of maternal employment on children's achievement? There are many reasons that parents work, and several possible ways, both positive and negative, in which employment could affect children's cognitive and academic development. An economic model of influence suggests that the income that maternal employment brings into the home will improve the standard of living, boost investment in children's education, and increase access to high quality goods and services (e.g., books, toys, extra lessons); this improvement may then facilitate positive cognitive and academic achievement. These benefits of the added income are hypothesized to be especially likely for children and families from less advantaged backgrounds. Mothers' earnings are vital to the well-being of many families, but they are especially critical when mothers are the heads of households or fathers are unemployed.

Mothers' work outside the home also introduces the possibility that work conditions will directly impinge on their parenting and therefore indirectly influence children. This parenting stress model suggests that less than ideal job conditions (e.g., instability, irregular schedules, limited autonomy) can be stressful for parents, and this stress can then compromise parenting in a way that renders children vulnerable to negative outcomes. Feeling as though there isn't enough time in the day can contribute to the felt stress of employed mothers; a recent survey found that 40% of working mothers feel rushed compared to 25% of employed dads and stay-at-home mothers. It is important to remember that work can impact parenting in positive ways, too. High quality jobs can provide positive opportunities for mothers in a way that can make them better parents and in that way support optimal development. An equal number of employed and stay-at-home moms report being very satisfied with their family life and with their life in general.

A third model, and one often cited by critics of maternal work, particularly when children are young, focuses on negative time effects due to lengthy time periods of separation each working day. The rationale here is that cognitive and academic development will be hampered when children have less of their mothers' time. When children are separated from their mothers, the quality of alternate care becomes an important factor to consider; alternate care that is less supportive than maternal care can be one way by which children's achievement can suffer (referred to as the lost resources hypothesis). Lack of maternal supervision can become a problem, particularly for older children. Together, these models highlight potential positive and negative effects of mothers working outside the home.

Studies have examined maternal employment in terms of categorical work status (employed versus not employed, full-time/part-time/not employed) or continuously, in terms of weekly hours of employment. Employment has been concurrently and prospectively linked with achievement outcomes; studies focusing on the prospective effects of maternal employment often focus on work when children are very young (referred to as early maternal employment). Typically, achievement has been measured based on performance on standardized tests (e.g., intelligence tests, formal tests of achievement), grades, teachers' or parents' reports of a child's academic achievement, and children's ultimate educational attainment. Studies in both the U.S. and other countries have examined these relations in diverse samples in terms of child age, ethnicity, family structure (e.g., one- or two-parent families), and socioeconomic status.

Overall, there are few main effects of employment on achievement; essentially, whether a mother works or not is often not associated with her children's achievement. This relation (or lack thereof) seems to be the same whether concurrent (Goldberg, Prause, Lucas-Thompson, & Himsel, 2008) or early employment (Lucas-Thompson, Goldberg, & Prause, 2010) is under investigation. Instead, the relation between maternal employment and children's achievement is complex and reflects various socioeconomic, familial, and contextual influences. For instance, maternal employment is most positive for families who are likely to be at risk socioeconomically, such as low-income families, families on welfare, or single-parent families. Maternal employment is more negative for families who are less at risk, such as middle- or upper-middle-class and two-parent families. For example, a recent longitudinal study found full-time maternal employment in the first year to be associated with lower scores on some measures of children's cognitive abilities only for non-Hispanic White children (Brooks-Gunn, Han, & Waldfogel, 2010).

There are also some suggestions that maternal employment is associated with more positive effects for girls than for boys. Role modeling opportunities would suggest stronger, more positive effects for daughters over sons. However, this latter finding depends in part on socioeconomic status: employment in middle- and upper-middle-class families is associated with decreases in achievement for boys, but boys in other economic conditions and girls are not affected in the same way. Gender effects may also depend on culture and what is considered normative for each sex. The timing and extent of employment also matter. Part-time work is associated with more optimal achievement than full-time work, and employment in the first year of life is associated with more negative achievement outcomes than later

employment. These findings highlight the importance of social context for understanding how maternal work may be associated with children's achievement: employment is important for achievement, but only under certain conditions and for certain subgroups of children and families.

Other factors are also important to consider. Individual characteristics can be important, such as the child's ability, parents' level of education, and fathers' employment. The quality of alternate (nonmaternal) care is another factor, which is particularly salient when considering early maternal employment . Children can be cared for in day care centers, on-site at schools, by relatives, by nonrelatives, or by some combination of arrangements. The number and quality of child care arrangements are important to consider, and can hinder or support optimal achievement independently and in conjunction with employment characteristics. For instance, child care that is of high quality can improve children's learning and language (Vandell et al., 2010). Also important to consider is the potential for selection biases. More specifically, it is possible that differences in achievement outcomes between the children of employed versus not employed mothers could actually reflect preexisting differences associated with which mothers join the labor force. Employed and nonemployed mothers differ on a variety of socioeconomic, demographic, psychological, and other characteristics that can determine who is employed and who is not. These differences may then render children more or less vulnerable to negative achievement outcomes. For instance, employed mothers are typically better educated and in smaller families with higher income levels. Of course, attitudes about work and parenting also tend to be different between these two groups of women. These factors need to be considered for if we are to truly understand the association between maternal work outside the home and children's achievement. Some studies do in fact suggest that associations are smaller once these factors are controlled for; however, most of the associations discussed previously are evident with and without such controls.

Summary and Recommendations

Mothers in the United States are in the labor force in large numbers; most of them return to work soon after birth and most work full-time. Despite the fact that maternal employment is becoming increasingly normative, it remains controversial. Public opinion commonly assumes that young children will not reach their full potential if their mothers are employed; however, research points to both positive and negative effects. Also, mothers being employed or not is not the primary determinant of how well children achieve; instead, the effects of employment depend on familial, contextual, and socioeconomic characteristics and the contributors to children's achievement are many, as this volume illustrates. The importance of the extent and timing of maternal employment suggest that young children and parents may benefit from additional institutional support in the way of federal paid parental leaves, more workplace flexibility, and subsidized high-quality child care. Social changes such as these may enable mothers to be employed while giving families choices and enabling children to reach their full potential.

References

Brooks-Gunn, J., Han, W-J., & Waldfogel, J. (2010). First-year maternal employment and child development in the first 7 years. *Monographs of the Society for Research in Child Development, 75*, 1–147.

Goldberg, W. A., Prause, J. A., Lucas-Thompson, R., & Himsel, A. (2008). Maternal employment and children's achievement in context: A meta-analysis of four decades of research. *Psychological Bulletin, 134*, 77–108.

Lucas-Thompson, R. G., Goldberg, W. A., & Prause, J. A. (2010). Maternal work early in the lives of children and its distal associations with achievement and behavior problems: A meta-analysis. *Psychological Bulletin, 136*, 915–942.

Pew Research Center. (2009). *The harried life of the working mother.* Retrieved from http://pewresearch.org/pubs/1360/working-women-conflicted-but-few-favor-return-to-traditional-roles].

Treas, J., & Drobnic, S. (Eds.). (2010). *Dividing the domestic: men, women, and household work in cross-national perspective*. Stanford, CA: Stanford University Press.

U.S. Census Bureau. (2002). *Statistical abstracts of the United States: 2002* (122nd ed.). Washington, DC: Author.

Vandell, D. L., Belsky, J., Burchinal, M., Steinberg, L., Vandergrift, N., & NICHD Early Child Care Research Network. (2010). Do effects of early child care extend to age 15 years? Results from the NICHD Study of Early Child Care and Youth Development. *Child Development, 81*, 737–756.

3.8

Television and Academic Achievement

Andrew J. Martin
University of Sydney

Introduction

Despite the rise of computers and other modern electronic mediums, television is still the most time-consuming leisure activity in which children and young people engage. Recent estimates suggest there are three or more television sets in most Western homes and that children aged 8 to 17 years watch an average of just under 2 hours of television per day (Australian Communications and Media Authority, 2007). Television is, then, a major presence in school-aged children's lives and its impact on achievement is important to understand. Hypotheses about the effects of television viewing on achievement take three forms: inhibiting (negative effects), facilitating (positive effects), and null hypotheses.

Turning to inhibiting perspectives first, it seems that displacement hypotheses receive most attention. Broadly, these state that television displaces important developmental and learning activities, thus inhibiting achievement. There has also been a distinction between quantitative and qualitative displacement, with the former referring to the hours of television viewing that directly displace time spent on schoolwork and the latter referring to poorer performance on academic tasks (e.g., homework, assignments) because they are conducted while the television is turned on (for reviews, see Beentjes & van der Voort, 1988; Hofferth, 2010; Neuman, 1988).

Another form of displacement is suggested under the subject depreciation hypothesis which argues that children's enjoyable experiences with television reduce their energy and interest in academic subject matter, leading to lower achievement. Related to this is the gratification (or, antischool) hypothesis that television provides drama, action, and excitement that is instantly gratifying, giving rise to the erroneous perception on the part of students that all schoolwork should be the same—and when it is not, disengagement and lower achievement follows (see Beentjes & van der Voort, 1988; Ennemoser & Schneider, 2007;

Koolstra, van der Voort, & van der Kamp, 1997; Razel, 2001 for summaries).

Brain-based and cognitive hypotheses have also predicted inhibiting effects of television on achievement. For example, the hemispheric specialization hypothesis suggests that some parts of the brain are overstimulated by television viewing and other parts of the brain responsible for much learning and achievement are underutilized and underactive. The joint operation of the two is suggested to result in poor academic achievement. A cognitive perspective on inhibition is developed under the passivity hypothesis. This holds that children learn best thorough active manipulation of environment/subject matter and that television is a passive interaction requiring low mental effort that does not foster learning. Also in the cognitive domain, the concentration deterioration hypothesis states that the fast pace and rapid content shifts in television negatively affect children's ability to concentrate on the school learning that is important for achievement. Similarly, the information processing hypothesis suggests that television trains students to process information in a particular way that is different from what is required on school tasks (for reviews, see Beentjes & van der Voort, 1988; Ennemoser & Schneider, 2007; Hofferth, 2010; Razel, 2001; Salomon, 1984;).

Under facilitating perspectives, schema theorists have suggested potential benefits of television for achievement. They argue against the notion of the zombie viewer, instead suggesting there is active cognitive engagement with much television material. With particular focus on reading achievement, some researchers have suggested the book-reading promotion hypothesis—where television promotes an interest in reading a particular book or series—thus developing reading achievement. Also connected with reading is the on-screen reading hypotheses—that television programs (particularly educational ones) comprise much on-screen text (including subtitles for many languages) that the viewer learns to read (see Beentjes & van der Voort, 1988; Neuman, 1988 for summaries).

Finally, null effect hypotheses suggest various perspectives on nonsignificant or counterbalanced effects of television on achievement. One version of this hypothesis is that there are no effects of television on achievement. Another version is that there may be an apparent effect but that after controlling for relevant background factors, there is no significant effect. A third version is that overall null effects may be evident but that for subgroups of children there are opposite or nonlinear effects that counterbalance to give the appearance of a null result. For example, mainstreaming perspectives argue for small positive effects of television viewing for students low in socioeconomic status (SES) and negative effects for high SES students, averaging to a null effect. This perspective argues that television may provide cognitively rich and language-intensive material beyond what low SES circumstances might provide, thus leading to positive effects on achievement. On the other hand, students high in SES stand to lose from television viewing as it provides a lower quality medium of cognitive and language material than what their circumstances might otherwise provide. Likewise, threshold hypotheses may apply such that there are positive effects for low amounts of viewing but negative effects for longer hours of viewing, with these curvilinear effects averaging to zero as a linear effect (for summaries, see Comstock & Scharrer, 1999; Beentjes & van der Voort, 1988; Ennemoser & Schneider, 2007; Razel, 2001).

Research Evidence

Before moving to the relative complexity of findings, it is appropriate to recognize that the predominant top-line effect of television viewing on academic achievement appears to be negative, but generally small (Beentjes & van der Voort, 1988; Comstock & Scharrer, 1999; Ennemoser & Schneider, 2007). In a synthesis of meta-analyses of television effects (based on 3 meta-analyses, 37 studies, 540 effects, and over 1 million participants), Hattie (2009) found a small negative effect (–.18) for the association between television and achievement. That said, it is evident there are important nuances and complexities that shed further light on the issue and provide direction for educational and parenting practice (discussed below). Understanding these complexities is probably best achieved by examining the various factors that seem to moderate the effects of television viewing on achievement. These moderators encompass the nature of television content, number of viewing hours, age of viewer, SES of viewer, and even the type of achievement under focus.

In terms of viewing content, there is a clear differentiation between educational and entertainment material. The research suggests that viewing educational content can lead to positive achievement effects whereas viewing entertainment content yields a negative (or no) effect on achievement (for summaries, see Australian Communications and Media Authority, 2007; Ennemoser & Schneider, 2007; Hofferth, 2010; Koolstra, van der Voort, & van der Kamp, 1997).

Educational programs may also increase students' motivation to read, knowledge of subject domains, and problem solving in mathematics and science. Interestingly, this content effect may vary with age, with relatively stronger effects for younger children receiving high quality content (Schmidt & Vandewater, 2008).

In terms of viewing hours, there appears to be a curvilinear relationship such that initial viewing time is positively associated with achievement, but longer hours are negatively associated with achievement (Ennemoser & Schneider, 2007; Hofferth, 2010; Neuman, 1988; Schmidt & Vandewater, 2008; Williams, Haertel, Haertel, & Walberg, 1982). Importantly, this curvilinear relationship seems to vary by age, with the optimal number of television hours decreasing as children get older—declining from 1 to 2 hours for young children to 30 minutes for 17 year olds (Razel, 2001; see also Neuman, 1988). In relation to age, findings have suggested that positive correlations with achievement exist for young children but not for older children (Australian Communications and Media Authority, 2007; Ennemoser & Schneider, 2007).

As discussed in relation to the mainstreaming hypothesis, SES seems relevant to the television–achievement link such that longer viewing by advantaged children is associated with declines in achievement whereas there is a positive or null effect for disadvantaged children (Schmidt & Vandewater, 2008). Also related to home context, when parents watch television with their children and talk about the content viewed, children's comprehension of the relevant subject matter is improved (Schmidt & Vandewater, 2008).

Other research has suggested that the effects of television viewing on achievement are generally null when relevant covariates are accommodated. For example, after accounting for prior achievement and personal background characteristics, Hofferth (2010) suggests no negative effects of television on achievement. Similarly, whereas cross-sectional associations between television and achievement are found, when appropriate longitudinal models are analyzed, this relationship drops to non-significance. However, this too may be moderated by the content viewed, with Ennemoser and Schneider (2007) finding negative effects for viewing entertainment material (distinct from educational material) after controlling for prior achievement and other background covariates. Also important to note is that an abundance of nonsignificant but consistently negative effects are suggestive of an overall negative effect worth recognizing (Ennemoser & Schneider, 2007; Razel, 2001).

The nature of the achievement measure is also important to consider. For example, whilst students may be able to reproduce knowledge from the television content to academic tasks directly related to that content, there has been some question about transfer (i.e., students' capacity to apply that knowledge to new situations and tasks). Some research has shown that although children understand the content of an educational program, they are unable to transfer central principles to problems involving a different set of stimuli (Schmidt & Vandewater, 2008). Notwithstanding this, other studies have shown successful transfer (Schmidt & Vandewater, 2008), with some suggesting it may be moderated by age and content, with older viewers able to transfer more effectively than younger viewers and when concepts are explicitly evident through the narrative (Schmidt & Vandewater, 2008).

Summary and Recommendations

The relationship between television viewing and achievement is complex. Although there appears to be a small negative relationship between television viewing and achievement, such effects can vary as a function of television content, viewer's age, viewer's SES, amount of television consumed, achievement types, and interactions between these factors. These complexities are especially important to recognize when considering recommendations for practice and research. In terms of practice, it is clear that the effects of television are not overwhelmingly favorable and so appropriate monitoring of viewing habits in the home is required. Findings also indicate that it is important to adjust viewing hours as children get older, with fewer hours of viewing as students move into and through high school. The nature of material children and young people watch is important to regulate, with different viewing limits for educational (relatively more hours per week) and entertainment (relatively fewer hours per week) content. In relation to SES, whilst it is encouraging that television does not seem to adversely affect disadvantaged students' achievement, it is important not to rely on television as a means of their educational development; instead, providing targeted educational intervention is likely to yield larger effect sizes for achievement.

There are also methodological implications. The importance of longitudinal work is evident, as it controls for prior achievement and thus can better assess the unique effects of television on achievement. Better measurement is needed. Television research comprises poor measurement of viewing hours and content (Ennemoser & Schneider, 2007). Greater retention of participants in studies is also needed. Problems of attrition abound, with children who drop out tending to watch more television and scoring lower in achievement than those who remain in studies, thus, leading to possible underestimation of television's negative effects (Ennemoser & Schneider, 2007; Koolstra et al., 1997). Finally, with the rise of handheld and mobile computing devices, the effects of television on achievement must be monitored and juxtaposed with the effects of these other media (Hattie, 2009). Taken together, there are complex television viewing effects that require ongoing attention in research and practice in order for practitioners and parents to optimally foster students' academic achievement and academic development.

References

Australian Communications and Media Authority (2007). *Media and communications in Australian families: Report of the Media and Society Research Project.* Canberra, ACT: Australian Communications and Media Authority.

Beentjes, J. W. J., & van der Voort, T. H. A. (1988). Television's impact on children's reading skills: A review of research. *Reading Research Quarterly, 23,* 389–413

Comstock, G., & Scharrer, E. (1999). *Television: What's on, who's watching, and what it means.* San Diego, CA: Academic Press.

Ennemoser, M., & Schneider, W. (2007). Relations of television viewing and reading: Findings from a 4-year longitudinal study. *Journal of Educational Psychology, 99,* 349–368.

Hattie, J. (2009). *Visible learning.* Oxford, England: Routledge.

Hofferth, S.L. (2010). Home media and children's achievement and behavior. *Child Development, 81,* 1598–1619.

Koolstra, C. M., van der Voort, T. H. A., & van der Kamp, L. J. T. (1997). Television's impact on children's reading comprehension and decoding skills: A 3-year panel study. *Reading Research Quarterly, 32,* 128–152.

Neuman, S. B. (1988). The displacement effect: Assessing the relation between television viewing and reading performance. *Reading Research Quarterly, 23,* 414–440.

Razel, M. (2001). The complex model of television viewing and educational achievement. *Journal of Educational Research, 94,* 371–379.

Salomon, G. (1984). Television is "easy" and print is "tough": The differential investment of mental effort in learning as a function of perceptions and attributions. *Journal of Educational Psychology, 76,* 647–658.

Schmidt, M. E., & Vandewater, E. A. (2008). Media and attention, cognition, and school achievement. *The Future of Children, 18,* 63–85.

Williams, P. A., Haertel, E. H., Haertel, G. D., & Walberg, H. J. (1982). The impact of leisure-time television on school learning: A research synthesis. *American Educational Research Journal, 19,* 19–50.

Section 4

Influences from the School

Catherine P. Bradshaw
Johns Hopkins University

4.1

Charter Schools and Academic Achievement

ANN ALLEN
The Ohio State University

Introduction

Charter schools are public schools that operate under their own governing boards. As schools of choice, charter schools compete with local district schools for student enrollment. Several countries have employed independent market-based public schools for a decade or more. The United States, New Zealand, Great Britain, and the Canadian province of Alberta incorporate some use of a market-based model of public schooling. Charter schools are typically authorized by a public agency, but under some state governing policies, they can be managed by private organizations. The idea behind these differences in organization—independent schools and independent boards—is that without the bureaucratic constrictions associated with traditional school districts, charter school leaders have the freedom to better respond to the needs of students and help students succeed. Creating smaller schools independent of large bureaucracies ideally provides parents and students opportunities for engagement they would not get in a larger system (Mintrom, 2003). Charter schools are also discussed as a way to experiment with education and produce innovative practices that then could transfer back to district schools (Nathan, 1996). Furthermore, the ability of students and parents to choose schools is intended to create pressure on all schools to improve.

Research Evidence

Research on charter schools does not present a clear picture of whether charter schools lead to increased student achievement. Part of the difficulty in gaining a clear understanding of the effects of charter schooling on achievement is that the nature of charter schools as independent public schools that are encouraged to be innovative in their approach to education creates a level of variability that makes generalizations difficult (Betts & Tang, 2008). Charter schools also vary considerably in how they are governed. In the United

States, where there are more than 5,000 charter schools serving more than 1 million students, charter schools are governed according to state policies, which differ in relation to regulation and oversight. Nevertheless, researchers have attempted to understand the effects of charter schooling on student achievement through a number of national studies.

Research on the effectiveness of charter schools suggests the charter school reform has not yet fulfilled its promise of increased achievement, although there are studies that point to some promising results for certain students in certain locations. For example, Betts and Tang (2008), in an analysis of 70 studies on charter schools and achievement, found only 13 studies that tested achievement gains using a lottery approach (comparing charter school lottery winners to charter school lottery losers) or a value-added approach, taking into account a student's past test scores. From the 13 studies, they concluded there was more evidence that charter schools outperformed traditional public schools, particularly at the elementary and middle school level, than evidence that they underperformed. At the high school level, the researchers found charter schools lagged behind the traditional public schools, especially in math achievement. Results from other studies are also mixed. For example, researchers who conducted national studies using longitudinal student-level test data on math and reading found on average no difference in learning gains between charter school students and their traditional public school counterparts (Center for Research on Education Outcomes [CREDO], 2009; Gleason, Clark, Tuttle, Dwoyer, & Silverberg, 2009; Zimmer et al., 2009). However, there is some indication that charter schools that serve more low-income or low-achieving students showed gains in math, whereas charter schools that serve high-income students who have had prior achievement showed drops in math achievement scores (Gleason et al., 2010).

Another systematic study of charters was conducted by the Rand Corporation (Zimmer et al., 2009) using longitudinal student-level math and reading test data from Ohio,

Texas, and Florida and the cities of Chicago, San Diego, Philadelphia, Denver, and Milwaukee. The researchers found that for middle and high school students in most of the locations, there was significantly no difference in achievement than what is found in traditional public schools, and that in some locales like Chicago and Texas, charter schools compared negatively to their traditional public school counterparts. The researchers also found that when data from kindergarten-entry charter schools was accounted for in the analysis, it affected only one location's results, "dramatically" lowering Ohio's achievement effects. When the K-entry schools were not included in the analysis, Ohio's results looked similar to other sites in the study. Researchers attributed the difference to the use of virtual or online charter schools in Ohio, which use technology to deliver education directly to students in their homes. Researchers found virtual schools constitute a large portion of K-entry charter schools in the state. Researchers also found greater variation in achievement among charter schools in Ohio than in other states. They suggest part of this variation may be related to the large diversity of organizations that can authorize charter schools and to financial constraints that limit charter school resources in the state (Zimmer et al., 2009). The study also found some evidence that students who attend charter schools for both middle and high school grades have greater graduation and college entry rates.

Other researchers have found that learning gains in charter schools are higher for elementary students in relation to reading and for middle schools in relation to math (Betts & Tang, 2008; CREDO, 2009), but high school students in charter schools show negative results in reading and math (CREDO, 2009). CREDO's study, also employing longitudinal student-level data of charter schools in 15 states and the District of Columbia, yielded positive results for 17% of the charter schools, negative results for 37% of the charter schools, and no discernible difference in achievement for nearly 50% of the charter schools in the study. CREDO (2009) researchers also found that English Language Learners tended to fare better in charter schools than traditional public schools. Yet, there appear to be some geographic areas in the United States where charter schools show more academic gains and innovation than others (CREDO, 2009; Hoxby, Murarka, & Kang, 2009; Nicotera, Mendiburo, & Berends, 2010), which suggests the policies that govern charter schools may influence the success of charter schools at improving achievement.

The difficulty in measuring student gains in charter schools is consistent across countries. In New Zealand, where public education was decentralized in 1997 as part of a national reform effort, the Ministry of Education sets guidelines and distributes funding to the country's primary and secondary schools, which are governed by their own separate boards. Researchers have noted the difficulty in measuring student learning gains related to the use of independent schools in New Zealand because there is no nationwide testing system, and less than half of the elementary schools administer a Ministry of Education-

sponsored progressive achievement test (Morphis, 2009). In England, there has been some research to suggest achievement increased with the introduction of grant-maintained independent schools, but given the host of initiatives aimed to raise academic achievement in the nation's schools, it is difficult to determine that the use of independent grant-maintained schools was the cause of increased achievement (Walford, 2000). In Alberta, Canada, where there are only a few charter schools, researchers who have used longitudinal student data (Bosetti, Foulkes, O'Reilly, & Sande, 2000) and aggregate school data (Da Costa, Peters, & Violato, 2002) have found that achievement results of charter school students are comparable to those of traditional public school students. In some cases, these researchers have found some learning gains. However, Thomson (2008) cautions that the favorable results may not account for the selection bias inherent in charter school admissions in Alberta, particularly in schools that do not have the resources to serve special-needs students. Admission bias may also appear in schools where there are criteria set for admission or where certain populations of students (e.g., special education) are unable to attend because they cannot access the transportation needed to get to the charter school.

There are several factors, such as admission policies, that must be considered when looking at the effect of charter schools on achievement. The charter school model provides greater choice to parents but accessing that choice also means student mobility, and researchers have noted that there is typically a dip in achievement when students move to a new school (Gleason et al., 2009; Hoxby et al., 2009). The study by Zimmer et al. (2009) suggests that researchers might get a more accurate picture of student achievement in charter schools if they look at students who have been in the school for a year or more.

The decentralization of schooling through the use of charter schools also creates resource challenges for independent schools. Wylie (2009) noted that one of the initial problems with the use of independent schools in New Zealand was the lack of linkages within the schooling system, which led to a lack of resources for schools. New Zealand has since worked to create stronger linkages among schools, such as providing greater curriculum support and direction.

Finally, researchers bring-up broader issues with the use of independent schools, which, while they may not have a direct influence on student achievement, have an effect on the overall mission of public education. For example, there is some evidence that charter schools have a segregationary effect on schooling, which works against public school aims for social cohesion (Fiske & Ladd, 2000; Rapp & Estes, 2007). Thomson (2008) notes that the reason why the use of charter schools is limited in Canada is probably because of that country's commitment to social cohesion.

Summary and Recommendations

Charter schools are popular with parents. They offer the promise of public education in a more responsive environment. With nearly 20 years of experience with charter schools, researchers are still working to identify effective ways to assess achievement gains across schools. The variability in the governance and design of individual charter schools, confounding factors such as student mobility, admissions, and school resources, and the different aims of schooling make it difficult to assess the achievement gains of students in charter schools over those in traditional public schools. The reliance on test scores over time as a means for determining success of charter schooling allows researchers to see achievement gains and compare those gains to students in traditional schools, but longitudinal test data can be problematic in that test scores may not reflect achievement gains for all students, particularly those in early grades (Zimmer et al., 2009) and may not capture all of the benefits of charter schooling on student success (Betts & Tang, 2009). Researchers are beginning to move away from reliance on test data only to capture the full effect of charter schooling on student achievement. But given the research-to-date, the question of whether students achieve at a higher rate in charter schools over traditional public schools is still unanswered.

Note

1. Data retrieved from the Center for Education Reform: http://www.edreform.com/Issues/Charter_Connection/?All_About_Charter_Schools

References

Betts, J. R. & Tang, Y. E. (2008). *Value-added and experimental studies of the effect of charter schools on student achievement.* Seattle, WA: National Charter School Research Project, Center on Reinventing Public Education, University of Washington, Bothell. Retrieved from http://www.crpe.org/cs/crpe/download/csr_files/pub_ncsrp_bettstang_dec08.pdf

Bosetti, L., Foulkes, E., O'Reilly, R., & Sande, D. (2000). *Canadian charter schools at the crossroads: A final report.* Kelowna, BC, Canada: Society for the Advancement of Excellence in Education.

Center for Research on Education Outcomes (CREDO). (2009). *Multiple choice: Charter performance in 16 states.* Stanford, CA: Stanford University. Retrieved from http://credo.stanford.edu/.

Da Costa, J., Peters, F., & Violato, C. (2002). *Achievement in Alberta's charter schools: A longitudinal study* (SAEE Research Series, 13). Kelowna, BC, Canada: Society for the Advancement of Excellence in Education.

Fiske, E. B., & Ladd, H. F. (2000). *When schools compete: A cautionary tale.* Washington, DC: Brookings Institution Press.

Gleason, P., Clark, M., Tuttle, M. C., Dwoyer, E., & Silverberg, M. (2010). *The evaluation of charter school impacts: Final report.* Washington, DC: Institute of Education Science, U.S. Department of Education.

Hoxby, C. M., Murarka, S., & Kang, J. (2009, September). *How New York City's charter schools affect achievement, August 2009 report.* Cambridge, MA: New York City Charter Schools Evaluation Project.

Mintrom, M. (2003). Market organizations and deliberative democracy: Choice and voice in public service delivery. *Administration and Society, 35,* 52–81.

Morphis, E. (2009). *The shift to school choice in New Zealand* (National Center for the Study of the Privatization of Education, Paper No. 179). Retrieved from http://www.ncspe.org/list-papers.php

Nathan, J. (1996). *Charter schools: Creating hope for American education.* San Francisco, CA: Jossey-Bass.

Nicotera, A., Mendiburo, M., & Berends, M. (2010). Charter school effects in an urban school district: An analysis of student achievement gains in Indianapolis. National Center of School Choice, Nashville, TN. Retrieved from http://www.vanderbilt.edu/schoolchoice/documents/briefs/brief_Nicotera_COMPLETE.pdf

Rapp, K., & Eckes, S. (2007). Dispelling the myth of "white flight": An examination of minority enrollment in charter schools. *Educational Policy, 21*(4), 615–661.

Thomson, K. (2008). *An evaluation of the charter school movement in Alberta, Canada* (National Center for the Study of the Privatization of Education, Paper No.159). Retrieved from http://www.ncspe.org/list-papers.phpWalford, G. (2003). School choice and educational change in England and Wales. In D. N. Plank & G. Sykes (Eds.), *Choosing choice: School choice in international perspective* (pp. 68–91). New York: Teachers College Press.

Wylie, C. (2009). *What can we learn from the last twenty years: Why tomorrow's schools could not achieve key purposes and how we can do things differently with self-managed schools.* Herbison Lecture. Retrieved from www.nzcer.org.nz/pdfs/learn-last-20-years.pdf

Zimmer, R., Gill, B., Booker, K., Lavertu, S., Sass, T. R., & Witte, J. (2009). *Charter schools in eight states: Effects on achievement, attainment, integration, and competition.* Santa Monica, CA: RAND. Retrieved from http://www.rand.org/pubs/monographs/MG869/

4.2

Ability Grouping

ED BAINES
Institute of Education, London

Introduction

Grouping students on the basis of some estimate of their academic ability is a widely used approach in many countries to the organisation of pupils for instructional purposes, though its exact nature varies between and within countries. This review examines the nature and rationale for the use of ability grouping; it also summarises findings relating to academic achievement and explanatory processes.

Organising pupils in groups on the basis of ability provokes strong debates amongst educators, politicians, and parents. Its use is based on a belief that all students' attainment can be increased if instruction, learning support, the curriculum, resources, teacher expertise, and so on, are targeted at students according to similar ability level. However, many concerns are expressed about the potentially negative effects of ability grouping, particularly in relation to equality of opportunity, and access to curriculum, resources, and instructional expertise. Homogenous ability grouping can inadvertently organise students by socioeconomic background (SEB) and across racial lines (Oakes, 2005). It may thus exacerbate existing societal divisions.

Homogenous ability grouping can take different forms and be present at different organisational levels within the school system. Students may be grouped by ability *within* classrooms (within-class ability grouping) and may receive differentiated instruction. Tracking or streaming refers to the allocation of students to different classes on the basis of similar ability levels for all academic subjects. The curriculum offered may differ between tracks/streams to match the perceived level. Another form of ability grouping, setting or regrouping, is similar to tracking but is particular to the curriculum area studied and therefore allows students to be in different ability group levels for different academic subjects. The same curriculum is usually accessed by all students. The opposite of ability grouping is heterogeneous ability grouping in which group composition reflects the

school intake. This review will only consider literature relating to ability grouping within schools and classes. Readers interested in other forms of ability grouping, should refer elsewhere (e.g., Schoffield, 2010).

Research Evidence

There is a long history of research on ability grouping, including several meta-analyses and literature reviews. Findings from recent international studies, particularly the ongoing triennial PISA research, indicate consistent effects of ability grouping in relation to performance in reading, mathematics, and science assessments. The PISA studies involved data collections from 15-year-old students and their schools across up to 65 countries. This research compared the academic performance of students that had experienced homogenous ability grouping for all curricula, with those that experienced some ability grouping or none at all, and found that the more schools grouped by ability the lower the overall performance. Findings also indicate that the earlier that differentiation starts the greater the gap in achievement becomes by SEB, without any improvement in achievement overall. After controlling for student and school SEB, the latest PISA study found no independent relation between the grouping of students by ability and reading performance. The PISA research concludes that "school systems that seek to cater to different students' needs through a high level of differentiation in the institutions, grade levels and classes have not succeeded in producing superior overall results, and in some respects they have lower-than-average and more socially unequal performance" (Organisation for Economic Co-operation and Development [OECD], 2010, p. 13).

International comparison studies are limited by their cross-sectional and correlational nature and are unable to offer causal explanations. Analyses are limited to crude comparisons of types/levels of ability grouping and are unable to determine the effects of more flexible or informal systems as used in many schools or of uncontrolled variables (e.g. curriculum coverage, student composition, teacher expertise/experience and so on).

Meta-analyses of experimental and correlational studies examining the effect of homogenous ability grouping on achievement also show little overall benefit for the achievement of all students and where trends are reported, effect sizes are small (Kulik & Kulik, 1982; Slavin, 1987, 1990). Studies of tracked systems and comparisons of the achievement performance of high, middle, and low ability students show inconsistencies in reported effect sizes, though most are generally small (Hattie, 2002). However, the majority of studies on ability grouping tend to involve the different groups undertaking broadly the same curriculum and part of the purpose of ability grouping is to enable differentiation. Research that focuses on the co-occurrence of tracking and a differentiated curriculum shows more marked effects, which suggests that gifted and high ability students tend to perform better in homogeneous ability classes, whereas those in the low ability range tend to fare worse in ability groups than in heterogeneous classes (Hallinan & Kubitschek, 1999; Schoffield, 2010).

Few studies have focused on the practice of "setting" in schools, yet there are advantages to this approach over tracking, most notably a greater flexibility in reassignment and potentially a closer match between instruction and individuals' level of ability. Slavin's (1987) meta-analysis included seven studies comparing setting and heterogeneous grouping at elementary school level in terms of performance in reading or mathematics. Results were inconclusive. More recently a naturalistic longitudinal study of the impact of setting on 6,000 secondary school students, from 45 UK comprehensive schools, found that the strength of setting experienced within a curriculum (from entirely mixed ability to rigorous setting experiences across the 3 years examined) showed no effect on student's performance in national English, mathematics, and science assessments at 13 to 14 years and in a follow-up at 15 to 16 years (Ireson & Hallam, 2001; Ireson, Hallam, & Hurley, 2005). Similarly there was little evidence of an increased achievement gap. However, at 13 to 14 years, low ability students in mathematics made slightly more progress in response to mixed ability grouping and high ability students benefited from a more rigorous setting. Analyses controlled for SEB, previous attainment, and other background variables.

Studies of the effects of within-class ability grouping on achievement are rare. The advantage of within-class grouping over between-class grouping is its closer relationship with learning and teaching purposes, greater flexibility in reassignment, and greater opportunity for sustained interaction with teachers and peers. Meta-analyses indicate that within-class ability grouping may have modest to marked effects on student achievement in comparison to nongrouping or heterogeneous grouping (Lou et al., 1996). Consistent with other findings on ability grouping, low ability students appear to benefit most from mixed ability grouping. With average effect sizes varying markedly between studies and within meta-analyses, the effects of within-class ability grouping are unclear. This may be due to variations in task, instruction and interaction type and the group sizes that students within these groups experience (Baines, Blatchford, & Kutnick, 2003). As within-class ability grouping can be utilized for a range of pedagogic purposes (e.g., group instruction, peer-interactive learning) and may be embedded within a lesson involving other pedagogic practices, it is difficult to identify effects on performance beyond small scale experimental designs (Blatchford, Kutnick, Baines, & Galton, 2003). Studies of within-class grouping with an enriched curriculum (e.g., for use with talented students) suggest more substantial effect sizes than heterogeneous grouping (Lou et al., 1996), though this may be due to the different curricula undertaken.

Potential Causal Mechanisms.   Although there is some disagreement in quantitative analyses about the impact of ability grouping between classrooms on academic achievement, effect sizes seem uniformly small to absent, suggesting that there is little to be explained (Hattie, 2002). Interestingly though, qualitative studies have illustrated how student experiences vary between low, middle, high, and heterogeneous ability groups, thus providing insights into explanatory processes.

Qualitative studies suggest that teachers have higher expectations of students in higher ability groups and lower expectations of students in lower ability groups (Boaler, Wiliam, & Brown, 2000). These expectations are reflected in curriculum and examination demands and through teacher–pupil interaction. Expectations may have marked effects on student motivation with some students benefitting from the pressure of high expectations while others are turned off learning by low expectations. Interestingly, studies have found that when students are located in ability groups above their achievement level they tend to make better progress than students of equivalent ability in groups that are at approximately the right level (Ireson et al., 2005). Placement in a lower group depresses students' academic progress regardless of attainment level.

Studies also indicate that teachers alter their pedagogic approach according to their expectations about the ability range of the classes they teach (Boaler et al., 2000). This, of course, is part of the point of homogeneous ability grouping, but when accompanied by low expectations it may function to lower the challenging and motivating nature of teaching and learning. Research conveys a depressing picture of the low level and fragmented nature of teaching and learning in low ability groups. By contrast higher ability classes experience more interactive, challenging, sustained, and responsive teaching. They may also have more highly experienced/qualified teachers (Oakes, 2005). Studies suggest that where setting is accompanied by didactic instruction there is a wider disparity in academic performance across sets than when within-class groups and individualised instruction are used alongside setting (e.g. Wiliam & Bartholomew, 2004). Varying pedagogic approaches may go some way to explaining the variable effects associated with ability grouping.

Summary and Recommendations

Although there are seemingly obvious advantages to homogenous ability grouping, the evidence is less convincing. Some studies report marked variability between schools thus explaining inconsistent findings. Either way research suggests that it is not the activity of between-class ability grouping per se that leads to the observed small effects on achievement but rather its interaction with curriculum, classroom, and student characteristics.

A key attraction to the use of between-class ability grouping is that it enables instruction at a single level and direct instruction. However, ability groups are never completely homogenous and treating them as such can be problematic. A one-size-fits-all approach to instruction will tend to meet the needs of some students in the class while either constraining the learning of others or making them struggle to keep up. Without efficient and flexible structures to allow students to change groups, students may become disenchanted with learning. Research suggests that more could be done to make strategic and flexible use of within-class grouping practices for learning purposes. This may mean sometimes strategically mixing abilities for particular activities (e.g., peer-interactive learning) and at other times sustaining a more homogenous ability range to enable differentiation and support for students of all ability levels (e.g., through small-group instruction). When enmeshed with other pedagogic practices, such an approach may provide motivating, challenging, and mutually reinforcing instructional contexts that enhance student learning whilst engaging constructively with student diversity.

References

Baines, E., Blatchford, P., & Kutnick, P. (2003). Grouping practices in classrooms: Changing patterns over primary and secondary schooling. *International Journal of Educational Research, 39*, 9–34.

Blatchford, P., Kutnick, P., Baines, E., & Galton, M. (2003). Toward a social pedagogy of classroom group work. *International Journal of Educational Research, 39*, 153–172.

Boaler, J., Wiliam, D., & Brown, M. (2000). Students' experiences of ability grouping: Disaffection, polarisation and the construction of failure, *British Educational Research Journal, 26*, 631–648.

Hallinan, M. T., & Kubitschek, W. N. (1999). Curriculum differentiation and high school achievement. *Social Psychology of Education, 2*, 1–22.

Hattie, J. A. C. (2002). Classroom composition and peer effects. *International Journal of Educational Research, 37*, 449–481.

Ireson, J., & Hallam, S. (2001). *Ability grouping in education*. London: Chapman.

Ireson, J., Hallam, S., & Hurley, C. (2005). What are the effects of ability grouping on GCSE attainment? *British Educational Research Journal, 31*, 443–458

Kulik, C.-L., & Kulik, J. (1982). Effects of ability grouping on secondary school students: A meta-analysis of evaluation findings. *American Educational Research Journal, 19*, 415–428.

Lou, Y., Abrami, P., Spence, J., Chambers, B., Poulsen, C., & d'Apollonia, S. (1996). Within-class grouping: A meta-analysis. *Review of Educational Research, 66*, 423–458.

Oakes, J. (2005). *Keeping track: How schools structure inequality*. New Haven, CT: Yale University Press.

Organisation for Economic Co-operation and Development (OECD). (2010). *PISA 2009 Results: What makes a school successful? Resources, policies and practices* (Vol. 4). Paris: Author. Retrieved from http://dx.doi.org/10.1787/9789264091559-en

Schoffield, J. W. (2010). International evidence on ability grouping with curriculum differentiation and the achievement gap in secondary schools, *Teachers College Record, 112*, 1492–1528.

Slavin, R. (1987). Ability grouping and student achievement in the elementary schools: A best-evidence synthesis. *Review of Educational Research, 57*, 293–336.

Slavin, R. (1990). Ability grouping in secondary schools: A best-evidence synthesis. *Review of Educational Research, 60*, 471–499.

Wiliam, D., & Bartholomew, H. (2004). It's not which school but which set you're in that matters: the influence of ability grouping practices on student progress in mathematics. *British Educational Research Journal, 30*, 279–295.

4.3

Evaluating and Improving
Student–Teacher Interactions

Anne H. Cash and Bridget K. Hamre
School of Education, Johns Hopkins University

Introduction

School administrators today are charged with the challenging task of selecting and supporting a workforce of effective teachers. With the increased focus on teacher accountability there is much discussion and debate about how to identify effective teachers. As schools move away from the failed teacher evaluation systems in which almost all teachers are labeled as proficient (Weisberg et al., 2009), they have focused primarily on how to incorporate student test scores into teacher evaluation. Although there is clearly a need to hold teachers accountable for what students are learning, basing teacher evaluation solely on these metrics is problematic for several reasons. Most notably, student performance data do not provide guidance to administrators or teachers on what aspects of teacher practices need improvement. In this chapter, we describe data-based systems that school administrators can use to both identify and increase teacher practices that are associated with student achievement.

In recent years, research has shed light on exactly how and why teachers matter for students' achievement. Although some teacher practices are grade- or content-specific, other practices are crucial for students' development across contexts. For example, the nature and quality of teachers' interactions with students are linked to students' academic and social outcomes in the United States (Pianta, Belsky, Vandergrift, Houts, & Morrison, 2008) and internationally (Cadima, Leal, & Burchinal, 2010). Students who experience positive, supportive interactions with teachers and peers in the classroom make greater academic gains and exhibit fewer behavior problems (Mashburn et al., 2008). When teachers engage students in discussions that require higher order thinking skills, students understand concepts better (Peterson & French, 2008) and have increased language skills (Mashburn et al., 2008).

The challenge for school principals, then, is to harness what is known about good teaching and to build it into systems for teacher evaluation and professional development. Ideally, they would use validated evaluation tools that are based in research on effective teaching practices. Instead, in the United States and internationally, teacher evaluation often occurs informally, through activities like unstructured classroom observations and looking over lesson plans (Dymoke & Harrison, 2006; Weisberg et al., 2009). Observations are typically short and infrequent, and rarely are they tied to decisions on hiring, professional development, or compensation (Weisberg et al., 2009). In turn, professional development opportunities for in-service teachers vary widely in format, duration, and content, and relatively few demonstrate effectiveness in changing teacher practices or student outcomes (Garet, Porter, Desimone, Birman, & Yoon, 2001).

Research Evidence

Better tools for evaluation and professional development are available. A number of standardized and validated approaches for observing classrooms have been developed. Some of these are subject-specific, like the Protocol for Language Arts Teaching Observation (PLATO; Grossman et al., 2010). Other tools focus on teaching practices more broadly. The Classroom Assessment Scoring System (CLASS; Pianta, La Paro, & Hamre, 2008) is used to observe the quality of interactions among teachers and students and the climate of the classroom environment. Importantly, research documents the ways in which these observational systems assess components of the classroom setting that are linked to student achievement (Grossman et al., 2010; Pianta, Mashburn, Downer, Hamre, & Justice, 2008).

A number of professional development approaches that focus explicitly on teachers' classroom practices demonstrate effectiveness in changing practices and, in some cases, show corresponding effects on student achievement (e.g. Domitrovich et al., 2009; Mashburn, Downer, Hamre, Justice, & Pianta, 2010). Many of these systems include factors that teachers themselves report as important in changing practice—opportunities for active learning (such as opportunities to observe or be observed, plan implementation, review student work, or present to peers), alignment with state and district standards and assessments, and opportunities for professional discussions among teachers (Garet et al., 2001).

Given the existence of validated systems for observing teachers and a variety of approaches for increasing teachers' use of effective practices, an opportunity exists for schools to build data-based, integrated systems for evaluation and professional development. Administrators can use validated observation systems with confidence that the practices they are looking for are linked to student outcomes. They can also select formats for professional development that have demonstrated effectiveness for changing teacher practice. Importantly, active efforts to align evaluation and professional development systems across an entire school can facilitate discussion among teachers and administration about effective practices and create a context for improvement. Evaluation becomes more transparent and less intimidating when it is tied to practicable ideas for change that will improve the results of future evaluations. Professional development opportunities can be more engaging when teachers know that the material is both research-based and important for their evaluations.

As one example of how this type of system can work we will briefly describe work conducted by Pianta and colleagues in developing an aligned system of evaluation and improvement tools for schools. This work is based on an observational tool, the CLASS, which has been used in research for the past 10 years. The CLASS provides a framework for organizing the types of interactions teachers have with students that are mostly closely aligned with students' academic and social outcomes. The CLASS sorts these multifaceted interactions into three broad domains—Emotional Support, Classroom Organization, and Instructional Support—a conceptual structure which is supported by observational data in over 4,000 preschool and elementary classrooms (Hamre et al., 2011). Emotional Support captures the quality of relationships among teachers and students, teachers' awareness and responsiveness to students' emotional and academic needs, and support for students' interests and autonomy. Classroom Organization reflects teachers' use of proactive strategies to make behavioral expectations clear, skill at managing instructional time, and ability to promote and sustain student engagement and learning. Instructional Support incorporates teachers' strategies to develop students' content knowledge and higher order thinking skills, provide students with feedback, and facilitate instructional conversations. Importantly, the CLASS can be used across grades and subject matter within a school for two reasons. First, student–teacher interactions in this framework can be observed regardless of curricula or programs that are already in place. Second, there are separate versions of the CLASS available to observe prekindergarten, lower elementary, upper elementary, and secondary classroom settings. The versions share common domains of interactions but differ in more detailed descriptions of what the interactions look like by grade level.

The CLASS has been incorporated into several professional development approaches targeting student–teacher interactions. Three models have been developed and evaluated so far: coursework, coaching, and an online video library. Across all three formats, there is a focus on observing teaching practices of self and others in specific ways. This is in line with recent research showing that teachers can develop skills in observing their own and other teachers' classroom practice and that these observational skills are related to teachers' classroom interactions (Hamre, Pianta, Burchinal, & Downer, 2010). Similar work demonstrating the importance of observation has been conducted with preservice teachers in Italy (Santagata, Zannoni, & Stigler, 2007).

One form of professional development introduces teachers to the specific classroom practices assessed by the CLASS in a 14-week course (Hamre et al., 2010). Teachers study the importance of teacher-student interactions in promoting learning and learn to identify specific teacher-student interactions in observations of other teachers' practices. In-service prekindergarten teachers who took the course, compared to those randomly assigned to a control group, demonstrated more effective teaching (Hamre et al., 2010).

Another form of professional development, which was developed to align with the CLASS, is the MyTeaching-Partner (MTP) Coaching model. MTP uses the CLASS framework for the basis of ongoing, targeted discussion between coaches and teachers. Prekindergarten teachers exposed to this model showed increased use of effective teacher–student interactions (Pianta, Mashburn, Downer, Hamre, & Justice, 2008) and their students showed greater gains in language and literacy outcomes (Mashburn et al., 2010).

Opportunities for teachers to develop observation skills are also embedded in an online video library that provides video clips of effective teacher-student interactions. The CLASS provides the language to describe the teacher-student interactions evident in each real-world video exemplar. Exposure to the video library alone is associated with improvements in use of effective interactions (Pianta, Mashburn et al., 2008).

Although these professional development models have been primarily designed and tested in early childhood education settings, the formats are easily adapted for older grades using the elementary and secondary versions of the CLASS materials. A version of the MyTeachingPartner consultancy program is currently being evaluated for use in secondary school settings. The point here is that professional development can take a variety of formats—coursework, coaching, or even independent work on the web—each of which has demonstrated effectiveness. What has worked well in these cases is alignment of professional development with the CLASS, a validated observation tool, and a focus on observing and replicating effective teacher-student interactions.

Summary and Recommendations

Standardized, validated systems for observing and supporting teachers can be very useful for administrators seeking to increase teachers' use of effective practices schoolwide. They provide a platform for school staff to observe, identify, and discuss effective teaching. Instead of relying on what can be overwhelming amounts of information on what qualifies as "good" teaching, administrators who choose validated observational systems can focus on key practices with demonstrated links to student achievement. The benefits of a validated system often outweigh those of district- or school-specific measures because there is a greater chance that validated approaches will lead to student outcomes of interest.

There is still research to be done to determine best practices for aligning observation systems with systems for improvement. For example, most observation systems do not currently recommend specific scores for which teachers should be hired, supported, or fired. But validated systems of observation do provide rich information about teacher practices across grade levels and opportunities to increase teacher effectiveness as well as student achievement.

References

Cadima, J., Leal, T., & Burchinal, M. (2010). The quality of teacher–student interactions: Associations with first graders' academic and behavioral outcomes. *Journal of School Psychology, 48*(6), 457–482. doi: 10.1016/j.jsp.2010.09.001

Domitrovich, C. E., Gest, S. D., Gill, S., Bierman, K. L., Welsh, J. A., & Jones, D. (2009). Fostering high-quality teaching with an enriched curriculum and professional development support: The Head Start REDI program. *American Educational Research Journal, 46*(2), 567–597. doi:10.3102/0002831208328089

Dymoke, S., & Harrison, J. K. (2006). Professional development and the beginning teacher: Issues of teacher autonomy and institutional conformity in the performance review process. *Journal of Education for Teaching, 32*(1), 71–92.

Garet, M. S., Porter, A. C., Desimone, L., Birman, B. F., & Yoon, K. S. (2001). What makes professional development effective? Results from a national sample of teachers. *American Educational Research Journal, 38*(4), 915–945.

Grossman, P., Loeb, S., Cohen, J., Hammerness, K., Wyckoff, J., Boyd, D., & Lankford, H. (2010). *Measure for measure: The relationship between measures of instructional practice in middle school English language arts and teachers' value-added scores* (No. 45). Washington, DC: National Center for Analysis of Longitudinal Data in Education Research.

Hamre, B. K., Pianta, R. C., Burchinal, M., & Downer, J. T. (2010). *A course on supporting early language and literacy development through effective teacher–child interactions: Effects on teacher beliefs, knowledge and practice.* Washington, DC: Society for Research on Educational Effectiveness.

Hamre, B. K., Pianta, R. C., Downer, J. T., Hakigami, A., Mashburn, A. J., Jones, S. M., ... Brackett, M. A. (2011). *Teaching through interactions—Testing a developmental framework of teacher effectiveness in over 4,000 classrooms.* Manuscript submitted for publication.

Mashburn, A. J., Downer, J. T., Hamre, B. K., Justice, L. M., & Pianta, R. C. (2010). Teaching consultation and children's language and literacy development during pre-kindergarten. *Applied Developmental Science, 14*(4), 179–198.

Mashburn, A. J., Pianta, R. C., Hamre, B. K., Downer, J. T., Barbarin, O. A., Bryant, D., ... Howes, C. (2008). Measures of classroom quality in prekindergarten and children's development of academic, language, and social skills. *Child Development, 79*(3), 732–749.

Peterson, S. M., & French, L. (2008). Supporting young children's explanations through inquiry science in preschool. *Early Childhood Research Quarterly, 23*(3), 395–408.

Pianta, R. C., Belsky, J., Vandergrift, N., Houts, R., & Morrison, F. J. (2008). Classroom effects on children's achievement trajectories in elementary school. *American Educational Research Journal, 45*(2), 365–397. doi:10.3102/0002831207308230

Pianta, R. C., La Paro, K. M., & Hamre, B. K. (2008). *Classroom assessment scoring system.* Baltimore, MD: Brookes.

Pianta, R. C., Mashburn, A. J., Downer, J. T., Hamre, B. K., & Justice, L. (2008). Effects of web-mediated professional development resources on teacher–child interactions in pre-kindergarten classrooms. *Early Childhood Research Quarterly, 23*(4), 431–451. doi: 10.1016/j.ecresq.2008.02.001

Santagata, R., Zannoni, C., & Stigler, J. W. (2007). The role of lesson analysis in pre-service teacher education: An empirical investigation of teacher learning from a virtual video-based field experience. *Journal of Mathematics Teacher Education, 10*(2), 123–140.

Weisberg, D., Sexton, S., Mulhern, J., Keeling, D., Schunk, J., Palcisco, A., & Morgan, K. (2009). *The widget effect: Our national failure to acknowledge and act on differences in teacher effectiveness.* Brooklyn, NY: The New Teacher Project.

4.4

Mixed-Grade Elementary-School Classes and Student Achievement

LINLEY CORNISH
University of New England

Introduction

The entrenched and widespread lockstep system of schooling, where students are locked into a year or grade based on age and "step" forward with their age peers, means there is a general perception that single-grade classes are the norm. Yet mixed-grade classes of one sort or another have always been common and typically still account for one quarter to one third of all classes in developed countries and more in developing countries. Such classes are mostly formed by necessity, because of insufficient students (as in remote rural areas), insufficient teachers, or uneven grade enrolments. Some mixed-grade classes, however, are formed by choice.

The issue of terminology is particularly pertinent when trying to separate findings for the different types of mixed-grade class in elementary schools: nongraded, multiage, multigrade, composite, and stage classes. Each has different contextual characteristics that could potentially influence student achievement. Yet characteristics of these classes have traditionally not been well described in research publications; therefore, it is not always possible to clarify which type of class is being studied. Although secondary schools also sometimes have mixed-age, mixed-grade classes (e.g., vertical semester organisation), they are not discussed here.

Research Evidence

Nongraded Classes. Nongraded classes are formed by choice because of a belief in the educational benefits of diversity, including interactions with younger and older classmates, and of learning based on individual need or preference. Students are not identified by their age or grade. Achievement in nongraded classes seems on the whole to be better than achievement in single-grade classes, as perhaps should be expected from a concentration on individual learning needs and developmentally appropriate curriculum.

For example, Kim (1996, unpublished EdD thesis cited in Hattie, 2009) found low positive effects for nongraded classes in 98 studies. Anderson and Pavan (1993) analyzed 64 studies from 1968 to 1990 comparing nongraded and graded classes; in 58% of studies, academic achievement was better in nongraded classes, in 33% there were no differences related to the type of class, and in 9% achievement was better in graded classes: "boys, blacks, underachievers, and students of lower socioeconomic status were more likely to perform better…the longer pupils were in nongraded programs, the greater the improvement in their achievement scores in relation to ability" (p. 53). Pavan conducted an (unpublished) update to 86 studies in 2000 and to 91 in 2004 and found "that my earlier conclusions have not been challenged" (personal communication August 23, 2010).

Gutiérrez and Slavin (1992) published a best-evidence synthesis for four different types of nongraded programs:

1. In Joplin Plan arrangements, students were ability grouped for one subject (most commonly reading). There were "substantial positive results in favor of the nongraded program. The median effect size (ES) for the four best-quality studies was +.50; for all studies from which effect sizes could be estimated, it is +.46" (p. 13).

2. In comprehensive programs, multiple subjects were ability-grouped. Results again consistently favored the nongraded program with "higher positive differences related to increase in duration of the program" (Lloyd, 1999, p. 193).

3. No significant differences were found for programs which incorporated individualized instruction in the form of learning centers, activity packages, programmed instruction, or one-on-one tutoring. Better results were obtained for longer lasting programs, as well as for older students.

4. Individually Guided Education (IGE) was a more developed form of (3), involving individualized learning plans. Whereas overall results did not favor IGE, Gutiérrez and Slavin cautioned that the degree of implementa-

tion of IGE varied a lot and some studies reported very favorable results (one with an ES of +.80).

Multiage Classes.   Multiage classes are a less-developed form of nongraded classes. They consist of children from at least two but commonly three school grades or years. Students usually have the same teacher for 2 or 3 years as they progress from being a younger to a middle to an older learner. A student's association with grade is nominal only, though some grade-specific activities do occur (e.g., standardized tests, grade excursions). The permanence of the class and the teacher are crucial, allowing for an ongoing focus on each child's learning needs. Thus students work up or down or at their nominal grade level for different subjects, in flexible learning groups which are usually mixed age. A teacher might use ability groups for some mathematics and perhaps language lessons but heterogeneous groups with open-ended learning tasks are common. Since students all progress at different speeds based on their current learning needs and development, they are not prepared for grade-based tests in the way that students in a single-grade class are, which makes comparisons of achievement potentially problematic. There have been two major reviews of worldwide multiage classes, both by Simon Veenman: a best-evidence synthesis (1995) and a meta-analysis of the same data with a few extra studies (1996). In both cases, the result of an essentially zero effect size was found; that is, there was no significant difference in achievement between multiage and single-grade classes.

Multigrade Classes.   Multigrade classes are formed by necessity. They are typically found in rural schools and are usually permanent because the total enrolment in the school is never large enough to form single-grade classes. A multigrade school might have only one seventh-grade class or several two- to fifth-grade classes varying from very small to full-sized. Students usually have the same teacher and many of the same classmates for a number of years.

Veenman's reviews also included analyses for multigrade classes. In his 1995 analysis of 38 studies (1938 to 1995), Veenman reported "no consistent differences" between achievement in multigrade and single-grade classes; for the 34 studies from which ESs could be estimated, he found a median ES of .00 (Veenman, 1995). His reanalysis in 1996 included 45 studies. A series of analyses that included and excluded outliers and zeros did "not drastically alter the mean effect sizes. Overall, the results show that there is no significant difference" in achievement between multigrade and single-grade classes (Veenman, 1996, p. 329).

Veenman did find some between-country differences, with a small positive effect for studies conducted in the United States ($d = .05$) and Canada ($d = .08$) and a small negative effect for studies conducted in Europe ($d = -.05$) (Veenman, 1996, p. 331). Differences were also found for grade level ($N = 34$), with a small positive effect for lower grades (K-2), an essentially zero effect for middle grades

(3-4) and a small negative effect for higher grades (5-6) (Veenman, 1996, p. 333).

Composite or Combination Classes.   Composite or combination classes are a subset of multigrade classes, usually found in urban and suburban schools. They are also formed by necessity when the formation of full-sized classes results in some leftover students who are then combined into a composite/combination class. The temporary nature of the classes means they are viewed with suspicion or hostility by parents (Cornish, 2006; Pratt & Treacy, 1986). To appease parents, principals often deliberately select particular students or teachers for composite classes (Burns & Mason, 1998). The selection bias is based on ability and maturity, with a strong preference for medium to high ability students who can work independently and not be disruptive. When this happens, claims about achievement need even more careful interpretation, not only because the composite class is specially selected but also because single-grade classes in the same school are concomitantly disadvantaged. Yet details about how the composite class was formed are rarely provided in reported studies.

Veenman (1995) was criticized by Mason and Burns (1996) who argued that there is a negative effect on achievement in composite classes (1996, 1997a, 1997b) and that the "no difference" result is obtained because the negative effects on achievement are balanced out by positive effects resulting from selection bias of students and possibly also of teachers. Their claims of reduced achievement were largely based on the increased difficulty of teaching a composite class and reduced teacher time with each grade. They reported five U.S. empirical studies where the combination classes were formed by "nonpurposeful assignment"; that is, with no selection bias. Four of the studies "provided some evidence favoring single-grade classes, with the other study showing no difference" (estimated ES = −.1) (1997a, p. 40). The small number of studies and the lack of strong evidence favoring single-grade classes do not conclusively support their argument that the more difficult teaching environment in combination classes leads to a decrease in student achievement.

Studies of multigrade classes, including Veenman's analyses, usually include composite classes, as evidenced by descriptions of "urban multigrade classes." However Veenman's reanalysis (1996) showed only very small differences between rural multigrade classes ($d = +.10$) and (sub)urban composite classes ($d = +.06$) (p. 335).

Sims (2008) provides strong support for Mason and Burns's hypothesis of a decrease in achievement in composite classes. His analysis of second- and third-grade results in the mathematics and language sections of state-wide standardized tests in California showed that "combination classes have an unambiguously negative effect on student achievement and the effect is greater for third graders than second graders" (p. 477).

On the other hand, Wilkinson and Hamilton (2003) tested 484 students from grades 2 to 6 in nine different schools in New Zealand, with one composite and one single-grade class from each school and no selection bias in allocation of students to classes. Differences between the single-grade and composite classes were minimal. The authors concluded that their findings "call into question Mason and Burns's theory concerning the possible negative effects of multi-grade classes … and they are consistent with Veenman's conclusion that the effects are benign" (p. 234).

Stage Classes.   Stage classes are formed by choice when syllabus documents are written for 2-year stages rather than 1-year grades. Classes based on 2 years give more stability as enrolments change (Lloyd, 1997; Sims, 2008), more continuity because a teacher usually stays with the class for 2 years, and economic benefits because fewer classes need to be formed. There are no published achievement studies which clearly relate to stage classes, so very little can be noted with confidence about them.

Summary and Recommendations

Studies of achievement in mixed-grade classes show that achievement is not negatively affected by being in such a class. Unless the particular type of mixed-grade class is specified, however, particular claims need to be interpreted with caution. What goes on inside the classroom is more important than the type of class. Because of the different contextual factors related to the different types of mixed-age class, what goes on inside the classroom differs. The results for nongraded classes are positive. Results from the other types of mixed-grade class show essentially "no difference" from single-grade classes, though there is dispute about achievement in composite classes. Readers need to exercise caution when interpreting the different studies and researchers need to clearly distinguish multigrade classes from their subset composite classes, and to determine whether there was selection bias in the formation of the classes.

References

Anderson, R. H., & Pavan, B. N. (1993). *Nongradedness: Helping it to happen*. Lancaster, PA: Technomic.

Burns, R. B., & Mason, D. A. (1998). Class formation and composition in elementary schools. *American Educational Researcher, 35*(4), 739–772.

Cornish, L. (2006). Parents' views of composite classes in an Australian primary school. *The Australian Educational Researcher, 33*(2), 123–142.

Gutiérrez, R., & Slavin, R. E. (1992). *Achievement effects of the nongraded elementary school: A retrospective review* (pp. iii, 1–46). Baltimore, MD: Johns Hopkins University, Center for Research on Effective Schooling for Disadvantaged Students.

Hattie, J. A. C. (2009). *Visible learning; A synthesis of over 800 meta-analyses relating to achievement*. London: Routledge.

Lloyd, L. (1997). Composite classes and teachers' beliefs. *Asia-Pacific Journal of Teacher Education, 25*(3), 225–259.

Lloyd, L. (1999). Multi-age classes and high ability students. *Review of Educational Research, 69*(2), 187–212.

Mason, D. A., & Burns, R. B. (1996). "Simply no worse and simply no better" may simply be wrong: A critique of Veenman's conclusion about multigrade classes. *Review of Educational Research, 66*(3), 307–322.

Mason, D. A., & Burns, R. B. (1997a). Reassessing the effects of combination classes. *Educational Research and Evaluation, 3*(1), 1–53.

Mason, D. A., & Burns, R. B. (1997b). Toward a theory of combination classes. *Educational Research and Evaluation, 3*(4), 281–304.

Pratt, C., & Treacy, K. (1986). *A study of student grouping practices in early childhood classes in Western Australian government primary schools* (pp. 1–60). Co-operative Research Series Report No.9. Perth: Education Department of Western Australia.

Sims, D. (2008). A strategic response to class size reduction: Combination classes and student achievement in California. *Journal of Policy Analysis and Management, 27*(3), 457–478.

Veenman, S. (1995). Cognitive and noncognitive effects of multigrade and multi-age classes: A best-evidence synthesis. *Review of Educational Research, 65*(4), 319–381.

Veenman, S. (1996). Effects of multigrade and multi-age classes reconsidered. *Review of Educational Research, 66*(3), 323–340.

Wilkinson, I. A. G., & Hamilton, R. J. (2003). Learning to read in composite (multigrade) classes in New Zealand: Teachers make the difference. *Teaching and Teacher Education, 19*(2), 221–235.

4.5

School-Based Mental Health

Erin Dowdy, Matthew P. Quirk, and Jenna K. Chin
University of California, Santa Barbara

Introduction

The term *school-based mental health* generally refers to the delivery of any type of mental health services within a school setting. However, the term is in need of a clearer conceptual framework due to the variety of settings in which services are offered, including within classrooms, entire schools, or through external programs linked to schools, and due to the variety of personnel providing services, such as psychologists, social workers, psychiatric nurses, therapists, and counselors (Adelman & Taylor, 2003). More fundamentally, the term *mental health* is plagued with ambiguity. Although mental "health" is a positive concept, it is often used in reference to mental illness and encompasses services provided to those with diagnosable mental disorders or other serious psychopathology. Emerging research on "dual-factor" models of mental health suggest that mental illness and mental wellness are not on a single continuum, but rather are separate, complementary constructs (Suldo & Shaffer, 2008). Thus, an individual's "mental health" may be best understood when considering both strengths as well as deficits, and school-based mental health services should encompass both wellness-enhancing and symptom-reduction goals.

Despite the lack of definitional clarity, the perceived need for and establishment of school-based mental health services exists across nations. Schools often become the de facto mental health care system for many children and adolescents (Farmer, Burns, Phillips, Angold, & Costello, 2003). Since children in many countries are required to attend schools, behavioral and emotional difficulties often become apparent and impact functioning within the school setting. Currently, school based mental health services are the most commonly accessed services for youth with mental health problems in the United States (Farmer et al., 2003) due to both accessibility and perceived acceptability (Leaf, Schultz, Kiser, & Pruitt, 2003).

Research Evidence

Research conducted over the past decade has provided evidence supporting the efficacy of multiple school-based mental health service delivery frameworks, including systems of care (Leaf et al., 2003), three-tiered models (Bradley, Doolittle, & Bartolotta, 2008), and policy vision frameworks (Adelman & Taylor, 2003). This research, along with recent legislation, advocacy efforts, and changes to educational policies (e.g., International Alliance for Child and Adolescent Mental Health and Schools, 2003), has resulted in an increased focus on addressing children's mental health needs in schools. School-based mental health services have since been established for a variety of purposes including prevention, crisis intervention, early intervention, treatment, and the promotion of positive emotional and social development (Adelman & Taylor, 2003).

The increased attention on school-based mental health has also been driven, at least in part, by research clearly showing relations between children's social and emotional well-being and academic achievement. Students with emotional and behavioral disorders experience low overall academic achievement, as measured by achievement test scores (Bradley et al., 2008). The academic differences between students functioning well (in terms of their behavioral and emotional health) and those that are not functioning well are quite drastic. Specifically, estimates suggest that 75% of students with significant emotional and behavioral problems in the United States are achieving below expected grade levels in reading and 97% are below expected grade levels in math (Bradley et al., 2008). International studies have found similar results demonstrating moderate correlations between emotional and behavioral problems and poor academic performance (e.g., Lipps et al., 2010). Therefore, the inverse relation between academic achievement and mental health problems appears to be pervasive across nations.

Whereas behavioral and emotional problems are significant barriers to academic achievement, positive behavioral and emotional health is associated with academic success (e.g., Ryland, Lundervold, Elgen, & Hysing, 2010). Yet these relations should not be interpreted in isolation. Meta-analyses show that learning is influenced by a variety of both proximal (e.g., psychological, instructional, and home environments) and distal (e.g., economic, organizational, and policy) factors (Wang, Haertel, & Walberg, 1993) and that academic success can be attributed to the constellation and interplay of multiple variables. Studies have suggested some specific moderating variables that further explain the relation between behavioral and emotional problems and academic achievement. For example, students who have stronger relationships with their teachers and higher classroom engagement (Hughes, Luo, Kwok, & Loyd, 2008) experience more favorable academic outcomes. In addition, international studies have found that academic outcomes are influenced by peer dropouts (Rosenblum, Goldblatt, & Moin, 2008), student-reported problems with teachers (Rodrigo et al., 2010), and low perceived parental support (Siziya, Muula, & Rudatsikira, 2007). Students with higher intellectual functioning have also been shown to have a "protective effect" for mental health, being significantly less likely to have a psychiatric disorder compared to students with lower intellectual functioning (Ryland et al., 2010). These variables, among others, should be considered in the conceptualization of emotional and behavioral problems, as well as in the formulation of interventions.

Although it is difficult to determine if behavioral problems lead to underachievement or vice versa (Bradley et al., 2008), the relation can be explained, in part, by examining the reduced exposure to instruction that often co-occurs with emotional and behavioral difficulties. Students with emotional and behavioral problems exhibit behaviors which often lead to less instructional exposure. For example, students with emotional and behavioral problems experience higher rates of suspensions (Bradley et al., 2008). Research has replicated these trends internationally showing that youth with emotional and behavioral problems suffer from missed instructional time manifested by lower school enrollment rates and higher rates of truancy (e.g., Siziya et al., 2007). Additionally, students with emotional and behavioral problems drop out of school at alarmingly higher rates than the general population. For example, U.S. national longitudinal studies show that more than half of students identified as having significant emotional or behavioral problems leave the educational system by dropping out, and of those that do remain in school, only 42% graduate with a diploma (Bradley et al., 2008). Studies conducted in other countries have found similar relations, demonstrating that students with psychological problems are more likely to drop out (e.g., Borovoy, 2008).

Summary and Recommendations

Despite the growing support for the provision of school-based mental health services, there remain some criticisms. Critics often express concerns that schools are not the appropriate place for mental health services, claiming that they fall outside of the scope of the educational system (Adelman & Taylor, 2003). These concerns stem from fears that academic instructional time may be compromised by time spent dealing with mental health issues and that the mental health of students should not be a primary concern of educators. However, if services are not provided within the schools many students will not receive mental health treatment; research implies that this can lead to significant emotional and financial costs for children, families, schools, and society (Bradley et al., 2008). In fact, research consistently shows that school mental health programming leads to improved educational outcomes, such as decreased absences, discipline referrals, and improved test scores (Collaborative for Academic, Social, and Emotional Learning [CASEL], 2008). Critics also fear that familial rights and values could be infringed upon (Adelman & Taylor, 2003). However, schools are advised to collaborate with families, as they are essential partners when providing mental health services within the schools (Leaf et al., 2003).

In response to common criticisms of school-based mental health services, Adelman and Taylor (2003) suggest that to potentially have the greatest impact on educational reform, a policy rationale connecting with the mission of schools is needed. The recommendation is that while schools may not be required to address the mental health needs of all students, when the mental health needs directly affect student learning then schools must intervene. Specifically, schools are responsible for addressing barriers to student learning (Adelman & Taylor, 2003; Leaf et al., 2003). By adopting a unified and cohesive policy approach, school-based mental health services can continue to benefit students in need.

Schools, teachers, parents, and researchers acknowledging the importance of mental health services are advised to: provide a comprehensive array of services (i.e., not only services for mental illness), provide individualized services to reduce the child's barriers to learning, promote early identification and early intervention services, provide services within the least restrictive environment, involve families in the planning and delivery of services, and integrate all services provided through various agencies both within the school and community (Leaf et al., 2003). Additionally, the importance of classroom climate and connectedness, which can be achieved as part of the continuum of mental health services provided, deserves attention as findings support a relation with improved academic performance (Hughes et al., 2008). In summary, a variety of research supports that school-based mental health services positively affect academic outcomes (e.g., CASEL, 2008) and the delivery of these services should be advocated for to improve the overall functioning of students and schools.

References

Adelman, H. S., & Taylor, L. (2003). Toward a comprehensive policy vision for mental health in schools. In M. D. Weist, S. W. Evans, & N. A. Lever (Eds.), *Handbook of school mental health: Advancing practice and research* (pp. 23–43). New York: Kluwer Academic/Plenum .

Borovoy, A. (2008). Japan's hidden youths: Mainstreaming the emotionally distressed in Japan. *Culture, Medicine, and Psychiatry, 32*, 552–576. doi: 10.1007/s11013-008-9106-2

Bradley, R., Doolittle, J., & Bartolotta, R. (2008). Building on the data and adding to the discussion: The experiences and outcomes of students with emotional disturbance. *Journal of Behavioral Education, 17*, 4–23. doi:10.1007/s10864-007-9058-6

Collaborative for Academic, Social, and Emotional Learning (CASEL). (2008). *Benefits of SEL.* Retrieved http://casel.org/why-it-matters/benefits-of-sel/_

Farmer, E. M. Z., Burns, B. J., Phillips, S. D., Angold, A., & Costello, E. J. (2003). Pathways into and through mental health services for children and adolescents. *Psychiatric Services, 54*, 60–66. doi:10.1176/appi.ps.54.1.60

Hughes, J. N., Luo, W., Kwok, O., & Loyd, L. K. (2008). Teacher–student support, effortful engagement, and achievement: A 3-year longitudinal study. *Journal of Educational Psychology, 100*(1), 1–14. doi:10.1037/0022-0663.100.1.1

International Alliance for Child and Adolescent Mental Health and Schools. (2003). Retrieved from http://www.intercamhs.org/

Leaf, P. J., Schultz, D., Kiser, L. J., & Pruitt, D. B. (2003). School mental health in systems of care. In M. D. Weist, S. W. Evans, & N. A. Lever (Eds.), *Handbook of school mental health: Advancing practice and research* (pp. 239–256). New York: Kluwer Academic/Plenum.

Lipps, G. E., Lowe, G. A., Halliday, S., Morris-Patterson, A., Clarke, N., & Wilson, R. N. (2010). The association of academic tracking to depressive symptoms among adolescents in three Caribbean countries. *Child & Adolescent Psychiatry & Mental Health, 4*(16), 1–10. doi:10.1186/1753-2000-4-16

Rodrigo, C., Welgama, S., Gurusinghe, J., Wijeratne, T., Jayananda, G., & Rajapakse, S. (2010). Symptoms of anxiety and depression in adolescent students: A perspective from Sri Lanka, *Child and Adolescent Psychiatry and Mental Health, 4*(10), 1–3. doi: 10.1186/1753-2000-4-10

Rosenblum, S., Goldblatt, H., & Moin, V. (2008). The hidden dropout phenomenon among immigrant high-school students: The case of Ethiopian adolescents in Israel—A pilot study. *School Psychology International, 29*(105), 105–127. doi: 10.1177/0143034307088506

Ryland, H. K., Lundervold, A. J., Elgen, I., & Hysing, M. (2010). Is there a protective effect of normal to high intellectual function on mental health in children with chronic illness? *Child and Adolescent Psychiatry & Mental Health, 4*(3), 1–8.

Siziya, S., Muula, A. S., & Rudatsikira, E. (2007). Prevalence and correlates of truancy among adolescents in Swaziland: findings from the Global School-Based Health Survey. *Child and Adolescent Psychiatry and Mental Health, 1*(15), 1–8. doi:10.1186/1753-2000-1-15

Suldo, S. M., & Shaffer, E. J. (2008). Looking beyond psychopathology: The dual-factor model of mental health in youth. *School Psychology Review, 37*, 52–68.

Wang, M. C., Haertel, G. D., & Walberg, H. J. (1993). Toward a knowledge base for school learning. *Review of Educational Research, 63*(3), 249–294. doi:10.2307/1170546

4.6

Achievement in Faith-Based Schools

L. MICKEY FENZEL
Loyola University Maryland

Introduction

In response to a growing concern about the continuing decline in the number of faith-based (also referred to as parochial) schools, the U.S. Department of Education issued a report from the White House in 2008 that underscored the benefits to communities and students, particularly students in urban, low-income communities, provided by faith-based K-12 schools. According to this report, these schools provide a safe and structured environment and academic rigor that leads to high levels of academic achievement for children placed at risk.

This document reported that, according to the National Center for Education Statistics, in the 2005–2006 school year, there were more than 22,000 faith-based schools in operation and that these schools represented 17% of the K-12 schools in the United States, more than three times the number of nonreligious affiliated private schools. Assuring strong faith-based schools was noted in the report as essential also to stabilizing communities and attracting new families and jobs.

Research Evidence

Led by the early work of Coleman, Hoffer, and Kilgore (1982), considerable research over the past 30 years has sought to determine whether students who attend religious and other private schools achieve at higher levels than do students at public schools and, if such differences exist, what characteristics of these schools account for the achievement differences. Whereas some research (e.g., Bryk, Holland, & Lee, 1993; Coleman et al., 1984; Jeynes, 2005, 2008) has identified an academic achievement advantage for private schools over public schools, even when controlling for student background characteristics, other studies (e.g., Braun, Jenkins, & Grigg, 2006; Wenglinski, 2007) suggest that such differences either do not exist or are minimal.

The work of Wenglinski (2007) is particularly noteworthy for two reasons: it provides a longitudinal analysis for predicting 12th-grade achievement using 8th-grade achievement scores (using data from the National Educational Longitudinal Study; NELS) and it recognizes several categories of nonpublic schools, including Catholic diocesan, Catholic religious order, non-Catholic religious, and independent private schools. Controlling for family socioeconomic status and parental involvement indicators, this research found no general private school benefit in 12th-grade achievement, except for Catholic religious order schools in reading, mathematics, and history achievement. Additional analyses showed that students in Catholic religious order schools and independent private schools outperformed public school students on verbal SAT college entrance exams, after controlling for family background characteristics.

Two studies (Braun et al., 2006; Jeynes, 2008) examined effects of different types of religious schools on student achievement. In their examination of differences in National Assessment of Education Progress (NAEP) scores of fourth and eighth graders, Braun et al. found that average difference in adjusted mean mathematics scores was significantly higher for Lutheran schools and significantly lower for Conservative Christian schools when compared to all public schools. Catholic school scores in mathematics were higher than those of public schools only when adjustments for student characteristics were not included. With respect to overall reading achievement, both Catholic and Lutheran schools scored higher than public schools with and without adjustments.

Jeynes (2008), in a meta-analysis of 41 studies, found an overall religious school advantage over public schools in student achievement with most effect sizes in the .15 to .30 range, with similar advantages for Catholic and Protestant school students. Further analyses showed that Protestant school students generally performed better on standardized achievement tests (with most studies reporting large national data sets such as NELS and NAEP) and less well on nonstandardized achievement measures when compared to Catholic school students. Jeynes (2008) argued that examining differences in achievement and educational practices in Catholic and Protestant schools could inform educators of best practices that could contribute to further improvement of faith-based education, as well as public education. However, the racial/ethnic, socioeconomic, and geographic diversity of these schools and their students may make it difficult to identify best practices that would be effective in different schools.

The faith-based school advantage is not limited to the United States, as research in Great Britain (Morris, 2009), Australia (Marks, 2009), and Denmark (Schindler Rangvid, 2008) has shown. For example, students in Australian Catholic schools and other private schools scored higher on university entrance exams when compared to students in government schools, and Danish students in Catholic, but not Protestant, schools attained higher levels of education when compared to public schools. The British study (Morris, 2009) cited the ability of Catholic schools to generate an environment more favorable to academic achievement as a possible reason for the consistently greater performance of primary and secondary Catholic school students on government measures of school success.

In an earlier meta-analytic study using NELS data, Jeynes (2005) found that students in the lowest SES quartile who attended religious schools achieved at higher levels when compared to low SES students in public schools. In addition, the religious school advantage was significantly greater for students in the lowest SES quartile than for students in other SES groups, as well as for students in middle school and high school.

Determining just what characteristics of faith-based schools contribute to higher student achievement and achievement gains, to the extent to which these exist, has been a difficult task, although several researchers have identified or suggested some of the school characteristics. For example, from their analyses of the 1980 National Center for Educational Statistics (NCES) High School and Beyond study data, Coleman et al. (1982) found that the characteristic with the greatest influence on student achievement was students' perceptions of the behavioral climate of the school with respect to lower levels of student absenteeism, fighting, and threatening behavior toward teachers. The amount of homework assigned reported by students was also related to achievement.

In his review of the research literature on the factors that contribute to the higher levels of academic achievement of students in faith-based schools, Jeynes (2002) identified five school traits—school atmosphere (including a "positive school spirit" and teachers who showed interest in students), more homework assigned, lower levels of violence and the threat of violence, a higher level of racial harmony, and the kinds of discipline employed. His analysis of 1992 NELS data for 12th graders showed, first, that religious (or faith-based) schools differed significantly from secular schools

(both private and public) on measures of all five traits, with the largest effects for racial harmony and school atmosphere. In addition, when these five factors were included in multivariate analyses, more assigned homework, greater racial harmony, and less school violence were significantly related to academic achievement. Further analyses conducted by Jeynes (2002) suggested that religious schools may be better than public schools in urban settings in promoting greater racial harmony and reducing school violence. In addition, Morris (2009) identified Catholic schools as generally providing an environment that students perceive as being more supportive, mission focused, and oriented toward academic success.

Consistent with the research (Jeynes, 2005) that suggests a particular academic (and social) benefit for urban students of color from high poverty neighborhoods who attend religious or faith-based schools, is research on NativityMiguel middle schools (Fenzel, 2009; Fenzel & Monteith, 2008; Podsiadlo & Philliber, 2003). These schools, which number over 60 throughout the United States educate urban children who are at risk, and who are placed in small schools with small classes, with an extended day and year for additional study and academic support. They also engage parents and support their graduates through high school and into college. A study of 11 NativityMiguel schools in seven cities found that the students achieved at higher levels on national standardized tests of verbal and mathematical achievement, and demonstrated greater gains in achievement, when compared to students at urban public and diocesan Catholic schools (Fenzel, 2009; Fenzel & Monteith, 2008). In addition, this research suggested that school climate factors that favored the NativityMiguel schools over the comparison schools and contributed to higher levels of academic engagement and success included students' perceptions of the school as being enjoyable with rules that were fair, peer relationships as being friendly and supportive, and their teachers as supportive, task-oriented, and caring. In addition, analyses showed that the supportive climate of NativityMiguel schools contributed to students' perceptions of their intrinsic motivation for school work and their academic engagement and success (Fenzel & O'Brennan, 2007).

A report from the Fordham Institute (Hamilton, 2008) cited several examples of independent network and diocesan efforts that have provided high-quality Catholic schools that educate urban children and adolescents placed at risk because of economic poverty. In addition to acknowledging NativityMiguel schools among these effective endeavors, the report (Hamilton, 2008; Meyer, 2008) also identified Cristo Rey high schools as highly successful faith-based initiatives that raise the levels of academic achievement and attainment of low-income urban students of color. In addition to small class sizes, a rigorous college preparatory course of study, and effective instruction and individual attention, Cristo Rey schools provide a unique corporate work study program. The Fordham report identified these successful urban initiatives as examples of ways that Catholic schools are contributing much to improving the levels of academic achievement and attainment of Catholic and non-Catholic urban children and adolescents.

Summary and Recommendations

The growing body of research on faith-based schools suggests that schools sponsored by religious orders are particularly effective at improving academic achievement and attainment of students—and urban children and adolescents from low-income families in particular. Factors that distinguish these schools are small classes for instruction, a rigorous curriculum, and extended school day and year that provide needed support to help students advance their academic skills. In addition, these schools, such as NativityMiguel and Cristo Rey schools, provide a supportive and violence-free environment that enables students to focus on academic skill development and develop a stronger motivation to succeed.

References

Braun, H., Jenkins, F., & Grigg, W. (2006). *Comparing private schools and public schools using hierarchical linear modeling* (NCES 2006-461). Washington, DC: U.S. Department of Education.

Bryk, A. S., Holland, P. B., & Lee, V. E. (1993). *Catholic schools and the common good.* Cambridge, MA: Harvard University Press.

Coleman, J., Hoffer, T., & Kilgore, S. (1982). Cognitive outcomes in public and private schools. *Sociology of Education, 55*, 65–76. Retrieved from http://www.jstor.org/stable/2112288

Fenzel, L. M. (2009). *Improving urban middle schools: Lessons from the Nativity schools.* Albany, NY: State University of New York Press.

Fenzel, L. M., & Monteith, R. H. (2008). Successful alternative middle schools for urban minority children: A study of Nativity schools. *Journal of Education for Students Placed at Risk, 13*, 381–401. doi: 10.1080/10824660802427686

Fenzel, L. M., & O'Brennan, L. M. (2007, April). *Educating at-risk urban African American children: The effects of school climate on motivation and academic achievement.* Paper presented at the annual meeting of the American Educational Research Association, Chicago.

Hamilton, S. W., Ed. (2008). *Who will save America's urban Catholic schools?* Washington, DC: Thomas Fordham Institute. Retrieved from http://www.edexcellence.net

Jeynes, W. H. (2002). Why religious schools positively impact the academic achievement of children. *International Journal of Education and Religion, 3*, 16–32.

Jeynes, W. H. (2005). The impact of religious school on the academic achievement of low-SES students. *Journal of Empirical Theology, 18*, 22–40.

Jeynes, W. H. (2008). The effects of Catholic and Protestant schools: A meta-analysis. *Catholic Education: A Journal of Inquiry and Practice, 12*, 255–275.

Marks, G. (2009). Accounting for school-sector differences in university entrance performance. *Australian Journal of Education, 53*, 19–38.

Meyer, P. (2008). Independent networks: NativityMiguel & Cristo Rey. In S. W. Hamilton (Ed.), *Who will save America's urban Catholic schools?* Washington, DC: Thomas Fordham Institute. Retrieved from http://www.edexcellence.net

Morris, A. B. (2009). A few hard facts and a great deal of conjecture: Catholic schools in England. *Journal of Education & Christian Belief, 13*, 65–80.

Podsiadlo, Rev. J. J., S. J., & Philliber, W. W. (2003). The Nativity Mission Center: A successful approach to the education of Latino boys. *Journal of Education for Students Placed at Risk, 8*, 419–428. doi: 10.1207/S15327671ESPR0804_3

Schindler Rangvid, B. (2008). Private school diversity in Denmark's national voucher system. *Scandinavian Journal of Educational Research, 52*, 331–354.

U.S. Department of Education. (2008). *Preserving a critical national asset: America's disadvantaged students and the crisis in faith-based urban schools*, Washington, DC: Author. Retrieved from http://www.ed.gov/admins/comm/choice/faithbased/

Wenglinsky, H. (2007, October). *Are private high schools better academically than public high schools?* Washington, DC: Center on Education Policy. Retrieved from http://www.cep-dc.org/

4.7

Class Size

JOHN HATTIE
University of Melbourne

Introduction

It is not difficult to find claims for both sides of the argument about whether or not reducing class sizes leads to enhancements in learning outcomes. One side argues that reducing class size leads to more individualized instruction, higher quality instruction, greater scope for innovation and student-centered teaching, increased teacher morale, fewer disruptions, less student misbehavior, and greater ease in engaging students in academic activities. On the other side, there is a voluminous literature that does not support the claim that learning outcomes are markedly enhanced when class sizes are reduced. Hattie (2007) located 14 major reviews and meta-analyses (based on 164 studies, 40,000+ teachers, and about 1 million students, and the overall average effects were very small ($d = .13$; there were positive indicators that reducing class size does enhance achievement but these effects are quite small. The 14 major reviews represent a variety of designs including meta-analysis, longitudinal studies, cross-cohort studies and they are from several countries (United States, United Kingdom, Israel, Bolivia); from across all grades; and use some of the most sophisticated statistical methods available. There is remarkable consistency across the effect sizes from these many diverse studies.

Research Evidence

Glass and Smith (1978) completed the first meta-analysis on this topic synthesizing 77 studies, and found that when classes are reduced from 25 to 15 the effects were, on average, very small (.09). They also synthesized 59 studies covering 371 effects relating to class size and nonachievement based outcomes such as self-concept, interpersonal regard, engagement, quality of instruction, teacher attitude, and school climate (Smith & Glass, 1980)—and the effects were similarly "negligible."

The best known study is Project Student–Teacher Achievement Ratios (STAR), which involved a random assignment of about 6,500 students in 329 classrooms in 79 schools entering kindergarten. Teachers and students were assigned for 3 years to a regular class (22–26 students), or small class (13–17 students; Achilles & Finn, 2000). The overall effects (.15 to .27) increased as students spent additional years in a small class (about .12 for each year), were double for minority students, but there were no effects for motivation and self-concept. In follow-up studies of these students, there remained small effects favoring those from smaller classes in achievement, engagement in learning, and higher graduation rates, and with less dropouts (Finn, Gerber, & Boyd-Zaharias, 2005).

Other large scale studies have found similar low effects: the Wisconsin study (Molner at el., 1999), Connecticut (Hoxby, 2000), California (Jepsen & Rivkin, 2002), as have various econometric studies (Hanushek, Rivkin, & Taylor, 1996; Krueger, 1999), and value-added studies (Ludwig & Bossi, 1999). Akerhielm (1995) used the National Education Longitudinal Study (NELS), based on a U.S. nationally representative sample of over 24,000 eighth graders. She found an overall effect size of .18 for science and .13 for history, and concluded that "the incremental benefits may not surpass the incremental costs of decreasing class size" (p. 239).

Similar findings have been reported in non-Western countries. Fuller (1987) reviewed nine studies in developing countries (Botswana, Thailand, India, Chile, Iran, Egypt, Kenya, Malaysia, Puerto Rico, Tanzania, Bolivia, and Argentina), and found no difference in learning outcomes relating to class size. Wößmann and West (2002) investigated the effect of class size on student achievement across many countries using the Third International Mathematics and Science Study (TIMSS) data. They were unable to detect a statistically significant effect of class size on student achievement for most school systems. Indeed, many of the countries where class sizes were greatest were among the highest performers across the comparable countries (including most Western countries).

Across all these studies, there is a high degree of overlap in the effects between larger and smaller classes. Some teachers are more effective than others, almost irrespective of the class size. Analyses of interactions across differing class sizes has shown few differences in the percent of student-initiated questions, the percent of student-initiated comments, the percent of students off-task, student engagement, or in time waiting for help. There are slight increases in on-task behavior, in social interaction, but more direct teacher and whole group instruction in smaller classes. The typical arguments supporting smaller classes is that they increase in on-task behavior, allow greater amounts of individual attention and less whole class teaching, more prosocial interactions, peer interactions, and student imitated questions, and greater curricula coverage—although there is more evidence not supporting than supporting these claims (Evertson & Folger, 1989). Finn, Gerber, Achilles, and Boyd-Zaharias, (2001), for example, found that teachers in STAR small classes spent increased time in direct instruction, although less time on managerial organizational tasks. Bourke (1986) found no relationship between class size and student engagement, more whole-class teaching, and not more individualization in smaller classes; and in smaller classes there were fewer teacher–student interactions and fewer student questions.

Finn et al. (2001) undertook the most comprehensive review of potential reasons to account for the small overall effect size when reducing class sizes. Their claim was that the major effects of smaller class sizes related to the "visibility of the individual"—in smaller classes there is increased pressure to participate: "students in a small class can't easily avoid being noticed and the teacher cannot readily ignore any pupil(s) even if s/he would like to" (p. 10). As a consequence they are more likely to take responsibility for their learning, be less involved in social loafing, have a greater sense of belonging, and higher levels of group cohesiveness. Thus, if any effects accrue from smaller classes, the reasons relate to what students rather than teachers do in smaller versus larger classes (see also Blatchford, 2011).

The cost of class size reduction is high (teacher salaries, buildings) and ongoing, and compared with many other innovations, prohibitive. Brewer, Krop, Gill, and Reichardt (1999) estimated the costs of reducing class sizes to 18 students in Years 1 to 3 in the United States would require hiring an additional 100,000 teachers at a cost of $U.S.5 to 6 billion per year, and an additional 55% more classrooms. To reduce again from 18 to 15 students would cost a further $U.S. 5 to 6 billion per year. Instead, they estimate that this investment could, instead, be used to raise teachers' salaries by $20,000 per year (see also Blatchford, Goldstein, Martin, & Browne, 2002).

Summary and Recommendations

The conclusion is that it may be more effective to ask: "Why, given the seemingly obvious advantages for reducing class size, has it *not* led to the expected substantial positive impacts on student achievement?" The major reason seems to be that teachers of smaller classes seem to adopt the same teaching methods as they were using in larger classes and thus not optimizing the opportunities presented by having fewer students. Glass, Cahen, Smith, and Filby (1982) reported that the nature of the instruction rarely changed when classes were reduced from 40 to 20 students. A poor/good teacher with 30 students may remain a poor/good teacher even only with 20 students. Even in smaller classes teachers continue to teach as if there were 30 students in front of them. In a sense, why should they not: What has worked for them (successfully at least in their eyes) in one context is surely adaptable for many other situations. There is little change in instructional practices in smaller classes—in the structure of lessons, teaching practices, opportunities, or content coverage. Perhaps retraining would change this (but see Stasz & Stecher, 2000).

The effects of reducing class size are small, which should not be surprising when teachers appear to not change their teaching behaviors even when provided with opportunities in smaller classes to teach in different ways. The major issue is less whether class size makes a difference (as it appears not), but whether there are teaching strategies that optimize student learning in smaller classes. The slight increase, for example, for the junior classes may be that teachers of these classes are more likely to adopt the teaching principles and behaviors that optimize small-group learning. Given the enormous costs and the high levels of advocacy by teachers and parents for lower class size, it is necessary to rephrase the key question from does class size reduction positively influence student achievement toward how can we optimize teaching in small classes.

References

Achilles, C. M., & Finn, J. D. (2000). Should class size be a cornerstone for educational policy? In M. C. Wang & J. D. Finn (Eds.), *How small classes help teachers do their best* (pp. 299–324). Philadelphia, PA: Temple University Center for Research in Human Development in Education.

Akerhielm, K. (1995). Does class size matter? *Economics of Education Review, 14*(3), 229–241.

Blatchford, P. (2011). Three generations of research on class-size effects. In K. R. Harris, S. Graham, & T. Urdan (Eds.), *APA educational psychology handbook: Vol. 2. Individual differences and cultural and contextual factors* (pp 529–554). Washington, DC: American Psychological Association.

Blatchford, P., Goldstein, H., Martin, C., & Browne, W. (2002). A study of class size effects in English school reception year classes. *British Educational Research Journal, 28(2),* 169–185.

Bourke, S. (1986). How smaller is better: Some relationships between class size, teaching practices, and student achievement. *American Educational Research Journal, 23*(4), 558–571.

Brewer, D. J., Krop, C., Gill, B. P., & Reichardt, R. (1999). Estimating the cost of national class size reductions under different policy alternatives. *Educational Evaluation and Policy Analysis, 21*(2), 179–192.

Evertson, C. M., & Folger, J. K. (1989, March). *Small class, large class: What do teachers do differently?* Paper presented at American Educational Research Association, San Francisco, CA.

Finn, J. D., Gerber, S. B., Achilles, C. M., & Boyd-Zaharias, J. (2001). The enduring effects of small classes. *Teachers College Record, 103*(2), 145–183.

Finn, J. D., Gerber, S. B., & Boyd-Zaharias, J. (2005). Small classes in the early grades, academic achievement, and graduating from high school. *Journal of Educational Psychology, 94,* 214–223.

Fuller, B. (1987). What school factors raise achievement in the third world? *Review of Educational Research, 57*(3), 255–292.

Glass, G. V., & Smith, M. L. (1978). *Meta-analysis of research on the relationship of class size and achievement.* San Francisco, CA: Far West Laboratory for Educational Research & Development.

Glass, G. V., Cahen, L. S., Smith, M. K., & Filby, N. N. (1982). *School class size: Research and policy.* Beverly Hills, CA: Sage.

Hanushek, E. A., Rivkin, S. G., & Taylor, L. L. (1996). Aggregation and the estimated effects of school resources, *Review of Economics and Statistics, 78,* 611–627.

Hattie, J. A. C. (2007). The paradox of reducing class size and improved learning outcomes. *International Journal of Education, 42,* 387–425.

Hoxby, C. M. (2000). The effects of class size on student achievement: New evidence from population variation. *Quarterly Journal of Economics, 115*(4), 1239–1285.

Jepsen, C., & Rivkin, S. (2002). *What is the trade-off between smaller classes and teacher quality?* (NBER Working Paper Series 9205). Retrieved from http://www.nber.org/papers/w9205

Krueger, A. B. (1999). Experimental estimates of education production functions'. *Quarterly Journal of Economics, 114*(2), 497–532.

Ludwig, J., & Bossi, L. J. (1999). The puzzling case of school resources and student achievement. *Educational Evaluation and Policy Analysis, 21*(4), 385–403.

Smith, M. L., & Glass, G. V. (1980). Meta-analysis of research on class size and its relationship to attitudes and instruction. *American Educational Research Journal, 17*(4), 419–433.

Stasz, C., & Stecher, B. M. (2000). Teaching mathematics and language arts in reduced size and non-reduced size classrooms. *Educational Evaluation and Policy Analysis, 22*(4), 313–329.

Wößmann, L., & West, M. R. (2002). *Class-size effects in school systems around the world: Evidence from between-grade variation in TIMSS.* Retrieved from ftp://repec.iza.org/RePEc/Discussionpaper/dp485.pdf

4.8

Financing Schools

Eric A. Hanushek
Stanford University

Introduction

Around the world, schools are overwhelmingly controlled and operated by governments, and governmental policies directly affect much of what goes on in schools. The financing of schools has traditionally been addressed from two different perspectives. For the longest period, the central issues have revolved around how money for schools is raised and how it is distributed to local schools. These issues fit naturally into the policy debates around where a society's resources should be invested, along with the related question of how much is spent on schools. Over the past half century, however, a second perspective has entered into the debates, namely, how student performance relates to the financing of schools. This latter perspective has dramatically shifted the policy discussions about school finance. It has also made it clear that finance discussions cannot be separated from broader educational policy discussions because it is important to integrate finance incentives with other policies designed to improve achievement.

Research Evidence

The new finance focus comes from investigations of the impact of finance on student outcomes. Hundreds of estimates using accepted statistical approaches provide a clear picture of the relationship between resources and achievement. Although they do not always agree, the majority of the studies have found that differences in either the absolute spending level or spending increases bear little or no consistent relationship to student achievement (e.g., Hanushek, 2003, 2006). Perhaps the best known study on this issue was one of the first, *Equality of Educational Opportunity* (Coleman et al., 1966), the "Coleman Report." This report was one of the first attempts to apply statistical analyses to student achievement in what is now commonly referred to as "educational production functions." In 1964, The U.S. Congress funded this massive study to assess the reasons

for the continued failure to close the Black–White achievement gap. The report suggested that variation in school resources had little or nothing to do with differences in student achievement, and that almost all the test score gap was attributable to the widely varying social and economic conditions of Black and White citizens.

The findings of the Coleman Report were extremely controversial, but, since its publication in 1966, a vast literature has confirmed many of the original conclusions. Studies have examined spending and related resources, such as class size, teacher experience, teacher education, teacher credentials, and other possible school inputs– all without finding a consistent or systematic influence on student achievement. For example, with regard to pupil–teacher ratios, almost three-quarters of all studies report no significant relationship with achievement. The studies that do indicate a statistically significant relationship are evenly divided between those showing the expected negative impact of a higher pupil–teacher ratio and those showing a positive impact on achievement (Hanushek, 2003, 2006). Even though the now-famous STAR study from Tennessee found positive impacts in a random assignment experimental study during the 1980s (Word et al., 1990), the Tennessee STAR study is balanced not only by hundreds of other studies reaching the opposite conclusion, but also the disappointing results of California and many other U.S. states that have introduced programs for reducing class sizes in grades K-3 and other grades (see the research in Ehrenberg, Brewer, Gamoran, & Willms, 2001). Similarly, there is no support for any consistent relationship between the level of a teacher's education and student achievement (Hanushek & Rivkin, 2006). Less than 10% of the studies on this topic find a statistically significant positive impact of additional teacher education on student achievement. Teacher experience has historically shown a stronger relationship with performance, but recent studies have consistently found that the impact of experience is concentrated in the first year or two of teaching with little or no positive impact resulting from additional experience.

It is important to highlight these issues in the discussion of finances because class size reductions and increases in teacher salaries have been very important over the past half-century in the tremendous increases in real expenditure per pupil in schools (Hanushek & Rivkin, 1997). Class size reduction programs have been very popular even though they are perhaps the most expensive of all school reform programs and even though research suggests that they are unlikely to be generally associated with improved student achievement. Because the primary determinants of teacher pay—experience and education level—do not have a consistent link with achievement, what teachers are paid also shows little consistent relationship with achievement. A teacher who has been successful in improving her students' achievement is as likely to have a low salary as a high salary (Hanushek & Rivkin, 2004). Further, since salaries make up the largest component of school district expenditures, variations in instructional expenditures also have little consistent relationship with achievement.

Some studies have found statistically significant positive effects of school spending, and people who wish to advocate for more spending tend to cite just these. Nonetheless, particularly with the spending studies, the relatively few studies finding a positive relationship with achievement tend to be the lowest quality studies. These studies disproportionately rely on aggregate state evidence, where omission of any measures of state policy differences is likely to introduce bias in the estimated effects of spending differences (Hanushek,2003). Further, these results are not simply a peculiarity of the United States. The same results are found across countries, as reviewed by Woessmann (2007a). Quite consistently, the analysis of performance on international achievement tests suggests that things other than resources are most important for student outcomes (Hanushek & Woessmann, 2011).

Another line of research has examined teacher quality measured on an outcome basis as a potentially important influence on student achievement. As opposed to assessing quality on the basis of measured teacher characteristics such as teacher education or experience, this work has concentrated on whether some teachers consistently produce more gains in student achievement than other teachers. Working with extensive longitudinal data on individual students from different U.S. states, these studies have confirmed large differences among teachers in terms of outcomes in the classroom (see Hanushek & Rivkin, 2010). This research, which also finds that differences in teacher effectiveness are not closely related to commonly observed characteristics of teachers, leads to a different conclusion from the Coleman Report. Teachers and schools differ dramatically, but, as found in the Coleman Report, it is not the simple measured characteristics that are important.

The inability to identify specific teacher qualities makes it difficult to regulate having high-quality teachers in classrooms. It also contributes to a conclusion that changes in

the institutional structure and incentives of schools are fundamental to improving school outcomes. The simplest statement is: *if one is concerned about student performance, one should gear policy to student performance.* Perhaps the largest problem with the current organization of most schools in most countries is that nobody's job or career is closely related to student performance. Relatedly, popular input policies, such as lowering class size, do nothing to change the structure of incentives.

One potential alternative is to alter the structure of school finance to include performance incentives for teachers and other school personnel. Existing international evidence suggests some clear general policies related to institutional structure of schools that are important, and these have direct ramifications for the structure of school finance (Hanushek & Woessmann, 2011). Foremost among these, the performance of a system is affected by the incentives that actors face. That is, if the actors in the education process are rewarded (extrinsically or intrinsically) for producing better student achievement, and if they are penalized for not producing high achievement, then achievement is likely to improve. The incentives to produce high-quality education, in turn, are created by the institutions of the education system—the rules and regulations that explicitly or implicitly set rewards and penalties for the people involved in the education process.

From existing work, three interrelated institutional policies come to the forefront: promoting more competition, so that parental demand will create strong incentives to individual schools; autonomy in local decision making, so that individual schools and their leaders will take actions to promote student achievement; and, an accountability system that identifies good school performance and leads to rewards based on this. The evidence is summarized in Woessmann (2007b). It is also a central part of considerations of why some nations have done better in terms of international test scores (Mourshed, Chijioke, & Barber, 2010). One of the key channels by which these institutions affect performance is clearly through ensuring a strong teacher force in the schools. Each of the institutions provides incentives to improve on student outcomes, and the most direct way to do this comes through improving the effectiveness of teachers.

The exact form of such incentives will vary across different countries. For example, the United States relies considerably on individual states to organize and to finance the schools. Historically, the states have differed considerably, but none of them has relied very much on incentives for performance. It is easy, however, to establish a school finance system that emphasizes performance incentives (Hanushek & Lindseth (2009).

One of the big issues in doing this is thinking about performance incentives for teachers, even though these have not proved popular in many places where they are discussed. One reason for the general resistance by teachers to incentive systems like performance pay is a concern about what will be rewarded. Research shows, for example, that families make a huge difference in the education of students. An implication of this is that the finance system should not reward or punish teachers for the portion of education they are not responsible for. If some students come to school better prepared than others, their teachers should not receive extra rewards. Similarly, if students come from disadvantaged backgrounds that leave them less well prepared for schools, we should not punish their teachers.

Pursuing this approach requires an aggressive system of performance measurement. It is necessary to track the progress of individual students and to relate this progress to the teachers that are responsible for it. This does not necessarily mean a system of individual rewards as opposed to group rewards for teachers in a school, but it does mean accurately measuring the performance of schools. Nor does it mean that test-based measures should be exclusively used. This area—designing accountability systems—is an obvious area for governmental leadership (although not necessarily ignoring local preferences and capacity).

The international evidence again suggests that countries that rely more on performance rewards for teachers show higher achievement, other things being equal (Woessmann, 2011). Whereas the evaluations of specific forms of performance pay are just now beginning to be developed (Podgursky & Springer, 2007), there are signs that schools are generally moving to experiment with such ideas.

Summary and Recommendations

The main message of current research is thus that school finance questions must be put into a larger context. It is not possible to expect higher achievement of students from simply providing extra resources to schools. Some specific thought must be given to how any resources affect the incentives of people in the schools. One cannot expect to improve student achievement and outcomes simply by putting more resources into the existing schools. Thus, the traditional focus of school finance policy on the flows of resources is misguided, because it conflicts with an outcome basis for decision making. While there is some uncertainty about the specific details of programs, the most promising school finance policies and institutions are ones that promote higher achievement (instead of simply providing more resources to schools). The modern way to view school finance is how the support of schools relates to incentives.

References

Coleman, J. S., Campbell, E. Q., Hobson, C. J. ,McPartland, J., Mood, A. M., Weinfeld, F. D., & York, R. J. (1966). *Equality of educational opportunity*. Washington, DC.: U.S. Government Printing Office.

Ehrenberg, R. G., Brewer, D. J., Gamoran, A., & Willms, J. D. (2001). Class size and student achievement. *Psychological Science in the Public Interest, 2*(1),1–30.

Hanushek, E. A. (2003). The failure of input-based schooling policies. *Economic Journal, 113*(485), F64–F98.

Hanushek, E. A. (2006). School resources. In E. A. Hanushek & F. Welch (Eds.), *Handbook of the economics of education* (pp. 865–908). Amsterdam, Netherlands: North Holland.

Hanushek, E. A., & Lindseth, A. A. (2009). *Schoolhouses, courthouses, and statehouses: Solving the funding-achievement puzzle in America's public schools*. Princeton, NJ: Princeton University Press.

Hanushek, E. A., & Rivkin, S. G. (1997). Understanding the twentieth-century growth in U.S. school spending. *Journal of Human Resources, 32*(1), 35–68.

Hanushek, E. A., & Rivkin, S. G. (2004). How to improve the supply of high quality teachers. In D. Ravitch (Ed.), *Brookings papers on education policy 2004* (pp. 7–25). Washington, DC: Brookings Institution Press.

Hanushek, E. A., & Rivkin, S. G. (2006). Teacher quality. In E. A. Hanushek & F. Welch (Eds.), *Handbook of the economics of education* (pp. 1051–1078). Amsterdam, Netherlands: North Holland.

Hanushek, E. A., & Rivkin, S. G. (2010). Generalizations about using value-added measures of teacher quality. *American Economic Review, 100*(2),267–271.

Hanushek, E, A., & Woessmann, L. (2011). The economics of international differences in educational achievement. In E. A. Hanushek, S. Machin, & L. Woessmann (Eds.), *Handbook of the economics of education* (Vol. 3, pp. 89–200). Amsterdam, Netherlands: North Holland.

Mourshed, M., Chijioke, C., & Barber, M. (2010). *How the world's most improved school systems keep getting better*. New York: McKinsey.

Podgursky, M. J., & Springer, M. G.. (2007). Teacher performance pay: A review. *Journal of Policy Analysis and Management, 26*(4), 909–949.

Woessmann, L. (2007a). International evidence on expenditure and class size: A review. In *Brookings papers on education policy 2006/2007* (pp. 245–272). Washington, DC: Brookings.

Woessmann, L. (2007b). International evidence on school competition, autonomy and accountability: A review. *Peabody Journal of Education, 82*(2–3), 473–497.

Woessmann, L. (2011). Cross-country evidence on teacher performance pay. *Economics of Education Review, 30*(3), 404–418.

Word, E., Johnston, J. Bain, H. P., DeWayne Fulton, B., Zaharies, J. B., Lintz, M. N., ... Breda, C. (1990). *Student/teacher achievement ratio (STAR), Tennessee's K-3 class size study: Final summary report, 1985–1990*. Nashville, TN: Tennessee State Department of Education.

4.9

Influences of School Layout and Design on Student Achievement

C. Kenneth Tanner
The University of Georgia

Introduction

Recently, the intricate activity of relating an official learning environment, such as a school building layout, to students' learning and behavior is receiving increased emphasis in research and formal writing. This is in contrast to the traditional "nuts and bolts" commentary on facilities of bygone years. A significant issue is how do we capture consistency of measurement of school design and then relate it to a student's acquisition of knowledge? Researchers at the School Design and Planning Laboratory (SDPL) at the University of Georgia in Atlanta, stipulate that measurement should, as Flygt suggests, include objective–subjective assessments representative of both the functional/technical and the ethical/aesthetical dimensions of a facility (Flygt, 2009).

The SDPL research ties aspects of the interplay of knowledge, beliefs, behaviors, and actions in reference to a place (the school) to cognition or acquisition of knowledge (measured by standardized scores on tests for cognition). Researchers independent of the SDPL have linked these two areas, simultaneously. For example, Rollero and De Piccoli (2010) maintain that affective and cognitive dimensions, defined as place attachment and identification, characterize the relationship between people and places. Their timely study shows that the affective and the cognitive dimensions (a) are directly predicted by different demographical and psychosocial variables and (b) are strictly associated with the perception of the place and its inhabitants. Furthermore they contend, and I certainly agree, that cognitive and affective dimensions are two distinct but correlated components.

Beginning in 1997, the SDPL associates discovered that no valid and reliable measurements existed that would indicate if or how much the school's physical environment contributes to or influences the student's cognitive learning. Hence, we set out, tolerating colleagues' pointed skepticism, to explore a way to link place and cognitive learning. Up until then, we discovered that school environments were usually built on whims, standardized codes, and

unsupported "best practices," or hearsay evidence among educational planners and decision makers. To strengthen our argument, we encouraged educators to examine the issue of "best practices in building schools," which often goes unchallenged regarding whose best practices and what, when, where, and how they might influence various educational and cultural settings (Tanner & Lackney 2006, pp. 263–322). Our conclusion is to avoid using best practices as a basis for planning and designing schoolhouses.

Early studies at SDPL began with identifying aspects of places where students learn; these are called "design patterns," after Alexander, Ishikawa, and Silverstein (1977), from their masterwork, *A Pattern Language*. Our primary assumption was that design patterns in the school's physical environment influence student achievement; therefore, "Each pattern describes a problem which occurs over and over again in our environment, and then describes the core of the solution to that problem, in such a way that you can use this solution a million times over, without ever doing it the same way twice" (Alexander et al. 1997, p. x). That is, we assumed that place and cognitive dimensions are related in various ways. Readers interested in more detail on the physical environment as we have defined it may refer to additional works such as Sommer (1969), Tanner and Lackney (2006, pp. 263–322), and Tanner (2009).

Research Evidence

Beginning as early as 1997, characteristics of design patterns were identified and debated among educational leaders attending graduate level classes offered in the SDPL. The purpose of these discussions was to validate each "education related design pattern" based on need and relevance to teaching and learning. Three broad areas are identified below that represent a fraction of our findings.

Movement Classifications. For many years, researchers in the field of environmental psychology have been interested in research on movement classifications, described as links to main entrances, pathways with goals, circulation patterns, density or freedom of movement, personal space, and social distance. In our validation process we always asked questions about too much or too little space and then referred to issues of social and personal distance to develop a stem for a measurement scale to be used in assessing existing places and spaces for learning.

Regarding personal and social distance, Wohlwill and Van Vliet (1985) summarized the effects of high student density as a hindrance to movement. "It appears as though the consequences of high-density conditions that involve either too many children or too little space are: excess levels of stimulation; stress and arousal; a drain on resources available; considerable interference; reductions in desired privacy levels; and loss of control" (pp. 108–109). Works such as this have led to the assertion that a high-density school has a negative influence on achievement (Weinstein & David, 1987). Our decision about freedom of movement has been consistent: An overcrowded school is not conducive to teaching and learning. It is not the size of the school that plays the positive or negative role in student achievement so much as it is the density—number of students per square and cubic unit of measurement.

Some other major conclusions from our research at the SDPL are summarized as follows: The issue of density may be viewed through psychological implications implied in "territoriality of place." Since the school is a social system within the cultural environment, social distance as it relates to crowding and density is a function of school design. This line of reasoning should be made for school size and the size of classrooms. Special attention should be given to circulation classifications that permit student traffic to flow quickly from one part of the building to another. Movement within the school should be a conscious and perceptible environmental exchange; and complex structures that cause crowding should be avoided. School design should include pathways both inside and outside of the building. Pathways may link structures together and lead into the natural environment.

Architectural Design. Fiske (1995) indicated that the organization of space has a profound effect on learning, and students feel better connected to a building that anticipates their needs and respects them as individuals. When children attend a school designed with their needs in mind, they notice it and demonstrate a more natural disposition toward respectful behavior and a willingness to contribute to the classroom community (Herbert, 1998). The process used in planning greatly influences school layout.

Collaboration among stakeholders in planning and designing a school is a significant step in achieving the right design. Both the planner and the stakeholders (including parents and students) learn from each other. Participation can lead to the ultimate agreement about what the future should look like and includes awareness and perception. Awareness involves persuading participants to speak the

same language; perception takes awareness forward to the next milestone because it facilitates an understanding of the physical, social, cultural, and economic ramifications for the project outcomes (Sanoff, 1994).

The need exists for the development of spaces that engage, challenge, and arouse a student's imagination. Brain-compatible learning requires much more interaction with the environment than current facilities allow. Taylor and Vlastos (1975) suggested that educational architecture is a "three-dimensional textbook." This means that the learning environment is a functional art form, a place of beauty, and a motivational center for learning. School buildings are visual objects, and as such they can be stimulating both in terms of their intrinsic design and their use.

Architectural design should include a friendly entrance that is age appropriate and highly visible. Huge, overpowering entrances are intimidating to young children, for example. The entrance should evoke a welcoming feeling not instill fear (Alexander et al., 1977). To stakeholders, the school administrative offices should be centralized for convenience and connection. Main buildings have an obvious reference point, a feature that heightens the sense of community. Variation of ceiling heights and intimacy gradients help blend public and private places in schools and give the effect of drawing people into an area.

The issue of scale must be emphasized in planning the school layout. Meek (1995) contributed to the issue of scale when she wrote about Crow Island School: "Then you are at the front door, and what you notice is that the door handle is too low. Too low for you, just right for children" (p. 53).

Daylight and Views. The presence of natural light in classrooms improves student learning. An extensive research effort, including a controlled study of over 21,000 students in California, Washington, and Colorado found that students with the most "day lighting" in their classrooms progressed 20% faster on mathematics and 26% faster on reading tests over a period of one year than students having less daylight in their classrooms (Heschong Mahone Group, 1999). "We also identified another window-related effect, in that students in classrooms where windows could be opened were found to progress 7–8% faster than those with fixed windows. This occurred regardless of whether the classroom also had air conditioning" (p. 62). Rather than being a distraction, which disrupts the learning process, an argument often used from the "conventional wisdom" side, windows provide a necessary relief for students (Kuller & Lindsten, 1992).

Exposing children to harmful forms of lighting in poorly designed schools is reason enough for us to seriously consider Alexander's et al. (1977) notion of "wings of light." Windows (views) overlooking life is another positive aspect of design amenable to translation from the theories of "pattern language" to the school environment.

Light is the most important environmental input, after food and water, in controlling bodily functions (Wurtman, 1975). Lights of different colors affect blood pressure, pulse, respiration rates, brain activity, and biorhythms. Full-spectrum light, required to influence the pineal gland's synthesis of melatonin, which in turn helps determine the body's output of the neurotransmitter serotonin, is critical to a child's health and development (Ott, 1973). To help reduce the imbalances caused by inadequate exposure to the near ultraviolet and infrared ends of the spectrum, full-spectrum bulbs that approximate the wavelengths provided by sunshine should replace standard bulbs. There is ample evidence that people need daylight to regulate circadian rhythms (Alexander et al., 1977, p. 527). Poorly lit and windowless classrooms can cause students to experience a daily form of jet lag, while forms of florescent lighting may affect some students and teachers by causing mild seizures.

Summary and Recommendations

In conclusion, the following are selected physical characteristics of learning environments that research suggests will improve student performance: Allow ample space for learning to avoid overcrowding; design for abundant circulation patterns; maintain scale as a guide; require plenty of natural light in the classroom; and demand extensive stakeholder participation in planning and designing a school.

References

Alexander, C., Ishikawa, S., & Silverstein, M. (1977). *A pattern language.* New York: Oxford University Press.

Fiske, E. B. (1995). Systematic school reform: Implications for architecture. In A. Meek (Ed.), *Designing places for learning* (pp. 1–10). Alexandria, VA: ASCD.

Flygt, E. (2009) Investigating architectural quality theories for school evaluation: A critical review of evaluation instruments in Sweden. *Educational Management, Administration & Leadership, 37*(5), 645–666.

Herbert, E. A. (1998). Design matters: How school environment affects children. *Educational Leadership, 56,* 69–70.

Heschong Mahone Group (1999). *Daylighting in schools.* Fair Oaks, CA: Author. (11626 Fair Oaks Blvd. #302, Fair Oaks, CA 95628)

Kuller, R., & Lindsten, C. (1992). Health and behavior of children in classrooms with and without windows. *Journal of Environmental Psychology, 12,* 305–317.

Meek, A. (Ed.). (1995). *Designing places for learning.* Alexandria, VA: ASCD.

Rollero, C., & De Piccoli, N. (2010). Place attachment, identification and environment perception: An empirical study. *Journal of Environmental Psychology, 30*(2), 198–205.

Ott, J. (1973), *Health and light.* New York: Simon & Schuster.

Sanoff, H. (1994). *School design.* New York: Van Nostrand Reinhold.

Sommer, R. (1969). *Personal space.* Englewood Cliffs, NJ: Prentice-Hall.

Tanner, C. K. (2009). Effects of school design on student outcomes. *Journal of Educational Administration, 47*(3), 376–394.

Tanner, C. K., & Lackney, J. A. (2006). *Educational facilities planning: Leadership, architecture, and management.* Boston, MA: Allyn & Bacon.

Taylor, A. P., & Vlastos, G. (1975). *School zone: Learning environments for children.* New York: Van Nostrand Reinhold.

Weinstein, C. S., & David, T. G. (Eds.). (1987). *Spaces for children: The built environment and child development.* New York: Plenum Press.

Wohlwill, J. F., & van Vliet, W. (1985). *Habitats for children: The impacts of density.* Hillsdale, NJ: Erlbaum.

Wurtman, R. J. (1975). The effects of light on the human body. *Scientific American, 233,* 68–77.

4.10

Grade Retention

SHANE R. JIMERSON AND JACQUELINE A. BROWN
University of California, Santa Barbara

Introduction

Grade retention is the practice where a student who has been in a specific grade level for a full school year is required to remain at that level for a subsequent school year (Jackson, 1975; Jimerson, 2001). In the United States, the practice of grade retention as an intervention for students who struggle is a controversial topic that has been examined since the early 1900s. With the No Child Left Behind federal legislation passed in 2001, U.S. states increasingly use performance on tests to evaluate schools and make decisions about grade promotion. In other countries, grade promotion is not always tied to standardized assessments, yet retention is used at varying rates in countries around the world (e.g., Guèvrement, Roos, & Brownell, 2007; Uysal, 2010). Although individual differences exist among retained students, factors that are often associated with an increased risk of retention include living in poverty, frequent changes in school or chronic absenteeism, reading and behavior problems, and difficulties with peer relationships (Jimerson & Skokut, 2008).

Because of potential short- and long-term effects that grade retention can have on student achievement and socioemotional outcomes, it remains a controversial topic in research and practice. Those who advocate its use claim that it enables students making inadequate academic progress to catch up, supports students who are emotionally immature, and increases academic homogeneity within the classroom (Ehmke, Drechsel, & Carstensen, 2010; Lorence, 2006). On the other hand, those opposed to grade retention emphasize the deleterious outcomes (e.g., achievement, motivation to learn, and self-concept) revealed in multiple meta-analyses (Holmes & Matthews, 1984; Jimerson, 2001). Researchers also contend that although educators may choose to retain students because it is a fairly easy approach to implement, thorough assessment is not always conducted to determine whether students should repeat the entire grade curriculum or if they would be unable to perform specific academic and cognitive activities if promoted to the following grade level (Hong & Yu, 2007). The following reviews key articles and meta-analyses that inform this debate, examines moderators and causal factors that play a role in grade retention, offers a brief summary of some existing critiques of grade retention research, and provides recommendations for future research and practice.

Research Evidence

There have been four seminal reviews that have examined the effects of grade retention on student achievement. Throughout these reviews, academic achievement was generally measured using achievement test scores, grades, or standardized norm referenced achievement tests. One of the first systemic reviews examining the efficacy of grade retention was conducted by Jackson (1975), and included 30 studies published between 1911 and 1973. The purpose of the review was to determine whether students suffering academically or socioemotionally would benefit from grade retention. Jackson concluded that there is no evidence to support the use of grade retention over promotion. Two meta-analyses conducted by Holmes and colleagues (Holmes, 1989; Holmes & Matthews, 1984) also examined studies published on grade retention and included comparison samples matched on various dimensions such as intelligence, achievement tests, and socioeconomic status (SES). The results of both meta-analyses found that there were negative effects associated with grade retention, including lower academic achievement, higher socioemotional maladjustment, and lower self-concept. Similar results were found by two more recent meta-analyses (Allen, Chen, Willson, & Hughes, 2009; Jimerson, 2001). Although the results of Allen and colleagues did not find advantages to retaining students, they also did not find negative effects.

Research conducted outside of the United States has also yielded similar results. Guèvrement, Roos, and Brownell (2007) utilized a large sample of students in kindergarten through eighth grade as well as students retained in third grade within a given year in Manitoba, Canada. Results indicated that there were no short-term improvements in standardized test scores for the majority of third grade students and that ninth grade students who had been retained were significantly more likely to withdraw from school. Research conducted in Germany (e.g., Ehmke, Drechsel, & Carstensen, 2010) has also found that there are no academic differences between matched groups that are retained and those promoted with respect to math and science achievement, suggesting that it would be more beneficial to promote students and provide them with additional academic support.

Because of the research designs used in grade retention research, researchers have commented upon the inability to make conclusions about the causal effects of grade retention, because random assignment to different treatment conditions is typically needed to assess causality (Allen, Chen, Willson, & Hughes, 2009; Lorence, 2006). This limitation will be further discussed below when examining the critiques of grade retention research. One of the studies that examined the causal effects of grade retention on different school outcomes (Uysal, 2010) found that grade retention has a worsening effect on student educational achievement, leading to increases in dropout rates and decreased grades in mathematics and German. On the other hand, researchers have been more successful at examining factors that moderate the effect of grade retention on student achievement. These include school setting, peer interactions, teacher effectiveness, grade level, limited English language proficiency, home–school relationships, children's externalizing problems, number of school changes per year, and socioeconomic status (Guèvrement, Roos, & Brownell, 2007; Hong & Yu, 2007; Wu, West, & Hughes, 2008).

Existing Critiques of Grade Retention Research. Despite the longstanding focus on grade retention, there are various critiques of the existing research. One main critique of both early and more recent research involves methodological concerns and a dearth of empirical evidence (Alexander, Entwisle, & Dauber, 2003; Allen et al., 2009; Jackson, 1975; Lorence, 2006). These researchers found that many studies do not use a control group of nonretained students and that a potential decline in performance may instead be due to general changes that exist for any group. They also emphasized that the most effective way to assess the effects of such practices would be to first match students on various factors (e.g., age, SES, sex) and then randomly assign them to different treatment conditions to take into account initial differences in academic achievement, but that such an experimental design does not align with parent and teacher beliefs and school-based practices.

Another critique is the use of group comparison strategies such as same-age or same-grade comparisons (Lorence, 2006), as the specific method of comparison used may bias results. Research using same-grade comparisons has initially supported grade retention with positive effects

declining after a few years, and results using same-age comparisons often indicate that promoted students have higher scores than retained students. Lorence also suggests that many sample sizes used in grade retention research are too small to yield sufficient power and valid results, and that they are not always representative of the population (e.g., students from different social, economic, and cultural backgrounds). However, there has been an increased emphasis on addressing these concerns, particularly with respect to methodological concerns (e.g., Uysal, 2010; Wu, West, & Hughes, 2008).

Summary and Recommendations

Because research has shown that grade retention is not associated with academic growth, other interventions have been suggested in the literature. Although no single intervention will address the needs of every low-achieving student, evidence-based practices can be incorporated into general education to facilitate academic success. Recommended practices include parental involvement through regular contact with teachers and homework supervision, early reading and developmental programs to support low-achieving students and enhance language and social skills, school-based mental health programs to support children in their social and emotional adjustment, as well as tutoring and mentoring programs and other interventions that target specific academic skills (Ehmke, Drechsel, & Carstensen, 2010; Jimerson & Skokut, 2008). It has also been suggested that more attention be paid to the transition from elementary school to middle school or from middle school to high school, because higher rates of retention have been found in seventh and eighth grade (Guèvrement, Roos, & Brownell, 2007). Consequently, such practices not only focus on remediation for struggling students, but also on preventing problems by supporting all students. These practices emphasize the importance of collaboration between all educational professionals, families, and students to facilitate student success.

Further research is warranted, including additional studies that examine factors that moderate the effect of retention on student achievement, the role that attrition may play in explaining retention effects, and focus on the psychometric properties of achievement measures (Allen, Chen, Willson, & Hughes, 2009). Because much of the research has focused on the negative effects of retention, some researchers also suggest that future research examine potential positive effects (Lorence, 2006). Although it may be valuable to further expand upon grade retention research, it is also important to remember that neither social promotion nor grade retention will resolve all the tribulations of education. Consequently, it may be more beneficial for future research and practice to focus upon specific remedial intervention strategies that facilitate the socioemotional and academic success of youth, decreasing the need for retention (Jimerson, 2001).

In summary, the confluence of research examining

academic and adjustment outcomes associated with grade retention indicates that there are no benefits to student retention over promotion. Some studies reveal negative effects of grade retention, including lower academic achievement, higher socioemotional maladjustment, and increased risk for school withdrawal. Limitations of the existing grade retention literature include methodological concerns, use of age or grade norms, and sample size. Future studies addressing these concerns are therefore warranted, although additional emphasis on fostering student success is also recommended. This includes parent–teacher collaboration, early reading and developmental programs to identify concerns early and improve chances for success, and academic interventions (Jimerson & Skokut, 2008). Implementing these strategies into educational practices will help foster academic and socioemotional improvement for all students.

References

Alexander, K. L., Entwisle, D. R., & Dauber, S. L. (2003). *On the success of failure: A reassessment of the effects of retention in the primary grades* (2nd ed.). Cambridge, England: Cambridge University Press.

Allen, C. S., Chen, Q., Willson, V. L., & Hughes, J. N. (2009). Quality of research design moderates effects of grade retention on achievement: A meta-analytic multi-level analysis. *Educational Evaluation and Policy Analysis, 31,* 480–499. doi: 10.3102/0162373709352239.

Ehmke, T., Drechsel, B., & Carstensen, C. H. (2010). Effects of grade retention on achievement and self-concept in science and mathematics. *Studies in Educational Evaluation, 36,* 27–35. doi:10.1016/j.stueduc.2010.10.003

Guèvremont, A., Roos, N. P., & Brownell, M. (2007). Predictors and consequences of grade retention: Examining data from Manitoba, Canada. *Canadian Journal of School Psychology, 22,* 50–67. doi: 10.1177/0829573507301038

Holmes, C. T. (1989). Grade-level retention effects: A meta-analysis of research studies. In L. A. Shepard & M. L. Smith (Eds.), *Flunking grades: Research and policies on retention* (pp. 16–33). London: Falmer Press.

Holmes, C. T., & Matthews, K. M. (1984). The effects of nonpromotion on elementary and junior high school pupils: A meta-analysis. *Reviews of Educational Research, 54,* 225–236. doi: 10.3102/00346543054002225

Hong, G., & Yu, B. (2007). Early-grade retention and children's reading and math learning in elementary years. *Educational Evaluation and Policy Analysis, 29,* 239–261. doi: 10.3102/0162373707309073

Jackson, G. B. (1975). The research evidence on the effects of grade retention. *Review of Educational Research, 45,* 613–635. doi: 10.3102/00346543045004613

Jimerson, S. R. (2001). Meta-analysis of grade retention research: Implications for practice in the 21st century. *School Psychology Review, 30,* 420–437. Retrieved from http://www.nasponline.org/publications/spr/sprissues.aspx

Jimerson, S. R., & Skokut, M. (2008). Retention in grade. In S. Mathison, & R. E. Wayne (Eds.), *Battleground schools* (Vol. 1, pp. 520–525). Westport, CT: Greenwood.

Lorence, J. (2006). Retention and academic achievement research revisited from a United States perspective. *International Education Journal, 7,* 731–777.

Uysal, S. D. (2010). *The effect of grade retention on school outcomes: An application of doubly robust estimation method* (Discussion Paper 2010-01). Retrieved from http://www.uni-konstanz.de/cms/papers/publications.htm

Wu, W., West, S. G., & Hughes, J. N. (2008). Effect of retention in first grade on children's achievement trajectories over 4 years: A piecewise growth analysis using propensity score matching. *Journal of Educational Psychology, 100,* 727–740. doi: 10.1037/a0013098

4.11

Inclusive Education

GEOFF LINDSAY
University of Warwick

Introduction

Inclusive education, or mainstreaming, is the dominant policy internationally for educating students with special educational needs and disabilities (SEND), as indicated by the endorsement of the *Salamanca statement* (UNESCO, 1994), signed by representatives from 92 countries. Unlike other topics in this book, inclusive education is not simply, or arguably *even*, a matter of effectiveness when considering academic achievement. Rather, there is a strong tradition of a focus on students' rights to be educated in the main-. stream. Although energised also by concerns about the lack of evidence for superior outcomes from special education, the rights argument focuses on other matters, in particular the right not to be segregated from typically developing peers. Indeed, historically children and young people with severe and complex SEND have been excluded by law from the education systems of many countries. Furthermore, the rights debate concerning SEND may be seen as part of a broader discourse concerning antidiscrimination and social exclusion, particularly on grounds of ethnicity, gender, and socioeconomic status as well as disability.

This focus on rights has tended to distract from developing a sound evidence base as proponents have often argued that as inclusive education is a right therefore students *ought* de facto to be mainstreamed: from this perspective, empirical evidence is secondary (even redundant) to philosophy (ideology). Interestingly, Dunn's 1968 paper questioning special education, the most referenced in the field of learning disabilities (cited by McLeskey, 2004), is primarily an opinion piece with only a brief section on evidence; it also addresses only students with mild learning problems who had been labeled as mentally retarded. But there are also major methodological issues to address when attempting to evaluate the effectiveness of inclusive education and especially attempts to generalise findings. There are important differences between types of SEND: for example, in England there are 11 primary categories of SEND and

recognition that students may also have secondary and other needs. Within each category there are also variations of severity and persistence. Comparison of samples is made problematic by the use of different classificatory/definitional systems. Countries differ in their use of a diagnostic approach or a needs-based system for classifying needs (Desforges & Lindsay, 2010). Within the former, classificatory systems differ.[1] Also, comparing inclusion with special education is problematic as there are different forms of special provision (e.g., special school, class, unit, integrated resource, resource base) and mainstream education has also become more varied with the development of, for example, charter schools (U.S.) and academies, subject specialist schools, and federations of schools (UK). There are also challenges in determining the nature of inclusive education as an intervention. Unlike a reading program, for example, inclusive education is a pervasive educational intervention addressing a student's total educational experience. Consequently, outcome measures have included not only academic achievement but also social integration, self-esteem, and other factors. Furthermore, within an inclusive education approach there will be variations between schools in their use of specific programs, class sizes may vary, and models of inclusion within the school may also differ. Other variations include the expertise of teachers in the education of students with one or more different forms of SEND in their classes, their continuing professional development to address any training shortfall, and support from paraprofessionals (teaching assistants) and expert professionals (e.g., psychologists, speech and language therapists) who may visit or work permanently on site.

Research Evidence

In short, evaluating academic effectiveness and inclusive education is a huge challenge, and the research community has had limited success. Despite multiple studies, relatively few have adopted rigorous research designs, in particular the randomized control trial (RCT). Research is often characterized by descriptive examples of practice whose indicative effectiveness, as claimed by the researchers, is often difficult to evaluate and whose generalizability may be unknown; correlational and nonrandomization designs provide indicative evidence but are inferior approaches to evaluate effectiveness.

During the 1980s and 90s several reviews, using different methodologies (e.g., meta-analysis, narrative reviews), summarized the accumulating evidence of inclusive education on academic achievement drawn from studies with different levels of rigor. Carlberg and Kavale (1980) examined 50 pre-1980 studies and estimated a mean effect size (Cohen's *d*) of 0.15. Wang and Baker (1985–1986) estimated a mean effect size of 0.44 from 11 studies dating from 1975 to 1984. Baker (1994, cited in Baker, Wang, & Walberg, 1995), however, found a mean effect size of 0.11 for 11 studies (1983–1992). Hence the range of effect sizes from these three reviews was 0.11 to 0.44. However, the inclusion of studies with different designs (and levels of rigor) poses a challenge to interpretation; for example, including nonrandomized studies tends to bias the results to favor inclusive education (Slavin, 1984). Madden and Slavin (1983), who compared full-time special class and part-time resource programs with full-time mainstream class provision, acknowledge the limited number of rigorous studies but highlight two studies with individualised instruction which produced very large effect sizes of inclusive over special class provision of 1.24 and 2.56, respectively.

More recently, Lindsay (2007) reviewed 1,373 papers published in eight major special education journals but could identify only 14 comparative outcome studies. Importantly, none was an RCT and only nine compared performance of students with SEND in inclusive against special provision. Of these nine, just four provided academic outcome comparisons: three showed superiority of inclusive education, with important caveats in one case.

The tentative conclusion from this evidence is that inclusive education *can* be more effective than special provision in terms of academic achievement. However, this must be treated with great caution. The studies reviewed have tended not to have been RCTs. Furthermore, most have comprised of samples of students with mild/moderate learning difficulties. There is a lack of evidence on most types of SEND. Given that there are important reasons for an inclusive system based on consideration of children's rights to be part of mainstream society, and that this general policy is now well-embedded across the world, the major task is to identify the more specific aspects of practice that indicate improved academic progress for students with SEND.

It is also important to examine the interaction between factors such as type of disability, age, and the severity of the child's needs with different forms of provision. For example, Mills, Cole, Jenkins, and Dale (1998) found no overall differences in placement effects for groups of preschool children with disabilities, but higher performing children benefited more from integrated special education class placements, whereas lower performing children benefited more from mainstream or segregated placements. Teacher expertise and confidence are necessary for working effectively with students with each type of SEND: initial training is generally limited so continuing professional development is crucial. The innovative Inclusion Development Programme in England (http://nationalstrategies.standards. dcsf.gov.uk/node/116691 accessed 16 June 2011; Lindsay et al., 2011) was a national initiative to provide basic support for mainstream teachers for students with dyslexia, speech language and communication needs, autism spectrum disorder and behavioral emotional and social difficulties.

Teacher attitudes are also fundamental (Avramidis & Norwich, 2002; Scruggs & Mastropieri, 1996). Teachers tend to have differential attitudes to different types of SEND. Support from paraprofessionals (teaching assistants: TAs) has grown greatly in some countries and this has the potential to enhance achievement but to date the evidence is disappointing: a large scale study by Blatchford, Bassett, Brown, and Webster (2009) indicated a negative effect of TA support. This suggests that teachers and TAs are not developing a systematic collaboration with clear objectives and differential practices. Indeed, ultimately it is classroom practice that is the key. Individualized (personalized) instruction has been identified as important. This includes the integration of specific programs into the students' curriculum but goes further, and beyond an individual educational plan. It requires implementation of the appropriate, planned, and carefully monitored intervention program in the fullest sense. Flexibility is also necessary; TAs can help teachers with this as well as provide practical assistance.

Improving achievement also requires having high expectations of each student and a reconciling of the tension between developing an inclusive and effective school—a challenge when schools are increasingly judged by achievement outcomes. However, there is evidence that if social disadvantage is taken into account by the use of value added analyses, schools that promote inclusion can also be judged as effective in general and their non-SEND students are not disadvantaged (Kalambouka, Farrell, Dyson, & Kaplan, 2007). Indications of a general improvement of achievement of students with SEND are shown by the percentage of students in England achieving the expected outcome at age 11 years (level 4 in the national curriculum assessments). This has increased from 28.3% in 2006 to 33.5% in 2009, an increase of 5.2 percentage points compared with an increase of 2.8 percentage points (81.6% to 84.4%) for non-SEND students over this period (Department for Education, 2010).

Summary and Recommendations

The complexities of evaluating inclusive education for students with SEND are formidable. There is, at best, indicative evidence that for the most common form of mild/ moderate learning difficulties, inclusive education can be associated with better academic achievement. However, the issue of location is no longer central (Zigmond, 2003). The priority now is to explore the implementation of an *inclusive system* and hence the detailed examination of factors for which there is already indicative evidence. This requires national, local, district, and school action, both planning and implementation, using the best available evidence, but in a spirit of inquiry, testing out and accumulating further evidence of effective practice. Inherent is a need for flexibility which includes appreciation of different forms of location; the interaction between kinds of provision with factors such as type of disability, age, and severity of need; and the harnessing and optimal deployment of resources.

Note

1. The main systems are currently the *International Classification of Diseases* (ICD-10). (2010). Geneva, Switzerland: World Health Organization; and the *Diagnostic and Statistical Manual of Mental Disorders* (DSM-IV-TR). (2000). Washington, DC: American Psychiatric Press.

References

Avramides, E., & Norwich, B. (2002). Teachers' attitudes towards integration/inclusion: A review of the literature. *European Journal of Special Needs Education, 17*, 129–147.

Baker, E. T., Wang, M. C., & Walberg, H. J. (1994). The effects of inclusion on learning. *Educational Leadership, 52*, 33–35.

Blatchford, P., Bassett, P., Brown, P., & Webster, R. (2009b) The effect of support staff on pupil engagement and individual attention. *British Educational Research Journal, 35*(5), 661–686.

Carlberg, C., & Kavale, K. (1980). The efficacy of special versus regular class placement for exceptional children: A meta-analysis. *Journal of Special Education, 14*, 295–309.

Department for Education. (2010, October 19). *Children with special educational needs 2010: An analysis.* Retrieved from http://www.education.gov.uk/search/results?q=Children+with+special+educational+needs+2010%3A+An+analysis+19+October+2010.

Desforges, M., & Lindsay, G. (2010). *Procedures used to diagnose a disability and to assess special educational needs: An international review. NCSE Research Report No 5.* Trim, Ireland: National Council for Special Education. Retrieved from http://www.ncse.ie/research/researchreports.asp.

Dunn, L. M. (1968). Special education for the mildly retarded—Is much of it justifiable? *Exceptional Children, 35*, 5–22.

Lindsay, G. (2007). Educational psychology and the effectiveness of inclusive education/mainstreaming, *British Journal of Educational Psychology, 77*, 1–24.

Lindsay, G., Cullen, M. A.., Cullen, S., Dockrell, J., Strand, S. D., Arweck, E., … Goodlad, S. (2011). *Evaluation of impact of DfE investment in initiatives designed to improve teacher workforce skills in relation to SEN and disabilities* (DFE-RR115). London: Department for Education. Retrieved from https://www.education.gov.uk/publications/RSG/AllRsgPublications/Page3/DFE-RR115.

Madden, N. A., & Slavin, R. E. (1983). Mainstreaming students with mild handicaps: Academic and social outcomes. *Review of Educational Research, 53*, 519–569.

McLeskey, J. (2004). Classic articles in special education. *Remedial and Special Education, 25*, 79–87.

Mills, P. E., Cole, K. N., Jenkins, J. R., & Dale, P. S. (1998). Effects of differing levels of inclusion on preschoolers with disabilities. *Exceptional Children, 65*, 79–90.

Scruggs, T. E., & Mastropieri, M. A. (1996). Teacher perspectives of mainstreaming-inclusion, 1958–1995: A research synthesis. *Exceptional Children, 63*, 59–74.

Slavin, R. E. (1984). A rejoinder to Carlberg et al. *Educational Researcher, 13*(8), 24–27.

UNESCO (1994). *The Salamanca statement and framework for action on special needs education.* Paris: UNESCO

Wang, M. C., & Baker, E. T. (1985–1986). Mainstreaming programs: Design features and effects. *Journal of Special Education, 19*, 503–521.

Zigmond, N. (2003). Where should students with disabilities receive special education services? Is one place better than another? *Journal of Special Education, 37*, 193–199.

4.12

School-Wide Positive Behavior Interventions and Supports and Academic Achievement

Kent McIntosh
University of Oregon

Sophie V. Ty
University of British Columbia

Robert H. Horner
University of Oregon

George Sugai
University of Connecticut

Introduction

School-wide Positive Behavior Interventions and Supports (SWPBIS; also known as Positive Behaviour Support, Positive Behaviour for Learning, or Positive Behavior, Interactions and Learning Environment in School [PALS]) is a systems-level approach to enhancing student outcomes through redesigning the school environment and teaching students social competencies (Sugai & Horner, 2009). Defining features of SWPBIS are (a) a school-wide focus on preventing problem behavior as much as responding to it; (b) instruction in and recognition of expected behavior; (c) instructional consequences for problem behavior; (d) multiple tiers of intervention intensity to meet the needs of all students; and (e) collection and use of data for decision making. The primary goal of SWPBIS is to build a positive school social culture that makes the school a more effective learning environment.

SWPBIS is based on the empirical foundation of applied behavior analysis. Interventions implemented within SWPBIS vary depending on the school context. More than 16,000 schools are implementing SWPBIS in the United States, with widespread implementation in a number of other countries, including Australia (Yeung, Mooney, Barker, & Dobia, 2009), Canada (McIntosh, Bennett, & Price, 2011), and Norway (Sørlie & Ogden, 2007).

Although a focus on student social behavior as a means of addressing academic achievement may seem tangential, school personnel are more likely to improve academic achievement when they create a social context that supports effective teaching and learning. For example, results from a number of studies demonstrate that academic achievement

and social behavior are highly related (e.g., Durlak, Weissburg, Dymnicki, Taylor, & Schellinger, 2011). Therefore, the purpose of this chapter is to describe how implementing a SWPBIS approach to behavior support can lead to improved academic engagement and achievement.

Research Evidence

A growing evidence base, including experimental single case designs and randomized controlled trials, confirms the effectiveness of SWPBIS when implemented by typical school personnel. SWPBIS implementation is associated with significant decreases in problem behavior and increases in prosocial behavior (Nelson, Martella, & Marchand-Martella, 2002; Sørlie & Ogden, 2007), decreases in use of office discipline referrals and suspensions (Bradshaw, Mitchell, & Leaf, 2010), increases in school safety (Horner et al., 2009), and enhancements in organizational health (Bradshaw, Koth, Thornton, & Leaf, 2009). In addition, studies have found significant effects of SWPBIS on academic achievement, in terms of performance on standardized achievement measures (Nelson et al., 2002), proportion of students meeting expectations on provincial/state achievement tests (Horner et al., 2009; McIntosh et al., 2011), and academic self-concept (Yeung et al., 2009).

In terms of academic effects, SWPBIS may be considered as a mediator between effective instruction and academic achievement. SWPBIS is primarily an instructional approach to teaching social behavior, including academic engagement, which is necessary but not sufficient for improved academic achievement. SWPBIS can improve academic engagement, but academic engagement is insufficient to produce academic achievement. Without access to quality academic instruction, enhanced achievement is unlikely. SWPBIS indirectly improves academic achievement through the following mechanisms: (a) reducing use of exclusionary discipline, (b) enhancing academic engagement, and (c) enhancing teacher efficacy.

Reducing Use Of Exclusionary Discipline. Exclusionary discipline practices, such as office discipline referrals, detentions, and suspensions, have been shown to reduce time spent in instruction and increase the risk of further problem behavior, school dropout, and criminality (Hemphill, Toumbourou, Herrenkohl, McMorris, & Catalano, 2006). SWPBIS has been shown to reduce the use of office referrals and suspensions (Bradshaw, Mitchell, & Leaf, 2010), reduce risks of school dropout, and increase time spent receiving instruction in the classroom (Scott & Barrett, 2004).

Enhancing Academic Engagement. Quality of instructional environment and level of academic engagement are two primary mediators of the effectiveness of academic instruction (Ponitz, Rimm-Kaufman, Grimm, & Curby, 2010). In classrooms where instruction is disrupted by problem behavior, students are exposed to less academic instruction. SWPBIS reduces levels of problem behavior and emphasizes explicit instruction in and reinforcement of on-task behavior, enabling increased levels of academic engagement (K. Algozzine & Algozzine, 2007). Moreover, as SWPBIS leads to a safer, more predictable school environment (Horner et al., 2009), students can focus less on physical and social safety and more on learning.

Enhancing Teacher Efficacy. Teacher efficacy, the belief that one can positively enhance student outcomes, is strongly related to student achievement (Caprara, Barbaranelli, Steca, & Malone, 2006). Several recent studies have shown that implementation of SWPBIS is related to enhanced teacher efficacy (Kelm & McIntosh, 2012; Ross, Romer, & Horner, 2012). The effects of SWPBIS on teacher efficacy may be due to three phenomena. First, because SWPBIS is an instructional approach, the explicit instructional techniques used in SWPBIS may generalize to teaching academic skills (Kelm & McIntosh, 2012). Second, observing the positive effects of SWPBIS on social behavior may enhance feelings of efficacy for academic achievement as well. Third, efficacy may be enhanced by a shared vision and sense of purpose among school staff, a key component of organizational health. SWPBIS has been shown to enhance organizational health (Bradshaw et al., 2009), thereby increasing general teaching efficacy.

Summary and Recommendations

Although successful replication of SWPBIS implementation continues to be documented, some concerns have been expressed about SWPBIS use in school settings.

Some opposition is based on philosophical reasons, including the use of praise and tangible rewards as "bribes" and overemphasizing compliance (Lorhmann, Forman, Martin, & Palmieri, 2008). Other arguments question the effectiveness of a positive approach to addressing chronic problem behavior, and instead call for greater emphasis on exclusionary discipline and aversive punishment. Although important to consider, these concerns have not been well documented, whereas there is strong evidence supporting these practices. The strategic use of praise and other forms of extrinsic reinforcement have been shown to be effective, with little, if any detriment (Akin-Little, Eckert, Lovett, & Little, 2004), and an overemphasis on punitive disciplinary practices has been associated with increases in dropout rates and juvenile delinquency (Hemphill et al., 2006).

Given the strong evidence for improved academic engagement and achievement, enhanced perceptions of school safety, and reduced disciplinary referrals, adoption of school-wide behavior support approaches, such as SWPBIS, is recommended. However, SWPBIS can only create an effective context for academic instruction and has not consistently been shown to enhance achievement on its own (B. Algozzine, Wang, & Violette, 2011). Schools that invest in both high quality academic instruction and behavior support are more likely to experience high levels of student engagement and achievement (McIntosh, Chard, Boland, & Horner, 2006). Effective systems for both areas include quality instruction for all students, a continuum of evidence-based support for those who require it, a team-based approach, and use of data to monitor implementation, adjust practices, and measure outcomes.

References

Akin-Little, K. A., Eckert, T. L., Lovett, B. J., & Little, S. G. (2004). Extrinsic reinforcement in the classroom: Bribery or best practice. *School Psychology Review, 33,* 344–362.

Algozzine, K., & Algozzine, B. (2007). Classroom instructional ecology and school-wide positive behavior support. *Journal of Applied School Psychology, 24,* 29–47. doi: 10.1300/J370v24n01_02

Algozzine, B., Wang, C., & Violette, A. S. (2011). Reexamining the relationship between academic achievement and social behavior. *Journal of Positive Behavior Interventions, 13,* 3–16. doi: 10.1177/1098300709359084

Bradshaw, C. P., Koth, C. W., Thornton, L. A., & Leaf, P. J. (2009). Altering school climate through school-wide positive behavioral interventions and supports: Findings from a group-randomized effectiveness trial. *Prevention Science, 10,* 100–115. doi: 10.1007/s11121-008-0114-9

Bradshaw, C. P., Mitchell, M. M., & Leaf, P. J. (2010). Examining the effects of schoolwide positive behavioral interventions and supports on student outcomes: Results from a randomized controlled effectiveness trial in elementary schools. *Journal of Positive Behavior Interventions, 12,* 133–148. doi: 10.1177/1098300709334798

Caprara, G., Barbaranelli, C., Steca, P., & Malone, P. (2006). Teachers' self-efficacy beliefs as determinants of job satisfaction and students' academic achievement: A study at the school level. *Journal of School Psychology, 44,* 473–490. doi: 10.1016/j.jsp.2006.09.001

Durlak, J. A., Weissburg, R. P., Dymnicki, A. B., Taylor, R. D., & Schellinger, K. B. (2011). The impact of enhancing students' social and emotional learning: A meta-analysis of school-based universal interventions. *Child Development, 82,* 405–432. doi: 10.1111/j.1467-8624.2010.01564.x

Hemphill, S. A., Toumbourou, J. W., Herrenkohl, T. I., McMorris, B. J., & Catalano, R. F. (2006). The effect of school suspensions and arrests on subsequent adolescent antisocial behavior in Australia and the United States. *Journal of Adolescent Health, 39*, 736–744.

Horner, R. H., Sugai, G., Smolkowski, K., Eber, L., Nakasato, J., Todd, A. W., & Esperanza, J. (2009). A randomized, wait-list controlled effectiveness trial assessing school-wide positive behavior support in elementary schools. *Journal of Positive Behavior Interventions, 11*, 133–144. doi: 10.1177/1098300709332067

Kelm, J. L., & McIntosh, K. (2012). Effects of school-wide positive behavior support on teacher self-efficacy. *Psychology in the Schools, 49*, 137–147.

Lorhmann, S., Forman, S., Martin, S., & Palmieri, M. (2008). Understanding school personnel's resistance to adopting schoolwide positive behavior support at a universal level of intervention. *Journal of Positive Behavior Interventions, 10*, 256–269.

McIntosh, K., Bennett, J. L., & Price, K. (2011). Evaluation of social and academic effects of school-wide positive behaviour support in a canadian school district. *Exceptionality Education International, 21*, 46–60.

McIntosh, K., Chard, D. J., Boland, J. B., & Horner, R. H. (2006). Demonstration of combined efforts in school-wide academic and behavioral systems and incidence of reading and behavior challenges in early elementary grades. *Journal of Positive Behavior Interventions, 8*, 146–154.

Nelson, J. R., Martella, R. M., & Marchand-Martella, N. (2002). Maximizing student learning: The effects of a comprehensive school-based program for preventing problem behaviors. *Journal of Emotional and Behavioral Disorders, 10*, 136–148. doi: 10.1177/10634266020100030201

Ponitz, C. C., Rimm-Kaufman, S. E., Grimm, K. J., & Curby, T. W. (2010). Kindergarten classroom quality, behavioral engagement, and reading achievement. *School Psychology Review, 38*, 102–120.

Ross, S. W., Romer, N., & Horner, R. H. (2012). Teacher well-being and the implementation of School-wide Positive Behavior Interventions and Supports. *Journal of Positive Behavior Interventions, 14*, 118–128.

Scott, T. M., & Barrett, S. B. (2004). Using staff and student time engaged in disciplinary procedures to evaluate the impact of school-wide pbs. *Journal of Positive Behavior Interventions, 6*, 21–27. doi: 10.1177/10983007040060010401

Sørlie, M. A., & Ogden, T. (2007). Immediate impacts of PALS: A school-wide multi-level programme targeting behaviour problems in elementary school. *Scandanavian Journal of Educational Research, 52*, 471–492. doi: 10.1080/00313830701576581

Sugai, G., & Horner, R. H. (2009). Defining and describing schoolwide positive behavior support. In W. Sailor, G. Dunlap, G. Sugai, & R. H. Horner (Eds.), *Handbook of positive behavior support* (pp. 307–326). New York: Springer.

Yeung, A. S., Mooney, M., Barker, K., & Dobia, B. (2009). Does school-wide positive behaviour system improve learning in primary schools? Some preliminary findings. *New Horizons in Education, 57*, 17–32.

4.13

School Connectedness

CLEA MCNEELY
University of Tennessee, Knoxville

Introduction

This entry has two goals. First, it describes the relation between school connectedness and academic achievement. Although the research literature is not large, some key findings do emerge. School connectedness is positively associated with student engagement, attendance, grades, and high school graduation. However, it does not seem to predict academic performance as assessed by standardized tests unless there is a concomitant and strong emphasis on academic achievement. Second, this chapter describes the research that explores how schools can influence students' connectedness. Features of schools associated with school connectedness include an orderly classroom environment, high rates of participation in extracurricular activities, and fair and consistently enforced discipline policies.

Research Evidence

School Connectedness. School connectedness has been defined in many ways, including, but not limited to social belonging, group solidarity, teacher support, school attachment, school bonding, emotional engagement, and student satisfaction (Libbey, 2004). Empirical research is beginning to demonstrate that these multiple conceptualizations of connectedness, although related, are not interchangeable (McNeely & Falci, 2004). Student connectedness to adults at school appears to promote health, prosocial behaviors, and academic achievement (for reviews see McNeely, Whitlock, & Libbey, 2009; Osterman, 2000). In contrast, connection to peers can negatively impact these outcomes, depending on one's choice of peers. Therefore, this chapter focuses on definitions of connectedness that emphasize relationships with adults. The research reviewed in this chapter measured one or more dimensions of supportive relationships with adults, including support for autonomy, respect, fairness, caring, belonging, and warmth.

Multiple cross-sectional studies show small or moder-

ate correlations between connectedness and academic achievement (Osterman, 2000). Longitudinal studies also find modest correlations between school connectedness and four academic outcomes: attendance, dropout, self-reported grades, and perceived academic competence (Archimbault, Janosz, Fallu, & Pagani, 2009; Bond et al. 2007; Crosnoe, Johnson, & Elder, 2004; Hughes, Luo, Kwok, & Loyd, 2008; Wang & Holcombe, 2010). These studies test and find empirical support for the hypothesis that when students feel supported by adults at school, they feel more motivated to engage in class and do their homework, and they are more likely to value school. The slow process of academic disconnection that can lead to dropping out is forestalled or reversed.

Only a few studies have examined the association between school connectedness and standardized assessments of academic performance. These studies suggest that school connectedness may not improve test scores. In a sample of Australian adolescents from 26 secondary schools, Bond et al. (2007) found that school connectedness measured in eighth grade positively predicted high school completion, but it did not predict performance on the university entrance exam. They measured school connectedness as a composite of commitment to school, perceptions that teachers are fair, attachment to peers, a sense of belonging, and perceptions of student autonomy within the school. Battistitch, Solomon, Kim, Watson, and Schaps (1995) examined the relation of students' sense of community in third- to sixth-grade students in six school districts in the United States. Student perceptions of the sense of community positively predicted academic engagement and motivation. However, a sense of community did not predict gains in performance on standardized reading, writing, or math tests. Battistitch et al. (1995) measured each school's sense of community with a scale that assessed students' perceptions of caring relationships and their perception of the extent to which students participated in setting classroom policy and making decisions.

Interestingly, when researchers utilize teacher reports of student–teacher relationships, positive relationships with teachers do predict performance on standardized assessments of reading and math, at least in elementary school (Hamre & Pianta, 2001; Hughes et al., 2008). These divergent findings suggest that teacher and student assessments of the supportiveness of the relationship may not be measuring the same thing.

The Role of Academic Press. In a seminal paper, Lee and Smith (1999) offer one explanation for the lack of association between school connectedness and performance on standardized tests: that school connectedness cannot improve academic performance unless there is an emphasis on academic press. Hoy, Sweetland, and Smith (2002) describe schools with academic press as follows: "teachers set high but achievable goals, they believe in the capability of their students to succeed, the school environment is orderly and serious, and students, teachers, and principals all respect academic achievement and work for success" (p. 79).

Using data from sixth and eighth grade students in 304 schools in Chicago, Lee and Smith (1999) found that in schools with a strong academic press, students who felt supported had higher math and reading scores one year later than did students who did not experience support. However, in schools with no academic press, even students with high social support did not experience gains in math and reading. Lee and Smith measured social support as a composite of perceived support for learning from parents, teachers, peers, and the community.

Factors that Foster School Connectedness. A question commonly posed by educators is how to increase students' feelings of connectedness to school. To date, interventions and research have focused on four dimensions of school climate as potential candidates for improving school connectedness: the physical space and size of the school, interpersonal relationships within the school, principal leadership, and academic emphasis (Battistich et al., 1995; Bond et al., 2007; Monahan, Oesterle, & Hawkins, 2010). Together, these dimensions affect how a school is experienced. Schools can feel safe, respectful, and academically challenging, or, conversely, they can feel unsafe, exclusionary, or chaotic.

In general, the more domains in which a school has a positive climate, the more connected students feel to school (Whitlock, 2006). This is because developmental supports operate cumulatively. That said, certain dimensions of school climate appear to be more predictive of school connectedness than others (McNeely, Nonnemaker, & Blum, 2002; Waters, Cross, & Shaw, 2010; Whitlock 2006).

The following aspects of school climate have been empirically linked to school connectedness:

- Calm, orderly classrooms;
- Teaching practices that foster cooperative and participatory learning;

- Discipline policies that have adults respond with tolerance to the first infraction of school rules;
- Opportunities and support for students to be involved in ongoing decision making within the school (often called support for autonomy);
- Teachers' beliefs that students are worthy of respect and capable of learning;
- High rates of participation in extracurricular activities.

Neither class size nor school size are strongly correlated with a student's sense of school connectedness (McNeely et al., 2002).

Other dimensions of school climate have been theoretically linked to school connectedness, but these relations have not been empirically tested. These dimensions include the degree to which teachers are allowed to contribute to decision making, the degree to which teachers are respected and treated fairly, the degree to which teachers feel supported, and the physical appearance of the school. Moreover, almost all research to date is cross-sectional. Research that documents the association between school climate and *changes* in connectedness over the course of a school year would help distinguish causal effects of school climate.

Summary and Recommendations

Study Academic Performance. Schools are under pressure to increase school completion rates and improve student academic performance. The research reviewed above demonstrates that school connectedness can help forestall or reverse the disengagement process that leads to school dropout. However, researchers generally have not studied what is to educators the most important outcome—standardized assessments of academic performance. Future research should include data on student performance as well as comprehensive measures of the academic dimensions of the school climate, including specific teacher practices, to understand the ways that connectedness and academic strategies interact to produce gains in learning. Ideally, this research will examine bidirectional associations between academic performance and connectedness.

Monitor School Connectedness with Measures That Guide Practice. Increasingly, educators are incentivized or mandated to monitor school climate and connectedness and implement strategies to improve them. Although there is unlikely to be agreement on a single conceptualization of connectedness and its subdomains, education policy makers will continue to make choices about how to define and measure connectedness. Results of ongoing monitoring efforts will have a greater impact—and hence justify the investment—if two strategies are followed. First, connection to different actors within the school should be distinguished, as they do not correlate similarly with academic adolescent outcomes. Measures to monitor school connectedness should focus on the adult–student relationships because connection to adults positively predicts academic outcomes (except test scores). Second, the different types of supportive relationships should be distinguished, such as support for autonomy, relatedness, and competence (Connell & Wellborn, 1991), because these types of support are not equivalent in their nature or their effect.

Future Measures of Connectedness Should Be Linked to Theory and Should Ask About Specific Actions by Specific Actors. For example: "teachers respect students in this school" (teacher support for autonomy) or "teachers in this school think all students can learn" (teacher support for competence). These measures are not only more theoretically precise, but they provide better guidance for educators who are seeking to change the dimensions of school connectedness that are positively and strongly linked to achievement.

Recommendations for Schools and Teachers. Several consensus panels and organizations have published recommendations for improving school connectedness. These include, among others, the National Research Council and Institute of Medicine (2004), the Centers for Disease Control and Prevention (2009), and the Wingspread Declaration on School Connectedness (Blum & Libbey, 2004). The recommendations from each of these groups are similar, and include the following.

- Implement high academic standards and expectations, and provide academic support to all students;
- Apply discipline policies that are collectively agreed upon and fairly and consistently enforced;
- Foster trusting and respectful relationships among teachers, staff, students, administrators, and families;
- Hire and support capable teachers skilled in content, teaching techniques, and classroom management strategies;
- Ensure that every student has one supportive adult at school they can turn to for help;
- Foster high family expectations for school performance; and
- Welcome families into the school.

In addition, a small number of interventions to increase school connectedness have been longitudinally evaluated (Bond et al., 2007; Monahan et al., 2010). These strategies should help schools increase attendance and grades and reduce dropout. The pay-off of school connectedness for academic performance has been more elusive, but the evidence is promising that connectedness can magnify the positive effects of academic press.

References

Archambault, I., Janosz, M., Fallu, J.-S., & Pagani, L. S. (2009). Student engagement and its relationship with early high school dropout. *Journal of Adolescence, 32*, 651–670.

Battistich, V., Solomon, D., Kim, D.-il., Watson, M., & Schaps, E. (1995). Schools as communities, poverty levels of student populations, and students' attitudes, motives, and performance: A multilevel analysis. *American Educational Research Journal, 32*, 627–658.

Blum, R. W., & Libbey, H. (2004). School connectedness: Strengthening health and educational outcomes for teens: Executive summary. *Journal of School Health, 74*, 231–234.

Bond, L., Butler, H., Thomas, L., Carlin, J., Glover, S., Bowes, G., & Patton, G. (2007). Social and school connectedness in early secondary school as predictors of late teenage substance use, mental health, and academic outcomes. *Journal of Adolescent Health, 40*(357), e9–18.

Centers for Disease Control and Prevention. (2009). *School connectedness: Strategies for increasing protective factors among youth.* Atlanta, GA: Author.

Connell, J. P., & Wellborn, J. G. (1991). Competence, autonomy, and relatedness: A motivational analysis of self-system processes. In M. R. Gunnar & L. A. Sroufe (Eds.), *Self- processes and development: The Minnesota symposia on child development* (Vol. 23, pp. 43–77). Hillsdale, NJ: Erlbaum.

Crosnoe, R., Johnson, M., K., & Elder, G. M., Jr. (2004). Intergenerational bonding in school: The behavioral and contextual correlates of student-teacher relationships. *Sociology of Education, 77*, 60–81.

Hamre, B. K., & Pianta, R. C. (2001). Early teacher–child relationships and the trajectory of children's school outcomes through eighth grade. *Child Development, 72*, 625–638.

Hoy, W., Sweetland, , K., Scott, R., & Smith, P. A. (2002). Toward an organizational model of achievement in high schools: The significance of collective efficacy. *Educational Administration Quarterly, 38*, 77–93.

Hughes, J. N., Luo, W., Kwok, O.-M., & Loyd, L. K. (2008). Teacher–student support, effortful engagement, and achievement: A 3-year longitudinal study. *Journal of Educational Psychology, 100*, 1–14.

Lee, V. E., & Smith, J. B. (1999). Social support and achievement for young adolescents in Chicago: The role of school academic press. *American Educational Research Journal, 36*. 907–945.

Libbey, H. (2004). Measuring student relationships to school: Attachment, bonding, connectedness and engagement. *Journal of School Health, 74*, 274–283.

McNeely, C. A., & Falci, C. (2004). School connectedness and the transition into and out of health risk behaviors among adolescents: A comparison of social belonging and teacher support. *Journal of School Health, 74*, 284–292.

McNeely, C. A., Nonnemaker, J., M., & Blum, R. W. (2002). Promoting connectedness to school: Evidence from the National Longitudinal Study of Adolescent Health. *Journal of School Health, 72*, 138–146.

McNeely, C. A., Whitlock, J., & Libbey, H. (2009). School connectedness and adolescent well being. In S. Christianson & A. L. Reschly (Eds.), *Handbook on school-family partnerships*. New York: Erlbaum.

Monahan, K. C., Oesterle, S., & Hawkins, J. D. (2010). Predictors and consequences of school connectedness: The case for prevention. *The Prevention Researcher, 17*, 3–6.

National Research Council and Institute of Medicine. (2004). *Engaging schools: Fostering high school students' motivation to learn*. Washington, DC: National Academy Press.

Osterman, K. F. (2000). Students' need for belonging in the school community. *Review of Educational Research, 70*, 323–367.

Wang, M., & Holcombe, R. (2010). Adolescents' perceptions of school environment, engagement, and academic achievement in middle school. *American Education Research Journal, 47*(3), 633–662.

Waters, S., Cross, D., & Shaw, T. (2010). Does the nature of schools matter? An exploration of selected school ecology factors on adolescent perceptions of school connectedness. *British Journal of Educational Psychology, 80*, 381–402.

Whitlock, J. L. (2006). Youth perceptions of life at school: Contextual correlates of school connectedness in adolescence. *Applied Developmental Science, 10*, 13–29.

4.14

Teacher Mentoring, Coaching, and Consultation

Elise T. Pas
Johns Hopkins University

Daniel S. Newman
National-Louis University

Introduction

There is widespread concern nationally regarding the impact of teacher preparation and the resulting ability to adequately meet the academic and behavioral needs of students. In addition, issues of teacher turnover (nearly half of all American teachers leave the field within 5 years) have implications for student achievement. More specifically, in the 2007–2008 school year, 15% of American teachers overall left their schools and 8% left the profession altogether. Meanwhile, nearly one-quarter of beginning teachers (i.e., those with 1 to 3 years of experience) left their school in 2007–2008 (9% left the field; Keigher & Cross, 2010). In response to these rising concerns, many schools implement a variety of initiatives which are meant to provide teachers with direct and ongoing support and seek to foster teacher learning and performance.

This embedded support is often provided to teachers through the vehicles of mentoring, teacher induction (i.e., mentoring specifically targeting new teachers), coaching, and consultation. Though the approaches and focus of each type of support vary, in every case, support is embedded within the school as part of in-service training and supervision practices (i.e., teachers supporting other teachers, an internal coach providing support). The goal is to improve teacher practice first, and ultimately, student achievement. The purpose of this chapter is to define these constructs, discuss the research base on these models' effects on student achievement, and provide recommendations for practice. Although there is a burgeoning research base on teacher professional development in general, much of this research is beyond the scope of this chapter because it does not include embedded support.

Defining Teacher Mentoring, Coaching, and Consultation. In most cases, differentiation between support provided to teachers is less apparent when grouped by these categories, than when looking at the rigor within each ap-

proach. In general, within each approach, there are low rigor, low intensity, and nonformalized initiatives—"mentoring," "coaching," or "consultation"—and in each case, there are formal, structured, and intense versions of these same activities. For example, in the mentoring and induction literature, one can differentiate between (a) regularly provided induction that is low intensity and lacks structured training and time to provide mentoring and (b) comprehensive induction, which provides these elements as well as classroom observation and feedback (Glazerman et al., 2010).

Similarly, consensus is lacking in the field over what coaching entails and therefore how it is defined and implemented. In fact, many different approaches of coaching have been outlined and subsequently categorized (see Denton & Hasbrouck, 2009 for a full review). Currently, the most complete and comprehensive categorization system was put forth by the American Institutes for Research (AIR, 2004) and delineated the following coaching models: (a) technical coaching which targets novice teachers' instruction through an expert model of professional development (i.e., the coach is an expert teacher); (b) collaborative problem solving in which a coach helps teachers address the needs of a student of concern through facilitating problem-solving stages (i.e., problem identification, identifying and prioritizing goals, developing an action plan, and evaluating the outcomes); (c) reflective coaching in which the coach prompts reflective and critical thinking about teaching practices to change behavior; (d) team-building coaching which utilizes reflective coaching techniques within a group-context, and (e) reform or change coaching which targets whole-school (rather than individual teacher) improvement.

When organized through the above heuristic, overlap with research on school consultation emerges, such that both coaching and consultation "programs" or models utilize one or more of these overall approaches. Finally, within the consultation literature, there are a variety of models utilized which differ based on the focus of the problem solving, the level of the intervention, and the communicative approach (Denton & Hasbrouck, 2009). To a greater extent than in the mentoring, induction, or coaching literature, there are named consultation approaches which have been theoretically developed and studied; for example, Behavioral/Problem Solving Consultation (BPSC; Bergen, 1977), Instructional Consultation (IC; Rosenfield, 1987), and Conjoint Behavioral Consultation (CBC; Sheridan & Kratochwill, 2007).

Research Evidence

To date, much of the published literature in mentoring, coaching, and consultation has been theoretical or correlational, rather than causal. In addition, the vast majority of studies have come out of the United States, with consultation literature found more commonly than coaching or mentoring literature in other countries. Part of the reason there is limited research is that the constructs of "mentoring," "coaching," and "consultation" are not representative, in and of themselves, of an intervention; rather they represent a cluster of approaches which range from low intensity and unstructured to rigorous, clearly defined interventions. Within each of these areas, there are isolated randomized, controlled trials examining initiatives which have been well-defined. These studies are very recent and in some cases, are ongoing.

The theoretical mechanism through which embedded support interventions impact student achievement is by way of improving teacher practice. Therefore, a short-term outcome is teacher practice and student achievement is a long-term outcome for these initiatives. Thus, multiyear studies are needed to evaluate and detect student achievement outcomes.

Induction. In a randomized, controlled trial examining the impacts of comprehensive teacher induction and support, positive impacts on student achievement were found in the third year of the study, following 2 years of teacher exposure to comprehensive supports. There were no effects on teacher or student outcomes when teachers only received one year of teacher induction supports. Despite student achievement gains, no impacts were found on teacher satisfaction or retention (Glazerman et al., 2010), although these effects may take longer than 3 years to emerge. In a correlational study using the national Schools and Staffing Survey (SASS) data, induction programs were also found not to be significantly related to teacher retention (Smith & Ingersoll, 2004), although this represents all induction initiatives, not only those that are comprehensive. An international review of successful teacher induction reports that key components include training for mentors and in-service training for beginning teachers which is provided in a supportive environment and allows for teacher reflection on practice (Howe, 2006).

Coaching. In the case of coaching, the most rigorous studies are actually on professional development (PD)

initiatives targeting specific academic content and incorporate coaching (e.g., reading, math, or science; e.g., AIR, 2004). For example, the Reading First initiative utilized Reading First coaches as part of an effort to improve reading instruction and student achievement. The effects of coaching in particular have not been isolated in this case, but regardless, the results are mixed. Overall, Reading First had an impact on teacher practice and student decoding at one grade level, but not on broader student achievement (Gamse et al., 2008). The Early Reading PD Interventions Study did isolate the effects of coaching specifically by utilizing an experimental design with two, 1-year treatment conditions: a summer institute for teachers as a first treatment condition, and the same institute plus coaching as a second treatment condition. In both conditions, there were significant impacts on teacher knowledge of empirically-based instruction practices; however, no gains on student achievement emerged (Garet et al., 2008). It should be noted that one year may represent too short a timeline to observe such effects. Interestingly, coaching also did not account for statistically significant gains in teacher practice over the other treatment condition.

Consultation. Finally, though much literature has been published regarding school-based consultation models in the United States and in many other countries, much of it has been theoretical in nature or focused only on process variables. For example, a randomized controlled trial was conducted of the IC model. Although the final report of this study is not yet publicly available, data from an early stage of the IC study (i.e., after 1.5 years) indicated a positive and significant effect of IC on teacher efficacy, but not instructional practices or job satisfaction (Vu et al., 2011). Prior to this randomized controlled trial the most rigorous study of IC was a quasi-experimental study which indicated that classrooms within schools receiving IC support had significantly higher reading achievement (i.e., classroom averages) than classrooms in schools without IC (Silva, 2007).

Consultation is elusive to study given challenges for researchers such as identifying causality in a multiparty system (i.e., consultant, consultee, and client) and defining and measuring treatment integrity (Erchul & Martens, 2002). However, some authors have suggested that there exists an ample amount of evidence to demonstrate that consultation is an effective treatment (for example, see Erchul & Martens, 2002; Erchul & Sheridan, 2008).

Summary and Recommendations

The research on school change suggests that practitioners seeking to improve student achievement via embedded teacher support interventions need to provide enough time within the school day for these interventions to be implemented *and* enough years for the intervention to translate into improvements in student achievement. In addition, comprehensive interventions that build a structure (e.g., time, adequate training, and support from administration) for these models is of utmost importance. Finally, teacher support needs to be ongoing and scheduled regularly – and those providing the mentoring, coaching, or consultation need to also receive ongoing training and supervision to ensure their effectiveness.

In recent years, the U.S. Department of Education has specifically targeted the rigorous study of these school-based embedded teacher support interventions from which some promising findings are demonstrated. Research suggests that school change can take at least 3 to 5 years, which would imply that the existing studies are not of long-enough duration to adequately capture a long-term outcome like student achievement. There is a clear need for greater research which considers: (a) an agreement and clarity within each of these subareas (i.e., mentoring, coaching, and consultation) on observable, measurable intervention components with a clearer theory of action and (b) clarity on the level of intervention these represent (Erchul & Sheridan, 2008).

It is likely that many schools practice less rigorous versions of each of these approaches, which may be caused by and reflective of the literature that is lacking rigorous studies. In addition, outside of the issue of duration, the presented studies treat mentoring, coaching, and 6+consultation as school-level interventions yet struggle to detect school-level effects. The extent to which these interventions are applied school-wide must be considered; it is likely that not *all* teachers receive the intervention in a school, therefore, it would be harder to affect (and therefore, detect) school-level outcomes. With outside eyes looking more critically at education than ever before, particularly on teachers' impact on student learning, the question of how best to support teachers to promote positive outcomes for children is increasingly important. This review suggests that when conducted in a comprehensive way which embeds the proper support and training, mentoring, coaching, and consultation models can improve student achievement. By studying consultation, coaching, and mentoring with increased rigor we learn how to help teachers help children achieve.

References

American Institutes for Research. (2004). Conceptual overview: Coaching in the Professional Development Impact Study. Unpublished manuscript.

Bergen, J. R. (1977). *Behavioral consultation*. Columbus, OH: Merrill.

Denton, C. A., & Hasbrouck, J. (2009). A description of instructional coaching and its relationship to consultation. *Journal of Educational and Psychological Consultation, 19,* 150–175.

Erchul, W. P., & Sheridan, S. M. (2008). Overview: The state of scientific research in school consultation. In W.P. Erchul & S.M. Sheridan (Eds), *Handbook of research in school consultation* (pp. 3–12). New York: Erlbaum.

Erchul, W. P., & Martens, B. K. (2002). *School consultation: Conceptual and empirical bases of practice* (2nd ed.). Springer-Verlag: New York.

Gamse, B. C., Jacob, R. T., Horst, M., Boulay, B., Unlu, F., Bozzi, L, … Rosenblum, S. (2008). *Reading First impact final report* (Report number NCEE 2009-4039). Washington, DC: U.S. Department of Education. Retrieved from http://ies.ed.gov/ncee/pdf/20094038.pdf.

Garet, M.S., Cronen, S., Eaton, M., Kurki, A., Ludwig, M., Jones, W., … Silverberg, M. (2008). *The impact of two professional development interventions on early reading instruction and achievement* (Report number NCEE 2008-4030). Washington, DC: U.S. Department of Education. Retrieved from http://ies.ed.gov/ncee/pdf/20084030.pdf.

Glazerman, S., Isenberg, E., Dolfin, S., Bleeker, M., Johnson, A., Grider, M., & Ali, M. (2010). *Impacts of comprehensive teacher induction: Final results from a randomized controlled study* (Report number NCEE 2010-4027). Washington, DC: U.S. Department of Education. Retrieved from http://ies.ed.gov/ncee/pubs/20104027/pdf/20104027.pdf.

Howe, E. R. (2006). Exemplary teacher induction: An international review. *Educational Philosophy and Theory, 38,* 287–297.

Keigher, A., & Cross, F. (2010). *Teacher attrition and mobility: Results from the 2008-09 Teacher Follow-up Survey* (Report number NCES 2010-353). Washington, DC: U.S. Department of Education. Retrieved from http://nces.ed.gov/pubs2010/2010353.pdf .

Rosenfield, S. (1987). *Instructional consultation*. Hillsdale, NJ: Erlbaum.

Sheridan, S. M., & Kratochwill, T. R. (2007). *Conjoint behavioral consultation: Promoting family-school connections and interventions.* New York: Springer.

Silva, A. (2007). *A quasi-experimental evaluation of reading and special education outcomes for English language learners in Instructional consultation teams schools* (Unpublished dissertation). University of Maryland, College Park,

Smith, T. M., & Ingersoll, R. M. (2004). What are the effects of induction and mentoring on beginning teacher turnover? *American Educational Research Journal, 41,* 681–714.

Vu, P., Bruckman, K., Koehler, J., Kaiser, L., Rosenfield, S., Nelson, D., & Gottfredson, G. D. (2011). *The effects of Instructional Consultation Teams on teacher beliefs and instructional practices.* Manuscript submitted for publication.

4.15

The Link between Student Mobility and Academics

Bess Rose and Catherine P. Bradshaw
Johns Hopkins University

Introduction

The term *student mobility* refers to the transferring of students between schools. Although some school moves are expected or scheduled (i.e., normative), such as promotion from elementary school to middle school, mobility typically refers to nonpromotional transfers, such as the moving between schools at normally unscheduled times (i.e., nonnormative) (Mehana & Reynolds, 2004). The focus of the current paper is on nonnormative moves because these are the types of transitions which research has generally linked with reduced academic performance. One of the most common reasons for school mobility is change in family residence, which itself can be due to a variety of factors, such as the family experiencing some type of change or instability, as in the case of divorce/marriage, loss of employment, unstable housing, residential moves, migration, and employment related transfers (e.g., military base transfers). Other reasons for school mobility include school closures or merges, redistricting, and family choice (Schacter, 2001). Much of the research on student mobility has focused on urban and low income families because urban schools tend to be disproportionately affected by student mobility. However, there are also studies examining the impact of strategic moves, which are potentially beneficial (Rumberger, 2003). Such "upward mobility" can result in improved living conditions, and thus school environments (Deluca & Dayton, 2009; Hanushek, Kain, & Rivkin, 2004).

Research Evidence

Measuring Student Mobility. In order to understand the relationship between student mobility and academic achievement, it is first necessary to examine the different ways in which mobility can be measured. Mobility can be considered as both an individual factor influencing the performance of the student who moves, as well as an aggregate factor, such as a school- or classroom-level factor, which reflects the concentration of mobile students. There are a variety of methods for calculating student mobility as a school compositional characteristic. They often vary as a function of the importance placed on students transferring into a school (entrants or "inward mobility"), as opposed to those transferring out (withdrawals or "outward mobility"). Many schools and districts use a combination of both entrants and withdrawals to calculate mobility statistics. Some researchers posit that this statistic can be misleading, since it is the entrants, not the withdrawals, who impose the bulk of administrative, instructional, and socioemotional burden on the school (Lash & Kirkpatrick, 1990; Rogers, 2004). A similar approach can be used at the classroom level, to examine its more proximal influences on student achievement and other outcomes. There also has been considerable research examining student mobility as an individual-level characteristic.

Effects of Mobility. Not surprisingly, mobility has been negatively linked with academic achievement at the school, classroom, and individual student levels. For example, a meta-analysis by Mehana and Reynolds (2004) examined the impact of mobility on elementary reading and math achievement, and found a moderate composite effect size (–.25 for reading, –.24 for math), controlling for variables, such as socioeconomic status (SES) and grade level. This effect was interpreted as a 4-month difference between mobile and nonmobile students. However, the study did have some limitations; it included both expected and unexpected school transfers, and did not control for prior achievement, thereby limiting the ability to draw causal inferences, particularly with regard to the impact of nonnormative school moves. Rumberger and Larson (1998) further examined this issue using the National Educational Longitudinal Survey (NELS: 88) data. Controlling for gender, race/ethnicity, prior academic achievement and engagement, socioeconomic status, and family and school characteristics, they found that students who made a non-

155

promotional school transfer between 8th and 12th grades were less likely to complete high school than those with no unscheduled school moves; those who made two or more nonpromotional school transfers were also more likely to get a GED than nonmobile students.

Analysis at the classroom-level has demonstrated a potential influence of mobility on both mobile and nonmobile students. For example, Rogers (2004) used retrospective longitudinal data on students in grades 5, 8, and 12. After controlling for classroom poverty and suspension rates, mobility accounted for an additional small but significant amount of the variance in classroom academic outcomes, as measured by state standardized tests, attendance, promotion rates, and grade point average (Rogers, 2004). At the school level, there is evidence that even students who are not themselves mobile but attend schools with high mobility rates, have significantly lower standardized test scores than their nonmobile peers in low-mobility schools (Rumberger et al., 1998). Similarly, Hanushek, Kain, and Rivkin (2004) found that school quality was adversely affected by new student entry, especially during the school year.

Yet, there is some disagreement among researchers as to the specific role that mobility plays in academic achievement. For example, although mobile students overall perform worse on measures of academic achievement than nonmobile students, several researchers have suggested that much of this gap is explained by the students' background characteristics, especially socioeconomic status (e.g., Rumberger, 2003). Some studies suggest that it is a combination of family poverty, prior achievement, and family structure, not mobility, that account for the lower academic performance of mobile students (Alexander, Entwisle, & Dauber, 1996; Tucker, Marx, & Long, 1998). However, other studies have found a significant contribution of mobility when controlling for socioeconomic status and other background factors (Rogers, 2004; Rumberger & Larson, 1998; Wood, Halfon, Scarlata, Newacheck, & Nessim, 1993).

Further consideration of some potential mechanisms by which student mobility might impact student achievement could help elucidate this association. For example, a study of 21 classrooms in an urban elementary school identified some of the ways that mobility affects teachers and classrooms (Lash & Kirkpatrick, 1990). New students, who were usually admitted to class without any advance notice to the teacher, caused interruptions to class activities and functioning, because teachers needed to review material that the other students had already learned. From a behavioral perspective, new students also are unfamiliar with the school-wide and classroom norms and expectations for behaviors, thus making the environment less predictable for all students (Bradshaw, Sawyer, & O'Brennan, 2009).

With regard to the impact of strategic residential mobility on student achievement, much of this work has been conducted in the context of evaluations of housing policies and voucher programs. For example, DeLuca and Dayton (2009) reviewed the impact of housing voucher programs that enable poor families to move to neighborhoods that are safer, less disadvantaged, and less segregated. They found that some of these programs do appear to improve academic achievement of participating students in the short term. Another study found that students who moved within the same region but to a new district experienced a significant improvement in school quality; however, those who remained within the same district or changed regions did not gain in school quality (Hanushek, Kain, & Rivkin, 2004).

Summary and Recommendations

Issues related to student mobility can be addressed through both preventing mobility before it occurs, and mitigating its effects after it has occurred. With regard to prevention, schools and districts should implement policies aimed at promoting stability, such as allowing students who change residence across school boundaries to remain at the same school, at least for the current school year. Other research emphasizes the importance of improving the quality of education and climate of high-mobility schools in an effort to reduce the likelihood of other students relocating (Rumberger, 2003).

In terms of mitigating the effects of mobility, there are a number of strategies that administrators and teachers can use to help new students adjust to the school environment (e.g., (Bradshaw, Sudhinaraset, Mmari, & Blum, 2010; Lash & Kirkpatrick, 1990; Rumberger, 2003). For example, a recent study of mobile military students—those students who moved multiple times as a result of a parent's involvement in the military—found that lacking basic information about the school, such as the class schedule, where to sit at lunch, or layout of the school building can be very stressful (Bradshaw et al., 2010). Therefore, providing these materials about the school in the form of a new student packet is helpful in the early phases of the transition process. Student to student programs (e.g., buddy programs) also can help mobile students transition more efficiently into a new school environment. In schools with high rates of student mobility, new student and new family social events, such as picnics, should be offered periodically throughout the school year, not just at the beginning of the year (Bradshaw et al., 2010). Much of the disruption for the new student and the receiving classroom alike hinges on the lack of prior notice from the incoming family or the sending school. Therefore, strategies for promoting school and family collaboration and communication are critical to a smooth transition process. Demie, Lewis, and Taplin (2005) described a process for analyzing student data to identify achievement patterns related to mobility and to target student interventions appropriately. It is also critical to address the issue of mobility in teacher preparation and training programs in order to better prepare teachers for working with mobile populations (Lash & Kirkpatrick, 1990).

There are also a number of implications of these findings for educational researchers, the most obvious of which is careful consideration of the different methods for calculating mobility indices. School and classroom mobility data should also be closely examined in order to understand mobility patterns more accurately (Lash & Kirkpatrick, 1990). Longitudinal studies will inevitably have missing data due to students having moved. A close examination of this issue by Grady and Beretvas (2010) demonstrates that commonly utilized practices to deal with these missing records, such as deleting cases of mobile students or assigning students belonging to more than one school to the first school of membership, can considerably impact the pattern of findings. Researchers should also keep in mind that school and classroom enrollments fluctuate across the school year (Lash & Kirkpatrick, 1990), which may also influence school-based research studies of various educational interventions and curricula. Longitudinal analyses also should account for mobility using analytic procedures such as multiple membership random effects models (Grady & Beretvas, 2010). Moreover, even if mobility is not explicitly a question of interest, any type of school-based longitudinal study should carefully consider the impact of student mobility.

References

Alexander, K. L., Entwisle, D. R., & Dauber, S. L. (1996). Children in motion: School transfers and elementary school performance. *Journal of Educational Research, 90*, 3–12.

Bradshaw, C. P., Sawyer, A. L., & O'Brennan, L. M. (2009). A social disorganization perspective on bullying-related attitudes and behaviors: The influence of school context. *American Journal of Community Psychology, 43*(3–4), 204–220.

Bradshaw, C. P., Sudhinaraset, M., Mmari, K., & Blum, R. W. (2010). School transitions among military adolescents: A qualitative study of stress appraisal and coping. *School Psychology Review, 39*(1), 84–105.

DeLuca, S., & Dayton, E. (2009). Switching social contexts: The effects of housing mobility and school choice programs on youth outcomes. *Annual Review of Sociology, 35*, 457–491.

Demie, F., Lewis, K., & Taplin, A. (2005). Pupil mobility in schools and implications for raising achievement. *Educational Studies, 31*, 131–147.

Grady, M. W., & Beretvas, S. N. (2010). Incorporating student mobility in achievement growth modeling: A cross-classified multiple membership growth curve model. *Multivariate Behavioral Research, 45*, 393–419.

Hanushek, E. A., Kain, J. F., & Rivkin, S. G. (2004). Disruption versus Tiebout improvement: The costs and benefits of switching schools. *Journal of Public Economics, 88*, 1721–1746.

Lash, A., & Kirkpatrick, S. (1990). A classroom perspective on student mobility. *Elementary School Journal, 91*, 171–191.

Mehana, M., & Reynolds, A. J. (2004). School mobility and achievement: A meta-analysis. *Children and Youth Services Review, 26*(1), 93–119.

Rogers, L. (2004). *Student mobility in Maryland: A report to The Annie E. Casey Foundation.* Baltimore, MD: Maryland State Department of Education.

Rumberger, R. W. (2003). The causes and consequences of student mobility. *Journal of Negro Education, 72*(1), 6–21.

Rumberger, R. W., & Larson, K. A. (1998). Student mobility and the increased risk of high school dropout. *American Journal of Education, 107*, 1–35.

Schacter, J. (2001). Why people move: Exploring the March 2000 current population series. Current Population Reports. Washington, DC: U.S. Census Bureau.

Tucker, C. J., Marx, J., & Long, L. (1998). "Moving on": Residential mobility and children's school lives. *Sociology of Education, 71*, 111–129.

Wood, D., Halfon, N., Scarlata, D., Newacheck, P., & Nessim, S. (1993). Impact of family relocation on children's growth, development, school function, and behavior. *Journal of the American Medical Association, 270*, 1334–1338.

4.16

Service-Learning

SHELLEY H. BILLIG
RMC Research Corporation

Introduction

Service-learning is an instructional practice wherein youth master educational objectives by performing a service to meet an authentic community need. For example, high school students may build playground structures for elementary students or for the neighborhood park as a way of learning and applying geometry knowledge and skills. Middle school aged students may learn about local history by cleaning up cemeteries and learning about the individuals who are buried there by researching local archives and interviewing relatives. Elementary school students may conduct a nutrition campaign by learning about healthy foods and lifestyles and presenting an analysis of their nutritional intake to their parents and friends.

Ideally, service-learning has four components: *investigation*, where youth choose a social issue, investigate its expression in their community or in the world, determine what they can do to address the issue, and establish a baseline; *planning and preparation*, where youth decide exactly how they will tackle the issue and operationalize their thinking through an activity plan; *action*, where youth provide the community service; reflection, where adults facilitate youth writing, discussing, representing, or otherwise thinking about their service activities, the impact of their service on those being served, and the meaning the service has for themselves; and *demonstration/celebration*, where youth show others what they have accomplished and sometimes ask for changes in policy or practice from decision makers.

Service-learning can take place during the school day as a part of the traditional curriculum, during extended school hours, or as a community-based volunteer activity that is not associated with the school. School-based service-learning can be found at all grade spans, prekindergarten through graduate school. As of 2009, service-learning could be found in approximately one third of all K-12 public schools (Corporation for National and Community Service, 2009). In addition, service-learning can be found in many countries other than the United States, most notably Argentina, Canada, Germany, Israel, Japan, Mexico, and Singapore. In countries other than the United States, service-learning is known as community-engaged learning or another term indicating the link to the community.

Service-learning has its roots in the work of John Dewey who wrote about the importance of experiential education as a key teaching and learning strategy. Initially, the emphasis in service-learning was on having students provide community service and perhaps meet a requirement for provision of a certain amount of service hours. Over time, the practice has evolved to become more closely linked to curriculum, with a stronger balance between the service and the learning.

Research Evidence

There is a paucity of published research on service-learning, and most of what is available reflects the results of program evaluations. There were no meta-analyses published as of 2010, though there have been several published summaries of the research.

The leading summaries of service-learning impacts in the United States tend to be published once a decade in a themed issue of the *Phi Delta Kappan* (Billig, 2000; Conrad & Hedin, 1991; Furco & Root, 2010). In all of these articles, authors showed that results of primarily quasi-experimental studies of service-learning yielded significant positive impacts on students' academic engagement, civic engagement, and areas in the social-emotional learning realm.

In the academic domain, studies show that service-learning is strongly associated with academic engagement (e.g., Billig, 2010; Billig, Root, & Jesse, 2005; Furco, 2002). Increased interest in specific content, such as mathematics or science, is associated with students' willingness to attend class and persist with challenging content. Students develop a stronger sense of self-efficacy for learning (e.g., Billig, 2000; Furco & Root, 2010; Melchior, 1998). In a few quasi-experimental studies, service-learning was associated with increases in academic performance on state assessments (Billig, Jesse, & Grimley, 2008; Meyer, Billig, & Hofschire, 2004).

In the civic domain, service-learning is associated with the development of an ethic of service, intention to vote; awareness of social issues; and a range of civic activities and behaviors, such as forming relationships with civically engaged adults, reading the news more often and discussing current events with friends and family, and other aspects of civic responsibility (e.g., Billig et al., 2005; Kahne & Middaugh, 2009; Melchior & Bailis, 2002).

In the social-emotional learning domain, research consistently shows that participation in service-learning is linked with increases in self-management, ability to resolve conflicts without resorting to violence, and likelihood of displaying prosocial behaviors (e.g., Billig, 2011; Melchior, 1998; Yamauchi, Billig, Meyer, & Hofschire, 2006).

Nearly all of the studies from the past decade include discussions of the moderators of outcomes, and without exception, the studies show that quality matters. Studies in the 1990s showed that quality was defined as duration, youth voice in decision making, and link to curriculum. Starting in 2008, standards and indicators for K-12 service-learning quality were published (National Youth Leadership Council, 2008) and since that time, most studies use the standards as the definition of quality. These standards address: duration and intensity, link to curriculum, meaningful service, youth voice, community partnerships, respect for diversity, cognitively challenging reflection, and progress monitoring. As a group, these standards have consistently been shown to have a strong association with outcomes (e.g., Billig, 2010), although some of the standards and indicators, such as duration and intensity and link to curriculum, have a stronger connection than others. Many studies show that without quality defined in this way, there is little or no impact of participation other than developing an ethic of service (Billig, 2000, 2009; Furco & Root, 2010).

Other associations often found in the literature are that direct contact with those being served has a stronger impact than indirect contact. Females typically show stronger gains than males, whereas youth from disadvantaged backgrounds typically experience strong outcomes in the realms of academics and civics. Teachers with at least 2 years of experience in facilitating service-learning have stronger impacts than those with less experience. In addition, service-learning is much more likely to have impacts and be sustained when there is strong leadership support and when service-learning is addressed in state or local policies.

The literature is rife with critiques of the research in the field. In addition to the paucity of research, many of the studies have been criticized for their lack of rigor in the design, sampling, and analysis, and their relative lack of use of "hard data" to make their case. The studies cited here tend to be among the best in the field.

Summary and Recommendations

Though the research in this field is scarce, the practice of service-learning is promising, primarily because it is based on so many of the factors shown in the research to be associated with academic and civic engagement and performance. The hands-on nature of the approach and the strong emphasis on transfer of knowledge are both factors associated with increased achievement. The focus on collaboration, goal attainment, constructive feedback, and autonomy, which are features of service-learning, are similarly correlated with positive youth development outcomes.

References

Billig, S. H. (2000, May). Research on K–12 school-based service-learning: The evidence builds. *Phi Delta Kappan, 81*(9), 658–664.

Billig, S. H. (2009). Does quality really matter? Testing the new K-12 service-learning standards for quality practice. In B. E. Moely, S. H. Billig, & B. A. Holland (Eds.), *Advances in service-learning research: Vol. 9. Creating our identities in service-learning and community engagement* (pp. 131–157). Charlotte, NC: Information Age.

Billig, S. H. (2010, Summer/Fall). Why is service-learning such a good idea? Explanations from the research. *Colleagues Magazine, 5*(1), 8–11.

Billig, S. H. (2011, February). Making the most of your time: Implementing the K-12 service-learning standards for quality practice. *The Prevention Researcher, 18*(1), 8–13.

Billig, S. H., Jesse, D., & Grimley, M. (2008). Using service-learning to promote character development in a large urban district. *Journal of Research in Character Education, 6*(1), 21–34.

Billig, S. H., Root, S., & Jesse, D. (2005). The relationship between quality indicators of service-learning and student outcomes: Testing professional wisdom. In S. Root, J. Callahan, & S. H. Billig (Eds.), *Advances in service-learning research: Vol. 5. Improving service-learning practice: Research on models to enhance impacts* (pp. 97–115). Greenwich, CT: Information Age.

Conrad, D., & Hedin, D. (1991). School-based community service: What we know from research and theory. *Phi Delta Kappan, 72*(10), 743–749.

Corporation for National and Community Service (2009). *Volunteering in America: State and city trends and rankings.* Washington DC: Author.

Furco, A. (2002). Is service-learning really better than community service? A study of high school service program outcomes. In A. Furco & S. H. Billig (Eds.), *Advances in service-learning research: Vol.1. Service-learning: The essence of the pedagogy* (pp. 23–50). Greenwich, CT: Information Age.

Furco, A., & Root, S. (2010). Research demonstrates the value of service-learning. *Phi Delta Kappan, 91*(5), 16–20.

Kahne, J., & Middaugh, E. (2009). *Democracy for some: The civic opportunity gap in high school.* In J. Youniss & P. Levine (Eds.), *Engaging young people in civic life* (pp. 29–58). Nashville, TN: Vanderbilt University Press.

Melchior, A. (1998). *National evaluation of Learn and Serve America school and community based programs: Final report.* Washington DC: Corporation for National and Community Service.

Melchior, A., & Bailis, L. N. (2002). Impact of service-learning on civic attitudes and behaviors of middle and high school youth: Findings from three national evaluations. In A. Furco & S. H. Billig (Eds.), *Advances in service-learning research:Vol.1. Service-learning: The essence of the pedagogy* (pp. 201–222). Greenwich, CT: Information Age. Retrieved from http://www.service-learning.org/wg_php/library/?action=detailed&item=4277

Meyer, S. J., Billig, S. H., & Hofschire, L. (2004). The impact of k-12 school-based service-learning on academic achievement and student engagement in Michigan. In M. Welch & S. H. Billig (Eds.), *Advances in service-learning research: Vol. 4. New perspectives in service-learning: Research to advance the field* (pp. 61–85). Greenwich, CT: Information Age.

National Youth Leadership Council. (2008). *K-12 service-learning stan-dards for quality practice*. St. Paul, MN: National Youth Leadership Council.

Yamauchi, L. A., Billig, S. H., Meyer, S., & Hofschire, L. (2006). Student outcomes associated with service-learning in a culturally relevant high school program. *Journal of Prevention and Intervention in the Community, 32*(1/2), 149–164.

4.17

Single-Sex Schools and Academic Achievement

Shirley L. Yu and Isabel Rodriguez-Hejazi
University of Houston

Introduction

Grouping students according to sex is a prominent school organizational and reform effort. Two such alternatives include *single-sex instruction* or *single-sex classes*, in which students are grouped by sex for classes in certain subjects within larger coeducational school settings, and *single-sex schools* or *single-sex education*, in which the entire student body is one sex (Hoffman, Parker, & Badgett, 2008; Mael, Alonso, Gibson, Rogers, & Smith, 2005). This entry focuses on single-sex schools at the elementary and secondary level, with particular attention to their influence on academic achievement.

In the United States, the earliest schools were for boys only, and starting in the 1700s, boys and girls were taught separately for much of the period until the early 20th century, when coeducational schools became the norm. However, up until the early 1970s, schools still followed some single-sex curricula in their coeducational setting, providing such courses as home economics, garment making, and secretarial work for girls, and geography, mechanics, and industrial arts for boys (American Council for CoEducational Schooling, n.d.). These practices changed in 1972 with the passing of Title IX of the Education Amendments, which prohibited sex discrimination in federally funded education programs and activities (American Council for CoEducational Schooling, n.d.). Because of this amendment, public schools were prohibited from differentiating between sexes in their curriculum, and single-sex public education had become almost nonexistent by the 1980s.

Recently, interest has grown substantially for public single-sex education in the U.S. The No Child Left Behind Act of 2001 authorized school districts to use local or innovative program funds to offer single-sex schools and classrooms consistent with applicable laws. In 2006, Title IX regulations were amended by the U.S. Department of Education, providing school districts additional flexibility to implement single-sex programs. This amendment encouraged public schools to create innovative programs, including single-sex classes, in order to increase learning in the classroom. This amendment also emphasized that schools providing single-sex classes for one gender must offer the same opportunities for the other gender. In addition, parents and students are given the choice of whether students enroll in these classes (American Association of University Women, 2009; Riordan et al., 2008).

Single-sex schools have been and are predominantly offered as a private school option in the United States, including private day and boarding schools that are either religiously affiliated or independent (Salomone, 2003). Indeed, the majority of single-sex research studies have been conducted in Catholic single-sex schools (Mael et al., 2005). In other countries, single-sex schooling has had a long history, and studies on this topic come from countries such as Great Britain, Ireland, and Australia. In Australia, almost 25% of students in their final year of secondary school are enrolled in single-sex settings, a feature in a national context that is described as being in an intermediate position between rare and regular (Ainley & Daly, 2002). Single-sex schooling has been part of public education in many parts of the world. New Zealand has a great number of single-sex public schools. Because they are regarded highly by the community, demand for public single-sex schools exceeds the available enrollment spaces in the larger towns and cities in New Zealand (Harker, 2000).

Single-sex schools have been proposed and implemented for a variety of reasons (Campbell & Sanders, 2002), including potential benefits for differing groups: girls, particularly in the science, technology, engineering, and mathematics (STEM) subjects; boys; and disadvantaged youth, especially ethnic minority boys. Their very existence and the recent resurgence of interest is the subject of vigorous debate and differences in philosophical values, including but not limited to issues of gender equity, gender role stereotypes, and whether separate can be equal (Ewing, 2006; Salomone, 2003). Both proponents and opponents of single-sex schools have made claims based more upon theoretical beliefs and philosophical argument than empirical research findings. Thus, it is important to identify well-designed studies of the effects of single-sex schools.

Research Evidence

A comprehensive, systematic quantitative literature review of studies examining single-sex schools was conducted for the U.S. Department of Education (Mael et al., 2005). Utilizing a clearly outlined and rigorous set of inclusion criteria, 2,221 initial studies were reduced to 40 that compared single-sex and coeducational schools in English-speaking or Westernized countries and included statistical controls for individual difference factors (e.g., SES, ability, age), school and class differences. These studies were reviewed in terms of outcomes in the domains of concurrent academic achievement (i.e., all subjects, mathematics, science, verbal and English, and social studies achievement tests), long-term academic accomplishment, adaptation and socioemotional development, perceived school culture, and satisfaction. For each outcome, studies were coded in terms of whether findings across studies were in support of single-sex schooling, in support of coeducational schooling, null (no differences), or mixed (supporting both single-sex and coeducational schooling) (Mael et al., 2005). Findings across studies were further reported by outcome for girls and boys separately.

For all subject achievement test scores, the majority of the nine studies examined reported positive effects for both girls and boys in single-sex schools, specifically at the high school level. For the eight studies comparing single-sex and coeducational schooling for girls, five (63%) supported single-sex schooling. For the four studies comparing boys in the two types of schools, three (75%) supported single-sex schooling (Mael et al., 2005).

For mathematics achievement test scores, 8 of 14 studies (56%), all at the high school level, found null results, with equal numbers of studies (3 each, 22%) in support of single-sex or having mixed results, and none in favor of coeducation. For the 11 studies comparing single-sex and coeducational schooling for girls, only 3 (27%) supported single-sex schooling, with the majority (8, 73%) reporting null results, and none favoring coeducation. Of the 9 studies comparing boys in the two types of schools, 3 (33%) supported single-sex schooling, with 4 (44%) finding null results, and 2 (23%) favoring coeducation (Mael et al., 2005).

Results were similar for science achievement test scores: 5 of 8 studies (62%) at the high school level found null results, with 2 (25%) and 1 (13%) in support of single-sex or having mixed results, respectively. For girls, 2 of 5 studies (40%) supported single-sex schooling, with the other 2 (40%) reporting null results. For boys, 1 of 3 studies (33%) supported single-sex schooling, with 2 (67%) finding null results (Mael et al., 2005).

With respect to verbal and English achievement test scores, 7 of 10 studies (70%) at the high school level reported null results, and 3 (30%) were supportive of single-sex schooling. For girls, only 1 of 8 studies (12.5%) supported single-sex schooling, with the majority (6, 75%) reporting null results, and 1 (12.5%) with mixed results. For boys, 2 of 6 studies (33%) favored single-sex schooling, with 3 (50%) finding null results, and 1 (17%) mixed findings (Mael et al., 2005). Only one study, again at the high school level, examined social studies achievement, and it supported single-sex schools for girls, with null findings for boys (Mael et al., 2005).

Overall, for concurrent academic achievement, the results of Mael et al.'s (2005) systematic review supported positive effects of single-sex schools on all-subject achievement tests. For mathematics, science, English, and social studies, about one-third of the studies supported single-sex schools, with null and mixed results found in the remaining studies. Mael et al. describe the overall findings for concurrent academic achievement as a split between positive findings for single-sex (SS) schooling and no differences or null findings, with little support for coeducational (CE) schooling (p. xv). This "small to medium support" (p. 83) for single-sex schooling applies to both males and females at the elementary and high school levels, although males are underrepresented in this research.

Few studies have examined the long-term impact of single-sex schooling. Two studies (Marsh, 1989; Riordan, 1990) in Mael et al.'s (2005) review examined protracted effects of single-sex compared to coeducational school attendance in high school. For both college graduation and graduate school attendance one study (Marsh, 1989) found null results. For graduate school admissions tests, one study favored single-sex schools for both boys and girls and one found null results. Another longitudinal study examining long-term academic accomplishment of a sample of British people born in 1958 found beneficial effects of single-sex schooling for girls at age 16, with no effects for either sex at later ages. Single-sex schooling was also associated with attainment in gender-atypical subject areas for both sexes during the school years as well as later in life (Sullivan, Joshi, & Leonard, 2010)

Aside from achievement, single-sex schooling has also been implemented and investigated in terms of impact on attitudinal and socioemotional outcomes. Based upon Mael et al.'s (2005) review, studies examining self-concept, locus of control, school track and subject preferences were split between those supporting single-sex schooling and studies indicating no statistical difference. For higher educational and career aspirations, single-sex schools had positive effects for girls. Further, female graduates of single-sex high schools reported higher academic engagement and confidence in mathematics and computer skills in one of the studies reviewed (Sax, 2009).

Summary and Recommendations

Overall, the available research on the effectiveness of single-sex schools on a variety of outcomes is mixed. There is some evidence that single-sex schooling can be helpful, in particular for outcomes such as academic achievement and positive academic aspirations. However, for many outcomes (e.g., gender equitable classroom treatment, school climate or culture, later college performance), there are no studies or too few studies meeting the review criteria to allow for any conclusions (Mael et al., 2004, 2005). In terms of future research, more experimental and quasi-experimental studies with adequate controls are needed in order to provide more definitive evidence of any benefits of single-sex schools, as many of the studies in the literature are considered flawed and limited in quality (Mael et al., 2005). More studies on public single-sex schools in the United States are needed, especially at the elementary level. In addition, research examining the actual mechanisms by which single-sex schools may provide benefits over coeducation is needed. For example, if fewer distractions are indeed a hallmark of single-sex schools as widely perceived, then research is needed to support this contention. Further, studies are needed to examine important moderators, or variables that have potential differential effects for single-sex schooling, such as socioeconomic status or ethnicity (Mael et al., 2005). Currently, many of the claims of the benefits of single-sex schools are based more on perception or opinion than on scientific evidence; accordingly, research is needed to support these claims.

In recognition that single-sex schooling will likely increase and that families will continue to explore this option, a number of recommendations for practice should be considered. The main recommendation cited by multiple experts is the need for more professional development for teachers on meeting the needs of their students in single-sex schools (Cable & Spradlin, 2008; Riordan et al., 2008). To be effective, single-sex schooling cannot be simply the segregation of boys and girls. Effective teaching strategies and a school culture where teachers can share experiences without fear of threat need to be developed. Some advocate that gender differences must be taken into account, and educators must be trained in how to successfully explore these differences in the classroom to influence academic achievement (Gurian, Stevens, & Daniels, 2009; National Association for Single Sex Public Education, n.d.), whereas others argue that effective teaching is not gender-specific.

In order for single-sex education to succeed, there must be clear commitment and support of the approach from administrators, educators, parents, students, and community members, which includes keeping stakeholders fully informed of the rationale behind the school's approach and its benefits (Younger & Warrington, 2006). This involves establishing a rapport among educators of shared respect and commitment to single-sex education. This rapport must be extended to the community and to the students themselves, so together they demonstrate a strong commitment to the school's aspirations. Further, administration and staff must make efforts over time to sustain, monitor, and evaluate the effects of single-sex schools (Younger & Warrington, 2006).

References

Ainley, J., & Daly, P. (2002). Participation in science courses in the final year of high school in Australia: The influences of single-sex and coeducational schools. In A. Datnow & L. Hubbard (Eds.), *Gender in policy and practice: Perspectives on single-sex and coeducational schooling* (pp. 243–262). New York: RoutledgeFalmer.

American Association of University Women. (2009). *Separated by sex: Title IX and single-sex education.* AAUW Public Policy and Government Relations Department. Retrieved from http://www.aauw.org/act/issue_advocacy/actionpages/upload/single-sex_ed111.pdf

American Council for CoEducational Schooling (n.d.). History: A short history of the coeducation of youth in the U.S. Retrieved from http://lives.clas.asu.edu/acces/history.html

Cable, K., & Spradlin, (2008). *Single-sex education in the 21st century* (Education Policy Brief, 6[9]). Bloomington, IN: Indiana University Center for Evaluation and Education Policy. Retrieved from http://www.eric.ed.gov/PDFS/ED503856.pdf

Campbell, P. B., & Sanders, J. (2002). Challenging the system: Assumptions and data behind the push for single-sex schooling. In A. Datnow & L. Hubbard (Eds.), *Gender in policy and practice: Perspectives on single sex and coeducational schooling* (pp. 31–46) New York: RoutledgeFalmer.

Ewing, E. T. (2006). The repudiation of single-sex education: Boys' schools in the Soviet Union, 1943–1954. *American Educational Research Journal, 43,* 621–650.

Gurian, M., Stevens, K., & Daniels, P. (2009). *Successful single-sex classrooms: A practical guide to teaching boys and girls separately.* San Francisco, CA: Jossey-Bass.

Harker, R. (2000). Achievement, gender and the single-sex/coed debate. *British Journal of Sociology of Education, 21,* 203–218.

Hoffman, B. H., Parker, R. P., & Badgett, B. A. (2008). The effect of single-sex instruction in a large, urban, at-risk high school. *The Journal of Educational Research, 102,* 15–35.

Mael, F., Alonso, A., Gibson, D., Rogers, K., & Smith, M. (2005). Single-sex versus coeducational schooling: A systematic review. Washington, DC: U.S. Department of Education, Office of Planning, Evaluation, and Policy Development, Policy and Program Studies Service. Retrieved from http://www2.ed.gov/rschstat/eval/other/single-sex/single-sex.pdf

Mael, F., Smith, M., Alonso, A., Rogers, K., & Gibson, D. (2004). *Theoretical arguments for and against single-sex schools: A critical analysis of the explanations.* Washington, DC: American Institutes for Research. Retrieved from http://www.air.org/files/SSX_Explanatory_11-23-04.pdf

Marsh, H. W. (1989). Effects of attending single-sex and coeducational high schools on achievement, attitudes, behaviors, and sex differences. *Journal of Educational Psychology, 81,* 70–85.

National Association for Single Sex Public Education (NASSPE). (n.d.). *About NASSPE.* Retrieved from http://www.singlesexschools.org/home-nasspe.htm

Riordan, C., Faddis, B. J., Beam, M., Seager, A., Tanney, A., DiBiase, R., &Valentine, J. (2008). *Early implementation of public single-sex schools: Perceptions and characteristics.* Washington, DC: U.S. Department of Education, Office of Planning, Evaluation and Policy Development. Retrieved from http://www2.ed.gov/rschstat/eval/other/single-sex/characteristics/characteristics.pdf

Salomone, R. C. (2003). *Same, different, equal: Rethinking single-sex schooling.* New Haven, CT: Yale University Press.

Sax, L. J. (2009). *Women graduates of single-sex and coeducational high schools: Differences in their characteristics and the transition to college.* Los Angeles, CA: The Sudikoff Family Institute for Education and New Media, UCLA Graduate School of Education and Information Studies.

Sullivan, A., Joshi, H., & Leonard, D. (2010) Single-sex schooling and academic attainment at school and through the lifecourse. *American Educational Research Journal, 47,* 6–36.

Younger, M. R., & Warrington, M. (2006). Would Harry and Hermione have done better in single-sex classes? A review of single-sex teaching in coeducational secondary schools in the United Kingdom. *American Educational Research Journal, 43,* 579–620.

4.18

Summer School and Student Achievement in the United States

JORDAN D. MATSUDAIRA
Cornell University

Introduction

Summer school has long been a feature of elementary and secondary education in the United States, but since the mid-1990s it has become a prominent school strategy for improving student achievement. The first summer school programs were created in the early 1900s to provide organized recreational activities for children left idle in the wake of labor laws that prevented children from working (Cooper, Charlton, Valentine, Muhlenbruck, & Borman, 2000). Over time, however, educators began to embrace the potential for such programs to improve student achievement, either by providing more educational time for enrichment activities or for remedial education for children falling behind.

The interest in summer school as a remedial strategy increased markedly in response to building evidence on summer learning loss—the phenomenon that children, especially those from low-income families, lose about one month's worth of achievement gains over the summer vacation months. In the past decade, many districts have adopted accountability policies that force students not meeting yearly achievement targets in key subject areas to attend summer school as a condition for promotion to the next grade. Chicago Public Schools were the first to implement such a policy in 1996, but many other large districts followed close behind, including New York City, Los Angeles, Philadelphia, Boston, and Washington, DC. This article briefly reviews some of the research in the United States that motivated this public policy interest in summer school, and presents results from the best of the many research studies that evaluate its effectiveness in promoting student achievement.

Research Evidence

Much of the interest in summer school is motivated by the finding that students tend to lose some of their achievement gains during the summer. Cooper, Nye, Charlton, Lindsay, and Greathouse (1996) reviewed 39 studies dating back to 1906 and conducted a meta-analysis of 13 more recent studies of the effects of summer vacation on achievement. Their meta-analysis suggests that summer vacation reduces achievement by an overall average of one month on a grade-level equivalent scale, or by about one tenth of a standard deviation relative to Spring test scores (Cooper et al. 1996, p. 227). One of the most influential studies in this literature is Entwisle and Alexander (1992), who showed that summer setback occurs primarily for students from a low socioeconomic background (SES)—indeed, nonpoor children exhibited summer achievement gains—and thus contributes to Black–White achievement gaps since minority students are differentially poor. Alexander, Entwisle, and Olson (2007) found that early differences in summer learning manifest themselves in SES related differences in long-term outcomes such as high school completion and 4-year college attendance.

What does the literature have to say about the effectiveness of summer school in preventing these types of learning losses? The Sustaining Effects Study was one of the earliest serious attempts to evaluate the achievement effects of summer school. Started in 1975, the study tracked about 120,000 students across 300 elementary schools for 3 years. Carter (1984) reports that the study found that there were no achievement effects from attendance at summer school on math or reading achievement. While this finding led to a pessimistic view of summer school for some years after its publication, an important caveat is that at the time of the study summer school programs were not well tailored to increase achievement, particularly in math and reading, and so the null finding might not be surprising. In the three decades since the Sustaining Effects Study, as summer school programs grew in prevalence—Borman (2001) suggested their prevalence approximately doubled—they also became more focused on providing remedial instruction in academic subjects, and so may have become more effective in bolstering student achievement.

Cooper et al. (2000) conducted a meta-analysis of 54 published studies of summer school programs. Most of the studies (41) reviewed were described as remedial programs, and seven described their goal as acceleration. For the remedial programs, Cooper et al. (2000) found an average effect size of .26 standard deviations. The average effects were positive for most subgroups identified, but tended to be larger for students in higher grades relative to those in lower grades, and for middle class students relative to low SES students. This latter result seems at odds with the summer learning loss literature, but Cooper et al. (2000) speculate that it may be due to differences in the quality of the summer school programs to which students from different SES backgrounds have access. The overall average impact of acceleration programs on achievement was quantitatively similar, but less precisely estimated.

A major limitation of the studies reviewed by Cooper et al. (2000) is that the research designs are generally weak, often based on simple pretest–posttest comparisons or designs lacking an equivalent comparison group. The direction of bias in such designs is hard to pin down in general, as it depends on the nature of student selection into summer school. If programs are voluntary, a reasonable guess is that differentially motivated students will be more likely to enroll in summer school leading to a positive bias (summer school programs will appear more effective than they actually are). On the other hand, with mandatory programs the selection might be just the opposite if teachers choose students to attend summer school who are struggling differentially. Indeed, the average effect size found in the five reviewed studies employing random assignment was substantially lower at .14 standard deviations, suggesting that these selection effects are indeed important.

Several studies in the past decade have better addressed these methodological issues, and provide the best evidence on the effects of summer school on student achievement. Borman and Dowling (2006) report on a randomized evaluation of a multiyear summer school intervention starting in 1999 called Teach Baltimore, which was designed to proactively prevent summer learning loss by enrolling students in summer school starting the year following kindergarten or first grade. Starting with a group of students who voluntarily applied, the program randomly assigned students to either attend summer school for three consecutive years, or to a no treatment control condition. While the program revealed no significant achievement effects of being randomized to attend summer school, there was significant noncompliance with only one in three students attending all 3 years of the treatment. The authors report, however, statistically significant instrumental variable estimates of summer school attendance on achievement for "compliers"—defined as those students participating at an above average attendance rate for at least two summers—of about .3 standard deviations each for vocabulary, comprehension, and reading. While encouraging, the effect for noncompliers might be significantly lower than this and so the overall effects of the program might be more modest. Another caveat about

their study is that some of the achievement gaps between treatment and control students become pronounced during the school year, rather than during the summer as one would expect if the effects are driven primarily by differences in exposure to summer school. This might suggest some failure of randomization, or perhaps an endogenous response of teachers to students' participation in summer school.

As described above, for most students in recent years summer school is not an option chosen voluntarily as in Teach Baltimore, but rather a mandatory consequence for students not meeting achievement standards on high-stakes tests. Two studies have implemented quasi-experimental evaluations of these types of mandatory programs in two large urban school districts. Matsudaira (2008) evaluated the mandatory summer school policy adopted in a large urban school district in the Northeast that is similar to the programs implemented by many other urban districts, requiring all students in grades 3 to 8 failing end of year exams in math or reading to attend summer school. In principle, students attending summer school received targeted instruction in the subject(s) they failed and were required to get a satisfactory score on a similar test at the end of the summer in order to be promoted to the next grade.[3] In practice, however, few students were retained in the district.

Note that the rule requiring students to attend summer school creates a stark problem for evaluating the effect of summer school, as now the students who attend summer school are by design lower achieving than students who do not attend. Since achievement scores are correlated over time, it would be very surprising then if the scores of students who attended summer school were not lower than the scores of students not attending, leading to the spurious conclusion that summer school was ineffective or harmful to achievement. Matsudaira (2008) overcomes this problem with a regression-discontinuity research design that essentially compares the subsequent achievement of students scoring just below and just above the passing thresholds on the end of year exams. Since students in this narrow range of scores on the end of year exam are similar to each other in terms of other factors that might affect achievement but students barely failing the exam are much more likely to attend summer school, the difference in their later year achievement scores can be causally attributed to summer school. Using this design, Matsudaira (2008) finds an average effect of summer school attendance across all grades of about .12 standard deviations for both math and reading.

As noted above, a common feature of recent summer school programs, particularly in urban districts, is the addition of testing at the end of the summer: many districts require students who fail to score above a minimum proficiency threshold at the end of the summer session to repeat a grade. This high-stakes environment may make students more engaged and thus increase summer school's potential for increasing achievement, but if retention has an independent impact on achievement as some research has shown (Eide & Showalter 2001; Holmes 1989), then coupling a policy of sending students to summer school with a probability of retention might have different effects than summer school alone.

Using a research design similar to Matsudaira (2008), Jacob and Lefgren (2004) evaluated the summer school program implemented by Chicago Public Schools in 1996. In Chicago, between 10 and 20% of students mandated to attend summer school were eventually retained. Overall, the study finds a positive net effect on third grade achievement of summer school and grade retention equal to about 20% of a year's worth of learning for both math and reading, and finds that achievement measured 2 years later is about 25 to 40% less. For 6th grade, the measured effects were not significantly different from zero. Somewhat surprisingly, the study finds fairly large positive effects of grade retention that apparently account for nearly half of the net effects (of summer school and grade retention) on achievement.

Summary and Recommendations

Overall, there is broad research consensus that summer school programs have a modest positive impact on student achievement. The best studies of remedial programs—the randomized studies surveyed by Cooper et al. (2000), Matsudaira (2008), and Jacob and Lefgren (2004)—suggest effect sizes on the order of .14 standard deviations. This appears quite substantial when compared to the effects of benchmark successful interventions like the Project Star class-size reduction, especially given the relatively short duration and low cost of summer school. There is not much credible evidence that these programs are more effective for low-income youth, as predicted by the literature on summer learning loss, but that should not take away from the evidence that programs targeted at low-income youth have clearly been demonstrated to be effective.

One clear implication for education policy is that there is a human capital return to investing in summer school programs, and that targeting such programs to low-income youth is one way to decrease class-based disparities in academic achievement. That said, allocating scarce resources to programs targeting summer learning should take into account the effectiveness of summer school relative to some other strategies. Kim (2006) and Kim and White (2011) have shown that simply providing students with books in a voluntary summer reading program is a low-cost way of increasing reading achievement. And Lehman (2011) provided tentative evidence that switching to a year-round school calendar, whereby the long summer break is replaced with several shorter breaks during the academic year, in-creased the number of students passing year-end exams in Chicago Public Schools.

Future research in this area would do a service by comparing the cost-effectiveness of these other strategies to summer school.

Note

1. Students who did not meet minimum attendance thresholds or who received unsatisfactory teacher reviews of their coursework were also required to attend summer school, but in practice few students passing end of year exams were required to attend for these reasons.

References

Alexander, K. L, Entwisle, D. R , & L. S Olson. (2007). Lasting consequences of the summer learning gap. *American Sociological Review, 72*(2), 167–180.

Borman, G. D. (2001). Summers are for learning. *Principal, 80*(3), 26–29.

Borman, G. D., & Dowling, N. M. (2006). Longitudinal achievement effects of multiyear summer school: Evidence From the Teach Baltimore randomized field trial. *Educational Evaluation and Policy Analysis, 28*(1), 25–48.

Carter, L. F. (1984). The sustaining effects study of compensatory and elementary education. *Educational Researcher, 13*(7), 4–13.

Cooper, H., Charlton, K., Valentine, J. C., Muhlenbruck, L., & Borman, G. D. (2000). Making the most of summer school: A meta-analytic and narrative review. *Monographs of the Society for Research in Child Development, 65*(1), 1–127.

Cooper, H., Nye, B., Charlton, K., Lindsay, J., & Greathouse, S. (1996). The effects of summer vacation on achievement test scores: A narrative and meta-analytic review. *Review of Education Research, 66*, 227–268.

Eide, E. R., & Showalter, M. (2001). The effect of grade retention on educational and labor market outcomes. *Economics of Education Review, 20*, 563–576.

Entwisle, D. R., & Alexander, K. L. (1992). Summer setback: Race, poverty, school composition and mathematics achievement in the first two years of school. *American Sociological Review, 57*, 72–84.

Holmes, C. T. (1989). Grade level retention effects: A meta-analysis of research studies. In L. A. Shepard & M. L. Smith (Eds.), *Flunking grades: Research and policies on retention* (pp. 16–33). London: Falmer Press.

Jacob, B. A., & Lefgren, L. (2004). Remedial education and student achievement: A regression-discontinuity analysis. *Review of Economics and Statistics, 86*(1), 226–244.

Kim, J. (2006). Effects of a voluntary summer reading intervention on reading achievement: Results from a randomized field trial. *Educational Evaluation and Policy Analysis, 28*(4), 335–355.

Kim, J. S., & White, T. G. (2011). Solving the problem of summer reading loss. *Phi Delta Kappan, 92*(7), 64–67.

Lehman, D. (2011). *Year-round education and student achievement: The effectiveness of year-round education in Chicago* (Senior Thesis). Princeton University, Princeton, NJ.

Matsudaira, J. D. (2008). Mandatory summer school and student achievement. *Journal of Econometrics, 142*(2), 829–850.

4.19

Within Class Grouping

Arguments, Practices, and Research Evidence

YIPING LOU
University of South Florida

Introduction

Whether and how to group students within class for effective learning is a question that teachers, researchers, and policy makers have asked for several decades. Two of the most common and contentious within-class grouping practices are homogeneous ability grouping and heterogeneous ability grouping. Each has its enthusiastic advocates and strong critics.

The main argument for homogeneous within-class ability grouping is that when students are grouped by ability, teachers can have greater flexibility in adjusting learning objectives and the pace of instruction to meet individual learning needs, especially in a diverse classroom (Chorzempa & Graham, 2006). For example, teachers can increase the pace and level of instruction for high achievers and provide more individual attention, repetition, and review for low achievers. Most of the studies on the effects of within-class homogeneous ability grouping on student achievement were conducted in the late 1950s and 1960s. Similar to critics of between-class ability grouping, critics of within-class ability grouping argue that separating students into different ability groups may serve to increase divisions along ethnic, racial, and class lines (Rosenbaum, 1976), have detrimental psychological effects such as lower self-concept (Rogers, Smith, & Coleman, 1978) on lower ability students due to social comparison (Reuman, 1989), low expectation from their teachers and therefore lower learning opportunity (Dreeben & Barr, 1988), and consequently lower achievement (Chorzempa & Graham, 2006).

Heterogeneous within-class ability grouping became more popular in the 1980s and 1990s when social constructivist learning theory became more widely accepted in all levels of education. The primary goal of heterogeneous grouping tends to be the emphasis of social interaction, cooperative and collaborative learning (Lou et al., 1996). Cooperative learning is a more structured form of small-group instruction that utilizes both positive interdependence and individual accountability to encourage students to learn (Abrami et al., 1995). Advocates of heterogeneous ability learning argue that such grouping encourages more peer helping and cognitive elaboration among group members. Critics of heterogeneous within-class ability grouping, on the other hand, are concerned that higher ability students are denied the opportunity to learn in heterogeneous ability groups because they have already mastered most of the material, and the pace and level of learning tend to be below their capacity, so that their main role in the group becomes that of teacher rather than learner (Lou et al., 1996).

Both forms of within-class grouping continue to be used today in the United States, Britain, and other countries, although the preference of use appears to differ for different subject areas and levels of education. In a survey across the United States, Chorzempa and Graham (2006) found that 63% of the participating elementary teachers employed within-class ability grouping in reading, especially in schools with diverse student characteristics. One difference the researchers noticed is that the groups were smaller and more flexible than those formed in the past. The primary reason teachers gave for using within-class ability grouping was to better meet students' needs in a diverse classroom. In Britain, Hallam, Ireson, Lister, Chaudhury, and Davies's (2003) survey found that homogeneous within-class ability grouping was most widely used in the core subjects of mathematics and English; in all other subjects, the most prevalent grouping structure was mixed ability groups within mixed ability classes. At the secondary level in Britain, students are often assigned to work in small groups of four to six students during parts of a lesson in science and English to discuss ideas and processes; in mathematics classes, the most common organization is whole class teaching and individual seat work with occasional small-group learning (Kutnick, Blatchford, Clark, MacIntyre, & Baines, 2005).

Research Evidence

Several meta-analyses have been conducted synthesizing empirical studies that compared the effects of within-class grouping versus no grouping on student achievement and other outcomes (see Table 4.19.1). Although the magnitude of the effect sizes appear to vary across the syntheses, the results showed an average small to moderate positive effect of grouping based on empirical studies that used experimental or quasi-experimental comparisons. Early meta-analyses (Kulik & Kulik, 1987, 1991; Slavin, 1987) focused on the effects of homogeneous within-class ability grouping. The average effect sizes were +0.32, +0.25, and +0.17, respectively, indicating small positive effects of within-class grouping on student achievement.

Lou et al. (1996) conducted a more comprehensive synthesis, addressing two research questions: (a) the effects of within-class grouping versus no grouping and (b) the effects of homogeneous ability grouping versus heterogeneous ability grouping. For the first comparison, their results were based on 145 independent findings from 66 studies. On average, within-class grouping has a small, significantly positive effect over no grouping on student achievement (weighted mean ES = +0.17). The effect sizes were similar for homogeneous ability grouping versus no grouping (ES = +0.16) and heterogeneous ability grouping versus no grouping (ES = +0.19). There was no significant difference in student self-concept between grouped and ungrouped classes. Students in the within-class grouping condition on average had more positive attitudes toward the subjects they were learning. A number of study features significantly moderated the effects of within-class grouping on student achievement. Within-class grouping effects on student achievement were larger: (a) when outcomes were measured by locally developed tests and geared to instruction, (b) when teachers received training on small-group instruction, (c) when more or different instructional materials and rewards were used in small-group instruction, (d) when grouping basis used standardized tests or mixed sources, (e) when cooperative learning strategies were used, and (f)

for lower ability students although effects of within-class grouping were positive for students at all ability levels, in all subjects and at all grade levels.

In the studies that directly compared homogeneous within-class ability grouping versus heterogeneous within-class ability grouping, the mean effect size was +0.12 favoring homogeneous ability grouping based on 20 independent findings from 12 studies (Lou et al., 1996). The significant moderating factors include subject area and relative ability of students. In mathematics and science classes, types of group ability composition did not appear to make a significant difference on student achievement; in reading, students appeared to learn more in homogeneous ability groups than heterogeneous ability groups. Low ability students appeared to benefit more in the heterogeneous ability groups; medium ability students appeared to learn more in the homogeneous ability groups; and high ability students learned equally well in either homogeneous or heterogeneous ability groups. Two more recent studies (Meijnen & Guldemond, 2002; Saleh, Lazonder, & Jong, 2005) comparing homogeneous and heterogeneous within-class ability grouping on achievement for students at different ability levels found the same pattern of results.

Springer, Stanne, and Donovan (1999) synthesized a total of 39 studies on the effects of heterogeneous small-group cooperative or collaborative learning in undergraduate mathematics, technology, and engineering (STEM) education. They found an average moderate positive effect of small-group cooperative or collaborative learning on college students' achievement, persistence, and attitudes (weighted effect size = +0.51, +0.46, and +0.55, respectively). Effects on student achievement were more pronounced: (a) for underrepresented groups such as African Americans and Latinos than for Whites and heterogeneous groups, (b) when small-group learning took place outside of class rather than in class, and (c) when achievement was measured by locally developed exams or grades rather than standardized tests. There was no difference on achievement whether groups followed more structured cooperative learning strategies or a less structured collaborative learn-

Chapter 4.19.1 Table 1 Meta-Analyses on the Effects of Within-Class Grouping

Authors	Outcomes	Number of studies (independent findings)	Focus	Effect Size
Slavin (1987)	Achievement	7	Homogeneous ability grouping in elementary schools	+0.32
Kulik & Kulik (1987)	Achievement	15	Homogeneous ability grouping	+0.25
Kulik & Kulik (1991)	Achievement	11	Homogeneous ability grouping	+0.17
Lou et al. (1996)	Achievement	66 (145)	Grouping vs no grouping	+0.17*
	Attitudes	21 (30)	Grouping vs no grouping	+0.18*
	Self-concept	10 (12)	Grouping vs no grouping	+0.09
	Achievement	12 (20)	Homogeneous vs. heterogeneous ability	+0.12*
Springer et al. (1999)	Achievement	37 (49)	Small group learning in undergraduate STEM	+0.51*
	Persistence	9 (10)	Small group learning in undergraduate STEM	+0.46*
	Attitudes	11 (12)	Small group learning in undergraduate STEM	+0.55*

*p<.05

ing approach and whether random placement into groups was employed.

Several recent studies attempted to examine and identify patterns of mediating processes in homogeneous and heterogeneous ability groups that may explain the differential impact on student achievement and motivation. Meijnen and Guldemond (2002) compared patterns of social reference and achievement in homogeneous and heterogeneous groups for students of different ability levels. They found that method of grouping does influence the reference processes that develop in the class. In homogeneous groups, students tend to set their academic reference points to those working at a similar level as themselves; whereas in heterogeneous groups, this correlation appears to be weak. This appears to be most detrimental to lower-achievers, whose performance was half standard deviation lower in homogeneous groups than in heterogeneous groups. They argue that by grouping students in homogeneous groups, the teacher is clearly expressing different expectations and demands for different students and such expectations are then adopted by the students, leading to lower performance for low-achievers.

Saleh, Lazonder, and Jong (2005) investigated patterns of social interaction in explaining the differential effects of homogeneous and heterogeneous ability grouping on achievement for students at different ability levels. They categorized episodes of student interaction into two major types: individual elaboration and collaborative elaboration. Individual elaboration refers to interaction episodes where a single individual answered a question, resolved a conflict, or engaged in reasoning. Collaborative interaction refers to interaction episodes where more than one individual added to the conversation. They found that homogeneous grouping produced a higher proportion of collaborative elaborations for average and high ability students but not for low ability students who, in the absence of more capable peers, give and receive very few elaborated explanations among themselves. Heterogeneous grouping produced more individual collaboration overall, often in the form of teacher–learner dialogue between high and low ability students with average ability students rarely contributing in elaborate explanations.

Summary and Recommendations

Research evidence over several decades showed that within class small-group learning, whether homogeneous or heterogeneous ability, is more effective than no grouping on student achievement at all education levels. The effects of within-class grouping are positive for students at all ability levels, especially for lower ability students. However, low ability students tend to achieve significantly more in heterogeneous ability groups than in homogeneous ability groups. This may be due to the opportunity of low ability

students to ask more questions and receive more elaborate elaboration from higher ability students, higher expectation, motivation, and self-concept in heterogeneous ability groups. Contrary to critics' fears, heterogeneous ability grouping does not seem to hinder the achievement of high ability students who appear to learn equally well in either homogeneous or heterogeneous groups. Average ability students, on the other hand, appear to benefit more in homogeneous ability groups than heterogeneous groups, which may be due to more opportunity of collaborative dialogue in homogeneous groups. To be maximally effective for all students, within-class grouping requires the adaptation of instructional methods such as cooperative and collaborative learning and materials for small-group learning.

References

Abrami, P. C., Chambers, B., Poulsen, C., De Simone, C., D'Apolonia, S., & Howden, J. (1995). *Classroom connections: Understanding and using cooperative learning.* Toronto, Canada: Harcourt Brace.

Chorzempa, B. F., & Graham, S. (2006). Primary-grade teachers' use of within-class ability grouping in reading. *Journal of Educational Psychology, 98,* 529–541.

Dreeben, R., & Barr, R. (1988). Classroom composition and the design of instruction. *Sociology of Education, 61,* 129–142.

Hallam, S., Ireson, J., Lister, V., Chaudhury, I. A., & Davies, J. (2003). Ability grouping practices in the primary schools: A survey. *Educational Studies, 29,* 69–83.

Kulik, J. A., & Kulik, C.-L. C. (1987). Effects of ability grouping on student achievement. *Equity and Excellence, 23,* 22–30.

Kulik, J. A., & Kulik, C.-L. C. (1991). *Research on ability grouping: Historical and contemporary perspectives.* University of Connecticut, National Research Center and Gifted and Talented. (ERIC Document Reproduction Service No. ED 350 777)

Kutnick, P., Blatchford, P., Clark, H., MacIntyre, H., & Baines, E. (2005). Teachers understandings of the relationship between within-class (pupil) grouping and learning in secondary schools. *Educational Research, 47,* 1–24.

Lou, Y., Abrami, P. C., Spencer, J. C., Poulsen, C., Chambers, B., & d'Apollonia, S. (1996). Within-class grouping: A meta-analysis. *Review of Educational Research, 66,* 423–458.

Meijnen, G. W., & Guldemond, H. (2002). Grouping in primary schools and reference processes. *Educational Research and Evaluation, 8,* 229–248.

Reuman, D. A. (1989). How social comparison mediates the relation between ability grouping practices and students' achievement expectancies in mathematics. *Journal of Educational Psychology, 81,* 178–189.

Rogers, C. M., Smith, M. D., & Coleman, J. M. (1978). Social comparison in the classroom: the relationship between academic achievement and self-concept. *Journal of Educational Psychology, 70,* 50–57.

Rosenbaum, J. E. (1976). *Making inequality: The hidden curriculum of high school tracking.* New York: Wiley.

Saleh, M., Lazonder, A. W., & Jong, T. D. (2005). Effects of within-class ability grouping on social interactions, achievement, and motivation. *International Science, 33,* 105–119.

Slavin, R. E. (1987). Ability grouping and student achievement in elementary schools: A best-evidence synthesis. *Review of Educational Research, 57,* 293–336.

Springer, L., Stanne, M. E., & Donovan, S. S. (1999). Effects of small group learning on undergraduates in science, mathematics, engineering, and technology: A meta-analysis. *Review of Educational Research, 69,* 21–51.

4.20

Special Education and Academic Achievement

BENJAMIN ZABLOTSKY AND MICHAEL S. ROSENBERG
Johns Hopkins University

Introduction

Special education is the process of delivering specially designed instruction to meet the unique needs of students with disabilities. However, defining special education need is not straightforward and often a function of international context and nation specific policy decisions (Florian, 2007). In the United States, according to the Individuals with Disabilities Education Act of 2004 (IDEA), the most recent iteration of the historic Education of All Handicapped Children Act of 1975, students who have one or more of 13 identified disabilities (including autism, developmental disability, intellectual impairment, emotional and/or behavioral disability, speech and language disability, deaf-blind, visual impairment, hearing impairment, orthopedic or physical impairment, attention deficit disorder, traumatic brain injury, and/or multiple disabilities) are entitled, regardless of the severity of their disability, to a free public education in the least restrictive environment, preferably in the general education classroom. An Individualized Education Plan (IEP) is the formal document used to inform and guide the delivery of instruction and the provision of related services (e.g., psychological services, occupational therapy, etc.). Although categories differ across nations, factors that make special education "special" include the (a) intensity of instruction provided, (b) structure of content being presented, (c) collaboration among myriad of professional experts, and (d) increased frequency of performance monitoring and assessment (Kauffman & Hallahan, 2005).

Research Evidence

In our current era of enhanced standards and increased accountability, it is not surprising that schools and educators are held responsible for the academic outcomes of their students with special education needs. With approximately 11.2% of school-aged students in the United States identified with disabilities receiving special education services

(U.S. Department of Education, 2010) and longstanding doubts about certain special education practices, there is a justifiable appetite for valid and reliable reports of special education efficacy as it relates to essential academic skills and content (e.g., Edmonds & Spradlin, 2010). The great majority of students with disabilities, 97% of those identified, are held to the same academic performance standards as their nondisabled peers. Still, only two studies have been found that have investigated systematically the global impact of special education on the academic achievement of students with disabilities, with, at best, inconclusive results. Reynolds and Wolfe (1999) found that special education services had limited success for large numbers of elementary students with disabilities in the Chicago Public Schools. Specifically, significant improvements in reading and math achievement were noted only for students in primary grades (grades 1–3) and only for those students who had disabilities other than learning disabilities. In contrast, Hanushek, Kain, and Rifkin (1998) examined fourth and fifth grade students in Texas and found that special education increased the reading and math achievement of students with disabilities, particularly those identified as having learning disabilities.

The limited and discrepant findings of these efforts are likely due to both conceptual and methodological shortcomings associated with conducting global evaluations of special education services. Special education is based on the assumption of individualization, with varied and broad-based instructional and support activities directed toward the unique learning characteristics and needs of students. Consequently, the characteristics of students in special education, being both heterogeneous and idiosyncratic, can interact with certain aspects of testing and accountability, thereby limiting the accuracy and generality of outcome data (Schulte & Villwock, 2004). Moreover, views of what constitutes a desirable outcome for students with disabilities often go beyond assessments of basic reading and math skills and can include achievement in advanced content areas (e.g., science, algebra, literature), which require a range and intensity of supports and accommodations. Moreover, many special education efforts go beyond academics and focus on long-term goals that center on functional life skills, social competence, and transition skills associated with post-school outcomes, such as finding employment and living independently. If global standardized tests of basic skills are the only metric used to assess special education efficacy, the true value of special education on academic and nonacademic outcomes will not be captured.

Perhaps the most useful way of assessing special education efficacy is to look at methods and metrics that address the individualized nature of students' learning challenges. Growing in popularity as a comprehensive, highly individualized tiered service delivery framework, Response to Intervention (RTI) is built on a foundation of simplicity and a tightly coordinated organizational structure: Effective instruction is delivered to prevent problems from occurring and evidence-based interventions are applied to address problems that do arise (Baker, Fien, & Baker, 2010). Briefly, RTI involves actively monitoring the performance of all students who receive a high-quality universal general education program that employs research-based instructional practices, and subsequently identifying nonresponders and those "at-risk" for failure. Those identified as poor performers in general education, many of whom were previously referred for special education, are assigned to more intensive Tier-2 interventions that often include repeated practice, differentiated instruction, or flexible grouping. Children who fail to respond to Tier-2 interventions receive highly intensive and specialized Tier-3 instruction, usually delivered by special educators. The goal of the RTI is to provide students with the appropriate level of support necessary for academic success depending on their level of impairment or disability. Ideally, students will respond to supported instruction and benefit from staying in the general classroom. These concepts of inclusion, tiered levels of instruction, and RTI, are not unique to the United States and has gained ground internationally in recent decades with a number of United Nations Educational, Scientific, and Cultural Organization (UNESCO) reports and initiatives (e.g., *The Salamanca Statement and Framework for Action; Developing Sustainable Inclusion policies and Practices*) (Peters, 2007).

Several studies have found that tiered RTI service delivery can increase the reading and math performance of at-risk and special education elementary students, as well as reduce the number of students who are referred for special education services. For example, in a large scale implementation of an RTI model using the Reading First program with students in Grades K–3, the percentage of students with significant reading difficulties was reduced by 30% and the rate of students identified as having a learning disability dropped by 81% (Torgesen, 2009). Similar findings were reported by Vaughn, Wanzek, Linan-Thompson, & Murray (2007) who found that both elementary Tier-2 and Tier-3 responders assigned to the RTI condition outperformed control students on several critical measures of reading effectiveness. Still, at secondary school levels,

RTI is less established, with initial findings suggesting that additional work is needed in modifying the framework to account for the entrenched history of academic problems encountered by students with disabilities (Vaughn et al., 2010). Interestingly, research efforts that have applied RTI to the social behavior of students are encouraging (e.g., Cheney, Flower, & Templeton, 2008). In short, although more needs to be known about the nature and outcome of Tier-3 interventions, it is clear that a significant number of students do respond to the intensive Tier-2 interventions and fewer students are identified for special education services.

Many RTI efforts use a standard protocol approach in which specific evidence-based practices are linked to the various tiers or intensities of instruction. Procedures are standardized, meaning that students who respond inadequately to instruction and behavioral expectations during general class instruction would receive preselected prescribed interventions. Although a range of evidence-based programs or methods are available, several of the more prominent are (a) direct (or explicit) instruction, particularly for basic numeracy and phonological awareness skills (e.g., Adams & Engelmann, 1996); (b) cooperative and peer-mediated learning activities in which students work together in structured ways to tutor each other (e.g., Slavin & Lake, 2007); and (c) learning strategies and content enhancements, a broad array of techniques that teachers and students use to promote understanding and use of higher order secondary content knowledge (e.g., Deshler & Kennedy, 2009).

Summary and Recommendations

In summary, the individualized nature of special education makes assessments of its efficacy challenging. Global efforts that have utilized standardized tests as outcome measures have been limited and inconsistent. RTI, which is built on a foundation of a tiered organizational structure, can be a more useful way of evaluating the aggregated effects of special education while at the same time considering the individualized nature of students' learning challenges and controlling for contextual differences among nations. Existing outcome studies of RTI have been promising and a catalog of effective instructional practices continues to evolve.

References

Adams, G. L, & Engelmann, S. (1996). *Research in direct instruction: 25 Years beyond DISTAR*. Seattle, WA: Educational Achievement Systems.

Baker, S. K., Fien, H., & Baker, D. (2010). Robust reading instruction in the early grades: Conceptual and practical issues in the integration and evaluation of tier 1 and tier 2 instructional supports. *Focus on Exceptional Children, 42*(9), 1–20.

Cheney, D., Flower, A., & Templeton, T. (2008). Applying response to intervention metrics in the social domain for students at risk of developing emotional or behavioral disorders. *Journal of Special Education, 42*(2), 108–126.

Deshler, D., & Kennedy, M. (2009). Struggling adolescent readers. *Better: Evidence-based Education, 1*(1), 10–11.

Edmonds, B. C., & Spradlin, T. (2010). What does it take to become a high performing special education planning district? A study of Indiana's special education delivery service system. *Remedial and Special Education, 31*(5), 320–329.

Florian, L. (2007). Reimagining special education. In L. Florian (Ed.), *The Sage handbook of special education* (pp. 7–20). London: Sage.

Hanushek, E. A., Kain, J. F., & Rivkin, S. G. (1998). *Does special education raise academic achievement for students with disabilities?* (Working Paper No. 6690). Cambridge, MA: National Bureau of Economic Research.

Kauffman, J., & Hallahan, D. (2005). *Special education: What is it and why we need it?* Boston, MA: Pearson Education.

Peters, S. (2007). Inclusion as a strategy for achieving education for all. In L. Florian (Ed.), *The Sage handbook of special education* (pp. 117–130). London: Sage.

Reynolds, R. J., & Wolfe, B. (1999). Special education and school achievement: An exploratory analysis with a central-city sample. *Educational Evaluation and Policy Analysis, 21*(3), 249–269.

Schulte, A. C., & Villwock, D. N. (2004). Using high-stakes tests to derive school-level measures of special education efficacy, *Exceptionality, 12*(2), 107–126.

Slavin, R. E., & Lake, C. (2007). Effective programs in elementary mathematics: A best-evidence synthesis. *Best Evidence Encyclopedia*. Retrieved from http://www.bestevidence.org/word/elem_math_Feb_9_2007.pdf

Torgesen, J. K. (2009). The response to intervention instructional model: Some outcomes from a large-scale implementation in reading first schools. *Child Development Perspectives, 3*(1), 38–40.

Vaughn, S., Wanzek, J., Linan-Thompson, S., & Murray, C. S. (2007). Monitoring response to supplemental services for students at risk for reading difficulties: High and low responders. In S. R. Jimerson, M. K. Burns, & A. M. VanDerHeyden (Eds.), *Handbook of response to intervention: The science and practice of assessment and intervention* (pp. 234–243). New York: Springer.

Vaughn, S., Cirino, P. T., Wanzek, J., Wexler, J., Fletcher, J. M., Denton, C. D., & Francis, D. J. (2010). Response to intervention for middle school students with reading difficulties: Effects of a primary and secondary intervention. *School Psychology Review, 39*, 3–21.

U.S. Department of Education (2010). *Individuals with Disabilities Education (IDEA) data.* Retrieved from http://ideadata.org

4.21

Social and Emotional Learning and Academic Achievement

Jessika Zmuda and Catherine P. Bradshaw
Johns Hopkins University

Introduction

Student social and emotional development is considered by many to be intrinsically linked with academic learning and achievement (Durlak, Weissberg, Dymnicki, Taylor, & Schellinger, 2011). Social skills are critical building blocks because learning is directed, motivated, and facilitated by positive relationships with teachers, peers, and parents. A student's ability to recognize and regulate emotions is also essential, as unmanaged emotional stress can detract from engagement in learning opportunities and hinder academic progress over time (Elias et al., 1997). Waters and Sroufe (1983) highlighted the significance of social and emotional competence with regard to students' ability to "generate and coordinate flexible, adaptive responses to demands and generate and capitalize on opportunities in the environment" (p. 80); these factors in turn are linked with academic achievement.

Schools' emphasis on teaching social and emotional skills can be traced back to the 1960s. At the time, much of the programming focused on civic responsibility and moral character development. Over the last two decades the promotion of social and emotional learning (SEL) through school-based universal preventive interventions has emerged as an approach to fostering academic success (CASEL, 2005). The SEL framework incorporates competence-promotion and positive youth development perspectives, and focuses on strengthening protective mechanisms and mitigating risk factors (Catalano, Berglund, Ryan, Lonczak, & Hawkins, 2002; Guerra & Bradshaw, 2008).

The broader SEL framework features both individual and school-level strategies. At the individual level, SEL programming provides instruction in mastering five interconnected, core competencies: self-awareness, self-management, social awareness, relationship skills, and responsible decision-making (CASEL, 2005; Elias et al., 1997). SEL programs provide the opportunity and structure for students to learn to "recognize and manage emotions, care about others, make good decisions, behave ethically and responsibly, develop positive relationships, and avoid negative behaviors" (Zins, Bloodworth, Weissberg, & Walberg, 2007, p. 192). At the level of the school, the SEL framework can be used to promote social and emotional conditions as necessary for learning and academic achievement (Osher et al., 2007), including physical and emotional safety, school connectedness, social emotional learning, and a climate of high expectations for achievement and behavior. Implementation of SEL programming at the individual and school level is expected to provide a foundation for improved test scores and grades, as well as reductions in behavior problems (Greenberg, 2006).

Research Evidence

Several studies have been conducted over the last 15 years to examine the effects of universal SEL programs on various academic, behavioral, and attitudinal outcomes. A series of meta-analyses and reviews have concluded that universal school-based interventions are generally effective across a diverse range of outcomes, including academic performance (see CASEL, 2005; Catalano et al., 2002; Wilson, Gottfredson, & Najaka, 2001; Zins et al., 2007; cf. Social and Character Development Consortium, 2010). For example, the Collaborative for Academic, Social, and Emotional Learning (CASEL, 2005) reviewed outcomes on 80 SEL programs, with the goal of providing guidance to educators in selecting appropriate SEL programs. Roughly a third of the programs reviewed included components which integrated SEL with academic curricula. All the programs examined produced positive academic outcomes, and 83% resulted in academic gains (Zins et al., 2007). In a meta-analysis of 165 published outcome studies of school-based prevention programs, Wilson and colleagues (2001) found that SEL-oriented programs resulted in reduced drop-out and improved attendance. In another review of 25 school-based prevention programs, Catalano and colleagues (2002) found that 19 (76%) resulted in statistically significant improvements in academic achievement. The U.S. Department of Health and Human Services, Substance Abuse and Mental Health Services Administration (SAMHSA; 2002) report on model prevention programs supporting academic achievement has also documented increased grade point averages, improvements in standardized test scores, and improved reading, writing, and math skills resulting from school-based prevention programs including SEL components.

More recently, a large-scale meta-analysis was conducted of 213 universal, school-based SEL programs serving approximately 270,000 kindergarten through high school students (Durlak et al., 2011). The meta-analysis investigated the effects of interventions to promote social and emotional development on multiple outcomes, including academic achievement. Academic performance measures included grade point averages and standardized reading or math achievement tests. The results demonstrated a significant, 11 percentile-point gain in academic achievement ($p \leq .05$) in comparison to controls. A secondary goal of the meta-analysis was to determine whether existing school personnel could successfully implement SEL interventions; the authors found that SEL programs delivered by teachers were effective across all outcome categories, including academic achievement. While programs delivered by other school staff (e.g., counselors) were effective across fewer outcome categories, those delivered by nonschool staff were least effective and did not significantly improve academic performance.

Although the findings regarding the impacts of SEL programming on academic outcomes have generally been favorable, a recent multisite randomized trial of seven different SEL programs did not demonstrate impacts on student academic achievement, behavior, or social-emotional development (Social and Character Development Consortium, 2010). The report highlighted the importance of the fidelity with which SEL programs are implemented, as prior research documents a clear association between high quality implementation and student outcomes (Domitrovich et al., 2008; Durlak et al., 2011). For example, Durlak and colleagues found that implementation quality was an important moderator of program impact, such that programs implemented with high fidelity produced significant effects across all outcome categories, including academic achievement. In contrast, those programs that experienced implementation problems failed to achieve a positive effect on academic performance and a number of other outcome categories. Further, the authors found that adherence to the following four evidence-based practices moderated program impact: a step-by-step training approach (S), using active forms of learning (A), focusing sufficient time on skill development (F), and having explicit learning goals (E). Programs following all four "SAFE" procedures demonstrated significant effects across all outcome categories, including academic performance, whereas those programs that did not follow all four procedures were only effective in about half of the outcomes.

More empirical research is needed to identify the specific mediators of the impact of SEL programs on enhancing academic outcomes (Durlak et al., 2011). For example, the available research suggests that executive function, a set of cognitive skills necessary for goal-directed behavior such as inhibition and planning, may play an important role by improving cognitive-affect regulation in the prefrontal cortex (Greenberg, 2006). Beyond the individual-level, SEL programs may enhance school environmental supports (e.g., a climate of high expectations for academic performance, and safe, orderly classrooms), teacher practices, and student–teacher relationships, which in turn may translate into improved academic achievement (Catalano et al., 2002; Durlak et al., 2011). There is also a need for additional research on SEL programs at the middle and high school levels, as there are comparatively fewer programs which have been created to be developmentally appropriate for adolescents.

Summary and Recommendations

The research base on SEL and academic achievement has grown over the last two decades and generally presents a strong rationale for educators, policymakers, teachers, and the public to consider incorporating SEL programming into standard educational practice. Empirical findings from several studies and recent meta-analyses indicate that SEL-oriented interventions can directly improve academic performance and related outcomes for student success, such as attendance and drop-out. As a result, there is growing support for SEL programming in U.S. federal legislation, such as the reauthorization of the Elementary and Secondary Education Act.

It is important to keep in mind that these positive outcomes are the result of carefully planned, well-implemented, teacher-taught SEL interventions. To optimize effectiveness, selection of research-based interventions responsive to the target population is key. The CASEL (2005) publication may be a useful starting place to select an appropriate intervention. Schools may also consider training teachers and staff to implement SEL programs, rather than hiring outside implementers, as research indicates that SEL programs taught by teachers and school staff produce the most positive results (Durlak et al., 2011). Schools should also receive adequate technical assistance or coaching when implementing programs in order to ensure high implementation quality (Domitrovich et al., 2008), as implementation problems have been found to significantly diminish the effects of SEL interventions. Finally, schools may consider integrating SEL programming with academic material, as this approach capitalizes on the interdependence of multiple dimensions of human development (Durlak et al., 2011; Zins et al., 2007).

References

Collaborative for Academic, Social, and Emotional Learning (CASEL). (2005). *Safe and sound: An educational leader's guide to evidence-based social and emotional learning programs—Illinois edition.* Chicago, IL: Author. Retrieved from http://www.eric.ed.gov/PDFS/ED505373.pdf

Catalano, R. F., Berglund, M. L., Ryan, J. A. M., Lonczak, H. S., & Hawkins, J. D. (2002). Positive youth development in the United States: Research findings on evaluations of positive youth development programs. *Prevention & Treatment, 5,* Article 15.

Domitrovich, C. E., Bradshaw, C. P., Poduska, J., Hoagwood, K., Buckley, J., Olin, S., … Ialongo, N. S. (2008). Maximizing the implementation quality of evidence-based preventive interventions in schools: A conceptual framework. *Advances in School Mental Health Promotion: Training and Practice, Research and Policy, 1*(3), 6–28.

Durlak, J. A., Weissberg, R. P., Dymnicki, A. B., Taylor, R. D., & Schellinger, K. B. (2011). The impact of enhancing students' social and emotional learning: A meta-analysis of schoo-based universal interventions. *Child Development, 82*(1), 405–432.

Elias, M. J., Zins, J. E., Weissberg, R. P., Frey, K. S., Greenberg, M. T., Haynes, N. M., … Shriver, T. P(1997). *Promoting social and emotional learning: Guidelines for educators.* Alexandria, VA: Association for Supervision and Curriculum Development.

Greenberg, M. T. (2006). Promoting resilience in children and youth: Preventive interventions and their interface with neuroscience. *Annals of the New York Academy of Science, 1094,* 139–150.

Guerra, N. G., & Bradshaw, C. P. (2008). Linking the prevention of problem behaviors and positive youth development: Core competencies for positive youth development and risk prevention. *New Directions for Child and Adolescent Development, 122,* 1–17.

Osher, D., Sprague, J., Weissberg, R., Axelrod, J., Keenan, S., Kendziora, K., & Zins, J. (2007). A comprehensive approach to promoting social, emotional, and academic growth in contemporary schools. In A. Thomas & J. Grimes (Eds.), *Best practices in school psychology* (Vol. 5, pp. 1263–1278). Bethesda, MD: National Association of School Psychologists.

Social and Character Development Research Consortium. (2010). *Efficacy of schoolwide programs to promote social and character development and reduce problem behavior in elementary school children* (NCER 2011–2001). Washington, DC: National Center for Education Research, Institute of Education Sciences, U.S. Department of Education.

U.S. Department of Health and Human Services, Substance Abuse and Mental Health Services Administration. (2002). *SAMHSA model programs: Model prevention programs supporting academic achievement.* Washington, DC: Author.

Waters, E., & Sroufe, L. (1983). Social competence as a developmental construct. *Developmental Review, 3*(1), 79–97.

Wilson, D. B., Gottfredson, D. C., & Najaka, S. S. (2001). School-based prevention of problem behaviors: A meta-analysis. *Journal of Quantitative Criminology, 17*(3), 247–272.

Zins, J. E., Bloodworth, M. R., Weissberg, R. P., & Walberg, H. J. (2007). The scientific base linking social and emotional learning to school success. *Journal of Educational & Psychological Consultation, 17*(2–3), 191–210.

4.22

Middle School Transitions

ERIC M. ANDERMAN
Ohio State University

Introduction

The transition from schools that serve young children into schools that serve early adolescents has been a topic of interest for education researchers and policy makers for many years. This is an important area of research, because transitions between schools during the early adolescent years often occur at the onset of puberty. Thus these transitions occur while students, parents, and teachers are simultaneously dealing with the academic, social, and motivational issues that occur during the adolescent years. It is important for educators, policy makers, researchers, and parents to understand this transitional period, so that effective learning environments can be provided for early adolescents. For many students, the transition represents a time when motivation and achievement noticeably change, often in a negative direction.

Research Evidence

Results of most studies of academic achievement at the transition indicate that in general, achievement declines for most students as they move into new school settings during early adolescence. In particular, when students attend schools that primarily serve early adolescents (e.g., schools with grade configurations of sixth through eighth grade or seventh through ninth grade in many countries), academic achievement is often lower than it was for the same students during elementary school; thus achievement declines for many students as they move into these new school environments. Most studies indicate that both standardized test scores and teacher-assigned grades are lower for students who attend schools that primarily serve early adolescents, compared to other schools (e.g., schools that serve both young children and early adolescents together, such as schools with kindergarten through grade 8 configurations) (Gutman & Midgley, 2000; Simmons

& Blyth, 1987; Warburton, Jenkins, & Coxhead, 1983). Although many of the studies of achievement across the transition have been conducted in the United States, studies conducted in England have yielded similar findings (Warburton et al., 1983).

Many studies of school transitions have examined achievement in terms of students' motivation toward academic achievement. Several researchers have found that students' attitudes toward achievement become particularly negative during grades 6 through 8, immediately after the transition (e.g., Eccles, Midgley, & Adler, 1984). Specifically, students report that they perceive school to be less interesting, useful, and important than they did when they were in elementary school. These shifting attitudes toward school are related to the changes in achievement that occur for many students.

The transition from elementary school into middle school coincides with the onset of adolescent physical, cognitive, and psychological development (Patrick & Drake, 2009). Students and their social worlds are changing rapidly, and these changes are related to academic achievement in important ways. Physically, adolescents are going through puberty; their bodies are growing and changing rapidly. They are growing taller, weighing more than they did in the past, and developing adult sexual characteristics. Cognitively, adolescents are developing the ability to think about more complex topics; they are now able to entertain abstract possibilities, and engage in more cognitively complex academic work at school. Socially, adolescents are becoming more involved with their peers, more self-conscious, and more interested in dating and sexuality. Although in the past, many researchers attributed the declines in achievement and motivation specifically to the physiological changes associated with puberty, research conducted in recent years has demonstrated that these negative shifts in academic behaviors are not attributable to pubertal development (Anderman, 2012, for a review). Rather, these shifts often are attributable to the types of academic environments and instructional practices of middle schools.

In general, although adolescents are going through many major changes during the same period when they move from elementary schools into middle grade schools, the new school environments often do not meet these students' needs. When adolescents' developmental needs are not met, motivation and achievement suffer. Researchers have argued and demonstrated that this is a problem of "stage-environment fit": adolescents are at a stage of development where they would benefit from specific types of educational environments that many middle grade schools do not provide (Eccles & Midgley, 1989).

More specifically, researchers have argued that early adolescents are best served by school environments that provide (a) warm, caring relationships with teachers; (b) cognitively challenging academic work; (c) the opportunity to express autonomy and make choices during the school day; and (d) a sense of belonging in the school community. However, research indicates that many (although certainly not all) middle grade schools are characterized by environments in which teachers and students have poor, confrontational relationships; in which students often are asked to complete many worksheets and given undemanding, repetitive assignments; in which students do not get the opportunity to make choices about how they spend their time or about the academic tasks with which they engage; and in which students often do not feel like they "belong" (Anderman, 2012). This mismatch between what adolescents need from a developmental perspective, and what they are provided with in schools, causes many of them to become disengaged with school; this disengagement adversely affects their motivation and ultimately their achievement. Although schools have changed somewhat in response to research on this topic, there is still room for improvement (Juvonen, Le, Kaganoff, Augustine, & Constant, 2004).

One of the other reasons often cited for declines in achievement across this transition is the increasing focus on grades, competition, and relative ability that is prominent in schools serving early adolescents. As students enter into middle schools, grading practices become more focused on ability and less on effort than they were during elementary school (Anderman & Maehr, 1994). Studies indicate that during elementary school, students often report that the purpose of schooling is to truly learn and master academic material; however, after the transition, students perceive that the mastery of academic content is less important than during elementary school; rather, obtaining high grades and demonstrating one's academic ability rise in importance after the transition (Anderman & Midgley, 1997). Thus performance on "tests" becomes much more important to students, teachers, and parents after the transition. Increased focus on grades and ability during adolescence is an international phenomenon, as suggested by studies conducted in the United States, as well as in South Korea (Bong, 2009), and in China (Liu, 2003). Many students become less engaged with school after the transition be-

cause for many, learning is simply no longer an enjoyable enterprise; whereas learning was "fun" during elementary school, it often becomes competitive and provokes anxiety after the transition.

One of the reasons why grades and ability differences become particularly salient after the transition is due to the increased emergence of between-class ability grouping. During the elementary grades, students generally spend most of the day in the same classroom, with the same students and teacher. Although sometimes elementary educators engage in teaming practices wherein different teachers will instruct the students in different subjects (e.g., reading, social studies), most grouping of students occurs within the classroom. However, the entry into middle schools often marks the beginning of between-class ability grouping; students often are separated into remedial, basic, or advanced tracks. Research indicates that such practices may be detrimental to the achievement-related attitudes of students, particularly those who are in the lower ability tracks (Oakes & Lipton, 1990). Thus the achievement of lower ability students in particular may be adversely affected after the transition.

Students' ability beliefs and achievement values also change across the transition. Research indicates that after the transition, students report liking many school subjects less than they did in elementary school. In addition, for some students, their beliefs about their abilities in certain school subjects decline (Wigfield, Eccles, Mac Iver, Reuman, & Midgley, 1991). For example, students in particular often report losing confidence in their abilities in mathematics after they move into the middle grades. Students' intrinsic motivation to learn (i.e., learning for the sake of learning) also decreases as students move from elementary schools into middle schools (Harter, Whitesell, & Kowalski, 1992).

These decrements in ability beliefs, achievement values, and intrinsic motivation are important, because they affect future achievement for adolescents. Students' beliefs about their abilities in specific subject areas are predictive of their subsequent achievement in those areas; for example, a student who believes that she is an outstanding science student is likely to continue to get high science grades in the future, whereas a student who does not believe that she has the ability to learn science well will quite likely not obtain good science grades in the future. In addition, students' valuing of academic subjects during early adolescence is predictive of subsequent involvement with those subjects; for example, students who value mathematics are more likely to choose to enroll in math courses later in adolescence, when those courses often become electives (Wigfield & Eccles, 1992).

Summary and Recommendations

In summary, research indicates that in general, academic achievement declines across school transitions that occur during early adolescence. Although most research has been conducted in the United States, studies that have been conducted in other countries generally also indicate that students become more focused on grades and extrinsic outcomes after the transition. Many students become less interested in their academic subjects after the transition, and this lack of interest can affect their achievement. In addition, many students' beliefs about their abilities decline after the transition. Many of these unfortunate changes in motivation, ability beliefs, and achievement are attributed to the fact that the environments provided by many middle level schools do not meet the developmental needs of early adolescents. Nevertheless, decrements in achievement and motivation are not inevitable; when schools utilize instructional practices that are developmentally appropriate, achievement and motivation do not necessarily need to decline (Anderman, Maehr, & Midgley, 1999; Simmons & Blyth, 1987).

References

Anderman, E. M. (2012). Adolescence. In K. Harris & S. G. T. Urdan (Eds.), *APA handbook educational psychology,* Vol. 3: *Applications to learning and teaching* (pp. 43–61). Washington DC: American Psychological Association.

Anderman, E. M., & Maehr, M. L. (1994). Motivation and schooling in the middle grades. *Review of Educational Research, 64*(2), 287–309.

Anderman, E. M., Maehr, M. L., & Midgley, C. (1999). Declining motivation after the transition to middle school: Schools can make a difference. *Journal of Research and Development in Education, 32,* 131–147.

Anderman, E. M., & Midgley, C. (1997). Changes in achievement goal orientations, perceived academic competence, and grades across the transition to middle-level schools. *Contemporary Educational Psychology, 22*(3), 269–298.

Bong, M. (2009). Age-related differences in achievement goal differentiation. *Journal of Educational Psychology, 101*(4), 879–896.

Eccles, J. S., & Midgley, C. (1989). Stage-environment fit: Developmentally appropriate classrooms for young adolescents. In C. Ames & R. Ames (Eds.), *Research on motivation in education: Goals and cognitions* (Vol. 3, pp. 139–186). New York: Academic Press.

Eccles, J. S., Midgley, C., & Adler, T. F. (1984). Grade-related changes in the school environment: Effects on achievement motivation. In J. G. Nicholls & M. L. Maehr (Eds.), *Advances in motivation and achievement: The development of achievement motivation* (pp. 283–331). Greenwich: JAI.

Gutman, L. M., & Midgley, C. (2000). The role of protective factors in supporting the academic achievement of poor African American students during the middle school transition. *Journal of Youth and Adolescence, 29,* 223–248).

Harter, S., Whitesell, N. R., & Kowalski, P. S. (1992). Individual differences in the effects of educational transitions on young adolescents' perceptions of competence and motivational orientation. *American Educational Research Journal, 29*(4), 777–807.

Liu, P. (2003). Transition from elementary to middle school and change in motivation: An examination of Chinese students. *Journal of Research in Childhood Education, 18*(1), 71–83.

Oakes, J., & Lipton, M. (1990). Tracking and ability grouping: A structural barrier to access and achievement. In J. I. Goodlad & P. Keating (Eds.), *Access to knowledge: An agenda for our nation's schools* (pp. 187–204). New York: College Entrance Examination Board.

Patrick, H., & Drake, B. M. (2009). Middle school. In E. M. Anderman & L. H. Anderman (Eds.), *Psychology of classroom learning* (Vol. 2, pp. 775–778). Detroit, MI: Cengage.

Simmons, R. G., & Blyth, D. A. (1987). *Moving into adolescence: The impact of pubertal change and school context.* New York: Aldine de Gruyter.

Warburton, S., Jenkins, W. L., & Coxhead, P. (1983). Science achievement and attitudes and the age of transfer to secondary school. *Educational Research, 25,* 177–183.

Wigfield, A., & Eccles, J. S. (1992). The development of achievement task values: A theoretical analysis. *Developmental Review, 12*(3), 265–310.

Wigfield, A., Eccles, J. S., Mac Iver, D., Reuman, D. A., & Midgley, C. (1991). Transitions during early adolescence: Changes in children's domain-specific self-perceptions and general self-esteem across the transition to junior high school. *Developmental Psychology, 27*(4), 552–565.

Section 5

Influences from the Classroom

EDITOR: JULIANNE TURNER
University of Notre Dame

5.1

Classroom Instructional Contexts

Debra K. Meyer
Elmhurst College

Introduction

Context refers to the whole that is created when interrelated parts are woven together to give meaning. Research that explains *how* teaching and learning are interrelated with student outcomes as well as research that describes *why* students in the same classroom have different or similar experiences are essential for understanding instructional contexts. Because classrooms encompass so much—relations and interactions among students, teachers, their classroom interactions as well as their interactions outside of the classroom—*instructional contexts* must be conceptualized as more than the sum of their parts. For more than two decades researchers such as Brophy and Good (1986) and Hattie (2009) have arrived at similar conclusions: that the success of students depends on teachers' abilities to "respond to contextual features of the classroom situation" (Hattie, 2009, p. 261). The dynamic qualities of classrooms have intrigued and perplexed researchers and practitioners for decades, but there is little research that explicitly addresses achievement in relation to instructional contexts, and fewer conceptual frameworks for understanding any correlations that exist.

Research Evidence

In reviewing the literature that connects "classroom instructional contexts" and "achievement" there are significant overlaps with research focusing on simultaneous influences such as teacher expectations, class size, grouping structures, and student characteristics (Hattie, 2009), which are the topics of other reviews in this volume. Therefore, in this entry, the review of the literature shifts to examples from twin studies and comparative research to illustrate how longitudinal and cross-cultural research expand our understanding of instructional contexts. Both research paradigms closely link classroom features to student achievement, and help to answer two complementary questions: How similar are

students' experiences in the same classroom in relation to their achievements? What common characteristics across instructional contexts have been associated with differences in achievement?

Do Similar Students Experience Similar Instructional Contexts?

Studies of twins provide a natural "matched pair" design for exploring how similar students experience the same and different classrooms. In this way, twin studies uniquely address questions about the home environment's role in achievement and motivation at school. Twin studies also typically involve longitudinal datasets when investigating classroom experiences, an element that is frequently missing in research on classrooms that often uses a snapshot approach of comparing classrooms with different students and teachers.

A recent example of a twin study that revealed links between instructional context and achievement is Asbury, Almeida, Hibel, Harlaar, and Plomin's (2008) study of 61, 10-year-old, year 5, twin pairs (38 female) in the United Kingdom. Asbury et al. investigated the relations among classroom characteristics, student happiness, and English, mathematics, and science achievement. A daily diary method was used to capture the classroom characteristics of social and academic stressors, student relationships with teachers, and levels of engagement or "positivity." Academic achievement was measured on a 5-point scale using the national curriculum ratings. These researchers found that twins experienced the same classrooms differently and that these differences were associated with their achievement score. A major difference was the importance of enjoyment of school and its relation to higher mathematics and science achievement. This twin study highlighted several important features of instructional contexts: (a) that emotional and motivational factors were important, but that these relationships (b) were not shared by twins in the same classrooms, and (c) did not hold true across all disciplines (i.e., enjoyment in English was not a predictor of achievement, with more similar achievement outcomes for twins).

In addition to examining instructional contexts within a grade level, twin researchers typically examine how experiences over time impact student outcomes. An example of such work is Byrne et al.'s (2010) longitudinal investigation of twins' literacy achievements from kindergarten through second grade. Using data collected from Australia and the United States, twins were followed as some pairs shared the same classrooms while others were assigned to different classrooms. Literacy achievement was measured using an early word and nonword reading assessment, a standardized reading comprehension passage, and a developmental spelling test. Bryne et al. found that the majority of differences between twins in literacy achievements could *not* be attributed to their classroom assignments. Twins in the same classroom experienced different reading outcomes more than twins assigned to different classrooms, which further highlights the complexity of instructional contexts.

Moreover, findings suggesting that twins experience different instructional contexts when assigned to the same classroom (e.g., Asbury et al., 2008; Byrne et al., 2010) underscore that teacher-assignment and classroom-assignment are not synonymous. Byrne et al. (2010) discussed how classroom features other than the teacher also influence student achievement. For example, they described that twins' early literacy development in the same classroom could be influenced by different social networks, different perceptions of classroom climate (cf. Asbury et al., 2008), and different forms of support, such as their interactions with other adults in the classroom. The intricacy of twins' experiences in the same classroom provides compelling support for the assumption that similar students may experience different instructional contexts with the same teacher and further calls attention to how difficult it is to isolate a direct teacher effect on student achievement.

As teachers often note, instructional context is influenced by factors outside the classroom in important ways. Twin research provides a natural control for the influence of home, but home influences are not the only external contributors to instructional contexts. For example, Bryne et al. (2010) emphasized that twin studies often render classroom placement less important due to shared home influences, which also makes any twin findings of classroom differences more persuasive. Sibling interactions at home can ameliorate some differences in class assignments, providing twins with the benefit of each other's classroom experiences, social networks, or additional forms of support. In addition, instructional contexts could be influenced by the common practice of clustering teachers with similar characteristics within schools and grade levels (Byrne et al., 2010). Such teaming practices might explain why classroom effects appear less significant in some years because the instructional contexts actually may be more homogeneous within a particular age/grade level due to factors such as high team competence, efficacy, and collaboration. Another way that twin studies reveal how instructional contexts involve

more than a single classroom stems from their longitudinal nature. For example, Byrne et al. (2010) emphasized that genetics and learning experiences both influence students' development and instructional contexts in ways that ebb and flow over time. Thus instructional context is more than a specific set of classroom characteristics at one point in time; each successive classroom assignment is influenced by the experiences that preceded it. Seemingly "peripheral" influences on instructional contexts suggest that some of the most powerful effects on achievement could stem from continuity of quality instruction within teaching teams and across years.

What Common Characteristics of Classrooms are Associated with Achievement? While instructional context effects on student achievement may seem highly nuanced, comparative researchers have identified instructional context features that are related to achievement across national boundaries (e.g., Osborn's, 2001, study of classroom contexts in England, France, and Denmark). The best known comparative research programs are the large-scale collaborative studies examining instructional contexts in relation to achievement, motivational, and socioemotional factors across countries, such as the Trends in International Mathematics and Science Study (TIMISS) and the Program for International Student Assessment (PISA). A major contribution of these research programs is that their findings can offer generalizations about the most essential and common classroom characteristics associated with achievement, usually within specific disciplinary contexts (e.g., What is needed for female students to be successful in science classrooms?).

An example of research utilizing cross-national differences in mathematics is Else-Quest, Shibley Hyde, and Linn's (2010) meta-analysis of gender differences in using 2003 TIMSS and PISA data. They found that gender differences in mathematics achievement had complex associations with student attitudes about learning mathematics. The instructional contexts in which females demonstrated the highest achievement were in countries that reflected greater societal valuing of mathematics and of gender equity (e.g., proportion of women in science and politics; number of girls enrolled in mathematics classes). In this meta-analysis, achievement was defined as a combination of three (TIMSS) to four (PISA) content domain scales, but like the twin studies analyses also included student attitudes and affect. The TIMSS data provided student reports of self-confidence in and valuing of mathematics and the PISA data included measures of intrinsic and extrinsic motivation, anxiety, self-concept, and self-efficacy. Else-Quest et al. (2010) reported that gender equity is important for mathematics achievement because of its association with increases in girls' valuing of and confidence in the discipline. They recommended that for instructional contexts to be effective for female students in mathematics, girls and women must be (a) "encouraged to succeed" within classroom and cultural contexts with high value and expectations," (b) have "the necessary educational tools," such as quality instruction and challenging curriculum opportunities, and (c) experience "visible role models excelling in mathematics," like female teachers, balanced female–male enrollment in classes, and professional women in science (p. 125).

In addition, cross-cultural research can help explain how cultural similarities between school and home are important for achievement. An example of comparative research that illustrates the importance of congruence between the school and home culture is Hess and Azuma's (1991) literature synthesis of their research program comparing school experiences in Japan and the United States. Hess and Azuma's work examined cultural ways in which teachers attempt to engage students in learning. In Japan, teachers support students in learning how to adapt to the instructional context, whereas in the United States teachers are more likely to modify the instructional context for them. Furthermore, the cultural congruence between school and home depends on how parents and teachers socialize and reinforce children's interactions and beliefs. Hess and Azuma (1991) also argued that culturally based values regarding achievement motivation may be an equally important factor because performance may be valued differently. In this way, instructional contexts would be influenced both by whether parents believe that the child must adapt to the instructional context and by the value parents place on performance outcomes such as measures of achievement (e.g., grades, test scores, etc.). Such findings from comparative research about the importance of home–school congruence are difficult to rectify with twin research that suggests twins may have different experiences in the same classroom. These are not as much contradictory findings as they are complementary answers that further highlight the complexities of instructional context and the multiple factors that impact achievement.

Summary and Recommendations

There exists a growing, yet disconnected, research literature on the relationships among classroom instructional contexts and student achievement. The largest gaps appear to be an absence of conceptual models and research dedicated to defining the concept of "instructional context." New models of instructional context that are discipline specific seem essential, like Guthrie and Cox's (2001) model of contexts for engaged reading. Such frameworks demand more complexity, which means no single research program will be able to fully test them. Rather, a combination of qualitative and quantitative work that is interconnected with conceptual coherence will be critical for improving our understanding of instructional contexts and their relations to achievement (Bempechat & Drago-Severson, 1999).

New Ways of Describing and Thinking about Instructional Contexts. One way to approach rethinking instructional contexts is to integrate what is often termed "teacher effects" into classroom instructional contexts. As Marshall

and Weinstein (1986) argued with respect to teacher expectations, and Bryne et al. (2010) reiterated, teacher effects cannot be separated from classroom-level effects. Similarly, Rubie-Davies's (2007) qualitative teacher expectation research described how a classroom's instructional context is not separate from what we often label "classroom climate." Conceptual clarity and integration are needed theoretically as well as empirically.

At the same time, theory and research also must situate instructional context within classrooms, in schools, in homes and communities, and societies. Findings from cross-national studies and twin studies illustrate that classroom contexts include intricate social networks of peers, families, and culture; and that successful outcomes involve both psychological well-being *and* academic progress. New conceptual frameworks and future classroom research, therefore, must integrate the social, psychological, and cultural with learning and achievement outcomes to describe and explain the relations among instructional contexts and a variety of student outcomes, including different ways of defining achievement (e.g., Else-Quest et al., 2010; Hess & Azuma, 1991; Osborn, 2001).

Making the "Messiness" of Instructional Contexts Clearly Relevant. For educational policy makers and teachers, these complexities must be parsed to render them practical while not oversimplifying any of them as "silver bullets." Research on instructional context needs to include learning and achievement outcomes to effectively guide practice and policy. For example, researchers already could deconstruct the current climate of blaming teachers as the primary reason for student failure on measures of achievement (Baker et al., 2010). As Byrne et al. (2010) concluded: "To the degree that classroom effects are not due to teachers, the case for basing high-stakes decisions about teacher accountability on them must remain less secure" (p. 40). Rather than remain embedded in research articles, research programs are needed that intentionally investigate differential achievement effects within classrooms and schools over time and connect them to factors at multiple levels. Moreover, both quantitative and qualitative research is essential—quantitative to support which relationships statistically exist, and qualitative to describe what this *looks like* in classrooms.

In closing, it seems remarkable, yet disconcerting, that in the last two decades we have yet to clearly define, systematically study, or understand the role of classroom instructional contexts in ways that have positively influenced educational policies, teaching practices, or student outcomes. In 1986, Brophy and Good reviewed a then emerging body of classroom research that highlighted teacher effects on student achievement, and their conclusions appear to still be relevant:

> In the past, when detailed information describing classroom processes and linking them to outcomes did not exist, education change efforts were typically based on simple theoretical models and associated rhetoric calling for "solutions" that were both over-simplified and overly rigid. The

data reviewed here should make it clear that no such "solution" can be effective because what constitutes effective instruction (even if attention is restricted to achievement as the sole outcome of interest) varies with context. (p. 331)

In today's increasingly diverse classrooms, this challenge has been heightened. Research-based conceptual frameworks and programs are needed more than ever before to inform teachers about which students are most likely to experience different outcomes and to correct the common public misperception that there can be a one-size-fits-all approach to determining an effective instructional context.

References

Asbury, K., Almeida, D., Hibel, J., Harlaar, N., & Plomin, R. (2008). Clones in the classroom: A daily diary study of the nonshared environmental relationship between monozygotic twin differences in school experience and achievement. *Twin Research and Human Genetics, 11*, 586–595. doi:10.137/twin.11.6.586

Baker, E. L., Barton, P. E., Darling-Hammond, L., Haertel, E., Ladd, H. F., Linn, R. L., ... Shepard, L. A. (2010). *Problems with the use of student test scores to evaluate teachers* (Briefing Paper #278). Washington, DC: Economic Policy Institute.

Bempechat, J., & Drago–Severson, E. (1999). Cross–national differences in academic achievement: Beyond etic conceptions of children's understandings. *Review of Educational Research, 69*, 287–314.

Brophy, J. E., & Good, T. L. (1986). Teacher behaviour and student achievement. In M. Wittrock (Ed.), *Handbook of research on teaching* (3rd ed., pp. 328–375). New York: Macmillan.

Byrne, B., Coventry, W., Olson, R., Wadsworth, S., Samuelsson, S., Petrill, S., ... Corley, R. (2010). "Teacher effects" in early literacy development: Evidence from a study of twins. *Journal of Educational Psychology, 102*, 32–42. doi:10.1037/a0017288

Else–Quest, N. M., Shibley Hyde, J. & Linn, M. C. (2010). Cross–national patterns of gender differences in mathematics: A meta–analysis. *Psychological Bulletin, 136*, 103–127.

Guthrie, J. T., & Cox, K. E. (2001). Classroom conditions for motivation and engagement in reading. *Educational Psychology Review, 13*, 283–302.

Hattie, J. (2009). *Visible learning: A synthesis of over 800 meta-analyses relating to achievement*. New York: Routledge.

Hess, R. D., & Azuma, H. (1991). Cultural support for schooling: Contrasts between Japan and the United States. *Educational Researcher, 20*(9), 2–8, 12.

Marshall, H. H., & Weinstein, R. S. (1986). Classroom context of student–perceived differential teacher treatment. *Journal of Educational Psychology, 78*, 441–453.

Osborn, M. (2001). Constants and contexts in pupil expectations of learning and schooling: Comparing learners in England, France and Denmark. *Comparative Education, 37*, 267–278.

Rubie–Davies, C. M. (2007). Classroom interactions: Exploring the practices of high- and low-expectation teachers. *British Journal of Educational Psychology, 77*, 298–306.

5.2

Academic Motivation and Achievement in Classrooms

LYNLEY H. ANDERMAN
University of Ohio

Introduction

Motivation is one of the processes that initiates and directs behavior. In the classroom, students' academic motivation explains their willingness and promptness in beginning academic tasks and the amount of effort they put forth (initiation and investment), as well as their persistence with academic work in the face of obstacles and distractions, and their selection of various tasks or courses of study.

Current research on students' motivation represents a wide range of theoretical perspectives, with many different aspects of motivation studied. Generally, however, current research focuses on students' cognitions—thoughts and beliefs—that shape and influence their engagement. These can include, for example, students' perceptions of how interesting (e.g., Ainley, Hidi, & Berndorff, 2002), important, or useful (Eccles, 1983) they find a specific subject or activity; how competent and confident they feel to perform a task satisfactorily (Bandura, 1997); their beliefs about the reasons for their own successes and difficulties (Weiner, 1985); and the degree to which they are focused on the goal of understanding and mastering content versus a focus on the external indicators of success, such as grades and rewards (Ames, 1992). Although all of these beliefs and thought-processes are linked in some way to students' learning and achievement, the current chapter will discuss two bodies of research in which effects on achievement have been a particular focus of attention: students' expectancies of success and sense of efficacy (e.g., Wigfield, 1994), and students' sense of autonomy and perceptions of autonomy support (e.g., Reeve, 2002).

Research Evidence

Students' Expectancy Beliefs. Of all motivation-related cognitions that have been studied, those related to students' perceptions of their own competence, expectancies of success, and sense of efficacy have proven to be particularly robust predictors of achievement. Some researchers examine expectancies of success at the level of a particular class setting (e.g., "How well do you expect to do in your math/ English class this year"; Wigfield & Eccles, 2000, p. 70), whereas others focus on much more specific expectancy beliefs (typically referred to as efficacy beliefs) in reference to a particular task or type of task (e.g., Bandura, 1997).

In terms of students' expectancies of success in specific classes, there is considerable evidence from several large-scale studies that students' expectancies are positively related to their course-specific achievement. These studies utilize students' self-reported expectancies of success from large-scale surveys to predict achievement, usually measured in terms of teacher-assigned grades (Eccles, 1983; Wigfield, 1994). Much of this work has focused on understanding students' performance in math classes, although similar findings have also been reported in other academic domains. Much of the research in this area is cross-sectional in design, but these effects also have been demonstrated longitudinally, even over several years of schooling (Wigfield, 1994). Furthermore, a study of fifth grade students in Germany demonstrated that students' expectancies of success predicted teacher-assigned grades, in both math and German classes, even after students' IQ and previous achievement scores were taken into account (Koller, 2010). Generally, adolescent more than younger students' expectancies show stronger associations with their actual achievement. This pattern probably reflects older students' increased experience with schooling and greater awareness of their past performance, which lead to more stability in their self-evaluations. In contrast, younger children's self-reported expectancies of success tend to be less stable and less reliably associated with later achievement.

In contrast to a general expectation that one will do well in a particular class, the sense of self-efficacy is more narrowly defined. Efficacy refers to individuals' judgments of their own skills for performing specific actions, solving particular types of problems, or achieving a desired outcome.

Students with a strong sense of efficacy have been shown to be more willing to take on and persist with challenging tasks, to expend more effort, and to demonstrate greater academic performance. Furthermore, the positive effects of high efficacy have been demonstrated across a range of age groups and nationalities (e.g., Bong, 2001; Multon, Brown, & Lent, 1991; Pintrich & de Groot, 1990). In a meta-analysis, Multon et al. reported an effect size of .38 for the relation between students' self-efficacy beliefs and academic performance. In other words, across a range of student ages and settings, efficacy beliefs accounted for approximately 14% of the variance in academic performance, most typically measured using tests of basic skills. The effect size was significantly smaller for elementary-aged students than for those in high school or college. Thus, as with more general expectancy beliefs discussed earlier, young children's self-judgments are less reliable predictors of their achievement than is true for older students.

In the classroom, students' sense of self-efficacy for various tasks and types of problems can be supported through practices that help students recognize their own progress and learning. For example, teaching students to set short-term, achievable goals and to evaluate and record their own progress toward those goals can help to build a sense of efficacy. In addition, feedback that links students' successes to a combination of effort and ability (as opposed to other causes, such as good luck or teacher kindness) also has been shown to enhance students' self-efficacy (see Schunk & Zimmerman, 2006, for a review).

Sense of Autonomy and Autonomy Support.   A number of studies have investigated the extent to which students experience a sense of autonomy and self-direction while engaging in academic tasks, and their successful learning and performance of those tasks. In this research, the focus is not so much on the quantity of students' motivation (i.e., how motivated is this student?) as on the quality or type of motivation students experience. That is, students are assumed to benefit from particular types of motivation—autonomous, self-directed reasons for engaging—rather than motivation based on external incentives, demands, rewards, and constraints (Deci, Vallerand, Pelletier, & Ryan, 1991). In this work, autonomy is defined as "self-governance" and represents a continuum that ranges from having one's behavior completely regulated by external forces to complete self-regulation, where one's behaviors are personally valued and consistent with one's beliefs (Ryan & Deci, 2006, p. 1562). In the classroom, this sense of autonomy would manifest itself in students' sense that they engage in tasks and activities that reflect their personal values and sense of themselves as individuals, rather than because of compulsion, coercion, or feelings of guilt. Of particular importance in educational settings is the extent to which students perceive that their teachers are supportive of student autonomy and self-direction, as compared to emphasizing teacher control and external rewards or punishments for learning-related behavior.

A number of studies have demonstrated correlational associations between students' perceptions of autonomy support in their classes and indicators of student achievement. For example, Black and Deci (2000) measured college students' perceptions of autonomy support in a chemistry course. These perceptions were associated with higher exam scores and overall course grades, particularly for those students who reported low levels of self-direction for learning chemistry at the beginning of the course. In addition, a number of studies have demonstrated effects using experimental and quasi-experimental approaches. Grolnick and Ryan (1987) randomly assigned fifth-grade students to different groups for reading instruction in a learning laboratory. Students were tested on their rote and conceptual recall of the story they had read. Students who received noncontrolling instruction (deemphasizing external contingencies for learning) demonstrated greater interest and conceptual learning than did those who received controlling instruction (i.e., providing an incentive or pressure for learning). This difference was not evident, however, in students' rote recall of the story, although those who received controlling instruction demonstrated greater deterioration in their recall at a one-week follow-up. Thus, these findings suggest that experiencing a greater degree of autonomy in the instructional setting particularly supported students' comprehension and higher-order learning of material, more than surface and short-term memorization. A similar pattern of findings has been reported in other studies, with a variety of student populations, including college students' performance on analytic reasoning problems (Boggiano, Flink, Shields, Seelbach, & Barrett, 1993), fourth grade students' solving of anagrams and spatial relationship problems (Flink, Boggiano, & Barrett, 1990), and Belgian early adolescents' test scores in a health and nutrition class (Vansteenkiste, Simons, Lens, Soenens, & Matos, 2005).

Given the apparent importance of students' perceptions of autonomy support from teachers, some researchers have focused on the types of instructional practices that promote this perception. Teacher practices such as encouraging students to solve problems in their own way, focusing on the quality of students' performance, acknowledging students' feelings, and spending more time listening than talking have been identified as elements of autonomy-supportive instruction. In contrast, requiring students to solve problems in a particular way, the use of directive or commanding statements, and using coercive techniques including rewards and punishments, are elements of a controlling teaching style (Black & Deci, 2000; Reeve, 2002).

Summary and Recommendations

In summary, students' motivation matters for their academic achievement. Two factors that have been shown to be particularly important in relation to achievement are that students believe they can be successful with the tasks assigned to them and that they perceive some autonomy and self-direction in their activities. To promote these beliefs in their students, it is important that teachers help students set realistic, appropriately challenging academic goals and monitor their own progress. In terms of supporting students' sense of autonomy, teachers can provide students with choices over things like the topics and procedural aspects of tasks but probably more important is helping students feel ownership over their own learning. This can include supporting students in exploring multiple and unique ways to solve problems and requiring them to defend their strategies and solutions (Stefanou, Perencevich, DiCintio, & Turner, 2004).

Finally, as noted at the beginning of this chapter, students' expectancies, efficacy beliefs, and autonomy—motivations in general—are not the only or even necessarily the most important influences on achievement outcomes. No amount of efficacy or autonomy will compensate for a lack of necessary skills or content knowledge or for poor quality instruction. Motivation does, however, have an important role in determining the quantity and quality of students' engagement with learning activities and, thus, indirectly their achievement in classrooms.

References

Ainley, M., Hidi, S., & Berndorff, D. (2002). Interest, learning, and the psychological processes that mediate their relationship. *Journal of Educational Psychology, 94,* 545–561.

Ames, C. (1992). Classrooms: Goals, structures, and student motivation. *Journal of Educational Psychology, 84,* 261–271.

Bandura, A. (1997). *Self–efficacy: The exercise of control.* New York: Freeman.

Black, A. E., & Deci, E. L. (2000). The effects of instructors' autonomy support and students' autonomous motivation on learning organic chemistry: A self-determination theory perspective. *Science Education, 84,* 740–756.

Boggiano, A. K., Flink, C., Shields, A., Seelbach, A., & Barrett, M. (1993). Use of techniques promoting students' self-determination: Effects on students' analytic problem-solving skills. *Motivation and Emotion, 17,* 319–336.

Bong, M. (2001). Role of self-efficacy and task-value in predicting college students' course performance and future enrollment intentions. *Contemporary Educational Psychology, 26,* 553–570.

Deci, E. L., Vallerand, R. J., Pelletier, L. G., & Ryan, R. M. (1991). Motivation and education: The self-determination perspective. *Educational Psychologist, 26,* 325–346.

Eccles, J. S. (1983). Expectancies, values and academic behaviors. In J. T. Spence (Ed.), *Achievement and achievement motives* (pp. 75–146). San Francisco, CA: Freeman.

Flink, C., Boggiano, A. K., & Barrett, M. (1990). Controlling teaching strategies: Undermining children's self-determination and performance. *Journal of Personality and Social Psychology, 59,* 916–924.

Grolnick, W. S., & Ryan, R. M. (1987). Autonomy in children's learning: An experimental and individual difference investigation. *Journal of Personality and Social Psychology, 52,* 890–898.

Koller, O. (2010, September). *The predictive power of motivation on achievement beyond intelligence and prior knowledge.* Paper presented at the International Conference on Motivation, Porto, Portugal.

Multon, K. D., Brown, S. D., & Lent, R. W. (1991). Relation of self–efficacy beliefs to academic outcomes: A meta–analytic investigation. *Journal of Counseling Psychology, 38,* 30–38.

Pintrich, P. R., & de Groot, E. V. (1990). Motivational and self-regulated learning components of classroom academic performance. *Journal of Educational Psychology, 82,* 33– 40.

Reeve, J. (2002). Self–determination theory applied to educational settings. In E. L. Deci & R. M. Ryan (Eds.), *Handbook of self–determination research* (pp. 183–203). New York: University of Rochester Press.

Ryan, R. M., & Deci, E. L. (2006). Self–regulation and the problem of human autonomy: Does psychology need choice, self-determination, and will? *Journal of Personality, 74,* 1557–1585.

Schunk, D. H., & Zimmerman, B. J. (2006). Competence and control beliefs: Distinguishing the means and ends. In P. A. Alexander & P. H. Winne (Eds.), *Handbook of educational psychology* (2nd ed., pp. 349–367). Mahwah, NJ: Erlbaum.

Stefanou, C. R., Perencevich, K. C., DiCintio, M., & Turner, J.C. (2004). Supporting autonomy in the classroom: Ways teachers encourage student decision making and ownership. *Educational Psychologist, 39,* 97–110.

Vansteenkiste, M., Simons, J., Lens, W., Soenens, B., & Matos, L. (2005). Examining the motivational impact of intrinsic versus extrinsic goal framing and autonomy-supportive versus internally controlling communication style on early adolescents' academic achievement. *Child Development, 76,* 483–501.

Weiner, B. (1985). An attributional theory of achievement motivation and emotion. *Psychological Review, 92,* 548–573.

Wigfield, A. (1994). Expectancy-value theory of achievement motivation: A developmental perspective. *Educational Psychology Review, 6,* 49–78.

Wigfield, A., & Eccles, J. S. (2000). Expectancy-value theory of achievement motivation. *Contemporary Educational Psychology, 25,* 68–81.

5.3

Elementary Classroom Management

Inge R. Poole and Carolyn M. Evertson
Vanderbilt University

Introduction

Classrooms are complex social and cultural entities in which multiple simultaneous events occur among a variety of individuals who have potentially conflicting goals. Therefore managing and organizing classrooms well requires the orchestration of events, individuals, materials, and goals in order to maximize student academic achievement. The term, *classroom management*, is often defined as discipline and control of student behavior, but can be more effectively understood as "the actions teachers take to create an environment that supports and facilitates both academic and social-emotional learning" (Evertson & Weinstein, 2006, p. 5).

Research Evidence

Comparison of more and less effective classroom managers recognizes the importance of teachers starting the year with attention to classroom routines, and possessing awareness of what is occurring in the classroom, who is doing what, and whether and how to respond. In fact, classroom management is consistently ranked as a significant influence on student learning and achievement (Hattie, 2009). Its importance is documented by a strong research base across multiple areas of education (Evertson & Weinstein, 2006). A major theme of classroom management research is that teachers who are effective classroom managers demonstrate an ethos of "warm demander"; that is, these teachers signify to all that they care for their students and simultaneously hold high expectations for their academic, social, and continued success. The following five specific tasks illustrate the complex nature of a warm demander's role.

Develop Caring and Supportive Relationships with and among Students. Students' learning is maximized when they are part of a learning community in which positive teacher–student and peer–peer relationships are present (Brophy, 2000). Such cohesive communities impact students' achievement in positive ways (Hattie, 2009). Unfortunately, not all students have equitable access to a caring learning community. Various factors counteract the development of positive relationships. For example, as students move through school, the incongruity between their needs for emotional support and the structures of departmentalization can inhibit desirable teacher–student relationships (Pianta, 2006). A teacher's overly dominating or oppositional style of management can hinder the development of positive teacher–student relationships and students' academic achievement (Wubbels, Brekelmans, den Brok, & van Tartwijk, 2006). Low-achieving students are particularly at risk for a downward cycle of poor academic performance and negative teacher–student relationships (Jerome & Pianta, 2008).

When classrooms are characterized by positive teacher–student relationships, student achievement increases. In particular, students' "higher-quality relationships with kindergarten teachers predicts [sic] greater academic success and classroom participation both in kindergarten and continuing throughout eighth grade" (Jerome & Pianta, 2008, p.162), whereas negativity in kindergarten relates to lower eighth grade achievement scores (Pianta, 2006). Classroom management also influences peer–peer relationships. Peers' perceptions of peers are informed by a teacher's interactions with these students. At transitions between schools, student achievement falls, and peer–peer relationships are particularly important: If children make friends in the first month of the transition, the decrease in their achievement levels is reduced (Galton, 1995). Where low peer acceptance exists, warm demanders can intervene by communicating their own acceptance of each child. Teachers can also encourage the formation of healthy student friendships by establishing procedures that prevent exclusion, such as turn-taking on the playground.

Organize and Implement Instruction to Optimize Students' Access to Learning. Students "learn more when most of the available time is allocated to curriculum-related activities and the classroom management system emphasizes maintaining their engagement in those activities" (Ladson-Billings, 1994, p. 11). The way instruction is planned and presented communicates teachers' expectations to students. Teacher expectations of student learning affect student achievement in the expected directions (Hattie, 2009; Pianta, 2006). Certain student populations are more vulnerable to insufficient or negative teacher expectations: students who belong to minority groups, those with lower socioeconomic status, seeming unattractiveness, with certain cultural stereotypes, and those bearing diagnostic labels (Rubie-Davies, 2008). A warm demander's responsibility, then, includes planning and enacting lessons that incorporate and challenge all students as well as establishing a classroom that is culturally responsive. This is particularly important at the elementary level since research identifies that "by the age of eight, disparities between the cultural values and patterns of communication of the home and the school can diminish the desire of young people to learn and to believe in their own capacity to learn"(Vavrus, 2008, p. 51).

There are at least three aspects of culturally responsive teaching in connection with classroom management: curriculum, instruction, and community (Gay, 2006). First, the curriculum values students' cultural knowledge as a source for instruction (e.g., the Māori *Te Marautanga o Aotearoa* national curriculum of New Zealand, see http://tinyurl.com/yhvd2b8). Second, the instruction itself incorporates students' familiar ways of interacting and reflects more accurately the structure of their cultural environment (e.g., African American students increase learning by pursuing multiple, overlapping goals, such as content, character, and social activism; Ladson-Billings, 1994). Third, culturally responsive teaching is coherent with classroom community through student collaboration. Building community through student small-group interactions advances student achievement "irrespective of ethnicity, race, gender, or ability groupings" (e.g., the "talk-story" of the KEEP Program for Native Hawaiian primary students; Gay, 2006, p.362).

Use Group Management Methods that Encourage Students' Engagement in Academic Tasks. While some classrooms have been documented with effective classroom management, high student engagement, but a paucity of content instruction (Weade & Evertson, 1988), warm demanders focus group structures on academic content. Differing group structures require distinct group management methods to help students learn, and these various structures have unique effects on student achievement (Hattie, 2009). Techniques that are pertinent to all group structures include feedback, clarity, and classroom routines. Feedback involves communicating with students about their understanding of content, their performance on tasks, and their interactions with others. Feedback is bidirectional in nature and influences student academic achievement in par-

ticular when teachers connect student effort with outcome and when students connect teachers' instructional efforts with student understanding (Hattie, 2009). For example, a teacher may use praise to identify a student's success on a long-term project: "Your careful attention to each step of this project helped you complete it accurately and on time. Great job!" The student's reply, "I just followed the checklist you gave us," may inform the teacher, in turn, of the success and potential future use of the instruction provided.

Clarity refers mainly to how the learning environment is structured, lessons are presented, examples are offered, and practice is completed. The presentation of clear and coherent content enables students to construct meaningful learning and to retain it (Brophy, 2000). For example, in small-group settings, students increase their interactions over content when they use a reporter form to clarify their task.

Patterns of interaction that are taught, practiced, and consistently enforced to the point of fluid use becoming *classroom routines*. One critical area for routines is transitions. Classroom shifts between activities, content, and locations, comprise approximately 15% of the school day (Carter & Doyle, 2006). These transitions can be a source or catalyst for student misbehavior. Warm demanders effectively manage transitions through the use of cues to signal students that the transition is about to take place (e.g., music, lighting, designated phrase), monitoring to know how students are making the transition, and consistently using transition routines (Carter & Doyle, 2006). Classroom routines help students to become self-regulating.

Promote the Development of Students' Social Skills and Self-Regulation. Specific instruction for students in social skills is associated with academic achievement in that it increases students' abilities to interact positively with peers, comply promptly with teacher directions, and participate successfully in the "discourses of power" (Delpit, 1995). Students are more likely to become self-regulating when they have teacher modeling and explicit teaching on the strategies of "propositional knowledge (what to do), procedural knowledge (how to do it) and conditional knowledge (when and why to do it)" (Brophy, 2000, p. 25). Strategy teaching implies making visible the management systems that permeate students' learning of content. Teachers can help students enhance strategy learning through cognitive modeling (e.g., self-verbalization) and providing corrective feedback. For example, if a student is unable to complete the assigned independent work, a warm demander may ask the student what location in the room he or she could find the assignment posted; how the student might use the displayed example problem; what time period is being provided to complete the work; or other questions to help the student identify the available supports within the classroom and choose an appropriate path toward completion.

Self-regulation additionally can impact student achievement through the fact that a portion of learning occurs distinct from the structures of the classroom (Nuthall, 2005).

Self-regulation is an end-goal for classroom management: "to create an environment in which students behave appropriately, not out of fear of punishment or desire for reward, but out of a sense of personal responsibility, respect, and regard for the group" (Woolfolk-Hoy & Weinstein, 2006, p. 210). However, warm demanders must prepare for the eventuality that students do misbehave even while working toward this goal.

Use Appropriate Interventions to Assist Students with Behavior Problems.   Disruptive students can have negative effects on their own and on all other students' achievement (Hattie, 2009). Responsive classroom management is not a mere off-the-cuff reaction to student misbehavior; rather, it includes understanding why the student is misbehaving, selecting a response that promotes a positive return to instruction, and utilizing interventions to advance student maturation (Emmer & Stough, 2008). Interventions can include conversational (e.g., student or parent conferences, verbal feedback on un/desirable behavior, drawing students back into the lesson with questions); physical (e.g., making eye contact, increasing proximity, rearranging seating to separate students); and written responses (e.g., behavior contracts; student explanation of misbehavior, effects, and goals for improvement).

Less effective teachers may feel challenged by students' misbehaviors and establish a classroom management system that is so rigid and focused on compliance it dampens student motivation, strangles the sense of community, and makes the risk-taking of learning too high-stakes. Students "may become less interested in subjects taught by teachers who display anger, mistarget and punish innocent students, and do not provide warnings before issuing punishments" (Lewis, 2006, p.1203). Whereas, "more effective teachers monitored student behavior closely, intervened to correct inappropriate behavior before it escalated, and made fewer empty threats and warnings when dealing with misbehavior," it was their social, emotional, and cultural effectiveness that led to increased student academic achievement (Evertson, 1997, p. 254).

Summary and Recommendations

Classroom management has long been a concern of teachers and continues to play a significant role in teachers' and students' experiences with learning. The concept of the "warm demander" is a powerful construct through which to consider effective classroom management and its connection with student academic achievement. While all teachers may not yet be able to effectively demonstrate the five tasks outlined and to prompt a related increase in achievement, it is possible for them to learn how and to engender the achievement increase. Professional development, reflection, and continued practice provide opportunities for teachers to increase their skill in classroom management. Developing collections of the storied experiences (Carter & Doyle, 2006) of warm demanders also could help novice

and struggling teachers build contrast sets and move toward more effective classroom management for themselves and for their students.

Future research on effective classroom management could utilize these storied collections to test the construct of the warm demander, further refine it, and propose beneficial directions for teacher training. Additionally, the collections could be used in future research to consider a multiple goals perspective of classroom management: how the multiple areas of students' lives that are influenced by classroom management, including student academic achievement, inform one another. Finally, future research could seek evidence within the collections connecting effective classroom management with students' academic achievement beyond standardized testing to include students' deep understandings of content.

References

Brophy, J. (2000). *Teaching: Educational practice series* (Vol. 1). Geneva, Switzerland: International Bureau of Education.

Carter, K., & Doyle, W. (2006). Classroom management in early childhood and elementary classrooms. In C. M. Evertson & C. S. Weinstein (Eds.), *Handbook of classroom management: Research, practice, and contemporary issues* (pp. 373–406). Mahwah, NJ: Erlbaum.

Delpit, L. (1995). *Other people's children: Cultural conflict in the classroom.* New York: New Press.

Emmer, E. T., & Stough, L. M. (2008). Responsive classroom management. In T. Good (Ed.), *21st century education: A reference handbook* (Vol.1, pp. 140–148). Thousand Oaks, CA: Sage.

Evertson, C. M. (1997). Classroom management. In H. J. Walberg & G. D. Haertel (Eds.), *Psychology and educational practice* (pp. 251–273). Berkeley, CA: McCutchan.

Evertson, C. M., & Weinstein, C. S. (2006). Classroom management as a field of inquiry. In C. M. Evertson & C. S. Weinstein (Eds.), *Handbook of classroom management: Research, practice, and contemporary issues* (pp. 3–15). Mahwah, NJ: Erlbaum.

Galton, M. J. (1995). *Crisis in the primary classroom.* London: D. Fulton.

Gay, G. (2006). Culturally responsive teaching. In C. M. Evertson & C. S. Weinstein (Eds.), *Handbook of classroom management: Research, practice, and contemporary issues* (pp. 343–370). Mahwah, NJ: Erlbaum.

Hattie, J. (2009). *Visible learning: A synthesis of over 800 meta-analyses relating to achievement.* London: Routledge.

Jerome, E. M., & Pianta, R. C. (2008). Teacher–student relationships. In T. Good (Ed.), *21st century education: A reference handbook* (Vol.2, pp. 158–165). Thousand Oaks, CA: Sage.

Ladson-Billings, G. (1994). *The dreamkeepers: Successful teachers of African American children.* San Francisco, CA: Jossey-Bass.

Lewis, R. (2006). Classroom discipline in Australia. In C. M. Evertson & C. S. Weinstein (Eds.), *Handbook of classroom management: Research, practice, and contemporary issues* (pp. 1193–1214). Mahwah, NJ: Erlbaum.

Nuthall, G. A. (2005). The cultural myths and realities of classroom teaching and learning: A personal journey. *Teachers College Record, 107*(5), 895–934.

Pianta, R. C. (2006). Classroom management and relationships between children and teachers: Implications for research and practice. In C. M. Evertson & C. S. Weinstein (Eds.), *Handbook of classroom management: Research, practice, and contemporary issues* (pp. 685–709). Mahwah, NJ: Erlbaum.

Rubie-Davies, C. (2008). Teacher expectations. In T. Good (Ed.), *21st century education: A reference handbook* (Vol. 1, pp. 254–262). Thousand Oaks, CA: Sage.

Vavrus, M. (2008b). Culturally responsive teaching. In T. Good (Ed.),

21st century education: A reference handbook (Vol. 2, pp. 49–57). Thousand Oaks, CA: Sage.

Weade, R., & Evertson, C. M. (1988). The construction of lessons in effective and less effective classrooms. *Teaching and Teacher Education, 4*, 189–213.

Woolfolk-Hoy, A., & Weinstein, C. S. (2006). Student and teacher perspectives. In C. M. Evertson & C. S. Weinstein (Eds.), *Handbook of classroom management: Research, practice, and contemporary issues* (pp. 181–219). Mahwah, NJ: Erlbaum.

Wubbels, T., Brekelmans, M., den Brok, P., & van Tartwijk, J. (2006). An interpersonal perspective on classroom management in the Netherlands. In C. M. Evertson & C. S. Weinstein (Eds.), *Handbook of classroom management: Research, practice, and contemporary issues* (pp. 1161–1191). Mahwah, NJ: Erlbaum.

5.4

Emotion and Achievement in the Classroom

Thomas Goetz
University of Konstanz and Thurgau University of Teacher Education

Nathan C. Hall
McGill University

Introduction

With the exception of extensive research on test anxiety since the 1950s (Sarason & Mandler, 1952; Zeidner, 2007) and on emotions in achievement settings based on attribution theory (Weiner, 1985), empirical educational research has largely neglected students' emotions. Over the past decade, however, a discernible increase in theoretical and empirical contributions on emotions in education is reflected in numerous special issues and edited volumes (Efklides & Volet, 2005; Linnenbrink, 2006; Linnenbrink-Garcia & Pekrun, 2011; Lipnevich & Roberts, 2012; Schutz & Lanehart, 2002; Schutz & Pekrun, 2007). Nonetheless, with the exception of research on anxiety/achievement relations (e.g., Hembree, 1988; Ma, 1999; Seipp, 1991), there exist only scattered empirical findings on relations between other emotions and academic achievement (Pekrun, 2006). This lack of emphasis is reflected in a recent PsychINFO search (January 2011) for manuscript titles including "achievement" *and* "anxiety" (532) as compared to "enjoyment" (10), "hope" (14), "pride" (7), "anger" (8), "shame" (8), or "boredom" (3). In contrast to 1,015 titles including "achievement" *and* "self-concept," the relatively small number of publications in the field of emotions as compared to self-concept research is clearly evident.

Research Evidence

Strength of Emotion/Achievement Relations

Anxiety—Meta-analyses. Concerning the magnitude of emotion/achievement relations, there exist three seminal meta-analyses in which academic anxiety is exclusively evaluated. In his meta-analysis of 562 North American studies (1952–1986), Hembree (1988) explored the correlates, causes, effects, and remediation of test anxiety. The studies consisted of samples from upper elementary school to high school and included various achievement measures includ-

ing test scores, course grades, and GPA. Results showed test anxiety to have typically moderate negative relations with achievement, for example, with grades in mathematics ($r = -.22$), natural sciences ($r = -.21$), and social sciences ($r = -.25$). In Seipp (1991), a similar meta-analysis of 126 European and North American studies (1975–1988) revealed generally moderate negative relations between anxiety and academic performance, as indicated in a population effect size of $-.21$ (range $= -.36$ to $-.07$). The third domain-specific meta-analysis by Ma (1999) explored anxiety and achievement relations concerning mathematics across 26 studies of elementary and secondary students, finding once again a modest population correlation of $-.27$ (range $= -.60$ to $-.12$). Taken together, meta-analyses findings consistently demonstrate significant, albeit moderate, negative relations typically ranging from $-.20$ to $-.25$ between anxiety and achievement outcomes.

Discrete Emotions—Single Studies. Empirical findings on relations between discrete emotions and academic achievement are clear with respect to emotion valence: Pleasant emotions (e.g., enjoyment, pride) are positively related to achievement whereas unpleasant emotions (e.g., anxiety, boredom) are negatively related (Pekrun, 2006). Further, cumulative research indicates that emotion/achievement relations are best understood as linear and not curvilinear in nature (e.g., inverted-U relationship as in Yerkes & Dodson, 1908; see Zeidner, 1998, 2007). Concerning the strength of discrete emotions/achievement relations, recent studies indicate differences with respect to emotion type and academic domain. Goetz et al. (2012; grades 8/11) found the mean and median within-domain relation between discrete classroom-related emotions (enjoyment, pride, anxiety, anger, boredom) and grades in multiple subject domains (mathematics, physics, German, English) to be |.25| (range $= .04$ to $.40$; $SD = .08$). These values are consistent with related studies on emotion/achievement relations in high-school and university students (e.g., Goetz, Cronjaeger, Frenzel, & Lüdtke, 2010; Goetz, Frenzel, Hall, & Pekrun, 2008; Goetz, Frenzel, Pekrun, Hall, & Lüdtke, 2007; Pekrun, Elliot, & Maier, 2009; Pekrun, Goetz, Daniels, Stupnisky, & Perry, 2010). To summarize, single studies indicate mean discrete emotions/achievement relations of approximately |.25|.

Mediating Factors in Emotion/Achievement Relations. There exist few theoretical approaches in which the mechanisms underlying discrete emotion/achievement relations are addressed. Of these models, the most prominent is a comprehensive model outlined by Pekrun, Frenzel, Goetz, and Perry (2007) that incorporates social-cognitive emotion theories as well as empirical findings concerning discrete emotions in achievement settings. In Pekrun's model, it is assumed that emotion/achievement relations are mediated by cognitive resources, motivation, strategy use, and self-regulated learning such that specific emotions impact these variables that, in turn, predict achievement outcomes. Further, the effects of emotions on mediating variables and achievement are assumed to be additionally complicated by the emotional dimensions of valence (pleasant vs. unpleasant) and activation (activating vs. deactivating). Based on these dimensions, four groups of emotions can be distinguished: positive activating emotions (e.g., enjoyment, hope, pride, gratitude); positive deactivating emotions (e.g., relaxation, contentment, relief); negative activating emotions (e.g., anger, frustration, anxiety, shame); and negative deactivating emotions (e.g., boredom, sadness, disappointment, hopelessness). In most conditions, it is assumed that positive activating emotions exert positive effects on achievement whereas negative deactivating emotions exert negative effects, in contrast to positive deactivating and negative activating emotions that are assumed to have ambivalent effects on motivation and cognitive processing (Pekrun, 2006). Nevertheless, there exists little research in which these proposed mediation mechanisms are examined, competitively evaluated, or explored with respect to reverse causality (e.g., cognitive resources as mediators of emotion/achievement relations vs. emotions as mediators of cognitive resources/achievement relations; Pekrun, Goetz, Titz, & Perry, 2002a; Turner & Waugh, 2007).

Moderators of Emotion/Achievement Relations. Findings on emotion/achievement relations typically show a wide range of relations for both (test) anxiety and other discrete emotions. Moreover, there exist numerous studies in research on anxiety (Zeidner, 1998, 2007) and other discrete emotions (e.g., Pekrun et al., 2002a; Goetz, Cronjaeger et al., 2010; Goetz, Frenzel, Hall, & Pekrun, 2008; Goetz et al., 2007) that taken together suggest three primary moderators of emotion/achievement relations:

1. Relations are stronger when emotions and achievement are assessed within a specific domain (e.g., math anxiety and math achievement vs. learning anxiety and GPA).

2. Relations are stronger in the math and science domains as compared to verbal domains.
3. Emotion valence determines relation valence: Pleasant emotions are positively related with achievement and unpleasant emotions are negatively related.

Research on test anxiety and achievement relations suggests additional moderating variables (Zeidner, 1998, 2007), including those that increase these relations (e.g., evaluative settings, negative feedback) and decrease these relations (e.g., structured conditions, social support). Although often cited as a possible moderator, gender has not been found to substantially moderate anxiety/achievement relations (Zeidner, 1998, 2007). Empirical findings concerning gender effects on discrete emotion/achievement relations are presently lacking. With respect to causal ordering, it is important to note that reciprocal relations between emotions and achievement can also be assumed (Pekrun et al., 2002a; for test anxiety, see Zeidner, 1998, 2007). More specifically, achievement can impact emotions (e.g., good grades predict enjoyment) directly or via academic self-concept (e.g., good grades predict perceived competence which predicts enjoyment; Goetz, Frenzel, Hall, & Pekrun, 2008).

Relevance of Academic Emotions for Academic Achievement. Studies indicate that emotion/achievement relations are, on average, weak to moderate in magnitude (cf., academic self-concept/achievement: average $r = .50$ to .70; Marsh & Craven, 2006). However, even relatively weak effects of emotions on academic achievement may have a strong cumulative impact on students' long-term achievement. The findings outlined above further suggest considerable variability in emotion/achievement relations as a function of emotion type and academic discipline, highlighting the potential for notably stronger relations for specific emotions in specific academic settings (e.g., anxiety in natural science classes). In addition, whereas academic emotions are of relevance to achievement outcomes, their effects also generalize to salient developmental outcomes including health, subjective well-being, career choice, and lifelong learning (Pekrun, 2006). Finally, in light of the dominance of anxiety research, relatively unexplored positive academic emotions have also received recent attention. According to Pekrun, Goetz, Titz, and Perry (2002b), positive emotions "help to envision goals and challenges, open the mind to thoughts and problem-solving, protect health by fostering resiliency, create attachments to significant others, lay the groundwork for individual self-regulation, and guide the behavior of groups, social systems, and nations" (p. 149).

Summary and Recommendations

Given the importance of academic emotions with respect to achievement outcomes as well as student development, and accounting for the status quo of research in this field, the following research activities are recommended:

- Research on emotion/achievement relations should focus on discrete emotions, such as enjoyment, hope, pride, gratitude, relaxation, contentment, relief, anger, frustration, anxiety, shame, boredom, sadness, disappointment, and hopelessness in addition to test anxiety.
- Given the domain-specificity of academic emotional experiences and subject domain as a moderator of the strength of emotion/achievement relations, domain-specific investigations are warranted.
- As most research on emotion/achievement relations has focused on testing situations (i.e., anxiety) and the classroom setting, future studies on homework-related emotions remains relatively unexplored and may yield intriguing findings (cf., Dettmers et al., 2011).
- Empirical research examining the assumed causal relations between emotions and achievement is needed (e.g., longitudinal, experimental, intervention designs).
- The continued development of domain- and age-specific instruments for the assessment of discrete emotions other than (test) anxiety is required to adequately explore emotion/achievement relations (e.g., domain-general and domain-specific measures in the Achievement Emotions Questionnaire; Pekrun, Goetz, Frenzel, Barchfield, & Perry, 2011).

Concerning implications of research on emotion/achievement relations for teaching and teacher education programs, possible recommendations include:

- The impact of academic emotions on learning and achievement should be highlighted in teacher education curricula.
- Antecedents of academic emotions should also be addressed in teacher education curricula to facilitate teachers' understanding of how students' emotions are affected by the mediating and moderating variables outlined above.
- Based on knowledge of emotion antecedents, teachers should acknowledge their potential to impact students' emotions and attempt to foster pleasant and reduce negative emotions; for example, by enhancing students' academic self-concept (Goetz et al., 2008), adopting an enthusiastic teaching style (Frenzel, Goetz, Lüdke, Pekrun, & Sutton, 2009), or fostering students' emotion regulation competencies (e.g., for coping with test anxiety, see Zeidner, 1998, 2007; for coping with boredom, see Nett, Goetz, & Hall, 2011).
- Teachers should also be aware of their own emotional experiences and attempt to optimize their emotions concerning instruction so as to promote students' emotions and achievement (Frenzel et al., 2009; Schutz & Zembylas, 2009).

It is essential that ongoing empirical research on students' emotions be consistently incorporated into teacher education programs and informed by educational practice.

In this manner, researchers and educators alike will be better able to identify and develop instructional strategies and intervention programs that optimize student's academic emotional experiences and thereby facilitate not only learning and academic achievement, but also critical developmental outcomes including health and psychological well-being.

References

Dettmers, S., Trautwein, U., Lüdtke, Goetz, T., Frenzel, A. C., & Pekrun, R. (2011). Students' emotions during homework in mathematics: Testing a theoretical model of antecedents and achievement outcomes. *Contemporary Educational Psychology*, *36*(1), 25–35.

Efklides, A., & Volet, S. (2005). Feelings and emotions in the learning process [Special issue]. *Learning and Instruction, 15,* 377–380.

Frenzel, A. C., Goetz, T., Lüdtke, O., Pekrun, R., & Sutton, R. E. (2009). Emotional transmission in the classroom: Exploring the relationship between teacher and student enjoyment. *Journal of Educational Psychology, 101*(3), 705–716.

Goetz, T., Cronjaeger, H., Frenzel, A. C., Lüdtke, O., & Hall, N. C. (2010). Academic self-concept and emotion relations: Domain specificity and age effects. *Contemporary Educational Psychology, 35,* 44–58.

Goetz, T., Frenzel, C. A., Hall, N. C., & Pekrun, R. (2008). Antecedents of academic emotions: Testing the internal/external frame of reference model for academic enjoyment. *Contemporary Educational Psychology, 33,* 9–33.

Goetz, T., Frenzel, C. A., Pekrun, R., Hall, N. C., & Lüdtke, O. (2007). Between- and within-domain relations of students' academic emotions. *Journal of Educational Psychology, 99*(4), 715–733.

Goetz, T., Nett, U., Martiny, S., Hall, N. C., Pekrun, R., Dettmers, S., & Trautwein, U. (2012). Students' emotions during homework: Structures, self–concept antecedents, and achievement outcomes. *Learning and Individual Differences, 22*(2), 225–234.

Hembree, R. (1988). Correlates, causes, effects, and treatment of test anxiety. *Review of Educational Research, 58,* 7–77.

Linnenbrink, E. A. (2006). Emotion research in education: Theoretical and methodological perspectives on the integration of affect, motivation, and cognition [Special issue]. *Educational Psychology Review, 18,* 307–314.

Linnenbrink-Garcia, E. A., & Pekrun, R. (2011). Students' emotions and academic engagement [Special issue]. *Contemporary Educational Psychology, 36*(1), 1–3.

Lipnevich, A. A., & Roberts, R. D. (2012). Noncognitive skills in education: Emerging research and applications in a variety of international contexts. *Learning and Individual Differences, 22*(2), 173–177.

Ma, X. (1999). A meta-analysis of the relationship between anxiety toward mathematics and achievement in mathematics. *Journal for Research in Mathematics Education, 30*(5), 520–540.

Marsh, H., W., & Craven, R. G. (2006). Reciprocal effects of self–concept and performance from a multidimensional perspective: Beyond seductive pleasure and unidimensional perspectives. *Perspectives on Psychological Science, 1*(2), 133–163.

Nett, U. E., Goetz, T., & Hall, N. C. (2011). Coping with boredom in school: An experience sampling perspective. *Contemporary Educational Psychology, 36*(1), 49–59.

Pekrun, R. (2006). The control-value theory of achievement emotions: Assumptions, corollaries, and implications for educational research and practice. *Educational Psychology Review, 18,* 315–341.

Pekrun, R., Elliot, A. J., & Maier, M. A. (2009). Achievement goals and achievement emotions: Testing a model of their joint relations with academic performance. *Journal of Educational Psychology, 101,* 115–135.

Pekrun, R., Frenzel, A. C., Götz, T. & Perry, R. P. (2007). The control-value theory of achievement emotions: An integrative approach to emotions in education. In P. A. Schutz & R. Pekrun (Eds.), *Emotion in education,* (pp. 13–36). San Diego, CA: Academic Press.

Pekrun, R., Goetz, T., Daniels, L. M., Stupnisky, R. H., & Perry, R. P. (2010). Boredom in achievement settings: Exploring control-value antecedents and performance outcomes of a neglected emotion. *Journal of Educational Psychology, 102*(3), 531–549.

Pekrun, R., Goetz, T., Frenzel, A. C., Barchfeld, P., & Perry, R. P. (2011). Measuring emotions in students' learning and performance: The achievement emotions questionnaire (AEQ). *Contemporary Educational Psychology, 36*(1), 36–48.

Pekrun, R., Goetz, T., Titz, W., & Perry, R. P. (2002a). Academic emotions in students' self–regulated learning and achievement: A program of qualitative and quantitative research. *Educational Psychologist, 37*(2), 91–105.

Pekrun, R., Goetz, T., Titz, W., & Perry, R. P. (2002b). Positive emotions in education. In E. Frydenberg (Ed.), *Beyond coping: Meeting goals, visions, and challenges* (pp. 149–173). Oxford, England: Oxford University Press.

Sarason, S. B., & Mandler, G. (1952). Some correlates of test anxiety. *Journal of Abnormal and Social Psychology, 47*(4), 810–817.

Schutz, P. A., & Lanehart, S. L. (Eds.). (2002). Emotions in education [Special issue]. *Educational Psychologist, 37*(2).

Schutz, P. A., & Pekrun, R. (Eds.). (2007). *Emotions in education.* San Diego, CA: Elsevier.

Schutz, P. A., & Zembylas, M. (Eds.). (2009). *Advances in teacher emotions research: The impact on teachers lives.* San Diego, CA: Academic Press.Seipp, B. (1991). Anxiety and academic performance: A meta–analysis of findings. *Anxiety Research, 4,* 27–41.

Turner, J. E., & Waugh, R. M. (2007). A dynamical systems perspective regarding students' learning processes: Shame reactions and emergent self–organizations. In P. A. Schutz & R. Pekrun (Eds.), *Emotion in education* (pp. 125–145). San Diego, CA: Academic Press.

Weiner, B. (1985). An attributional theory of achievement motivation and emotion. *Psychological Review, 92*(4), 548–573.

Yerkes, R. M., & Dodson, J. D. (1908). The relation of strength of stimulus to rapidity of habit–formation. *Journal of Comparative and Neurological Psychology, 18,* 459–489.

Zeidner, M. (1998). *Test anxiety: The state of the art.* New York: Plenum Press.

Zeidner, M. (2007). Test anxiety: Conceptions, findings, conclusions. In P. A. Schutz & R. Pekrun (Eds.), *Emotion in education* (pp. 165–184). San Diego, CA: Academic Press.

5.5

Secondary Classroom Management

ANNE GREGORY AND JENNIFER R. JONES
Graduate School of Applied and Professional Psychology, Rutgers University

Introduction

Teachers with effective classroom management in secondary schools both promote positive achievement-oriented behavior and successfully intervene with off-task and rule-breaking behavior. They are skilled at establishing a caring and respectful environment and sustaining student engagement, which ensures that less effort is needed for enforcing rules and reducing disruptive behavior (Evertson & Weinstein, 2006). Theory would suggest that effective managers are able to increase student engagement, which may in turn increase student achievement. That said, few rigorous studies have directly examined how effective management leads to achievement gains in high school. Moreover, most classroom management research has been conducted in the elementary grades.

Secondary teachers interact with youth in a developmental phase characterized by the increasing role of peers. The draw to peers can be challenging for teachers as they try to balance adolescents' need for peer affiliation and autonomy with adult demands. Another challenge relates to the well-documented pattern that ethnic minority students tend to be issued referrals for discipline at higher rates than majority students (Gazeley, 2010; Gregory, Skiba, & Noguera, 2010). This pattern raises questions about whether a universal conceptualization of good secondary classroom management can be used to understand how to elicit cooperation with *all* students, including those from minority racial/ethnic backgrounds. Perhaps some teacher practices serve some groups more than others, which would suggest a consideration of culturally relevant classroom management.

Past approaches to understanding what comprises good classroom management have been driven by competing theoretical stances on human development and behavioral change (Evertson & Weinstein, 2006). Behavioral theory emphasizes that disruptive or cooperative behavior in classrooms increases or decreases depending on whether positive or negative stimuli are applied or removed (Osher,

Bear, Sprague, & Doyle, 2010). Social learning theory posits that students learn to cooperate by observing others and internalizing rules of conduct (Evertson & Weinstein, 2006). Derived from Rogerian principles, a person-centered approach to management emphasizes building trust and shared responsibility for the functioning of the classroom (Freiberg & Lamb, 2009). Students become invested in maintaining a positive climate, and as a result, become self-disciplined. An ecological approach emphasizes the importance of instructional momentum in keeping students actively participating. Currently, there are efforts to synthesize theories and develop a more comprehensive understanding of effective classroom management (Osher et al., 2010). A synthesis recognizes the utility of (a) reinforcing positive behavior and (b) explicitly developing social/emotional capacities, while building trusting and individualized relationships with students (Osher et al., 2010). This is a promising guide to conceptualizing secondary classroom management given that cooperation with adolescent-aged students may require more than behavioral contingencies and include the fostering of trusting relationships.

Research Evidence

There is a growing body of research that suggests an emphasis on relationship building in the classroom is linked to the welfare of adolescents. Drawing on 119 studies, a meta-analysis showed that teacher practices that emphasized relationship building and responsiveness to individual student needs were correlated with positive student outcomes related to cognition (e.g., grades, critical thinking) and behavior (motivation, attendance, engagement; Cornelius-White, 2007). The meditational links between such practices and increased achievement have not been empirically established. Yet, a vast body of research shows that students who are more engaged tend to have higher achievement compared to their less engaged peers. Logically, the more students are engaged and on-task, the more students will successfully achieve in their academics. This suggests that good managers effectively engage students, which enables them to accomplish academic tasks.

There have been demonstrations of the link between effective classroom management in middle and high schools and student engagement (Evertson & Weinstein, 2006). One study observed teachers in seventh and eighth grade at the beginning of their school year, and found that effective managers had low levels of disruptive behavior throughout the school year, compared to ineffective managers whose students exhibited more inappropriate behavior across the year. Better managers were more explicit about expectations, offered detailed directions about how to meet those expectations, and dealt with inappropriate behavior in a prompt fashion. They made accurate and timely desists when students got off-task or broke a rule. Further, secondary teachers who use hands-on and competency-enhancing activities tend to have more engaged and motivated students (Evertson & Weinstein, 2006). Productive classrooms keep students on-task through a strong "program of action" (Osher et al., 2010). Recent intervention research demonstrates that teachers can improve in these areas of effective management. For instance, the *MyTeachingPartner* professional development program pairs secondary teachers with consultants who view videotapes of teachers' instruction and guide them in developing new instructional strategies and behavior management approaches (Allen et al., 2011).

Classrooms and schools may also benefit from whole school and classroom-based interventions that target aggression and disruption. A recent meta-analysis of 249 experimental or quasi-experimental studies showed that universal violence prevention programs (engaging all students regardless of risk) had a mean effect size of 0.21 and selected/indicated programs (engaging at-risk students) had a mean effect size of 0.29 (Wilson & Lipsey, 2007). While these programs had small effect sizes, they were practically significant in substantially reducing aggression and disruption in schools. Importantly, the different treatment orientations (e.g., behavioral, cognitive, social skills) produced similar effects. This suggests that teachers can effectively reduce disruption using programs that focus on increasing students' socioemotional abilities (a social skills approach) or reinforcing positive behaviors (a behavioral approach). One such behavioral program is called the *Good Behavior Game*, in which students work in teams to reach collective behavioral goals. According to Embry (2004) approximately 20 independent studies across different grade levels, settings, and different types of students determined that the *Good Behavior Game* shows consistent impact on lowering impulsive and disruptive behaviors of children and teens.

Another widely used program is called *Positive Behavior Support* (PBS), which is implemented across a school setting. In PBS, behavioral expectations are explicitly defined and taught to all students. Positive reinforcement in the form of reward tickets is regularly issued to students for meeting expectations. In addition, a continuum of consequences for problem behavior is developed along with a comprehensive system to monitor and make data-driven decisions about patterns in problem behavior. There have been some mixed results as to whether *all* students benefit from this program. On the one hand, a 3-year longitudinal study of PBS in a single middle school (mostly comprised of Black and Latino students) showed that each year of program implementation there was a significant reduction in long-term suspensions (Lassen, Steele, & Sailor, 2006). On the other hand, a national sample of schools at the elementary and middle school level implementing PBS for at least a year, found significant disciplinary disproportionality for Black and Latino students in office disciplinary referrals, which are mostly generated by teachers in response to a perceived rule infraction (Skiba et al., 2008). These results raise questions about the effectiveness of programs that do not take into consideration racial dynamics, economic stressors, or other influences related to diversity in the classroom. Moreover, universal approaches to educational practice have frequently been critiqued if they do not specifically address student differences in the classroom.

The critique of universal approaches can be applied to conceptualizations of effective classroom management that do not consider diversity in the classroom. In response to such critique, Weinstein and colleagues (Weinstein, Tomlinson-Clarke, & Curran, 2004) offer a theory of culturally responsive classroom management, which occurs when teachers recognize their own ethocentricism, build caring classroom communities, draw on knowledge of their students' cultural backgrounds, use classroom management strategies in sync with those backgrounds, and understand broad social, economic, and political issues facing their students. The theoretical framework is promising but has yet to be tested through intervention research. Lacking are causal connections between multicultural training or teacher professional development opportunities and ethnic minority students' engagement and behavior. In fact, whether teachers' cultural responsiveness is linked to their classroom management practices is unknown (Alviar-Martin & Ho, 2010).

Universal approaches to effective management may also suffer from a lack of consideration of students' developmentally specific needs. Eliciting cooperation from elementary students may differ from eliciting cooperation from secondary students (Campbell et al., 2009). With adolescent students, teachers may need to consider specific peer dynamics in the classroom. Adolescents have a need for peer approval and affiliation, which may result in strong peer cliques and group attitudes toward the teachers' authority (Evertson & Weinstein, 2006). Teachers may need to foster positive peer pressure to maintained student engagement in academic tasks. In addition, teens have greater needs for autonomy and leadership in classrooms than younger children (Hay, 2009). Effective management may require more opportunities for adolescent decision making and self-determination.

Summary and Recommendations

In sum, school practitioners are challenged to elicit cooperation and engagement from their adolescent students. Engaged students are less likely to disrupt instruction and more likely to achieve. Effective management requires that teachers implement dynamic lesson plans, reinforce positive behavior, and intervene with misbehavior early and efficiently. With adolescents, school practitioners also need to develop trusting relationships and offer leadership roles so students take a shared responsibility in maintaining a well-functioning classroom. A focus on dynamic instruction, reinforcement of behavior, relationship building, and adolescent developmental needs combines a range of theories (e.g., behavioral, person-centered, ecological, developmental). Future research needs to test whether a synthesis of theories is most useful in capturing the complexity of managing both groups and individual students in secondary school classrooms. In addition, given differential disciplinary outcomes for certain racial and ethnic student groups, theory on culturally responsive classroom management needs to be rigorously tested. In the meantime, it is important that school practitioners identify whether the way they manage their classrooms benefit some groups of students over others. Teachers need to focus on engaging individual students (especially those at-risk for repeated disciplinary action) as well as the group as a whole.

References

Allen, J. P., Pianta, R. C., Gregory, A., Mikami, A., & Lun, J. (2011). An interaction-based approach to enhancing secondary school instruction and student achievement. *Science, 19,* 1034–1037.

Alviar-Martin, T., & Ho, Li-Ching, (2010). "So, where do they fit in?" Teachers' perspectives of multi-cultural education and diversity in Singapore. *Teaching and Teacher Education.* Retrieved from http://www.elsevier.com/wps/find/ journaldescription.cws_home/224/description#description.

Campbell, C., Deed, C., Drane, S., Faulkner, M., McDonough, A., Mornane, A., Prain, V., … Sullivan, P. (2009). Junior secondary students' perceptions of influences on their engagement with schooling. *Australian Journal of Education, 53,* 54–68.

Cornelius-White (2007). Learner-centered teacher–student relationships are effective: A meta-analysis. *Review of Educational Research, 77,* 113–143.

Evertson, C., & Weinstein, C. (2006). *Handbook of classroom management: Research, practice, and contemporary issues.* Mahwah, NJ: Erlbaum.

Embry, D. D. (2004). Community-based prevention using simple, low cost, evidence-based kernels and behavior vaccines. *Journal of Community Psychology, 32,* 575–591.

Freiberg, H. J. & Lamb, S. M. (2009). Dimensions of person-centered classroom management. *Theory into Practice, 48,* 99–105.

Gazeley, L. (2010). The role of school exclusion processes in the reproduction of social and educational disadvantage. *British Journal of Educational Studies, 1,* 1–17.

Gregory, A., Skiba, R. J., & Noguera, P. A. (2010). The achievement gap and the discipline gap: Two sides of the same coin? *Educational Researcher, 39,* 59–68.

Hay, P. J. (2009). Students' perceptions of schooling in a senior secondary system. *Australian Journal of Education, 53,* 54–68.

Lassen, S. R., Steele, M. M., & Sailor, W. (2006). The relationship of school-wide positive behavior support to academic achievement in an urban middle school. *Psychology in the Schools,* 701–712.

Osher, D., Bear, G. G., Sprague, J. R., & Doyle, W. (2010). How can we improve school discipline? *Educational Researcher, 39,* 48–58.

Skiba, R. J., Simmons, A. B., Ritter, S., Gibb, A. C., Rausch, M. K., Cuadrado, J., … Chung, C. (2008). Achieving equity in special education: History, status, and current challenges. *Exceptional Children, 74,* 264–288.

Weinstein, C. S., Tomlinson-Clarke, S., & Curran, M. (2004). Toward a conception of culturally responsive classroom management. *Journal of Teacher Education, 55*(1), 25–38.

Wilson, S. J., & Lipsey, M. W. (2007). School-based interventions for aggressive and disruptive behavior: Update of a meta-analysis. *American Journal of Preventive Medicine, 33,* 130–143.

5.6

Homework and Academic Achievement

Jianzhong Xu
Mississippi State University

Introduction

Typically defined as "tasks assigned to students by school teachers that are meant to be carried out during nonschool hours" (Cooper, 1989, p. 7), homework is a "complicated thing" (Corno, 1996), influenced by more factors than any other instructional activities (Cooper, 2001). It is a widespread educational activity extending across cultures, ages, and ability levels (Chen & Stevenson, 1989; Warton, 2001). Indeed, for most school-age children, homework is an important part of their daily routine (Cooper, Robinson, & Patall, 2006). It is also an issue of tremendous everyday importance for parents and teachers alike (Trautwein, 2007). Not surprisingly, homework has been a perennial topic of public interest and an active area of investigation among educational researchers (Cooper et al., 2006).

Research Evidence

Reviews of homework research (e.g., Cooper, 1989; Cooper et al., 2006; Keith, 1986; Walberg, 1991) provide generally consistent evidence for a positive influence of homework on academic achievement. In their recent synthesis of 69 studies conducted in the United States, Cooper et al. (2006) found, with rare exceptions, that homework had a positive effect on academic achievement. They categorized the 69 studies into three basic design types. The first type included six studies that used experimental designs to compare homework and no-homework conditions. The six studies all revealed a positive effect of homework on unit tests, with effect sizes varying between $d = .39$ and $d = .97$.

The second type used data from 31 cross-sectional studies (e.g., the National Education Longitudinal Study), most using multiple regression analyses or structural equation modeling. The large majority of these studies revealed positive and generally significant relationships between the amount of homework and achievement when various potentially confounding variables were controlled.

The third type involved the calculation of a simple bivariate correlation between the time the student spent on homework and the measure of achievement. These 32 studies included 69 separate correlations based on 35 separate samples of students. Of the 69 correlations, 50 were in a positive direction and 19 in a negative direction, with a weighted average correlation of $r = .24$.

In addition, Cooper et al. (2006) examined whether the magnitude of the correlation between homework and academic achievement was moderated by other variables (e.g., grade level, achievement measure, and subject matter). They found that a stronger correlation existed at the middle and high school levels than at the elementary school level.

Cooper et al. (2006) noted design flaws in most of the studies reviewed. However, they also noted that these studies tended not to share the same flaws. Given that a wide variety of students have provided data, that the studies have controlled for or tested many plausible rival hypotheses in various combinations, and that the effects of homework have been tested in multiple subject areas, they concluded that homework has a positive influence on academic achievement.

More recently, a number of studies suggest that there is a critical need to pay attention to other important variables that influence the effect of homework on academic achievement, including homework quality (e.g., Dettmers, Trautwein, Lüdtke, Kunter, & Baumert, 2010), homework effort (e.g., Trautwein, 2007), and self-efficacy beliefs (e.g., Zimmerman & Kitsantas, 2005). Dettmers et al. (2010) examined the association of two indicators of homework quality (i.e., homework selection and homework challenge) with mathematics achievement. The homework selection scale assessed how well-prepared and interesting homework assignments were perceived to be, whereas the homework challenge scale assessed the extent to which homework assignments were perceived to be cognitively challenging. Multilevel modeling was used to analyze longitudinal data from a representative sample of 3,483 students in grades

9 and 10 in Germany. The study revealed that mathematics achievement was positively related to both homework selection and homework challenge at the class level. In addition, mathematics achievement was negatively related to homework challenge at the student level. On the other hand, after controlling confounding variables (e.g., gender, prior achievement, and cognitive abilities), homework time was not related to mathematics achievement.

In another study, Trautwein (2007) examined the associations between homework effort and mathematics achievement, based on data from 483 eighth graders in Germany. A homework effort scale assessed homework compliance and effort invested in homework (e.g., "I do my best in my mathematics homework"). The study revealed that, after controlling for prior achievement, homework effort positively and statistically significantly predicted both mathematics grades and mathematics test scores.

Zimmerman and Kitsantas (2005) examined the meditational role of two self-efficacy beliefs (learning and perceived responsibility) between students' homework practices and academic achievement, based on the data from 179 high school girls in the United States. Self-efficacy for learning assessed students' perceived self-efficacy regarding performing various forms of academic learning (e.g., reading, note-taking, testing, writing, and studying). The perceived responsibility for learning scale assessed whether the participants perceived the student or the teacher as more responsible for various learning tasks or outcomes, such as student motivation (e.g., going through the motions without trying), deportment (e.g., fooling around in class), and learning processes (e.g., not taking notes in class). Path analyses showed significant paths (a) from homework experiences to the girls' self-efficacy for learning beliefs and their perception of student responsibility for academic outcomes, and (b) from these two beliefs to the girls' grade point average (GPA) at the end of the school term. Specifically, the results showed that the direct effect of the girls' prior achievement on their GPA was small ($p = .18$), but the indirect effect was larger ($p = .39$), indicating most of the variance in prior achievement is mediated through homework-related variables in the model (i.e., quality of homework, and self-efficacy for learning and perceived responsibility).

Summary and Recommendations

Many previous studies have examined the relationship between academic achievement and homework using variables such as the amount of homework assigned, time spent on homework, and the amount of homework completed. Results from these studies generally support the notion that the relationship between homework and academic achievement is a positive one for students in grades 7 to 12. More recently, a number of studies indicate that other factors may play a more important role in academic achievement than homework time, including homework quality, homework effort, and self-efficacy.

Consequently, instead of focusing on the quantity of homework, there is a critical need for teachers to improve the effectiveness of their instruction by designing more interesting, well-selected, and adequately difficult and challenging homework assignments (Dettmers et al., 2010; Epstein & Van Voorhis, 2001). This is particularly important, as engaging and interesting homework assignments can boost students' self-efficacy and responsibility for learning (Ramdass & Zimmerman, 2010), and as homework quality is positively related to students' homework effort (Dettmers et al., 2010).

Also it would be important to pay more direct attention to the effort students put into homework, as various homework distractions (e.g., TV viewing, online chatting, text messaging, and blogging) may interfere with their attempt to follow through on their homework assignments (Xu, 2010) and as spending a lot of time on homework may signify a rather inefficient, unmotivated homework style (Trautwein, 2007). In addition, it would be important for teachers to model and provide students with explicit instructions on how better to manage their homework, including organizing the workspace, setting priorities, managing time, monitoring motivation, and coping with negative emotions (Xu, 2009). Finally, it would be important to listen to students' perspectives about what teachers can do to help them better manage homework, which would enable educators to provide more appropriate support in their effort at homework management (e.g., by making homework more interesting and by providing individualized homework feedback). This, in turn, will further promote students' self-efficacy, self-regulatory skills, and responsibility for managing their own homework.

References

Chen, C., & Stevenson, H. W. (1989). Homework: A cross–cultural examination. *Child Development, 60*, 551–561.

Cooper, H. (1989). *Homework*. White Plains, NY: Longman.

Cooper, H. (2001). *The battle over homework: Common ground for administrators, teachers, and parents* (2nd ed.). Thousand Oaks, CA: Corwin Press.

Cooper, H., Robinson, J. C., & Patall, E. A. (2006). Does homework improve academic achievement? A synthesis of research, 1987–2003. *Review of Educational Research, 76*, 1–62.

Corno, L. (1996). Homework is a complicated thing. *Educational Researcher, 25*(8), 27–30.

Dettmers, S., Trautwein, U., Lüdtke, O., Kunter, M., & Baumert, H. (2010). Homework works if homework quality is high: Using multilevel modeling to predict the development of achievement in mathematics. *Journal of Educational Psychology, 102*, 467–482.

Epstein, J. L., & Van Voorhis, F. L. (2001). More than minutes: Teachers' roles in designing homework. *Educational Psychologist, 36*, 181–193.

Keith, T. Z. (1986). *Homework*. West Lafayette, IN: Kappa Delta Pi.

Ramdass, D., & Zimmerman, B. J. (2011). Developing self–regulation skills: The important role of homework. *Journal of Advanced Academics, 22*, 194–218.

Trautwein, U. (2007). The homework–achievement relation reconsidered: Differentiating homework time, homework frequency, and homework effort. *Learning and Instruction, 17*, 372–388.

Walberg, H. J. (1991). Does homework help? *School Community Journal, 1*(1), 13–15.

Warton, P. M. (2001). The forgotten voices in homework: Views of students. *Educational Psychologist, 36*, 155–165.

Xu, J. (2009). School location, student achievement, and homework management reported by middle school students. *School Community Journal, 19*(2), 27–43.

Xu, J. (2010). Predicting homework distraction at the secondary school level: A multilevel analysis. *Teachers College Record, 112*, 1937–1970.

Zimmerman, B. J., & Kitsantas, A. (2005). Homework practices and academic achievement: The mediating role of self-efficacy and perceived responsibility beliefs. *Contemporary Educational Psychology, 30*, 397–417.

5.7

The Role of Formative Assessment in Student Achievement

ARYN C. KARPINSKI
Kent State University

JEROME V. D'AGOSTINO
The Ohio State University

Introduction

Formative assessment (FA) involves the appraisal of student attributes, and most importantly, the use of the appraisal information to guide instruction and to enhance student learning. Black and Wiliam (1998b) state that FA encompasses "all those activities undertaken by teachers, and/or by their students, which provide information to be used as feedback to modify the teaching and learning activities in which they are engaged. Such assessment becomes formative assessment when the evidence is actually used to adapt the teaching to meet student needs" (p. 8). Some key elements of FA include: (a) identification of learning goals, outcomes, and criteria for achievement, (b) communication between teachers and students about students' current knowledge status and future directions, (c) active involvement of students in their own learning, and (d) teachers responding to feedback by modifying teaching strategies (e.g., Black & Wiliam, 1998a,b).

Reviews and research syntheses of FA studies (Black & Wiliam, 1998a; Natriello, 1987) have revealed that FA is a critical component of classroom effectiveness as reflected by the rather large effect sizes that result from good FA implementation. Prior research has demonstrated that proper implementation is not merely the process of collecting information on student learning through frequent assessment, or possessing knowledge of assessment concepts. The most critical aspects of FA are the teacher's skills at collecting meaningful student work and providing students constructive feedback to both monitor their learning and guide instructional decisions.

Though FA was discussed at least as early as the 1970s, it was not until more recently that the relationship between FA and improved student achievement was considered in greater depth (Black & Wiliam, 1998a). Paul Black and Dylan Wiliam published "Assessment and Classroom Learning" (1998a), which reviewed two earlier articles by Natriello (1987) and Crooks (1988). Natriello found previous research on the impact of assessment as misguided due to a lack of control over certain variables such as the quality and quantity of feedback. Crooks, focusing on the impact of evaluation on students, concluded that the summative function of evaluation has been too dominant, and more attention should be given to FA (Black & Wiliam, 1998a). The National Research Council (NRC) promoted FA as a key attribute in the classroom, and advocated an increase in the frequency of its use. In more recent years, FA theory and practice has become a more prominent topic of research and debate, offering strategies and solutions to the potential limitations of No Child Left Behind (NCLB; 2002).

Research Evidence

Research has highlighted the benefits of FA for learning and achievement. Many short-term benefits include: (a) encouraging active learning strategies, (b) providing knowledge of results and corrective feedback, (c) helping students monitor their own progress, and (d) fostering accountability (Brookhart, 2007). Long-term benefits are currently being researched; however, results have shown that regular classroom assessment (CA) improves overall academic achievement for most students, especially low-achieving and disabled students. Because FA is arguably the most cost-effective technique to improve student achievement, other long-term benefits entail higher lifetime earnings and general economic growth for society (Wiliam & Leahy, 2007).

Research Relating FA and Achievement. Meta-analyses have demonstrated that FA is a key factor in increasing student achievement. Focusing primarily on student performance and mean gains, Fuchs and Fuchs (1986) conducted a meta-analysis and found that when teachers reviewed (i.e., two to five times per week) classroom- and individual-level data from assessment activities with their elementary school students, a larger achievement effect size was noted ($d = .92$) compared to teachers who did not ($d = .42$). In one of the most widely cited reviews on FA, Black and Wiliam (1998a) examined classroom practices, student motivation and participation in assessment practices, learning theory, classroom strategies, and the properties of effective feedback. They concluded that FA has a profound effect on learning with effect sizes between .4 and .7 (see also Wiliam, Lee, Harrison, & Black, 2004). Additionally, FA practices tend to help low-achieving students more than high-achieving students.

In single studies of FA, Fontana and Fernandes (1994) examined 25 math teachers who were trained in self-evaluation methods. Frequent self-evaluation as part of the classroom assessment (CA) process has been theorized to be a key factor in enhancing student performance. After training the students (i.e., ages 8 to 14) in self-evaluation, the mean gain in math achievement for the younger students was about twice that of the control group. Similar findings in another study also demonstrated the value of self-evaluation in motivation and achievement. Schunk (1996) found that students who used frequent self-evaluation and focused on *how* to solve problems had raised achievement outcomes compared to students that merely solved for the correct answer.

More recent research on CA has demonstrated that students made significant learning gains and produced higher achievement scores when teachers implemented various FA strategies (e.g., feedback focused on learning and not grades, self-assessment). The achievement gains made were comparable to raising achievement from the lower quartile in performance on national achievement tests to above average (Wiliam et al., 2004). Likewise, Rodriguez (2004) investigated the effects of teacher CA practices on achievement in mathematics using data from the Third International Math and Science Study (TIMSS). Teacher CA practices were operationalized as the actual homework tasks assigned and the uses teachers employed for assigned homework. It was found that more frequent moderate levels of assigned homework were associated with higher performing classrooms (Rodriguez, 2004).

Ruiz-Primo and Furtak (2007) examined informal FA practices, which are FA practices that can take place during any teacher–student interaction and are not always planned. The results illustrated that using informal strategies (e.g., informal conversations between teachers and students focusing on the teachers' occurrences of eliciting, recognizing, and using information from their students) led to improved student performance compared to teachers that did not implement such strategies. In addition, Fox-Turnbull (2006) investigated the relation between "teacher knowledge of FA feedback" (i.e., teachers asking students higher-level or open-ended questions to extend their thinking) and student achievement. It was found that teacher knowledge had an impact on the use and quality of FA feedback, which had a positive influence on students' achievement.

Why is FA Related to Achievement Gains? The causal mechanisms behind the positive relation between FA and achievement are apparent by first examining summative assessment (SA), which is assessment done periodically to determine how much students know. SA is typically viewed as an accountability measure that is used as part of the grading process (i.e., usually at the end of a course or end of a year). Thus, due to the nature and timing of SA, it is not designed to provide teachers with feedback to improve student learning and achievement. SA is a means to gauge students' learning relative to content standards, which can only help in evaluating certain aspects of the learning process. It cannot provide information to make adjustments during the learning process, which is the purpose of FA. FA is part of the instructional process, and when incorporated into classroom practice, it provides the information needed to adjust teaching and learning while they are happening. These adjustments help to ensure students achieve targeted standards-based learning goals.

The research literature identifies some features of FA, or causal mechanisms, which allow for the positive relation between FA and student learning and achievement. Providing high quality feedback on student work (e.g., helping students identify gaps between their current knowledge base and learning goals) is a very powerful way to raise standards and achievement (Bangert-Drowns, Kulik, & Kulik, 1991; Black & Wiliam, 1998a). In addition, feedback should target the activity or assignment at hand (i.e., not the student), and the student must comprehend the feedback to implement it in future assignments and high-stakes tests (Black & Wiliam, 1998a).

Kluger and DeNisi (1996) reviewed several thousand manuscripts on teacher feedback, and found an average effect of .4. The effects varied considerably, however, and a number were negative. In attempting to account for variations in effect sizes, the authors identified certain features of feedback that either promoted or detracted from effectiveness in terms of increased student achievement. Feedback interventions that directed students' attention to the self through praise or other affective cues typically yielded negative effects. Efforts to focus students' attention toward the task, including emphasis on what students did correctly and where they needed improvement, tended to produce positive effects on learning. Thus, praise alone without substantive feedback was deleterious.

Little work has focused on exploring the natural variation in feedback skills among teachers, and on the degree to which actual, noninduced practices impact achievement. With regards to self-evaluation as part of FA, it has been found that teaching students to self-assess increases understanding and the quality of work. Additionally, engaging students' prior knowledge to support new learning (i.e., knowledge transfer and generalization) allows for a direct impact of FA on achievement. This transfer is supported when a variety of activities are used in assessing and instructing students. Additionally, studies have demonstrated that students who understand the learning goals and criteria for evaluation, and have opportunities to reflect on their work, show greater progress than those who do not (Fontana & Fernandes, 1994).

Summary and Recommendations

The reasons that FA is vital for teacher effectiveness are often misunderstood and not entirely known. It is known that some testing does provide students with practice on the skills necessary to achieve learning objectives, but too much testing (i.e., more than once or twice a week) actually can hinder learning (Bangert-Drowns et al., 1991). Nor is it likely that teachers' knowledge of conventional assessment concepts, such as reliability, validity, and item writing, can account for the positive effects of FA on students' achievement levels. For CA to have a dramatic impact on learning, teachers must collect useful information that indicates students' strengths and weaknesses, communicate students' progress to them, and modify instruction to address their weaknesses and build on their strengths.

Black and Wiliam (1998a,b) make several suggestions for the effective implementation of FA in the classroom in terms of having a positive impact on student achievement (i.e., the nature and timing of FA). For maximum achievement gains, FA should eliminate recall or rote activities in which the final grade or score on an assignment or test frequently becomes more important than the process of learning. Black and Wiliam (1998) also stress a cooperative atmosphere in the classroom over a competitive agenda, and that teachers should emphasize quality rather than quantity.

Offering students effective feedback based on student performance information perhaps is the most critical step in the FA process. Critical elements of productive feedback (Brookhart, 2007) include: (a) providing meaningful assessment activities linked to key objectives, (b) having a method of detecting strengths, weaknesses, and present performance level, (c) having a clear understanding of the reference levels for students to attain, (d) measuring the gap between the present and reference levels, (e) communicating the gap effectively to students, and (f) providing students follow-up activities to continually monitor progress toward closing the gap. Teacher education programs and professional development opportunities should focus on providing teachers the opportunity to cultivate effective FA skills.

References

Bangert-Drowns, R. L., Kulik, J. A., & Kulik, C. C. (1991). Effects of frequent classroom testing. *Journal of Educational Research, 85*, 89–99.

Black, P., & Wiliam, D. (1998a). Assessment and classroom learning. *Assessment in Education: Principles, Policy, and Practice, 5*(1), 7–74.

Black, P., & Wiliam, D. (1998b). Inside the black box: Raising standards through classroom assessment. *Phi Delta Kappan, 80*(2), 139–148.

Brookhart, S. M. (2007). Expanding views about formative classroom assessment: A review of the literature. In J. H. McMillan (Ed.), *Formative classroom assessment: Theory into practice* (pp. 43–62). New York: Teachers College Press.

Crooks, T. J. (1988). The impact of classroom evaluation practices on students. *Review of Educational Research, 58*, 438–481.

Fontana, D., & Fernandes, M. (1994). Improvements in mathematics performance as a consequence of self-assessment in Portuguese primary school pupils. *British Journal of Educational Psychology, 64*, 407–417.

Fox-Turnbull, W. (2006). The influences of teacher knowledge and authentic formative assessment on student learning in technology education. *International Journal of Technology & Design Education, 16*(1), 53–77.

Fuchs, L. S., & Fuchs, D. (1986). Effects of systematic formative evaluation: A meta-analysis. *Exceptional Children, 53*, 199–208.

Kluger, A. N., & DeNisi, A. (1996). The effects of feedback interventions on performance: a historical review, a meta-analysis, and a preliminary feedback intervention theory. *Psychological Bulletin, 119*, 254–284.

Natriello, G. (1987). The impact of evaluation processes on students. *Educational Psychologist, 22*(2), 155–175.

No Child Left Behind Act (2002). Pub. L. No. 107-110, 115 Stat. 1425.

Rodriguez, M. C. (2004). The role of classroom assessment in student performance on TIMSS. *Applied Measurement in Education, 17*(1), 1–24.

Ruiz-Primo, M. A., & Furtak, E. M. (2007). Exploring teachers' informal formative assessment practices and students' understanding in the context of scientific inquiry. *Journal of Research in Science Teaching, 44*(1), 57–84.

Schunk, D. H. (1996). Goal and self-evaluative influences during children's cognitive skill learning. *American Educational Research Journal, 33*, 359–382.

Wiliam, D., & Leahy, S. (2007). A theoretical foundation for formative assessment. In J. H. McMillan (Ed.), *Formative classroom assessment: Theory into practice* (pp. 29–42). New York: Teachers College Press.

Wiliam, D. Lee, C., Harrison, C., & Black, P. (2004). Teachers developing assessment for learning: Impact on student achievement. *Assessment in Education, 11*(1), 49–65.

5.8

Peer Influences in Elementary School

GARY W. LADD
Arizona State University

Introduction

Much of the research designed to explicate the precursors of children's school engagement and achievement has been focused on factors such as children's cognitive and linguistic skills, their physical-motor skills, and their socioeconomic and ethnic backgrounds. Only recently have researchers systematically explored children's behavior and relationships with classmates as predictors of their educational performance. This is surprising when one considers that many modes of instruction require that students relate with classmates. It has been estimated that nearly 80% of elementary school teachers use peer-mediated learning activities (e.g., peer collaboration, cooperative learning) in their classrooms. Moreover, it has been argued that "peers matter most," because children spend the majority of the school day interacting with age mates (Hymel, Comfort, Schonert-Reichl, & McDougall, 1996).

Recent theory and evidence on the interpersonal foundations of learning and achievement has elevated this topic's importance within the educational community. Greater investigative attention has been devoted to the hypothesis that peer relations in school shape children's school engagement and achievement (see Ladd, 2003). School engagement refers to child attitudes and behaviors that precede and promote learning and achievement. According to the school engagement hypothesis, children do not achieve in school unless they participate in classrooms in ways that promote learning.

Research Evidence

Aspects of Classroom Peer Relations that are Related to School Engagement and Achievement.

Accumulating evidence links classroom peer relationships with school engagement and achievement. Promising lines of investigation are based on the premise that peer relationships expose children to specific processes (e.g., support, instruc-

tion, exclusion, conflict; see Ladd, 2003, 2005). Because peer relationships bring different processes to bear upon children, they vary in the effects they have on children's school engagement and achievement (see Ladd, 2005). In the next three sections, evidence pertaining to the adaptive significance of three types of classroom peer relationships is considered.

Classroom Peer Acceptance and Rejection.

Peer rejection is defined as how disliked (versus liked) a child is by group members (Ladd, 2005). Early peer rejection has been shown to predict problems such as negative school attitudes, school avoidance, and underachievement in kindergarten and thereafter (Ladd, 1990). During the elementary years, peer rejection has been linked with behavior problems and academic deficits (Ladd, 2006; Ladd, Kochenderfer, & Coleman, 1997). Further, dropping out of school, truancy, and underachievement are forecast at an earlier stage by peer rejection in grade school (see Ladd, 2005).

Two overarching hypotheses have guided efforts to elucidate rejection's effects on children's engagement and achievement. Each hypothesis invokes differing, albeit related assumptions about rejection-related processes.

Rejection Limits Classroom Engagement and Participation.

It has been proposed that when peers dislike persons within their group, they act in rejecting ways toward these children (e.g., ignoring them, excluding them from activities), and these behaviors become observable indicators of rejection not only for rejected children, but also for the larger peer group (Buhs & Ladd, 2001; Buhs, Ladd, & Herlad, 2006). A related hypothesis is that rejection deprives children of social and academic supports (e.g., peer affirmation, tutoring, inclusion in learning activities, study groups, etc.) that facilitate learning and achievement (see Buhs & Ladd, 2001; Buhs et al., 2006).

Examination of these hypotheses is incomplete, but extant evidence shows that rejected children often disengage

205

from classroom activities (Buhs & Ladd, 2001; Buhs et al., 2006). In learning groups, for example, disliked children are often ignored or excluded by peers, even when assigned tasks by teachers. Regardless of whether rejection occurs early or later in grade school, children who suffer longer periods of rejection exhibit slower growth in classroom participation (Ladd, Herald-Brown, & Reiser, 2008). Peer rejection also has been linked with underachievement (i.e., Buhs & Ladd, 2001; Buhs et al., 2006).

Rejection Engenders Negative Self- and Peer Perceptions. Another influential hypothesis is that peer rejection causes children to develop negative beliefs about themselves and their classmates. These perceptions, in turn, interfere with their school engagement and achievement.

Evidence shows that children who are rejected in grade school tend to see themselves as socially and academically inept (Boivin & Begin, 1989). In turn, children who regard themselves as academically incompetent exhibit lower rates of achievement (Guay, Boivin, & Hodges, 1999).

Rejection also predicts children's perceptions of classmates. Betts and Rotenberg (2007) found that peer acceptance mediated the relation between children's trust of classmates and their school adjustment; children who saw peers as untrustworthy tended to be less accepted by classmates and less well-adjusted in the classroom.

Taken together, this evidence suggests that peer group rejection discourages participation in learning activities, and engenders beliefs that interfere with children's engagement and achievement.

Classroom Friendships. Most children form friendships in school. Unlike peer *group* relations (e.g., peer acceptance, rejection) friendships are *dyadic* and created by mutual consent. Investigated features include participation in friendships, number of friendships, quality and stability of friendships, and friendship processes (e.g., support, aid, conflict; see Ladd, 2005). Three principal premises have guided efforts to understand the role of friendships in school engagement and achievement.

Friendships Provide Emotional and Instrumental Support. It has been proposed that friendships contribute to academic engagement and achievement by providing children with emotional security and instructional support (Ladd, Kochenderfer, & Coleman, 1996; Wentzel, 1998). Consistent with these assertions, evidence shows that children who formed and maintained friendships in kindergarten classrooms developed more favorable school attitudes and performed better academically than those who did not (Ladd, 1990). Further, children who saw their friendships as offering support and instrumental aid tended to view their classrooms as supportive environments (Ladd et al., 1996). Likewise, in studies with adolescents, researchers find that friendship is associated with students' emotional well-being, and that emotional adjustment predicts classroom engagement and achievement (Wentzel, 1998).

Friendships Are a Source of Conflict. Studies of conflict processes in friendships show that children who experience higher levels of discord in classroom friendships are more likely to manifest negative school attitudes, disaffection during the school day, and classroom disruptiveness. Among kindergartners, it was discovered that those who reported more conflict in their classroom friendships liked school less (Ladd et al., 1996). In studies of adolescents, conflict in friendships anteceded gains in disruptiveness over the course of a school year (Berndt & Keefe, 1995).

Friends Model Social Behavior. The premise that friends motivate each other's school success by modeling socially acceptable behavior has received some corroboration. Data imply that children tend to align themselves with friends' goals. In one study, preadolescents who viewed their friends as having lofty academic goals behaved in ways that furthered their own achievement (Wentzel, Filisetti, & Looney, 2007).

These studies suggest that, in addition to peer group acceptance, friendships and friendship processes contribute to children's school engagement and achievement. For younger as well as older students, friendship may provide important emotional, instrumental, and motivational resources.

Peer Victimization. Efforts to identify and study victimized children in school contexts have expanded exponentially due to educators' and parents' concerns about school violence and safety. Accruing evidence suggests that peer harassment is a relatively age-invariant phenomenon, occurring at all levels of schooling, including grade school (Ladd, 2005). Two principal hypotheses have guided research on peer victimization and children's educational progress.

Peer Victimization Promotes Poor Mental Health. Peer victimization is seen as a stressor that fosters adjustment problems and weakens children's desire to participate in schooling. Studies suggest that harassment causes children to feel fearful and alienated in school, and these concerns promote school disengagement (Ladd et al., 1996). In studies with third and fourth graders, victimization forecasted depression, which, in turn, predicted lower grades and achievement scores (Schwartz, Gorman, Nakamoto, & Tobin, 2005). Likewise, studies with middle school children suggest that victimization causes psychological symptoms that interfere with school performance (i.e., lower GPAs, absenteeism; Juvonen, Nishina, & Graham, 2000). Taken together, the results of these studies suggest that victims of peer harassment are at risk for school maladjustment and that psychological difficulties are one of the mechanisms underlying victimization's negative effects on learning and achievement.

Peer Victimization Promotes Poor Physical Health. Victimization's impact on children's schoolwork may also be mediated through changes in their physical health. Findings show that the combination of peer victimization and chronic abdominal pain was predictive of academic difficulties (Greco, Freeman, & Dufton, 2006). It has also been shown that peer victimization forecasts declines in physical and psychological health, which, in turn, impair school functioning (e.g., absences, poor GPA; Nishina, Juvonen, & Witkow, 2005).

Victimization, it appears, has the capacity to provoke or exacerbate mental and physical ailments which, in turn, detract from children's school engagement and achievement. However, because children participate in many types of peer relationship in classrooms, it becomes important to consider the conjoint contributions of these ties.

Contributions of Multiple Classroom Relationships. In recent years, investigators have gathered data on multiple classroom relationships and examined the relative associations of these ties to children's educational progress. Findings suggest that relationships make differential contributions to children's school performance (Ladd, 2005).

Studies of grade school children suggest that classroom peer acceptance and friendships make distinct contributions to the prediction of school engagement and competence. With young children, Ladd (1990) found that friendship and peer acceptance uniquely predicted changes in kindergartners' school perceptions, avoidance, and academic readiness. In another study (Ladd et al., 1996), several types of peer relationships were examined after adjusting for shared predictive linkages, and some relationships were found to be better predictors of children's school performance than others. Peer victimization, for example, predicted gains in children's loneliness and school avoidance above and beyond associations that were attributable to friendship and peer group acceptance/rejection. In contrast, peer group acceptance uniquely predicted improvements in children's achievement. Overall, these findings were consistent with the view that peer relationships are both specialized in the types of resources or constraints they create for children, but also diverse in the sense that some resources may be found in more than one form of relationship.

Summary and Recommendations

In sum, there is empirical support for the premise that classroom peer rejection, friendships, and peer victimization bring different processes to bear upon children and have differing effects on their educational progress. Evidence indicates that classroom peer relationships are specialized in the types of resources or constraints they create for children. For example, in contrast to classroom friendships or peer group acceptance, peer victimization appears to be a stronger influence on the development of loneliness and school avoidance. Peer group acceptance, by comparison, appears to have greater sway over children's participation in classroom activities and subsequent achievement.

It also appears that the contributions of peer relationships to children's adjustment depends not only on the functional properties of particular peer relationships (e.g., the resources or constraints they confer upon children), but also upon the duration of children's participation in these relationships (i.e., their history of exposure to specific relationship processes). Extant findings (see Ladd et al., 2008) indicate that children's risk for educational difficulties is increased by longer exposures to relational adversities.

References

Berndt, T. J., & Keefe, K. (1995). Friends' influence on adolescent's adjustment to school. *Child Development, 66*, 1312–1319.

Betts, L.R., & Rotenberg, K. J. (2007). Trustworthiness, friendships and self-control: Factors that contribute to young children's school adjustment. *Infant and Child Development, 16*, 491–508.

Boivin, M., & Begin, G. (1989). Peer status and self-perception among early elementary school children: The case of the rejected children. *Child Development, 60*, 591–596.

Buhs, E. S., & Ladd, G. W. (2001). Peer rejection as antecedent of young children's school adjustment: An examination of mediating processes. *Developmental Psychology, 37*, 550–560.

Buhs, E. S., Ladd, G. W., & Herald, S. L. (2006). Peer exclusion and victimization: Processes that mediate the relation between peer group rejection and children's classroom engagement and achievement? *Journal of Educational Psychology, 98*, 1–13.

Greco, L. A., Freeman, K. E., & Dufton, L. (2006). Overt and relational victimization among children with frequent abdominal pain: links to social skills, academic functioning, and health service use. *Journal of Pediatric Psychology, 32*, 319–329.

Guay, F., Boivin, M., & Hodges, E. V. E. (1999). Predicting changes in academic achievement: A model of peer experiences and self–system processes. *Journal of Education Psychology, 91*, 105–115.

Hymel, S., Comfort, C., Schonert–Reichel, K., & McDougall, P. (1996). Academic failure and school dropout: The influence on peers. In J. Juvonen & K. R. Wentzel (Eds.), *Social motivation: Understanding children's school adjustment* (Cambridge Studies in Social and Emotional Development) (pp. 313–345). New York: Cambridge University Press.

Juvonen, J., Nishina, A., & Graham, S. (2000). Peer harassment, psychological adjustment, and school functioning in early adolescence. *Journal of Educational Psychology, 92*, 349–359.

Ladd, G. W. (1990). Having friends, keeping friends, making friends, and being liked by peers in the classroom: Predictors of children's early school adjustment? *Child Development, 61*, 1081–1100.

Ladd, G. W. (2003). Probing the adaptive significance of children's behavior and relationships in the school context: A child by environment perspective. In R. Kail (Ed.), *Advances in child behavior and development* (Vol. 31, pp. 43–104). New York: Wiley.

Ladd, G. W. (2005). *Children's peer relations and social competence: A century of progress.* New Haven, CT: Yale University Press.

Ladd, G. W. (2006). Peer rejection, aggressive or withdrawn behavior, and psychological maladjustment from ages 5 to 12: An examination of four predictive models. *Child Development, 77*, 822–846.

Ladd, G. W., Herald-Brown, S. L., & Reiser, M. (2008). Does chronic classroom peer rejection predict the development of children's classroom participation during the grade school years? *Child Development, 79*, 1001–1015.

Ladd, G. W., Kochenderfer, B. J., & Coleman, C. C. (1996). Friendship quality as a predictor of young children's early school adjustment. *Child Development, 67*, 1103–1118.

Ladd, G. W., Kochenderfer, B. J., & Coleman, C. C. (1997). Classroom peer acceptance, friendship, and victimization: Distinct relational systems that contribute uniquely to children's school adjustment? *Child Development, 68*, 1181–1197.

Nishina, A., Juvonen, J., & Witkow, M. R. (2005). Sticks and stones may break my bones, but names will make me feel sick: The psychosocial, somatic, and scholastic consequences of peer harassment. *Journal of Clinical Child and Adolescent Psychology, 34*, 37–48.

Schwartz, D., Gorman, A. H., Nakamoto, J., & Toblin, R. L. (2005). Victimization in the peer group and children's academic functioning. *Journal of Educational Psychology, 97,* 425–435.

Wentzel, K. R. (1998). Social relationships and motivation in middle school: The role of parents, teachers, and peers. *Journal of Educational Psychology, 90,* 202–209.

Wentzel, K. R., Filisetti, L., & Looney, L. (2007). Adolescent prosocial behavior: The role of self–processes and contextual cues. *Child Development, 78,* 895–910.

5.9

Acceleration for All

Henry M. Levin and Pilar Soler
Teachers College, Columbia University

Introduction

The movement toward acceleration for all students was established in the 1980s as an attempt to bring all students into the educational mainstream by accelerating learning through educational enrichment. It was a response to the failure of "remediation" to create successful learning outcomes for students who are at-risk of educational failure by virtue of family poverty and other difficult conditions for learning in homes and communities. Remediation has traditionally been chosen by schools as the appropriate educational strategy for such students by which curriculum content is simplified and the pace of instruction is reduced. The rationale behind remediation is that students need to master basic skills and facts before they can do more challenging work. But, many decades of experience have shown that the fruit of such an approach is that students get farther and farther behind the mainstream and find school to be dispiriting and defeating.

Accelerated schools represent an attempt to deepen the learning experience of such students by developing an enriched approach that builds upon experience, intrinsic curiosity, active involvement, and embedding the learning of basic skills in more challenging student involvement. In many respects it owes its spirit to John Dewey, as it aims to engage students on their own terms and experiences and expand their desire to learn through research, community projects, and artistic endeavors, while building mastery of basic skills through the motivation and challenge of deeper learning experiences and creativity. At its heart is an attempt to provide all students with the gifted and talented opportunities that are normally accorded to only a small and privileged group of students. Acceleration is based upon a deeper and more engaging learning approach.

As much as the overall goal and approach are compelling to many educators, the process of implementation has been found to be daunting. In contrast to approaches that focus only on changing individual teachers and classrooms, the Accelerated Schools Project undertakes to convert entire schools by transforming school culture to build on three principles: unity of purpose; responsibility for decisions and their consequences; and a pedagogy of enlisting student, teacher, and family strengths as a basis for instructional content and activities. Not only does this entail the widespread reconstruction of most school practices, but it also requires a profound shift in school culture from professional individualism of school staff to deep collaboration; to relegating responsibility for decision making, governance, and accountability to school staff, parents, and communities rather than compliance with rules, regulations, and administrative mandates (Finnan & Swanson, 2000); and to an instructional approach that aggressively identifies all available resources including those of parents and school community to build on the strengths of school participants rather than decrying and addressing weaknesses.

Research Evidence

Starting in 1986 the Stanford University project began to construct the process in two schools that had volunteered to participate (Levin, 1995). Through a combination of experimentation and application of the central ideas, the model was constructed and expanded to other schools, largely through regional networks. The Accelerated Schools Project also used its foundational principles for schools to work continuously on learning and improvement of practices. Much of the lessons of the initial phase are found in the *Accelerated Schools Resource Guide* (Hopfenberg et al., 1993) which summarized the transformation process and practices of accelerated schools. Although implementation was found to be highly challenging, requiring strong leadership, coaching, and commitment, the Accelerated Schools Project expanded rapidly, reaching about 1,000 schools in 41 states, 50 schools in Hong Kong, and a few experimental schools in other nations (e.g., Spain and Australia) by 2000.

The approach was designed to address a broad range of educational goals including the expansion of metacognition strategies of students and their full development in communicative, artistic, analytic, interpersonal, behavioral, and citizenship skills. Although test results are an important by-product of acceleration, the key academic outcomes were viewed as student performance in planning, implementing, and evaluating such undertakings as research projects, artistic endeavors, problem-solving challenges, and community service activities. These are much more multidimensional, far-reaching, and complex than can be assessed by conventional standardized tests in a few subjects. Nevertheless, given the currency of standardized testing, the external evaluations by independent entities mainly focused on these narrower attributes.

A brief listing of some of these independent evaluations follows. Twenty-five schools in Memphis, Tennessee that had adopted whole school change models were compared with a matched group of nonreform schools (Ross et al., 2001). The six Accelerated Schools showed the largest changes among all of the reform models—the effect-size for reading was 1.29, indicating gains from about the 30th percentile to the 70th percentile for a largely minority and poverty population. Across five subject areas the Accelerated Schools showed an average effect size of about .77.

A national assessment was carried out and financed independently by one of the most eminent evaluation organizations in the United States, MDRC (Bloom et al., 2001). The population of all 90 schools that had at least 5 years of Accelerated Schools involvement in the early 1990s was provided to the MDRC. MDRC randomly sampled this population of schools to obtain continuous and comparable test results for all third graders for a 10-year period, from 5 years before the advent of participation to 5 years following the adoption. Total sample size generated by this strategy was over 5,000 students from eight schools. It is also important to note that this was before the era of No Child Left Behind in the United States which started in 2001, where accountability pressure for raising test scores led to new practices including intensive test preparation. In this earlier period the test scores for schools with high concentrations of minorities and students from poverty were generally flat. The 5-year period was chosen because the first years require intensive implementation of new practices and transition to a new school culture. By the fifth year the average test results had increased in both mathematics and reading by about 8 percentiles or effect sizes from about .19 to .24 after adjustment for a large set of covariates for student backgrounds. Even this estimated effect is likely understated because about half of the students in the samples had been in attendance for less than 3 years rather than the full period from kindergarten through third grade. Most promising was that schools with the lowest initial test scores had the largest gains in achievement.

A rather different approach to acceleration is represented in a rigorous evaluation of a school district that decided to eliminate all remedial courses for slow achievers in its middle school and replace them with placement in mainstream courses and workshops in mathematics with heterogeneous grouping (Burris & Garrity, 2008; Burris, Heubert, & Levin, 2006). The goal was to bring all eighth graders into Algebra I by preparing them from school entry at sixth grade to succeed in mathematics, regardless of the level of mathematics performance they had achieved in fifth grade. The evaluation was also an interrupted time series comparing the high school accomplishments in mathematics of three cohorts of middle school graduates immediately prior to the accelerated reform with three cohorts that followed the reform. Two measures of outcome were used for the final year of high school: numbers of advanced mathematics courses taken and mathematics test scores in the final year of high school. Separate analyses were done by student race, socioeconomic background, gender, and baseline test scores in mathematics at grade 5.

Postreform students were found to take about twice as many advanced mathematics courses in high school as prereform students. Test scores increased for all defined groups except those with the highest math scores at the fifth grade baseline who were able to maintain their high standing, despite being placed in heterogeneous mathematics classes. The improvement in mathematics participation and test results in the accelerated district vastly outpaced those of districts in the state with similar demographics.

Summary and Recommendations

The Accelerated Schools approach has been used with success in Brazil to reduce the high rate of grade repetition, a very costly phenomenon (Luck & Parente, 2006). It was also used with varying degrees of success in Hong Kong, despite the intense focus of families, schools, and students on a regimen of test memorization that undermines motivation to transform schools for broader educational results (Lee, Levin, & Soler, 2005). The overall record for Accelerated Schools suggests that when implemented, the results are positive and strong; however, implementation is a challenge in a school culture that emphasizes remediation and test preparation in contrast to a focus on fuller student development through enrichment.

References

Bloom, H. S., Rock, J., Ham, S., Melton, L. O'Brien, J., with Doolittle, F. C., & Kagehiro, S. (2001). *Evaluating the accelerated schools approach: A look at early implementation and impacts on student achievement in eight elementary schools.* New York: MDRC. Retrieved from http://www.mdrc.org/publications/107/full.pdf.

Burris, C. C., & Garrity, D. T. (2008). *Detracking for excellence and equity.* Alexandria, VA: Association for Supervision and Curriculum Development.

Burris, C. C., Heubert, J. P., & Levin, H. M. (2006). Accelerated mathematics achievement using heterogeneous grouping. *American Educational Research Journal, 43*(1), 105–136.

Finnan, C., & Swanson, J. D. (2000). *Accelerating the learning of all students: Cultivating culture change in schools, classrooms, and individuals.* Boulder, CO: Westview Press.

Hopfenberg, W., Levin, H. M., Chase, C., Christensen, G., Moore, M. Soler, P., ...Rodriguez, G. (1993). *The accelerated schools resource guide*. San Francisco, CA: Jossey–Bass.

Lee, J. C., Levin, H. M., & Soler, P. (2005). Accelerated schools for quality education: A Hong Kong perspective. *The Urban Review, 37*(1), 63–81.

Levin, H. M. (1995). Accelerated schools: the background. In C. Finnan, E. P. St. John, J. McCarthy, & S. P. Slovacek (Eds.), *Accelerated schools in action: Lessons from the field* (pp. 3–23). Thousand Oaks, CA: Corwin Press.

Luck, H. & Parente, M. (2006). Using accelerated learning to correct student flows: The case of Parana, Brazil. Brasilia: Instituto de Pesquisa Economica Avancada. Retrieved from http://info.worldbank.org/etools/docs/library/236016/D3_Heloisa_Luck__Accelerated_learning_3.pdf.

No Child Left Behind Act (2002). Pub. L. No. 107-110, 115 Stat. 1425.

Ross, S., Sanders, W., Wright, S. P., Stringfield, S., Wang, L. W., & Alberg, M. (2001) Two and three year achievement results from the Memphis restructuring initiative. *School Effectiveness and School Improvement, 12*(3), 323–346.

5.10

Ability Grouping

Janet Ward Schofield
University of Pittsburgh

Introduction

A fundamental decision that all educational systems must make is whether and how to group their students. Some forms of grouping, such as grouping by age, are commonly taken so much for granted that they are hardly even recognized as an actual decision. However, other forms of grouping are subject to much more controversy. This entry focuses on one such practice, tracking or streaming, which is the division of students into specific sets of classes within a school based on assessment of their academic ability or achievement, so that students attend all their classes with others of a roughly similar academic level. The purpose of this practice is to provide students in each track with a curriculum suited to their current skills and their anticipated educational and career goals. For example, three tracks within a school might be named "academic," "general," and "vocational," or "basic," "college-prep," and "honors," reflecting the kinds of students they enroll and the subject matter taught. School systems vary widely with regard to the extent to which students' and parents' preferences can impact the particular track in which a student is enrolled.

Those who support tracking compared to heterogeneous classrooms argue that it increases learning by allowing teachers to target instruction more precisely to students' existing skills. Specifically, they contend that high- and average-achieving students are better off with tracking because the presence of low-ability students does not limit the kind of material taught or slow their progress and that lower achieving students are better off because they are spared the threat to their self-esteem posed by constant comparison with their higher achieving peers. In contrast, those opposing tracking point out numerous potential disadvantages. For example, sometimes factors like social class or racial/ethnic group membership play a role in track placement, further disadvantaging already disadvantaged students by unfairly concentrating them in stigmatized lower tracks. In addition, low-track students are sometimes taught by less skilled teachers than those in higher tracks, thus potentially further undermining their achievement.

Because tracking and its potentially differential impact on different groups of students has been so controversial, a substantial amount of research has been conducted to illuminate tracking's impact on learning. This is a complex task, presenting major methodological challenges. For example, comparing the academic growth of initially low- and high-achieving students in tracked schools to assess tracking's effect is problematic because initially high-achieving students might well learn more than initially low-achieving students even if they were all in the same classes, leading to misleading conclusions about the impact of tracking.

However, researchers have developed numerous ways to deal with such problems, at least partially. For example, sometimes it is possible to compare the progress of students in school systems using tracking to that of academically similar students in systems not using tracking or in systems that start tracking earlier in students' lives, which allows comparison between the learning of initially similar students in tracked and untracked environments. Also, new and relatively sophisticated statistical procedures have helped to clarify the extent to which any differences found between high- and low-achieving students in tracked schools are due to track effects rather than to initial differences between students.

Research Evidence

Influential reviews of the literature on tracking have quite consistently concluded that tracking widens the gap between initially high- and low-achievers by undermining the achievement of initially low-achieving students (Gamoran & Berends, 1987; Oakes, Gamoran, & Page, 1992). Some have also concluded that tracking further increases the achievement gap by increasing gains among initially high-achieving students (Hallinan & Kubitschek, 1999). Tracking appears to have little impact on average students' achievement, although this issue has received less attention than tracking's impact on high- and low-achieving students.

These conclusions are generally consistent with the results of research on the impact of both components of tracking: changes in the composition of classes and of the curriculum. Specifically, a substantial body of correlational research suggests that average peer achievement levels are related to individual achievement gains with higher achieving peers leading to more achievement gains, controlling for the individual's initial achievement (Schofield, 2010). Also, a more challenging curriculum itself is likely to be associated with more learning.

It is unfortunate that many studies of tracking do not address the broad issue of whether, overall, tracking increases or decreases achievement, focusing rather on the issue of its impact on the achievement gap between initially high- and low-achieving students. Perhaps this is partly because different forms of tracking may have quite different effects, making it hard to draw any overall conclusions about tracking's impact. For example, schools with less mobility between tracks produce greater inequality and lower academic achievement than tracked schools using more flexible practices.

However, two kinds of studies do speak to this issue. First, meta-analyses generally suggest that the *overall* impact of tracking is small to nonexistent (Kulik & Kulik, 1982; Noland & Taylor, 1986 cited in Wilkinson et al., 1999; Slavin, 1990). Second, studies employing data from large international studies like PISA, PIRLS, and TIMSS have explored the relationship between the age at which curriculum differentiation begins and students' overall achievement, as well as the achievement of different kinds of students. (Although *curriculum differentiation* was typically studied, normally students in these studies were placed in classes, tracks, or schools with different curricula on the basis of their achievement, making findings from these studies relevant here.) One of these studies concluded that both initially high- and low-achieving students are negatively affected by tracking, although low-achieving students were more negatively impacted (Hanushek & Woessmann, 2006). Other analyses of PISA data concluded that reading (but not math) scores are lower in countries that track students early in their educational careers than in those that track them later (Organization of Economic Co-operation and Development [OECD], 2004, 2005). Regarding the achievement gap, analysis of TIMSS data from 54 nations suggests that early tracking increases the achievement gap between students from different social class backgrounds (Schuetz, Ursprung, & Woessmann, 2005).

Overall, it appears that tracking tends to lower the achievement of initially low-achieving students and that in some cases it may increase the achievement of initially high-achieving ones. Thus, the question of what causes such effects arises. Numerous factors, from differences in the financial resources devoted to students in different tracks to the increase in social class and ethnic group homogeneity that commonly accompany tracking, have been suggested.

Another factor that may account for the differential impact of tracking on the achievement of high- and low-achieving students is the way in which tracking impacts teachers' behaviors. Indeed, a major review of the literature concluded that teachers' behaviors are influenced by students' social and academic background in a way that helps to explain school and class composition effects (Thrupp, Lauder, & Robinson, 2002). For example, teachers assign more homework in high-ability classes than in low-ability ones (Oakes, 2005).

An additional factor often implicated in tracking's impact on the achievement gap is the changes it creates in peer group processes. A massive review of the literature from many countries on this topic concludes that although the direct impact of peer effects is very modest, they often impact achievement indirectly by shaping many aspects of the instructional and social environment affecting achievement (Wilkinson et al, 1999)

Summary and Recommendations

The primary rationale for tracking is that it will improve student achievement by allowing teachers to adjust the content and pace of instruction to students' ability level. However, there is very little reason to believe that tracking improves achievement, except for high-achieving students in some cases. Indeed, evidence suggests that it frequently undermines the achievement of initially low-achieving students, thus increasing the achievement gap. Because low socioeconomic status and minority students are more likely to be found in lower tracks (Mickelson, 2001), tracking also decreases the potential of education to foster social equality.

Because of tracking's effects on the achievement gap, many school systems have de-tracked, creating more heterogeneous classrooms. However, consideration of such a change often mobilizes strong opposition on the part of the parents of high-achieving children. School systems concerned about the impact of tracking on the achievement gap that face strong pressures *not* to de-track should consider using flexible modes of ability grouping by subject matter. Schools maintaining tracking systems should (a) use a flexible tracking system that encourages movement between tracks, (b) raise the performance requirements in lower-achieving tracks by providing more challenging work there, (c) make sure that the teachers of lower-achieving students are at least as qualified and experienced as those teaching higher achieving students and that their approach to teaching is designed to stimulate student interest and involvement.

References

Gamoran, A., & Berends, M. (1987). The effects of stratification in secondary schools: Synthesis of survey and ethnographic research. *Review of Educational Research, 57*(4), 415–435.

Hallinan, M. T., & Kubitschek, W. N. (1999). Curriculum differentiation and high school achievement. *Social Psychology of Education, 2*, 1–22.

Hanushek, E. A., & Woessmann, L. (2006). Does educational tracking affect performance and inequality? Differences-in-differences evidence across countries. *The Economic Journal, 116*, 63–76.

Kulik, J. A., & Kulik, C. L. C. (1982). Effects of ability grouping on student achievement. *Equity and Excellence, 23*(1–2), 22–30.

Mickelson, R. A. (2001). Subverting Swann: First- and second-generation segregation in the Charlotte-Mecklenburg schools. *American Educational Research Journal, 38*(2), 215–252.

Oakes, J. (2005). *Keeping track: How schools structure inequality* (2nd ed.). New Haven, CT: Yale University Press.

Oakes, J. Gamoran, A., & Page, R. N. (1992). Curriculum differentiation opportunities, outcomes, and meanings. In P. Jackson (Ed.), *Handbook of research on curriculum* (pp. 570–608). New York: Macmillan.

Organization for Economic Co-operation and Development (OECD). (2004). *Learning for tomorrow's world: First results from PISA 2003*. Retrieved from http://www.pisa.oecd.org/dataoecd/1/60/34002216.pdf.

Organization for Economic Co-operation and Development (OECD). (2005). *School factors related to quality and equity: Results from PISA 2000*. Retrieved from http://www.oecd.org/dataoecd/15/20/34668095.pdf.

Slavin, R. E. (1990). Ability grouping in secondary schools: A best–evidence synthesis. *Review of Educational Research, 60*(3), 471–499.

Schofield, J. W. (2010). International evidence on ability grouping with curriculum differentiation and the achievement gap in secondary schools. *Teachers College Record, 112*(5), 1490–1526.

Schuetz, G., Ursprung, H. W., & Woessmann, L. (2005). *Education policy and equality of opportunity* (CESifo Working Paper 1518, Category 3: Social Protection). Retrieved from www.CESifo–group.de.

Thrupp, M., Lauder, H., & Robinson, T. (2002). School composition and peer effects. *International Journal of Educational Research, 37*, 483–504.

Wilkinson, I. A. G., Hattie, J. A., Parr, J. M., Townsend, M. A. R., Thrupp, M., & Lauder, H. (1999, November 5). *Influence of peer effects on learning outcomes: A review of the literature*. Final Report to the Ministry of Education. Wellington, New Zealand.

5.11

Collaboration in the Classroom

University of California, Los Angeles

Introduction

Recognizing that students can learn by working with and helping each other, school districts, state departments of education, national research organizations, and curriculum specialists have long recommended the use of collaborative group work in classrooms. Research reviews and meta-analyses showing positive effects of group collaboration on student achievement compared with other forms of instruction that involve little interaction between students (e.g., teacher-led whole-class instruction, individual work) date back several decades (Slavin, 1983). Even positive reviews, however, acknowledge that placing students in collaborative groups does not guarantee that learning will take place. Consequently, much research has explored the mechanisms by which working with other students' benefits or hinders student learning, and the many ways in which collaborative work might be orchestrated for maximum benefit (Esmonde, 2009; O'Donnell, 2006; Webb & Palincsar, 1996).

Research Evidence

Perspectives on the Benefits of Peer Interaction.
According to social-behavioral perspectives (Slavin, 1983), working with other students will lead to increased effort, greater learning, and more liking of the task and other students than instructional settings without such opportunities for peer engagement. When students work toward a common goal, especially a group or cooperative goal that group members can attain only if the group is successful, they will feel individually accountable and personally responsible for what happens in the group and, consequently, will work hard and encourage others to do the same. Socially cohesive groups motivate students to help each other because they care about the group and its members. To promote a sense of group identification and concern for others, some cooperative learning methods use teambuilding and development of social skills (e.g.,

active listening, stating ideas freely, taking turns, making decisions democratically) to help group members trust and support each other, communicate accurately and effectively, and resolve conflicts constructively.

Cognitive/developmental perspectives on learning from peers focus on the cognitive processes occurring during group collaboration. In the Piagetian perspective (Piaget, 1932), cognitive conflict arises when learners perceive a contradiction between their existing understanding and what they hear or see in the course of interacting with others. To resolve the conflict, learners reexamine and question their own ideas and beliefs, seek additional information, and try out new ideas, which leads to higher levels of reasoning and learning. In the Vygotskian perspective, learning can occur when a more expert person helps a less expert person (Vygotsky, 1978). Through a process sometimes called scaffolding or guided participation, the more skilled person enables the less competent person to carry out a task or solve a problem that the latter student could not perform without assistance. The less proficient student can internalize skills and knowledge that he or she has practiced and developed so that they become part of the individual's repertoire.

From a cognitive elaboration perspective (O'Donnell, 2006), giving and receiving explanations may lead students to restructure their own knowledge and understanding. Explaining material to others may promote learning by encouraging explainers to rehearse information, reorganize and clarify material in their own minds, recognize misconceptions and gaps in understanding, strengthen connections between new information and previously learned information, internalize and acquire new strategies and knowledge, and develop new perspectives and understanding (Chi, 2000). When they receive explanations, students can compare their own knowledge with what is being presented, correct misconceptions, and recognize and fill in gaps in their own knowledge. Maximum benefits will accrue when learners apply the explanations received to try to solve the problem or carry out the task themselves.

215

Through coconstruction of knowledge (Barron, 2000), students can collaboratively build knowledge and problem-solving strategies that no group member has at the start by acknowledging, clarifying, correcting, building upon, and connecting each other's ideas and suggestions. Coconstruction may require highly coordinated interaction among group members, characterized by students paying close attention to and acknowledging, repeating, and elaborating on each other's ideas.

Debilitating Interpersonal Processes. Groups may not function in ways that are optimal for learning (Webb & Palincsar, 1996): students can be left out of group collaboration; extroverted students may dominate group work at the expense of introverted students; and high-status students tend to be more active, assertive, talkative, and influential than low-status individuals. Other students may choose not to participate. They may engage in social loafing, or diffusion of responsibility, which arises when one or more group members sit back and let others do the work. This free rider effect may turn into a sucker effect when the group members who are working discover that they have been taken for a free ride and start to contribute less in order to avoid being suckers (Salomon & Globerson, 1989). To combat tendencies toward such unbalanced participation, cooperative learning methods often assign group members responsibilities for specific aspects of a group project, or require group members to learn and teach different portions of the material to each other.

Students may fail to seek help when they need it or fail to obtain effective help when they seek it (Nelson-Le Gall, 1992). Students may not be able to monitor their own comprehension well enough to realize they need help. Or they may decide not to seek help for fear of being judged academically or socially incompetent, to conform to perceived classroom norms to work independently, because they believe themselves unable to benefit from help, or because they believe others do not have the competence or knowledge to provide help. Students who do seek help may select potential helpers who are nice, kind, or who have high status, rather than those who have task-relevant skills. Or students may have ineffective help-seeking strategies, such as asking vague, indirect, confusing, or unfocused questions, rather than questions that are explicit, precise, and direct, and targeted to a specific aspect of the problem or task (the latter being easier for groups to answer).

Too Little or Too Much Conflict may be Detrimental. Infrequent conflict may reflect suppression of disagreements, either from the domination of one group member over the others or from social pressures not to challenge others. Too much conflict may prevent group members from moving forward, especially if they engage in an adversarial or conflictual style of argumentation instead of a coconstructive style in which they work together to critique suggestions and create new solutions.

Group functioning may also suffer from uncoordinated communication (Barron, 2000), marked by low levels of attention to, and uptake of, members' suggestions (even correct ones), and by students advocating and repeating their own positions and ideas, and ignoring or rejecting others' suggestions. Lack of coordination and joint attention may undermine many of the processes by which individuals can gain by collaborating with others, such as resolving conflicts and coconstructing knowledge, as well as reduce group cohesion and students' motivation to work together.

Other negative socioemotional processes, such as rudeness, hostility, and unresponsiveness, may also impede group members' participation and learning. Rudely disagreeing with others and ignoring their suggestions may prevent groups from solving problems correctly. Aggressiveness, hostility, and insulting behavior may lead to unconstructive and bitter arguments and may cause students to withhold knowledge and ideas from the group or to decide not to seek help.

Empirical evidence links these processes to learning outcomes. For example, explanation is consistently and positively related to learning outcomes (Howe et al., 2007), whereas rudeness or disagreement is negatively related (Chiu & Khoo, 2003). Learning measures in these studies typically consist of individually administered achievement tests, although the quality of the collaborative group's problem or task solution sometimes serves as the outcome measure.

Summary and Recommendations

Preparing Students for Collaboration. To promote beneficial peer interaction and inhibit detrimental group dynamics, teachers can carry out activities prior to collaboration, such as building students' communication skills. Students can receive instruction in taking turns speaking; engaging in active listening; asking clear and precise questions; making and asking for suggestions and explanations; expressing and requesting ideas and opinions; using persuasive talk; summarizing conversations; checking others' answers; and monitoring others' understanding and the progress of the group. Some programs focus on skills specifically related to explaining and high-level reasoning, including providing reasons to justify assertions, opinions, and suggestions; giving explanations rather than answers; anticipating objections; and challenging others with counterarguments (Mercer, Dawes, Wegerif, & Sams, 2004). To prevent low-status students from being marginalized in group interaction, teachers can alter high-status students' expectations about low-status students' competence. Methods include providing low-status students with academic and nonacademic skills that they then teach to high-status students, and having teachers point out the multiple abilities that are needed for task completion and highlighting special abilities that low-status students bring to the task (Cohen, 1994).

Structuring Collaborative Work. Some peer-learning approaches assign students roles to play or require students to carry out specific activities while collaborating: such as learning leader (or recaller) and active listener, in which the recaller summarizes material and the listener is responsible for detecting errors, identifying omissions and seeking clarification; and tutor, who gives explanations, corrections, and feedback to the tutee (Fuchs et al., 1997).

Specific activities to carry out during collaborative work may include asking each other high-level questions, jointly answering questions to help groups reflect on problems and strategies before solving them (King, 1997), and responding to written prompts to give elaborated explanations justifying answers and beliefs (Mevarech & Kramarsky, 2003). Sometimes the teacher takes a leadership role to model strategies (e.g., generating questions about the text they have read, summarizing the text, and generating predictions) before gradually helping students learn to carry them out in their groups. Collaborative work may also be structured as debates, in which groups are subdivided into teams who master material on different sides of an issue, debate the issue with the other team, and then work as a group to synthesize the two positions (Johnson & Johnson, 1994).

Teachers' Instructional Practices.   Teachers can monitor group collaboration and intervene when groups exhibit communication problems, such as some students dominating the interaction and preventing useful dialogue, or failing to justify their opinions and ideas. To improve communication, teachers can remind students about their obligations (e.g., share their thinking and solution methods with others, challenge each other's solutions) and make specific communication suggestions (e.g., stop another student and ask for help). Teachers can also increase the incidence of explaining in collaborative groups by asking students probing and clarifying questions, identifying discrepancies in students' work, and offering indirect hints about directions to take (Gillies, 2004), and by refraining from providing direct supervision (Galton & Williamson, 1992).

The nature of teacher discourse with students during whole-class instruction and the norms teachers negotiate with the class about expected interpersonal exchanges may also influence group collaboration. Pressing students to explain and justify their problem-solving strategies and generalizations, and elaborate on their ideas and opinions can increase the incidence of student explanations during group work as well as during classroom discussion. Teachers can negotiate norms for active student participation by discussing students' responsibilities to explain, defend, evaluate, and challenge their own and others' thinking when interacting with others, and discussing examples of genuine dialogue between students (Yackel, Cobb, & Wood, 1991).

Teachers can also encourage active participation of students through the use of complex tasks or open-ended problems without clear-cut answers or procedures that require the combined expertise of everyone in the group. Such tasks encourage groups to recognize and value the different contributions that students can make, whereas narrowly defined tasks or problems, especially those that can completed by one student with the requisite skills, may limit participation of some students (Cohen, 1994).

References

Barron, B. (2000). Achieving coordination in collaborative problem–solving groups. *Journal of the Learning Sciences, 9,* 403–436.

Chi, M. T. H. (2000). Self–explaining expository texts: The dual processes of generating inferences and repairing mental models. In R. Glaser (Ed.), *Advances in instructional psychology: Educational design and cognitive science* (pp. 161–238). Hillsdale, NJ: Erlbaum.

Chiu, M. M., & Khoo, L. (2003). Rudeness and status effects during group problem solving: Do they bias evaluations and reduce the likelihood of correct solutions? *Journal of Educational Psychology, 95,* 506–523.

Cohen, E. G. (1994b). Restructuring the classroom: Conditions for productive small groups. *Review of Educational Research, 64,* 1–35.

Esmonde, I. (2009). Ideas and identities: Supporting equity in cooperative mathematics learning. *Review of Educational Research, 79,* 1008–1043.

Fuchs, L. S., Fuchs, D., Hamlett, C. L., Phillips, N. B., Karns, K., & Dutka, S. (1997). Enhancing students' helping behavior during peer–mediated instruction with conceptual mathematical explanations. *Elementary School Journal, 97,* 223–249.

Galton, M., & Williamson, J. (1992). *Group work in the primary classroom.* London: Routledge.

Gillies, R. M. (2004). The effects of communication training on teachers' and students' verbal behaviours during cooperative learning. *International Journal of Educational Research, 41,* 257–279.

Howe, C., Tolmie, A., Thurston, A., Topping, K., Christie, D., Livingston, K., …Donaldson, C. (2007). Group work in elementary science: Towards organisational principles for supporting pupil learning. *Learning and Instruction, 17,* 549–563.

Johnson, D. W., & Johnson, R. T. (1994). *Learning together and alone: Cooperative, competitive, and individualistic learning* (4th ed.). Boston, MA: Allyn & Bacon.

King, A. (1997). ASK to THINK—TEL WHY: A model of transactive peer tutoring for scaffolding higher level complex learning. *Educational Psychologist, 32,* 221–235.

Mercer, N., Dawes, L., Wegerif, R., & Sams, C. (2004). Reasoning as a scientist: Ways of helping children to use language to learn science. *British Educational Research Journal, 30,* 359–377.

Mevarech, A. R., & Kramarski, B. (2003). The effects of metacognitive training versus worked-out examples on students' mathematical reasoning. *British Journal of Educational Psychology, 73,* 449–471.

Nelson-Le Gall, S. (1992). Children's instrumental help-seeking: Its role in the social acquisition and construction of knowledge. In R. Hertz-Lazarowitz & N. Miller (Eds.), *Interaction in cooperative groups: The theoretical anatomy of group learning* (pp. 49–68). New York: Cambridge University Press.

O'Donnell, A. M. (2006). The role of peers and group learning. In P. A. Alexander & P. H. Winne (Eds.), *Handbook of educational psychology* (pp. 781–802). Mahwah, NJ: Erlbaum.

Piaget, J. (1932). *The language and thought of the child* (2nd. ed.). London: Routledge & Kegan Paul.

Salomon, G., & Globerson, T. (1989). When teams do not function the way they ought to. *International Journal of Educational Research, 13,* 89–99.

Slavin. R. (1983). *Cooperative learning.* New York: Longman.

Vygotsky, L. S. (1978). *Mind in society: The development of higher psychological processes* (M. Cole, V. John–Steiner, S. Scribner, & E. Souberman, Eds. & Trans.). Cambridge, MA: Harvard University Press.

Webb, N. M., & Palincsar, A. S. (1996). Group processes in the classroom. In D. Berliner & R. Calfee (Eds.), *Handbook of educational psychology* (pp. 841–873). New York: Macmillan.

Yackel, E., Cobb, P., & Wood, T. (1991). Small–group interactions as a source of learning opportunities in second-grade mathematics. *Journal for Research in Mathematics Education, 22,* 390–408.

Section 6

Influences from the Teacher

EDITOR: ANITA WOOLFOLK HOY
Ohio State University

6.1

Teacher–Student Relationships

HEATHER A. DAVIS
North Carolina State University

Introduction

Since the early 1980s, a growing body of literature has documented the important relations of students' perceptions of teacher relationships to their classroom motivation, learning, performance, and school completion (Davis, 2003; Wentzel, 2009). In a meta-analysis, Cornelius-White (2008) found students' perceptions of supportive teacher relationships were correlated, on average, between .25 and .55 with academic and social outcomes including participation, satisfaction, self-efficacy, critical thinking, standardized achievement in math and language, increasing attendance, reduction in disruptive behavior, and higher grades. Conversely, findings suggest students' motivation and adjustment to school may be adversely affected when their relationships with teachers are distressed (Cornelius-White, 2008).

Teacher–student relationships have been conceptualized in many ways (Davis, 2003; Wentzel, 2009). The three dominant frameworks in the United States tend to be extensions of parenting styles (Reeve, 2006; Walker, 2008), teachers' beliefs (Woolfolk Hoy & Davis, 2005), and attachment theory (Pianta, 1999). Each of these frameworks posit that teachers, like parents, interact with children in ways that are more or less responsive, warm, and controlling. Findings are consistent across studies; when teachers respond to students in ways that are responsive to student needs, emotionally warm, and provide for student autonomy, students tend to not only feel more motivated in the classroom but also achieve at higher rates. Attachment frameworks further add to our understanding of the teacher relationship by arguing that within the context of the parent relationship, children develop generalized beliefs that they use to interpret their other nonparental social relationships (Davis, 2003). Findings from these studies suggest that students bring to the classroom prior ways of interacting with their teachers that may reflect their previous adult relationships and contribute to the quality of a given teacher–child relationship. More-

over, children who have, in the past, experienced positive relationships with teachers tend to recapitulate supportive relationships with teachers and experience benefits to learning and motivation (Davis, 2006).

Research Evidence

For over 25 years, Wubbels and colleagues (see Wubbels, Brekelmans, den Brok, & van Tartwijk, 2006 for review) define communication as broadly as possible, to encompass, "every behavior that someone displays in the presence of someone else … [this perspective] assumes that one cannot not communicate … whatever a person's intentions are, the others will infer meaning from [their] behavior" (p. 1162). Their model is particularly helpful for understanding the process by which teacher actions (and inactions) come to imbue meaning for students independently of a teacher's intent. In their model, interpersonal communication can be described by two dimensions: dominance-submission (or influence) and opposition-cooperation (or proximity). Underlying the influence dimension is the issue of who controls the communication. When teachers are directive and in control of the communication, they are said to be displaying dominant behavior. Underlying the proximity dimension is the matter of the tone of the communication. When teachers use a tone of patience and understanding, even if they are issuing a directive, they are said to be displaying a cooperative behavior. From these two dimensions Wubbels and colleagues created eight types of communication behaviors.

They argue that each type of communication behavior can play an important role in a teacher's repertoire of interpersonal and relationship building skills:

> Teachers can exhibit acceptable behavior in each sector. In the course of a day, or a week, most teachers will encounter classroom situations in which it is appropriate to be dissatisfied, or uncertain, or admonishing … one of the

fundamental ideas … is that communication behaviors continually change. Communication *styles* [however] emerge only after a great many behaviors have occurred and been observed. (Wubbels, Levy, & Brekelmans, 1997, p. 83)

Wubbels and colleagues have made several important contributions to the field of teacher–student interaction research. Specifically, their research program has identified the critical relation that dominant behaviors play in improving student learning outcomes such as attitude, achievement, and regulation of learning behaviors. The trend in their studies is that the more dominant the teacher, the more her students achieve. With that said, the more cooperative the teacher, the more positive attitudes her students will have. "These results create a dilemma…. If teachers want students to be both high-achieving and supportive, they may find themselves pulling in two directions: strictness correlates well with high achievement, while flexibility relates to positive attitudes" (Wubbels et al., 1997 p. 84). The amount of variance explained by the two dimensions, however, tends to vary by teaching context with each dimension making separate but distinctive contributions to both cognitive and motivational outcomes.

It had been thought that teachers' displays of influence had a more direct influence on cognitive outcomes, while teachers' displays of proximity operated indirectly though enhanced motivation. However, recent studies by den Brok, Wubbels, van Tartwijk, and Veldman (2010) examining the role of students' ethnicity in shaping their perceptions of teacher interpersonal behavior in multicultural classrooms indicate students' differentially interpret teachers' displays of influence and proximity based on their ethnic identity. Both dimensions of proximity and influence predicted subject matter attitudes and report card grades across six different ethnic groups. Yet, the amount of variance explained by each dimension and the pathways of direct and indirect influence varied by ethnic group.

Across several studies den Brok and colleagues suggest the amount of cultural diversity in the class might also contribute to students' perceptions of teacher communication style. Levy, Wubbels, Brekelmans, and Morganfield (1997) found "the greater the number of cultural backgrounds in a class, the more dominant and cooperative the perception of the teacher" (p. 45). The greater the percentage of U.S.-born students in the class, the more the students tended to perceive the teacher as submissive. den Brok, Levy, Wubbels, and Roderiguez (2003) also found students' language at home was significantly related to their perceptions of teachers' "understanding" behaviors. Students who spoke primarily Spanish at home tended to perceive more understanding from their teachers than their Asian American or African American peers. Students born outside of the United States perceived their teachers to be more admonishing and dissatisfied. Levy, den Brok, Wubbels, and Brekelmans (2002) also found the perception of teacher behavior varied as a function of students' gender and ethnicity, with African American males among the least

likely to perceive leadership behaviors and helpful/friendly behaviors from their teachers.

Findings from across these studies suggest *how* teachers exert influence in their classroom is critically important. Work by Middleton and colleagues (see Middleton & Midgley, 2002) suggests that when teachers adopt the dominant role as an instructional leader, they can exert different types of "press" on their students to engage with academic work. Middleton conceptualizes academic press as the enactment of teacher beliefs, motives, and values regarding their subject matter, teaching, and learning. This concept of the "press" of a context is not new to the field of child development (see also Davis, 2006). Press can be direct through the teacher's interactions with students or indirect through the climate they create around learning in their classroom. Press communicates not only a type of intensity in the relationship but depending on the kind of press, can connote the quality of influence displays students' perceive from their teachers. They identified three types of academic presses: press for understanding, press for performance, and press for competition. For example, when teachers press their students for understanding, they implicitly communicate to students their confidence in students' abilities to master content and their perception that students can be successful pursuing that type of career. Consistent across the field of motivation are findings that students are more engaged with academic content when they perceive their teachers are focused on understanding.

Summary and Recommendations

As teachers, Wubbels and colleagues offer us a lens for evaluating the messages we send to our students. We can begin by evaluating the ways in which we attempt to cultivate a sense of interpersonal warmth with our students. We can monitor our proximity behaviors: are we seeking eye contact and have we "checked in" with each and every student in the class, are we monitoring the levels of pleasant and unpleasant emotions we express, and do our verbal and nonverbal messages align? Simple measures to videotape our instruction and to journal students responses to our behavior can provide powerful insights into the emotional climate we are creating. Next, we can evaluate the methods we use to influence students to engage in the tasks we design. When interacting with students, what messages do we send to our students about authority and control? As with proximity behaviors, we can monitor the messages we send that press students toward understanding, performance, or competition. And, we can work to send messages that emphasize the importance of mastering material. During interim planning, we can evaluate lessons to identify ways that we can simultaneously communicate our authority as classroom leaders, the relevance and importance of the lesson, in addition to the opportunities students have to be autonomous and to choose to engage. Finally, as the language, ethnic, and socioeconomic status of students increasingly diverges from the background of many teachers, we can make special efforts to gain the knowledge about our students that allows for mutual respect and appropriate choices in instruction.

References

Cornelius–White, J. (2008). Learner–centered student–teacher relationships are effective: A meta–analysis. *Review of Educational Research, 77,* 113–143.

Davis, H. A. (2003). Conceptualizing the role of student–teacher relationships on children's social and cognitive development. *Educational Psychologist, 38,* 207–234.

Davis, H. A. (2006). Exploring the contexts of relationship quality between middle school students and teachers. *The Elementary School Journal: Special Issue on the Interpersonal Contexts of Motivation and Learning, 106,* 193–223.

den Brok, P., Levy, J., Wubbels, T., & Roderiguez, M. (2003). Cultural influences on students' perceptions of videotaped lessons. *International Journal of Intercultural Relations, 27,* 355–374.

den Brok, P., Wubbels, T., van Tartwijk, J., & Veldman, I (2010). The differential effect of the teacher–student interpersonal relationship on student outcomes for students with different ethnic backgrounds. *British Journal of Educational Psychology, 80,* 199–221.

Levy, J., den Brok, P., Wubbels, T., & Brekelmans, M. (2002). Students' perceptions of interpersonal aspects of the learning environment. *Learning Environments Research, 6,* 5–36.

Levy, J., Wubbels, T., Brekelmans, M., & Morganfield, B. (1997). Language and cultural factors in students' perceptions of teacher communication style. *International Journal of Intercultural Relations, 21,* 29–56.

Middleton, M. J., & Midgley, C. (2002). Beyond motivation: Middle school students' perceptions of press for understanding in math. *Contemporary Educational Psychology, 27,* 373–391.

Pianta, R. C. (1999). *Enhancing relationships between children and teachers.* Washington, DC: American Psychological Association.

Reeve, J. (2006). Teachers as facilitators: What autonomy–supportive teachers do and why their students benefit. *Elementary School Journal, 106,* 225–236.

Walker, J. (2008). Looking at teacher practices through the lens of parenting style. *Journal of Experimental Education, 76,* 218–240.

Wentzel, K. R. (2009). Students' relationships with teachers as motivational contexts. In K. R. Wentzel & A. Wigfield (Eds.), *Handbook of motivation* (pp. 301–322). New York: Routledge.

Woolfolk Hoy, A. E., & Davis, H. A. (2005). Teacher self–efficacy and its influence on adolescent achievement. In T. Urdan & M. F. Pajares (Eds.), *Adolescence and education: Vol. 5. Self–efficacy beliefs during adolescence* (pp. 117–137). Greenwich, CT: Information Age.

Wubbels, T., Brekelmans, M., den Brok, P., & van Tartwijk, J. (2006). Interpersonal perspective on classroom management in Secondary Classrooms in the Netherlands. In C. M. Evertson, & C. S. Weinstein (Eds.), *Handbook of classroom management: Research, practice, and contemporary issues* (pp. 1161–1191). Mahwah, NJ: Erlbaum.

Wubbels, T., Levy, J., & Brekelmans, M. (1997). Paying attention to relationships. *Educational Leadership, 54,* 82–86.

6.2

National Board for Professional Teaching Standards

Mary E. Dilworth
National Board for Professional Teaching Standards

Introduction

Teacher quality is the single most valuable predictor of student performance and as such defining *quality* is an important issue for both the policy and the educational communities (Cochran-Smith & Zeichner, 2005; Darling Hammond & Youngs, 2002; Dilworth & Aguerrebere, 2008). There are a host of proxies for teacher quality (e.g., degree acquisition, licensing, years of experience, and most importantly student learning, achievement, and outcomes). The National Board for Professional Teaching Standards (NBPTS) was established in 1987 as a measure of teaching quality (i.e., exceptional or accomplished teaching in the form of advanced certification). Conceived from a recommendation of the Carnegie Forum on Education and the Economy's seminal report, *A Nation Prepared: Teachers for the 21st Century,* the National Board was founded as a central component in a comprehensive effort to reform the way public education was structured in the United States (Tucker, 1995). It is a private, nongovernmental, nonpartisan entity designed to provide a voluntary process for identifying exemplary teaching practice. Its five core propositions, 25 discipline specific standards, and accompanying assessments were created with the assumption that the identification of advanced teaching knowledge and skills would be a significant contribution to the profession and to the achievement of students.

The founders of the National Board debated a number of factors considered pertinent to an advanced certification: What should be the assessment framework, the standards, and the prerequisites for application? They concluded that eligible candidates must be school based educators, and licensed by the state for 3 years. The process requires candidates to submit four portfolios demonstrating their practice and six 30-minute assessment center exercises to gauge subject matter knowledge.

The research that substantiates National Board certification as a viable assessment of accomplished teaching is equally divided—the first in the development of the standards and assessments, and the second focusing on matters of implementation and effect. This review focuses on the latter work most closely related to the impact of National Board certification on student learning and achievement.

Research Evidence

There are two recent comprehensive publications that directly address the body of work of the National Board and its influence on learning and achievement. Specifically, *The Impact of the National Board for Professional Teaching Standards: A Review of the Research* (Gitomer, 2007), and *Assessing Accomplished Teaching: Advanced-level Certification Programs* (National Research Council [NRC], 2008).

Gitomer (2007) offers an extensive annotated literature review that is organized around five questions that have dominated the NBPTS research. Specifically, to what extent does the NBPTS certification process identify strong instructional practice; identify teachers who differ in terms of their students' academic achievement; enhance teacher effectiveness; are schools more effective due to the influence of NBCTs on the practice of their non-NBCT colleagues; and does NBPTS contribute to the equitable distribution of teachers?

The Committee on the Evaluation of Teacher Certification by the National Board for Professional Teaching Standards (NBPTS) was established by the National Research Council (NRC) and was charged, by congressional mandate, to examine similar issues: the impact of NBPTS on teachers who obtain National Board Certification, teachers who attempt but are unsuccessful, and teachers who do not apply; the extent to which National Board Certification makes a difference in the academic achievement of students; and the cost effectiveness of advanced-level certification as a means for improving teacher quality.

Although each of these compilations has different purposes and approaches, they are consistent in the criteria that they use for studies included in their work. The criteria include but are not limited to a clear study design, defensible methodology, sufficiently described sample, appropriate measures, and sound conclusions. Each volume provides a critical analysis of all factors. Together, Gitomer and the NRC address 12 studies as the basis for their conclusions regarding the impact of NBPTS on student learning, achievement and outcomes. They rely heavily on Cantrell, Fullerton, Kane, and Staiger (2008); Cavalluzzo (2004); Clotfelter, Ladd, and Vigdor (2004, 2006); Goldhaber and Anthony (2007); Harris and Sass (2007); Sanders, Ashton, and Wright (2005) but also include comments on Amrein-Beardsley and Berliner (2006); Bond, Smith, Baker, and Hattie (2000); McColskey et al. (2005); Stone (2002); and Vandervoort, Amrein-Beardsley, and Berliner (2004).

The abundance of research on National Board Certified Teachers' (NBCT) impact on achievement focuses on student performance at the elementary level, is situated in North Carolina, and compares those who have achieved National Board Certification with those who have not achieved it or with those who have not pursued NB Certification. By and large, the studies focus on student test results in reading and mathematics. When taken as a whole, the weight of research evidence indicates a positive impact of National Board Certification on student achievement. The research clearly indicates that National Board certification distinguishes or "signals," more effective teachers from less effective teachers (NRC, 2008) with respect to student achievement and those students of National Board Certified Teachers (NBCTS) tend to learn more than students taught by others (Gitomer, 2007).

Goldhaber and Anthony (2004, 2007) sought to answer the question, "To what extent do students of teachers who eventually become NBCTs at some point demonstrate greater achievement gains than those who do not?" Using a North Carolina sample of approximately 400,000 student records matched to 9,000 teachers over a 3-year period, they examined third to fifth grade student test gains by looking at National Board Certified Teachers' (NBCT) effectiveness prior to the year in which they attained certification. Their findings indicated that students of NBCTs demonstrate more learning than do students of teachers who were not NBCTs. Specifically, they found NBCTs were more effective in reading, but not in math; future NBCTs were more effective than other teachers; current applicants showed a decline in effectiveness during the first year of certification; and effects for students receiving free or reduced price lunch (FRPLs) were approximately twice the size for non-FRPLs.

Harris and Sass (2007) conducted a study in Florida over a 5-year time frame and examined teachers in elementary, middle, and high schools. The authors' teacher dataset was substantially larger than Goldhaber and Anthony, with more than 1,500 and 1,700 NBCTs used in the analysis of mathematics and reading scores, respectively. Their study addressed four key questions: are NBCTs more effective than others; does the NBPTS process influence teacher effectiveness; do NBCTs affect performance of fellow teach-

ers; and does certification provide additional information about effectiveness beyond other available teacher quality indicators?

In Florida, students take two standardized achievement tests annually as part of the Florida Comprehensive Assessment Test (FCAT). One battery of tests is the SAT-9, a national standardized norm-referenced test, FCAT-NRT, and the second battery, known as the FCAT-SSS, is a criterion-referenced test based on the Sunshine State Standards (SSS). Thus, the FCAT-SSS is directly linked to state standards and is used to meet federal accountability requirements. In their review of FCAT-NRT the authors looked across grades 3 through 10. They found no overall effect for National Board certification in either mathematics or reading. When disaggregated by grade levels, there was a small significant and positive effect in mathematics for middle and high school, but no apparent effects in reading.

Harris and Sass then conducted the same series of analyses with the same students and teachers, using the FCAT-SSS test battery as the outcome measure. In this analysis they found that the overall NBCT effect for reading across grades 3 through 10 was positive and significant for the FCAT-SSS; for reading, the effect was significant for both precertification and postcertification; and for mathematics, there was a marginally significant positive effect of precertification NBCTs only. In addition, grade-level results for the FCAT-SSS are notably discrepant from those for the FCAT-NRT. For instance, the authors find what was low-achievement postcertification is now mostly positive. For elementary teachers, effects remain nonsignificant or marginal, but, in middle school, one now sees significant positive effects prior to NBPTS-certification in reading. Further, in high school, post certification effects show positive for the FCAT-SSS, significantly for mathematics.

Cavalluzzo's (2004) work is titled *Is National Board Certification an Effective Signal of Teacher Quality?* While similar in focus to Goldhaber and Anthony (2007) as well as Harris and Sass (2007) this study is distinguished from others in a variety of ways. Specifically, the research focuses on a single discipline, mathematics; at the high school level; has a large and diverse sample of 107,997 high school students with 2,137 NBCTs and non-NBCTs and a larger set of student and teacher variables than were presented in other state-wide and cross-district studies.

Cavalluzzo compared student achievement of NBCTS with that of the larger teacher population, and with those who pursued and failed or withdrew from the National Board Certification process. Employing a range of statistical models, the author found: students whose teachers were currently NBCT applicants scored significantly higher than those students whose teachers had no participation with NBPTS; the test scores of students whose teachers were National Board Certified (NBCT) were significantly higher than students whose teachers had no participation with NBPTS; students whose teachers applied for NBPTS certification but failed to be certified scored significantly lower than students whose teachers had no participation with NBPTS; and Black and Hispanic students benefited from NBCTs more so than did other students.

Cantrell, Fullerton, Kane, and Staiger (2007) offer the first empirical study of NBCTs and their impact on student achievement that employs random assignment in its methodology. The approach provides a control for preexisting differences among the groups of students assigned to National Board certified and non-National Board certified teachers. In addition, the authors used each applicant's NBPTS scaled score (not just whether the candidates achieved certification) to test whether the score is related to teacher impacts.

Data were collected from the Los Angeles Unified School District (LAUSD) for the years 2003-2004 and 2004-2005 and compared the performance of third through fifth grade students randomly assigned to NBPTS applicants and to comparison teachers. The sample included 99 matched pairs of NB certification applicants and non-National Board certified teachers.

The study indicates that teachers who applied but were unsuccessful in their bid for National Board Certification are less effective than those teachers who never pursued this designation. At the same time, the authors found that teachers who accomplished National Board Certification were more effective than those teachers who were unsuccessful in their attempts for National Board Certification. Generally, differences between NBCTs and nonapplicants were not significant; but differences between NBCTs and unsuccessful applicants were significant

The research team of Clotfelter, Ladd, and Vigdor (2006, 2007, 2010) offers several studies, situated in North Carolina, that contribute to understanding NBCTs impact on student achievement. In their earliest research (2006) the authors found that NBCTs were more effective that others in reading and math and that effectiveness declined during the year of application; comparisons prior to and following certification showed mixed results. In their 2007 work the authors conclude that the consistency of effects for NBCTs across multiple models for both mathematics and reading provides compelling evidence that the cohort of NBCTS in North Carolina between 1995 and 2004 raised achievement test scores more than other teachers. In their most recent work (2010), "Teacher Credentials and Student Achievement in High School: A Cross-Subject Analysis with Student Fixed Effects" the authors find that the National Board Certification process appears to identify effective teachers but does not make them more effective.

Lastly, Sanders, Ashton, and Wright (2005) compared results from two large North Carolina school districts using four different models. Grades 4 through 8 were each analyzed separately using a database that included 4 years of data (1999–2000 to 2002–2003). Teachers were classified as NBCTs, unsuccessful candidates, current applicants, and no affiliation with NBPTS. Comparisons are made across these groupings to evaluate the same kinds of claims investigated by other studies. The authors' work is distinguished from others in that they take the impact

of *nesting* of students i.e., learning gains associated with a teacher may be attributable to shared characteristics of students in that particular classroom. The findings of this study indicate that for this group of teachers and students, NBCTs produce student gains varying in significance by grade and subject tested. However, the study also found that NBCTs account for significant achievement gains for students in some grades and subject areas; and NBCTs produce positive impact on the academic performance of children in minority groups. On most indicators, students of NBCTs do better, although the differences seldom rise to the level of statistical significance.

Summary and Recommendations

The relationship of NBCTs to student achievement can be summarized as follows:

- Studies that compare test score gains for students of teachers who were and were not successful in earning NB Certification consistently found statistically significant differences between groups (NRC, 2008)
- Results from comparisons of test scores for students of NBCTs and nonapplicants were less consistent (NRC, 2008).
- NBCTs tend to have students who have stronger historical records of achievement. When assignment factors are controlled, students of NBCTs still tend to learn somewhat more, but the findings are quite modest in magnitude (Gitomer, 2007).
- There are no strong methodological studies that use any outcome measures other than student standardized achievement scores (Gitomer, 2007).

There are scores of studies that support the notion that National Board certification has a positive impact on student achievement. Even though the limitation of subject area, grade level, and vicinity prevent generalizations, there is a large body of work that contributes to the student achievement literature.

References

Bond, L.S., SmithT. Baker, T.,., & Hattie, J. (2000). The certification system of the National Board for Professional Teaching Standards: A construct and consequential validity study (NBPTS Report). Arlington, VA, NBPTS. Retrieved from http://www.nbpts.org/UserFiles/File/validity_1__UNC_Greebsboro_D_-_Bond.pdf

Cantrell, S., Fullerton, J., Kane, T. J., & Staiger, D. (2008, December). National Board certification and teacher effectiveness: Evidence from a random assignment experiment (NBER Working Paper No. w14608). Retrieved from http://ssrn.com/abstract=1320853

Carnegie Forum on Education and the Economy-Task Force on Teaching as a Profession (1986) A nation prepared: Teachers for the 21st century. New York: Carnegie Corporation of New Yorkr

Cavalluzzo, L. (2004). Is National Board certification an effective signal of teacher quality? National Science Foundation and the National Board of Professional Teaching Standards. Alexandria, VA: CNA Corporation

Clotfelter, C. T., Ladd, H. F., & Vigdor, J.L. (2004). Teacher quality and minority achievement gaps (Working Paper Series San04-04). Durham,

NC: Duke University. Retrieved from http://www.pubpol.duke.edu/research/papers/SAN04–04.pdf

Clotfelter, C. T., Ladd, H. F., & Vigdor, J. L. (2006). Teacher–student matching and the assessment of teacher effectiveness (NBER Working Paper #11936). *Journal of Human Resources.*

Clotfelter, C. T., Ladd, H. F. & Vignor, J. L. (2007, March) : *How and why teachers' credentials matter in student achievement?* Working paper 2. National Center for Analysis of Longitudinal Data in Education Research. Washington, DC: AIR

Clotfelter, C. T., Ladd, H. F., & Vigdor, J. (2010) Teacher credentials and student achievement in high school: A cross-subject analysis with student fixed effects. *Journal of Human Resources, 45*(3), 655–681.

Cochran-Smith, M., & Zeichner, K. M. (Eds.). (2005). *Studying teacher education: The report of the AERA Panel on Research and Teacher Education.* Mahwah, NJ: Erlbaum.

Darling–Hammond L., & Youngs, P. (2002). Defining "highly qualified teachers": What does "scientifically–based research" actually tell us? *Educational Researcher, 31*(9), 13–25.

Dilworth, M. E., & Aguerrebere, J. (2008). NCLB's highly qualified teacher: A placeholder definition. *National Journal of Urban Education and Practice, 1*(2).

Gitomer, D. (2007, July). *ETS research report: The impact of the National Board for Professional Teaching Standards: A review of the research* (RR-07-33). Princeton, NJ: ETS.

Goldhaber, D., & Anthony, E. (2007) Can teacher quality be effectively assessed? National board certification as a signal of effective teaching. *Review of Economics and Statistics, 89*(1), 134–150.

Goldhaber, D., & Anthony, E (April 2004) Can teacher quality be effectively assessed? Washington, D.C.: Urban Institute

Harris, D. N., & Sass, T. R. (2007, March). *The effects of NBPTS-certified teachers on student achievement* (Working Paper No. 4). Washington, DC: National Center for Analysis of Longitudinal Data in Education Research, Urban Institute. Retrieved from http://www.caldercenter.org/PDF/1001060_NBPTS_Certified.pdf

McColskey, W., Stronge, J. H., Ward, T. J. Tucker, P. D., Howard, B., Lewis, K., & Hindman, J. L. (2005). Teacher effectiveness, student achievement, and National Board Certified Teachers (NBPTS Report).

National Research Council. (2008). *Assessing accomplished teaching: Advanced-level certification programs.* Committee on Evaluation of Teacher Certification by the National Board for Professional Teaching Standards. Milton D. Hakel, Judith Anderson Koenig, and Stuart W. Elliot, editors. Board on Testing and Assessment, Center for Education, Division of Behavioral and Social Sciences Education. Washington, DC: The National Academies Press.

Sanders, W. L., Ashton, J. J., & Wright, S. P. (2005). *Comparison of the effects of NBPTS certified teachers with other teachers on the rate of student academic progress* (NBPTS Report) (pp. 1–37). Arlington, VA: NBPTS.

Stone, J. E. (2002). *The value-added gains of NBPTS-certified teachers in Tennessee: A brief report.* Arlington, VA: NBPTS. (ERIC Document Reproduction Service ED 472 132137)

Tucker, M. (1995) A Nation Prepared: Teachers for the 21st Century: The Report of the Carnegie Forum on Education and the Economy's Task Force on Teaching as a Profession (1995) In (Eds.) R. Ginsberg and D. Plank Commissions, reports, reforms, and educational policy (pp. 41-46). Westport, CT: Praeger Publishing.

Vandevoort, L. G., Amrein-Beardsley, A., & Berliner, D. (2004). National Board Certified Teachers and their students' achievement. *Education Policy Analysis Archives, 12*(46), 1–117.

6.3

Classroom Management and Student Achievement

H. Jerome Freiberg
College of Education, University of Houston

Introduction

Classroom management is the gatekeeper of learning and is framed by social, cultural, instructional, and organizational contexts. It provides teachers and students with the opportunity to participate and build a positive framework of interpersonal and academic interactions. As teaching, learning, and society in general become more complex, classroom management provides a source to navigate this complexity. The term is often used synonymously with *student behavior* and *discipline* and spans a continuum from compliance and obedience to student reflection and self-discipline. Student achievement may be one result of classroom management, because effective management enables the teaching and learning process within the unique educational social context. Achievement outcomes range from high-stakes national, regional, and local testing to end of year examinations to course content grades to formal and informal formative and summative assessments. The connection between classroom management and student achievement is undergoing increased global attention as educators, parents, and policy makers seek ways to improve student engagement and academic success.

The study of classroom management has a trend line stretching across multiple decades and nations. In the United States, the idea of classroom management was often discussed during the 20th century. Educators such as Bagley (*Classroom Management,* 1907), Perry (*The Management of a City School*, 1908), and Breed (*Classroom Organization and Management*, 1933) proffered some of the earliest ideas on the ability of classroom management to increase student success, reduce financial costs, and improve test scores. Public opinion polls of education in the United States conducted by the Gallup Organization and reported by *Phi Delta Kappan* have consistently ranked "school discipline" in the top three concerns from the late 1960s until the present; often it is the primary educational concern for parents and the public.

Research Evidence

Studies about the management and organization of classrooms became more specialized in the second half of the 20th century as specific elements of the learning process were analyzed. Behaviorist-based or Skinnerian research in the 1950s and 1960s explored the ability of a rewards and punishment (stimulus/response) system to trigger predictable positive responses. Ecological studies, beginning in the late 1950s, treated classrooms as ecological systems where settings and activities can be altered to create a more conducive environment for learning (as cited by Brophy, 2006). Key areas of research include teacher awareness "withitness," multitasking, lesson engagement, student engagement, and assignment variability. Process-outcome (product) studies of the 1960s and 1970s examined the relationship between classroom processes and student outcomes, particularly related to student achievement gains (Emmer & Evertson, 1982).

Wang, Haertel, and Walberg (1993) considered the influence of educational, psychological, and social factors on general learning. Their meta-analysis collected data from over 11,000 unique relations and found that proximal variables such as psychological, instructional, and home influence forces are more impactful than outlier variables such as demographics, policy, and organizational factors. Their analysis identified classroom management as the most important of five factors influencing school learning and student achievement.

Person-centered classroom studies (those that examine teacher/student interpersonal interactions) turned attention toward the direct social and emotional needs of individual students and teachers and how interpersonal relationships can improve student achievement. Cornelius-White (2007) conducted a far-reaching meta-analysis beginning in the 1940s through 2004 and concluded that learner and person-centered classrooms facilitate higher achievement and positive learning environments (creativity/critical thinking, math/verbal achievement, student participation, student satisfaction/self-esteem, and reduction in absences, disruptive behavior, and dropouts) with stronger teacher-student relationships than teacher-centered or traditional classrooms.

Brophy noted in examining the history of classroom management research that a general consensus was being reached in the 1980s on interconnectedness between classroom management and student learning and achievement. However, researchers continued exploring unique and particular aspects of student learning (e.g. gender, social constructivist, sociocultural, and grade-level differences) (Brophy, 2006). By the 1990s, the emphasis on school reform rose to the center of attention and intensified interest in teacher development and student achievement. Researchers at the start of the 21st century revisited the importance of classrooms in the broader milieu. Even though not all agree on the appropriateness or practicality of individual investigations and research findings, studies generally reach a consensus on the significance and potential positive impacts of classroom management. Among those are: increased instruction time, increased student achievement, improved learning environments, teacher preparation, and student–teacher connectedness.

In a series of three studies that spanned two decades, which are described below, strong evidence demonstrates that classroom management (particularly programs or approaches that engage students in the management of the classroom) can produce statistically and educationally significant achievement gains as measured by national and state assessments for students from low income and minority communities. The implications of matching person-centered (prosocial) management approaches with an active learning curriculum provide a comprehensive view of classroom management's role in student achievement. In the area of student learning, Freiberg, Prokosch et al. (1990) found that a prosocial management program (Consistency Management & Cooperative Discipline® [CMCD]) improved student performance on the Texas Education Assessment of Minimal Skills (TEAMS) against control schools (d = 0.51) and increased passing rates by 17% compared to the 2% decrease in nonprogram schools. Freiberg, Connell, and Lorentz (2001) studied the same prosocial program's impact on mathematics and found greater gains in student achievement than the math-based curriculum implemented singularly with significantly greater achievement gains (d = 0.33) against the four comparison schools with the same mathematics curriculum. Freiberg, Huzinec, and Templeton (2009) provided additional evidence of increased student achievement as students in classroom management schools outperformed control students in both reading (64th percentile) and mathematics (67th percentile) assessments in a 2-year period compared to control students (50th percentile in both categories). Advances in classroom management can create a significant pathway to student achievement by emphasizing effective and efficient use of instructional time, the building of student self-discipline, student engagement in the operations of the classroom, and enabling greater student involvement in more complex academic learning.

Links between classroom management strategies and overall school environment, including student and staff satisfaction, discipline problems, and levels of active learning, are further evidenced by Opuni's (2006) studies of the prosocial CMCD management program over multiple years in different regions. His study revealed improvement in teacher–student relationships (with the majority rising above national mean averages), significant declines in student referrals, and students significantly outperforming comparison cohorts in math and reading standardized test scores. Also crucial was the increase in available instructional time created as a result of decreased attention spent on classroom disruptions. With more instructional time, students showed increased academic performance and greater levels of learning.

The international applications of classroom management are also gaining increased attention throughout Europe, Asia, and the Middle East. In northern Italy, Chiari (1994) found that classrooms with management systems are more conducive to student learning because students individually assume responsibility for their learning and develop a sense of school connectedness. When students display ownership of the environment, the social, emotional, and learning climates are all improved resulting in increased higher order cognitive processes. Harwood (2007) in England continued with this focus, finding that the classroom management program CMCD, implemented in the London Challenge schools, was indeed a powerful tool in transforming, not just managing, both positive and negative student behavior. A decrease in student expulsions coupled with increased academic attainment validated its role in linking classroom management and student achievement. Creemers (1994) conducted a study of educational systems that included the Dutch Educational Priority Policy that sought an increase in effective instruction and effective schools, particularly within low income student groups. He found that effective learning environments are universally most valuable to student achievement and that consistency, achieved in part through classroom management, is a main component of such environments. If teachers establish consistent, effective classrooms, students are more apt to demonstrate higher academic attainment levels.

There is much support for linking student-centered classroom management and increased student achievement, both academically and socially. Lewis, Romi, Katz, and Qui (2008) studied educational institutions in Australia, China, and Israel and identified a connection between student participation in maintaining classroom discipline and a corresponding decrease in distractions and disciplinary issues. Ben-Peretz, Eilam, and Yankelevitch (2006) provided a synthesis of classroom management research undertaken across grade levels in multicultural and heterogeneous classrooms in present-day Israel. Their research highlighted the shift in classroom emphasis toward teacher autonomy and student-oriented teaching. Similar studies on the impact of classroom learning environments in Asia also exhibit increased attention to classroom environments including classroom management and the ability to move away from traditional classrooms into more nuanced settings that grant students the ability to become engaged, participatory learners working collaboratively both inside and outside of the formal classroom setting (Chionh & Fraser, 2009; Nishioka, 2006).

Summary and Recommendations

With the number of international and national studies increasing, classroom management programs for schools have proliferated, offering different approaches to improving classroom cultures. Freiberg and Lapointe (2006) completed a study utilizing the reviews of 14 external groups and organizations of over 800 discipline classroom management and other behavioral intervention programs, identifying "research-based" and "research-tested" programs that prevent or reduce classroom discipline problems as well as improve student achievement. They found few classroom management programs have external, third-party evaluations or longitudinal studies to validate their program's effectiveness, complicating the already difficult decision of selecting which program will lead to the greatest postimplementation improvements. However, of the 800 programs there were only a few that reported gains in student achievement. As countries see the need to educate youth for a more complex society and world, classroom management models that have proved successful at improving student achievement in a range of settings need to be brought to the table of educational transformation. Their exact manifestation will vary, whether ecological, prosocial, or person-centered, but it is clear that even the best attempts at curricular improvements will be needlessly hampered without a corresponding plan for managing the day-to-day operations of any school or classroom.

References

Bagley, W. C. (1907). *Classroom management: Its principles and techniques.* New York: Macmillan.

Ben–Peretz, M., Eilam, B., & Yankelevitch, E. (2006). Classroom management in Israel: multicultural classrooms in an immigrant country. In C. M Evertson & C. S. Weinstein (Eds.), *Handbook of classroom management: Research, practice, and contemporary issues* (pp. 1121–1140). Mahwah, NJ: Erlbaum.

Breed, F. (1933). *Classroom organization and management.* Yonkers-on-Hudson, NY: World Book Co.

Brophy, J. (2006). History of research on classroom management. In C. M. Evertson & C. S. Weinstein (Eds.), *Handbook of classroom management: Research, practice, and contemporary issues* (pp. 17–43). Mahwah, NJ: Erlbaum.

Chiari, G. (1994). *Climi di classe e apprendimento* [Class and learning climates]. Milan, Italy: FrancoAngeli.

Chionh, Y. H., & Fraser, B. J. (2009). Classroom environment, achievement, attitudes and self-esteem in geography and mathematics in Singapore. *International Research in Geographical and Environmental Education, 18*(1), 29–44.

Cornelius-White, J. (2007). Learner–centered teacher–student relationships are effective: A meta–analysis. *Review of Educational Research, 77*(1), 113–143.

Creemers, B. (1994). *The effective classroom.* London: Cassell.

Emmer, E. T., & Evertson, C. M. (1982). Effective classroom management at the beginning of the school year in junior high school classes. *Journal of Educational Psychology, 74,* 485–498.

Freiberg, H. J., Connell, M. L., & Lorentz, J. (2001). Effects of consistency management on student mathematics achievement in seven chapter 1 elementary schools. *Journal of Education for Students Placed at Risk, 6*(3), 249–270.

Freiberg, H. J., Huzinec, C., & Templeton, S. M. (2009). Classroom management—A pathway to student achievement. *Elementary School Journal, 110*(1), 64–80.

Freiberg, H. J., & Lapointe, J. M. (2006). Research-based programs for preventing and solving discipline problems. In C. M. Evertson & C. S. Weinstein (Eds.), *Handbook of classroom management: Research, practice, and contemporary issues* (pp. 735–786). Mahwah, NJ: Erlbaum.

Freiberg, H. J., Prokosch, N., Tresister, E. S., & Stein, T. (1990). Turning around five at-risk elementary schools. *Journal of School Effectiveness and School Improvement, 1*(1), 5–25.

Harwood, P. (2007). *A review of Consistency Management & Cooperative Discipline in the UK.* London Challenge Behaviour Adviser. Unpublished evaluation submitted to the *London Challenge,* Dept. for Education and Skills, London, England.

Lewis, R., Romi, S., Katz, Y. J., & Qui, X. (2008). Students' reaction to classroom discipline in Australia, Israel, and China. *Teaching and Teacher Education, 24*(3), 715–724.

Nishioka, K. (2006). Classroom management in post-war Japan. In C. M. Evertson & C. S. Weinstein (Eds.), *Handbook of classroom management: Research, practice, and contemporary issues* (pp. 1215–1237). Mahwah, NJ: Lawrence Erlbaum Associates.

Opuni, K. A. (2006). *The effectiveness of the consistency management & cooperative discipline (CMCD) model as a student empowerment and achievement enhancer: The experiences of two K-12 inner-city school systems.* Paper presented at the 4th Annual Hawaii International Conference of Education, Honolulu, Hawaii.

Perry, A. (1908). *The management of a city school.* New York: Macmillan.

Wang, M. C., Haertel, G. D., & Walberg, H. J. (1993). Toward a knowledge base for school learning. *Review of Educational Research, 63,* 249–294.

6.4

Fostering Student Creativity in the Era of High-Stakes Testing

BREE FRICK
Columbus State Community College

Introduction

Promoting creativity among students within the educational context of high-stakes testing presents complex dilemmas for educators. In the past 20 years, an increasingly competitive international marketplace and the development of new technologies have reshaped the world economy. Finding innovative strategies for solving complex world problems has become essential in order for industrialized nations to stay globally competitive (Florida, 2002) and has caused departments of education around the world to introduce changes in school curricula and especially evaluation. Ranking systems like the Program for International Student Assessment (PISA) that compare mathematics and reading competence in 15-year-old students in over 65 countries have fueled a push for accountability systems in the form of standardized, high-stakes tests (HST) in most industrialized nations. For example, the United States, England, Germany, Japan, and Singapore all have implemented high-stakes tests in schools (Fleischman, Hopstock, Pelczar, & Shelley, 2010; Rotberg, 2006). In the United States, the No Child Left Behind Act (NCLB), a reauthorization of the 1965 Elementary and Secondary Education Act (ESEA), requires the implementation of assessment tests for students in public schools to "ensure students are meeting challenging state academic achievement and content standards" (NCLB, 2002, p. 17).

Literature addressing problems with HST continues to grow worldwide, but is prominent in the United States in particular where a large public debate roars over issues of test equality and academic effectiveness (Mons, 2009). Cross-national comparison between different nations' testing methods has shown that assessment often is not a reliable tool for measuring a nations' ranking in student ability, nor is it an appropriate tool for affecting policy change (Rotberg, 2006). Whereas most agree that encouraging creativity and innovation in students will lead to a more flexible and competent workforce, HST may weaken students' ability to think flexibly and creatively (Hennessey

& Amabile, 2010). Although the volume of worldwide research related to the effects of HST on student innovation is limited, current findings across various fields—particularly research in motivation theory and teacher practices—serve as a guide to how student creativity and innovative ability can flourish in spite of HST.

Research Evidence

Recent research on student motivation has shown that emphasis placed on HST in recent years has affected the ways in which students approach learning in the classroom (Ryan & Weinstein, 2009), as well as teacher ability to foster creativity in students (Bunting, 2007). Even though cultural differences that may exist from country to country in how learning in classrooms is structured, motivation theory can apply to most learning situations. According to self-determination theory (SDT), individuals may be motivated to do tasks either intrinsically (doing an activity for its inherent satisfactions), or extrinsically (doing an activity for its instrumental value) (Deci & Ryan, 1985). Performance-oriented atmospheres created by HST—a focus on student scores, rote memorization and drills—can decrease students' intrinsic motivation and ability to think creatively (Amabile, 1999; Deci & Ryan, 1985). External factors (such as an emphasis on test scores) can actually "kill" creativity in individuals (Amabile, 1999). Hennessey (2000) claims this "creative death" occurs because students learn that rewards are usually paired with required activities that are sometimes perceived as aversive. As a result, rewards may cause students to react negatively, especially when their actions are controlled by socially imposed factors, like tests.

Other motivational theories also support the finding that HST may be detrimental to students' ability to think innovatively. Achievement goal theory examines the types of goal structures that influence student motivation. Mastery-focused goal structures promote a deep understanding of subject matter. Students in a classroom in which mastery goals are promoted are more likely to express an interest in learning the material because it is useful and interesting to them. On the other hand, performance goal structures (e.g., a test-driven curriculum) can lead to the utilization of surface-level learning strategies that promote self-handicapping strategies, as well as cheating (Meece, E. M. Anderman & L. Anderman, 2006). According to Kaplan, Middleton, Urdan, and Midgley (2002), mastery goal structures refer to the need for understanding, mastering, and improving upon tasks. Performance goal structures, however, involve self-involvement, a desire for successful outcomes with little effort, and avoidance of demonstrating lack of ability. Because many schools adopt performance goal structures to address the demands of HST, mastery of subject matter can diminish within classrooms.

Motivation theory has led us to a deeper understanding of how HST can affect our students' approaches to learning, and these effects are amplified by the many changes schools have implemented to allow HST to take center stage. In England, students are required to sit for over 70 tests in their school careers. As a result, testing has become a priority in the school day (Mons, 2009). In the United States, 77% of school districts in one study reported that they have reduced instructional time in other subject areas to make more time for reading and mathematics (Center on Education Policy, 2007, p. 42). Research in Swedish schools indicated that teachers are increasingly concerned for their students' stress levels as a result of a test-centered curriculum (Mons, 2009). Nichols and Berliner's (2006) extensive report on the effects of NCLB on the U.S. curriculum reveals that many schools have done away with recess, shortened lunch periods, and removed untested subject areas from the school schedule. Innovative, diverse activities—field trips, community outreach, creative writing, and problem-based learning activities—were all reported by teachers as having been cut to make more time for testing. The activities being cut are the same teaching methods tools that enhance student creativity—varied learning experiences that present content matter in real-life contexts (Hennessey & Amabile, 2010).

Not only has the variety of school curricula suffered under the weight of HST, but its quality has diminished as well. Often HST requires that curriculum be taught with particular, predetermined content in mind, often leading to a "scripted" style of instruction. This type of instruction advocates only one "right way" to complete a task or solve a problem. In many Asian countries, tests structure every aspect of the curriculum, leading teachers to rely on rote memorization so that students can memorize all the information required to pass tests (Rotberg, 2006). In the United States, Nichols and Berliner (2006) reported that many teachers use drills, exercises, and worksheets in place of more involved classroom work in order to cover all of the tested material. Whereas it may save time, a narrowed curriculum also narrows student focus toward learning only what will be tested, only for the sake of performing well on the test.

Even though these research findings may sound discouraging, it is possible for teachers to support student innovation, creativity, and subject mastery while also meeting the demands of HST. Research on teachers' instructional methodologies has helped isolate various teaching techniques that can enhance student learning despite testing pressures. For example, introducing Problem-Based Learning (PBL) activities into the classroom can enrich students' ability to apply their knowledge in a specific subject area while also cultivating their creative capacities. In PBL, students are provided with realistic problems which they must solve using both their current knowledge of the material and new knowledge that they access during the PBL process (Howard-Jones, 2002). The implementation of divergent thinking activities, in which students must quickly generate many ideas for solving one problem, is yet another method for fostering student creativity in the classroom, and can be easily incorporated into existing lessons. Encouraging students to think divergently (i.e., prompting students to compile a list of every possible use for a common object, such as a paper clip or a test tube or asking students to brainstorm many solutions to a real problem such as insufficient parking space at school) can be implemented in lessons across the curriculum (Hong, Hartzell, & Greene, 2009).

Analyses of teachers' classroom practices have led some researchers to propose that teachers who find ways to promote learning mastery goals in their classrooms will simultaneously foster student creativity. Hong et al. (2009) explored the relationships between teachers' epistemological beliefs, motivation, and goal orientation and their instructional practices that lead to enhanced student creativity. One of the strongest predictors of the use of instructional practices that foster creativity was the promotion of mastery goals by teachers. Specifically, those teachers were more likely to provide experiential learning for their students, such as labs or group projects, and stressed the importance of understanding over test performance. According to Hong et al., these teachers are more likely to enjoy their work, and in turn, to provide creative instruction that inspires student creativity. Additionally, these teachers reflected more frequently on their instructional practices, and were more likely to employ a wide range of teaching methods.

Bunting (2007) suggests that teachers can foster student creativity and teach passionately while continuing to follow the required "scripts" imposed upon them by HST policies, if teachers engage in self-reflection, whether it be revisiting their reasons for becoming a teacher in the first place, their love for teaching, their desire for order and purpose, or their desire to share their own creativity. This self-reflection can help maintain balance between external demands and quality teaching. Bunting also suggests that teachers seek out models—other educators who are successfully juggling external demands while remaining true to their sense of purpose—and take the time to observe them, discuss their concerns, and share solutions to problems.

Summary and Conclusions

The pressures and limitations that HST have placed on classroom learning worldwide create a question of balance. Some wonder if it will ever be possible to mend the gap between standards-based accountability and a more holistic teaching approach, in which more importance is placed on student creativity and learning goals. The research reviewed here indicates it is indeed possible to maintain creativity-fostering practices in the classroom while meeting the demands of HST, as long as teachers are willing to change their approach to the material they are required to teach, and the ways in which they teach it.

Even though standardized testing will continue to have a role in education policy, many nations are suggesting that changes and additions be made to the nature of standardized assessments. In recent years, education reform in Singapore, China, and Japan has called for a new emphasis on creativity and expression in schools, despite difficulty due to the massive amount of information those countries' standardized tests requires students to memorize (Rotberg, 2006). In the United States, the National Forum to Accelerate Middle Grades Reform (2002) proposes that although tests are important, deeper, more authentic assessment needs to be legitimized as well, including the creation of portfolios, performances, and demonstrations to measure student success. According to Houston, the struggle between external pressures for performance and accountability and the need for good teaching will continue to create tension worldwide until changes are implemented that would result from broader, deeper thinking about making the most out of the talent of our citizens (2007). Fittingly, Ryan and Weinstein (2009) suggest that an intrinsically oriented approach, where school stakeholders, parents, administrators, teachers, and students "work together to identify barriers to change and the goals to which they aspire, and to actively empower and support change from within.... Not only does this result in greater engagement and knowledge, it also models the democratic processes and responsibilities schools should prepare all students to assume" (p. 231). Research interest surrounding the effect of high-stakes testing on classroom creativity continues to grow worldwide at a steady pace. As this research synthesis suggests, it is possible to address the challenges of fostering students' innovative abilities in the face of HST as long as educators remain flexible in their classroom practices. Supporting creativity in an era of difficult problems and complex solutions will build the skills students need to compete in a rapidly changing global economy.

References

Amabile, T. (1999) *How to kill creativity.* Boston, MA: Harvard Business School Press.

Bunting, C. (2007). Teachers get personal about teaching to survive NCLB. *Phi Delta Kappan, 88,* 76–78.

Center on Education Policy. (2007). *Answering the question that matters most: Has student achievement increased since No Child Left Behind?* Washington, DC: Center on Education Policy.

Deci, E., & Ryan, R. (1985). *Intrinsic motivation and self–determination in human behavior.* New York: Plenum.

Fleischman, H. L., Hopstock, P. J., Pelczar, M. P., & Shelley, B. E. (2010). *Highlights From PISA 2009: Performance of U.S. 15–Year–old students in reading, mathematics, and science literacy in an international context.* Washington, DC: National Center for Education Statistics, U.S. Department of Education.

Florida, R. (2002). *The rise of the creative class and how it's transforming work, community and everyday life.* New York: Basic Books.

Hennessey, B. (2000). Self-determination theory and the social psychology of creativity. *Psychological Inquiry, 11*(4), 293.

Hennesey, B., & Amabile, T. M. (2010). Creativity. *Annual Review of Psychology, 61,* 59–98.

Hong, E., Hartzell, S., & Greene, M. (2009). Fostering creativity in the classroom: Effects of teachers' epistemological beliefs, motivation, and goal orientation. *Journal of Creative Behavior, 43*(3), 192–110.

Houston, P. (2007). The seven deadly sins of no child left behind. *Phi Delta Kappan, 88*(10), 744–748.

Howard-Jones, P. (2002). A dual-state model of creative cognition for supporting strategies that foster creativity in the classroom. *International Journal of Technology and design Education, 12,* 21–226.

Kaplan, A., Middleton, M. J., Urdan, T., & Midgley, C. (2002). Achievement goals and goal structures. In C. Midgley (Ed.), *Goals, goal structures, and patterns of adaptive learning* (pp. 21–53). Mahwah, NJ: Erlbaum.

Meece, J., Anderman, E., & Anderman, L. (2006). Classroom goal structure, student motivation, and academic achievement. *Annual Review of Psychology, 57,* 487–503.

Mons, N. (2009). *Theoretical and real effects of standardised assessment.* Background paper to the study: National Testing of Pupils in Europe, Eurydice Network. Retrieved from http://eacea.ec.europa.eu/education/eurydice/documents/thematic_reports/111EN.pdf

National Forum to Accelerate Middle Grades Reform. (2002). Our vision statement. Retrieved from http://www.mgforum.org/vision.asp

Nichols, S. L., & Berliner, D. C. (2005). *The inevitable corruption of indicators and educators through high–stakes testing.* Lansing, MI: The Great Lakes Center of Education Research & Practice.

No Child Left Behind Act (2002). Pub. L. No. 107-110, 115 Stat. 1425.

Rotberg, I. C. (2006). Assessment around the world. *Educational Leadership, 64*(3), 58–63.

Ryan, R. M., & Weinstein, N. (2009). Undermining quality teaching and learning: A self–determination perspective on high–stakes testing. *Theory and Research in Education, 7,* 224–233.

6.5

Nontraditional Teacher Preparation

Belinda G. Gimbert
Educational Administration, The Ohio State University

Introduction

In many countries, policy makers, in response to calls from the public and practitioners in hard-to-staff school districts, have attempted to relieve teacher shortages in core academic subjects through legislative provision and financial support for nontraditional teacher preparation programs (Ingersoll, 2004). The expansion of alternative (or nontraditional) teacher preparation that began in the late 1980s has continued into the 21st century. However, accompanying the proliferation of nontraditional teacher preparation programs is a growing controversy that surrounds the manner in which teachers are trained to attain the teacher quality required by many state and national mandates for teacher licensure. Student achievement as an outcome of an effective nontraditional teacher preparation has attracted much attention. Several researchers studying global teacher education programs and related issues of teacher licensure/certification have aggressively debated the relation between teacher preparation and student performance. The question of how teacher characteristics affect student academic learning has long been of concern to global educational community.

Internationally teacher educators are challenged to increase the number of program completers by creating innovative pathways to certification, simultaneously producing teachers of quality who can effectively foster the academic achievement of all students. Currently, in the United States, for example, all 50 states and the District of Columbia have legislated nontraditional teacher preparation programs (Feistritzer, 2007). These programs are delivered by school districts, educational service agencies, universities, 4-year colleges, 2-year community colleges, for profit and nonprofit organizations, or partnerships of these entities. Also included are national programs like Troops to Teachers, which focuses on military personnel moving into teaching positions, and Teach for America (TFA), which focuses on new college graduates who did not major in education. As is the case with most educational concepts that become popular over a rather short period of time, programs of alternate pathways to teacher licensure appear to have more differences than similarities.

Research Evidence

Among those who study international teacher education programs and related issues of teacher licensure/certification, the relation between teacher preparation and student performance is one of the most aggressively debated issues. Whereas K-12 institutions worldwide face teacher shortages in specific content areas such as mathematics, science, and special education, researchers, policy makers, and practitioners contest the most effective ways to prepare new teachers. However, very little empirical work has examined the consequences of teachers' training on students' outcomes. Some research efforts to assess the impact of teacher training on K-12 student achievement have applied analytical procedures to aggregated data from multiple state and national databases situated in different countries. For example, U.S. studies (Darling-Hammond, Berry, & Thoreson, 2001; Goldhaber & Brewer, 2000) have analyzed data from the National Assessment of Educational Progress (NAEP), the National Educational Longitudinal Study (NELS), Longitudinal Study of American Youth (LSAY), and Schools and Staffing Surveys (SASS). Other studies have analyzed data from a survey conducted by the French Ministry of Education (Bressoux, 1996), and also from the Jerusalem Schools Authority, Israel (Angrist & Lavy, 2001). Individually, the results of these studies have yielded conflicting and at times confusing evidence about the relation between type of teacher certification and student achievement for both policy makers and practitioners. Collectively, an in-depth review of the more recent empirical large-scale empirical studies reveals some consistent findings.

Across studies using different units of analysis and different measures of preparation, a significant relation between teacher qualification and student achievement has been documented and accepted. In a study of data from the National Educational Longitudinal Study (NELS, 1998), Goldhaber and Brewer (2000) examined the relations between 12th-grade students' performance in mathematics and science and teacher certification (3,786 mathematics students; 2,524 science students; 2,098 mathematics teachers; and 1,371 science teachers). First, students of teachers with mathematics degrees or certification in mathematics achieved better than the students of teachers without subject matter preparation. Second, student test scores in mathematics were higher when the teacher of record held professional or full state certification relative to the students' scores when taught by a teacher who was certified out of subject or held private school certification. Third, students taught by teachers with bachelor's or master's degrees in mathematics outperformed the students taught by teachers who were not credentialed in the same field. Fourth, students taught by an uncertified science teacher or a science teacher who held a private school certification showed lower scores. Fifth, measurement of student achievement growth revealed no significant differences between mathematics or science students' test scores for teachers with emergency certification and those traditionally certified. In their conclusion, Goldhaber and Brewer argued that "at the very least," the study's outcomes "cast doubt on the claims of the educational establishment that standard certification should be required of all teachers" (p. 145).

In their critique, Darling-Hammond et al. emphasized that some of the results for emergency and temporary certification generated by Goldhaber and Brewer's statistical model were generated from a very small sample and were not statistically significant (Birkeland & Peske, 2003). In their reanalysis of these data, Darling-Hammond et al. claimed that only about one-third of the NELS sample teachers who held temporary or emergency licenses were new entrants to teaching with little or no educational background. Further, these researchers demonstrated that many of the 24 science teachers (of 3,469 in Goldhaber and Brewer's study sample) with temporary or emergency certificates were similar in years of teaching and subject matter knowledge compared to the certified teachers in the sample. The findings revealed high school students taught by the subsample of teachers on temporary or emergency certification and who were new to teaching attained smaller achievement gains than those who had attained full state certification through a traditional pathway.

Greenberg, Rhodes, Ye, and Stancavage (2004) analyzed data from the NAEP 2000 Grade 8 mathematics assessment to examine how teacher qualifications were related to student achievement in mathematics among students enrolled in U.S. public schools. In this study, four specific teacher qualifications were defined accordingly: teacher certification, academic major or minor, highest postsecondary degree, and years of teaching experience. Although relying on cross-sectional NAEP background data for measures of student achievement, they found, in-

dependent of other factors and teaching credentials, teacher certification and holding a degree in mathematics were the teacher qualifications associated with higher mathematics achievement among eighth-grade public school students. Interestingly, a second finding pertained to economically disadvantaged eighth-grade students who were less likely to have a mathematics teacher with a degree in mathematics than their more affluent counterparts. A third finding revealed that students in high-ability mathematics classes were more likely to have teachers with a major or minor in mathematics or mathematics education than students in mixed- or low-ability mathematics classes. No relations between having a major or minor in education and student achievement were found.

A study conducted by Boyd, Grossman, Lankford, Loeb, and Wyckoff (2006) assessed how changes in entry requirements altered the teacher workforce and affected student achievement. To conduct the analysis of the relation between six different types of pathways into teaching, nontraditional and traditional, and student achievement, the researchers constructed a student database "with student exam scores, lagged scores and characteristics of students and their peers linked to their schools, teachers and characteristics of those teachers, including indicators of the pathway into teaching" (p. 8). Specifically, this study addressed whether students of teachers who enter the classrooms with reduced coursework preparation and limited clinical experiences achieve gains that differ significantly from students who are taught by traditionally certified or temporary licensed teachers. They found that, relative to other estimated effects, pathway differences were of moderate importance. Specifically, for elementary mathematics and English/language arts (ELA), they found that students of nontraditional teachers achieved as well as those of college-recommended pathways by the end of the third year of teaching. Likewise, for middle school mathematics, similar results have indicated that initially, there is no significant difference between pathways of preparation. However, middle school mathematics students of teachers in one particular nontraditional pathway, Teaching Fellows, made significantly greater improvement between their second and third years of teaching, outperforming the students of college-recommended teachers.

Constantine and colleagues (Constantine et al., 2009) studied 87 alternatively certified (AC) teachers and 87 traditionally certified (TC) teachers from 62 schools in 20 districts and seven states. Within each school, students in the same grade were randomly assigned to either an AC teacher or a TC teacher. There were no statistically significant differences between the math and reading performance of students with the TC or AC teachers. The researchers concluded that there was also no correlation between increased teacher training coursework and a teachers' effectiveness in the classroom (see also Gimbert, Cristol, & Sene, 2007). Kane, Rockoff, and Staiger (2007) noted that "teachers vary considerably in the extent to which they promote student learning, but whether a teacher is certified or not is largely irrelevant to predicting their effectiveness" (p. 629). When comparing certified teachers with teachers in teaching fellows programs and certified teachers with uncertified teachers, no significant differences were found in student math achievement scores between the different groups. However, the same study found that students with teachers who were teaching fellows and uncertified teachers underperformed in reading when compared to certified teachers. Finally, Kane et al. observed that both certified and alternatively certified teachers' effectiveness improves with the first few years of experience. Additional findings suggest that initial classroom performance was a more reliable predictor of teacher effectiveness in the future than certification status of teachers (p. 615).

Summary and Recommendations

Despite the available global research that has investigated national and state data sets to ascertain the impact of teacher qualifications, surprisingly little research exists that links the qualification of an individual teacher to the performance of students at both the classroom-level and the individual student level. Policy makers and practitioners have recognized that reliable measures and valid disaggregated data procedures are vital to providing trustworthy indices of teacher effectiveness. In summary, although findings from studies around alternative and traditional certified teachers that have attempted to compare teacher quality and effectiveness with student achievement are more often than not inconsistent and in some cases, inconclusive, a 2010 report, *Preparing Teachers: Building Evidence for Sound Policy*, released by the National Academy of Sciences, has concluded that there is insufficient evidence to suggest that teachers who take alternative pathways into the classroom have any greater or lesser effect on students' academic performance in reading, mathematics, and science.

References

Angrist, J. D., & Lavy, V. (2001). Does teacher training affect pupil learning? Evidence from matched comparison on Jerusalem Public Schools. *Journal of Labor Economics, 19*(2), 343–369.

Birkeland, S. E., & Peske, H. G. (2003). *Meeting competing demands: The shifting approach to ensuring teacher quality in one alternative certification program site.* Paper presented at the American Educational research Association annual meeting, Chicago, IL.

Boyd, D., Grossman, P., Lankford, H., Loeb, S., & Wyckoff, J. (2006, April). *How changes in entry requirements alter the teacher workforce and affect student achievement.* Paper presented at the American Education Research Association annual meeting, San Francisco, CA.

Bressoux, P. (1996). The effects of teachers' training on pupils' achievement: The case of elementary schools in France. *School Effectiveness and School Improvement, 7*(3), 252–279.

Constantine, J., Player, D., Silva, T., Hallgren, K., Grider, M., & Deke, J. (2009, February). *An evaluation of teachers trained through different routes to certification* (Final report. NCEE 2009–4043). Jessup, MD: National Center for Education Evaluation and Regional Assistance. (ERIC Document Reproduction Service No. ED504313)

Darling–Hammond, L., Berry, B., & Thoreson, A. (2001). Does teaching certification matter? Evaluating the evidence. *Educational Evaluation and Policy Analysis, 23*(1), 57–77.

Feistritzer, E. (2007). *Building a quality teaching force: Lesson learned from alternative routes.* Upper Saddle River, NJ: Prentice Hall.

Gimbert, B. G., Cristol, D., & Sene, A. M. (2007, September). The impact of teacher preparation on student achievement in algebra in a "hard to staff" urban pre-K-12-university partnership. *School Effectiveness and School Improvement, 18*(3), 245–272.

Goldhaber, D. B., & Brewer., D. (2000). Does teacher certification matter? High school teacher certification and student achievement. *Educational Evaluation and Policy Analysis, 22*(2), 129–145.

Greenberg, E., Rhodes, D., Ye, X., & Stancavage, F. (2004, April). Prepared to teach: Teacher preparation and student achievement in eighth-grade mathematics. Paper presented at the Annual Meeting of the American Educational Research Association, San Diego, CA. Retrieved from http://www.air.org/news_events/documents/AERA-2004PreparedtoTeach.pdf

Harrison, A. G. (2006, May). *Recruiting and educating science teachers in Australia.* Paper presented at the Science, Technology, Engineering and Math—Alternative Certification for Teachers Conference, Arlington, VA. Retrieved from http://www.stemtec.org/act/

Ingersoll, R. (2004). *Why do high–poverty schools have difficulty staffing their classrooms with qualified teachers?* Washington, DC: Center for American Progress.

Kane, T. J., Rockoff, J. E., & Staiger, D. O. (2007). What does certification tell us about teacher effectiveness? Evidence from New York City. *Economics of Education Review, 27*(6), 615–631.

National Academy of Sciences. (2010). *Preparing teachers: Building evidence for sound policy.* Washington, DC: National Academy of Sciences Press.

Vázquez-Abad, J., & Charland, J. (May 2006). *Preparing science teachers for Québec's high–school at Université de Montréal.* Paper presented at the Science, Technology, Engineering and Math—Alternative Certification for Teachers Conference, Arlington, VA. Retrieved from http://www.stemtec.org/act/

6.6

Quality of Teaching

LAURA GOE
Educational Testing Service

Introduction

Quality of teaching has been defined and measured in a number of ways—by politicians, researchers, and teachers themselves. Quality of teaching is something of a moving target, with dramatic changes in recent years, in part because of the increasing availability of data linking teachers to their students' achievement test scores. In some research, the focus is on the quality of *teacher practice* (i.e., observed teachers' performance in the classroom, or artifacts of that performance such as lesson plans, assignments, and reflections on practice). Others may use the term *quality of teaching* to mean *successful teaching*; that is, teaching which can be directly linked to improvements in student learning (Fenstermacher & Richardson, 2005). Although the term *teacher quality* is often used interchangeably with *teaching quality*, *teacher* quality is more broadly viewed as not only teacher practice but also teachers' credentials (such as degrees, subject matter knowledge, license, etc.), and teachers' characteristics (gender, race, self-efficacy, resiliency, etc.). Thus, *teaching* quality can be viewed as a subset of *teacher* quality that focuses chiefly on teachers' instruction—both knowledge and delivery—and instructional artifacts. Further, *teaching* and *teacher* quality are also linked in research policy to a fairly new concept, *teacher effectiveness*, which is consistently defined as a teacher's contribution to measurable student learning.

Research Evidence

Recently, the conversation around teacher quality has taken an interesting turn. There are now many more requests for the inclusion of student achievement in teacher evaluation systems: Teachers are deemed effective if students achieve one year's growth in learning over the course of a school year.

Observing teaching practice and making some type of record of what was observed has been the standard method of evaluating teacher quality in most states and districts in the United States as well as many other countries. How that observation is done varies widely, from a drop-in evaluation lasting only minutes to a formal evaluation that is scheduled in advance and may include pre- and postobservation conferences between the teacher being observed and the evaluator. The instruments used by those observing teacher practice also vary greatly, from one-page checklists where a simple "yes" or "no" can be checked to indicate the presence or absence of something in the classroom or in the teacher's behavior and actions, to complex rubrics with multiple indicators and three to seven "levels" of performance. Other performance measures evaluate artifacts of teacher practice such as lesson plans, reflections on the lesson, and professional activities undertaken outside the classroom.

The attractiveness of using observation rubrics as the primary determinant of teaching quality may be changing in light of research. Studies on the relationship between teacher observation and actual student learning results have been mixed in terms of the correlation between scores on observation instruments and student achievement growth (for a review of research, see Goe, Bell, & Little, 2008). Concerns about how well teacher observation identifies good and poor teaching have been raised in such studies as the "Widget Effect" which examined results from teacher observations in several U.S. states and found that most teachers performed at the two highest levels on the observation instrument, despite large differences in achievement among these teachers' students (Weisberg, Sexton, Mulhern, & Keeling, 2009). Whether the observation instruments are not capturing what is important, or whether those conducting the observations are not adequately trained to recognize meaningful variations in teacher practice is open to debate. A study using observation data collected by highly trained observers did find some significant correlations between teachers' observation ratings and student achievement growth (Kane, Taylor, Tyler, & Wooten, 2010), suggesting that observer training is important in accurately differentiating among teachers.

Better measures and systems of measures may be needed to accurately capture differences in teaching quality. The CLASS instrument, developed at the University of Virginia, focuses on capturing differences among teachers that include the emotional supports teachers provide to students rather than just the instructional supports. In one of the CLASS studies, emotional supports were found to positively impact achievement, suggesting that instructional supports may be only part of what accounts for differences in teacher quality (Pianta, Belsky, Vandergrift, Houts, & Morrison, 2008), a conclusion in agreement with the finding by Kane et al. (2010) that the "learning environment" correlates more highly with student achievement than "instruction."

Other efforts are being made internationally to develop and pilot better measures of teacher quality. Formulated as a rejection of the inspectorate method as "not objective, reliable, or functional," an evaluation system developed in Turkey was designed to be "multiple data-driven, participatory, transparent, functional, objective, and reliable" (Koçak, 2006, p. 799).

There have been a number of studies that have reviewed the research on teacher quality relative to student outcomes (e.g., Goe, 2007; Wayne & Youngs, 2003). Reviewers examined qualifications, teacher characteristics, instructional practices, and student learning as measured by standardized test scores. Teacher experience up to 5 years, and mathematics expertise (as indicated by teaching certification in mathematics, a college major in mathematics, or number of mathematics courses in college) were correlated with higher achievement, but no other variables showed strong and consistent patterns across studies. Day, Sammons, Kingston, and Gu (2006) conducted research in England and found that two characteristics, teachers' commitment and resiliency, were correlated with student achievement. Research that focused on specific teacher practices and their connection to student learning include a study using data from the Third International Mathematics and Science Study. One result was that in classrooms where students had more opportunities to work collaboratively or to do actual experiments, achievement was higher (House, 2006).

With so much emphasis on assessing teaching quality and holding teachers accountable for not only their performance but also their students' success, there are some who worry about whether teachers are becoming demoralized by the constant scrutiny of their efforts. Larsen (2005) analyzed evaluation practices in the United States, Australia, England, and Canada and concluded that many evaluation models focus on the limited part of teachers' knowledge and practice that can be efficiently captured, ignoring the complex nature of teaching and inhibiting teachers' creativity, risk-taking (trying new teaching strategies) and flexibility in the classroom, as well as lowering morale and contributing to stress and anxiety among teachers. A study in Greece showed that teachers' perceptions of various measures used in the evaluation process varied by whether the measures were used for formative or summative purposes (Kyriakides, Demetriou, & Charalmbous, 2006). Teachers were most likely to rate measures negatively that focused on accountability, whereas they were more positive about measures used to examine their teaching processes.

Summary and Recommendations

The Gates Foundation has funded several large-scale studies in an attempt to get a better sense of the relationships among various measures of teacher qualifications, characteristics, and instructional practices (Gates Foundation, 2010). When the results of those studies are compiled, it should be possible to get a more accurate and nuanced view of the relationship among teacher qualifications, characteristics, practices, and student achievement growth. These studies include several observation instruments, tests of teachers' knowledge for teaching in particular subjects, measures of teacher self-efficacy, student surveys, student work samples, pre- and posttests, standardized achievement tests, and more. In recent years, researchers from around the world have demonstrated that there are large differences in the quality of teaching as evidenced by student achievement linked to specific teachers. However, much less is known about the underlying reasons for those differences. The future of research in this area will be in the complex, classroom-level work of sorting out what makes some teachers more effective than others.

Teacher quality may be enhanced by several aligned strategies:

- **Teacher preparation** programs should consider establishing "feedback loops" that will allow them to gather information on their graduates' performance in their placement schools and then use that information to improve the program. Working directly with schools where their teachers are placed as well as with novice teachers' principals and mentors, the preparation programs should gather information about whether the novice teachers are well-prepared for the contexts and challenges they teach in, and whether they are able to effectively deliver instruction, engage students, and create a structured learning environment. In addition, results from novice teachers' evaluation (such as observation scores) and their students' achievement results should inform teacher preparation programs' strategies for improving preparation.
- **Professional development** varies widely in topic and delivery, but there is limited evidence of its impact on teaching quality, which may be partly due to poor study design and measures (Desimone, 2009). However, some types of professional development may be more likely to lead to changes in teacher practice than others. A study by the Teacher Training Center for International Educators (2007) determined that professional development was more likely to lead to change in teacher practice if it was job-embedded and aligned with school priorities.

To better understand the role of professional development in improving teaching quality, it is necessary to conduct studies that link participation in professional development to changes in teacher practice and then to changes in student achievement.

- **Teacher evaluation** should include multiple measures of teacher performance (such as observations, student achievement, surveys, portfolios, student work samples, etc.) rather than just one measure (Goe et al., 2008). There is no single measure that alone captures everything that is important in the complex activity of teacher and learning. Teachers are expected not only to ensure that students learn at high levels, they are also responsible for instilling values such as cooperativeness, respect for others, and citizenship. By using multiple measures, a more complete picture of individual teachers' and groups of teachers' strengths and weaknesses across the full scope of their responsibilities can be developed, and professional growth plans targeted to teachers' specific needs can be more accurately created.

References

Day, C., Sammons, P., Kington, A., & Gu, Q. (2006). Methodological synergy in a national project: The VITAE story. *Evaluation and Research in Education, 19*(2), 102–125.

Desimone, L. M. (2009). Improving impact studies of teachers' professional development: Toward better conceptualizations and measures. *Educational Researcher, 38*(3), 181–199.

Fenstermacher, G. D., & Richardson, V. (2005). On making determinations of quality in teaching. *Teachers College Record, 107*(1), 186–213.

Gates Foundation. (2010). *Measures of effective teaching (MET) Project: Working with teachers to develop fair and reliable measures of effective teaching.* Seattle, WA: Author.

Goe, L. (2007). *The link between teacher quality and student outcomes: A research synthesis.* Washington, DC: National Comprehensive Center for Teacher Quality.

Goe, L., Bell, C., & Little, O. (2008). *Approaches to evaluating teacher effectiveness: A research synthesis.* Washington, DC: National Comprehensive Center for Teacher Quality.

House, J. D. (2006). The effects of classroom instructional strategies on science achievement of elementary–school students in Japan: Findings from the Third International Mathematics and Science Study (TIMSS). *International Journal of Instructional Media, 33*(2), 217–229.

Kane, T. J., Taylor, E. S., Tyler, J. H., & Wooten, A. L. (2010). *Identifying effective classroom practices using student achievement data.* Cambridge, MA: National Bureau of Economic Research.

Koçak, R. (2006). The validity and reliability of the teachers' performance evaluation scale. *Educational Sciences: Theory & Practice, 6*(3), 799–808.

Kyriakides, L., Demetriou, D., & Charalmbous, C. (2006). Generating criteria for evaluating teachers through teacher effectiveness research. *Educational Research 48*(1), 1–20.

Larsen, M. A. (2005). A critical analysis of teacher evaluation policy trends. *Australian Journal of Education, 49*(3), 292–305.

Pianta, R., Belsky, J., Vandergrift, N., Houts, R., & Morrison, F. J. (2008). Classroom effects on children's achievement trajectories in elementary school. *American Educational Research Journal, 45*(2), 365–397.

Teacher Training Center for International Educators (2007). Professional development that makes a difference. *International Educator, 22*(2), 33.

Wayne, A. J., & Youngs, P. (2003). Teacher characteristics and student achievement gains: A review. *Review of Educational Research, 73*(1), 89–122.

Weisberg, D., Sexton, S., Mulhern, J., & Keeling, D. (2009). *The widget effect: Our national failure to acknowledge and act on differences in teacher effectiveness.* Brooklyn, NY: The New Teacher Project.

6.7

Methods for Studying Teacher and Teaching Effectiveness

ALEXANDER GRÖSCHNER AND TINA SEIDEL
Technische Universität, München, Germany

RICHARD J. SHAVELSON
Stanford University

Introduction

Although there is only limited empirical evidence of direct effects of teachers and teaching on student learning (D'Agostino & Powers, 2009; Nye, Konstantopoulos, & Hedges, 2004), there have been substantial advances in teacher- and teaching-effectiveness models, research designs, and corresponding statistical methods over the past 50 years. These changes, once again, demonstrate that developments in theory and method go hand-in-hand in moving a field forward. We suspect that these advances will lead to improvements in our capacity to explain processes of teachers and teaching that link to student learning.

Research Evidence

Whereas the 1960s research on teacher effectiveness concentrated on aspects of teacher personality, the 1970s and 1980s were characterized by a strong focus on teaching and teacher behavior in classrooms. In the process-product paradigm, teacher behavior was modeled as process variables (teacher use of reinforcement, higher-order questioning, etc.), whereas student characteristics and outcomes were included as presage and product variables (e.g., Shavelson, Webb, & Burstein, 1986). As Seidel and Shavelson (2007) pointed out, almost all reviews and meta-analyses in teacher- and teaching-effectiveness research have been based on this model. During the 1990s research shifted toward opportunity-to-learn models based on the assumption that learning is a set of constructive processes in which the individual student activates, elaborates, and organizes knowledge in a self-regulated way. Teaching, from this perspective, is considered to be providing opportunities for students to be actively engaged in activities that promote higher-order learning. Teacher characteristics in this model influence the way learning opportunities are constructed

in the process of teaching. Effects of teachers on student learning, thus, are modeled as being mediated by the process of teaching.

Taking into account recent models of teacher and teaching effectiveness it is necessary to distinguish between methods for studying *teacher effectiveness* and *teaching effectiveness*. Due to the focus on methodological approaches in this entry we are limited in describing these fields of study and empirical findings. Therefore, we concentrate on key findings including outlines and analyses of methodical approaches and research designs. Before proceeding, we want to clarify some vocabulary. We speak of *teacher effectiveness* when we refer to teacher characteristics and qualifications as predictors of teaching and student achievement. We speak of *teaching effectiveness* when referring to the effects of teaching on student learning.

Methods for Studying Teacher Effectiveness.
A chapter about methods for studying teacher effectiveness should capture quantitative as well as qualitative approaches. In this chapter we will focus on quantitative methods that predominantly use standardized measures to investigate teacher effectiveness. Furthermore, we focus on the interplay between theoretical concepts about expected effects of teachers on student learning and research designs and instruments used for measurement.

Teacher effectiveness methods have long been focused on rather distal indicators such as state certification, teacher qualifications (college ratings, test scores, degrees) and course attendance (Wayne & Youngs, 2003). Thereby, teacher characteristics are considered as prerequisites and interpreted in relation to their effectiveness on student achievement. The designs are typically correlational. In "value-added" models, however, it is assumed that teachers add to students' progress during a certain period of time (e.g. between a pre- and posttest). But teacher effects in this model need to be carefully considered with regard to the kind of effects that reasonably can or cannot be estimated with this approach (National Research Council [NRC]/ National Academy of Education [NAE], 2010). Wayne and Youngs (2003) summarize that in the case of teachers' college ratings and test scores positive relations with student achievement exist, whereas in the case of degrees, coursework, and certification findings are mostly inconclusive (Wayne & Youngs, 2003, p. 107).

In contrast to these distal measures and causal interpretations, teacher effectiveness research increasingly is focused on teacher variables proximal to supporting students' executive learning activities (Hill, Rowan, & Ball, 2005). Based on opportunity-to-learn models, mediating processes between teacher knowledge, teaching in classrooms, and student learning are considered in research designs and analytic methods. An example for this kind of research is represented in the study of Baumert and colleagues (2010), in which student progress is measured by means of a pre- and posttest, teacher knowledge by means of a standardized test on teacher content knowledge (CK), and pedagogical content knowledge (PCK), and teaching by means of standardized student questionnaires on teaching quality. By using a multilevel structural equation model these researchers found that content knowledge is systematically related to pedagogical content knowledge, that teacher knowledge positively and directly is related to teaching quality, and teaching quality also is related to student progress in mathematics. The findings in this field indicate that the complexity of teaching and learning in classrooms requires high rigor in developing models and applying appropriate research designs. Furthermore, concerted effort is required in developing instruments that assess teacher competencies in a valid and reliable way.

Methods for Studying Teaching Effectiveness. In teaching effectiveness research a number of teaching variables have been identified repeatedly that show substantial impact on student learning. These refer to teaching components that were shown empirically to impact student learning such as structure and coherence, feedback, adaptive instruction, time-on-task, and teacher support and guidance. Seidel and Shavelson (2007) highlight the necessity of disentangling the rather heterogeneous research designs and methods as applied in teaching effectiveness research. By disentangling results of a meta-analysis based on research design and methods, two main streams of teaching effectiveness research were found, one focusing on large-scale surveys including a variety of teaching and student variables, and a second using experimental and quasi-experimental designs with a focus on single teaching components. With regard to effects of teaching on student learning Seidel and Shavelson concluded that studies with a focus on supporting domain-specific learning activities of students (e.g., mathematical argumentation, scientific inquiry) show the strongest effects on student learning. These studies were mainly conducted by means of quasi-experimental or experimental research designs.

In applying opportunity-to-learn models, recent studies use complex research designs in which teaching, for example, is measured by means of different perspectives (teacher, students, experts), by multiple data sources (video, questionnaires, interviews) and multiple measuring points (during a school year, term, teaching unit). In addition, student learning is assessed by multiple criteria referring to learning processes, cognitive outcomes, and motivational-affective outcomes. An example for such an approach is the study of Seidel, Rimmele, and Prenzel (2005) in which video analysis of lesson clarity and coherence is systematically linked to student perceptions of the supportiveness of this learning environment, learning motivation and student progress in knowledge and interest over the course of one school calendar. They found that high lesson clarity and coherence was systematically related to the students' perception of the learning environment as supportive, intrinsic learning motivation, and achievement progress.

Given that teaching effectiveness research represents a rather heterogeneous field with distinctive research designs and methods, a trend toward reviews of specific teaching components can be observed. These teaching components, for example, refer to cooperative learning (Slavin, 1998), feedback (Hattie & Timperley, 2007), or inquiry-based science instruction (Minner, Levy, & Century, 2010). These reviews and meta-analyses contribute to a specific analysis of advances in the field and help to interpret and explain findings in the complex setting of teaching and learning.

Summary and Recommendations

The aim of this entry was to describe the state-of-art of methodical approaches in studying teacher and teaching effectiveness. A key development in the field is the use of complex models of teaching and learning, representing the relations between teachers, teaching, and student learning. These models are applied by using comprehensive research designs and including multiple indicators and measurement instruments. Recent meta-analyses and reviews emphasize that it is worth this effort because methods and indicators of measurement drive the effect sizes to be yielded in research studies. For future research an expansion of the single focus on student achievement towards the multi-dimensionality of student learning is emphasized. As research has shown, practitioners are challenged when managing complex teacher-student interactions. Scientific knowledge may help teachers develop adaptive strategies to scaffold student learning as well as to motivate teachers when they attend professional teacher development programs.

References

Baumert, J., Kunter, M., Blum, W., Brunner, M., Voss, T., Jordan, A., … Tsai, Y.-M. (2010). Teachers' mathematical knowledge, cognitive activation in the classroom, and student progress. *American Educational Research Journal, 47*(1), 133–180.

D'Agostino, J. V., & Powers, S. J. (2009). Predicting teacher performance with test scores and grade point average: A meta-analysis. *American*

Educational Research Journal, 46(1), 146–182. Hattie, J., & Timperley, H. (2007). The power of feedback. *Review of Educational Research, 77*(1), 81–112.

Hill, H. C., Rowan, B., & Ball, D. L. (2005). Effects of teachers' mathematical knowledge for teaching on student achievement. *American Educational Research Journal, 42*(2), 371–406.

Minner, D. D., Levy, A. J., & Century, J. (2010). Inquiry-based science instruction—What is it and does it matter? Results from a research synthesis years 1984 to 2002. *Journal of Research in Science Teaching, 47*(4), 474–496.

National Research Council (NRC) and National Academy of Education (NAE). (2010). *Getting value out of value-added: Report of a workshop*. Washington, DC: National Academies Press.

Nye, B., Konstantopoulos, S., & Hedges, L. V. (2004). How large are teacher effects? *Educational Evaluation and Policy Analysis, 26*(3), 237–257.

Shavelson, R. J., Webb, N. M., & Burstein, L. (1986). Measurement of teaching. In M. Wittrock (Ed.), *Handbook of research on teaching* (pp. 50–91). New York: Macmillan.

Seidel, T., Rimmele, R., & Prenzel, M. (2005). Clarity and coherence of lesson goals as a scaffold for student learning. *Learning and Instruction, 15*, 539–556.

Seidel, T., & Shavelson, R. (2007). Teaching effectiveness research in the past decade: The role of theory and research design in disentangling meta-analysis results. *Review of Educational Research, 77*(4), 454–499.

Slavin, R. E. (1998). Research on cooperative learning and achievement: What we know, what we need to know. *Contemporary Educational Psychology, 21*(1), 43–69.

Wayne, A. J., & Youngs, P. (2003). Teacher characteristics and student achievement gains: A review. *Review of Educational Research, 73*(1), 89–122.

6.8

Teachers' Expectations

LEE JUSSIM
Rutgers University

Introduction

Research on teacher expectations has sparked a slew of controversies that are reviewed here in order to identify what is (and is not) well-established on the basis of the evidence. The term *teacher expectations* has referred to a family of related constructs, including predictions about students' future performance, beliefs about students' current levels of ability or performance, and beliefs about "normative" behavior. Teacher expectations, however they are defined, can relate to student achievement in three distinct ways: accuracy, bias, and self-fulfilling prophecy.

Accuracy refers to teacher expectations predicting or reflecting student achievement without having caused that achievement. For example, students' achievement in prior years typically correlates about .4 to .8 with current year teacher expectations (Brophy, 1983; Jussim & Harber, 2005). Similarly, teacher expectations predict *without causing* future student achievement far more than they cause future achievement; that is, the main reason teacher expectations predict student achievement is that they are accurate (e.g., Trouilloud, Sarrazin, Martinek, & Guillet, 2002).

Bias occurs when teachers' expectations unduly influence or distort teachers' own evaluations of students. For example, if a teacher overestimates a student's academic competence, that teacher may evaluate the student's performance more positively than the same teacher evaluates identical work produced by a student whose academic competence the teacher underestimates. These types of expectancy biases influence *the teacher's judgments* about students' learning or achievement, but they do not influence students' actual learning or achievement. Nonetheless, bias can influence *apparent* achievement, because, if teachers' expectations influence their evaluations, they can also influence grades (e.g., Jussim, 1989; Williams, 1976).

A *self-fulfilling prophecy* occurs when a perceiver's originally false expectation leads to its own actual (not merely perceived) confirmation (Merton, 1948). In educational contexts, this refers to a teacher's erroneous expectation leading to its own fulfillment. This occurs when the erroneous expectation leads the teacher to behave differently toward high and low expectancy students, and when those students' achievement changes from what it otherwise would have been to confirm the teacher's expectation. Thus, the high expectancy students achieve at higher levels, and the low expectancy students achieve at lower levels (or learns less) than they would have had a self-fulfilling prophecy not occurred. The overwhelming majority of research on teacher expectations has examined their potentially self-fulfilling effects.

Research Evidence

The study of teacher expectations was launched by the classic and controversial Pygmalion study (Rosenthal & Jacobson, 1968). Rosenthal and Jacobson led teachers to believe that some students in their classes were "late bloomers" who were destined to show dramatic increases in IQ over the year. In fact, these students had been selected at random. Results showed that, especially in the earlier grades, the "late bloomers" gained more in IQ. Teacher expectations created a self-fulfilling prophecy.

Rosenthal and Jacobson's study (1968) received considerable attention in some circles and in the popular press because it seemed to provide a powerful explanation for the low achievement of "disadvantaged" students. However, it was also criticized on conceptual, methodological, and statistical grounds (see Jussim, Robustelli, & Cain, 2009; Wineburg, 1987 for reviews).

Much of the controversy over the existence of self-fulfilling prophecies was resolved by Rosenthal and Rubin's (1978) meta-analysis of experimental studies of interpersonal expectancy effects. The expectancy effect size was equal to a correlation of about .30 between teacher expectations and achievement, and the probability of finding the observed expectancy effects, if the phenomenon did not exist, was essentially zero.

The Rosenthal and Rubin (1978) left open the question of the extent to which self-fulfilling prophecies occur naturally, without experimental intervention. To what extent, then, do naturally occurring teacher expectations create self-fulfilling prophecies? Jussim et al. (2009) reviewed the effect sizes obtained in every published naturalistic study of teacher expectations within a school. Nearly all of these studies used standardized achievement tests as an objective outcome. On average, two conclusions are warranted by these reviews: (a) self-fulfilling prophecies have been found sufficiently often in naturalistic research that it currently seems reasonable to conclude that they are indeed very widespread; and (b) under naturalistic conditions, the effect size is typically quite modest (e.g., an effect size of $r = .1$ means that a one standard deviation increase in teacher expectations would produce, on average, the equivalent of about a 10 point increase on the SATs).

The most stunning claim that emerged from Rosenthal and Jacobson's (1968) study was that teacher expectations have self-fulfilling effects on intelligence (rather than mere achievement). This claim remains controversial today, with some scientists concluding that there is no self-fulfilling effect on intelligence (e.g., Snow, 1994; Wineburg, 1987) and others concluding that the effect is real (e.g., Raudenbush, 1984). Regardless of which conclusion one believes, one thing is certain: There is no evidence that teacher expectations generally have large and dramatic effects on IQ.

Self-sustaining prophecies are a subtype of self-fulfilling prophecies in which teachers' expectations lead students to continue to perform at a level which otherwise would have changed. Researchers have periodically speculated that such effects might be more likely to occur than those that involve changing students' achievement (Cooper, 1979; Kuklinski & Weinstein, 2002). Although this may be true, it is also true that in naturalistic studies, the effect size for self-sustaining prophecies can be no larger than the effect size for self-fulfilling prophecies. This must be true for a set of logical and statistical reasons that can only be summarized here: (a) Self-sustaining effects occur because prior achievement affects teacher expectations, which in turn affect future achievement. (b) Both relationships (of prior achievement to teacher expectations, and of teacher expectations to future achievement) are always partial and imperfect (teachers do not hold equally high expectations for all students with equally high prior achievement; high teacher expectations do not produce identically high future achievement among all students); so that (c) the combined effect (of prior achievement on teacher expectations, and of expectations on future achievement) must be lower (for the statistically inclined, this functions just as do conditional probabilities) than the effect, by itself, of teacher expectations on students' future achievement (see Jussim, 1991). Thus, although self-sustaining effects undoubtedly occur, in general, they are probably even more modest than the already modest average self-fulfilling prophecy effect sizes found in most naturalistic research.

Moderators: Under What Conditions are Teacher Expectations Most (and Least) Likely to Produce Self-Fulfilling Prophecies?

Timing of False Expectations. Studies that induce false teacher expectations experimentally are considerably more likely to produce self-fulfilling prophecies if that induction takes place very early in the school year (e.g., Raudenbush, 1984). This probably occurs because teachers can be more readily influenced by false information before they get to know their students; once teachers do get to know their students, the false information has little effect on their expectations.

Age and New Situations. Raudenbush's (1984) meta-analysis also found that the strongest teacher expectation effects occurred in first, second, and seventh grades. A simple "younger children are more susceptible" hypothesis can account for the grades 1 and 2 effect, but not for the grade 7 effect. Another possibility is that people are most susceptible to self-fulfilling prophecies when they enter new situations—and people in general may be more vulnerable to all sorts of social influences in situations with which they are not familiar (see Jussim & Harber, 2005, for a review). In the classroom, however, even these relatively more powerful effects between first, second, and seventh graders only averaged about $r = .2$.

Positive versus Negative Expectancy Effects. The social science and educational literature is peppered with suggestions that the self-fulfilling prophecies produced by teacher expectations typically do more harm than good (e.g., Jussim & Harber, 2005; Weinstein, Gregory, & Strambler, 2004). Unfortunately, the evidence does not support such a pessimistic conclusion. This is primarily because that evidence is quite sparse, and because even that sparse evidence provides a decidedly mixed picture, with a handful of small studies showing negative effects are indeed more powerful, and one large-scale study showing that positive effects are more powerful (see Jussim & Harber, 2005, for a review).

Student Stigmatization. Students who belong to stigmatized groups may be particularly vulnerable to self-fulfilling prophecies. This seems to be true of both low achievers and students belonging to stigmatized demographic groups. Erroneously high teacher expectations for previously low achieving students, produced self-fulfilling prophecy effect sizes of $r = .3.4$, but self-fulfilling prophecy effect sizes of near zero among high achievers. Similarly, teacher expectations produced self-fulfilling prophecy effects of near zero for White or middle SES students, but effects of $r = .2$ to $.6$ among low SES, African American, and low achieving/low SES students (see Jussim & Harber, 2005). There have, however, only been a handful of studies and, clearly, more research is needed.

Accumulation. Many reviews and perspectives have suggested that empirical studies underestimate self-fulfilling prophecies, because expectancy effects may accumulate over time or over multiple perceivers .(see Jussim & Harber, 2005 for a review). Many targets may be subjected to the same or similar erroneous expectations over and over again. If those expectations are consistently self-fulfilling, effects that are small in one context can become huge over long periods. Despite the compelling nature of the accumulation story, the evidence does not support it (see Jussim & Harber, 2005). Research has distinguished between two types of accumulation. *Concurrent accumulation* refers to accumulation of self-fulfilling prophecies over multiple teachers at the same time. The typically modest self-fulfilling prophecy effects found in studies between a teacher and a student fully capture the accumulation of self-fulfilling prophecy effects across all teachers (i.e., even those whose expectations were not directly assessed) sharing that teacher's erroneous expectation at the same time (explaining why, statistically, this is inherently true is beyond the scope of this entry, but is explained in Jussim & Harber, 2005). Thus, even if self-fulfilling prophecies do accumulate across multiple teachers, the total effects are quite modest.

Accumulation over time occurs when a self-fulfilling prophecy process triggered by a teacher's expectations at one time continues so that a teacher's initial false belief more strongly influences students over time. The evidence regarding accumulation over time is even clearer: it has never been found. Every study that has assessed whether the self-fulfilling prophecies produced by teacher expectations accumulate over time has, instead, found that they dissipate over time. Although such self-fulfilling prophecies dissipate rather than accumulate over time, their effects can be quite long-lasting, detectable (to a lesser extent) many years after they first occurred (see Jussim & Harber, 2005).

Processes. Self-fulfilling prophecies start with inaccurate expectations. Although teacher expectations are generally quite accurate (Brophy, 1983; Jussim et al, 2009), they are rarely perfectly accurate. Social stereotypes, unjustified diagnostic labels, and bona fide student changes can all be sources of inaccuracy in expectations. These effects should not be overstated, because the existing research strongly suggests that, for the most part, teachers' perceptions of differences between students from different demographic groups are quite accurate, and labels (e.g., "learning disabled") are usually applied appropriately. When applied inappropriately, however, they can be sources of inaccurate expectations.

Self-fulfilling prophecies occur, in large part, because teachers hold high expectancy students to higher standards of performance and, at the same time, provide a warmer and more supportive environment to them (Jussim et al., 2009). Differential treatment can lead to self-fulfilling prophecies through either or both of two general routes. High standards means providing high expectancy students with more opportunities to master difficult material. When

coupled with the support for doing so, highs may simply learn more material more quickly.

In addition, however, differential treatment also may indirectly affect achievement, by enhancing or undermining motivation. The logic of student motivation at least partially mediating effects of teacher expectations on student achievement is clear and compelling. High standards and emotional support are likely to increase students' psychological investment in school, intrinsic motivation, and self-expectations, all of which have well-established beneficial effects on achievement. Despite the apparent obviousness of such a process, it has, in fact, been extraordinarily difficult for research to empirically demonstrate that student motivation actually does mediate very much of the effect of teacher expectations on student achievement (Jussim et al, 2009). Whether this is the case because motivation is unimportant (which seems very unlikely) or because empirical research has not yet discovered the important motivational processes, is currently unclear.

Summary and Recommendations

First, teachers should take considerable comfort from the empirical evidence that, in contrast to some of the more extreme claims, shows that, in general, expectancy effects are small, fragile, and fleeting, rather than large, pervasive, and enduring. Second, any recommendation suggesting that teachers should simply adopt high expectations for all students would be oversimplified, unworkable, and probably dysfunctional. High expectations *can* work at raising student achievement, but only if they are backed up with the resources and institutional supports to do so.

The most constructive lessons to be learned for teachers from the research are the following:

1. Hold expectations flexibly. You might be wrong. The student's label might be wrong. Also, students change.
2. Holding high standards without providing a warm environment is merely harsh. A warm environment without high standards lacks backbone. But if you can create a combination of high standards with a warm and supportive environment it will benefit all students, not just the high achievers.
3. High expectations will mean different things for different students. Attaining average performance might be high for one student and low for another. If teachers want to purposely harness expectancy effects to maximize student achievement, they need to couple a high expectation (for that student) with a clear plan for how that student will maximize his or her learning and achievement.

References

Brophy, J. (1983). Research on the self–fulfilling prophecy and teacher expectations. *Journal of Educational Psychology, 75,* 631–661.
Cooper, H. (1979). Pygmalion grows up: A model for teacher expectation

communication, and performance influence. *Review of Educational Research, 49,* 389–410.

Jussim, L. (1991). Social perception and social reality: A reflection–construction model. *Psychological Review, 98,* 54–73.

Jussim, L., & Harber, K. (2005). Teacher expectations and self–fulfilling prophecies: Knowns and unknowns; resolved and unresolved controversies. *Personality and Social Psychology Review, 9,* 131–135.

Jussim, L., Robustelli, S., & Cain, T. (2009). Teacher expectations and self–fulfilling prophecies. In A. Wigfield & K. Wentzel (Eds.), *Handbook of motivation at school* (pp. 349–380). Mahwah, NJ: Erlbaum..

Merton, R. K. (1948). The self–fulfilling prophecy. *Antioch Review, 8,* 193–210.

Raudenbush, S. W. (1984). Magnitude of teacher expectancy effects on pupil IQ as a function of the credibility of expectancy inductions: A synthesis of findings from 18 experiments. *Journal of Educational Psychology, 76,* 85–97.

Rosenthal, R., & Jacobson, L. (1968a). *Pygmalion in the classroom: Teacher expectations and student intellectual development.* New York: Holt, Rinehart, & Winston.

Rosenthal R., & Rubin, D. B. (1978). Interpersonal expectancy effects: The first 345 studies. *The Behavioral and Brain Sciences, 3,* 377–386.

Snow, R. E. (1995). Pygmalion and intelligence? *Current Directions in Psychological Science, 4,* 169–171.

Trouilloud, D., Sarrazin, P., Martinek, T., & Guillet, E. (2002). The influence of teacher expectations on students' achievement in physical education classes: Pygmalion revisited. *European Journal of Social Psychology, 32,* 1–17.

Weinstein, R. S., Gregory, A., & Strambler, M. J. (2004). Intractable self–fulfilling prophecies: Fifty years after Brown v. Board of Education. *American Psychologist, 59,* 511–520.

Williams, T. (1976). Teacher prophecies and the inheritance of inequality. *Sociology of Education, 49,* 223–236.

Wineburg, S. S. (1987). The self–fulfillment of the self–fulfilling prophecy: A critical appraisal. *Educational Researcher, 16,* 28–40.

6.9

Teacher Enthusiasm and Student Learning

Melanie Keller
University of Konstanz, Germany

Knut Neumann
Leibniz Institute for Science and Mathematics Education, Germany

Hans E. Fischer
University of Duisburg-Essen, Germany

Introduction

When asking preservice teachers which characteristics comprise an effective teacher, "enthusiasm for teaching" comes up as the second most important factor, surpassed only by "being student-oriented" (Witcher & Onwuegbuzie, 2001). Preservice teachers describe enthusiasm as the possession of an unwavering love of the subject and of teaching and demonstrating commitment to the job. This view of the importance of enthusiasm is shared by many researchers, and consequently, enthusiasm is listed as a key determinant of effective teaching in major reviews of related research (e.g., Brophy & Good, 1986). In university settings, where student ratings are used for evaluation of instructors, enthusiasm is not only a common aspect of multifaceted teacher evaluation instruments (e.g., Marsh, 1994) but even more so a desirable and defining characteristic of good teachers.

Usually, teacher enthusiasm is considered to be a special mode of delivering information to students (cf. Kunter et al., 2008). A teacher is perceived as being enthusiastic when he or she succeeds in communicating excitement about the subject to students. Notions of enthusiasm can vary considerably: most of them consider only the "delivery" aspect and adopt a behavioral approach that relates enthusiasm mainly to a teacher's expressiveness (such as gestures, vocal delivery, or facial expressions; e.g., Collins, 1978). Other notions define enthusiasm as a component of a teacher's personal characteristics or even an aspect of professional competence and view expressive behaviors only as the manifestation of an underlying quality or characteristic of enthusiasm (Kunter et al., 2008; see also Frenzel, Goetz, Lüdtke, Pekrun, & Sutton, 2009 on the relation between teacher *enjoyment* and enthusiasm).

Teacher enthusiasm is considered to be an important component of classroom life, not merely because teachers, researchers, and students all believe that it is, but more tangibly because it has the power to positively influence student outcomes (Brigham, Scruggs, & Mastropieri, 1992; Patrick, Hisley, & Kempler, 2000; Rosenshine, 1970).

Research Evidence

In Rosenshine's (1970) review of research on teacher enthusiasm prior to 1970, it is clear that student achievement was the focus for the studies included. Two research designs were distinguished: high inference and low inference studies. In the high inference studies, the level of a teacher's enthusiasm is determined via students' perceptions or external observers; this is usually done on high-inferential indicators such as bipolar adjectives (e.g., dull vs. stimulating). Teachers deemed more enthusiastic were compared to less enthusiastic ones with regard to students' achievement. Findings favored enthusiastic teachers: student achievement was higher for students of more enthusiastic teachers. Summarizing the low-inference studies, three types of behaviors corresponding to enthusiastic teaching could be identified: teachers' expressiveness, praise, and the types of questions a teacher asked in class.

Researchers made important advances in identifying these low-inference behaviors by defining eight indicators for enthusiasm in reference to teachers' expressiveness: varying the speed and tone of voice; maintaining eye contact with the group; using demonstrative gestures; movements of the body and in space; exhibiting a lively facial expression; choosing highly descriptive and illustrative words; being eager in accepting students' ideas and feelings; and maintaining general vitality and drive throughout the lesson (Collins, 1978). The majority of the following studies used these enthusiasm indicators and employed them in experimental settings. Teachers were trained to perform high or low on particular enthusiasm indicators and behaviors. After ascertaining the effectiveness of the training, students were assigned to either a trained and therefore enthusiastic teacher or alternatively to a teacher with no training. Again, with respect to achievement, results favored those students in the enthusiastic condition (e.g., Brigham et al., 1992). There have been studies, however, that fail to demonstrate the expected relation between teacher enthusiasm and student achievement, but this failure has been attributed to design-related and methodological issues rather than to the construct of enthusiasm itself (e.g., Bettencourt, Gillet, Gall, & Hull, 1983). Nevertheless, a general positive influence of teacher enthusiasm on students' achievement seems to be an established relation, even though research investigating this effect is rather old. This positive effect is also supported by ample evidence that enthusiastic teachers are perceived by students to be more effective (cf. Feldman, 2007). Further studies show that teacher enthusiasm positively influences not only students' achievement, but also their behavioral (e.g., on-task behavior, Brigham et al., 1992) and affective outcomes (e.g., intrinsic motivation, Patrick et al., 2000).

Although research has supported the conclusion that enthusiasm influences student outcomes, exactly how this dynamic works remains unclear; there is not yet any empirical evidence conveying such a mechanism. However, various ideas and explanations can be found throughout literature, essentially highlighting three possible mechanisms. One is that enthusiastic teacher behaviors increase student attention, which serves as a mediator between enthusiasm and student achievement. One possibility is that teaching in an enthusiastic way provides "stimulus characteristics likely to attract and hold the attention of students" (Bettencourt et al., 1983, p. 446). This explanation is especially likely when enthusiastic behaviors are defined mainly as expressive, nonverbal behaviors because the attention-commanding role of such behaviors is established (cf. Bettencourt et al., 1983). In a second possible mechanism (see also Frenzel et al., 2009), the teacher serves as a kind of role model for his or her students; thereby, students are able to adopt the teachers' attitudes (e.g. enjoyment and enthusiasm) for themselves and "therefore concentrate more, think about the topic more, associate more positive feelings toward the subject, and consequently achieve more" (Brigham et al., 1992, p. 73). A third suggestion is that students "catch" their teachers' emotions and consequently experience these emotions themselves (*emotional contagion*; cf. Hatfield, Cacioppo, & Rapson, 1994). When it comes to achievement, the influence of enthusiasm is possibly twofold: the nonverbal part of teacher enthusiasm has a positive effect on students' attention, whereas the enthusiastic teacher, serving as a role model in exhibiting enjoyment and engagement, has a positive effect on students' motivation and academic emotions. Therefore, student behaviors and states related both to attention and motivation might serve as conduits through which the influence of enthusiasm on achievement can be explained.

Concerning the causal relation between teacher enthusiasm and student achievement, experimental studies conducted to evaluate the effect of enthusiasm on students support the idea that the direction of causality is from enthusiasm to achievement. In this kind of study, indicators for enthusiasm are set in advance for teacher training. In parallel, observers rate the teachers' behavior on these indicators before and after the teacher training to ascertain its effectiveness. In an experimental control group design, the effect of teacher enthusiasm on students' outcomes is investigated. The majority of these studies report successful training of teachers' enthusiasm, with the experimental group outperforming the control group in terms of their respective students' outcomes (e.g. Bettencourt et al., 1983; Brigham et al., 1992; Patrick et al., 2000).

Correspondingly, the reverse effect of student achievement and motivation on teachers' enthusiasm seems intuitive: a teacher, who is confronted with highly interested, motivated high-achievers, would be presumably more enthusiastic than a teacher confronted with less interested, lower-achieving students (Stenlund, 1995). Other authors also suggest that students' behavior, achievement, and motivation may affect teachers' enthusiasm (e.g. Frenzel et al., 2009; Patrick et al., 2000). As with most human interactions, the effects are likely reciprocal.

Summary and Recommendations

The evidence presented in this chapter supports the importance of teacher enthusiasm when considering effective teaching and fostering meaningful learning. Regarding student achievement, however, the research results are rather old and new investigations are warranted. With respect to research on teacher enthusiasm in general, there are also limitations, especially related to how teacher enthusiasm is conceptualized. As mentioned before, the majority of the research considers enthusiasm as mainly expressive behavior whereas only one investigation explicitly conceptualizes it as a traitlike teacher characteristic (Kunter et al., 2008). Even though a relationship between the two notions is posited, it is not exactly supported empirically. Regarding conceptualization, one may inquire about the object of enthusiasm: what is a teacher enthusiastic *about* (cf. Kunter et al. 2008)? A behavioral notion, naturally, cannot provide insight into this question. Furthermore, the question of whether enthusiasm is something subject-specific also emerges: Can a teacher who teaches two subjects, for instance, be more enthusiastic about teaching one subject over the other? Does being enthusiastic about teaching have the same implications as being enthusiastic about the subject? Kunter et al. (2008) demonstrated that enthusiasm about teaching is a more powerful predictor when it comes to various teacher behaviors; in any case, more studies are needed investigating the relations between enthusiastic behaviors and a possible trait of enthusiasm.

In light of the research presented here, future studies

would need to consider an integrated model of teacher enthusiasm with a trait-like component as the "source." This component would need to be considered subject-specific and may also be tied to other teacher characteristics, such as subject matter knowledge or resilience (c.f. Kunter et al., 2008). Such personal traitlike enthusiasm manifests itself in nonverbal, expressive behaviors. Therefore, this manifestation and possible conditions for a successful transfer between traitlike and behavioral components need to be carefully investigated.

As presented at the beginning, expressive behaviors of teachers positively influence students, and trainings thereof have been successfully accomplished. As a possible practical application of these findings, teachers can be made aware and trained to be more expressive in order to engage their students. Teachers should understand that their positive attitude and feelings are transported to students (*emotional contagion*); a good and effective way of showing one's enthusiasm is being (nonverbally) expressive, perhaps excessively so, for example by using gestures to accentuate or illustrate some contents, exhibiting a lively facial expression, and avoiding being physically withdrawn (behind the desk or rigid posture). However, enthusiasm as expressive behavior is unlikely to hold student engagement over a long time if the students are otherwise not supported in their motivation and learning (cf. Patrick et al., 2000). Expressive behavior could, however, foster students' motivation and learning when first confronted with new subject matter, or could help bridge an otherwise dry topic (c.f. Frenzel et al., 2009). To identify possible long-term applications of enthusiasm in classroom practice, other ways enthusiasm manifests, in addition to expressiveness, need to be investigated. It seems plausible that enthusiasm could also be expressed through other engagement-, motivation- and contextualized teaching strategies. Once these potential means of expression are identified, they can be considered for the development of future teacher training.

References

Bettencourt, E. M., Gillet, M. H., Gall, M. D., & Hull, R. E. (1983). Effects of teacher enthusiasm training on students' on-task behavior and achievement. *American Educational Research Journal, 20*(3), 435–450.

Brigham, F. J., Scruggs, T. E., & Mastropieri, M. A. (1992). Teacher enthusiasm and learning disabilities classrooms: Effects on learning and behavior. *Learning Disabilities Research & Practice, 7*, 68–73.

Brophy, J., & Good, T. L. (1986). Teacher behavior and student achievement. In M. Wittrock (Ed.), *Handbook of research on teaching* (pp. 340–370). New York: Macmillan.

Collins, M. L. (1978). Effects of enthusiasm training on preservice elementary teachers. *Research in Teacher Education, 29*, 53–57.

Feldman, K. A. (2007). Identifying exemplary teachers and teaching: Evidence from student ratings. In R. P. Perry & J. C. Smart (Eds.), *The scholarship of teaching and learning in higher education: An evidence-based perspective* (pp. 93–143). Dordrecht, Netherlands: Springer.

Frenzel, A. C., Goetz, T., Lüdtke, O., Pekrun, R., & Sutton, R. E. (2009). Emotional transmission in the classroom: Exploring the relationship between teacher and student enjoyment. *Journal of Educational Psychology, 101*(3), 705–716.

Hatfield, E., Cacioppo, J. L., & Rapson, R. L. (1994). *Emotional contagion*. Cambridge, England: Cambridge University Press.

Kunter, M., Tsai, Y.-M., Klusmann, U., Brunner, M., Krauss, S., & Baumert, J. (2008). Students' and mathematics teachers' perceptions of teacher enthusiasm and instruction. *Learning and Instruction, 18*, 468–482.

Marsh, H. W. (1994). Weighting for the right criteria in the instructional development and effectiveness assessment (IDEA) system: Global and specific ratings of teaching effectiveness and their relation to course objectives. *Journal of Educational Psychology, 86*(4), 631–648.

Patrick, B. C., Hisley, J., & Kempler, T. (2000). "What's everybody so excited about?": The effects of teacher enthusiasm on student intrinsic motivation and vitality. *The Journal of Experimental Education, 68*(3), 217–236.

Rosenshine, B. (1970). Enthusiastic teaching: A research review. *School Review, 78*(4), 499–514.

Stenlund, K. V. (1995). Teacher perceptions across cultures: the impact of students on teacher enthusiasm and discouragement in a cross-cultural context. *The Alberta Journal of Educational Research, 41*(2), 145–161.

Witcher, A. E., Onwuegbuzie, A. J., & Minor, L. C. (2001). Characteristics of effective teachers: perceptions of preservice teachers. *Research in the Schools, 8*(2), 45–57.

6.10

Teachers' Cultural and Professional Identities and Student Outcomes

Revathy Kumar and Linda Alvarado
University of Toledo

Introduction

Teachers are members of cultural communities defined by, but not restricted to, nationality, race, ethnicity, class, religion, and language. Membership within these communities defines cultural identity and informs values, behaviors, and attitudes. Cultural identity develops over time within family, community, and school environments set within social and political contexts. Thus complex and multifaceted, it is simultaneously stable and shifting. The stable aspects of cultural identity stem from years of socialization. Consequent internalization of, and identification with, beliefs and values during their early stages of life are therefore resistant to change. Thus, choices that teachers make, actions they take, and experiences they value inside and outside the classroom are informed by past experiences, knowledge base, and learned value beliefs—their socialized cultural identities.

The study of teachers' cultural and professional identities draws from several disciplines, including developmental, educational, social, and cultural psychology; anthropology; sociology; and sociolinguistics. All adopt sociocultural perspectives of identity development. Several theories, among them social constructivist and sociocultural theories (e.g., Shewder, 1990), social-identity theory (Tajfel, 1978), and self-construal and possible-selves theory (Markus & Kitayama, 1991) view identity development as an ongoing process shaped through interactions in specific cultural contexts.

Research Evidence

Teachers bring cultural identities, values, and beliefs to school practice. The professional identity, "teacher," is embedded within subjective cultural identities. Teachers' identity construction is a process as, in the context of teaching, they negotiate long-held beliefs and values within their socially defined and institutionalized professional role as teachers. The two identities—cultural and profes-sional—are interwoven: Professional identity builds on the "relatively stable and enduring constellation of attributes, beliefs, values, motives, and experiences in terms of which people define themselves in a professional role" (Ibarra, 1999, pp. 764–765). Teachers' cultural identities (including prejudices toward, and biases regarding students different from themselves that influence classroom actions) do not necessarily result from conscious and rational decision-making processes. However, the values teachers promote in the classroom; cultural models they adopt for classroom discourses; and attributions they make for the successes and failures of students from varied backgrounds—all expressions of cultural and professional identities—profoundly affect students' academic achievements and psychological well-being.

White Teachers' Cultural Identity in the United States and Western Countries and Implications for Student Achievement. Dissonance between teachers' and students' cultural identities is a source of major concern for educators, because minority (e.g., ethnic, religious, lingual, and socioeconomic) and immigrant student populations are growing in North America (Canada and the United States), Europe, and Australia. Mainstream White teachers in these nations tend to be ill-equipped to meet these students' needs (Sleeter, 2001). Demographers predict that by 2035, half the United States' school-age population will be students of color. In contrast, the majority of teachers will be White, monolingual, middle-class women (U.S. Department of Education, National Center for Education Statistics, 2007). Many White teachers experience a deep ambivalence toward minority and immigrant students (Hollins & Torres-Guzman, 2005) not merely because teachers' and students' cultural identities differ; they feel ill-prepared to meet academic and psychosocial needs of minority and immigrant students because of how different cultural identities play out within the classroom context (Ladson-Billings, 2000).

Evidence indicates White teachers' cultural identity manifests in academic and behavioral expectations of students who differ culturally from mainstream identity. Across several Western countries (Tenenbaum & Ruck, 2007) student characteristics such as socioeconomic status, ethnicity, age, and motivation influenced teachers' susceptibility to biased achievement expectations. For example, Dutch teachers' expectations mediated the interaction between teachers' implicit prejudiced attitudes and students' ethnicity (Turkish, Moroccan, Dutch) on students' standardized math and text comprehension scores. Further, students who experienced negative teacher expectation bias were, after 5 years, in lower educational tracks, whereas students who experienced positive expectation bias were in higher educational tracks (van den Bergh, Denessen, Hornstra, Voeten, & Holland, 2010). Results of a study juxtaposing teachers' and students' ethnic identities (Rubie-Davis, Hattie, & Hamilton, 2006) found that White teachers in New Zealand significantly augmented White students' but not Māori students' achievement by providing more challenging tasks. Findings suggest that the difficulty White teachers experience in understanding their biases can debilitate student learning and achievement.

Social Reconstructionist and Sociocultural Perspectives of White Teachers' Cultural Identity.

In the United States, social scientists describe White identity as an invisible, taken-for-granted normative identity rooted in institutionalized social and economic privilege. Consequently, few White teachers think of extending cultural identity to themselves as a majority privileged group. This lack of reflection results in unquestioned acceptance and promotion of dominant cultural values present in texts and other curricular material.

According to the sociocultural perspective, learning involves a dynamic and integrated constellation of cultural practices wherein learners engage in collaborative activities to coconstruct knowledge of the world. Thus students' cognition and learning are dependent on understanding cues and processes embedded within cultural contexts. This perspective assumes shared cultural understanding of meditational tools between teachers and taught; but this may not always be the case when mainstream White teachers and their students use different cultural systems to make meaning of the world. This lack of shared cultural understanding can create feelings of dissonance. Students who experienced such dissonance because beliefs and behavioral expectations at home and school conflicted were more angry and self-deprecating, felt less academically efficacious, and had lower grade point averages than did low dissonance students (Arunkumar [Kumar], Midgley, & Urdan, 1999).

White teachers are socialized into the Western ethic of ability and hard work as the basis for success, and into cultural norms that value capitalism and individualism. These societal values inform teachers' cultural identity and give rise to specific egocentric ways of thinking and feeling (Shewder, 1990) that promote individual needs and self-enhancing (rather than social) goals. Either consciously or unconsciously, White teachers in public schools often attempt to transfer these values to students via classroom practices and policies.

There is, though, a growing awareness that in contemporary multicultural society many students have interdependent self-construals that emphasize fitting in with others and maintaining harmonious relationships. The cultural scripts for the two self-construal systems are very different and have important implications for individuals' cognition, emotion, and motivation (Markus & Kitayama, 1991). White teachers with independent construals strive to create motivational learning environments that promote opportunities for self-enhancing expression of unique and autonomous selves. This environment may not motivate students with interdependent self-construals who strive to fit in and foster connection to others. Teachers who fail to account for differing self-processes among students, such as self-affirmation, self-verification, self-evaluation, and self-presentation, and with independent and interdependent self-construals actually risk promoting cultural conflict in the classroom to the detriment of students' motivation to learn. While this issue is not confined to White teachers, a majority of teachers are White, whereas the number of students of color and immigrant students with interdependent construals is on the rise.

Tharp for example, demonstrated how dissonance between teachers' and students' cultural identities interfered with native Hawaiian students' learning in traditional American schools. Changes in classroom structure that incorporated group learning centers and peer collaboration similar to Hawaiian students' community, and emphasized sharing and cooperation facilitated their adjustment to school and promoted better learning opportunities (Tharp, Estrada, Dalton, & Yamayuchi, 2000). Similar issues regarding the educational and psychological consequences of cultural incompatibility between home and school cultures for native, immigrant, and minority groups are reported in many countries, as are efforts to address these incompatibilities or suggestions for addressing them (cf., Saha & Dworkin, 2009, sections 6 and 7).

Cultural and Professional Identity of Minority Teachers.

Some case study and ethnographic research explores the cultural identity and teaching experiences of minority faculty, primarily African Americans, in predominantly White schools (Gee, 2000,). Minority teachers often experience a lack of support as they negotiate sociocultural issues. An underrepresented group in the predominantly White teaching force, they remain highly visible, yet silenced (Mabokela & Madsen, 2007). They often feel constrained by the "minority representative" label thrust upon them, and report that their identity and efficacy as a teacher is frequently called into question by school administrators, colleagues, and students both mainstream and minority. Close scrutiny of their work is accompanied by feelings of stereotype threat and subsequent burnout (Milner & Woolfolk Hoy, 2003).

Cultural Values, Minority Teachers' Self-Construals, and Student Outcomes.   Many minority teachers view teaching as social justice work. They perceive their responsibility, defined by cultural identity, as combating stereotypes about minorities and acting as advocates for minority students. They tap into cultural resources to act as cultural brokers and role models for ethnic minority children, motivating them to higher levels of academic achievement, encouraging them to think about possible career aspirations, and supporting them to challenge and overcome negative sociocultural stereotypes. However, it is simplistic to assume that a cultural match, particularly if narrowly defined in terms of ethnicity, is sufficient for the academic advancement of minority students. Match in student–teacher self-construals is mediated through class, language, color, educational opportunities, cultural capital, and schooling experiences. Achinstein and Aguirre (2000) give the example of some middle-class Latino teachers who resented working with low socioeconomic status students and of some Latino teachers from low socioeconomic backgrounds who resented teaching Latino children who came from more affluent families. As Quincho and Rios (2000) indicate, being a person of color does not translate into increased effectiveness when teaching students of color. Minority teachers need support if they are to harness their cultural resources to develop more multicultural, rather than monocultural, teacher identities and better serve culturally diverse student bodies.

Summary and Recommendations

Teacher identity—cultural and professional—is not static and unchangeable. To enable teachers and preservice teachers to develop truly multicultural identities, it is important to stop viewing White/majority identity as ubiquitous and privileged and minority identity as monocultural and marginalized. Process-oriented identity development theories suggest that though mainstream teachers may start with a taken-for-granted and foreclosed identity, and minority teachers (e.g., African Americans) may either reject the meaningfulness of race in their lives, experience self-hatred (Cross, 1991), or develop an oppositional identity, it is possible for all of them to become more reflective, understanding, and appreciative regarding their own and their students' cultural identities.

To this end, several scholars (e.g., Townsend & Bates, 2007) emphasize the importance of supporting active and preservice teachers to engage in self-reflection, bringing to consciousness their often unconscious attitudes and belief systems, enabling them to achieve an honest understanding and acknowledgment of personal prejudices and biases. This self-reflective process and the ensuing cognitive dissonance will pave the way for teachers—mainstream and minority—to achieve a truly multicultural identity, one that

acknowledges individual differences as well as the influences of the collective cultural identity.

A multicultural professional teacher identity will enable teachers to critically reflect on and rethink attitudes, beliefs, and actions; become aware of how cultural identity influences beliefs and actions; understand the role of language and culture in students' learning and development; translate knowledge of cultural groups and individual students into curricular and instructional strategies; and work collaboratively with professionals, families, and communities to share knowledge, resources, and support students (Flores, 2007). Ultimately, expanding the repertoire of teachers' cultural and professional identity is essential to improve students' achievement and meet the academic needs of a culturally diverse student body.

References

Achinstein, B., & Aguirre, J. (2000). Cultural match or cultural suspect: How new teachers or color negotiate sociocultural challenges in the classroom. *Teachers College Record, 110,* 1505–1540.

Arunkumar (Kumar), R., Midgley, C., & Urdan, T. (1999). Perceiving high or low home–school dissonance: Longitudinal effects on adolescent emotional and academic well–being. *Journal of Research on Adolescence, 4,* 441–466.

Cross, W. E. Jr. (1991). *Shades of Black.* Philadelphia, PA: Temple University Press.

Flores, M. A. (2007). Navigating contradictory communities of practice in learning to teach for social justice. *Anthropology and Education Quarterly, 38,* 308–402.

Gee, J. P. (2000). Identity as an analytic lens for research in education. *Review of Research in Education, 25,* 99–125.

Hollins, E. R., & Torres–Guzman, M. A. (2005). Research on preparing teachers for diverse populations. In M. Cochran–Smith & K. M. Zeichner (Eds.), *Studying teacher education: A report of the AERA panel on research and teacher education* (pp. 477–548). Mahwah, NJ: Erlbaum.

Ibarra, H. (1999). Provisional selves: Experimenting with image and identity in professional adaptation. *Administrative Science Quarterly, 44,* 764–791.

Ladson-Billings, G. (2000). Fighting for our lives: Preparing teachers to teach African American students. *Journal of Teacher Education, 51,* 206–214.

Mabokela, R. O., & Madsen, J. A. (2007). African American teachers in suburban desegregated schools: Intergroup differences and the impact of performance pressures. *Teachers College Record, 109,* 1171–1206.

Markus, H., & Kitayama, S. (1991). Culture and self: Implications for cognition, emotion, and motivations. *Psychological Review, 98,* 224–253.

Milner, H. R., & Woolfolk Hoy, A. (2003). A case study of an African American teacher's self–efficacy, stereotype threat, and persistence. *Teaching and Teacher Education 19,* 263–276.

Quincho, A., & Rios, F. (2000). The power of their presence: Minority group teachers and schooling. *Review of Educational Research, 70,* 485–528.

Rubie–Davis, C., Hattie, J., & Hamilton, R. (2006). Expecting the best for students: Teacher expectations and academic outcomes. *British Journal of Educational Psychology, 76,* 429–444.

Saha, L. J., & Dworkin, A. G. (2009). *International handbook of teachers and teaching (Sections 6 & 7).* New York: Springer.

Shewder, R. A. (1991). *Thinking through cultures: Expeditions in cultural psychology.* Cambridge, MA: Harvard University Press.

Sleeter, C. E. (2001). Preparing teachers for culturally diverse schools: Research and the overwhelming presence of Whiteness. *Journal of Teacher Education, 52,* 94–123.

Tajfel, H. (1978). *Differentiation between social groups: Studies on social psychology of intergroup relations.* London: Academic Press.

Tennenbaum, H. R., & Ruck, M. D. (2007). Are teachers' expectations different for racial minority than for European American students? A meta–analysis. *Journal of Educational psychology, 99,* 253–273.

Tharp, R., Estrada, P., Dalton, S., & Yamayuchi, L. (2000). *Teaching transformed: Achieving excellence, fairness, inclusion, and harmony.* Boulder, CO: Westview.

Townsend T., & Bates, R. (2007). *Handbook of teacher education: Globalization, standards, and professionalism in times of change.* Dordrecht, Netherlands: Springer.

U.S. Department of Education, National Center for Education Statistics (2007). Retrieved from http://www.nces.ed.gov/

van den Bergh, L., Denessen, E., Hornsha, L., Voeten, M., & Holland, R. W. (2010). The implicit prejudices attitudes of teachers: Relations to teacher expectation and achievement gap. *American Educational Research Journal, 47,* 497–527.

6.11

Teacher Intelligence

What Is It and Why Do We Care?

Andrew J. McEachin
University of Virginia

Dominic J. Brewer
University of Southern California

Introduction

Over the past several decades, few topics have been discussed and researched more than the decline or stagnation of the U.S. K-12 public education system. The *Coleman Report* (Coleman et al., 1966) was one of the first attempts to parse out the causes and consequences of achievement disparities between the rich and poor and Caucasians and members of racial and ethnic groups. Although the methods used in the report have been widely debated, a key finding was that teachers' aptitude, or verbal intelligence, was highly correlated with student achievement. In the report, teachers were given a short assessment measuring their verbal abilities at the end of a survey. The teachers' score on the assessment was highly correlated with the academic performance of their students (Ehrenberg & Brewer, 1995). Since then, researchers, policy makers, and district officials have tried to measure *teacher intelligence* using a variety of proxies: SATs, college selectivity, licensure exams, and undergraduate major (e.g., Angrist & Guryan, 2008; Clotfelter, Ladd, & Vigdor, 2007; Goldhaber & Hansen, 2010). In this chapter we first broadly define intelligence, and discuss the different ways it has been measured and used. We then focus on how measures and proxies of teacher intelligence have been used in education and their relationship with student achievement. We close with comments on the use of measures of teacher intelligence in staffing and policy decisions.

What is Intelligence? In a perfect world, one assessment could derive an error-free measure of intelligence which would be correlated with outcomes of interest; for example, labor productivity, credit worthiness, voting patterns. In our imperfect world, however, intelligence cannot be properly evaluated by a single measure, nor can it be measured without error. We instead have to settle for proxies of intelligence. Furthermore, before one can meaningfully measure any latent traits (e.g., intelligence), one must first develop a meaningful construct. In other words, one must clearly define what is meant by "intelligence."

Similar to a traditional K-12 public schools system where the difficulty of tasks and knowledge acquired build over time, intelligence is a hierarchical construct (see Shavelson & Huang, 2003 for more detail). At the lowest level is contextualized domain specific knowledge (e.g., 10th grade physics) and at the highest level is a decontextualized general ability, which is often referred to as intelligence quotient (IQ) or "G." Even though measures of intelligence are neither perfect nor deterministic (Shavelson & Huang, 2003), they can serve as useful predictors of future success. Broad abilities, the categories between domain specific knowledge and "intelligence," such as verbal, quantitative, and spatial reasoning, are commonly measured proxies for intelligence. For example, admission offices in colleges and universities around the world heavily rely on measures of broad abilities (e.g., SAT, GRE, LSAT).

Domain specific measures of intelligence are less generalizable than broad abilities measures. Replacing a board exam with an MCAT score would be a foolhardy policy. Whereas the latter may predict the future success in medical schools by assessing one's verbal, quantitative, and spatial reasoning, it does not measure the specific knowledge required to be a doctor. Depending on the construct of interest, measures of intelligence are used in two ways: as screens and signals. Often measures of intelligence are used as *screens*, mechanisms that keep unqualified individuals from entering professions or other uniform communities. Doctors, lawyers, plumbers, and many other professionals must first attain a passing score on a licensing exam. One is only interested in whether the applicant attained a passing score, not the actual magnitude of the score. Domain specific measures of intelligence are the most commonly used screens. Conversely, the magnitude of an intelligence measure can be used as a *signal* for future success. Both domain specific (Praxis) and broad abilities (general GRE, MCAT) are often used as predictors for success in postsecondary education and job performance.

Research Evidence

Research has demonstrated that teachers are the single most important school-input in the education production process (Coleman et al., 1966; Hanushek, Kain, O'Brien, & Rivkin, 2005) For example, students with a teacher in the 85th percentile of teacher quality outperform students with a teacher at the median of teacher quality by .22 standard deviations (Hanushek et al., 2005). But how would one go about measuring teacher quality? In many circumstances, educational stakeholders use proxies of teacher intelligence as screens and signals of teacher quality. The research on the relationship between teacher ability, or characteristics, and student achievement often falls into five groups: the rating of teachers' undergraduate institutions, course taking and degrees, certification status, test scores, and other (Wayne & Young, 2003). In this review, we focus on proxies of teacher intelligence: achievement and licensure tests (e.g., SAT, Praxis, CBEST). Starting with the Coleman report and ending with more recent literature on teacher licensure exams, we briefly review the teacher intelligence literature as it pertains to student achievement.

Teacher Testing. Researchers have used both decontextualized general measures of ability and domain specific knowledge as proxies for teacher intelligence. The first strand of literature dating back to the 1960s relied more on general measures of teachers' verbal intelligence (Coleman et al., 1966; Ehrenberg & Brewer, 1995), while the more recent research focuses on the teacher licensure exams which are measures of domain specific knowledge. Although both may be referred to *measures of intelligence*, they measure different skill sets and may therefore be differentially related to student achievement.

The Coleman report released in the 1960s started a wave of research attempting to connect measures of teacher intelligence to student achievement (Coleman et al, 1966). Early research found a positive link between teacher ability, as measured by an achievement test, and student achievement (Ehrenberg & Brewer, 1995. A specific association was found between teachers' verbal ability, as measured by a short assessment at the end of the Coleman survey, and student achievement (Ehrenberg & Brewer, 1995). College admission tests and selectivity have also been used as proxies for teacher intelligence or ability. Schools with teachers from more selective universities, a proxy for intelligence, had higher gains in student achievement than schools with lower average selectivity (Ehrenberg & Brewer, 1994).

A more recent wave of literature exploits the rise in the number of states requiring teacher-licensure exams. Since the passage of No Child Left Behind (2002), states require teachers to meet certain requirements before applying for a teaching credential (Angrist & Guryan, 2008; Goldhaber, 2007; Goldhaber & Hansen, 2010). Recent research in the United States has begun to use student level longitudinal data to examine the relation between teacher characteristics and student achievement (Clotfelter, Ladd, & Vigdor, 2007; Goldhaber, 2007). A one standard deviation increase in teachers' Praxis scores yields only a 1 to 2% of a standard deviation increase in student achievement (Clotfelter et al, 2007). The results do not appear to be specific to just the United States. A similar positive relation exists between teacher licensure exams and higher average student achievement in Mexico (Santibanez, 2007).

Furthermore, one can assess the quality of the Praxis both in terms of its ability to act as a *signal* of future teacher quality and as a *screen* for entering the teaching profession (Goldhaber & Hansen, 2010). The authors take advantage of a unique dataset that includes observations for teachers who initially failed the Praxis but were still allowed to teach, assuming they passed the Praxis within a calendar year. On average, the Praxis serves as a weak signal of teacher quality. There is a no relationship between passing the Praxis and students' English scores and a small, positive relationship with math scores. Although the Praxis was not established to serve as a *signal*, the authors note that individuals involved in the teacher hiring process may use the scores when deciding between candidates. On average, the Praxis did not serve as a *signal* of teacher quality. Research also demonstrates that Black teachers had a positive statistically significant effect on Black students, regardless of their Praxis scores (Goldhaber & Hansen, 2010). Therefore, the interpretation of teachers' Praxis score in North Carolina cannot be removed from other characteristics. Researchers have also explored the use of California licensure exams (CSET, CBEST, and RICA) as a signal for future teacher performance. The scores on the CA licensure exams had no significant relationship with levels or gains in student ELA or Math achievement (Buddin & Zamarro, 2009). There is also no significant difference in student achievement gains between teachers who initially failed the California Licensure exams compare to teachers who passed the first time.

Developing research suggests that principals may devalue measures of teacher ability or intelligence during the interview process because they assume that credentialed teachers have met certain intellectual requirements during the credentialing process (Harris, Rutledge, Ingle, & Thompson, 2010). A conflict in the hiring process may well exist if the professional *screens* used by many states and districts are unrelated with student achievement. Furthermore, unless a more unified approach is taken, the relationship between teacher licensure exams and student achievement will be heterogeneous across states.

To make matters more muddled, research suggests that the presence of teacher licensure exams has failed to raise the quality of the teaching profession. Using state-level variation in teacher licensure requirements, researchers find that the presence of teacher licensure exams does not raise the quality of individuals entering the teaching profession (Angrist & Guryan, 2008). The cost of studying for, and the presence of measure error in, the exams can actually keep high-quality teachers from entering the profession. Furthermore, as noted above, licensure exams may also keep minority teachers kept out of the profession since they are more likely to fail the exam (Goldhaber, 2007). Other researchers have found that the quality of teachers, as measured by high school class ranking, college admission tests, and degree type has declined over the past few decades, with the most notable changes at the tails of the quality distribution (Corcoran, Evans, & Schwab, 2004).

Summary and Recommendations

In this review we focused on the relationship between teacher ability, as a predictor of teacher quality, and student achievement. As noted by the above discussion, observable teacher characteristics, "Although not a complete measure of teacher quality, teacher ability is clearly a quantifiable predictor of teacher effectiveness in the classroom" (Pelayo & Brewer, 2010, p. 180). The question now becomes: "How do we validly and reliably measure teacher ability as a predictor of future teacher quality?" (Pelayo & Brewer, 2010, p. 180) The prior literature paints a confusing picture for policy makers and education stakeholders. The relationship between teachers' grades, test scores, university selectivity, and other observable factors are loosely related to student achievement. Yet, teachers have a large impact on student learning (Hanushek et al., 2005). Policy makers and educational stakeholders would benefit from a more objective, unified measure of teacher ability.

References

Angrist, J. D., & Guryan, J. (2008). Does teacher testing raise teacher quality? Evidence from state certification requirements. *Economics of Education Review, 27*, 483–503.

Buddin, R., & Zamarro, G. (2009). Teacher qualifications and student achievement in urban elementary schools. *The Journal of Urban Economics, 66*(2), 103–115.

Clotfelter, C. T., Ladd, H. F., Vigdor, J.L. (2007). *How and why do teacher credentials matter for student achievement?* (NBER Working Paper no. 12828). Boston, MA: National Bureau of Economic Research.

Coleman, C. T., Campbell, E., Hobson, C., McPartland, J., Mood, A. M., Weinfeld, F.D., & York, R. L. (1966). *Equality of educational opportunity*. Washington, DC: Department of Health, Education, and Welfare.

Corcoran, S. P., Evans, W. N., & Schwab, R. M. (2004). Women, the labor market, and the declining relative quality of teachers. *Journal of Policy Analysis and Management, 23*(3), 449–470.

Ehrenberg, R. G., & Brewer, D. J. (1994). Do school and teacher characteristics matter? Evidence from high school and beyond. *Economics of Education Review, 13*(1), 1–17.

Ehrenberg, R. G., & Brewer, D. J. (1995). Did teachers' verbal ability and race matter in the 1960s? *Coleman* revisited. *Economics of Education Review, 14*(1), 1–21.

Goldhaber, D. (2007). Everyone's doing it, but what does teacher testing tell us about teacher effectiveness? *Journal of Human Resources, 42*(4), 765–794.

Goldhaber, D., & Hansen, M. (2010). Race, gender, and teacher testing: How informative a tool is teacher licensure testing? *American Educational Research Journal, 47*(1), 218–251.

Hanushek, E. A., Kain, J. F., O'brien, D. M., & Rivkin, S. G. (2005). *The market for teacher quality* (NBER Working Paper 11154). Boston, MA: National Bureau of Economic Research.

Harris, D. N., Rutledge, S., Ingle, W., & Thompson, C. (2010). Mix and match: What principals really look for when hiring teachers. *Education Finance and Policy, 5*(2), 228–246.

No Child Left Behind Act (2002). Pub. L. No. 107-110, 115 Stat. 1425.

Pelayo, I., & Brewer, D. J. (2010). Teacher quality in education production. In D. Brewer & P. McEwan (Eds.), *International encyclopedia of education* (pp. 178–182). New York: Elsevier.

Santibanez, L. (2006). Why we should care if teachers get A's: Teachers test scores and student achievement in Mexico. *Economics of Education Review, 25*, 510–520.

Shavelson, R. J., & Huang, L. (2003). Responding responsibly to the frenzy to assess learning in higher education. *Change, 35*(1), 10–19.

Wayne, A. J., & Youngs, P. (2003). Teacher characteristics and student achievement gains: A review. *Review of Educational Research, 73*(1), 89–122.

6.12

Pedagogical Content Knowledge

JULIE GESS-NEWSOME
Williamette University

Introduction

What teachers know should affect classroom practice and thus student learning. Research linking teachers' characteristics to student achievement, however, has not supported this assumption. Teacher content knowledge as traditionally measured by standardized tests, courses taken, and grade point average, has only weak positive relationships to student achievement (Ferguson & Womack, 1993). See and Gröschner, Seidel, and Shavelson (Entry 6.7 this volume) for more complete discussions of teacher characteristics and content knowledge.

Such findings have puzzled researchers for nearly 40 years. In considering the dilemma, Shulman (1986) proposed a "missing paradigm" in educational research. The construct, pedagogical content knowledge, challenged past practices of examining knowledge of subject matter and pedagogy separately. Instead, pedagogical content knowledge (PCK), recognizes the melding of subject matter expertise with pedagogical strategies and knowledge of the learner to produce high quality classroom practice. For Shulman and the researchers that followed, PCK is a unique knowledge base held by teachers that allows them to consider the structure and importance of an instructional topic, recognize the features that will make it more or less accessible to students, and justify the selection of teaching practices based on learning needs. With PCK, neither content knowledge nor generic teaching skills alone are sufficient to be an effective teacher.

Research Evidence

Nature of PCK. Since 1986, research concerning PCK focused on defining its nature and constituent parts. Shulman (1987) defined PCK as one of seven professional knowledge bases needed for teaching. Other knowledge bases included subject matter knowledge, pedagogical knowledge, curricular knowledge, knowledge of students,

knowledge of context, and knowledge of educational goals. Building from earlier work (Grossman, 1990; Wilson, Shulman, & Rickert, 1988) and applied to the field of science, Magnusson, Krajcik, and Borko (1999) defined PCK as the transformation of subject matter knowledge and beliefs, pedagogical knowledge and beliefs, and knowledge and beliefs about context into a distinct knowledge base for teaching. In their model, PCK included orientations to teaching (such as inquiry, didactic, and conceptual change) that shaped and were shaped by knowledge of science curricula, knowledge of students' understanding of science, knowledge of instructional strategies, and knowledge of assessment of scientific literacy.

Although variations exist, most definitions of PCK include the following components:

- *Content knowledge,* including depth, breadth, and accuracy of content knowledge; connections within and between topics and the nature of the discipline; and fluency with multiple modes of representation or examples of a topic;
- *Pedagogical knowledge,* including a rationale linking teaching strategies to learning; strategies for eliciting student prior understandings; and strategies to promote student examination of their own thinking;
- *Contextual knowledge,* including understanding how student variations, such as student prior conceptions, impact instructional decisions (Gess-Newsome, Carlson, Gardner, & Taylor, 2010).

There is mounting evidence that PCK exists on a continuum, both across and within teachers, and influences teaching. Working from the assumption that depth of content knowledge is a precursor to PCK, early studies examined the differences between teachers. Some examined teaching practice resulting from varying teacher preparation programs (Grossman, 1990). Others compared teaching practices in self-described high and low knowledge areas, or examined teacher planning for content topics within and outside their area of specialization (Hashweh, 1987) or across experience levels (Borko & Livingston, 1989). These studies demonstrated that depth of content knowledge resulted in differing teaching practices, providing initial support for the PCK construct. When teaching high knowledge areas, teachers were more likely to present new information, ask high-level questions, review student work, encourage open-ended and student-initiated activities, recognize student misconceptions, and vary from or augment curricular materials. In low knowledge areas, classroom practices were more teacher and curriculum-centered with fewer opportunities for student directed instruction. Student questioning in low knowledge areas was infrequent and student misconceptions ignored or reinforced (Gess-Newsome, 1999).

When examining the development of PCK over time, the results are mixed. Hashweh (1987) compared how biology and physics teachers went about planning a topic in their content area and one outside their area. Teachers had a richer, more integrated knowledge base for the topics that they taught, indicating that PCK develops with the experience of teaching a topic multiple times. Such findings reinforce those of other studies that examine the impact of professional development on PCK (Barnett & Hobson, 2001; van Driel, Verloop, & deVos, 1998). Many of these studies note that examining student work or misconceptions are particularly effective means of increasing teachers' careful consideration of content and pedagogical knowledge on classroom practice. In contrast, studies in Germany (Baumert et al., 2010; Krauss, Baumert, & Blum, 2008) found limited growth in PCK and CK across a teacher's career. Through looking at natural variation in teacher preparation programs in Germany, the most rigorous programs that included mathematics preparation similar to a master's degree produced teachers with CK (multitopic mathematical content knowledge) and PCK scores that exceeded those of teachers who received less rigorous content preparation. Interestingly, CK and PCK scores did not change with years of teaching experience following graduation. An analysis across preservice teachers within a preparation program showed that two-thirds of the growth occurred during formal university coursework with the last third occurring during the final 18-month apprentice teaching. The authors suggest that such perplexing results point to the idea of deliberate practice theory (Ericsson, Krampe, & Tesch-Römer, 1993). This theory proposes that change does not come with simple repetition of a task, but from thoughtful reflection, motivation to grow, and guidance through expert feedback. While the authors note that such professional development does not commonly exist in Germany, preservice preparation programs often include such characteristics, as do some of the professional development opportunities reported in other studies.

PCK and Student Achievement. Two large studies in mathematics are among the few to provide initial evidence that teachers with strong PCK are more likely to increase student achievement. In a study of how the mathematical knowledge needed for teaching impacts student achievement, Hill, Rowan, and Ball (2005) examined U.S. elementary mathematics teachers' knowledge in the first and third grades. Key to this study was a multiple-choice test that assessed teacher mathematical knowledge of commonly taught topics: number concepts, operations, patterns, functions, and algebra. The test focused specifically on the knowledge that teachers use in the classroom rather than general mathematical knowledge, and included tasks that involved mathematical explanations, alternative representations of mathematical ideas, and unusual solution methods. For example, one task asked teachers to examine and assess three different approaches to a multidigit multiplication problem, 35 x 25. The goal of the task was to capture both common mathematical knowledge and knowledge specialized for teaching. Teachers' content knowledge for teaching mathematics (CKT-M) significantly and positively predicted student achievement at both grade levels. CKT-M was the strongest teacher-level predictor of academic achievement exceeding teacher background characteristics such as number of mathematics and methods courses, certification, and years of teaching experience. The only variable that approached CKT-M in explaining student achievement was student socioeconomic status (SES). Teachers in the lowest 20 to 30% of CKT-M scores had significantly lower student achievement gains, though further increases in teacher knowledge did not additionally influence student gains. Such findings suggest that there is a minimum threshold of CK needed to improve student achievement, but diminishing returns beyond that point.

In the Baumert et al. (2010) study described previously, 13 open-ended content items on various mathematics topics assessed profound mathematical content knowledge taught in school and measured secondary mathematics teacher content knowledge. The test represented a content knowledge level that fell between that of a good secondary student and the knowledge taught at the university. Three knowledge dimensions defined PCK of mathematics: mathematical tasks, student thinking, and multiple representations. PCK scores predicted a higher quality of instruction, defined by student thinking (called cognitive activation), lesson correspondence to the grade-appropriate curriculum, individual student learning support, and classroom management, which in turn predicted student achievement. In fact, PCK scores explained 39% of student achievement variance. The importance of PCK for student achievement was more important in low SES students than for high SES students.

The Baumert et al. study (2010) further examined the interaction of the various categories of knowledge related to PCK. Content knowledge was not a predictor of high quality instruction, supporting the hypothesis that PCK and CK are theoretically and empirically distinct. Content knowledge was highly correlated to PCK scores and the correlation increased with teacher expertise. This finding suggests that CK may be a precursor to PCK and that expertise results in more coherent knowledge structures. As noted before, neither PCK nor CK increased with teaching experience in this population. Such research helps clarify the definition of PCK as well as provide initial evidence for how to support its growth.

Summary and Recommendations

With limited correlations of traditional measures of teacher knowledge to student achievement, it is important to find alternative measures to understand what teachers know and do. With such knowledge, we have the opportunity to more carefully, effectively, and efficiently support teacher growth and ultimately improve student achievement. While many of the findings discussed are promising, additional research is needed. First, consensus on PCK and CK definitions and measurements is critical to future research. Both in-depth case study measures and standardized tools used for large samples are required to confirm and expand emerging results for both teacher PCK and CK. Second, research must attend to the links between teacher thinking, teacher practice, and student achievement. While it is appealing to believe that one knowledge type transfers seamlessly to the next, past research has shown that this is not the case. Third, as evidence of PCK mounts, particularly as it affects student achievement, there needs to be a more thoughtful consideration of and research into the effectiveness of teacher preparation and professional development programs. A recent outcome of this research is the growth in content-specific teacher preparation programs, such as the UTeach program developed at the University of Texas at Austin (http://uteach.utexas.edu). This program purposefully blends content knowledge with attention to student learning and powerful instructional strategies. Teacher and student learning results need to be compared to more traditional programs where little time or attention is given to content specific preparation. Finally, while current evidence is not sufficient to support policy recommendations, further examination of PCK will help identify the nature of the knowledge needed for teaching as well as the methods through which we can assist teachers into translating this knowledge into classroom practices that improve student learning.

References

Barnett, J., & Hodson, D. (2001). Pedagogical context knowledge: Toward a fuller understanding of what good science teachers know. *Science Education, 85*, 426–453.

Baumert, J., Kunter, M., Blum, W., Brunner, M., Voss, T., Jordan, A., … Tsai, Y. (2010). Teachers' mathematical knowledge, cognitive action in the classroom, and student progress. *American Educational Research Journal, 47*, 133–180.

Borko, H., & Livingston, C. (1989). Cognition and improvisation: Differences in mathematics instruction by expert and novice teachers. *American Educational Research Journal, 26*(4), 473–498.

Ericsson, K. A., Krampe, R. T., & Tesch–Römer, C. (1993). The role of deliberate practice in the acquisition of expert performance. *Psychological Review, 100*, 363–406.

Ferguson, P., & Womack, S. T. (1993). The impact of subject matter and educational coursework on teaching performance. *Journal of Teacher Education, 44*(1), 55–63.

Gess-Newsome, J. (1999). Secondary teachers' knowledge and beliefs about subject matter and its impact on instruction. In J. Gess-Newsome & N. G. Lederman (Eds.), *Examining pedagogical content knowledge: The construct and its implications for science education* (pp. 51–94). Dordrecht, Netherlands: Kluwer Academic.

Gess–Newsome, J., Carlson, J., Gardner, A., & Taylor, J. (2010). *Project PRIME: Building science teachers' pedagogical content knowledge through educative curriculum materials and professional development.* Retrieved from BSCS.org\ProjectPRIMEPapers.

Grossman, P. L. (1990). *The making of a teacher: Teacher knowledge and teacher education.* New York: Teachers College Press.

Hashweh, M. Z. (1987). Effects of subject matter knowledge in the teaching of biology and physics. *Teaching and Teacher Education, 3*(2), 109–120.

Hill, H. C., Rowan, B., & Ball, D. L. (2005). Effects of teachers' mathematics knowledge for teaching on student achievement. *American Educational Research Journal, 42*, 371–406.

Krauss, S., Baumert, J., & Blum, W. (2008). Secondary mathematics teachers' pedagogical content knowledge and content knowledge: Validation of the COACTIV constructs. *The International Journal on Mathematics Education, 40*(5), 873–892.

Magnusson, S., Krajcik, J., & Borko, H. (1999). Nature, sources, and development of pedagogical content knowledge for teaching. In J. Gess–Newsome & N. G. Lederman (Eds.), *Examining pedagogical content knowledge: The construct and its implications for science education* (pp. 95–132). Dordrecht, Netherlands: Kluwer Academic.

Shulman, L. S. (1986). Those who understand: Knowledge growth in teaching. *Educational Researcher, 15*(2), 4–14.

Shulman, L. S. (1987). Knowledge and teaching: Foundations of the new reform. *Harvard Educational Review, 57*(1), 1–22.

van Driel, J. H., Verloop, N., & DeVos, W. (1998). Developing science teachers' pedagogical content knowledge. *Journal of Research in Science Teaching, 35*, 673–695.

Wilson, S. M., Shulman, L. S., & Rickert, A. E. (1988). 150 different ways of knowing: Representations of knowledge in teaching. In J. Calderhead (Ed.), *Exploring teacher thinking* (pp. 104–124). Sussex, England: Holt, Rinehart, & Winston.

6.13

Teacher Beliefs about Teaching and Learning

The Role of Idea-Oriented Pedagogy

Richard Prawat
Michigan State University

Introduction

Since the early 1970s, educational researchers have recognized the importance of teacher cognitions and beliefs, especially as they relate to what have been called the commonplaces of teaching—the what, who, where, and how of teaching. These commonplaces reflect the fact that teaching is always about some content that is taught to someone in some context using some pedagogical strategy or technique. As Lee Shulman argued (1987), many experienced teachers create their own amalgam of beliefs about the commonplaces of teaching. He singled out what may be the most important example of this kind of hybrid teacher knowledge, the now well-known category called "pedagogical content knowledge" (PCK). PCK represents knowledge of content *for teaching* and thus is distinct from content knowledge per se, which is typically measured by performance on subject-matter tests (Shulman, 1986, p. 9).

Pedagogical content knowledge is hard won on the part of those teachers who acquire it, marking the end point of sorts of what is often a lengthy intellectual journey. Because of the importance of this type of knowledge, which epitomizes the kind of deep yet applicable understanding evidenced by the best of our teachers (see Hill, Rowan, & Ball, 2005), educators need to understand the factors that may contribute to its development, which is what I intend to do in this entry. The question addressed here can be stated as follows: What classroom content beliefs—what ways of construing and acting toward subject matter in the classroom—are related to teachers' willingness to undertake the journey that leads to the acquisition of pedagogical content knowledge?

Research Evidence

Shulman points to one key notion that may serve as an impetus for this quest: The belief that teaching, at its core, involves the exchange of ideas. This belief, if embraced by PCK-minded teachers, points to what may be a unique appreciation on their part of the role that ideas play in the disciplines. Dewey viewed ideas as nothing less than the connective tissue that holds mind and world together. "Ideas direct operations," he wrote (1910/1988, p. 134). "The operations have a result in which ideas are no longer abstract, mere ideas, but where they *qualify sensible things*" [emphasis added]. Ideas open up important phenomena—a work of history viewed as "story," for example, which means it is told from some perspective and often has heroes, or number in mathematics seen through the lens of the big idea of additive composition. Ideas reveal the regularities that help explain phenomena (Prawat, 2003).

Teachers who appreciate the role of big ideas in disciplinary knowledge, research demonstrates, bring a unique perspective to bear in thinking about the role of knowledge (Prawat, 1993): They appear to value knowledge as a *trans*formative rather than what might be termed a merely *in*formative interaction with the world. The informative approach, in its most enlightened, constructivist form, still views knowledge as primarily instrumental in nature. Knowledge informs the individuals about situations they encounter that are potentially problematic in the sense that they block progress toward important goals. Knowledge thus helps people figure out and deal with problematic situations; these situations can be straightforward, like those presented on a mathematics worksheet or incredibly complex, like a personal relationship that is unraveling.

The disciplines, in this view, turn up knowledge that helps people get on with their lives. Progressive teachers try to strip education from the schoolroom and make it instrumental in students' everyday life—helpful, in other words, in dealing with what Dewey terms the problems "already stirring in the child's experience" (1910/1997, p. 199). There is, however, a danger associated with the endorsement of a problem-solving orientation to disciplinary knowledge that in most cases cannot be avoided. It casts the role of knowledge as being essentially negative in nature:

Knowledge is a tool that enables us to deal with obstacles or difficulties in life. Thus, students are told that they have to learn the valuable task of taking number apart and putting it back together in early elementary school so that they can avoid being cheated at the grocery store or avoid failing mathematics at the next grade level.

There is a second, nontraditional way of thinking about the role of disciplinary knowledge in a person's life. Big ideas developed in the disciplines can open up new elements or facets of the world to the novice learner. They make life more interesting. In an earlier piece (1993), I used an example from one of Molière's plays, that of the newly rich but unschooled Jourdain who suddenly discovered, to his great delight, that whenever he spoke, he spoke prose: "I am speaking Prose!" he exclaimed. "I have spoken Prose throughout my whole life." The idea that he possesses a tool used by the great authors, the ability to construct prose, excites Jourdain beyond measure.

Shulman writes that a trait shared by teachers who value pedagogical content knowledge is that of turning ideas around in their heads. Not only do these teachers examine ideas, they take them for a ride so to speak. An example might be reflecting on the notion in biology that structure dictates function, and then seeing how many specific things in and outside the domain of biology can be viewed through the lens provided by this idea. It is big ideas developed within disciplines, according to Goodwin (1994, p. 608), that allow those in different professions to transform the world into what he calls the "phenomenal categories" that make up their work environment. Disciplinary ideas can thus open one up to the power of possibility. Viewed from this perspective, knowledge is associated less with what Maxine Greene (1986, p. 74) calls "negative freedom"—being free from obstacles or entanglements—and more with "positive freedom" defined as "the capacity to create new experiences."

Viewing the world through the lens of disciplinary ideas transforms it for students, allowing them to live more meaningfully, more richly, in the world. Teachers who view knowledge in this way differ, of course, from traditional teachers who think of themselves as dispensers of knowledge, the so-called sage on the stage. Teachers who focus on ideas also, however, differ from problem or inquiry-oriented teachers in how they organize classrooms and expose students to content (Prawat & Schmidt, 2006). Inquiry-oriented teachers are often described as being those who prefer to play an indirect role in teaching and learning, the proverbial "guide on the side."

As this last statement indicates, inquiry-oriented teachers place a premium on students being "partners" in the active, hands-on knowledge construction process. Traditional teachers assign much less importance to the student activity dimension in learning. Despite this difference, however, both groups of teachers, research and theory shows, subscribe either explicitly or implicitly to what, in debates that can be traced back to the Middle Ages, has historically been termed a *nominalist* view of knowledge. (In fact, this view

was so predominant at the time that those who disagreed with it were considered "dunces," a term derived from the chief proponent of the minority view of epistemology, John *Duns* Scotus.)

Nominalism, also called inductionism, was, until quite recently, the view of knowledge endorsed by those thought to be in the best position to know, practicing scientists—those who actually produce new knowledge. Science historians, drawing on the unofficial record, now understand that theories like Darwin's or Einstein's emerged from an act of creative intelligence so dramatic that it represented, according to Jacob Bronowski, an "explosion" of thought (R. Root-Bernstein & M. Root-Bernstein, 1999, p. 145). One of Darwin's notions, that of "nature selecting," sprung to his mind as a metaphor. Being an English countryman, Darwin was well acquainted with the notion that man can create new species (i.e., of dogs and sheep) through selective breeding. This metaphor, he realized, was the perfect lens for viewing the process of species creation in nature.

Teachers who appreciate the power of disciplinary ideas must, at least implicitly, share this second view of knowledge discovery: That it represents a creative insight that points to an important regularity in the world. I have elsewhere contrasted the approach to teaching and learning that would best fit this view of knowledge as a hybrid of the two divergent roles described above—"the guide on the side" and the "sage on the stage" (2003). The teacher who truly appreciates the eye-opening role that ideas play in a student's life would be less likely to see the value in either extreme—passive guidance or frontal presentation—as they relate to the presentation of powerful concepts in the classroom. The teacher's inclination would be to use big ideas to foster a transactive relationship between student and world. This notion fits well with Shulman's concept of pedagogical content knowledge.

The teacher's role in the above scenario is more like that of a tour guide, a "sage on the side" in other words (or, more properly, "a sage *along*side"). This sort of PCK-oriented teacher is excited about the specifics of what his or her professional vision reveals about important aspects of the world. As a result, he or she is eager to equip students with a similar set of lens. At this point, we must assume that this kind of pedagogical stance in American education, given the U.S. commitment to the nominalist theory of knowledge, is "caught by" rather than "taught to" teachers. If research has demonstrated anything about progressive teaching in the United States, it is the ubiquity of the distinction between process and content in disciplinary domains, a classic nominalist position on this issue (Prawat, 2003).

The importance of this distinction in American education, as a number of commentators have noted, does not mean that content and process are viewed as equal partners, especially in inquiry learning in science and mathematics. Content, defined as disciplinary facts and concepts, is typically viewed by U.S. teachers as being *in service* of process, defined as induction—reasoning from the particular to the general. The search for examples about how to cultivate an alternative to nominalist thinking on the part of teachers is thus best conducted away from American shores, in countries where students typically perform very well on international comparisons of science and mathematics achievement (Prawat & Schmidt, 2006). Teachers in countries like Singapore and Japan, for example, are much more inclined than those in the United States to employ strategies that directly engage the student with core scientific ideas. As described in a middle-school science document in Japan, the goal of instruction is to focus on the use of big ideas to "deepen students' understanding of natural events and phenomena" (Schmidt, 1996, p. 156).

There is little doubt about the need for teachers in the United States to change their practice, especially in the core curricular areas of literacy, science, and mathematics. A 2005 NAEP study (Grigg, Lauko, & Brockway, 2006) documents this need: Less than a third of our eighth graders were able to reach the proficient level in science; among economically disadvantaged youth, only 16% were able to reach the proficient level at the eighth grade. Despite studies that contrast pedagogical practices and beliefs in the United States—particularly those related to the teaching of content—with those in high performing countries, the commitment to fostering problem-based or inquiry-oriented pedagogy remains undiminished in science and mathematics.

This preference for inquiry-based approaches in core disciplinary domains comes through loud and clear in a recent study commissioned by the National Research Council that makes recommendations about the learning and teaching of science in grades kindergarten through eighth grade (Duschl, Schweingruber, & Shouse, 2006). While the authors attempt to address some of the shortcomings associated with earlier versions of the inquiry approach by calling for greater clarity about the outcomes of investigations, they do endorse what they describe as a "science as practice" orientation. This approach involves students in extended investigations about topics like global warming. Such investigations, of course, have their place in the classroom but not as the primary means of teaching to content standards.

Summary and Recommendations

Idea-centered teaching of the sort advocated here starts with the process of grounding students in the big ideas developed within disciplinary domains by teaching the ideas first. The notion here is that one "looks *with* ideas, not *for* ideas." Given the nature of scientific discovery, described by Miller as an imaginative act of vision (2000, p. 252), the obvious starting point in presenting a big idea in a content domain is figuring out how to concretize or instantiate the core or gist of the idea. This would, of necessity, involve

the use of metaphor, visualization, or physical enactment, the kind of understanding that appears to lie at the heart of pedagogical content knowledge. If idea oriented teaching and learning becomes more the norm than the exception in U.S. education, it will increase the likelihood that graduates of the system, and thus those who teach in it, will embrace a belief that is at the core of this unique kind of professional knowledge: The view that disciplinary knowledge allows students to be in the world in a richer way, one that is more attuned to the wondrous possibilities that reside there.

References

Dewey, J. (1929/1988). The quest for certainty. In J. A. Boydston (Ed.), *John Dewey: The later works, 1925–1953* (Vol. 4). Carbondale, IL: Southern University Press.

Dewey, J. (1997). *How we think.* Mineola, NY: Dover. (Original work published 1910)

Duschl, R. A., Schweingruber, H. A., & Shouse, A. W. (Eds.). (2006). *Taking science to school: Learning and teaching science in grades K–8.* [pre-publication copy]. Board on Science Education, Center for Education, Division of Behavioral and Social Science and Education). Washington, DC: National Academies Press.

Goodwin, C. (1994). Professional vision. *American Anthropologist, 96*(3), 606–633.

Greene, M. (1986). Reflection and passion in teaching. *Journal of Curriculum and Supervision, 2,* 68–81.

Grigg, W. S., Lauko, M. A., & Brockway, D. M. (2006). *The Nation's Report Card: Science 2005* (NCES 2006–466). U.S. Department of Education, National Center for Education Statistics. Washington, DC: U.S. Government Printing Office.

Hill, H. C., Rowan, B., & Ball, D. L. (2005). Effects of teachers' mathematical knowledge for teaching on student achievement. *American Educational Research Journal, 42*(2), 371–406.

Hill, H. C., Rowan, Ball, D. L., & Shilling, S. G. (2008). Unpacking pedagogical content knowledge: Conceptualizing and measuring teachers' topic-specific knowledge of students. *Journal for Research in Mathematics Education, 39*(2), 372–400.

Miller, A. I. (2000). *Insights of genius: Imagery and creativity in science and art.* Cambridge, MA: MIT Press.

Prawat, R. S. (1993). The value of ideas: Problems versus possibilities in learning. *American Educational Research Journal, 22*(6), 5–16.

Prawat, R. S. (2003). Is realism a better belief than nominalism? Reopening the ancient debate. In J. Raths & A. C. McAninch (Eds.), *Advances in teacher education: Vol 6. Teacher beliefs and classroom performance: The impact of teacher education* (pp. 65–97). Charlotte, NC: Information Age.

Prawat, R. S., & Schmidt, W. H. (2006). Curriculum coherence: Does the logic underlying the organization of subject matter matter? In S. J. Howie & T. Plomp (Eds.), *Contexts of learning mathematics and science: Lessons learned from TIMSS* (pp. 265–276). Lisse, Netherlands: Swets & Zeitlinger.

Root-Bernstein, R., & Root-Bernstein, M. (1999). *Sparks of genius.* Boston, MA: Houghton–Mifflin.

Schmidt, W. H.(Ed.). (1996). *Characterizing pedagogical flow.* Dordrecht, Netherlands: Kluwer.

Shulman, L. S. (1986). Those who understand: Knowledge growth in teaching. *Educational Researcher, 15*(2), 4–14.

Shulman, L. S. (1987). Knowledge and teaching: Foundations of the new reform. *Harvard Educational Review, 57*(1), 1–22.

6.14

School Reform

LINDA VALLI AND CARLA FINKELSTEIN
University of Maryland

Introduction

Since the 1980s, there has been a distinct trend in school reform efforts that emphasizes accountability. This is clearly seen in the United States, where the passage of the No Child Left Behind (NCLB; 2002) legislation marked a significant turn from applying standards to using high-stakes tests as the primary tool of reform. With a few notable exceptions, similar trends are apparent in countries throughout the world (Sahlberg, 2007). In this chapter, we review the empirical research on these two primary types of reform—standards-based reform (SBR) and high-stakes accountability (HSA)—that aim to influence teaching practices and student achievement. We examine what is meant by teaching practices and student achievement as well as ways in which these two phenomena are studied and measured. We conclude with recommendations for future reform initiatives.

The standards-based reform (SBR) movement in the United States, which began in the late 1980s, has sought to raise the achievement of all students to specific, articulated standards. Partly in response to the 1983 publication of *A Nation at Risk*, states and content area associations such as the National Council for Teachers of Mathematics have developed standards detailing what students ought to know and be able to do. In mathematics education, by promoting active learning opportunities, higher order thinking, nonroutine problem solving, and connections beyond the classroom, these new standards demanded new proficiencies from teachers as well as students. The same was true when other content area associations produced new standards and professional development (PD) became a driver of reform. The theory of action behind SBR was that by providing a coherent instructional guidance system of standards, curriculum materials, assessments, and opportunities to learn, teachers could improve their teaching practices and student achievement. Accountability was not an explicit part of this

system beyond the implicit notion of professional accountability to high standards of teaching and learning.

Research Evidence

Evaluations of early standards-based reform (SBR) efforts primarily examined the effectiveness of reforms on teacher beliefs and practices through teacher self-report surveys indicating their engagement in PD activities and changes in their instructional practices. A few studies did attempt to make empirical connections between standards-based reform implementation, teacher practices, and student achievement. An investigation of a statewide mathematics reform through analysis of teacher surveys and student test scores found a high correlation between teachers who attended reform-oriented PD, increases in reform-oriented mathematics teaching practices such as having students do problems with more than one solution, and decreases in conventional practices such as teaching primarily from a textbook (Cohen & Hill, 2000). Results also showed a "modest relationship" between schools with higher average student test scores and teachers who participated in curriculum-based PD, as well as with teachers who reported implementation of reform math practices.

At the school district level, researchers collaborated with administrators and teachers to create and implement a constructivist, inquiry-based science curriculum for 8,000 middle school students in an urban district (Fishman, Marx, Best, & Tal, 2003). Through qualitative analysis of classroom observations, researchers reported that most teachers implemented the strategy modeled during PD workshops. They found that "our design approach to professional development enabled us to make reasoned and substantial improvements in both teacher learning and subsequent student performance" (p. 655). Noting that nationally normed or state-mandated assessments may fail to capture the particular impact of local systemic reforms, the authors emphasized the importance of student assessment remaining proximal to the curricular and instructional approach of the reform. In this case, for example, the researchers themselves constructed the assessments used to measure student progress.

One of many studies of the literacy reform in New York's Community School District No. 2 used case study methods to investigate what may account for improved student performance on standardized reading tests (Stein & D'Amico, 2002). Based on 100 classroom observations and teacher interviews, the authors found a strong relationship between years of experience in the district and implementation of reform literacy practices (such as appropriately matching students to leveled texts). Although most teachers newer to the district implemented structural features of the reform (such as classroom arrangement), their teaching practices were less aligned with underlying instructional goals. The study concluded that "parallels between how district children learn to read and district teachers learn to teach" (p. 1317)—such as modeling and scaffolding—are significant to the reform's successful implementation.

Studies from this period emphasize the importance of aligning curriculum frameworks, instructional materials, assessments, and school organization with reform-oriented conceptualizations of teacher learning and teaching practice. As such, these studies implicitly illustrate the methodological challenges in disentangling the various components of the reform. As explained in one study, "the more successful agencies are at 'aligning' the instruments of a given policy, the more headaches analysts will have in discerning the extent to which they operate jointly or separately" (Cohen & Hill, 2000, p. 322).

In contrast to SBR, high-stakes accountability (HSA) is an outcome rather than an input model of school reform. Its theory of action is that student achievement will improve if schools and teachers are held accountable for that improvement. With growing concern about the achievement of U.S. students relative to students in other countries, as well as the achievement gap between groups of U.S. students, HSA was written into federal policy in the 2002 No Child Left Behind legislation. Researchers, especially economists working in production function frameworks, have examined the direct relationship between accountability policies and student test scores, with no measures of teaching practice. Not surprisingly, many of these studies show increases in test scores. A meta-analysis of "76 effect-size estimates" from 14 selected "cross-state causal-comparative and correlational studies" concluded that high-stakes testing had modest positive effects on reading and mathematics achievement (Lee, 2008). Comparing the impact of high-stakes to low-stakes tests, the study determined that student gain was greater under high-stakes conditions: equivalent to approximately 2 to 3 months of learning, depending on subject matter and grade level.

But because of the differences in tests and proficiency standards across the states, many researchers and policymakers have urged the use of a common assessment, such as the National Assessment of Educational Progress (NAEP), as a more accurate indicator of progress in student achievement. In a recent report, a panel of researchers concluded that, for the most part, pre-NCLB achievement gains were greater than post-NCLB gains and that NAEP scores rarely reflected the achievement gains shown on state tests (Baker et al., 2010). These findings raise a crucial question: Are scores on NAEP lower because it is a low-stakes test—suggesting that high-stakes tests are a more accurate indicator of student learning—or because high-stakes test scores are unduly inflated due to coaching, drilling, and teaching to the test (Lee, 2008)? Qualitative research that includes participant observation, in-depth interviews, and artifact analysis strongly suggests the latter. For example, a meta-synthesis of 49 studies that examined the impact of high-stakes tests on teaching practices and that included 740 teachers, 96 schools, 38 districts, and 19 states, found that, in the vast majority of cases, teaching practices narrowed the curriculum, fragmented knowledge to correspond to tested content, and became more teacher-centered (Au, 2007). Because teachers aligned their practices to the high-stakes tests, curriculum content was "increasingly taught in isolated pieces and often learned only within the context of the tests themselves" (p. 263).

A series of studies from the Rand Corporation and the Center for Educational Policy (CEP) indicate that HSA can have positive outcomes. Teachers report, for example, increased expectations for student learning, more focused attention on low-performing students and groups, instructional alignment with standards, and data-based decision making (Hamilton, Stecher, Russell, & Miles, 2008). But, by and large, the impact seems to be what most educators would consider negative. Survey data, case studies, classroom observations, and interviews from educators across a wide range of states and school districts find a narrowing of the curriculum to tested topics and greater emphasis on test taking skills (Hamilton, Stecher, Marsh et al., 2007; Hamilton, Stecher, Russell et al., 2008; CEP, 2009). Although administrators report data-driven decision making, teachers often say they do not know how to use the data to guide their day-to-day decision making (CEP, 2009), but feel pressure to make instructional changes to align with tests, even when those changes are inconsistent with their beliefs about teaching (Hamilton, Stecher, Russell et al., 2008). And although more attention is given to some students, teachers express concern that this attention is too frequently on the "bubble-kids" (those just below the proficiency standard) and that other students are being neglected (Hamilton, Stecher, Marsh et al., 2007).

Although high-stakes tests are supposedly aligned with content standards and should, in theory, promote SBR, this review of the research indicates the contrary. High-stakes tests seem to influence teaching practices in a more narrow and limiting direction, with questionable benefits to student learning. Further, the current U.S. interest in shifting accountability from school-level proficiency goals to teacher-level value-added measures (VAM) of student learning is unlikely to be the answer. Although some countries have begun using VAM for performance-related pay incentives (Atkinson et al., 2009), a broad range of researchers agree that these measures are neither valid nor reliable at the teacher level and that using these measures to evaluate teachers will continue to erode good teaching practices as well as discourage teachers from working with the neediest students (Baker et al., 2010).

This does not necessarily mean, however, that external exams should be discarded as a tool in education reform efforts. Comparative international studies using PISA and TIMMS data find that the institutionalized practice of giving external, national exams positively correlates with student achievement in the areas of mathematics, science, and reading (Collier & Millimet, 2009; Fuchs & Wößmann, 2007). But in these high achieving countries, external exams are used sparingly before high school, are not used as teacher evaluation and accountability tools, and include open-ended tasks (Sahlberg, 2007). This indicates that the nature and use of exams, rather than testing frequency, are key elements in a reform model. As noted in the previously cited meta-analyses, poorly designed and narrowly focused tests negatively impact teaching practices, whereas well-designed tests have the potential to do the opposite (Au, 2007). Because teachers align their practices with the test, some external exams encourage curricular expansion, knowledge integration, and student-centered pedagogies.

But such changes in instructional practice are not easy to bring about. Evidence from a number of studies, including a comparative study of England, Wales, and the United States, indicates that changing instructional approaches is more difficult than changing curriculum coverage and that teachers need considerable guidance to do this (Firestone & Mayrowetz, 2000; Hamilton, Stecher, Russell et al., 2008). These findings suggest the importance of a sustained instructional guidance system such as those recommended in early SBR efforts as well as other comprehensive approaches to school reform. Pre-NCLB studies of Chicago's public elementary schools, for example, find that five essential supports are necessary to improve student learning in reading and mathematics: school leadership, parent/community ties, professional capacity, a student-centered learning climate, and an instructional guidance system. In their analysis, the researchers argue that removing any one of these elements so weakens the entire structure that little sustained gain occurs in student outcomes (Bryk, Sebring, Allensworth, Luppescu, & Easton, 2010).

Summary and Recommendations

Collectively, the research reviewed in this chapter provides little evidence that high-stakes accountability contributes to improved teaching practices or student achievement. Although there is some indication that HSA has an im-

mediate impact on student test scores, these achievement score gains are likely to reflect relatively shallow, non-transferable and short-lived learning. In contrast, there is increasing evidence that using standards and assessments within a coherent instructional guidance system, investing in fewer but better tests as indicators of learning rather than sanctioning tools, and having a comprehensive approach to school improvement are the reform strategies most likely to improve teaching practices and student learning.

References

Atkinson, A., Burgess, S., Croxson, B., Gregg, P., Propper, C., Slater, H., & Wilson, D. (2009). Evaluating the impact of performance-related pay for teachers in England. *Labour Economics, 16*(3), 251–261.

Au, W. (2007). High-stakes testing and curricular control: A qualitative metasynthesis. *Educational Researcher, 36*(5), 258–267.

Baker, E., Barton, P., Darling-Hammond, L., Haertel, E., Ladd, H., Linn, R., … Shepard, L. (2010). *Problems with the use of student test scores to evaluate teachers.* Washington, DC: Economic Policy Institute.

Bryk, A., Sebring, P., Allensworth, E., Luppescu, S., & Easton, J. (2010). *Organizing schools for improvement: Lessons from Chicago.* Chicago, IL: University of Chicago Press.

Center for Education Policy. (2009). *How state and federal accountability policies have influenced curriculum and instruction in three states.* Washington, DC: Author.

Cohen, D., & Hill, H. (2000). Instructional policy and classroom performance: The mathematics reform in California. *Teachers College Record, 102*(2), 294–343.

Collier, T., & Millimet, D. (2009). Institutional arrangements in educational systems and student achievement: A cross–national analysis. *Empirical Economics, 37*(2), 329–381.

Firestone, W., & Mayrowetz, D. (2000). Rethinking "high–stakes": Lessons from the United States and England and Wales. *Teachers College Record, 102*(4), 724–749.

Fishman, B., Marx, R., Best, S., & Tal, R. (2003). Linking teacher and student learning to improve professional development in systemic reform. *Teaching and Teacher Education, 19*(6), 643–658.

Fuchs, T., & Wößmann, L. (2007). What accounts for international differences in student performance? A re–examination using PISA data. *Empirical Economics, 32*(2–3), 433–464.

Hamilton, L., Stecher, B., Marsh, J., McCombs, J., Robyn, A., Russell, J., … Barney, H. (2007). *Standards–based accountability under No Child Left Behind: Experiences of teachers and administrators in three states.* Santa Monica, CA: Rand.

Hamilton, L., Stecher, B., Russell, J., Marsh, J., & Miles, J. (2008). Accountability and teaching practices: School-level actions and teacher responses. In B. Fuller, M. Henne, & E. Hannum (Eds.), *Strong state, weak schools: The benefits and dilemmas of centralized accountability* (pp. 31–66). St. Louis, MO: Emerald.

Lee, J. (2008). Is test-driven external accountability effective? Synthesizing the evidence from cross-state causal-comparative and correlational studies. *Review of Educational Research, 78*(3), 608–644.

National Commission on Excellence in Education. (1983). *A nation at risk: The imperative for educational reform.* Washington, DC: Author.

No Child Left Behind Act (2002). Pub. L. No. 107-110, 115 Stat. 1425.

Sahlberg, P. (2007). Education policies for raising student learning: The Finnish approach. *Journal of Education Policy, 22*(2), 147–171.

Stein, M. K., & D'Amico, L. (2002). Inquiry at the crossroads of policy and learning: A study of a district-wide literacy initiative. *Teachers College Record, 104*(7), 1313–1344.

6.15

Teacher Efficacy

JOHN A. ROSS
University of Toronto

Introduction

Teacher efficacy refers to teachers' confidence in their professional abilities, specifically, teachers' expectations that they will be able to perform the actions that lead to student learning. Teacher efficacy influences professional behavior through cognitive processes (especially goal setting), motivational processes (especially attributions for success and failure), affective processes (especially control of negative feelings), and selection processes (choices about physical and social environments, activities, etc.) (Bandura, 1997). Teachers with high levels of teacher efficacy anticipate that they will be successful. They choose more challenging goals for themselves and their students, are more likely to take responsibility for outcomes, and persist in the face of failure. Teacher efficacy crystallizes in the early career years when teachers are learning to teach (Woolfolk Hoy & Spero, 1995) and remains relatively stable unless disturbed by a change in working conditions such as assignment to an unfamiliar grade or subject or curriculum restructuring.

Research Evidence

The substantial evidence supporting claims about the importance of teacher efficacy has been summarized in three substantive narrative reviews. The first examined the antecedents and consequences of teacher efficacy, focusing on the implications for school improvement and building the argument that enhancing teachers' beliefs plays a key role in school improvement (Ross, 1998). The second reviewed the theoretical underpinnings of the construct, reconceptualizing teacher efficacy as perception of task difficulty combined with assessment of personal teaching competence (Tschannen-Moran, Woolfolk Hoy, & Hoy, 1998). The third reviewed studies of collective teacher efficacy; that is, teachers' perceptions of the ability of their fellow faculty members to bring about student learning (Goddard, Hoy, & Woolfolk Hoy, 2004). The latter review found that collective and individual efficacy were highly correlated but conceptually distinct. The evidence is consistent: few teacher characteristics have as much impact on instructional practice and student outcomes as teacher efficacy.

Although no quantitative meta-analysis has been published, teacher efficacy is a strong predictor of student achievement at the individual and collective teacher levels. The causal mechanisms linking teacher efficacy to achievement include many factors, the most salient are these five:

Professional Learning. Teachers with higher teacher efficacy are more willing than other teachers to participate in professional learning opportunities (Geijsel, Sleegers, Stoel, & Kruger, 2009) and to experiment with new teaching ideas, particularly techniques that are difficult, involve risks, and require control to be shared with students. Such teachers are willing to improve their skills and implement new approaches because they believe that they can make a difference to students. By acquiring new skills, teachers with high efficacy beliefs become more effective in the classroom, creating higher achievement. There is a reciprocal relation that can create an upward spiral of success: high teacher efficacy enables teachers to seek out and acquire new instructional skills; such skills contribute to greater student learning and success in the classroom strengthens teachers' beliefs in their effectiveness.

Difficult-to-Teach Students. Teachers with higher teacher efficacy are more likely than teachers with lesser confidence to focus on lower achievers, take responsibility for students with exceptionalities rather than referring them to special classes, and hold high academic and social expectations for even inattentive and aggressive children (Tournaki & Podell, 2005). High efficacy teachers are also less likely to label incoming students as problematic (Munthe & Thuen, 2009). Giving more attention to hard-to-teach students and being resilient in the face of teaching challenges raises the low end of the achievement distribution.

266

Classroom Management and Emotional Control. Teachers with high efficacy beliefs rely less on custodial than on humanistic student management approaches. The latter techniques promote self-regulation, a strong contributor to student achievement. Teacher efficacy mediates between perceived student misbehavior and emotional exhaustion (Tsouloupas, Carson, Matthews, Grawitch, & Barber, 2010) such that high efficacy teachers are less likely to experience burnout from dealing with challenging students. The insulation from emotional enervation provided by self-efficacy beliefs and the higher emotional intelligence of high efficacy teachers enable these teachers to channel more of their emotional energy into interactions focused on learning rather than on confronting violations of classroom rules. Because frequent, negative interaction with misbehaving children is the leading job stressor for teachers, emotional control contributes to high efficacy teachers experiencing high levels of job satisfaction (Caprara, Barbaranelli, Borgogni, & Steca, 2003), exhibiting greater enthusiasm for teaching and continuing in the profession. In addition, because job satisfaction is linked to lower absenteeism and professional commitment, high teacher efficacy contributes to enhanced student achievement.

Student Self-Efficacy. Teacher efficacy contributes to student self-efficacy: confident teachers engender confidence in their students. Student self-efficacy predicts achievement directly through goal setting and indirectly through persistence. Student self-efficacy has a greater effect on student achievement than student ability and other motivational variables (Pajares, 1996).

Enabling School Culture. Teacher efficacy contributes to the professional commitment of teachers (Ross & Gray, 2006), the maintenance of collaborative school culture, teacher influence on instructional issues (Goddard, 2002), and faculty trust. Each of these school culture variables enhances the ability of teachers to work together as a cohesive team to promote student learning, contributing to higher achievement through vertical and horizontal integration of instructional practice.

Summary and Recommendations

Critiques of teacher efficacy research focus on researchers' reliance on cross-sectional designs, an issue given the reciprocal nature of teacher efficacy-achievement relationships. There are professional development treatments developed from social cognition theory that elevate teacher efficacy but few of these interventions simultaneously examine the impact of teacher efficacy changes on student achievement or track the achievement impact of changes in teacher efficacy that occur when students move from one classroom to another. Many studies have identified mediators and moderators of teacher efficacy but very few have found or even searched for moderators of the teacher efficacy–achievement relationship. In addition, researchers have favored between-teacher designs with less attention devoted to identifying predictors of teacher efficacy variations within-teachers.

The findings from teacher efficacy research provide consistent evidence of the construct's impact on student achievement. Schools should consider teachers' professional confidence when making selection decisions: it is not just the overall level of confidence but its foundation in realistic self-appraisal. For experienced teachers, strengthening teacher efficacy through professional learning and organizational enhancement should be a core element of school improvement plans. Principals can play a key role by helping teachers recognize their success and attributing student outcomes to teachers' professional abilities; for example, by guiding teachers' interpretation of classroom and external assessments (Ross & Bruce, 2007), by facilitating access to skill development in-service, by creating school structures that enable teachers to learn from one another, and by emphasizing the collective capacity at the school as a stimulus to individual renewal.

References

Bandura, A. (1997). *Self-efficacy: The exercise of control*. New York: Freeman.

Caprara, G. V., Barbaranelli, C., Borgogni, L., & Steca, P. (2003). Efficacy beliefs as determinants of teachers' job satisfaction. *Journal of Educational Psychology, 95*, 821–832.

Geijsel, F. P., Sleegers, P. J. C., Stoel, R. D., & Kruger, M. L. (2009). The effect of teacher psychological and school organizational and leadership factors on teachers' professional learning in Dutch schools. *Elementary School Journal, 109*(4), 406–427.

Goddard, R. D. (2002). Collective efficacy and school organization: A multilevel analysis of teacher influence in schools. *Theory and Research in Educational Administration, 1*, 169–184.

Goddard, R. D., Hoy, W. K., & Woolfolk Hoy, A. (2004). Collective efficacy beliefs: Theoretical developments, empirical evidence, and future directions. *Educational Researcher, 33*(3), 3–13.

Munthe, E., & Thuen, E. (2009). Lower secondary school teachers' judgements of pupils' problems. *Teachers and Teaching: Theory and Practice, 15*(5), 563–578.

Pajares, F. (1996). Self–efficacy beliefs in academic settings. *Review of Educational Research, 66*(4), 543–578.

Ross, J. A. (1998). The antecedents and consequences of teacher efficacy. In J. Brophy (Ed.), *Research on Teaching* (Vol. 7, pp. 49–74). Greenwich, CT: JAI Press.

Ross, J. A., & Bruce, C. (2007). Self–assessment and professional growth: The case of a grade 8 mathematics teacher. *Teaching and Teacher Education, 23*(2), 146–159.

Ross, J. A., & Gray, P. (2006) Transformational leadership and teacher commitment to organizational values: The mediating effects of collective teacher efficacy. *School Effectiveness and School Improvement, 17*(2), 179–199.

Tournaki, N., & Podell, D. M. (2005). The impact of student characteristics and teacher efficacy on teachers' predictions of student success. *Teaching and Teacher Education, 21*, 299–314.

Tschannen–Moran, M., Wolfolk Hoy, A., & Hoy, W. K. (1998). Teacher efficacy: Its meaning and measure. *Review of Educational Research, 68*(2), 202–248.

Tsouloupas, C. N., Carson, R. L., Matthews, R., Grawitch, M. J., & Barber, L. K. (2010). Exploring the association between teachers' perceived student misbehaviour and emotional exhaustion: The importance of teacher efficacy beliefs and emotion regulation. *Educational Psychology, 30*(2), 173–189.

Woolfolk Hoy, A., & Spero, R. B. (2005). Changes in teacher efficacy during the early years of teaching: A comparison of four measures. *Teaching and Teacher Education, 21*, 343–356.

6.16

Teachers' Epistemological Beliefs and Achievement

Gregory Schraw
University of Nevada, Las Vegas

Joanne Brownlee
Queensland University of Technology

Lori Olafson
University of Nevada, Las Vegas

Introduction

Epistemology is the study of beliefs about the origin and acquisition of knowledge. Research since the early 1980s has focused more on the structure and development of college students' epistemological beliefs, although there has been an increased interested in teachers' epistemological beliefs since 2000. There is clear evidence that teachers' epistemological beliefs influence instructional practice and achievement of learning outcomes for their students.

Research Evidence

There seem to be at least four separate epistemological beliefs (Schommer-Aikins, 2002). One is *simple knowledge,* which refers to the belief that knowledge is discrete and unambiguous. Students and teachers who score high on this dimension believe that learning is equivalent to accumulating a vast amount of factual knowledge in an encyclopedic fashion. A second belief is *certain knowledge,* which pertains to the assumption that knowledge is constant: Once something is believed to be true, it remains true forever. A third belief is *fixed ability*, which holds that one's ability to learn is inborn and cannot be improved through either effort or strategy use. A fourth belief is *quick learning,* which refers to the belief that learning occurs quickly or not at all.

These beliefs are assumed to develop over time across three possible stages or positions, which include *dualist/absolutist* (i.e., belief that there is one right authority), *multiplist* (i.e., belief that different personal viewpoints exist), and *relativist/evaluativist* (i.e., belief that knowledge and values are contextual and evaluated). These stages map loosely onto Perry's (1970) developmental positions of dualism, relativism, and commitment to relativism. There is evidence that individuals at the evaluativist stage are

better problem solvers and reasoners, in part because they use more and better evidence to construct arguments from integrated perspectives (Kuhn, 1991).

Epistemological Beliefs and Teaching Practices. Since 2000, researchers have investigated teachers' epistemological beliefs using interviews and the self-report scales. Teachers characterized by multiplist and evaluativist views are more likely to promote constructivist learning activities in their classroom (Olafson & Schraw, 2006). These studies have reported that teachers' epistemological beliefs influence teaching practices (Brownlee & Berthelsen, 2005). One consistent finding is that teachers with more sophisticated epistemological beliefs are more likely to endorse student-centered instructional practices that emphasize critical reasoning. In contrast, teachers with less sophisticated beliefs are more likely to focus on traditional curriculum, student testing, and mastery of basic concepts. In addition, teachers with more sophisticated personal epistemologies used a greater number of pedagogical strategies in their classrooms that are designed to promote deeper learning and reflection, including generating, constructing, and reconstructing. Such teaching practices are likely to influence the learning outcomes or achievement of students in their classrooms.

Research also provides evidence that teachers' epistemological beliefs affect how they model their beliefs and views to students. Teachers holding the view that ability is fixed and cannot be changed may inadvertently discourage students from setting ambitious learning goals. In contrast, teachers who believe that ability is less critical to learning may indirectly encourage students to set higher goals and to be less troubled by temporary failures in the classroom. For example, Jordan, Schwartz, and McGhie-Richmond (2009) found that teachers who believe that learning is not quick, and that knowledge is constructed by taking on others' perspectives, were more likely to use dialogue to promote thinking in children. In these classrooms that were epistemologically based, students were encouraged to embrace the complexity and evolution of knowledge. The teacher recognized the importance of developing students' epistemological beliefs and adapted instruction in order to promote development. Rather than requiring students to memorize facts, for example, the teacher asked students to synthesize knowledge and apply this knowledge to challenging tasks (Schommer-Aikins, 2002).

Conversely, teachers who believe that knowledge is absolute and can be passively received, and that ability is more or less fixed, used more teacher centered, traditional approaches to teaching. Several other studies have demonstrated that teachers with sophisticated constructivist beliefs focus on higher order thinking in the classroom and have higher expectations for student performance and achievement (Maggioni & Parkinson, 2008).

Epistemological Beliefs and Learning Outcomes. Teachers' epistemological beliefs have an impact on student epistemological development and learning outcomes, and shape students' emerging conceptions of knowledge (Lidar, Lundqvist, & Ostman, 2005; Marra, 2005). Teachers' beliefs in simple knowledge negatively affected complex problem solving in the classroom. As beliefs in complex, incremental knowledge increased, problem solving improved. Similarly, epistemological beliefs differed across academic disciplines among college undergraduate and graduate students. Students in "soft" disciplines, such as the humanities, were more likely to believe that knowledge is uncertain than students in "hard" disciplines, such as physics. Compared with undergraduates, graduate students were more likely to believe that knowledge is uncertain and develops incrementally (they did not believe in quick learning).

In seminal work, Kuhn (1991) found that epistemological beliefs are related to one's ability to argue persuasively and that sophisticated argumentation increases as students become better educated and exposed to evaluativist world views. In this program of research, individuals were classified as an *absolutist* (one who believes that knowledge is absolutely right or wrong), a *multiplist* (one who believes that knowledge is completely relative), or an *evaluativist* (one who believes that knowledge is evaluated and constrained by contextual factors such as commonly accepted rules) based on their beliefs about the certainty of knowledge. Evaluativists were more likely than absolutists to provide legitimate evidence in support of an argument. In addition, compared with absolutists, evaluativists generated a greater number of plausible alternative theories and provided better counterarguments.

Changing Epistemological Beliefs. Beliefs appear to develop slowly, although more sophisticated beliefs and a greater level of development have been observed in graduate students compared to preservice undergraduate students.

However, a number of studies report that preservice teachers who were enrolled in a program based on multiplist teaching perspectives experienced more growth in sophisticated epistemological beliefs as compared with preservice teachers in a skills-based approach, suggesting that critical inquiry and exposure to a variety of epistemological perspectives during preservice training is beneficial to students. As an example, Marra (2005) reported how constructivist instruction affected the development of graduate student teachers at a university. Teachers reported a variety of changes after the course, but especially changes in epistemological and pedagogical beliefs. Teachers adopted constructivist beliefs that emphasized the role of student interactions. In addition, graduate student teachers adopted stronger contextualist beliefs about the complexity and certainty of knowledge. A number of recent studies indicate that collaborative discussion, journals, and reflection logs in the context of preservice teacher education are effective ways to promote awareness of beliefs and facilitate epistemological development.

Nevertheless, discrepancies between teachers' espoused and enacted beliefs are commonly noted in the research. In particular, it seems that although preservice teachers indicate a preference for constructivist beliefs based on a multiplist epistemology, they find it difficult to put these beliefs into practice once they enter the teaching profession (Ozgun-Koca & Sen, 2006). Discrepancies have been reported at all grade levels in a variety of domains. Several explanations have been put forth, including administrative pressure to adopt transmission pedagogy; that is, the role of high-stakes testing that emphasizes proficiency rather than higher order reasoning, and lack of time.

Summary and Recommendations

There is clear evidence that how teachers think about knowledge and knowing does affect their classroom practices and student learning outcomes. We are starting to understand more about how such explicit reflections might influence changes in beliefs. For example, Valinides and Angeli (2005) showed that changes in preservice teachers' epistemological beliefs could be affected by explicit reflection on the process of critical thinking. Another potential area of research that sheds light on explicit reflections relates to calibration training. Calibration involves helping preservice teachers to analyze their own epistemological beliefs and decide which beliefs are more likely to lead to effective teaching practices. Maggioni and Parkinson (2008) suggest that simply reflecting on personal epistemology is not enough. There needs to be some understanding of how these beliefs measure up and relate to effective practice. Explicit reflection on epistemological beliefs, particularly through the use of calibration training, provides an interesting new line of inquiry for how to promote epistemological beliefs in teachers.

Promoting explicit discussion of epistemological beliefs and their impact on learning and teaching should also be a part of the educational curriculum in general, not just teacher preparation (Brownlee & Berthelsen, 2005). Collaborative learning and active reflection are excellent ways to promote such epistemological awareness and development in classrooms and also for preservice teachers in teacher education programs (Olafson & Schraw, 2006). However, while we know that such approaches may promote better learning outcomes for students in classrooms, we also know that even skilled teachers find it difficult at times to put into practice constructivist pedagogy consistent with sophisticated epistemological beliefs. Teachers should be prepared to face these challenges in the classroom.

References

Brownlee, J., & Berthelsen, D. (2005). Personal epistemology and relational pedagogy in early childhood teacher education programs. *Early Years, 26,* 17–29.

Hofer, B. (2004). Exploring the dimensions of personal epistemology in differing classroom contexts: Student interpretations during the first year of college. *Contemporary Educational Psychology, 29,* 129–163.

Jordan, A., Schwartz, E., & McGhie-Richmond, D. (2009). Preparing teachers for inclusive classrooms, *Teaching and Teacher Education, 25,* 535–542.

Kuhn, D. (1991). *The skills of argument.* New York: Cambridge University Press.

Lidar, M., Lundqvist, E., & Ostman, L. (2005). Teaching and learning in the science classroom: The interplay between teachers' epistemological moves and students' practical epistemologies. *Science Education, 90,* 148–163.

Maggioni, L., & Parkinson, M. (2008). The role of teacher epistemic cognition, epistemic beliefs, and calibration in instruction. *Educational Psychology Review, 20*(4), 445–461.

Marra, R. (2005). Teacher beliefs: The impact of the design of constructivist learning environments on instructor epistemologies. *Learning Environments Research, 8,* 135–155.

Olafson, L. J., & Schraw, G. (2006). Teachers' beliefs and practices within and across domains. *International Journal of Educational Research, 45,* 71–84.

Ozgun-Koca, S., & Sen, A. (2006). The beliefs and perceptions of pre–service teachers enrolled in a subject–area dominant teacher education program about "effective education." *Teaching and Teacher Education, 22,* 946–960.

Perry, W. G., Jr. (1970). *Forms of intellectual and ethical development in the college years.* New York: Academic Press.

Schommer–Aikins, M. (2002). An evolving theoretical framework for an epistemological belief system. In B. K. Hofer & P. R. Pintrich (Eds.), *Personal epistemology: The psychology of beliefs about knowledge and knowing* (pp. 103–118). Mahwah, NJ: Erlbaum.

Valinides, N., & Angeli, C. (2005). Effects of instruction on changes in epistemological beliefs. *Contemporary Educational Psychology, 30,* 314–330.

6.17

Teacher Motivation and Student Achievement Outcomes

H. M. G. WATT AND P. W. RICHARDSON
Monash University

Introduction

Motivation theorists share the view that motivation is an internal state that initiates, regulates, and sustains behaviour. There are various theoretical models of motivation that focus on different components and processes. Until recently, researchers have predominantly focused on student motivations, and their relation to student participation, learning, and achievement. Lately, theories and concepts developed in the student motivation literature have been fruitfully applied to the study of teacher motivation (Richardson & Watt, 2010).

Teacher motivations impact teacher behaviours, and thereby students' own motivations. In turn, students' motivations impact their participation, effort, aspirations, learning and achievement (c.f., Section 2 this Handbook). In his seminal review, Brophy (1986) included choice, sincere praise, reinforcement, enthusiasm, guidance, modelling, and interest induction as teacher behaviours that promote student motivation and achievement. Public competition, frequent drill and practice, and insincere teacher praise and criticism tend to undermine student interest and motivation (e.g., Turner et al., 2002).

Research Evidence

The major teacher motivation theories are currently self-efficacy theory, self-determination theory (SDT), expectancy-value theory, and goal theory. Of these, teacher self-efficacy research has the longest history; it refers to "the teacher's belief in her and his ability to organize and execute the courses of action required to successfully accomplish a specific teaching task in a particular context" (Tschannen-Moran, Woolfolk Hoy, & Hoy, 1998, p. 233). Teachers who have high self-efficacy are more likely to try new teaching strategies, implement classroom management methods which enhance student autonomy, provide particular assistance to low achievers, build student competence beliefs, set attainable student goals, persist in the face of failure, be more committed to the profession, and experience less burnout (c.f., Ross, Entry 6.15 this volume). On the other hand, exaggerated levels of self-efficacy can impede innovation, learning new skills, and encumber critical reflection (Wheatley, 2002). Self-efficacy is most malleable early in learning (Bandura, 1997) but resistant to change once established; it has been found to increase through teacher education then decrease during early career teaching, possibly due to reduced social and structural supports. Beyond the individual, collective teacher efficacy is an emergent group-level factor which is a relatively stable attribute of school culture, and once established, is resistant to change (Woolfolk Hoy, Hoy, & Davis, 2009). It interacts with individual teacher self-efficacy to motivate increased effort, persistence, resilience, and consequently, student outcomes. The mechanisms by which teacher self-efficacy beliefs can bring about consequences for students are not yet clear, nor, whether causal inferences are warranted.

Self-determination theory (SDT) posits a general theory of basic human needs based on autonomy, competence, and relatedness (Deci & Ryan, 2000). Autonomy supportive teachers facilitate and encourage students in their goal pursuit, providing choice, rationales, empathy, and structure, while avoiding high levels of control (Reeve, Bolt, & Cai, 1999). Teachers who are engaged, committed, and enjoy their work, provide greater autonomy support to their students, who exhibit higher intrinsic motivation, self-regulated learning, and achievement. Specifically, teacher involvement (affection, attunement, dependability), structure (clarity of expectations, adjustment of teaching strategies), and autonomy support (respect, relevance) have been found to affect students' behavioral engagement and emotions (Skinner & Belmont, 1993). Different student characteristics also elicit different teacher behaviours, highlighting the need to intervene into teacher-student interactions. Otherwise teachers tend to magnify students' initial levels of motivation, producing increased motivation for the already motivated, but decreased levels for the initially unmotivated.

Competence. Teachers' expectancies for students (see Jussim, Entry 6.8 this volume) can have profound influences on students' perceptions of competence, learning, and achievement. These expectations are often communicated nonverbally and unintentionally, but students nonetheless perceive and internalise them, with direct consequences for self-efficacy, motivation, effort, and achievement. Implicit teacher prejudices shape teacher expectancies; for example, teachers who evaluate their students as less intelligent through the lens of prejudiced attitudes, engender negative achievement consequences (c.f., Bishop, Entry 2.18 this volume).

Relatedness. Relatedness is fostered by teacher warmth and affect to students. This acutely influences how students experience their classrooms, their subsequent goals and achievement. When interactions and relationships are emotionally supportive, nurturing, and facilitative of goal achievement through the provision of help and instruction, students come to value and pursue the academic and social goals conveyed by their teachers (Wentzel, 2009). High expectations for student achievement in combination with teacher caring and support are essential ingredients to positive relationships.

Expectancy-Value Theory. Expectancy-value theroy (Eccles, 2005) has provided a powerful lens through which to understand the complexity of teacher motivations, the enduring impact they have on career persistence and satisfaction, consequences for teachers' psychological well-being, and implications for student achievement. Motivations most endorsed for choosing teaching as a career include intrinsic value, perceived teaching abilities, to make a social contribution, work with youth, and shape the future of youth. Those initial career motivations subsequently have a positive impact on beginning teachers' career satisfaction and plans to persist in the profession. In contrast, negative longitudinal correlations occur as a result of entering teaching as a "fallback" career motivation; and, personal utility motivations (job security, time for family, job transferability) exhibit negative or nonsignificant relationships. A typology of beginning teachers has been identified, who hold particular constellations of motivations even at the outset of their careers (see Watt & Richardson, 2008).

Goal Theory. Recent work using the conceptual framework of goal theory, has demonstrated that the classroom is an achievement arena for teachers too, predicting teacher behaviours and thereby student outcomes. Teacher mastery and ability-avoidance goals have been respectively related to their positive and negative patterns of classroom communication and behaviour (Butler & Shibaz, 2008), while relational goals are the most critical.

Summary and Recommendations

Similar elements have been identified at the school level as at the class level that shape student, and presumably, teacher motivations. Environments characterised by centralised control and high levels of bureaucracy and compliance serve to dampen the positive effects which teacher motivations can otherwise have. Whereas, a decentralised model of decision making, a school climate reflecting feelings of unity, pride, trust, cooperation, acceptance of differences, security, shared goals, and a supportive school leadership, allow the space and opportunity for skilled and motivated teachers to be more effective (Rowan, Chiang, & Miller, 1997). Motivated teachers are more likely to support and implement progressive reforms, experience higher career satisfaction, and remain in the profession longer. But, when teachers perceive pressures from above (e.g., curriculum and performance standards) and below (e.g., demanding students), they become less self-determined toward their work, and more controlling with their students, which negatively impacts student intrinsic motivation and sense of autonomy (Pelletier, Seguin-Levesque, & Legault, 2002; Roth, Assor, Kanat-Maymon, & Kaplan, 2007). Although we know working with children and adolescents is consistently strongly endorsed as a reason for wanting to be a teacher, policy measures designed to increase teacher accountability, through measuring student achievement, have significantly changed the nature of teachers' work and reduced the time which can be spent in teacher–student interactions. Under these circumstances, teacher motivation is a double-edged sword that can lead to reduced engagement if highly valued goals are not attained (de Jesus & Lens, 2005).

Teachers exhibit higher levels of job stress than those in other professions (Stoeber & Rennert, 2008). Teachers who maintain their high motivations in situations where their goals cannot be attained are more likely to experience burnout (de Jesus & Lens, 2005), a condition linked to teacher turnover, low professional commitment, poor coping strategies, low work satisfaction and well-being. In contrast, *worn out* teachers reduce their effort and occupational engagement to cope with chronic stressors, and are no longer personally invested in performing well. Three times as many teachers were worn out than burned out (Stephenson, 1990). Teachers worn down by their work exhibit reduced work goals, lower responsibility for work outcomes, lower idealism, heightened emotional detachment, work alienation, and self-interest (Burke & Greenglass, 1995). When teachers become burned out, or worn out, their students' achievement outcomes are likely to suffer because they are more concerned with their personal survival. In contrast, motivated teachers, working in contexts which allow them to achieve their goals, will promote student motivations, learning, and achievement outcomes.

References

Bandura, A. (1997). *Self-efficacy: The exercise of control.* New York: Freeman.

Brophy, J. (1986). Teacher influences on student achievement. *American Psychologist, 41,* 1069–1077.

Burke, R. J., & Greenglass, E. R. (1995). A longitudinal examination of the Cherniss model of psychological burnout. *Social Science Medicine, 40,* 1357–1363.

Butler, R., & Shibaz, L. (2008). Achievement goals for teaching as predictors of students' perceptions of instructional practices and students' help seeking and cheating. *Learning and Instruction, 18,* 453–467.

de Jesus, S. N., & Lens, W. (2005). An integrated model for the study of teacher motivation. *Applied Psychology—An International Review (Psychologie Appliquée—Revue Internationale), 54*(1), 119–134.

Deci, E. L., & Ryan, R. M. (2000). The "what" and "why" of goal pursuits: Human needs and the self–determination of behaviour. *Psychological Inquiry, 11,* 227–268.

Eccles, J. S. (2005). Subjective task value and the Eccles et al. model of achievement-related choices. In A. J. Elliot & C. S. Dweck (Eds.), *Handbook of competence and motivation* (pp. 105–121). New York: Guilford.

Pelletier, L. G., Seguin–Levesque, C., & Legault, L. (2002). Pressure from above and pressure from below as determinants of teachers' motivation and teaching behaviors. *Journal of Educational Psychology, 94*(1), 186–196.

Reeve, J., Bolt, E., & Cai, Y. (1999). Autonomy-supportive teachers: How they teach and motivate students. *Journal of Educational Psychology, 91*(3), 537–548.

Richardson, P. W., & Watt, H. M. G. (2010). Current and future directions in teacher motivation research. In T. C. Urdan & S. A. Karabenick (Eds.), *Advances in motivation and achievement: Vol. 16B. The decade ahead: Applications and contexts of motivation and achievement* (pp. 139–173). Bingley, England: Emerald.

Roth, G., Assor, A., Kanat–Maymon, Y., & Kaplan, H. (2007). Autonomous motivation for teaching: How self–determined teaching may lead to self–determined learning. *Journal of Educational Psychology, 99,* 761–774.

Rowan, B., Chiang, F.–S., & Miller, R. J. (1997). Using research on employees' performance to study the effects of teachers on students' achievement *Sociology of Education, 70*(4), 256–284.

Skinner, E. A., & Belmont, M. J. (1993). Motivation in the classroom: Reciprocal effects of teacher behaviour and student engagement across the school year. *Journal of Educational Psychology, 85,* 571–581.

Stephenson, D. (1990). Affective consequences of teachers' psychological investment. *Journal of Educational Research, 84*(1), 53–57.

Stoeber, J., & Rennert, D. (2008). Perfectionism in school teachers: Relations with stress appraisals, coping styles, and burnout. *Anxiety, Stress, & Coping, 21,* 37–53.

Tschannen–Moran, M., Woolfolk Hoy, A., & Hoy, W. K. (1998). Teacher efficacy: Its meaning and measure. *Review of Educational Research 68*(2), 202–248.

Turner, J. C., Midgley, C., Meyer, D. K., Gheen, M., Anderman, E. M., Kang, Y., & Patrick, H. (2002). The classroom environment and students' reports of avoidance strategies in mathematics: A multimethod study. *Journal of Educational Psychology, 94*(1), 88–106.

Watt, H. M. G., & Richardson, P. W. (2008). Motivations, perceptions, and aspirations concerning teaching as a career for different types of beginning teachers. *Learning and Instruction, 18,* 408–428.

Wentzel, K. (2009). Students' relationships with teachers as motivational contexts. In K. Wentzel & A. Wigfield (Eds.), *Handbook of motivation at school.* New York: Routledge.

Wheatley, K. F. (2002). The potential benefits of teacher efficacy doubts for educational reform. *Teaching and Teacher Education, 18,* 5–22.

Woolfolk Hoy, Hoy, & Davis, (2009). Teachers' self-efficacy beliefs. In K. Wentzel & A. Wingfield (Eds.), *Handbook of motivation at school* (pp. 627–654). New York: Routledge,

6.18

The Relation of Teacher Characteristics to Student Achievement

XIN MA
University of Kentucky

Introduction

A large body of studies examines the relation of teacher characteristics to student achievement, often referred to as teacher effects. Although teacher characteristics are defined with variation across studies, student achievement usually refers to a form of standardized achievement test (e.g., ACT). The goal of research on teacher effects is to identify effective teacher characteristics that promote growth (gains) in student outcomes. Researchers seek to determine the extent of the relation between teacher characteristics and student outcomes to establish an order of importance among teacher characteristics.

Research Evidence

According to early research on school effectiveness (e.g., Coleman et al., 1966), variables that could be manipulated (e.g., the nature of school curriculum) had very limited effects on student achievement when compared with the effects of family background. These early contentions led to the pessimistic conclusion that schools do not make any difference in schooling outcomes and have provoked vigorous research on school effects. The relation of teacher characteristics to student achievement has been part of this research effort.

Do Teachers Matter Revisited. Recent advances in research on school effects have led to a general agreement that schools do provide some "added value." Teachers are certainly one of the most critical elements of this valued-added system with its causal mechanism commonly assumed as teaching influencing learning. For example, as the most proximal factors to students, teacher characteristics determine student outcomes (more than both school characteristics and district characteristics that are much more distant to students) (Stringfield, 1994).

Some studies in econometrics attempt to estimate what can be referred to as "net" teacher effects. For example, Rockoff (2004) used panel data from elementary school students and teachers to estimate teacher effects with control over student characteristics and classroom specific variables. He found large and statistically significant differences among teachers. A one standard deviation increase in teacher quality (teacher effects) raises reading and mathematics test scores by a quarter of one standard deviation on a nationally standardized scale. Two propositions are revealed in these studies. First, teachers can be dramatically different in their effectiveness in teaching. Second, teachers can be reasonably responsible for gains in student achievement. Therefore, it does matter to which teacher a student is assigned.

Teacher Education, Experience, and Certification. Most studies search for unique teacher quality (education background, performance on licensure examinations, certification status, and teaching experience) in relation to student achievement to bear specific implications for education policy and practice. Any simple inspection of this research literature, however, would reveal abundant divergence not only in empirical findings but also in attempts to synthesize existing research literature.

In 2002, the U.S. Department of Education released its own review of the research literature on teacher quality. Several propositions are relevant to the relation between teacher quality and student achievement, including that "researchers have found that some teachers are much more effective than others" (p. 7), that "studies have consistently documented the important connection between a teacher's verbal and cognitive abilities and student achievement" (p. 7), and that "there is little evidence that education school course work leads to improved student achievement" (p. 19).

Darling-Hammond and Youngs's (2002) review presented both similar and different propositions on the same relation:

74

[Several] aspects of teachers' qualifications have been found to bear some relationship to student achievement. These include teachers' (a) general academic and verbal ability; (b) subject matter knowledge; (c) knowledge about teaching and learning as reflected in teacher education courses or preparation experiences; (d) teaching experience; and (e) the combined set of qualifications measured by teacher certification, which includes most of the preceding factors. (p. 16)

In fact, Darling-Hammond and Youngs (2002) claimed effects (on student achievement) of these teacher quality factors at all levels (teacher, school, district, and state).

Wayne and Youngs (2003) attempted to reconcile the divergent empirical findings by carefully linking knowledge claims with the qualities of research methods. They concluded confidently that "mathematics students learn more when their teachers have standard mathematics certification (as compared with private school mathematics certification or no mathematics certification)" (pp. 105–106) and "high school students learn more mathematics when their mathematics teachers have additional degrees or coursework in mathematics" (p. 103). They chose to leave out the relation of teacher experience to student achievement, believing that methodological concerns make "the relationships that emerge between experience and student achievement… difficult to interpret" (p. 107). They suggested with caution that students learn more from teachers with higher test scores and teachers who graduate from colleges with higher ratings.

Several large-scale studies based on representative samples or vigorous experimental designs have been added to the research literature after Wayne and Youngs (2003), which is the latest review on the issue. RAND (2010) investigated the relation of teacher quality (experience, education, and scores on licensure examinations) to student achievement by analyzing 5 years of reading and mathematics standards tests. There is no evidence that these traditional standards of teacher quality have substantial effects on student achievement across elementary, middle, and high schools. Using teacher surveys from a congressionally mandated national study of the Title 1 program (Prospects), Jepsen (2005) reported that teacher quality (education, certification, and experience) is an insignificant predictor of student achievement, especially for the lower elementary grades. Nye, Konstantopoulos, and Hedges (2004) employed a 4-year experimental design in which teachers and students are randomly assigned to classes to estimate how large teacher effects are. They concluded "the estimated relation of teacher experience with student achievement gains is substantial, but is statistically significant only for 2nd-grade reading and 3rd-grade mathematics" (p. 237). Using data also from Prospects, Rowan, Correnti, and Miller (2002) reported a negative effect of teachers' holding master's degrees on (elementary) student achievement. Rowan et al. also stated that the impact of teacher certification on the performance of elementary students reveals little discernible effect.

Assessing Characteristics of Teachers and Teaching. Hill, Rowan, and Ball (2005) classified research programs that have measured characteristics of teachers and teaching. What has been discussed in this chapter falls into what they call "teachers in the educational production function literature" (p. 374) that examines teacher preparation and experience as well as teacher performance on certification examinations or other tests of subject matter competence to focus on teacher characteristics that relate to student achievement.

Teacher Behaviors.   Classified as "teachers in the process-product literature" (p. 373), another set of studies focuses on classrooms to examine the relationship between teacher behavior (curricular and instructional characteristics of a teacher's classroom practice) and student achievement. Moving beyond the impact of appearance and enthusiasm, researchers take the stand that what teachers do in their classrooms affects student achievement. Hill et al. (2005) concluded that:

[There is] substantial evidence that certain teaching behaviors did affect students' achievement gains. For example, focusing class time on active academic instruction rather than classroom management, student choice/game time, personal adjustment, or nonacademic subjects was found to be a consistent correlate of student achievement gains, as were presenting materials in a structured format via advance organizers, making salient linkages explicit, and calling attention to main ideas. (p. 373)

Teacher Knowledge.   Finally, Hill et al. (2005) presented what they call "teachers in the teacher knowledge literature" (p. 376). Focused directly on teacher knowledge, this alternative literature asks what teachers must know about subject matter content in order to teach it to students for maximum gains in achievement. "In this research program, researchers propose distinguishing between the ways in which academic content must be known to teach effectively and the ways in which ordinary adults know such content" (p. 376).

The general expectation is that teachers' ability to understand three types of knowledge affects student achievement. *Content knowledge* is facts and concepts; *pedagogical content knowledge* is representations of specific content ideas and an understanding of what makes the learning of a specific topic difficult or easy for students; and *curriculum knowledge* is awareness of how topics are arranged both within a school year and over time and ways of using curriculum resources (e.g., textbooks) to organize a program of study for students (see Hill et al., 2005).

This alternative approach to understand teacher characteristics in relation to student achievement is promising: "Until now, however, it has not been possible to link teachers' professionally usable knowledge of their subjects to student achievement" (Hill et al., 2005, p. 377). These researchers have started this line of research, reporting that

Teachers' mathematical knowledge was significantly related to student achievement gains in both first and third grades after controlling for key student- and teacher-level covariates. This result, while consonant with findings from the educational production function literature, was obtained via a measure focusing on the specialized mathematical knowledge and skills used in teaching mathematics. (p. 371).

Summary and Recommendations

Research syntheses have generated recommendations for both education policy and classroom practice. Wayne and Youngs (2003) stated that "policymakers should encourage better screening of prospective teachers [and] may wish to require that teachers hold degrees from institutions with particular quality characteristics" (p. 97). In addition they noted that, "teacher compensation systems [that] reward teachers for holding advanced degrees [are likely] a wise policy [and] policymakers [may use] their power to specify coursework and degree requirements for different assignments" (p. 103).

Reynolds and Teddlie (2000) recommend firstly the management of time to ensure lessons start and finish on time, secondly the importance of clarity of lessons based on adequate preparation, and thirdly teacher effective behavior including questioning, having a limited focus in lessons (avoiding spreading out to several different curriculum areas), maintaining task orientation, keeping rapid lesson pace, ensuring that classroom routines and rules are well understood to reduce the need of students to seek out teachers for guidance, and having a warm and accepting classroom climate.

Focusing on education research, Wayne and Youngs (2003) concluded that "there is a need for research on the relationship between student achievement and teachers' performance on tests currently in use [and] researchers should take note of the recent implementation of new approaches to teacher performance assessment" (p. 101), that "studies that use subject-specific measures of teacher preparation and that distinguish between subject preparation and preparation in the methods of teaching a subject would provide valuable new information" (p. 104), and that "researchers need to design studies that take into consideration the particular requirements associated with particular certification types used in individual states [and] parallel research efforts are needed to examine differences in retention rates among teachers with different types of certification" (p. 106).

Nye et al. (2004) have demonstrated the importance of contextual characteristics in education research on teacher effects:

Our estimates of teacher effects on achievement gains are similar in magnitude to those of previous econometric stud-

ies, but we find larger effects on mathematics achievement than on reading achievement…. We also find much larger teacher effects variance in low socioeconomic status (SES) schools than in high SES schools. (p. 239)

As early as 1971, Hanushek found that teachers do not account for Hispanic students in that different teachers and classroom compositions do not affect their achievement outcomes. Methodologically, at the current stage, the most essential issue about which researchers should be mindful is context—teacher effects may differentiate among students of different characteristics (e.g., ability and SES), among school subjects (e.g., reading and mathematics), among schools of different characteristics (e.g., level and SES), and among geographic regions (e.g., state and country).

References

Coleman, J. S., Campbell, E. Q., Hobson, C. J., McPartland, J., Mood, A. M., Wienfield, F. D., & York, R. L. (1966). *Equality of educational opportunity.* Washington, DC: U.S. Government Printing Office.

Darling-Hammond, L., & Youngs, P. (2002). Defining "highly qualified teachers": What does "scientifically-based research" actually tell us? *Educational Researcher, 31*(9), 13–25.

Hanushek, E. (1971). Teacher characteristics and gains in student achievement: Estimation using micro data. *American Economic Review, 61,* 280–288.

Hill, H. C., Rowan, B., & Ball, D. L. (2005). Effects of teachers' mathematical knowledge for teaching on student achievement. *American Educational Research Journal, 42,* 371–406.

Jepsen, C. (2005). Teacher characteristics and student achievement: Evidence from teacher surveys. *Journal of Urban Economics, 57,* 302–319.

Nye, B., Konstantopoulos, S., & Hedges, L. V. (2004). How large are teacher effects? *Educational Evaluation and Policy Analysis, 26,* 237–257.

RAND. (2010). *What teacher characteristics affect student achievement? Findings from Los Angeles public schools.* Santa Monica, CA: Author.

Reynolds, D., & Teddlie, C. (2000). The process of school effectiveness. In C. Teddlie & D Reynolds (Eds.), *The international handbook of school effectiveness research* (pp. 134–159). London: Falmer.

Rockoff, J. E. (2004). The impact of individual teachers on student achievement: Evidence from panel data. *American Economic Review, 94,* 247–252.

Rowan, B., Correnti, R., & Miller, R. J. (2002). What large-scale, survey research tells us about teacher effects on student achievement: Insights from the Prospects student of elementary schools. *Teachers College Record, 104,* 1525–1567.

Stringfield, S. (1994). The analysis of large databases in school effectiveness research. In D. Reynolds, B. P. M. Creemers, P. S. Nesselrodt, E. C. Schaffer, S. Stringfield, & C. Teddlie (Eds.), *Advances in school effectiveness research and practice* (pp. 55–72). London: Pergamon.

U.S. Department of Education. (2002). *Meeting the highly qualified teachers challenge: The Secretary's annual report on teacher quality.* Washington, DC: U.S. Department of Education, Office of Postsecondary Education, Office of Policy, Planning, and Innovation.

Wayne, A. J., & Youngs, P. (2003). Teacher characteristics and student achievement gains: A review. *Review of Educational Research, 73,* 89–122.

Section 7

Influences from the Curriculum

EDITOR: RAYNE SPERLING
Pennsylvania State University

7.1

Values Education Programs

TERENCE LOVAT
The University of New Castle, Australia and Oxford University, UK

Introduction

Values education and associated variants (e.g., character education, moral education) have in common a primary concern for the whole development of students, including emotional, aesthetic, and spiritual, but especially personal and social-moral development. In particular, they tend to focus on the issue of values-rich teaching environments and explicit values discourse as being crucial ways in which this whole development is best achieved. Values education does not connote a firm set of doctrines and procedures, being constituted rather by a coalition of researchers and practitioners engaged in a multiplicity of projects and curricula directed toward the common goal of whole development as defined above.

The history of values education can be traced to ancient times, including reference to the philosophical perspectives of Aristotle and Confucius, thereafter to Thomas Aquinas and Thomas More in the West and the Sufi mystic Abu al-Ghazali in the Islamic world. All of these figures referred to learning being an essentially moral enterprise and requiring a level of personal inculcation and commitment. Thomas More, for instance, argued that "true education," in contrast with mere "instruction," was about the development of personal integrity and the conforming of one's actions to the common good. The tradition continued in more modern times with John Dewey suggesting that education was principally a means of instilling moral judiciousness and Richard S. Peters, who drew the distinction between instrumentalist education and holistic education, in which the distinguishing feature was around values. It was only education related to "what is of value" that allowed education to be of value at all:

> According to R. S. Peters, education implies that something worthwhile is being intentionally transmitted in a morally acceptable manner…values should be present in all educational practices … I agree with John Dewey that all education is, and should be, moral education. (Raulo, 2002, p. 507)

Values education has often been associated more with religious than public schooling and as being, at best, a partial or optional attachment to mainstream education. Defined as above, however, it is proposed to be an essential artefact to effective education wherever it functions. Hence, its role in facilitating student achievement becomes of central importance.

Research Evidence

Values education research of the past has not been replete with reference to student academic achievement per se or with experimental work directed at proving a connection. Indeed, when understood merely to pertain to easily testable and measurable outcomes, academic achievement has often been cast as being in opposition to the holistic intentions implicit in values education (Noddings, 1992; Peters, 1981). In more recent times, however, a persistent theme has emerged of academic achievement being among the consequences of values education interventions (Arthur, 2010; Berkowitz & Bier, 2005; Lovat, Dally, Clement, & Toomey, 2011; Lovat, Toomey, & Clement, 2010; Nucci & Darvaez, 2008). This has led to concerted work exploring the link between the phenomena entailed in values education and effective learning, work that covers the spectrum of philosophy, neuroscience, and pedagogy.

In philosophy, Carr (2006) has revived the case of Dewey and Peters in arguing that it is teachers who model integrity and practice their profession in ways that entail sound relationships and moral interchange with their students who are most likely to inspire students to learn and achieve. In the neurosciences, insights into the greater coherence of cognition, affect, and sociality have been used to illustrate why it is that the values-rich environment is more likely to stimulate cognitive powers than routine teaching settings (Immordino-Yang & Faeth, 2010). Additionally, Newmann and Associates' (1996) "pedagogical dynamics" required for effective teaching included three that are central to values education: "catering for diversity" concerned the need for a respectful relationship between teacher and student; "school coherence" was about the school that is committed by word and deed to the good of the students above all else; and, "trustful, supportive ambience" referred to the ethics and aesthetics of the learning environment.

Work of this sort has led in turn to seeing values education and effective teaching as being in a synergistic relationship, working together in the interests of student achievement, including academic achievement. Benninga, Berkowitz, Kuehn, and Smith (2003) engaged in fine-tuned empirical work that demonstrated the link between values education and strengthened academic focus. Benninga et al. traced the accumulated effects over 4 years (1999–2002) of enhanced performance in basic skills tests when allied with the roll-out of a values education (character education) program in 120 Californian primary schools. The results included evidence of a steady and progressive positive correlation ($p = .053$ to $p = .09$) between the identified values education factors and specified academic results. Tirri (2010) summarizes an array of empirical work that has demonstrated the centrality of values education to the establishment of effective learning environments, characterized by moral leadership, caring and trusting relationships, ethical practice, and explicit pedagogical values. Neil Hawkes (2010) provides empirical evidence, combining doctoral research and professional practice, of the holistic effects of values education, including on student academic improvement, a claim ultimately endorsed by the UK inspectorial process, Ofsted.

The link between values education and student achievement was further evidenced in teacher testimony about strengthened academic diligence being among the effects of the various interventions that functioned under the umbrella of the Australian Values Education Program between 2003 and 2009. As the projects developed from pilot work to large-scale, longitudinal and multisite work, this testimony became more assured through the nature of the evidence. In the end, 381 schools, 100,000 students, 10,000 teachers, and 50 university researchers were involved in this work. Testimony of improved outcomes, enhanced engagement and "doing well" began as persistent anecdotal evidence in the earlier projects and led progressively to empirical evidence being established in the final project. This evidence is summarized below.

In the largest, two-stage project, *Values Education Good Practice Schools Project*, the first stage report (Department of Education and Science Training [DEST], 2006) identified an array of effective learning features that, it was claimed, were strengthened by the intervention. These included: enhanced intellectual depth; greater student engagement in mainstream curricula and more complex thinking across the curriculum. Such testimony rarely stood alone, typically being encased in more generalized statements about improved classroom relationships, better student behaviour, and calmer classroom environments. Typical of such testimony is the following: "by creating an environment where these values were constantly shaping classroom activity, student learning was improving, teachers and students were happier, and school was calmer" (p. 120).

Evidence in the second stage report (Department of Education, Employment and Workplace Relations [DEEWR], 2008) was characterized by greater specificity about the types of positive behaviour normally associated with student academic improvement. These behaviours were also presented in ways that pointed to the potential for them to be tested and measured: "improved relationships ... improved student attendance, fewer reportable behaviour incidents ... ocused classroom activity, calmer classrooms with students going about their work purposefully" (p. 27).

Empirical work that followed up on the above projects took the form of the *Project to Test and Measure the Impact of Values Education on Student Effects and School Ambience* (Lovat, Toomey, Dally, & Clement, 2009). This project was characterized by intensive quantitative and qualitative work. The mixed methods approach employed followed a sequential explanatory design in which quantitative data were collected over two time-periods and analysed, with qualitative data collected during the second phase and analysed separately to help explain and elaborate on the quantitative results. There was a particular focus on the many anecdotal claims made in earlier projects about improvements in student academic learning and the kinds of behaviour that accompanied such improvements. In this report, evidence was elicited that, as a result of the values education intervention, students were putting greater effort into their work and trying harder and striving to achieve their best (Lovat, Toomey, Dally, & Clement 2009, pp. 29, 78, 98, 99, 100). Students were also more engaged in learning (p. 13), taking greater responsibility for their learning and working together more co-operatively (p. 45), and were more willing to ask for help and to help each other (p. 100). They were also engaging at a greater intellectual depth (pp. 65, 100), taking more responsibility for their own learning, and recognizing the importance of respecting others' right to learn (p. 10). The executive summary of the report concluded:

> there was substantial quantitative and qualitative evidence suggesting ... observable and measurable improvements in students' academic diligence, including increased attentiveness, a greater capacity to work independently as well as more cooperatively, greater care and effort being invested in schoolwork and students assuming more responsibility for their own learning as well as classroom "chores". (p. 6)

Summary and Recommendations

In summary, the link between values education and student academic achievement has not been proven definitively but an array of research findings seems to provide strong indications of a connection. It presents as one of a number of contemporary research fields that underline the complexity and multivariate nature of student achievement. As such, it would seem to be important that values education be given some priority in initial teacher education, ongoing teacher professional development, leadership training and funded research.

References

Arthur, J. (2010). *Of good character: Exploration of virtues and values in 3–25 year–olds*. Exeter, England: Imprint Academic.

Benninga, J., Berkowitz, M., Kuehn, P., & Smith, K. (2003). The relationship of character education implementation and academic achievement in elementary schools. *Journal of Research in Character Education, 6,* 19–32.

Berkowitz, M., & Bier, M. (2005). *What works in character education: A research driven guide for educators*. Washington, DC: Character Education Partnership.

Carr, D. (2006). Professional and personal values and virtues in education and teaching. *Oxford Review of Education, 32,* 171–183.

Department of Education, Employment and Workplace Relations (DEEWR). (2008). *At the heart of what we do: Values education at the centre of schooling* (Report of the Values Education Good Practice Schools—Stage 2). Melbourne, Australia: Curriculum Corporation. Retrieved from http://www.curriculum.edu.au/verve/_resources/VEGPSP-2_final_3_execsummary.pdf

Department of Education, Science and Training (DEST). (2006). *Implementing the national framework for values education in Australian schools* (Report of the Values Education Good Practice Schools Project—Stage 1). Melbourne, Australia: Curriculum Corporation. Retrieved from http://www.curriculum.edu.au/verve/_resources/VEGPS1_FINAL_REPORT_081106.pdf

Hawkes, N. (2010). Values education and the national curriculum in England. In T. Lovat, R. Toomey, & N. Clement (Eds.), *International research handbook on values education and student wellbeing* (pp. 225–238). Dordrecht, Netherlands: Springer.

Immordino-Yang, M., & Faeth, M. (2010). Building smart students: A neuroscience perspective on the role of emotion and skilled intuition in learning. In D. Sousa (Ed.), *Mind, brain and education* (pp. 66–81). Bloomington, IN: Solution Tree Press.

Lovat, T., Dally, K., Clement, N., & Toomey, R. (2011). *Values pedagogy and student achievement: Contemporary research evidence.* Dordrecht, Netherlands: Springer.

Lovat, T., Toomey, R., & Clement, N. (Eds.), (2010). *International research handbook on values education and student wellbeing.* Dordrecht, Netherlands: Springer.

Lovat, T., Toomey, R., Dally, K., & Clement, N. (2009). *Project to test and measure the impact of values education on student effects and school ambience*: Report for the Australian Government (DEEWR). Retrieved from http://www.curriculum.edu.au/verve/_resources/Project_to_Test_and_Measure_the_Impact_of_Values_Education.pdf

Newmann, F., & Associates. (1996). *Authentic achievement: Restructuring schools for intellectual quality.* San Francisco, CA: Jossey–Bass.

Noddings, N. (1992). *The challenge to care in schools: An alternative approach to education.* New York: Teachers College Press.

Nucci, L., & Narvaez, D. (2008). *Handbook of moral and character education.* New York: Routledge.

Peters, R. S. (1981). *Moral development and moral education.* London: George Allen & Unwin.

Raulo, M. (2002). Moral education and development. *Journal of Social Philosophy, 31,* 507–518.

Tirri, K. (2010). Teacher values underlying professional practice. In T. Lovat, R. Toomey, & N. Clement (Eds.), *International research handbook on values education and student wellbeing* (pp. 153–162). Dordrecht, Netherlands: Springer.

7.2

Activity-Based Learning Strategies

KIRA J. CARBONNEAU AND SCOTT C. MARLEY
University of New Mexico

Introduction

Teacher education textbooks frequently suggest that activity-based learning strategies are effective instructional strategies that promote student achievement (e.g., Billstein, Libeskind, & Lott, 2009). Often described by practitioners and researchers as "hands-on learning," activity-based learning strategies emphasize the manipulation of concrete objects to represent abstract concepts. The present overview of activity-based learning strategies consists of the following: (a) a definition and examples of activity-based learning strategies; (b) a review of theoretical explanations for the efficacy of activity based-learning strategies; (c) a review of the empirical evidence regarding activity-based learning strategies and student achievement; and, (d) a discussion of future directions of research.

Definition and Examples of Activity-Based Learning Strategies. Activity-based learning strategies are instructional approaches where children are encouraged to physically interact with objects that represent concepts under study. Examples of activity-based learning strategies from the domains of language, mathematics, and science are instructing children to perform actions described by a story with manipulatives representing story characters and settings (Biazak, Marley, & Levin, 2010); calculating the amount of money one should receive from a financial transaction with manipulatives that represent money (McNeil, Uttal, Jarvin, & Sternberg, 2009); and, designing an experiment that tests the effects of various materials on the rate an object sinks in water (Chen & Klahr, 1999), respectively.

Theoretical Explanations. Contemporary developmental theories propose that individuals construct meaning via interacting with their environment. Piaget (1962) and Bruner (1964) both proposed that children's cognitive skills emerge in a sequential manner with more complex cognitive skills developing over time. These cognitive skills are often de-

scribed in terms of capability to manipulate various mental representations. For example, according to Bruner (1964), three forms of mental representation exist. The first form of mental representation, enactive representation, consists of memory for physically experienced events (i.e., motor learning). The second form of mental representation, iconic representation, is comprised of mental images. Information at this level is often described as being held in the "mind's eye" or as imagination. The third form of mental representation, symbolic representation, is information stored as abstract symbols (i.e., words and numbers).

Bruner proposed that one's competence with the three forms of mental representation improves with age. In addition, according to this developmental perspective, it is expected that when a higher form of representation fails to facilitate construction of meaning the activation of a lower form of representation may result in beneficial cognitive consequences. For example, elementary-aged children who struggle to learn the abstract concept of regrouping with symbolic representations (i.e., numbers) may benefit from manipulating (enactive representation) or viewing images (iconic representation) of base-10 blocks to embody borrowing from a higher place value. Piaget (1962) offers a comparable perspective of cognitive development that provides an analogous theoretical explanation for the assumed benefits of hands-on learning strategies.

Research Evidence

A robust empirical finding associated with activity-based learning is that promoting relevant motor activity during study improves memory in a range of learning situations. For example, relative to free study controls or alternative learning strategies, participants who utilize activity-based learning strategies have exhibited marked improvements in recall of lists of nouns and phrases describing actions (Mangels & Heinberg, 2006). Unfortunately, there is a paucity of scientifically based research that examines the effects of activity-based learning strategies on standardized outcome measures related to student achievement. The lack of studies examining achievement outcomes in relation to activity-based learning has resulted in a knowledge base largely consisting of learning as measured by experimenter-created measures. Therefore, conclusions regarding the efficacy of activity-based learning strategies at improving student achievement in the content domains must be made cautiously due to the known problem with experimenter-created outcome measures. With this limitation in mind the following sections review current evidence regarding the efficacy of activity-based learning strategies in the domains of language, mathematics and science.

Language. Examinations of activity-based learning strategies have uncovered learning benefits for students' listening and reading comprehension. Manipulating objects as directed by a narrative has been found to improve memory for spatial relationships, text inconsistencies, and story events (Biazak, Marley, & Levin, 2010). Furthermore, the ability to benefit from imagery instruction has been associated with manipulatives. For example, Glenberg and associates (2004) found with elementary-age children that interacting with text-relevant objects during reading instruction could gradually be replaced with instructions to imagine manipulating the objects. This finding has been replicated in studies with children from samples representing diverse populations (Marley, Szabo, Levin, & Glenberg, 2011).

Mathematics. The use of mathematic manipulatives is recommended to teachers as an efficacious activity-based learning strategy. This recommendation is emphasized as a developmentally appropriate teaching practice for early elementary-age children. However, debates about the efficacy of these strategies have persisted since the 1960s, and have been continually spurred by conflicting empirical findings (McNeil & Jarvin, 2007; Sowell, 1989). Based on discrepant findings in the literature, Sowell (1989) performed a meta-analysis of 60 studies purporting to examine the efficacy of activity-based learning strategies applied to mathematics. Sowell's results indicated a moderate effect size in favor of curricula that utilized activity on basic computation skills and students' attitudes toward math when the studies were conducted over an entire school year. However, no statistical differences on retention and transfer of students' mathematical knowledge were found in favor of activity-based strategies.

More recently, McNeil and Jarvin (2007) have cautioned that additional research is needed before learning strategies that utilize manipulatives are declared effective. In their own words, McNeil and Jarvin recommend that studies are needed to "uncover the mechanisms by which manipulatives influence performance" (p. 314). Their cautionary note should be given ample consideration because several inconsistencies exist in the empirical research with studies finding manipulation of objects: to be beneficial (Gürbüz,

2010); finding no benefit (Scott & Neufeld, 1976); as well as uncovering negative outcomes (McNeil, Uttal, Jarvin, & Sternberg, 2009).

Science. Activity-based learning strategies have been seen as effective techniques for teaching scientific concepts. A meta-analysis of learning strategies in science education supports the effectiveness of "hands-on" learning (Schroeder, Scott, Tolson, Huang, & Lee, 2007). A portion of this meta-analysis examined studies of "manipulation strategies" that required teachers to provide students with the opportunity to engage in physical interactions with manipulatives. Studies which utilized these strategies yielded a large standardized effect size on measures of student achievement in favor of activity-based learning participants relative to participants who studied using alternative learning strategies.

Summary and Recommendations

Future research concerning activity-based learning strategies will have important scientific and educational implications. The literature examining the effects of activity-based learning strategies on student achievement has several limitations. First, very few studies examine the effects of these strategies on standardized measures of student achievement. Second, the literature largely consists of studies that lack strong experimental controls. Third, the studies that do compare activity-based strategies to appropriate and relevant controls tend to utilize experimenter-created outcomes. These and other limitations of the literature restrict the ability of researchers to make endorsements regarding the efficacy of activity-based learning strategies at improving student achievement. Research is needed that examines activity-based learning strategies at the classroom level. These future studies should be designed with adequate experimental controls and outcome measures that are not too tightly aligned with the interventions.

Additional scientifically based research that examines the role of developmental differences is necessary. Age-related differences in the ability to capitalize from activity-based strategies have been identified within the language literature base (e.g., Glenberg, Guttierrez, Levin, Japuntich, & Kaschak, 2004). With the ability to benefit from learning strategies that utilize concrete manipulatives being attenuated for younger children (for relevant discussion in math, see McNeil & Jarvin, 2007) these findings contradict predictions derived from contemporary developmental theory. However, there is a scarcity of empirical studies examining these developmental differences within all content areas and further research is required to understand the efficacy of activity-based learning with young children.

In terms of educational implications, future research investigating activity-based learning strategies and their impact on student achievement are warranted. Currently, observers of activity-based programs in India, supported by the United Nations Children's Fund (UNICEF), is beginning to notice an improvement in children's learning (Thangav-elu, 2006). Yet, more research is necessary to determine if observations from these types of programs align with standardized measures of student achievement. To further impact education, the collection of international data will be vital in understanding how and when activity-based learning strategies are effective for students.

Teacher education textbooks (Billstein et al., 2009) often suggest that activity-based learning strategies are effective strategies that facilitate learners' active construction of meaning. Furthermore, developmental theorists have advocated activity-based learning as an effective learning strategy (Bruner, 1964; Piaget, 1962). The current empirical evidence contains several inconsistencies, with studies finding the strategies result in positive cognitive consequence and other studies finding no or negative effects. Age-related differences (Glenberg et al., 2004) and the nature of the outcome measures (Sowell, 1989) have been examined as explanations for these differential findings. Before strong prescriptive statements can be made regarding the effectiveness of activity-based learning strategies in improving student achievement further systematic examinations are necessary.

References

Biazak, J. E., Marley, S. C., & Levin, J. R. (2010). Does an activity-based learning strategy improve preschool children's memory for narrative passages? *Early Childhood Research Quarterly*, 25, 515–526.

Billstein, R., Libeskind, S., & Lott, J. (2009). *Problem solving approach to mathematics for elementary school teachers*. Menlo Park, CA: Benjamin/Cummings.

Bruner, J. S. (1964). The course of cognitive growth. *American Psychologist*, 19, 1–15.

Chen, Z., & Klahr, D.(1999). All other things being equal: Acquisition and transfer of the control of variables strategy. *Child Development*, 70(5), 1098–1120.

Glenberg, A. M., Gutierrez, T., Levin, J. R., Japuntich, S., & Kaschak, M. P. (2004). Activity and imagined activity can enhance young children's reading comprehension. *Journal of Educational Psychology*, 96(3), 424–436.

Gürbüz, R. (2010). The effect of activity-based instruction on conceptual development of seventh grade students in probability. *International Journal of Mathematical Education in Science and Technology*, 41(6), 743–767.

Mangels, J. A., & Heinberg, A. (2006). Improved episodic integration through enactment: Implications for aging. *Journal of General Psychology*, 133, 37–65.

Marley, S. C., Szabo, Z., Levin, J. R., & Glenberg, A. M. (2011). Investigation of an activity-based text–processing strategy in mixed-age child dyads. *The Journal of Experimental Education*, 79(3), 340–360.

McNeil, N., & Jarvin, L. (2007). When theories don't add up: Disentangling the manipulatives debate. *Theory Into Practice*, 46(4), 309–316.

McNeil, N. M., Uttal, D. H., Jarvin, L., & Sternberg, R. J. (2009). Should you show me the money? Concrete objects both hurt and help performance on mathematics problems. *Learning and Instruction*, 19(2), 171–184.

Piaget, J. (1962). *Play, dreams, and imitation in childhood*. New York: Norton.

Schroeder, C. M., Scott, T. P., Tolson, H., Huang, T. Y., & Lee, Y. H. (2007). A meta-analysis of national research: Effects of teaching strategies on student achievement in science in the United States. *Journal of Research in Science Teaching*, 44(10), 1436–1460.

Scott, L. F., & Neufeld, H. (1976). Concrete Instruction in elementary school mathematics: Pictorial vs. manipulative. *School Science and Mathematics*, 76(1), 68–72.

Sowell, E. (1989). Effects of manipulative materials in mathematics instruction. *Journal of Research in Mathematics Education*, 20(5), 498–505.

Thangavelu, S. (2006). *Activity-based Learning—A radical change in primary education*. UNICEF: India. Retrieved from http://www.unicef.org/india/education_1546.htm

7.3

Bilingual Education Programs and Student Achievement

MetaMetrics and University of North Carolina at Chapel Hill

JACKIE EUNJUNG RELYEA-KIM
University of North Carolina at Chapel Hill

Introduction

The term, *bilingual education program*, refers to school-based instruction in which students' first language and another language, sometimes the societal language, are used. There are many forms and labels for bilingual education programs including dual-language, one- or two-way dual-language, bilingual immersion education, developmental bilingual education, and transitional bilingual education. Program labels typically depend on the timing of instructional introduction and cessation of either native or new language and on the extent to which each language is emphasized.

Over 6,000 languages are spoken in the world, and perhaps 60 to 75% of the world's population is bilingual (Lewis, 2009). Reasons for bilingual education vary and depend on factors such as linguistic heterogeneity of a country, desire to promote national identity or cultural heritage, or political will for national participation in, or leadership of, global citizenship or a competitive economy. In many parts of the world, bilingualism has been a culturally important standard for thousands of years. The research and practice literature is replete with support for the important personal and societal benefits of bilingualism. For example, bilingual children, on average, may outperform monolinguals on cognitive and metalinguistic tasks (e.g., Bialystok & Martin, 2004). However, bilingual education in many parts of the world is not without critics. For instance, in the United States, where language-minority children represent a fast-growing segment of the school-age population, use of minority language in schooling and bilingual education programs is controversial.

Sound bilingual education program implementation and policy depend in part on data-based studies. However, situational factors surrounding bilingual education program implementation, as well as challenges in accomplishing bilingual education research, make attribution of outcome effects to program characteristics, and synthesis across studies, difficult. Unfortunately, these challenges are not well addressed in much of the current research literature on bilingual education effectiveness. The most salient research design challenges include the following: (a) studying effectiveness of potentially contributory variables within "packages" of instructional delivery; (b) conducting true experiments with random assignment; (c) documenting student growth over reasonably long periods of time; and (d) inclusion of researcher-designed and curriculum-based measures which may provide additional insight into students' progress in ways that provide practical import. Additional challenges for research syntheses include researcher failure to report: (a) comparison program description and implementation fidelity; (b) societal, political, and cultural contexts that might impact students' language-learning motivation identity formation, or academic performance (e.g., Marsh, Hau, & Kong, 2000); (c) extensive descriptions of student variables such as length of time living in the country or level of native- and new-language oracy and literacy; and (d) clear and complete description of outcome measures, including information about test score reliability and validity.

Research Evidence

Three, large-scale, longitudinal, quasi-experimental U.S. studies, which resulted in comparable conclusions, are frequently cited in the literature. Ramírez and colleagues (Ramírez, Yuen, Ramey, & Pasta, 1991) and Thomas and Collier (1997) reported that young students learning English as a new language who were in earlier-exit bilingual programs, on average, made similar or greater progress in English reading, English language arts, and mathematics as compared to counterparts in English-immersion programs or to norms reported for standardized tests. However, after third grade (through sixth or twelfth, respectively), students who were enrolled in earlier-exit programs demonstrated decelerated rate of performance while those in maintenance,

285

late-exit, or dual-language programs, on average, made more positive academic strides. Thomas and Collier (2002) later reported similar findings and cautioned that students with low levels of English proficiency should only be placed in long-term dual-language or maintenance programs.

In addition to the three large-scale studies, a handful of narrative or quantitative meta-analytic research syntheses on the topic of bilingual education program achievement effects are also widely cited by researchers, practitioners, and policy makers (e.g., Baker & de Kanter, 1981; Greene, 1998; Rolstad, Mahoney, & Glass, 2005; Rossell & Baker, 1996; Slavin & Cheung, 2003; Willig, 1985). For example, Willig (1985) and Greene (1998) conducted meta-analyses using strict criteria for study inclusion and Rolstad and colleagues (2005) conducted a meta-analysis using broad criteria for inclusion, resulting in reviews of 23, 11, and 17 studies, respectively. All three sets of researchers concluded that bilingual education was more advantageous for English-language learners' academic and language learning when compared to various other programs. As an example, Rolstad and colleagues (2005) reported that, overall, bilingual education was more beneficial for English-language learners than all-English approaches, and over the long run, dual-language bilingual education resulted in better English and native-language learning when compared to short-term transitional bilingual education. Achievement areas studied included reading, oral language, mathematics, and to a lesser extent, writing/spelling, social studies, and science.

However, on the other hand, conclusions from three often-cited narrative research syntheses were mixed. Baker and de Kanter (1981), Rossell and Baker (1996), and Slavin and Cheung (2003), each used relatively strict criteria for study inclusion, resulting in reviews of 28, 72, and 16 studies of English-language learners, respectively. Only one set of researchers, Slavin and Cheung (2003), concluded that, on the whole, the evidence favored bilingual approaches, especially dual-language programs. Baker and de Kanter (1981) reported mixed results. Students in transitional bilingual education sometimes outperformed counterparts in other types of programs. However, sometimes students in English-as-a-second-language pullout programs outperformed those in other programs. Rossell and Baker (1996) updated the Baker and de Kanter (1981) study, and concluded there was no consistent research support for transitional bilingual education as a superior instructional program for students learning English.

In addition to the meta-analyses and syntheses, over the last 25 years, many studies have investigated bilingual education in the United States and internationally. However, using criteria commonly accepted as a minimum standard for rigorous quasi-experimental or experimental research (e.g., August & Shanahan, 2006), a search of the research literature yielded only 14 rigorously conducted studies (5 international, 9 United States) for close analysis. Across the 14 studies, a few consistent differences were apparent between international studies and U.S. investigations. For example, the international studies tended to include high school students whereas U.S. studies mainly targeted younger learners. As would be expected, new and native languages varied across international studies; for example, whereas English was the new language in the U.S. studies, Spanish was the native language most frequently studied.

However, findings across the two bodies of research were similar in that mixed results were reported for both the international and the U.S. studies. In a majority of the studies, some form of bilingual education was related to greater student growth when compared to peers' growth for selected native or new language oracy, literacy, or math measures (e.g., Barnett, Yarosz, Thomas, Jung, & Blanco, 2007; Durán, Roseth, & Hoffman, 2010; Harley, Hart, & Lapkin, 1986; Marsh et al., 2000; Medrano, 1987; Rodríguez, Díaz, Duran, & Espinosa, 1995; Tong, Irby, Lara-Alecio, & Mathes, 2008; van der Leij, 2010; Winsler, Díaz, Espinosa, & Rodríguez, 1999). However, it was also not uncommon for researchers to report *no effect* of bilingual education for student growth on other achievement measures in native or new language oracy or literacy. The conflicting findings often occurred within the same study (Barnett et al., 2007; Durán et al., 2010; Marsh et al., 2000; Medrano, 1987; Rodríguez et al., 1995; Tong, Irby et al., 2008; van der Leij, 2010; Winsler et al., 1999). In a few cases, some researchers also concluded that students enrolled in more intense bilingual education or transitional bilingual education demonstrated *less growth* on selected achievement outcomes as compared to students enrolled in less intense bilingual education (Marsh et al., 2000) or English immersion (de Ramírez & Shapiro, 2006; López & Tashakkori, 2004a, 2004b).

There was also inconsistency across studies regarding which types of outcomes were affected. For instance, some researchers who reported positive bilingual education effects, noted benefits for aspects of oracy or reading in the new language (primarily English) (Harley, Hart, & Lapkin, 1986; Marsh et al., 2000; Rodríguez et al., 1995; Tong, Irby et al., 2008; van der Leij, 2010; Winsler et al., 1999). But others found no comparative effects on the same or similar outcomes (Admiraal, Westhoff, & de Bot, 2006; Barnett et al., 2007; Durán et al., 2010; Medrano, 1987; Rodríguez et al., 1995; Tong, Irby et al., 2008; Tong, Lara-Alecio et al., 2008; van der Leij, 2010; Wagner, Spratt, & Ezzaki, 1989; Winsler et al., 1999). Too few studies comparing different forms of bilingual education were located to support synthesis across studies about whether particular forms of bilingual education were superior to others. As an example, however, Tong, Irby, and colleagues (2008) found positive advantages for developmental bilingual education as compared to transitional bilingual education. In another case, no differences were found between transitional bilingual education and structured immersion (Tong, Lara-Alecio et al., 2008).

A pressing policy issue in some countries is related to whether any advantages witnessed in new-language learning in bilingual situations simultaneously negatively affect maintenance of native language. The majority of the rigorously conducted studies included measures of students' native-language growth. In most cases, bilingual education enhanced students' native language growth on some aspects of oracy or reading above and beyond that of students in the comparison groups (Barnett et al., 2007; Durán et al., 2010; Marsh et al, 2000; Tong, Irby, et al., 2008; van der Leij, 2010). In no case was student growth on any measure of native language diminished, as compared to peers'.

Summary and Recommendations

In part because of great variability in program definition and in research design, conclusions from research and research syntheses are mixed. Rather than address the "does bilingual education work" question, perhaps more will be learned by asking, "What desirable learning outcomes are well achieved under which kinds of conditions and for which kinds of students?" To accomplish such research, however, there is a great need to give more attention to at least three factors. First, researchers must attend to theoretical reasoning, rationale, and hypothesizing about potential factors and critical mechanisms at play in studies. Such attention might provide an important stage both for research design and interpretation of results (cf. Marsh et al, 2000). For instance, researchers could address potential aptitude-by-treatment interactions under conditions where student outcomes may be functions of student characteristics such as language background and motivation, sociocultural factors, and educational program characteristics (e.g., Cummins, 1996). Few investigators, as yet, approach research of bilingual programs with such hypotheses. Second, mixed-methods studies might lead to better understanding of program results in relation to program, sociocultural, and student characteristics. Third, increased research activity worldwide, especially with regard to both native- and new-language program emphases and outcomes, could greatly enhance our understanding of program impact on student achievement in varying social contexts.

References

*14 studies in 15 reports reviewed for synthesis in the present article

*Admiraal, W., Westhoff, G., & de Bot, K. (2006). Evaluation of bilingual secondary education in the Netherlands: Students' language proficiency in English. *Educational Research and Evaluation, 12,* 75–93.

August, D., & Shanahan, T. (2006). *Developing literacy in second–language learners: Report of the national literacy panel on language minority children and youth.* Mahwah, NJ: Erlbaum.

Baker, K., & de Kanter, A. A. (1981). *Effectiveness of bilingual education: A review of the literature* (Final draft report). Washington, DC: Department of Education, Office of Planning, Budget, and Evaluation.

*Barnett, W. S., Yarosz, D. J., Thomas, J., Jung, K., & Blanco, D. (2007). Two-way and monolingual English immersion in preschool education: An experimental comparison. *Early Childhood Research Quarterly, 22,* 277–293.

Bialystok, E., & Martin, M. M. (2004). Attention and inhibition in bilingual children: Evidence from the dimensional change card sort task. *Developmental Science, 7,* 325–339.

Cummins, J. (1996). Bilingual education: What does the research say? In J. Cummins (Ed.), *Negotiating identities: Education for empower-*

ment in a diverse society (pp. 97–133). Los Angeles, CA: California Association for Bilingual Education.

*de Ramírez, D. R., & Shapiro, E. S. (2006). Curriculum-based measurement and the evaluation of reading skills of Spanish-speaking English language learners in bilingual education classrooms. *School Psychology Review, 35,* 356–369.

*Durán, L. K., Roseth, C., & Hoffman, P. (2010). An experimental study comparing English-only and transitional bilingual education on Spanish-speaking preschoolers' early literacy development. *Early Childhood Research Quarterly, 25*(2), 207–217.

Greene, J. P. (1998). *A meta-analysis of the effectiveness of bilingual education.* Claremont, CA: Thomas Rivera Policy Institute.

*Harley, B., Hart, D., & Lapkin, S. (1986). The effects of early bilingual schooling on first language skills. *Applied Psycholinguistics, 7,* 295–321.

Lewis, M. P. (Ed.). (2009). *Ethnologue: Languages of the world.* Dallas, TX: SIL International.

*López, M. G., & Tashakkori, A. (2004a). Effects of a two-way bilingual program on the literacy development of students in kindergarten and first grade. *Bilingual Research Journal, 28,* 19–34.

*López, M. G., & Tashakkori, A. (2004b). Narrowing the gap: Effects of a two-way bilingual education program on the literacy development of at-risk primary students. *Journal of Education for Students Placed at Risk, 9,* 325–336.

*Marsh, H. W., Hau, K–T., & Kong, C–W. (2000). Late immersion and language of instruction in Hong Kong high schools: Achievement growth in language and non-language subjects. *Harvard Educational Review, 70,* 302–346.

*Medrano, M. F. (1987). The effects of bilingual education on reading and mathematics achievement: A longitudinal case study. *Equity and Excellence in Education, 23,* 17–19.

Ramírez, D. J., Yuen, S. D., Ramey, D. R., & Pasta, D. J. (1991). *Final report: National longitudinal study of structured English immersion strategy, early-exit and late-exit transitional bilingual education programs for language–minority children* (Vols. 1–2). San Mateo, CA: Aguirre International.

*Rodríguez, J. L., Díaz, R. M., Duran, D., & Espinosa, L. (1995). The impact of bilingual preschool education on the language development of Spanish-speaking children. *Early Childhood Research Quarterly, 10,* 475–490.

Rolstad, K., Mahoney, K., & Glass, G. V. (2005). The big picture: A meta-analysis of program effectiveness research on English language learners. *Educational Policy, 19*(4), 572–594.

Rossell, C. H., & Baker, K. (1996). The educational effectiveness of bilingual education. *Research in the Teaching of English, 30*(1), 7–74.

Slavin, R. E., & Cheung, A. (2003). *Effective reading programs for English language learners: A best–evidence synthesis.* Baltimore, MD: Johns Hopkins University Center for Research on the Education of Students Placed at Risk (CRESPAR).

Thomas, W. P., & Collier, V. (1997). *School effectiveness for language minority students.* Washington, DC: National Clearinghouse for Bilingual Education.

Thomas, W. P., & Collier, V. (2002). *A national study of school effectiveness for language minority students' long-term academic achievement: Final report.* Washington, DC: Center for Research on Education, Diversity & Excellence.

*Tong, F., Irby, B. J., Lara-Alecio, R., & Mathes, P. G. (2008). English and Spanish acquisition by Hispanic second graders in developmental bilingual programs: A 3-year longitudinal randomized study. *Hispanic Journal of Behavioral Science, 30,* 500–529.

*Tong, F., Lara-Alecio, R., Irby, B., Mathes, P., & Kwok, O. (2008). Accelerating early academic oral English development in transitional bilingual and structured English immersion programs. *American Educational Research Journal, 45,* 1011–1044.

*van der Leij, A. (2010). Acquiring reading and vocabulary in Dutch and English: The effect of concurrent instruction. *Reading and Writing, 23,* 415–434.

*Wagner, D. A., Spratt, J. E., & Ezzaki, A. (1989). Does learning to read in a second language always put the child at a disadvantage? Some counterevidence from Morocco. *Applied Psycholinguistics, 10,* 31–48.

Willig, A. C. (1985). A meta–analysis of selected studies on the effectiveness of bilingual education. *Review of Educational Research, 5*(3), 269–318.

*Winsler, A., Díaz, R. M., Espinosa, L., & Rodríguez, J. L. (1999). When learning a second language does not mean losing the first: Bilingual language development in low-income, Spanish-speaking children attending bilingual preschool. *Child Development, 70,* 349–362.

7.4

Intelligent Tutors—Strategy Types

Bonnie J. F. Meyer
Pennsylvania State University

Introduction

Broadly defined, an intelligent tutoring system provides instruction by a computer system without the help of human instructors (Psotka, Massey, & Mutter, 1988). This includes computer-based learning environments (CBLEs; Aleven, Roll, McLaren, & Koedinger, 2010; Azevedo, Cromley, & Seibert, 2004) and automated interventions to improve reading comprehension strategies (McNamara, 2007). The use of computer-based tutors can alleviate the problems related to expense, competence, and access of trained human tutors, as well as help classroom teachers individualize instruction. Intelligent, computer-based, and agent-based tutoring are new fields of research with great promise in reaching new audiences, providing immediate feedback and consistency, and delivering effective tutoring (Anderson, Corbett, Koedinger, & Pelletier, 1995; Graesser et al., 2004; Woolf, 2009).

Frequently "intelligent tutors" refer to a subset of CBLEs that involve software designed to guide students as they learn complex skills or strategies through practice. They usually involve four main components (Aleven et al., 2010). First, there is an interface component for the student to interact with the intelligent tutor. One or more virtual characters, avatars, or pedagogical agents (Kramer, 2010) often direct this interaction with students. The second component is based on an expert's understanding of the strategy/skill to be taught. The third component is a representation of the student's understanding that can be compared to the expert's understanding. Such comparisons range from simple key-word searches to the use of latent semantic analysis (LSA) or Bayesian reasoning. Intelligent tutors often help to scaffold student performance by providing hints matched to student competence or requests for help. Mismatches between the expert and student models of understanding drive the fourth component for an intelligent tutor. This component provides feedback customized to the student and further individualization through selection of a subsequent lesson to best meet a student's needs (e.g., levels of remediation, enrichment; see Meyer, Wijekumar, & Lin, 2011).

Research Evidence

Most research with intelligent tutors has focused on teaching skills in well-structured domains, such as mathematics (e.g., Kalyuga & Sweller, 2005). However, there are growing numbers of intelligent tutoring systems directed at strategy instruction. Strategies are optimal ways to process information or perform a task in an effort to reach a goal. Good strategy instruction usually provides direct instruction, modeling, scaffolding, and reduction of hints and help with increasing student proficiency. These components of strategy instruction mesh well with the four main components of intelligent tutors.

Intelligent Tutoring of the Structure Strategy (ITSS), a reading comprehension strategy (Meyer & Wijekumar, 2007), is described as an example of intelligent tutors and their effects on achievement. The structure strategy focuses on common patterns used by authors to organize expository texts and to convey main ideas. These patterns build on one another to convey the logical structure of a text. ITSS explicitly teaches learners how to follow the logical structure through strategic use of knowledge about text structures. Students learn how to use these structures to increase comprehension and organize their writing about what they remember from reading. For example, students learn about certain vocabulary words, called signaling words ("however") that can clue readers into arguments often made in expository text. The structure strategy showed strong effects on performance in randomized control studies in traditional classroom settings (e.g., Meyer & Poon, 2001). Teaching of the structure strategy transitioned from classroom settings to online tutoring of children by adults ($d = .92$ for delayed posttest between strategy group and regular school reading program; Meyer et al., 2002). The lessons and interactions between children and human tutors served as models for the development of the intelligent tutor, ITSS.

Two recent studies examined variations to the feedback component of ITSS. Meyer et al. (2010) investigated the effect of type of feedback versions (elaborated versus simple feedback) on fifth- and seventh-grade students' reading achievement, as measured by writing main ideas, recalling ideas after reading texts, and a standardized reading comprehension test. In the elaborated feedback version, the animated, pedagogical agent provided elaborated feedback with scaffolding to improve performance on subsequent trials, while the other feedback version involved the same agent providing only simple feedback about the correctness of a student's response. In the elaborated feedback-ITSS only, students with deficient performance on a third trial received a model response to improve writing of main ideas. Students who received elaborated feedback performed better on a standardized test of reading comprehension than students who received simple feedback. Next, Meyer, Wijekumar, and Lin (2011) varied the extent of individualization of instruction between versions of ITSS (individualized or standard). The more individually tailored ITSS was developed to provide remediation or enrichment lessons matched to the individual needs of each student, as determined by rapid online comparison of a model of student performance to a key aspect of the expert model. Students in the individualized condition made greater improvements from pretest to posttest on a standardized reading comprehension test ($d = .55$) than students in the standard condition ($d = .30$). Additionally, students who received more individualized instruction demonstrated higher mastery achievement goals when working in the lessons, greater improvement using signaling words, better work in lessons, and more positive posttest attitudes toward computers than students receiving standard instruction. The two studies point to two critical components of effective strategy-type intelligent tutors that affect reading achievement: personalized, elaborated feedback and individualized practice. Currently, thousands of children from grades 4 through 8 are using ITSS twice a week for 45 min over a 6 month period in Pennsylvania, Minnesota, or California. An interface for teachers in ITSS helps to keep teachers informed about the progress of each of their students.

Historically, the self-explanation strategy appears to be the initial strategy used in an intelligent tutoring context. Aleven and Koedinger (2002) found that students using a self-explanation version of an intelligent tutor for geometry were better able to provide accurate explanations and could better transfer to novel geometry problems than students using the intelligent tutor to learn geometry without the self-explanation strategy. More recently, Koedinger and colleagues (e.g., Aleven, Roll et al., 2010) have examined the effects of help seeking (Help Tutor), a self-regulated learning strategy. The Help Tutor was embedded in a Geometry Cognitive Tutor. The Help tutor resulted in improved help seeking, but did not affect geometry achievement over the Geometry Cognitive Tutor without the Help Tutor.

The self-explanation strategy also was combined with reading strategies in a computer-based reading program at the high school level, called iSTART (McNamara, O'Reilly, Rowe, Boonthum, & Levinstein, 2007). In iSTART, self-explanation is combined with five reading strategies: paraphrasing, comprehension monitoring, predicting, bridging (interrelating concepts in text and fostering inferences), and elaboration. One avatar in iSTART models strategy use and another virtual character provides scaffolded feedback. Students select one of the five reading strategies and self-explain after each sentence in a science text. Reading achievement is assessed by self-explanation of a science text and comprehension questions to two types (text-based and bridging). McNamara, O'Reilly, Best, and Ozuru (2006) showed that iSTART increased reading comprehension over a control group, but different types of questions increased for different types of readers. Less strategic readers performed better on text-based questions than controls, but not bridging questions, while more strategic readers performed better on bridging questions than controls, but not text-based questions. Due to the multiple strategies taught in iSTART, the cause of improvements for different types of readers is currently undetermined.

McNamara's (2007) edited volume about strategies includes seven computer-automated interventions. One, Summary Street (e.g., Caccamise, Franzke, Eckhoff, Kintsch, & Kintsch, 2007), is a computerized summary writing trainer that teaches a strategy for writing summaries. Summary Street uses LSA to analyze students' summaries by judging the similarity in meaning between summaries and the texts. In Summary Street, students receive immediate feedback about irrelevant sentences in summaries as well as spelling errors, copying, and redundancy. Feedback is presented in the form of a graphic display that shows scores for different text sections and a bar indicating the length of the summary. Caccamise and colleagues (2007) indicated that students working with Summary Street write better summaries and recall more gist information than students in control groups compared in quasi-experimental studies.

Another, promising intervention included in the McNamara book (2007) is *Thinking Reader* (Dalton & Proctor, 2007; Dalton & Strangman, 2006). Students using *Thinking Reader* read three novels and could have words or passages read with synchronized highlighting. There also were background knowledge links, a multimedia glossary, and embedded strategy instruction about predicting, clarifying, questioning, summarizing, and visualizing. Students received individualized feedback to their responses. Virtual animated characters served as strategy coaches by providing hints and modeled responses. Through a quasi-experimental research design, the investigators compared traditional instruction (novels in print and classroom strategy instruction) to *Thinking Reader* with struggling middle school readers. After statistical control of gender and initial reading achievement, students in *Thinking Reader* scored significantly higher on a standardized reading achievement test than the traditional group (about a half a grade level higher in reading achievement gain). Findings suggested greater gains for certain types of students: specifically, students with vocabulary scores higher than their comprehension scores.

Summary and Recommendations

Due to the complexity, duration, and immersion in classrooms of the new strategy-type intelligent tutors, overall effects on achievement vary. Most commonly, evaluations on achievement have been measured by gains on experimenter-designed materials, but some studies have examined effects on standardized achievement tests. Additionally, because multiple components or strategies are involved in the recent interventions with these strategy tutors, critical components or dosages for many are yet to be identified.

Recent developments with intelligent tutors hold promise for teachers in classrooms to use strategy tutors as tools for managing more individualization of instruction. Most strategy tutors can be used independently, while others need some teacher input (e.g., formal grading of essays). Use of intelligent tutors of the strategy type can provide powerful tools to teachers as they help students to transfer the strategies to classroom learning and increase academic achievement.

References

Aleven, V., & Koedinger, K. R. (2002). An effective metacognitive strategy: Learning by doing and explaining with a computer-based cognitive tutor. *Cognitive Science, 26*, 147–179.

Aleven, V., Roll, I., McLaren, B. M., Koedinger, K. R. (2010). Automated, unobtrusive, action-by-action assessment of self-regulation during learning with an intelligent tutoring system. *Educational Psychologist, 45*(4), 224–233

Anderson, J. R., Corbett, A. T., Koedinger, K. R., & Pelletier, R. (1995). Cognitive tutors: Lessons learned. *Journal of the Learning Sciences, 4*, 167–207.

Azevedo, R., Cromley, J. G., & Seiber, D. (2004). Does adaptive scaffolding facilitate students' ability to regulate their learning with hypermedia? *Contemporary Educational Psychology, 29*, 344–370.

Caccamise, D., Franzke, M., Eckhoff, A., Kintsch, E., & Kintsch, W. (2007). Guided practice in technology–based summary writing. In D. McNamara (Ed.), *Reading comprehension strategies: Theories, interventions, and technologies* (pp. 375–396). Mahwah, NJ: Erlbaum.

Dalton, B., & Proctor, C. P. (2007). Reading as thinking: Integrating strategy instruction in a universally designed digital literacy environment. In D. S. McNamara (Ed.), *Reading comprehension strategies: Theories, interventions, and technologies* (pp. 421–440). Mahwah, NJ: Erlbaum.

Dalton, B., & Strangman, N. (2006). Improving struggling readers' comprehension through scaffolded hypertexts and other computer-based literacy programs. In M. C. McKenna, L. D. Labbor, R. D. Kieffer, & D. Reinking (Eds.) *International handbook of literacy and technology* (Vol. 2, pp. 75–92). Mahwah, NJ: Erlbaum.

Graesser, A. C., Lu, S., Jackson, G. T., Mitchell, H. H., Ventura, M., Olney, A., & Louwerse, M. M. (2004). AutoTutor: A tutor with dialogue in natural language. *Behavior Research Methods, Instruments, and Computers, 36*, 180–192.

Kalyuga, S., & Sweller, J. (2005). Rapid dynamic assessment of expertise to improve the efficiency of adaptive e-learning. *Educational Technology, Research and Development, 53*(3), 83–93.

Kramer, N. C. (2010). Psychology research on embodied conversational agents: The case of pedagogical agents. *Journal of Media Psychology, 22*, 47–51.

McNamara, D. S. (2007). *Reading comprehension strategies: Theories, interventions, and technologies*. Mahwah, NJ: Erlbaum.

McNamara, D. S., O'Reilly, T., Best, R., & Ozuru, Y. (2006). Improving adolescent students' reading comprehension with iSTART. *Journal of Educational Computing Research, 34*, 147–171.

McNamara, D. S., O'Reilly, T., Rowe, M., Boonthum, C., & Levinstein, I. B. (2007). iSTART: A web–based tutor that teaches self-explanation and metacognitive reading strategies. In D. S. McNamara (Ed.), *Reading comprehension strategies: Theories, interventions, and technologies* (pp. 397–421). Mahwah, NJ: Erlbaum.

Meyer, B. J. F., Middlemiss, W., Theodorou Brezinski, K. L., McDougall, J., & Bartlett, B. J. (2002). Effects of structure strategy instruction delivered to fifth-grade children via the Internet with and without the aid of older adult tutors. *Journal of Educational Psychology, 94*, 486–519.

Meyer, B. J. F., & Poon, L. W. (2001). Effects of structure strategy training and signaling on recall of text. *Journal of Educational Psychology, 93*, 141–159.

Meyer, B. J. F., & Wijekumar, K. (2007). A web-based tutoring system for the structure strategy: Theoretical background, design, and findings. In D. S. McNamara (Ed.), *Reading comprehension strategies: Theories, interventions, and technologies* (pp. 347–375). Mahwah, NJ: Erlbaum.

Meyer, B. J. F., Wijekumar, K. K., & Lin, Y. (2011). Individualizing a web-based structure strategy intervention for fifth graders' comprehension of nonfiction. *Journal of Educational Psychology, 103*(1), 140–168.

Meyer, B. J. F., Wijekumar, K., Middlemiss, W., Higley, Lei, P., K., Meier, C., & Spielvogel, J. (2010). Web-based tutoring of the structure strategy with or without elaborated feedback or choice for fifth– and seventh–grade readers. *Reading Research Quarterly. 45*(1), 62–92.

Psotka, J., Massey, L. D., & Mutter, S. A. (1988). *Intelligent tutoring systems: Lessons learned*. Hillsdale, NJ: Erlbaum.

Woolf, B. P. (2009). *Building intelligent interactive tutors: Student-centered strategies for revolutionizing e–learning*. Burlington, MA: Elsevier.

7.5

Creativity and Creativity Programs

Heather L. Hammond, Lauren E. Skidmore, Amanda Wilcox-Herzog, and James C. Kaufman
California State University at San Bernardino

Introduction

Creativity is not a new concept. Plato, Aristotle, Freud, Vygotsky, and Jung all addressed the topic (Kaufman, 2009), whereas Guilford (1950) has been credited with spurring the advancement of creativity research with a speech given as president of the American Psychological Association and was responsible for developing the structure of intellect theory which identified different components of intellect. One of these components spoke to creativity and included the idea of divergent and convergent thinking. Additionally, Guilford developed assessment tools to measure intelligence and creativity. Divergent Thinking (DT) can be thought of as the cognitive processes used to produce multiple responses to open-ended questions or problems. DT is often contrasted with convergent thinking, the cognitive processes used to find the best solution to a given problem (Kaufman, Plucker, & Baer, 2008). Although today there are many working definitions of creativity, most include the twin concepts of novelty and appropriateness (Kaufman, 2009). One definition of creativity based on a synthesis of literature is "the interaction among aptitude, process, and environment by which an individual or group produces a perceptible product that is both novel and useful as defined within a social context" (Plucker, Beghetto, & Dow, 2004, p. 90). Creativity scholars generally agree that creativity continues to develop throughout the lifespan (Hendrick, 2001). Creativity can involve play (exploration and imagination), cognitive abilities (imagination and divergent thinking), and experience (personal and social) which are associated with overall academic achievement, particularly in areas of language (written and oral) and cognition (science, math, word problems, and technology) (Hendrick, 2001).

These efforts to operationalize creativity and thinking have led scholars to consider additional aspects of creativity such as developmental progression, facilitation, and creative motivation. For instance, both domestic and cross-cultural researchers are interested in what types of creativity pro-

grams are more effective, how to teach creativity, how to motivate creativity, how to enhance creativity, and how creativity impacts achievement.

Research Evidence

Early childhood educators dispute the effectiveness of various curricula types to promote student academic achievement. One side suggests that play-based curriculum supports optimal development (particularly creative development) by presenting learning through an active, child-directed approach. Such an approach emphasizes divergent thinking and encourages teachers to assist and guide children as needed (Frost, Wortham, & Reifel, 2005). Research has shown that play-based programs are related to less juvenile delinquency (Schweinhart & Weikart, 1998), and positive self-esteem and social interaction (Marcon, 2002). Play-based programs have also been linked to creative thinking (divergent and convergent thinking) across the lifespan (Lloyd & Howe, 2003).

Furthermore, play-based programs have been associated with higher academic achievements. Marcon's (2002) longitudinal study compared 183 children from three preschool programs: play-based, direct instruction, and a combination of the two types. She found that children in play-based programs had the highest grade point averages (4% higher than the combination program and 14% higher than the direct instruction); the differences amongst play-based and direct instruction were moderate (effect size =.38). Montie, Xiang, & Schweinhart's (2006) longitudinal study examined 10 countries (United States, Finland, Greece, Hong Kong, Indonesia, Ireland, Italy, Poland, Spain, and Thailand) on the International Association for Evaluation of Educational Achievement (IEA) Preprimary Project which was investigating preschool experiences and the outcomes on cognitive and language performances at age 7. Results indicated that elements of play-based programs were associated with higher cognitive performance (i.e., small group activities and variety of materials provided), higher language performance (i.e., child-initiated activities) and increased amount of years in preschool also increased language and cognitive performance in all countries. Huffman and Speer (2000) also concluded that urban classrooms (Head Start/Public School Transition Project) that incorporated higher levels of play-based curricula had students score higher in the Woodcock-Johnson Tests of Achievement, particularly in letter/word identification and word problems, than classrooms with lower levels of play-based curricula. However, Miller and Bizzell (1984) had mixed results when comparing play-based and direct instruction preschool programs on language and math performance based on gender differences. Males from play-based programs performed higher on language and math scales (Comprehensive Test of Basic Skills) than males from direct instruction programs, whereas females from direct instruction programs scored higher on language and math than females from play-based programs. This gender variation should be considered since males and females may learn differently, therefore, some programs may be more suited for one gender than the other.

Research related to direct instruction with young children shows that direct-instruction supports academic achievement through strategies that involve rote memorization, quick retrieval of that memorized information, and convergent thinking (Feeney, Galper, & Seefeldt, 2009). This approach tends to focus on meeting state mandated educational standards with less emphasis on divergent thinking. With regard to child outcomes, although direct instruction programs emphasize academic skills, research shows that over time, gains made academically may "fade-out" and that children do not outperform children in play-based programs (Marcon, 2002). Marcon's (2002) study on preschool aged children indicated that participants from direct instruction programs and play-based scored higher on academic performance (GPA) than the combination (direct instruction and play-based) program. However, when revisited, during fifth grade, academic performance (GPA) did not have any significant differences amongst the three types of programs, but by sixth grade, students from direct instruction programs performed lower than play-based and the combination approach (Macron, 2002).

Creativity and Teaching. In addition to an ongoing debate regarding which educational program best enhances children's development (including creative development), there is also an ongoing debate regarding how to teach creativity. Some scholars advocate teaching creativity directly, whereas others suggest that creativity should be taught in a more indirect manner. For example, an indirect approach emphasizes process in which children engage in creative activities for the pleasure of doing so, whereas a direct approach emphasizes creation of a product (Jeffrey & Craft, 2004). The direct approach incorporates teacher-directed projects or crafts in an effort to encourage children's creativity. This approach encourages similarity among children and convergent thinking. The indirect approach stresses the

process of creativity over the final product. This approach allows children to freely explore creative activities and emphasizes divergent thinking. Research supports that creativity is best learned indirectly through the encouragement and feedback of the teacher (Beghetto & Kaufman, 2007). Creativity is best encouraged when teachers engage in behaviors that scaffold rather than direct children's activities, adopt attitudes supportive of exploration and free choice, and offer creative activities. Additionally, teachers need to create an environment that is psychologically safe for students to explore ideas. This includes allowing for mistakes to be made and tolerating ambiguity in the classroom (Hendrick, 2001). Cross-cultural research demonstrates that countries outside of the United States also struggle with the best way to teach and implement creativity. According to Tan (2000), Singapore has expressed a serious commitment to promoting creativity by increasing creativity curricula and creative thinking in the classroom, which mostly relies on teachers to accomplish these tasks with their students. Tan (2000) indicates that enhancing creativity is linked to higher socioeconomics, greater advancements in technology, and higher educational advancement. However, Tan pointed out that there is little structure, limited education for these teachers to teach creativity, and limited research on creativity in Singapore. Additionally, research suggests that children and college students from Singapore perform poorly on creativity measures compared to others from other countries (Tan, 2000). Tan suggested that these findings can be attributed to lingering feelings about direct instruction in Singapore and lack of support in teaching creativity. In Germany, Freund and Holling (2008) investigated the influence of classroom type, creativity, and reasoning ability on academic performance in 1,133 high school students. They concluded that creativity and reasoning ability were highly significant as predictors of higher academic performance; reasoning ability was a slightly higher predictor. However, in Germany, students are assigned to schools based on their cognitive abilities, which have different levels of difficulty and their own standards per school. Therefore, classroom type was not predictive of academic performance. The authors suggested that schools' individual standards and teacher's personal values on creativity in the classroom may be associated with the lack of significance of classroom type on academic performance.

Creativity and Motivation. In addition to instruction type, motivation can promote creativity. Promotion of motivation includes attentions to both extrinsic and intrinsic factors. A person who is extrinsically motivated does a task for external reasons, such as obtaining a reward. Intrinsic motivation comes from an internal love of a task: passion fuels the productivity. Amabile (1996) found that intrinsic motivation bolsters creativity more than extrinsic motivation. People driven by personal enjoyment will be more creative than if motivated by rewards or praise. Beghetto and Kaufman (2010) acknowledge that creativity is best fostered through intrinsic motivation but argue that a balance between the two types of motivation can be useful. Additionally, motivation style influences academic achievement. Corpus, McClintic-Gilbert, and Hayenga (2009) indicated that intrinsic motivation and higher academic achievement influenced each other bidirectly amongst third through eighth grade students (N = 1051) but lower academic performance was not linked to extrinsic motivation.

Extrinsic motivators (tokens, extra credit, etc.), for example, should be used during certain activities, whereas intrinsic motivators are best used during other activities. The key is to know the goal of the activity. If facts and figures need to be learned, then it may be necessary to take the risk of using reward and depleting the creativeness of the task. However, if the task is to improve creative writing, for example, then encouraging intrinsic motivation is appropriate. The ability to choose the type of motivation to use is important if educators are to have the most impact during activities (Beghetto & Kaufman, 2010). Sarsani (2009) divided teenage students in India into three groups based on their levels of creative thinking (high, average, and low). Sarsani concluded that a high percentage of all three creative groups valued their academic performance—yet they were extrinsically motivated by grades and viewed academic failure as a disastrous.

Creativity and Feedback. Finally, creative development also depends on the type of feedback one receives. According to the Goldilocks Principle, creative development depends on positive feedback which includes developmentally appropriate criticism and encouragement (Beghetto & Kaufman, 2007). Positive feedback assists children in reaching their full creative potential. The Goldilocks Principle also states that negative or "harsh" feedback causes children's creative development to falter and may lead to inhibition of the creative process. Additionally, passive feedback (wherein children receive too much praise without real evaluation or suggestive criticism) can affect the creative process in children. Passive feedback can lead to disconnection from essential societal and personal evaluations which may cause the development of creativity to be stifled. In other words, lack of authentic positive feedback may hinder a child's ability to eventually reach their full creative potential (Beghetto & Kaufman, 2007). Sarsani (2008) concluded that highly creative students (which were also associated to higher intelligence) reported that their teachers provided positive feedback and motivation regarding their academic performance, whereas low creative thinking students reported to have less supportive feedback and motivation.

Summary and Recommendations

Although early childhood programs utilizing direct instruction continue to proliferate, domestic and cross-cultural research suggests that play-based programs tend to more effectively promote creativity and academic achievement than do direct instruction programs. Additionally, research

suggests teachers should lean toward indirect teaching strategies and intrinsic motivators in order to best promote divergent and convergent thinking, and academic performance amongst their students. Therefore, teachers should refrain from evaluating their students' creative projects, but rather allow children to experience the process of creativity and not heavily promote the end product of a creative activity. In addition, teachers should be aware of their feedback regarding their students' creativity and academic performance and aim for developmentally appropriate criticism and encouragement (positive feedback) which allows children to reach their full creative and academic potential. Teachers should not harshly criticize their students' creative projects and academic performance because that may result in lack of motivation in participating in that particular task. Lastly, teachers need to take into consideration the cultural values and beliefs of their pupils and try to balance creativity, accountability, and standards, in order to promote optimal development and academic performance for their students.

References

Amabile, T. M. (1996). *Creativity in context: Update to "The social psychology of creativity."* Boulder, CO: Westview Press.

Beghetto, R. A., & Kaufman, J. C. (2007) Intellectual estuaries: Connecting learning and creativity in programs of advanced academics. *Journal of Advanced Academics, 20,* 296–324.

Beghetto, R., & Kaufman, J. (Eds.). (2010). *Nurturing creativity in the classroom.* New York: Cambridge University Press.

Corpus, J. H., McClintic-Gilbert, M. S., & Hayenga, A. O. (2009). Within-year changes in children's intrinsic and extrinsic motivational orientations: Contextual predictors and academic outcomes. *Contemporary Educational Psychology, 34,* 154–166.

Frost, J. L., Wortham, S. C., & Reifel, S. (2005). Play and the curriculum. In J. Trawick-Smith (Eds.), *Play and child development* (2nd ed., pp. 212–245). Upper Saddle River, NJ: Pearson Education.

Feeney, S., Galper, A., & Seefeldt, C. (2009). *Continuing issues in early childhood education* (3rd ed.). Upper Saddle River, NJ: Pearson.

Freund, P. A., & Holling, H. (2008). Creativity in the classroom: A multilevel analysis investigating the impact of creativity and reasoning ability on GPA. *Creativity Research Journal, 20,* 309–318.

Guilford, J. P. (1950). Creativity. *American Psychologist, 5*(9), 444–454.

Hendrick, J. (2001). *The whole child: Developmental education for the early years* (7th ed.). Upper Saddle River, NJ: Merrill Prentice-Hall.

Huffman, L. R., & Speer, P. W. (2000). Academic performance among at-risk children: The role of developmentally appropriate practices. *Early Childhood Research Quarterly, 15,* 167–184.

Jeffrey, B., & Craft, A. (2004). Teaching creatively and teaching for creativity: Distinctions and relationships. *Educational Studies, 30,* 77–87.

Kaufman, J. C. (2009). *Creativity 101.* New York: Springer.

Kaufman, J. C., Plucker, J. A., & Baer, J. (2008). *Essentials of creativity assessment.* New York: Wiley.

Lloyd, B., & Howe, N. (2003). Solitary play and convergent and divergent thinking skills in preschool children. *Early Childhood Research Quarterly, 18,* 22–41.

Marcon, R. A. (2002). Moving up the grades: Relationship between preschool model and later school success. *Early Childhood Research & Practice, 4,* 1–20.

Miller, L. B., & Bizzell, R. P. (1984). Long-term effects of four preschool programs: Ninth and tenth-grade results. *Child Development, 55,* 1570–1587.

Montie, J. E., Xiang, Z., & Schweinhart, L. J. (2006). Preschool experience in 10 countries: Cognitive and language performance at age 7. *Early Childhood Research Quarterly, 21,* 313–331.

Plucker, J. A., Beghetto, R. A., & Dow, G. T. (2004). Why isn't creativity more important to educational psychologists? Potential, pitfalls, and future directions in creativity research. *Educational Psychologists, 39,* 83–96.

Sarsani, M. R. (2008). Do high and low creative children differ in their cognition and motivation? *Creativity Research Journal, 20,* 155–170.

Schweinhart, L. J., & Weikart, D. P. (1998). Why curriculum matters in early childhood education. *Educational Leadership, 55,* 57–60.

Tan, A. (2000). A review on the study of creativity in Singapore. Journal of Creative Behavior, 34, 259–284.

7.6

Outdoor Education

Justin Dillon
King's College, London

Introduction

Outdoor education is a broad term encompassing activities such as work in the school grounds; visits to the local park; urban studies; rural studies; nature study; residential fieldwork; heritage study; and outward bound courses. Its breadth reflects its origins in curriculum subjects as diverse as geography, physical education, and science. The term would not normally be used to refer to visits to galleries, museums, and science centers although visits to farms and botanic gardens might be included. The broader term *learning outside the classroom* would include all the activities above and its use is becoming more common. A related term gaining in popularity in England is *learning in natural environments* (LINE).

In the past, outdoor education might have been associated with the term *informal learning*; however, growing dissatisfaction with the false dichotomy of informal/formal learning (since learning is learning) has led to the use of terms such as *learning in informal contexts*. Even then, the range of pedagogies used outdoors and the vast array of contexts used by educators outdoors makes the use of formal/informal somewhat redundant.

The history of outdoor education, in modern times, at least, can be traced back to the 19th century with the advent of organised camping. The birth of the Scouting movement in the early 20th century laid the foundation for movements such as Outward Bound. The recent growth of forest schools in countries such as Denmark and Wales points to increased awareness of the value of outdoor education. Many of the outdoor education movements reflect philosophical positions such as the value of experiential learning and the need to empathise with nature. This point was recognised in the 1950s by two U.S. researchers, Donaldson and Donaldson, who saw outdoor education as "education *in*, *about* and *for* the outdoors" (1958, p. 17).

Research Evidence

Because of the diversity of the area, relevant research reviews include those looking at environmental education (Hart & Nolan, 1999); adventure education and outward bound (Hattie, Marsh, Neill, & Richards (1997); and school grounds as sites for learning (Malone & Tranter, 2003). The overlap between the reviews varies considerably in terms of the quality of the research examined and the contexts in which the studies described were carried out.

As one example, Rickinson et al. (2004) critically examined 150 pieces of research on outdoor learning published in English between 1993 and 2003. The research reviewed covered outdoor education in elementary, middle, and high schools as well as colleges and universities. The studies were grouped by contexts: fieldwork (e.g., river water quality monitoring) and outdoor visits; outdoor adventure education; and school grounds/community projects. They concluded that "Substantial evidence exists to indicate that fieldwork, properly conceived, adequately planned, well taught and effectively followed up, offers learners opportunities to develop their knowledge and skills in ways that add value to their everyday experiences in the classroom" (2004, p. 5). More recently, the UK Office for Standards in Education (Ofsted) noted that "When planned and implemented well, learning outside the classroom contributed significantly to raising standards and improving pupils' personal, social and emotional development" (2008, p. 5).

Outdoor education often complements and extends learning in the classroom. Evidence for this claim comes from, inter alia, a study of high school students from 11 Californian schools (State Education and Environment Roundtable [SEER], 2000). Students who undertook outdoor environmental learning scored higher in 72% of the academic assessments (reading, science, mathematics, higher attendance rates, and grade point averages) as compared with students from traditional schools in research by the California State Education and Environment Roundtable. In another study, Eaton (2000) found that outdoor learning experiences were more effective for developing cognitive skills than classroom-based learning. Such comparative studies, though important, are rare and very difficult to carry out.

One of the most important studies in this area is that of Nundy (1999) who looked at the role and effectiveness of residential fieldwork on UK upper primary school students. He highlighted three major benefits: a positive impact on long-term memory due to the memorable nature of the fieldwork setting; affective benefits of the residential experience, such as individual growth and improvements in social skills; reinforcement between the affective and the cognitive, with each influencing the other and providing a bridge to higher order learning. Nundy concluded that "Residential fieldwork is capable not only of generating positive cognitive and affective learning amongst students, but this may be enhanced significantly compared to that achievable within a classroom environment" (Nundy, 1999, p. 190). Nundy's study is important because it drew attention to the possibility of outdoor education adding value to conventional school-based education.

Studies (e.g., Thom, 2002) point to a range of benefits of outdoor adventure programs which include improvements in a range of outcomes including: general and specific academic skills; independence; locus of control; communication skills; and group cohesion and teamwork. However, substantial variation has been found in outcomes depending on factors such as the course aims and pedagogy. Compared to fieldwork and visits, outdoor adventure education tends to have less of a focus on developing knowledge and skills. The diversity of studies, while they suggest the impacts of outdoor education may be varied and possibly generalizable, have tended to lack any overall coherence nor have they led to the development of any overarching theoretical frameworks.

Two meta-analyses, one by Cason and Gillis (1994) and the other by Hattie et al. (1997) reported substantial evidence not only of positive effects of outdoor adventure education in the short term, but also continued gains in the long term. Hattie et al. examined the findings of 96 studies (1,728 effect sizes, and 151 samples) and reported that "the overall immediate effect size from these various adventure programs is 0.34" (1997, p. 55). The authors note that this meta-analysis suggests that 65% of students who participate in an adventure programme exceed the learning of those who do not participate in such a programme. Cason and Gillis (1994) had reported similar findings after they had carried out a meta-analysis of 43 studies of adolescent adventure programs. The authors reported an average effect size of 0.31 (that is, a 12.2% improvement in the rate of learning for the average participant).

Rickinson et al. (2004) examined the literature on school grounds and community projects, an area of outdoor education that has the capacity to link with most curriculum areas. They identified specific examples of benefits stemming from this area as being gains in science process skills and improved understanding of design and technology-related issues. Again, in the affective domain, important impacts included "greater confidence, renewed pride in community, stronger motivation toward learning, and greater sense of belonging and responsibility" (p. 6).

Rickinson et al.'s review (2004) supports particular kinds of outdoor education, specifically, programs which: "(i) provide longer, more sustained outdoor experiences than is often provided; (ii) incorporate well-designed preparatory follow-up work; (iii) use a range of carefully structured learning activities and assessments linked to the school curriculum; (iv) recognise and emphasise the role of facilitation in the learning process and (v) develop close links between programme aims and programme practices" (p. 7). Their advice to policy makers is unequivocal: "Those with a statutory and non-statutory responsibility for policy relating to outdoor education should be in no doubt that there is a considerable body of empirical research evidence to support and inform their work" (p. 7).

In terms of gaps in the research, relatively few studies have looked at the experiences of specific groups such as girls or students with special educational needs. A potential weakness of the existing research literature is that it has far too frequently been assumed that the reported barriers to outdoor education, such as health and safety concerns, time and cost, are the most fundamental challenges. If that was the case, then how is it that so many teachers and schools do take children beyond the classroom?

Summary and Recommendations

Rickinson et al. (2004) note a need to improve the methodological rigor of research and evaluation in outdoor education. They also suggest a need to improve and deepen the research based understandings of the outdoor learning *process*: "To put it simply, there is still much to be learnt about how and why programmes work or not" (p. 8). They also identify a number of 'blind spots' "(i) the nature of the 'learning' in outdoor education; (ii) the relationship between indoor learning and outdoor learning; and (iii) the historical and political aspects of outdoor education policy and curricula" (p. 8).

Traditionally, barriers to outdoor education include concerns over health and safety; cost; shortage of space in the curriculum; lack of teacher confidence and competence; travelling time; and lack of provision. However, Dillon (2011, p. 7) has argued that another set of barriers "must exist to explain the differences between individual teachers and schools" in terms of access and provision. Dillon claims that these barriers are centred around the following factors: teachers' view of the nature of their subject; teachers' views of the role of education; teachers' views of effective pedagogy; teachers' self-efficacy; teachers' working practices (planning, teaching, and evaluation); teachers' and school leaders commitment to school-community links; the relationship between schools and providers

References

Cason, D., & Gillis, H.L. (1994). A meta-analysis of outdoor adventure programming with adolescents. *Journal of Experiential Education, 17*(1), 40–47.

Dillon, J. (2010). *Beyond barriers to learning outside the classroom in natural environments* (A briefing paper for Natural England). Reading, England: Natural England.

Donaldson, G. W., & Donaldson, L. E. (1958). Outdoor education: A definition. *Journal of Health, Physical Education and Recreation, 29,* 17–63.

Eaton, D. (2000). Cognitive and affective learning in outdoor education. *Dissertation Abstracts International—Section A: Humanities and Social Sciences, 60*(10-A), 3595.

Hart, P., & Nolan, K. (1999). A critical analysis of research in environmental education. *Studies in Science Education, 34,* 1–69.

Hattie, J., Marsh, H. W., Neill, J. T., & Richards, G. E. (1997). Adventure education and outward bound: Out-of-class experiences that make a lasting difference. *Review of Educational Research, 67*(1), 43–87.

Malone, K., & Tranter, P. J. (2003). School grounds as sites for learning: Making the most of environmental opportunities. *Environmental Education Research, 9*(3), 283–303.

Nundy, S. (1999). The fieldwork effect: the role and impact of fieldwork in the upper primary school, *International Research in Geographical and Environmental Education, 8*(2), 190–198.

Office for Standards in Education (Ofsted). (2008). *Learning outside the classroom: How far should you go?* London: Ofsted.

Rickinson, M., Dillon, J., Teamey, K., Morris, M., Choi, M. Y., Sanders, D., & Benefield, P. (2004). *A review of research on outdoor learning.* Preston Montford, England: Field Studies Council.

State Education and Environment Roundtable (SEER). (2000). *The effects of environment-based education on student achievement.* Retrieved from http://www.seer.org/pages/csap.pdf

Thom, G. (2002). *Evaluation of pilot summer activities programme for 16 Year Olds* (DfES Research Report 341). London: DfES.

7.7

Role of Discussion in Reading Comprehension

IAN A. G. WILKINSON AND KATHRYN NELSON
Ohio State University

Introduction

Engaging students in classroom discussions about texts is thought to be a powerful approach to deepening their understanding of the texts and fostering their general comprehension abilities. Martin Nystrand (2002), one of the leading proponents of discussion as a means of enhancing reading comprehension, defined discussion as the "free exchange of information among students and/or between at least three participants that lasts longer than 30 seconds" (p. 30). However, discussion can be defined more generally as the open-ended, collaborative exchange of ideas among a teacher and students or among students for the purpose of furthering students' thinking, understanding, learning, or appreciation of text (Wilkinson, 2009). Participants present multiple points of view on the topic, respond to the ideas of others, and reflect on each other's ideas in an effort to build their knowledge, understanding, or interpretation of text. Engaging students in discussion about texts may provide an alternative means of fostering students' reading comprehension abilities beyond the explicit teaching of comprehension strategies (Wilkinson & Son, 2011).

To illustrate, the following excerpt is taken from a discussion between a teacher and a small group of 4th-grade students about a story called *Victor*, by James Howe. The story is about a young boy, named Cody, who is incapacitated, lying in a coma in a hospital bed. Cody creates an imaginary world ("The Land Above") inspired by the ceiling tiles in the hospital to help him get through the illness. During his stay in hospital, a mysterious man named Victor visits Cody and tells Cody stories about what his life will be like when he grows up. The teacher and students are trying to understand who Victor is:

Michelle: I think Victor's an angel.
Teacher: You think Victor's an angel? Can you tell me why you think so?
Michelle: Because he, well maybe he comes from like the land above, and that's where he's talking to him. And that's why maybe Cody can't see Victor 'cause he's from the land above and he's talking to him from up there.
Nancy: Maybe's he's just a figure, but he always has this thing on his face that he doesn't have…
Matt: But he, Cody kept saying "three tiles up, two to the left."
Teacher: That was interesting
Andrew: You mean "three tiles down, two to the left."
Nancy: Yeah, he was talking about the ceiling.
Sam: He thought it was a real place where people lived and stuff, but he said the funny thing about it was, he never gave them a name.
Andrew: And also, the reason why I don't think Victor was in the land above, well how could he be talking from the land above because remember when Cody said he could hear him, hear the screeching on the floor from when Victor was pulling up a chair to keep Cody company.
Teacher: So that's. Are you saying that's evidence?
Andrew: Yeah.
Teacher: Interesting.
Andrew: So how could he be from the land above? I mean he could be from the land above, but how could he be talking from the land above?
Matt: But how do you know people can't travel from and to [the] land above?
Nancy: This isn't realistic. This isn't like nonfiction, so anything can happen.

Note that the students had considerable responsibility for constructing their understanding and interpretation of the story. Michelle stated her opinion and the teacher asked a question that probed for the reason for her opinion ("Can you tell me why you think so?") that elicited a variety of responses. Most of the contributions came from students and there were many consecutive exchanges among students with only brief, occasional comments from the teacher. The students appear to have been genuinely interested in exploring the issue of who is Victor, they asked questions that built on each other's responses, and they challenged each other's views, often using evidence from the text, in a collective effort to make sense of the story. This kind of exchange stands in contrast to the traditional recitation model or I-R-E pattern of classroom discourse in which the teacher *Initiates* a question, students *Respond*, and the teacher *Evaluates* the response. In a recitation model, the teacher controls the direction of the discussion and has interpretative authority. Students take a passive role as the teacher shapes and guides the students' learning.

Research Evidence

The origins of discussion as a teaching method can be traced back to Socrates and Plato, though research on discussion about text as a means of enhancing students' abilities and learning has a shorter history. One of the first empirical studies on the topic was a doctoral dissertation by Casper (1964) on the effects of the Junior Great Books discussion program with gifted fifth-grade students, as measured by a test of intellectual operation based on the work of J. B. Guilford. The 1980s and 1990s saw a proliferation of approaches to conducting high-quality discussion about text. There are now a large number of discourse-intensive pedagogies that serve to disrupt the traditional I-R-E pattern of classroom discourse in favor of more open-ended, collaborative exchanges of ideas among participants for the purpose of improving students' comprehension of text (e.g., Beck & McKeown, 2006; Beck, McKeown, Hamilton, & Kucan, 1997).

Several major studies have shed light on the incidence of discussion about text in teaching of language arts. Commeyras and DeGroff (1998) surveyed the teaching practices of a random sample of 1,519 K-12 U.S. literacy teachers and related professionals and found that only 33% of respondents reported that they frequently or very frequently had students meet in small groups to discuss literature in their classrooms. Commeyras and DeGroff also found that discussions were more common in elementary and middle school classes than they were in high school classes. In a large observational study of eighth-grade and ninth-grade language arts and English classes in eight Midwestern communities in the United States, Nystrand (1997) found that open-ended, whole-class discussion averaged only 52 seconds per class in eighth grade and only 14 seconds per class in ninth grade. Similarly, in an observational study of 64 middle and high school English classrooms in five U.S. states, Applebee, Langer, Nystrand, and Gamoran (2003) found that the amount of time spent on open discussions averaged only 68 seconds per class. Discussions also seem to be relatively uncommon in UK classrooms (Alexander, 2006). Thus, despite educators' recognition that discussion has potential value, discussions about text are quite rare.

What does research show about the effects of discussion on reading comprehension? There have been three major reviews of the role of discussion in shaping students' reading comprehension. Nystrand (2006) provided a broad, narrative review of the role of discussion in promoting reading comprehension. Murphy, Wilkinson, Soter, Hennessey, and Alexander (2009) conducted a meta-analysis of 42 studies of the effects of nine approaches to conducting text-based discussions on measures of teacher and student talk and individual student comprehension and learning outcomes. Murphy, Wilkinson, and Soter (2011) followed up with a review of the literature on the role of discussion in enhancing students' comprehension, focusing on the results of studies in which researchers assessed the effects of discussion on measures that are independent of the texts discussed. Collectively, these reviews show that the effects of discussion vary depending on the nature of the discussion and the type of study. Many approaches to discussion are effective at promoting students' literal and inferential comprehension, producing effects as large as 3.0 standard deviations for single-group design studies and 0.8 standard deviations for multiple-group studies. Some approaches are effective at promoting students' critical thinking, reasoning, and argumentation about text, producing effects as large as 2.5 standard deviations for single-group studies and 0.4 standard deviations for multiple-group studies.

The effects of discussion also vary by type of outcome measure. The effects of discussion have been assessed on measures of teacher and student talk, researcher-developed measures, including complex writing tasks (e.g., persuasive essays), and commercial, standardized tests of reading comprehension. By and large, the effects are greatest on measures of student and teacher talk—student talk increases and teacher talk decreases—they are smaller on researcher-developed measures of comprehension, and they are smaller still on commercial, standardized assessments of comprehension.

A number of other factors seem to moderate the effects of discussion on reading comprehension. One factor is the kind of talk. Increases in student talk do not necessarily result in concomitant increases in student comprehension; rather, it seems that a particular kind of talk is necessary to promote comprehension (cf. Wells, 1989). Productive discussions are structured and focused yet not dominated by the teacher. Students hold the floor for extended periods of time and they are prompted, either by the teacher or by other students, to discuss texts through open-ended and authentic questions. In productive discussions, there is a high degree of uptake where the teacher or students incorporate the ideas of others into their questions and build on each other's ideas. Another moderating factor is students' reading ability. The benefits of discussion seem to be more potent for students of below-average ability than for students of average or above-average ability, presumably because students of higher ability levels already possess the skills needed to comprehend stories. Yet another factor is time spent discussing texts. Interestingly, it seems that the greatest effects of discussion become apparent in the first three weeks in which discussions are implemented.

Why does discussion seem to benefit students' reading comprehension? As reviews of the research suggest, the key agent is the talk in the discussion. But what does the talk accomplish? The views of scholars who do research on discussion differ on this issue. Some scholars argue that the talk in discussion fosters greater student engagement in making sense of the text (e.g., McKeown, Beck, & Blake, 2009). They contend that the talk serves as a tool to help students organize their thoughts, make inferences, reason, and reflect on the meaning of the text. Some scholars take a more social view of learning and argue that the talk makes students' thinking public, enabling them to learn how others think about the text and prompting them to come to terms with different points of view (e.g., Almasi, 1994). Some scholars take an even more social view of learning and argue that the talk enables students to coconstruct knowledge and understandings together (e.g., Wells, 2007). According to this view, the talk functions as a vehicle that enables students to combine their intellectual resources to collectively make sense of the text. Neil Mercer (2000), a British psychologist who studies language use in the classroom, calls this process "inter-thinking."

Regardless of which perspective on talk is taken, the talk in discussions seems to be especially productive when students are encouraged to consider others' perspectives and to explain, elaborate, and defend their positions; that is, to argue constructively about the issues raised by the text. Students come away from such discussions knowing not only how to think critically and reflectively about the text they have discussed but also, it is hoped, how to apply these ways of thinking to other texts in other reading situations (Reznitskaya et al., 2008).

Taken together, the level of evidence on the effects of discussion on reading comprehension might best be described as moderate (Kamil et al., 2008). Although current studies suggest that discussion improves reading comprehension, producing some medium to large effect sizes, more experimental and quasi-experimental studies of the topic are needed. Much of the research consists of single group pretest-posttest design studies or multiple-group studies with criterion measures that afford little confidence in the veracity of the outcomes. It is important to seek evidence of the effects of discussion beyond measures of the effects on learning and comprehension of texts that were the subject of the discussion—measures of students' abilities to comprehend new, unfamiliar texts and to perform novel comprehension-related tasks. It stands to reason that enabling students to engage in discussions about texts should improve their comprehension of those same texts. The more interesting and important question is whether the discussion enables students to acquire the habits of mind to transfer their comprehension abilities to new texts and novel tasks (Wilkinson & Son, 2011).

It is also important to compare the effects of discussion to those of explicit instruction in comprehension strategies (cf. McKeown, Beck, & Blake, 2009)—the currently favored approach to teaching comprehension. There is ample research showing that instruction in small repertoires of comprehension strategies produces robust gains in students' comprehension, especially for students with learning disabilities, and that the benefits can transfer to new texts and novel tasks (Wilkinson & Son, 2011). If discussion-based approaches to teaching comprehension are to gain traction in classroom instruction, more research is needed that compares discussion about text with explicit strategy instruction.

Summary and Recommendations

For teachers, professional development is fundamental to the implementation of productive discussions. As indicated earlier, there is considerable consensus about what is involved in conducting productive discussion about text. But conducting these discussions is not easy (perhaps this why they are so rare in classrooms). Although there is good understanding of their general framework, there is no one way of conducting discussions; there are no prescribed moves that can be applied with all texts and all topics because what a teacher needs to do depends on the momentary ebb and flow of discussion. For most teachers, implementing productive discussions about text requires a substantial shift in their knowledge and beliefs about their role as a teacher and about the role of talk in learning and its potential benefit for students' comprehension. It also requires a deep conceptual understanding of what constitutes productive talk about text. For these reasons, sustained and scaffolded professional development is fundamental to the implementation of productive discussions about text

References

Alexander, R. J. (2006). *Towards dialogic teaching: Rethinking classroom talk* (3rd ed.). York, England: Dialogos.

Almasi, J. F. (1994). The nature of fourth graders' sociocognitive conflicts in peer-led and teacher-led discussions of literature. *Reading Research Quarterly, 30*(3), 314–351.

Applebee, A. N., Langer, J. A., Nystrand, M., & Gamoran, A. (2003). Discussion-based approaches to developing understanding: Classroom instruction and student performance in middle and high school English. *American Education Research Journal, 40*(3), 685–730.

Beck, I. L., & McKeown, M. G., (2006). *Improving comprehension with questioning the author: A fresh and expanded view of a powerful approach.* New York: Scholastic.

Beck, I. L., McKeown, M. G., Hamilton, R. L., & Kucan, L. (1997). *Questioning the Author: An approach for enhancing student engagement with text.* Newark, NJ: International Reading Association.

Casper, T. P. (1964). *Effects of the Junior Great Books program at the fifth grade level on four intellectual operations and certain of their component factors as defined by J. P. Guilford.* (Unpublished doctoral dissertation). Saint Louis University, St. Louis.

Commeyras, M., & DeGroff, L. (1998). Literacy professionals' perspectives on professional development and pedagogy: A national survey. *Reading Research Quarterly, 33*, 434–472.

Kamil, M. L., Borman, G. D., Dole, J., Kral, C. C., Salinger, T., & Torgesen, J. (2008). *Improving adolescent literacy: Effective classroom and intervention practices: A practice guide* (NCEE #2008-4027).

Washington, DC: National Center for Education Evaluation and Regional Assistance, Institute of Education Sciences, U.S. Department of Education.

McKeown, M. G., Beck, I. L., & Blake, R. G. K. (2009). Rethinking reading comprehension instruction: A comparison of instruction for strategies and content approaches. *Reading Research Quarterly, 44*(3), 218–253.

Mercer, N. (2000). *Words and minds: How we use language to think together*. London: Routledge.

Murphy, P. K., Wilkinson, I. A. G., & Soter, A. O. (2011). Instruction based on discussion. In R. E. Mayer & P. A. Alexander (Eds.), *Handbook of research on learning and instruction* (pp. 221–234).New York: Routledge.

Murphy, P. K., Wilkinson, I. A. G., Soter, A. O., Hennessey, M. N., & Alexander, J. F. (2009). Examining the effects of classroom discussion on students' high-level comprehension of text: A meta-analysis. *Journal of Educational Psychology, 101,* 740–764.

Nystrand, M. (1997). *Opening dialogue: Understanding the dynamics of language and learning in the English classroom*. New York: Teachers College Press.

Nystrand, M. (2002). *CLASS 4.0 User's manual: A Windows laptop computer system for the in-class analysis of classroom discourse*. Madison, WI: Wisconsin Center for Education Research.

Nystrand, M. (2006). Research on the role of classroom discourse as it affects reading comprehension. *Research in the Teaching of English, 40*(4), 392–412.

Reznitskaya, A., Anderson, R. C., Dong, T., Li, Y., Kim, I.-H., & Kim, S.-Y. (2008). Learning to think well: Applications of argument schema theory. In C. C. Block & S. Parris (Eds.), *Comprehension instruction: Research-based best practices* (pp. 196–213). New York: Guilford.

Wells, G. (1989). Language in the classroom: Literacy and collaborative talk. *Language and Education, 3*, 251–273.

Wells, G. (2007). Semiotic mediation, dialogue and the construction of knowledge. *Human Development, 50*(5), 244–274.

Wilkinson, I. A. G. (2009). Discussion methods. In E. M. Anderman & L. H. Anderman (Eds.), *Psychology of classroom learning: An encyclopedia* (pp. 330–336). Detroit, MI: Gale/Cengage.

Wilkinson. I. A. G., & Son. E. H. (2011). A dialogic turn in research on learning and teaching to comprehend. In M. L. Kamil, P. D. Pearson, E. Moje, & P. Afflerbach (Eds.), *Handbook of reading research* (Vol. 4, pp. 359–387). New York: Routledge.

7.8

The Impact of Calculators on Student Achievement in the K-12 Mathematics Classroom

AIMEE J. ELLINGTON
Virginia Commonwealth University

Introduction

In the United States in 1974, the National Council of Teachers of Mathematics (NCTM) issued its first official statement on technology strongly encouraging the use of calculators in mathematics instruction. Skepticism about the role that calculators play in the classroom—most specifically their impact on students' paper-and-pencil skills—has been a catalyst for debate in the mathematics education community since the early 1970s. In the early years, mathematics educators questioned the educational relevance of calculators. As they became standard devices in classrooms, the discussion shifted to how to maximize the benefits of using calculators in the study of mathematics. Now, early in the 21st century, calculators are commonplace in K-12 classrooms. In particular, a national survey revealed that basic four function calculators are used in 62% of American elementary schools and in 82% of middle schools (Weiss, Banilower, & Smith, 2001). Also, 49% of middle school teachers say that they incorporate scientific calculators in their mathematics instruction on a regular basis (Weiss et al., 2001). According to the Trends in International Mathematics and Science Study (TIMSS), calculators are used by three-fourths of eighth grade students around the world. However, the purpose for using them and the frequency of use varies from country to country (Beaton et al., 1997).

When graphing calculators were introduced in the 1980s, the NCTM (1989) gave the technology credit for "the emergence of a new classroom dynamic in which teachers and students become natural partners in developing mathematical ideas and solving mathematical problems" (p. 128). Currently, graphing calculators are incorporated in instruction by 26% of middle school teachers in American classrooms, whereas 78% of high school mathematics teachers routinely use them in their classrooms (Weiss et al., 2001). Technology, particularly graphing calculators, has had a significant impact on how students learn and

what they learn when studying mathematics (Roschelle & Singleton, 2008). These devices provide students with numeric, symbolic, and graphic data for a wide variety of numeric tasks. With this type of information quickly and readily available, teachers can place more emphasis on the conceptual aspects of mathematics content and less time on computational skills. However, it should be noted that experts in the field do not condone calculator use totally replacing paper-and-pencil work in the mathematics classroom (Roschelle & Singleton, 2008).

The results of more than 170 quantitative research studies on calculator use in K-12 classrooms have been synthesized through meta-analysis (Ellington, 2003, 2006; Hembree & Dessart, 1986, 1992; Khoju, Jaciw, & Miller 2005; Nikolaou, 2001; Smith, 1996). Narrative reviews (some examples are Burrill et al., 2002; Penglase & Arnold, 1996; Roschelle & Singleton, 2008) of quantitative and qualitative graphing calculator-based research have expanded on the findings of the meta-analyses. Fifteen percent of the studies that were analyzed were conducted in classrooms outside of the United States. The results of these efforts are outlined below.

Research Evidence

The quantitative studies analyzed through the meta-analysis process typically applied a quasi-experimental research design in which a treatment group with access to calculators was compared to a control group without access to calculators (e.g., Harskamp, Suhre, & Van Streun, 1998). In the majority of cases, the instruction provided to both groups was the same (e.g., Graham & Thomas, 2000), although some studies investigated the use of instructional materials designed especially for use with calculators (e.g., Szetela & Super, 1987). Achievement was measured by students' ability to demonstrate mathematical skills on an assessment of mathematical procedures or concepts. The skills these instruments were designed to assess can be organized into three categories: (a) *computational* or procedural skills (i.e., those necessary to apply an algorithm or complete a procedure; e.g., Burnett, 1985); (b) *conceptual* skills (i.e., those required to understand mathematical concepts; e.g., Ruthven, 1990); and (c) *problem solving* skills (i.e., the skills used to apply mathematical concepts or procedures to solving applications or word problems; e.g., Szetela & Super, 1987). The type of calculator incorporated in instruction ranged from basic four function calculators or scientific calculators typically used in elementary mathematics classes (e.g., Szetela & Super, 1987), to graphing calculators typically used in teaching algebra, precalculus, and other advanced mathematics courses in secondary and postsecondary schools (e.g., Graham & Thomas, 2000). Computer algebra systems (either calculator or computer software) were not used in the research studies summarized here.

It should be noted that in the early days of calculator-based research, the role of the calculator was primarily functional (i.e. drill and practice, checking work, etc.). Rarely were calculators fully integrated into mathematics instruction. In later years (i.e., studies conducted after 1990) calculators became an integral part of the instruction process (e.g., Ruthven, 1990). In a few cases, primary studies were conducted with students of low or high ability level. Where possible, results for these groups are noted. However, most studies were conducted in mixed ability classrooms. The meta-analyses do not report results for students of specific gender, race, or socioeconomic status but some results are reported for specific grade levels.

Two meta-analyses (Ellington, 2006; Khoju et al., 2005) considered only studies in which the graphing calculator was used in the classroom. The other meta-analyses (Ellington, 2003, Hembree & Dessart, 1986, 1992; Nikolaou, 2001; Smith, 1996) were conducted with research using all varieties of calculators.

All Types of Calculators (Basic, Scientific, and Graphing).

Two meta-analyses (Nikolaou, 2001; Smith, 1996) did not provide separate results based on whether or not the calculator was part of the assessment process. Smith (1996) analyzed 23 research reports and found that calculators had a positive effect on students' conceptual understanding and also helped improve their problem solving skills. He also determined that calculators had no effect on students' computational skills. The results were more favorable for high school students as compared to students in elementary classrooms. Since most of the high school studies used graphing calculators, Smith surmised that the type of technology may have been the reason for the difference. Nikolaou's (2001) meta-analysis of 24 original studies found that the use of calculators improved students overall achievement in mathematics. Nikolaou's (2001) work also supported the previous finding (Smith, 1996) that calculators had a positive impact on students' problem solving skills.

Other meta-analyses (Ellington, 2003; Hembree & Dessart, 1986, 1992) differentiated results based on whether or not students were allowed to use calculators during the testing process. Based on the analysis of over 120 studies in which calculators were part of both testing and instruction, the skills of students in all three categories (procedural, conceptual, and problem solving) improved (Ellington, 2003; Hembree & Dessart, 1986, 1992). Calculators also had a positive impact on students' ability to select the appropriate strategies to solve problems (Hembree & Dessart, 1986). With respect to both of these findings, low and average ability students realized the most gains (Hembree & Dessart, 1986). For high ability students, procedural and problem solving skills were neither helped nor hindered from the use of calculators. The benefit of calculator use for students of all ability levels was greatest from long term calculator use (i.e., 9 or more weeks) and when the device used was a graphing calculator (Ellington, 2003). The impact of calculators on problem solving skills was most significant when curriculum materials were designed specifically for use with the calculator (Ellington, 2003).

When students used calculators during instruction but did not have access to them during testing, the procedural and problem solving skills of average ability students improved in all grades except fourth grade (Hembree & Dessart, 1986). In fact, calculators had a negative impact on the computational skills of fourth grade students (Hembree & Dessart, 1986). Ellington (2003) found that even though students did not use calculators on tests, their ability to select the appropriate problem solving strategy improved after they used calculators during instruction. Under these same instructional conditions, the conceptual understanding of students of all ability levels was neither helped nor hindered by calculator use (Ellington, 2003).

Graphing Calculators.

Both meta-analyses (Ellington, 2006; Khoju et al. 2005) that solely analyzed studies of graphing calculator use considered those without computer algebra system capabilities. Khoju et al. (2005) evaluated graphing calculator use in four research studies conducted in algebra classrooms and found that graphing calculators improved student performance in algebra when they were incorporated with instructional materials specifically designed for calculator use. Ellington (2006) evaluated students' procedural and conceptual skills in all subject areas using 42 empirical studies that were conducted in mixed ability classrooms. While instruction involved a wide variety of mathematical content at the level of Algebra I and above, most of the studies were conducted in algebra and precalculus classes. When graphing calculators were used in instruction but not included in testing, students experienced gains in their conceptual understanding of the topic they were learning. Under these same conditions, the calculator had no effect on students' procedural skills. When the graphing calculator was an integral part of both mathematics instruction and testing, students' procedural and conceptual skills improved with calculator use. In more general terms, students performed better on tests of overall mathematics achievement when compared with students who did not have access to graphing calculators.

The narrative reviews of graphing calculators use provide some interesting results related to specific content and demographic groups. With respect to overall student achievement (Burrill et al., 2002), low ability students realized larger gains on tests of mathematical achievement after using graphing calculators when compared with the results of average or high ability students. Narrative reviews also provide results about learning specific content. Graphing calculators were useful tools for students who were developing an understanding of the function concept (Penglase & Arnold, 1996). The research evaluated by Burrill et al. (2002) supported this result and also found that graphing calculators benefitted students in the study of variables, the interpretation of graphs, and when working on application problems involving algebraic skills and concepts. Burrill et al. (2002) reported that students were more willing to try a variety of solution strategies and incorporate the algebraic, numeric, and graphic views provided by the calculator in their work. With respect to the time devoted to different types of tasks, students with graphing calculators spent more time problem solving and conducting mathematical investigations when compared with students without access to calculators (Burrill et al., 2002).

Critics of Calculator Use.   The primary concern of critics of calculator use is that students will use the device as a crutch and, consequently, will have weaker computational and reasoning skills. With respect to the mathematics taught in lower grades, critics often quote the result of the Hembree and Dessart (1986) meta-analysis regarding the decline of paper-and-pencil skills of fourth grade students after calculator use. This finding was based on research conducted before 1982. Meta-analyses on studies conducted after 1982 (Ellington, 2003; Nikolaou, 2001; Smith, 1996) neither support nor refute this result. In spite of the lack of statistical results to support the fact, critics question students' computational abilities as well as their abilities to understand and interpret the data supplied by the calculator in upper grades as well.

Summary and Recommendations

The results of the research summarized above support the following recommendations for teachers, administrators, and other decision makers. Calculators should be part of instruction in mathematics courses at all educational levels (elementary, middle, and high school). Calculator use should be limited to experimentation and concept development activities in the early grades. The duration of calculator use should increase as students move through the higher grades. However, at all levels of the educational hierarchy, calculators should not replace the development of paper-and-pencil skills, mental calculations, and number sense skills in students. Class time must be spent on a variety of noncalculator activities including, but not limited to, work with the basic operations, estimation, and algebraic manipulation.

The emphasis of calculator-based work should be on problem solving activities and helping students develop their conceptual understanding. Calculators may be useful in reducing the cognitive load which allows (a) instructional time to focus on the conceptual aspect of mathematical tasks and (b) real-world examples that involve "messy" numbers to be part of the educational experience. To be most effective, calculators should be included in all aspects of mathematical instruction including assessment. To that end, assessments must be written to evaluate more than just procedural skills.

Graphing calculators coupled with instructional materials that emphasize the connections between numerical, symbolic, and graphic representations should be used to teach mathematics content at the level of Algebra I and above. Helping students understand the rich relations between the various representations is extremely important for the technology to be used effectively. Class time should also be spent on sense making activities. In particular, students must be taught how to interpret the information that the calculator provides as well as the limitations of the information that the graphing calculator presents.

With respect to calculators, professional development for mathematics teachers should focus on three areas: (a) helping teachers determine the appropriate balance between paper-and-pencil tasks and calculator explorations; (b) effective ways to help students incorporate the graphic, numeric, and symbolic data into mathematical investigations; and (c) appropriate assessments of student understanding when they have access to calculators during the testing process.

Concerns about calculator use are mostly related to how the technology is incorporated into instruction, not whether calculators have a role in the educational process. Calculators should not replace paper-and-pencil calculations (Roschelle & Singleton, 2008). Students must work with the basic operations with all types of real numbers (whole numbers, fractions, decimals, integers, etc.). This is a significant part of the elementary and middle school curriculum and it is work in which calculators should not play a significant role. In the upper grades, students must also conduct basic algebraic manipulations by hand. At all levels, extensive time should be devoted to the development of number sense and reasoning skills. Teachers should spend class time helping students interpret the results provided by the calculator and understanding the limitations of the technology. Simply put, educators must work toward a balance between paper-and-pencil activities and calculator-based activities so that the two complement each other throughout the learning process (Waits & Demana, 2000).

Future research should consider the specifics of the calculator's role in the instruction process, which content areas to emphasize, and the benefits of calculator use to different demographic groups. Research should be conducted on calculator use by teachers who have participated in professional development activities on effective instructional approaches especially with graphing calculators.

References

Beaton, A., Mullis, I., Martin, M., Gonzalez, E., Kelly, D., & Smith, T. (1997). *Mathematics achievement in the middle school years: IEA's Third International Mathematics and Science Study (TIMSS)*. Chestnut Hill, MA: TIMSS International Study Center.

Burnett, C. M. (1985). The effectiveness of using a hand-held calculator as an instructional aid in the teaching of fraction to decimal conversion to sixth-grade students. *Dissertation Abstracts International, 46*, 2174A.

Burrill, G., Allison, J., Breaux, G., Kastberg, S., Leatham, K., & Sanchez, W. (2002). *Handheld graphing technology in secondary mathematics: Research findings and implications for classroom practice*. Dallas, TX: Texas Instruments.

Ellington, A. J. (2006). The effects of non-CAS graphing calculators on student achievement and attitude levels in mathematics: A meta-analysis. *School Science and Mathematics, 106*(1), 16–26.

Ellington, A. J. (2003). A meta-analysis of the effects of calculators on students' achievement and attitude levels in pre-college mathematics classes. *Journal for Research in Mathematics Education, 34*(5), 433–463.

Graham, A., & Thomas, M. (2000). Building a versatile understanding of algebraic variables with a graphic calculator. *Educational Studies in Mathematics, 41*, 265–282.

Harskamp, E., Suhre, C., & Van Streun, A. (1998). The graphics calculator in mathematics education: An experiment in the Netherlands. *Hiroshima Journal of Mathematics Education, 6*, 13–31.

Hembree, R., & Dessart, D. (1986). Effects of hand-held calculators in precollege mathematics education: A meta-analysis. *Journal for Research in Mathematics Education, 17*, 83–99.

Hembree, R., & Dessart, D. (1992). Research on calculators in mathematics education. In J. Fey (Ed.), *Calculators in mathematics education* (pp. 23–32). Reston, VA: National Council of Teachers of Mathematics.

Khoju, M., Jaciw, A., & Miller, G. I. (2005). *Effectiveness of graphing calculators in K-12 mathematics achievement: A systematic review*. Palo Alto, CA: Empirical Education.

National Council of Teachers of Mathematics. (1974, December). NCTM Board approves policy statement on the use of minicalculators in the mathematics classroom. *NCTM Newsletter, 11*, 3.

Nikolaou, C. (2001). Hand-held calculator use and achievement in mathematics: A meta-analysis. *Dissertation Abstracts International, 62*(08), 2707.

Penglase, M., & Arnold, S. (1996). The graphics calculator in mathematics education: A critical review of recent research. *Mathematics Education Research Journal, 8*, 58–90.

Roschelle, J., & Singleton, C. (2008). Graphing calculators: Enhancing math learning for all students. In J. Voogt & G. Knezek (Eds.), *International handbook of information technology in primary and secondary education* (pp. 951–959). New York: Springer.

Ruthven, K. (1990). The influence of graphic calculator use on translation from graphic to symbolic forms. *Educational Studies in Mathematics, 21*, 431–450.

Smith, B. (1996). A meta-analysis of outcomes from the use of calculators in mathematics education. *Dissertation Abstracts International, 57*, 787A. (University Microfilms No. DA9724626)

Szetela, W., & Super, D. (1987). Calculators and instruction in problem solving in grade 7. *Journal for Research in Mathematics Education, 18*, 215–229.

Waits, B., & Demana, F. (2000). Calculators in mathematics teaching and learning: Past, present and future. In M. J. Burke (Ed.), *Learning mathematics for a new century* (pp. 51–66). Reston, VA: National Council of Teachers of Mathematics.

Weiss, I., Banilower, E., & Smith, P. S. (2001). *Report of the 2000 national survey of science and mathematics education*. Chapel Hill, NC: Horizon Research.

7.9

Second Language Vocabulary

Yongqi Gu
Victoria University of Wellington

Introduction

For thousands of students going through the schooling challenge in a nonnative language of instruction, the hurdle to academic success includes not only subject knowledge, but also a working ability in the second language (L2) itself. Vocabulary being the carrier of meaning is crucial for academic success (Corson, 1997), and it is even more so for succeeding academically in a second language (August & Shanahan, 2006). The overwhelming research attention on L2 vocabulary has focused on English as a second language (ESL). However, the ESL research reviewed in this chapter will be relevant to similar contexts where another second language is used as the language of instruction.

Students entering an English-medium education system with English not being their native language are often referred to as English language learners (ELLs). The academic achievement of these students has remained a major concern for parents, educators, and governments (Herman, 2009), despite evidence on the unfairness of most content-based tests that are linguistically challenging (Abedi, Hofstetter, & Lord, 2004). Given the Herculean challenge ELLs face (August & Shanahan, 2006) in gaining not only general English competence, but also academic English proficiency as well as content mastery, considerable efforts have gone into the explanation of the academic achievement gap between ESL and English only learners. Other attention has been directed at closing this gap. Second language vocabulary has emerged as one of the main explanations and a major proposed solution to the ELLs' school achievement problem (August & Shanahan, 2006).

Research Evidence

Vocabulary in Academic Achievement. Vocabulary is situated at the very core of academic meaning systems, and therefore is essential to academic success at school (Corson, 1997). There is enough evidence suggesting

that "vocabulary diversity is the most consistently used marker of proficiency in education" (p. 673). Interestingly, a student's vocabulary, which is so important for academic literacy at school, is very much socioculturally divided. In other words, vocabulary development and achievement gaps are related to socioeconomic status (Corson, 1997).

Not all words are equally important for academic achievement. In any language, a small number of high-frequency words cover a large amount of texts. In English, for example, the 2,000 most frequently used words constitute around 80 to 87% of running words in English texts (Nation, 2001). Besides these words, certain words appear in school texts much more often than they do elsewhere. These words are referred to as "academic vocabulary." Coxhead (2000) identified 570 of these words, which cover 8 to 10% of running words in academic texts across various disciplines. Given the high utility value of high-frequency words and academic vocabulary, it is inconceivable that children who have problems with these two types of words would be able to achieve academically at school.

Second Language Vocabulary and Academic Achievement. Indeed, vocabulary has been found to be a major problem for L2 learners, so much so that researchers have identified a "vocabulary gap" in school achievement between L2 learners and other learners (August, Carlo, Dressler, & Snow, 2005). Both the breadth and the depth of L2 vocabulary have been found to be considerably below the norm of other students. For example, August et al. (2005) reported that ELLs not only knew fewer English words than monolingual English speakers, but also knew less about the meanings of these words (p. 51). This of course doesn't mean that the ELLs' language or conceptual development necessarily falls behind that of English only students. In fact, there is evidence showing the advantage of bilingual over monolingual learners in the total conceptual store of both a receptive and productive nature (Allman, 2005). What the gap means is that these

307

ELLs' deficiency in English vocabulary will put them at a disadvantage in learning through the medium of English. In one of the classic studies, for example, Saville-Troike (1984) examined various aspects of linguistic knowledge and their relation to academic achievement and found that "vocabulary knowledge is the single most important area of L2 competence when learning content through that language is the dependent variable" (p. 199).

For many L2 learners who are seen as underachieving at school, the real problem may well be a lack of conceptual development in the academic aspects of the L2. In a widely accepted distinction between conversational fluency, or basic interpersonal communicative skills (BICS) and academic language proficiency, or cognitive academic language proficiency (CALP), Cummins (2008) stresses a crucial point many classroom teachers may overlook, that the conversational proficiency (the BICS) of L2 children may be acquired relatively easily, normally within 2 years of exposure in the target language. This pseudoproficiency, as it were, may mask the lack of academic language proficiency (the CALP) which requires at least 5 to 7 years for immigrant children to reach mainstream norms (Cummins, 2008). The idea is straightforward: Basic conversation language is context-embedded and cognitively undemanding, whereas schooling from upper primary school onwards frequently demands thinking and abstract ideas that require decontextualized and cognitively demanding use of language. Much of academic achievement at this level is tied to cognitive and conceptual growth, with academic language in general and academic vocabulary in particular being the carrier of knowledge. In other words, the academic deficiency of L2 learners may well have resulted from a lack of CALP, the development of which is dependent upon conceptual growth related to the academic vocabulary in L2.

Teaching and Learning Second Language Vocabulary. The next natural questions to ask are: Is vocabulary instruction effective in vocabulary learning and academic reading? Are there instruction methods that are better than other methods? Perhaps the most comprehensive answers to these questions come from Stahl and Fairbanks's (1986) meta-analysis of 52 studies of vocabulary instruction. The review concluded that in general, direct instruction of vocabulary has "a significant effect on the comprehension of passages containing taught words," and a "slight but significant effect on comprehension of passages not necessarily containing taught words" (p. 100).

Many more recent vocabulary intervention studies have also revealed the usefulness of vocabulary intervention; and a number of studies involving L2 learners have revealed similar results. For example, Carlo et al. (2004) designed a 15-week vocabulary intervention program for 254 bilingual and monolingual children in the United States. The study found that both direct instruction of words and the teaching of word learning strategies were effective in improving reading comprehension and word knowledge, for both ELL

and English only learners. Townsend and Collins (2008) taught 60 frequent words on Coxhead's (2000) Academic Word List to a group of 52 ELLs in a middle school in Southern California in a 20-session vocabulary intervention program. The study found that the intervention was successful in helping these students learn the target words, and that students with higher initial general English proficiency had greater gains. In another study (Kelley, Lesaux, Kieffer, & Faller, 2010), an 18-week academic vocabulary intervention programme was designed for 476 sixth graders (346 L2 learners and 130 English native speakers) in seven urban middle schools in the United States. Text-based multiple and planned exposures to selected "high-impact academic words" were found to be effective in developing the students' depth of vocabulary knowledge and in their reading comprehension. Moreover, the intervention was found to be equally beneficial for both L2 learners and native speaker learners.

One of the major principles for vocabulary instruction is to include vocabulary learning strategies (Kelley et al., 2010). Many studies have explored how L2 learners strategically maximise their own learning results. In general, strategic learning of vocabulary has been found to be highly related to the growth of lexical competence and of general proficiency in L2 (Gu, 2003). A few studies (e.g., Kelley et al., 2010) have included the instruction of a number of vocabulary learning strategies (e.g., contextual inferencing, morphological analysis). Both teachers and learners have found the strategy instruction empowering.

Summary and Recommendations

For many learners taught in a second language at school, underachievement can often be attributed to a deficiency in the second language. Their fluency in daily communications often masks their lack of "cognitive academic language proficiency" (Cummins, 2008), which in turn is very much dependent on the vocabulary competence in the L2 of instruction.

Direct instruction of selected high-utility words (e.g., academic vocabulary) has been found effective both in enhancing word knowledge and in boosting reading comprehension and learning through an L2. In addition, vocabulary learning strategies ensure that students will be able to know what to learn and how to learn it beyond the classroom.

References

Abedi, J., Hofstetter, C. H., & Lord, C. (2004). Assessment accommodations for English language learners: Implications for policy-based empirical research. *Review of Educational Research*, 74(1), 1–28.

Allman, B. (2005). Vocabulary size and accuracy of monolingual and bilingual preschool children. In J. Cohen, K. T. McAlister, K. Rolstad, & J. MacSwan (Eds.), *Proceedings of the 4th International Symposium on Bilingualism* (pp. 5–71). Somerville, MA: Cascadilla Press.

August, D., Carlo, M., Dressler, C., & Snow, C. (2005). The critical role of vocabulary development for English language learners. *Learning Disabilities Research and Practice*, 20(1), 50–57.

August, D., & Shanahan, T. (2006). *Developing literacy in second-language learners: Report of the National Literacy Panel on Language-Minority Children and Youth*. Mahwah, NJ: Erlbaum.

Carlo, M., August, D., McLaughlin, B., Snow, C., Dressler, C., Lippman, D., Lively, T., … Snow, C. (2004). Closing the gap: Addressing the vocabulary needs of English-language learners in bilingual and mainstream classrooms. *Reading Research Quarterly*, *39*(2), 188–215.

Corson, D. (1997). The learning and use of academic English words. *Language Learning*, *47*(4), 671–718.

Coxhead, A. (2000). A new academic word list. *TESOL Quarterly*, *34*(2), 213–238.

Cummins, J. (2008). BICS and CALP: Empirical and theoretical status of the distinction. In B. Street (Ed.), *Encyclopedia of language and education: Vol. 2. Literacy* (2nd ed., pp. 71–83). New York: Springer.

Gu, Y. (2003). Vocabulary learning in a second language: Person, task, context and strategies. *TESL-EJ*, *7*(2). Retrieved from http://tesl-ej.org/ej26/a4.html

Herman, J. (2009). Introduction [Special issue]. *Educational Assessment*, *14*(3), 119–121.

Kelley, J. G., Lesaux, N. K., Kieffer, M. J., & Faller, S. E. (2010). Effective academic vocabulary instruction in the urban middle school. *The Reading Teacher,* *64*(1), 5–14.

Nation, I. S. P. (2001). *Learning vocabulary in another language*. Cambridge, England: Cambridge University Press.

Saville-Troike, M. (1984). What really matters in second language learning for academic achievement? *TESOL Quarterly*, *18*(2), 199–219.

Stahl, S. A., & Fairbanks, M. M. (1986). The effects of vocabulary instruction: A model-based meta-analysis. *Review of Educational Research*, *56*, 72–110.

Townsend, D., & Collins, P. (2008). Academic vocabulary and middle school English learners: An intervention study. *Reading and Writing*, *22*(9), 993–1019.

7.10
Language Teaching Curricula

ELI HINKEL
Seattle University

Introduction

English Language Learners (ELLs) represent a large majority of those who set out to learn a language other than their mother tongue in school systems in English-speaking countries. These students work to acquire English as a second language (ESL) in the process of their schooling. According to the U.S. Census, in 2011, more than 30% of all students in U.S. schools are ELLs who are speakers of approximately 500 languages. In practically all school systems in various world regions, such as Australia, Canada, New Zealand, or the United Kingdom, ELLs come from a wide variety of backgrounds. These students can be recent immigrants, children of guest workers, or children of employees of multinational companies, or other types of sojourners, as well as individuals raised in families or communities where English is not used for communication. In the regions where English is the primary language of schooling, extensive resources are dedicated to providing ELLs with the essential proficiencies that are fundamental to their schooling (e.g., listening comprehension, speaking, reading, and writing). These resources include supplementary instruction in language and skill development, teacher preparation, education, and special training, curricula, textbooks, or teaching materials, time, and the financial means to accomplish these resources. Due to the fact that the number of ELLs in school systems in various countries is expected to grow, extensive and intensive efforts have been undertaken to meet their language learning needs.

Research Evidence

To date, an enormous amount of data has established that a dramatic divide persists in the academic achievement of ELLs and other groups of students (e.g. Genesee, Lindholm-Leary, Saunders, & Christian, 2006; Miller, Kostogriz, & Gearon, 2010; Thomas & Collier, 2002). Data consist of test and examination scores, graduation rates, a broad range of language proficiency measures, and a vast body of research. A key reason for the prominent and persistent achievement divide stems from the fact that ELLs need to develop their language proficiencies simultaneously while attaining and demonstrating knowledge of content in school subjects, such as social studies, history, and math. Currently, there is no empirical validation of the effectiveness of curriculum designs developed specifically for ELLs (e.g., Genesee et al., 2006; Hinkel, 2011; What Works Clearinghouse, 2009). For this reason, the remainder of this overview will take a brief look at the two most predominant and widely adopted curricular models for teaching ELLs language and content simultaneously.

At present, two different types of curricula that seek to combine instruction in both language and school subjects are prevalent in various world regions. Content-based language and subject-matter instruction is commonly adopted in U.S. and Canadian school curricula; whereas genre-based language teaching predominates in the UK, Australia, and New Zealand.

The main principles of *content-based curricula* consist of integrating second language reading, writing, and language instruction with subject-matter content, such as history or math (e.g., Snow, 2005; Snow & Brinton, 1997). For example, integrated instruction in content and language can pivot on thematically selected readings or writing tasks, with the attendant language teaching that focuses on the uses of grammar and contextualized vocabulary. In some cases, content-based instruction can also have supplementary foci on other academic skills, such as critical thinking, library research, or information gathering (Hinkel, 2006).

Content-based teaching in the form of sheltered instruction observation protocol (SIOP) has been widely adopted in U.S. schools that enroll large numbers of ELLs. The SIOP model in effect represents a framework for teaching school subjects and language in mainstream classes. To this end, SIOP also deals with various classroom strategies and techniques for teachers who work with ELLs in their schools (e.g., Echevarría, Vogt, & Short, 2008). Under the auspices of the U.S. Department of Education, the What Works Clearinghouse has examined eight studies of the SIOP effectiveness. According to this review (What Works Clearinghouse, 2009, p. 1), none of the eight empirical studies of SIOP effectiveness meet "evidence standards," and thus no conclusions can be made "based on research about the effectiveness or ineffectiveness of SIOP" (p. 1).

Outside the United States as well, several important and practical concerns have been widely noted regarding content-based instruction and the teaching of language at the same time. One of these, for instance, pertains to the level of expertise in matters of content and language expected of mainstream or language teachers who work within content-based curricular models. Many empirical reports indicate that language teachers are trained to deal with language pedagogy, but are far less trained in the areas of content and school subjects (e.g., Met, 1998; Snow, 2005). On the other hand, in the context of language-centered curricula, it may be difficult to determine what content should be included for the purposes of language development. Additionally, in content-based instruction, research has not yet established what content needs to be taught in order to advance students' language skills (e.g., Swan, 2005). In light of the fact that a great deal of preparation and work is required for teaching content to ELLs, in many cases, the teaching of the language, for example, grammar or writing, is often neglected. As an outcome, a vast majority of instructional materials on content-based teaching consistently emphasize the need for intensive and focused language instruction (e.g., Hinkel, 2004; Snow, 2005).

In the UK, New Zealand, and Australia in particular, *genre-based curricular models and approaches* predominate among methodological schools of thought on language and subject-matter instruction. Genre-based curricula, similar to content-based teaching, also seek to integrate the teaching of language with instruction in reading and writing. The genre-based approach and teaching techniques draw on the foundations of systemic functional linguistics and genre theory. These analytical approaches serve as the basis for teaching the language required of ELLs in school subjects. To this end, genre-based language instruction centers on the features of language employed in a diverse range of spoken and written genres, such as school textbooks, academic speaking and writing, or subject-matter assignments that require both reading and writing. This curricular model addresses a broad array of genres from news reports to textbooks and formal written prose. The overarching objective of genre-based pedagogy is to enable ELLs to analyze school discourse while reading and writing in order to produce written prose typically expected in the context of schooling (e.g., Cope & Kalantzis, 2000).

In genre-based curricula, language teaching endeavors to address the features of discourse and text in the social and practical contexts where the written prose is produced and the purposes which it is expected meet. To achieve this goal, teaching activities may represent an analysis of written prose in such genres as textbooks in social sciences or history, or math story problems. Classroom teaching is designed to increase students' awareness of particular grammar and vocabulary elements found in school texts or other contexts (e.g., Schleppegrell, 2004).

However, as with the content-based curricular design, the effectiveness of genre-based curricula and teaching methods has not been established empirically. Many experts in the teaching and learning of language and second language contend that genres and their linguistic features may be subjective, culture-bound, vaguely defined, or even irrelevant to diverse types of ELLs (e.g., see Leki, 2007 for a thorough discussion). For example, Henry Widdowson, one of the prominent world-class authorities on language teaching (Widdowson, 2003, p. 69) states that "the conception of genres as stable entities is only a convenient fiction: they are in reality sociocultural processes, continually in flux." According to Widdowson, the findings of genre analyses represent impressionistic judgments about their distinctiveness, and therefore, such findings simply have limited validity. Thus, given that genres are far from well-defined, the pedagogic viability of genre-based curricula and the attendant teaching of genre-defined discourse and language features is in fact "limited" (p. 70).

Summary and Recommendations

Valid research is urgently needed to identify language skills and teaching methodologies to help bridge the unmistakable achievement divide between ELLs and other cohorts of students. In the final count, the overarching objective of empirically-grounded and principled curricular designs is to provide ELLs with access to educational opportunities and to enable these students to communicate effectively in a broad range of educational and social contexts.

References

Cope, B., & Kalantzis, M. (Eds.). (2000). *Multiliteracies: Literacy learning and the design of social* futures. London: Routledge.

Echevarría, J., Vogt, M., & Short, D. (2008). *Making content comprehensible for English learners: The SIOP model*. Boston, MA: Pearson.

Genesee, F., Lindholm-Leary, K., Saunders, W., & Christian, D. (2006). *Educating English language learners: A synthesis of research evidence.* Cambridge, England: Cambridge University Press.

Hinkel, E. (2004). *Teaching academic ESL writing: Practical techniques in vocabulary and grammar*. Mahwah, NJ: Erlbaum.

Hinkel, E. (2006). Current perspectives on teaching the four skills. *TESOL Quarterly, 40*(1), 109–131.

Hinkel, E. (Ed.). (2011). *Handbook of research in second language teaching and learning* (Vol. 2). New York: Routledge.

Leki, I. (2007). *Undergraduates in a second language: Challenges and complexities of academic literacy development*. New York: Routledge.

Met, M. (1998). Curriculum decision-making in content-based teaching. In F. Genesee & J. Cenoz (Eds.), *Beyond bilingualism: Multilingualism and multilingual education* (pp. 35–63). Clevedon, England: Multilingual Matters.

Miller, J., Kostogriz, A., & Gearon, M, (Eds.). (2010). *Culturally and linguistically diverse classrooms: New dilemmas for teachers*. Clevedon, England: Multilingual Matters.

Schleppegrell, M. (2004). *The language of schooling*. Mahwah, NJ: Erlbaum.

Snow, M. (2005). A model of academic literacy for integrated language and content instruction. In E. Hinkel (Ed.), *Handbook of research in second language teaching and learning* (pp. 693–712). Mahwah, NJ: Erlbaum.

Snow, M., & Brinton, D. (1997). *The content-based classroom: Perspectives on integrating language and content*. London: Longman.

Swan, M. (2005). Legislation by hypothesis: The case of task-based instruction. *Applied Linguistics, 26*(3), 376–401.

Thomas, W., & Collier, V. (2002). *A national study of school effectiveness for language minority students' long-term academic achievement: Final report*. Santa Cruz, CA: Center for Research on Education, Diversity & Excellence.

What Works Clearinghouse. (2009). *WWC intervention report: Sheltered instruction observation protocol (SIOP)*. Washington, DC: Institute of Education Sciences, U.S. Department of Education.

Widdowson, H. (2003). *Defining issues in English language teaching*. Oxford, England: Oxford University Press.

7.11

Measurement of History Achievement in the United States and Europe

MARK SMITH, JOEL BREAKSTONE, AND SAM WINEBURG
Stanford University

Introduction

Any discussion of history achievement must start with an acknowledgment of the diverse ways in which it is measured. The United States and European nations have devised very different systems for gauging student achievement. Consequently, it is difficult to make comparisons regarding student achievement across nations. Local circumstances have influenced the form, content, and goals of history tests. To illustrate some of the different approaches to assessment, we briefly examine history testing in the United States, the Netherlands, and England.

Research Evidence

United States. Large-scale efforts to measure history achievement in the United States are nearly a century old. In 1917, J. Carleton Bell, managing editor of the American Psychological Association's *Journal of Educational Psychology*, sought to define the "historic sense." Bell and his colleague David F. McCollum (1917) proposed five characteristics: (a) understand present events in light of the past, (b) sift through the documentary record and construct an account, (c) appreciate the historical narrative, (d) generate reflective answers to "thought questions" on a given historical situation, and (e) answer factual questions about people and events. Interested in measuring the historic sense, Bell and McCollum administered a test of factual recall to students ($N = 1500$) in Texas in 1915–1916. They found that elementary students answered only 16% of the items correctly, high school students managed only 33%, and university students fell short of half (49%). Bell and McCollum were alarmed by these findings, but their method of measurement was perhaps even more consequential than their results. Although they acknowledged that the ability to answer factual questions was the least important dimension of the "historic sense," they settled on this aspect because it was "most readily tested" (p. 258). Their decision to narrow

the focus of achievement to factual recall has been widely followed in the United States ever since.

Bell and McCollum's research took place just as a new testing method was emerging. The first multiple-choice item appeared in the Kansas Silent Reading Test in 1914 (Samelson, 1990). The U.S. Army, in an effort to screen thousands of recruits for World War I, quickly adopted the format (Kevles, 1968). The Army's broad implementation of multiple-choice tests received widespread news coverage and spawned a host of multiple-choice intelligence tests. Achievement tests that used this format appeared soon after. In 1926 the College Entrance Examination Board created the Scholastic Aptitude Test, signaling a broader shift in the American educational system. Samelson explains the transformation. "The multiple-choice test—efficient, quantitative, objective, capable of sampling wide areas of subject matter and easily generating data for complicated statistical analyses—had become the symbol or synonym for American education" (1990, p. 122). Most information about history achievement in the United States since Bell and McCollum's study has been based on student performance on multiple-choice tests (Wineburg, 2004; Wineburg & Fogo, 2010). Today, each of the 23 states that administer a statewide test of history achievement use multiple-choice questions, and 14 of these states use only multiple-choice questions (Grant & Horn, 2006; Martin, Schneider, Fogo, & Kon, 2008). The National Assessment of Educational Progress (NAEP) U.S. History test also relies heavily on discrete multiple-choice questions to gauge student achievement. Results from NAEP, known as the "Nation's Report Card," are widely reported as evidence of American students' historical knowledge or lack thereof (e.g., Ravitch & Finn, 1987).

The heavy reliance on multiple-choice questions has been criticized by educators who believe that these tests measure little more than factual recall and that achievement in history encompasses aspects that cannot be captured by a blackened bubble on a test form (Rabb, 2007). Despite widespread dissatisfaction with multiple-choice history tests, few researchers have sought to document what they actually measure. A study by Gabriel Reich (2009) is a rare example. Reich had 10th grade history students (N = 13) in New York "talk aloud" as they worked through selected multiple-choice items from the New York *Global History and Geography Regents Examination*. He found that the selected items measured student mastery of history content, basic literacy, and test-wiseness, but did not elicit more complex aspects of historical thinking. Reich's study is an important first step in the examination of the validity of multiple-choice exams, but more research is needed to examine the validity of multiple-choice tests for measuring history achievement. If multiple-choice questions are limited in their ability to measure higher-order skills, then educators and policy makers in the United States will have to consider alternative forms of assessment.

The Netherlands. In the Netherlands, history testing has sought for some time to include skills beyond factual recall. In contrast to the United States, which lacks a unified history testing system, many European nations have national achievement tests. Arie Wilschut (2010) has detailed the evolution of the Dutch testing system. Although there was no subject-specific test, national examination guidelines created in 1965 required that students be "familiar with dealing with historical documents" (Wilschut, 2010, p. 709). Dutch legislators soon decided that students' history achievement deserved greater attention and in 1968 mandated a national written history exam, similar to those already required in other subject areas. After teachers expressed reservations about the examination, the Dutch Secretary of Education created the Commission on Experiments in Final Examination in History to examine its feasibility. After extended study, the commission concluded that an effective history examination could be drafted. It debuted in 1981, but did not include higher order thinking skills because the Commission had concluded that it would be too difficult to measure students' abilities in these areas. Almost immediately, many teachers criticized the new exam for failing to address historical thinking. Despite the extended process for formulating the exam, a second commission was created to explore possible alternatives. After nearly a decade of work, a revised test was implemented in 1993. Rather than a fixed body of content (i.e., names, dates and events), the test focused on "historical skills" and "approaches to history" (Wilschut, 2010, p. 710). The exam's actual historical content changed from year to year.

In the late 1990s, public debate in the Netherlands prompted a reconsideration of the national history exam structure and another commission was created to revisit the requirements for history education. Many observers expected that this commission would produce a list of names and dates for students to memorize, akin to the kinds of examination used in the United States. Instead, the commission established a framework of 10 historical eras,

but left it to individual schools and teachers to determine the specific examples of names, dates, and events to define the different eras. The purpose of the chronological framework was to improve students' historical understanding, rather than to emphasize rote memorization. As a result, the national examination would be based on these 10 eras and historical thinking skills. The public response to the commission's plan was markedly negative. National history had become broadly popular in the Netherlands and calls for a Dutch "canon" led the Education Council to create yet another commission. The van Oostrom Commission generated a list of 50 persons and events that "every Dutchman should know" (Wilschut, 2010, p. 716). This list of facts now awaits approval by the Dutch parliament. Its approval could prompt another revision to the national history test and perhaps move it closer to the American model, which emphasizes factual recall and recognition.

England and Wales. History tests in England have traditionally emphasized broader aspects of disciplinary skills over factual recall. These history assessments have been heavily influenced by the work of the Schools Council History 13-16 Project (today known as the Schools History Project). Established with government funding in 1972, the SCHP was charged with revising the history curriculum for 13- to 16-year-old students. The SCHP "took as its starting point the nature of history" (Booth, 1994, p. 63). Rather than a curriculum focused on teaching discrete facts about the past in chronological order, the SCHP stressed the skills and "forms of knowledge" that are characteristic of the discipline of history (Booth, 1994; Shemilt, 1983). This curricular shift had a dramatic effect on the history curriculum in England. The History National Curriculum, which was developed and implemented in the late 1980s, prescribed disciplinary achievement outcomes like the use of historical sources as evidence and the ability to understand various interpretations of the past (Booth, 1994). The legacy of the SCHP is evident to this day. The Key Stage 3 (ages 11–14) of the History National Curriculum, for example, calls for students to learn "Key Processes" like "Historical Enquiry" and "Using Evidence," and to understand "Key Concepts" like "Significance" and "Interpretation" (Qualifications and Curriculum Authority, 2007).

The National Curriculum Assessments for history are designed to measure these disciplinary skills rather than mastery of specific dates or facts. For example, the General Certificate of Secondary Education (GCSE), which is an exam offered for students at the end of Key Stage 4 (ages 14–16), requires students to reason about historical sources to establish facts or compare interpretations. The GSCE also requires students to use source fragments to reason about disciplinary concepts such as causation or continuity and change (Wilschut, 2010). Moreover, the format of these exams requires students to formulate their thoughts in complete sentences, thus emphasizing written expression and argument.

Summary and Recommendations

That history assessments vary greatly in form, content, and goals makes it difficult to compare history achievement across nations. More work is needed to better understand how these assessments function as measures of history achievement. Especially needed are studies that examine the validity of these various approaches for measuring disciplinary skills. Only then can we have a discussion about the best approaches to measuring history achievement and begin to develop common assessments to better examine history achievement across nations.

References

Bell, J. C., & McCollum, D. F. (1917). A study of the attainment of pupils in United States history. *Journal of Educational Psychology, 8*(5), 257–274.

Booth, M. (1994). Cognition in history: A British perspective. *Educational Psychologist, 29*(2), 61–69.

Grant, S., & Horn, C. (2006). The state of state-level history tests. In S. Grant (Ed.), *Measuring history: Cases of state-level testing across the United States* (pp. 9–27). Greenwich, CT: Information Age.

Kevles, D. (1968). Testing the Army's intelligence: Psychologists and the military in World War I. *Journal of American History, 55*(3), 565–581.

Martin, D., Schneider, J., Fogo, B., & Kon, J. (2008). *A report on the state of U.S. history education: State programs and national policies as of 2008.* National History Education Clearinghouse. Retrieved from http://teachinghistory.org/system/files/NHEC_Report.pdf

Qualifications and Curriculum Authority. (2007). *History: Programme of study for Key Stage 3 and attainment target.* Retrieved from http://curriculum.qcda.gov.uk/uploads/QCA-07-3335-p_History3_tcm8-189.pdf

Rabb, T. (2007, November 28). Assessments and standards: The case of history. *Education Week, 27*(13), 27–36.

Ravitch, D., & Finn, C. (1987). *What do our 17-year-olds know?: A report on the first National Assessment of History and Literature.* New York: Harper & Row.

Reich, G. (2009). Testing historical knowledge: Standards, multiple-choice questions and student reasoning. *Theory and Research in Social Education, 37*(3), 325–360.

Samelson, F. (1990). Was early mental testing (a) racist inspired, (b) objective science, (c) a technology for democracy, (d) the origin of multiple-choice exams, (e) none of the above? (mark the right answer). In M. Sokal (Ed.), *Psychological testing and American society, 1890–1913* (pp.113–127). New Brunswick, NJ: Rutgers University Press.

Shemilt, D. (1983). The devil's locomotive. *History and Theory, 22*(4), 1–18.

Wilschut, A. (2010). History at the mercy of politicians and ideologies: Germany, England, and the Netherlands in the 19th and 20th centuries. *Journal of Curriculum Studies, 42*(5), 693–723. doi: 10.1080/00220270903049446

Wineburg, S. (2004). Crazy for history. *Journal of American History, 90*(4), 1401–1414.

Wineburg, S., & Fogo, B. (2010). Testing in history. In P. Peterson, E. Baker, & B. McGaw (Eds.), *International encyclopedia of education* (Vol. 4, pp. 175–180). London: Elsevier.

7.12

Reading

Phonics Instruction

WILLIAM E. TUNMER AND ALISON W. ARROW
Massey University

Introduction

Phonics has been defined as "an approach to, or type of, reading instruction that is intended to promote the discovery of the alphabetic principle, the correspondences between phonemes and graphemes, and phonological decoding" (Scarborough & Brady, 2002, p. 20). The alphabetic principle refers to the fundamental concept that in alphabetic orthographies letters and letter combinations are used to represent the phonemes (sounds) of spoken words. For example, a beginning student who writes *color* as KLR clearly grasps the alphabetic principle.

Phonological decoding is the cognitive ability to translate letters and letter patterns into phonological forms and differs from phonics rules in four important ways (Tunmer & Nicholson, 2011). First, the rules of phonics can be stated explicitly (e.g., the letter *f* makes the "fuh" sound), whereas phonological decoding "rules" are implicit. Much, if not most, of what children learning to read in English come to know about the orthography is acquired through implicit learning (Snow & Juel, 2005; Tunmer & Nicholson, 2011; Venezky, 1999). The second difference is that the rules taught in phonics are relatively few, whereas phonological decoding rules number in the hundreds. There are simply too many letter–sound relationships for children to acquire by direct instruction. Third, phonics rules are slow and laborious to apply, whereas phonological decoding rules operate very quickly and (seemingly) effortlessly. Skilled readers can rapidly and easily pronounce nonwords like *jit, med, dut, prew, thrain,* and *fruice.* Fourth, in contrast to letter–sound correspondences acquired by direct phonics instruction, which are largely context-free (i.e., involve one-to-one correspondences between single letters/digraphs and single phonemes), letter–sound correspondences acquired by implicit learning are mostly context-sensitive (i.e., depend on position-specific constraints or the presence of "marker" letters). For example, the letter *y* makes one sound in final position of 2-syllable words (e.g., *baby,*

happy), another sound at the beginning of words (e.g., *yes, you, yogurt*), and yet another sound in single open syllable words (e.g., *by, my*).

Research on how children learn to read indicates that achievement in reading comprehension performance depends on the ability to recognize the words of text accurately and quickly, and that the development of automaticity in word recognition in turn depends on the ability to make use of letter–sound relationships in identifying unknown words. The latter process, which is promoted by phonics instruction, provides the basis for constructing the detailed orthographic representations required for the automatization of word recognition, or what Ehri (2005) calls *sight word* knowledge.

Although children must rely increasingly on induction to acquire the spelling–sound relationships necessary for learning to read, explicit phonics instruction plays an important role in helping to "kick-start" the process by which beginning readers acquire untaught spelling–sound relationships through implicit learning. Venezky (1999) argued that "phonics is a means to an end, not an end itself" (p.231). Because of the nature of English orthography, one of the main functions of phonics instruction is to provide beginning readers with a process for generating approximate phonological representations of unknown words that gets them close enough to the correct phonological form that, with context, the correct identification can be made. Children learn to use their knowledge of spelling-to-sound relationships acquired through phonics instruction to produce approximate phonological representations, or partial decodings, for unknown words, especially those containing irregular, polyphonic (e.g., *ear* as in *bear* and *hear*), or orthographically complex spelling patterns. The phonological representations provide the basis for generating alternative pronunciations of target words until one is produced that matches a word in the child's lexical memory and makes sense in the context in which it appears. Additional spelling–sound relationships, especially context-sensitive patterns, can then be induced from the stored orthographic representations of words that have been correctly identified (Tunmer & Chapman, 2012).

Phonics instruction is useful not because of the specific letter–sound correspondences taught (which are limited in number), but because it instills in beginning readers a firm grasp of the alphabetic principle, and gives them practice in looking closely at word spelling (Snow & Juel, 2005). For children encountering difficulty in developing the ability to perceive intuitively the redundant patterns and connections between speech and print, explicit instruction in alphabetic coding skills is likely to be crucial. In support of these claims is a large body of research indicating that explicit, systematic instruction in the code relating spellings to pronunciations positively influences reading achievement, especially during the early stages of learning to read (Brady, 2011; Hattie, 2009; National Reading Panel, 2000; Snow, Burns, & Griffin, 1998).

Instruction in the alphabetic code varies along several dimensions, including the degree of explicitness, systematicity, and intensity with which letter–sound relationships are taught (Brady, 2011). In typical phonics programs children's attention is directed to specific letter–sound patterns, the patterns are presented in a particular sequence, instruction focuses on both consonant and vowel graphemes and also on more advanced spelling patterns, and instruction in orthographic patterns is a major ongoing component of the early literacy curriculum. In contrast, the whole language approach to teaching literacy assumes that children require little or no direct instruction in spelling–sound patterns (Pressley, 2006). A shortcoming of this approach, however, is that it stresses the importance of using information from many sources in identifying words without recognizing that skills and strategies involving phonological information are of primary importance in beginning literacy development (Tunmer & Nicholson, 2011).

Research Evidence

The strongest evidence supporting the effectiveness of systematic phonics instruction over nonsystematic or no phonics instruction (e.g., whole language or whole word approaches) comes from large-scale meta-analyses. The National Reading Panel (2000) reported the results of 66 treatment-control comparisons from 38 studies that satisfied strict criteria. The cognitive achievement outcomes examined in the studies included recognizing regularly spelled words, correctly pronouncing pseudo-words, recognizing real words that included both regular and irregular spellings, comprehending text, orally reading connected text, and spelling words correctly (Ehri, 2004). Results indicated that the overall mean effect size at the end of training was .41; that the effectiveness of systematic phonics instruction was greater among kindergarteners and first graders ($d = .55$) than second through sixth grades ($d = .27$); that first grade children at risk benefited more from phonics instruction ($d = .74$) than normally achieving first graders ($d = .48$);

and that systematic phonics instruction had larger effects for children from low SES backgrounds ($d = .66$) than for children from middle SES backgrounds ($d = .44$). Comparisons of the positive effects of three different types of phonic programs did not yield significant differences, which is consistent with the suggestion that the primary function of systematic phonics instruction, regardless of the form it takes, is to initiate the process of inducing letter–sound correspondences without explicit instruction.

More recently, Hattie (2009) reported even stronger effects for phonics instruction. He summarized 14 meta-analyses involving 12,000 students and found that phonics had a significant effect on learning to read, with a mean effect size of .60. In contrast, he summarized four meta-analyses of whole-language teaching involving 630 students and found that it had almost no effect. The mean effect size was only .06.

Although research has firmly established that phonics is more effective than other methods of teaching beginning reading, it is not sufficient for acquiring fast, accurate word recognition ability. Many children, possibly up to 10%, fail to learn to read through phonics instruction. To benefit from phonics, children must acquire phonemic awareness, the ability to reflect on and manipulate the phonemic elements of spoken words. The phonemically aware child knows that the spoken word "feet" has three sounds, that "eat" is what remains when the first sound (e.g., /f/) of "feet" is deleted, and that "fee" is what remains when the final sound (e.g., /t/) is deleted. To discover mappings between spelling patterns and sound patterns, children must be able to segment spoken words into subcomponents. Beginning readers who experience ongoing difficulties in detecting phonemic sequences in words will not be able to fully grasp the alphabetic principle and discover spelling-to-sound relationships. In support of the claim that phonemic awareness is causally related to learning to read is a considerable amount of research evidence indicating that training in phonemic awareness during or before reading instruction produces significant experimental group advantages in reading achievement, especially when combined with letter–sound training (Ehri, 2004; National Reading Panel, 2000; Pressley, 2006).

Systematic phonics instruction is also likely to be more effective among children with higher levels of oral vocabulary knowledge at school entry for two reasons (Tunmer & Nicholson, 2011). First, vocabulary growth during the preschool years causes words to become more fully differentiated in lexical memory. Prior to that point, words are stored in only partially differentiated form. Because deficiencies in vocabulary growth are accompanied by more poorly specified phonological representations of spoken words, the development of phonemic awareness is likely to be impaired in children with poorly developed vocabulary knowledge at the beginning of school. As a consequence, these children will lack the basis for understanding the alphabetic principle and discovering letter–sound relationships. Second, children with poorly developed vocabulary knowledge will have trouble identifying and assigning appropriate meanings to unknown printed words, especially partially decoded or irregularly spelled words, if the corresponding spoken words are not in their listening vocabulary. This in turn will limit the development of their phonological decoding skills, as additional spelling–sound relationships can be induced from words that have been correctly identified (Tunmer & Chapman, 2012).

Recent research on phonics instruction has focused on two questions; first, is phonics more effective under some circumstances than others, and second, is phonics more effective for some children than others? Regarding the first question, the research discussed earlier clearly indicates that providing beginning and struggling readers with explicit and systematic instruction in orthographic patterns and word identification strategies outside the context of reading connected text is more effective than only teaching word analysis skills incidentally (i.e., "as the need arises") during text reading. However, research also indicates that superior outcomes are achieved when systematic phonics instruction is accompanied by rich and varied opportunities for children to practice and receive feedback on applying their newly acquired word analysis skills while actively engaged in the processes of reading and writing (Brady, 2011). Phonics instruction needs to be fully integrated within the literacy curriculum, not segregated from it.

Regarding the second question, recent research indicates that the amount of explicit instruction in phonemic awareness and phonemically based decoding skills needed to initiate the process of inducing letter–sound relationships varies considerably across children. Some beginning readers seem to grasp the idea after having had only a few spelling–sound correspondences explicitly taught to them, whereas other children require a fairly structured and teacher-supported introduction to reading (Snow & Juel, 2005; Tunmer & Nicholson, 2011). Supporting an interaction between student characteristics and method of teaching reading are the results of a study by Connor, Morrison, and Katch (2004) examining the effects of different instructional emphases on children possessing varying amounts of literacy-related skills (oral vocabulary, letter identification, letter–sound correspondence) at school entry. They found that children who began first grade with below-average reading-related skills made larger reading gains in classrooms that provided greater amounts of teacher-managed, code-focused instruction throughout the year than in classrooms that provided greater amounts of child-managed, meaning-focused instruction. In contrast, for children with higher reading-related skills at school entry, greater growth in reading was achieved in classrooms that provided lesser amounts of teacher-managed, code-focused instruction and greater amounts of child-managed, meaning-focused instruction. These findings suggest that instructional strategies that may be effective with some students may be less effective when applied to other students with different skills. In support of this claim, Conner et al. (2009) reported that children in first-grade classrooms that individualized reading instruc-

tion by taking into account child-by-instruction interactions made greater gains in reading achievement than children in control classrooms.

Summary and Recommendations

To ensure that teaching phonics is optimally effective, greater attention needs to be placed on differential instruction, where teachers used research-based assessment procedures and instructional strategies to cater to the different skill needs of beginning readers from the outset of schooling. The ability to determine the amount and form of code instruction that works best for which children will require high levels of teacher knowledge and professionalism. Currently, many practicing teachers exhibit weaknesses in concepts pertaining to the structure of language and nature of English orthography that are central to code-based instruction (Brady, 2011). Research also suggests that the instructors responsible for the training of preservice and in-service teachers are generally not well informed about the body of knowledge required to teach systematically phonemically based word-level skills and strategies (Joshi et al., 2009). Focusing greater attention on enhancing the quality of teacher preparation and professional development is likely to be the key to increasing the effectiveness of phonics instruction.

References

Brady, S. (2011). Efficacy of phonics teaching for reading outcomes: Indications from Post-NRP research. In S. Brady, D. Braze, & C. Fowler (Eds.), *Explaining individual differences in reading: Theory and evidence* (pp. 69–76). New York: Psychology Press.

Connor, C. M., Morrison, F. J., & Katch, L. E. (2004). Beyond the reading wars: Exploring the effect of child-instruction interactions on growth in early reading. *Scientific Studies of Reading, 8,* 305–336.

Connor, C. M., Piasta, S. B., Fishman, B., Glasney, S., Schatschneider, C., Crowe, E., … Morrison, F. (2009). Individualizing student instruction precisely: Effects of child x instruction interactions on first graders' literacy development. *Child Development, 80,* 77–100.

Ehri, L.C. (2004). Teaching phonemic awareness and phonics: An explanation of the National Reading Panel meta-analyses. In P. McCardle & V. Chhabra (Eds.), *The voice of evidence in reading research* (pp. 153–186). Baltimore, MD: Brookes.

Ehri, L. C. (2005). Development of sight word reading: Phases and findings. In M. J. Snowling & C. Hulme (Eds.), *The science of reading: A handbook* (pp. 135–154). Oxford, England: Blackwell.

Hattie, J. A. (2009). *Visible learning: A synthesis of over 800 meta-analyses relating to achievement.* London: Routledge.

Joshi, R. M., Binks, E., Hougen, M., Dahlgren, M., Ocker-Dean, E., & Smith, D. (2009). Why elementary teachers might be inadequately prepared to teach reading. *Journal of Learning Disabilities, 42,* 392–402.

National Reading Panel. (2000). *Teaching children to read: An evidence-based assessment of the scientific research literature on reading and its implications for reading instruction.* Washington, DC: National Institute for Child Health and Human Development.

Pressley, M. (2006). *Reading instruction that works: The case for balanced teaching.* New York: Guilford.

Scarborough, H. S., & Brady, S. A. (2002). Toward a common terminology for talking about speech and reading: A glossary of the *"Phon"* words and some related terms. *Journal of Literacy Research, 34,* 299–334.

Snow, C. E., Burns, M. S., & Griffin, P. (1998). *Preventing reading difficulties in young children.* Washington, DC: National Academy Press.

Snow, C. E., & Juel, C. (2005). Teaching children to read: What do we know about how to do it? In M. J. Snowling & C. Hulme (Eds.), *The science of reading: A handbook* (pp. 501–520). Oxford: Blackwell.

Tunmer, W. E., & Chapman, J. W. (2012). Does set for variability mediate the influence of vocabulary knowledge on the development of word recognition skills? *Scientific Studies of Reading, 16,* 122–140.

Tunmer, W. E., & Nicholson, T. (2011). The development and teaching of word recognition skill. In M. L. Kamil, P. D. Pearson, E. B. Moje, & P. Afflerbach (Eds.), *Handbook of reading research* (Vol. 4, pp. 405–431). New York: Routledge.

Venezky, R. L. (1999). *The American way of spelling: The structure and origins of English orthography.* New York: Guildford.

7.13

Repeated Reading

WILLIAM J. THERRIEN AND SARAH J. WATT
University of Iowa

Introduction

Repeated reading is a "supplemental reading program that consists of re-reading a short and meaningful passage until a satisfactory level of fluency is reached" (Samuel, 1979, p. 404). The program is geared toward improving reading fluency (i.e., the ability to read with speed, accuracy, and proper expression; Kuhn & Stahl, 2003). Fluency is an essential reading skill (National Institute of Child Health and Human Development [NICHHD], 2000) that is significantly correlated with reading comprehension (Fuchs, Fuchs, Hosp, & Jenkins, 2001). Repeated reading was originally conceptualized in the late 1970s (Samuels, 1979) but research on the most beneficial techniques for implementation and overall effectiveness continues to be evaluated today.

Research Evidence

The use of meta-analyses to evaluate the effectiveness of interventions and make practice recommendations for students has increased over the last decade. Results of meta-analyses are often evaluated using the following effect size (ES) guidelines: Small effect ES = below .50; Medium effect ES = .50-.80; and Large effect ES = above .80 (Cohen, 1988). Therrien (2004) conducted a meta-analysis of 18 research studies to determine the effectiveness of repeated reading and identify essential components of the program. The meta-analysis indicated that, on average, repeated reading programs had an ES increase of .5 on fluency and .25 on comprehension measures (Therrien, 2004). Three instructional components maximized the effectiveness of repeated reading: (a) providing corrective feedback on word errors, (b) having students reread passages until they achieve a certain fluency rate (e.g., certain number of correct words per minute), and (c) requiring students to set goals (e.g., student sets a fluency goal for each reading or instructional session) (Morgan & Sideridis, 2006; Therrien, 2004). Re-

peated reading programs that included these instructional components were over two times (fluency ES = 1.37) more effective (Therrien, 2004).

Repeated reading has been an effective intervention for improving fluency for normal achieving students (Rasinski, Padak, Linek, & Sturtevant, 1994), students with learning disabilities (Bryant et al., 2000), and deaf students (Schrimer, Schaffer, Therrien, & Schrimer, in press). Students with instructional reading levels between first and third grade are most likely to benefit from repeated reading (Kuhn & Stahl, 2003). Fluency gains are also more likely if passages that contain a high degree of word overlap are used during program implementation (Rashotte & Torgesen, 1985).

The effectiveness of repeated reading is explained by the theory of automaticity (LaBerge & Samuels, 1974). It is hypothesized that poor reading fluency is primarily due to difficulty with word recognition. Slow decoding in turn hampers students' comprehension. Repeated reading improves reading fluency by providing students multiple opportunities to master individual words, phrases, sentences, and paragraphs in a passage. By rereading, students' fluency gradually improves on the reread passages. Through extended program implementation, increased fluency attained on reread passages transfers to novel passages.

Although extensive research has been conducted on repeated reading, its veracity as a reading program remains in question. One concern is that repeated readings impact on comprehension. Although repeated reading programs have been shown to significantly impact fluency on both reread and novel passages, the program often has little to no impact on comprehension (Therrien, 2004). Repeated reading may, therefore, best be implemented in combination with a comprehension instructional component such as summarization.

Second, it remains unknown whether it is necessary to reread passages in order to improve students' reading fluency. Critics (Kuhn & Stahl, 2003; Pressley, 2006) contend that improvements in reading fluency attained through repeated reading have little to do with rereading but instead are due to simple practice effects. They argue that students can make similar gains by reading aloud with corrective feedback. Several studies have compared repeated reading to oral reading of nonrepetitive texts and found no significant differences (Homan, Klesius, & Hite, 1993; O'Connor, White, & Swanson, 2007; Van Bon, Boksebeld, Font Freide, & Van den Hurk, 1991). If repetition is not needed to improve reading fluency, it likely makes more sense to have students read passages only once because reading novel passages instead of the same one multiple times will increase student exposure to additional vocabulary words, topics, and genre (Homan et al., 1993).

Summary and Recommendations

Despite the questions about repeated reading delineated above, practitioners should view this method as a potentially effective program for students with instructional reading levels between first and third grade who struggle with reading fluency. In order to maximize the program's effectiveness, the essential instructional components of providing corrective feedback on word errors, having students reread each passage until a set criterion is reached, and requiring students to set goals should be included in program implementation. While implementing repeated reading, student progress needs to be monitored via a curriculum based fluency measure with program modifications being made if the student demonstrates little to no progress. Additional research examining the necessity of passage repetition and the interaction between reading fluency and comprehension needs to be conducted.

References

Bryant, D. P., Vaughn, S., Linan-Thompson, S., Ugel, N., Hamff, A., & Hougen, M. (2000). Reading outcomes for students with and without reading disabilities in general education middle-school content area classes. *Learning Disability Quarterly, 23*, 238–252. doi: 10.2307/1511347

Cohen, J. (1988). *Statistical power analysis for the behavioral sciences* (2nd ed.) Hillsdale, NJ: Erlbaum.

Fuchs, L. S., Fuchs, D., Hosp, M. K., & Jenkins, J. R. (2001). Oral reading fluency as an indicator of reading competence: A theoretical, empirical, and historical analysis. *Scientific Studies of Reading, 5*(3), 239–256. doi: 10.1207/S1532799XSSR05033

Homan, S. P., Klesius, J. P., & Hite, C. (1993). Effects of repeated readings and nonrepetitive strategies on students' fluency and comprehension. *Journal of Educational Research, 87*(2), 94–99. doi: 10.1080/00220671.1993.9941172

Kuhn, M. R., & Stahl, S. A. (2003). Fluency: A review of developmental and remedial practices. *Journal of Educational Psychology, 95*(1), 3–21. doi: 10.1037/0022-0663.95.1.3

LaBerge, D., & Samuels, S. J. (1974). Toward a theory of automatic information processing in reading. *Cognitive Psychology, 6*, 293–323. doi: 10.1016/0010-0285(74)90015-2

Morgan, P. L., & Sideridis, G. D. (2006). Contrasting the effectiveness of fluency interventions for students with or at risk for learning disabilities: A multilevel random coefficient meta-analysis. *Learning Disabilities Research and Practice, 21*, 191–210. doi: 10.1111/j.1540-5826.2006.00218.x

National Institute of Child Health and Human Development (NICHD). (2000). *Teaching children to read: An evidence-based assessment of the scientific literature on reading and its implications for reading instruction.* Washington, DC: U.S. Government Printing Office.

O'Connor, R., White, A., & Swanson, H. (2007). Repeated reading versus continuous reading: Influences on reading fluency and comprehension. *Exceptional Children, 74*, 31–46.

Pressley, M. (2006, April 29). *What the future of reading research could be.* Paper presented at the International Reading Association's Reading Research 2006, Chicago, IL.

Rashotte, C., & Torgesen, J. (1985). Repeated reading and reading fluency in learning disabled children. *Reading Research Quarterly, 20*(2), 180–188. doi: 10.1598/RRQ.20.2.4

Rasinski, T., Padak, N., Linek, W., & Sturtevant, E. (1994). Effects of fluency development on urban second-grade readers. *Journal of Educational Research, 87*(3), 158–165. doi: 10.1080/00220671.1994.9941237

Samuels, S. (1979). The method of repeated readings. *The Reading Teacher, 32*(4), 403–408.

Schrimer, B. R., Schaffer, L., Therrien, W. J., & Schirmer, T. N. (In Press). Reread-Adapt and Answer-Comprehend Intervention with deaf readers: Effect on fluency and reading achievement. American Annals of the Deaf.

Therrien, W. J. (2004). Fluency and comprehension gains as a result of repeated reading: A meta-analysis. *Remedial and Special Education, 25*(4), 252–261. doi: 10.1177/07419325040250040801

Von Bon, W. H. J., Boksebeld, L. M., Font Freide, T. A. M, & Van Den Hurk, A. J. M. (1991). A comparison of three methods of reading-while- listening. *Journal of Learning Disabilities, 24*(8), 471–476.

7.14

Reading

Sentence Combining: Grammar Programs

BRUCE SADDLER AND NICOLE BAK
University at Albany

Introduction

High profile reports by the National Commission on Writing (2005) and for the Carnegie Corporation (Graham & Perin, 2007) underscore the importance and the challenge of writing. Communication in writing, though an essential skill for students to develop while in school and an important factor for success in many careers, is an incredibly complex process to teach and learn (Scardamalia & Bereiter, 1986). Writers must manage several skills while writing, including the planning, organizing, revising, and editing of prose. Of these skills, composing interesting sentences that communicate ideas clearly to a reader can be particularly challenging. Sentences are the vehicles for the writers' ideas, and the ability to construct complex and varied sentence structures facilitates the writers' ability to communicate those ideas to a reader.

During the 1960s and 1970s, grammar was the preferred instructional method to increase students' sentence writing ability in the United States. Often this instruction focused on explicitly teaching parts of speech, sentence types, and the diagramming of sentences to identify relationships between constituent elements. Although widely taught, a seminal writing meta-analysis by Hillocks (1987) revealed that the study of grammar contributed nothing to the quality of a student's writing, nor did grammar instruction have a significant impact on the use of proper mechanics (Hillocks, 1987). One reason for this outcome may have been because traditional grammar instruction afforded students few opportunities to engage in the authentic application of these skills within their own writing. Dissatisfaction with the outcomes of grammar instruction led researchers to seek alternative methods to improve sentence level writing ability. One such method was sentence combining.

On the most rudimentary level, sentence combining involves explicitly teaching students how to manipulate or rewrite short, syntactically simple sentences into sentences that are more varied in terms of style, as revealed in the arrangement of words and word choice, and complexity represented by length and syntactic structure (Saddler, 2009). For example, simple sentences such as: "The coffee was black. The coffee was hot. The cup was torn. The cup was leaking." could be combined in a multitude of ways depending on the author's style, for example: "The hot, black coffee leaked from the torn cup."

Combining sentences in frequent sessions where the exercises are carefully modeled and openly discussed can expose writers to a variety of syntactic structures they can utilize while composing or revising to convey their ideas more effectively. In addition, such practice can also provide writers with a systematic method to explore language without the need to generate content/ideas thus reducing some of the cognitive burden associated with the composing process. The exercises can provide a venue for playing with words and ideas while also providing focused, interesting language experiences. In comparison to grammar instruction, such practice represents practical applied knowledge of syntax rather than knowledge about syntax and grammatical rules.

Research Evidence

Sentence combining has a well-established research base. In fact, over 85 studies conducted during the last 45 years have demonstrated that sentence combining is an effective method for helping students produce more syntactically complex sentences (cf. Hunt, 1965; O'Hare, 1973) and may lead to improvements in overall writing quality (cf. Perron, 1974). In fact, in Hillocks's meta-analysis (1987), sentence combining was highlighted as being twice as effective as other methods such as free writing and grammar instruction in enhancing the quality of students' writing.

More recently, two high-profile reports underscored sentence combining's effectiveness. First, an extensive meta-analysis of the effect of grammar teaching on writing development by Andrews and colleagues (2006) found little evidence supporting the effectiveness of grammar, whereas sentence combining was determined to have a much more positive effect on writing. In addition, in *Writing Next: A Report to the Carnegie Corporation* (Graham & Perin, 2007), sentence combining had a consistently positive and moderate effect on writing and was listed among the practices recommended for inclusion within effective writing programs. Three recent studies provide further support for sentence combining practice while extending prior research in several important ways.

For example, in several recent studies, Saddler and colleagues investigated the role of peer-assisted instruction in sentence combining. Saddler and Graham (2005) was the first study that investigated the effects of sentence combining practice using a peer assisted grouping arrangement versus traditional grammar instruction. They reported that those students taught to combine sentences in mixed-ability dyads were twice as likely to produce correct sentences when compared to students in grammar-focused dyads. Further, after revising, the sentence combining group improved the quality of their stories to a statistically significant degree over the grammar group.

In a second, single-subject replication and extension study, Saddler, Behforooz, and Asaro (2008), found that students in low-ability dyads who were taught sentence combining, demonstrated an improvement in their ability to combine basic sentences. Further, sentence combining instruction also had an effect on the overall quality of stories written by all the students in terms of ideation, organization, grammar, sentence, structure, word choice, and mechanics. The sentence combining strategy also had an effect on the complexity of the sentences and increased the students' use of constructions taught during the intervention from pretest to posttest.

Saddler, Asaro, and Behforooz (2008) included a peer-editor checklist as they studied the effect of the sentence combining strategy and peer assisted grouping strategy in another single subject design. The participants in this study included four writers who were identified as having a learning disability. Theoretically, sentence combining may be particularly effective for individuals with learning disabilities as they typically produce sentences that are shorter, less syntactically complex, more error filled, and less vocabulary rich than normally developing writers (e.g., Houck & Billingsley, 1989; Myklebust, 1973; Newcomer & Barenbaum, 1991).

Their findings contributed to the research base supporting sentence combining as an effective instructional technique in several ways. Participants were able to correctly combine sentences after treatment, they increased the quality of their writing, and after intervention increased in their attempts to revise their writing when compared to baseline. These three studies provide further support for the use of sentence combining as a method to improve sentence construction ability and overall writing quality. Furthermore, these studies demonstrate that sentence combining is effective with young writers at various ability levels, including writers

with disabilities, and may favorably impact the quality and quantity of revisions. These studies also reveal that peer grouping can be an effective instructional arrangement during sentence combining practice.

Summary and Recommendations

In conclusion, research indicates that sentence combining is a viable strategy to use in place of traditional grammar instruction, can be utilized with writers with different abilities, and can be practiced in peer learning structures. As one component of a writing program, sentence combining practice can help writers improve the quality, variety, and complexity of their sentences while also improving the quality of their prose.

References

Andrews, R., Torgerson, C., Beverton, S., Freeman, A., Locke, T., Low, G., … Zhu, N. (2006). The effect of grammar teaching on writing development. *British Educational Research Journal, 32,* 39–55.

Graham, S., & Perin, D. (2007). *Writing next: Effective strategies to improve writing of adolescents in middle and high schools—A report to Carnegie Corporation of New York.* Washington, DC: Alliance for Excellent Education.

Hillocks, G. (1987). Synthesis of research on teaching writing. *Educational Leadership, 44*(8), 71–82.

Houck C. K., & Billingsley, B. S. (1989). Written expression of students with and without learning disabilities: Differences across the grades. *Journal of Learning Disabilities, 22,* 561–575.

Hunt, K. W. (1965). *Grammatical structures written at three grade levels.* (Research Report No. 3). Champaign, IL: National Council of Teachers of English.

Myklebust, H. R. (1973). Development and disorders of written language. *Studies of normal and exceptional children* (Vol. 2, pp. 99–110). New York: Grune & Stratton.

National Commission on Writing. (2005). *Writing: A powerful message from state government.* Retrieved from http://www.writingcommission.org/report/html

Newcomer, P. L., & Barenbaum, E. M. (1991). The written composing ability of children with learning disabilities: A review of the literature from 1980 to 1990. *Journal of Learning Disabilities, 24,* 578–593.

O'Hare, F. (1973). *Sentence combining: Improving student writing without formal grammar instruction.* Champaign, IL: National Council of Teachers of English.

Perron, J. D. (1974). An exploratory approach to extending the syntactic development of fourth grade students through the use of sentence-combining methods. *Dissertation Abstracts International, 35,* A4316.

Saddler, B. (2009, Summer). Sentence combining. *The International Dyslexia Association: Perspectives on Language and Literacy, 3,* 27–29.

Saddler, B., Asaro, K., & Behforooz, B. (2008). The effects of peer-assisted sentence combining practice on four young writers with learning disabilities. *Learning Disabilities: A Contemporary Journal, 6*(1), 17–31.

Saddler, B., Behforooz, B., & Asaro, K. (2008). The effects of sentence combining instruction on the writing of fourth grade students with writing difficulties. *Journal of Special Education, 42,* 79–90. doi: 10.1177/0022466907310371

Saddler, B., & Graham, S. (2005). The effects of peer-assisted sentence combining instruction on the writing performance of more and less skilled young writers. *Journal of Educational Psychology, 97*(1), 43–54. doi:10.1037/0022066397143

Scardamalia, M., & Bereiter, C. (1986). Research on written composition. In M. C. Wittrock (Ed.), *Handbook of research on teaching* (3rd ed., pp. 778–803). New York: Macmillan.

7.15

Extracurricular Activities in Secondary Schools

Boaz Shulruf and Grace Ying Wang
University of Auckland

Introduction

Student performance at secondary school is the main determinant for enrolment in tertiary education. As part of their school daily life, and in response to students' and parents' demands, many secondary schools offer a wide variety of activities over and above core curricular classroom teaching and learning, which are usually referred to as cocurricular or extracurricular activities (ECA). In addressing this demand, whether from students or other stakeholders, secondary schools allocate considerable resources to the extracurricular material. It is acknowledged that ECAs have been integrated into primary education in some countries, such as the United States, Australia, and New Zealand, suggesting potentially positive effects for social and cognitive development (Annemarie & Seiler, 2011).

Research into the impact of extracurricular activities on students dates back to the 1930s with studies documenting the range of activities being offered in schools and questioning whether participation in certain high school activities could be related to higher achievement at college (Baxter, 1936; M. N. Holland, 1933). However, despite a raft of studies on ECA participation being undertaken over nearly eight decades (Shulruf, in press), little is known or understood about the causal effect between participation in such activities and educational outcomes.

Research Evidence

In 1987, Holland and Andre carried out a review of literature relating to extracurricular participation and adolescent development with the aim of providing a critique of methodological approaches and possible directions for future research (A. Holland & Andre, 1987). However, while this review was relatively comprehensive, it was said to lack the evidence needed to support the conclusions drawn, and it had no theoretical framework or definitions of its key terms (Taylor & Chiogiojl, 1988). Notwithstanding, this study did

raise the profile of extracurricular activity and exposed it as an area in need of additional research.

Extracurricular studies examine a multitude of activities. Some authors take a broad-based approach and examine participation across a range of activities, both school-sponsored and outside-of-school activities, whereas others nominate and examine particular extracurricular areas, such as participation in athletics or in academically related activities (for details see Shulruf, in press). Nonetheless, studies that only focus on school-sponsored activities tend to be the exception rather than the rule. In the last 15 years there has been a move toward examining extracurricular activities within school programs and their impact on student learning outcomes. McNeal (1995), for example, examined student involvement in "formal" extracurricular school activities and their impact on student retention, and Broh (2002) studied the educational impact of participation in both sport-related and non-sport-related school-sponsored activities. Their results suggest that academic achievement was greater for athletes compared to their peers who participated in nonathletic extracurricular activities.

A comprehensive review of the literature on ECA for high school students in the United States (Feldman & Matjasko, 2005) found that while extracurricular activities are viewed as highly important "developmental settings for adolescents," little is understood about the "contextual influences" affecting that development, or the relation between participation and outcomes (pp. 160–161). Studies such as Lewis's (2004) meta-analysis of extracurricular participation conclude that the best academic and social outcomes for students are gained through well-designed, developmentally appropriate activities, but they are unable to describe or pinpoint the particular characteristics contributing to these outcomes. Furthermore, only limited evidence was suggested to support the commonly held justification for carrying out extracurricular activities. The effect size of sports activity participation on academic endeavours was $d = .10$ for all studies and $d = .13$ for longitudinal studies).

Many studies have set out to examine how participation in such activities is beneficial for students. For example, Melnick, Sabo, and Vanfossen (1992) examined the educational effects of interscholastic participation on African American and Hispanic boys and girls. They found that while high school athletic participation was for many a means of being included in social youth groups, it was not necessarily related to grades and standardized test scores. Others found a strong link between participation in athletics and the likelihood of students dropping out of school (McNeal, 1995); and still more have found that participation in sports is linked to improved school attendance, academic outcomes, including school grades, coursework selection, homework, educational and occupational aspirations, social relationships, and self-esteem (e.g., Marsh & Kleitman, 2003). Furthermore, participation in extracurricular activities was associated with high educational attainment and high grades, low dropout rate, gaining cultural capital, and enrolment in tertiary education (Buoye, 2004; Shulruf, in press; Shulruf, Tumen, & Tolley, 2008; Stearns & Glennie, 2010)

Many studies emphasise the impact of moderating factors such as gender, ethnicity, and socioeconomic status on the level and type of outcome achieved (Brown & Evans, 2002; Shulruf et al., 2008). Davalos, Chavez, and Guardiola (1999), for example, found that both ethnicity and gender were important moderating factors on the impact of extracurricular activities on school retention; non-Hispanic students were more likely than Hispanic students to participate in ECA, and boys were more likely to participate in sports than girls. In examining the association between extracurricular activities and academic achievement, Valentine, Cooper, Bettencourt, and DuBois (2002) suggested that although academic achievements are associated with ECA, the association is mediated through student self-beliefs. Self-beliefs refer to cognitive representations of what the individual might become in the future. Self-beliefs may act as casual agents in academic achievement, which can be positive (honour student) or negative (dropout) (Valentine et al., 2002). Thus, when engaging out-of-school activities that promote a positive academic self-concept, a student will be more likely to view these academic activities as congruent with the self and make more effort in academic work (Valentine et al., 2002).

More recently, Shulruf (in press) conducted a critical review and meta-analysis of the literature and investigated what it is about ECA participation that supports positive educational outcomes. Twenty-nine studies met the search criteria for inclusion in his analysis. The findings from studies on participation in extracurricular activity and students' outcomes suggest a positive relation between participation in school-sponsored activities and achievement. However, it is unclear exactly what it is about these types of activities that causes the learning-related outcomes, or indeed whether there is a causal relation at all. In many instances effect sizes were low, indicating that there was no meaningful association. Meaningful effect sizes were found in only two instances: the effect of general extracurricular activities on aspiration to tertiary studies; and the effect of student council participation on GPA. For example, sport was the most commonly investigated extracurricular activity across the 29 studies; however, the effect of sports activities across the range of learning outcomes was minimal, and ranged between –.01 to .31.

Shulruf (in press) noted that there are limitations in the collection of data from studies on ECA due to the widely varied approaches taken, the multiplicity of outcomes, and the varying definitions of outcomes. For example, studies used a wide range of academic outcome measures, including: GCSE in the United Kingdom; and GPA, SAT scores, grades for single core curriculum subjects, course credits, and self-reports/teacher ratings in the United States.

Studies on associations between ECA and academic outcomes also focused on a range of different core curriculum areas; some examined English, some science, some maths, and others a mixture or all three. Interestingly most of the studies on ECA did not measure level of activity attendance and none were found to measure the quality of participation.

Further examination of the approaches used in studies based on secondary source data revealed more methodological issues. For example, Marsh and Kleitman (2003) used NELS:88 for their study and sampled 12,084 students from the 1988 cohort. However, on closer examination, their study included only 4,250 students (35%) with valid data for all the variables considered in the analysis. Moreover, students who transferred or dropped out of school were excluded from the main analyses. Lack of an analysis of missing data, and exclusion of the students who had left school, raises a critical question about whether or not the effects found in this analysis are only artifacts. Alternatively, the results could be overturned if all the data were included in the analysis. For example, one might assume that there were many students, among the 65% who were excluded from the study, who participated in ECA but left school for various reasons, including poor outcomes.

None of the other studies that used NELS:88 revealed any analyses of missing data. In addition, it was found that the data used excluded students who changed schools and those who did not complete questionnaires (or whose parents did not complete them). The vulnerability for bias is great because students with low grades are more likely to drop out or change schools and their parents are less likely to be engaged in school life. Excluding these students from the analysis, while it is known that the majority of students are active in ECA (Cooper, Valentine, Nye, & Lindsay, 1999), is likely to bias the reported results upwards.

These methodological issues have major implications should one wish to develop evidence based policy around ECA in schools. The major issue is the lack of robust evidence suggesting causal effect of ECA on educational outcomes. If causal effects are not evident, the inference is that increasing public investment in ECA puts resources where they are not needed as the more privileged students would benefit the most.

Summary and Recommendations

The aim of this chapter was to ascertain what it is about ECA participation that supports positive academic outcomes and why, and to consider how the common assumptions about the benefits of ECA participation can be validated. It appears that the current knowledge on ECA participation does not suggest that extracurricular activities universally affect student educational outcomes either positively or negatively. It is therefore considered essential that further research be carried out to unravel how participation in extracurricular activities contributes to students' outcomes and why these might be. Such research should investigate aspects of participation, including what motivates participation, how and why students participate, and how such participation impacts on their outcomes.

Lack of evidence for causality strongly suggests that the fundamental question that should be asked is: "Do extracurricular activities have any effect on students' academic outcomes?" It is therefore recommended that further studies try to identify the effects of ECA on students' outcomes by including measures for causality in their study design. Although the best measures for causal effects are established by prospective randomized controlled trials (Abramson, 1995), it is noted that undertaking such studies is very difficult in the social sciences, particularly in respect to ethical issues. Thus, the second-best option is to apply quasi-experimental methods with an emphasis on causal effects; that is, collecting data which enables assessment of as many causality criteria as possible. Implementing such measures in the ECA research is important. Schools in most countries spend significant resources on extracurricular activities but, as this review has found, there is no robust evidence supporting the effectiveness of that expenditure. Thus, research in this area is crucial, particularly if one wishes to improve school effectiveness and student academic outcomes.

References

Abramson, H. J. (1995). *Survey methods in community medicine*. New York: Churchill Livingstone.

Annemarie, S. D., & Seiler, R. (2011). Extra-curricular sport participation: A potential buffer against social anxiety symptoms in primary school children. *Psychology of Sport and Exercise, 12*(4), 347–354.

Baxter, S. G. (1936). Intelligence and the extra-curriculum activities selected in high school and college. *The School Review, 44*(9), 681–688.

Broh, B. A. (2002). Linking extracurricular programming to academic achievement: Who benefits and why? *Sociology of Education, 75*(1), 69–95.

Brown, R., & Evans, W. P. (2002). Extracurricular activity and ethnicity: Creating greater school connection among diverse student populations. *Urban Education, 37*(1), 41–58.

Buoye, A. J. (2004). *Capitalizing in the extra curriculum: Participation, peer influence, and academic achievement*. University of Notre Dame, Indiana.

Cooper, H., Valentine, J. C., Nye, B., & Lindsay, J. J. (1999). Relationships between five after-school activities and academic achievement. *Journal of Educational Psychology, 91*(2), 369–378.

Davalos, D. B., Chavez, E. C., & Guardiola, R. J. (1999). The effects of extracurricular activity, ethnic identification, and perception of school on student dropout rates. *Hispanic Journal of Behavioral Sciences, 21*(1), 61–77.

Feldman, A. F., & Matjasko, J. L. (2005). The role of school-based extracurricular activities in adolescent development: A comprehensive review and future directions. *Review of Educational Research, 75*(2), 159–210.

Holland, A., & Andre, T. (1987). Participation in extracurricular activities in secondary school: What is known, what needs to be known? *Review of Educational Research, 57*(4), 437–466.

Holland, M. N. (1933). Extra-curriculum activities in high schools and intermediate schools in Detroit. *The School Review, 41*(10), 759–767.

Lewis, C. P. (2004). *The relation between extracurricular activities with academic and social competencies in school age children: A meta-analysis*. Texas A&M University.

Marsh, H. W., & Kleitman, S. (2003). School athletic participation: Mostly gain with little pain. *Journal of Sport & Exercise Psychology, 25*(2), 205–228.

McNeal, R. B. (1995). Extracurricular activities and high school dropouts. *Sociology of Education, 68*(1), 62–80.

Melnick, M. J., Sabo, D. F., & Vanfossen, B. (1992). Educational effects of interscholastic athletic participation on African-American and Hispanic youth. *Adolescence, 27*(106), 295–308.

Shulruf, B. (in press). Do extra-curricular activities in schools improve educational outcomes? A critical review and meta-analysis of the literature *International Review of Education*.

Shulruf, B., Tumen, S., & Tolley, H. (2008). Extracurricular activities in school, do they matter? *Children and Youth Services Review, 30*(4), 418-426

Stearns, E., & Glennie, E. J. (2010). Opportunities to participate: Extracurricular activities' distribution across and academic correlates in high schools. *Social Science Research, 39*(2), 296–309.

Taylor, J. L., & Chiogiojl, E. N. (1988). The Holland and Andre Study on extracurricular activities: Imbalanced and incomplete. *Review of Educational Research, 58*(1), 99–105.

Valentine, J. C., Cooper, B., Bettencourt, A., & DuBois, D. L. (2002). Out-of-school activities and academic achievement: The mediating role of self-beliefs. *Educational Psychologist, 37*(4), 245–256.

7.16

Improving Academic Achievement with Social Skills

FRANK M. GRESHAM, MICHAEL J. VANCE, AND JEFFREY CHENIER
Louisiana State University

Introduction

Social skills are learned behaviors that allow an individual to interact appropriately with others and to avoid behaviors that result in negative social interactions (Gresham & Elliott, 1990, p. 1). Social skills can include a number of verbal and nonverbal behaviors such as appropriately asking for help, listening to others, getting along with others, doing nice things for others, taking turns when you talk, and disagreeing appropriately. Though not frequently seen as the primary purpose of education, various research studies conducted worldwide and across a variety of students have documented the relationship between social skills/prosocial behaviors and academic achievement as measured by achievement test scores and grade point average (i.e., Ray & Elliott, 2006; Rutherford, Dupaul, & Jitendra, 2008; Sonja, Melita, Milena, Jana, & Cirila, 2009; Wentzel & Watkins, 2002; Wight & Chapparo, 2008; Xinyin, Hongyun, Lei, & Yunfeng, 2008). Though social skills aren't intuitively related to academic success, Caprara, Barbaranelli, Pastorelli, Bandura, & Zimbardo (2000) found that teacher ratings of third grader's social behavior were better predictors of their eighth grade academic achievement scores than their third grade academic achievement scores.

Social skills have been shown to be related to behaviors associated with academic success such as problem solving, motivation, and strong peer relationships both for students who are typically developing and those with disabilities. This close relationship has led some to call social skills "academic enablers," which are nonacademic behaviors that can lead to academic achievement (DiPerna & Elliott, 2002). While there is some discussion of whether academic achievement leads to increased social skills or good social skills lead to higher levels of academic achievement, there is research to suggest that there are mechanisms that allow for appropriate social skills to aid in the learning process such as their ability to reduce instances of problem behaviors

(Gresham, 2009) and improve teacher–student interactions (Del Prette & Del Prette, 2009), suggesting there is probably a reciprocal relationship (Welsh, Parke, Widaman, & O'Neil, 2001). Given this critical link, the accurate assessment of social skills is imperative and appropriate social skills instruction is seemingly a necessary part of the general education curriculum.

Research Evidence

With a plethora of interventions available aimed at teaching social skills, there have been numerous meta-analyses and reviews of social skills training programs conducted over the past 25 years both for studies utilizing group and single subject designs. Recently there have been two mega analyses (analyses of meta-analyses) that combined examined 370 peer-reviewed studies working with over 25,000 school-aged children and adolescents and were aimed at examining the effectiveness of social skills training for individuals with or at risk for emotional and behavioral disorders (Cook, Gresham, Kern, Barrerras, Thornton, & Crews, 2008; Gresham, Cook, Crews, & Kern, 2004).

Gresham, Cook, et al. (2004) over a series of six meta-analyses showed that social skills training is an effective strategy for reducing aggressive externalizing behaviors, improving internalizing behaviors, and reducing antisocial behavior patterns in children and youth. Within these analyses, students in social skills training groups had a grand mean effect size of $r = .29$ and a BESD of .65 suggesting that 65% of individuals in social skills training groups improved in these studies as compared to only 35% of students in control groups. In the second analyses, Cook et al. examined results related specifically to secondary students (ages 11 and up) who had or who were at risk for emotional behavior disorders. Similar to the Gresham et al. analyses, Cook et al. found that across five meta-analyses there was a grand mean effect size of $r = .32$ and a BESD of .66 suggesting that 66% of individuals in social skills training improve as compared to only 34% of individuals in control groups.

While these two mega-analyses dealt with meta-analyses composed primarily of Western based samples, they both have promising results related to the ability to increase social skills (through explicit social skills training) with difficult students. Though future meta-analytic research should be conducted with non-Western samples, research worldwide has repeatedly shown that social skills/prosocial behaviors are related to academic achievement (Del Prette & Del Prette, 2009; Sonja et al., 2009; Xinyin et al., 2008), thus making social skills training one evidence based option for what could be a very serious problem.

Summary and Recommendations

Students not engaging in appropriate social skills could be engaging in improper behavior for one of two reasons: (a) They have not yet had the opportunity to learn appropriate skills ("can't do" or acquisition deficit) or (b) appropriate social skills were learned but were not aptly reinforced in previous settings ("won't do" or performance deficit). For students with acquisition deficits, it is necessary to teach appropriate social skills and then reinforce their occurrence; but for students who have previously engaged in appropriate skills, additional social skills training may not be necessary. School personnel dealing with students with performance deficits would be better suited to increase the reinforcement value of engaging in appropriate social skills in a way that would make appropriate behaviors more reinforcing than inappropriate ones.

Since school personnel typically don't know what is considered appropriate behavior for students at home, it may be necessary to determine what social skills are necessary for increasing academic achievement and what those behaviors would look like at school, and teach them explicitly. Within a public health model, this would be similar to providing all individuals with a vaccination; students may not be susceptible to a particular influenza (inappropriate social skills), but explicitly teaching and reinforcing appropriate social skills for the entire school could act as a safeguard. For example, if school personnel believe that appropriately asking for help when encountering difficulties is a necessary social skill related to academic achievement, teachers could actively teach and reinforce appropriate behaviors related to asking for help (raising hand, submitting questions in writing, etc.) while not responding to inappropriate behaviors aimed at the same result (yelling questions out, cheating on tests, etc.). For students who have additional problems (engage in inappropriate social skills), additional training or reinforcement could be warranted.

Given the close relationship between social skills and academic achievement as measured in GPA and achievement test scores, it is important to have a clear set of ex-

pectations for appropriate social skills in the school setting. Since research has shown that social skills training can be effective even for the most difficult students, it seems worthwhile to explicitly teach appropriate social skills at the school level. For students who do not respond to universal social skills instruction but who have exhibited appropriate skills in the past, additional reinforcement should be provided for appropriate social skills behavior as well as additional social skills training more germane to the school setting when required.

References

Caprara, G. V., Barbaranelli, C., Pastorelli, C., Bandura, A., & Zimbardo, P. G. (2000). Prosocial foundations of children's academic achievement. *Psychological Science, 11*, 302–306.

Cook, C. R., Gresham, F. M., Kern, L., Barreras, R. B., Thornton, S., & Crews, S. (2008). Social skills training for secondary students with emotional and/or behavioral disorders: A review and analysis of the meta-analytic literature. *Journal of Emotional & Behavioral Disorders, 16*(3), 131–144.

Del Prette, Z. A. P., & Del Prette, A. (2009). *Psicologia das habilidades sociais na infância: Teoria e Prática* (4th ed.) [Psychology of social skills in childhood: Theory and practice]. Petrópolis, Rio de Janeiro, Brazil: Vozes.

DiPerna, J. C., & Elliott, S. N. (2002). Promoting academic enablers to improve student achievement: An introduction to the miniseries. *School Psychology Review, 31*, 293–297.

Gresham, F. M. (2009). Análise do comportamento aplicada às habilidades sociais [Behavior analysis applied to social skills]. In A. Del Prette & Z.A.P. Del Prette (Eds.), *Psicologia das habilidades sociais: Diversidade teórica e suas implicações* (pp. 17–66) [The psychology of social skills: Multiple theories and their implications]. Petrópolis, Rio de Janeiro, Brazil: Vozes.

Gresham, F. M., Cook, C. R., Crews, S., & Kern, L. (2004). Social skills training for children and youth with emotional and behavioral disorders: Validity considerations and future directions. *Behavioral Disorders, 30*(1), 32–46.

Gresham, F. M., & Elliott, S. N. (1990). *Social skills rating system.* Circle Pines, MN: American Guidance Service.

Ray, C. E., & Elliott, S. N. (2006). Social adjustment and academic achievement: A predictive model for students with diverse academic and behavior competencies. *School Psychology Review, 35*(3), 493–501.

Rutherford, L. E., Dupaul, G. J., & Jitendra, A. K. (2008). Examining the relationship between treatment outcomes for academic achievement and social skills in school-age children with attention-deficit hyperactivity disorder. *Psychology in the Schools, 45*(2), 145–157.

Sonja, P., Melita, P., Milena, V., Jana, K., & Cirila, P. (2009). Students' social behaviour in relation to their academic achievement in primary and secondary school: Teacher's perspective. *Psihologijske teme/ Psychological Topics, 18*(1), 55–74.

Welsh, M., Parke, R. D., Widaman, K., & O'Neill, R. (2001). Linkages between children's social and academic competence: A longitudinal analysis. *Journal of School Psychology, 39*(6), 463–481.

Wentzel, K. R., & Watkins, D. (2002). Peer relationships and collaborative learning as contexts for academic enablers. *School Psychology Review, 31*, 366–377.

Wight, M., & Chapparo, C. (2008). Social competence and learning difficulties: Teacher perceptions. *Australian Occupational Therapy Journal, 55*(4), 256–265.

Xinyin, C., Hongyun, L., Lei, C., & Yunfeng, H. (2008). Effects of the peer group on the development of social functioning and academic achievement: A longitudinal study in Chinese children. *Child Development, 79*(2), 235–251.

7.17

Visual Perception Programs

BARBARA HANNA WASIK, ADRIENNE N. VILLAGOMEZ, SHEENA BERRY, AND SANDRA B. EVARRS
University of North Carolina, Chapel Hill

Introduction

Consider the following classroom scenario: Stacy, a 7-year-old girl, is recommended to the school psychologist by her second grade teacher because she is having a difficult time distinguishing words that look similar (run, ran) and she has trouble remembering sight words (of, the, have). The teacher is concerned with Stacy's achievement and thinks that Stacy is unmotivated and inattentive.

The concerns with Stacy may suggest some difficulty in visual discrimination skills and possibly some visual memory difficulties. Interest in perceptual concerns of this nature dates back many years. Although early theories in the field of psychology noted links between perceptual development and conceptual development (e.g., Gestalt theory, Piagetian theory, Hebb's theory), beginning in the 1960s, considerable research was focused on visual and auditory perception skills and their relation to achievement. *Visual perception* is an umbrella term that encompasses eight different skills. In addition to visual discrimination and visual memory, the following are recognized as specific skills that are includeed under visual perception: visual closure, figure–ground discrimination, visual–spatial relationships, visual association, visual–motor integration, and visual–auditory integration (Kavale, 1982).

In this chapter, we briefly examine the relation of visual perception to achievement and learning disabilities as well as the results of several meta-analyses on this relation, followed by an analysis of visual perception programs and controversies. We conclude with recommendations regarding assessment and educational interventions for children with visual perception difficulties.

Research Evidence

A causal link between visual perception skills and academic achievement seems intuitive, especially for reading and mathematics where visual discrimination of letters, numbers, symbols, and patterns is essential for mastery of skills. Visual discrimination, the ability to organize and interpret visual sensory stimuli, is one of the most studied skills under visual perception. Difficulties in visual perception manifest in behaviors that may lead to concerns with a visual perceptual disorder or a learning disability.

Various visual perceptual skill deficits may impact all areas of academic achievement, such as reading, mathematics, spelling, and writing. The relation of visual perception to academic achievement is likely to be most influential during early reading acquisition (Scheiman & Rouse, 2006), and may be presented as deficits in visual memory of letters and words, tracking, and maintaining attention to reading text. The area of written expression affected by visual perception deficits may result in weak letter formation, letter reversals, and difficulty with the organization of worksheets and text. A student experiencing difficulties in visual perception may exhibit the following mathematic impairments: reversals of numbers, misaligning both horizontal and vertical series of numbers, weak mental math visualization, and difficulties with geometric concepts. Other negative effects can be difficulty with the ability to transition between a worksheet, book, or blackboard.

Research in the 1960s and 1970s was influenced by beliefs of a causal relation between that of perceptual development and conceptual development. Focusing on distinct visual perception skills, researchers examined how difficulties in visual perception influenced reading and math performance. This research was characterized by a wide range of instruments used to identify visual perception skill deficits and assess achievement, and led to interventions focused on one or more aspects of visual perception. In his first review of these studies, Kavale (1982) performed a meta-analysis that included empirical research findings from 161 correlational, comparative, and predictive studies to measure the relation between visual perception skills and reading ability. He included research on all eight component skills identified earlier for visual perception, investigating the relation between these component visual perceptual skills with six reading skills found within the literature: general reading, reading readiness, word recognition, reading comprehension, vocabulary, and spelling. Each of the eight visual perceptual skills was found to account for 6% to 20% of variance in reading ability with the highest association occurring among visual memory and visual discrimination with reading ability. Findings suggested that visual perception is an important correlate of reading achievement, but the proportion of explained variance in reading skills was contingent on the particular combination of visual and reading variables considered. When intelligence was controlled, the correlation between visual perceptual skills and reading ability decreased, yet remained significant for visual memory, visual discrimination, visual closure, and visual–motor integration.

In Kavale and Forness's 2000 review of visual perceptual skills and reading, again using a meta-analysis to integrate the literature on auditory and visual perception with reading achievement, they concluded that there was some justification for early conceptualizations that emphasized perception in learning disabilities. Perceptual processes, however, no longer needed to be considered primary factors in predicting reading ability given the limitations surrounding the magnitude and nature of the relation between perceptual skills and reading, as well as recent advances showing other processes that hold greater promise for explaining reading disability.

Moving beyond the questions Kavale first raised about the relation between visual perception and achievement, other research has focused on visual perception programs, asking whether these programs and practices have a valid basis. These questions follow many years of children participating in interventions that have not been substantiated through empirical investigations. Kavale and Mattson (1983) examined 180 studies of perceptual motor programs and found little evidence for their effectiveness. Furthermore, a publication of the Council for Learning Disabilities (1987) advised against the use of perceptual-motor testing and training to improve academic performance or perceptual and perceptual-motor functions. Some of the current treatment programs are based upon theories that, for example, propose to improve the ability of the cerebellum to process information, or focus on primitive reflexes that might impede normal development related to the brain, but these newer approaches have not been validated (Hyatt, 2007).

Such findings have fueled a highly controversial debate in the field regarding the efficacy of interventions used to treat visual perception disorders. In 1998, the American Academy of Pediatrics (AAP), the American Academy of Ophthalmology (AAO), and the American Association for Pediatric Ophthalmology and Strabismus (AAPOS) collaborated in a position paper to make recommendations related to vision and learning disabilities. The position paper regarded the two deficits as separate dysfunctions and explicitly stated that there was no scientific support for treatment such as visual training, organizational training, and perceptual training to improve academic abilities among children with learning disabilities. In response, Bowman (2002) addressed several assumptions, inconsistencies, and allegations of this position paper to provide evidence of both positive correlations between learning disabilities and vision deficits, as well as evidence of effective treatment. Individual research studies during the past two decades (e.g., Kulp, Edwards, & Mitchell, 2002; Goldstand, Koslowe, & Parush, 2005) do continue to find relations between different visual perception skills and academic achievement, but the evidence for treatment efficacy has not been positive.

This controversial debate on the role of visual perceptual interventions continues, with increasingly compelling evidence calling into question educational practices and prompting writers to reach out to educators, psychologists, physicians, occupational therapists, parents, and other professionals to alert them to the "nonvalidated practices in the treatment of individuals with disabilities" (e.g., Jacobson, Foxx, & Mulick, 2005; see also Hyatt et al., 2009, p. 4). Hyatt and colleagues (2009) conducted a meta-analysis on perceptual motor programs, sensory integration, and tinted lenses. Here we will report the results of their meta-analysis on perceptual motor programs and sensory integration because of the implications for visual perception disorders and the use of such programs with children in educational settings. Perceptual-motor training addresses difficulties in visual, auditory, and kinesthetic perception, and programs such as the Doman-Delacto patterning program continue to be available, though they have not been validated (AAP et al., 1998; Jacobson et al., 2005). Sensory integration, first popularized in the 1970s, continues to receive considerable attention as an intervention, based on the belief that achievement would improve with sensory integrative therapy (Vargas & Camilli, 1999). Its theoretical base assumes that higher-level functions, including those involved in academic skills, are dependent upon lower-level processing of sensory information (Hoehn & Baumeister, 1994). Yet, as Hyatt et al. (2009) conclude from published reviews of research (e.g., Vargas & Camilli, 1999), sensory integration therapy is an unproven intervention and is unlikely to be supported in the future.

Summary and Recommendations

Given the paucity of evidence for intervention programs, where does that leave teachers, psychologists, and parents who seek ways to help children? First, it should be noted that the research on visual perception does not rule out a correlation between visual perceptual difficulties and achievement. Rather, the research outcomes call for recognition that other factors might be making more significant contributions to the difficulties noted in achievement, such as the roles of intelligence, motivation, or other environmental factors. Second, educators, psychologists, and parents need to know how visual perceptual difficulties may be manifest in the classroom. For example, students with perception issues may exhibit poor automatic letter- and word recognition, difficulty computing simple mathematic operations, and struggle with remembering how visual stimuli may be sequenced or classified based on their visual characteristics. Within the school setting, a classroom teacher may assess a student's visual perception through examination of work products and careful observation in the learning setting. Writing artifacts, evaluation of visual spatial ability, fine motor control when manipulating items, and categorization can all be considered when a student is experiencing perceived learning difficulties. The teacher may also refer the student to the school psychologist or occupational therapist for further evaluation. Such evaluations may include clinical observations, standardized assessments, and criterion referenced assessments to help rule out other difficulties and to assist with the development of interventions.

Educational interventions can include both *compensatory strategies* and *educational modifications* and may be most appropriate for children in the early elementary grades. Many compensatory strategies for children with visual perception disorders, such as visual discrimination, visual closure, or visual memory, can help increase the likelihood that children will be able to perform better academically (Griffin, 2004). Teachers can monitor the child's progress and skill acquisition and modify the instruction and environmental factors as needed. Providing multiple modes of presentation is also an effective strategy. For example, if the assignment is listed on a board at the front of the classroom, the teacher can also read the instructions as well as check for understanding by requesting that the student describe the assignment prior to attempting it. Teachers can also assist the student in insuring proper seating and appropriate use of writing implement or scissors. Additional techniques include allowing the student to copy materials placed on his or her desk rather than from a distant board, providing materials at close range, which allows the child to manipulate hands on, and providing extra time to complete tasks which require visual perceptual skills.

In addition, specific practice on areas of difficulty can be included by the teacher as part of classroom work. This specific practice would focus on tasks that are closely aligned with the areas of weakness, such as providing additional help with letter discrimination by giving tasks that require letter discrimination, in contract to providing instruction that address the assumed processed of visual perception disorders.

Children who experience reading difficulties may benefit from enlarged print books, papers, worksheets, or other materials. For writing, providing additional structure and guidelines to a student's paper by making lines more visible and distinct, dividing the paper into sections, and providing paper with raised lines which provides kinesthetic feedback can be helpful. Strategies which may assist students in mathematics include manipulatives and guided visualization. Simple graph construction and interpretation can also help build a student's visual perceptual and discrimination skills. Teachers can obtain information on children's performance before, during, and after modifications in order to gain information on their value for the individual child.

The overwhelming outcome of major research reviews has called into question the provision of interventions that focus on processes, and national associations have called for an end to such interventions, fueling a controversy over the past 30 years. Indeed, the controversy raises serious concerns about the misleading information provided to parents and professionals. These interventions continue in the field, especially for children diagnosed with learning disorders, perceptual disorders, or pervasive developmental delays, raising concerns that children are not being provided with more effective interventions.

Teachers and other professionals do have resources to help these children, in particular, making modifications within the classroom and providing practice on the specific skill areas. The prevalence of children identified with difficulties in visual perception underscores the need for continued research on variables that contribute to visual perception difficulties and specific studies on interventions that enhance children's learning.

References

American Academy of Pediatrics (AAP), American Academy of Ophthalmology (AAO), & American Association for Pediatric Ophthalmology and Strabismus (AAPOS). (1998). Learning disabilities, dyslexia, and vision: A subject review. *Pediatrics, 102,* 1217–1219.

Bowman, M. D. (2002). Learning disabilities, dyslexia, and vision: A subject review. A rebuttal, literature review, and commentary. *Optometry, 73,* 553–575.

Council for Learning Disabilities. (1987). The CLD position statement. *Journal of Learning Disabilities, 20* (6), 349–350.

Goldstand, S., Koslowe, & Parush, S. (2005). Vision, visual-information processing, and academic performance among seventh-grade schoolchildren: A more significant relationship than we thought? *The American Journal of Occupational Therapy, 59,* 377–389.

Griffin, S. (2004). Contributions of central conceptual structure theory to education. In A. Demetriou & A. Raftopoulos (Eds.), *Cognitive developmental change: Theories, models, and measurement* (pp. 264–295). Cambridge, England: Cambridge University Press

Hoehn, T. P., & Baumeister, A. A. (1994). A critique of the application of sensory integration therapy to children with learning disabilities. *Journal of Learning Disabilities, 27*(6), 338–350.

Hyatt, K. (2007). Building stronger brains or wishful thinking? *Remedial and Special Education, 28,* 117–124.

Hyatt, K. J., Stephenson, J., & Carter, M. (2009). A review of three controversial educational practices: Perceptual motor programs, sensory integration, and tinted lenses. *Education and Treatment of Children, 32,* 313–342

Jacobson, J. W., Foxx, R. M., & Mulick, J.A. (Eds.). (2005). *Controversial therapies for developmental disabilities.* Mahwah, NJ: Erlbaum.

Kavale, K. (1982). Meta-analysis of the relationship between visual perceptual skills and reading achievement. *Journal of Learning Disabilities, 15,* 42–51.

Kavale, K. A., & Forness, S. R. (2000). Auditory and visual perception processes and reading ability: A quantitative reanalysis and historical reinterpretation. *Learning Disability Quarterly, 23,* 253–270.

Kavale, K., & Mattson, P. D. (1983). One jumped off the balance beam, *Meta-Analysis of Perceptual-Motor Training Journal, 16*(3),165–173.

Kulp, M. T., Edwards, K. E., & Mitchell, G. L. (2002). Is visual memory predictive of below-average academic achievement in second through fourth graders? *Optometry and Vision Science, 79,* 431–434.

Scheiman, M. M., & Rou*se*, M. W. *(2006). Optometric management of learning-related vision problems* (2nd ed.). St. Louis, MO: Mosby-Elsevier.

Vargas, S., & Camilli, G. (1999). A meta-analysis of research on sensory integration treatment. *American Journal of Occupational Therapy, 53,* 189–198.

7.18

Reading

Vocabulary Programs

A. WILSON, R. JESSON, AND S. MCNAUGHTON
University of Auckland

Introduction

Vocabulary is highly related to reading comprehension (Stahl & Fairbanks, 1986) and, more generally, as students' understanding of words becomes more nuanced they learn to think in more sophisticated ways. However, the extent to which vocabulary knowledge can be separated from reading comprehension is unclear.

Word learning involves more than knowing definitions. It includes knowing relationships of words to other words, connotations in different contexts, and knowing transformations into different morphological forms. Fully knowledgeable use of words includes more than understanding in reading and listening, but also productive use in speaking and writing. Thus developing vocabulary knowledge requires not only increasing breadth (numbers of words) but also increasing depth (more information about each word).

Whereas estimates of the breadth of word knowledge and word learning vary, it is clear that students need to learn a large number of words. Disparities in the vocabulary development of different groups of learners are a major issue. Hart and Risley (1995) estimated that by 3 years of age low SES children had learned about 500 of the approximately 10 million words they had been exposed to, whereas higher SES children have learned 1,100 of the over 30 million words they have been exposed to. These early language and vocabulary differences widen across the primary school years such that by the end of Grade 2 there exists a gap of roughly 2 years acquisition of vocabulary between SES groups (Biemiller & Boote, 2006). Vocabulary programs in schools are often less than ideal, with limited instructional time targeted for vocabulary learning (Blachowicz, Fisher, Ogle, & Watts-Taffe, 2006). To meet the need for more effective vocabulary instruction, a variety of models have been researched.

Research Evidence

Incidental Learning. Most of the words children know are learned incidentally through many exposures to words in many contexts, rather than through formal teaching. Incidental learning through reading is particularly important as children's books have many more new words than conversation and at school most new word learning comes from reading. Optimising incidental learning in the classroom requires deliberate programming (Pressley, Disney, & Anderson, 2007).

The average probability of learning an unknown word while reading or listening to stories has been calculated to be 15%, although this varies with student factors such as grade level, reading ability, as well as assessment and text factors (Swanborn & de Glopper, 1999). With instructional intervention, this can be increased, by on average 9% with repetition of the stories (Biemiller & Boote, 2006), and with teacher explanation of vocabulary meanings during story reading (Penno, Wilkinson, & Moore, 2002), increasing the probability to an average of 26%. By adding in review of learned words and ensuring that all definitions were given by the teacher (rather than other children) Biemiller and Boote (2006) were able to raise this to 41%.

However, incidental learning even with teacher elaboration is relatively inefficient with learners expending considerable energy making inferences that may only yield a vague or inaccurate understanding of the word meaning because of variable contextual information (Baumann, Kame'enui, & Ash, 2003, p. 759). Similarly, because differential amounts of reading due to differences in reading ability predict vocabulary knowledge, a reliance on incidental learning is likely to exacerbate disparities.

To be effective, programs need to ensure that texts offer enough opportunities for students first to meet new words, but then to remeet them enough times to learn them in depth. Gardner (2004) noted that expository texts provide more new words more often than narratives and contain higher percentages of academic high frequency words and unique words, as well as being lexically denser. Collections of expository texts on the same theme offer more opportunities to remeet words than themed narrative collections. Moreover, conceptual understanding for content area and disciplinary learning is interdependent with vocabulary knowledge (Harmon, Hedrick, & Wood, 2005). Thus, wide reading of self-chosen stories in itself will not suffice for the vocabulary necessary for schooling success.

Explicit and Direct Instruction. Explicit and direct vocabulary instruction can be more efficient than incidental learning (Beck & McKeown, 1991). Meta-analyses show that explicit vocabulary instruction, which has two general formats, can have a significant effect on the comprehension of passages containing the taught words but a more modest effect on standardised measures of reading comprehension (Fukkink & de Glopper, 1998; Stahl & Fairbanks, 1986).

Teaching Specific Words. Because more targeted instruction produces greater word learning, researchers have sought to identify the words to teach which will produce greatest gains in reading. Biemiller (2005) demonstrated that students learn words in roughly the same order, thus it should be possible to identify the words known by most children at a specific grade level (and then teach them to those who do not know them). Others suggest that target words should be those that are needed for understanding specific texts or concepts, and those that will be useful or frequently encountered in the literate and specialized linguistic contexts required at school (Beck & McKeown, 1991). Although no one method has yet been empirically established as superior, it is clearly important for teachers to make careful decisions about which words to teach.

Procedures for teaching specific words include memory techniques such as the *key word method*, which entails learners constructing an interactive visual image between the new word and a familiar word that shares some common features (Pressley et al., 2007). Whereas some words can be learned effectively this way, Baumann et al. (2003) question whether students would be able to retain mnemonic keys for large numbers of words, and whether the strategy would become tiresome over time.

Providing students with definitions is another procedure but traditional dictionaries are poor tools for learning the meanings of words by themselves (Scott, Nagy, & Flinspach, 2008). However, providing definitions becomes more effective when combined with other active processing such as adding contextual information, writing, or rich manipulation of words (Blachowicz et al., 2006).

A number of multicomponent programs place more emphasis on deep understanding of words. Interactive techniques which increase depth of learning include requiring students to make semantic connections among words,

and explaining the connections. In addition, self-selection of words to study also results in increased word learning, arguably through increased student engagement (see Blachowicz et al., 2006).

A repeated finding is that students need multiple exposures to new words. However, even after relatively intensive instruction not all taught words are remembered. This finding together with the observation that not all words needed can be learned through specific direct instruction has led to a second approach.

Teaching Word Learning Strategies. It is inevitable that students will come across novel words in texts (Scott et al., 2008). Thus, some researchers advocate teaching word learning strategies that students can use to take the most advantage of contextual and morphological information available.

The strategy of deriving meanings from context is teachable (Fukkink & de Glopper, 1998). Programs designed to teach comprehension strategies more generally have shown this too in three waves of research (Wilkinson & Son, 2011). Single strategy instruction in the first wave was followed in the second wave by instruction focused on multiple strategies which showed more sizable effects on experimenter developed tests but smaller effects on standardized tests of reading comprehension. In the third wave of comprehension strategy research Pressley and his colleagues developed transactional strategies instruction (TSI) (Pressley et al., 1992). The TSI program emphasised flexible use of a small repertoire of strategies, including strategies to make meaning from unfamiliar words, and it has been found to have robust effects on measures of comprehension, including standardized tests.

Scott and colleagues (2008) also advocate the need for flexible strategy use coordinated with a high level of comprehension monitoring. The specific vocabulary strategy of morphological analysis, especially when part of a more general multicomponent *word consciousness* program, has been shown to benefit comprehension (Baumann et al., 2003) and science and social studies learning (Harmon et al., 2005). An even more embedded approach to vocabulary can be seen within concept oriented reading instruction (CORI), which aims to improve reading comprehension and increase engagement within thematic science learning. The reading comprehension aims include fluency, vocabulary, self-monitoring, and "fix-up strategies" (Guthrie, McRae, & Klauda, 2007, p. 242). Thus the vocabulary teaching is embedded within reading strategy instruction, which itself is embedded in an authentic learning context.

Wilkinson and Son (2011), however, point out problems with this line of research. The first is that it is not clear whether it is the strategies per se that produce the change, or increased engagement and interaction with texts. Second, there is a risk with strategy instruction of it becoming too mechanical with reduced effects over time (see also Lai, McNaughton, Amituanai-Toloa, Turner, & Hsiao, 2009). Third, the evidence suggests that the programs are difficult to implement across many classrooms. Wilkinson and Son (2011) suggest dialogic approaches for a more productive fourth wave of research.

Summary and Recommendations

Because so many factors influence comprehension with different texts and different learners, a balanced approach to teaching literacy is often advocated in the context of vocabulary this typically includes teaching of selected word meanings in context alongside independent word learning strategies and developing word consciousness (e.g., Baumann et al., 2003; Nagy & Scott, 2000).

The evidence suggests that the most effective programs for vocabulary learning will be comprehensive, multicomponent, long term, and targeted (Pressley et al., 2007). Such programs will provide for both immersion in vocabulary rich environments and explicit forms of instruction with extensive practice, deliver articulated knowledge of specific words, and promote productive strategies for solving and learning new words. The optimal format may be more discursive programs. Effective vocabulary programs will be embedded in extensive literacy instruction and be part of effective literacy programs generally.

There are two implications of this latter conclusion for analyses of multicomponent vocabulary programs. The first is that specific causal relationships of components will be difficult to untangle. The second implication is that the most effective programs also will be determined by properties of effective teachers, especially those identified for teaching culturally and linguistically diverse and poorer students. Systematic analysis of these properties is missing from the research. Current models predict effective programs would build teacher knowledge and their expertise. The research reviewed suggests that effective instruction requires considerable content knowledge relating to words and their uses in comprehending school related topics and texts. It requires considerable flexibility in using evidence based programs. It requires predispositions to playfulness and inventiveness with words and their uses as a part of classroom pedagogy if these are to be modelled for children (Pressley et al., 2007). Also, current models would predict teaching would be based on a robust and coherent process of collective inquiry using evidence of learning, teaching, and achievement patterns to enable flexible and evidence based practices (Lai & McNaughton, 2009).

References

Baumann, J. F., Kame'enui, E. J., & Ash, G. E. (2003). Research on vocabulary instruction: Voltaire redux. In *Handbook of research on teaching the English language arts* (2nd ed., pp. 752–785). Mahwah, NJ: Erlbaum.

Beck, I. L., & McKeown, M. G. (1991). Conditions of vocabulary acquisition. In R. E. Barr, M. L. E. Kamil, P. Mosenthal, & P. Pearson (Eds.), *Handbook of reading research* (Vol. 2, pp. 789–814). Hillsdale, NJ: Erlbaum.

Biemiller, A. (2005). Size and sequence in vocabulary development: Implications for choosing words for primary grade vocabulary instruction. In A. Hiebert & M. Kamil (Eds.), *Teaching and learning vocabulary: Bringing research to practice* (pp. 223–242). Mahwah, NJ: Erlbaum.

Biemiller, A., & Boote, C. (2006). An effective method for building meaning vocabulary in primary grades. *SO—Journal of Educational Psychology, 98*(1), 44–62.

Blachowicz, C. L. Z., Fisher, P. J. L., Ogle, D., & Watts-Taffe, S. (2006). Theory and research into practice: Vocabulary: Questions from the classroom. *Reading Research Quarterly, 41*(4), 524–539.

Fukkink, R. G., & de Glopper, K. (1998). Effects of instruction in deriving word meaning from context: A meta-analysis. *Review of educational research, 68*(4), 450–469.

Gardner, D. (2004). Vocabulary input through extensive reading: A comparison of words found in children's narrative and expository reading materials. *Applied Linguistics, 25*(1), 1–37.

Guthrie, J. T., McRae, A., & Klauda, S. L. (2007). Contributions of concept-oriented reading instruction to knowledge about interventions for motivations in reading. *Educational Psychologist, 42*, 237–250.

Harmon, J. M., Hedrick, W. B., & Wood, K. D. (2005). Research on vocabulary instruction in the content areas: Implications for struggling readers. *Reading & Writing Quarterly, 21*(3), 261–280. doi:10.1080/10573560590949377

Hart, B., & Risley, T. R. (1995). *Meaningful differences in the everyday experience of young American children*. Baltimore, MD: Brookes.

Lai, M. K., McNaughton, S., Amituanai-Toloa, M., Turner, R., & Hsiao, S. (2009). Sustained acceleration of achievement in reading comprehension: The New Zealand experience. *Reading Research Quarterly, 44*(1), 30–56.

Nagy, W. E., & Scott, J. A. (2000). Vocabulary processes. In M. L. Kamil, P. Mosenthal, P. D. Pearson, & R. Barr (Eds.), *Handbook of reading research* (Vol. 3, pp. 269–284). Mahwah, NJ: Erlbaum.

Pearson, P. D., Hiebert, E. H., & Kamil, M. L. (2007). Vocabulary assessment: What we know and what we need to know. *Reading Research Quarterly, 42*(2), 282–296.

Penno, J. F., Wilkinson, I. A. G., & Moore, D. W. (2002). Vocabulary acquisition from teacher explanation and repeated listening to stories: Do they overcome the Matthew Effect? *Journal of Educational Psychology, 94*(1), 23–33.

Pressley, M., Disney, L., & Anderson, K. (2007). Landmark vocabulary instructional research and the vocabulary instructional research that makes sense now. In R. K. Wagner, A. E. Muse, & K. R. Tannenbaum (Eds.), *Vocabulary acquisition: Implications for reading comprehension* (pp. 205–232). New York: Guilford.

Pressley, M., Beard El-Dinary, P., Gaskins, I., Schuder, T., Bergman, J. L., Almasi, J., & Brown, R. (1992). Beyond direct explanation: Transactional instruction of reading comprehension strategies. *The Elementary School Journal, 92*(5), 513–555.

Scott, J. A., Nagy, W. E., & Flinspach, S. L. (2008). More than merely words: Redefining vocabulary learning in a culturally and linguistically diverse society. In A. Farstrup & J. Samuels (Eds.), *What research has to say about vocabulary instruction* (pp. 574–593). Newark, DE: International Reading Association.

Stahl, S. A., & Fairbanks, M. M. (1986). The effects of vocabulary instruction: A model-based meta-analysis. *Review of educational research, 56*(1), 72–110.

Swanborn, M. S. L., & de Glopper, K. (1999). Incidental word learning while reading: A meta-analysis. *Review of Educational Research, 69*(3), 261–285.

Wilkinson, I. A. G., & Son, E. H. (2011). A dialogic turn in research on learning and teaching to comprehend. In M. L. Kamil, P. D. Pearson, E. B. Moje, & P. Afflerbach (Eds), *Handbook of reading research* (Vol. IV). New York: Routledge.

7.19

Achievement in Adolescent Health Education

MEGAN SANDERS, RASHEA HAMILTON, AND ERIC M. ANDERMAN
The Ohio State University

Introduction

The area of health education is unique: whereas performance on standardized examinations is used to evaluate success in most academic domains, demonstrating factual knowledge often does not subsequently correspond to the desired outcomes of health education. For example, many adolescents and adults know that it is important to eat healthy foods and to exercise, but nevertheless continue to engage in unhealthy behaviors (e.g., eating unhealthy foods) despite having this knowledge. Similarly, smokers often fail to quit the habit, even though most have heard reports about the risks and dangers of smoking. Although these individuals possess factual knowledge about how to live healthier lives, that knowledge often does not translate to a change in attitudes and behavior.

Thus, given this inconsistent relation between knowledge and behavior, "achievement" within health education needs to be assessed and evaluated somewhat differently than the way it is measured in most other academic domains. Specifically, in addition to factual knowledge, other important outcome variables must be considered. These other outcomes include enhanced efficacy to engage in safe behaviors and to refuse to participate in dangerous or risky activities; improved attitudes and motivation to avoid dangerous and unhealthy situations; increased intentions to engage in healthful behaviors; and actual engagement in healthy and nonrisky activities. Health education programs may be effective to the extent that they encourage achievement in terms of such outcomes.

Therefore, in the present entry we review some of the characteristics of effective health education and make recommendations for health educators based on these characteristics. In our review, we focus in particular on adolescents, because adolescence represents a period of development in which individuals are particularly likely to engage in risky activities and to develop unhealthy habits

(e.g., smoking, poor nutrition, lack of exercise, and alcohol and drug use) that may persist into adulthood and lead to serious long-term health risks (Rew, 2005).

Research Evidence

Before exploring characteristics of effective health education programs, it is first important to note that achievement is represented by various outcome variables across different domains of health. For example, in studies of pregnancy prevention, outcome variables can include sexual activity, contraceptive use, pregnancy rates, and childbirth (Franklin, Grant, Corcoran, Miller, & Bultman, 1997). In studies of HIV prevention, outcomes may include sexual intentions, knowledge, attitudes, behaviors, and motivation (Anderman et al., 2009). Thus examinations of achievement in health education must be sensitive to the fact that outcome measures vary greatly based on the focus of the program and the types of measures that were employed within studies.

Despite the variability in outcome measures, effective health education programs have many features in common. One area of commonality is that most of these programs are focused on prevention (e.g., prevention of engagement in risky behaviors) and are designed to prevent the initiation of unhealthy behaviors. In a review of effective prevention programs (i.e., programs that lead to achievement), Nation et al. (2003) identified five characteristics demonstrated by effective prevention programs across four different domains of health education (substance abuse, risky sexual behavior, school failure, and delinquency). Specifically, effective programs (a) are comprehensive in nature (i.e., they incorporate multiple interventions that occur across multiple settings); (b) incorporate a variety of teaching methods (e.g., interactive instruction and opportunities to practice newly learned skills); (c) are delivered with sufficient dosage (i.e., participants are exposed to sufficient amounts of the program); (d) are informed by theory, and

(e) promote positive relationships (e.g., between participants and their peers) (see also Dusenbury & Falco, 1995; Kirby et al., 1994).

Research has also cited the timing in which students are exposed to programming as influencing effectiveness. Somers and Surmann (2005) reported that later and decreased exposure to sex education was predictive of more sexual activity. Similarly, Mueller, Gavin, and Kulkarni (2008) reported that sex education may be more effective if provided prior to initiation of sexual activity. Other researchers support this argument noting that students that are younger and not active sexually may be easier to influence (Franklin & Corcoran, 2000).

There is also a research base that also notes the importance of peers in enhancing program effectiveness. Mellanby, Newcombe, Rees, and Tripp (2001) reported that although peers may not be as effective as adults in imparting information to students, peers are more effective in helping establish norms and attitudes related to sex. In previous studies, peers were seen as better models of behavior than teachers (Walcott, Meyers, & Landau, 2008). Additionally, peer-leaders have been demonstrated to enhance acceptability of health-related information, promote more accurate self-reports, and encourage attitude change (Valente, Unger, Ritt-Olson, Cen, & Johnson, 2006; Vuttanont, Greenhalgh, Griffin, & Boynton,2006; Walcott et al., 2008).

Effective programs also utilize a theory-based approach to change student behavior and attitudes. In their exploration of school-based health promotion programs, Peters, Kok, Ten Dam, Buijs, and Paulussen (2008) reported that theory-based programs were more effective across the three domains of substance abuse, sexual behavior, and nutrition than were non-theory-based programs. Franklin and Corcoran (2000) found similar results in their review of programs' effectiveness in preventing pregnancy. Both of these reviews specifically cite curriculum based on social cognitive theory as being particularly effective in impacting outcome variables.

Other research has also highlighted the relevance of program content as an important characteristic of effective health education programs. For example, research suggests that programs (e.g., HIV prevention programs) are particularly effective when they are designed or adjusted to be relevant to the culture in which the program is being implemented (Halperin et al., 2004; Nation et al., 2003). Similarly, programs that are fitted to participants' developmental stages (Nation et al., 2003) and that address the concerns of that particular age group (Dusenbury & Falco, 1995) are also particularly effective. Thus a health program that is effective in one culture or with one developmental group may not necessarily be equally as effective in another context.

Another key characteristic of effective programs that lead to achievement is the mode of presentation of health-related information, which is an important predictor of acquiring health-related knowledge (Donohew, Lorch, & Palmgreen, 1998). One of the practices that most strongly distinguish effective from ineffective health education programs is the use of interactive techniques to communicate information (Dusenbury & Falco, 1995; Herbert & Lohrmann, 2010). More specifically, a review of 10 effective health curricula used with adolescent populations indicated that five communication strategies were common across many of these programs, including the use of role playing, group activities, interactive technologies (e.g., websites), team games, and small-group discussions (Herbert & Lohrmann, 2010). Instructional approaches that utilize diverse presentation techniques are likely to be particularly effective (Nation et al., 2003; Park, 2006; Vuttanont et al., 2006; Walcott et al., 2008).

Finally, effective health education programs are also distinct in their implementation. Research suggests that well-trained teachers are integral to effective programs (Nation et al., 2003; Peters et al., 2008; Vuttanont et al., 2006) and that teaching educators how to use interactive techniques may be a particularly important component of this training (Dusenbury & Falco, 1995). However, initial training is not enough; effective programs also provide continuing support for teachers (Dusenbury & Falco, 1995). One way that programs provide this support is through feedback to instructors; such feedback helps educators to evaluate and improve the program effectiveness (Nation at al., 2003).

Summary and Recommendations

Achievement in health education needs to be defined broadly to include behavioral and attitudinal/motivational outcomes, in addition to factual knowledge. We briefly reviewed the program characteristics that are related to this expanded understanding of achievement. Research suggests that programs that are comprehensive in nature, attempt to intervene with youth as early as possible, incorporate peers in the implementation of programming, driven by theory, culturally and developmentally relevant to the participants, interactive in nature, and applied in appropriate dosages lead to desired and beneficial outcomes. Additionally, sufficient training and support for educators are also important factors for the success of these programs.

The implications of these conclusions for the professional development of health educators are particularly important. As we suggested before, teaching that encourages achievement in broader terms is different from teaching that frames achievement more narrowly as demonstrating factual knowledge. In light of these conclusions, it is clear that health educators need to consider the perspectives and concerns of the participating students in order for programs to be maximally effective. Furthermore, health educators must also acknowledge that the ways in which they communicate and reinforce health-related information to these adolescent populations can have important effects on health-related outcomes. Simply presenting information and asking students to memorize it for a test is less effective in health education than techniques that allow students to come to deeply understand and value the information and skills that are being acquired (Anderman et al., 2011).

References

Anderman, E. M., Cupp, P. K., Lane, D. R., Zimmerman, R., Gray, D., & O'Connell, A. (2011). Classroom goal structures and HIV/pregnancy prevention education in rural high school health classrooms. *Journal of Research on Adolescence, 21*, 904–922.

Anderman, E. M., Lane, D. R., Zimmerman, R., Cupp, P. K., & Phebus, V. (2009). Comparing the efficacy of permanent classroom teachers to temporary health educators for pregnancy and HIV prevention. *Health Promotion Practice, 10*, 597–605.

Donohew, L., Lorch, E. P., & Palmgreen, P. (1998). Applications of a theoretic model of information exposure to health interventions. *Human Communication Research, 24*, 454–468.

Dusenbury, L., & Falco, M. (1995). Eleven components of effective drug abuse prevention curricula. *Journal of School Health, 65*, 420–425.

Franklin, C., & Corcoran, J. (2000). Preventing adolescent pregnancy: A review of programs and practices. Social Work, *45*(1), 40–52.

Franklin, C., Grant, D., Corcoran, J., Miller, P. O. D., & Bultman, L. (1997). Effectiveness of prevention programs for adolescent pregnancy: A meta-analysis. *Journal of Marriage and the Family, 59*, 551–567.

Halperin, D. T., Steiner, J. J., Cassell, M. M., Green, E. C., Hearst, N., Kirby, D., … Cates, W. (2004). The time has come for common ground on preventing sexual transmission of HIV. *The Lancet, 364*, 1913–1915.

Herbert, P. C., & Lohrmann, D. K. (2010). It's all in the delivery! An analysis of instructional strategies from effective health education curricula. *Journal of School Health, 81*, 258–264.

Kirby, D., Short, L., Collins, J., Rugg, D., Kolbe, L., Howard, M., …Zabin, L. S. (1994). School-based programs to reduce sexual risk behaviors: A review of effectiveness. *Public Health Reports, 109*, 339–360.

Mellanby, A. R., Newcombe, R. G., Rees, J., & Tripp, J. H. (2001). A comparative study of peer-led and adult-led school sex education. *Health Education Research, 16*(4), 481–492.

Mueller, T. E., Gavin, L. E., & Kulkarni, A. (2008). The association between sex education and youth's engagement in sexual intercourse, age at first intercourse, and birth control use at first sex. *Journal of Adolescent Health, 42*(1), 89–96.

Nation, M., Crusto, C., Wandersman, A., Kumpfer, K. L., Seybolt, D., Morrissey-Kane, E., & Davino, K. (2003). What works in prevention: Principles of effective prevention programs. *American Psychologist, 58*, 449–456.

Park. E. (2006). School-based smoking prevention programs for adolescents in South Korea: A systematic review. *Health Education Research Theory and Practice, 21*(3), 407–415.

Peters, L. W. H., Kok, G., Ten Dam, G. T. M., Buijs, G. J. & Paulussen, T. G. W. M. (2009). Effective elements of school health promotion across behavioral domains: A systematic review of reviews. *Biomedical Public Health, 9*(182), 1–14.

Rew, L. (2005). *Adolescent health: A multidisciplinary approach to theory, research, and intervention.* Thousand Oaks, CA: Sage.

Somers, C. L., & Surmann, A. T. (2005). Sources and timing of sex education: Relations with American adolescents sexual attitudes and behavior. *Educational Review, 57*(1), 37–54.

Valente, T. W., Unger, J. B., Ritt-Olson, A., Cen, S. Y. & Johnson, A. (2006). The interaction of curriculum type and implementation method on 1-year smoking outcomes in a school-based prevention program. *Health Education Research Theory and Practice, 21*(3), 315–324.

Vuttanont, U., Greenhalgh, T., Griffin, M. & Boynton, P. (2006). "Smart boys" and "sweet girls"—Sex education needs in Thai teenagers: A mixed-method study. *Lancet, 368*, 2068–2080.

Walcott, C. M., Meyers, A. B., & Landau, S. (2008). Adolescent sexual risk behaviors and school-based sexually transmitted infection/HIV prevention. *Psychology in the Schools, 45*(1), 39–51.

7.20

Writing Achievement

Mark Torrance
Nottingham Trent University, England

Raquel Fidalgo
University of León, Spain

Introduction

Achievement in writing, in educational contexts at least, is marked by the ability to produce text that extends across a number of paragraphs, that coheres—sentences and paragraphs are tied into a meaningful whole—and that accommodates the needs of potential readers. Achieving writers will be able to do this in a number of different textual genres (stories, persuasive letters, expository essays, and so forth) and for a range of audiences. Learning to write, in this sense, occurs almost exclusively within school. This is in contrast to learning to communicate in speech which is rarely a direct focus of formal education. Writing pervades learning and assessment across the curriculum in large part because it generates a permanent output that is relatively straightforward to assess.

Writing ability comprises a number of component skills which interact in complex and poorly understood ways. Some of these skills are imported from speech: beginning writers bring with them knowledge of vocabulary and morphology that can be applied directly to writing. Children suffering from general language impairment will therefore tend also to be struggling writers (Dockrell, Lindsay, & Connelly, 2009). They are also likely to bring implicit knowledge of typical content and structure of certain types of texts, although this will rarely extend beyond simple narratives. There is some evidence that being read to at home has positive effects on students' writing in school (Sylva, Scott, Totsika, Ereky-Stevens, & Crook, 2008). Beginning writers also require sufficiently well-developed motor skills and hand-eye coordination to make handwriting possible. (It remains the case that nearly all early writing within schools is by hand rather than by keyboard.)

All other component skills need to be taught. Initially, and most obviously, beginning writers need to learn how to form letters and how to spell. However mastering these low-level skills is not sufficient for writing achievement.

Students also need to move beyond communication skills that have developed in the context of spoken interaction and learn to communicate in the absence of an immediate and present audience. This involves the ability to monitor the possible communicational effect of what is being written (e.g., "Will my readers know what I'm talking about? Will this entertain them?") without the instant feedback that is available in conversation. Writers also need to have their own strategies for generating content for their text. Writing, particularly in educational contexts, rarely starts with the writer having specific content to communicate. In conversation the other speaker's utterances provide an ongoing source of cues to support the retrieval of appropriate things to say. This is absent in writing. Writers therefore need not only to decide how to structure their ideas within the text, but also to determine what these ideas should be.

The strategies that writers adopt in searching for and selecting what to say, is one of the defining features of writing achievement. Novice writing (and expert writing in some contexts) is characterised by "knowledge telling" (Scardamalia & Bereiter, 1991). This involves allowing either the text-just-produced or existing text schemas to cue what to say next. Students at this stage of development might, for example, write stories with a very linear structure: "She did this, then she did that, then she…" and so forth. If asked to think aloud while writing, nearly everything that they say will appear as text. There is little or no evidence of reflection. Sophisticated and complex "knowledge transforming" strategies are used by expert writers for determining content. These involve consideration of audience needs, and of the characteristics of the genre of the text that is being produced. In Scardamalia and Bereiter's terms, decisions about what to say derive from a dialectic between content space (what the writer knows that is relevant to the topic) and discourse space (rhetorical knowledge relevant to how this content might be expressed). Expert writers' think-aloud protocols therefore typically include considerable evaluation of possible content options, and reflection about how these might best be expressed. In a reverse of novice practice, most of what is thought does not appear on the page.

Writing achievement therefore involves development of both low level transcription and formulation skills necessary for making grammatically correct sentences appear on the page and higher level metacognitive skills associated with determining content and structure necessary to create effective text that communicates the writer's ideas. Developing competence typically takes at least the duration of formal schooling, and expertise is probably not achieved by the majority of students. One of the reasons for this is, arguably, that the various different decisions and processes associated with producing good text, such as forming letters, spelling, planning syntax, determining content, word choice, determining macrostructure, considering audience response, potentially converge within the writers mind at the same (or similar) time. Students' minds, and particularly young students' minds, do not have the resources to cope with these multiple demands. Several researchers have identified limitations in cognitive processing capacity (often labelled loosely as "working memory capacity") as a dominant reason for writing being both difficult to learn and, even in experts, difficult to do. Writing achievement is therefore partly dependent (a) on the processing resources that the student brings to the task, (b) on the extent to which the student has automatized writing's component processes, and (c) on whether or not the student can sequence or schedule the writing process in such a way as to avoid cognitive overload (Torrance & Galbraith, 2006). As children develop there is a general, cross-domain increase in the ability to maintain information in working memory. With practice and instruction, spelling and handwriting move from requiring explicit and conscious processing ("I must carefully form my letters," "Now how do I spell that word?") to being implicit and automatic. This liberates processing resources which can then be allocated to higher level processes, and particularly those associated with evaluating and developing the text's rhetorical impact. However, anecdotally at least, even older writers with well-developed basic literacy still run the risk of overload. Success therefore is also likely to require the use of explicit strategies for managing what they think about, and when. This is one possible reason why instructing writers to produce a plan in advance of producing full texts tends to result in a better final product (e.g., Kellogg, 1990).

So, in broad terms, becoming a competent writer requires (a) mastery of spelling and handwriting, so that low-level production processes do not interfere with higher-level thinking and problem solving, (b) possessing appropriate discourse knowledge so that text can be tailored to reader needs, and (c) possessing appropriate metacognitive control strategies to schedule the writing process in such a way that content and rhetorical decisions interact whilst at the same time avoiding cognitive overload. In addition to these, writers obviously also require (d) motivation to apply these strategies to their own writing, independently of teacher prompts. This strategy-plus-motivation combination is captured in the concept "writing self-regulation."

Research Evidence

There is, as might be expected, a robust relationship between both handwriting ability and spelling ability and more general measures of writing ability. Graham, Berninger, Abbot, Abbot, and Whitaker (1997) estimated that in a sample of first to sixth grade students, between 25% and 41% of variance in composition quality, and a higher proportion of variance in writing fluency, was predicted by independent measures of handwriting and spelling ability. This relationship decreases with age. A recent longitudinal study (Abbott, Berninger, & Fayol, 2010) suggests that, for handwriting, the relationship is only strong in the first 2 years of formal education, weakening through the rest of primary (elementary) grades. Spelling ability, on the other hand, remained a strong predictor of writing ability throughout the first 7 years of schooling.

These findings are consistent with the idea that lack of competence in low level processes reduces resources available for higher-level "knowledge transforming" processing. This suggests that training in spelling and handwriting might have knock-on benefits for higher-level (discursive/rhetorical) features of students' texts. Evaluations of interventions targeted specifically at students' handwriting and spelling provide some support this hypothesis. Berninger and coworkers (Berninger et al., 1997) found that various kinds of handwriting training given to Grade 1 students with poor handwriting skills, resulted in improved composition skills. Graham, Harris, and Fink (2000) found similar benefits in Grade 2 students, both with and without handwriting difficulties. In both cases these effects were achieved over a relatively large number of short training sessions (24 x 10 minute sessions, and 27 x 15-minute sessions respectively). The benefits of spelling instruction for composition quality are less clear cut, however. Graham, Harris, and Chorzempa (2002) found that writing fluency can be temporarily improved by 48 x 20-minute sessions of spelling instruction, but that these effects were not sustained. Berninger et al. (2002) also found evidence of increased fluency from teaching spelling alone, but no benefit on quality of composition.

In their meta-analysis of intervention studies sampling students in Grades 4 to 9, Graham and Perin (2007) identified 11 different forms of instruction that had been evaluated in a minimum of four or more methodologically robust studies. Most of these could be categorised as one of two kinds. Some interventions were designed to scaffold production, and therefore to have immediate effect on the writing of a particular text. For example several studies compared the quality of texts written with and without the requirement of first producing a written outline. Other interventions were aimed at developing writing skills in students that they can then, independently, apply to their own texts. Interventions of this form are successful if after instruction students spontaneously apply the new skill or skills to their writing, with a resulting increase in text quality.

In terms of scaffolding, both setting specific goals for the finished text ("your text should include the following features…") and writing collaboratively give relatively strong positive effects. Graham and Perin (2007) found smaller but still significant benefits of requiring that students engage is specific prewriting activities (e.g., producing a structured outline before composing the full text), of engaging students in various inquiry activities in which they explore content relevant to the writing task, and of requiring that they read and analyse good models of the type of text that they are about to produce. Research that has compared students given extensive practice at writing using a word processor suggest that this may also result in an improvement in text quality (e.g., Lowther, Ross, & Morrison, 2003, but see Dybdahl, Shaw, & Blahous, 1997). Clearly these forms of scaffolding are not mutually exclusive, and greater gains in writing quality are likely to be achieved if they are sensibly combined.

Arguably, however, simply changing the conditions under which a particular writing task is performed does not directly tap writing achievement. Achieving writers should be able to produce good text independently of teacher prompts. Interventions that achieve this will aim to develop skills that students will then apply regardless of the writing context. Graham and Perin (2007) identified five interventions of this type. They found no evidence that traditional grammar instruction improves student writing. Teaching sentence combining (taking two or more short sentences and using them to create a single, grammatically more sophisticated sentence; e.g., Saddler & Graham, 2005) shows a moderate positive effect.

The two most effective skill-focused interventions, both giving average effect sizes of .82—greater than for any of the scaffolding interventions—were teaching summary writing (e.g., Chang, Sung, & Chen, 2002; although in this and other studies outcome was evaluated in terms of students' ability to write summaries rather than compose full text) and strategy focused instruction. Strategy-focused interventions deliver a package of instruction aimed at developing in students explicit metacognitive strategies for controlling the writing processes (e.g., for generating and organising ideas, considering audience, and reviewing and revising what they write). A thoroughly evaluated example of this kind of intervention is self-regulated strategy development (SRSD; e.g., De La Paz & Graham, 2002). Evaluations of SRSD typically give effect sizes relative to control in excess of 1 in both typically developing students and struggling writers and in students ranging from midprimary (midelementary) to midsecondary grades. Interventions similar to SRSD have proved successful outside of North America, with similarly large effects found in evaluations in both Germany and Spain, and effects appear remarkably enduring (Fidalgo, Torrance, & Garcia, 2008). The success of strategy-focused interventions is usefully contrasted with instruction based in the process approach to instruction that dominates primary (elementary) writing instruction in the United States. This involves a combination of inquiry and extended writing practice with a focus on peer collaboration and meaningful tasks, but without a strategy focus. Evaluations of the process writing approach give a mean effect size of .32 (Graham & Perin, 2007).

Summary and Recommendations

Writing is a highly complex cognitive ability which comprises a range of different cognitive processes. It includes low-level processes focused on handwriting and spelling and higher level processes associated with determining and structuring content in such a way as to meet the demands of the reader. Unlike speech, writing is late-developing and requires protracted instruction and practice. Achievement in writing is partly dependent on home environment, and particularly how much the child reads. However the nature of the instruction that students receive probably plays a dominant role in predicting their success.

Enhancing writing achievement requires explicit and direct instruction focused on handwriting and spelling. Fluency in basic processes frees cognitive resources that can then be devoted to content generation and structuring. However, mastering spelling and handwriting is not enough for developing students' writing competence. Developing writers require metacognitive control strategies that regulate their production. These will probably involve both explicit discourse knowledge—schemas that represent how specific texts are structured—and process strategies that organise how and when the student thinks about different aspects of his or her text (generate ideas, identify reader goals, read through what has been written, and so forth). Interventions that include these strategy-focused methods tend to be more effective than other forms of instruction.

References

Abbott, R. D., Berninger, V. W., & Fayol, M. (2010). Longitudinal relationships of levels of language in writing and between writing and reading in grades 1 to 7. *Journal of Educational Psychology, 102*(2), 281–298.

Berninger, V. W., Vaughan, K., Abbott, R. D., Begay, K., Coleman, K. B., Curtin, G., … Graham, S. (2002). Teaching spelling and composition alone and together: Implications for the simple view of writing. *Journal of Educational Psychology, 94*(2), 291–304.

Berninger, V. W., Vaughan, K. B., Graham, S., Abbott, R. D., Abbott, S. P., Rogan, L. W., … Brooks, A.(1997). Treatment of handwriting problems in beginning writers: Transfer from handwriting to composition. *Journal of Educational Psychology, 89*(4), 652–666.

Chang, K. E., Sung, Y. T., & Chen, I. D. (2002). The effect of concept mapping to enhance text comprehension and summarization. *Journal of Experimental Education, 71,* 5–23.

De La Paz, S., & Graham, S. (2002). Explicitly teaching strategies, skills, and knowledge: Writing instruction in middle school classrooms. *Journal of Educational Psychology, 94*(4), 687–698.

Dockrell, J. E., Lindsay, G., & Connelly, V. (2009). The impact of specific language impairment on adolescents' written text. *Exceptional Children, 75*(4), 427–446.

Dybdahl, C. S., Shaw, D. G., & Blahous, E. (1997). The impact of the computer on writing: No simple answers. *Computers in the Schools, 13*(3/4), 41–53.

Fidalgo, R., Torrance, M., & Garcia, J. N. (2008). The long-term effects of strategy-focused writing instruction for grade six students. *Contemporary Educational Psychology, 33*(4), 672–693.

Graham, S., Berninger, V. W., Abbot, R. D., Abbot, S. P., & Whitaker, D. (1997). Role of mechanics in composing of elementary school students: A new methodological approach. *Journal of Educational Psychology, 89*(1), 170–182.

Graham, S., Harris, K. R., & Chorzempa, B. F. (2002). Contribution of spelling instruction to the spelling, writing, and reading of poor spellers. *Journal of Educational Psychology, 94*(4), 669–686.

Graham, S., Harris, K. R., & Fink, B. (2000). Is handwriting causally related to learning to write? Treatment of handwriting problems in beginning writers. *Journal of Educational Psychology, 92*(4), 620–633.

Graham, S., & Perin, D. (2007). A meta-analysis of writing instruction for adolescent students. *Journal of Educational Psychology, 99*(3), 445–476.

Kellogg, R. T. (1990). Effectiveness of prewriting strategies as a function of task demands. *American Journal of Psychology, 103*(3), 327–342.

Lowther, D. L., Ross, S. M., & Morrison, G. M. (2003). When each one has one: The influences on teaching strategies and student achievement of using laptops in the classroom. *Educational Technology, Research and Development, 51*(3), 23–44.

Saddler, B., & Graham, S. (2005). The effects of peer-assisted sentence combining instruction on the writing performance of more and less skilled young writers. *Journal of Educational Psychology, 97*, 43–54.

Scardamalia, M., & Bereiter, C. (1991). Literate expertise. In K. A. Ericsson & J. Smith (Eds.), *Toward a general theory of expertise: Prospects and limits* (pp. 172–194). Cambridge, England: Cambridge University Press.

Sylva, K., Scott, S., Totsika, V., Ereky-Stevens, K., & Crook, C. (2008). Training parents to help their children read: A randomized control trial. *British Journal of Educational Psychology, 78*, 435–455.

Torrance, M., & Galbraith, D. (2006). The processing demands of writing. In C. MacArthur, S. Graham, & J. Fitzgerald (Eds.), *Handbook of writing research* (pp. 67–82). New York: Guilford.

7.21

Reading

Comprehension Programs

Janice F. Almasi
University of Kentucky

Barbara Martin Palmer
Mount St. Mary's University

Introduction

In 1975, the "cognitive revolution" ushered in a robust period of research in which readers were viewed as active participants in the meaning construction process. Experimental studies of this era offered promising findings in that strategies-based interventions were generally found to be successful at enhancing comprehension. Recent reviews identified several historical "waves" of strategy instruction research. The first wave consisted of teaching students to use individual strategies and the second wave consisted of teaching students to use multiple strategies (e.g., reciprocal teaching, direct explanation strategy instruction) (Pressley, 2000). Wilkinson and Son (2011) distinguished transactional strategies instruction as a third wave because it extended multiple strategies instruction to include flexible strategy use while readers transact with text. Wilkinson and Son noted that recent research on strategies instruction has taken a "dialogic turn" producing a fourth wave in which dialogic approaches either embed strategy instruction in content domains or use classroom discussion to foster comprehension.

For the purposes of this entry we define a reading comprehension program as classroom instruction that focuses on reader, text, and context as active coparticipants in the meaning making process. In research such programs might be identified as interventions that teach single comprehension strategies, sets of comprehension strategies, or multicomponent interventions that include word level or fluency instruction *and* comprehension instruction. As well we define reading strategies as "deliberate, goal-directed attempts to control and modify the reader's efforts to decode text, understand words, and construct meanings of text" (Afflerbach, Pearson, & Paris, 2008, p. 368). Thus, selecting reading strategies (e.g., summarizing, questioning, visual-izing, predicting, monitoring) requires active engagement, conscious choice, and agency on the part of the reader.

Research Evidence

In their meta-analysis of 13 intervention studies conducted with struggling readers in Grades 6 through 12, Edmonds et al. (2009) found that students in treatment conditions outperformed their counterparts in comparison conditions on standardized and researcher-developed measures of reading comprehension ($ES = 0.89$). This finding suggests that struggling readers can be taught to comprehend; however, it does not explain the effect of different types of interventions on comprehension.

Therefore, Edmonds et al. (2009) also examined whether type of intervention was a predictor of effect size. Within the examined studies three types of interventions were used to enhance comprehension: (a) fluency/word study interventions; (b) comprehension interventions (e.g., teaching single strategies, multiple strategies, or using graphic organizers); and (c) multicomponent interventions, which included either word study and comprehension or fluency and comprehension. The average weighted effect sizes of fluency ($ES = -0.03$) and word study interventions ($ES = 0.34$) were not significantly different from zero. The average weighted effect sizes of multicomponent and comprehension interventions were significantly different from zero, and the effect size was large ($ES = 0.84$) for multicomponent interventions and very large for comprehension interventions ($ES = 1.23$). Bonferroni post hoc contrasts revealed significant differences in effects between multicomponent and comprehension interventions but not between multicomponent and word study interventions. This finding suggests that comprehension interventions were superior to all other forms of intervention.

Many interventions in Edmonds et al. (2009) taught single strategies with large effects on measures similar to the intervention, but smaller effects on transfer measures of comprehension. Other reviews of research found similar results for experimental and qualitative studies of narrative comprehension interventions for at-risk students (Almasi, Palmer, Madden, & Hart, 2011) and for students with learning disabilities (Gersten, Fuchs, Williams, & Baker, 2001). Their findings were consistent whether interventions used narrative or expository text. It is evident that teaching single strategies, while effective for short-term comprehension effects, are ineffective in terms of transfer.

It is clear that the most effective interventions are those that teach multiple strategies; however, it is unclear for whom they work best. Edmonds et al. (2009) examined the effects on comprehension by student population and found largest effects for students with disabilities ($ES = 1.50$), and moderate effects for samples that included both struggling students and students with disabilities ($ES = 0.68$) or samples that only included struggling readers ($ES = 0.45$).

Similar findings are reported in studies of students with learning disabilities. For example, Mastropieri, Scruggs, Bakken, and Whedon's (1996) meta-analysis of 68 studies found an overall effect size of 0.98 with the largest effects for interventions focused on self-questioning or cognitive strategies (e.g., using prior knowledge, self-questioning, self-monitoring, summarization) ($ES = 1.33$). Interventions focused on text enhancement (e.g., using illustrations, highlighting/underlining, using graphic organizers) had a mean effect size of 0.92. Interventions focused on skill training (e.g., vocabulary, repeated readings, placement of teacher questions) had the smallest effect size (0.62).

Vaughn, Gersten, and Chard (2000) categorized effective comprehension interventions into two clusters: (a) comprehension monitoring and (b) self-questioning. Their synthesis revealed that comprehension is enhanced when interventions teach students to be active readers who persevere when reading tasks get difficult. Two components were essential to include in interventions: multiple strategies and opportunities to verbalize. Interventions that included opportunities for students to verbalize their learning and graphically represent ideas while reading helped students to persevere, a finding confirmed by Swanson and Hoskyn's (1998) meta-analysis.

In a similar vein, Sencibaugh (2007) conducted a meta-analysis of 15 studies published from 1985 to 2005 in which interventions were aimed at enhancing the reading comprehension of students with learning disabilities. Findings revealed that auditory/language dependent strategies (e.g., summarization, self-questioning, retelling) had a greater impact ($ES = 1.18$) on reading comprehension skills than visually dependent strategies ($ES = 0.94$) (e.g., using illustrations, using semantic organizers). This finding suggests that students with learning disabilities benefit more when taught cognitive or metacognitive strategies that foster auditory/language processing.

Whereas previous meta-analyses examined type of interventions and strategies, Swanson (1999) examined programs that included elements of strategy instruction (SI), direct instruction (DI), or a combination of both. Results of the meta-analysis of 58 studies revealed that a prototypical intervention study had an effect size of 0.72 for reading comprehension. Studies using combinations of SI and DI had the largest effect sizes (M = 1.15). A number of intervention features increased the predictive power of treatment effectiveness: (a) dialogic interaction/questioning, (b) controlling the difficulty of the processing demands of the task, (c) elaborated explanations of procedural steps, (d) teacher modeling of steps, (e) small-group instruction that included verbal interaction, and (f) strategy cuing.

Many meta-analyses examined various reading comprehension programs and features of interventions that yield substantive effects, but for some programs meta-analyses were conducted of the entire body of work (e.g., Concept-Oriented Reading Instruction (CORI), Reciprocal Teaching, Reading Recovery). Each incorporates characteristics of the most effective comprehension interventions, and they include providing explicit instruction, teaching students how to use multiple strategies with authentic texts, and teaching students how to monitor and regulate their comprehension.

Guthrie, McRae, and Klauda's (2007) meta-analysis of 11 CORI studies found a large effect size of 0.91 on third and fifth graders' reading comprehension when measured by standardized tests. Large and moderate effect sizes were also found on researcher-designed measures of comprehension including multiple text comprehension ($ES = 0.93$), informational text comprehension ($ES = 0.73$), and narrative comprehension ($ES = 0.65$). In a composite measure of students' strategy use that included a performance assessment and a self-report measure, a mean effect size of 0.91 was reported across 9 studies.

In their review of 16 studies of reciprocal teaching, Rosenshine and Meister (1994) found a median effect size of .32 on standardized tests and a larger effect size of .88 when researcher-developed comprehension measures were used.

Finally, Elbaum, Vaughn, Hughes, and Moody (2000) examined the effectiveness of Reading Recovery (RR), an intensive tutorial intervention designed to develop the literacy skills of low-performing first-grade students, as part of a larger meta-analysis of one-to-one tutoring programs in the United States and other countries such as Canada and New Zealand. Based on weighted effect sizes for all students combined, RR was as or more effective than the other interventions included in their review.

Overall results of these meta-analyses suggest that struggling readers and those with disabilities can improve their comprehension, particularly when they are provided with interventions that include explicit comprehension strategy instruction in which students are taught to be active readers who monitor their understanding, self-question, and regulate their reading. Studies that taught students to flexibly use strategies in combination with one another (e.g., monitoring, summarizing, tapping background knowledge, predicting, identifying text structure, questioning) had significant impacts on proximal and distal measures of reading comprehension.

In their review, Wilkinson and Son (2011) noted that it is unclear why teaching students to use strategies enhances comprehension. They contend that two explanations account for the effect: (a) students become more actively engaged when taught to use strategies, and (b) strategies are a tool that enables students to talk about text. However, McKeown, Beck, and Blake (2009) argued that teaching students text content yields greater impacts on comprehension than teaching strategies, suggesting that content knowledge, not strategic knowledge, is essential to comprehension. Wilkinson and Son also noted that strategy instruction is often mechanical and does not reflect the desire for students to flexibly use strategies in a self-regulated manner. Almasi and Hart (2011) suggested that the primary reason is that such mechanical instruction does not focus on readers' agency. That is, instruction tends to focus on what the strategies are rather than on teaching students to become strategic. Wilkinson and Son concluded that teaching students to become strategic is difficult.

Summary and Recommendations

Reading comprehension programs are most successful when they teach children to be active, engaged readers who are able to monitor their comprehension and self-regulate their reading. As part of this process it is essential to provide explicit instruction in which students are taught a set of powerful strategies to use flexibly while reading, including: visualization, summarization, monitoring comprehension, self-questioning, tapping background knowledge, predicting and recognizing narrative and expository text structure. As part of the instruction it is also essential to include an explanation of when, where, and why to use particular strategies.

Findings also suggest that programs focused on word recognition or fluency are not appropriate for enhancing comprehension. Rather, achievement for proficient readers, struggling readers, and readers with learning disabilities is enhanced when students are taught multiple comprehension strategies, given opportunities to employ those strategies, and encouraged to verbalize their thinking related to such strategy use. Such instruction occurs best in small interactive groups in which teachers think aloud and model strategy use for students, provide procedural steps that teach readers how to employ strategies, and reduce processing demands for students.

Many of the meta-analyses showed larger effect sizes on researcher-designed measures than on standardized measures. Larger effect sizes came about because the constructs being measured were more closely aligned to the goals of the program creating a proximal measure of impact. Another dilemma with strategies instruction is

that transferring strategy knowledge from one context to another is difficult. By including instruction that focuses on transferring strategy use to multiple contexts and using more distal measures of reading comprehension, researchers will be able to assess long-term impacts of instruction on student learning. Future research would do well to include both researcher-designed and standardized measures to measure both near and far transfer.

References

Afflerbach, P., Pearson, P. D., & Paris, S. G. (2008). Clarifying the differences between reading skills and strategies. *The Reading Teacher, 61*(5), 364–373.

Almasi, J. F., & Hart, S. (2011). Best practices in comprehension. In L. M. Morrow & L. B. Gambrell (Eds.), *Best practices in literacy instruction* (4th ed. pp. 250–275). New York: Guilford.

Almasi, J. F., Palmer, B. M., Madden, A., & Hart, S. (2011). Interventions to enhance narrative comprehension. In R. Allington & A. McGill-Franzen (Eds.), *Handbook of reading disability research* (pp. 329–344). New York: Routledge.

Edmonds, M. S., Vaughn, S. Wexler, J., Reutebuch, C., Tackett, K. K., & Schnakenberg, J. W. (2009). A synthesis of reading interventions and effects on reading comprehension outcomes for older struggling readers. *Review of Educational Research, 79*(1), 262–300.

Elbaum, B., Vaughn, S., Hughes, M., & Moody, S. (2000). How effective are one-to-one tutoring programs in reading for elementary students at risk for reading failure? A meta-analysis of the intervention research. *Journal of Educational Psychology, 92*(4), 605–619.

Gersten, R., Fuchs, L. S., Williams, J. P., & Baker, S. (2001). Teaching reading comprehension strategies to students with learning disabilities: A review of research. *Review of Educational Research, 71*(2), 279–320.

Guthrie, J. T., McRae, A., & Klauda, S. L. (2007). Contributions of concept-oriented reading instruction to knowledge about interventions for motivations in reading. *Educational Psychologist, 42*(4), 237–250.

Mastropieri, M. A., Scruggs, T. E., Bakken, J. P., & Whedon, C. (1996). Reading comprehension: A synthesis of research in learning disabilities. *Advances in Learning and Behavioral Disabilities, 10B*, 201–227.

McKeown, M. G, Beck, I. L., & Blake, R. G. K. (2009). Rethinking reading comprehension instruction: A comparison of instruction for strategies and content approaches. *Reading Research Quarterly, 44*(3), 218–253.

Pressley, M. (2000). What should comprehension instruction be the instruction of? In M. Kamil, P. B. Mosenthal, P. D. Pearson, & R. Barr (Eds.), *Handbook of Reading Research* (Vol. 3, pp. 545–561). Mahwah, NJ: Erlbaum.

Rosenshine, B., & Meister, C. (1994). Reciprocal teaching: A review of the research. *Review of Educational Research, 64*(4), 479–530. doi: 10.3102/00346543064004479

Sencibaugh, J. M. (2007). Meta-analysis of reading comprehension interventions for students with learning disabilities: Strategies and implications. *Reading Improvement, 44*, 6–22.

Swanson, H. L. (1999). Reading research for students with LD: A meta-analysis of intervention outcomes. *Journal of Learning Disabilities, 32*(6), 504–532.

Swanson, H. L., & Hoskyn, M. (1998). Experimental intervention research on students with learning disabilities: A meta-analysis of treatment outcomes. *Review of Educational Research, 68*(3), 277–321.

Vaughn, S., Gersten, R., & Chard, D. J. (2000). The underlying message in LD intervention research: Findings from research syntheses. *Exceptional Children, 67*(1), 99–114.

Wilkinson, I. A. G., & Son, E. H. (2011). A dialogic turn in research on learning and teaching to comprehend. In M. L. Kamil, P. D. Pearson, E. B. Moje, & P. P. Afflerbach (Eds.), *Handbook of reading research* (Vol. 4, pp. 359–387). New York: Routledge.

7.22

Response to Intervention

The Sum is Greater than Its Parts

PAUL J. RICCOMINI
Pennsylvania State University

GREGORY W. SMITH
Hartwick College

Introduction

Pertaining to the education of students with disabilities, the international trend of Western countries has been influenced by rights-based principles inherent in the reports, declarations, and treaties of the United Nations (UN), the United Nations Educational, Scientific and Cultural Organization (UNESCO), and the Organization for Economic Co-operation and Development (OECD) (O'Brien, Shevlin, O'Keefe, Fitzgerald, Curtis, & Kenny, 2009). By putting into place systems of compensatory education, remedial education, and special education, many countries around the world have responded to the issue of difficulties in learning and achievement (van Kraayenoord, 2010). In the United States, legal mandates allow for the use of response to intervention (RTI) as a way to meet the unique educational needs of students who struggle with the curriculum, and how it is presented. Although there are variations, RTI utilizes four main elements: (a) evidenced based instruction, (b) interventions with increasing levels of intensity, (c) monitoring of academic progress, and (d) a problem-solving approach to determine what to teach and how to teach it (Batsche et al., 2005; Reynolds, Wheldall, & Madelaine, 2009; Riccomini & Smith, 2011). Although RTI is largely a U.S. initiative, components of RTI are evident internationally.

For students with LD, a lack of academic ability in reading and mathematics reflects inefficiencies in intellectual processes that have far-reaching implications across cognitive domains; the need for effective interventions to support such students is paramount (Graham, Bellert, Thomas, & Pegg, 2007; Hughes & Dexter, 2011b). For children experiencing difficulties in learning, early identification is essential for the implementation of a timely and effective intervention (Leung, Lindsay, & Loc, 2007). Historically (and across disciplines), target-setting, progress monitoring, and program evaluation are identified as crucial components for cultivating improvement in student learning outcomes (Davies et al., 1999).

Internationally, the goal to raise educational standards has been guided by explicit policies (Norwich, 2009). In the United States, one such policy is a mandate to implement RTI in public schools in an attempt to facilitate the early identification of students with learning disabilities (LD). Consequently, over 70% of U.S. school districts are implementing RTI (Spectrum K12, 2009) and RTI is gaining attention and interest within the international educational community. However, there remain many unanswered questions and conflicting opinions regarding the overall effectiveness and research support of RTI models for academic achievement and identification of students with learning disabilities (Burns, Appleton, & Stehouwer, 2005; Hughes & Dexter, 2011a).

A typical model of RTI is represented by a multilevel intervention system that increases in intensity across the tiers (Hallahan, Kaufmann, & Pullen, 2009). The primary goal of RTI is twofold: (a) to provide interventions that struggling students require to become successful in the general education curriculum, and (b) if the interventions are not successful, to provide school districts with enough progress monitoring data to make a well-informed decision to either implement different interventions, or initiate a referral for special education eligibility testing (Martinez & Young, 2011). In order for an intervention program to be sustainable, it needs to be cost effective and beneficial to all participants (Dawkins, Ritz, & Louden, 2009). RTI serves as a bridge to link evidenced based practice with a practical and efficient decision making process for determining special education eligibility; by doing so, RTI remains efficient, practical, and sustainable.

Research Evidence

As educational systems struggle with the challenges of educating a rapidly growing student population comprised of varied educational needs, educators seek research-based instructional models and programs. With the growing popularity of RTI (at least in the United States), educators and researchers are looking for evidence to support the overall effectiveness of RTI. We provide a brief overview of research on RTI related to academic achievement and eligibility decisions for students with learning disabilities.

In a review of field studies employing RTI models, Hughes and Dexter (2011a) reviewed and synthesized the findings of 16 studies. The complete review is available from RTI Action Network (www.rtinetwork.com). Broadly speaking, their conclusions are best summarized with their own words: "we characterize the research base for establishing the impact of various models of approaches to RTI as emerging…" (p.10).

Specifically, four main conclusions were ascertained from their review. First, "emerging evidence" from the studies suggests that academic gains are possible within a RTI model; however, this finding is limited in that there are significant concerns regarding the research designs and procedures used. Second, improving mathematics performance through an RTI model has "tentative" support in the research because of the limited number of studies and small sample sizes used. Third, there is "emerging data" that suggest the number of placements in special education can be reduced; however, the studies that demonstrated these findings have limitations with specific aspects of how students who did not respond were identified and procedures used to establish eligibility. Finally, common themes emerged across all 16 studies reviewed regarding the various system factors that are essential to the efficacy of RTI models and included: (a) high quality and continuous professional development, (b) system and building level administrative support, (c) teacher acceptance and adjustment to different instructional roles, (d) full participation of all school staff, and (e) appropriate time for meeting (Hughes & Dexter, 2011a).

In contrast, a meta-analysis conducted by Burns et al. (2005) found the use of RTI models reduced the number of referrals to special education and increased overall reading scores. Interestingly, one of the authors of the meta-analysis (Burns, 2010), cautions against "summative" statements regarding the effectiveness of RTI models given that research is currently continuing to evolve. More specifically, Burns stressed his cautionary point by stating: "because of the nature of RTI as a school wide initiative there are no studies that examine the model in its entirety using a randomized design…" (p. 1).

As the RTI research evolves, a clearer picture of effective and less effective RTI models should become more apparent. Given the conflicting conclusions and limitations of the current research on RTI, it is obvious that much more work with carefully controlled research is warranted to fully examine the many variables involved with the process of response to intervention.

Summary and Recommendations

The process of RTI is the combination of well-established educational practices that together form a systematic and effective approach to improving the instructional programs for all students as well as possibly a more complete manner in which to diagnose students with learning disabilities. Although, largely a U.S. led initiative, the components are grounded in educational practices that occur across international educational systems. Scholars around the world have initiated research to examine RTI and components of RTI. Additional future research, however, is necessary to explicate components of effective RTI.

References

Batsche, G., Elliott, J., Graden, J. L., Grimes, J., Kovaleski, J. F., Prasse, D., … Seege, M. (2005). *Response to intervention policy considerations and implementation.* Reston, VA: National Association of State Directors of Special Education.

Burns, M. K. (2010). Response-to-intervention research: Is the sum of the parts as great as the whole? Retrieved from www.rtinetwork.org/learn/research/response-to-intervention-research-is-the-sum-of-the-parts-as-great-as-the-whole.

Burns, M. K., Appleton, J. J., & Stehouwer, J. D. (2005). Meta-analysis of response-to-intervention research: Examining field-based and research-implemented models. *Journal of Psychoeducational Assessment, 23,* 381–394.

Davies, D. D., Lee, J., Postlethwaite, K., Tarr, J., Thomas, G., & Yee, W. C. (1999). After inspection and special schools: Action planning and making progress. *British Journal of Special Education, 26*(3), 130–135.

Dawkins, S., Ritz, M. E., & Louden, W. (2009). Evaluating the practicability and sustainability of a reading intervention programme, using preservice teachers as trained volunteers. *Australian Journal of Language and Literacy, 32*(2), 136–147.

Graham, L., Bellert, A., Thomas, J., & Pegg, J. (2007). QuickSmart: A basic academic skills intervention for middle school students with learning difficulties. *Journal of Learning Disabilities, 40*(5), 410–419.

Hughes, C. A., & Dexter, D. D. (2011a). Field studies of RTI Programs, Revised. Retrieved from www.rtinetwork.org/learn/research/field-studies-rti-programs.

Hughes, C. A., & Dexter, D. D. (2011b). Response to intervention: A research-based summary. *Theory into Practice, 50,* 4–11.

Hallahan, D. P., Kauffman, J. M., & Pullen, P. C. (2009). *Exceptional learners: An introduction to special education.* Boston, MA: Allyn & Bacon.

Leung, C., Lindsay, G., & Loc, S. K. (2007). Early identification of primary school students with learning difficulties in Hong Kong: The development of a checklist. *European Journal of Special Needs Education, 22*(3), 327–339

Martinez, H., & Young, A. (2011). Response to intervention: How is it practiced and perceived? *International Journal of Special Education, 26*(1), 44–52.

Norwich, B. (2009). Dilemmas of difference and the identification of special educational needs/disability: International perspectives. *British Educational Research Journal, 35*(3), 447–467.

O'Brien, P., Shevlin, M., O'Keefe, M., Fitzgerald, S., Curtis, S., & Kenny, M. (2009). Opening up a whole new world for students with intellectual disabilities within a third level setting. *British Journal of Learning Disabilities, 37*(4), 285–292.

Reynolds, M., Wheldall, K., & Madelaine, A. (2009). The devil is in detail regarding the efficacy of Reading Recovery: A rejoinder to Schwartz,

Hobsbaum, Briggs, and Scull. *International Journal of Disability, Development and Education, 56*(1), 17–35.

Riccomini, P. J., & Smith G. W. (2011). Introduction of response to intervention in mathematics. In R. Gersten & R. Newman-Gonchar (Eds.), *Understanding RTI in mathematics: Proven methods of applications* (pp 1–16). Baltimore, MD: Brookes.

Spectrum K12. (2009). *Response to intervention (RTI) adoption survey 2009*. Towson, MD: Author.

van Kraayenoord, C. E. (2010). Response to intervention: New ways and wariness. *Reading Research Quarterly, 45*(3), 363–376.

7.23

Successful Mathematics Achievement Is Attainable

PATTI BROSNAN AND AARON SCHMIDLIN
The Ohio State University

MELVA R. GRANT
Old Dominion University

Introduction

Success in mathematics achievement is a goal shared by nations worldwide. Understanding how educational systems can best help students to succeed is a central challenge facing education policy makers, school administrators, and teachers today. Herein we will provide readers with research indicating how the early research focused on predictors of successful mathematics achievement and then we will review some of the current and future directions of research related to this topic and provide policy makers with concrete recommendations for improving student mathematics performance. Whereas the data do not allow causal inference, the results of international studies highlight key differences between mathematics education systems that perform well and those that do not. It is hoped that continued examination of these results would serve as a catalyst for conversations amongst educational researchers worldwide as a means to define venues for improving mathematical achievement among learners.

We acknowledge that achievement in mathematics might be interpreted in a variety of ways, drawing from various data sources based on one's own paradigm and stance. For the purpose of this essay, we define mathematical achievement to correspond with the current views suggested by various international organizations. These views include, success in meeting both mastery of basic skills as well as the command of thinking tools and problem-solving skills that assure success in navigating the subject area, including mathematical problem solving, mathematical meaning making depicted through appropriate use of tools when solving novel problems, and the ability to use mathematics in unfamiliar contexts.

Research Findings

Scholars had initially defined predictors of mathematics achievement as those factors that organized students into categories according to sex, race, and socioeconomic status (Gonzales et al, 2008). Accordingly, studies were reported on student success on various measures of achievement according to these criteria. In brief, the difference scores between males and females have decreased dramatically over time, with males having a small gain over females in the highest performing countries. Differences between racial/ethnic groups have shown little improvement with the minority populations scoring lower. Socioeconomic status remains the greatest challenge as the difference scores remained consistently lower for students living in poverty. Over time, other predictors such as background knowledge, immigrant student language development, students with disabilities, parental income and parental education, as well as community type, home background, and motivation were included in studies as a means to expand analysis of factors contributing to mathematics achievement among various groups (Gonzales et al, 2008; Organisation for Economic Co-operation and Development (OECD), 2010a). Collectively, the focus on student characteristics and their influence on achievement did produce results that showed performance gaps among student groups. For instance, disproportionate numbers of poor and racial minority students consistently provided evidence of low performance on high-stakes tests of mathematical competency (National Action Committee for Minorities in Engineering, 1997).

It has been recognized that the reliance on high-stakes testing for making instructional and policy decisions regarding mathematics is not without its limitations. Shepard (2001) reviewed the effects of high-stakes accountability pressures. Her findings contend that these measures mostly focus on mathematics skills resulting in: "(a) inflated test score gains, (b) curriculum distortion, and (c) loss of intrinsic motivation to learn" (p. 1). Given the pressures of high-stakes testing, many teachers feel that they must focus on skills-based mathematics instruction and therefore fail to provide students with access to the quality of learning that expands their capacity to think and problem solve.

Furthermore, Stipek's (1996) research on motivation and instruction in mathematics concludes that when teachers

348

emphasize preparation for high-stakes testing, there is a corresponding decrease in students' intrinsic motivation toward and interest in learning mathematics. When students are faced with this kind of pressure, they become less engaged in learning tasks and are much less likely to persist in solving difficult problems. These data seem to indicate that the way teachers and administrators go about meeting the mathematics achievement standards before them can be determinant in student success.

According to Schoenfeld (2002), meeting the goal of securing higher levels of student achievement in mathematics, education professionals must commit to delivering a high quality curriculum; securing a stable, knowledgeable, and professional teaching community; using high quality assessment that is aligned with curricular goals; and establishing stability and mechanisms for the evolution of curricula, assessment, and professional development. Current research indicates that there is hope for mathematics educators who are seeking to improve their students' performance. Large-scale reform-oriented research projects have shown the ability to diminish gaps in performance experienced by minorities and other underrepresented groups.

Characteristics of High-Achieving Programs. International mathematics assessments indicate that, high performing mathematics education programs include curricula that focus on developing higher order thinking skills, empowered and competent classroom-based professionals, and effective accountability systems that hold schools and administrators responsible for student performance (OECD, 2010b). Under this model, an empowered staff has the freedom to make decisions about mathematics curriculum and instruction and is provided with the support necessary to implement the curriculum effectively (OECD, 2010b).

Senk and Thompson (in press) confirm that a focus on instructional practices that aim to advance students' mathematical thinking, instead of mastery of skills, leads to higher performance on measures of achievement on all levels. Additionally, the data indicate that when mathematics standards, assessment, curriculum, and professional development are appropriately aligned, historically low-performing groups manage to outperform other groups, on all measures of achievement.

Curricula. Educational theorists argue that researchers and policy makers must seek to implement curricula for students that are robust in mathematics content; a pedagogy that is student-centered and challenging; and utilize assessment that is formative and summative. To do so, mathematics educators need to develop a deep knowledge of subject matter, child development, learning theories, curriculum trajectory, and teaching methods (Darling-Hammond, 1999). Decades of research and thought have been directed toward developing successful curriculum for school mathematics.

High performing mathematics education programs empower classroom-based professionals and administrators to make decisions about curriculum and instruction for effective implementation and should serve to inform policy makers and educational leaders seeking to implement successful educational programs (OECD, 2010b). A top-down model of reform and implementation wherein policy makers and educational leaders make all curricular decisions has long proven futile in assuring success in nurturing growth among teachers or students. Consensus exists that grounding teacher growth and development in knowledge about student thinking can result in more effective mathematics practice that, in turn, produces higher student mathematics achievement at all levels (Fennema et al., 1996).

A mathematics instructional model that has shown tremendous promise is the cognitively guided instruction (CGI) program. In various forms, a CGI model operates on the theory that if teachers understand how students think and learn mathematics, they can better predict what their students need and match their instruction accordingly. Research has shown consistently that students in CGI classrooms demonstrated higher level problem-solving abilities and greater recall of number facts, while CGI teachers more often emphasized problem-solving skills, listened to students, and had greater knowledge of students' thinking when compared to control-group students and teachers (Carpenter, Fennema, Peterson, Chiang, & Loef, 1989).

While programs like CGI empower teachers to be more successful in the mathematics classroom, sustained support is needed to effectively navigate demands of student centered curriculum and instruction. International assessments indicate that student mathematics performance can be negatively impacted when teachers are not adequately prepared, supported, or accountable when making curricular decisions for their students (OECD, 2010b). Clearly, any attempt to implement an effective mathematics education program must include staff capable of providing it.

Prerequisite Support for Implementation. International assessment results and their associated inquiries indicate that, high performing mathematics education programs include teaching professionals that are sufficiently supported to implement the curriculum effectively (OECD, 2010b). One characteristic of nations that are high achieving in mathematics is commitment to professional learning for teachers and the research literature supports the effectiveness of these practices. This suggests a connection among opportunities for teacher learning, quality of teaching, and student learning of mathematics. This characteristic focus on supporting teachers should not be surprising. In their systematic review of 1,300 studies on the effectiveness of teachers' in-service professional learning, Yoon and colleagues (Yoon, Duncan, Lee, Scarloss, & Shapley, 2007) analyzed the findings from six studies that offered substantial contact hours of professional learning in mathematics education (ranging from 30 to 100 hours in total) spread out over 6 to 12 months showed a positive and significant effect on student mathematics achievement gains. Across the studies, the levels of professional learning that offered an average of 49 hours in a year boosted student mathematics achievement by approximately 21 percentile points. Thus studies indicate that supporting teachers in their development as professionals is critical to building successful educational programs in mathematics.

While qualitative studies have sought to examine how professional communities in mathematics are formed and how they operate, a number of large-scale studies have illustrated how collaborative, classroom-embedded, professional learning that is focused on student performance has resulted in changed practices and improved student mathematics achievement (Calkins, Guenther, Belfiore, & Lash, 2007; Goddard, Goddard & Tschannen-Moran, 2007).

One strategy that features classroom-embedded professional development is school-based coaching. Coaching models recognize that if professional development is to take root in teachers' practice, ongoing and specific follow-up is necessary to help teachers incorporate new knowledge and skills into mathematics classroom practice (Garet, Porter, Desimone, Birman, & Yoon, 2001; Guskey, 2000).

Summary and Recommendations

Understanding how educational systems can best help students to succeed in mathematics is a central challenge facing education policy makers, school administrators, and teachers today. Older research in the field of mathematics education sought to categorize and track students to understand why certain groups of students were more likely to succeed or fail. International research indicates that this focus on students as the problem may be misguided. As internationally successful mathematics programs continue to show lower differences in student performance than is observed in less successful programs it is becoming clearer that the presence or absence of this gap in student mathematics performance seems to be dependent upon the educational system students happen to find themselves in (OECD, 2010b). This indicates that the problem is not the result of individual student deficiencies but rather the result of deficiencies in the system they attend. Recognizing this possibility is a good first step to improving student mathematics performance in any educational system.

Recommendations, on the basis of international research, suggest that increasing student mathematics achievement cannot be accomplished in the absence of robust educational programs for teacher development. Primarily, in order for our educational systems to be successful in mathematics, teachers need to be able to respond to students' needs. This cannot occur unless teachers are allowed to adjust curriculum in response to the needs of their students; are able to understand student-learning needs; and are provided the time, the peer support, and the classroom-embedded training necessary to perform these functions well. When mathematics teachers are well supported in teaching for understanding and have good curricular materials to use, children really do learn mathematics problem solving skills, and racial and SES differences in performance diminish. Given this, the policy issue that needs to be addressed is

what kinds of systemic support structures will promote the successful implementation of mathematics curricula and their progressive refinement over time?

Further research needs to be conducted into how teachers and students may be assisted in establishing a platform for success in ways that both groups contribute to and benefit from quality mathematics education. While mathematics may be a civil rights issue, clearly educational programs cannot succeed unless they account for the needs of their participants (Schoenfeld, 2002).

References

Calkins, A., Guenther, W., Belfiore, G., & Lash, D. (2007). *The turnaround challenge: Why America's best opportunity to dramatically improve student achievement lies in our worst performing schools*. Boston, MA: Mass Insight Education & Research Institute.

Carpenter, T. P., Fennema, E., Peterson, P. L., Chiang, C. P., & Loef, M. (1989). Using knowledge of children's mathematics thinking in classroom teaching: An experimental study. *American Educational Research Journal, 26*(4), 499–531.

Darling-Hammond, L. (1999). *Teacher quality and student achievement: A review of state policy evidence*. Seattle, WA: Center for the Study of Teaching and Policy, University of Washington.

Fennema, E., Carpenter, T., Franke, M., Levi, L., Jacobs, V., Empson, S. (1996). A longitudinal study of learning to use children's thinking in mathematics instruction. *Journal for Research in Mathematics Education, 27*(4), 403–434.

Garet, M., Porter, A., Desimone, L., Birman, B., & Yoon, K. S. (2001). What makes professional development effective? Results from a national sample of teachers. *American Educational Research Journal, 38*(4), 915–945.

Goddard, Y. L., Goddard, R. D., & Tschannen-Moran, M. (2007). Theoretical and empirical investigation of teacher collaboration for school improvement and student achievement in public elementary schools. *Teachers College Record, 109*(4), 877–896.

Gonzales, P., Williams, T., Jocelyn, L., Roey, S., Kastberg, D., & Brenwald, S. (2008). *Highlights from TIMSS 2007: Mathematics and science achievement of U.S. fourth- and eighth-grade students in an international context*. Jessup, MD: National Center for Education Statistics.

Guskey, T. G. (2000). *Evaluating professional development*. Thousand Oaks, CA: Corwin Press.

National Action Committee for Minorities in Engineering. (1997). *Engineering and affirmative action: Crisis in the making*. New York: Author.

Organisation for Economic Co-operation and Development (OECD). (2010a). PISA 2009 Results: Overcoming social background—Equity in learning opportunities and outcomes (Vol. 2). Retrieved from http://dx.doi.org/10.1787/9789264091504-en

Organisation for Economic Co-operation and Development (OECD). (2010b). PISA 2009 Results: Learning to learn—Student engagement, strategies and practices (Vol. 3). Retrieved from http://dx.doi.org/10.1787/9789264083943-en

Schoenfeld, A. (2002). Making mathematics work for all children: Issues of standards, testing, and equity. *Educational Researcher, 31*(1), 13–25

Senk, S., & Thompson, D. (Eds.). (In press). *Standards-oriented school mathematics curricula: What does the research say about student outcomes?* Mahwah, NJ: Erlbaum.

Shepard, L. (2001). *Protecting learning from the harmful effects of high-stakes testing*. Paper presented at the annual meeting of the American Educational Research Association, Seattle, WA.

Stipek, D. J. (1996). Motivation and instruction. In D. C. Berliner & R. C. Calfee (Eds.), *Handbook of educational psychology* (pp. 85–113). New York: Macmillan.

Yoon, K. S., Duncan, T., Lee, S. W.-Y., Scarloss, B., & Shapley, K. (2007). Reviewing the evidence on how teacher professional development affects student achievement (Issues & Answers Report, REL 2007–No. 033). Retrieved from http://ies.ed.gov/ncee/edlabs/regions/southwest/pdf/REL_2007033.pdf

Section 8

Influences from Teaching Strategies

EDITOR: CHRISTINE RUBIE-DAVIES
University of Auckland

Note: An entry entitled "Cognitive Task Analysis" by Kenneth A. Yates and Richard E. Clark was inadvertently omitted from Section 8 and can be found on the Routledge Website at www.routledge.com/9780415879019.

Yates, K. A., and Clark, R. E. (2012). Cognitive task analysis. In J. Hattie and E. M. Anderman (Eds.), *International guide to student achievement.* New York: Routledge.

8.1

Goal Orientation

ANDREW J. MARTIN
University of Sydney

Introduction

This discussion examines the link between academic goals and academic achievement (operationalized through indices such as course grades, class achievement, standardized test scores, literacy, and numeracy proficiency). Different types of goal constructs have been implemented in psychoeducational research including goal setting, goal orientations, and goal structures (Anderman & Wolters, 2006; Grant & Dweck, 2003; Maehr & Zusho, 2009). Goal orientation generally refers to the reasons *why* students do what they do. Goal setting tends to be concerned with *what* students are aiming for. Goal structures refer to the goal-related messages made salient in the classroom, including motivation climates (Anderman & Wolters, 2006; Maehr & Zusho, 2009). This discussion is focused on the two student-based goal constructs, goal setting and goal orientation, and what evidence says about their links to academic achievement.

The classic (or normative) goal orientation perspective focuses on mastery and performance goals, positing that mastery goals are adaptive for achievement outcomes and performance goals are inimical to achievement. More recent work has suggested a revised or multiple goals perspective that incorporates avoidance and approach dimensions, positing that performance goals can assist learning and achievement and seeking to articulate the conditions and ways this occurs (see Anderman & Wolters, 2006; Elliot, 2005; Maehr & Zusho, 2009; Martin, Marsh, Debus, & Malmberg, 2008 for summaries and reviews).

Mastery orientation is focused on factors and processes such as effort, self-improvement, skill development, learning, and the task at hand. Performance orientation is focused more on demonstrating relative ability, social comparisons, and outperforming others (Martin et al., 2008). When integrated with approach–avoidance dimensions, mastery approach is focused on learning, improving, and understanding; mastery avoidance is focused on avoiding misunderstanding and not being able to learn; performance approach is focused on outperforming others and appearing competent; and, performance avoidance is focused on avoiding appearing incompetent (Elliot, 2005). Thus, there are three salient models: the classic two-goal model (mastery and performance) and the subsequent three-goal (mastery, performance approach, and performance avoidance) and four-goal (mastery approach, mastery avoidance, performance approach, and performance avoidance) models. The two- and three-goal models are the most validated (Maehr & Zusho, 2009) and are the focus of the present discussion.

Research Evidence

The link between mastery orientation and most academic factors and processes is generally quite clear: it is positively related to persistence, interest, choice, effort, self-regulation, and deep processing; it is negatively related to maladaptive factors such as self-handicapping, avoidance, and disengagement (Anderman & Wolters, 2006). In terms of achievement, however, the evidence is mixed, with some research finding no significant connection to achievement (see Anderman & Wolters, 2006 for a summary) and other research suggesting greater effects but under particular conditions such as in experimental settings (Linnenbrink-Garcia, Tyson, & Patall, 2008). Moreover, although correlational analyses show significant associations with achievement (Linnenbrink-Garcia et al., 2008), when prior achievement is taken into account, regression analyses suggest no major role for mastery orientation in achievement outcomes (Church, Elliot, & Gable, 2001).

In explaining these findings, some have suggested it is inappropriate to expect mastery orientation to directly map onto achievement in noteworthy ways because that is not what mastery is about; mastery is about learning, not about normative grading standards and performance (Maehr & Zusho, 2009). Moreover, recent meta-analysis has suggested that the specific content and focus of mastery goals may also be influential in affecting achievement. Hulleman and colleagues (Hulleman, Schrager, Bodmann, & Harackie-wicz, 2010), for example, found that mastery goals with a goal-relevant focus evinced a negative relationship with performance (course grades, exam scores) whereas mastery goals without a goal focus were positively associated with performance.

Other meta-analyses have demonstrated positive achieve-ment effects for mastery goals, but also suggest moderating factors. For example, Utman (1997) found that adaptive effects for mastery goals may be stronger for relatively complex tasks and relatively limited in the achievement of young children. Assessing factors in the three-goal model, meta-analysis by Payne, Youngcourt, and Beaubien (2007) found the strongest effect for mastery goals.

In wrestling with the sometimes inconsistent link be-tween mastery and achievement, it has been recognized that mastery goals may need "something more or different" (Brophy, 2005, p. 172) to more directly and powerfully pre-dict performance outcomes. According to Brophy, this may entail rote learning, drill, deliberate practice, last-minute cramming, and even some shallow processing strategies that are aligned with test conditions and demands. Martin (2006, 2011; Martin & Liem, 2010) has also suggested something more or different in the form of personal best (PB) goals that seek to integrate mastery and performance approach goals, discussed more fully in a subsequent chapter.

Performance Orientation. Particularly in relation to achievement, researchers have emphasized the need to differentiate performance approach and avoidance goals. Performance avoidance goals are quite consistently nega-tively associated with achievement (e.g., Anderman & Wolters, 2006; Elliot, 2005; Maehr & Zusho, 2009; Payne et al., 2007). Interestingly, when considering performance approach goals, research has more consistently (relative to performance avoidance) found positive links to achieve-ment. The extent to which performance approach goals positively link to achievement, however, can depend on the context or the individual. In terms of context, Harackiewicz and colleagues find that in highly competitive circum-stances, performance approach is associated with academic achievement (Harackiewicz, Barron, Pintrich, Elliott, & Thrash, 2002). In terms of individual factors, performance approach goals are associated with achievement for students high in self-efficacy and for students also high in mastery goals (Midgley, Kaplan, & Middleton, 2001).

As noted above, a recent meta-analysis has suggested that the specific content and focus of goals may also be influential in affecting achievement. Hulleman et al. (2010) found that normative performance approach goals (e.g., comparisons with others; outperform others) were positively associated with performance (course grades) whereas performance goals with an appearance or evalua-tive component (e.g., wanting to appear smart) were nega-tively associated with performance. This is consistent with earlier work by Grant and Dweck (2003) who suggested that resolving some of the ongoing controversies in goal

orientation research may require clearly and consistently distinguishing between goals with a comparison component and goals with a content component. Perhaps reflecting the counterbalancing of different performance goal content, Payne et al.'s (2007) meta-analysis found a null relationship between performance approach goals and achievement. Similarly, Utman's (1997) meta-analysis found no compel-ling link between performance approach and achievement, particularly under experimental conditions. Another view suggests that students with a performance approach are more likely to have a history of positive achievement and it is this that is associated with subsequent achievement, not the performance goal (Brophy, 2005).

Brophy (2005) raised other concerns with performance goals. For example, a focus on peer comparisons and competition distracts students from attending to what is needed to achieve on assessment tasks. He also suggested that performance approach goals render the student at risk of shifts to performance avoidance goals (that are known to negatively impact achievement). This shift is more likely when performance approach students do not perform well or are under disproportionate pressure of weighty and difficult schoolwork because then there is a risk that performance avoidance will ensue. For these reasons, Brophy (2005) suggests teachers should abandon performance goals that involve peer comparisons and instead promote performance goals directed to actual achievement.

Summary and Recommendations

Probably the most consistent aspect of achievement effects under goal orientation is the size of the associations. Irre-spective of whether mastery and performance goals do or do not positively or negatively associate with achievement, the effects are generally small, yielding relatively little ex-plained variance in achievement. Specific studies, reviews, and encompassing meta-analyses generally yield absolute correlations of up to approximately $r = .20$ (e.g., see Brophy, 2005; Hulleman et al., 2010; Payne et al., 2007). Hence, although the debate as to the relative advantages and draw-backs of performance orientation in the context of a mastery orientation is ongoing (see Brophy, 2005; Harackiewicz et al., 2002; Kaplan & Middleton, 2002), there can be little vigorous debate as to the overarching aggregate range of ab-solute effects. This is not to dismiss the more powerful role of goal orientations for other valued educational processes and factors (e.g., effort, interest, persistence, valuing), but it is perhaps prudent to have appropriate perspective in relation to actual achievement effects.

Research into the link between goal orientation and achievement has also identified issues relevant to education-al practice. In the main, it appears educational advice would lean toward mastery more than performance approaches. Nevertheless, research has also identified adaptive nuances relevant to each that are of potential use for educators. First, it is important that educators be clear about the effects of goal orientation; for example, as a result of promoting mastery, expecting gains in motivation and engagement is perhaps more feasible than expecting gains in achievement. Second, understanding the role of goal orientation in simple and complex tasks is important. For example, mastery may be more appropriate for complex tasks. Third, there may be a need to alert students to times when nonmastery strategies are needed—such as rote learning, cramming, and drill leading up to a test. Fourth, in terms of performance goals, it is evident that some performance goals are not inimical to performance whereas others that have a heavy evaluative component may be. Fifth, performance goals directed to achievement itself more than the comparative aspects of achievement may have their place. Finally, some recent research has suggested personal growth goals as a possible means of reconciling mastery and performance goals—a subsequent chapter on personal best (PB) goals deals with this. Taken together, a vast volume of research has been conducted in this area and provided considerable insight into the precise nature of goal orientation, its effects, and its implications for educators.

References

Anderman, E. M., & Wolters, C. A. (2006). Goals, values, and affect: Influences on student motivation. In P. A. Alexander & P. Winne (Eds.), *Handbook of educational psychology* (pp. 369–389). Mahwah, NJ: Erlbaum.

Brophy, J. (2005). Goal theorists should move on from performance goals. *Educational Psychologist, 40*, 167–176.

Church, M. A., Elliot, A. J., & Gable, S. L. (2001). Perceptions of classroom environment, achievement goals, and achievement outcomes. *Journal of Educational Psychology, 93*, 43–54.

Elliot, A. J. (2005). A conceptual history of the achievement goal construct. In A. J. Elliot & C. S. Dweck (Eds.), *Handbook of competence and motivation* (pp. 52–72). New York: Guilford.

Grant, H., & Dweck, C. (2003). Clarifying achievement goals and their impact. *Journal of Personality and Social Psychology, 85*, 541–553.

Harackiewicz, J., Barron, K., Pintrich, P., Elliot, A., & Thrash, T. (2002). Revision of achievement goal theory: Necessary and illuminating. *Journal of Educational Psychology, 94*, 638–645.

Hulleman, C. S., Schrager, S. M., Bodmann, S. M., & Harackiewicz, J. M. (2010). A meta-analytic review of achievement goal measures: Different labels for the same constructs or different constructs with similar labels? *Psychological Bulletin, 136*, 422–449.

Kaplan, A., & Middleton, M. (2002). Should childhood be a journey or a race? Response to Harackiewicz et al. (2002). *Journal of Educational Psychology, 94*, 646–648.

Linnenbrink-Garcia, L., Tyson, D. F., & Patall, E. A. (2008). When are achievement goal orientations beneficial for academic achievement? A closer look at moderating factors. *International Review of Social Psychology, 21*, 19–70.

Maehr, M. L., & Zusho, A. (2009). Achievement goal theory: The past, present, and future. In K. R. Wentzel & A. Wigfield (Eds.), *Handbook of motivation at school* (pp. 77–104). New York: Routledge.

Martin, A. J. (2006). Personal bests (PBs): A proposed multidimensional model and empirical analysis. *British Journal of Educational Psychology, 76*, 803–825.

Martin, A. J. (2011). Personal best (PB) approaches to academic development: Implications for motivation and assessment. *Educational Practice and Theory, 33*, 93–99.

Martin, A. J., & Liem, G. A. (2010). Academic personal bests (PBs), engagement, and achievement: A cross-lagged panel analysis. *Learning and Individual Differences, 20*, 265–270.

Martin, A. J., Marsh, H. W., Debus, R. L., & Malmberg, L-E. (2008). Performance and mastery orientation of high school and university/college students: A Rasch perspective. *Educational and Psychological Measurement, 68*, 464–487.

Midgley, C., Kaplan, A., & Middleton, M. (2001). Performance-approach goals: Good for what, for whom, under what circumstances, and at what costs? *Journal of Educational Psychology, 93*, 77–86.

Payne, S. C., Youngcourt, S. S., & Beaubien, J. M. (2007). A meta-analytic examination of the goal orientation nomological net. *Journal of Applied Psychology, 92*, 128–150.

Utman, C. H. (1997). Performance effects of motivational state: A meta-analysis. *Personality and Social Psychology Review, 1*, 170–182.

8.2

Goal Setting and Personal Best Goals

Andrew J. Martin
University of Sydney

Introduction

Goal setting refers to *what* students are aiming for (Anderman & Wolters, 2006; Maehr & Zusho, 2009). Various goal setting models have been developed that seek to articulate the many goals toward which students strive. Ford's (1992) motivational system theory, for example, outlines a taxonomy of 24 content goals: intrapersonal goals comprising affective goals, cognitive goals, and subjective organization goals; and person-environment goals comprising self-assertive social relationship goals, integrative social relationship goals, and task goals. Lemos (1996) has suggested four basic content goals students try to meet: compliance, working, mastery, and evaluation goals. Carver and Scheier (1996) have considered the hierarchical organization of goals with high-level abstract goals at the apex (e.g., universal human goals and values), subsumed by midlevel goals (Ford's and Lemos's goals are good examples), further subsumed by low-level specific goals that are needed to attain the midlevel goals (e.g., to try harder on a particular task, to be more organized in a particular task).

Research Evidence

In drawing together numerous meta-analyses of content goals, Hattie (2009) found an overall effect size of .56 (that typically ranges in meta-analyses between .52 and .82; Locke & Latham, 2002). Interestingly, the size of effects varies as a function of difficulty and importance/commitment. For example, more difficult and challenging goals yielded larger effect sizes (*d* = .66; Hattie, 2009). According to Locke and Latham (2002), difficult goals are more closely connected to achievement because they encapsulate a clearer idea of success and direct attention to the relevant behaviors needed to attain the goal. There is also variability on the nature of difficulty effects, with research suggesting the need for an optimal balance of known to unknown material. For example, as students ac-

quire new skills and knowledge, it seems important to have a high ratio of known to unknown material. In cases where 90% of material is known, there is an effect size of 1.19 for achievement. Where only 50% of material is known, there is an effect size of .49 (Hattie, 2009).

There is also a significant effect of goal commitment on achievement, but this seems to be more the case for special education students (Hattie, 2009). It also seems as though the achievement effects of goal setting level off when the limits of ability are reached or when commitment to the goal lapses (Locke & Latham, 2002). Another factor relevant to goal attainment is the belief that one can attain the goal (Locke & Latham, 2002), with greater self-efficacy associated with goal attainment.

According to Locke and Latham (2002), goal setting affects achievement through a number of functions and mechanisms. First, they have a directive purpose that helps an individual direct attention and effort toward goal-relevant tasks and activities. Second, goals can have an energizing capacity. Third, goals impact persistence. Fourth, goals lead to the task-relevant knowledge and skills required for goal attainment. Finally, goals create a dissonance between current and desired attainment and motivate the individual to reduce that dissonance. Locke and Latham (2002) further articulate a specific model of the goal–achievement link, as follows: (a) specific and difficult goals lead to (b) achievement and this relationship is moderated by (c) goal commitment, goal importance, task complexity, and self-efficacy with these processes all operationalized through (d) specific mechanisms such as persistence, strategies, and effort.

Personal Best (PB) Goals. One of the most recent goal constructs introduced to the psycho-educational literature is that representing "personal best" approaches to schoolwork. Personal best (PB) goals are defined as specific, challenging, competitively self-referenced targets toward which individuals strive. Although typically applied in the sporting domain (Martin, 2006), academic examples include scoring better than on a previous test, spending longer on the current assignment than the previous assignment, or preparing more for a test than one would typically prepare. Sample items in prior research are: "When I do my schoolwork I try to do it better than I've done before"; and "When I do my schoolwork I try to get a better result than I've got before" (Martin, 2006; Martin & Liem, 2010).

Martin (2006, 2011) suggests PB goals may lend clarity to recent debates focused on mastery and performance orientations in achievement contexts. As described above, although evidence demonstrates adaptive properties of mastery and performance goals, there is not always consistency regarding specific effects on achievement. It has been suggested that personal best (PB) goals may represent an adaptive blend of mastery and performance orientations (Martin, 2006, 2011; Martin & Liem, 2010). Specifically, they reflect a mastery orientation because they are self-referenced and self-improvement based and yet hold a sufficient element of performance orientation in that the student is competitive, but with his or her own previous performance. Furthermore, it may be that PB goals are a means by which students coordinate multiple goals in the classroom. Whilst it has been suggested that students can hold both mastery and performance goals (Heyman & Dweck, 1992), there remain questions as to whether they can successfully do so in reality (Brophy, 2005). PB goals may be a way to facilitate students' integration of mastery and performance goals.

Two studies investigating the link between PB goals and academic outcomes are summarized here. The first is a cross-sectional study (Martin, 2006) of 1,016 high school students that validated a model of academic PB goals comprising goals that are specific, challenging, competitively self-referenced, and self-improvement focused. This study also demonstrated the positive yield of PB goals for school engagement, including educational aspirations, enjoyment of school, class participation, and persistence. The second study (Martin & Liem, 2010) is a longitudinal cross-lagged analytic investigation that examined the effects of pursuing PB goals on a wider set of engagement and achievement factors with a larger sample of high school students ($N =$ 1,866). Cross-lagged path models showed that academic PB goals predicted subsequent literacy achievement, numeracy achievement, test effort, enjoyment of school, persistence, class participation, homework completion, educational aspirations, and (negatively) disengagement. This second study was significant not only because it found significant effects of PB goals across time (after controlling for prior variance in the outcome variable) but also because it extended prior research to show PB goals also predict actual achievement.

Summary and Recommendations

In the main, goals are significantly associated with achievement. However, the extent to which this is the case depends on the goal construct, its dimensions, its moderators, and the methodological and analytical rigor with which the association is investigated. Current and promising future directions in relation to achievement appear to be in the area of assessment—and the integration of goal perspectives in achievement assessment. Anderman and colleagues (E. M. Anderman, L. Anderman, Yough, & Gimbert, 2010), for example, have sought to integrate goal theory with growth and value-added models of achievement assessment, arguing that of all the motivation constructs, goal orientation may be the one most closely aligned with value-added approaches to achievement. Indeed, PB goals may represent a goal construct that is even more closely aligned with growth and value-added models of achievement, with their explicit emphasis on personal progress. Along these lines, Martin (2006) described the concept of a Personal Best Index (PBI). The PBI is calculated on the basis of a student matching or exceeding a previous level of performance. Researchers such as Betebenner (2009) have subsequently discussed Student Growth Percentiles (SGPs), that estimate a student's observed growth and compare this with the growth of students with a similar level of prior achievement. Both growth indices (PBI and SGP) can be a basis for students setting achievement targets.

In educational practice aimed at teaching growth-oriented goal setting, educators can encourage students to focus less on comparisons with others, less on competition, and more on individually progressive standards of excellence (Martin, 2011). It has also been suggested that students might be taught how to develop plans for targets that are accessible, clear, specific, self-improvement based, challenging, and competitively self-referenced (Martin, 2006, 2011). There is also advice on the types of goals that are possible. For instance, a student might choose to pursue a "product" goal such as a specific grade or he or she may pursue a "process" goal that comprises effort and skill development (Martin, 2011). Collectively, these are all evidence-based applications of goal research that hold the potential to offer very real and exciting contributions to educational practice, educational assessment, and academic achievement.

References

Anderman, E. M., Anderman, L., Yough, M., & Gimbert, B. (2010). Value-added models of assessment: Implications for motivation and accountability. *Educational Psychologist, 45,* 123–137.

Anderman, E. M., & Wolters, C. A. (2006). Goals, values, and affect: Influences on student motivation. In P. A. Alexander & P. Winne (Eds.), *Handbook of educational psychology* (pp. 369–389). Mahwah, NJ: Erlbaum.

Betebenner, D. (2009). *Growth, standards and accountability.* Dover, NH: Center for Assessment.

Brophy, J. (2005). Goal theorists should move on from performance goals. *Educational Psychologist, 40,* 167–176.

Carver, C. S., & Scheier, M. F. (1996). *Perspectives on personality.* Needham Heights, MA: Allyn & Bacon.

Ford, M. E. (1992). *Motivating humans: Goals, emotions, and personal agency.* Newbury Park, CA: Sage.

Hattie, J. (2009). *Visible learning.* Oxford, England: Routledge.

Heyman, G. D., & Dweck, C. S. (1992). Achievement goals and intrinsic motivation: Their relation and their role in adaptive motivation. *Motivation and Emotion, 16,* 231–247.

Lemos, M. (1996). Students' and teachers' goals in the classroom. *Learning and Instruction, 2,* 151–171.

Locke, E. A., & Latham, G. P. (2002). Building practically useful theory of goal setting and task motivation. *American Psychologist, 57,* 705–717.

Maehr, M. L., & Zusho, A. (2009). Achievement goal theory: The past, present, and future. In K. R. Wentzel & A. Wigfield (Eds.), *Handbook of motivation at school* (pp. 77–104). New York: Routledge.

Martin, A. J. (2006). Personal bests (PBs): A proposed multidimensional model and empirical analysis. *British Journal of Educational Psychology, 76,* 803–825.

Martin, A. J. (2011). Personal best (PB) approaches to academic development: Implications for motivation and assessment. *Educational Practice and Theory, 33,* 93–99.

Martin, A. J., & Liem, G. A. (2010). Academic personal bests (PBs), engagement, and achievement: A cross-lagged panel analysis. *Learning and Individual Differences, 20,* 265–270.

8.3

Keller's Personalized System of Instruction

ERIC J. FOX
FoxyLearning LLC, Las Vegas

Introduction

Keller's personalized system of instruction (PSI)—also called "The Keller Plan," "The Keller Method," or simply the personalized system of instruction—emerged in the 1960s as an alternative to lecture-based college teaching (Keller, 1968). The model was initially developed by Fred S. Keller, J. Gilmour Sherman, Rodolpho Azzi, and Carolina Martuscelli Bori in 1963 while founding the department of psychology at the new University of Brasília, with early implementations also occurring at Columbia University and Arizona State University. PSI is a general course model that emphasizes individualized mastery learning and de-emphasizes the use of group lectures. Its key features include requiring the demonstration of mastery on a unit of instruction before advancing to the next, self-pacing (necessary to accommodate the mastery requirement), the use of lectures for motivational purposes (rather than delivery of course content), an emphasis on the written word and textual materials, and the use of peer proctors for individual tutoring, scoring, and feedback (Keller, 1968). Interest in PSI grew quickly after its introduction, and by 1979 over 3,000 papers, articles, and research reports on PSI had been published and over 5,000 PSI courses were known to be in existence (Sherman, 1982). Although interest in PSI peaked in the 1970s (Buskist, Cush, & DeGrandpre, 1991), adoption and research continued into the 21st century and the system seems to have gained newfound relevance as an attractive model for distance and online education (Grant & Spencer, 2003).

Students in a prototypical PSI course use a study guide and textbook to individually work through small units of material until they feel they are ready to demonstrate mastery. An assessment is then administered and a proctor—usually a student who has already completed the course or an advanced student in the same class—scores it and provides feedback and individual tutoring to the student. If the student meets the mastery criterion for the unit, he or she is free to continue on to the next unit; if not, the student will be required to complete the assessment (or a parallel version thereof) again until mastery is achieved. Students are allowed to complete the assessment as many times as necessary without penalty. This cycle is repeated for each unit of the course, with the student progressing at his or her own pace, until all of the units in the course have been mastered. Other activities such as lectures, demonstrations, and laboratory exercises may be used in the course, but they are not the primary method for delivering course content. Actual implementations of PSI often contain slight variations of the core features, such as using deadlines to reduce student procrastination, completely eliminating lectures, using computers to administer and score assessments, modifying or eliminating the role of the proctor, and modifying the size of the instructional unit (Kulik, Jaksa, & Kulik, 1978).

Research Evidence

Despite the variability in the details of its implementation, PSI has an exceptionally large research base supporting its positive impact on student achievement. In 1992, Sherman estimated that over 2,000 studies on PSI had been conducted, with the vast majority of them demonstrating that students in PSI courses learn the course content better, remember it longer, and like the experience more than students in traditional courses. While research on PSI definitely slowed after the 1970s, mostly due to issues unrelated to student achievement (as will be described later), reports of its implementation and effectiveness continue to emerge (e.g., Chase & Houmanfar, 2009). Most PSI studies focus on student performance on traditional course exams, including both unit exams and comprehensive final exams, while measures of student satisfaction, course completion/withdrawal rates, and student study time are also frequently collected. Given the expansive nature of the PSI literature, it can be useful to summarize the several published reviews and analyses of this literature.

Two of the earliest reviews were published in 1976. Taveggia (1976) examined the results of 14 studies includeing courses from introductory psychology, learning, cultural anthropology, chemistry, electrical engineering, mechanical engineering, and nuclear engineering. In summarizing the impact on average student scores on course exams, the author concluded that PSI "has proven superior to the conventional methods with which it has been compared" (p. 1032). A more extensive review of over 400 PSI studies was published by J. A, Kulik (1976) and found only two reports that favored traditional course formats over PSI. Only 31 of the studies in this review were found to provide systematic and methodologically sound comparisons of PSI to other methods, and in 25 of those studies PSI resulted in significantly higher final exam scores (the remaining six studies found no statistically significant difference between the scores of students in PSI courses and those of students in traditional courses). Kulik also found support for PSI in all six of the studies focusing on retention scores, all four of the studies focusing on transfer effects, and in six of the seven studies focusing on student attitudes about the course.

A meta-analysis of 72 studies comparing PSI to conventional instruction was conducted by J. A. Kulik, Kulik, and Cohen (1979). Focusing only on studies that did not have "crippling" methodological or design flaws, the authors found positive results for PSI on several different outcome measures. Students in PSI courses had final exam scores that were, on average, about 8 percentage points higher than those of students in lecture-based classes (indicating an average effect size of .5). Moreover, this difference increased to 14 percentage points for retention exams administered several months after the end of a course. Final course grades in PSI courses averaged nearly a full letter grade higher (0.8 using a traditional 4.0 grading scale) than final grades in other courses. PSI also outperformed traditional courses in measures of student satisfaction, receiving higher ratings in most studies for overall quality, learning, overall enjoyment, and work load. Course completion rates and estimates of student workload were found to be similar in PSI and conventional classes.

Another meta-analysis of mastery learning programs (C. C. Kulik, Kulik, & Bangert-Drowns, 1990) included a strong emphasis on PSI, with 72 of the 108 studies examined focusing on PSI in college-level courses. Again, PSI was found to have a strong, positive effect on student achievement. Final exam scores were higher for PSI students in 62 of 67 studies, and 69% of these results were statistically significant. On average, PSI improved exam scores by .48 standard deviations, which is a relatively strong effect in education research. The authors of this review noted that "few educational treatments of any sort were consistently associated with achievement effects as large as those produced by mastery teaching" (C. C. Kulik et al., 1990, p.

292). Although this analysis reported a slightly slower completion rate for PSI classes, an analysis of the 29 studies for which data on both course completion and achievement were reported revealed that exam scores were higher in PSI courses regardless of completion rate. Students in PSI courses were also found to spend slightly more time studying, but achievement boosts did not appear to result from increases in study time alone.

Because PSI is a general course model consisting of a "package" of features, a great deal of research has been conducted attempting to determine which of its features are most critical for success (see Fox, 2004; J. A. Kulik et al., 1978; Sherman, Ruskin, & Semb, 1982 for summaries of many of these studies). These component analyses have revealed that features such as unit mastery and the immediate feedback typically provided by peer proctors (but also deliverable via computer) seem key to producing positive results. The use of lectures for "motivational purposes," on the other hand, does not seem to have any clear effect on either student achievement or motivation. One of the most controversial and challenging components of PSI is self-pacing. Most of the research indicates that self-pacing in and of itself does not impact student learning (J. A. Kulik et al., 1978), and there is some evidence that mastery programs that limit self-pacing may actually produce superior achievement (C. C. Kulik et al., 1990). Some degree of self-pacing is required to implement the vital mastery component of PSI, but without constraints it can lead to student procrastination. The research on the value of peer proctoring in PSI (beyond the provision of immediate scoring and feedback) has generated mixed results, but there is a larger body of research on peer tutoring suggesting it can be a very effective instructional technique. To capitalize on the extensive research on the components of PSI and advances in information technology, Fox (2004) suggested that the key features of PSI be updated and redefined as unit mastery, flexible pacing, on-demand course content, immediate feedback, and peer tutoring.

Summary and Recommendations

Despite the strong empirical support and early enthusiasm for PSI, it is not a dominant form of teaching today. Likely reasons for the decline in interest in PSI have been offered by a variety of authors (Buskist et al., 1991; Grant & Spencer, 2003; Sherman, 1992) and include the educational establishment's resistance to change, the time required to develop and manage an effective PSI course, the reporting of ineffective teaching methods inaccurately labeled as "PSI," the difficulty in adapting a self-paced teaching model to a traditional academic calendar, and misunderstandings and misconceptions about PSI in the literature. Some misconceptions, such that PSI is not suitable for teaching higher order thinking skills, seem to persist despite evidence to the contrary (see Crone-Todd & Pear, 2001). Others believe that PSI is only suitable for higher education, where it clearly has had the greatest impact, but it has also proven effective with elementary and secondary students and many other populations (see Sherman et al., 1982).

Educators interested in implementing PSI have the advantage of several decades of research and case studies to guide their efforts (see Fox, 2004). Using this research as a guide, it is recommended that PSI courses include, at the very least, the components that enjoy the most empirical support: unit mastery and immediate feedback. The feedback can be delivered effectively via an automated, computerized system, though some PSI purists might argue that peer tutors should remain involved to enhance the personalization of the student's learning experience. Implementing the unit mastery component requires some degree of self-pacing for students, but it is recommended that measures be taken to prevent procrastination (e.g., awarding bonus points for mastering a unit by a specified deadline or using contingency contracting). Units should be relatively small and appear manageable to students, and it can be helpful to gradually increase the unit difficulty level to help build student confidence early in the course. Unit mastery tests should be well-aligned with the unit learning objectives, be as brief as possible (some students will be taking them multiple times), and be easily scored (either via computerized means or a human proctor). It can be helpful to have several variants of each unit test to reduce cheating and rote memorization by students who require repeated attempts to master the unit. Finally, technology can be used to both greatly expand the range of on-demand materials available to students (we no longer need to rely solely on textual materials to replace ephemeral lectures) and ease the administrative burden of PSI on instructors. A good learning management system, for example, can help you automate the mastery testing process, provide constant access to student grades and records, facilitate tutoring and collaboration among students, and deliver any manner of digital content.

Although we may never know for certain the reasons PSI fell from favor, we can be well-assured that lack of positive impact on student achievement was not one of them. Indeed, it would be difficult to find a teaching method with a stronger research base than PSI. Any educator or researcher looking for a more effective alternative to traditional group lectures is encouraged to consider PSI. Several decades of research provide guidance on how to implement PSI's features most effectively, and the model seems to be a strong foundation on which to build increasingly important online and distance education programs.

References

Buskist, W., Cush, D., & DeGrandpre, R. J. (1991). The life and times of PSI. *Journal of Behavioral Education, 1*(2), 215–234.

Chase, J. A., & Houmanfar, R. (2009). The differential effects of elaborate feedback and basic feedback on student performance in a modified personalized system of instruction course. *Journal of Behavioral Education, 18*, 245–265.

Crone-Todd, D. E., & Pear, J. J. (2001). Application of Bloom's taxonomy to PSI. *Behavior Analyst Today, 3*, 204–210.

Fox, E. J. (2004). The Personalized System of Instruction: A flexible and effective approach to mastery learning. In D. J. Moran & R. W. Malott (Eds.), *Evidence-based educational methods* (pp. 201–221). San Diego, CA: Elsevier Academic Press.

Grant, L. K., & Spencer, R. E. (2003). The personalized system of instruction: Review and applications to distance education. *The International Review of Research in Open and Distance Learning, 4*. Retrieved from http://www.irrodl.org/index.php/irrodl/article/view/152/705

Keller, F. S. (1968). "Goodbye teacher…". *Journal of Applied Behavior Analysis, 1*, 79–89.

Kulik, C. C., Kulik, J. A., & Bangert-Drowns, R. L. (1990). Effectiveness of mastery learning programs: A meta-analysis. *Review of Educational Research, 60*, 265–299.

Kulik, J. A. (1976). PSI: A formative evaluation. In B. A. Green, Jr. (Ed.), *Personalized instruction in higher education: Proceedings of the second national conference* (pp. 140–145). Washington, DC: Center for Personalized Instruction.

Kulik, J. A., Jaksa, P., & Kulik, C. C. (1978). Research on component features of Keller's Personalized System of Instruction. *Journal of Personalized Instruction, 3*(1), 2–14.

Kulik, J. A., Kulik, C. C., & Cohen, P. A. (1979). A meta-analysis of outcome studies of Keller's personalized system of instruction. *American Psychologist, 34*(4), 307–318.

Sherman, J. G. (1982). PSI today. In F. S. Keller & J. G. Sherman (Eds.), *The PSI handbook: Essays on personalized instruction* (pp. 72–78). Lawrence, KS: TRI.

Sherman, J. G. (1992). Reflections on PSI: Good news and bad. *Journal of Applied Behavior Analysis, 25*(1), 59–64.

Sherman, J. G., Ruskin, R. S., & Semb, G. B. (Eds.). (1982). *The Personalized System of Instruction: 48 seminal papers*. Lawrence, KS: TRI.

Taveggia, T. C. (1976). Personalized instruction: A summary of comparative research, 1967–1975. *American Journal of Physics, 44*, 1028–1033.

8.4

Concept Mapping

Joseph D. Novak
Cornell University

Introduction

Concept maps are a knowledge representation tool developed in our research program at Cornell University in the early 1970s (Rowell, 1975). Based on Ausubel's (1963, 1968) assimilation theory for cognitive learning and a constructivist epistemology (Novak, 1977, 1993;Toulmin, 1972), concept maps show a hierarchical arrangement of concepts and propositions as seen in Figure 8.4.1.

Developed initially to observe changes in children's understanding of basic science concepts as they progressed from first through 12th grade, we soon found that concept maps were also a powerful tool to aid meaningful learning in any subject matter domain, from preschool to university

or corporate research teams (Novak, 1998; Novak & Gowin, 1984). With the development (at the Florida Institute for Human and Machine Cognition in the 1990s) of excellent, free software (http://cmap.ihmc.us) for constructing and using concept maps, new opportunities for the use of this tool are being observed all over the world. Concept maps are now being used extensively in corporations and governmental organizations to enhance research efforts, capture and archive expert knowledge, and resolve organizational problems (Moon, Hoffman, Novak, & Cañas, 2011).

The principal problem in most educational settings is that learners engage primarily in rote learning strategies, and thus fail to build deep understanding of basic concepts and to organize their knowledge hierarchically as is charac-

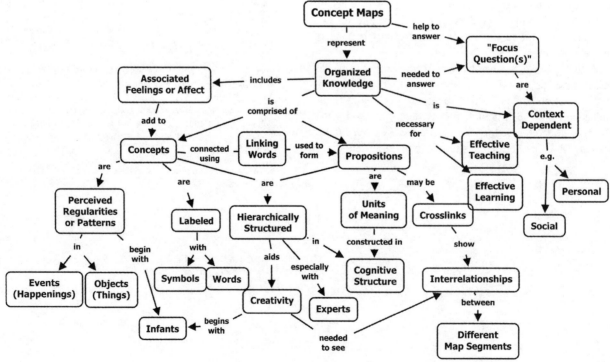

Figure 8.4.1

teristic of experts (Chi, Feltovich, & Glaser, 1981; Novak 2010; Novak & Gowin, 1984). When concept maps are used in instruction and assessment, they require learners to move toward meaningful learning strategies (Mintzes, Wandersee, & Novak, 1998; Nesbit & Adesope, 2006). The use of concept maps also enhances learners' confidence in their learning and leads to enhanced self-concept (Novak, 2010). Concept maps are also useful for identifying student misconceptions and facilitating the remediations of misconceptions (Miller et al., 2009; Novak, 2002.

Research Evidence

Many studies using concept maps as an assessment tool either use a scoring scheme suggested by Novak and Gowin (1984) or some modification of this scheme. Table 8.4.1 presents the criteria suggested, and Figure 8.4.2 illustrates application of this scoring scheme. It was suggested that researchers modify this scheme to place greater emphasis on those aspects of learning most critical in a given study. For example, when Achterberg (1991) evaluated consumer understanding of U.S. Department of Agriculture dietary guidelines they gave extra weight to those concepts that were critical dietary concepts, such as low density and high density cholesterol. These modifications can lead to higher validity and reliability in scoring, with interrater reliabilities exceeding 0.9 (Achterberg, 1991). Although no meta-analyses for assessment were found for what we call concept maps, there are some good reviews of the subject, such as Novak and Wandersee (1990) and Stoddart, Abrams, Gasper, and Canaday (2000).

Issues of validity and reliability must be considered with any evaluation method, and this is certainly true

Table 8.4.1   A Suggested Scoring Scheme for Concept Maps

1   *Propositions.*   Is the meaning relationship between two concepts indicated by the connecting line and linking word(s)? Is the relationship valid? For each meaningful, valid proposition shown, socre 1 point. (See scoring model below.)

2   *Hierarchy.*   Does the map show hierarchy? Is each subordinate concept more specific and less general than the concept drawn above it (in the context of the material being mapped)? Socre 5 points for each valid level of the hierarchy.

3   *Cross links.*   Does the map show meaningful connections between one segment of the concept hierarchy and another segment? Is the relationship shown significant and valid? Score 10 points for each cross link that is both valid and significant and 2 points for each cross link that is valid but does not illustrate a synthesis between sets of related concepts or propositions. Cross links can indicate creative ability and special care should be given to identifying and rewarding its expression. Unique or creative cross links might receive special recongition, or extrat points.

4.   *Examples:*   Specific events or objects that are valid instances of those designated by the concept label can be scored 1 point each. (These are not circled because they are not concepts.)

5.   In addition, a criterion concept map may be constructed, and scored, for the material to be mapped, and the student scores divided by the criterion map score to give a percentage for comparison. (Some students may do better than the criterion and receive more than 100% on this basis.)

Novak &Gowin, 1984, p. 36.

with the use of concept maps. Moreover, learners must have sufficient experience with concept mapping to build some skill in the use of this tool for learning before it can be used reliably and validly for assessment. Some of the poor results reported for achievement using concept maps are more likely a failure to give adequate instruction and practice in the use of this tool prior to its use for assessment. Ruiz-Primo and Shavelson (1996; Ruiz-Primo, Schultz, Li,

Scoring Model

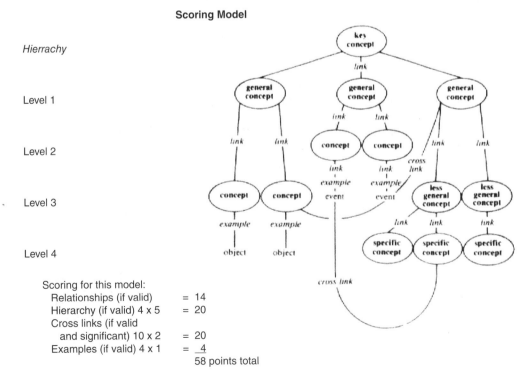

Figure 8.4.2 A concept map scoring scheme suggested by Novak and Gowin (1984, p. 37)

& Shavelson 2001; Ruiz-Primo, Shavelson, Li, & Schultz, 2001) and her colleagues have studied the problem of reliability and validity of concept maps as assessment tools. In general, these and other studies show that concept maps can be both valid and reliable assessment tools (Shavelson & Ruiz-Primo, 2000). However, adding constraints to the kind or size of concept maps produced may increase reliability but reduce validity of concept maps for assessment. Similarly, adding constraints to the kinds of linking words that can be used may increase reliability and possibilities for computer scoring, but substantially reduce validity. The extent of directions provided to students can also affect reliability and validity (Ruiz-Primo, 2010).

Based on the higher cognitive demands with the use of concept maps for assessing the quality of knowledge organization acquired by students, we would expect that correlations with traditional tests would be lower for recall types of items and higher for those questions that require some restructuring or application of knowledge. This has been found to be the case in studies by Hingmanshu and Widera (2010) and Wilson (1993).

Summary and Recommendations

There is increasing interest in assessments that provide data on students' affective response to instruction and assessment. From our earliest work with concept maps, we found that their effect on enhancing meaningful learning provided an additional positive benefit of enhancing student's self-confidence and positive attitudes toward the discipline (Novak & Gown, 1984). While traditional true-false and multiple-choice exam success measures primarily rote or near rote learning and provides some *extrinsic* motivation to learners, use of concept maps in learning and assessment can lead to strong *intrinsic* motivation and a sense of mastery of the subject matter. Studies by Okebukola (1990), Thompson and Mintzes (2002) and Barney, Minzes, and Yen (2005) show that when used in conjunction with appropriate Likert-type questionnaires, concept maps can elicit strong positive affective changes that can have long-term benefits to learners.

Compared with the thousands of studies that have been done on the psychometric characteristics of more traditional tests, research on the use of concept maps for assessment is still in its infancy. Nevertheless, the work that has been done strongly supports the value of concept maps as learning assessment tools.

References

Achterburg, C. (1991). Consumer interpretation of US dietary guidelines. *Proceedings of the Nutritional Society of New Zealand, 16*, 15–30

Ausubel, D. P. (1963). *The psychology of meaningful verbal learning.* New York: Grune & Stratton.

Ausubel, D. P. (1968). *Educational psychology: A cognitive view.* New York: Holt, Rinehart & Winston.

Barney, E. C., Minzes, J. J., & Yen, C-F, (2005). Assessing knowledge,

attitudes and behavior toward charismatic megafauna: The case of Dolphin. *Journal of Environmental Education, 36*(2), 41–53.

Chi, M. T. H., Feltovich, P. J., & Glaser, R. (1991). Categorization and representation of physics knowledge by experts and novices. *Cognitive Science, 5*, 121–152.

Himangshu, S., & Widera, A. C. (2010). Beyond individual classrooms: How valid are concept maps for large scale assessment? In A. Sanchez, A. J. Cañas, & J. D. Novak (Eds.), *Proceedings of the Fourth International Conference on Concept Mapping.* Viña del Mar, Chile. This Proceedings was published by the conference organizers

Miller, K. J. Koury, K. A., Fitzgerald, G. E., Hollingsead, C., Mitchem, K.J., Tsai, H-H., & Park, M. K. (2009). Concept mapping as a research tool to evaluate conceptual change related to instructional methods. *Teacher Education and Special Education, 32*(4), 365–378.

Mintzes, J. J, & Quinn, H. J. (2007). Knowledge restructuring in biology: Testing a punctuated model of conceptual change. *International Journal of Science and Mathematics Education, 5*(2), 281–306.

Mintzes, J. J., Wandersee, J. H., & Novak, J. D. (1998). Teaching science for understanding. San Diego, CA: Academic Press.

Moon, B. M., Hoffman, R. R., Novak, J. D., & Cañas, A. J. (2011). *Applying concept mapping: Capturing, analyzing, and organizing knowledge.* New York: CRC Press.

Novak, J. D. (1977). *A theory of education.* Ithaca, NY: Cornell University Press.

Novak, J. D. (1993). Human constructivism: A unification of psychological and epistemological phenomena in meaning making. *International Journal of Personal Construct Psychology, 6*, 167–193.

Novak, J. D. (1998). *Learning, creating, and using knowledge: Concept maps as facilitative tools in schools and corporations.* Mahwah, NJ: Erlbaum.

Novak, J. D. (2002). Meaningful learning: The essential factor for conceptual change in limited or appropriate propositional hierarchies (LIPHs) leading to empowerment of learners. *Science Education, 86*(4), 548--571

Novak, J. D. (2010). *Learning, creating, and using knowledge: Concept maps as facilitative tools in schools and corporations.* New York: Routledge.

Novak, J. D., & Gowin, D. B. (1984). *Learning how to learn.* New York: Cambridge University Press.

Novak, J. D., & Wandersee, J. H. (1990). Perspectives on concept mapping [Special issue]. *Journal of Research in Science Teaching, 27*(10), 921–1075.

Okebukola, P. A. (1990). Attaining meaningful learning of concepts in genetics and ecology: An examination of the potency of the concept-mapping technique. *Journal of Research in Science Teaching, 27*(5), 493–504.

Rowell, R. M. (1975, March 19). *Children's concept of natural phenomena: Use of concept mapping to describe these concepts.* Paper presented at the NARST annual conventions.

Ruiz-Primo, M. A. (2010). Evaluating concept maps as formative assessment tools. *Proceedings of the Fourth International Conference on Concept Mapping.* J. Sánchez, A. J. Cañas, & J. D. Novak (Eds.). Viña del Mar, Chile.

Ruiz-Primo, M. A., Schultz, S. E., Li, M., & Shavelson, R. J. (2001). Comparison of the reliability and validity of scores from two concept-mapping techniques. *Journal of Research in Science Teaching, 38*, 260–278.

Ruiz-Primo, M. A., & Shavelson, R. J. (1996). Problems and issues in the use of concept maps in science assessment. *Journal of Research in Science Teaching, 33*, 569–600.

Ruiz-Primo, M. A., Shavelson, R. J., Li, M., & Schultz, S. E. (2001). On the validity of cognitive interpretations of scores from alternative concept-mapping techniques. *Educational Assessment, 7*, 99–141.

Shavelson, R. J., & Ruiz-Primo, M. A., (2000). On the psychometrics of assessing science understanding. In J. Mintzes, J. Wandersee, & J. Novak (Eds.), *Assessing science understanding* (pp. 303–341). San Diego, CA: Academic Press.

Stoddart, T., Abrams, R. Gasper, E., & Canaday, D. (2000). Concept maps as assessment in science inquiry learning—A report of methodology. *International Journal of Science Education, 22*(12), 1221–1246.

Thompson, T. L., & Mintzes, J. J. (2002). Cognitive structure and the affective domain: On knowing and feeling in biology. *International Journal of Science Education, 45*(6), 645–660.

Toulmin, S. (1972). *Human understanding: Vol. 1. The collective use and evolution of concepts.* Princeton, NJ: Princeton University Press.

Wilson, J. M. (1993). *The predictive validity of concept-mapping: Relationships to measures of achievement.* Paper presented at Third International Seminar on Misconceptions and Educational Strategies in Science and Mathematics, Ithaca, NY.

8.5

Direct Instruction

GREGORY ARIEF D. LIEM AND ANDREW J. MARTIN
University of Sydney

Introduction

This chapter provides an overview of the yields of direct instruction on academic achievement. Direct instruction (DI), which originated in the work of Engelmann and colleagues in the 1960s, is a systematic model of teaching that focuses on a sequenced and incremental mastery of curriculum-based competence and a capacity to apply generalizable skills to tackle other similar questions/problems (Adams & Engelmann, 1996). DI is implemented through carefully planned lessons in which students are provided with substantial, and yet gradually reduced, guidance (i.e., mediated scaffolding). Key features of DI lie in the clear and explicit teacher-scripted instruction and all students having multiple, and relatively equal, opportunities to respond—more so than the more limited opportunities that a relatively few individual students may have in traditional classes (Adams & Engelmann, 1996). To ensure high-quality instructional interactions for students of all skill levels, DI involves careful and flexible differentiation of students in lessons that are appropriate to their current instructional needs. Hence, DI is appropriate for all students, including those in at-risk groups.

DI is underpinned by basic philosophies and assumptions that all students are teachable and have the potential to improve academically; lower-performing and less advantaged students should be taught at an accelerated pace to catch up with their higher-performing peers; all teachers can be trained to conduct DI; and the implementation of DI has to be controlled and standardized in order to minimize student misinterpretation and maximize instructional effects (Barbash, 2011; Engelmann & Carnine, 1991). As reviewed by Hattie (2009), specific implementation of DI involves seven carefully organized major steps including to: (a) communicate learning goals and orient students to learn; (b) examine if students possess the knowledge and skills needed to understand the new lesson; (c) present key principles of the new lesson through clear instruction; (d) check student

mastery and understanding by posing questions, providing examples, and correcting misconceptions; (e) provide opportunities for guided practice; (f) assess performance and provide feedback on the guided practice; and (g) provide opportunities for independent practice through group or individual work in class or homework. Thus, guided intensive learning, in the forms of deliberate practice and worked examples, is at the heart of DI. As our reviews below suggest, DI is regarded as a highly effective instructional model that brings about significant improvements in student academic achievement and also positive changes in student affective and behavioral outcomes. This review is focused on the DI method and its principal components (e.g., guided practice, worked examples) and what research evidence says about their links to academic achievement. Further information can be found at the National Institute of Direct Instruction website (www.nifdi.org).

Research Evidence

Evidence for the yields of DI on academic achievement is seen in the empirical studies demonstrating the effectiveness of various DI programs relative to other programs. In this line of research, investigators typically compare academic performance of students in a DI program with that of students in control or other intervention groups or measure achievement scores gained by students before and after exposure to a DI program. Evidence for the effectiveness of DI can also be seen in studies showing the yields of various components, strategies, and techniques emphasized in DI practices (e.g., spaced practice, worked examples).

Adams and Engelmann (1996) provided one of the first comprehensive and systematic reports on DI. Their report focused on the implementation of the Project Follow Through, a national project considered to be the largest experimental study conducted in a naturalistic setting involving 72,000 early childhood students over 10 years (1965–1975). The Project aimed to examine the effectiveness of nine major educational approaches, including DI, on a myriad of key educational outcomes. The findings showed that DI was the only program with consistently positive effects (with effect sizes or $d > .25$) on basic skills (e.g., word recognition, spelling, math computation), cognitive skills (e.g., reading comprehension, math problem solving), and affective outcomes (e.g., self-concept, attributions to success). In a follow-up study of participants in the Project, Meyer (1984) showed that, compared to students in non-DI control schools, students in DI schools reported higher rates of graduation and acceptance to college, lower rates of dropping out, and higher ninth-grade scores on reading ($d = 0.43$) and math ($d = 0.28$).

Adams and Engelmann (1996) also reported on meta-analysis based on 37 DI studies. They found DI had large effect sizes for various groups of students, including regular ($d = 1.27$) and special education students ($d = 0.76$), younger ($d = .087$) and older students ($d = 1.50$), and across different academic domains, including reading ($d = 0.69$), social studies ($d = 0.97$), math ($d = 1.11$), spelling ($d = 1.33$), and science ($d = 2.44$). In support of this range of findings, a meta-analysis conducted by Hass (2005) suggested that, compared with other instructional methods (e.g., problem-based teaching), the most effective method of teaching algebra is DI ($d = 0.55$). He attributed this finding to the fact that DI focuses on desired learning outcomes, gradual improvement, appropriate pacing, curriculum-based competence, and mastery for all students. Moreover, a great amount of opportunities for students to practice that are emphasized in DI—both guided and independent practice—seem to be effective in optimizing student mastery of the curriculum. Indeed, as a meta-analysis conducted by Donovan and Radosevich (1998) showed, students in spaced or distributed practice conditions performed better than those in massed practice conditions ($d = 0.46$) because spaced practice provides students with time to reorganize their knowledge (i.e., integrating, adjusting, correcting).

In one of the most ambitious reviews, Borman and colleagues (Borman, Hewes, Overman, & Brown, 2003) conducted a meta-analysis of the effectiveness of 29 school reform programs. They concluded that DI, with an average effect size of $d = 0.21$, is an instructional program with the strongest systematic evidence of effectiveness (based on 49 DI studies and 182 effect sizes)—outperforming all the other programs including Success for All ($d = 0.18$) and School Development Program ($d = 0.15$).

DI has also been found to be effective in optimizing learning and achievement in special education settings. Forness and colleagues (Forness, Kavale, Blum, & Lloyd, 1997) conducted a mega-analysis of prior meta-analyses and demonstrated that DI was the only one of seven intervention programs for special education students with convincing effect sizes for both reading ($d = 0.85$) and math ($d = 0.50$). In a similar vein, a comprehensive analysis of interventions for learning disabled students by Swanson (2000) indicated that whilst an emphasis on DI alone generated a large effect ($d = 0.72$), programs that integrate DI with learning strate-

gies enhancement were even more effective in maximizing student achievement ($d = 0.84$).

In a synthesis of four meta-analyses involving over 42,000 students across 304 DI studies and 597 effects, Hattie (2009) found an average effect size of $d = 0.59$ which ranked 26th out of 138 effects on achievement. He also noted that DI should not be confused with didactic teaching relying on a one-way teacher-directed instruction or transmission teaching characterized by acquisition of knowledge through mere repetition or rote learning. Hattie concluded, "the very successful DI method... and the underlying principles of DI place it among the most successful outcomes" (pp. 204–205).

Ongoing debates (see e.g., Kirschner, Sweller, & Clark, 2006; Mayer, 2004; Tobias & Duffy, 2009) have contrasted the achievement yield of DI and its various procedural components with that of minimally guided instructional approaches, including discovery learning, problem-based learning, and enquiry-based learning. The preponderance of empirical findings apparently points to effectiveness of DI methods relative to the other approaches. A meta-analysis by Alfieri and colleagues (Alfieri, Brooks, Aldrich, & Tenenbaum, 2011), for example, showed that explicit instruction, of which DI is one form, was more beneficial for student achievement than unassisted discovery ($d = 0.38$). They also found that the effectiveness of explicit instruction differed across academic subjects, with a significantly larger average effect size for verbal and social skills ($d = 0.95$) than for problem solving ($d = 0.48$), science ($d = 0.39$), or math ($d = 0.16$). The relative advantage of explicit instruction over unassisted discovery-based instructions was also moderated by age, with the mean effect size for adolescents ($d = 0.53$) significantly greater than that for adults ($d = 0.26$). Furthermore, the benefits of explicit instruction also differed as a function of the outcomes considered, with a mean effect size for acquisition scores ($d = 0.95$) relatively larger than those for posttest scores ($d = 0.35$) and solution time ($d = 0.21$). Interestingly, the specific instructional techniques emphasized in DI also moderated the findings, with participants provided with worked examples ($d = 0.63$), feedback ($d = 0.46$), direct teaching ($d = 0.29$), and explanations ($d = 0.28$) performing better than those in pure discovery groups. These findings are consistent with Hattie's (2009) synthesis suggesting the relatively small achievement effects of problem-based learning ($d = 0.15$) and enquiry-based teaching ($d = 0.31$)—two major forms of minimally guided instruction (see also Kirschner et al., 2006; Mayer, 2004; Tobias & Duffy, 2009).

Considered together, our reviews support the view that instructional methods that allow teachers to be activators of student learning (e.g., reciprocal teaching, explicit instruction, $d = 0.60$; Hattie, 2009) have an overall effect size that is larger than instructional methods in which teachers predominantly serve as facilitators of student learning (e.g., enquiry-based teaching, problem-based learning, $d = 0.17$; Hattie, 2009). This is possible as the intensive guidance provided in DI alleviates cognitive demands and allows working memory and executive functioning to more effectively process the presented information using higher order thinking skills (e.g., reorganizing, inferring, integrating) (see Alfieri et al., 2011; Kirschner et al., 2006). Indeed, the high-level cognitive processing needed to construct knowledge and solve problems can be promoted through intensive guidance emphasized in DI (Mayer, 2004).

Summary and Recommendations

A consistent pattern identified in our reviews points to the effectiveness of Direct Instruction (DI), a specific teaching program, and of specific explicit instructional practices underpinning the program (e.g., guided practice, worked examples) in maximizing student academic achievement. Collectively, studies, reviews, and encompassing meta-analyses (e.g., Borman et al., 2003; Hattie, 2009) show that DI has significantly large effects on achievement. Although these effects may vary as a function of various moderating factors (e.g., academic subjects, types of performance outcome, specific instructional practices, age groups, expertise levels), a bulk of evidence supports the benefits of DI and its key instructional practices relative to minimally guided or unassisted instructions. However, this is not to dismiss the constructivist view of learning—which is often believed to be supported by minimally guided instructions—because DI principles and practices are indeed useful to promote the process of knowledge construction. Importantly, though, it seems constructivist approaches are better assisted by direct and structured input from the teacher that systematically and unambiguously builds the knowledge and skills needed to subsequently engage in meaningful discovery, problem-based, and enquiry-based learning. If we may, the horse must be well and truly before the cart when it comes to effective instruction and learning.

Research evidence into the links between DI and academic achievement has also pointed to relevant educational implications and recommendations. As a general point, teachers can be encouraged to follow DI steps in their lessons. Specifically, this can be done by meeting each of the following conditions and implementing its more specific facilitating strategies. First, teachers ought to ensure that students see that the task to be learned is achievable and manageable. This can be done by stating the lesson goals explicitly, separating the task into smaller subtasks, and communicating optimism to the class. Second, teachers can carefully prepare, plan, and sequence lessons that comprise appropriately scripted/well-thought-through instructions. Third, teachers can look to better ensure student understanding of the lesson by posing questions and

modeling the use of procedures and strategies effective to solve problems. Fourth, teachers can provide students with opportunities to deliberately and purposefully practice the skills and knowledge they are to learn. This can be done by assigning students an adequate amount of assisted practice (e.g., worked examples) and then, allowing for appropriately monitored independent practice (e.g., homework). Fifth, teachers should continually assess student mastery of lessons and subject matter by evaluating how they perform during practice and providing immediate feedback. Finally, direct and explicit remediation is needed when vital skills and knowledge have not been learnt. Taken together, these evidence-based applications of DI research hold important educational implications in optimizing student achievement.

References

Adams, G., & Engelmann, S. (1996). *Research on direct instruction: 25 years beyond DISTAR.* Seattle, WA: Educational Achievement Systems.

Alfieri, L., Brooks, P. J., Aldrich, N. J., & Tenenbaum, H. R. (2011). Does discovery-based instruction enhance learning? *Journal of Educational Psychology, 103,* 1–18.

Barbash, S. (2011). *Clear teaching: With direct instruction, Siegfried Engelmann discovered a better way of teaching.* Arlington, VA: Education Consumers Foundation.

Borman, G. D., Hewes, G. M., Overman, L. T., & Brown, S. (2003). Comprehensive school reform and achievement: A meta-analysis. *Review of Educational Research, 73,* 125–230.

Donovan, J. J., & Radosevich, D. J. (1998). A meta-analytic review of the distribution of practice effect: Now you see it, now you don't. *Journal of Applied Psychology, 84,* 795–805.

Engelmann, S., & Carnine, D. (1991). *Theory of instruction: Principles and applications.* Eugene, OR: ADI Press.

Forness, S. R., Kavale, K. A., Blum, I. M., & Lloyd, J. W. (1997). Mega-analysis of meta-analyses: What works in special education. *Teaching Exceptional Children, 29,* 4–9.

Haas, M. (2005). Teaching methods for secondary algebra: A meta-analysis of findings. *NASSP Bulletin, 89,* 24–46.

Hattie, J. (2009). *Visible learning: A synthesis of over 800 meta-analyses relating to achievement.* New York: Routledge.

Kirschner, P. A., Sweller, J., & Clark, R. E. (2006). Why minimal guidance during instruction does not work: An analysis of the failure of constructivist, discovery, problem-based, experiential, and inquiry-based teaching. *Educational Psychologist, 41,* 75–86.

Mayer, R. E. (2004). Should there be a three-strikes rule against pure discovery learning? The case for guided methods of instruction. *American Psychologist, 59,* 14–19.

Meyer, L. A. (1984). Long-term effects of the Direct Instruction Project follow through. *Elementary School Journal, 84,* 380–394.

Swanson, H. L. (2000). What instruction works for students with learning disabilities? Summarizing the results of a meta-analysis of interventions studies. In R. M. Gersten, E. P. Schiller, & S. Vaughn (Eds.), *Contemporary special education research: Syntheses of the knowledge base on critical instructional issues* (pp. 1–30). Mahwah, NJ: Erlbaum.

Tobias, S., & Duffy, T. M. (Eds.). (2009). *Constructivist instruction: Success of failure?* New York: Routledge.

8.6
Reciprocal Teaching

ANNEMARIE SULLIVAN PALINCSAR
University of Michigan

Introduction

Reciprocal teaching (RT) is an instructional procedure designed to enhance students' reading comprehension. The procedure typically engages teachers and students in a dialogue, the purpose of which is to jointly construct the meaning of the text. The dialogue is supported with the use of four strategies: question generating, summarizing, clarifying, and predicting. When students are initially introduced to RT, the teacher models the application of these strategies for both actively bringing meaning to the text and monitoring one's own thinking and learning from text. Over the course of time, the students assume increased responsibility for leading the dialogues. By focusing on the processes requisite to successful comprehension, RT provides students with tools for learning from text independently.

Reciprocal teaching has a long history; it was Palincsar's dissertation study (1982), conducted in the early 1980s at the Center for the Study of Reading (University of Illinois, Urbana-Champaign), and was the focus of a number of studies by Palincsar and Brown over several decades. In addition, as the references suggest, there have been numerous replications of RT with diverse groups of students.

Research Evidence

The majority of research regarding RT has been conducted in reading and listening comprehension by general, remedial, and special educators. Approximately 300 middle-school students and 400 primary grade students participated in the research conducted by Palincsar and Brown on RT. Designed especially for students who were at-risk for academic difficulty, or who were already identified as remedial or special education students, participants in the research typically scored below the 40th percentile on norm-referenced measures of reading achievement. To evaluate the success of the intervention, criterion-referenced measures of text comprehension were administered as one of several assessments of student learning. These assessments were designed to evaluate students' ability to recall information, draw inferences, identify the gist of the passage, and apply information presented in the text to a novel situation. The criterion level of performance was defined as the ability to score 75% to 85% on four out of five consecutive assessments. Prior to instruction, students typically scored approximately 30% on these criterion-referenced measures of text comprehension (averaging 3 of 10 questions correct). However, at the conclusion of instruction (typically 20 days) approximately 80% of both the primary and middle-school students achieved the criterion level of performance. Furthermore, participants demonstrated maintenance of these gains for up to 6 months to a year following instruction (Palincsar & Brown, 1984, 1988).

Rosenshine and Meister (1994) completed a meta-analysis of 16 studies of RT, conducted with students from age 7 to adulthood, in which RT was compared with: traditional basal reading instruction, explicit instruction in reading comprehension, and reading and answering questions. They determined that when standardized measures were used to assess comprehension, the median effect size, favoring RT, was .32. When experimenter-developed comprehension tests were used, the median effect size was .88. Furthermore, the researchers found no significant relationship between the number of sessions (which ranged from 6 to 25), nor for the size of the instructional group (which ranged from 2 to 23). In addition, reciprocal teaching has been found effective in teaching children with mild disabilities in resource room programs (Marston, 1995) and in inclusion classrooms (Lederer, 2000), with deaf and hard-of-hearing students (Al-Hilawani, 2003), with high school students (Alfassi, 1998; Westera & Moore, 1995), with bilingual students (Padron, 1992), and with English learners in countries other than the United States (Fung, Wilkinson, & Moore, 2002).

The Causal Mechanisms. There are at least two categories of mechanisms: (a) the role of the strategies in promoting comprehension and comprehension monitoring, and (b) the affordances of the participation structure for both the teacher and children .

There are four RT strategies: summarizing, questioning, clarifying, and predicting. When students first begin RT dialogues, they are encouraged to use the strategies with each segment of text; later, as the students become more familiar with the strategies and the purposes for each, the strategies are used opportunistically.

- *Summarizing*: Summarizing engages students in identifying, paraphrasing, and integrating important information in the text. Students ask themselves: "What is the gist of the text? What is the most important information? "Why did the author write this part?" The reader then puts the answers to these questions into their own words.
- *Questioning*: Students can be taught to generate and ask questions about the text at many levels. For example, questions can be raised that recall details in the text; others engage the students in drawing inferences from the text, or in applying information in the text to a novel problem or situation (questions that may or may not have a single, agreed-upon answer).
- *Clarifying*: Clarifying is particularly useful when working with students who may believe that the purpose of reading is merely to correctly identify the words, not necessarily to make sense of them. Clarifying engages students in attending to the many reasons why text may be difficult to understand (e.g., unfamiliar vocabulary, challenging concepts, awkward structure, unclear referent words, idiomatic expressions). Students are taught to be alert to such situations, and most importantly, to take some measures to restore meaning when the text is unclear (e.g., rereading, reading ahead, asking for help).
- *Predicting*: Predicting requires students to hypothesize about what the author might discuss next in the text. There are several approaches that students can take to predicting; one is to think about what one already knows about the topic; another is to attend to text features (e.g., headings, embedded questions), or text structure; that is how the text is organized (e.g., as a chronology, in terms of problems and solutions, or causes and effects.) Students make predictions and then read for the purpose of confirming or disproving their hypotheses.

Using the Strategies in RT Dialogues.

A typical discussion might follow this pattern: The group reads a section of text silently or reading along as someone in the group reads orally (depending upon the decoding skills of the students). The discussion leader (a teacher or student) generates a question to which the other members respond. Other members of the group are invited to ask questions they thought of while reading the text. The leader then summarizes the text and asks the group if they would like to elaborate upon or revise the summary. Necessary clarifications may be discussed throughout the dialogue or all at once. Finally, in preparation for moving on to the next segment of text, the group makes predictions.

In summary, in the context of RT, strategies are being taught in meaningful contexts, that is, while reading extended text, rather than in isolation using artificial tasks (e.g., "underline the main idea"). In addition, students are encouraged to use the strategies flexibly and opportunistically; in other words students learn to use the strategies as opportunities arise in which they will assist comprehension, rather than routinely applying the strategies. Finally, the strategies are taught as a means for enhancing comprehension, rather than as an end in themselves.

The Learning Principles Underlying the Use of RT and How These Relate to the Participant Structure.

Underlying the model of RT is the notion that expert-led social interactions play an important role in learning and can provide a major impetus to cognitive development. This idea, found in the writings of Vygotsky, Dewey, and Piaget, emphasizes the role of guided practice in the context of social interaction as a key to developmental change. Dialogue is a critical element of socially mediated instruction, since it provides the means by which experts provide and adjust support to novice learners, and novice learners have the opportunity to "try out" the use of the tools they are learning about (in this case, the strategies and the dialogue).

Socially mediated instruction is sometimes referred to as scaffolded instruction to the extent that a scaffold provides support that is both temporary and adjustable. In the initial phase of RT, teachers provide considerable support to students as they learn the strategies and their application to understanding text. Scaffolding may take the form of teachers' explaining, modeling through the use of think-aloud, or prompting (e.g., supplying an appropriate interrogative with which to start a question). Over the course of instruction, there is a conscious effort on the part of the teacher to gradually decrease the amount of support provided to students, so that eventually, teachers provide minimal support and act more in the role of coach providing feedback and prompting only as necessary. This approach encourages the teacher to differentiate scaffolding; some students may need more sustained assistance than others.

Metacognitive strategy instruction has also informed RT. Metacognition refers to: (a) the knowledge we have about ourselves as learners, the demands of learning tasks, and the strategies we employ to achieve tasks successfully, and (b) the ability to monitor and regulate learning. Metacognitive knowledge is developmental in nature since it is acquired over time and is influenced by our experiences in the same way that we acquire and use any kind of knowledge. As students participate in RT dialogues, they acquire more awareness about themselves as readers and how they interact with texts that have different demands.

Finally, RT takes into consideration the influence of motivation on student learning and the kinds of attributions that students who have a history of academic difficulty typically make. Students who are anxious and feel helpless in school are inclined to attribute success with a task to "luck," while attributing failure with a task to their own lack of ability. Students making these kinds of attributions need to make connections between engaging in strategic activity and the outcomes of this activity. Reciprocal Teaching enhances motivation by increasing student awareness of the kinds of factors that influence learning outcomes; furthermore, as students become experienced with RT dialogues, they come to appreciate the relationship between their activity as readers and the outcomes of this activity. RT also enhances motivation since students typically enjoy interacting with their peers and collaborating with their teachers.

Summary and Recommendations

Comparative studies have been conducted to determine the essential features of RT. Specifically, the studies were designed to evaluate the role of dialogue in teaching students to be self-regulated learners and to determine whether all four strategies were needed to improve students' comprehension of text. To compare RT with other kinds of instruction that focused on teaching the same set of strategies, not in dialogic manner, students were randomly assigned to one of four conditions; (a) modeling, in which the teacher demonstrated how to use the strategies while reading text and the students observed and responded to the teacher's questions; (b) isolated skills practice, in which students were taught the RT strategies using worksheet activities with extensive teacher feedback regarding their performance; (c) RT/independent practice, in which students were taught RT for only 4 days, followed by 8 days of independently applying the strategies in writing while reading text. Only the traditional RT procedure that incorporated dialogic instruction was effective in bringing about large and reliable changes in student performance (Brown & Palincsar, 1987).

A second comparative study was conducted to determine if all four strategies were needed to improve students' comprehension abilities or whether a subset would suffice. The performance of students who were taught 10 days of reciprocal questioning along, and students who were taught ten days of reciprocal summarizing alone, were compared with 10 days of the traditional RT procedure, in which students were taught all four strategies concurrently. Neither of the individual strategy conditions was as effective as the full set of strategies (Brown & Palincsar, 1987).

The developer has designed a website to support educators and researchers who wish to conduct professional development or research regarding RT: http://edr1.educ. msu.edu/CompStrat/login.asp (Username: demo; Password: demo).

References

Alfassi, M. (1998). Reading for meaning: The efficacy of reciprocal teaching in fostering reading comprehension in high school students in remedial reading classes. *American Educational Research Journal, 35*(2), 309–332.

Al-Hilawani, Y. A. (2003). Clinical examination of three methods of teaching reading comprehension to deaf and hard-of-hearing students: From research to classroom applications. *Journal of Deaf Studies and Deaf Education, 8*(2), 146–156.

Brown, A. L., & Palincsar, A. (1987). Reciprocal teaching of comprehension strategies: A natural history of one program for enhancing learning. In J. Day & J. Borkowski (Eds.), *Intelligence and exceptionality: New directions for theory, assessment, and instructional practices* (pp 81–131). Norwood, NJ: Ablex.

Fung, I. Y. Y., Wilkinson, I. A. G., & Moore, D. W. (2002). L-1-assisted reciprocal teaching to improve ESL students' comprehension of English expository text. *Learning and Instruction, 13*(1), 1–31.

Lederer, J. M. (2000). Reciprocal teaching of social studies in inclusive elementary classrooms. *Journal of Learning Disabilities, 33*(1), 91–106.

Marston, D. (1995). Comparison of reading intervention approaches for students with mild disabilities. *Exceptional Children, 62*(1), 20–37.

Oczkus, L. D. (2003). *Reciprocal teaching at work: Strategies for improving reading comprehension.* Newark, DE: International Reading Association.

Padron, Y. N. (1992). The effect of strategy instruction on bilingual students' cognitive strategy use in reading. *Bilingual Research Journal, 16*(3–4), 35–51.

Palincsar, A. S. (2003). Collaborative approaches to comprehension instruction. In A. S. Sweet & C. E. Snow (Eds.), *Rethinking reading comprehension* (pp. 99–114). New York: Guilford.

Palincsar, A. S., & Brown, A. (1984). Reciprocal teaching of comprehension-fostering and comprehension-monitoring activities. *Cognition and Instruction, 1*(2), 117–175.

Rosenshine, B., & Meister, C. (1994). Reciprocal teaching: A review of the research. *Review of Educational Research, 64*(4), 479–530.

Westera, J., & Moore, D. W. (1995). Reciprocal teaching of reading comprehension in a New Zealand high school. *Psychology in the Schools, 32*(3), 225–232.

8.7

Cooperative, Competitive, and Individualistic Learning Environments

DAVID W. JOHNSON AND ROGER T. JOHNSON
University of Minnesota

Introduction

Learning environments reflect the overall structure of the learning goals, which in turn largely determine the daily routines, the social and emotional atmosphere, and the moment-to-moment interaction among the teacher and students and among the students themselves. There are three ways in which the learning goals may be structured—cooperatively, competitively, and individualistically. *Cooperative learning* is the instructional use of small groups so that students work together to maximize their own and each other's learning. Within cooperative situations, individuals seek outcomes that are beneficial to themselves and beneficial to all other group members. *Competitive learning* is students working against each other to achieve an academic goal such as a grade of "A" that only one or a few students can attain. Within competitive situations, individuals seek outcomes that are beneficial to themselves but detrimental to all other group members. *Individualistic learning* is students working by themselves to accomplish learning goals unrelated to those of the other students. In individualistic situations, individuals seek outcomes that are beneficial to themselves, ignoring as irrelevant those of others. In cooperative and individualistic learning, teachers evaluate student efforts on a criteria-referenced basis, while in competitive learning teachers grade students on a norm-referenced basis. There are limitations on when and where teachers may use competitive and individualistic learning appropriately, teachers may structure any learning task cooperatively in any subject area with any curriculum.

There are three types of cooperative learning: formal cooperative learning, informal cooperative learning, and cooperative base groups (Johnson, Johnson, & Holubec, 2008). *Formal cooperative learning* consists of students working together, for one class period to several weeks, to achieve shared learning goals and complete jointly specific tasks and assignments (such as problem solving, completing a curriculum unit, writing a report, conducting an experiment, or having a dialogue about assigned text material). Any course requirement or assignment may be structured to be cooperative. *Informal cooperative learning* consists of having students work together to achieve a joint learning goal in temporary, ad hoc groups that last from a few minutes to one class period. Students engage in brief dialogues or activities in temporary, ad hoc groups in response to a limited number of questions about what is being learned. *Cooperative base groups* are long-term, heterogeneous cooperative learning groups with stable membership whose primary responsibilities are to provide support, encouragement, and assistance to make academic progress and develop cognitively and socially in healthy ways as well as holding each other accountable for striving to learn.

Cooperative learning has powerful effects on academic achievement. It is directly based on social interdependence theory, there are hundreds of research studies validating its effectiveness, and there are clear operational procedures for educators to use. In this chapter, therefore, the nature of cooperative, competitive, and individualistic learning will be briefly defined, the nature of social interdependent theory will be discussed, and the research demonstrating the impact of cooperative learning on achievement will be presented.

Research Evidence

History of Social Interdependence Theory. Cooperative, competitive, and individualistic learning have their roots in social interdependence theory (Deutsch, 1949, 1962; Johnson & Johnson, 1989, 2005). Theorizing on social interdependence began in the 1900s, in the 1930s, Kurt Koffka (1935) proposed that groups were dynamic wholes in which the interdependence among members could vary. One of his colleagues, Kurt Lewin (1935) refined Koffka's notions from the 1920s and 1930s while stating that (a) the essence of a group is the interdependence among members (created by common goals) which results in the group being a "dynamic whole" so that a change in the state of any member or subgroup changes the state of any other member or subgroup, and (b) an intrinsic state of tension within group members motivates movement toward the accomplishment of the desired common goals. For interdependence to exist there must be more than one person or entity involved, and the persons or entities must have impact on each other in that a change in the state of one causes a change in the state of the others.

In the late 1940s, Morton Deutsch, extended Lewin's reasoning about social interdependence and formulated a theory of cooperation and competition (Deutsch, 1949, 1962). Deutsch conceptualized two types of social interdependence—positive and negative. Deutsch's basic premise was that the type of interdependence structured in a situation determines how individuals interact with each other, which, in turn, largely determines the outcomes. Positive interdependence tends to result in promoting interaction and negative interdependence tends to result in oppositional interaction. No interdependence tends to result in an absence of interaction. The relationship between the type of social interdependence and the interaction pattern it elicits is assumed to be bidirectional: each may cause the other. Deutsch's theory has served as a major conceptual structure for this area of inquiry since 1949.

Essential Elements of Cooperation.

Simply placing students in groups and telling them to work together does not in and of itself create effective cooperation. There are many ways in which group efforts can go wrong (Johnson & F. Johnson, 2009). The barriers to effective cooperative learning are avoided when it is properly structured. Effective cooperative learning is dependent on five basic elements being structured in each cooperative lesson (Johnson, Johnson, & Holubec, 2008). The first and most important element is *Positive interdependence* which exists when group members perceive that they are linked with each other in such a way that one member cannot succeed unless everyone succeeds (Deutsch, 1962). If one fails, all fail. The second essential element of cooperative learning is *individual and group accountability*. The group must be accountable for achieving its goals. Each member must be accountable for contributing his or her share of the work (which ensures that no one "hitch-hikes" on the work of others). The third essential component is *promotive interaction*, which occurs when members share resources and help, support, encourage, and praise each other's efforts to learn. Cooperative learning groups are both an academic support system (every student has someone who is committed to helping him or her learn) and a personal support system (every student has someone who is committed to him or her as a person). The fourth essential element of cooperative learning is teaching students the required *interpersonal and small-group skills*. In cooperative learning groups students are required to learn academic subject matter (taskwork) and also to learn the interpersonal and small-group skills required to function as part of a group (teamwork), such as

leadership, decision making, trust building, communication, and conflict management (Johnson, 2009; Johnson & F. Johnson, 2009). The fifth essential component of cooperative learning is *group processing*, which exists when group members discuss how well they are achieving their goals and maintaining effective working relationships. Groups need to describe what member actions are helpful and unhelpful and make decisions about what behaviors to continue or change.

Social Interdependence and Achievement.

A meta-analysis of all relevant studies found that the average person cooperating performed at about 2/3 a standard deviation above the average person performing within a competitive (effect size = 0.67) or individualistic situation (effect size = 0.64). Individuals from all ability levels achieved higher in cooperative situations than they did in competitive or individualistic situations. In addition, no significant differences were found among studies for (a) published and unpublished studies, (b) size of the group, (c) gender, (d) academic subject area, (e) socioeconomic class of participants, (f) age of subject, (g) sample size, (h) ethnic and cultural background of participants, (i) duration of the study, (j) type of reward (symbolic or tangible), and (k) the setting in which the research took place (i.e., research laboratory or field settings).

An important aspect of school life is engagement in learning. One indication of engagement in learning is time on task. Cooperators spend considerably more time on task than do competitors (effect size = 0.76) or students working individually (effect size = 1.17), and competitors tended to spent more time on task than participants working individualistically (effect size = 0.64). In addition, students working cooperatively tended to be more involved in activities and tasks, attach greater importance to success, and engage in more on-task behavior and less apathetic, off-task, disruptive behaviors. Finally, cooperative experiences, compared with competitive and individualistic ones, have been found to promote more positive attitudes toward the task and the experience of working on the task (effect-sizes = 0.57 and 0.42 respectively). Cooperative experiences promoted more frequent insight into and use of higher-level cognitive and moral reasoning strategies than did competitive (effect size = 0.93) or individualistic efforts (effect size = 0.97). Cooperation also tends to promote more accurate perspective taking than do competitive (effect size = 0.61) or individualistic (effect size = 0.44) efforts.

Another component of achievement is process gain, which occurs when new ideas, solutions, or efforts are generated through group interactions that are not generated when persons work alone. Process gain (as opposed to process loss) and collective induction tend to occur more frequently in cooperative than in competitive or individualistic efforts (Johnson & Johnson, 1989, 2005). Several studies have also examined transfer of learning. *Group-to-individual transfer* occurs when individuals demonstrate mastery of the material studied in a subsequent task done individually. The evidence generally indicates that cooperative efforts result in greater transfer to new tasks than do competitive or individualistic efforts (Johnson & Johnson, 1989, 2005). In other words, group-to-individual transfer tends to be greater than individual-to-individual transfer.

Finally, the more students participated in cooperative learning experiences, and the more cooperatively they perceived their classes, the more they believed that everyone who tried had an equal chance to succeed in class, that students got the grades they deserved, and that the grading system was fair (Johnson & Johnson, 1989, 2005).

Competitiveness and Achievement. There are conditions when competition may be constructive (Johnson & Johnson, 1989, 1999, 2005; Stanne, Johnson, & Johnson, 1999; Tjosvold, Johnson, Johnson, & Sun, 2009). First, negative goal interdependence must exist in the current situation. Second, competition must take place within a cooperative context that clearly specifies the specifics of the competition, including where it is to take place, its boundaries (when it begins and ends), the criteria for winning, the rules of conduct, and the judges. Third, the task should be practicing well-learned skills, reviewing well-learned material, or performing simple, unitary/nondivisible, overlearned activities. Fourth, participants should be homogeneously matched in terms of ability and training. Competitors must believe that they have a reasonable chance of winning and losing. Fifth, participants must be able to audit and monitor progress of competitors to determine who is ahead and who is behind and how much effort needs to be expended to win. Sixth, it should be relatively unimportant whether one wins or loses. Seventh, participants should have the social skills to be good winners and good losers. This means winning with humility, pleasure, and modesty, and being gracious when you lose. Finally, participants should ***not*** overgeneralize the results of the competition. Winning does not make a person more worthwhile and losing does not make a person less worthwhile.

Individualistic Efforts and Productivity. No interdependence typically results in no interaction, which in turn results in relatively reduced productivity and achievement.

There are conditions, however, under which individualistic efforts may be constructive (Johnson & Johnson, 1999). The conditions include when unitary, nondivisible, simple tasks need to be completed; the directions for completing the learning task are clear and specific; the goal is perceived to be important; and individuals expect to be successful in achieving the goals. Individualistic learning may work best when it is part of a larger cooperative lesson.

Summary and Recommendations

The implications of this research are clear. Teachers should structure learning situations cooperatively the majority of the time. Appropriate competitive and individualistic lessons may be used for fun changes of pace and to provide some variety in instructional situations.

References

Deutsch, M. (1949). A theory of cooperation and competition. *Human Relations, 2,* 129–152.

Deutsch, M. (1962). Cooperation and trust: Some theoretical notes. In M. R. Jones (Ed.), *Nebraska symposium on motivation* (pp. 275–319). Lincoln: University of Nebraska Press.

Johnson, D. W. (2009). *Reaching out: Interpersonal effectiveness and self–actualization* (10th ed.). Boston, MA: Allyn & Bacon.

Johnson, D. W., & Johnson, R. (1989). *Cooperation and competition: Theory and research.* Edina, MN: Interaction.

Johnson, D. W., & Johnson, R. (1999). *Learning together and alone: Cooperative, competitive, and individualistic learning* (5th ed.). Boston, MA: Allyn & Bacon.

Johnson, D. W., & Johnson, R. (2005). New developments in social interdependence theory. *Psychology Monographs, 131*(4), 285–358.

Johnson, D. W., & Johnson, F. (2009). *Joining together: Group theory and group skills* (10th ed.). Boston, MA: Allyn & Bacon.

Johnson, D. W., Johnson, R., & Holubec, E. (2008). *Cooperation in the classroom* (7th ed.). Edina, MN: Interaction.

Koffka, K. (1935). *Principles of gestalt psychology.* New York: Harcourt, Brace.

Lewin, K. (1935). *A dynamic theory of personality.* New York: McGraw–Hill.

Stanne, M., Johnson, D. W., & Johnson, R. (1999). Social interdependence and motor performance: A meta–analysis. *Psychological Bulletin, 125*(1), 133–154.

Tjosvold, D., Johnson, D. W., Johnson, R., & Sun, H. (2003). Can interpersonal competition be constructive within organizations? *Journal of Psychology, 137*(1), 63–84.

8.8
Peer Tutoring School-Age Children

DILARA DENIZ CAN
University of Washington

MARIKA GINSBURG-BLOCK
University of Delaware

Introduction

Peer tutoring is a form of peer assisted learning (PAL). In general, PAL can be defined as the acquisition of knowledge and skill through active helping and supporting among status equals or matched companions (Topping, 2001). PAL involves people from similar social groupings who are not professional teachers helping each other to learn and learning themselves by so doing. PAL includes dyadic peer tutoring, peer modeling, peer monitoring, peer assessment, reciprocal peer coaching, small-group cooperative learning interventions, and peer education and counseling (Ginsburg-Block, Rohrbeck, & Fantuzzo, 2006; Slavin, 1995; Topping, 2001).

Specifically, peer tutoring is an instructional strategy that employs peer interaction for the purpose of teaching and learning (Ginsburg-Block, Rohrbeck, & Fantuzzo, 2006; Topping, 2001). Peer tutoring may involve same/ cross-age and same/cross-ability students. Through peer tutoring, peers act as one-on-one teachers, and employ a class of practices and strategies to provide each other with individualized instruction, practice, repetition, and clarification of concepts (Utley & Mortweed, 1997). Peer tutoring facilitates greater engagement, successful practice, and reinforcement of core skills for both the tutor and tutee (Ginsburg-Block, Rohrbeck, & Fantuzzo, 2006; Thurston & Topping, 2007). Peers are defined as individuals of comparable stature, such as school age children, and peer tutoring is characterized by specific role taking as tutor or tutee, with high focus on curriculum content and usually specific procedures for interaction in which participants are trained (Topping, 2001). As students engage each other in the process of learning, every student finds the opportunity to receive individual attention and immediate feedback, which the teacher cannot possibly provide during whole-class instruction. Peer tutoring, therefore, provides the teachers with an excellent strategy for classroom management, and allows the teachers to share the responsibility of instruction with students, resulting in role change from primary deliverer of instruction to facilitator (Slavin, 1995).

The theoretical mechanisms that underlie the peer tutoring research posit that socialization experiences with peers have a powerful influence on student academic motivation and achievement (Ginsburg-Block, Rohrbeck, Lavigne, & Fantuzzo, 2008; Rohrbeck, Ginsburg-Block, Fantuzzo, & Miller, 2003). Social learning opportunities positively affect students' cognition, behavior, and motivation (Ginsburg-Block et al., 2006). Social-interactionist, sociocultural, or social constructivist views provide the theoretical cornerstones of peer assisted learning, in general (Topping, 2001). Supported or scaffolded exploration through social and cognitive interaction with a more experienced peer in relation to a task of a level of difficulty within the tutee's "zone of proximal development" serves as one underlying mechanism for peer assisted learning (Topping & Ehly, 1998; Tymms, Merrell, Thurston, Andor, Topping & Miller, 2011; Vygotsky, 1978). Contemporary achievement motivation theorists (e.g., Ryan & Deci, 2000) suggest that students continually strive to establish self-regulation and mastery of newly learned concepts. Academic environments organized to achieve these goals (e.g., student centered instructional strategies such as peer tutoring) have been linked to positive student achievement as well as affective outcomes (e.g., self-efficacy, motivation).

Research Evidence

Several meta-analyses and reviews of the peer-assisted learning literature have been conducted within the past few decades. For example, Topping and Lindsay (1992) reviewed paired reading interventions from 60 small-scale intervention studies, and reported that paired readers improved three to four times the expected rate in terms of reading accuracy and reading comprehension. A more meta-analytic review of 81 group comparison design studies evaluating peer-assisted learning (PAL) interventions with elementary school students produced positive weighted effect sizes ($d = 0.33$), indicating increases in achievement across content areas (Rohrbeck et al., 2003). PAL strategies outperformed traditional methods with a large effect size of .59 for academic outcomes (Rohrbeck et al., 2003). In this meta-analysis, there were no differences in effects between peer tutoring and small-group procedures such as cooperative learning, with both yielding comparable positive results (Rohrbeck et al., 2003). In a more recent research synthesis in which literature with middle and high school students was reviewed, peer tutoring was reported as effective for special education students in both general and special education settings attending grades 6 through 12 (Okilwa & Shelby, 2010). Each of the 12 studies reviewed implemented peer tutoring in at least one content area (e.g., language arts, math, science, and social studies) and moderate to high effect sizes were reported for the learning of such basic skills (Okilwa & Shelby, 2010).

While an abundance of research evidence suggests that peer tutoring strategies are associated with academic (e.g., reading fluency and comprehension, spelling, math computation) and cognitive gains (Fuchs, Fuchs, & Burish, 2000; Ginsburg-Block, Rohrbeck, Fantuzzo, & Lavigne, 2006), they have been frequently related to nonacademic outcomes, as well. Those include gains in social skills (e.g., improved social interactions, making friends), self-concept, behavior (e.g., being on-task), academic motivation, self-efficacy, and self-esteem (i.e., self-worth and competence) (Ensergueix, 2010; Ginsburg-Block, Rohrbeck, & Fantuzzo, 2006; Ginsburg-Block et al., 2008; Miller, Topping, & Thurston, 2010). In a meta-analysis by Ginsburg-Block, Rohrbeck, and Fantuzzo (2006), 36 studies on PAL (e.g., peer tutoring, peer teaching, small-group learning) were reviewed that examined social, self-concept, and behavioral outcomes of PAL. Consistent with Rohrbeck et al. (2003) results, PAL interventions were reported to be more effective for low-income versus high income, urban versus suburban-rural, minority versus nonminority, and Grades 1 to 3 students versus Grades 4 to 6 students (Ginsburg-Block, Rohrbeck, & Fantuzzo, 2006). Overall, results suggested that PAL interventions that focused on academics also improved social and self-concept outcomes (Ginsburg-Block, Rohrbeck, & Fantuzzo, 2006).

Along with meta-analyses that document the power of peer tutoring as an intervention, the effectiveness of several peer tutoring models has been established through multiple well-controlled experimental research studies such as Classwide Peer Tutoring (CWPT), Peer Assisted Learning Strategies (PALS), and Reciprocal Peer Tutoring (RPT). CWPT engages entire classrooms in peer tutoring, student pairs rotate weekly, and are either assigned randomly or matched by ability (Greenwood, Delquadri, & Hall, 1989). During tutoring, students switch roles, allowing each other to participate in both the tutor and tutee roles. Consistent with CWPT, PALS follows a reciprocal tutoring format in each session, while adding ongoing computerized curriculum-based measurement procedures that provide teachers with information about student performance (Fuchs et al., 2000). RPT employs same-age student pairs of comparable ability, with the primary objective of keeping students engaged in constructive academic activity. Each session involves a 20-minute problem solving session in which students alternate between the role of teacher and student. Implementation of RPT involves preparation, teamwork training, and supervision, all of which involve the participation of the classroom teacher. Such evidence-based models have been successfully applied across content areas, grade levels, and diverse learners (Ginsburg-Block, Rohrbeck, & Fantuzzo, 2006).

While studies have shown peer tutoring strategies to be effective in general for vulnerable groups of students including low-income, minority, urban, English Language Learners, and students with disabilities elementary through adolescent years (Duran, Blanch, Thurston, & Topping, 2010; Scheeler, Macluckie, & Albright, 2010), it is important to note that some peer tutoring strategies may be more effective than others. Several effective components of peer tutoring have been identified. Peer tutoring strategies that allow for the individualization of tasks and evaluation standards according to student performance, that provide opportunities for student autonomy and a structure for peer interactions, and that use interdependent group reward contingencies have yielded significantly better results than strategies lacking these components (Ginsburg-Block, Rohrbeck, & Fantuzzo, 2006; Rohrbeck et al., 2003). Specifically, interventions that used interdependent reward contingencies, ipsative evaluation procedures, and provided students with more autonomy had higher effect sizes (Rohrbeck et al., 2003). In addition, one very important factor that enables efficient collaboration between students is the existence of a climate of trust. The success of peer tutoring interventions is increased by strategies that help create trustful relationships (Ginsburg-Block et al., 2008). For example, group contingencies help achieve trusting relationships between tutors and tutees by fostering collective responsibility for one another (Ginsburg-Block et al., 2008).

Summary and Recommendations

Previous peer tutoring research documents several issues to be mindful of regarding the application of the research conducted in this field to practice (e.g., teacher practices in classrooms, cost-effectiveness, the issue of fairness, etc.). For instance, research-based PAL strategies in the current literature are not widely used by educators (Rohrbeck et al., 2003). In a survey of classroom teachers, although two thirds of teachers used opportunities for weekly student interaction, less than one fifth used the specific empirically supported PAL strategies (Henke, Chen, & Goldman, 1999). It appears that there is lack of continuity between the research literature and teacher practices in the classrooms. Therefore, the question remains how best to develop PAL interventions in collaboration with practitioners to maximize those interventions' use, integrity, and effectiveness (Rohrbeck et al., 2003).

Ecological validity, the degree to which PAL programs reflect teacher and classroom realities, should be considered while designing PAL interventions. Indicators of ecological validity in PAL interventions that have been associated with enhanced intervention effectiveness include intervention integrity, satisfaction, and collaboration between program developers and classroom teachers. For example, in a study by Tymms et al. (2011), in a district-wide study of peer tutoring intervention in which comprehensive teacher training was offered on intervention procedures (e.g., via professional development sessions, delivery of intervention manuals, opportunities for active engagement such as taking part in project evaluation, etc.), a high proportion of the teachers (92.5%) reported that they followed the implementation guidelines of paired reading and math interventions without any problems for most or all of the time. Thus, effective training of teachers and other staff and their active participation in the intervention process help increase the implementation integrity or compliance to intervention techniques. Such indicators are associated with increased likelihood of interventions being adopted by practitioners (Lamb-Parker, Greenfield, Fantuzzo, Clark, & Coolahan, 2000). Among other factors that can be monitored to make peer tutoring interventions more widely used are the arrangement of the intervention intensity and possible inclusion within already established school curricula. Intensive interventions might not be feasible to conduct (e.g., difficult to manage, boring for students, etc.) while lighter interventions (i.e., fewer sessions per week) may be more manageable and enjoyable (Tymms et al., 2011). There is research evidence that when peer tutoring interventions are made part of school curricula (e.g., Success for All, PALS), their implementation may be easier and more feasible (Ginsburg-Block et al., 2008).

In addition, research suggests that organizational condition (i.e., same-age versus cross-age peer tutoring) as well as the role played (i.e., acting as the tutor, tutee, or both) are important factors while designing dyadic peer tutoring interventions. For example, in a study by Tymms et al. (2011) cross-age peer tutoring positively enhanced cognitive attainment for reading and math in two differently aged cohorts for both tutors and tutees. In a study by Miller et al. (2010), the experimental group of 10- to 11-year-old children who participated in a randomized trial of paired reading over 15 weeks demonstrated higher levels of self-esteem (i.e., improved beliefs about competence) in both same-age and cross-age conditions following the intervention; however, gains in self-worth were only reported for older children who tutored younger children, and not in the same-age group. Such new information might have significance for schools interested in designing peer tutoring interventions.

In summary, overall benefits of peer tutoring include superiority to traditional models, effectiveness in promoting academic as well as affective outcomes such as self-efficacy and self-motivation, effectiveness with vulnerable student populations, and versatility and cost-effectiveness. While designing peer tutoring interventions, it is recommended to (a) include practitioner perspectives, (b) carefully determine tutor/tutee roles and age categorizations,(c) establish trust between the tutors and tutees, (d) successfully monitor the intensity and duration of interventions, (e) make the interventions part of the school curricula if feasible, and (f) include the participants (e.g., teachers, parents, etc.) in the evaluation process. Incorporating these procedures will likely increase the use of evidence-based peer tutoring strategies in classrooms and ultimately student achievement.

References

Duran, D., Blanch, S., Thurston, A., & Topping, K. (2010). Online reciprocal peer tutoring for the improvement of linguistic abilities in Spanish and English. *Journal for the Study of* Education *and Development, 33,* 209–222.

Ensergueix, P. J. (2010). Reciprocal peer tutoring in a physical education setting: Influence of peer tutoring training and gender on motor performance and self-efficacy outcomes. *European Journal of Psychology of Education, 25,* 222–242.

Fuchs, D., Fuchs, L. S., & Burish, P. (2000). Peer–assisted learning strategies: An evidence-based practice to promote reading achievement. *Learning Disabilities Research & Practice, 15,* 85–91.

Ginsburg-Block, M., Rohrbeck, C., & Fantuzzo, J. W. (2006). A meta-analytic review of social, self–concept, and behavioral outcomes of peer assisted learning. *Journal of Educational Psychology, 98,* 732–749.

Ginsburg-Block, M., Rohrbeck, C., Fantuzzo, J. W., & Lavigne, N. C. (2006). Peer assisted learning strategies. In G. Bear & K. Minke (Eds.), *Children's needs: Vol. 3. Understanding and addressing the developmental needs of children* (pp. 631–645). Bethesda, MD: National Association of School Psychologists.

Ginsburg-Block, M., Rohrbeck, C., & Lavigne, N., & Fantuzzo, J. W. (2008). Peer assisted learning: An academic strategy for enhancing motivation among diverse students. In A. E. Gottfried & C. Hudley (Eds.), *Academic motivation and the culture of school in childhood and adolescence* (pp. 247–273). New York: Oxford University Press.

Greenwood, C. R., Delquadri, J. C., & Hall, R. V. (1989). Longitudinal effects of class wide peer tutoring. *Journal of Educational Psychology, 81,* 371–383.

Henke, R. R., Chen, X., & Goldman, G. (1999). *What happens in classrooms? Instructional practices in elementary and secondary schools, 1994–1995.* Washington, DC: U.S. Department of Education, National Center for Education Statistics.

Lamb-Parker, F., Greenfield, D. B., Fantuzzo, J. W., Clark, C., & Coolahan, K. C. (2000). Shared decision making in early childhood research: A foundation for successful community–university partnerships. *NHSA Dialog, 3,* 234–257.

Miller, D. Topping, K., & Thurston, A. (2010). Peer tutoring in reading: The effects of role and organization on two dimensions of self-esteem. *British Journal of Educational Psychology, 80,* 417–433.

Okilwa, N. S., & Shelby, L. (2010). The effects of peer tutoring on academic performance of students with disabilities in grades 6 through 12: A synthesis of the literature. *Remedial and Special Education, 31,* 450–463.

Rohrbeck, C., Ginsburg-Block, M., Fantuzzo, J., & Miller, T. (2003). Peer assisted learning interventions with elementary school students: A meta-analytic review. *Journal of Educational Psychology, 95*(2), 240–257.

Ryan, R. M., & Deci, E. L. (2000). Self-determination theory and the facilitation of intrinsic motivation, social development, and well–being. *American Psychologist, 55,* 68–78.

Scheeler, M. C., Macluckie, M., & Albright, K. (2010). Effects of immediate feedback delivered by peer tutors on the oral presentation skills of adolescents with learning disabilities. *Remedial and Special Education, 31,* 77–86.

Slavin, S. E. (1995). *Cooperative learning: Theory, research, and practice.* Needham Heights, MA: Allyn & Bacon.

Thurston, A., & Topping, K. J. (2007). Peer tutoring in schools: Cognitive models and organizational typography. *Journal of Cognitive Education and Psychology, 6,* 356–372.

Topping, K. J. (2001). *Peer assisted learning: A practical guide for teachers.* Cambridge, MA: Brookline Books.

Topping, K. J., & Ehly, S. (Eds.). (1998). *Peer assisted learning.* Mahwah, NJ: Erlbaum.Topping, K. J., & Lindsay, G. A. (1992). Paired reading: A review of the literature. *Research Papers in Education, 7,* 199–246.

Topping, K. J., & Lindsay, G. A. (1992). Paired reading: A review of the literature. *Research Papers in Education, 7,* 199–246.

Tymms, P., Merrell, C., Thurston, A., Andor, J., Topping, K., & Miller, D. (2011). Improving attainment across a whole district: School reform through peer tutoring in a randomized controlled trial. *School Effectiveness and School Improvement, 22,* 265–289.

Utley, C. A., & Mortweet, S. L. (1997). Peer–mediated instruction and interventions. *Focus on Exceptional Children, 29,* 1–23.

Vygotsky, L. S. (1978). *Mind in society: The development of higher psychological processes.* Cambridge, MA: MIT Press.

8.9

Problem Solving

R. Taconis
Eindhoven School of Education

Introduction

Problem solving is "any goal-directed sequence of cognitive operations" (Anderson, 1980, p. 257). Problems may vary in a multitude of dimensions such as: familiarity, complexity, being open or closed, the amount of information available, and the type of cognitive activities required (or useful) to solve the problem (Jonassen, 2000; Taconis, Ferguson-Hessler, & Broekkamp, 2001). Problems may be ill-defined or well-defined: Ill-defined problems may consist of just a rough and incomplete description or may even require that the problem is extracted from a context by the problem solver.

It is important to note that the term *problem* in many cases is relative. A situation may be a problem to one person in the sense that it requires a goal directed sequence of cognitive operations, but may be immediately apparent to an expert. It strongly depends on the distance between the knowledge, skills, and metacognition required to solve the problem, and the problem solver's resources. Moreover, different kinds of problems may require different mental resources (Jonassen, 2000). Solving a problem typically is a complex, demanding, and lengthy process (Sweller & van Merriënboer, 2005), and thus persistent effort may be needed to keep all necessary cognitive resources available, and high levels of concentration and confidence. This is particularly so when faced with a large scale, ill-defined, complex problem, without others providing much cognitive emotional support.

Research Evidence

Teaching students adequate cognitive strategies and bringing them to use these in a systematic way in order to solve school problems, turns out to be quite difficult. A large number of researchers who have focused on problem solving have a background in cognitive psychology. They usually focus on fundamental and general aspects of problem solving often employing problems of a general nature. This has led to a range of general theoretical approaches such as: the gestalt approach (Duncker), the behaviorist approach (Skinner), the cultural-historical approach (Vygotsky), and cognitive psychological approaches (Simon, Newell). Much attention has been paid to the process of problem solving, its (desired) sequencing, problem solving strategies, and heuristics for solving problems. Besides this, a large group of researchers have investigated problem solving from a domain-bound perspective. Often the way experts solve problems is investigated and compared to the approach taken by novices in order to find ways to facilitate or teach expertlike behavior (Chi, Glaser, & Farr, 1988).

More recently, cognitive research, brain research, artificial intelligence, and computer modeling have contributed insight into problem solving. The cognitive load approach employs aspects of information processing theory and emphasizes the inherent limitations of working memory. Individuals differ in cognitive processing capacity, and instructional designers may need to limit cognitive load, as overload makes problems difficult to solve, and ineffective for the acquisition of knowledge and understanding (Sweller, 1988).

Cognitive Outline: Skills Base and Knowledge Base. Obviously, problem solving activities need to be practiced before the student becomes fluent and makes few errors. Practice strengthens both the structure of the so-called skills base, and leads to automation. However, school subjects such as physics, mathematics, or geography are semantically rich domains meaning that the performance of cognitive strategies strongly depends on the domain knowledge and the understanding of these domains. Therefore, it seems just as necessary to work on the perfection of the knowledge and understanding of the domain as on the problem solving skills.

Both skills and knowledge range from general to specific. Some may be general (such as reading skills, or general knowledge of what determines valid arguments); others may be more generic (such as the need for proof in mathematics, or knowledge of science words) or even specific to a small class of problems (such as skills in solving differential equations, or knowledge of Einstein's general relativity). Successful problem solving in semantically rich domains requires both skills (the ability to perform) and an adequate knowledge base (knowing what, when, and how) (Taconis et al., 2001). For example, analyzing a problem (skill) can only be performed in a semantically rich domain when one has knowledge of what to look for and what information to discard. Since problem solving implies a complex and prolonged effort involving the coordinated use of a variety of cognitive activities, problem solving also requires strategic knowledge (knowledge of the approaches that could be fruitful in a particular situation), as well as metacognitive (regulative) abilities.

Analyzing the scarce evidence in a quantitative meta-study comparing the actual learning results on science (school) problem solving obtained in a range of empirical studies (1980–1996), Taconis et al. (2001, p. 43) asked the question: "Which learning activities contribute to the learning of science problem solving?" They focused on three characteristics of the treatments: (a) the learning tasks and its relation to the task of problem solving (same, akin, different, only a specific part of the problem solving process); (b) the type of knowledge focused on; and (c) the learning conditions. The problems involved in this study were of varying complexity, from various science domains, and required different types of cognitive activities.

Effects on Cognitive Factors.   Treatments concentrating on problem solving strategy without giving attention to the knowledge used in the solution, tended to have little or no learning effect. When parallel attention was given to the quality of the knowledge base, however, the effect increased. Treatments focusing on the quality of the knowledge base of the subjects were the most effective. This conclusion appears to be valid for school problems of varying complexity, requiring either problem solving skills or skills in formulation and testing of hypotheses (Taconis et al., 2001). Tasks that strengthen the knowledge base (e.g., help the construction of adequate schemata) contribute to the mastery of problem solving more effectively. Examples of such tasks include: eliciting information, removing misconceptions, qualitative analysis, assessing possible solutions, categorizing problems, concept mapping (Nesbit & Adesope, 2006), and particularly powerful is studying worked examples or explaining worked examples to other students (Sweller, 2006).

Learning Conditions.   Learning conditions include immediate feedback to the learners and external guidelines on *what to do* and explicit criteria for *what to reach*. Having students work in small groups does not improve problem solving education unless the group work is combined with other measures that have been shown to be effective, such as attention for schema construction, external guidelines, and immediate feedback. Group work may even show a significantly negative effect, and it may be that collaborative learning is only beneficial for very complex tasks. Among the don'ts of problem solving education are: focusing too much on isolated aspects of problem solving or phases within the problem solving process, denying guidance, criteria, or feedback to students, particularly in unstructured group work.

Metacognition, Self-Regulation, and Epistemological Beliefs.   Both aspects of metacognition are clearly important in problem solving: that is, metacognitive knowledge and awareness (e.g., insight into the progress being made, a view of the difficulties ahead related to the resources available, and criteria for an adequate and complete solution), as well as metacognitive control (the ability to adapt plans if necessary) (Shin, Jonassen & McGee, 2003). Lesh and Zawojewski (2007) conclude that the way metacognitive skills steer mathematical problem solving, for example, depends on the phase of the problem solving process. Pajares (1996), however, finds that self-regulation has no direct effect on mathematical problem solving, but has an indirect effect through self-efficacy only. Thus it is important that students need opportunities to experience successes in solving problems, both to learn from and to build up a self-efficacy high enough to energetically and effectively encounter new challenges. In the background to self-regulation, epistemological beliefs are active. For example, inadequate personal beliefs, such as that problem solving ability in science is a gift, it cannot be learned, may hinder the acquisition of problem solving achievement.

Motivational and Emotional Factors.   Theories on problem solving have not always emphasized the role of motivation (Mayer, 1998 p. 56). Given that problem solving is often a long and demanding process it may be that interest, motivation, and self-efficacy will be critically important when solving problems.

Task Perception, Task Valuing, and Interest.   Students learn more meaningfully when they are interested, when they consider a problem as meaningful, worth solving, will engage more completely/deeply in solving it, and can mobilize their cognitive resources more effectively (Jonassen, 2000).

Cultural Issues and Beliefs.   Processes like problem solving are interwoven with various aspects of cultures (Nisbett, Peng, Choi, & Norenzayan 2001). One's cultural heritage may emphasize particular problem solving approaches (Guss & Wiley, 2007) that may or may not line up with Western modern science. What if, for instance, the idea of individually isolating a problem in order to subsequently solve it analytically is alien from a student's (indigenous) cultural background? Cultural issues may hinder collaboration in teams, asking for help, or may comprise (epistemological) beliefs contrasting with those enclosed in the school problems that are usually embedded in the culture of Western modern science.

Summary and Recommendations

Optimizing students' achievement in problem solving should aim at a balanced mix of various factors. It can be fostered most effectively if the teacher:

- Ensures that there is enough understanding *before* demanding that students solve (difficult) problems, thus fostering self-efficacy and preventing cognitive overload.
- Programs exercises aimed at building an adequate knowledge base, such as concept mapping and studying worked examples.
- Uses problems that are interesting, worthwhile, and manageable in the eyes of the students, and that match their individual cognitive resources. Since students differ in their cognitive capacities, style, and preferences, this points in the direction of an adaptive, individual approach in which the problems are tuned to the actual competence of the students.
- Variation in problems (their types and their presentation) will probably help learning.
- Provides ample social and emotional support, adequate guidelines on what to do, and criteria for the result (what to aim at).
- Gives instructions (and feedback) that focuses on knowledge and understanding *as well as* on the strategies, skills, the self-regulation necessary for problem solving.
- Has a keen eye for individual and cultural differences between students.

Adaptive computer training programs using problems perceived as relevant and manageable by the learner could be a practical approach. It could be the medium for delivering a variety of learning tasks, worked problems, and exercise problems that focus on strengthening the knowledge base and thinking skills. Guidelines and immediate feedback could be implemented to create an adequate learning environment for science problem solving.

References

Anderson, J. R. (1980). *Cognitive psychology and its implications*. New York: Freeman.

Chi, M. T. H., Glaser R., & Farr, M. J. (Eds.). (1988). *The nature of expertise*. Hillsdale, NJ: Erlbaum.

Guss, C. D., & Wiley, B. (2007). Meta cognition of problem solving strategies in Brazil, India, and the United States. *Journal of Cognition and Culture, 7*, 1–25.

Jonassen, D. H. (2000). Toward a design theory of problem solving. *Educational Technology Research and Development, 48*(4), 63–85.

Lesh, R., & Zawojewski, J. (2007). Problem solving and modeling. In F. K. Lester (Ed.), *Second handbook of research on mathematics teaching and learning* (pp. 763–804). Reston, VA: National Council of Teachers of Mathematics

Mayer, R. E. (1998). Cognitive, meta-cognitive, and motivational aspects of problem solving. *Instructional Science, 26*, 49–63.

Nesbit, J. C., & Adesope, O. O. (2006). Learning with concept and knowledge maps: A meta-analysis. *Review of Educational Research, 76*, 413–448.

Nisbett, R. E., Peng, K., Choi, I., & Norenzayan, A. (2001). Culture and systems of thought: Holistic versus analytic cognition. *Psychological Review, 108*(2), 291–310.

Pajares, F. (1996). Self-efficacy beliefs and mathematical problem-solving of gifted students. *Contemporary Educational Psychology, 21*, 325–344.

Shin, N., Jonassen, H. D., & McGee, S. (2003). Predictors of well-structured and ill-structured problem solving in an astronomy simulation. *Journal of Research in Science Teaching, 40*(1), 6–33.

Sweller, J., (1988). Cognitive load during problem solving: Effects on learning. *Cognitive Science, 12*, 257–285.

Sweller, J. (2006). The worked example effect and human cognition. *Learning and Instruction, 16*(2), 165–169.

Sweller, J., & van Merriënboer, J. J. G. (2005). Cognitive load theory and complex learning: Recent developments and future directions. *Educational Psychology Review, 17*(2), 147–177.

Taconis, R., Ferguson-Hessler, M. G. M., & Broekkamp, H. (2001). Teaching science problem solving: An overview of experimental work. *Journal of Research in Science Education, 38*, 442–468.

8.10

Problem-Based Learning

David Gijbels
University of Antwerp

Piet Van den Bossche
University of Antwerp and Maastricht University

Sofie Loyens
Erasmus University, Rotterdam

Introduction

Originally developed for medical training in Canada at Mc-Master University, the orthodox version of problem-based learning (PBL) has been modified and applied globally in many disciplines. Many curricula or parts thereof are modelled on the basis of problem-based learning. Nowadays, PBL can be considered as "one of the few curriculum-wide educational innovations surviving since the sixties" (Schmidt, van der Molen, te Winkel, & Wijnen, 2009, p. 2). In the literature, PBL has been defined and described in different ways. Based on the original method as developed at McMaster University, Barrows (1996) described six core characteristics of PBL. The first characteristic is that learning needs to be student-centred. Second, learning has to occur in small student groups under the guidance of a tutor. The third characteristic refers to the tutor as a facilitator or guide. Fourth, authentic problems are primarily encountered in the learning sequence, before any preparation or study has occurred. Fifth, the problems are used as a trigger for students' prior knowledge, which leads to the discovery of knowledge gaps. Finally, these knowledge gaps are overcome through self-directed learning.

The aim of schools and colleges implementing PBL is to educate students so that they are able to understand and solve complex problems in a changing world (Gijbels, Dochy, Van den Bossche, & Segers, 2005). Therefore, if one ponders the implementation of PBL, a major question is: Do students, using PBL, reach these goals in a more effective way than students who receive conventional instruction? Albanese and Mitchell (1993, p. 56) pose this question as follows: "Stated bluntly, if problem-based learning is simply another route to achieving the same product, why bother with the expense and effort of undertaking a painful curriculum revision?" The interest in this question has produced, until now at least, nine systematic reviews of the effects of problem-based learning. Three of these were published in the same year and in the same journal (Albanese & Mitchell, 1993; Berkson, 1993; Vernon & Blake, 1993). Colliver (2000) and Smits, Verbeek, and Buisonjé (2002) undertook a systematic review, each from a different point of view. Dochy, Segers, Van den Bossche, and Gijbels (2003) and Gijbels et al. (2005) looked to students' achievement in problem-based learning and how the effects of PBL are moderated. Walker and Leary (2009) have built on the latter two meta-analyses in a more recent systematic review on problem-based learning in which they looked at differences across problem types, disciplines, and assessment models. Finally, Schmidt and colleagues (2009) have performed a meta-analysis on the effects of a single, medical PBL curriculum in the Netherlands.

Research Evidence

The review by Albanese and Mitchell (1993) is probably the most widely known. The core question in this review, "What are the effects of problem-based learning?" is investigated by means of five subquestions: (a) What are the costs compared with lecture-based instruction? (b) Do PBL-students develop the cognitive scaffolding necessary to easily assimilate new basic sciences information? (c) To what extent are PBL students exposed to an adequate range of content? (d) Do PBL students become overly dependent on a small-group environment? (e) Do faculty dislike PBL because of the concentrated time commitment required? The study categorises and lists the qualitative results of studies in medical education from 1972 to 1993. The results are presented in a review that reports effect sizes and *p*-values with the institutions as the units of analysis. The main results from this review are that PBL is more nurturing and enjoyable and that PBL graduates perform as well, and sometimes better, on clinical examinations and faculty evaluations than students in more conventional instruction. However, PBL students score lower on basic science examinations and view themselves as less well prepared in the basic sciences in comparison to their conventionally trained counterparts. Further, PBL-graduates tend to engage in backward reasoning rather than the forward reasoning experts engage in. Finally, the costs of PBL are high when class sizes are larger than 100.

At the same time, Vernon and Blake (1993) synthesised all available research from 1970 through 1992 comparing PBL with more conventional methods of medical education. Five separate statistical meta-analyses resulted in the following main results: PBL was found to be significantly superior with respect to students' attitudes and opinions about their programs and measures of students' clinical performance. Contrary to the previous reviews findings, the results of PBL students did not significantly differ from conventionally taught students on miscellaneous tests of factual knowledge and tests of clinical knowledge. However, students from conventional education performed significantly better than their PBL counterparts on the National Board of Medical Examiners (NBME), a standardized test administered to medical students in the United States.

Berkson (1993) also searched for evidence of the effectiveness of PBL in the medical PBL literature up until1992. Six topics on the effectiveness of PBL compared to conventional curricula underlie this narrative meta-analysis in the medical domain: problem solving, the imparting of knowledge, students' motivation to learn medical science, the promotion of self-directed learning skills, student and faculty satisfaction, and the financial costs. The results showed no distinction between graduates from PBL and conventional instruction, but found PBL can be stressful for both students and faculty and a PBL curriculum may be unreasonably expensive. Subsequently, Colliver (2000) questioned the educational superiority of PBL relative to standard approaches. Colliver focused on the credibility of the claims about the ties between PBL and educational outcomes and the magnitude of the effects. He conducted a review of medical education literature, starting with the three reviews published in 1993 and moving on to research published from 1992 through 1998 in the primary sources for research in medical education. For each study, a summary was written, which included the study design, outcomes measures, effect sizes, as well as further information relevant to the research conclusion. Colliver concluded that there was no convincing evidence that PBL improves the student's knowledge base and clinical performance, at least not of the magnitude that would be expected given the resources required for a PBL curriculum. Nevertheless, PBL may provide a more challenging, motivating, and enjoyable approach to medical education.

A later review by Smits et al. (2002) is limited to the effectiveness of PBL in continuing medical education. This review only included controlled evaluation studies in continuing medical education from 1974 to 2000. In short, Smits and colleagues concluded that there was limited evidence for PBL to increase participants' knowledge, performance, and patients' health. However, there was only moderate evidence that doctors were more satisfied with PBL.

The review by Dochy et al. (2003) was the first review searching for studies beyond the domain of medical education. The main question was similar, but much more itemised than the other reviews: What are the main effects of PBL on students' knowledge and knowledge application and what are the potential moderators of the effect of PBL? The results of this meta-analysis suggested that PBL has statistically and practically significant positive effects on students' knowledge application. The effects of PBL on students' knowledge base tended to be negative. However, this effect was found to be strongly influenced by outliers and the moderator analysis suggested that students in a PBL environment can rely on a more structured knowledge-base.

In order to further investigate the moderating effect of the method of assessment on the effects of PBL, a second meta-analysis was set up (Gijbels et al., 2005). In this meta-analysis, the influence of assessment was the main independent variable. The goal of this study was to describe the effects of PBL from the angle of the underlying focal constructs being measured with the assessment. Using Sugrue's model (1995) as a frame of reference, the research questions were: What are the effects of PBL when the assessment of its main goals focuses on respectively (a) the understanding of concepts, (b) the understanding of the principles that link concepts, and (c) the linking of concepts and principles to conditions and procedures for application? In order to be congruent with its educational goals and resulting instructional principles and practices, the assessment of the application of knowledge when working with authentic problems is at the heart of the matter in PBL. Therefore, it was expected that students in PBL would perform better at the third level when compared to students in more traditional learning environments. The results of the meta-analysis showed a difference in the reported effects of PBL between each of the three levels. However, contrary to expectations that the effects of PBL would be larger when the method of assessment was more capable of evaluating complex levels, the effect size for the third level of the knowledge structure was smaller compared to the effect size of the second level and not statistically significant. Moreover, in only 8 of the 40 studies included in the meta-analysis was the assessment focused at the third level. Most studies (N = 31) assessed at the level of understanding of concepts. PBL had the most positive effects when focal constructs being assessed were at the second level, understanding the principles that link concepts. These results imply an implicit challenge for PBL to pay more attention to the third level of the knowledge structure, both during the learning activities that take place and students' assessment.

A meta-analysis by Walker and Leary (2009) builds upon the studies by Dochy et al. (2003) and Gijbels et al. (2005). They performed a meta-analysis that crossed disciplines as well as categorized the types of problems used, the PBL approach employed, and the level of assessment. Across 82 studies and 201 outcomes, their findings favored PBL ($d = 0.13$) with sufficient heterogeneity to that warrants a closer examination of moderating factors.

Finally, Schmidt and colleagues (2009) conducted a meta-analysis of curricular comparisons, using a single, PBL medical school in the Netherlands. This school was compared with traditional medical schools in the Netherlands. Medical knowledge was one of the outcome variables in this meta-analysis and was measured by medical students' scores on the so-called progress test consisting of 200 to 300 questions dealing with medicine as a whole. The overall weighted effect size averaged over the 90 comparisons involving the PBL curriculum under study and various Dutch medical schools was equal to $d = .07$. This implies a small, positive effect.

Summary and Recommendations

Considering the numerous reviews of research on PBL, we can concur with the two tendencies that have been noted earlier by Strobel and Van Barneveld (2009, p. 53): The first is that traditional learning approaches tended to produce better outcomes on assessment of basic science knowledge; however, this was not always the case. A second trend noted was that a PBL approach tended to produce better outcomes for clinical knowledge and skills. This suggests that PBL fosters an accessible and connected knowledge base.

We would like to highlight that, although PBL is implemented in a large variety of disciplines, the research evidence discussed above is almost exclusively based on research in medical education because other research is not available or does not meet the quality criteria that are used in meta-analyses. Future research on the effects of PBL should therefore take a cross-disciplinary focus. Another important finding is that the more recent meta-analyses point to the important role of several mediating variables such as the type of problem tasks or the level of assessment in explaining the effects of PBL. When implementing or investigating PBL much more attention needs to be paid to these conditions under which the effects of PBL can be maximised in a wide range of disciplines.

References

Albanese, M. A., & Mitchell, S. (1993). Problem-based learning: A review of literature on its outcomes and implementation issues. *Academic Medicine, 68,* 52–81.

Barrows, H. S. (1996). Problem-based learning in medicine and beyond. In L. Wilkerson & W. H. Gijselaers (Eds.), *Bringing problem-based learning to higher education: Theory and practice* (pp. 3–13) (New Directions for Teaching and Learning, No. 68). San Francisco, CA: Jossey-Bass.

Berkson, L. (1993). Problem-based learning: Have the expectations been met? *Academic Medicine, 68*(10), S79–S88.

Colliver, J. A. (2000). Effectiveness of problem-based learning curricula: Research and theory. *Academic Medicine, 75*(3), 259–266.

Dochy, F., Segers, M., Van den Bossche, P., & Gijbels, D. (2003). Effects of problem-based learning: A meta-analysis. *Learning and Instruction, 13,* 533–568.

Gijbels, D., Dochy, F, Van den Bossche, P., & Segers, M. (2005). Effects of problem-based learning: A meta-analysis from the angle of assessment. *Review of Educational Research, 75*(1), 27–61.

Schmidt, H. G., Van der Molen, H. T., te Winkel, W. W. R., & Wijnen, W. H. F. W (2009). Constructivist, problem-based learning does work: A meta-analysis of curricular comparisons involving a single medical school. *Educational Psychologist, 44,* 1–23.

Smits, P. B. A., Verbeek, J. H. A. M., & De Buisonje, C. D. (2002). Problem based learning in continuing medical education: A review of controlled evaluation studies. *British Medical Journal, 321,* 153–156

Strobel, J., & Van Barneveld, A. (2009). When is PBL more effective? A meta-synthesis of meta-analyses comparing PBL to conventional classrooms. *The Interdisciplinary Journal of Problem-Based Learning, 3,* 44–58.

Sugrue, B. (1995). A theory-based framework for assessing domain-specific problem solving ability. *Educational Measurement: Issues and Practice 14*(3), 29–36.

Vernon, D. T. A., & Blake, R. L. (1993). Does problem-based learning work? A meta-analysis of evaluative research. *Academic Medicine, 68,* 550–563.

Walker, A., & Leary, H. (2009). A problem based learning meta-analysis: Differences across problem types, implementation types, disciplines, and assessment levels. Interdisciplinary *Journal of Problem-Based Learning, 3*(1), 12–43.

8.11

The Search for the Key for Individualised Instruction

Catherine Scott
Research Cairn Millar Institute

Introduction

Interest in individual differences has had a long history in educational psychology. From early days researchers sought the personal attribute(s) that would explain variations in educational attainment: to many the most obvious candidate was intelligence. Variations in measured intelligence (IQ) were regarded as significant not only for how much children could learn but how they should be taught. During the 1960s and 1970s this belief led to the search for the correct educational treatment (teaching methods) for children with differing levels of IQ. The expectation was that educational outcomes would be dependent on aptitude-treatment interactions (ATI); that is, the interplay between differing levels of ability and specific teaching methods. At the time this enterprise was regarded as particularly important for the education of students with below normal IQ; currently, tailoring teaching to ability is found mostly in discussions of education for those categorized as gifted and talented.

Despite a couple of decades of investigations and experimentation ATI were found to be a theoretical and practical dead end. As Bracht (1970, p. 627) noted: "Although there is an increasing interest in the topic of ATI among educational psychologists, very little empirical evidence has been provided to support the concept". Glass (1970, p. 210) proposed that he knew of no other statement that has been confirmed so many times by so many people. A few years later Cronbach and Snow (1977, p. 6) also observed that well-substantiated findings regarding ATI are scarce. More recently, meta-analyses by Hattie (2009) demonstrated that individualising instruction is, at best, an inefficient strategy for increasing student attainment (mean effect size for all interventions = .40; effect size for individualising instruction = .23).

Research Evidence

When One Intelligence Is Not Enough: Multiple Intelligences and Learning Styles. In the 1980s not only ATI fell from favour: The notion of intelligence as measured by an IQ test also fell into disrepute in many quarters. Standard IQ measurement was regarded as doing no justice to the considerable variety of human abilities and talents. Theories that claimed to better capture these became increasingly popular, particularly Gardner's theory of multiple intelligences (MI; 1983) and assorted theories of learning styles.

Neither, however, has proven to be either a sound theory of human ability or a firm basis for designing effective instruction. Even MI's founder, Gardner, admits that empirical evidence in support of it is lacking. As Waterhouse (2006) observes:

> To date there have been no published studies that offer evidence of the validity of the multiple intelligences. In 1994 Sternberg reported finding no empirical studies. In 2000 Allix reported finding no empirical validating studies, and at that time Gardner and Connell conceded that there was "little hard evidence for MI theory" (2000, p. 292). In 2004 Sternberg and Grigerenko stated that there were no validating studies for multiple intelligences, and in 2004 Gardner asserted that he would be "delighted were such evidence to accrue" (p. 214), and he admitted that "MI theory has few enthusiasts among psychometricians or others of a traditional psychological background" because they require "psychometric or experimental evidence that allows one to prove the existence of the several intelligences" (2004, p. 214). (p. 208)

Learning Styles. Learning styles as a concept is widely endorsed and has become the basis for a new theory about the necessity and efficacy of tailoring teaching to individual attributes, in this case, student's learning style. While the term *learning style* has commonsense appeal, investigating the field reveals that it is characterised by considerable conceptual confusion and the lack of any generally accepted definition of what these styles may be. As Cassidy notes (2004, p, 440): "there exist almost as many definitions as there are theorists in the area". A multitude of models exists, vying for prominence in a very crowded field. Coffield, Moseley, Hall, and Ecclestone (2004) reported finding 71 different theories of learning style in current circulation in the UK. Models are also based on a dizzying variety of perceptual, cognitive, and physiological factors, including preferring to work alone or in groups, in the evening in the morning, when the temperature is high or low, while eating or otherwise, and so on. Not surprisingly, in his overview of learning styles theory, Cassidy (2004) describes the field as "fragmented and disparate" (p. 419).

A few prominent examples of theories in current use include Kolb's (1984) four-way typology (converger, diverger, assimilator, accommodator); Mills's (2002) four-way typology, based on the work of Gregorc (1984) (concrete sequential, abstract random, abstract sequential, concrete random), and the Felder and Silverman's (1988) four-dimensional model. In Australian schools the most popular models are those that derive from Fleming's VARK theory (2009), which divides learners into originally four but now most commonly three groups: visual, auditory, or tactile/kinaesthetic. One is tempted to note that these categories are reassuringly concrete, unlike the others already mentioned, and apparently discernible by simply observing children.

Attempts to discover commonality across the many models are rare, but the results of those that are conducted lead to the conclusion that they are not accessing the same constructs. Ferrell (1983) performed factor analytic studies on four commonly used instruments: the Grasha-Riechmann Student Learning Style Scales, Kolb Learning Styles Inventory, Dunn Learning Style Inventory, and Johnson Decision Making Inventory and concluded that "the instruments were clearly not measuring the same thing" (p. 33). To speak of learning styles is thus to attempt to shoehorn a mix of theories and models into one category in which they do not fit. Those who promote the concept speak as if there is but one, accepted model: theirs, one assumes. In such a context even if empirical evidence for the effectiveness of basing pedagogy on one discrete model of learning styles could be found this cannot be said to provide proof of the efficacy of learning styles as they are currently conceived.

Scanning the literature also demonstrates that learning styles are frequently conflated with other ways of categorising human mental function; for example, personality typologies and cognitive styles. As an example, Ford and Chen (2001) claimed to have found support for matching learning style to teaching method; however, the construct they used, field dependence/independence, is commonly regarded as a measure of cognitive style; that is, a person's habitual way of perceiving, thinking, and remembering.

It would be surprising if so conceptually confused a field

generated measurement instruments with good psychometric properties. Investigations of the properties of a variety of scales have revealed that even the most widely used are inadequate in this regard. Garner (2000) noted, of the studies of the psychometric properties of Kolb's Learning Styles Inventory published from the 1970s through to the late 1990s, "results indicated that test retest measurements for the LSI did not reliably assess the learning styles of any learners" (p. 346). Duff and Duffy (2002) investigated Honey and Mumford's Learning Style Questionnaire (LSQ), Kolb's Learning Style Inventory (LSI), and a later refined version (LSI-1985) and reported that:

> Exploratory and confirmatory factor analysis failed to support the existence of the two bipolar dimensions proposed by Kolb, and four learning styles hypothesised by Honey and Mumford. An item analysis and pruning exercise failed to raise the internal consistency reliability to a satisfactory level, or provide adequate model fit to the data. The results of a structural equation model finds no consistent relationship between scores on the four learning style scales, two bipolar dimensions and academic performance. (p. 147)

Kappe, Boekholt, den Rooyen, and Van der Flier (2009) conducted a study of the predictive validity and reliability of the Learning Styles Questionnaire with a sample of Dutch students. They reported that:

> Although learning styles were matched to correspondingly suitable learning criteria, the LSQ revealed no predictive validity, however we can report good test–retest reliabilities over a two year time period. Given the lack of positive findings, using the LSQ to stimulate learning in college students is debatable. (p.464)

Coffield et al. (2004) investigated the 13 most popular learning styles models and concluded that these models, their measurement, and application have little offer as guides for the design of instruction. The authors noted the considerable conceptual difficulties in the field and continuing issues with the reliability and validity of existing measurement instruments. They also commented that even within the one model the diagnosis of a learner's style can depend on which instrument is used, which makes organising teaching around the results problematic, even if there were evidence for the effectiveness of this strategy.

Most recently Hattie (2009), in his compendium of meta-analyses of studies of effects on student learning, has meta-analysed results from 411 studies on learning styles and found that many were characterised by conceptual confusion (frequently conflating learning styles with learning strategies, for example) and significant measurement and methodological flaws. He sums up the evidence thus:

> The argument defended in this chapter is that successful learning is a function of the worthwhileness and clarity of the learning intentions, the specifications, and the success criteria; the power of using multiple and appropriate teaching strategies with a particular emphasis on the presence of feedback focussed at the right level of instruction (acquisi-

tion or proficiencies); seeing learning and teaching from the students' perspective; and placing reliance on teaching study skills and strategies of learning. *Emphasising learning styles,* coaching for tests, mentoring and *individualised instruction are noted for their lack of impact* [emphasis added]. (p. 199)

Recent studies of the utility of learning styles as guides for teaching practice have reached the same conclusions as those from earlier decades that investigated aptitude-treatment interactions: learning styles have fared no better than any other hypothesised characteristic in well-designed studies of their utility (Hargreaves, 2005; Reynolds, 1997; Snider, 1992; Stahl, 2002). Failure to find evidence for the utility of tailoring instruction to individuals' learning styles has not prevented this term from being frequently included in discussions about and recommendations on pedagogy. It also continues to influence what teachers do in their day-to-day work. Practitioners from preschool school to university level attempt to apply the theory in classrooms, administering the unreliable tests, criticised by so many, to their students, using the results as a guide to classroom practice and encouraging or requiring students to apply the results to understanding, controlling, and explaining their own learning. If nothing else, these activities represent a waste of precious teaching and learning time.

Harmful Effects of Labelling: Cultural Differences and Stereotyping.

Consideration of the empirical evidence leads to the conclusion that the search for ATI in various guises is of enduring interest; however, the utility of these as a guide for practice has been questioned and refuted. Attempting to adapt pedagogy to supposed individual differences is not a harmless strategy, at least in part because it distracts practitioners from those aspects of teaching practice that have proven benefits for children's learning. It also encourages a cultural tendency to look for explanations for behaviour and attainment in the wrong place, in individual traits and dispositions in isolation from the contexts in which these operate: The best predictor of what a student will learn is prior learning opportunities; that is, what the student already knows, rather than some aspect of his or her ability level, cognitive style, or perceptual preference (Nuthall, 2007).

On the second point, those who promote learning styles and other ways to categorise students are furnishing yet another way to stereotype and to form damaging expectations of students. Gutiérrez and Rogoff (2003) have commented on the ways in which learning styles, instead of liberating children from minority cultures from stereotyping, have become another way to confine them within expectations and to define what they can or cannot do and how they are supposed do it. Those "styles" said to be properties of certain ethnic groups, according to Gutierrez and Rogoff, "reside not as traits of individuals or collections of individuals but as proclivities of people with certain histories of engagement with specific cultural activities" (p. 19).

What appear to be individual or cultural traits are the results of learning experiences, which do not of themselves define the limits of the possible in terms of what and how members of any particular culture can learn. Given what is known about the effects, positive and negative of teachers' expectations (Rubie-Davies, 2005, 2008), anything that licenses differing expectations for individual students or categories of students is to be deplored.

Evidence would suggest that children in classes or school systems where learning styles are in favour and who appear to be having difficulties with academic learning are likely to be labelled as tactile/kinaesthetic learners (Rubie-Davies, personal communication, August 2011). Working with practising teachers has yielded many observations along the lines that "at our school we have a lot of kids with problems with reading and spelling, because of different learning styles" (Scott & Dinham, 2008). It appears that instead of careful diagnosis and targeted remediation these children are likely to be subjected to "instruction" purportedly tailored to their "style", in short to teaching that is not informed by sound pedagogy.

Summary and Recommendations

Interest in individual differences as guides to pedagogical decision making has a long history in English-speaking cultures. In the 1960s it spawned a research endeavour that failed to find any support for tailoring teaching to IQ. Subsequent attempts to widen the definition of "aptitude" to include other "intelligences" or theoretical cognitive attributes have had no more success as aids to effective pedagogical decision making. In contrast, knowledge is increasing about the generic teaching methods that assist all students to learn effectively and efficiently.

References

Bracht, J. (1970). Experimental factor relating to aptitude-treatment interactions. *Review of Educational Research, 40*(5), 627–645.

Cassidy, S. (2004). Learning styles: An overview of theories, models, and measures. *Educational Psychology, 24*(4), 419–444.

Coffield, F., Moseley, D., Hall, E., & Ecclestone, K. (2004). *Learning styles and pedagogy in post-16 learning. A systematic and critical review.* London: Learning and Skills Research Centre.

Cronbach, L. J., & Snow, R. E. (1977). *Aptitudes and instructional methods: A handbook for research on interactions.* New York: Irvington.

Duff, A., & Duffy T. (2002). Psychometric properties of Honey & Mumford's Learning Styles Questionnaire (LSQ). *Personality and Individual Differences, 33*(1), 147–163. References and further reading may be available for this article. To view references and further reading you must purchase this article.

Felder, R. M., & Silverman, L. K (1988). Learning and teaching styles in engineering education. Engineering Education, 78(7), 674–681.

Ferrell, Barbara G. (1983). A factor analytic comparison of four learning-styles instruments. *Journal of Educational Psychology, 75*(1), 33–39.

Fleming, N. (2009). A guide to learning styles. Retrieved from http://www.vark-learn.com/english/index.asp

Ford, N., & Chen. S. Y. (2001). Matching/mismatching revisited: An empirical study of learning and teaching styles. *British Journal of Educational Technology, 1*, 5–22.

Gardner, H. (1983). *Frames of mind: The theory of multiple intelligences.* New York: Basic Books.

Garner, I. (2000). Problems and inconsistencies with Kolb's learning styles. *Educational Psychology, 20*(3), 341–348

Glass, G. (1970). Discussion. In M. C. Wittrock & D. El Riley (Eds.), *The evaluation of instruction: Issues and problems* (pp. 210–211). New York: Holt, Rinehart & Winston.

Gregorc, A. F. (1984). Style as symptom: A phenomenological perspective. *Theory into Practice, 23*(1), 51–55.

Gutiérrez, K. D., & Rogoff, B. (2003). Cultural ways of learning: Individual traits or repertoires of practice. *Educational Researcher, 32*(50), 19–25.

Hargreaves, D. (Chair). (2005). *About learning: Report of the Learning Working Group.* London: Demos.

Hattie, J. (2009). *Visible learning.* London: Routledge. References and further reading may be available for this article. To view references and further reading you must purchase this article.

Kappe, F. R., Boekholt, L., den Rooyen, C., & Van der Flier, H. (2009). A predictive validity study of the Learning Style Questionnaire (LSQ) using multiple, specific learning criteria. *Learning and Individual Differences, 19*(4), 464–467.

Kolb, D. (1984). *Experiential learning: Experience as the source of learning and development.* Englewood Cliffs, NJ: Prentice-Hall.

Mills, D. W. (2002). *Applying what we know: Student learning styles.* Retrieved from http://www.csrnet.org/csrnet/articles/student-learning-styles.html

Nuthall, G. (2007). *The hidden lives of learners.* Wellington, NZ: NZCER Press.

Reynolds, M. (1997). Learning styles: A critique. *Management Learning, 28*(2), 115–133.

Rubie-Davies, C. M. (2005, December). *Exploring class level teacher expectations and pedagogical beliefs.* Paper presented at the NZARE conference, Dunedin, New Zealand.

Rubie-Davies, C. M. (2008). Teacher beliefs and expectations: Relationships with student learning. In C. M. Rubie-Davies & C. Rawlinson (Eds.), *Challenging thinking about teaching and learning* (pp. 25–39). Hauppauge, NY: Nova.

Scott, C., & Dinham, S. (2008). Born not made: The nativist myth and teachers' thinking. *Teacher Development, 12*(2), 115–124.

Snider, V. (1992). The name assigned to the document by the author. This field may also contain sub-titles, series names, and report numbers. Learning styles and learning to read: A critique. *The entity from which ERIC acquires the content, including journal, organization, and conference names, or by means of online submission from the author. Remedial and Special Education, 13*(1), 6–18.

Stahl, S. A. (2002). Different strokes for different folks? In L. Abbeduto (Ed.), *Taking sides: Clashing on controversial issues in educational psychology* (pp. 98–107). Boston, MA: McGraw-Hill.

Waterhouse, L. (2006). Multiple intelligences, the Mozart effect, and emotional intelligence: A critical review. *Educational Psychologist, 41*(4), 207–225.

8.12

Instructional Simulations

JENNIFER J. VOGEL-WALCUTT, NAOMI MALONE, AND SAE SCHATZ
University of Central Florida

Introduction

Simulations are tools that, when used for instruction, allow learners to practice in a repeatable, focused environment (Aldrich, 2004). Instructional computer-based simulations employ a systematic instructional methodology (e.g., scenario-based training) and accurately represent a problem-solving domain (Oser, Cannon-Bowers, Dwyer, & Miller, 1997). This combination enables learners to practice integration of their skills and to perform under realistic conditions, such as environmental distractions, stress, and time pressure (Beaubien & Baker, 2004). Simulations can be utilized across multiple learning domains, from STEM-focused education to arts and humanities; and for a variety of purposes, such as problem solving or studying phenomena not visible to the human eye (Reigeluth & Schwartz, 1989). Additionally, extensive literature exists examining the use of simulations for education, investigating most levels of instruction (from elementary to adult) and spanning many different instructional strategies (West, Snellen, Tong, & Murray, 1991).

Research Evidence

Broadly defined, computer-based instruction (CBI) refers to all guided collections of interactive multimedia instruction (IMI), whether they employ drill-and-practice tutoring, computer-managed instructions (such as online learning management systems), or presentation of illustrative simulations (Kulik & Kulik, 1991). From its early days, CBI has been generally hailed for its substantial time-savings. Studies indicate that, on average, CBI reduces teaching time by one-third compared to conventional instruction (Kulik & Kulik, 1991). Additionally, students show a moderate to large improvement in learning achievement when using CBI as compared to those in a traditional classroom (Waxman, Lin, & Michko, 2003).

Despite its efficiency and (in some cases) greater effectiveness, however, the most commonly used CBI is didactic in nature; it generally employs a behaviorist approach, in which the educational experience engenders recall and concept definition, but is insufficient for more sophisticated abilities (Dede, 2007; National Research Council, 2000, pp. 6–8). This is partially evidenced by CBI's diminishing effectiveness at higher levels of education; that is, in elementary schools it shows a 0.46 average effect size over traditional instruction, but the effect size drops to 0.26 for college students (Niemiec & Walberg, 1987). Thus, it is reasonable to conclude that "[CBI programs] have apparently been less successful in teaching the higher order skills emphasized at higher educational levels" (Kulik & Kulik, 1991, p. 76). Or, to put it more bluntly: CBI systems appear to be best suited for imparting "factual knowledge and recipe-like procedures" (Dede, 2008, p. 47).

Simulations are a specialized form of CBI that offer several advantages over traditional computer-based multimedia instruction. Simulations provide a virtual environment that facilitates realistic experiential learning, more effectively supporting the teaching of complex knowledge, skills, and attitudes (Cannon-Bowers & Salas, 1998). Simulations also respond dynamically and provide intrinsic feedback (i.e., immediate cause-and-effect responses), allowing learners to witness the outcomes of their actions, to safely make mistakes and observe the results, and to explore (and correct) their misconceptions (Ross, Phillips, Klein, & Cohn, 2005). Finally, instructional simulations can accept concurrent participation, which provides a platform for group or vicarious learning. Learning group-work skills within a simulation produces better results than teaching these skills in a traditional lecture-style classroom (e.g., Lassiter, Vaughn, Smaltz, Morgan, & Salas, 1990).

When used carefully, simulations can support effective learning (e.g., Klein et al., 2005). However, currently, to capitalize on these benefits, expert teachers must be involved in their application (e.g., Smith-Jentsch, John-ston, & Payne, 1998). That is, teachers must facilitate the instructional tasks and assist in the learning process (Jones, Hennessy, & Deutsch, 1985). Some argue that a good teacher is the primary determinant of the effective-ness of simulation-based learning (Jones et al., 1985) or that "simulators without instructors are virtually useless for training" (Stottler, & Pike, 2002, p. 4). The heavy reliance upon teachers creates a bottleneck that makes simulation-based learning more challenging for less experienced teach-ers and limits replicability of the instructional experience from class to class.

Another significant barrier to the use of computer simula-tions in education is the intimidation felt by nontechnical educators. In addition to their educational duties, teachers may also need to serve as technological experts, performing tasks such as simulation set-up or content authoring. How-ever, most teachers are not equipped to deal with the design and development considerations of simulations (Hanson & Shelton, 2008). Similarly, students also face a technological learning curve; they must invest time determining how to operate the system (Kirriemuir & McFarlane, 2004). Finally, to successfully implement simulations into classrooms, buy-in must be attained, not only from students, but also from parents, administrators, and other support staff. Without a supportive social environment, teachers will find it difficult to integrate instructional simulations into their curricula (Kirkland & Sutch, 2009).

Summary and Recommendations

To make simulations more accessible to educators, teachers need to understand the types of technologies available, and identify those simulations that best meet their instructional goals. For example, Aldrich (2005) categorized simulations into four genres: branching stories, interactive spreadsheets, game-based models, and virtual labs/virtual products. Branching stories involve sequential multiple-choice deci-sions by students that impact their progression through the narrative toward a successful or unsuccessful conclusion. This genre is easy to use and deploy, making it favorable for entry-level students and employees. Interactive spread-sheets are useful for teaching abstract concepts or complex systems in all disciplines and can involve multiplayer or group environments. Game-based models are built with the intention of making learning fun, and although more study is needed in this area, Aldrich suggests that it increases student satisfaction and effectiveness. Finally, virtual labs and products focus on visually accurate, full or partial representations of instructional objects, allowing learners to practice a range of tasks. Another option for teachers to explore is to search out existing instructional simulations (e.g., via the Internet). Currently, multimedia resource re-positories (such as MERLOT, www.merlot.org, or SERC, serc.carleton.edu) include some simulation listings and vari-ous discipline-specific resources that can provide teachers with accessible options. Other specialized resources, such

as NASA's educator website (education.nasa.gov), also offer recommendations for K-12 classrooms.

Instructional simulations can be used across multiple domains, disciplines, purposes, and modalities. They sup-port higher order skill acquisition, provide dynamic and immediate feedback, and can support collaborative instruc-tion. As educators consider the use of simulations, these technologies should be viewed not just as higher-fidelity CBI platforms but as unique instructional tools. Simulations enable students to acquire and synthesize information, test out their theories, and see the outcomes of their decisions. Beyond serving as an adjunct to a curriculum, simulations can provide distinct educational experiences that better en-able students to assimilate and later apply their knowledge in the real world. However, teachers face several challenges as they attempt to incorporate simulations into their class-rooms. They may feel intimidated by a lack of technical skills, and they may feel overwhelmed by the quantity of available simulation options that, as a whole, have not been systematically vetted. Despite these challenges, the potential learning gains offered by instructional simulations warrant the time and effort required by teachers to invest in their effective use.

References

Aldrich, C. (2004). *Simulations and the future of learning: An innovative (and perhaps revolutionary) approach to e-learning.* San Francisco, CA: Pfeiffer.
Aldrich, C. (2005). *Learning by doing: A comprehensive guide to simula-tions, computer games, and pedagogy in e-learning and other educa-tional experiences.* San Francisco, CA: Pfeiffer.
Beaubien, J. M., & Baker, D. P. (2004). The use of simulation for train-ing teamwork skills in health care: How low can you go? *Quality and Safety in Health Care, 13,* i51–i56.
Cannon-Bowers, J. A., & Salas, E. (1998). Team performance and train-ing in complex environments: recent findings from applied research. *Current Directions in Psychological Science, 7*(3), 83–87.
Dede, C. (2007). *Reinventing the role of information and communications technologies in education* (Yearbook of the National Society for the Study of Education), *106,* 11–38.
Dede, C. (2008). Theoretical perspectives influencing the use of infor-mation technology in teaching and learning. In J. M. Voogt & G. A. Knezek (Eds.), *International handbook of information technology in primary and secondary education* (pp. 43–62). New York: Springer.
Hanson, K., & Shelton, B. (2008). Design and development of virtual real-ity: Analysis of challenges faced by educators. *Educational Technology & Society, 11*(1), 118–131.
Kirkland, K., & Sutch, D. (2009). Overcoming the barriers to educational innovation: A literature review. Futurelab. Retrieved from http://www.futurelab.org.uk/
Kirriemuir, J., & McFarlane, A. (2004). *Literature review in games and learning.* Futurelab. Retrieved from http://telearn.archives-ouvertes.fr/docs/00/19/04/53/PDF/kirriemuir-j-2004-r8.pdf
Klein, C., Salas, E., Burke, C. S., Goodwin, G. F., Halpin, S., Diaz-Granados, D., & Badum, A. (2005). Does team training enhance team processes, performance, and team member affective outcomes? A meta-analysis. *Human Factors, 50*(6), 903–933.
Kulik, C., & Kulik, J. A. (1991). Effectiveness of computer-based instruc-tion: An updated analysis. *Computers in Human Behavior, 7*(1–2), 75–94.
Lassiter, D. L., Vaughn, J. S., Smaltz, V. E., Morgan, B. B., Jr., & Salas, E. (1990). A comparison of two types of training interventions on team

communication performance. In M. E. Wiklund (Ed.), *Proceedings of the 34th Annual Meeting of HFES* (pp. 1372–1376). Santa Monica, CA: HFES.

Jones, E. R., Hennessy, R. T., & Deutsch, S. (Eds.). (1985). *Human factors aspects of simulation.* Committee on Human Factors, National Research Council. Washington, DC: National Academy Press.

National Research Council, Committee on Developments in the Science of Learning and Committee on Learning Research and Educational Practice, (2000). J. D. Bransford, A. Brown, & R. Cocking (Eds.), *How people learn: Brain, mind, experience, and school.* Washington, DC: National Academy Press.

Niemiec, R., & Walberg, H. J. (1987). Comparative effects of computer assisted instruction: A synthesis of reviews. *Journal of Educational Computing Research, 3,* 19–37.

Oser, R. L., Cannon-Bowers, J. A., Dwyer, D. J., & Miller, H. (1997, June). *An event based approach for training: Enhancing the utility of joint service simulations.* Paper presented at the 65th Military Operations Research Society Symposium, Quantico, VA.

Reigeluth, C. M., & Schwartz, E. (1989). An instructional theory for the design of computer-based simulations. *Journal of Computer-Based Instruction, 16*(1), 1–10

Ross, K. G., Phillips, J. K., Klein, G., & Cohn, J. (2005). Creating expertise: A framework to guide simulation-based training.Technical Report Contract M67854-04-C-8035. Washington, DC: Office for Naval Research.

Smith-Jentsch, K. A., Johnston, J. H., & Payne, S. C. (1998). Measuring team-related expertise in complex environments. In J. A. Cannon-Bowers & E. Salas (Eds.), *Making decisions under stress* (pp. 61–87). Washington, DC: American Psychological Association.

Stottler, R. H. & Pike, B. (2002). An embedded training solution: FBCB2/ tactical decision making intelligent tutoring system. In *Proceedings of I/ITSEC,* Orlando, FL: NTSA.

Waxman, H.C., Lin, M.-F., & Michko, G.M. (2003). *A meta-analysis of the effectiveness of teaching and learning with technology on student outcomes.* Naperville: IL: North Central Regional Educational Laboratory.

West, C., Snellen, J., Tong, K., & Murray, S. (1991). *A report on the research and development of instructional simulation.* (ERIC Document Reproduction Service, No. ED340362)

8.13

Programmed Instruction

DEBORAH V. SVOBODA, ANDREA L. JONES, KIMBERLY VAN VULPEN, AND DONNA HARRINGTON
University of Maryland

Introduction

Programmed instruction is a term with many different definitions. Today, it may mean computer-based learning in many forms, including distance learning techniques (e.g., televised instruction to remote locations, software programs developed for use by students independent of traditional classroom courses), use of online course management systems (e.g., Blackboard), and hybrids of traditional classroom and distance learning applications. Historically, however, programmed instruction has a very specific definition rooted in the history of American pedagogy and psychology. As classroom-based education was developing in the early 20th century, psychologist Edward Thorndike conducted animal research and concluded that satisfying reinforcement following a correct response would increase the likelihood that a behavior would be repeated (Kulhavy & Wager, 1993). Thorndike's law of effect became central to the theory of learning that underpins programmed instruction.

Influenced by Thorndike's work, Sidney Pressey developed the first mechanical testing device in the early 1920s. Set within a cultural context reflective of the ascendance of science and inventions, automated testing machines allowed for student testing independent of teacher oversight, thereby making more efficient use of classroom teacher time (Petrina, 2004). Pressey's automated teaching machines and programs enabled students to use the device to test themselves, answering multiple choice questions, and receiving immediate feedback from the device as to whether their answer was correct. Feedback served as a reinforcer, meeting the basic tenet of Thorndike's law of effect and established behavioral constructs in American pedagogy (Kulhavy & Wager, 1993).

B.F. Skinner (1986) elaborated upon the work of Thorndike and Pressey, applying his own tenets of operant conditioning to education and developed programmed instruction approaches consisting of: (a) frames of instructional material delivered in small increments in order to reduce error and arranged by level of complexity, (b) questions posed to students regarding material presented, (c) a student response requirement, and (d) feedback on the student response either confirming the correct answer or providing knowledge of the correct answer (Kulhavy & Wager, 1993; Molenda, 2008). Prompting correct responses as frequently as possible established feedback as reinforcer and motivator (Kulhavy & Wager, 1993). Educational research of the time supported Skinner's programmed instruction model; programs and equipment proliferated, and programmed instruction found its way into textbooks. However, overprompting on programmed instruction devices led to student reliance on the technology and to student reports of boredom and lack of stimulation (McDonald, Yanchar, & Osguthorpe, 2005). Programmed instruction began to fall out of favor as the technology proved inflexible to individual student needs at times reducing educational material to the lowest common denominator. Programmed instruction materials were also expensive to change and update. Wallin (2005) describes a similar rise and fall of the use of educational technology in Sweden from 1960 to 1980. Finally, research of the time found more successful learning with the use of mixed teaching methods (McDonald et al., 2005).

These historical and theoretical foundations of programmed instruction can still be seen in the evolution of distance and computer-based learning of today. Bandura's social learning theory also had a significant impact on the early development of computer instruction (Cruthirds & Hanna, 1997). Drawing from the principle assumption that people learn from observing others, social learning theory supported the use of computers as a valid avenue for providing this learned experience. Computer-based learning today is more interactive and student directed, and instruction is creatively planned by the course developer to encourage student interaction through the use of available technology such as CD-ROMS, videos, Internet, and photographs (Cruthirds & Hanna, 1997). Today, programmed tutoring, direct instruction, and personalized systems of instruction

(PSI) (Molenda, 2008) all contain adapted elements of programmed instruction and extensive research has been done on this topic.

Research Evidence

Kulik, Kulik, and Cohen (1980) conducted a meta-analysis of 312 evaluation studies of five different technologies used in college classroom instruction over a 25-year period. Technology programs studied included 74 studies of PSI, 59 on computer-based instruction (CBI), 48 on Postlethwait's Audio-Tutorial Approach (A-T), 57 on programmed instruction (PI), and 74 on visual-based instruction (VBI). Overall, instructional technology had a positive effect size of .28 on student achievement on exam scores, with wide variation among the five technology programs examined. PSI had the highest effect on student achievement (ES = 0.55); CBI and PI were next with small effect sizes just over 0.20; A-T and VBI had less than 0.20 ES. The use of technology instruction in the "soft" disciplines (social sciences and humanities) had an average effect of .38 and an average effect of .21 for the "hard" disciplines, and technology enhanced student achievement in the introductory courses less than in advanced level courses.

At the secondary school level (grades 7 through 12), however, programmed instruction was not found to be more effective than conventional instruction in improving teaching in Kulik and colleagues' meta-analysis of 48 studies of the effectiveness of programmed instruction (Kulik, Schwalb, & Kulik, 1982). Programmed instruction on average did not significantly raise students' average achievement on final examinations, increase students' positive attitudes toward the subject matter and instruction, promote retention of material learned, or decrease the correlation between students' aptitude and achievement. However, Kulik et al. (1982) found significant effects of programmed instruction over conventional instruction on student achievement in final examinations in some areas. Programmed instruction had a large effect size of .57 in comparison to conventional instruction of social sciences, but very small to no effect for instruction in science (ES = .11) and math (ES = -.01); average effect sizes for programmed instruction on student achievement increased over time with average effect sizes of -.01, .14, and .28 for studies published in 1961 to 1965, 1966 to 1970, and 1971 to 1975, respectively (Kulik et al., 1982).

J. A. Kulik, Bangert, and Williams (1983) conducted a meta-analysis of 51 evaluations of computer-based teaching for students in grades 6 through 12 that examined five different types of computer-based instruction, including drill and practice, tutoring, computer-managed teaching, simulation, and programming the computer to solve problems. Computer-based instruction had a positive median effect on final exams of .32, but varied by type of instruction utilized. Students' attitudes toward the subject matter and computers were more positive for those students in the computer-based instruction courses in comparison to their peers in courses with conventional teaching. Students in the computer-based instruction courses spent less time learning the material relative to comparable courses attended by their peers, with a 39% savings in time in one study (ES = .78) and 88% savings in time in a second study. Kulik and colleagues concluded that overall computer-based instruction positively affects final examination scores for students in secondary level classes.

In a later meta-analysis, Kulik and Kulik (1991) reviewed 254 studies of kindergarten through college settings evaluating the effectiveness of computer-based instruction (CBI) in comparison to conventional teaching in increasing student academic performance in test scores, retention of subject material measured by follow-up exams, student attitudes toward computers and instruction, course completion (postsecondary instruction), and time spent in CBI settings (postsecondary studies). Kulik and Kulik found that CBI increased student performance on tests, with an average effect size of 0.30 compared to control group instruction, although effects differed across other factors: (a) studies published in journals reported larger average effect sizes than those published as technical reports and dissertations; (b) CBI used for short duration (4 weeks or less) had a larger average effect on student test scores than CBI used for longer durations; and (c) studies controlling for teacher effects reported lower average effect sizes than those studies that did not control for teacher effects. Kulik and Kulik did not find a difference in the average effect of CBI on student performance in relationship to year of publication of the study. Three different CBI methods were identified as computer-managed instruction (CMI), computer-enriched instruction (CEI), and computer-assisted instruction (CAI). Overall, CEI programs did not contribute to an increase in student performance; there were no significant differences in student performance at the postsecondary level; and CAI and CMI were moderately effective at the precollege level. Studies reporting larger average positive effects were in education, psychology, and music education (Kulik & Kulik, 1991).

In a more recent study, J. A. Kulik (2003) examined 27 controlled evaluation studies conducted since 1990 in elementary and secondary school settings on the use of technology in reading instruction. The studies examined six different types of programs: integrated learning systems (ILS, 16 studies); writing-based reading programs (12 studies); reading management programs (3 studies); word processing and Internet resources (10 studies); microcomputer-based laboratories (8 studies); and science tutoring and simulations (12 studies). Achievement effect size for Integrated Learning Systems (ILS) for mathematics ranged from 0.14 to 1.05, with an average effect on student achievement of 0.40 in comparison to students receiving conventional teaching in mathematics. The achievement effect size for ILS reading ranged from 0.00 to 0.44, with an average effect size on the reading subtests of 0.06. J. A. Kulik (2003) found three key factors to improving the effectiveness of ILS: (a) students who spent the curriculum recommended time in ILS instruction significantly increased their performance on average in both subjects; (b) teachers who integrated ILS into classroom curriculum as a mutually supportive method significantly increased their students' mathematics scores; and (c) students who were paired in their learning in ILS instruction appear to increase their mathematics scores in comparison to their peers who engage in ILS as an individual activity. J. A. Kulik (2003) concluded ILS instruction has positive effects on students' achievement with an overall achievement effect size of 0.28, which is educationally meaningful.

Twelve evaluation studies of the writing-based program, Writing to Read (WTR) were analyzed for their effect on reading scores for students in kindergarten through Grade 4, with an effect of 0.84 standard deviations for kindergarten student reading scores and an average effect size of 0.40 in Grade 1 reading scores (J. A. Kulik, 2003). Beyond Grade 1, Kulik found mixed effects across five studies with an average effect size of 0.25; the studies beyond Grade 1 were diverse in their design, the technology program used, the grade at which the study began, and the grade at which testing occurred, which may explain the differences in effects found.

The third technology program reviewed by J. A. Kulik (2003) was accelerated reading (AR) with few evaluation studies available for analysis. Correlational studies conducted in three states in the United States reported an effect of 0.43 on increased student reading scores in Grades 3 through 8 for students in school districts that owned the AR program. However, Kulik notes these same districts also had higher math scores, and cautions the interpretation of the results from correlation studies.

Kulik's (2003) meta-analysis also included 12 controlled studies on the effects of technology (e.g. word processing, computer writing prompts, and computer enrichment) on students' writing. The overall effect of the word processing programs on writing skills was 0.30 in four studies of students in Grades 5 through 8. Word processing plus programs (writing prompts) were examined in two evaluation studies, with ES = 1.34 on student writing skills in Grades 6 and 9; the ES of the second study could not be calculated from the information provided in the study. Kulik suggests the effectiveness of the writing prompts was related to the manner in which the prompts were delivered to the students.

Computer enrichment technology was the final area examined by Kulik (2003) in relationship to student writing skill level in elementary and secondary school. The studies had diverse methods of implementing enrichment of computer access for their students' writing instruction. Five out of the six evaluation studies found positive effects of computer enrichment on students' writing skills, with effects ranging from -0.10 to 0.46, with an average ES = 0.34 (Kulik, 2003).

Jaehnig and Miller (2007) reviewed 33 studies that reported the feedback pattern utilized in programmed instruction and concluded that knowledge-of-response feedback was *not* recommended, whereas knowledge-of-correct-response feedback was somewhat effective, although further

research "is needed to determine the situations in which it is useful" (p. 228) and what types of feedback are most effective (e.g. elaboration feedback, post-feedback delays with question, and feedback in view). Camnalbur and Erdoğan (2008) reviewed 78 studies conducted in Turkey from 1998 to 2007 for primary school level education. The studies examined the effectiveness of computer-assisted instruction compared to traditional instruction in improving student academic success with an average effect size of 0.95 in fixed effects, and 1.05 ES in random effects model. The two models found student academic success was higher in computer-assisted instruction compared to traditional instruction.

Summary and Recommendations

Across the many studies conducted on programmed instructions, there is evidence that it can improve student achievement, at least under some circumstances and in some content areas. Many researchers in the field of online instruction recommend a constructivist approach to course development (Huang, 2002), which allows for consideration of different learning theories including those that explore learning through action, reasoning, and existing knowledge. Frailich, Kesner, and Hofstein (2007) found that achievement, attitudes, and interest were better when a web-based learning component was added to a 10th grade chemistry course. However, they concluded that "the success in integrating web-based learning is very much dependent on the teachers. The professional development of teachers and the support given to them is crucial when implementing such a new learning environment" (p. 194).

Advanced technologies in online and computer-based instruction have now made it possible to further develop the vision of those who pioneered programmed instruction in its beginnings (Cruthirds & Hanna, 1997). With this advancement, however, new challenges have presented themselves. In its original form, programmed instruction had a rigid approach to teaching and learning (McDonald et al., 2005) and the "locus of control" was held by the instructional program itself (Cruthirds & Hanna, 1997). With current technology, programmed instruction looks very different and allows for a more interactive and flexible form of instruction. This flexibility is considered a positive change from the rigidity of the past (McDonald et al., 2005); however, it brings with it the need for further professional development for teachers who will implement it, as well as additional research to answer the new questions that this advancement in technology is creating in the field of programmed instruction (Cruthirds & Hanna, 1997).

References

Camnalbur, M., & Erdoğan, Y. (2008). A meta-analysis on the effectiveness of computer-assisted instruction: Turkey sample. *Educational Sciences: Theory & Practice, 8*(2), 497–505. Retrieved from http://eric.ed.gov/ERICDocs/data/ericdocs2sql/content_storage_01/0000019b/80/43/7f/8d.pdf

Cruthirds, J., & Hanna, M. S. (1997). Programmed instruction and interactive multimedia: A third consideration. Retrieved from http://www.natcom.org/ctronline2/96-97pro.htm

Frailich, M., Kesner, M., & Hofstein, A. (2007). The influence of web-based chemistry learning on students' perceptions, attitudes, and achievements. *Research in Science & Technological Education, 25*(2), 179–197.

Huang, H-M. (2002) Toward constructivism for adult learners in online learning environments. *British Journal of Educational Technology, 33*(1), 27–37. Retrieved from http://web.ebscohost.com.proxy-hs.researchport.umd.edu/ehost/pdfviewer/pdfviewer?vid=4&hid=112&sid=8bc07a73-d008-4f1d-82b4-77486a9ebe27%40sessionmgr104

Jaehnig, W., & Miller, M. L. (2007). Feedback types in programmed instruction: A systematic review. *The Psychological Record, 57,* 219–232. Retrieved from http://search.ebscohost.com.proxy-hs.researchport.umd.edu/login.aspx?direct=true&db=buh&AN=24658186&site=ehost-live

Kulik, C.-L. C., & Kulik, J. A. (1991). Effectiveness of computer-based instruction: An updated analysis. *Computers in Human Behavior, 7,* 75–94. doi:10.1016/0747-5632(91)90030-5

Kulik, C.-L. C., Kulik, J. A., & Cohen, P. A. (1980). Instructional technology and college teaching. *Teaching of Psychology, 7*(4), 199–205. doi:10.1207/s15328023top0704_1

Kulik, C.-L. C., Schwalb, B. J., & Kulik, J. A. (1982). Programmed instruction in secondary education: A meta-analysis of evaluation findings. *The Journal of Educational Research, 75*(3), 133–138. Retrieved from http://www.jstor.org/stable/27539881

Kulik, J. A. (May 2003). *Effects of using instructional technology in elementary and secondary schools: What controlled evaluation studies say: Final report* (SRI Project Number P10446.001). Arlington, VA: SRI International. Retrieved from http://www.ssa.sri.com/policy/csted/reports/sandt/it/Kulik_ITinK-12_Main_Report.pdf

Kulik, J. A., Bangert, R. L., & Williams, G. W. (1983). Effects of computer-based teaching on secondary school students. *Journal of Educational Psychology, 75*(1), 19–26. doi:10.1037/0022-0663.75.1.19

Kulkavy, R., & Wager, W. (1993). Feedback in programmed instruction: Historical context and implications for practice. In J. Dempsey & G. Sales (Eds.), *Interactive instruction and feedback* (pp. 3–20). Englewood Cliffs, NJ: Educational Technology. Retrieved from http://books.google.com/books?id=ss3fz-5WC6gC&Ipb=PA3&ots=uw4HtsG814&dq=%22programmed%20instruction%22&pg=PA3#v=onepage&q=%22programmed%20instruction%22&f=false

McDonald, J., Yanchar, S., & Osguthorpe, R. (2005). Learning from programmed instruction: Examining implications for modern instructional technology. *Educational Technology Research and Development, 53*(2), 84–98. doi: 10.1007/BFO2504867

Molenda, M. (2008). The programmed instruction era: When effectiveness mattered. *TechTrends, 52*(2), 52–58. doi:10.1007/s11528-008-0136-y

Petrina, S. (2004). Sidney Pressey and the automation of education, 1924–1934. *Technology and Culture, 45*(2), 305–330. doi: 10.1353/tech.2004.0085

Skinner, B. (1986). Programmed instruction revisited. *The Phi Delta Kappan 68*(2), 103–110. Retrieved from http://www.jstor.org/stable/400060743

Wallin, E. (2005). The rise and fall of Swedish educational technology 1960–1980. *Scandinavian Journal of Educational Research, 49*(5), 437–460.

8.14

Multimedia Learning

RICHARD E. MAYER
University of California, Santa Barbara

Introduction

Multimedia learning refers to learning with words and pictures (Mayer, 2005, 2009). The words may be spoken (delivered live or via speakers) or printed (delivered on a page, board, or screen); the pictures may be static graphics (such as illustrations, charts, maps, or photos delivered on a page or screen) or dynamic graphics (such as animation or video delivered on a screen). Examples of multimedia instruction include a narrated animation, a computer-based educational game, a PowerPoint presentation, or an illustrated textbook. Figure 8.3 shows frames and spoken words from a narrated animation on how a pump works.

For hundreds of years the primary vehicle for instruction has been words, such as lectures or textbooks. Advances in computer and communication technologies now allow instructors to supplement verbal modes of instruction with visual modes of instruction, including dazzling graphics that students can interact with. Research on multimedia learning provides encouraging evidence that under appropriate circumstances, students learn better from words and pictures than from words alone with a median effect size of $d = 1.39$ based on transfer tests in 11 experimental comparisons (Mayer, 2005, 2009).

What Is the Historical Context of Multimedia Learning? More than 350 years ago in 1658, John Amos Comenius published the world's first and most popular illustrated textbook, *Orbis Pictus* (The World in Pictures). Each page contained a line drawing (such as a tailor's shop, the parts of a house, or the planets) with each part labeled with a name and description both in the reader's first language and in Latin (Comenius, 1658/1887). As the first book to combine words and pictures in order to promote learning, *Orbis Pictus* is a forerunner of today's illustrated textbooks and multimedia instruction in general. Other milestones in the evolution of multimedia learning include the initial educational use of motion pictures in the early 1920s, tele-

vision in the 1950s, personal computers in the 1960s, and the Internet in the 1990s.

Research Evidence

The *cognitive theory of multimedia learning* is based on three principles of how people learn within the human information processing system: *dual channels*—humans have separate information processing channels for words and pictures (Paivio, 1986); *limited capacity*—within each channel people can engage in a only a small amount of cognitive processing at one time (Plass, Moreno, & Brunken, 2010; Sweller, 1999); and *active processing*—meaningful learning depends on the learner's cognitive processing during learning, including attending to relevant incoming verbal and pictorial information, mentally organizing it into a coherent verbal or pictorial representation, and integrating them with each other and with knowledge activated from long-term memory (Mayer, 2005, 2009). Three kinds of cognitive processing during learning are *extraneous processing*—cognitive processing that does not support the instructional objective and is caused by poor instructional design; *essential processing*—cognitive processing that is required to mentally represent the presented words and pictures and is caused by the complexity of the essential material; and *generative processing*—cognitive processing that involves mentally organizing and integrating the material for deep understanding and depends on the motivation of the learner to exert effort. Given the limits on information processing capacity, three important goals of instructional design are to reduce extraneous processing, manage essential processing, and foster generative processing.

What Are the Effects of Multimedia Instruction on Student Achievement? Researchers have identified evidence-based principles for how to design effective multimedia instruction that are consistent with cognitive theories of how people learn from words and pictures. Techniques intended to reduce extraneous processing include the coherence principle, signaling principle, redundancy principle, spatial contiguity principle, and temporal contiguity principle. The *coherence principle* is that people learn better when extraneous words, sounds, and pictures are excluded from a multimedia lesson. In a meta-analysis based on 14 experimental comparisons, Mayer (2009) reported a median effect size of $d = 0.97$. The *signaling principle* is that people learn better from a multimedia lesson when cues highlight the essential material. In a meta-analysis based on 6 experimental comparisons, Mayer (2009) reported a median effect size of $d = 0.52$. The *redundancy principle* is that people learn better from graphics and narration than from graphics, narration, and onscreen text. In a meta-analysis based on 5 experimental comparisons, Mayer (2009) reported a median

effect size of $d = 0.72$. The *spatial contiguity principle* is that people learn better when corresponding printed words and pictures are presented near each other on the screen or page. In meta-analyses, Mayer (2009) reported a median effect size of $d = 1.19$ based on 5 experimental comparisons, and Ginns (2006) reported a weighted mean effect size of $d = 0.72$ based on 37 experimental comparisons. The *temporal contiguity principle* is that people learn better when corresponding words and pictures are presented at the same time. In meta-analyses, Mayer (2009) reported a median effect size of $d = 1.31$ based on 8 experimental comparisons, and Ginns (2006) reported a weighted mean effect size of $d = 0.72$ based on 13 experimental comparisons.

Techniques aimed at managing essential processing are the segmenting principle, the pretraining principle,

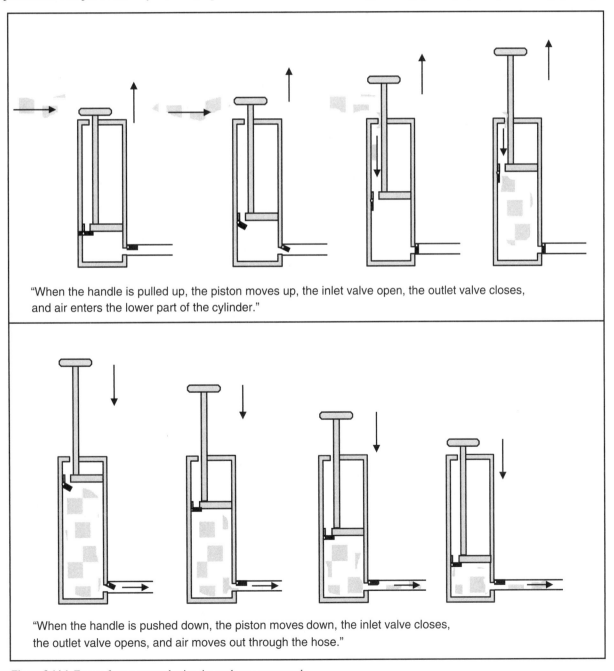

"When the handle is pulled up, the piston moves up, the inlet valve open, the outlet valve closes, and air enters the lower part of the cylinder."

"When the handle is pushed down, the piston moves down, the inlet valve closes, the outlet valve opens, and air moves out through the hose."

Figure 8.14.1 Frames from a narrated animation on how a pump works

and the modality principle. The *segmenting principle* is that people learn better when a multimedia lesson is presented in user-paced segments rather than as a continuous presentation. In a meta-analysis involving 3 experimental comparisons, Mayer (2009) reported a median effect size of $d = 0.98$. The *pretraining principle* is that people learn better from a multimedia lesson when they receive pretraining in the names and characteristics of the main concepts. In a meta-analysis involving 5 experimental comparisons, Mayer (2009) reported a median effect size of $d = 0.85$. The *modality principle* is that people learn better from graphics and narration than from animation and onscreen text. In a meta-analysis involving 17 experimental comparisons involving system-paced presentation, Mayer (2009) reported a median effect size of $d = 1.02$, whereas Ginns (2005) reported a weighted mean effect size of $d = 0.93$ based on 31 experimental comparisons with system-paced presentation.

Techniques intended to foster generative processing include the multimedia principle, personalization principle, and voice principle. The *multimedia principle* is that people learn better from words and corresponding pictures than from words alone. Based on 11 experimental comparisons, Mayer (2009) reported a median effect size of $d = 1.39$.

The *personalization principle* is that people learn better from multimedia lessons when words are in conversational style rather than formal style. Based on 11 experimental comparisons, Mayer (2009) reported a median effect size of $d = 1.11$. The *voice principle* is that people learn better from multimedia lessons when words are spoken with a human voice rather than a machine voice. Based on 3 experimental comparisons, Mayer reported a median effect size of $d = 1.02$.

Techniques that do not appear to improve multimedia learning include increasing the visual realism of the graphics, adding a static image of the instructor on the screen, or changing a series of static frames into an animation when the presentation is under system pacing (Clark & Mayer, 2008; Lowe & Schnotz, 2008; Mayer, 2009; Mayer, Hegarty, Mayer, & Campbell, 2005).

Summary and Recommendations

There is evidence that some of the effects are strongest for low-knowledge learners rather than high-knowledge learners, for tests of transfer rather than retention, and when the material is unfamiliar and presented at a fast pace (Mayer, 2009). For example, Kalyuga (2005) reported evidence for the *expertise reversal effect* in which some multimedia instructional design principles that are effective for novices are not effective for experts and may even be detrimental.

Most of the studies on multimedia learning involve short lessons with immediate tests in laboratory contexts. It would be useful to determine the extent to which multimedia design principles apply to more authentic learning environments, and to pinpoint the boundary conditions under which the principles are most effective in improving student achievement.

The primary practical recommendation for improving student achievement is that people can understand material better when it is presented with words and pictures rather than with words alone. In creating multimedia lessons that promote student achievement, instructors should be guided by evidence-based principles of multimedia design.

References

Comenius, J. A. (1887). *The Orbis Pictus.* Syracuse, NY: C. W. Bardeen. (Original work published 1658)

Clark, R. C., & Mayer, R. E. (2008). *e-Learning and the science of instruction* (2nd ed.). San Francisco, CA: Pfeiffer.

Ginns, P. (2005). Meta-analysis of the modality effect. *Learning and Instruction, 15,* 313–332.

Ginns, P. (2006). Integrating information: A meta-analysis of spatial contiguity and temporal contiguity effects. *Learning and Instruction, 16,* 511–525.

Kalyuga, S. (2005). The prior knowledge principle in multimedia learning. In R. E. Mayer (Ed.), *The Cambridge handbook of multimedia learning* (pp. 325–338). New York: Cambridge University Press.

Lowe, R., & Schnotz, W. (Eds.). (2008). *Learning with animation.* New York: Cambridge University Press.

Mayer, R. E. (Ed.). (2005). *The Cambridge handbook of multimedia learning.* New York: Cambridge University Press.

Mayer, R. E. (2009). *Multimedia learning* (2nd ed.). New York: Cambridge University Press.

Mayer, R. E., Hegarty, M., Mayer, S., & Campbell, J. (2005). When static media promote active learning: Annotated illustrations versus narrated animations in multimedia learning. *Journal of Experimental Psychology: Applied, 11,* 256–265.

Paivio, A. (1986). *Mental representations: A dual-coding approach.* Oxford, England: Oxford University Press.

Plass, J. L., Moreno, R., & Brunken, R. (2010). *Cognitive load theory.* New York: Cambridge University Press.

Sweller, J. (1999). *Instructional design in technical areas.* Camberwell, Australia: ACER Press.

8.15

Technology-Supported Learning and Academic Achievement

PETER REIMANN AND ANINDITO ADITOMO
University of Sydney

Introduction

Computer technologies have been introduced into schools since about 1960, with large scale deployment starting in the 1980s once personal computers became widely available and affordable. A second wave of deployment saw the networking of computers, first in the form of classroom based local-area network (LAN), and more recently the connection to the Internet. More recent trends include such developments as the introduction of interactive whiteboards into classrooms, and the establishment of 1:1 computing (one digital device per student) in some systems. However, the major meta-analyses available at this time do not address these more recent developments—one might also add the increasing interest in mobile and cloud computing amongst them—but focus on the classic question: Do students in classes where computers are used profit from this compared to students in classes where no computers are used?

Concerning our question, of whether technologies make a difference for education, more than 60 meta-analyses have appeared since 1980, covering thousands of individual comparative studies. Most of the meta-analyses have focused on questions specific to certain types of technologies, subject matter, or grade level. However, a secondary meta-analysis has been published (Tamim, Bernard, Borokhosvski, Abrami, & Schmid, 2011) that aggregates the data from 25 meta-analyses. We will use Tamin et al. (2011) to answer the general question; we complement this by drawing from more recent meta-analyses, most of them not covered in Tamim et al. (2011), to address more specific questions regarding the effects on important learning areas (mathematics, reading, writing, language learning). Notably absent from the literature are meta-analyses of technology use for science learning.

Although space does not permit us to report on the effectiveness of specific types of educational technology, it is worth mentioning what types are typically included in the label "computer technology" (CT). What is covered in

these studies are CT applications that can be categorized fairly well into five types (Li & Ma, 2010): (a) tutorials: programs that directly teach by providing information, demonstration, and opportunities for (drill and) practice; (b) communication media, such as e-mail, web-browsers, video conferencing tools that provide access to information and opportunities for communication, including student-to-student communication; (c) exploratory environments, including simulations, hypermedia environments, web quests; (d) tools, in particular productivity tools (word processors, presentations tools), media manipulation software, such as for digital imaging and music, and (data) analysis tools, such as spreadsheet programs; (e) programming languages, ranging from general purpose ones (e.g., Java, Prolog) to those with a didactic function (e.g., Logo). It is important to keep this variety of meanings of CT in mind when looking at the field through the lens of meta-analyses.

Research Evidence

The most comprehensive review currently available is provided by Tamim and colleagues (2011). They employed a second-order meta-analysis procedure to summarize 25 meta-analyses, which together cover 1,055 primary studies and more than 100,000 students. This represents 40 years of research activity addressing the question of whether students in face-to-face classrooms that use (CT) obtained higher achievement than those in classrooms without technology. The study found that technology had a positive but relatively small effect ($d = 0.35$) on student achievement. The effect was larger for K-12 ($d = 0.40$) compared to postsecondary classrooms ($d = 0.29$). Another recent meta-analysis (Schmid et al., 2009), not included in Tamim et al.'s review, found a very similar effect size ($d = 0.28$) for postsecondary classrooms. A further moderating variable identified by Tamim et al. was related to *how* technology is used: it had a larger effect when used to support instruction ($d = 0.42$) than when used to deliver content ($d = 0.31$).

Again, this was consistent with the findings of Schmid et al., which showed that technology for cognitive support ($d = 0.41$) was more beneficial than technology for presentation support ($d = 0.10$). To go beyond this broad picture, we now review evidence for specific content areas.

Li and Ma (2010) performed a meta-analysis of 85 independent effect sizes extracted from 46 primary studies involving a total of 36,793 learners that indicated statistically significant positive effects of CT on *mathematics* achievement ($d = 0.28$). In addition, several characteristics of primary studies were identified as having effects. For example, CT showed advantage in promoting the mathematics achievement of elementary over secondary school students. As well, CT showed larger effects on the mathematics achievement of special need students than that of general education students. The positive effect of CT was greater when combined with a constructivist approach to teaching than with a traditional approach to teaching, and studies that used nonstandardized tests as measures of mathematics achievement reported larger effects of CT than studies that used standardized tests.

Another meta-analysis on the effect of computers on mathematics was reported by Cheung and Slavin (2011). The total sample size was 56,886 students at both the elementary (n = 31,555) and secondary (n = 25,331) levels. Technology had a positive but small effect (0.15 standard deviations) on students' scores in standardized math tests. In terms of other variables that moderated the effect, Cheung and Slavin found that computers had a larger effect when used more than 30 minutes/week. The effect also varied depending on the type of intervention, with supplemental computer assisted instruction having larger impacts than "comprehensive models" and "computer-managed learning". Furthermore, the authors also reported that larger effects were more often found in quasi-experiments ($d = 0.19$) compared to randomized experiments ($d = 0.10$), and in smaller sample studies ($d = 0.26$) compared to larger sample studies ($d = 0.12$).

A meta-analysis reported by Cheung and Slavin (2012) reviewed 85 studies on the effect of various CTs on *reading* achievement. This included students at the kindergarten (n = 2,068), elementary (n = 34,200), and secondary levels (n = 24,453). They found an average effect size of $d = 0.16$, indicating a small positive impact on reading achievement. This effect varied depending on how technology was used: When technology was used just to supplement traditional classroom instruction, the effect was only $d = 0.11$. But when technology was used in a more integrated manner, the effect increased to $d = 0.28$. Technology's impact was also greater for low ability ($d = 0.37$) compared to high ability ($d = 0.08$) students, and for secondary ($d = 0.31$) than elementary students ($d = 0.10$). In addition, the authors found that some methodological features influenced the effect size, with large-scale randomized experiments finding smaller effects of technology, compared to smaller-scale quasi-experiments.

The meta-analysis reported by Goldberg, Russell, and Cook (2003) examined the question of whether word processing software positively impacted K-12 students' *writing*. Included were 26 independent studies published between 1992 and 2002 (sample sizes were not reported). On writing quantity, the analysis found an average effect size of 0.54, indicating a moderate positive impact of word processing technology on the length of students' writing. The study also looked into writing quality, which was measured using various indicators such as coherence, organization, tone, voice, and creativity. On measures of quality, word processors also had a positive effect ($d = 0.40$) on students' writing. The effects on both quantity and quality were stable across students with varying prior computer experience and prior achievement. In addition, the availability of writing support (keyboard training, technical assistance, teacher feedback, and peer editing) made little difference to the effect of computers on students' writing.

Goldberg and colleagues also examined studies that provided information on students' writing processes. Six studies found that students made more changes between drafts when using word processors. Other studies showed that when using computers, students' writing became more collaborative, with more peer editing and discussions. Furthermore, a study found that students' writing when using paper-and-pencil followed a linear process from brainstorming, outlining, and drafting to revising. When using computers, however, this process became less linear, with students iterating between producing and revising their texts.

Zhao (2003) reported a meta-analysis of 9 studies on technology-supported (second) *language learning* in postsecondary classrooms. These studies covered 419 students and a variety of target languages (English, German, Spanish, French, and Arabic). The analysis found a large average effect size of $d = 1.12$. Unfortunately, probably because of the limited number of studies examined, the analysis did not examine potential moderating variables which may influence the effect.

The last study we include sheds light on a tendency reported in various of the meta-analyses described above: that the pedagogy employed along with CT use in classrooms plays an important role. Rosen and Salomon (2007) made this the focus of their meta-analysis by comparing studies along the dimension constructivist pedagogy versus traditional pedagogy. By analyzing 32 studies that varied on this dimension—all of them in mathematics education—they found that while the mean effect size across all studies was medium ($d = 0.46$), it rose to 0.90 in favor of constructivist learning environments when constructivist-appropriate measures were used (i.e., those that assess creativity and collaboration, as opposed to just computation fluency). But even in cases where traditional pedagogy was used and assessed only with traditional learning measures for math achievement, traditional education yielded poorer or similar outcomes when compared with constructivist use of CT.

Summary and Recommendations

Table 8.2 summarizes the findings from the meta-analyses included in this chapter by learning area. It seems safe to

Table 8.15.1 Summary of Studies by Learning Area

Achievement area	Effect size (d)	Moderating variables		
		Use of technology	Education level	Methodological features
Overall	0.35	Support instruction > Deliver content	K-12 > Postsecondary	Not examined
Mathematics	0.15 – 0.28	Constructivist > Traditional pedagogy	Elementary > Secondary	a) Randomized exp. > Quasi-experiment b) Small sample > Large sample
Reading	0.16	Integrated > Traditional pedagogy	Secondary > Elementary	a) Randomized exp. > Quasi-experiment b) Small sample > Large sample
Writing	0.54 (quantity) 0.40 (quality)	Not examined	Not examined	Not examined
Second language	1.12	Not examined	Not examined	Not examined

conclude that, most of the time, ICT does have a positive, albeit relatively small, impact on students' achievement across many content areas. The effect of computer technology seems to be particularly small in studies that use either large samples or randomized control groups. Thus, claims that any particular technology, in and of itself, will bring large, radical, or revolutionary impact on achievement should be met with skepticism. But at the very least, these findings show that technology does not have detrimental effects on learning.

The key pedagogical message resulting from the research reviewed is that CT use in classrooms will more likely be supporting learning if it is employed for the purpose of students interacting with content and interacting with peers rather than solely distributing and presenting content. There are quantitative variations across different content areas, with the effects on writing seemingly the strongest. But it is particularly difficult to discern, with meta-analyses, the extent to which this can be attributed to a general effect of text processing technology (that usually includes spell checkers and basic grammar checking), as different from (additional) effects on editing, revising, organizing text, and other deep features of writing.

The rapid development of technology will mean that there will always be new gadgets to be trialed in the classroom, ever tempting researchers and educators to conduct yet again another technology/nontechnology study. But we argue that it's time to end technology vs. non-technology studies, because (a) it is unlikely that there are students left who do not use ICT (outside of the classroom at least), and (b) there is strong evidence, some of which is summarized above, showing that what matters more is *how* rather than *whether* technology is used in the classroom. The second aspect has been argued famously by Richard E. Clark (1983), who considered CT to No CT comparisons meaningless (for learning with media) because it makes little sense to look at a tool/medium without considering how the tool is used, what messages are conveyed, and what the use context is. While we do not want to end on so

skeptical a note, it needs to be considered to what extent it continues to make sense to ask the CT versus No CT question in its most general variant. To us at least, it seems more appropriate for future meta-analytical work to look at the *differential* effects of different types of technologies, given the vast differences between CT use for communication and collaboration compared to problem solving or media construction, for instance.

References

Cheung, A., & Slavin, R. E. (2011). *The effectiveness of educational technology applications for enhancing mathematics achievement in K-12 classrooms: A meta-analysis.* Baltimore, MD: Johns Hopkins University, Center for Research and Reform in Education, Retrieved from http://www.bestevidence.org/word/tech_math_Apr_11_2012.pdf.

Cheung, A., & Slavin, R. E. (2012). *The effectiveness of educational technology applications for enhancing reading achievement in K-12 classrooms: A meta-analysis.* Baltimore, MD: Johns Hopkins University, Center for Research and Reform in Education, Retrieved from http://www.bestevidence.org/word/tech_read_Apr_25_2012.pdf.

Clark, R. E. (1983). Reconsidering research on learning from media. *Review of Educational Research, 53*, 445–449.

Goldberg, A., Russell, M., & Cook, A. (2003). The effect of computers on student writing: A meta-analysis of studies from 1992–2002. *Journal of Technology, Learning, and Assessment, 2*, 3–51.

Li, Q., & Ma, X. (2010). A meta-analysis of the effects of computer technology on school students' mathematics learning. *Educational Psychology Review, 22*(3), 215–243.

Rosen, Y., & Salomon, G. (2007). The differential learning achievements of constructivist technology-intensive learning environments as compared with traditional ones: A meta-analysis. *Journal of Educational Computing Research, 36*, 1–14

Schmid, R. F. et al. (2009). Technology's effect on achievement in higher education: A stage I meta-analysis of classroom applications. *Journal of Computing in Higher Education, 21*, 95–109.

Tamim, R. M., Bernard, R. M., Borokhosvski, E., Abrami, P. C., & Schmid, R. F. (2011). What forty years of research says about the impact of technology on learning: A second-order meta-analysis and validation study. *Review of Educational Research, 81*(1), 4–28.

Zhao, Y. (2003). Recent developments in technology and language learning: A literature review and meta-analysis. *CALICO Journal, 21*(10), 7–27. Retrieved from https://www.calico.org/html/article_279.pdf

8.16

Feedback

HELEN TIMPERLEY
University of Auckland

Introduction

Feedback is information provided by an agent to a learner about aspects of performance or understanding (Hattie & Timperley, 2007). Usually, feedback follows instruction. For example, a student might be taught a new mathematical concept, attempt some examples that demonstrate misconceptions about that concept, and a peer, teacher, or parent will correct these misconceptions by giving feedback. Alternatively, the learner looks up the answers and analyses the errors, thus providing feedback to him- or herself. More recently, feedback has become integrated into formative assessment processes (Allal, 2010), so some forms of feedback could more accurately be seen as new instruction. In these situations, feedback takes the form of extending students' understandings and fills gaps between what is understood and what is aimed to be understood. Whichever way it is thought about, it is most powerful when it addresses faulty interpretations, not a lack of understanding (Kulhavy, 1977). Feedback must have something on which to build.

Interest in feedback is high because the effects on student achievement can be high. Feedback itself ranks 10th on the contributions to student achievement in Hattie's (2009) meta-analysis on the effects of a variety of influences on student achievement. Its power comes partly from clustering with other strategies associated with effective feedback including student self-report grades (rank 1), formative evaluation (rank 3), and teacher clarity (rank 8). Effective feedback is usually embedded in these other strategies.

Research Evidence

A number of meta-analyses have assessed the influence of feedback. In order of the effect sizes these studies include: Skiba, Casey, and Center (1985–1986) with an ES of 1.24 for special education students; Lysakowski and Walberg (1982) with an ES of 1.13 for cues and corrective feedback; Walberg (1982) with an ES of 0.81 on cues, motivational

influences, and reinforcement; Tenenbaum and Goldring (1989) with an ES of 0.74 on cues, participation, reinforcement, feedback, and correctives; Rummel and Feinberg (1988) with an ES of 0.6 on extrinsic feedback and rewards; Yeany and Miller (1983) with an ES of 0.52 on diagnostic feedback in science; Kluger and DeNisi (1996) with an ES of 0.38 on feedback in general; L'Hommedieu, Menges, and Brinko (1990) with an ES of 0.34 on student ratings; Moin (1986) with an ES of 0.29 on feedback in general; Bangert-Drowns, Kulik, Kulik, and Morgan (1991) with an ES of 0.28 on testing; Kulik and Kulik (1988) with an ES of 0.28 on immediate versus delayed feedback; Getsie, Langer, and Glass (1985) with an ES of 0.14 on rewards and punishments, and Wilkinson (1981) with an ES of 0.12 on teacher praise.

As can be seen from this summary, the effects are not consistent. Some types of feedback are clearly more effective than others and a more detailed analysis of individual studies shows that some forms can actually be negative. Those forms of feedback with positive effects provide information to the learner about the task, the processes needed to understand or perform the tasks, and self-regulation of learning. Those much less effective are focused on forms of feedback that do not provide task-related information. Lipnevich and Smith (2009), for example, identified that providing students with a tentative grade and no comments on a piece of work near the beginning of a course depressed future performance. Deci, Koestner, and Ryan (1999) found a negative correlation between extrinsic rewards and task performance because these kinds of rewards undermine intrinsic motivation.

Hattie and Timperley (2007) developed a model from a synthesis of meta-analyses on feedback. They proposed that the main purpose of feedback is to reduce discrepancies between current understandings or performance, and a goal. The conditions under which feedback is most likely to be effective in improving learning is when the goal is clear and the feedback leads to increased effort to tackle more challenging tasks or goals (Kluger & DeNisi, 1996). It can be effective in improving error detection skills when students seek better strategies to complete tasks or obtain more information from which they can then solve problems. Alternatively, feedback can lead to strategies that are ineffective in improving learning such as abandoning goals, disengaging in the pursuit of further goals, blurring the goals or combining them with so many others that the learner can pick and choose those goals they attain and ignore the others. These alternative responses are more likely to happen when goals are unclear, or are seen to be unmanageable (Sweller, 1990).

To reduce the discrepancy between current performance and a desired goal, a student must be able to answer three questions. The first relates to the goal itself with the student asking, "Where am I going?" The answer to this question might be thought of as "feed up." The second relates to information about current performance with the student asking, "How am I doing?" The answer to this question takes the traditional form of feedback. The third relates to information about how to reduce the discrepancy between current performance and a goal, with the student asking, "Where to next?" or feed forward.

Answering the question "How am I going?" provides information relative to a task or performance goal. Even anticipating this kind of feedback can have a positive effect on task performance (Vollemyer & Rheinberg, 2005). It is effective when it consists of information about progress, and / or how to proceed. It is ineffective when it fails to convey to the student information that helps them to understand how they are going in ways that provide guidance for the next question of "Where to next?" If the feedback takes the form of a test mark, for example, it typically provides little information to the student about what to do to close the gap between current performance and a goal. Alternatively, feedback that provides this information leads to greater possibilities for learning, enhanced challenges, more self-regulation over the learning process, deeper understanding, and more information about what is and what is not understood. Thus answering this feed forward question potentially provides rich opportunities for learning.

The three questions do not work in isolation from one another but work together in iterative cycles of understanding goals, working out progress toward them and identifying better strategies for achieving them. Hattie and Timperley (2007) identified how the three questions influenced feedback at four levels, three of which are effective and one ineffective. The three effective levels are feedback about the task, process, and self-regulation. The less effective level is focused on the self that includes personal evaluations, praise, and affect about the learner.

Feedback about the task usually provides information about whether work is correct or incorrect and may include directions to acquire more, different, or correct information. Positive evaluative feedback (is correct) has more impact on motivation than negative evaluative feedback (is incorrect) but not necessarily on achievement (Rakoczy, Klieme,

Bügermeister, & Harks (2008). One of the problems with too much feedback at the task level is that students may focus on the immediate goal and not the strategies to attain the goal. It seems likely that task-focused feedback is most beneficial when it helps students reject wrong strategies and provides cues for searching and strategising; that is, leading to the second level of feedback about the processing of the task.

This second level of feedback about the process used to create a product or task may be at a surface level that involves the acquisition, storing, reproduction, and use of knowledge. At a deeper level it includes information about relations in the environment, relations perceived by a person, and relations between the environment and the person's perceptions (Balzer, Doherty, & O'Connor, 1989). This kind of feedback addresses cognitive processes, and transference to other more difficult or untried tasks (Purdie, Hattie, & Douglas, 1996). Feedback about the process can also include students' strategies for error detection because some of the most powerful feedback is when a learner develops error detection strategies and so is able to provide feedback to him or herself. Thus, feedback about this second level is particularly effective when it includes feedback for self-regulation.

This third self-regulation level addresses the way students monitor, direct, and regulate their actions toward the learning goal. It implies autonomy, self-control, self-direction, and self-discipline and can have significant effects on achievement when carefully scaffolded (Nicol, 2009). When students create internal feedback and self-assess, they need to have the confidence or willingness to invest effort into seeking and dealing with the feedback information.

The final level of feedback to self as a person is only referred to here because of the high frequency of its use in classrooms, particularly in the form of personal praise. Typically, it is not effective because it contains little task-related information and is rarely converted into more commitment to learning goals, enhanced self-efficacy or understanding of the task. The circumstances under which praise might be effective occur when it is directed to the effort, self-regulation, engagement, or processes relating to the task and its performance. The litmus test is the amount of information that is given about reducing discrepancies between current performance and the desired goal with a focus on strategies and effort, not on perceptions of ability.

Summary and Recommendations

It appears that teachers find it difficult to provide feedback on the first three levels. Hattie (2009) notes in his analysis that, in reality, teachers provide little task, process, and self-regulated feedback. A study by Timperley and Parr (2009) examined the increase in use of three formative assessment strategies within a professional development project. Teachers introduced the first two strategies, articulating learning intentions and working with students to develop success criteria, relatively consistently. Feedback, on the other hand, was only rarely given and feed forward was almost absent.

The research on feedback presents an unsolved dilemma. Potentially, feedback can have high effects on student learning and achievement when it helps students reduce the discrepancies between current understandings and performance and goals. Yet the most common forms of feedback in classrooms, test marks and personal praise, are those least likely to produce these effects. Shifting these teacher behaviours appears to be very difficult. The key question needs to shift from, "What kinds of feedback are effective?" to "How can we encourage teachers to use the kinds of feedback known to be effective?"

References

Allal, L. (2010) Assessment and the regulation of learning. *International Encyclopaedia of Education* (pp. 348–352). New York: Elsevier.

Balzer, W. K., Doherty, M. E., & O'Connor, R., Jr. (1989). Effects of cognitive feedback on performance. *Psychological Bulletin, 106*(3), 410–433.

Bangert-Drowns, R. L., Kulik, C. L., Kulik, J. A., & Morgan, M. T. (1991). The instructional effect of feedback in test-like events. *Review of Educational Research, 61*, 213–237.

Deci, E. L., Koestner, R., & Ryan, M. R. (1999). A meta-analytical review of experiments examining the effects of extrinsic rewards on intrinsic motivation. *Psychological Bulletin, 125*, 627–668.

Getsie, R. L., Langer, P., & Glass, G. V. (1985). Meta-analysis of the effects of type and combination of feedback on children's discrimination learning. *Review of Educational Research, 55*(1), 9–22.

Hattie, J. (2009). *Visible learning a synthesis of over 800 meta-analyses relating to achievement.* New York: Routledge.

Hattie, J., & Timperley, H. (2007). The power of feedback. *Review of Educational Research, 77*(1), 81–112.

Kluger, A. N., & DeNisi, A. (1996). The effects of feedback interventions on performance: A historical review, a meta-analysis, and a preliminary feedback intervention theory. *Psychological Bulletin, 119*(2), 254–284.

Kulhavy, R. W. (1977). Feedback in written instruction. *Review of Educational Research, 47*(1), 211–232.

Kulik, J. A., & Kulik, C. C. (1988). Timing of feedback and verbal learning. *Review of Educational Research, 58*(1), 79–97.

Lipnevich, A., & Smith, J. (2009). Effects of differential feedback on students' examination performance. *Journal of Experimental Psychology. 15*(4), 319–333.

L'Hommedieu, R., Menges, R. J., & Brinko, K. T. (1990). Methodological explanations for the modest effects of feedback from student ratings. *Journal of Educational Psychology, 82*(2), 232–241.

Lysakowski, R. S., & Walberg, H. J. (1982). Instructional effects of cues, participation, and corrective feedback: A quantitative synthesis. *American Educational Research Journal, 19*, 559–578.

Moin, A. K. (1986). *Relative effectiveness of various techniques of calculus instruction: A meta-analysis* (Unpublished doctoral dissertation). Department of Mathematics, University of Syracuse, Syracuse, New York.

Nicol, D. (2009). Assessment for learner self-regulation: Enhancing achievement in first year using learning technologies. *Assessment and Evaluation in Higher Education, 34*(3), 335–352.

Purdie, N., Hattie, J. A., & Douglas, G. (1996). Student conceptions of learning and their use of self-regulated learning strategies: A cross-cultural comparison. *Journal of Educational Psychology, 88*, 87–100.

Rakoczy, K., Klieme, E., Bügermeister, A., & Harks, B. (2008). The interplay between student evaluation and instruction. *Journal of Psychology, 216*(2). 111–1124.

Rummel, A., & Feinberg, R. (1988). Cognitive evaluation theory: A meta-analytic review of the literature. *Social Behavior and Personality, 16*(2), 147–164.

Skiba, R., Casey, A., & Center, B. A. (1985-1986). Nonaversive procedures in the treatment of classroom behaviour problems. *Journal of Special Education, 19*, 459–481.

Sweller, J. (1990). Cognitive processes and instruction procedures. *Australian Journal of Education, 34*(2), 125–130.

Tenenbaum, G., & Goldring, E. (1989). A meta-analysis of the effect of enhanced instruction: Cues, participation, reinforcement and feedback and correctives on motor skill learning. *Journal of Research and Development in Education, 22*, 5–64.

Timperley, H. S., & Parr, J. M. (2009). What is this lesson about? Instructional processes and student understandings in writing classrooms. *The Curriculum Journal, 20*(1), 43–60.

Vollemyer, R., & Rheinberg, F. (2005). A surprising effect of feedback on learning. *Learning and Instruction, 15*, 589–602.

Walberg, H. J. (1982). What makes schooling effective? *Contemporary Education Review, 1*, 1–34.

Wilkinson, S. S (1981). The relationship of teacher praise and student achievement: A meta-analysis of selected research. *Dissertation Abstracts International, 41*, (9-A), 3998.

Yeany, R. H., & Miller, P. A. (1983). Effects of diagnostic/remedial instruction on science learning: A meta-analysis. *Journal of Research in Science Teaching, 20*, 19–26.

8.17

Individualized Instruction

HERSH C. WAXMAN, BEVERLY L. ALFORD, AND DANIELLE B. BROWN
Texas A&M University

Introduction

Individualized instruction refers to the idea that each student learns differently and thus in order to accommodate these differences, instruction should be personalized, matched, or adapted to the experiences, aptitudes, and interests of each individual student. This concept emphasizes the importance of teachers viewing learning from the students' personal viewpoint or "eyes of the student" and then personalizing instruction in order to maximize the individual needs of students (Nuthall, 2005).

Individualized instruction has been referred to and described by a number of different constructs such as "adaptive instruction," "differentiated instruction," and "personalized learning." Individualizing or differentiating instruction for students of different abilities within the same classroom, operates on several key assumptions, all of which are crucial when considering effective instruction: (a) students differ in their interests and readiness to learn, (b) student differences are critical in the education process, (c) learning has to occur "within" students, rather than "to" them, (e) students need teachers who identify and build upon their strengths and weaknesses, (f) effective teachers create and modify instruction for the various students within the classroom, and (g) effective classrooms do not treat all students the same; rather, they ensure students receive what they need (Tomlinson, 2006).

Individualized instruction has a long history (Washburne, 1925) and there have been several articles that have traced the psychological roots of individualized programs back to two traditions: the continental tradition (e.g., Rousseau, Froebel, & Piaget) and the Anglo-American tradition (e.g., Hobbes, Darwin, & Thorndike; cf., Walberg, 1975). About 25 years ago, there were many individualized instruction programs that were widely implemented in schools (Wang & Walberg, 1985). Most of these programs, however, have disappeared over the past few decades, primarily due to the lack of research evidence of their effectiveness.

Research Evidence

There have been several meta-analyses that have focused on the effects of individualized instruction on student learning (Hattie, 2009). Waxman, Wang, Anderson, and Walberg's (1985) meta-analysis of 38 studies, for example, examined the effects of adaptive instruction on students' cognitive, affective, and behavioral outcomes. They found a weighted effective size of 0.45 suggesting that the average student in individualized or adaptive learning programs scores at the 67th percentile of control group distributions. They also found that the effects were consistent across grade levels, socioeconomic levels, races, community types, and difference types of research studies.

Other meta-analyses, however, have found very slight overall effects for individualized instruction. Bangert, Kulik, and Kulik's (1983) meta-analysis of 53 studies, for example, found that an individualized teaching system has only a small effect on student outcomes in secondary school courses. They found that individualized teaching systems did not contribute significantly to students' performance ($d = 0.10$), attitudes toward subject ($d = 0.14$), critical thinking ability ($d = 0.26$), or student self-esteem ($d = 0.26$). Horak's (1981) meta-analysis investigated the effects of individualized instruction on mathematics achievement at the elementary, middle, and high school levels. She found that the overall average effect size was -0.07 which means that the average student in an individualized program achieved 0.07 of a standard deviation less than that of the average student in a traditional program. She also found that the longer duration of the study (> 8 months), the less likely it was to find a noticeable difference in students' achievement.

Hattie's (2009) meta-synthesis of nine meta-analyses on individualized instruction included 600 studies, 1,146 effects, and 9,380 participants and yielded a very modest effective size ($d = 0.23$) that ranked 100th out of 138 teaching, learning, and curricular approaches he synthesized. Although the evidence on the effectiveness of individualized instruction is disappointing, it should be pointed out that the only research summarized in the meta-analyses is quantitative which excludes all of the qualitative studies in this area.

Current Areas in Individualized Instruction. Early childhood education (ECE) is one area where individualized instruction continues to be prominently emphasized. ECE generally focuses on the critical balance between providing instruction based on what is known about children's social, emotional, and cognitive development with meeting those expectations that are the result of an ever-increasing shift toward educational standardization and answerability. Understanding and recognizing instructional issues unique to each learner has moved toward the forefront of early childhood education policy and learning.

Perhaps one of the best known contributors to early childhood education, Maria Montessori championed a theoretical and practical approach to learning which recognized the individuality of each child—particularly in connection with developmental characteristics and challenges. A prominent advocate of individual instruction, Montessori was among the first to offer teachers of young children and elementary students an alternative to whole-class teaching (Brehony, 2000). The Montessori approach operates on the philosophy that children learn by way of their own activities and adaptations. She placed huge emphasis on the prepared environment (e.g., classroom arrangement, learning materials, instructional flexibility, and student freedom), much of which underscores the tenets of individualized instruction (Jensen, 2004). Some additional and enduring elements of Montessori's program include: sensitive periods, or windows of opportunity for growth; auto-education, or children working on their own; mixed aged grouping; and self-paced activities (Wolfe, 2002).

Young children and students in elementary school differ greatly in their learning abilities and needs; and if educators intend to optimally maximize students' individual potential, they must address these differences (Tomlinson, 2000). The National Association for the Education of Young Children (NAEYC) espoused that learning proceeds "at varying" and "uneven rates across different areas of a child's individual functioning" (Copple & Bredekamp, 2009, p. 11). Additionally, pertaining to students in primary grades, NAEYC advised that practitioners ought to "adapt instruction for individual children who are having difficulty and also for those who are capable of more advanced levels of competence" (p. 295).

Another specific type of individualized instruction that has been shown to enhance student achievement, while also allowing teachers to overcome some of the obstacles associated with individualizing at the secondary level, is computer-assisted instruction (CAI). CAI is capable of individualizing instruction for a large number of diverse learners across multiple subject areas (Azevedo & Bernard, 1995). In addition, students are more motivated to participate in computer instruction purely for the fact that they are allowed to use a computer (Barley et al., 2002). A key component of individualized instruction, immediate and frequent feedback, can also be provided with CAI. From these formative assessments, CAI can modify instruction accordingly to what best suits the needs of the student. Although the overall effects of computer-assisted instruction ($d = 0.37$) have been found to be only slightly higher than that for individualized instruction, there are several aspects of CAI such as students "controlling" the learning and optimizing the feedback that hold promise for improving student learning (Hattie, 2009).

Summary and Recommendations

During the current high-stakes testing and accountability era, there have been few individualized instructional models implemented in schools. It has been argued, for example, that teachers are racing against the clock to cover the standards before a test, instead of pacing instruction to meet the needs of individual students (Tomlinson, 2000). Several educators, however, argue that individualized instruction has the greatest potential for improving instruction in today's standards-based environment (Corcoran & Silander, 2009). In order to provide individualized instruction to students, teachers need to be highly skilled in providing this type of instruction to meet students' needs while also preparing them for high-stakes tests (Brimijoin, 2005).

As our schools become more culturally and linguistically diverse, individualized instruction may become more important as a teaching and learning strategy. In classrooms where instruction is individualized, students are generally highly engaged and actively participate in their own learning. In addition, this type of instructional environment provides equitable learning opportunities for *all* students.

Although the theoretical and practical arguments for enhancing student achievement through individualized instruction are convincing, more research needs to examine how recent approaches to individualized instruction impact student outcomes. Instructional programs today are generally bounded by the constraints of the school organization and budget. Matching instructional objectives and activities to the experiences, aptitudes, and interests of individual students does not appear to be a high priority in the 21st century, but we may see increased interest in areas such as early childhood education and computer-assisted instruction.

References

Azevedo, R., & Bernard, R.N. (1995). Assessing the effects of feedback in computer-assisted learning. *British Journal of Educational Technology, 26*(1), 57–58.

Bangert, R. L., Kulik, J. A., & Kulik, C. L. C. (1983). Individualized systems of instruction in secondary schools. *Review of Educational Research, 53*(2), 143–158.

Barley, Z., Lauer, P. A., Arens, S. A., Apthrop, H. S., Englert, K. S., Snow, D., & Akiba, M. (2002). *Helping at-risk students meet standards: A synthesis of evidence-based classroom practices.* Aurora, CO: Mid-continent Research for Education and Learning.

Brehony, K. J. (2000). Montessori, individual work and individuality in the elementary school classroom. *History of Education, 29*(2), 115–128.

Brimijoin, K. (2005). Differentiation and high-stakes testing: An oxymoron? *Theory into Practice, 44*(3), 254–261.

Copple, C., & Bredekamp, S. (2009). *Developmentally appropriate practice in early childhood programs.* Washington, DC: National Association for the Education of Young Children.

Corcoran, T., & Silander, M. (2009). Instruction in high schools: The evidence and the challenge. *The Future of Children, 19*(1), 157–183.

Hattie, J. (2009). *Visible learning: A synthesis of over 800 meta-analyses relating to achievement.* London: Routledge.

Horak, V. M. (1981). A meta-analysis of research findings on individualized instruction in mathematics. *Journal of Educational Research, 74*(4), 249–253.

Jensen, S. J. (2004). One individual at a time: Instruction in the Montessori classroom. *Montessori Life, 16*(4), 46–49.

Nuthall, G. A. (2005). The cultural myths and realities of classroom teaching and learning: A personal journey. *Teachers College Record, 107*(5), 895–934.

Tomlinson, C.A. (2000). Reconcilable differences? Standards-based teaching and differentiation. *Educational Leadership, 58*(1), 6–11.

Tomlinson, C. A. (2006). An *educator's guide to differentiating instruction.* Boston, MA: Houghton Mifflin.

Walberg, H. J. (1975). Psychological theories of educational individualization. In H. Talmage (Ed.), *Systems of individualized education* (pp. 5–26). Berkeley, CA: McCutchan.

Wang, M. C., & Walberg, H. J. (Eds.). (1985). *Adapting instruction to individual differences.* Berkeley, CA: McCutchan.

Washburne, C. W. (Ed.). (1925). *Adapting the schools to individual differences* (24th yearbook of the National Society for the Study of Education, Part 2). Chicago, IL: University of Chicago Press.

Waxman, H. C., Wang, M. C., Anderson, K. A., & Walberg, H. J. (1985). Adaptive education and student outcomes: A quantitative synthesis. *Journal of Educational Research, 78*(4), 228–236.

Wolfe, J. (2002). *Learning from the past: Historical voices in early childhood education.* Mayerthorpe, Alberta: Piney Branch.

8.18

Worked Examples

PAUL AYRES AND JOHN SWELLER
University of New South Wales

Introduction

Over the last three decades, cognitive load theory (Sweller, Ayres, & Kalyuga, 2011) has been used to identify a number of effects that directly implicate teaching, learning, and instructional design. The most widely investigated is the worked example effect, which has been shown to lead to better learning outcomes than solving equivalent problems. This chapter describes the worked example effect and some of the associated empirical research. Variations and additions to the basic worked example design are also described, showing how modifications can support the development of problem solving skills.

A worked example provides a step-by-step solution to a problem. Worked examples are often known under synonyms such as *learning from examples*, *example-based learning*, *learning from model answers,* and *studying expert solutions*. The following is a worked example to a quadratic equation:

Problem: solve $x^2 - x - 12 = 0$
Solution: $x^2 - x - 12 = 0$
$(x - 4)(x + 3) = 0$
$x - 4 = 0$, or $x + 3 = 0$
$x = 4$, or $x = -3$.

In a traditional textbook approach to teaching mathematics, worked examples are often initially presented followed by extensive practice on solving similar and dissimilar (transfer) problems. Students may only be shown further worked examples after failing to find solutions to some of the problems. As a consequence learners are required to spend a significant amount of time on problem solving.

Showing students step-by-step solutions to mathematical problems, or explaining in detail how some scientific or economic principle works is not new. Teachers have always employed such techniques. However, in more recent times such methods have been questioned. An ongoing debate in education questions how much explicit help should be given to the learner by the teacher? A variety of views have emerged that range from advocating discovery learning or problem solving to explicit instruction. Constructivists view explicit instruction as a form of knowledge transmission, which is considered ineffective. But as Kirschner, Sweller, and Clark (2006) observed, methods such as discovery learning and problem solving have a weak theoretical base with little supporting empirical evidence. In contrast, the use of worked examples, which are a form of explicit instruction, has a very strong theoretical and empirical research base. Considerable evidence (e.g., Oksa, Kalyuga, & Chandler, 2010) exists that worked examples are a highly effective way of teaching learners, particularly those with little domain-specific prior knowledge (novices).

Research Evidence

The evidence in support of worked examples has come from randomised controlled experiments. Two groups of learners are chosen at random from a sample of students. One group receives instructional guidance through a set of worked examples; the second group spends the same amount of time on the same problem set but it is asked to solve the problems themselves. For example, using the quadratic equations example above, after an initial period where both groups receive some introductory information, including a limited number of worked examples, the worked example group receives a set of problem pairs in which the first member of each pair is a worked example while the second is a similar problem. The problem solving group receives the same set of problem pairs, but is required to solve all problems. Following this acquisition phase, both groups are asked to solve a different set of problems or tasks without any further practice or guidance. Typically, the worked example group will outperform the problem-solving group on similar and transfer problems (e.g., Cooper & Sweller, 1987).

The Empirical Evidence in Support of Worked Examples. The early evidence for the worked example effect came from learning mathematics. Sweller and Cooper (1985) used algebraic manipulation problems (e.g., for the expression x = ax - b, make x the subject) to show that worked examples required less time to process than solving the equivalent, conventional problems during the learning phase, and led to quicker solution times and improved test performance on similar test problems. In a second study, Cooper and Sweller (1987) replicated these results with word problems. They also demonstrated that transfer could be achieved with extra learning time. It was found that given a longer acquisition phase, worked examples were better able than problem solving practice to automate problem-solving operators sufficiently to transfer knowledge to other, novel problems. Following this early work, researchers replicated the worked example effect in many other mathematical and scientific domains (for more extensive summaries see Sweller et al., 2011). Furthermore, worked examples have been shown to be effective over a substantial period of time (2 years; Zhu & Simon, 1987) and in group work settings (Retnowati, Ayres, & Sweller, 2010).

More recent research has focused on less mathematical and scientific domains. As a consequence, it has been shown that worked examples can be effective in second language acquisition (Diao, Chandler, & Sweller, 2007), visual arts (Rourke & Sweller, 2009), and English literature (Oksa et al., 2010). A notable feature of the Oksa et al. study was that novices were presented with extracts from Shakespearean plays, with explanatory notes integrated into the original text. Providing model answers or interpretations of the text led to better comprehension than asking students to make their own interpretations (problem solving equivalent).

Theoretical Explanation for the Worked Example Effect. The studies reported above are a sample of the evidence in support of the worked example effect. But what are the cognitive processes that underpin this phenomenon? Cognitive load theory has articulated a strong theoretical argument (see Sweller et al., 2011). When students are required to learn through problem solving, they often solve the problem but fail to learn from the experience. When faced with a novel problem to solve, novice learners rely on general problem solving strategies (Newell & Simon, 1972) that require problem solvers to constantly consider and search for the differences between the given information and the goal, and the problem solving operators that might reduce those differences. This process results in very high levels of cognitive load that overtaxes a limited capacity human working memory (Miller, 1956), thus reducing learning. In contrast, studying worked examples does not require a constant search and a continuous alignment between goal and problem states because solutions are explicitly shown. The learner is better able to recognise the best solution paths and corresponding problem states without taxing working memory resources to the same extent as problem solving. Hence appropriate knowledge

structures are built in long-term memory in the form of schemas. A schema is a cognitive construct that allow us to recognise and solve related problems (Chi, Glaser, & Rees, 1982). A central aim of learning is to develop highly sophisticated schemas that enable us to solve complex problems. The worked example effect has shown repeatedly that worked examples are a highly effective method of building schematic knowledge.

Modifications to Worked Examples as Expertise Increases. As argued above, asking novices to problem-solve does not facilitate optimum schema acquisition because the learner's working memory resources are inefficiently occupied. However, as expertise develops, working memory is better able to deal with problem solving methods because highly developed schemas enable the learner to process greater chunks of information in working memory, allowing more resources to be directed to learning while problem solving. As a consequence, a problem solving strategy can be effective for learners with high levels of relevant domain specific knowledge. Furthermore, for such learners, worked examples can become ineffective in an example of the expertise reversal effect (see Kalyuga, Ayres, Chandler, & Sweller, 2003). The expertise reversal effect occurs when a strategy effective for novices becomes ineffective or harmful for learners with higher levels of knowledge. In the case of worked examples, studies have shown that the advantages of worked examples over learning by problem solving disappear, or reverse, as expertise develops. This effect has been shown in quite different domains, for example on mathematical tasks (Kalyuga & Sweller, 2004) and English literature (Oksa et al., 2010).

The underlying reason underpinning the expertise reversal effect is that asking more knowledgeable learners to follow direct instructional guidance designed for novices is redundant (Sweller et al., 2011). More knowledgeable learners do not need such guidance, and these learners spend precious working memory resources processing unnecessary information.

To help the transition from worked examples to problem solving practice, completion tasks have been used (van Merriënboer, 1990; Paas & van Merriënboer, 1994). A completion task omits steps in the solution, or explanation, which the learner is required to complete, representing a worked example/problem-solving hybrid. More sophisticated uses of completion problems have been implemented based on a fading strategy, which gradually decreases the levels of instructional guidance as learner expertise develops (Atkinson, Derry, Renkl, & Wortham, 2000). In a fading strategy the steps in a worked example are gradually faded out as learner knowledge increases, until finally, full problems are presented. Hence, the learner is required to use more problem solving as expertise develops. With this gradual fading strategy, increases in knowledge are used to overcome the demands on working memory made by a greater exposure to problem solving. Considerable evidence has been collected demonstrating the effectiveness of the fading strategy as expertise develops (see Renkl, Atkinson, & Große, 2004).

Summary and Recommendations

Substantial evidence has been collected in support of the worked example effect. Learners, particularly those in the initial stages of learning, benefit more from studying worked examples than equivalent episodes of problem solving. Studying worked examples provides a highly effective method of learning in a novel domain. In contrast to a commonly held educational belief, asking novices to problem solve does not lead to optimum learning outcomes, including problem solving proficiency. However, as expertise develops, a greater exposure to problem solving is required, and this exposure can be scaffolded by modifying worked examples to include, completion and fading examples. There are no shortcuts to acquiring problem solving skills. Students must develop their domain specific knowledge sufficiently to enable their working memories to cope with higher processing demands. A well-structured course of worked examples can assist problem-solving competence.

References

Atkinson, R. K., Derry, S. J., Renkl, A., & Wortham, D. (2000). Learning from examples: Instructional principles from the worked examples research. *Review of Educational Research, 70,* 181–214.

Chi, M., Glaser, R., & Rees, E. (1982). Expertise in problem solving. In R. Sternberg (Ed.), *Advances in the psychology of human intelligence* (pp. 7–75). Hillsdale, NJ: Erlbaum.

Cooper, G., & Sweller, J. (1987). Effects of schema acquisition and rule automation on mathematical problem-solving transfer. *Journal of Educational Psychology, 79,* 347–362.

Diao, Y., Chandler, P., & Sweller, J. (2007). The effect of written text on comprehension of spoken English as a foreign language. *American Journal of Psychology, 120,* 237–261.

Kalyuga, S., Ayres, P., Chandler, P., & Sweller, J. (2003). The expertise reversal effect. *Educational Psychologist, 38,* 23–31.

Kalyuga, S., & Sweller, J. (2004). Measuring knowledge to optimize cognitive load factors during instruction. *Journal of Educational Psychology, 96,* 558–568.

Kirschner, P. A., Sweller, J., & Clark, R. E. (2006). Why minimal guidance during instruction does not work: An analysis of the failure of constructivist, discovery, problem-based, experiential, and inquiry-based teaching. *Educational Psychologist, 46,* 75–86.

Miller, G. A. (1956). The magical number seven, plus or minus two: Some limits on our capacity for processing information. *Psychological Review, 63,* 81–97.

Newell, A., & Simon, H. A. (1972). *Human problem solving.* Englewood Cliffs, NJ: Prentice Hall.

Oksa, A., Kalyuga, S., & Chandler, P. (2010). Expertise reversal effect in using explanatory notes for readers of Shakespearean text. *Instructional Science, 38,* 217–236.

Paas, F. G. W. C., & van Merriënboer, J. J. G. (1994). Variability of worked examples and transfer of geometrical problem-solving skills: A cognitive-load approach. *Journal of Educational Psychology, 86,* 122–133.

Renkl, A., Atkinson, R. K., & Große, C. S. (2004). How fading worked solution steps works—A cognitive load perspective. *Instructional Science, 32,* 59–82.

Retnowati, E., Ayres, P., & Sweller, J. (2010). Worked example effects in individual and group work settings. *Educational Psychology, 30,* 349–367.

Rourke, A., & Sweller, J. (2009). The worked-example effect using ill-defined problems: Learning to recognise designers' styles. *Learning and Instruction, 19,* 185–199

Sweller, J., Ayres, P., & Kalyuga, S. (2011). *Cognitive load theory.* New York: Springer.

Sweller, J., & Cooper, G. A. (1985). The use of worked examples as a substitute for problem solving in learning algebra. *Cognition and Instruction, 1,* 59–89.

Van Merriënboer, J. J. G. (1990). Strategies for programming instruction in high school: Program completion vs. program generation. *Journal of Educational Computing Research, 6,* 265–285.

Zhu, X., & Simon, H. A. (1987). Learning mathematics from examples and by doing. *Cognition and Instruction, 4,* 137–166.

8.19
Spaced and Massed Practice

DOMINIC A. SIMON
New Mexico State University

Introduction

Perhaps one of the most overused adages concerning learning is the old saw that practice makes perfect. Like most pieces of advice, there is a ring of truth to it, but it is not an unqualified truth about how people (or other animals) learn. Of course, it is not that practice is *unimportant*; for almost all forms of learning practice is very valuable. However, it is the *right kind* of practice that matters. In keeping with the observation that many of these right kinds of practice are more demanding of learners than intuition would often suggest, Bjork (1994) has referred to them as involving "desirable difficulties." A number of such desirable difficulties have been identified, but one of the oldest and most reliable surrounds the distributed practice effect which was first reported by the "father" of memory research, Hermann Ebbinghaus (1885/1964). In short, distributing exposure to information benefits learning.

Research Evidence

Normally, when people talk of distributed practice effects they are really referring to two closely related phenomena, the spacing effect and the lag effect. Consider a simple list of words, perhaps a shopping list (albeit a slightly strange one where some items appear once and others twice): "marmalade, bread, milk, butter, butter, bread, marmalade, flour." A typical person who reads such a list and then attempts to remember the items a short time later will, other things being equal, be more likely to remember words that are presented twice in the list (e.g., marmalade, bread), rather than those presented once (e.g., milk, flour). An exception occurs for items like butter that occur twice in immediate succession or in a "massed" fashion. In general, massed words are not better remembered than once-presented items: thus, contrary to most people's intuitions, number of repetitions per se is not usually critical to learning.

Does that mean that repetition is never valuable for learning? Not at all: the spacing effect refers to the finding that items presented twice but with the presentations spaced out (e.g., bread, marmalade), are generally better remembered that massed items (e.g., butter). Also, items with a longer lag between initial presentation and later repetition (e.g., marmalade) are generally better remembered than items with shorter lags (e.g., bread): This finding of superior learning with more spacing is called the lag effect. Together, the spacing and the lag effects are known under the collective term of *distributed practice effects* (Cepeda, Pashler, Vul, Wixted, & Rohrer, 2006).

When learning, after the first exposure to new information, we have options as to how to interact with that information on subsequent occasions. We can either be passively exposed to it again (i.e., have another study opportunity), or we can be tested on the information with or without feedback. While it is true that repeated *study* opportunities help learning, at least when spaced out in time, there is a growing literature suggesting that spaced *testing* opportunities are powerful aids to learning. Roediger and colleagues in particular, have demonstrated repeatedly and with a variety of different materials that spaced tests act as potent learning events (Kornell & Bjork, 2008; Roediger & Karpicke, 2006). Of course, this is quite counterintuitive to most people, who tend to think that a test is simply a means of seeing whether learning has taken place. The act of retrieving information from memory, or upon failing to do so, getting feedback about the correct answer, both seem to strongly influence the probability of later being able to retrieve that same information. In a recent paper, with very practical application, Karpicke and Blunt (2011), have shown exactly these kinds of effects with material from science textbooks. They demonstrated that both recall of facts and inference questions were better answered after engaging in retrieval practice than after an equivalent amount of time on the commonly recommended practice of creating concept maps after reading the text passages.

A large number of studies of distribution of practice effects have been published in the century or so since they were first discovered and using a widely diverse set of learning materials such as simple word lists, lists of paired words (e.g., foreign-English vocabulary items), simple and complex motor tasks, and mathematical problems. In a promising example of the potential of distributed practice to foster something beyond simple learning, Kornell and Bjork (2008) had people study a number of examples of paintings from different artists in either a massed fashion, where all the examples for a given artist were seen in close succession, or in a distributed fashion where the examples from each artist were intermingled with those of other artists. After a brief delay the participants were shown paintings by the same artists that not been presented earlier. The authors initially expected that massing would be more helpful to the process of induction, learning to extract and thus recognize the painters' respective styles, although they knew that memory would be helped by spacing. People in the spaced condition, however, were better able to identify which artists had painted the new paintings than were people in the massed condition. Such a finding implies that the potential benefits of spacing are far broader than the traditional studies in which memory is the primary measure would suggest.

Notably in the Kornell and Bjork painting study, the learners themselves did not predict the outcome. Indeed the majority of them expected that massed practice would be better than spaced. Likewise Karpicke and Blunt found that learners' predictions about the efficacy of their experiences were opposite to their objective learning outcomes. These are not new findings: Across a number of studies, learners young and old have shown a reliable tendency to expect that massed practice will serve them better than will distributed practice (Benjamin & Bird, 2006; Son, 2004, 2010). This metacognitive deficit whereby judged and actual benefits are at odds might be part of the reason that distributed practice does not figure more prominently in formal and informal learning experiences.

The general finding of the lag effect might imply that the longer the separation between presentations the better. Indeed some research articles have suggested exactly that. However, when potentially confounding factors are taken into consideration, such as total exposure to learned materials, it appears that there is a complex relationship between lag and the delay until the information is critically required. In a comprehensive review of the literature, Cepeda, Vul, Rohrer, Wixted, and Pashler (2008) identified some basic generalities with regard to this complex relationship and used them in their attempts to model it. Among these is that increasing the spacing between presentations does not lead to a continuous increase in learning benefits. That is, although in general longer retention delays call for increased spacing, for a given delay before testing, there is an optimum spacing and increasing that spacing beyond

the optimum level tends to make retention of the information decline.

These observations suggest that maximal gains necessarily rely on a sense of what the ideal retention test delay will be. Clearly for a formal examination, this delay can be judged very accurately, but for predicting when a given piece of information is likely to be needed in general life is much harder to predict. Work still needs to be done to determine the ideal compromises between the factors of study distribution and a realistic estimate of what an average retention delay ought to be aimed for. Fortunately, as Cepeda et al. (2008) pointed out, one need not be obsessively concerned about finding the optimum because, while using a study lag that is too long is of less benefit than the optimum, the relative costs for too long a lag are generally smaller than for using too small a lag.

Why does spacing work? Oddly for such a (relatively) long studied effect it is surprising that more definitive explanations of the phenomena have not been established. Candidate accounts have included such notions as: diminished processing of massed items (less attention may be paid to a piece of information that was just seen, than to one that has not been seen for a while); and retrieval practice (the act of retrieving information from memory, for example, in study-phase testing, acts to strengthen it and make it more accessible for future occasions). Note that this is at odds with typical notions of artificial recording devices, such as cameras and sound recorders, that are expected to store information and allow repeated retrieval of it unmodified by that retrieval process); reminding (repetitions of information serve to strengthen the stored memory trace of an item thereby reducing their rates of future decay); and differential processing (the mental and material contexts in which a first and a second exposure to a piece of information are likely to be more different when those exposures are separated in time. Thus there may be two distinct memory traces to call upon at retrieval, raising the probability that at least one of them will be accessible in the future; Benjamin & Tullis, 2010). At various times evidence consistent with each of these explanations has been put forward. It may well be that the effects are a complicated combination of several if not all of them.

Summary and Recommendations

One clear recommendation is that one should experience repeated exposure to materials that are to be learned; so long as it is distributed in time. It is remarkable, how often students admit to not reading their textbook even once during a semester. Some are better and have read the book, or at least sections of it, *once*. However, very few claim to have reread anything. Perhaps students see reading texts as like watching movies: Once they've seen them once, they know the story? Unfortunately, much of the knowledge and skills that educational systems are designed to impart are not so readily acquired.

Interestingly, few people seem to have the same attitude toward, say, health: most people seem to acknowledge that repeated efforts are needed to maintain, for example, cardiovascular health. For some reason though, students often behave as if information will be acquired and retained after a single sitting, this despite their firsthand experience to the contrary on examinations and such (though in part this may be related to a belief in endowment rather than effort as the critical determinant of academic success). The repetition and testing opportunities can be distributed throughout a course unit, across units, and arguably in a well-designed curriculum, across one's whole formal education. This can be done formally in class and curriculum planning, as well as informally by educating students about the benefits of distributed practice and self-testing.

At a specific level of implementation it follows from the basic premise of distributed practice that peppering problems from older units throughout each successive unit in, say, a mathematics class would be a productive way of taking advantage of spacing effects to foster a continued readiness to solve a variety of problem types. This same practice gives students practice in identifying problem types independently of hints such as chapter headings and the surrounding problems. Training students to identify problem types is an oft overlooked component of their mathematical education but it is a central skill both for taking tests and for applying one's mathematical knowledge to problems in the world.

It should be noted that there is nothing new in the attempt to bring distributed practice effects to the attention of educators. Indeed a paper by Dempster (1988) about spacing effects was subtitled "A Case Study in the Failure to Apply the Results of Psychological Research." Research psychologists have known about the value of distributed practice for over a century, but for a variety of reasons, distribution of practice has not been as widely adopted as it ought to be. Of course studying is not seen as a universally enjoyable experience, but if one is going to study, then one ought to invest one's time wisely and distributing practice helps to do just that.

References

Benjamin, A. S., & Bird, R. D. (2006). Metacognitive control of the spacing of study repetitions. *Journal of Memory and Language, 55*, 126–137.

Benjamin, A. S., & Tullis, J. (2010). What makes distributed practice effective? *Cognitive Psychology, 61*, 228–247.

Bjork, R. A. (1994). Memory and metamemory considerations in the training of human beings. In J. Metcalfe & A. P. Shimamura (Eds.), *Metacognition: Knowing about knowing* (pp. 185–205). Cambridge, MA: MIT Press.

Cepeda, N. J., Pashler, H., Vul, E., Wixted, J. T., & Rohrer, D. (2006). Distributed practice in verbal recall tasks: A review and quantitative synthesis. *Psychological Bulletin, 132*, 354–380.

Cepeda, N. J., Vul, E., Rohrer, D., Wixted, J. T., & Pashler, H. (2008). Spacing effects in learning: A temporal ridgeline of optimal retention. *Psychological Science, 19*, 1095–1102.

Dempster, F. N. (1988). The spacing effect: A case study in failure to apply the results of psychological research. *American Psychologist, 43*, 627–634.

Ebbinghaus, H. (1964). *Memory: A contribution to experimental psychology*. New York: Dover. (Original work published 1885)

Karpicke, J. D., & Blunt, J. R. (2011). Retrieval practice produces more learning than elaborative studying with concept mapping, *Science, 331*, 772–775.

Kornell, N., & Bjork, R. A. (2008). Learning concepts and categories: Is spacing the "Enemy of induction"? *Psychological Science, 19*, 585–592.

Roediger, H. L., & Karpicke, J. D. (2006). The power of testing memory: Basic research and implications for educational practice. *Perspectives on Psychological Science, 1*, 181–210.

Son, L. K. (2004). Spacing one's study: Evidence for a metacognitive control strategy. *Journal of Experimental Psychology: Learning, Memory and Cognition, 30*, 601–604.

Son, L. K. (2010). Metacognitive control and the spacing effect. *Journal of Experimental Psychology: Learning, Memory and Cognition. 36*, 255–262.

8.20

Questioning

SCOTTY D. CRAIG
Arizona State University, Polytechnic

Introduction

Questions are a primary component that facilitates academic achievement. Indeed, over the years researchers have claimed that questioning is one of the processing components that underlies comprehension (Collins, Brown & Larkin, 1980), problem solving (Reisbeck, 1988), reasoning (Graesser, Baggett & Williams, 1996), creativity (Sternberg, 1987), and learning (Pashler et al., 2007). The question literature can be divided into two broad categories: question exposure and question generation. Question generation will not be the current focus of this entry (see Rosenshine, Meister, & Chapman, 1996 for a review).

Research Evidence

Questions help guide the learning process. First, they serve as a prompt to encourage active processing of material, thus increasing the likelihood that discrepancies will be detected. Second, they serve to focus the learner's processing by providing activation to the learner's larger network of knowledge. When the question is presented to the learner, it sets up expectations based on his or her previous knowledge. This activated knowledge is reconstituted and compared to the new experience or new information (Derry, 1996). If there are no inconsistencies between the active mental representation and the information, then no learning occurs (i.e., the content is already known). Questions are important when discrepancies are present because the questions encourage attempts to understand the new information in the face of expectation violations (Schank, 1986), cognitive disequilibrium (Graesser, Lu, Olde, Cooper-Pye, & Whitten, 2005), or other types of events that cause confusion (Bjork & Bjork, 2006) or curiosity (Jang, 2009). Without the question, the learner is less prone to bother rectifying the conceptual violations (Eakin, 2005). When discrepancies are detected, there is a need for explanation, which results in a modification to the learner's mental model and a deeper comprehension of the material. The learner detects discrepancies between previous knowledge and the new content, they have the opportunity to recompose existing knowledge and bring them into correspondence with the new content (Chi, 2000).

Some questions are more effective than others. Questions must encourage sufficient processing of the information for discrepancies to be identified. So, presenting a statement, while it might activate previous knowledge, would not always encourage learning. Likewise, simple or shallow questions that do not require much processing may also not increase learning (Ge, Chen, & Davis, 2005; Lin et al., 2005). While shallow questions might help students to learn factual knowledge, they do not help at deeper conceptual levels (e.g., conceptual relationships or misconception correction; Craig, Graesser, & Gholson, 2009). A deep question is a question integrated with content that builds links between understanding and the mechanisms and components described in materials to be learned. These questions are aligned with the higher levels of Bloom's taxonomy (1956) and the long-answer question categories in the question taxonomy proposed by Graesser and Person (1994). In order to illustrate the difference between deep questions and shallow questions, consider an example of each. An example of a shallow question, according to Graesser and Person (1994), would be a verification question (e.g., "Can I just kind of trace this?"), in which the student is referring to a diagram of the heart. The purpose for categorizing this type of question as shallow is because it does not take much intrinsic thought on the student's part. It is a simple "yes" or "no" question. In contrast, another example of a deep-reasoning question would be a casual antecedent question (e.g., "Why is it that your arteries clog based upon your cholesterol level but your veins don't?"). The reason for categorizing this question as "deep" is because the student must take the knowledge he or she knows about the circulatory system, and make a connection and compare the differences between the two.

414

Driscoll and colleagues (2003) provided evidence for this distinction. In a laboratory experiment with college students, they demonstrated that only participants who observed dialogs with deep level questions showed improved learning over a simple presentation of the information. Presentation of a simple statement or a shallow question on the same content at the same point in the presentations did not improve learning. This effect has been shown to hold in both college students and middle school students and has been shown to be as effective as an interactive tutoring system (Craig, Sullins, Witherspoon, & Gholson, 2006) and human teachers (Gholson, Coles, & Craig, 2010).

Implementation of questions by teachers can be equally as important to the learning process as student generation of questions. Silliman and Wilkinson (1994) investigated the elements of classroom dialogue traditionally used by teachers to guide and evaluate novice learners. They found that question-answer dialogs were often implemented by teachers in traditional classroom settings. When implemented, this was an effective method by which teachers could identify student knowledge deficits (Silliman & Wilkinson, 1994) and improve feedback from the student to the teacher so that the teacher can tailor explanations to the students (Aguiar, Mortimer, & Scott, 2010). In a controlled classroom experiment, deep question–answer dialogs led by a teacher have been shown to improve students' learning on classroom tests by as much as a letter grade (Gholson, Graesser, & Craig, 2009).

Summary and Recommendations

Questions can play an important role in the learning process by activating previous knowledge and guiding the integration of new knowledge. During this process, deep questions are more effective for facilitating complex knowledge acquisition. Deep questions have been effectively used during learning by inducing question asking by students via questions stems or observational models and by good question explanation dialogs led by teachers.

References

Aguiar, O. G., Mortimer, E. F., & Scott, P. (2010). Learning from and responding to students' questions: The authoritative and dialogic tension. *Journal of Research in Science Teaching, 47*, 174–193.

Bjork, R. A., & Bjork, E. L. (2006). Optimizing treatment and instruction: Implications of a new theory of disuse. In L.-G. Nilsson & N. Ohta (Eds.), *Memory and society: Psychological perspectives* (pp. 116–140). New York: Psychology Press.

Bloom, B. S., Engelhart, M. D., Furst, E. J., Hill, W. H., & Krathwohl, D. R. (Eds.). (1956). *Taxonomy of educational objectives: The classification of educational goals. Handbook 1: Cognitive domain.* New York: Academic Press.

Chi, M. T. H. (2000). Self-explaining expository texts: The dual processes of generating inferences and repairing mental models. In R. Glaser (Ed.), *Advances in instructional psychology* (pp. 161–238). Hillsdale, NJ: Erlbaum.

Collins, A., Brown, J. S., & Larkin, K. M. (1980). Inference in text understanding. In R. J. Spiro, B. C. Bruce, & W. F. Brewer (Eds.), *Theoretical issues in reading comprehension* (pp. 385–407). Hillsdale, NJ: Erlbaum.

Craig, S. D., Graesser, A. C., & Gholson, B. (2009, May). *Integration of vicarious learning environments into high school and middle school classrooms.* Paper presented at the 21st Annual Convention of the Association for Psychological Science, San Francisco, CA.

Craig, S. D., Sullins, J., Witherspoon, A., & Gholson, B. (2006). Deep-level reasoning questions effect: The role of dialog and deep-level reasoning questions during vicarious learning. *Cognition and Instruction, 24*, 565–591

Derry, S. J. (1996). Cognitive schema theory in the constructivist debate. *Educational Psychologist, 31*(3–4), 163–174.

Driscoll, D., Craig, S. D., Gholson, B., Ventura, M., Hu, X., & Graesser, A. (2003). Vicarious learning: Effects of overhearing dialog and monolog-like discourse in a virtual tutoring session. *Journal of Educational Computing Research, 29*, 431–450.

Eakin, D. K. (2005). Illusions of knowing: Metamemory and memory under conditions of retroactive interference. *Journal of Memory and Language, 52*, 526–534.

Ge, X., Chen, C., & Davis, K. (2005). Scaffolding novice instructional designers' problem-solving processes using question prompts in a web-based learning environment. *Journal of Educational Computing Research, 33*, 219–248.

Gholson, B., Coles, R., & Craig, S. D. (2010). Features of computerized multimedia environments that support vicarious learning processes. In M. S. Khine & I. M. Saleh (Eds.), *New science of learning: Cognition, computers and collaboration in education* (pp. 53–78). New York: Springer.

Gholson, B. Graesser, A. C., & Craig, S. D. (2009, June). *IDRIVE project summary: An overview of our randomized classroom experiments in the Memphis city schools.* Poster presented at the 4th Annual Institute of Educational Sciences Research Conference, Washington, DC.

Graesser, A. C., Baggett, W., & Williams, K. (1996). Question-driven explanatory reasoning. *Applied Cognitive Psychology, 10*, S17–S32.

Graesser, A. C., Lu, S., Olde, B. A., Cooper-Pye, E., & Whitten, S. (2005). Question asking and eye tracking during cognitive disequilibrium: Comprehending illustrated texts on devices when the devices break down. *Memory & Cognition, 33*, 1235–1247.

Graesser, A. C, & Person, N. (1994). Question asking during tutoring. *American Educational Research Journal, 31*, 104–137.

Jang, H. (2009). *Cultivating curiosity to promote students' learning.* Paper presented at the 2009 convention of the American Educational Research Association, San Diego, CA.

Lin, H., Kidwai, K., Munyofu, M., Swain, J., Ausman, B., & Dwyer, F. (2005). The effect of verbal advance organizers in complementing animated instruction. *Journal of Visual Literacy, 25*, 237–248.

Pashler, H., Bain, P., Bottge, B., Graesser, A., Koedinger, K., McDaniel, M., & Metcalf, J. (2007). *Organizing instruction and study to improve student learning* (NCER 2007-2004). Washington, DC: National Center for Education Research, Institute of Education Sciences, U.S. Department of Education. Retrieved from http://ncer.ed.gov.

Reisbeck, C. K. (1988). Are questions just function calls? *Questing Exchange, 2*, 17–24.

Rosenshine, B., Meister, C., & Chapman, S. (1996). Teaching students to generate questions: A review of the intervention studies. *Review of Education Research, 66*, 188–221.

Schank, R. C. (1986). *Explanation patterns: Understanding mechanically and creatively.* Hillsdale, NJ: Erlbaum.

Silliman, E. R., & Wilkinson, L. C. (1994). Discourse scaffolds for classroom intervention. In G. P. Wallach & K. G. Butler (Eds.), *Language learning disabilities in school-aged children and adolescents* (2nd ed., pp. 27–52). Boston, MA: Allyn & Bacon.

Sternberg, R. J. (1987). Questioning and intelligence. *Questing Exchange, 1*, 11–13.

8.21

Effects of Testing

Jaekyung Lee
State University of New York at Buffalo

Young-Sun Lee
Columbia University

Introduction

This entry focuses on testing designed to measure and monitor students' academic achievement in school settings. Although there are controversies about whether testing enhances student learning and achievement, it is critical to understand not only the effectiveness of testing, but also how, when, and why it works. To answer this, a consideration of testing attributes and conditions such as teacher-developed formative assessments versus standardized summative assessments must be examined. While an evaluation of testing effects call for scientifically based evidence, derived from experimental and correlational studies, it is also necessary to understand both the social and educational context of testing in which the research has been embedded.

The origin of public testing dates as far back as the 2nd century BCE when civil service exams were used during the Han dynasty of China (206 BCE–220 CE) to select elite government officials. Over time, modern external examinations have grown as instruments of control over educational systems in many countries (Eckstein & Noah, 1993); the history of educational testing and assessment reveals underlying assumptions and beliefs about human learning and teaching (Madaus & O'Dwyer, 1999; Shepard, 1991). While teacher-made tests, assignments, or observations remain a dominant form of classroom assessment, standardized testing with reliance on short multiple-choice questions has facilitated objective, reliable, and efficient evaluation on a large scale.

It is critical to differentiate between formative and summative assessments due to their different testing functions, effects, and causal mechanisms. While formative assessments involve repeated testing or other evaluation procedures by teachers *during* instruction, summative assessments occur after the completion of instruction for a summary evaluation of student achievement. The key function of formative assessments for both students and teachers is feedback; it provides students with opportuni-

ties to improve learning and allows teachers to improve teaching based on test results. The benefits of formative assessments as an effective instructional intervention have been demonstrated on various occasions with a moderate to large effect size that ranges 0.4 to 0.7 in standard deviation units (Black & Wiliam, 1998; Crooks, 1988; Fuchs & Fuchs, 1986; Shute, 2008). An example of formative assessments is curriculum-based measurement (CBM) that employs repeated, frequent measurements of student performance in basic skills by classroom teachers. It also underlies a mastery learning model in which a major component of its effectiveness arises from additional feedback (Crooks, 1988; Kulik & Kulik, 1987).

In contrast, summative assessments are designed and used for selection and end of course evaluation purposes, including high-stakes accountability with consequences for students (e.g., grades, promotion/retention, graduation) or for teachers and schools (e.g., school report cards, financial rewards, sanctions). One example of such high-stakes tests is the annual reading and math testing requirement as mandated by the No Child Left Behind Act (NCLB; 2002) in the United States. Evidence on the effects of external standardized tests, high-stakes testing in particular, on student achievement has been inconsistent and remains controversial (Lee, 2008; National Research Council, 2011; Phelps, 2005). The average effect size of high stakes test-driven external accountability in the United States was 0.08 with a wide range of mixed results (Lee, 2008).

Research Evidence

Generalization about the average testing effect is difficult to make, since the effects of testing tend to vary among different achievement levels of students under different characteristics and conditions of testing. Formative interpretations help low achieving students the most, and the effectiveness of formative feedback depends on several detailed features of its quality (Black & Wiliam, 1998; Crooks, 1988; Shute,

2008). There are various factors that interact with formative feedback to influence student success. First, testing effects are greater when evaluation standards are high, but attainable enough to optimize learning (Betts & Grogger, 2003; Figlio & Lucas, 2004). The caveat is that higher standards and high-stakes testing may reduce educational attainment for students at high risk of academic failure even when they increase achievement as measured by test scores. Second, the timing and frequency of testing matter. In general, assessments immediately following the instruction of a subject matter improve student learning and retention (Crooks, 1988). However, the level of student achievement dictates the optimal time to give formative feedback: low-achieving students may benefit from immediate feedback, whereas high-achieving students may prefer or benefit from delayed feedback (Shute, 2008). A moderate frequency of testing is desirable, and more frequent testing may produce further modest benefits (Crooks, 1988). A mixed form of frequent assessments may work even better (e.g., short, frequent in-class tests as well as homework assignments and a few longer less-frequent in-class tests) (Black & Wiliam, 1998). Third, the point of reference for evaluation interacts with student achievement level. For low-performing students, norm-referenced formative feedback causes students to attribute failures to their lack of ability and lowers their expectation and motivation for future task performance (Kluger & DeNisi, 1996), whereas self-referenced feedback induces greater motivation than norm-referenced feedback (McColskey & Leary, 1985).

The causal mechanisms by which testing influences achievement also vary according to the nature and type of testing. Formative assessments rely on feedback (information provided as a result of testing) as a primary mechanism for behavioral modification and instructional improvement. In contrast, summative assessments, high-stakes tests in particular, rely more on incentives (expected grades, rewards/sanctions) as a mechanism to affect learning and achievement. Formative assessments are expected to cause the following (Crooks, 1988): (a) the perception by the learner and teacher of a gap between a desired goal and his or her present state of knowledge and skill; (b) the action taken by the learner and the teacher to close that gap in order to attain the desired goal. Summative assessments can have similar effects, but their feedback and correction functions are highly limited due to restricted frequency and timing of testing. Since summative assessments count more than formative assessments in final grading and evaluation, they may stimulate learning motivation and efforts at the cost of increased test anxiety and academic pressure. The logic of high-stakes testing for external accountability draws upon rationalistic and behavioristic views of human behavior by positing that holding schools, teachers, or students accountable for academic performance as measured by standardized tests, with incentives such as rewards and sanctions, will inform, motivate, and reorient the behavior of schooling agents toward the goal of academic improvement (Benveniste, 1985; Lee, 2008).

One critical issue is whether the feedback and summative purposes of student evaluation are incompatible and thus should be separated (Crooks, 2010). Those who support clear separation of the two argue that where evaluations count significantly toward the student's final grade, the student tends to pay less attention to the feedback, and thus to learn less from it. This negative effect should be reduced if only the final evaluation counts for a grade, as is generally the case in mastery learning procedures. A counterargument for considering more evaluations in grading is to improve the reliability of the grading process and to raise student motivation for working harder throughout the whole process of instruction. A problem occurs when the same test serves as both an intervention tool and an evaluation tool at the same time. For example, if students are tested more often for grading, they will simply focus on what is expected to appear on the test and their test score may improve as an artifact of testing practice without concomitant gain in learning. Similarly, teachers may narrow curriculum and teach to the test in response to external high-stakes testing. To avoid this problem, evaluation of high-stakes testing effects requires an independent low-stakes test to demonstrate that achievement gains are transferrable (Lee, 2008). Clearly, this problem is reduced in case of formative assessments which does not count at all or much less for final grading or evaluation purpose.

Summary and Recommendations

The tension between the goals of instructional improvement (formative) and grading or accountability (summative) has been intensified in the current test-driven accountability policy environment, although these two goals are not necessarily incompatible and appropriate design and uses of testing can help meet both goals (Baker, 2007). Tests themselves are neither valid/effective nor invalid/ineffective, but the validity or efficacy depends on how test results are interpreted and used. Educators need to acknowledge both potential benefits and limitations of different types of testing for different groups of students. Common criticisms of teacher-made formative assessments include the lack of reliability and objectivity as well as relatively low grading standards, whereas external standardized tests often suffer from misalignment with local curriculum as well as potential negative effects such as curriculum distortion, test score inflation, student disengagement, and dropout. Educators also need to be fully aware of potential test biases and stereotype threats related to standardized test performance for certain groups, particularly racial/ethnic minority and female students (Spencer, Steele, & Quinn, 1999; Steele & Aronson, 1995).

References

Baker, E. L. (2007). The end(s) of testing. *Educational Researcher, 36*(6), 309–317.

Benveniste, G. (1985). The design of school accountability systems. *Educational Evaluation and Policy Analysis, 7*(3), 261–279.

Betts, J. R., & Grogger, J. (2003). The impact of grading standards on student achievement, educational attainment, and entry-level earnings. *Economics of Education Review, 22*, 343–352.

Black, P., & Wiliam, D. (1998). Inside the black box: Raising standards through classroom assessment. *Phi Delta Kappan, 80*(2), 139–148.

Crooks, T. J. (1988). The impact of classroom evaluation practices on students. *Review of Educational Research, 58*(4), 438–481.

Eckstein, M. A., & Noah, H. J. (1993). *Secondary school examinations: International perspectives on policies and practices.* New Haven, CT: Yale University Press.

Figlio, D. N., & Lucas, M. E. (2004). Do high grading standards affect student performance? *Journal of Public Economics, 88*, 1815–1834.

Fuchs, L. S., & Fuchs, D. (1986). Effects of systematic formative evaluation: A meta-analysis. *Exceptional Children, 53*, 199–208.

Kluger, A. N., & DeNisi, A. (1996). The effects of feedback interventions on performance: A historical review, a meta-analysis, and a preliminary feedback intervention theory. *Psychological Bulletin, 119*(2), 254–284.

Kulik, C-L. C., & Kulik, J. A. (1987). Mastery testing and student learning: A meta-analysis. *Journal of Educational Technology Systems, 15*, 325–345.

Lee, J. (2008). Is test-driven external accountability effective? Synthesizing the evidence from cross-state causal-comparative and correlational studies. *Review of Educational Research, 78*(3), 608–644.

Madaus, G. F., & O'Dwyer, L. M. (1999). A short history of performance assessment. *Phi Delta Kappan, 80*(9), 688–695.

McColskey, W., & Leary, M. R. (1985). Differential effects of norm-referenced and self-referenced feedback on performance expectancies, attribution, and motivation. *Contemporary Educational Psychology, 10*, 275–284.

National Research Council. (2011). *Incentives and test-based accountability in education.* Washington, DC: National Academies Press.

No Child Left Behind Act (2002). Pub. L. No. 107-110, 115 Stat. 1425.

Phelps, R. P. (2005). The rich, robust research literature on testing's achievement benefits. In R. P. Phelps (Ed.), *Defending standardized tests* (pp. 55–90). Mahwah, NJ: Erlbaum.

Shepard, L. A. (1991). Psychometricians' beliefs about learning. *Educational Researcher, 20*(7), 2–16.

Shute, V. J. (2008). Focus on formative feedback. *Review of Educational Research, 78*(1), 153–189.

Spencer, S. J., Steele, C. M., & Quinn, D. M. (1999). Stereotype threat and women's math performance. *Journal of Experimental Social Psychology, 35*, 4–28.

Steele, C. M., & Aronson, J. (1995). Stereotype threat and the intellectual test performance of African Americans. *Journal of Personality and Social Psychology, 69*, 797–811.

8.22

Metacognitive Strategies

Linda Baker
University of Maryland, Baltimore County

Introduction

A primary goal of education is to help students become independent, autonomous, and effective learners. Fostering students' metacognitive knowledge and control is a means toward this goal. Metacognitive knowledge includes knowledge about the skills, strategies, and resources that are needed to perform a task effectively, and metacognitive control is the use of strategies to ensure successful task completion, such as planning, evaluating, and monitoring.

Research on metacognition has its roots in the 1970s work of cognitive developmental psychologists John Flavell and Ann Brown, whose interests in memory development led them to ask what children know about their memory and how they learn to control it. Researchers soon turned to investigations of metacognition in relation to student achievement, and today this topic is a significant area of inquiry across the globe. An indicator of its popular appeal is that a Google search for "metacognition and achievement" yielded 646,000 hits in June 2011.

One reason metacognition has received so much attention is that younger and less successful students do not use metacognitive strategies effectively, if at all, and they have limited knowledge of when, where, and why to use those strategies. A second and more compelling reason is that these strategies can be taught and doing so leads to increases in achievement. Much contemporary research on metacognition is framed within the broader context of self-regulated learning, which acknowledges the inextricable connections among cognitive and metacognitive strategies, affect and motivation.

The distinction between cognitive and metacognitive strategies is not always explicitly articulated in research and practice, but one way of thinking about the distinction is that cognitive strategies enable us to make progress on a given task, whereas metacognitive strategies enable us to control progress. For example, cognitive strategies for learning include rehearsal (e.g., underlining), elaboration (e.g., summarizing), and organization (e.g., creating a concept map). Metacognitive strategies include planning (e.g., allocating resources), monitoring (e.g., self-testing to check understanding), and evaluating (e.g., making judgments about the effectiveness of one's efforts).

Metacognitive strategies can be applied productively in any content domain, as shown by considering three phases of a generic problem-solving task. Before starting to solve the problem, students think about what they already know to set goals and develop a solution plan. Then, during problem solving, they monitor their cognitive activities and compare progress against expected goals. After reaching a solution, they evaluate the adequacy and reasonableness of outcomes and revise accordingly if necessary.

Research Evidence

The comprehensive *Handbook of Metacognition in Education* provides theoretical perspectives and reviews of empirical research on metacognition in reading, writing, science, and mathematics, as well as chapters on the role of technology in fostering metacognition (Hacker, Dunlosky, & Graesser, 2009). *Trends and Prospects in Metacognitive Research* focuses on contemporary European research (Efklides & Misailidi, 2010). Other recent books devoted exclusively to metacognition include those with a focus on young children (Larkin, 2010), on strategies and instruction (Waters & Schneider, 2010), on literacy (Israel, Block, Bauserman, & Kinnucan-Welsch, 2005), and on mathematics (Desoete & Veenman, 2006). The journal *Metacognition and Learning* has published scholarly articles since 2006. Practical resources for teachers are increasingly available in print and electronic media.

In order to determine what students know about metacognition, researchers rely primarily on questionnaires that assess declarative, procedural, and conditional knowledge about strategies (that is, what they are, how they are used, and under what conditions) and that assess reported use of strategies to control one's own cognitive processes. These instruments consistently reveal relations between students' metacognitive awareness and academic achievement, from the earliest years of schooling through postgraduate education. Two instruments that have been widely used, translated, or adapted are the Metacognitive Awareness Inventory (Schraw & Dennison, 1994) and the Metacognitive Awareness of Reading Strategies Inventory (Mokhtari & Reichard, 2002).

Early evidence that metacognitive strategies could be taught under controlled conditions stimulated interest in implementing metacognitive interventions in classroom contexts (Baker, 2008). Most intervention studies provide instruction of multiple strategies that have been well-validated as effective. These interventions typically have both teacher-led and student-centered components, such as explicit explanation of how, when, and why to use metacognitive strategies, modeling, guided practice, and peer collaboration. The typical sequence is for teacher-led explicit instruction to be followed by a gradual release of responsibility to the students themselves. The studies have shown that students who are taught to use a variety of cognitive and metacognitive strategies have greater gains in metacognitive awareness and academic achievement than students who do not receive the training. Successful outcomes have been obtained in reading, writing, mathematics, and science, from early primary grades to secondary and tertiary education levels. Two illustrative studies are described below, followed by a summary of findings from a recent meta-analysis (Dignath & Buttner, 2008).

A project carried out in the Netherlands examined the extent to which classroom teachers could enhance students' reading comprehension and metacognitive knowledge about reading strategies (Houtveen & van de Grift, 2007). Participants were 10-year-old students enrolled in 20 schools that either implemented the intervention or offered standard instruction. Teachers in the intervention schools provided instruction in cognitive and metacognitive strategies using approaches documented as effective. Strategies included: (a) reading selectively and making decisions about the reading process (what to read carefully, what to read quickly, what not to read, what to reread); (b) drawing from, comparing, and integrating prior knowledge with material in the text; and (c) monitoring understanding of the text. Students were tested before the intervention was implemented, after it ended, and at the beginning of the next school year. Results showed that intervention students gained more in metacognitive knowledge and in reading achievement on a standardized test both immediately and the following year. The delayed test results are an important demonstration that strategies instruction can have long-term benefits.

Research has shown positive effects of metacognitive strategy instruction on mathematics achievement as well. For example, researchers in Israel developed a method where secondary school students are trained to ask themselves a series of questions: (a) Comprehension: "What is the problem all about?" (b) Connection: "What are the similarities and differences between the problem at hand and problems that you have solved in the past?" (c) Strategies: "What strategies are appropriate for solving the problem?" (d) Reflection: "Does the solution make sense? Can I solve the problem differently? Did I consider all the relevant information?" Across several studies, participants who received this month-long intervention demonstrated greater knowledge of metacognitive regulation and they received higher math scores than those in classes receiving traditional instruction. Moreover, in one study, students in the intervention condition reportedly transferred their metacognitive strategies to a high-stakes assessment taken several months later (Mevarech & Amrany, 2008).

The number of well-designed and well-executed studies that include metacognitive strategies instruction has increased dramatically in the 21st century, prompting several teams of researchers to conduct meta-analyses. A particularly informative meta-analysis (Dignath & Buttner, 2008) included interventions in different content domains (math, reading/writing, and other), at different grade levels (primary, secondary), and with different instructional components (cognitive strategies, metacognitive strategies, metacognitive reflection, and motivation). Following are some of the key findings.

Strategy instruction yields greater benefits for students in secondary schools than in primary schools (Dignath & Buttner, 2008). This reflects in part that older students have already acquired some metacognitive knowledge from their more extensive schooling history and so are better able to build on prior experiences. The developmental difference may also have neurobiological underpinnings: the brain's prefrontal lobes, which are involved in higher order cognitive processes and executive control, are more fully mature in adolescence.

Intervention effects were stronger at primary and secondary levels when metacognitive reflection was included in the training (Dignath & Buttner, 2008). It is not enough to instruct metacognitive strategies; students also need feedback about their strategy use, knowledge about effective strategies, and conditions under which they are most useful. At the primary school level, effects on achievement were stronger if interventions included metacognitive strategies, whereas at the secondary school level, effects were stronger if metacognitive reflection was a component of instruction. Developmentally, adolescents are more proficient at abstract thinking, including thinking about their own thought processes. Effects at both levels were stronger when cognitive strategies and metacognitive strategies were the joint focus of instruction (Dignath & Buttner, 2008).

Individual studies typically focus on one academic domain, but because meta-analyses synthesize effects across studies, they allow for comparisons across subject areas. Results revealed stronger effects for younger students in the math interventions than in the reading/writing interventions (Dignath & Buttner, 2008). If children do not yet have fluency in the basic processes of reading and writing, they must allocate limited cognitive resources to decoding and transcription rather than to evaluating and regulating. Lack of fluency in basic math processes (e.g., fact retrieval) does not seem to interfere with learning metacognitive strategies to the same extent.

Classroom-based intervention programs vary in length considerably, ranging from a few weeks up to 6 months are more. The meta-analysis revealed that programs were more effective the longer they were implemented (Dignath & Buttner, 2008). Learning to use metacognitive strategies effectively does not happen quickly. Students need ample time to practice the strategies, to receive feedback on their use, and to take on full responsibility for their application. The likelihood of transfer of strategies to new contexts also increases with more instructional time.

Summary and Recommendations

The research summarized in this entry has shown that metacognitive strategies enhance achievement across core subject areas and that these strategies can be successfully taught. Research converges on the following instructional practices for fostering metacognitive knowledge and control:

- Explicit teaching and modeling of metacognitive strategies;
- Gradual transition from external regulation (by the teacher/ tutor) to self-regulation (by the students);
- Informative feedback on strategy implementation;
- Opportunities for students to elaborate, discuss, and assess the effectiveness of their own strategies;
- Instruction that explicitly links the quality of performance with the strategies used so that students see the value of using strategies;
- Opportunities for students to transfer their metacognitive knowledge across areas of the curriculum.

The effects on achievement are stronger when students have the opportunity to reflect on their metacognitive processes. One way teachers can help students engage in self-assessment of their cognition is to use a metacognitive questionnaire, several of which are appropriate for classroom use (Mokhtari & Reichard, 2002, Schraw & Dennison, 1994). Teachers will gain a greater understanding of their students' metacognitive strengths by reviewing the questionnaire responses, and they will learn of areas in need of further attention. Sharing results with the class will give students greater awareness of their own cognitive processes and enhance their understanding of metacognitive strategy use.

Effects of strategy training are stronger when it is provided by researchers rather than classroom teachers (Dignath & Buttner, 2008). This suggests that teachers should receive enhanced professional development to give them the knowledge and skills to foster metacognition as part of their regular instructional practice. Metacognitive strategies

instruction is still not commonly observed in most primary and secondary classrooms, and interviews with teachers have revealed limited knowledge about metacognition and how to foster it.

The common element in all of the approaches for teaching students to use metacognitive strategies is that teachers make explicit their own planning, monitoring, and evaluating processes. Yet many teachers find that modeling thinking processes is difficult. Increasing teachers' own metacognitive awareness of their cognitive processes is an important first step in preparing them to increase students' awareness. Providing opportunities for teachers to talk with one another about their own thinking can be helpful in fostering such understandings (Baker, 2004).

Worldwide, educational policy makers now recommend attention to metacognition in the classroom. That particular term may not always be used, but the underlying idea of fostering independence in learning is apparent. In numerous countries including Belgium, Finland, Singapore, Turkey, and the United States, national standards call for students to be taught effective metacognitive strategies in literacy, math, and science. The evidence that metacognitive strategies impact academic achievement is too strong to ignore.

References

Baker, L. (2004). Reading comprehension and science inquiry: Metacognitive connections. In E. W. Saul (Ed.), *Crossing borders in literacy and science instruction: Perspectives on theory and practice* (pp. 239–257). Newark, DE: International Reading Association; Arlington, VA: National Science Teachers Association.

Baker, L. (2008). Metacognition in comprehension instruction: What we've learned since NRP. In C. C. Block & S. R. Parris (Eds.), *Comprehension instruction: Research-based best practices* (2nd ed., pp. 65–79). New York: Guilford.

Desoete, A., & Veenman, M. (Eds.). (2006). *Metacognition in mathematics education.* Hauppauge, NY: Nova Science.

Dignath, C., & Buttner, G. (2008). Components of fostering self-regulated learning among students. A meta-analysis on intervention studies at primary and secondary school level. *Metacognition and Learning, 3,* 231–264.

Efklides, A., & Misailidi, P. (Eds.). (2010). *Trends and prospects in metacognition research.* New York: Springer.

Hacker, D. J., Dunlosky, J., & Graesser, A. (2009). *Handbook of metacognition in education.* New York: Routledge.

Houtveen, A. A. M., & van de Frift, W. J. C. M. (2007). Effects of metacognitive strategy instruction and instruction time on reading comprehension. *School Effectiveness and School Improvement, 18,* 173–190.

Israel, S. E., Block, C. C., Bauserman, K. L., & Kinnucan-Welsch, K. (Eds.). (2005). *Metacognition in literacy learning: Theory, assessment, instruction, and professional development.* New York: Erlbaum.

Larkin, S. (2010). *Metacognition in young children.* New York: Routledge.

Mevarech, Z. R., & Amrany, C. (2008). Immediate and delayed effects of meta-cognitive instruction on regulation of cognition and mathematics achievement. *Metacognition and Learning, 3,* 147–157.

Mokhtari, K., & Reichard, C. A. (2002). Assessing students' metacognitive awareness of reading strategies. *Journal of Educational Psychology, 94,* 249–259.

Schraw, G. & Dennison, R. S. (1994). Assessing metacognitive awareness. *Contemporary Educational Psychology, 19,* 460–475.

Waters, H. S., & Schneider, W. (Eds.). (2010). *Metacognition, strategy use, and instruction.* New York: Guilford.

8.23

Mentoring

Queensland University of Technology

BRIAN HANSFORD AND LISA CATHERINE EHRICH

Introduction

Research relating to mentoring has burgeoned in the last two decades and, as might be expected, there is immense variation in the nature and rigour of this research. For some, mentoring seems to be a panacea for many societal problems as the studies have focussed on juvenile crime, teenage pregnancy, academic performance, drug usage, school dropout rates, teacher attributes, parental relationship, heightened self-confidence, general "at risk" children, and issues of gender, ethnicity, socioeconomic status, and equity. Rather than being a panacea, it would be more accurate to suggest that in specific circumstances mentoring has the potential to be associated with beneficial outcomes.

Research Evidence

Jacobi (1991) provided a seminal review that explored mentoring and undergraduate success, and found that many studies focused more on processes than outcomes. She concluded that while there was no direct support for the link that mentoring promotes academic success, she identified several studies that indicated mentoring as providing some indirect support. McPartland and Nettles (1991) concluded that there were improvements in academic achievement as measured by grade point averages by "at risk students" who had been mentored. By way of contrast, Slicker and Palmer (1993) found no such improvement in academic achievement. The extensive evaluation of the "Big Brothers Big Sisters" programs concluded among other things positive changes in grades and perceived academic competence as a consequence of mentoring (Grossman & Tierney, 1998). However, Rhodes (2001) in commenting on this much reported study suggested the results are promising but cautions against generalizing the outcomes to other mentoring studies. This caution relates to the selection of mentors: in this program mentors are carefully screened, trained, and supported. Quality control is high and "the program requires

a year's commitment…they provide at least six hours of training and ongoing supervision" (Rhodes, 2001, p. 2). In Rhodes's view this level of commitment to mentors is not characteristic of many mentoring programs. Commenting on the role of mentors, Rhodes, Grossman, and Resch (2000) suggested that in acting as role models, mentors may convey messages concerning the value of schooling and stimulate the attitudes of youth toward school achievement and perceived academic competence. They further suggest that competent mentors may impinge on the beliefs of youth relating to a link between educational attainment and future workplace opportunities.

The complexity of mentoring research findings is indicated by Campbell and Campbell (2000) in a faculty/student mentoring program of undergraduate students where higher GPAs were reported for mentored students. Yet, Blakely, Menon, and Jones (1995) indicated grades were impacted sporadically by mentoring and Aseltine, Dupre, and Lamlein (2000) suggested there was no relationship between mentoring and grades. Such apparently disparate results tend to reflect the nature and method of sample selection, the mentoring program implemented, and the rigour of research design, including the evaluation program utilized.

Rhodes et al. (2000) used a sample of 959 young adolescents who had applied to Big Sister Big Brother programs. These were randomly assigned to treatment and control groups and a study was implemented to explore whether mentoring outcomes on achievement were mediated through improvements in parental relationships. The benefits of mentoring interventions to improve perceived parental relationships were shown to be important mediators of change in adolescents' academic outcomes and behaviours. It is important to note that the outcomes were based on perceptions.

Hansford, Tennent, and Ehrich (2003) reported an analysis of 159 articles relating to mentoring in educational contexts. This study drew articles from the United States (61%), United Kingdom (19%), Australia (16%), and the remaining studies were from Canada, Belgium, South Africa, and South East Asian countries. The authors intended to conduct a meta-analysis but only a small number of studies included quantitative results. As a consequence the study focussed on an analysis of beneficial and negative outcomes of mentoring in educational contexts. This relative lack of quantitative studies is evident in many areas of mentoring research. Additional to this was that of the 159 educational studies coded only 22 identified and discussed to some extent the conceptual or theoretic underpinnings of the particular study (Hansford et al., 2003). A number of beneficial outcomes for mentors, mentees, and the organisations involved were identified. However, the "dark side" of mentoring was also evident as a number of negative outcomes were recorded. In terms of the potential for a relationship to exist between mentoring and achievement the study reported only 10 of the 159 educational studies contained data that addressed this topic. These 10 studies indicated that the educational organisation, that is, the school, the governing body, or educational authority, reported beneficial outcomes in terms of the educational grades, attendance, or behaviour of students. In summarising the study it appeared that much of the mentoring research in educational contexts was qualitative or descriptive; many studies lacked theoretical or conceptual frameworks and few studies had as their focus mentoring and achievement.

In recent years more mentoring studies have considered achievement as a significant variable. In particular, several of these studies have focussed on samples from "at-risk" students. DuBois, Holloway, Valentine, and Cooper (2002) conducted an in-depth meta-analysis which reviewed 55 evaluations of mentoring programs on youth. These evaluations produced a total of 575 separate estimates of effect sizes. The study had two aims and these were: (a) to assess the overall effects of mentoring on youth programs and (b) to examine the possibility of variations in program effects relating to the design and implementation of mentoring programs, youth characteristics, mentor-mentee relationships, and program outcomes. The overall effect-size was .18 which led DuBois et al. to conclude that the "findings provide evidence of only a modest or small benefit of program participation for the average youth" (p.168).

The study of DuBois et al. (2002) also found that many factors were not moderators of this overall small effect. These factors included: gender, race, and ethnicity of mentors, the geographical location of the program, the setting where the mentoring took place, and the compensation of mentors, the screening of mentors and the matching of mentors and youth, the frequency of mentor and youth contact and the length of a mentoring relationship, none of which significantly moderated effect size. The impact of mentoring on academic and educational measures tended not to provide strong evidence of any of the other four outcome variables: emotional or psychological, problem or high-risk behaviour, social competence and career or employment.

The focus of the meta-analysis conducted by Eby, Allen, Evans, Thomas, and DuBois (2009) was to determine the effect size associated with regard to three types of mentoring; namely, youth, academic, and workplace mentoring. A database of 112 studies provided 116 independent samples for the analysis. Overall, the effect sizes associated with the three types of mentoring were considered small. Youth mentoring was associated with effect sizes ranging from .03 to .14, academic mentoring with effect sizes of .11 to .36, and workplace mentoring with effect sizes ranging from .03 to .19. Youth mentoring was more likely to affect school attitudes and less likely to affect performance. Academic mentoring was more likely to affect performance and school attitudes. Workplace mentoring was more likely to enhance helping behaviour, situational satisfaction, and interpersonal relationships and less likely to result in gains in job performance. The results suggest that mentoring is more likely related to attitudes than to behaviour, health, and career outcomes.

Studies from countries other than the United States show trends similar to those reported above, namely a diversity of outcomes. A study by Rodger and Tremblay (2003), for example, reported on the effects of a peer mentoring program on academic success among first year university students in Canada. Nine hundred and eighty-three students completed an academic motivation inventory and of these 537 were randomly assigned to participate in a mentoring program with the remainder serving as a control group. The researchers found only partial support for the hypothesis that mentoring would have a positive effect on student achievement. Another Canadian study by Campbell and Campbell (1997) of 339 undergraduate students used a matched pairs design that indicated mentored students obtained higher GPAs and that the amount of mentor-protégé contact was positively correlated with GPAs.

In a comprehensive review of mentoring literature, Hall (2003) noted the major difference between United Kingdom and United States research was the relative lack of large-scale quantitative studies in the United Kingdom. It is further pointed out that many of the youth mentoring studies in the United Kingdom report positive outcomes such as fewer school absences, better attitudes, and improvement in parental relationships. However, these positive outcomes do not always include improvements in academic achievement.

A study conducted by Vazsonyi and Snider (2008) involved 2,735 adolescent apprentices from Switzerland (who attended school part-time) and 368 adolescent students who worked part-time in the United States. The researchers sought to determine the impact of mentoring on adolescent developmental outcomes. They found that high quality experiences were positively associated with employment skills, self-esteem, well-being, and negatively associated with alcohol use, drug use, and delinquency. An important limitation of this study was that data came from participant self-reports.

In an Australian study, Muckert (2002) examined groups

of first year tertiary students and used a pre-and posttest design. Students were assigned to either a peer-mentoring or a control group. Peer-mentoring had a positive effect on reenrolment intentions, persistence intentions, academic performance, and self-reported adjustment. However, in a number of instances these apparent gains did not achieve statistical significance.

In a 6-year New Zealand study of high ability high school students, Irving, Moore, and Hamilton (2007) found that students believed they had gained skills during a mentoring program but the statistical analysis did not provide evidence of significant gains in academic achievement. Sundi (2007), in a Norwegian study focussing on teacher education, raised some of the potential "dark side" issues of mentoring. It was pointed out variables such as power, control, dependence, and intimacy were frequently not considered in mentoring research. Further it was suggested that mentoring can obstruct the development of reflection.

Summary and Recommendations

From the aforementioned discussion, it appears that the research linking mentoring and achievement does provide some evidence of a positive association. However, the level of this association is small and in many studies the outcomes or effects reported cannot be taken as a causal relationship. Although the outcomes are rather modest there is evidence that the average effects from mentoring remain relatively constant (and small) when a number of possible mediating factors are considered.

A number of comments can be made regarding the existing research. First, there is, as in other mentoring research, concern about the defining of the term *mentor* or the concept of mentoring. Second, there is a need for additional studies to build on the notion that theory-based and empirically based mentoring studies produce more positive outcomes. In looking at the literature there are still many simplistic studies that are poorly designed and rather lacking in rigorous evaluative procedures. Third, when achievement is included as a variable in mentoring studies its measurement is often based on perceptions. There seems to be a place for studies that consider both the perceptions and reality of achievement. Fourth, studies that consider developmental stages of the youth involved, strength of peer associations, and the features of the contextual setting warrant consideration.

References

Aseltine, R., Dupre, M., & Lamlein, P. (2000). Mentoring as a drug prevention strategy: An evaluation across ages. *Adolescent and Family Health, 1,* 11–20.

Blakely, C. M., Menon, R., & Jones, D. J. (1995). *Project belong: Final report.* College Station, TX: Public Policy Research Institute, Texas A&M University.

Campbell, T. A., & Campbell, D. E. (1997). Faculty/student mentor program: Effects on academic performance and retention. *Research in Higher Education, 38*(6), 727–742.

DuBois, D. L., Holloway, B. E., Valentine, J. C., & Cooper, H. (2002). Effectiveness of mentoring programs for youth: A meta- analytic review. *American Journal of Community Psychology, 30*(2), 157–197.

Eby, L. T., Allen, T. D., Evans, S. C., Thomas, D., & DuBois, D. (2009). Does mentoring matter? A multidisciplinary meta-analysis comparing mentored and non-mentored individuals. *Journal of Vocational Behavior, 72*(2), 254–267.

Grossman, J. B., & Tierney, J. P. (1998). Does mentoring work? An impact study of the Big Brothers Big Sisters program. *Evaluation Review, 22,* 403–426.

Hall, J. C. (2003). *Mentoring and young people: A literature review* (SCRS Research Report 114). Glasgow, Scotland: The SCRS Centre, University of Glasgow.

Hansford, B., Tennent, L., & Ehrich, L. C. (2003). Educational mentoring: Is it worth the effort? *Educational Research and Perspectives, 30*(1), 51–62

Irving, S. E., Moore, D. W., & Hamilton, R. J. (2003). Mentoring for high ability high school students. *Education and Training, 52*(2), 100–109.

Jacobi, M. (1991). Mentoring and academic success: A literature review. *Review of Educational Research, 61*(4), 505–532.

McPartland, J. M., & Nettles, S. M. (1991). Using community adults as advocates or mentors for at-risk middle school students: A two-year evaluation of program raise. *American Journal of Education, 99*(4), 568– 586.

Muckert, T. D. (2002). *Investigating the student attrition process and the contribution of peer-mentoring interventions in an Australian first year university program.* Australian Digital Theses Program. Retrieved from http://www4gu.edu.au:8080/adt-root/public/adt-QGU20030226.171200/

Rhodes, J. (2001, Summer). Youth mentoring in perspective. *The Centre.* Retrieved from http://www.fourh.umn.edu/educators/research/center/.

Rhodes, J. E., Grossman, J. B., & Resch, N. L. (2000). Agents of change: Pathways through which mentoring relationships influence adolescents, adjustment. *Child Development, 71*(6), 1662–1671.

Rodger, S., & Tremblay, P. F. (2003). The effects of a peer mentoring program on academic success among first year university students. *Canadian Journal of Higher Education, 33*(3), 1–17.

Slicker, E. K., & Palmer, D. J. (1993). Mentoring at-risk high school students: Evaluating a school-based program. *School Counselor, 40,* 327–334.

Sundi, L. (2007). Mentoring a new mantra for education. *Teaching and Teacher Education, 23*(2), 201–204.

Vazsonyi, A., & Snider, J. B. (2008). Mentoring competencies, and adjustment in adolescents: American part-time employment and European apprenticeships. *International Journal of Behavioral Development, 32*(1), 46–55.

8.24

Teacher Immediacy

ANN BAINBRIDGE FRYMIER
Miami University

Introduction

The concept of immediacy was introduced by psychologist Albert Mehrabian (1971) and refers to the degree of perceived physical or psychological closeness between people in a relationship. He defined the immediacy principle in terms of the implicit messages that people use to signal approach and avoidance. Specifically, "people are drawn toward persons and things they like, evaluate highly, and prefer; and they avoid or move away from things they dislike, evaluate negatively, or do not prefer" (Mehrabian, 1971, p. 1). While immediacy is a perception, it has been operationalized primarily by a set of nonverbal behaviors, and to a lesser extent verbal behaviors. Communication behaviors that have been shown to enhance perceptions of immediacy include, but are not limited to, closer distances, increased eye contact, smiling, vocal variety, more direct body orientation, more open, relaxed, and accessible postures, forward leans, and decreased occurrences of arms akimbo. These nonverbal behaviors reflect liking and are perceived as being warm, active, inviting, approachable, dynamic, and engaging.

Research Evidence

Andersen (1979) conducted the first research that examined the relationship between teacher immediacy and student achievement. She hypothesized that students would learn more from more highly immediate teachers. Anderson found a relationship between teacher immediacy and affective learning; that is, students reported liking and valuing the teacher and the content more when the teacher engaged in more immediacy behaviors. However, she did not find a relationship with cognitive learning, which was measured with a typical content exam. Much was made about the lack of relationship between immediacy and cognitive learning. Critics characterized immediacy as simply a means for teachers to win popularity contests. Later research

using Richmond, McCroskey, Kearney, and Plax's (1987) cognitive learning scale and Frymier and Houser's (1999) learning indicators scale, along with research using traditional experimental designs provided stronger evidence that immediacy had a positive impact on affective and cognitive learning (Comstock, Rowell, & Bowers, 1995; Frymier & Houser, 1998; Witt, Wheeless, & Allen, 2004).

Over 250 articles and dissertations have examined teacher immediacy in some fashion. Witt, Wheeless, and Allen (2004) conducted a meta-analysis and reviewed 55 studies that tested the relationship between affective learning and nonverbal immediacy, and reported an average correlation of .49. Using Richmond et al.'s (1987) cognitive learning measure, researchers repeatedly found a positive relationship with teacher immediacy. Witt et al. (2004) reviewed 44 studies that examined the relationship between nonverbal immediacy and students' perceived cognitive learning (on the Richmond scale) and found an average correlation between perceived cognitive learning and immediacy was .51.

Using students' self-reports of learning have been routinely criticized and in response a number of experimental studies were conducted where cognitive learning could be measured in a more valid way. The first of these studies was conducted by Kelley and Gorham (1988) who reported a correlation of .30 between recall and teacher immediacy. Witt et al. (2004) reviewed 11 studies using tests of recall/knowledge as a measure of cognitive learning and reported an average correlation of .17 with teacher nonverbal immediacy. After 30 years of research and nearly 300 studies, it is clear that the use of nonverbal immediacy behaviors has a positive impact on students' affective and cognitive learning. The impact is small to moderate, but significant and worthwhile.

Several causal explanations have been put forth to explain the relationship between immediacy and learning. The first was put forth by Kelley and Gorham (1988) who proposed that immediacy gained students attention. This explanation received little support. Christophel (1990) and

425

Frymier (1994) both provided support for a motivation explanation; that immediacy enhanced students' motivation to study which in turn enhanced learning. Rodriguez, Plax, and Kearney (1996) proposed the affective learning model that proposed affective learning as a mediator between immediacy and learning. Taken together, these models present evidence that immediacy behaviors create a positive response in students that can be described as motivation, liking, or affect, which in turn facilitates students' learning, particularly the feeling that they have learned more.

Over 300 published studies have supported the notion that teacher immediacy has a positive impact on students. Scholars have argued over the exact nature of the influence, but with few exceptions, the research has concluded that students benefit when teachers use nonverbal immediacy behaviors in their teaching. The research also clearly indicates that immediacy alone is not sufficient; nonverbal immediacy behaviors must accompany other teacher behaviors that facilitate learning. Immediacy appears to "grease the skids" of learning. When teachers use immediacy behaviors it creates a positive relationship with students that support students' learning.

Summary and Recommendations

On the surface, advising teachers to smile, use vocal variety, make eye contact, and use positive gestures with students seems rather insubstantial. Most people who lack formal training in communication respond to such advice by rolling their eyes. However, the research that has been reviewed in this entry clearly indicates that these nonverbal behaviors consistently have a positive impact on students. So how is it that such seemingly mundane behaviors are so important?

First, communication is made up of both verbal and nonverbal messages that stimulate meaning in other people. Verbal messages involve words, which can be oral or written. Nonverbal messages, in contrast, encompass all of the behaviors that we use to communicate that do not involve words; such as vocal characteristics, facial expressions, hand gestures, head movements, posture, attire and appearance, eye contact, touch, physical distance, and the use of space. We use nonverbal messages in a variety of ways in conjunction with verbal messages. For instance we might emphasize a word by snapping our fingers, or to prevent someone from interrupting we might increase our loudness and speak faster. When we like someone we often move a little closer (but not too close) and when we dislike someone we often move a little further away. When we are further away from someone than we'd like to be, we often make more eye contact as a way of reducing the distance between ourselves and the receiver. That is, we use nonverbal messages to help our verbal messages make sense to others. A verbal message without nonverbal messages is confusing at best. Oral communication without nonverbal messages (which is impossible) is like written communication with no spaces or punctuation.

The nonverbal messages that convey immediacy enhance the meaning of the verbal messages they accompany. We use a speaker's nonverbal messages to help us understand the verbal message and to judge its value. If the speaker sounds bored and uninterested (conveyed by nonverbal behaviors) we are apt to believe that about the content. When a teacher uses nonverbal immediacy behaviors, he or she is communicating that the content is interesting and exciting and also conveys that the teacher likes the students. Classrooms are by definition evaluative environments. Being liked by the person who is evaluating us almost always makes us feel more at ease and more willing to take risks and do things like ask questions. Therefore these seemingly mundane nonverbal behaviors communicate powerful messages that accompany the content a teacher is sharing with students.

For most of us, when we are excited and interested about our topic and like the people with whom we are talking, we naturally use nonverbal immediacy behaviors as this conveys our enthusiasm and liking. There are a number of reasons why teachers may not feel excited or interested in what they are teaching and there is a similar list of reasons why teachers may not like their students. When this is the case, teachers are unlikely to exhibit nonverbal immediacy. So what do you do if you don't like your students or are bored with what you are teaching? Can you fake immediacy? Most of us can fake immediacy at least a little, but very few of us can fake it convincingly for any extended period of time. So what can you do? First, you can make changes in your lessons or teaching assignment so that you can be excited about what you are teaching and the students you are teaching. We may have limited control over these things and if you really do not like students, you should probably find a different profession. The second answer lies in your awareness of your own communication behaviors and the extent your behaviors match the message you're intending to send. While it can be uncomfortable, videotaping yourself teaching is the best way to assess your communication behaviors. You may discover that you do not smile nearly as much as you think you do or that your voice is much shriller than you thought. After videotaping yourself, view the video and look for the following immediacy behaviors:

- Gesturing while talking to the class.
- Using vocal variety when talking to the class.
- Looking at the class while talking.
- Smiling at the class while talking.
- A relaxed body position while talking to the class.
- Moving around the classroom while teaching.
- Moving closer to students while talking.
- Smiling at individual students in class.

How frequently do you use each behavior? How often do you use the opposite of each behavior such as having a tense body position or using a monotone voice? Are the behaviors you are using conveying the feelings you want to convey? Sometimes we have to make a conscious effort to "turn up the volume" on our nonverbal behaviors so that they have the desired impact. This is particularly true in large classes where the physical distance between the teacher and the students is great or when we are tired. At other times we may need to "psych ourselves up" before we teach so that we feel the necessary enthusiasm for the content and the class. This may be particularly important when our teaching assignment is difficult.

When reviewing your video of yourself teaching, really listen and look for what messages you are communicating. Some teachers may be afraid of their students or nervous that their students will know more than they do. Like all emotions, fear is communicated primarily through nonverbal behaviors. You may lack immediacy because of the fear or anxiety you feel about teaching. In this case you need to tackle the cause of the fear or anxiety. For most of us, we cannot display a relaxed posture until we feel relaxed.

To conclude, nonverbal immediacy is a set of related nonverbal behaviors that accompany verbal messages. In the teaching context, teachers are usually most focused on the content of their lesson and not on the subtle nonverbal behaviors used to communicate that content. However the nonverbal behaviors help teachers accomplish their teaching goals by communicating approach to students. While we can learn in negative environments, it is easier and more fun to learn from teachers who we believe like us. We are more apt to reciprocate the teacher's approach behaviors, and approach the teaching and the content ourselves.

References

Andersen, J. F. (1979). Teacher immediacy as a predictor of teaching effectiveness. In D. Nimmo (Ed.), *Communication yearbook* (Vol. 3, pp. 543–559). New Brunswick, NJ: Transaction.

Christophel, D. M. (1990). The relationship among teacher immediacy behaviors, student motivation and learning. *Communication Education, 39*, 323–340.

Comstock, J., Rowell, E., & Bowers, J. (1995). Food for thought: Teacher nonverbal immediacy, student learning, and curvilinearity. *Communication Education, 44*, 251–266.

Frymier, A. B. (1994). A model of immediacy in the classroom. *Communication Quarterly, 42*, 133–144.

Frymier, A. B., & Houser, M. L. (1998). Does making content relevant make a difference in learning? *Communication Research Reports, 15*, 121–129.

Kearney, P., Plax, T. G., & Wendt-Wasco, N. J. (1985). Teacher immediacy for affective learning in divergent college classes. *Communication Quarterly, 33*, 61–71.

Kelley, D. H., & Gorham, J. (1988). Effects of immediacy on recall information. *Communication Education, 37* 198–207.

Mehrabian, A. (1971). *Silent messages.* Belmont, CA: Wadsworth.

Richmond, V. P., & McCroskey, J. C. (1992). *Power in the classroom: Communication, control, and concern.* Hillsdale, NJ: Erlbaum.

Richmond, V. P., McCroskey, J. C., Kearney, P., & Plax, T. G. (1987). Power in the classroom VII: Linking behavior alteration techniques to cognitive learning. *Communications Education, 36*(1), 1–12.

Rodriguez, J. I., Plax, T. G., & Kearney, P. (1996). Clarifying the relationship between teacher nonverbal immediacy and student cognitive learning: Affective learning as the central causal mediator. *Communication Education, 45*, 293–305.

Witt, P. L., Wheeless, L. R., & Allen, M. (2004). A meta-analytical review of the relationship between teacher immediacy and student learning. *Communication Monographs, 71*, 184–207.

8.25

The Impact of Teaching Assistants on Pupils

Rob Webster and Peter Blatchford
Institute of Education, University of London

Introduction

The Growth of TAs Worldwide. Since the early- to mid-1990s, there has been a phenomenal growth in classroom- or pupil-based support staff. These adults are known in different countries by different names: *teaching assistant, classroom assistant,* and *learning support assistant* are common in the UK; *paraprofessional and paraeducator* in the United States; and *teacher aide* in Australia. In line with the UK Government, in this paper, we use the generic term *teaching assistant* (TA) to cover these equivalent roles.

A recent international survey reports a general increase in TAs employed in schools in the United States, Australia, Italy, Sweden, Canada, Finland, Germany, Hong Kong, Iceland, Ireland, Malta, and South Africa (Giangreco & Doyle, 2007). We are also aware of increases in use of TAs in New Zealand. The growth and numbers of TAs seem most pronounced in the UK. In 2011, TAs comprised a quarter of the total school workforce in state schools in England, and over half of all support staff. TAs are therefore now a sizeable part of the school workforce. It also seems numbers of TAs have been increasing at a faster rate than teachers. These data aside, it is difficult to obtain exact figures on the number of TAs and their proportion in the school workforce. There is an urgent need for international data on TA employment.

One principal reason for the growth in TAs worldwide is the way inclusion into mainstream schools has become the favoured means of educating children with special educational needs and disabilities. TAs are seen as integral to this process. Another reason, in the UK at least, was to help deal with problems with teacher workloads—a main contributory factor to the crisis in teacher retention during the 2000s. The English and Welsh Governments in 2003 implemented *The National Agreement,* as it was called, to raise pupil standards and tackle excessive teacher workload, in large part via new and expanded support roles and responsibilities for TAs and other support staff.

There is much debate about the appropriate role of TAs. There is ambiguity because in one sense TAs can help pupils *indirectly* by assisting the school to enhance teaching (e.g., by taking on teachers' administrative duties), but many TAs have a *direct* teaching role, interacting daily with pupils (mainly those with learning and behavioural needs), supplementing teacher input, and providing opportunities for one-to-one and small-group work. This direct instructional role affects boundaries between teaching and nonteaching roles and has been controversial in the UK (Bach, Kessler & Heron, 2004) and elsewhere (e.g., Finland, Takala, 2007; and the United States, Giangreco, 2010).

Given the scale of the increase in TAs, and their direct, educational role, it is vital to ask about the impact of TAs on pupils' educational progress. Worryingly, such evidence is very thin. This chapter, therefore, makes heavy use of the largest study yet conducted on TAs—the UK 5-year Deployment and Impact of Support Staff (DISS) project (Blatchford, Russell, & Webster, 2012)—which was set up to describe the characteristics and deployment of TAs and other school support staff, and to address, for the first time, their impact on teachers, teaching, and pupils.

Research Findings

Impact of TAs on Academic Outcomes. Reviews by Alborz, Pearson, Farrell, and Howes (2009) and Slavin, Lake, Davis, and Madden (2009) show that experimental studies that examined the effect of TAs who deliver specific curricular interventions (mostly in literacy), tend to have a positive impact on pupil progress when TAs are prepared and trained, and have support and guidance from the teacher and school about practice.

However, other experimental studies report negative results. Klassen (2001), in a study of 67 pupils who had a statement of special educational needs (SEN) for a specific literacy difficulty or dyslexia, and who were assigned additional support for literacy, found they made less progress than their unsupported peers. Finn, Gerber, Farber, and Achilles (2000) found that there was no compensatory effect of having TAs (extra to teachers) in larger ("regular") classes.

Curricular interventions led by TAs take up only a small part of pupils' school days, and a main limitation of research in this field is the lack of rigorous empirical studies of the impact of TAs when judged in relation to normal forms of deployment under everyday conditions over the school year. Such results were provided by the DISS study (see Blatchford, Bassett et al., 2011; Blatchford, Russell, & Webster, 2012). This used an alternative, longitudinal, and naturalistic design within which the analysis studied effects of TA support (based on teacher estimates and measures from systematic observation) on 8,200 pupils' academic progress in English, mathematics, and science under normal classroom conditions. Two cohorts of pupils in seven age groups in mainstream schools were tracked over one year each. Multilevel regression methods were used to address the independent effect of TA support on pupil outcomes, controlling for factors known to affect progress (and TA support), such as pupils' SEN status, prior attainment, eligibility for free school meals, English as additional language, deprivation, gender, and ethnicity.[1]

The results were striking: 16 of the 21 results were in a negative direction and there were no positive effects of TA support for any subject or for any year group. Those pupils receiving the most support from TAs made less progress than similar pupils who received little or no support from TAs, even after controlling for factors likely to be related to more TA support (e.g., prior attainment and SEN status). Furthermore, there is evidence from the DISS study that learning outcomes for pupils with the highest levels of need, who are typically those who receive the most support from TAs, are worse (Webster et al., 2010). These results are troubling, and we turn to likely explanations once we have looked at other effects.

Impact of TAs on Pupils' Behaviour, Motivation, and Approaches to Learning. It would seem to follow from reports of teachers (Blatchford, Bassett et al., 2011; Blatchford, Russell, & Webster, 2012) that assigning TAs to particular pupils, usually those with problems connected to learning, behavior, or attention, would give these pupils more individual attention and help them develop confidence and motivation, good working habits, and the willingness to finish tasks. Schlapp, Davidson, and Wilson (2003) identify the benefits of classroom assistants more in terms of the range of learning experiences provided and effects on pupil motivation, confidence, and self-esteem, and less in terms of pupil progress. The DISS study found the presence of TAs helped maintain classroom focus and discipline through an extra pair of eyes.

On the other hand, there are concerns that TAs can encourage dependency, because they prioritise outcomes of activities rather than encouraging pupils to think for themselves (Moyles & Suschitzky, 1997). Giangreco (2010) has argued that overreliance on one-to-one paraprofessional

support leads to a wide range of detrimental effects on pupils (e.g., in terms of interference with ownership and responsibility, and separation from classmates).

The DISS study examined the effect of the amount of TA support on eight scales representing so called Positive Approaches to Learning (PAL) (see Blatchford, Bassett et al., 2011; Blatchford, Russell, & Webster, 2012); that is, distractibility; task confidence; motivation; disruptiveness; independence; relationships with other pupils; completion of assigned work; and follows instructions from adults. The results showed little evidence that the amount of support pupils received from TAs over a school year improved these dimensions, except for those in Year 9 (13- to 14-year-olds), where there was a clear positive effect of TA support across all eight PAL outcomes.

Impact of TAs on Teachers and Teaching. Although effects of TAs on pupils' academic learning is worrying, it is worth noting that the DISS study consistently showed that TAs and other support staff had a strong positive effect on teachers' job satisfaction, levels of stress, and workload—chiefly by relieving teachers of many of their administrative duties (Blatchford, Bassett et al, 2011; Blatchford et al., 2012). Results from systematic observations also confirmed teachers' views that TAs had a positive effect in terms of reducing disruption and allowing more time for the teacher to teach.

Summary and Recommendations

How do we account for these negative results found by the UK DISS project? One obvious explanation might be that pupils given most TA support would in any case have been likely to make less progress. However, such explanations, in terms of preexisting characteristics of pupils, are unlikely because key pupil characteristics that typically affect progress (and TA support), such as SEN status, prior attainment, and measures of deprivation, were controlled for in the statistical analyses. To be of any consequence, any potential factor would need to be systemic across all year groups and subjects, and related to *both* attainment and TA support.

So, if pupil factors do not appear to be explaining the negative relationship between TA support and pupil progress, what is? The wider pedagogical role model (presented in Figure 8.4) was developed to summarise and interpret other results from the DISS study concerning the broader context within which TAs work, and which are likely to maximise or inhibit their effectiveness.

The WPR model has three key concepts:

1. *Preparedness.* Preparedness concerns the lack of training and professional development of TAs and teachers, and day-to-day aspects of planning and preparation before lessons, and feedback afterwards, which are likely to have a bearing on learning outcomes for pupils.
2. *Deployment.* The DISS study found TAs have a direct

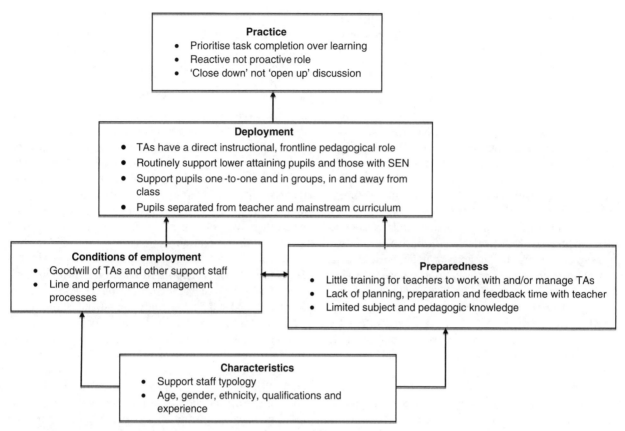

Figure 8.25.1 The wider pedagogical role model.

pedagogical role, interacting with pupils, usually in one-to-one and group contexts, and predominantly with pupils with SEN. The more severe a pupil's needs, the more interaction with a TA increases, and interaction with a teacher decreases. Pupils' interactions with TAs are much more sustained and interactive than those they have with teachers. This might seem pedagogically valuable, but it also means that TA-supported pupils become separated from the teacher, missing out on everyday teacher-to-pupil interactions and mainstream curriculum coverage (especially where TAs are given responsibility for leading interventions away from the classroom).

3. *Practice.* The DISS findings show that pupils' interactions with TAs are much lower in quality than those with teachers (Rubie-Davies, Blatchford, Webster, Koutsoubou, & Bassett, 2010). TAs are more concerned with task completion than learning; and inadequate preparation leads to TAs' interactions being reactive. In addition, teachers generally open up pupil talk, whereas TAs close down talk, both linguistically and cognitively (Radford, Blatchford, & Webster, 2011).

Conclusions

Though data are limited, there are signs of a huge increase in the use of paraprofessionals working in education, many with front line educational roles. The largest study to date of the impact of TAs on pupils' academic progress has shown

that there is a negative relationship between the amount of support from TAs and pupils' academic progress. The findings from DISS, and the work of Giangreco, show that TAs in the UK and the United States have a predominantly remedial role, supporting lower-attaining pupils and those with SEN. Teachers like this arrangement because they can then teach the rest of the class in the knowledge that the children in most need get more individual adult attention. But the more support pupils get from TAs, the less they get from teachers. It is perhaps unsurprising then that these pupils make less progress.

The WPR model summarises the most likely explanations for the DISS study findings. There are likely to be similarities with the ways in which TAs are deployed and prepared in other countries apart from the UK (e.g., Giangreco, 2010; Takala, 2007), although only the DISS project has so far been able to produce data on the effect of TA support on pupil attainment in such a large scale and systematic way.

Future research needs to examine the possible explanatory factors of preparedness, deployment, and practice of TAs in different countries, where TAs may have different characteristics and different systems for deploying TAs may operate.

It is the lowest achieving pupils who benefit most from high-quality teaching. As Giangreco. (2010) has argued, we would not accept a situation in which children without SEN are routinely taught by TAs instead of teachers. The present remedial role of TAs lets down the most disadvantaged children. There needs to be a reconsideration of the use of TAs in the context of the inclusion of pupils with SEN.

We have been careful to stress that these effects are not the fault of TAs. Instead, these effects are attributable to decisions made about them, often with the best of intentions, together with inadequate training for teachers on how to work with TAs, and a lack of opportunities for them to properly brief TAs before lessons. There is a clear need for a fundamental rethink of the appropriate pedagogical role of TAs. It is important to address untested assumptions that they help to raise standards. Should TAs have a primary, frontline instructional role? If so, what should this consist of? If not, what would a secondary nonpedagogical role consist of? It also means reexamining the role of teachers to ensure they adopt an inclusive pedagogy, are not reliant on TAs teaching on pupils with SEN.

Note

1. Further details on the rationale for this approach and further justification for claims about the causal role of TAs on pupil outcomes can be found in (Blatchford, Bassett et al., 2011).

References

Alborz, A., Pearson, D., Farrell, P., & Howes, A. (2009). *The impact of adult support staff on pupils and mainstream schools*. London: Dept. for Children, Schools and Families and Institute of Education.

Bach, S., Kessler, I., & Heron, P. (2004, April). *Support roles and changing job boundaries in the public services: The case of teaching assistants in British primary schools*. Paper presented at International Labour Process Conference, Amsterdam.

Blatchford, P., Bassett, P., Brown, P., Martin, C., Russell, A., & Webster, R. (2011). The impact of support staff on pupils' "positive approaches to learning" and their academic progress. *British Educational Research Journal, 37(3), 443–464*.

Blatchford, P., Russell, A., & Webster, R. (2012). *Reassessing the impact of teaching assistants: How research challenges practice and policy*. Abingdon, England: Routledge.

Finn, J. D., Gerber, S. B., Farber, S. L., & Achilles, C. M. (2000). Teacher aides: An alternative to small classes? In M. C. Wang & J. D. Finn (Eds.), *How small classes help teachers do their best* (pp. 131–174). Philadelphia, PA: Temple University Center for Research in Human Development.

Giangreco, M. F. (2010). One-to-one paraprofessionals for students with disabilities in inclusive classrooms: Is conventional wisdom wrong? *Intellectual and Developmental Disabilities, 4* (1), 1–13.

Giangreco, M. F., & Doyle, M. B. (2007). Teacher assistants in inclusive schools. In L. Florian (Ed.), *The SAGE handbook of special education* (pp. 429–439). London: Sage.

Klassen, R. (2001). After the statement: Reading progress made by secondary students with specific literacy difficulty provision. *Educational Psychology in Practice, 17*(2), 121–133.

Moyles, J., & Suschitzky, W. (1997, November). The employment and deployment of classroom support staff: head teachers' perspectives. *Research in Education, 58*, 21–34.

Radford, J., Blatchford, P., & Webster, R. (2011). Opening up and closing down: Comparing teacher and TA talk in mathematics lessons. *Learning and Instruction, 21*(5), 625–635.

Rubie-Davies, C., Blatchford, P., Webster, R., Koutsoubou, M., & Bassett, P. (2010). Enhancing learning?: A comparison of teacher and teaching assistant interactions with pupils. *School Effectiveness and School Improvement, 21*(4), 429–449.

Schlapp, U., Davidson, J., & Wilson, V. (2003). An "extra pair of hands"?: Managing classroom assistants in Scottish primary schools. *Educational Management and Administration, 31*(2) 189–205.

Slavin, R.E., Lake, C., Davis, S., Madden, N. (2009). *Effective programs for struggling readers: A best evidence synthesis*. Baltimore, MD: Center for Research and Reform in Education, Johns Hopkins University.

Takala, M. (2007). The work of classroom assistants in special and mainstream education in Finland. *British Journal of Special Education, 34*(1), 50–57.

Webster, R., Blatchford, P., Bassett, P., Brown, P., Martin, C., & Russell, A. (2010). Double standards and first principles: Framing teaching assistant support for pupils with special educational needs. *European Journal of Special Educational Needs, 25*(4), 319–336.

8.26

Time on Task

Tamara van Gog
Erasmus University, Rotterdam

Introduction

Time on task, which is counted among the most important factors affecting student learning and achievement, can be defined as the amount of time that students spend engaged in or paying attention to tasks that are related to outcome measures of learning or achievement (Berliner, 1991). This time can be spent either at school, or outside school (e.g., on self-study or homework activities).

Research Evidence

According to Carroll (1963), the degree of learning can be defined by the amount of time spent on a task, divided by the time a student requires to learn that task. Research has provided support for this model, indeed showing a positive association between time on task and students' learning and achievement in various educational contexts. For example, when fourth and fifth graders were allocated or spent less time on learning than they needed, their achievement was negatively affected (Gettinger, 1985), while the amount of time high school students spent on homework positively affected their grade (Keith, 1982), and the amount of time that medical students spent on self-study positively affected achievement (Gijselaers & Schmidt, 1995). Comparing two teaching methods in legal education, Admiraal, Wubbels, and Pilot (1999) demonstrated that a problem method led to increased time on task as well as higher achievement than the conventional case method.

The amount of time a student requires to learn a task up to a certain standard of performance may differ between students because of individual differences in ability (Anderson, 1976; Gettinger, 1984). In addition, how much time on task students are willing to invest is affected by, for instance, self-efficacy beliefs which influence students' persistence (e.g., Multon, Brown, & Lent, 1991). Finally, whether students invest sufficient time is influenced by their own metacognitive judgments of how much they have learned, which affect whether or not they will continue to study (e.g., Metcalfe, 2009).

It is important to distinguish time on task from allocated instructional time, that is, the time provided for instruction by policymakers, schools, or teachers (Berliner, 1991). Allocating insufficient instructional time can negatively affect learning (Gettinger, 1985), because it prevents students from spending sufficient time on a task to learn it. But even when sufficient time is allocated for instruction, students do not spend all of that time actually engaged in tasks that are relevant for learning (Karweit & Slavin, 1981). Some scheduled lessons may have to be canceled; for example, due to teacher illness or field trips. But time may also be lost during lessons, because teachers typically need to attend to organizational issues such as handing out materials, making off-topic announcements, or maintaining order, and students will spend some of the time on off-task behavior (i.e., not paying attention) because they are talking or daydreaming. A 1981 study by Karweit and Slavin in elementary school mathematics classes showed that students may be spending only 60% of the allocated time actually engaged in instructional activities.

Summary and Recommendations

Because time on task has a positive effect on achievement, it is an important variable to consider in educational research. Consider, for example, a researcher who wants to compare two instructional methods: one conventional method and one that involves additional support. Students in the condition with the additional support invest more time and attain higher achievement. Now, is the higher achievement a result of the additional support, or simply of the fact that these students spent more time on the task? Simons (1983) reviewed the effects of such instructional aids on time on task and performance and discusses ways in which these effects can be dealt with in educational research.

Moreover, time on task can play another, perhaps more interesting role in educational research, which is related to the individual differences in time needed to learn: it can enrich measures of learning. The more a particular task has been practiced, the faster it can be performed. This is known as the "power law of practice" (Newell & Rosenbloom, 1981). As a consequence, the amount of time a student needs to complete a particular task provides information on how well a student has learned that task. This information can be used in addition to other measures of performance (e.g., the number and type of errors made) to make judgments about individual students' learning by comparing time required to complete equivalent tasks at pretest and posttest. It can also be used to make judgments about the relative effectiveness of different instructional methods. For example, if instructional method A is compared to method B, and both methods lead to an equal number of errors made on a posttest, but students who had received method A are much faster, then method A has led to more efficient learning than method B (see Van Gog & Paas, 2008).

In sum, time on task is an important factor affecting students' performance, and should be carefully considered in educational practice as well as educational research.

References

Admiraal, W., Wubbels, T., & Pilot, A. (1999). College teaching in legal education: Teaching method, students' time on task, and achievement. *Research in Higher Education, 40*, 687–704.

Anderson, L. W. (1976). An empirical investigation of individual differences in time to learn. *Journal of Educational Psychology, 68*, 226–233.

Berliner, D. (1991). What's all the fuss about instructional time? In M. Ben-Peretz & R. Bromme (Eds.), *The nature of time in schools: Theoretical concepts, practitioner perceptions.* New York: Teachers College Press. Retrieved from http://courses.ed.asu.edu/berliner/readings/fuss/fuss.htm.

Carroll, J. B. (1963). A model of school learning. *Teachers College Record, 64*, 723–733.

Gettinger, M. (1984). Individual differences in time needed for learning: A review of the literature. *Educational Psychologist, 19*, 15–29.

Gettinger, M. (1985). Time allocated and time spent relative to time needed for learning as determinants of achievement. *Journal of Educational Psychology, 77*, 3–11.

Gijselaers, W. H., & Schmidt, H. G. (1995). Effects of quantity of instruction on time spent on learning and achievement. *Educational Research and Evaluation, 1*, 183–201.

Karweit, N. L., & Slavin, R. E. (1981). Measurement and modeling choices in studies of time and learning. *American Educational Research Journal, 18*, 157–171.

Keith, T. Z. (1982). Time spent on homework and high school grades: A large sample path analysis. *Journal of Educational Psychology, 74*, 248–253.

Metcalfe, J. (2009). Metacognitive judgments and control of study. *Current Directions in Psychological Science, 18*, 159–163.

Multon, K. D., Brown, S. D., & Lent, R. W. (1991). Relation of self-efficacy beliefs to academic outcomes: A meta-analytic investigation. *Journal of Counseling Psychology, 38*, 30–38.

Newell, A., & Rosenbloom, P. (1981). Mechanisms of skill acquisition and the law of practice. In J. R. Anderson (Ed), *Cognitive skills and their acquisition* (pp. 1–55). Hillsdale, NJ: Erlbaum.

Simons, P. R. J. (1983). How should we control time on task—or should we? *Instructional Science, 11*, 357–372.

Van Gog, T., & Paas, F. (2008). Instructional efficiency: Revisiting the original construct in educational research. *Educational Psychologist, 43*, 16–26.

8.27

Study Skills

Dale H. Schunk and Carol A. Mullen
The University of North Carolina at Greensboro

Introduction

Tonya and Kim are high school students in the same English class. Their homework is to study three chapters in Charles Dickens's *Great Expectations* for discussion and a quiz the next day. After dinner, each retreats to study. Tonya turns off her cell phone, TV, and social network webpage and assembles her book, class notebook, pencil, and highlighter. She leafs through the chapters, estimating about 2 hours for completing the task. While underlining relevant text and jotting points in her notebook, she pauses periodically, asking herself questions to prompt understanding of the content. After an hour she is more than halfway done, and feels confident about her grasp of the material. She takes a short break but finishes early. In contrast, Kim does not turn off electronic devices. While watching TV, she occasionally highlights text and does not take notes. She text-messages friends and hums along to tunes on her portable CD player. After an hour, she is not halfway done but quickly skims the remaining pages. She lacks confidence about doing well on the assigned work.

These vignettes illustrate differences in students' approaches to study skills and strategies used to learn information (Crespi & Bieu, 2005). Whereas Tonya effectively applies numerous skills, Kim—except for some text underlining—does not. One can surmise that Tonya will perform better in the class.

Research Evidence

There are different types of study skills: *Cognitive/metacognitive skills* include planning, organizing, rehearsing (e.g., memorizing, underlining), elaborating (e.g., note-taking, summarizing), monitoring comprehension, self-questioning, and technological skills (e.g., Internet search strategies). *Environmental/contextual skills* involve establishing a productive work environment, managing time, minimizing distractions, and seeking help when needed. *Motivational/affective skills* include setting goals, monitoring goal progress, feeling efficacious about learning, maintaining interest, making desirable attributions (i.e., perceived causes) for outcomes, and maintaining a positive attitude about learning. A *learning strategy* is a collection of skills that students use to attain a goal. Use of study skills is a central feature of *self-regulation*, which refers to self-generated thoughts, feelings, and actions directed toward reaching academic goals (Zimmerman, 1998).

For years, study skills have been emphasized in education, as in the case of the SQ3R (survey-question-read-recite-review) method for reading comprehension (Robinson, 1946). Interest in study skills accelerated in the 1980s and continues today. Researchers and practitioners are concerned about which study skills promote learning and how to teach them and encourage their use.

Various outcome measures have been investigated. At a basic level, researchers determine what skills students use, such as by observing students study and analyzing their work samples and questionnaire responses (e.g., Learning and Study Strategies Inventory—LASSI; Weinstein, Palmer, & Schulte, 1987). Researchers also compare students' use of study skills to their academic performances to determine how skill use relates to performance and whether some skills are more effective for learning particular content (Purdie & Hattie, 1999).

Reviews of the research generally show that use of study skills relates to better academic performance. Weinstein and Mayer (1986) found benefits for rehearsing, elaborating, organizing, monitoring comprehension, and maintaining a positive affective climate. Zimmerman (1998) obtained positive effects for cognitive/metacognitive skills, motivational/affective skills (e.g., goal setting, attributions, self-efficacy), and environmental/contextual skills (e.g., help seeking, time management). Purdie and Hattie (1999) found that students who used multiple study skills demonstrated higher performances, as did students who activated skills (e.g., organizing, note taking, elaborating) to process information at a deeper level.

These benefits of study skills on performance are consistent with predictions of cognitive and motivational theories. Information processing theories postulate that learning involves *encoding* or entering new information in the processing system and preparing it for storage (Matlin, 2009; Weinstein & Mayer, 1986). Encoding includes selection (attending to relevant information and transferring it to short-term memory); acquisition (transferring information from short- to long-term memory); construction (making connections between information in short-term memory); and integration (creating connections between information in short- and long-term memory). Study skills deal with these processes. Thus, rehearsing (e.g., repeating, underlining) addresses selection and acquisition, elaborating (e.g., rephrasing, summarizing) involves construction and integration, and monitoring comprehension may address all four processes.

Motivational researchers postulate that students enter learning situations with goals and *self-efficacy* (perceived competence) for attaining them (Schunk, 1990), especially when they understand how to use study skills. While working, they periodically assess their goal progress. Perceptions of progress strengthen self-efficacy and motivation. Learners who attribute their successes to effectively using study skills experience higher self-efficacy and motivation. Motivation may be involved in all mental encoding processes.

Developmental, sociocultural, and individual difference variables can moderate the influence of study skills on academic performances. Children's capabilities to process information improve with development (Matlin, 2009), as they are better able to sustain attention, encode, link, and retrieve information in memory, and monitor their comprehension. Younger children may learn study skills but not know when to use them (Alexander, Graham, & Harris, 1998). This *utilization deficiency* tends to diminish as cognitive capacities develop (Matlin, 2009).

Sociocultural variables such as peers, family members, and socioeconomic status (SES) influence students' use of study skills. Peers and family members are important models for students (Schunk, 1990). Students benefit when their peers value learning and demonstrate good study skills. Also important are family members who model study skills while reading and using technology (e.g., watching educational TV with children). SES includes social status (position, rank) and economic indicators (wealth, education). Higher SES families are more resource enriched with books, technology, games, travel, cultural experiences, and social connections. Greater access to resources and positive models can improve students' use of study skills, whereas lower SES families have fewer resources, some of which are not educational per se (e.g., entertainment on TV). A study of at-home use of media devices suggests that "media saturated" youth often infrequently use printed texts, have poor concentration when working with materials of substance, and low parental regulation (Rideout, Foehr, & Roberts, 2010).

Individual differences in abilities and learning strategies can affect how well students use study skills. Developmental disabilities can influence how effectively students process information (Matlin, 2009). Learners' preferred learning styles (e.g., auditory, visual), which vary across cultures (McInerney, 2008), also may affect their motivation and information processing.

Summary and Recommendations

Reviews of instructional programs suggest that students can be taught to use study skills and improve their performances (Alexander et al., 1998; Hattie, Biggs, & Purdie, 1996; Weinstein & Mayer, 1986). For low-level learning (e.g., facts, procedures), rehearsal and *mnemonics* (e.g., HOMES for the five Great Lakes) are useful. More complex skills such as summarizing and self-questioning are better when higher order learning (e.g., synthesis, analysis) is necessary.

To facilitate transfer of the skills beyond the training setting, it has been recommended that study skills instruction occur where learning is taking place rather than as a separate process (Hattie et al., 1996). Transfer is enhanced when students learn skills (e.g., metacognitive awareness) in conditions that are conducive to learning and when they have instructional support for using the requisite skills. Students should learn how to establish a productive work environment (Lens & Vansteenkiste, 2008). Pressley, Harris, and Marks (1992) recommended that teachers introduce a few skills at a time, stress the value of study skills, model skills, personalize feedback and teaching, use a distributed practice technique (producing many study sessions short in duration), provide opportunities for transfer, sustain motivation, and encourage reflection and planning.

Other issues involve differentiating instruction and time costs (Weinstein & Mayer, 1986). Students differ in their capacity to self-regulate. Some—especially those with learning problems—may benefit from explicit study skills instruction. Because using study skills takes time, learners who do not notice any learning improvements may feel discouraged. Given the pressures of standardized testing, teachers may prefer not to emphasize study skills. But teaching effective study skills helps students perform better, particularly when integrated with academic content.

References

Alexander, P. A., Graham, S., & Harris, K. R. (1998). A perspective on strategy research: Progress and prospects. *Educational Psychology Review, 10,* 129–154.

Crespi, T. D., & Bieu, R. P. (2005). Study skills. In S. W. Lee (Ed.), *Encyclopedia of school psychology* (pp. 539–543). Thousand Oaks, CA: Sage.

Hattie, J., Biggs, J., & Purdie, N. (1996). Effects of learning skills interventions on student learning: A meta-analysis. *Review of Educational Research, 66,* 99–136.

Lens, W., & Vansteenkiste, M. (2008). Promoting self–regulated learning: A motivational analysis. In D. H. Schunk & B. J. Zimmerman (Eds.),

Motivation and self–regulated learning: Theory, research, and applications (pp. 141–168). New York: Taylor & Francis.

Matlin, M. W. (2009). *Cognition* (7th ed.). Hoboken, NJ: Wiley.

McInerney, D. M. (2008). The motivational roles of cultural differences and cultural identity in self–regulated learning. In D. H. Schunk & B. J. Zimmerman (Eds.), *Motivation and self–regulated learning: Theory, research, and applications* (pp. 369–400). New York: Taylor & Francis.

Pressley, M., Harris, K. R., & Marks, M. B. (1992). But good strategy instructors are constructivists! *Educational Psychology Review, 4,* 3–31.

Purdie, N., & Hattie, J. (1999). The relationship between study skills and learning outcomes: A meta-analysis. *Australian Journal of Education, 43,* 72–86.

Rideout, V. J., Foehr, U. G., & Roberts, D. F. (2010). *Generation M²: Media in the lives of 8- to 18-year-olds* (pp. 1–79). Menlo Park, CA: Henry J. Kaiser Family Foundation Retrieved from http://www.kff.org/entmedia/upload/8010.pdf

Robinson, F. P. (1946). *Effective study.* New York: Harper.

Schunk, D. H. (1990). Goal setting and self-efficacy during self-regulated learning. *Educational Psychologist, 25,* 71–86.

Weinstein, C. E., & Mayer, R. E. (1986). The teaching of learning strategies. In M. C. Wittrock (Ed.), *Handbook of research on teaching* (3rd ed., pp. 315–327). New York: Macmillan.

Weinstein, C. E., Palmer, D. R., & Schulte, A. C. (1987). *LASSI: Learning and study strategies inventory.* Clearwater, FL: H & H.

Zimmerman, B. J. (1998). Academic studying and the development of personal skill: A self–regulatory perspective. *Educational Psychologist, 33,* 73–86.

8.28

Matching Style of Learning

STEVE HIGGINS
Durham University

Introduction

Matching teaching to an individual student's learning style is intuitively appealing. We are all different in our preferences and aptitudes so it seems reasonable that it would be more effective or more efficient to tailor or adapt instruction to an individual's preferences or personal needs. The idea resurfaces in education cyclically so teachers and schools try to identify these learning styles by asking learners what they prefer or what they think they need, or even by testing them, then matching teaching in some way in the belief that this will produce more effective learning. In particular the idea of visual, auditory, and kinaesthetic approaches to learning has proved very resilient with flurries of interest in each decade since the 1950s (Roberts & Coleman, 1958). Unfortunately the extensive research in this area has failed to find a convincing link between matching an individual's style of learning with teaching approaches so as to lead to better learning.

Research Evidence

Numerous studies over the years have looked at matching learning styles with teaching approaches and more recently addressed the idea of cognitive styles, but have not so far found a convincing link with sufficient evidence to warrant adopting the practice in schools. Studies targeting learning with activities that match an individual's identified learning style have not shown convincingly that there is any benefit, particularly for low attaining pupils (Kavale & Forness, 1987). The evidence of the lack of effectiveness of approaches such as visual, auditory, and kinaesthetic (VAK) has been available for decades (Arnold, 1968), yet the idea perennially reappears in both research and practice. In some studies controls even outperform the learning styles groups, relatively unusual in educational research, where most interventions show positive effects.

Overall the effect sizes in independent meta-analyses are low (0.14) or even negative (–0.03; Garlinger & Frank, 1986), suggesting that only one or two pupils in a class of 30 might benefit (or be harmed) from being taught in this way (Tamir, 1985). The evidence for the lack of impact (and in some cases detrimental effect) of using learning styles approaches has been demonstrated consistently in a number of research studies and meta-analyses. Positive effects are more likely to be reported by enthusiasts and in areas other than direct impact on learning outcomes, or where impact may be due to other factors, such as the use of technology (Slemmer, 2002). There is some evidence that cognitive style and task type may be connected (visualisation in some areas of mathematics is valuable, for example) and it is certainly helpful to have different representations of ideas when developing understanding, but it is unhelpful to assign learners to groups or categories on the basis of a learning style. Students who have not succeeded in early reading may well benefit from an approach which incorporates more physical movement, but this is not because they are kinaesthetic learners. The additional ingredients are more likely to be more engaged practice and more intensive tuition.

The second major issue is that the assessments used to identify particular are problematic. There is a very wide range of different "learning styles," with no overall agreement about exactly what this means. The unreliability of learning styles tests and assessments has also been the subject of a number of reviews (Coffield, Moseley, Hall, & Ecclestone, 2004; Pashler, McDaniel, Rohrer, & Bjork, 2008). We are not consistent in our preferences when tested from day to day and we do not always adopt the style we say we prefer when faced with learning activities. Tests based on self-reported preferences are therefore not very reliable guides to what we actually do. Overall the picture is consistent and robust that the evidence to support teaching to students' learning styles does not justify the practice in schools (Mayer, 2011).

It is also not clear logically, even if the tests were reliable, whether a teacher would only want to develop a student's strengths, or rather whether they should focus on areas for development and improvement (Klein, 2003). Some areas of the curriculum require specific forms of representation. Poetry and creative writing require verbal skills. If students are weak in verbal skills then encouraging them to develop their verbal strengths by using other areas of expertise (such as drama or concept mapping, for example) may be beneficial in developing the articulation they need to succeed verbally. However, it is important to remember that achievement in poetry and creative writing is assessed and evaluated through the written form. If it is an area they are not good at, it suggests they need more support and more effective practice. Similarly if a young person wants to be good at football it may be helpful to listen to their coach or to verbalise or visualise specific skills or a team's future success, but what counts is to be able to play the game physically and skillfully.

Another danger in adopting learning styles approaches is in labeling students. If a student is identified as a kinaesthetic learner at the age of 8, and as a result believes that he or she will not succeed at verbal or auditory tasks, then the child's motivation to engage in learning at school may well be damaged. Students need to believe that they can succeed through effort (Dweck, 1999). There may be some benefit in learners believing that they can succeed in a task if they can choose the particular approach they use, but it is important that they do not use the style they are labeled with as an excuse.

Summary and Recommendations

What is of interest in this area is that, despite the evidence, the idea of matching style of learning reemerges every few years in education. This suggests that when teachers use such approaches they get some positive feedback in classrooms from adopting a learning styles approach and that this encourages the practice. The evidence suggests, however, that this is not a direct benefit of matching teaching to learning style, rather it is an indirect result of the changes that have been introduced.

There is no doubt some benefit in making students feel valued by identifying their strengths, or in encouraging teachers to seek feedback by investigating how students respond to different teaching approaches, or by supporting students in finding a different (and successful) way of doing things. These may all be related to the way teachers use learning styles approaches. However, the key thing to remember is that it is not effective to match activities with students' preferred learning styles. It is more important for the teacher to have a range of ways of presenting and explaining ideas, to make students responsible for finding a successful way of doing their work, and for teachers actively to find out which approaches work for different students in different circumstances.

References

Arnold, R. D. (1968). Four methods of teaching word recognition to disabled readers. *The Elementary School Journal, 68(5),* 269–274.

Coffield, F., Moseley, D., Hall, E., & Ecclestone, K. (2004). *Learning styles and pedagogy in post-16 learning. A systematic and critical review.* London: Learning and Skills Research Centre.

Dweck. C. (1999). *Self-theories: Their role in motivation, personality and development.* Hove, England: Psychology Press.

Garlinger, D. K., & Frank, B. M. (1986). Teacher–student cognitive style and academic achievement: A review and a mini-meta analysis. *Journal of Classroom Interaction, 21(2),* 2–8.

Kavale K. A., & Forness S. R. (1987). Substance over style: Assessing the efficacy of modality testing and teaching. *Exceptional Children, 54(3),* 228–239.

Klein, P. D. (2003). Rethinking the multiplicity of cognitive resources and curricular representations: Alternatives to "learning styles" and "multiple intelligences." *Journal of Curriculum Studies, 35*(1), 45–81.

Mayer, R. E. (2011). Does styles research have useful implications for educational practice? *Learning and Individual Differences, 21,* 319–320.

Pashler, H., McDaniel, M., Rohrer, D., & Bjork, R. (2008). Learning styles: Concepts and evidence. *Psychological Science in the Public Interest, 9*(3), 106–119.

Roberts R. W., & Coleman J. C. (1958). An investigation of the role of visual and kinesthetic factors in reading failure. *The Journal of Educational Research, 51*(6), 445–451.

Slemmer, D. L. (2002).*The effect of learning styles on student achievement in various hypertext, hypermedia and technology enhanced learning environments: A meta-analysis.* (Unpublished doctoral dissertation). Boise State University, Boise, Idaho (ProQuest Dissertations and Theses)

Tamir, P. (1985). Meta-analysis of cognitive preferences and learning. *Journal of Research in Science Teaching, 22*(1), 1–17.

8.29

Two Types of Perceived Control over Learning

Perceived Efficacy and Perceived Autonomy

NIR MADJAR AND AVI ASSOR
Ben-Gurion University of the Negev

Introduction

Control over learning can have important effects on students' achievements, conceptual learning, and depth of processing. This entry refers to two aspects of control over learning: perceived *efficacy in attaining learning outcomes* and perceived *autonomy in learning*. Research on outcomes and contextual determinants is presented in relation to each type of control, with clear practical implications for educators interested in promoting these types of control.

Research Evidence

Control as Perceived Efficacy in Attaining Specific Outcomes.

Consider the following questions: Do you think you will be able to complete a crossword puzzle? Will you be able to comprehend scientific articles in quantum physics? How well will you succeed in learning a new language? Our confidence to engage and succeed reflects our self-efficacy in specific domains, and a vast number of studies have established high relationships between self-efficacy and academic achievements (Liem, Lau, & Nie, 2008). For example, students who perceive themselves as good in math are more likely to succeed in solving difficult problems they had never learned before, and more likely to persist longer when facing difficulty or failure (Bandura, 2002; Zimmerman & Campillo, 2003).

They are at least four sources that affect students' belief in their efficacy in specific tasks or domains (Bandura, 2002). The first and most influential source of self-efficacy is the actual outcome of past experiences. When we participate in a task our performance can inform us about our ability to handle that task, and this, in turn, shapes future expectations regarding our ability to succeed in similar tasks. The second is vicarious experiences, and this is obtained by observing similar others perform the task. The performance of others similar to us can inform us as to the likelihood of our success on a task. The third is verbal input or persuasion from significant other people. Others' opinion about our ability or chances of success can enhance or weaken our self-efficacy, especially if we highly respect their view (e.g., students may be influenced by the judgment of a teacher whom they look up to). The fourth source is one's affective state while facing a challenge. Feelings of excitement and anticipation may indicate the potential to perform well. However, people tend to appreciate high emotional arousal (particularly anxiety and hypervigilance) as debilitating; consequently, strong emotional arousal may be interpreted as indicating lack of competence.

Teacher and Classroom Attributes Promoting Self-Efficacy.

It appears that there are at least three educational practices which can help students' feel efficacious in learning tasks. The first is frequent optimal challenges. Students are likely to feel more efficacious if they face frequent optimal challenges that lead to continuing success (Schunk & Pajares, 2002). Tasks are experienced as optimally challenging when they allow students to succeed following investment of some effort (i.e., they are not too easy or too difficult), or when they involve concrete and short term goals (e.g., solving two specific algebra problems) rather than vague and distant goals (e.g., doing well in algebra this year). Another factor is when the standard for success is set in comparison to self or a criterion rather than compared to others. Determining success by comparing our performance to others' performance may undermine our perception that the challenge is optimal because we have considerably less control over factors affecting others' performance than our own. Thus, we may have no control over contextual factors that may help other people outperform us (e.g., others' getting extra help before the test).

The second practice is constructive feedback. While frequent success is essential for efficacy development, it is also important to have constructive feedback from valued others (teachers, parents) following one's performance, and in particular following failure. Constructive feedback has several features. Following failure it provides specific information on skills or concepts that are missing and ways of mastering these missing components (Butler, 1987). Feedback also can support thought processes that help students identify controllable sources of success and failure, and avoid the tendency to overattribute one's performance to uncontrollable factors. After we experience success or failure in a task, we usually make causal attributions (analyses of the causes of one's success or failure) that in turn shape our perceived efficacy for similar future tasks (Zimmerman & Campillo, 2003). Research by Dweck (1999) has shown that when we attribute our performance to uncontrollable factors such as luck or inborn fixed ability this is more likely to support the belief that we cannot change our poor efficacy, which in turn leads to a helpless response following failure. In contrast, attributing our failure mainly to lack of effort, prior knowledge, or appropriate skills fosters the perception that one can increase efficacy, which in turn leads to mastery oriented coping.

The third practice is nurturing coping resources. Stressful arousal often undermines perceived efficacy and performance (Bandura, 2002). To be able to deal with such stressful emotions, teachers would do well to help students develop various ways of coping with achievement related stress. Such coping could include observing successful coping and performance of similar others (Schunk & Zimmerman, 2007), developing various social cognitive coping strategies for reducing stress and anxiety, or training students in effective help seeking (Hayes, Luoma, Bond, Masuda, & Lisslis, 2006).

Control as Perceived Autonomy in Learning. While perceived efficacy refers to the extent to which we believe that we can attain certain learning ***outcomes*** (such as mastering various mathematical procedures), perceived autonomy refers to the degree to which we perceive that the learning outcomes are *valuable and the mode of learning is useful.* Accordingly, students are likely to feel autonomous while learning a certain subject if they perceive the subject as worth learning and the mode of learning builds on the strategies for learning that they already use. It is important to note that according to this view, the experience of autonomy emerges mainly from the feeling and the perception that one is engaged in actions that feel volitional because they make sense and are *coherent with one's goals and values.* This view of autonomy is based on self-determination theory (Assor, 2012; Ryan & Deci, 2000) which shows that perceived autonomy in learning predicts a wide variety of positive learning outcomes, including effort investment, grades, use of effective learning strategies, and positive emotions while learning (Assor, Kaplan, & Roth, 2002; Reeve, 2006).

Teacher and Classroom Attributes Promoting Sense of Autonomy. We can define autonomy as involving two major strivings: (a) the striving to be free from coercion and have optional choice, and (b) the striving for an inner

compass: direction giving, authentic, values, goals, and interests (Assor, 2012). The formation and existence of values, goals, and interests is very important because these entities provide inner criteria for making important decisions and for evaluating oneself and others. Direction giving goals, values, and interests also provide a basis for feeling that one's actions are coherent and meaningful. Indeed, when people do not have clear values, goals, and interests, the availability of choices might be a threat or a burden.

Summary and Recommendations

The focus of this entry is on teacher and classroom attributes that promote two aspects of control over learning: perceived efficacy and perceived autonomy. While perceived efficacy refers to the perception that one can attain specific learning outcomes, perceived autonomy refers to the perception that the outcome is inherently valuable and worth pursuing. The claim is that a sense of control in learning emerges only if students feel that they really want to study something because it is valuable (autonomy) and that they can also succeed in studying it (efficacy). There are at least seven types of teacher behaviors and classroom attributes which can directly undermine or support the need for autonomy as defined above.

1. *Minimizing controls.* This attribute refers to minimizing teachers' behaviors or features of the educational context which cause students to feel controlled from outside; such as, behaviors that pressure one to behave in a specific way in order to avoid unpleasant experiences; loss of material benefits and privileges; and pressure to behave in a specific way in order to feel worthy of love and esteem (Assor, Roth, & Deci, 2004).

2. *Perspective taking, openness to criticism, and respect when children do not behave in line with expectations or disagree.* This refers to teachers' inclination and ability to try to understand and to respect students perspective especially when students' positions are inconsistent with their views (even when they seem unreasonable or wrong). For example, when children do not want to engage in studying a certain topic, the teacher can first ask them why they do not wish to invest in this topic. If the students say that they are bored or that they do not believe that it is really important to know the information being studied, the perspective-taking teacher acknowledges those feelings, respects them, and then relies on additional autonomy supportive practices such as offering rationale and some choice.

3. *Providing rationale.* This refers to teachers' inclination and ability to provide a coherent, age appropriate, rationale for their expectations (and particularly the intention of the lesson). When students are provided with a clear and convincing rationale for actions they do not find particularly interesting or valuable, they feel less coerced. Moreover, when students understand and identify with the rationale for their school related

activities, they feel that the act of studying supports their need for autonomy because studying allows them to express and promote their values and goals.

4. *Supporting choice and initiation.* This attribute directly supports the striving for optional choice. Providing the choice is meaningful as this allows students to realize their goals and values and therefore their experience of perceived autonomy (Katz & Assor, 2007).

5. *Modeling engagement in learning.* Such modeling by teachers shows that learning is highly valuable, and increases the credibility of the educators' arguments that learning is valuable since they engage in it personally.

6. *Supporting value/goal/interest exploration.* This attribute is particularly relevant in high school. Adolescents are concerned with forming values, goals, and interests which can serve as guides for important decisions, future plans, and commitments. When students feel that being in their school helps them to form personal goals and values, this promotes a sense of autonomy and volition regarding school attendance and academic engagement, which in turn lead to increased investment in studying according to both teacher and students reports, as well as to increased students' vitality and well-being (Assor, 2012).

7. *Fostering inner-directed valuing processes (FIV).* This construct refers to a cluster of educators' behaviors which help students to pay attention to their *personal* values and needs more than attending to social pressure, so that they can make decisions based on these values and needs (Madjar, Assor, & Dotan, 2010). Thus, FIV can be viewed as training in decision making, which includes three components: Enhancing students' ability to withstand confusion and take their time before they make serious decisions; encouraging the examination of one's values and goals when faced with a difficult decision or social pressures; and encouraging the consideration of alternatives and relevant information before making a decision. FIV differs from general support for value exploration in that it is a socializing practice that is used when the child faces difficult decisions and social pressures and it provides "training" in decision making under stress. Further, adolescents' perceptions of their parents as high on FIV were found to predict identity exploration and the formation of commitments that are experienced as autonomous (Assor, 2012). FIV was also found to predict adolescents' capacity to experience anger and anxiety without losing control or immediately suppressing these feelings, as well as their tendency to try to understand the sources of these feelings and their implications for one's life and relationships.

References

Assor, A. (2012). Allowing choice and nurturing an inner compass: Educational contexts which fully support students' autonomy. In S. L. Christenson, A. L. Reschly, & C. Wylie (Eds.), *The handbook of research on student engagement* (pp. 421–439). New York: Springer Science.

Assor, A., Kaplan, H., & Roth, G. (2002). Choice is good, but relevance is excellent: Autonomy-enhancing and suppressing teacher behaviors predicting students' engagement in schoolwork. *British Journal of Educational Psychology, 72,* 261–278.

Assor, A., Roth, G., & Deci, E. L. (2004). The emotional costs of parents' conditional regard: A self-determination theory analysis. *Journal of Personality, 72,* 47–88.

Bandura, A. (2002). *Self-efficacy: The exercise of control.* New York: Freeman.

Butler, R. (1987). Task-involving and ego-involving properties of evaluation: Effects of different evaluation conditions on motivational perceptions, interest and performance. *Journal of Educational Psychology, 79,* 474–482.

Dweck, C. S. (1999). *Self-theories: Their role in motivation, personality, and development.* Philadelphia, PA: Psychology Press.

Hayes, S. C., Luoma, J. B., Bond, F. W., Masuda, A., & Lillis, J. (2006). Acceptance and commitment therapy: Model, processes and outcomes. *Behavior Research and Therapy, 44,* 1–25.

Katz, I., & Assor, A. (2007). When choice motivates and when it does not. *Educational Psychology Review, 19,* 429–442

Liem, A. D., Lau, S., & Nie, Y. (2008). The role of self-efficacy, task value and achievement goals in predicting learning strategies, task disengagement, peer relationship and achievement outcomes. *Contemporary Educational Psychology, 33,* 486–512.

Madjar, N., Assor, A., & Dotan, L. (2010, April). *Fostering value/goal formation and the capacity for inner valuing: Two under-emphasized aspects of autonomy support.* Paper presented at the American Education Research Association (AERA) Annual Conference, Denver, Colorado.

Reeve, J. (2006). Teachers as facilitators: What autonomy-supportive teachers do and why their students benefit. *The Elementary School Journal, 106,* 225–236.

Ryan, R. M., & Deci, E. R. (2000). Self–determination theory and the facilitation of intrinsic motivation, social development and well-being. *American Psychologist, 55*(1), 68–78.

Schunk, D. H., & Pajares, F. (2002). The development of academic self–efficacy. In A. Wigfield & J. Eccles (Eds.), *Development of achievement motivation* (pp. 16–31). San Diego, CA: Academic Press.

Schunk, D. H., & Zimmerman, B. J. (2007). Influencing children's self-efficacy and self-regulation of reading and writing through modeling. *Reading & Writing Quarterly, 23,* 7–25.

Zimmerman, B. J., & Campillo, M. (2003). Motivating self-regulated problem solvers. In J. E. Davidson & R. J. Sternberg (Eds.), *The nature of problem solving* (pp. 233–262). New York: Cambridge University Press.

8.30

Distance Education

Yong Zhao
University of Oregon

Jing Lei
Syracuse University

Introduction

Distance education, where learners and the instructor are separated by space or time has been in existence since the 19th century. The University of London established its International Programs and offered the first distance education degrees in 1858 (University of London, 2010). Educational institutions in other parts of the world gradually followed suit, such as the founding of the Society to Encourage Studies at Home, the first correspondence school in the United States, in 1873[1] and the establishment of the Department of Correspondence Studies at the University of Queensland in Australia in 1911 (White, 1982). These and many other correspondence learning programs marked the early stages of distance education.

The development of distance education has been constantly transformed by advances in information and communication technologies. The development of the modern postal service, for example, made correspondence learning possible for many who had previously been denied access to formal schooling. The invention of radio and television technology increased the spread, and in the last few decades, the Internet and other digital technologies have greatly enhanced and enriched distance learning. The rapid development and wide adoption of the Internet and multimedia technologies has brought fundamental changes in distance education and led to an "explosive" growth in online courses, online programs, and virtual schools in recent years (U.S. Department of Education, 2004). At the higher education level, distance education has evolved from a marginal form of education to a commonly accepted and increasingly popular alternative to traditional face-to-face education. As of fall 2007, online enrollment reached almost 4 million students in the United States, a 13% increase from fall 2006, and more than one third of faculty members had taught online (Allen & Seaman, 2008).

At the K-12 level, it is estimated that more than a million students in the United States alone took online courses in the school year 2007-2008, a 47% increase since 2005-2006 (Picciano & Seaman, 2009), and there are many new virtual schools offering a broad range of options. The courses vary from general K-12 curriculum to specific subjects; the targeted audience varies from all students to targeted groups of students; the level of curriculum varies from general courses and remedial courses to advanced courses and college preparation courses; and the pace varies from accelerated to standard to an extended learning pace (Muller & Ahearn, 2004).

Research Evidence

With the rapid growth of distance learning at all levels of education, there has also been a growing interest in the effectiveness of distance learning, and much research effort has been invested in examining whether or not, and to what degree, distance education is effective for student learning outcomes. Research has traditionally been dominated by comparison studies (Gunawardena & McIsaac, 2004; Lockee, Burton, & Cross, 1999; Zhao, Lei, Yan, Lai, & Tan, 2005). Typically these studies have compared the effectiveness of distance education with that of face-to-face education or the effectiveness of one technology over another. Findings from these individual studies have been inconclusive. Although some studies have found positive effects, their effects are then quickly balanced out by other studies that have found negative effects (Gunawardena & McIsaac, 2004), and many more studies report no significant differences in learning outcomes (Russell, 1999). Many comparison studies did not equate the distance course and the face-to-face course conditions being compared, such as the curriculum materials being used, pedagogical aspects, and learning time, even though research reveals that similarity in instruction and curriculum between the two settings affects differences in effectiveness (Means, Toyama, Murphy, Bakia, & Jones, 2009).

To overcome the limitations of individual studies and

to depict a large picture of the effectiveness of distance education, several synthesis studies, including summaries of primary studies and meta-analyses, have been conducted to analyze findings from individual comparison studies. The most influential and representative of such summary syntheses is Russell's annotated bibliography of studies of studies that showed no significant difference between face-to-face and distance education. These studies spanned almost a century, beginning in 1928 and ending in 1998. This impressive collection of 355 articles forcefully supported the *no significant difference phenomenon*, a term used by Russell to refer to effectiveness studies of distance education. Several meta-analysis studies have also come to essentially the same conclusion as Russell: there is no significant difference in student achievement between distance and face-to-face education (e.g., C. K. Cavanaugh, Gillan, Kromrey, Hess, & Blomeyer, 2004; C. S. Cavanaugh, 2001; Machtmes & Asher, 2000; Zhao et al., 2005).

These meta-analyses, however, reveal considerable differences among studies in terms of effect size, a measure of difference in learning outcomes between distance education and face-to-face education. Although as a whole, no significant difference is identified between distance education and face-to-face education, upon closer examination, these studies reveal that individual studies have indeed found important differences between the two.

Distance programs can vary a great deal in content, learner characteristics, instructor characteristics, and delivery method. Thus, it may be more meaningful to move "beyond the no-significant difference" (Twigg, 2001) to further examine the characteristics of individual studies and investigate these variables and the degree to which they differentially influence learning outcomes. Machtmes and Asher (2000), for example, reported that studies that employed two-way interactive technology were "the only type [of delivery] that had a positive effect size" (p. 38). With the advent of more cost-effective and efficient communication technologies such as the Internet, distance education programs have started to provide both synchronous and asynchronous communications that enable a broad range of interactions between students and instructors and among students. Distance education programs that have taken advantage of these tools have reported positive outcomes (i.e., Twigg, 2001; U.S. Department of Education, 2009; Zhao et al., 2005). Similarly, higher instructor involvement, or the presence of a "live" instructor, has been found to be important for effective distance education, and the degree of instructor involvement was a significant distinguishing quality of effective and ineffective distance education programs (Zhao et al., 2005). Several other factors, such as the content area or the curriculum, the type of learning environment, time spent on learning materials, and opportunities for collaboration, also seem to affect the effectiveness of distance education (Machtmes & Asher, 2000; Means et al., 2009; Zhao et al, 2005).

There appears to be more support for a hybrid, or blended model of distance education that combines both a face-to-face and a technology-mediated distance component. A meta-analysis demonstrated that blended instruction was more effective than face-to-face education or pure online education, and suggested that more effort was required to design and implement blended approaches (Means et al., 2009).

The rapid development of advanced multimedia and interactive technologies such as web 2.0 tools and the increasing use of these technologies in online distance education (particularly those that allow for more social interaction), has meant that online distance education has begun to show some advantages over traditional face-to-face education. More powerful delivery media and more sophisticated information and communication technologies enable the use of a combination of various technologies for teaching, learning, and interactions in distance education, making it easier than before to incorporate face-to-face learning elements into distance education. The widespread use of mobile technologies also is increasing the flexibility of access to distance education and the quality of interactions in distance learning (Koole, McQuilkin, & Ally, 2010). For example, Zhao et al. (2005) reported that comparison studies prior to 1998 found distance education to be less effective than face-to-face education, whereas those post-1998 found the opposite. A meta-analysis that reviews online learning studies from 1996 to 2008 reported that learning outcomes of students who did all or part of their studies online were better than those of students who took the same course in regular classroom settings (Means et al., 2009).

Summary and Recommendations

Distance education is in essence still education (Garisson & Shale, 1990). The same factors that have an impact on the effectiveness of distance education are often the same as those that affect the effectiveness of face-to-face education (Zhao et al., 2005). For example, time on task affects students' learning outcomes in face-to-face learning, so it is not surprising to find that "learners in the online condition who spent more time on task" had greater benefits from online learning (U.S. Department of Education, 2009).

Nevertheless, as the rapid development of information and communication technologies constantly provides new opportunities for distance education and at the same time poses new challenges to educational institutions, much research is needed to examine the unique characteristics of distance education (particularly as it can now combine interactions, well-structured lesson plans, and student engagement) and to develop a sound understanding of how to improve the effectiveness of teaching and learning at a distance.

Similar to face-to-face education, distance education programs vary greatly in many variables such as the curriculum, learner characteristics, instructor characteristics, types of interactions, pedagogical practices, the learning environment, and delivery method. By examining these variables and the degree to which they influence learning outcomes, we may be able to arrive at what distance education research is encouraged to do: find useful guidance for practice and research.

Note

1. The Society to Encourage Studies at Home was founded in 1873 by Anna Eliot Ticknor Agassiz, born June 1, 1823, died October 5, 1896.

References

Allen, I. E., & Seaman, J. (2008). Staying the course—Online education in the United States. Sloan

Cavanaugh, C., K., Gillan, J., Kromrey, J., Hess, M., & Blomeyer, R. (2004). *The effects of distance education on K-12 student outcomes: A meta-analysis.* Naperville, IL: Learning Point. Retrieved from http://www.ncrel.org/tech/distance/index.html.

Cavanaugh, C. S. (2001). The effectiveness of interactive distance education technologies in K-12 learning: A meta-analysis. *International Journal of Educational Telecommunications, 7*, 73–88.

Garrison, D. R., & Shale, D. (1990). *Education at a distance: From issues to practice.* Melbourne, FL: Krieger.

Gunawardena, C. N., & McIsaac, M. S. (2004). Distance education. In D. H. Jonassen (Ed.), *Handbook of research for educational communications and technology* (2nd ed., pp. 355–396). Mahwah, NJ: Erlbaum.

Koole, M., McQuilkin, J. L., & Ally, M. (2010). Mobile learning in distance education: Utility or futility? *Journal of Distance Education, 24*(2), 59–82.

Lockee, B., Burton, J., & Cross, L. (1999). No comparison: Distance education finds a new use for 'no significant difference. *Educational Technology, Research and Development, 47*(3), 33–42.

Machtmes, K., & Asher, J. W. (2000). A meta-analysis of the effectiveness of telecourses in distance education. *American Journal of Distance Education, 14*(1), 27–46.

Müller, E., & Ahearn, E. (2004). Virtual schools and students with disabilities. Alexandria, VA: Project Forum at the National Association of State Directors of Special Education (NASDSE).

Picciano, A. G., & Seaman, J. (2007). *K-12 online learning: A survey of U.S. school district administrators.* Boston, MA: Sloan Consortium. Retrieved from http://www.sloan-c.org/publications/survey/K-12_06.asp

Russell, T. L. (1999). *The no significant difference phenomenon.* Chapel Hill, NC: Office of Instructional Telecommunications, North Carolina State University.

Twigg, C. A. (2001). *Innovations in online learning: Moving beyond no significant difference.* Buffalo, NY: The Pew Learning and Technology Program.

University of London. (2010). University of London international programmes. Retrieved from http://www.londoninternational.ac.uk/about_us/facts.shtml

U.S. Department of Education. (2004). Toward a new golden age in American education: How the Internet, the law and today's students are revolutionzing expectations: The National Educational Technology Plan. Washington, DC: Author

U.S. Department of Education (2009). *Evaluation of evidence-based practices in online learning: A meta-analysis and review of online learning studies.* Washington, DC: Author.

White, M (1982). Distance education in Australian higher education — a history. *Distance Education, 3*(2), 255–278.

Zhao, Y., Lei, J., Yan, B., Lai, C., & Tan, H. S. (2005). What makes the difference? A practical analysis of research on the effectiveness of distance education. *Teachers College Record, 107*(8), 1836–1884.

8.31
Home School Programs

ANDREA CLEMENTS
East Tennessee State University

Introduction

Home schooling is a term used to refer to the education of children by their parents or guardians in a setting other than a public or private school; most often in their homes. Home schooling styles vary substantially and include, but are not limited to, the parent directly instructing the child, the child watching a video recording or satellite feed of an actual classroom, completing self-study workbooks or computer programs, some types of online instruction, or reading literature (Clements, 2004). Additional activities may include field trips, volunteering, scouting, organized sports, or taking classes through a home school cooperative in which parents teach groups of students. There is a practice often described as unschooling in which no traditional educational activities are employed, but students are encouraged to learn through life experiences. An example might be learning economics, physics, geometry, and architectural drawing, through the planning and construction of a structure such as a small home.

In the United States, the state of Oregon adopted a law requiring all children to be educated in public schools. In 1925, the U.S. Supreme Court ruled in *Pierce v. Society of Sisters* (268 U.S. 510) that private schools have the right to exist and that parents have the right to direct the upbringing and education of their children (Bloom, 1984), a decision which has commonly been used to support home schooling. After a period of governmental resistance to home schooling, repeated legal challenges from home schooling families have gradually influenced state legislatures to change their laws to permit the practice of home schooling. By 1993, home schooling in one form or another had become legal in all 50 states. Recent estimates of the number of home schooled children range from 1.5 million in 2007 (National Center for Education Statistics [NCES], 2009) to 2.04 million in 2010 (Ray, 2011). This represents roughly 2.5 to 3.0% of the K-12 population.

Home schoolers were once thought to consist primarily of very conservative or very liberal White families. Although currently the typical home schooled child in the United States comes from a White (77%), two-parent household (89%) (NCES, 2009), families from many religious and political persuasions are found among those who are home schooling. Compared with private school children, however, home school children tend to come from less affluent and more rural households. Collom (2005) found four primary reasons for families to choose home schooling: dissatisfaction with public schools, academic and pedagogical concerns, religious values, and family needs; however, none of these translated into distinct groups of home educators.

Research Evidence

Since the early 1980s, a few researchers have investigated the achievement of home schooled students, and the findings have been remarkably similar even though the number of students and the demographics of those students have changed appreciably. All have found the performance of home schooled students on various measures of achievement to be quite high. Lips and Feinberg (2008) reported that achievement test scores for home schooled students typically fall at the 70th to 80th percentile, meaning the home schooled students perform the same as or better than 70 to 80% of students in general, the majority of which are in public school. Virtually the same achievement level was found by Ray in 1997 and 2010 and Rudner in 1998. Rudner conducted a study of 20,760 home schooled children who took the Iowa Tests of Basic Skills or the Tests of Achievement and Proficiency in 1998. Both of these tests are widely used achievement tests. He found that the median scores for every subtest at every grade were well above those of public and private school students. Although between the time of Rudner's study and Ray's earlier study and the Lips and Feinberg study (2008) and the Ray (2011) study the

445

number of home schooled students increased greatly and home schooling families became much more diverse, the achievement advantage of home schooled students was virtually unchanged.

Additional findings from Rudner's study attesting to the benefits of home schooling were that almost 25% of home school students were enrolled one or more grades above their age-level peers in public and private schools; on average, home school students in grades 1 to 4 performed one grade level above their age-level public/private school peers; and the achievement test score gap between home school students and public/private school students widens from Grade 5 upwards. Achievement of home schooled students is much higher than achievement of public school students regardless of whether students are home schooled throughout their school careers or only for part of their schooling (Ray, 2010).

A well done, though smaller study of home schooled students in California found that neither student gender, amount of instructional time, household income, teaching experience, nor race predicted any differences in achievement for home schooled students (Collom, 2005). This is in stark contrast to findings for other forms of education in which race and class are very predictive of achievement. Three factors were found to predict home school achievement. Higher levels of parent education predicted higher achievement, conservative parents' (or right wing) children had higher achievement levels than liberal parents' (or more left wing) children, and children who were being home schooled because of special learning needs had lower achievement. This third reason is quite understandable as the need for which the student is home schooled would most likely be the cause of the lower achievement. For example, if a student were being home schooled because a parent felt that he or she would be better able to address a child's learning disability, that child would likely have lower achievement because of the learning disability rather than because of home schooling.

Achievement tests are excellent sources of information on current achievement, but the question remains as to the future performance of home schooled students. Jones and Gloeckner (2004) found that home schooled students perform as well as students who attended public schools on college entrance exams and first-year college grade point average. Van Pelt and colleagues (Van Pelt, Allison, & Allison, 2009), when following Canadian home schooled students over 15 years, found that home schooled adults were more likely than the comparable Canadian population to have completed an undergraduate degree, to be civically engaged, to value their religious beliefs, to have multiple income sources, to report income from self-employment, and to report high satisfaction with life. They were found to be physically active, to have higher average incomes than their peers, and were notably more engaged than the comparable population in a wide variety of cultural and leisure activities. They were equally likely not to be married, but unlike their Canadian counterparts, typically did not live in common-law arrangements, and they were less likely to have children early but tended to have larger than average families when they did have children. These studies attest to the benefits of home schooling beyond school age.

The home schoolers' achievements that have gained the most public attention have been spelling and geography bee wins in recent years. In 2001, the winner of the Scripps National Spelling Bee was the third winner in 5 years to have been home schooled. In 2000, eight of the finalists had been home schooled, with home schoolers taking the top three places. Once again, in 2007 the winner was home schooled, and five of the top 15 finalists were home schooled as well. In 2009, a home schooled student took second place. Similarly, in 2002 and 2003 home schooled students won the National Geography Bee. These statistics are significant given that home schoolers make up less than 3% of the student population.

Summary and Recommendations

There is much evidence that home schoolers' average achievement is higher than that of children who are not home schooled. There are several possible explanations for this. First, parental involvement has been shown to improve achievement and home schooling invariably involves parental involvement. Second, and closely related, would be the benefit of one-to-one instruction. When parents home school their children, there is a much lower student-teacher ratio than is found in either public or private schooling. This allows curriculum to be tailored to the student's needs and areas of confusion to be clarified more rapidly than in a traditional school setting. A third explanation for the success of home schooling, would be that home schooling parents tend to be more educated, on average, than other parents. These parents may be genetically more intelligent and this intelligence could be passed down to the children who then perform well academically. However, this could also be evidence that the parents were more motivated to seek education and therefore value it more than less educated parents, and they have passed this value to their children.

Applications of these reasons for success of home schooling are as follows. Parents being involved in their children's education, working with them on schoolwork, being aware of grades, and teaching or reteaching content should translate into achievement gains regardless of whether a child is being home schooled. Further, one-to-one instruction offers benefits because areas of specific misunderstanding and interest can be addressed for one student by one person rather than teaching in generalities to a group. The greatest drawback of one-to-one instruction is that it is cost prohibitive to implement it for every student in a public or private school setting. One-to-one instruction with nonparents might also be less effective than with parents because with a parent teaching his or her own child, the teacher actually loves and has a familial relationship with the child. Perhaps the love and care for the students is an additional cause of the effectiveness of home schooling, and increasing the love for and caring about students within public and private schools by teachers would positively impact achievement. Finally, while genetic transmission of intelligence is a possible way to affect student achievement, choosing teachers who are highly educated and who value the pursuit of education could be a way to affect student achievement.

Finally, because home schooling has been shown to result in such high achievement, it should be recommended in its own right for those with the wherewithal to accomplish it. While there may be many effective, achievement fostering components that make up home schooling, as mentioned above, what is clear is that home schooling itself is a very effective form of education.

References

Bloom, B. S. (1984). The 2 sigma problem: The search for methods of group instruction as effective as one-to-one tutoring. *Educational Researcher, 13*(6), 4–16.

Clements, A. D. (2004). *Homeschooling: A research-based how-to manual.* Lanham, MD: Scarecrow Education.

Collom, E. (2005). The ins and outs of homeschooling: The determinants of parental motivations and student achievement. *Education and Urban Society, 37,* 307–335.

Hammons, C. W. (2001). School@Home. *Education Next, 1*(4), 48–55.

Jones, P., & Gloeckner, G. (2004). First-year college performance: A study of home school graduates and traditional school graduates. *Journal of College Admissions, 183,* 17–20.

Lips, D., & Feinberg, E. (2008, April 3). Homeschooling: A growing option in American education. *Backgrounder* (No. 2122). Washington, DC: Heritage Foundation.

National Center for Education Statistics [NCES]. (2009). *Participation in education: Elementary/secondary education: Homeschooled students.* Washington, DC: U.S. Department of Education Institute of Education Sciences. Retrieved from http://nces.ed.gov/programs/coe/2009/section1/indicator06.asp

Ray, B. D. (1997). *Home education across the United States: Academic achievement, family characteristics, and longitudinal traits.* Salem, OR: National Home Education Research Institute.

Ray, B. D. (2010). Academic achievement and demographic traits of home school students: A nationwide study. *Academic Leadership Live: The Online Journal, 8*(1). Retrieved from http://www.academicleadership.org/article/Academic_Achievement_and_Demographic_Traits_of_Homeschool_Students_A_Nationwide_Study

Ray, B. D. (2011, January). *2.04 million home school students in the United States in 2010.* Salem, OR: National Home Education Research Institute.

Rudner, L. M. (1998). Scholastic achievement and demographic characteristics of home school students in 1998. *Education Policy Analysis, 7*(8). Retrieved from http://epaa.asu.edu/epaa/v7n8/

Van Pelt, D. A. N., Allison, P. A., & Allison, D. J. (2009). *Fifteen years later: Home-educated Canadian adults.* London, ONT: Canadian Centre for Home Education. Retrieved from http://www.hslda.ca/cche_research/2009Study.pdf

8.32

Evidence Based Reading Comprehension Programs for Students with Learning Disabilities

H. LEE SWANSON AND MICHAEL OROSCO
University of California-Riverside

Introduction

Reading comprehension difficulties are one of the most significant problems experienced by children identified with learning disabilities (LD). This is because reading comprehension underlies their performance in the majority of academic domains, as well as their adjustments to most school activities. Gertsen, Fuchs, Williams, and Baker (2001) provided one of the most comprehensive descriptive reviews of reading comprehension intervention for students with LD to date. In their review, they concluded that strategy instruction improves comprehension performance in students with LD. This finding complements several individual studies showing that students with LD do not efficiently monitor their learning or use of strategies (Canales, 2008; Jiménez, Rodrigo, Ortiz, & Guzmán, 1999). In contrast to their descriptive approach, however, this report relies on results from several meta-analyses to arrive at instructional conclusions.

Research Evidence

Before highlighting meta-analysis findings, it is important to note that several reviews concur with Gersten et al.'s (2001) observation on the importance of strategy instruction in the area of reading comprehension (e.g., Faggella-Luby & Deshler, 2008; Gajria, Jintendra, Sood, & Sacks, 2007; Jitendra, Hoppes, & Xin, 2000; Mastropieri, Scruggs, & Graetz, 2003). Strategy instruction is broadly defined as an experimental condition that uses teaching methods organized in such a manner as to help children with LD solve a problem. The teaching methods include two or more goal oriented *tactics*. A *tactic* reflects a single processing technique (such as elaboration, graphically organizing), or a means of monitoring information (such as reducing information processing load) that is usually mediated by the teacher, text, peers, or generated by the student (e.g., Kim, Vaughn, Wanzek, & Wei, 2004). Studies that used

methods that combine two or more goal oriented tactics (e.g., elaboration was coupled with verbal dialogue between teacher and students in a small group) are considered a form of strategy instruction. There are several excellent examples of strategy models in the literature applied to children with LD (e.g., Mastropieri & Scruggs, 1997; Wong, Harris, & Graham, 2003, for a review), with specific application to reading comprehension (e.g., Williams, Stafford, Lauer, Hall, & Pollini, 2009). The majority of these studies hold to the view that students with LD are inefficient processors of information and their access to information in long-term memory is underutilized unless they are explicitly prompted to use certain strategies (Swanson, 1993, for review, also see Vauras, Kinnunen, & Rauhanummi, 1999).

A major meta-analysis funded by the U.S. Department of Education to synthesize experimental intervention research over a 35-year period was conducted on children with LD (see Swanson, Hoskyn, & Lee, 1999; Swanson & Sachse-Lee, 2000). Swanson and several colleagues (e.g., Swanson & Deshler, 2003; Swanson & Hoskyn, 1998; Swanson, Hoskyn, & Lee, 1999), condensed over 3,000 effect sizes across several academic domains. In the domain of reading comprehension, a mean effect size of .72 was found for children with LD in the treatment condition versus children with LD in the control condition for group design studies (Swanson & Hoskyn, 1998) and .95 for single subject design studies (Swanson & Sachse-Lee, 2000). According to Cohen's (1988) classification system, the magnitude of the effect size was large.

Moderator Variables. Although the synthesis only included studies with control conditions, it is important to note that even the best evidence studies must be carefully scrutinized. For example, Simmerman and Swanson (2001) found a number of variables related to internal and external validity that when violated moderated the magnitude of treatment outcomes. Violations that were significantly related to treatment outcomes included:

- Teacher effects (studies that used the very same experimenter for treatment and control in administering treatments yield smaller effect sizes than those studies that used different experimenters in administering treatments);
- Reliance on experimental measures (studies that did not use standardized measures had much larger effect sizes than those which reported using standardized measures);
- Using different measures between pretest and posttest (larger effect sizes emerge for studies that used alternative forms when compared to those that used the same test);
- Using a heterogeneous sample in age (studies that included both elementary and secondary students yielded larger effect sizes than the other age level conditions);
- Using the correct unit of analysis (those studies that applied the appropriate unit of analysis yield smaller effect sizes than those that used the correct unit of analysis; that is, when small groups were presented with the interventions and the unit of analysis was groups instead of individuals).

Further, studies that left out critical information yielded inflated treatment outcomes. The underreporting of information related to ethnicity positively inflated the magnitude of treatment outcomes (studies that reported ethnicity yielded smaller effect sizes than those that did not report ethnicity); psychometric data (larger effect sizes occur when no psychometric information is reported when compared to the other conditions); and teacher application (studies that provide minimal information in terms of teacher implications and recommendations yielded larger effect sizes than those that did).

The magnitude of effect sizes was also influenced by whether studies reported using multiple definitional criteria in selecting their sample (studies that included multiple criteria in defining their sample yielded smaller effect sizes than those that did not report using multiple criteria). In addition, Simmerman and Swanson (2001)found that some methodological variables that influenced the magnitude of the effect size were not violations of internal or external validity, but rather were moderating variables related to the instructional setting (small instructional groups yield larger effect sizes than individual or large group instruction); direct teaching of transfer (studies that trained for transfer to different abstract skills yielded larger effect sizes than those that didn't); and treatment fidelity (studies that indicated the specific sessions in which treatment integrity was assessed yielded larger effect sizes than those that did not).

Instructional Variables. In the area of reading comprehension, a combination of both direction instruction and strategy instruction best predicted treatment outcomes (effect sizes). Consistent with direction instruction models, several studies focused on graduated sequences of steps with multiple opportunities for overlearning the content and skills in a reading program, cumulative review routines,

mass practice, and teaching of all component skills to mastery criterion. For the strategy aspect of the model, however, students focused on metacognitive issues, such as strategy implementation, strategy choice, and self-monitoring.

Summary and Recommendations

A metaregression was computed determining those instructional components necessary to predict reading treatment outcomes beyond an instructional core commonly found in the literature (Swanson, 1999). The instructional core included (a) daily reviews, (b) statements of an instructional objective, (c) teacher presentation of new material, (d) guided practice, (e) independent practice, and (f) formative evaluations and a *sequence of events*, such as the following:

1. State the learning objectives and orient the students to what they will be learning and what performance will be expected of them.
2. Review the skills necessary to understand the concept.
3. Present the information, give examples, and demonstrate the concepts/materials.
4. Pose questions (probes) to students and assess their level of understanding and correct misconceptions.
5. Provide group instruction and independent practice. Give students an opportunity to demonstrate new skills and learn the new information on their own.
6. Assess performance and provide feedback. Review the independent work and give a quiz.
7. Provide distributed practice and review.

Meta-analysis regression modeling assessed the independent contribution of each of these above components to effect size. Also considered were instructional components that contributed unique variance beyond the instructional core. For reading comprehension, those key instructional components (as stated in the treatment conditions) that contributed unique variance were:

1. *Directed Response/Questioning Treatment.* Description related to dialectic or Socratic teaching, the teacher directs students to ask questions, the teacher and student or students engage in reciprocal dialogue.
2. *Control Difficulty or Processing Demands of Task.* Treatment statements about short activities, level of difficulty controlled, teacher providing necessary assistance, teacher providing simplified demonstration, tasks sequenced from easy to difficult, or task analysis.
3. *Elaboration.* Statements in the treatment description about additional information or explanation provided about concepts, procedures, or steps, or redundant text or repetition within text.
4. *Modeling by the Teacher of Steps.* Statements or activities in the treatment descriptions which involve modeling by the teacher in terms of demonstration of processes or steps the students are to follow to solve the problem.

5. *Small Group Instruction.* Statements in the treatment description about instruction in a small group, or verbal interaction occurring in a small group with students or teacher.

6. *Strategy Cues.* Statements in the treatment description about reminders to use strategies or multiple steps, use of "think aloud models," or teacher presenting the benefits of strategy use or procedures.

In contrast, the important instructional components for word recognition that emerged from the regression analysis were:

1. *Sequencing.* Statements in the treatment description about breaking down the task, fading of prompts or cues, sequencing short activities, or using step-by-step prompts.

2. *Segmentation.* Statements in the treatment description about breaking down the targeted skill into smaller units, breaking into component parts, segmenting or synthesizing components parts.

3. *Advanced Organizers.* Statements in the treatment description about directing children to look over material prior to instruction, children directed to focus on particular information, providing prior information about task, and the teacher stating objectives of instruction prior to commencing.

The importance of these findings is that only a few components from a broad array of activities enhanced treatment outcomes for reading. The analysis found that only strategy cuing and small-group interactive instruction contributed significant variance to estimates of reading comprehension beyond the instructional core model for students with LD. There were no components that were significant beyond the instructional core when predicting word recognition outcomes.

In summary, combined strategy and direct instruction models do make a significant contribution to treatment outcomes in reading comprehension, and direct instruction is the preferred means of enhancing sight word recognition for children with LD. However, some instructional components are more important than others in predicting high effect size in reading comprehension, and those components differ from those that predict sight word recognition.

References

Canales, R. G. (2008). Procesos cognitivos y estrategias psicolingüísticas que intervienen en la lectora comprensiva: diseño y ejecución de un programa experimental en niños con problemas de aprendizaje [Psycholinguistic cognitive processes and strategies involved in understanding reading: Design and implementation of a pilot program for children with learning problems]. *Revista de Investigación en Psicología, 11*(1), 81–100.

Cohen, J. (1988). *Statistical power analysis for the behavioral sciences* (2nd ed.) Hillsdale, NJ: Erlbaum.

Faggella-Luby, M. N., & Deshler, D. D. (2008). Reading comprehension in adolescents with LD: What we know; what we need to learn. *Learning Disabilities Research & Practice, 23*(2), 70–78.

Gajria, M., Jitendra, A. K., Sood, S., & Sacks, G. (2007). Improving comprehension of expository text in students with LD: A research synthesis. *Journal of Learning Disabilities, 40*(3), 210–225.

Gersten, R., Fuchs, L. S., Williams, J. P., & Baker, S. (2001). Teaching reading comprehension strategies to students with learning disabilities: A review of research. *Review of Educational Research, 71*(2), 279–320.

Jiménez, J. E., Rodrigo, M., Ortiz, M. R., & Guzmán, R. (1999). Procedimientos de evaluación e intervención en el aprendizaje de la lectura y sus dificultades desde una perspectiva [Cognitive procedures for assessment and intervention in the learning of reading and its difficulties from a cognitive perspective]. *Infancia y Aprendizaje, 88*, 107–122.

Jitendra, A. K., Hoppes, M. K., & Xin, Y. P. (2000). Enhancing main idea comprehension for students with learning problems: The role of a summarization strategy and self-monitoring instruction. *The Journal of Special Education, 34*(3), 127–139.

Kim, A., Vaughn, S., Wanzek, J., & Wei, S. (2004). Graphic organizers and their effects on the reading comprehension of students with LD: A synthesis of research. *Journal of Learning Disabilities, 37*(2), 105–118.

Mastropieri, M. A., & Scruggs, T. E. (1997). Best practices in promoting reading comprehension in students with learning disabilities: 1976 to 1996. *Remedial and Special Education, 18*(4), 197–213.

Mastropieri, M. A., Scruggs, T. E., & Graetz, J. E. (2003). Reading comprehension instruction for secondary students: Challenges for struggling students and teachers. *Learning Disability Quarterly, 26*(2), 103–116.

Simmerman, S., & Swanson, H. L. (2001). Treatment outcomes for students with learning disabilities: How important are internal and external validity? *Journal of Learning Disabilities, 34*, 221–236.

Swanson, H. L. (1993). Principles and procedures in strategy use. In L. Meltzer (Ed.), *Strategy assessment and instruction for students with learning disabilities* (pp. 61–92). Austin, TX: PRO-ED.

Swanson, H. L. (1999). Reading research for students with LD: A meta-analysis in intervention outcomes. *Journal of Learning Disabilities, 32*(6), 504–532.

Swanson, H. L., & Deshler, D. (2003). Instructing adolescents with learning disabilities: Converting a meta-analysis to practice. *Journal of Learning Disabilities, 36*(2), 124–135.

Swanson, H. L., & Hoskyn, M. (1998). Experimental intervention research on students with learning disabilities: A meta-analysis of treatment outcomes. *Review of Educational Research, 68*(3), 277–321.

Swanson, H. L., Hoskyn, M., & Lee, C (1999). *Interventions for students with learning disabilities: A meta-analysis of treatment outcomes.* New York: Guilford.

Swanson, H. L., & Sachse-Lee, C. M. (2000). A meta-analysis of single-subject-design intervention research for students with LD. *Journal of Learning Disabilities, 33,* 114–136.

Vauras, M., Kinnunen, R., & Rauhanummi, T. (1999). The role of metacognition in the context of integrated strategy intervention. *European Journal of Psychology of Education. 14,* 555–569.

Williams, J. P., Stafford, K. B., Lauer, K. D., Hall, K. M., & Pollini, S. (2009). Embedding reading comprehension training in content-area instruction. *Journal of Educational Psychology, 101*(1), 1–20.

Wong, B., Harris, K., & Graham, S. (2003). Cognitive strategies instruction research in learning disabilities. In H. L. Swanson, K. Harris, & S. Graham (Eds.), *Handbook of learning disabilities* (pp. 295–305). New York: Guilford.

Section 9

Influences from an International Perspective

EDITOR: JULIAN G. ELLIOTT
DURHAM UNIVERSITY

9.1

Some Challenges to Educational Achievement in the Russian Federation since the End of the Soviet Union

JULIAN G. ELLIOTT
Durham University

Introduction

Despite the many political and economic difficulties that were encountered in the Soviet Union, education was long considered to be one of its success stories. Impressive standards of academic attainment in neighbourhood comprehensive schools, particularly in mathematics and science, were the product of high levels of motivation and discipline. Since the end of the Soviet period, however, there have been many events that have impacted significantly upon educational practice and achievement in Russia. Some key elements will be outlined and discussed in this present review.

Research Evidence

A striking aspect of the Soviet education system was its continuity and stability (Hufton & Elliott, 2000). Since the 1930s, a system of comprehensive schooling emphasised a highly structured academic and encyclopedic curriculum, well-developed pedagogic practices, and methods of assessment and reporting, that had all operated in a similar fashion over several generations. In addition to the high academic standards that pertained, what particularly impressed Western visitors were the high levels of motivation and behaviour that were routinely observed (e.g., Bronfenbrenner, 1970).

In the years immediately following the collapse of the Soviet Union, Russian schools appeared to continue in much the same vein as before. Despite the intense social, economic, and ideological changes within the wider society, there appeared to have been little impact upon everyday school practices (Alexander, 2000; Hufton & Elliott, 2000). Students continued to be largely hard-working, highly motivated, and compliant. Indeed, it seemed as if maintaining continuity in this way had a functional value in that the school appeared to serve as an enclave that could provide some respite from the massive social and economic unrest taking place outside its walls.

In a series of studies (see Elliott, Hufton, Illushin, & Willis, 2005) it was found that unlike their counterparts in the United States and England, Russian students' interest in education appeared to be less motivated by instrumental ends but, rather, was associated with the desire to be an educated person. Russian students, it was found, tended to see education as an important means of self-improvement; to be erudite and "cultured" was to be someone worthy of respect. Despite the social upheaval of the 1990s, children's orderly and disciplined classroom behaviour, a feature of the Soviet era (Bronfenbrenner, 1967; Elliott et al., 2005) largely persisted into the new millennium. In the Programme for International Student Assessment (PISA) study (Organisation for Economic Co-operation and Development [OECD], 2003), for example, Russian students were among those least likely to report that lessons were disrupted by noise and disorder, or that academic engagement was low.

Such behaviour was, in part, a product of longstanding socialisation experiences in which high levels of respect for teachers and schooling were reinforced by powerful peer processes. Following the work of Makarenko with abandoned and delinquent Soviet children in the 1920s and 30s, children's natural desire for affiliation and friendship was channelled through shared participation in tasks, and caretakers (parents and teachers) were tasked to develop the young child's social skills and attachment to collective ways of working. From the age of 3, most children were involved in group activities where, from within a supportive and caring environment, they were taught to cooperate, recognize, and respect the interests of the group and defer to the authority of adults (Tudge, 1991). Once in primary school, codes of behaviour were made very explicit and adult authority was strongly emphasised. The "collective" provided teachers with a powerful means of managing the classroom learning environment. Here, the class assisted in sharing standard-setting and exerting a positive influence on the behaviour and work rate of all the students.

453

As Bronfenbrenner (1970) noted, the peer group not only supported behaviour consistent with the values of the adult society, it also encouraged students to take personal initiative and responsibility for encouraging such behaviour in their classmates. Such processes were in marked contrast to those of many Western societies where peer influences often operate in a fashion that undermines the attitudes and behaviours that the school would wish to encourage.

However, it was not long after the end of the Soviet period before Russian schools were being exhorted to reform their practices in line with Western approaches. While recognising the achievements of the Soviet system, criticisms were voiced about the ideological nature of schooling and the authoritarian nature of student–teacher relations. These influences minimized debate and controversy, often undermined students' individuality, and resulted in passivity. To address these concerns, various reforms were advocated by major international bodies such as the World Bank, the Soros Foundation, the British Council, the Carnegie Foundation, and the U.S. Agency for International Development (USAID). Of course, behind such initiatives lay a political as well as an educational agenda. Such initiatives, often presented as value-free, technical approaches applicable to all modern forms of schooling, in actuality reflect a particular political worldview in which democratic pedagogy, learner-centredness, and individual autonomy are seen as necessary prerequisites for full participation in a capitalist society.

The 1992 Law on Education was a response to calls for greater emphasis upon personal self-determination, democratic relations, and "humanization" (i.e., responding to students as unique individuals with differing goals and potentials). However, given long-established Soviet practices, teachers were often unsure how to put these ideals into practice. Some argued that such changes were not appropriate means to address the challenges facing Russia; others paid lip-service while continuing in much the same vein as before (Eklof & Seregny, 2005). Not all parents were reassured either; one survey of parents found that nearly half of respondents did not support a more democratic school environment, seeing strictness and high demands as the most desirable qualities in teachers (Froumin, 2005). Many teachers were originally persuaded of the need for change but after a period, gradually reverted to their former modes of practice (Froumin, 2005). However, the rates of social and economic change are such that those who have sought to maintain the old Soviet educational practices and hierarchies are increasingly finding these ill-suited for contemporary school life.

There are few modern societies where the social and economic experiences of a nation have transformed so rapidly as that of Russia in the 1990s. From a society where, for generations, most young people had experienced relatively similar economic circumstances—expressed by the old Soviet joke that under capitalism, wealth was unevenly distributed, whereas under socialism, poverty was evenly distributed—huge disparities began to emerge. Newly enriched "New Russians" ostentatiously flaunted their wealth at a time when the majority of the populace was struggling to feed themselves. Many of those who were thriving appeared to prosper as a result of their entrepreneurial, streetwise skills, rather than because of any erudition. Students, becoming aware of the impoverishment of most teachers and academics, and perceiving little link between levels of scholarship and economic well-being, increasingly questioned whether existing school curricula were appropriate for the economic challenges they faced (Iartsev, 2000). At the same time, the important societal role of the teacher in the socialisation and acculturation of the child declined, not only because the perspectives of teachers no longer held such influence with young people but also because this process was seen as being associated with Soviet indoctrination.

Increasing materialism, instrumentalism, and individualism led to a questioning of traditional ideals and values that left many young people becoming anxious and alienated (Karpukhin, 2000). Commentators argued that as a result of the weakening of state and societal mechanisms of social regulation, the value systems of young people were increasingly being gleaned from intellectually undemanding mass culture (Zvonovskii & Lutseva, 2004). As faith in the strictures of society, and the guidance and influence of adults began to fade, peer subcultures became more significant. Unlike the Soviet period, where as a result of "explicit policy and practice" (Bronfenbrenner, 1967, p. 206), peer influences were harnessed in ways that promoted prevailing adult values, social commentators at the end of the millennium were voicing concerns that negative peer influences were undermining the moral fibre of youth, with greater prevalence of youth gangs and a growth in violent behaviour (Krug, Dahlberg, Mercy, Zwi, & Lozano, 2002). In the contemporary mass media, concerns are now being expressed that those in school today are the offspring of a lost generation whose lives were fundamentally impaired by the social turbulence and dislocation of the early 1990s

In more recent times, education has become highly valued once more. However, unlike students from previous generations (Elliott et al., 2005), the value of education as a means of individual growth has become less important and has been replaced by more instrumental goals whereby the kinds of knowledge and skills considered to be most worthy by students are those that bring material well-being.

Russian scholars and social commentators continue to express concerns about the education of the nation's youth. Education continues to be massively underfunded and, given the poor salaries (and as a consequence, the low status of teaching), too few of the nation's teachers are currently aged under 30. A sense that academic standards are insufficient has been fuelled by disappointing scores on recent PISA tests in reading, mathematics, and science (OECD, 2010). For a country with such strong traditions in mathematics and science, Russia's international position—significantly below the OECD average for both subjects—is disconcerting. However, in other respects, there are grounds for optimism. While the value of erudition as a means of gaining social approval has declined, there would appear to be high levels of enthusiasm for education as a means to socioeconomic advancement and a strong desire for university education. Despite concerns about poorer student behaviour, and some evidence from PISA data of a decline over the past decade, it would appear that this may be a matter of relative degree with Russian classrooms continuing to enjoy superior teacher–student relations and more orderly behavior than classrooms in most Western countries (OECD, 2010).

Summary and Recommendations

The Russian experience since the end of the Soviet Union has provided a natural experiment in which globalising (Western) influences have been variously embraced, accommodated, ignored, and resisted by children, their parents, and their teachers (Elliott & Tudge, 2007). While the picture in schools is variable, it would appear that in order to cope with the needs and expectations of students, teachers are now increasingly perceiving a need to adopt "modern" pedagogic practices and establish patterns of classroom relationships that are seemingly very different from those of a generation ago.

A distancing from traditional attachments and identities, an increase in individualism, and a greater resistance on the part of the young to the strictures of social institutions, are not purely contemporary Russian phenomena but rather, are features of all late-modern or postmodern societies. Such forces appear to be leading to changes in Russian students' educational orientations and behaviours. However, context does not operate solely in a unidirectional fashion upon individuals, and young people will continue to play an active role in the evolution of those proximal processes in classrooms and homes that are key to their intellectual and social development. Despite the tensions that have emerged within schools, it remains unclear how Russian students will navigate their educational and vocational futures in the light of the often opposing influences of their history and culture, and the forces of globalisation.

References

Alexander, R. (2000). *Culture and pedagogy: International comparisons in primary education*. Oxford, England: Blackwell.

Bronfenbrenner, U. (1967). Response to pressure from peers versus adults among Soviet and American school children. *International Journal of Psychology, 2*(3), 199–207.

Bronfenbrenner, U. (1970). *Two worlds of childhood*. New York: Russell Sage Foundation.

Canning, M., Moock, P., & Heleniak, T. (1999). *Reforming education in the regions of Russia* (World Bank technical paper no. 457). Washington DC: World Bank.

Eklof, B., & Seregny, S. (2005). Teachers in Russia: State, community and profession. In B. Eklof, L. Holmes, & V. Kaplan (Eds.), *Educational reform in post-Soviet Russia* (pp. 197–220). London: Cass.

Elliott, J.G., Hufton, N., Illushin, L., & Willis, W. (2005). *Motivation, engagement and educational performance*. London: Palgrave.

Elliott, J. G., & Tudge, J. R. H. (2007). The impact of the West on post-Soviet Russian education: Change and resistance to change. *Comparative Education, 43*(1), 93–112.

Froumin, I. D. (2005). Democratizing the Russian school: Achievements and setbacks. In B. Eklof, L. Holmes, & V. Kaplan (Eds.), *Educational reform in post-Soviet Russia* (pp. 129–152). London: Cass.

Hufton, N., & Elliott, J. (2000). Motivation to learn: The pedagogical nexus in the Russian school: Some implications for transnational research and policy borrowing. *Educational Studies, 26*, 115–136.

Iartsev, D.V. (2000). Characteristics of the socialisation of today's adolescent. *Russian Education and Society, 42*, 67–75.

Karpukhin, O. I. (2000). The young people of Russia: characteristics of their socialization and self determination. *Russian Education and Society, 42*(11), 47–57.

Krug, E. G., Dahlberg, L. L., Mercy, J. A., Zwi, A. B., & Lozano, R. (Eds.). (2002). *World report on violence and health*. Geneva, Switzerland: World Health Organisation.

Organisation for Economic Co-operation and Development (OECD). (2003). *Literacy skills for the world of tomorrow: Further results from PISA 2000*. Paris: Author.

Organisation for Economic Co-operation and Development (OECD). (2010). *PISA 2009 results: Learning trends: Changes in student performance since 2000* (Vol. 5). Retrieved from http://dx.doi.org/10.1787/9789264091580-en

Tudge, J. R. H. (1991). Education of young children in the Soviet Union: Current practice in historical perspective. *Elementary School Journal, 92*, 121–133.

Zvonovskii, V., & Lutseva, S. (2004). Young people's favourite leisure activities. *Russian Education and Society, 46*(1), 76–96.

9.2

Large-Scale Assessments of Achievement in Canada

KADRIYE ERCIKAN, MARIA ELENA OLIVERI, AND DEBRA SANDILANDS
University of British Columbia

Introduction

Canada is the world's second largest country by total area consisting of 13 jurisdictions (10 provinces and 3 territories) and shares the world's longest border with its neighbour to the south, the United States. Large-scale assessments of achievement in Canada have many similarities to those in the neighbouring United States but differ with respect to their roles and functions. As in the United States, each jurisdiction in Canada has its own large-scale assessment system; however, in Canada, results from these assessments are not used for high-stakes decisions such as rewarding, funding, or penalizing schools or teachers. At the pan-Canadian level, a national assessment is conducted by the Council of Ministers of Education Canada (CMEC), a consortium of ministries of education from all 13 jurisdictions. In addition, jurisdictions may choose to participate in international assessments such as the Trends in International Mathematics and Science Study (TIMSS) and the Programme for International Student Assessment (PISA). Even though these assessments are typically used for comparing performances of schools, jurisdictions, or Canada's performance with those of other countries, data from questionnaires accompanying these assessments are also used to understand contextual variables associated with learning and achievement. In the subsections below, we describe jurisdictional and national assessments of achievement in Canada and summarize research that utilizes data from these and international assessments for examining predictors of achievement.

Canada has one of the most decentralized education systems compared to those of other countries in North America and Europe. There is neither a national department, nor a ministry of education, nor federal funding for K-12 education (Klinger, DeLuca, & Miller, 2008; Klinger, Maggi, & D'Angiulli, 2011). Instead, under the Canadian constitution, education is a provincial or territorial responsibility. Thus, jurisdictions have autonomy in the organisation of school systems, curricula, educational policies, and in the development and management of large-scale assessments. Currently, every province and territory (except Nunavut) has at least one large-scale assessment program (Klinger et al., 2008). These assessment programs tend to be similar in form and function across the jurisdictions (Klinger et al., 2008). For example, all assessment programmes test reading, writing, and mathematics. They contain both multiple-choice and constructed-response items. Most are criterion-referenced, and are often developed and graded by Canadian teachers under the supervision and guidance of provincial/territorial assessment offices.

Provincial and territorial assessments serve two key functions: assessing achievement and certifying fulfillment of requirements for graduation from secondary schools. One set of provincial/territorial assessments is administered to all students within jurisdictions at select grades from elementary and secondary schools. These assessments are used to collect data for monitoring learning, evaluating the effectiveness of schools and districts, and planning instruction and curriculum to improve student learning. A second set of provincial/territorial assessments, administered as end-of-course examinations, plays a key role in certification of graduation from secondary schools (Ercikan & Barclay-McKeown, 2007).

Accountability in the Canadian context focuses on setting up school improvement plans that include identifying areas for improvement and developing and enacting initiatives and practices that will result in increased student achievement (Klinger et al., 2011). However, there are no sanctions if schools fail to demonstrate school improvement or meet the targets set out in their school improvement plans. Educators are not officially sanctioned for poor student performance and no bonus or merit pay incentives are attached to high test scores. Some of these assessments, however, have high-stakes consequences for students. Performance on the end-of-course assessments at the secondary levels comprise a significant percentage of students' final grades (i.e., typically between 20% and 50%) or serve as a graduation requirement or as an entrance requirement for postsecondary education (Klinger & Rogers, 2011).

Even though student performance on provincial or territorial assessments does not lead to rewards or penalties for teachers and schools, many educators teaching students assessed by these tests feel professionally responsible for their schools' results (Ercikan & Barclay-McKeown, 2007). There are reported cases of teachers requesting to teach students in grades that are not tested by provincial assessments, indicating that the stakes are perceived to be higher by these teachers (Klinger & Rogers, 2011). This is due to public scrutiny created by highly publicised school rankings of elementary and secondary schools developed by the Fraser Institute since 1998 (Ercikan & Barclay-McKeown, 2007). The school rankings are created using performance data from provincial assessments, unadjusted for intake or context, for comparing achievement across schools and subsequently publicized in national and provincial newspapers. These school rankings lead to inappropriate interpretations of test scores as indicators of school quality and effectiveness and shaming and penalizing of teachers and schools that have been providing education in, typically, the most challenging settings (Ercikan & Barclay-McKeown, 2007).

Research Evidence

Pan-Canadian Assessments.   The Pan-Canadian Assessment Programme (PCAP) conducted by the CMEC assesses 13- and 15-year-old students in reading, mathematics, and science and is intended to enable provinces and territories to improve their own assessments as well as validate their results against national assessment results. PCAP replaced the School Achievement Indicators Program (SAIP) which was the first attempt to arrive at a consensus on the elements of a national assessment. The PCAP was developed to have a more streamlined design and be more closely aligned with PISA. As in PISA, PCAP uses a major–minor domain design to assess reading, mathematics, and science. PCAP was first administered in 2007 to a student cohort who took PISA in 2009, thereby, enabling comparisons to be made between these two assessments. Performance results are reported at the provincial and national levels only.

In pan-Canadian assessments, all provinces and territories are involved in the development of the assessments. The provincial development teams review questions to ensure they are free from cultural and gender bias and stereotyping and that the assessment materials are a close match with provincial/territorial curricular objectives. A representative sample of Canadian students is selected to participate in PCAP, using a two-stage stratified random sampling. Schools are randomly selected and, within each school, students are randomly selected. Because of Canada's Official Languages Act, pan-Canadian assessments are administered in Canada's two official languages, English and French.

Predictors of Achievement in Canada.   In addition to assessing achievement, many large-scale assessments administer questionnaires to participating students, their teachers, and school principals. Data from these questionnaires allow educators, researchers, and policy-makers to examine correlations between achievement, contextual factors, self-reported attitudes, and teaching and learning strategies.

Despite consistent research indicating that much of the variation in achievement scores is associated with class-level variables, little research exists that can provide information about class-level correlates of achievement in Canada. Due to sampling designs, wherein students are randomly selected within schools, neither PCAP nor PISA provides data that allow for accurate analyses of class-level factors. Thus, typically, school and student-level variables are used in predicting achievement. Overall, school-level variables such as school climate and resources account for only approximately 20% of variance in achievement in Canada (Anderson et al., 2006; Organisation for Economic Co-operation and Development (OECD), 2001; Willms, 2004). This is significantly lower than the international average of 35% of variance accounted for at the school level for the OECD countries that took part in PISA 2000 (Anderson et al., 2006). These findings indicate that other factors such as student, classroom, or home contextual factors account for approximately 80% of variance in achievement in Canada (OECD, 2001).

Consistent with research in other countries, Canadian researchers have found a strong relation between student-level factors such as student beliefs, confidence, motivation, and student achievement. Using SAIP data, Anderson et al. (2006) found that student beliefs about mathematics showed a consistently strong positive relation with mathematics achievement that was stable across schools, suggesting that these perceptions or attitudes have a common influence across Canada. Based on TIMSS 1995 mathematics data, Ercikan et al. (2005a) found that confidence in mathematics was the strongest predictor of mathematics achievement. Using the PISA 2006 data, Areepattamannil, Freeman, and Klinger (2010) provided evidence that intrinsic motivation, such as enjoyment of science, and motivational beliefs such as self-efficacy and self-concept were strongly associated with adolescents' science achievement in Canada. As may be expected, achievement in Canada has also been shown to be positively correlated with student learning behaviours such as conscientiousness, and negatively correlated with behaviour problems such as inattention/hyperactivity, depression, and antisocial behaviour (Ellefsen & Beran, 2007).

As elsewhere, achievement in Canada is positively correlated with family socioeconomic status (SES). Students whose families have higher SES have a tendency to attain higher levels of achievement than those from less affluent backgrounds. However, studies have shown that there is a weaker relationship between SES and academic achievement of students in Canada compared to other OECD countries. For example, the achievement gap on PISA between students whose mothers have completed upper secondary school (an indicator of SES) and those whose mothers have not is smaller in Canada than in other countries (Anderson, Lin, Treagust, Ross, & Yore, 2007). Among the six English-speaking OECD countries examined in another study (Micklewright & Schnepf, 2004), Canada had the lowest difference in reading and math scores between students with more than 100 books in the home (another indicator of SES) and those with fewer than 100 books in the home. Two other family background factors have been shown to correlate with achievement in the Canadian context: family structure (with students from two-parent, nuclear families showing higher achievement than those from single-parent families) and immigrant status (with students who are native-born achieving higher than those born outside of Canada). As with studies of SES, these correlates appear to be associated with smaller gaps in achievement in Canada compared to other countries (Anderson et al., 2007; Micklewright & Schnepf, 2004). Thus, even though family factors, including SES, have been shown to correlate with academic achievement in Canada, the results of these studies suggest that these relationships are not as strong in Canada as in other countries.

As noted earlier, often only a small proportion of variance in achievement has been found to be attributable to school-level factors in Canada. At the school level, there is a positive relation between average school SES and student achievement in Canada. Schools serving students from higher SES backgrounds tend to perform higher than schools drawing from lower SES backgrounds. Willms (2004) notes that there is also a large "contextual effect" related to school SES: students in Canada who attend high SES schools are more apt to have higher academic achievement than students from comparable family SES backgrounds who attend low SES schools. In other words, high SES schools may attenuate the effects of low family SES, perhaps because high SES schools tend to have better resources and more positive school climates.

At the school level, instructional and leadership practices have been found to correlate with achievement in Canada. Areepattamannil et al. (2010) found that science teaching using hands-on activities was strongly associated with science achievement while science teaching using student investigations had the reverse association. Principals' vision and beliefs were found to be major determinants of writing achievement (Bouchamma, Lapointe, & Richard, 2007) and their transformational leadership practices were positively correlated with student achievement (Ross & Gray, 2006). Other research has identified an inverse relation between principal reported "limitations to learning" and achievement in mathematics and writing. This indicated that schools in which principals believe that student, home, and community characteristics constrain instructional effectiveness tended to have lower achievement scores (Anderson et al., 2006; Bouchamma et al. 2007). Other school-level factors that

account for meaningful proportions of variance in achievement in Canada include the use of formal assessment, teachers' qualifications, teacher autonomy, teacher–student relations, classroom climate, and students' use of school resources, with higher levels of these variables being associated with higher school achievement levels (Willms, 2004).

It is worth noting that predictors of achievement may vary for different student groups, such as gender, language, or ethnicity groups, in all countries. There is evidence that this is indeed the case in Canada. For example, research provides evidence that home environment and support for learning have differential association with achievement for gender groups. Home support for learning and parents' education level were identified as strong predictors of mathematics achievement on TIMSS 1995 for Canadian girls but not for Canadian boys (Ercikan et al., 2005a). Furthermore, these researchers have demonstrated that confidence in science was the strongest predictor of achievement for boys, whereas socioeconomic status related to parents' education level was the strongest predictor of achievement for girls (Ercikan, McCreith, & Lapointe, 2005b). Also within Canada, significant differences have been found when comparing students in Francophone minority and Francophone majority settings. Lack of human and material resources and deficits related to school-community-family relations in Francophone minority settings have been found to have a stronger relationship with achievement than in Francophone majority or Anglophone settings with similar shortages or deficits (Bouchamma, Lapointe, & Richard, 2007).

Summary and Recommendations

Challenges for the next generation of large-scale assessments of achievement in Canada are similar to those in many other countries. These include designing assessments that (a) improve learning and provide meaningful and useful information to students and teachers; (b) assess complex thinking of mathematics, reading, science, and history; and (c) provide useful data for policy and planning through well-constructed background questionnaires. Finally, in light of an increasingly diverse Canadian population, it is critical that the design of these assessments allow for well-designed statistical analyses and modeling of population heterogeneity to attain generalizations that apply to diverse subgroups.

References

Anderson, J. O., Lin, H. S., Treagust, D. F., Ross, S. P., & Yore, L.D. (2007). Using large-scale assessment datasets for research in science and mathematics education: Programme for International Student Assessment (PISA). *International Journal of Science and Mathematics Education, 5*(4), 591–614.

Anderson, J. O., Rogers, W. T., Klinger, D. A., Ungerleider, C., Glickman, V., & Anderson, B. (2006). Student and school correlates of mathematics achievement: Models of school performance based on pan-Canadian student assessment. *Canadian Journal of Education, 29*(3), 706–730.

Areepattamannil, S., Freeman, J. G., & Klinger, D. A. (2010). Influence of motivation, self-beliefs, and instructional practices on science achievement of adolescents in Canada. *Social Psychology of Education, 14*, 233–259.

Bouchamma, Y., Lapointe, C., & Richard, J. (2007). School determinants of achievement in writing: Implications for school management in minority settings. *Canadian Journal of Program Evaluation, 22*(3), 121–150.

Ellefsen, G., & Beran, T. N., (2007). Individuals, families, and achievement: A comprehensive model in a Canadian context. *Canadian Journal of School Psychology, 22*(2) 167–181.

Ercikan, K., & Barclay-McKeown. (2007). Design and development issues in large-scale assessments: Designing assessments to provide useful information to guide policy and practice. *Canadian Journal of Program Evaluation, 22(3),* 53–71.

Ercikan, K., McCreith, T., & Lapointe, V. (2005a). Factors associated with mathematics achievement and participation in advanced mathematics courses: An examination of gender differences from an international perspective. *School Science & Mathematics, 105*(1), 5–14.

Ercikan, K., McCreith, T., & Lapointe, T. (2005b). How are non-school related factors associated with participation and achievement in science? An examination of gender differences in Canada, the USA and Norway. In S. J. Howie & T. Plomp (Eds.), *Contexts of learning mathematics and science: lessons learned from TIMSS* (pp. 211–225). Lisse, Netherlands: Swets & Zeitlinger.

Klinger, D. A., DeLuca, C., & Miller, T. (2008). The evolving culture of large-scale assessments in Canadian education. *Canadian Journal of Educational Administration and Policy, 76(3)*, 1–34.

Klinger, D. A., Maggi, S., & D'Angiulli, A. (2011). School accountability and assessment: Should we put the roof up first? *The Educational Forum, 75*(2), 114–128.

Klinger, D. A., & Rogers, W. T. (2011). Teachers' perceptions of large-scale assessment programs within low–stakes accountability frameworks. *International Journal of Testing, 11*(2), 122–143.

Micklewright, J., & Schnepf, S. V., (2004). Educational achievement in English-speaking countries: Do different surveys tell the same story? (IZA Discussion Paper No. 1186). Retrieved from http://ssrn.com/abstract=562453.

Organisation for Economic Co-operation and Development (OECD). (2001). *Knowledge and skills for life: First results from the OECD Programme for International Student Assessment (PISA) 2000.* Paris: Author.

Ross, J. A., & Gray, P., (2006). School leadership and student achievement: The mediating effects of teacher beliefs. *Canadian Journal of Education/Revue canadienne de l'éducation, 29*(3), 798–822.

Willms, J. D. (2004). *Reading achievement in Canada and the United States: Findings from the OECD Programme for International Student Assessment* (OECD Report SP–601–05–04E). Paris: OECD.

9.3

Student Achievement in Israel

The Challenges of Ethnic and Religious Diversity

YARIV FENIGER

Department of Education, Ben-Gurion University of the Negev

Introduction

Israel is a multiethnic and multireligious society with a population of about 7.5 million inhabitants. The Jewish majority (about 80% of the total population) consists of three main origin groups: Ashkenazim (about 40%), who originated in Europe and America; Mizrachim (about 40%), who originated in the Middle East and North Africa; and new immigrants from the former Soviet Union. A much smaller group of new immigrants are Jews from Ethiopia. The Arab minority consists of a large Muslim majority (about 80%) and Christian and Druze minority groups, each comprising about 10% of the Arab population. Social research in Israel indicates that Ashkenazim are the most educationally and economically advantaged ethnoreligious group, whereas Muslims are the least advantaged.

Education in Israel is compulsory and free, from kindergarten to the end of secondary school (12th grade). Compulsory education culminates in matriculation (*Bagrut*) examinations administered by the Ministry of Education. The Jewish and Arab school sectors are almost completely separate. Most Arab students study in Arab state schools, where the language of instruction is Arabic and the staff are Arab. Jewish students study in either state, state-religious, or independent ultra-orthodox schools.

Research on student achievement in Israel has tended to focus on secondary education. This is mainly because data on elementary education are scarce while data on the matriculation examination are much more available. The absence of educational longitudinal data collection constrains research on students' achievement in Israel to primarily a reliance upon cross-sectional analyses. Recently, data from international tests, such as PISA, TIMSS, and PIRLS have become an important resource for research on educational achievement in Israel.

Research Evidence

Studies conducted in the last three decades have shown that Arab students in Israel tend to show lower achievement than Jewish students at all grade levels (Kennet-Cohen, Cohen, & Oren, 2005). Three main reasons can be adduced. The first, and most general, is the socioeconomic gap between Arab and Jewish families, with Arab families tending to be poorer and having lower levels of parental education. Yet, even after controlling for socioeconomic variables, the achievement of Muslim and Druze Arabs is usually lower than that of Jewish students (e.g., Ayalon & Shavit, 2004).

The second explanation is the longstanding discrimination in budget allocations. Studies show that, on average, schools in the Arab sector receive lower allocations per student and have fewer hours of instruction and a lower percentage of certified teachers than schools in the Jewish sector (Lavy, 1998). It is important to note, however, that in the last few years, allocations have been equalized as a consequence of a Supreme Court decision. The effects of the increased allocations for the Arab schools are, as yet, unknown.

The third explanation for the large gap is diglossia: a situation in which different dialects of the same language are used for different purposes. In Arabic the diglossia stems from the coexistence of modern standard Arabic, known as literary Arabic, which is used in writing, and a variety of spoken Arabic dialects which are used for everyday communication. The need to learn literary Arabic, in effect a second language, may slow down and complicate the learning process for Arab school children. Zuzovsky (2010), who analyzed data on fourth graders from the international PIRLS study, found that after controlling for socioeconomic background, achievement gaps between Jews and Arabs in reading remained large, while they disappeared or were reversed in mathematics and science. According to Zuzovsky, these findings support the hypothesis that the Arabic diglossia is a main cause of the lower reading achievement of Arab students.

Research has also revealed large disparities among students from different social groups within the Jewish majority. The most clearly documented disparity is between Jews of European or American origin (Ashkenazim) and Jews of Middle Eastern or North African origin (Mizrachim). Studies carried out in the 1950s and 1960s indicated that the achievement of Mizrachi elementary school children was, on average, much lower than that of Ashkenazi children. These researchers attributed the disparity to the more recent arrival of the Mizrachim in Israel and to the concomitant linguistic and socioeconomic difficulties with which they had to contend. The achievement gap during this period had far reaching educational consequences. Most Mizrachi youngsters were channeled into vocational tracks in secondary school, as a result of which relatively few of them obtained a matriculation certificate and went on to higher education (Shavit, 1990). Data from the 1990s and 2000s indicate that the Mizrachi–Ashkenazi achievement gap has decreased but not closed, and that Mizrachim are still overrepresented in lower-status high school programs which usually lead to lower attainment (Ayalon & Shavit, 2004; Mizrachi, Goodman, & Feniger, 2009).

Concerns about the Mizrachi–Ashkenazi educational gap led to attempts to better integrate the schools that served the two communities, along with the adoption and evaluations of means of making the integration work. One such means was cooperative learning, in which students work in groups to complete tasks collectively. Israeli studies found that cooperative learning helps students from underprivileged social groups to become more active participants in classroom activities and to attain higher test scores than students from similar background taught by traditional presentation-recitation methods (Shachar & Sharan, 1994).

As a country that has absorbed successive waves of immigrants, Israel has produced several studies on the incorporation of immigrants into the education system. In the last two decades this research has focused on new immigrants from the former Soviet Union (FSU) and Ethiopia. A recent study that covered several school subjects and grade levels has shown both similarities and differences between these groups of immigrants. In both groups, it took several years before immigrant students could reduce or close the achievement gap with comparable native-born Israelis. Yet, the achievement of the FSU immigrant students was much higher, especially in mathematics, than that of the immigrants from Ethiopia, and also showed faster achievement growth than Ethiopian students (Levin & Shohamy, 2008).

International comparisons such as PISA, TIMSS, and PIRLS have shown that the achievements of students in Israel are, on average, lower than those of students in other developed countries. Feniger and Shavit (2011), who analyzed PISA 2000 and PISA 2006 data, attribute the lower performance of Israeli students to the country's birth rate, which is the highest among the developed countries. As a result, students in Israel usually have more siblings than their counterparts in other developed countries, and their class sizes are often larger. Studies have shown that more siblings and larger classes have negative effects on achievement. Feniger and Shavit's (2011) study highlights the importance of the demographic context to the understanding of educational outcomes in comparative international studies.

Summary

The diversity and segmentation of Israeli society are a source of many social difficulties, but also make Israel a fertile ground for research on educational achievement. Research has demonstrated how sorting and grouping mechanisms (e.g., channeling students to vocational programs) preserve educational inequality while cooperative learning may help to reduce it. Research on the educational inequalities between Arabs and Jews highlights the importance of financial allocation to educational achievement and the impediment created by diglossia. Research on the integration of immigrant students highlights the need for awareness by school administrators and teachers of the fact that educational assimilation is a long process and that different groups of immigrants may progress at different rates. Finally, while researchers and policy makers usually attempt to explain why some countries do better than others by looking at differences in education policy, a recent Israeli study showed the importance of birthrate to the understanding cross-country educational disparities.

References

Ayalon, H., & Shavit, Y. (2004). Educational reforms and inequalities in Israel: The MMI hypothesis revisited. *Sociology of Education, 77*(2), 103–120.

Feniger, Y., & Shavit, Y. (2011). The demographic price: Fertility rate and achievement in international tests. *Israeli Sociology, 13*(1). (Hebrew).

Kennet-Cohen, T., Cohen, Y., & Oren, C. (2005). *Comparison of attainments in the Jewish sector and the Arab sector at different stages in the education system.* Jerusalem: National Institute for Testing and Evaluation. (Hebrew)

Lavy, V. (1998). Disparities between Arabs and Jews in school resources and student achievement in Israel. *Economic Development and Cultural Change, 47*(1), 175–192.

Levin, T., & Shohamy, E. (2008). Achievement of immigrant students in mathematics and academic Hebrew in Israeli schools: A large-scale evaluation study. *Studies in Educational Evaluation, 34*(1), 1–14.

Mizrachi, N., Goodman, Y. C., & Feniger, Y. (2009). "I don't want to see it": Decoupling ethnicity and class from social structure in Jewish Israeli high schools. *Ethnic and Racial Studies, 37*(7), 1203–1225.

Shachar, H., & Sharan, S. (1994). Talking, relating, and achieving: Effects of cooperative learning and. whole-class instruction. *Cognition and Instruction, 12*(4), 313–353.

Shavit, Y. (1990). Segregation, tracking, and the educational attainment of minorities: Arabs and Oriental Jews in Israel. *American Sociological Review, 55*(1), 115–126.

Zuzovsky, R. (2010). The impact of socioeconomic versus linguistic factors on achievement gaps between Hebrew-speaking and Arabic-speaking students in Israel in reading literacy and in mathematics and science achievements. *Studies in Educational Evaluation, 36*(4), 153–161.

9.4

Academic Achievement in Finland

Jennifer Chung
St. Mary's University College

Michael Crossley
University of Bristol

Introduction

This article examines factors that underpin the high academic achievement of students in Finland. This is done in the light of Finland's outstanding success in the Organisation for Economic Co-operation and Development's (OECD) international Program for International Student Assessment (PISA) survey. Attention is given to individual, professional, historical, and cultural factors, to the challenges levelled at international achievement studies, and to insights from its comparative educational research literature.

Research Evidence

Academic achievement in Finland has garnered much attention from the international community since the release of the first OECD's PISA scores in 2001. Finland came top in the PISA surveys of 2000, 2003, 2006, and 2009, demonstrating that Finnish students have high levels of proficiency in mathematics, science, and reading. International surveys carried out prior to PISA include the International Association for the Evaluation of Educational Achievement's (IEA) Trends in Mathematics and Science Survey (TIMSS), and Progress in Reading Literacy Survey (PIRLS). Finland, however, is not a frequent participant in the IEA's assessments (Chung, 2009). In the Second International Mathematics Study (SIMS), Finland ranked only average among the 18 participating countries (Sahlberg, 2007, p. 160). In the 1999 repeat of the Third International Mathematics and Science Study (TIMSS-R), 38 countries participated, and Finland ranked only slightly above average (Sahlberg, 2007, p. 161). PISA took a different approach from its counterparts in the IEA by reinventing the notion of literacy. This self-described "innovative" approach "is concerned with the capacity of students to extrapolate from what they have learned and to analyse and reason as they pose, solve and interpret problems in a variety of situations" (OECD, 2007, p. 3). This "forward looking" approach mea-

sures the ability of "young people to use their knowledge and skills in a variety of real-life situations, rather than merely on [sic] the extent to which they have mastered the school curriculum" (OECD, n.d., p. 6). PISA, therefore, does not use curricula from various countries as testing material; rather, it assesses the students' ability to *use* the knowledge gained in schools. PISA selects the testing age of 15 in order to measure "how far students approaching the end of compulsory education have acquired some of the knowledge and skills essential for full participation in the knowledge society" (OECD, n.d., p. 4). PISA has had a significant impact on educational policy making (Grek et al., 2004) and has helped to redefine educational goals by assessing what students can do with what they learn at school and not merely whether they can reproduce what they have learned. PISA's approach to assessing "literacy" and Finland's success in the survey illustrates the importance of the application of learning in Finnish education (Chung, 2009).

PISA has also attracted much criticism, which includes challenges to its research methodology. Many believe the methodology is too simplistic and insufficient; critics also denounce the age samples and questions asked (Chung, 2009). They also question the ability of PISA to provide comparability, given the large scale and disparity of cultural factors (e.g., Goldstein, 2004). The ability to fairly and equitably translate test materials into various languages is also a point of contention (e.g., Goldstein, 2004). Many also question if PISA fails to differentiate between the impact of cultural factors outside of schools, such as the role of the *juku* in Japan, and that of the education system itself (Goldstein, 2004; Sahlberg, 2007). Certainly such comparative studies enhance international competition and make education much more politically sensitive (Goldstein, 2004; Riley & Torrance, 2003). This politicization of education has created a "new education currency," and the dangerous possibility of simplistic, "off-the-shelf" solutions for educational improvement (Goldstein, 2004; Riley & Torrance,

2003, pp. 420–421). Comparativists have also long warned of the uncritical international transfer of educational policy and practice (Crossley & Watson, 2003; Phillips & Schweisfurth, 2006). Nevertheless, the allure of PISA and its credibility as an international achievement study perseveres.

Understanding Student Achievement in Finland. It can be argued that the structure of the Finnish education system contributes to high student achievement. Traditionally, Finnish education aimed to raise the level of the population's education and to encourage equality and egalitarian values (Chung, 2009). The system consists of a basic school sector, upper secondary school, and tertiary education. The vast majority of children attend preschool. The 2001 Basic Education Act stated that families had a right to preschool education and that local authorities are obligated to provide it. The Ministry sees preschool as an essential part of the education process and aids in achieving the goal of equal educational opportunities. Currently, approximately 96% of children partake in the preschool system (Chung, 2009). A transitional year for 6-year-olds provides a strong foundation for high-quality education at the next level (Sahlberg, 2007). Compulsory school begins at age 7 and lasts for 9 years. Compulsory schooling is broken down into two sections, the lower stage and the upper stage. The lower stage lasts 6 years and the upper for 3 years. Some 99.7% of students complete basic schooling in Finland, which gives it one of the lowest dropout rates in the world. In the 2006-2007 school year, the entire country had 350 compulsory school dropouts (Chung, 2009). After compulsory school, the students can choose between upper-secondary school and vocational school, and 97% of students completing compulsory education continue on to upper-secondary education. Approximately half of the continuing students choose upper-secondary school and half choose vocational education. Students applying to upper-secondary school fill out an *yhteishaku*, an application based on their marks from school, which also lists their preferences for upper-secondary school (Chung, 2009). Numbers in both sectors of upper-secondary education have increased in the past few decades. Students completing the vocational track of upper-secondary education sometimes enter the academic track after the completion of their course. The upper-secondary school culminates in a matriculation exam, which provides entry into university. This is the only national, standardized test that Finnish students undertake during their entire schooling. At the tertiary level, students can attend a university or a polytechnic. Polytechnics differ from universities in having a more practical, applied focus (Chung, 2009).

Finnish schools also provide extensive special needs education. Many attribute the high academic achievement of Finnish students to the strong support provided for weaker students. Schools provide special support for students with difficulties, disorders, and disadvantages and all students have the right to the same educational objectives and possibilities. Students with various difficulties, therefore, have the right to individual support. Furthermore, the Ministry of Education views it as better to keep a child in education rather than to fund exclusion later in life. The multiperson community involved in bringing a child to adulthood helps assess any problems that may arise and create preventative efforts such as remedial work for those in danger of dropping out (Chung, 2009).

Finland adheres to the principles of the Nordic welfare state, much like its Scandinavian neighbors. Many thus attribute some of Finland's academic success to the ethos of the welfare state (Chung, 2009). Welfare spending for Finland makes up more than 40% of the gross domestic product. The government spends money on unemployment benefits, education, pensions, health care, and social services. Although this is high compared to its OECD counterparts, Finland's spending on social welfare remains at a level similar to that of other Scandinavian countries. This affects education and educational achievement as all students study for free, have access to free medical and dental care, and attend university free of charge. Students who live far away from school are entitled to free transport (Chung, 2009). These egalitarian values allow all students, no matter of what socioeconomic background, to have equal chances in education. This commitment to equality and welfare is deeply rooted in the Finnish psyche. Furthermore, PISA data shows that academic achievement in Finland is very consistent; for example, the results of PISA 2000 (OECD, 2000) showed that Finland had the lowest between-school variance in scores, indicating high equality within the Finnish educational system and a relatively low influence of socioeconomic status on student performance (Chung, 2009). Academic achievement in Finland, therefore, does not have a large standard deviation, as indicated by PISA. Strong support for weaker students allows for a small range of scores and high achievement.

Finland's high academic achievement stems from the high quality of Finnish teachers. The history of Finnish teacher training indicates an "academic drift" of the profession (Kivinen & Rinne, 1994, p. 518). In 1934, the Jyväskylä College of Education trained teachers *after* the completion of secondary education. Even at this early time, teaching and teacher training held great respect in the nation. "It has been a very characteristic feature of Finnish teacher education that it has leaned on the legitimacy of the educational sciences…. Teacher training thus in fact eventually legitimated its gradually growing status by leaning on the established academic status of educational research" (Kivinen & Rinne, 1994, p. 519). In 1968, a committee determined that all teacher training courses require an upper-secondary school qualification and that they would consist of a 4-year course of study, culminating in a master's degree in education. This required that all teacher training would take place within the universities (Kivinen & Rinne, 1994) and in 1971, the Teacher Training Act moved all teacher training to the university level. Formal training for all teachers in Finland, including those of the primary school level, now leads to a master's degree (Sahlberg, 2007). Furthermore, "The interaction between teaching and research, it was hoped, would lead to an improved level of scholarship among the teachers" (Kivinen & Rinne, 1994, p. 522). These changes to teacher training professionalized and academized teacher training and the teaching profession, and also helped to close the gap between educational science and teacher training (Chung, 2009). A 2004 poll of upper-secondary students thus cited 26% of the sample naming teaching as the most sought-after profession (Sahlberg, 2007). Teaching is so popular that only 10% of applicants are accepted into teacher training programs (Chung, 2009). The esteem and strength of teacher training, therefore, generates high quality teachers, popularity for the profession, and master's degrees for all qualified teachers. Kivinen and Rinne (1994, p. 521) thus argue, "The long march of teachers from despised and underprivileged civil servants to the core of the academic elite has been more glorious and successful in Finnish society than in most other countries in the world" (Kivinen & Rinne, 1994, p. 521).

Summary

High quality teacher training is, therefore, seen as one of the most salient factors behind Finland's academic success (Chung, 2009). Furthermore, one can connect the respect for education in Finnish society to the high esteem in which teachers are held. As a result, a culture of trust exists in Finnish schools, underpinned by decentralization movements that delegated more responsibility to the municipal and school levels (Chung, 2009). The Finnish education system has also resisted adhering to global trends in education reform, such as emphasis on standards and accountability measures (Sahlberg, 2007; Webb, Vulliamy, Sarja, Hämäläinen, & Poikonen, 2009). The Finnish nationalist and independence movements also acknowledge the importance of education in the Finnish psyche. Finns hold education in high esteem and highlight "its significance for the development of society and the economy" (Herranen, 1995, p. 323). Furthermore, "there is in Finland a profound respect for an academic education and a profound desire to possess some form of degree" (Bacon, 1970, p. 210).

International achievement studies such as PISA clearly demonstrate that the Finnish education system generates high student academic achievement. The exact nature of these achievements deserves closer scrutiny but it will be interesting to see if, and how, other countries will try to learn from this experience, and to what extent Finland's success will influence policy developments elsewhere.

Acknowledgment

This entry draws upon Jennifer Chung's doctoral dissertation at the University of Oxford, and on comparative research on the nature of the influence of international comparisons of student achievement carried out by both authors.

References

Bacon, W. (1970). *Finland.* London: Hale.

Chung, J. (2009). *An investigation of reasons for Finland's success in PISA* (Unpublished doctoral dissertation). Oxford University, England.

Crossley, M., & Watson, K. (2003). *Comparative and international research in education: Globalisation, context and differences.* London: Routledge Falmer.

Goldstein, H. (2004). International comparisons of student attainment: Some issues arising from the PISA study. *Assessment in Education, 11*(3), 319–330.

Grek, S., Lawn, M., Lingard, B., Ozga, J., Rinne, R., Segerholm, C., & Simola, H. (2009). National policy brokering and the construction of the European education space in England, Sweden, Finland and Scotland. *Comparative Education, 45*(1), 5–21.

Herranen, M. (1995). Finland. In T. N. Postlethwaite (Ed.), *International encyclopedia of national systems of education* .pp. 2316–2324). Cambridge, England: Pergamon.

Kivinen, O., & Rinne, R. (1994). The thirst for learning, or protecting one's niche? The shaping of teacher training in Finland during the 19th and 20th centuries. *British Journal of Sociology of Education, 15*(4), 515–527.

Organisation for Economic Co-operation and Development (OECD). (n.d.). *PISA–The OECD programme for international student assessment.* Paris: Author.

Organisation for Economic Co-operation and Development (OECD. (2000). *Measuring student knowledge and skills: The PISA 2000 ssessment of reading, mathematical and scientific literacy.* Paris: Author.

Organisation for Economic Co-operation and Development (OECD). (2007). *PISA 2006: Science competencies for tomorrow's world: Executive summary.* Paris: Author.

Phillips, D., & Schweisfurth, M. (2006). *Comparative and international education: An introduction to theory, method and practice.* Trowbridge, Wiltshire, England: Cromwell.

Riley, K., & Torrance, H. (2003). Big change question: As national policy-makers seek to find solutions to national education issues, do international comparisons such as TIMSS and PISA create a wider understanding, or do they serve to promote the orthodoxies of international agencies? *Journal of Educational Change, 4*(4), 419–425.

Sahlberg, P. (2007). Education policies for raising student learning: The Finnish approach. *Journal of Education Policy, 22*(2), 147–171.

Webb, R., Vulliamy, G., Sarja, A., Hämäläinen, S., & Poikonen, P. (2009). Professional learning communities and teacher well-being? A comparative analysis of primary schools in England and Finland. *Oxford Review of Education, 35*(3), 405–422.

9.5

Ghana

DAVID PETERSON DEL MAR
Portland State University

Introduction

Ghana has a well-deserved reputation as one of Sub-Saharan Africa's most progressive nations. The first West African nation to achieve independence from colonial rule, it is one of the few nations on the continent to have established a cycle of presidential elections in which power changes hands peacefully, and it has avoided the major civil wars that have plagued so many of its neighbors.

Education has long played a key role in Ghana's development. Precontact societies trained children for roles characterized by both hierarchy and reciprocity. Arab and then European traders interacted with West Africans long before the British colonized the Gold Coast in the 19th and 20th centuries. British administrators hoped that education would Christianize Ghanaians and provide a steady stream of docile workers. But Ghanaians instead associated a Western education with upward mobility, with professional jobs—usually in the colonial government. By 1935 the Gold Coast (Ghana) had about 65,000 pupils, many more than much more populous Nigeria. Although classrooms were highly authoritarian and devoted to rote learning, they offered the prospect of future prosperity.

This pairing of high expectations and rigid pedagogies survived independence. The number of schools and pupils increased exponentially in the 1950s and 1960s, as Ghanaians took control of their own affairs, and the curriculum now addressed African and especially Ghanaian subjects. However, Kwame Nkrumah, Ghana's celebrated founder, used a highly structured curriculum to ensure that the young nation's schools were "teacher proof." More than a half-century later this pattern persists despite calls from academics and Government reports for teachers to develop student's critical-thinking skills. However measured, academic achievement lags far behind impressive participation rates.

Research Evidence

The proportion of young Ghanaians attending school has reached high levels since the federal government set out to make basic education free and compulsory in the 1990s. The net enrollment rate (the percentage of children of primary-school age enrolled in primary school) rose from less than three in five at the turn of the 21st century to well over four in five. The enrollment rate for junior secondary students has risen to roughly one half, though only about a third manage to complete 3 years and pass the entrance exam for senior high school. These impressive numbers mask some problems. Nearly one in three children begins primary school later than they should, and many have to repeat grades. The rapid expansion of Ghana's education system has pressed many untrained teachers into classrooms; by 2008 they constituted a majority in primary schools. Still, in terms of raw numbers, Ghana's schools have achieved a high level of success, relative both to its past and to the rest of Sub-Saharan Africa. Indeed, Ghana spends roughly one third of its budget on education, or 10% of its Gross National Product.

Student achievement has also risen but remains relatively low. In 2009, only 36 and 14% of students in the last year of primary school achieved proficiency in English and math, respectively, with proficiency defined as correctly answering just 55% of multiple-choice questions. A reading comprehension test administered at 50 primary schools revealed that over 30% were able to correctly answer 80% of the questions but that nearly as many were correct less than 18% of the time. Only 17% of 16-year-old Ghanaian students surpassed the modest benchmark for the 2007 Trends in International Math and Science Study, a lower figure than that achieved by nations with similar levels of economic development.

Case studies underscore these somewhat dispiriting

statistics. A study from a village in the Ashanti Region early in the 21st century found that its two primary and one junior-secondary school were characterized by apathetic students and teachers. Most of the students could speak only a few basic phrases in English, the principal mode of instruction. A study of several junior-secondary schools at Cape Coast, a more urban area, described teachers who were both authoritarian and uninterested. Likewise, another scholar, who observed a Primary 4 classroom in Kumasi, Ghana's second largest city, found teachers who insisted on rote learning and who had little patience for the many students who struggled to keep up.

A comparative study conducted in 2004–2005 found that Ghanaian classrooms were considerably less productive than those of Brazil, Morocco, or Tunisia. Ghanaian teachers were absent (43 days) or late (40 days) more than 40% of the time, an astonishing rate that is four to six times higher than for the other three countries. When Ghanaian teachers were present in school, they were more likely than the teachers of the other three countries to be out of the room or involved in organizational rather than teaching activities. In sum, learning activities consumed just 39% of the time set aside for that purpose, far less than the 71% average of the other counties.

Those learning activities, moreover, have remained highly passive and consist mainly of "chalk and talk." Teachers present factual material that students are expected to record and memorize for later regurgitation in the standardized exams that play such a large role in their educational futures. There is little discussion or other opportunities for student-based enquiry. It is a style of education, remarks anthropologist Cati Coe (2005, p. 148), that "makes teachers and the notes they provide the primary source of information," and "ways of knowing from observation and experience are largely closed off."

Educational achievement of course is influenced by many factors. The gender gap in access to schools has shrunk considerably over the past several decades, particularly for younger students. But region and especially social class remain very strong predictors of educational access and success. Rural, northern, and poor families are much less likely to invest in their children's educations, in part because their schools are considerably less effective. The best schools in Ghana are private institutions whose tuition fees exceed the incomes of most Ghanaians. All but a handful of these private schools resemble public schools in being highly authoritarian and emphasizing the mastery of facts. But they do a superior job of preparing students for the examinations that act as gateways to the best high schools, colleges, and careers. In 1997, for example, students from private schools were 10 to 15 times more likely to achieve high scores on their Basic Education Certificate Examinations, an extensive battery of tests which largely controls access to Ghana's top high schools, colleges, and occupations. A study completed at the turn of the 21st century found that one half of students admitted to study law, engineering, and other elite fields of study at its best

universities came from just 18 of its 504 senior-secondary schools. Public monies fund a large number of schools but spend much more per student at the university level, where students from prosperous families and private schools are overrepresented. Critics therefore argue that Ghana's education system is designed to give the appearance of opportunity for all (by opening and operating a large number of schools) while in fact reproducing privilege (by spending a large fraction of its budget on institutions that children from poor families are very unlikely to attend).

Structural factors explain much of Ghana's low level of student achievement. Although Ghana's overall economy has been improving, it remains a country with limited resources to devote to education and a growing gap between rich and poor. Even when the government covers the costs of school books, uniforms, and fees, poor parents are understandably reluctant to lose the precious income and other assistance that even young children contribute. Teaching remains a relatively low-paying occupation, and teachers may wait weeks or even months for their pay. Hence ambitious Ghanaians commonly use teaching as a stepping stone to more remunerative positions inside or outside of education.

Ghanaian education is also hampered by a deeply ingrained and widely shared conservatism. Respect for authority characterized Ghanaian societies even before colonization, and colonial schools were both highly popular and authoritarian. Children arrive at school predisposed to learn passively rather than actively, an inclination that few teachers challenge as they have usually attended teachers' colleges steeped in a tradition of "self-control, hard work, and obedience to elders." Even in-service training initiatives promoting innovative teaching approaches are typically taught in a highly authoritarian manner. Teachers are government employees, part of a system which tends to prize loyalty and conformity over initiative. This helps to explain why so many are tempted to approach their jobs as a sinecure (albeit a poorly paid one) rather than as an opportunity to challenge young minds to think independently.

Ghana is in fact becoming much less traditional, but Ghanaians commonly turn to their schools to counterbalance the effects of urbanization, conspicuous consumption, and an increasingly uninhibited popular culture. Administrators commonly cite immorality and indiscipline as the most common difficulty confronting schools, a concern unlikely to promote more student-focused styles of learning. National leaders have long feared that embedding local languages and other aspects of local culture in the schools would facilitate the sort of political fragmentation that has plagued so much of West Africa. Hence the curriculum is often insensitive to the requirements and sensibilities of particular villages or regions and is usually delivered by people raised and trained elsewhere.

Summary and Recommendations

There is much to be optimistic about in Ghanaian education. Participation rates have risen dramatically over the past generation and are now high. Scores on standardized tests are apparently up—though they remain modest. There are many highly dedicated teachers, and more leaders are talking about the importance of student-focused learning. Ghana is home to Ashesi University, an acclaimed private, liberal-arts college featuring enquiry-based education.

But poverty, inequality, and tradition combine to keep Ghana's student achievement far below its impressive rates of student participation. Teacher pay remains low. Only a tiny minority of poor students are able to use public schools as an avenue to good universities or well-paying jobs, in part because morale at such schools is generally low, the amount of time devoted to instruction is meager, and opportunities for student initiative are rare. Calls for reform are undercut by habits of deference cultivated before and during colonization and understandable fears that Ghanaian society in general and youth in particular require a larger dose of authoritarian social structures.

Future research on Ghanaian education could profitably focus on how to make teaching and learning more engaging and rewarding, a process that will require attention not just to popular attitudes and beliefs but to the complex cultural and social factors which foster and perpetuate them.

Bibliography

Abadzi, H. (2007). *Absenteeism and beyond: Instructional time loss and consequences*. Washington, DC: World Bank.

Addae-Mensah, I. (2000). *Education in Ghana: A tool for social mobility or social stratification?* Accra, Ghana: Institute for Scientific and Technological Information.

Akyeampong, K. (2009). Revisiting free compulsory university basic education (FCUBE) in Ghana. *Comparative Education, 45*, 175–195.

Akyeampong, K., Djangmah, J., Oduro, A., Seidu, A., & Hunt, F. (2007). *Access to basic education in Ghana: The evidence and the issues*. Brighton, England: Centre of International Education, University of Sussex; Winneba: University of Education, Winneba, Ghana.

Coe, C. (2005). *Dilemmas of culture in African Schools: Youth, nationalism, and the transformation of knowledge*. Chicago, IL: University of Chicago Press.

Darvas, P., & Krauss, A. (2011). *Education in Ghana: Improving equity, efficiency and accountability of education service delivery*. Washington, DC: World Bank.

Dei, G. J. S. (2004). *Schooling and education in Africa: The case of Ghana*. Trenton, NJ: Africa World Press.

Dull, L. J. (2006). *Disciplined development: Teachers and reform in Ghana*. Lanham, MD: Lexington.

Etsey, K., Smith, T. M., Gyamera, E., Koka, J., de Boer, J., Havi, E., & Heyneman, S. P. (2009). *Review of basic education quality in Ghana*. Washington, DC: U.S. Agency for International Development.

Folson, R. B. (1995). *The contribution of formal education to economic development and economic underdevelopment: Ghana as paradigm*. Frankfurt am Main, Germany: Peter Lang.

Opoku-Amankwa, K. (2009). "Teacher only calls her pets": Teachers' selective attention and the invisible life of a diverse classroom in Ghana. *Language and Education, 23*, 249–262.

Osei, G. M. (2009). *Education in post-Colonial Ghana: Teachers, schools and bureaucracy*. New York: Nova Science.

Pryor, J., & Ampiah, J. G. (2003). *Understandings of education in an African village*. Brighton, England: University of Sussex, Institute of Education.

9.6

Academic Achievement in South Africa

ANIL KANJEE
Tshwane University of Technology

Introduction

Academic achievement in South Africa has always been a high stakes political issue. Under the apartheid system academic achievement was the primary means to rank and sort people and to control the life chances of all South Africans. Mathonsi (1988) and Nzimande (1995) note that tests have been intentionally misused to deprive Blacks of access to resources and opportunity to higher education, and that their intellectual development has been stifled in a conscious and systematic manner to provide the White minority with a cheap source of labour. In the postapartheid system, academic achievement is used as an indicator for equity and redress, for effecting interventions to improve education quality and as a measure of progress. For example, the increase in the matriculation pass rates is regularly cited by the Department of Education as an indication that the education system is improving, while it has become standard practice to use learner performance levels to identify schools and districts in need of intervention.

Since the abolishment of the apartheid system in 1994, improving the low academic achievement of all learners, particularly poor, rural learners, the majority of whom are Black, has been one of the key goals of the education department. Despite some progress, this still remains a major challenge. This chapter provides an overview of academic achievement in South African schools, highlighting key findings and trends in performance since 1994, and notes the challenges and prospects for the future. However, any discussion of academic achievement in South African schools must be contextualised in relation to the dual education system within which learning and teaching take place and the research environment that dictates the availability and use of data on learner achievement.

Research Evidence

Prior to 1994, the apartheid policies of the South African state provided for higher state subsidies, better teachers, greater facilities, and more resources to schools serving White children while depriving those serving Black children of even the most basic resources (Kallaway, 2002). It is thus no surprise that there were huge disparities in the academic achievement levels of Black and White learners. The unequal and discriminatory nature of the education system was made possible by a system of testing and measurement in South Africa that was developed from within a tradition of psychology (Mathonsi, 1988; Nzimande, 1995). From the very beginning testing and measurement in South Africa have been used to produce theories of intellectual differences between races (Appel, 1989; Swartz, 1992). These practices laid the foundation of how assessment in education was to be conducted in South Africa in later years, which has taken the form of an elaborate system of tests and examinations by which control and entry into the economy was regulated (Swartz, 1992). Thus, examination results, the only source of information on the performance of learners, were used for selection into higher education as well as for entry into the world of work. Moreover, the limited capacity and expertise in the area of assessment and testing was restricted to a few, selected White researchers and academics (Cloete, Muller, & Orkin, 1986).

Matriculation Examinations. Until recently, the main source of data on academic achievement in South Africa was the matriculation examinations, a compulsory examination that is conducted in the final year (Grade 12) of secondary schooling. Over the last two decades, the format and content of the examinations have changed significantly. Prior to 1996, the matriculation examinations were administered separately by the 19 different education departments. In 1996, unified national examinations were introduced by implementing a single exam for all learners, irrespective of race or ethnicity. In practice, however, these examinations were independently set, administered, and graded by each of the nine provinces and the independent examinations board that catered to private schools. In the 2001 examinations, two significant changes were effected: (a) common national examination papers, in five subjects, mathematics, language, science, biology and accounting, were implemented for all examinees, and (b) the calculation of the final grade was changed to incorporate a year mark (which comprised 25% of the final grade). In 2009, the examination was again changed to reflect the new national curriculum. However, the practice of comparing results across different years continues unabated despite the significant differences in the examination papers between provinces and the changes in the calculation of the final grades across the different time periods (Kanjee, 2005). It is common practice to find reports and newspaper articles that uncritically compare changes in pass rates over time (from 58% in 1994, 47% in 1997, 62% in 2001, 73% in 2003, and declining to 61% in 2009) without accounting for how scores are calculated (Department of Education, 2003b; Thomson, 2010).

Assessment Surveys in South Africa. The first study to report on the national academic achievement of learners in South Africa was the Third International Mathematics and Science Studies (Kanjee, 2006). Although this was an international survey, it provided national data on mathematics and science achievement of Grade 8 learners. This study was followed by the Grade 9 longitudinal study, conducted by the Human Sciences Research Council in 1996, which assessed performance of learners in language, mathematics, and science. In 1999, the Monitoring Learning Achievement Study (MLA), was conducted by UNESCO and UNICEF to assess learner achievement at Grade 4 in language, life skills, and mathematics. The first national study conducted by the Department of Education was in 2001. Known as the Systemic Evaluation, this study assessed language, life skills, and mathematics achievement of Grade 3 learners. In the same year, South Africa also participated in the Southern African Consortium for Monitoring Education Quality (SACMEQ) regional study that assessed the performance of Grade 6 learners in language and mathematics. In 2004, the Grade 6 Systemic Evaluation study was conducted by the Department of Education followed by the second Grade 3 Systemic Study and the second SACMEQ Grade 6 study in 2007. All three studies assessed language and mathematics achievement.

Learner Performance Trends. A review of the data on learner achievement in South Africa reveals three key trends. First, across all provinces, in all content areas assessed and relative to other developing and developed nations, South African learners have extremely low levels of performance. The average scores in the Grade 3 study for

Table 9.6.1. SACMEQ II Mathematics and Reading Scores

Mathematics		Reading	
Mauritius	568	Seychelles	568
Kenya	548	Kenya	534
Seychelles	540	Tanzania	531
Mozambique	516	Mauritius	524
Tanzania	508	Swaziland	518
Swaziland	505	Botswana	510
Botswana	502	Mozambique	504
Uganda	495	South Africa	484
South Africa	492	Uganda	474
Lesotho	441	Lesotho	445
Namibia	426	Namibia	442
Average	500	Average	500

English was 36%, and 35% for mathematics (Department of Education, 2003a) while for Grade 6 it was 38% in English and 27% for mathematics (Department of Education, 2006). The SACMEQ study (see Table 9.6.1), involving 15 Southern African countries, revealed that South Africa ranked third from bottom in mathematics and fourth from bottom in reading, scoring below Mozambique, Swaziland, and Botswana (Moloi & Strauss, 2005). In the latest TIMSS survey that South Africa participated in, Grade 8 learners obtained the lowest mean mathematics mark and second lowest science mean mark compared to 46 other countries (Reddy, Kanjee, Diedericks, & Winnaar, 2006).

Second, academic achievement levels of learners have remained consistently low over time. While there have not been many trend studies, evidence from the TIMSS studies indicate no significant differences in learner scores over the 8-year period with mathematics scores of 278, 275, 264 and science scores of 263, 243, 244 respectively for the 1995, 1999, and 2003 studies. Similar trends were noted across the different provinces from the Grade 9 national assessment studies as noted in Figure 9.6.1.

Third, evidence from achievement scores indicates the existence of a two-tier system, distinguished by huge disparities between learners from different SES backgrounds, geographical regions, and language groups. As indicated in Table 9.6.2, achievement levels of Grade 6 learners from Quintile 1 schools, representing the poorest 20% schools in the country, is less than half of learners that attend the wealthier Quintile 5 schools. As reported by Reddy et al. (2006) similar trends are noted in the 1999 and 2002 TIMSS results (see Table 9.6.3), where the average scale scores of learners (in ex-House of Assembly schools) is over two standard deviations higher than that of average scale scores of learners (in ex-DET schools).[1] It must be noted that most of the Q1 to Q4 schools and ex-DET schools are in the rural areas.

Additional Studies. A limited number of studies have investigated the factors that contribute to the low achievement levels of learners in South Africa. Most of these

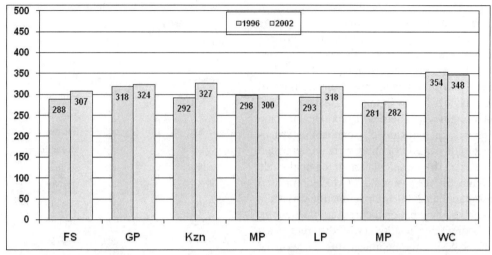

Figure 9.6.1 Comparison of Grade 9 mathematics performance in 1996 and 2002

Table 9.6.2 Grade 6 English and Mathematics Percentage Scores by Quintile Categories

	English	Maths
Q1	20	12
Q2	20	13
Q3	26	15
Q4	27	15
Q5	45	27

Table 9.6.3 TIMSS 1999 and 2003 Mathematics Scale Scores by Ex-Department

School type	1999 Average scale score	2003 average scale score
Ex-DET	238	227
Ex-HoR	348	314
Ex-HoD	406	366
Ex-HoA	442	468
Average	275	264

studies have applied regression and multilevel modelling to conduct their analysis while a number of qualitative studies have also been conducted (Department of Education, 2006; Kanjee, Molefe, Makgamatha, & Claassen, 2010; van der Berg, 2008). While a number of different factors have been identified from these studies, three key factors have regularly been linked to the poor achievement levels of South African learners. First, home level factors, which refers to the low SES of most learners, the limited exposure to the language of teaching due to different home languages, and a home learning environment where learners have limited or no access to adequate books and support for school work. Second, poor teacher quality; that is, limited teacher content knowledge, poor time management, as well as ineffective assessment and feedback practices. Third, poor curriculum leadership and support which refers to the limited support and materials provided to teachers by school principals and education officials to effectively implement the curriculum.

Summary and Recommendations

The last few years have seen a major increase in the implementation of large scale assessment studies in South Africa (Kanjee, 2006). In addition, the national assessment policy was recently revised to place greater emphasis on regular classroom assessments while the process of introducing an accountability system for schools began with census testing of all learners in Grade 1 to 6 and Grade 9 in 2011 and 2012. The impact of these changes and their implications on teacher, principal, and education department officials' practices, as well on the improvement of learning achievement is still unknown.

A critical weakness of the assessment system in South Africa is that achievement has been reduced to cognitive levels only, focussing on English and Mathematics. There is little or no emphasis on attitudes, skills, and behaviours that learners are expected to master. Another area that needs to be urgently addressed pertains to classroom assessment and teacher feedback skills. While the revised assessment policy does prioritise this aspect, there is limited focus on ensuring teachers are effectively equipped to meet the demands of learners so as to enhance improvement in learning. Finally, there is a need for a great deal more secondary analysis, specifically to address the challenge of limited capacity and skills to conduct these analyses as well as to improve access to available data.

The nature and form of how academic achievement is measured has undergone significant alteration in postapartheid South Africa. However, there is still much to be done to ensure that: (a) available information from assessment studies is effectively applied, and (b) there is a greater emphasis on assessment for learning as opposed to assessment of learning so that there is visible improvement in the achievement levels of learners in all South African schools, particularly those in which the most marginalised and disadvantaged find themselves.

Note

1. Ex-department refers to the previous racially based education departments under which schools were administered during the apartheid period.

    Ex-DET refers to schools for "Blacks"

    Ex-HoA refers to schools for "Whites"

    Ex-HoD refers to schools for "Indians"

    Ex-Hor refers to schools for "Coloureds" (or "mixed race")

References

Appel, S. W. (1989). "Outstanding individuals do not arise from ancestrally poor stock": Racial science and the education of Black South Africans. *Journal of Negro Education, 58*, 544–557.

Cloete, N., Muller, J., & Orkin, M. (1986). How we learned to stop worrying and love the HSRC. *Psychology and Society, 6*, 29–46.

Department of Education. (2003a). Grade 3 *national systemic evaluation report: Mainstream education.* Pretoria, South Africa: Author.

Department of Education. (2003b). *Speech by the Minister of Education, Professor Kader Asmal, MP, on the release of 2003 Senior Certificate Examinations results,* Cape Town, SA. Retrieved from http://www.polity.org.za/article/asmal-release-of-2003-matric-results-30122003-2003-12-30

Department of Education. (2006). *Grade 6 national systemic evaluation report.* Pretoria, South Africa: Author.

Kallaway, P. (Ed). (2002). *The history of education under apartheid 1948–1994.* Cape Town, South Africa: Pearson Education.

Kanjee, A. (2005). A matrix sampling model for monitoring performance trends in the matriculation exams. In V. Reddy (Ed.), *Marking matric: Overview and challenges.* Pretoria, South Africa: HSRC Press.

Kanjee, A. (2006). Improving learner achievement in schools: Applications of national assessments in South Africa. In *S. Buhlungu, J. Daniel, R. Southall, & J. Lutchman (Eds), State of the nation: South Africa 2007* (pp. 470–499). Pretoria, South Africa: HSRC Press.

Kanjee, A., Molefe, M. R. M., Makgamatha, M. M., & Claassen, N. C. W. (2010). *Teacher assessment practices in South African schools.* Pretoria, South Africa: HSRC Press. Unpublished report.

Mathonsi, E. N. (1988). *Black matriculation results: A mechanism of social control.* Johannesburg, South Africa: Skotaville.

Moloi, M., & Strauss, J. (2005). *The SACMEQ II Project in South Africa: A study of the conditions of schooling and the quality of education.* Harare, Zimbabwe: SACMEQ.

Nzimande, B. (1995, June). *To test or not to test.* Paper presented at the Congress of Psychometrics for Psychologists and Personnel Practitioners, Pretoria, South Africa.

Reddy, V., Kanjee, A., Diedericks, G., & Winnaar, L. (2006) *Mathematics and science achievement at South African schools in TIMSS 2003.* Cape Town, South Africa: HSRC Press.

Swartz, D. (1992). Issues in the reform of the system of certification South Africa. In E. Unterhalter, H. Wolpe, & T. Botha (Eds.), *Education in a future South Africa: Policy issues and transformation* (pp. 136–148). Trenton, NJ: Africa World Press.

Thomson, I. (2010). Equal education statement on the 2009 Matric results. Retrieved from http://blogs.uct.ac.za/blog/educblog/2010/01/08/equal-education-statement-on-2009-matric-results

Van der Berg, S. (2008). How effective are poor schools? Poverty and educational outcomes in South Africa. *Studies in Educational Evaluation, 34*(3), 145–154.

9.7

Educational Assessment and Educational Achievement in South America

JORGE MANZI AND DAVID D. PREISS
Pontificia Universidad Católica de Chile

Introduction

Since the early 1990s, there has been rapid progress in educational assessment in South America. This development has been fostered by the implementation across the region of several international assessment initiatives as well as national systems of educational assessment (NSEA; Martínez, 2010). Yet, the development of modern educational assessment in South America can be traced back to the late 1960s. In 1968, the first educational measurement center in Latin America—the Instituto Colombiano para la Evaluación de la Educación (ICFES)—was created in Colombia and put in charge of university admission tests. The first country that implemented a NSEA was Chile. In 1978, the Chilean government asked the Pontificia Universidad Católica de Chile to develop such a system, now known as Sistema de Medición de Calidad de la Educación (SIMCE; Martínez, 2008). Afterwards, following the global trend for a higher level of accountability and standardization, other South American countries have proceeded to establish their own NSEA as well as participate in a number of international assessment initiatives (Ferrer, 2006). In this entry, we shall review the main national and international assessment initiatives currently operating in the region and summarize what their implementation reveals about educational achievement.

Research Evidence

Three countries have well-established NSEA: Brazil, Colombia, and Chile. In Brazil, the Sistema de Avaliação da Educação Básica (SAEB) was established in 1990 (Crespo, Soares, de Mello, & Souza, 2000). Since 2005, the system has been comprised of two assessments, which are applied every 2 years. Both of these measures test Portuguese language and mathematics with a focus on problem solving. The Avaliação Nacional da Educação Básica (ANEB) tests a

sample of schools. The Avaliação Nacional do Rendimento Escolar (also known as Prova Brazil) is a national test for all students in two age cohorts. The ANEB is implemented in a sample of Brazil's fifth and ninth grade students as well as high school third year students. The results are reported at both the regional and national level. Prova Brazil is used to test Brazil's fifth and ninth grade students in all schools that have a minimum of 20 students enrolled in the class. Prova Brazil provides specific information for each municipality and school participant as well as a general report at the national level.

In 1991, the Colombian ICFES began developing assessments using representative samples of students. Since 2001, Colombia has operated a compulsory assessment system (SABER) administered by the ICFES that every 3 years tests all fifth and ninth graders in language, mathematics, and natural sciences. SABER is composed of two assessments: one that is operated by each school individually, and one that is run directly by the ICFES. The former is designed to inform the institutions locally, whereas the purpose of the latter is to provide national estimates of educational progress. In 2009, approximately 85% of students were assessed directly by their schools and 15% of students by ICFES. Reports are produced for both the school and district and regional level.

Chile's SIMCE is managed by the Education Ministry. Fourth graders are assessed each year for language, mathematics, and basic science achievement. Eighth graders and high school second-year students take language and mathematics assessments in alternate years. Eighth graders also take a social science and natural science assessment. SIMCE has recently implemented assessments in writing, English as a second language, and physical education. An assessment of competencies related to information technology use is in the making. Reports of national results as well as school level results are made publicly available and distributed to schools (administrators and teachers) and to families (Taut, Cortes,

472

Sebastian, & Preiss, 2008). In addition, detailed results for all the country's schools are provided online.

Argentina, Ecuador, Paraguay, Peru, and Uruguay have all implemented large-scale assessments of educational achievement. Most of these countries began implementing their NSEA during the mid-1990s. In Argentina, students have been tested by the Operativos Nacionales de Evaluación (ONE) since 1993. Ecuador began measuring educational achievement in 1996. Paraguay's Sistema nacional de evaluación del proceso educativo (SNEPE) was created in 1995 (Lafuente, 2009). Peru's NSEA started in 1996. In Uruguay, the Administración Nacional de la Educación Pública first established a unit responsible for educational measurement in 1995. A summary of the subject matters and years assessed for each country are referenced in Ferrer (2006) and Martínez (2008, 2010). The focus of all these systems is on mathematics and language. Natural and social sciences have also been assessed but not on a regular basis. Assessment in a language other than Spanish is undertaken in Peru. Although all of these countries measure educational achievement on a regular basis, the particular grades assessed have varied across the years, a practice that does not permit the operation of a systematic comparison of the achievement level reached by different cohorts of students. In some rounds of assessment, the evaluation performed within these countries has been universal (for a particular grade) and for other rounds it has been focused on specific samples (Argentina and Uruguay have used both). Some have evolved from measuring representative samples to universal assessments (Ecuador and Peru). Formative large-scale assessment has been also promoted (e.g., in 2010, the Uruguayan Departamento de Evaluación de los Aprendizajes implemented online tests of educational achievement with an emphasis placed upon their formative function).

Bolivia and Venezuela have each developed at least one large-scale measure but do not currently have a national system of educational assessment. In Bolivia, the Subsistema Nacional de Medición de la Calidad de la Educación Preescolar, Primaria y Secundaria (SIMECAL) was established in 1996. After 2005, SIMECAL was replaced by the Observatorio Plurinacional de la Calidad Educativa (OPCE). In 2010, this unit, together with UNICEF, assessed reading comprehension, social studies (or 'national reality') and logical reasoning in students from fifth, eighth grade, and high school fourth year. References in the literature to large scale educational assessments in Venezuela are limited to an assessment of language and mathematics achievement in sixth grade which was implemented in a sample of schools by the Sistema Nacional de Medición y Evaluación del Aprendizaje (SINEA), a unit that was dismantled in 2004 (Martínez, 2010).

In summary, NSEA vary across Latin American countries. Although all focus on the core curriculum subjects—language and mathematics—some countries include other subjects such as social and natural sciences. There are slight differences between countries in the grade levels assessed as well as the scope of, and audiences for, the reports they produce. Some NSEA seek to assess the performance of an entire population cohort, some assess samples, and others implement a mixed system. Their differences notwithstanding, the evidence concerning educational achievement produced by these systems indicates that all of the countries in the region have significant deficits in educational achievement, especially in language and mathematics (Murillo & Román, 2008). Those countries using cut-off scores to differentiate performance levels have reported that a large proportion of students perform below the expected standard. Where sociodemographic data enable comparative analyses, it has been noted that there exist significant educational gaps between differing socioeconomic and ethnic groups, rural and urban zones, as well as within the regions of the countries (Murillo & Román, 2008; Soares, 2006). Unfortunately, because most of the NSEA do not yield information about changes in achievement over time, or provide longitudinal comparisons, it is not possible to establish whether the deficits are developmental (i.e., performance levels change as children move through their school careers) or whether these differ between cohorts (Ravela et al., 2008).

In addition to the specific contribution of the NSEA, international testing programs have become major reference points in shaping educational policy. They are used for many purposes, including the assessment of the quality of education systems, the identification of successful initiatives, and the monitoring of educational progress. For these reasons, most South American countries are currently participating in at least one of the global testing programs: Programme for International Student Assessment (PISA), Trends in International Mathematics and Science Study (TIMSS) and International Civil and Citizenship Education Study (ICCS). They are also participating in a Latin-American initiative led by UNESCO: the Latin American Laboratory for Assessment of the Quality of Education (LLECE). Participation is strong in the LLECE (8 countries were included in the last round of this program, in 2006), and has increased in PISA (from 4 countries in 2000, to 6 in 2009). However, few countries were included in the ICCS study, and only one was part of the last round of TIMSS in 2007 (Colombia), where previously two other countries had been included (Argentina and Chile).

Global testing programs have consistently ranked South American countries below the international average in measures of knowledge or competence. The size of the gap in PISA, where a larger number of countries from the region have been included, indicates that 15-year-old participants are at least one full school year below the international average in language, mathematics, and science. However, during the last decade, the gap has been reduced, and two of the South American countries (Peru and Chile) achieved the largest increase in language from a 2000 baseline. Moreover, all countries that participated in the last two rounds of PISA showed stability or improvement in their average scores in language and mathematics.

South American countries are less consistently below the international average when attitudes are examined. For example, in the ICCS study, where the three participating countries (Chile, Colombia, and Paraguay) appeared in the bottom half of the civic knowledge distribution, performance was more diverse in attitudinal measures: below average in interpersonal trust, slightly above average in trust in government, and among the top countries in trust in schools.

The regional testing program (LLECE) was established by the Latin American and Caribbean countries to monitor the quality of education in three subject areas: language, mathematics, and sciences. It tests a sample of third and sixth graders in all participating countries. In the first two rounds of the program, the majority of South American countries appeared in the top half of the distribution.

Summary and Recommendations

Comparative testing programs have consistently shown that academic performance in each of the South American countries is strongly correlated with socioeconomic background (at the individual and school level). The challenge for the region is not only to raise performance so it becomes closer to the international average, but also to address the socioeconomic barriers that leave the majority of poor and indigenous students performing below acceptable standards. PISA 2009 indicated a degree of reduction of this gap for some of the South American countries but reducing such disparities remains as one of the main goals for educational policy in the region.

The poor performance of South American countries in international testing programs, combined with the large social and ethnic gaps in national and international test scores, have motivated educational policies aimed at improving school effectiveness especially in low performing schools with high levels of ethnic minority or socially disadvantaged students. Quality and equality are now at the center of educational policies in the region (Vegas & Petrow, 2008).

In spite of their recent progress, national testing programs in South America face important challenges. For some countries the most immediate goal is to reach some consistency and stability in terms of the subject area and grades covered, as well as the schedule of testing. Most countries have to address important technical requirements, such as the following:

1. To compare the performance of different cohorts tested at the same grade level as a means of monitoring the progress of the educational system. This will involve changes in the design of tests to make them compatible with equivalent requirements.
2. To introduce some follow-up studies of cohorts tested at different grades, ideally with vertically scaled tests.

These longitudinal designs are also useful for analysis of the relative efficacy of schools by using value added methods.

3. To define cut-off scores in order to inform educationalists about the proportion of students reaching curricular learning goals. These scores can also help to improve the public understanding of test results.
4. To design more effective delivery of information by establishing continuous monitoring of the understanding and use of test information for different stakeholders.
5. Finally, considering that many countries in the region are using tests for school and teacher accountability purposes, it is important to establish a well-designed plan for monitoring the influence and impact of accountability systems on the quality and validity of test results (Koretz, 2008).

References

Crespo, M., Soares, J. F., & de Mello e Souza, J. F. (2000). The Brazilian national evaluation system of basic education: Context, process, and impact. *Studies in Educational Evaluation, 26*(2), 105–125.
Ferrer, G. (2006). *Sistemas de Evaluación de Aprendizajes en América Latina: Balance y Desafíos* [Systems of learning assessment in Latin America: Balance and challenges]. Santiago, Chile: PREAL.
Koretz, D. (2008). *Measuring up: What educational testing really tells us.* Boston, MA: Harvard University Press.
Lafuente, M. (2009). La experiencia del Sistema Nacional de Evaluación del Proceso Educativo, SNEPE, en Paraguay: Aprendizajes y desafíos. [The experience of the national system of educational process assessment: Lessons and challenges]. *Revista Iberoamericana de Evaluación Educativa, 2*(1), 48–73.
Martínez, F. (2008). La evaluación de aprendizajes en América Latina [The assessment of learning performance in Latin America]. Cuadernos de Investigación. Retrieved from http://www.inee.edu.mx/index.php/publicaciones/resultados-de-investigacion/cuadernos-de-investigacion/3743
Martínez, F. (2010). Assessment in the context of educational policy: The case of Latin American countries. In P. Peterson, E. Baker, & B. McGaw (Eds.), *International encyclopedia of education* (pp. 479–485). Amsterdam, Netherlands: Elsevier.
Murillo, F. J., & Román, M. (2008). Resultados de Aprendizaje en América Latina a Partir de las Evaluaciones Nacionales [Learning results in Latin America according to the national assessments]. *Revista Iberoamericana de Evaluación Educativa, 1*(1), 7–35.
Ravela, P., Arregui, P., Valverde, G., Wolfe, R., Ferrer, G., Martínez Rizo, F.,... Wolf, L. (2008). Las evaluaciones educativas que América Latina necesita [The educational assessments that Latin America needs]. Retrieved from http://www.preal.org/BibliotecaN.asp?Pagina=2&Id_Carpeta=64&Camino=63|Preal%20Publicaciones/64|PREAL%20Documentos
Soares, J. F. (2006). Measuring cognitive achievement gaps and inequalities: The case of Brazil. *International Journal of Educational Research, 45*(3), 176–187.
Taut, S., Cortes, F., Sebastian, C., & Preiss, D. (2008). Evaluating school and parent reports of the national student achievement testing system (SIMCE) in Chile: Access, comprehension, and use. *Evaluation and Program Planning, 3,* 1–9.
Vegas, E., & Petrow, J. (2008). *Raising student learning in Latin America.* Washington, DC: World Bank.

9.8

Changing Definitions of Student Learning and Achievement in Postconflict Nepal

Shabnam Koirala-Azad
University of San Francisco

Introduction

This chapter focuses on challenges and achievements in student learning and achievement in postconflict Nepal. As one of the poorest countries in the world, Nepal tends to be a regular research site for studies on school quality and student learning in developing countries. While many studies (Agergaard et al., 2005; Carney, 2003; Subedi, 2003) focus on specific factors that affect student learning and achievement in the developing world context (lack of proper infrastructure, lack of resources and incentives, and gender disparities), studies situating student learning and achievement within the context of a civil war where the education sector has taken a hard hit, are just emerging. How is education both overtly and subtly affected by a fragmentation of political, economic, and social life? What are students learning within schools? How is "achievement" defined in a climate that is less than stable? What lessons can we learn from both the challenges and triumphs in student achievement within the current Nepali context?

Historical Context. Nepal has been a classic case of a society that was deliberately kept isolated by family rule for over a century between 1849 and 1951 CE. The Rana family determined that their rule would be perpetuated if the people were kept uneducated and the country remained cut off from the rest of the world (Sharma, 1990). When the country opened up to the outside world in 1951 with the introduction of a form of democracy, the education sector made significant advances.

However, lack of financial resources, trained teachers, and poor physical infrastructure, with the government responsible for implementing all educational programs, prevented much achievement in the field. A state of educational stagnation continued for over 30 years under the rule of the Shah family in the form of what was called the Panchayat System. Educational opportunities that existed for the privileged minority followed the "banking method"

of authoritarian education where testing was the primary indicator of student achievement (Freire, 1981).

The reintroduction of democracy in 1990 was an important landmark in the development of education, particularly given the forms of achievement required to cope with forces of globalization and neoliberal policies (Carney, 2003). The period from 1990 to 1996 was one that witnessed an unprecedented growth in the establishment of private schools that had as their goal the introduction of competitive education. This development was in part a response to the tendency for increasing numbers of Nepalese students to enroll in schools abroad, particularly in the United States, United Kingdom, Australia, and other European countries. Some private schools introduced curricula similar to that used in progressive schools in the West. Special stress was placed on achievement in English language, mathematics, and science so that students would be sufficiently competitive to apply for scholarships in schools abroad (Koirala, 2004).

Persistent Issues in Achievement Discourse and Practice. In all levels of Nepalese education, testing has been the primary indicator of student achievement with the burden of learning and achievement placed primarily on the shoulders of the student with success or failure resulting in strong psychosocial effects upon many. In contrast, there is a lack of systematic measures of accountability on the part of schools and teachers. Passing an exam, whether at the national or classroom level, not only determines the student's ability to "move up" but also determines which disciplines he or she might pursue. The highest value is placed on the sciences and mathematics, but only a fraction of the students that pass with honors gain entry into these fields.

In her research with Nepali high school students, Koirala-Azad (2008) found that failing the National School Leaving Certificate (SLC) exam three times (i.e., for three consecutive years) was commonplace for many students in poor urban schools. Gautam (2008) adds that the SLC passing rate of 63% in 2007, which marked one of the best rates in preceding years, demands careful attention to the 37% failure rate that indicated "a serious blow to the self-esteem of tens of thousands of youngsters, a huge loss of investment by poor families and a great waste of public funds" (p. 3). In this widely operationalized and accepted definition of achievement, students from the primary to university levels learn to "accept failure as normal." In 2010 the passing rate for the same exam was 64.31% (Office of Controller of Examinations, 2010), showing a consistent continuation of this worrying trend.

Nepal's national targets for the Millennium Development Goals are to achieve 100% enrollment in primary school, 100% completion rate to Grade 5, and 100% literacy among the 15- to 24-year-old group, by the year 2015 (Graner, 2006). While the country has made considerable progress in raising rates, especially at the primary school level, the unfortunate outcome of a stress on quantity, devoid of attention to quality, has meant the expansion of the "old" model of schools, negating possibilities for the incorporation of new, innovative, and child-centered methods of education that seek to include alternate definitions and practices of achievement. In his study on teachers in the 9th and 10th grade in 30 public and private schools in the Lalitpur District, Subedi (2003) confirmed that large, overcrowded classrooms with few resources had direct and negative effects on student achievement measured through scores on yearly exams.

Also missing from the achievement discourse are "38% of children from indigenous communities, 18% of Dalits and 1% of disabled children believed to be enrolled in primary education" (Gautam, 2008, p. 3). While the language of failure remains minimally contested and a significant part of educational discourse, a closer look at student achievement among "failures" shows that most are from traditionally marginalized groups and communities who already have limited access to education and resources. Dixit (2002) further stresses that Nepal currently has few methods of assessing student learning, even among those who pass, since examinations test "memorization abilities" over authentic understanding (p. 202).

Civil Conflict and Student Learning.

The 10-year Maoist conflict has disrupted the postdemocratic movement developments in education. The violent insurgency that engulfed the country of about 30 million people not only led to the loss of 13,000 innocent lives but left the educational sector in complete disarray. Schools were closed down for long periods of time due to frequent strikes and violence. A rise in cases of student abduction from schools, violence inflicted on teachers, and even recruitment of students into Maoist armies was paralleled with large numbers of students leaving Nepal to pursue their education elsewhere. Student learning became of less concern in comparison to the harmful politicization of educational spaces. For these reasons, according to recent statistics students with the means to do so have been leaving in search of more productive learning elsewhere. Nepalese students constitute the fifth largest group to enroll in colleges in the United States, in spite of the country being listed as one of the poorest.

While private schools, strengthened by a coalition, PAB-SON, fought to restore some peace within schools, public schools serving most of the country's young minds stagnated. The power and proliferation of these achievement-oriented private schools is further widening the gap between the rich and the poor. Those that have been affected by the decade-long violent conflict find it even more difficult to enroll their children in progressive schools, resorting to government schools marked by poor infrastructure (much of it destroyed during the conflict), lack of trained and capable teachers, little teaching material and community involvement.

With schools being used as spaces to further political agendas, or to incite fear in the general public, concerns around student learning were trampled over by more immediate concerns of separating the education sector from the political chaos that was all prevalent. Achievement, even in the traditional sense, was disrupted by political forces as parents found themselves struggling to engage children who had no choice but to be home than in school. Even new ideas based on child-centered approaches to achievement have been hindered due to a fragmentation of society, giving precedence to concerns about infrastructure redevelopment.

New Directions in Postconflict Nepal.

With a fragile peace process in place since November 2006 and with the abolition of the monarchy and the election of a constituent assembly to draft a new constitution based on parliamentary democracy, federalism, and secularism, the school system is arguably on the mend. The first effort began with a push to formally declare schools as "zones of peace." By protecting schools from the chaos and devastation outside, there was a drive to get students back in schools and to create an environment conducive to learning. Since then, several reports have advocated (Adhikari, 2009; Ministry of Education, 2006) child-centered learning, where the need to understand children's learning needs, to provide relevant education, and to assess accordingly is offered as an alternative to examination-oriented achievement. New partnerships, between private and government schools where resources and pedagogies are being shared, are providing new hopes for productive learning. One specific example is a teacher training program facilitated by Rato Bangla School (Kathmandu), Bank Street College of Education (New York), and Kathmandu University for teachers in private and government schools. While the innovation is noteworthy and hopeful, the reach of such initiatives is limited. At the university level, a partnership of several international nongovernment organizations (INGOs) and the Nepali government has led to the formation of Open University of Nepal (Dhakal Ramji, Ratanawijitrasin, & Srithamrongsawat, 2009), geared toward providing quality education for traditionally marginalized groups in Nepal, and seeking to bridge a persistent achievement gap.

Another promising development is the beginning of

conversations around the need to redefine key stakeholders in education. An effort to move the focus away from the government and donors to classrooms, teachers, and students is promising. Concern about the effects of conflict on students' long term learning abilities and overall well-being, has brought to light an urgent need to implement rights-based education and peace education, further stressing the need for a redefinition of "achievement" in the Nepalese educational context (Gautam, 2008; Graner, 2006).

Summary and Recommendations

Student learning and achievement in Nepali education have largely been measured by test scores and defined by the dichotomy of success and failure. Forces of globalization, neoliberal policies, and a push toward universal participation in education have created national education policies and practices driven by numerical goals. And while notable achievements have been made in this regard, critics bring to light two significant issues: the ongoing inaccuracies of testing methods and score reporting (Graner, 2006) and the achievement gap based on class, gender, ethnic group, and (dis)ability (Gautam, 2008). The end of Nepal's decade-long civil conflict, which stagnated education due to strikes and violence, has also marked a time for new possibilities in redefining education with a special focus on quality and achievement.

Since these efforts (private–public partnerships in progressive teacher training, creation of new institutions for the education of marginalized populations, student-centered pedagogies) are still fairly new, empirical mixed methods research that focuses on the experiences of students and teachers within classrooms, and which seeks to document implementation, student learning and achievement are currently few and desperately needed.

Teachers and students have supported the push toward declaring schools as "zones of peace." This depoliticization of education seems crucial in protecting schools from the types of political activities that directly affect student learning and achievement. At the policy level, a redefinition of key stakeholders in education seems imperative. New teacher training programs, informed by student-identified learning needs, and geared toward enhancing student learning, should offer training in various assessment methods so that this leads to a potentially slow but urgently needed departure from testing as the only measure of student achievement.

References

Adhikari, P. S. (2009). Child-centered approach: An imperative model for quality education in Nepal. Innovative Forum for Community Development. Retrieved from http://ifcd.org.np

Agergaard, J., Bista, M. B., & Carney, S. (2005, September). *Between global vision and local reality: Community managed schooling in Nepal.* Paper presented to the Oxford Conference on Education and Development, Oxford, England.

Carney, S. (2003). Globalisation, neo-liberalism and the limitations of school effectiveness research in developing countries: The case of Nepal. *Globalisation, Societies and Education, 1*(1), 87–101.

Dhakal, R., Ramji, R., Ratanawijitrasin, S., & Srithamrongsawat, S. (2009). Addressing the challenges to health sector decentralization in Nepal: an inquiry into the policy and implementation processes. *Nepal Medical College Journal, 11*(3), 152–157.

Dixit, S. (2002). Education, deception, state and society. In K. Dixit & S. Ramachandra (Eds.), *State of Nepal* (pp. 193-211). Kathmandu, Nepal: Himal Books.

Freire, P. (1981). The people speak their word: Learning to read and write in Sao Tome and Principe. *Harvard Educational Review,* 1981, *51,* 27–30.

Gautam, K. C. (2008, August 10). *Quality basic education as the foundation for Nepal's development.* Commencement Speech by former Assistant Secretary-General of the United Nations at graduation of ceremony of primary teacher training, Rato Bangla School, Kathmandu, Nepal.

Graner, E. (2006). Education in Nepal: Meeting or missing the millennium development goals? Retrieved from http://www.accessmylibrary.com/article-1G1-168162612/educationnepal-meeting-missing.html

Koirala, S. (2004). *Exploring solutions at the intersection of education, immigration and transnationalism: Efforts of the diaspora in Nepali social change* (Unpublished doctoral dissertation). University of California, Berkeley.

Koirala-Azad, S. (2008). Unraveling our realities: Nepali students as researchers and activists. *Asia Pacific Journal of Education, 28*(3), 24–38.

Ministry of Education and Sports, (2006). *National curriculum framework for school education (pre-primary to 12) in Nepal.* Retrieved from http://www.esat.org.np/documents/curriculum/ national.pdf

Office of Controller of Examination, Ministry of Education of Nepal. (n.d.). Retrieved from http://www.soce.gov.np/

Sharma, G. N. (1990). The impact of education during the Rana period in Nepal. *Himalayan Research Bulletin, 10*(2–3, 3–7).

Subedi, B. R. (2003). Factors influencing high school student achievement in Nepal. *International Education Journal, 4*(2), 98–107.

9.9

A Historical Perspective on Educational and Academic Achievement in Nigeria

CHARLES OKONKWO
The Ohio State University

RICHARD TABULAWA
University of Botswana

Introduction

The purpose of this review of students' academic achievement in Nigeria is to describe ways that individual differences, the diversity in social, political, and historical backgrounds, coupled with student/teacher/parent relationships, affect students' academic achievement and level of attainment. We first provide a context-specific social, cultural, environmental, and economic description of the conditions that form the analytical framework of this chapter.

Western forms of education were introduced in Nigeria by Christian missionaries in 1843 (Fafunwa, 1974). First promoted by missionaries in the southern part of the country, Western-style education was vigorously pursued in the northern part of Nigeria immediately before and following independence from the British Empire in 1960.

Currently, the educational system in Nigeria reflects a 6-3-3-4 model structure, with 6 years of primary school, 3 years of junior secondary schooling, 3 years of senior schooling, and 4 years of tertiary (college) education. There are 50,700 primary schools with an enrollment of 22.3 million, and 10,349 public secondary schools with an enrollment of 6.4 million. A further 900,000 students are enrolled in 218 tertiary institutions (i.e., 78 universities, 58 polytechnics, and 82 colleges of education) (Federal Ministry of Education, 2005).

Research Evidence

This review of factors that impact upon educational achievement highlights a number of core themes that are recurrent in national debates about educational policy in Nigeria. These are:

- Educational achievement as moderated by regional politics in Nigeria.
- The gender imbalance in educational access and achievement.
- Academic achievement as reflected in urban and rural locations.
- The effect of socioeconomic status (SES) on academic achievement.
- Other sociohistorical and physical factors that impact upon teaching, learning and achievement.

Educational Achievement as Moderated by Regional Politics in Nigeria. After Nigerian independence from the British Empire in 1960, three main regions (Northern, Eastern, and Western (the last two are often grouped together to form the Southern region) were formed. Regional politics in Nigeria have had a very extensive influence on educational achievement and attainment. Generally, there is a history of disparities in terms of educational achievement, access, and attainment in the country between the North and the South, with the latter faring better than the former. So serious have been these disparities that they have to a large measure shaped the country's successive postindependence educational policies. The Northern region's poorer performance has been explained in terms of its lukewarm receptivity of Western missionary education (Bassey, 1999); Northern Nigeria, being predominantly Muslim, viewed Christian missionary education as a means of conversion, which had to be resisted. This was later to prove disadvantageous to the Northern region. Postindependence educational policies sought to address this disadvantage, the aim being to equalize access and create incentives for ethnoregional mobilization. In 1979 the Nigerian government implemented the Federal Character program whose objective was to balance the educational gap between the North and the South. The program introduced a quota system for admission to federal government-run secondary schools, colleges, and universities. A government's review of admission into higher institutions (colleges, polytechnics, and universities) in 1992 resulted in the creation of a quota structure of: 40% merit, 30% catchment area, 20% disadvantaged states (which are mostly in the North) and 10% discretionary. This system appears to have proven successful in achieving greater regional equity in academic achievement (Aminu, 1988).

The Gender Imbalance and Educational Access and Achievement.
Despite the intentions of the 2000 millennium development goals (MDGs) that the formal and educational achievement gap between boys and girls should be closed, absentees from school continue to be disproportionately female in many developing countries, especially in Sub-Saharan Africa. In Nigeria in 2007, 64% of boys and 58% of girls of primary school age were in school. The gender imbalance is also reflected in the national literacy rates; 72% for men and 56% for women.

The gender imbalance is greater when one considers the educational pipeline (primary to secondary; secondary to university). Oanda and Akudolu (2010) posit that countries in Sub-Saharan Africa have female transition rates to secondary education that are generally less than 50%. In Nigeria, the primary school completion rate for males and females was 81% and 66% in 2006. The gross enrollment ratio (GER) for secondary schools stood at 38% for males and 32% for females within the same period with some variation in subject uptake (Egun & Tibi, 2010). In the tertiary institutions (colleges, universities, and polytechnics institutions), the female gross enrollment was recorded as 41%. Generally, the average rate of participation in higher education in Nigeria is at the very low rate of 6 to 9% (UNESCO, 2006).

Academic Achievement and Attainment as Reflected in Urban and Rural Locations.
One of the reasons for disparities in educational achievement concerns the differences in living standards between rural and urban areas. In Nigeria, the poverty rate is approximately 43.2% in urban areas and 63.3% in rural areas, with literacy rates of 89% and 62.1% respectively. Kaduna, one of the major states in Nigeria, for example, has a 34 percentage point gap in secondary gross enrollment ratio (GER) between urban and rural locations (96% compared to 62%).

Effect of Socioeconomic Status (SES) on Academic Achievement.
Nigeria is a country of inequities; the richest 10% of the population receives around half of the national income while the bottom 10% receives only 1.6%. Sixty percent of Nigerians live below the poverty datum line (Hardman et al. 2008). The Nigerian overall primary school net attendance (NAR) is relatively low at 60%; however, the students from the highest socioeconomic bracket have an 83% NAR whereas the NAR for those in the lowest socioeconomic bracket is merely 40%. The majority of school aged children in Nigeria who have never attended school are from the lowest socioeconomic bracket. Nigeria studies (see Ajila & Olutola, 2000) have shown a positive relationship between socioeconomic status and students' academic performance. Family structure also appears to be an important factor and significant differences have been found between the academic performance of students from single-parent family and those from two-parent family structures (Ichado, 1998).

Other Sociohistorical and Physical Factors that Impact Upon Teaching, Learning, and Achievement.
Nigeria is a resource-rich country. However, due to corruption and general economic mismanagement the country has struggled to provide for its people. In the area of education this has led to what Nwagwu (2002) refers to as a "crisis of confidence." This manifests itself in the form of overcrowded classrooms, overstretched (due to large teacher–student ratios) and poorly trained teachers, and inadequate resource materials for teaching (Bojuwoye, 2002).

The impact of HIV and AIDS on education in Sub-Saharan Africa is another critical factor. AIDS has orphaned around 12.3 million children in this region and the number is expected to rise substantially over the next decade. Orphaned and vulnerable children (OVCs) and child-headed households have grave consequences in that they increase attrition, dropout, and completion rates. Additionally, teacher absenteeism and high mortality rates of teachers and education administrators due to HIV/AIDS-related ailments destabilize the educational structure. The prevalence rate of HIV/AIDS among Nigeria's population has increased from 1.8% in 1988 to 5.8% in 2001. It is speculated that HIV/AIDS could have the following impacts on the education system: decrease in the supply of teachers; increase in the training costs for teachers; reduced public funding for schools; drop in school enrolment, especially for girls; and loss of financial, material, and emotional support for orphans.

Teaching and learning processes will clearly impact student achievement. Furthermore, the forms of social relations that pertain in the classroom can either demotivate or interest students in the activities being carried out. Teaching and learning in Sub-Saharan Africa in general (Tabulawa, 1997) and Nigeria in particular (Onocha & Okpala, 1990; Hardman et al. 2008) have been found to emphasize rote and teacher-led recitation. Calls are loud across the region to change to more participative learner-centred pedagogies. It is, however, accepted that this is not going to be easy, given (a) the embedded nature of teacher-centred pedagogies in the African historical, social, and cultural context (Tabulawa, 1997), and (b) technical problems (such as class size, lack of resources, and inadequately trained teachers).

Summary and Recommendations

Regional politics, gender, school location (whether rural or urban), socioeconomic status, and teaching and learning processes all appear to impact educational achievement and attainment in Nigeria. Obviously these factors do not function independently of one another nor are they the only ones impacting achievement. However, they seem to be the most salient in research on educational achievement in Nigeria. In view of this, it is recommended that:

1. Current efforts to reduce North–South disparities in educational achievement should be more widely implemented.
2. More attention should be paid to disparities. This amongst others requires a deeper understanding of the interaction between the gender gap in academic achievement and the presence of varying socioeconomic conditions.
3. Teacher training and in-service programs should be strengthened to emphasize more interactive and participative teaching methods.

References

Aminu, J. (1988). *The factors of centralization in two decades of Nigerian university development* (pp. 22–40). Lagos, NIgeria: National Universities Commission NUC Publication.

Ajila, C., & Olutola, A (2000). Impact of parents' socio-economic status on university students' academic performance. *Ife Journal of Educational Studies, 7*(1), 31–39.

Bassey, M. O. (1999). *Missionary rivalry and educational expansion in Nigeria 1885–1945*. New York: Mellen Press.

Bojuwoye, O. (2002). A case study of school-related factors affecting Nigerian secondary school pupils' academic performance. *Ilorin Journal of Education, 21,* 31–42.

Egun, A. C., & Tibi, E. U (2010). The gender gap in vocational education: Increasing girls' access in the 21st century in the Midwestern states of Nigeria. *International Journal of Vocational and Technical Education, 2*(2), 18–21.

Eweniyi, G. D (2002). The impact of family structure on university students' academic performance. *Ilorin Journal of Education, 21,* 20–28.

Fafunwa, A. B. (1974). *History of education in Nigeria*. London: Allen & Unwin.

Federal Ministry of Education. (2005). *Nigeria Education for all (EFA). Report card* [UNESCO High level group meeting]. Abuja: Federal Ministry of Education EFA Unit

Hardman, F., Abd-Kadir, J., & Smith, F. (2008). Pedagogical renewal: Improving the quality of classroom interaction in Nigerian primary schools. *International Journal of Educational Development, 28,* 55–69.

Ichado, S. M. (1998). Impact of broken home on academic performance on secondary school students in English language. *Journal of Research in Counselling Psychology, 4*(1), 84–87.

Nwagwu, C. C. (2002). Students' academic performance and the crisis of confidence in the Nigerian education system. *Ilorin Journal of Education, 21,* 10–19.

Oanda, I, & Akudolu, L-R. (2010). Addressing gender inequality in higher education through targeted institutional responses: Field evidence from Kenya and Nigeria. In Sabine O'hara (Ed). Higher education in Africa: Equity, access, opportunity. New York: Institute of International Education.

Onocha, C., & Okpala, P. (1990). Classroom interaction patterns of practicing and pre-service teachers of integrated science. *Research in Education, 43,* 23–31.

Tabulawa, R. (1997). Pedagogical classroom practice and the social context: The case of Botswana. *International Journal of Educational development, 17*(2), 189–204.

UNESCO. (2006). EFA global monitoring report 2007: Strong foundations: Early childhood care and education. Paris: Author. Retrieved from http://www.uis.UNESCO.org/ev.php?URL_ID=5187&URL_DO=DO_TOPIC&URL_SECTION=201

9.10

International Large-Scale Assessment Studies of Student Achievement

PETRA STANAT
Institute for Educational Quality Improvement, Humboldt University of Berlin

OLIVER LÜDTKE
Humboldt University of Berlin

Introduction

The quality and outcomes of educational systems are of considerable concern worldwide. In the 1950s, international organizations, such as the United Nations Educational, Scientific and Cultural Organization (UNESCO) and the Organization for Economic Co-operation and Development (OECD) began to collect and document comparative data on selected features of school systems (e.g., national curricula) in a number of countries. As an indicator of system effectiveness, the proportion of students reaching different levels of education in terms of certificates was used. Soon, however, researchers came to the realization that nominally comparable educational certificates may be associated with highly varying levels of student performance (Postlethwaite, 1999). A group of educational researchers therefore met in 1958 to discuss the possibility of assessing learning outcomes in an international context. This ultimately resulted in the First International Mathematics Study (FIMS) in which a total of 12 countries participated.

The First International Mathematics Study as well as the majority of subsequent international assessments, such as the more recent Trends in International Mathematics and Science Study (TIMSS) and the Progress in International Reading Literacy Study (PIRLS), were planned and conducted under the auspices of the International Association for the Evaluation of Educational Achievement (IEA)—an international foundation involving research institutions and government representatives of its member countries. At the beginning of the 21st century, the OECD began to assess student performance as well. The OECD's Programme for International Student Assessment (PISA) collects data on the achievement of 15-year-old students in the domains of reading, mathematics, and science every 3 years. In the first assessment carried out in 2000, the major domain was reading, followed by mathematics in 2003, and science

in 2006. In 2009, PISA came full circle and started a new assessment cycle with reading as the major domain. Thus, in the PISA 2009 reports it was possible to explore the extent to which changes in reading achievement occurred in participating countries over the previous 9 years (Klieme et al., 2010; OECD, 2010).

The primary goal of international large-scale assessment studies is to provide participating countries with comparative information on the achievement outcomes of their school systems. This endeavor is, of course, highly complex (Stanat & Lüdtke, 2008). One major challenge is to ensure cross-cultural and cross-linguistic equivalence of the assessment data. As a first step, the assessment domains have to be defined in a way that is meaningful in all participating countries. Two general approaches have been implemented in the past: The *curriculum-oriented approach*, which is used in most of the IEA studies, attempts to identify a common core of learning goals within the curricula of participating countries and to assess this common core with test items. The main criterion for the validity of the assessment, then, is the extent to which the test items match the internationally shared curriculum. The *literacy-oriented approach* aims at assessing knowledge and skills that are judged to be important for mastering authentic problems. Thus, literacy tests are based on normative assumptions about the relevance of knowledge and skills for students' lives. This approach is most consistently implemented in PISA.

In a second step, test items that are equivalent across countries have to be developed based on the definitions of the assessment domains. This requires the consideration of factors that may potentially bias students' responses and, as a result, the outcomes of the assessment, such as characteristics of language and culture-specific experiences. The task of developing cross-culturally equivalent items is particularly challenging for literacy tests which aim to ensure authenticity by embedding items in real-life contexts. Therefore, studies like PISA involve elaborate procedures designed to eliminate bias, such as comprehensive reviews of items carried out by national experts in each participating country, double translation of items and subsequent reconciliation of the two versions, standardized pretests combined with analyses of differential-item functioning (DIF) based on these pretest data (for an overview, see OECD, 2009).

Considerable care is also taken to ensure that test administration is standardized across participating countries and that the student samples are representative of the target population. Countries that fail to reach predefined participation rates at the school or student level are either excluded from the analyses or flagged in the reports.

Overall, international large-scale assessments have reached a high level of methodological sophistication (for critical discussions of selected methodological issues see, for example, Goldstein, 2004; Prais, 2003). They provide valuable data that can be used for both policy-related as well as basic research.

Research Evidence

Assessments like PISA offer information on the relative strengths and weaknesses of educational systems in terms of the examined outcomes. In addition to indicators capturing the level of achievement students reach in participating countries, the studies also provide indicators of educational equity, such as the strength of associations between achievement and students' socioeconomic background, achievement gaps between immigrant and native students, or gender differences. This allows national systems to compare themselves with international benchmarks indicating what other countries accomplish with respect to these outcomes. Because the assessments are repeated on a regular basis, moreover, they can be used to monitor changes over time.

Germany is a good example for the potential that international large-scale assessment studies like PISA can have for informing policy. In PISA 2000, Germany scored below the OECD average in all three assessment domains. The gap was most pronounced at the lower end of the performance distribution, with the weakest students performing more poorly in Germany than in most other countries. Moreover, the relationship between students' family background and performance was particularly strong in Germany, suggesting that its school system was less successful in promoting equity than the school systems of other countries. These findings have spurred a large number of educational reforms, such as the introduction of accountability systems, an increase in the number of whole-day schools, and targeted programs designed to improve instructional quality in the domains of mathematics, science, and reading. Although we cannot be sure of the extent to which these and other measures did, in fact, have the intended effects, the performance levels of students in Germany increased continually over the four PISA cycles, with the largest improvements occurring at the lower end of the distribution. As a result,

the disadvantages associated with students' immigrant background and with a low socioeconomic status decreased as well (Klieme et al., 2010).

With regard to international variations in student performance, one recurring pattern is that East Asian countries tend to reach high performance levels. In PISA 2009, for example, countries like Shanghai-China, Hong Kong-China, Korea, Singapore, or Japan were among the 10 highest scoring countries in all three test domains. Consistently high scores were also reported for Finland and, to a lesser degree, for Canada. The United States scored within the range of the OECD average in reading and science and below the OECD average in mathematics (OECD, 2010).

The between-country differences that are observed in large-scale assessments raise the question of their causes. Most quantitative investigations on this issue have focused on structural features of school systems. Applying an international production function model involving variables at the levels of students and their families, schools, school systems, and countries to PISA data, Fuchs and Woessmann (2007) for example found that external exams, several aspects of school autonomy (with regard to textbook choice, hiring of teachers, and within-school budget allocations), and private school management (but not private funding) were associated with higher levels of student performance. The positive effects of school autonomy were more pronounced in systems with external school leaving exams than in systems without such forms of assessment. Also, educational spending was positively related to achievement, yet the relationship was relatively weak and disappeared when four countries with very low levels of spending were excluded from the analyses.

Although analyses such as those performed by Woessmann and colleagues may provide some indication for potential causes of between-country differences in student achievement, their results need to be interpreted with caution. Countries differ with respect to numerous factors and these factors are often highly interrelated such that it is difficult (or even impossible) to disentangle them empirically. Among other things, analyses of structural variables typically ignore cultural characteristics, such as the extent to which the members of a society values education or share assumptions about teaching and learning processes. Based on the available data, moreover, it is impossible to take the complexity of school systems into account and to draw conclusions about causality. For example, the extent to which school autonomy will be effective is likely to depend on a variety of interrelated factors, such as the role school principals play within a system, the type of training they receive, and the employment status of teachers.

Summary and Recommendations

In sum, international large-scale assessment studies can provide countries with valuable information on the relative strengths and weaknesses of their school systems. Although the studies cannot determine what policy makers should do to improve the situation, they can pinpoint target points for interventions and monitor effects of educational reforms over time. In addition, researchers have used data from international large-scale assessment to explore a variety of basic research questions (e.g., Seaton, Marsh, & Craven, 2009; Baumert, Lüdtke, Trautwein, & Brunner, 2009).

In terms of explaining between-country differences in student achievement, several strategies for enhancing the explanatory potential of international large-scale assessment studies have been implemented in the past. One approach is to focus on selected countries and to perform in-depth analyses of their school systems and cultural contexts. A good example for this approach is the Michigan project on elementary school mathematics involving Japan, Taiwan, and the United States (Stevenson & Stigler, 1992). Particularly instructive are comparative video studies that provide insights into what actually happens in classroom instruction (e.g., Stigler, Gonzales, Kawanaka, Knoll, & Serrano, 1996). In addition, several countries have added national components to international large-scale assessment studies, such as longitudinal assessments (e.g., Knighton & Bussière, 2006) or measures of teacher competencies and background characteristics (Krauss, Baumert, & Blum, 2008).

New developments in international large-scale assessment studies include the introduction of technology-based testing. In PISA 2009, 25 countries adopted the international option of electronic reading assessment (ERA). The use of technology-based assessment offers opportunities for using new item formats and, potentially, implementing adaptive testing procedures.

In terms of theoretical developments, it would be highly desirable to expand existing models of student achievement to take into account cultural characteristics of countries (Winne & Nesbit, 2010). The challenge of developing such models is to identify the relevant cultural factors and to develop hypotheses about how they may impact teaching and learning in schools. Such an enriched framework would most likely help to provide a better understanding of student performance in relation to international comparison.

References

Baumert, J., Lüdtke, O., Trautwein, U., & Brunner, M. (2009). Large-scale student assessment studies measure the results of processes of knowledge acquisition: Evidence in support of the distinction between intelligence and student achievement. *Educational Research Review, 4*, 165–176.

Fuchs, L., & Woessmann, L. (2007). What accounts for international differences in student performance? A re-examination using PISA data. *Empirical Economics, 32*, 433–464.

Goldstein, H. (2004). International comparisons of student attainment: Some issues arising from the PISA study. *Assessment in Education: Principles, Policy and Practice, 11*, 319–330.

Klieme, E., Artelt, C., Hartig, J., Jude, N., Köller, O., Prenzel, M., … Stanat, P. (Eds.). (2010). *PISA 2009: Bilanz nach einem Jahrzehnt* [PISA 2009. Taking stock after one decade]. Münster: Waxmann.

Knighton, T., & Bussière, P. (2006). *Educational outcomes at age 19 associated with reading ability at age 15*. Ottawa: Statistics Canada.

Krauss, S., Baumert, J., & Blum, W. (2008). Secondary mathematics teachers' pedagogical content knowledge and content knowledge: Validation of the COACTIV constructs. *International Journal on Mathematics Education, 40*, 873–892.

Organisation for Economic Co-operation and Development (OECD). (2009). *PISA 2006: Technical report*. Paris: Author.

Organisation for Economic Co-operation and Development (OECD). (2010). PISA 2009: *What students know and can do: Student performance in reading, mathematics and science*. Paris: Author.

Postlethwaite, T. N. (1999). *International studies of educational achievement: Methodological issues*. Hong Kong, China: Comparative Education Research Centre.

Prais, S. J. (2003). Cautions on OECD's recent educational survey (PISA). *Oxford Review of Education, 29*, 139–163.

Seaton, M., Marsh, H. W., & Craven, R. G. (2009). Earning its place as a pan-human theory: Universality of the big-fish-little-pond effect across 41 culturally and economically diverse countries. *Journal of Educational Psychology, 101*, 403–419

Stanat, P., & Lüdtke, O. (2008). Multilevel issues in international large-scale assessment studies on student performance. In F. J. R. van de Vijver, D. A. van Hemert, & Y. H. Poortinga (Eds.), *Individuals and cultures in multilevel analysis* (pp. 315–344). Hillsdale, NJ: Erlbaum.

Stevenson, H. W., & Stigler, J. W. (1992). *The learning gap. Why our schools are failing and what we can learn from Japanese and Chinese education*. New York: Summit Books.

Stigler, J. W., Gonzales, P., Kawanaka, T., Knoll, S., & Serrano, A. (1996). *The TIMSS videotape classroom study: Methods and preliminary findings*. Washington, DC: National Center for Education Statistics, U.S. Department of Education.

Winne, P. H., & Nesbit, J. C. (2010). The psychology of academic achievement. *Annual Review of Psychology, 61*, 653–678.

9.11

Academic Achievement in Singapore

Pak Tee Ng
National Institute of Education, Nanyang Technological University

Introduction

Singapore is a young nation-state in South-East Asia. It gained its independence in 1965. It has a land area of only 700 square kilometers and a population of 4.5 million. Being a migrant society, it is racially and religiously diverse. Due to a lack of natural resources, human resources have become its competitive advantage in the global marketplace. Today, it has a strong economy and one of the highest per capita incomes globally. Singapore invests heavily in education to support its strategy of developing a knowledge-based economy, focusing on the lucrative high technology industries and high value-adding services. Its education system has gained a reputation for producing high academic achievements (Barber & Mourshed, 2007; Mourshed, Chijioke, & Barber, 2010).

Research Evidence

Students' Achievement in International Assessments. A good way of appreciating the academic achievement of Singapore students is to examine the results of those international assessments for primary and secondary school students that Singapore has participated in. These include the Trends in International Mathematics and Science Study (TIMSS), Progress in International Reading Literacy Study (PIRLS), and the Programme for International Student Assessment (PISA).

The academic achievement of Singapore students in the areas of mathematics and science is clearly reflected in the consistent and excellent results in TIMSS 1995, 1999, 2003, and 2007. TIMSS 1995 compared the performance of 45 countries at Grades 3, 4, 7, and 8 (Primary 3 and 4, and Secondary 1 and 2). In both mathematics and science, Singapore ranked first for Grades 7 and 8. Singapore ranked second for Grade 3 and first for Grade 4 in mathematics. Singapore came in seventh for both Grades 3 and 4 in science. TIMSS 1999 compared the performance of 38 countries for

Grade 8. Singapore ranked first in mathematics and second in science. TIMSS 2003 compared the performance of 49 countries for Grades 4 and 8. Singapore ranked first in both mathematics and science for both grades (Ministry of Education, 2004). TIMSS 2007 compared the performance of 59 countries for Grades 4 and 8. In science, Singapore emerged first for both Grades 4 and 8. In mathematics, Singapore ranked second and third, for Grade 4 and 8 respectively (Ministry of Education, 2008; see Table 9.11.1).

The academic achievement of Singapore students in the areas of reading literacy is reflected in the results of PIRLS 2001 and 2006. In PIRLS 2001, Singapore ranked 15th in the 35-country study. In PIRLS 2006, Singapore showed great progress by emerging fourth out of 45 education systems that participated in the study. Significantly, Singapore ranked top among the education systems in which pupils took their tests solely in English. When compared with education systems where English was one of the test languages, Singapore was placed second after Canada (Alberta) but ranked higher than the other Canadian provinces, the United States, England, New Zealand, and Scotland (Ministry of Education, 2007; see Table 9.11.2).

Results from PISA 2009 also affirm the high quality of education in Singapore (Ministry of Education 2010a). Out of 65 countries, Singapore ranked second in mathematics,

Table 9.11.1 TIMSS Results at a Glance

TIMSS	Level	Mathematics	Science
1995	Grade 3	2nd	7th
(45 countries)	Grade 4	1st	7th
	Grade 7	1st	1st
	Grade 8	1st	1st
1999	Grade 8	1st	2nd
(38 countries)			
2003	Grade 4	1st	1st
(49 countries)	Grade 8	1st	1st
2007	Grade 4	2nd	1st
(59 countries)	Grade 8	3rd	1st

Table 9.11.2 PIRLS Results at a Glance

PIRLS	Ranking
2001	15th /35 countries
2006	4th /45 countries

Table 9.11.3 PISA 2009 Result at a Glance

PISA 2009	Ranking
Mathematics	2nd/65 countries
Science	4th/65 countries
Reading	5th/65 countries

fourth in science, and fifth in reading. This is the first year that Singapore participated in this triennial study (see Table 9.11.3).

Key Factors For Current Success. The academic achievements of Singapore's education system may be attributed to various factors. First, there is strong central governmental control over the education system (Barber & Mourshed, 2007; Ng, 2008a), which aligns the various schools to a common goal. Under an umbrella vision of *Thinking Schools, Learning Nation* (Goh, 1997; Ng, 2005a), education policies are entwined with the economic plans and future needs of Singapore. This is coupled with a conscientious implementation of quality assurance models, which maintains standards in schools (Ng, 2008a, 2010).

Second, the government is committed to investing in education to enhance its human capacity. While some governments consider education as a source of expenditure, the Singapore government sees education as an important investment that is essential to its overall economic growth (Gopinathan, 2001). This translates into generous governmental support for continual improvements on educational infrastructure (Barber & Mourshed, 2007; Mourshed et al., 2010). Moreover, heavy investments are made in research for best practices and innovations in teaching, the results of which are implemented consistently across the system (Barber & Mourshed, 2007; Mourshed et al., 2010).

Third, there is a centralized and rigorous teacher selection, recruitment, and preservice training system (Barber & Mourshed, 2007). There is also a high societal regard for teaching as a profession, reflected in both remuneration and prestige, thus making it an attractive profession for the top 30% of the graduate cohort (Barber & Mourshed, 2007).

Fourth, there is a high cultural premium in education and strong home support for students' access to educational resources, including books and computers (Ministry of Education, 2000). As an example, shadow education, in the form of tuition classes and after school activities, arranged and paid for by parents, is a dominant feature in Singapore, reflecting this desire for academic achievement (Bray, 1999).

Fifth, there is a safe environment for students to learn in school. Interestingly, Singapore scores the highest percentage among all countries in the Index of Teachers' Perception of Safety in Schools for TIMSS 2003 (Ministry of Education, 2004).

Challenges for the Further Development of the System. Student academic achievements, measured through international assessments such as TIMSS and PIRLS, are still questionable in terms of their validity, reliability, and interpretation. However, the main challenge confronting the Singapore education system is that despite their good results, Singapore students generally rely on rote memory and repetitive learning as means to achieving high scores in examinations (Ng, 2005a). Such a mode of learning is insufficient for the 21st century as the demands of the knowledge economy require higher order thinking skills and creativity.

The Ministry of Education (MOE) has set out to address this situation. For example, in 2004, the MOE implemented the initiative "Innovation and Enterprise" to encourage the inculcation of a spirit of innovation and enterprise among schools and students (Ng, 2005b). In 2005, the Ministry of Education implemented the initiative "Teach Less Learn More" to transform the focus of learning from quantity to quality, and emphasizing curricular reform, pedagogical innovation, and student engagement (Ng, 2008b). More recently, the Ministry reiterated Singapore's need for a more holistic education with a new framework to identify 21st century competencies that schools should emphasize (Ministry of Education, 2010b).

A key government strategy to drive these educational reforms is to decentralize its power to the schools to encourage diversity and innovation. However, while doing so, the government still carries a great responsibility for achieving national outcomes and providing high value for public funding. Therefore, paradoxically, while schools are encouraged to be innovative, they must still be aligned to the national goals of social and economic development and conform to accountability systems (Ng, 2008a). Through such a centralized decentralization strategy, the government exerts strategic control on the schools while giving them tactical autonomy. Schools are asked to think out of the box while needing to do well within the box. This is no easy feat (Ng 2008a, 2010).

Summary

Because of its success in international assessments, the Singapore education system is often cited as an example that education systems in other countries could emulate. A key strength of the system is the awareness of policy makers that the education system cannot remain successful if it does not change with the times. This explains the presence of many initiatives to reform education. However, Ng (2008b, p. 14) notes: "While policy changes may have the right intentions, to really affect the core of learning in schools, changes need to go beyond the system-level structures and provisions to address deep and subtle issues." The greatest enemy of change is success. So, while there are initiatives to reform education, the subtle but great challenge is whether there is a willingness to let go of current success for a different success. The likelihood of a fundamental change in the nature of education in Singapore is rather remote. But the current robust system is definitely good at producing academic achievements in the foreseeable future.

References

Barber, M., & Mourshed, M. (2007). *How the world's best performing school systems come out on top*. London: McKinsey.

Bray, M. (1999). *The shadow education system: Private tutoring and its implications for planners*. (Fundamentals of Educational Planning Series, No. 61). Paris: UNESCO, International Institute for Educational Planning.

Goh, C. T. (1997, June 2). *Shaping our future: Thinking schools, learning nation*. Speech by Prime Minister Goh Chok Tong at the Opening of the 7th International Conference on Thinking, Singapore.

Gopinathan, S. (2001). Globalisation, the state and education policy in Singapore. In J. Tan, S. Gopinathan, and W. K. Ho (Eds.), *Challenges facing the Singapore education system today*. (pp. 35–49). Singapore: Prentice Hall.

Ministry of Education. (2000, November 28). *Singapore number one in mathematics again in the Third International Mathematics and Science Study 1999*. Singapore: Ministry of Education. Press Release.

Ministry of Education. (2004, December 14). *Singapore tops the Trends in International Mathematics and Science Study (TIMSS) 2003*. Singapore: Ministry of Education. Press Release.

Ministry of Education. (2007, November 29). *Singapore's performance in the Progress in International Reading Literacy Study (PIRLS) 2006*. Singapore: Ministry of Education. Press Release.

Ministry of Education. (2008, December 10). *Singapore performs well again in the latest Trends in International Mathematics and Science Study (TIMSS) 2007*. Singapore: Ministry of Education. Press Release.

Ministry of Education. (2010a. December 7). *International OECD study affirms the high quality of Singapore's education system*. Singapore: Ministry of Education. Press Release.

Ministry of Education. (2010b, March 9). *MOE to enhance learning of 21st century competencies and strengthen art, music and physical education*. Singapore: Ministry of Education. Press Release.

Mourshed, M., Chijioke, C., & Barber, M. (2010). *How the world's most improved school systems keep getting better*. London: McKinsey.

Ng, P. T. (2005a). Students' perception of change in the Singapore education system. *Educational Research for Policy and Practice, 3*(1), 77–92.

Ng, P. T. (2005b). Innovation and enterprise in Singapore schools. *Educational Research for Policy and Practice, 3*(3), 183–198.

Ng, P. T. (2008a). The phases and paradoxes of educational quality assurance: The case of the Singapore education system. *Quality Assurance in Education, 16*(2), 112–125.

Ng, P. T. (2008b). Educational Reform in Singapore: from quantity to quality. *Education Research Policy and Practice, 7*(1), 5–15.

Ng, P. T. (2010). The evolution and nature of school accountability in the Singapore education system. *Educational Assessment, Evaluation and Accountability, 22*(4), 275–292.

9.12

Academic Achievement in South Korea

Jongho Shin
Seoul National University, South Korea

Introduction

South Korean students are internationally well known for their high academic achievements. Compared with students in other countries, South Korea has ranked the highest, or one of the highest, in many international achievement assessments, such as the Trends in International Mathematics and Science Study (TIMMS) and the Program for International Student Assessment (PISA). In PISA 2009, South Korean students' academic performance was ranked first in reading and second in mathematics, and ranked between second and fourth in science (OECD, 2010b). So, how did South Korea achieve such success? In order to address this question several key factors must be discussed.

First, high academic achievement should be understood in relation to the sociohistorical context of the South Korean education system. Learning has significant meaning in the lives of South Koreans; academic achievement does not represent merely an ability that an individual possesses. Rather, South Koreans have an implicit understanding and knowledge of academic achievement that is closely tied to one's sense of self.

The origin of this perspective can be traced back to the Confucian tradition of the Korean Chosun Dynasty (1392–1910). An ideal person of this era was known as "Seon-Bi," someone who would be considered to be a classical scholar. Seon-Bi was expected to dedicate his efforts into the field of study in order to achieve the highest levels of competence and character to administer the world. Thus, learning was considered to be a process of not only acquiring knowledge but also attaining completeness as an individual, a whole, fine character (Educational Research Institute, Seoul National University, 1997).

Another important factor was the country's rapid growth and modernization. This provided numerous opportunities for social mobility and here a key factor was the individual's educational background (i.e., the level of education, and where one received one's education) (Kim, 1989; Lee, Kim, & Adams, 2010). Since then, a strong educational background has been considered to be an essential means to secure future success.

Research Evidence

Partly because of such rapid social change, parents' passion for, and involvement in, providing a better education for their children became a marked feature of the education system. Parental influence can help to explain a great deal of the educational successes of Korean students. Thus, in one study, 92.3% of South Korean parents indicated that they wished their children to be educated to college or graduate school level. Unsurprisingly, therefore, the nation's enrollment rate in higher education is higher than for most other developed countries. For example, the average rate of enrollment in college or above for an OECD member nation is 55%, whereas for South Korea it is 71% (OECD, 2010a).

High expectation of academic success also increases competition for entry into the most prestigious colleges and universities. This has resulted in significant personal financial investment in nonformal (shadow) education (e.g., personal-group tutoring and private after-school learning programs). According to Statistics Korea (2010), the average nonformal education expense per family in Seoul, the capital city of South Korea, is U.S.$500 per month. Considering that the average Korean monthly income per family is around $3,200, each family spends almost 15% of their income on nonformal education. An average participation rate in nonformal education for Korean students is 72%, far exceeding the OECD average of 47% (OECD, 2007). In most countries, nonformal education serves the function of supplementing what a student may fail to grasp in their formal education. However, the opposite is true in South Korea; the higher one's academic achievement, the greater the expenditure on nonformal education. This disparity reflects the national perception of education as a means to excel above others for social success (Park, Sung, Kim, Min, & Ham, 2009).

In addition to sociohistorical influences, a number of educational factors contribute to the nation's academic achievement, in particular, the amount of time spent on study. As President Obama noted, American children spend over a month less in school each year than children in South Korea. Park, Lee, Kang, and Hwang (2005) have shown that mathematical achievement was related to the number of hours that Korean students spent on independent study. They also reported that more than half of South Korean students (50.2%) believed they did not study enough despite the fact their country reports the greatest amount of study hours among OECD countries. According to PISA 2006 results, for example, South Korean students spent an average of 9.3 hours per week studying mathematics, whereas the OECD average was 6.6 hours (OECD, 2007).

A second key factor that explained high achievement in South Korea is the existence of a highly competitive learning atmosphere (Shin, Lee & Kim, 2009). As in other Northeast Asian countries, the number of prominent high schools and universities in South Korea is very limited and, as a result, competition to gain entry to such prestigious schools is very intense.

This competition serves as a strong source of extrinsic motivation. Students largely perceive their school work as an instrumental means to be successful in adult society (Shin, Hwang, & Seo, 2010). While South Korean students score lower in intrinsic motivation, subject interest, and academic self-efficacy when compared to Western students (OECD, 2007) this does not appear to have any significant impact on their high work rates or desire for academic success.

In addition to parental expectations, the involvement of parents in their children's education is another important factor. Although nonformal education is common in South Korea, this does not guarantee successful academic outcomes. It appears that this will only be productive when parents are interested and actively participate in their child's studies (Shin et al., 2010). In South Korea, academic work is not solely a personal concern for students, but rather, an issue for the entire family.

South Korean teachers and schools are considered to have less differential influence on academic achievement than is the case in other countries (Park, Sung et al., 2009; Sung, 2006). The reasons for this can be attributed to teachers being burdened with extra administrative duties that take time away from instructional preparation. Another unfortunate problem is that there are too few school programs that meet the differing needs of students. In1975, standardized curricula were applied to all elementary and secondary schools. As a result, with the exception of a few specialized high schools in science, foreign language, and arts, there is practically no difference in curriculum and instructional development and practices among South Korean schools,

surprisingly, not even between private and public schools (Sung, 2006).

Regrettably, under this system, the various talents, abilities, and needs of many students have tended to be neglected. Although South Korean students were positioned highly in PISA 2009, the proportion of high achieving students was not much larger than those for other OECD countries. When students at the highest level of achievement were compared, South Korean students were ranked at a dismal 14th place (OECD, 2010b).

Summary and Recommendations

So, how can South Korea advance from its current lopsided education system and develop a more complete approach? At the institutional level, students should be given more choice in their academic activities in school, a procedure that should have the effect of increasing the diversity of educational programs.

Additionally, teachers should be provided with the time necessary to develop their teaching expertise on an ongoing basis. Preparation time for all teachers could be supplemented by sabbatical leave for those who show exemplary instructional performance and achieve high levels of student academic success. They could then act as consultants to other teachers. Such a scheme is currently being planned by the Korean Ministry of Education, Science, and Technology.

Parents also need to play an active role in collaborating with teachers. Traditionally, South Korean parents have not cooperated well with schools or communities and, reflecting competitive drivers, have focused solely on their own children's education.

Competitive learning is the driving force for South Korean students. It is widely believed, however, that a key task for educators is to help students to become more intrinsically motivated. Studying should be seen as a lifelong enterprise that can enable one to fulfill one's own life goals beyond merely receiving good grades or gaining admission to desired schools.

In summary, South Korea's academic achievement has indeed proven noteworthy. However, concerns expressed about the current system including the conformity of school programs, the preoccupation of parents with the performance of their own children, and overstressed competition in education should not be neglected. Collaboration between parents, schools, and society as a whole is likely to be the most effective way to improve the nation's education system. As such, the small steps that are being taken in this respect are to be welcomed.

References

Kim, K. S.(1989). The expansion of secondary education. In S. I. Kim (Ed.), *Education in Korea*. Seoul, South Korea: Kyoyookkwahaksa.

Lee, C. J., Kim. S. Y., & Adams D. (2010). *Sixty years of Korean education*. Seoul, South Korea: Seoul National University Press.

Organisation for Economic Co-operation and Development (OECD).

(2007). *PISA 2006 Science competencies for tomorrow's world*. Paris: Author.

Organisation for Economic Co-operation and Development (OECD). (2010a). *Education at a glance: OECD indicators*. Paris: Author.

Organisation for Economic Co-operation and Development (OECD). (2010b). *PISA 2009 result: What students know and can do—Student performance in reading, mathematics and science*. Paris: Author.

Park, S. Y., Sung, K. S., Kim, J. Y., Min, B. C., & Ham, E. H. (2009). *The policy implications of PISA 2006* (Korean Education Development Institute [KEDI] Monograph). Seoul, South Korea: KEDI.

Seoul National University Education Research Institute. (1997). *History of education in Korea*. Seoul, South Korea: Kyoyookkwahaksa.

Shin, J., Hwang, H. Y., & Seo, E. J. (2010). The effect of private tutoring on students' academic achievement: Moderating effect of parental involvement and students' self-regulation. *Asian Journal of Education, 11*, 249–264.

Shin, J., Lee, H., & Kim, Y. (2009). Students and school factors affect mathematics achievement. *School Psychology International, 30*, 520–537.

Sung, K. (2006). A study on the middle school effect of Korea: Test of the Creemers' theoretical model of school effect. *Korean Journal of Sociology of Education, 16*(4), 93–114.

Statistics Korea. (2010). *Korean statistical information on education*. Daejeon, Korea.

9.13

An Overview of Student Achievement and the Related Factors in Taiwan

JENG LIU
Tunghai University

Introduction

Education is highly valued in Taiwan, as evidenced by the ancient Chinese saying "all pursuits except studying are of little value." As such, the average Taiwanese regards education as the only way to get ahead, and a person's academic achievements are commonly taken as a general index of success. Actually, education is given great importance throughout East Asia, as shown by past research indicating the high degree of academic success amongst students in Taiwan, mainland China, Japan, and Korea (Sun & Hwang, 1996; Zhou & Kim, 2006). The common denominator of East Asian culture is the widespread influence of Confucianism, which places great emphasis on education.

A wide range of factors influence the academic achievement of students in Taiwan, including the place of origin of one's ancestors; ethnicity; socioeconomic status; parental attitudes about learning; and area of residence. The following section probes into these factors and the influence they have on academic success. Additionally, some unique issues such as Taiwan's supplementary education and educational reform will be discussed.

Research Evidence

Background Factors. The population of Taiwan can be grouped into four communities distinct in terms of lifestyle, language, and livelihood: aboriginals; Taiwanese; Hakkas; and mainlanders. A number of studies (Lin & Hwang, 2009; Su & Hwang, 2009) in Taiwan have found that ethnicity and the place of origin of one's ancestors have an influence on academic achievement. Mainlanders have traditionally had the highest level of academic achievement, but the Hakkas are gradually overtaking them. The main reason for the high academic performance of mainlanders is that the government provides educational subsidies to the children of soldiers, civil servants, and teachers, posts mainly held by mainlanders.

In comparison with the other groups, Taiwan's aboriginals are at a distinct disadvantage in terms of educational and career opportunities, mainly due to their physical isolation in remote parts of the island, as well as cultural and linguistic differences. Apart from an insufficiency of facilities and teachers, the main reason for the relatively low level of academic achievement amongst aboriginals is the sense of cultural discontinuity they experience when participating in the mainstream educational system. Other factors include the comparatively low socioeconomic status of most aboriginals and a traditional lack of interest in formal education (Lin & Hwang, 2009).

With respect to family circumstances, it is generally believed that a stable family structure has a positive influence on academic achievement. Also, a student's academic performance has an influence on his or her parents' attitudes toward education: a high level of academic achievement engenders in the parents a more positive attitude toward education (J. J. Chen & Liu, 2001; Sun & Hwang, 1996). In addition, there is an inverse relation between academic achievement and the number of children in a family because families with many children have fewer resources available per child (Su & Hwang, 2009). Moreover, recent years have witnessed large numbers of Taiwanese marrying overseas nationals, and the academic achievement of the offspring of such marriages deserves special attention. Scholars have found that up to the junior high school level, the children of recent immigrants are less successful in their studies than other students, but the difference disappears at the high school level (J. J. Chen, 2010).

It has also been found that socioeconomic status is one of the most important factors influencing academic success. The relation between socioeconomic status and academic achievement becomes more apparent when examined from the perspective of Pierre Bourdieu's concept of cultural capital and James Coleman's concepts of social capital and financial capital. Research has shown that the higher the parents' socioeconomic status, the higher the academic achievement of their children (Hwang & Chen, 2008; Liu, 2009). In addition, scholars have pointed out that good interpersonal relationships have a positive influence on academic performance in all subjects (Chen & Liu, 2001; Y. G. Chen, Chen, & Hwang, 2006). Students who use an effective learning strategy and make connections between the different subjects they are studying have higher levels of academic achievement. With respect to differences related to gender, there is no consensus amongst the empirical studies which have been carried out (Hwang & Chen, 2008; Liu, 2011).

With respect to locality, studies have shown that there is no clear difference between the academic achievement of students living in the north, center, and south of Taiwan, but the students in these three areas have a higher level of achievement than those living in eastern Taiwan and the outlying islands (Lanyu, Mazu, etc.). A number of scholars have compared urban and rural elementary schools with respect to the allocation of educational resources (Chen & Liu, 2001; Su & Hwang, 2009). The results indicate that urban schools have better facilities and human resources than rural schools, showing that locality has a clear influence on academic achievement.

Taiwan's Educational Reform. The educational reforms carried out in recent years have also had an influence on student achievement. The curriculum reforms began to be carried out in 2000, and in 2001 the new "nine-year integrated curriculum" was put in place. The goals of the reforms include reducing student stress, simplifying teaching materials, and reducing the number of classroom hours. Yet, some have expressed concern that these measures may be tantamount to a lowering of academic standards. Moreover, scholars have pointed out that the related "diversified admission program" (which allows students to gain admission through application) is not only dubious with respect to fairness, but also causes students to doubt their skills and potential, issues bearing a close relationship to socioeconomic background and cultural capital (Chen & Liu, 2001).

The outcome of the reform measures is still not apparent, but it is clear that they have stimulated the rapid growth of supplementary education classes and increased student pressure (Hwang & Chen, 2008; Liu, 2009). Looking at it from the perspective of population ecology, if the educational reforms have succeeded in lowering student pressure, then the number of supplementary education classes should have decreased. Yet, statistics published by the Taiwan Institute of Economic Research indicate that the supplementary education industry has steadily grown, showing that despite the reforms the demand for such classes is actually increasing.

Supplementary Education. Also known as "cram schools" or "shadow education," supplementary education in a broad sense refers to any after-school educational activity, including art classes and skills training. In a more narrow sense, supplementary education refers to remedial education and exam preparation, including at-school after-class guidance, cram schools, and tutoring (Bray, 1999). Supplementary education is a time-honored institution in Taiwan whose role and functions have evolved over time. At present, cram schools are widespread throughout Taiwan, from the grade-school level all the way up to classes for graduate students and those preparing for professional licensing examinations (Liu, 2009).

A number of differences in the supplementary education phenomenon can be seen at different levels of education. At the elementary school level, most students attend supplementary classes related to their regular subjects, and it has been found that students who attend a number of talent classes (mainly in such subjects as art, music, languages, and computers) have better grades in school than students who only attend after-class daycare (Liu, 2009). At the junior high school level, students mainly participate in supplementary education to improve their grades, and it has been found that the educational level of the parents is an influential factor (Liu, 2011). The highest rate of participation is for students whose parents have an average income and level of education; there is no major different between families with very high and very low levels of income; and the rate is significantly lower for the children of parents with either very high or very low levels of education. At the high school level, supplementary education has a positive influence on grades, and the common experience serves to strengthen peer relationships (Liu, 2011). At the university level, students mostly participate in supplementary education in order to prepare for entrance exams, language tests required for studying abroad, or professional licensing exams (Hwang & Chen, 2008).

Scholars believe that the prevalence of supplementary education is mainly the result of the long-standing entrance exam system (Bray, 2003; Liu, 2009, 2011; Sun & Hwang, 1996). When carried out in a systematic fashion, supplementary education definitely does result in higher grades. Still, we need to weigh the overall benefits and drawbacks of such forms of additional provision. With respect to social stratification, since higher income families are able to enroll their children in more and better quality classes, supplementary education can be seen as a way of maintaining or even increasing social inequality. In addition, these classes are concentrated in urban centers, which in itself may place rural students at a distinct disadvantage (Liu, 2009; 2011).

The educational reforms carried out by the government have become the focus of a wave of criticism, leading parents to regard supplementary education as a good investment. Although supplementary education is not a part of the formal system of education, it has gradually evolved into an important institution which has already taken on many functions that were originally part of the formal education system. It also plays the essential role of imparting exam skills and helping people obtain diplomas, certifications, and specialized skills (Liu, 2009, 2011).

Summary and Recommendations

Scholars have suggested that Taiwan's overemphasis on academic degrees and rote memorization has turned schools into little more than test-preparation centers (Hwang & Chen, 2008; Liu, 2011). The result is that students appear to lack creativity and the ability to reflect and make insightful judgments. Despite the implementation of the 9-year integrated curriculum and the diversified admission program, supplementary education is as widespread as ever. Although this appears to increase academic achievement, it also has certain negative influences on learning. Supplementary education classes tend to focus exclusively on the main points of a subject, exam preparation, and rote memorization. This engenders a one-sided and passive attitude toward learning and can hamper student initiative and reflective ability.

Thus Taiwan is facing a serious problem in the field of education: an undue emphasis on rote memorization, exams results, and academic credentials. Despite a decade of educational reform measures in Taiwan, the exam culture remains firmly entrenched, and supplementary education continues to be a major growth industry. As mentioned above, the international honors garnered by Taiwanese students are mainly in certain fields such as mathematics competition. What is really needed, then, is the reform of an exam culture that tends to strangle the creative ability of Taiwanese students.

Finally, for those scholars who are interested in undertaking comparative studies, two large databases providing information on the academic success of Taiwanese students are currently accessible. One is the Taiwan Education Panel Survey (TEPS), a long-term project which collects data on students at junior high schools, senior high schools, vocational high schools, and vocational colleges throughout urban and rural Taiwan. The other database is the Taiwan Assessment of Student Achievement (TASA), which covers the main subjects taught at elementary schools, junior high schools, and senior high schools. The purpose of this database is to elucidate and analyze the prevailing trends relating to the academic success of students and to evaluate the effectiveness of the educational system and its policies. By continuing to investigate these topics, we can contribute to the accumulation of academic knowledge and policy development in this field more objectively and effectively.

References

Bray, M. (1999). *The shadow education system: Private tutoring and its implications for planners.* Paris: International Institute of Educational Planning.

Bray, M. (2003). *Adverse effects of private supplementary tutoring: Dimensions, Implications, and government responses.* Paris: International Institute of Educational Planning.

Chen, J. J. (2010). The effect of intermarriage on child's learning achievement. *NTTU Educational Research Journal, 21*(2), 61–89.

Chen, Y. G., Chen, M. T. & Hwang, Y. J. (2006). An empirical study on the relationship between multiple entrance program of senior high school and educational opportunity in Taiwan. *Journal of Education and Psychology, 29*(3), 433–459.

Chen, J. J. & Liu, J. (2001). The function of formal schooling revisited. *Journal of National Taitung University, 12,* 115–144.

Hwang, Y. J., & Chen, C. W. (2008). Academic cram schooling, academic performance, and opportunity of entering public universities. *Bulletin of Educational Research, 54*(1), 117–149.

Lin, H. M. & Hwang, Y. J. (2009). The study on relationship among the aborigines and Hans, cram schooling, and the academic achievement. *Contemporary Educational Research Quarterly, 17*(3), 41–81.

Liu, J. (2009). Cram schooling in Taiwan. *Journal of Youth Studies, 12*(1), 129–136.

Liu, J. (2011). Does cram schooling matters? Who goes to cram schools? Evidence from Taiwan. *International Journal of Educational Development, 32*(1), 46–62

Su, C. L., & Hwang, Y. J. (2009). Influence of cultural capital on academic performance through school social capital. *Bulletin of Educational Research, 55*(3), 99–129.

Sun, C. S., & Hwang, Y. J. (1996). Shadow education, cultural capital, and educational attainment. *Taiwanese Journal of Sociology, 19,* 95–139.

Zhou, M. & Kim, S. (2006). Community forces, social capital, and educational achievement: The case of supplementary education in the Chinese and Korean immigrant communities. *Harvard Education Review, 76,* 1–29.

Index